eCAADe 2021
Towards a New, Configurable Architecture

Volume 1

Editors
Vesna Stojaković, Bojan Tepavčević, University of Novi Sad, Faculty of Technical Sciences

1st Edition, September 2021
Towards a New, Configurable Architecture - Proceedings of the 39th International Hybrid Conference on Education and Research in Computer Aided Architectural Design in Europe, Novi Sad, Serbia, 8-10th September 2021, Volume 1. Edited by Vesna Stojaković and Bojan Tepavčević. Brussels: Education and Research in Computer Aided Architectural Design in Europe, Belgium / Novi Sad: Digital Design Center, University of Novi Sad.

Legal Depot
D/2021/14982/01

ISBN 978-94-91207-22-8 (volume 1), **Publisher** eCAADe (Education and Research in Computer Aided Architectural Design in Europe)

ISBN 978-86-6022-358-8 (volume 1), **Publisher** FTN (Faculty of Technical Sciences, University of Novi Sad, Serbia)

ISSN
2684-1843

Cover Design
Vesna Stojaković

Second edition printed by:
Tredition.com

eCAADe 2021
Towards a New, Configurable Architecture

Volume 1

Proceedings
The 39th Conference on Education and Research in Computer Aided Architectural Design in Europe

Hybrid Conference
8th-10th September 2021
Novi Sad, Serbia
Faculty of Technical Sciences
University of Novi Sad

Edited by
Vesna Stojaković
Bojan Tepavčević

ORGANIZATION

SPONSORS

Silver sponsor

Bronze sponsor

SUPPORTED BY

Министарство просвете, науке и технолошког развоја

Покрајински секретаријат за
високо образовање и научноистраживачку делатност

TECHNICAL SUPPORT

eCAADe SPECIAL SUPPORT

OpenConf (Martin Winchester)
ProceeDings (Gabriel Wurzer, Wolfgang Lorenz,
Bob Martens, Bojan Tepavčević, Vesna Stojaković)
CuminCAD (Bob Martens, Tomo Cerovsek)
Voting System (Martin Winchester)

FTN SPECIAL SUPPORT

Registration System (Dimitrije Nikolić)
Webpage (Marko Vučić)
IT support (Igor Zečević, Rade Lučić)

PREFACE

This is the first of two volumes, of the 39th eCAADe Proceedings, held as a hybrid event, from 8-10 September 2021 at the Department of Architecture, Faculty of Technical Sciences, University of Novi Sad, Serbia. The two volumes together contain 117 accepted papers. All papers are also available digitally at CumInCAD (Cumulative Index of Computer Aided Architectural Design) – http://papers.cumincad.org

Theme

"The problem of the house is a problem of the epoch. The equilibrium of society today depends upon it. Architecture has for its first duty, in this period of renewal, that of bringing about a revision of values, a revision of the constituent elements of the house."
Le Corbusier, Towards a New Architecture, 1923

Context

Almost a hundred years after the first edition of the book "Towards a New Architecture", the problem of architecture in the age of the Industrial Revolution is relevant again. A century ago Le Corbusier advocated for a new concept of architecture based on engineering logic of the Second Industrial Revolution and mass production. At the end of the 20th century, the Third Industrial Revolution brought a digital turn in architecture, reshaping the way of thinking and making. Today, industrial revolution is already changing architecture before our eyes towards a new, configurable architecture.

How we can describe the notion of configuration in architecture?

The notion of configuration can be described as a relative arrangement of elements in a particular system, form, figure, or other formations. Configuration represents the essence of the design process. The configurable architecture may include a process of abstract thinking through design and exploitation. It can be considered from different perspectives such as design analysis and critical thinking, creative process, digital fabrication, computational design, responsive architecture and environments, material-based design, autonomous assembly or interactive design visualization.

We are already witnessing the application of configurable products in other engineering disciplines that allow end users to participate in the design process and personalize products. How will the architecture in the 21st century respond to the challenges of a new configurable approach to design production and collaboration in the following years?

From mass-customization toward mass-personalization, configurable architecture is seeking for an answer to how architecture will adjust to habitual behavior of their users in the 21st century. What are the new lessons for architects in this new age, age of mass-customization? How parametric tools can enable every person to participate in the design process? What are the new tools for the design collaboration in architecture?

"Towards a new configurable architecture" critically questions the notion of configuration in architecture and how it can be applied to rethinking architectural ideas, design process, representation, fabrication and utilization process.

In order to specifically address some of the questions above, we have invited researchers, professors, experts and students to discuss topics such as:
Computational design
Rule based systems and shape grammar
Building Information Modeling
CAAD and education
CAAD, creativity and design thinking models
Smart cities, city modeling and GIS
Digital fabrication and robotics
Mass customization in design
Digital representation and visualization
VR, AR and interactive visualization
Agent-based modeling and machine learning in design
Simulation, prediction and evaluation in design
Structure optimization and material-based design
Bionics, bioprinting, living materials
Collaborative, participative or responsive design
Digital design for sustainable buildings
Performance based design
Digital heritage

The first volume of the proceedings contains 58 papers while the second volume contains 59 papers. In addition to the accepted papers, the first volume is preceded by Keynote papers including keynote speakers' contributions concerning the themes of their keynote lectures and the workshops organized the days before the Conference.

eCAADe 2021 conference chairs
Vesna Stojaković & Bojan Tepavčević

FOREWORD - eCAADe2021

Dear eCAADe friends,

The first eCAADe Hybrid conference Novi Sad 2021 "Towards a new configurable architecture" invites 'academicians, researchers, professionals and students to address how problem-formations in architecture, will be defined within the long lasting conditions (loss of valuable natural resources, construction waste, energy consumption, ect) that generate existence threatening problems for the planet earth and calls for the urgent action.
This year, our community was exited to meet with this challenging conference theme in city of Novi Sad for the 39th eCAADe conference in Europe. However, with still existing global crises, due to Covid outbreak, a joint decision was made to organize eCAADe 2021 Novi Sad conference in a Hybrid mode. The deep spirit of cooperation, and commitment of Novi Sad organization team gave a life to the eCAADe 2021 Hybrid Novi SAD Conference.
The theme "Towards a new configurable architecture" critically questions the notion of configuration in architecture and how it can be applied to rethinking architectural ideas, design process, representation, fabrication and utilisation process by seeing architecture in a particular way in which architecture system's components or services and their connectors or bindings are composed and structured into the resulting building system.
A conventional architecture design and construction is characterized by tightly coupled components, that are not configurable, modifiable, and reusable without harming the actual building system and generating construction waste. As a result, the AEC sector uses the most resources and generates the most waste that harms the planet earth.
This year's conference theme "Towards a new configurable architecture" that addresses these issue's within the frame work of eCAADe conference subjects is aligned with the Europe's "Circular Economy Action Plan for a Cleaner and More Competitive Europe".

Architecture by developing affinities and collaborations through multi-disciplinary, multi-scalar, and multi-centered approaches can transform the present and future condition of the Earth System. eCAADe conference is a unique environment for transforming tracks of thought by providing platforms for multi-disciplinary knowledge sharing. I'm looking forward to discussing these and other relevant issues in Novi Sad in physical and online environment.

The World PhD Workshop 2021, that is linked to Ecaade Novi Sad PhD workshop is aimed to build togetherness and collaboration among young researchers of sister organizations, of ACADIA, SiGradi, CAADRIA, ASCAD and eCAADe, will be held online at the 6th-7th-8th of December at Federal University of Juiz De Fora. The workshop provides an opportunity for young researchers of our communities to collaborate, to experience how PhD studies are conducted in various schools across the world, and gives an opportunity to meet with prominent researchers in the Architecture and Computing field.

I would like to thank to Novi Sad organization team who made eCAADe 2021 Hybrid conference event possible in this extended hard time of a global crisis. Especially, to Dr Vesna Stojaković and Dr Bojan Tepavčević, for their excellent organizational efforts, we feel welcome to Novi Sad.

Birgül Çolakoğlu
President of eCAADe

ON THE eCAADe HYBRID CONFERENCE 2021

Our eCAADe 2021 story started in 2016, when our research group, Digital Design Center at the Faculty of Technical Sciences, University of Novi Sad, got the opportunity to organize the eCAADe Regional International Symposium. The 4th eCAADe Regional International Symposium was successfully held in Novi Sad. In 2020 our school of architecture at the Faculty of Technical Sciences in Novi Sad was elected to serve as a host for the 2021 eCAADe.
We were aware that special circumstances of COVID-19 will bring us many challenges in the organizational process. However, we find valuable that it would be the first eCAADe conference organized in Southeastern part of Europe.

Development

Despite the global pandemic, eCAADe2021 conference in Novi Sad aroused a lot of attention and enthusiasm globally. In the first phase (call for abstracts) we received 334 abstracts from 42 countries. Abstracts were checked in accordance with the formal quality measures set out for submissions by eCAADe.

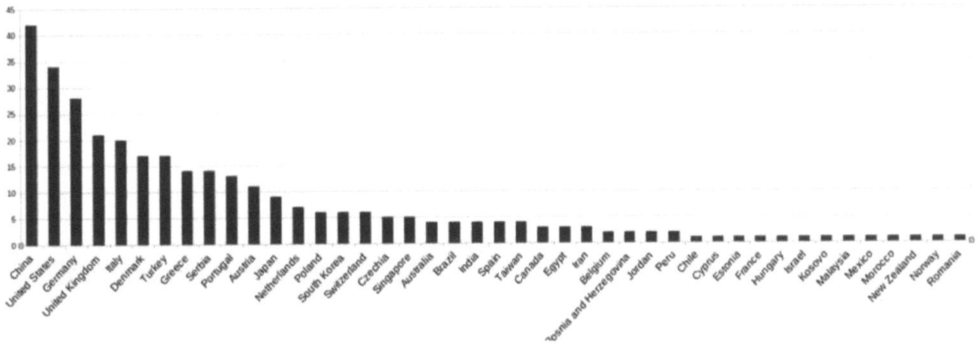

Abstracts were evaluated by three reviewers not affiliated with the authors to avoid a conflict of interest. After the abstract review process, 216 papers were accepted and invited for full paper submission for the second stage of the double blind-peer review process.

Due to the second wave rise of COVID-19 pandemics in Europe, 130 full papers were sumbitted for the second round of reviews. Papers were blind reviewed by three reviewers. After the second review stage, 117 full papers were accepted and authors were invited to submit camera-ready papers, which can be found in two volumes of this Proceedings as well as well as online on CumInCAD database.

Conference

eCAADe 2021 has been planned as a hybrid conference, hosted by the Faculty of Technical Sciences from 8-10th September 2021. Sessions are organized to frame the different specific session topics and to adapt to hybrid event organization. The four Keynotes were invited to provide specific, but complementary, visions addressing the spirit and theme of the event.

- Branko Kolarević, Dean and Professor Hillier College of Architecture and Design New Jersey Institute of Technology (NJIT)
- Ammar Mirjan, Gramazio Kohler Research, Professorship for Architecture und Digital Fabrication, ETH Zurich
- Hans Jakob Wagner, Research Associate at the ICD University of Stuttgart
- Ivan Tomović, Associate partner, project director and executive at Werner Sobek AG, Stuttgart, Germany

Professor Milena Stavrić from TU Graz, was asked to chair a round table on the topical area "configurable design": Architecture between digital and physical worlds in order to provide a particular opportunity for collective conversation. Along with the Conference sessions four online and six on-site workshops were organized bringing the opportunity to share practical development experiences.

eCAADe 2021 conference chairs
Vesna Stojaković & Bojan Tepavčević

ACKNOWLEDGEMENTS

First and foremost, we want to express our gratitude to all of the authors whose papers are included in the present proceedings, as well as the chairs of the sessions and roundtables, technical workshop tutors, the PhD workshop organizers and the keynote speakers, whose contributions can be regarded critical to the success of this conference. We are also grateful to the international Scientific Committee who evaluated 334 extended abstracts and 130 completed papers. Only because of eCAADe's access to the OpenConf System and the continuous support of Gabriel Wurzer and Martin Winchester was such a difficult task completed.

Organizing a hybrid eCAADe conference would not have been possible without the commitment of the eCAADe president Birgul Çolakoglu, council and committee members who kindly shared with us their experience and recommendations. It's never enough to express our special gratitude to Joachim Kieferle and Bob Martens who have always gave us decisive support and valuable suggestions. We would also like to thank Liss C. Werner, Armando Trento, Antonio Fioravanti and Jose Pedro Sousa who helped us by sharing experiences and valuable information regarding the organization of previous eCAADe conferences.

At the Faculty of Technical Sciences, we are thankful to Rade Doroslovački, the Dean of the Faculty and Jelena Atanacković Jeličić, the Head of Department of Architecture, who supported hosting the event from the beginning. We also want to express our gratitude to our local organizational team Marko Jovanović, Marko Vučić, Dimitrije Nikolić, Ivana Bajšanski, Jelena Kićanović and Miloš Obradović for their dedicated collaboration. We also wish to thank Igor Zečević and Rade Lučić from the IT center and other staff at Faculty of Technical Sciences.

Finally, we would like to thank our Silver sponsor - Bentley, and our Bronze sponsor - ABB for their support and our host Faculty of Technical Sciences, University of Novi Sad

Novi Sad, September 2021
Vesna Stojaković and Bojan Tepavčević *eCAADe 2021 Conference chairs*

SCIENTIFIC COMMITTEE

Achten Henri
Czech Technical University in Prague, Czechia
Agkathidis Asterios
University of Liverpool, United Kingdom
Aguiar Rita
Instituto Superior Técnico, Universidade de Lisboa, Portugal
Alaçam Sema
Faculty of Architecture, Turkey
Amorim Arivaldo
Federal University of Bahia, Brazil
Asanowicz Aleksander
Bialystok University of Technology, Poland
Atanackovic Jelicic Jelena
Faculty of Technical Sciences, Serbia
Azari Rahman
Pennsylvania State University, United States
Barczik Günter
Department Digital Design University of Applied Sciences Erfurt. Faculty of Architecture, Germany
Bernal Marcelo
Perkins&Will, United States
Bhatt Anand
ABA-NET/Architexturez Imprints, India
Bourdakis Vassilis
University of Thessaly, Greece
Braida Frederico
Federal University of Juiz de Fora (UFJF)/ Federal University of Technology - Paraná (UTFPR), Brazil
Braumann Johannes
UfG Linz / Robots in Architecture, Austria
Brown Andre
Victoria University Wellington, New Zealand
Cagdas Gulen
Istanbul Technical University, Turkey
Capone Mara
University of Naples Federico II, Italy
Cardoso Daniel
Federal University of Ceará, Brazil
Carl Timo
FRA-UAS, Germany
Carmo Pena Martinez Andressa
Universidade Federal de Viçosa, Brazil
Chronis Angelos
Austrian Institute of Technology, Austria
Colakoglu Birgul
ITU, Turkey
Coutinho Quaresma Filipe
DAU-ULHT, Portugal
De Luca Francesco
Tallinn University of Technology, Estonia
Dembski Fabian
High-Performance Computing Center Stuttgart, Germany
Devetaković Mirjana
University of Belgrade, Facuty of Architecture, Serbia
Di Mascio Danilo
The University of Huddersfield, United Kingdom
Dokonal Wolfgang
Graz University of technology, Austria
Dounas Theodoros
Robert Gordon University, Greece
Dragović Magdalena
Faculty of Civil Engineering, University of Belgrade, Serbia
Duarte Jose
Penn State University, United States

Eloy Sara
Instituto Universitário de Lisboa (ISCTE-IUL), ISTAR-IUL, Portugal
Erhan Halil
Simon Fraser University, Canada
Estévez Alberto T.
iBAG-UIC Barcelona, Spain
Figueiredo Bruno
University of Minho; Lab2PT, Portugal
Fioravanti Antonio
Sapienza University of Rome, Italy
Florio Wilson
Mackenzie University, Brazil
Fukuda Tomohiro
Osaka University, Japan
GARCIA ALVARADO RODRIGO
UBB, Chile
Gero John
UNCC, United States
Geyer Philipp
TU Berlin, Germany
Ghandi Mona
Washington State University, United States
Gomez Paula
Georgia Tech, United States
Gonenc Sorguc arzu
METU, Turkey
Gül Leman Figen
ITU, Turkey
Gursoy Benay
Pennsylvania State University, United States
Güzelci Orkan Zeynel
University of Porto, Portugal
Ham Jeremy
SurfCoast Architecture, Australia
Hernández Silvia Patricia
FAUD. UNC, Argentina
Herneoja Aulikki
University of Oulu, Oulu School of Architecture, Finland
Herrera Pablo C
Universidad Peruana de Ciencias Aplicadas, Peru
Hudert Markus
Aarhus University, Denmark
Jovanovic Marko
Faculty of Technical Sciences, Serbia
Jović Biljana
University of Belgrade, Faculty of Forestry, Department of Landscape Architecture and Horticulture, Serbia
Jowers Iestyn
The Open University, United Kingdom
Jutraz Anja
National Institute of Public Health, Slovenia
Juvancic Matevz
University of Ljubljana, Faculty of Architecture, Slovenia
Kepczynska-Walczak Anetta
Lodz University of Technology, Poland
Kieferle Joachim
Hochschule RheinMain, Germany
Kilian Axel
MIT, United States
Klinc Robert
University of Ljubljana, Faculty of Civil and Geodetic Engineering, Slovenia
Kocaturk Tuba
Deakin University | School of Architecture & Built Enviornment, Australia
Koch Volker
Karlsruhe Institute of Technology, Germany
Koering Dietmar
Arphneotype, Germany

Kontovourkis Odysseas
University of Cyprus, Cyprus
Kotnik Toni
Aalto University, Finland
Krasić Sonja
Faculty of Civil Engineering and architecture, university of Niš, Serbia
Langarica Rodrigo
Universidad Anáhuac Querétaro, Mexico
Lastra Alberto
University of Alcala, Spain
Lazić Marko
Fakultet tehničkih nauka, Serbia
Lee Hyunsoo
Yonsei University, South Korea
Leitao Carla
Rensselaer Polytechnic Institute, United States
Leitão António
Instituto Superior Tecnico, Portugal
Liapi Katherine
University of Patras, Greece
Ligler Heather
Pennsylvania State University, United States
Lima Fernando
Universidade Federal de Juiz de Fora, Brazil
Lombardi Davide
Xi'an Jiaotong - Liverpool University, China
Lorenz Wolfgang
TU Vienna, Austria
Marcus Adam
California College of the Arts, United States
Markovic Sladjana
Ministry of Education, Science and Technological Development, Republic of Serbia, Serbia
Martens Bob
TU Wien, Austria
Medić Saša
Faculty of Technical Sciences, University of Novi Sad, Serbia
Medjdoub Benachir
Nottingham Trent University, United Kingdom
Meneses-Carlos Fernando
Escuela Radical, Mexico
Meyboom AnnaLisa
School of Architecture & Landscape Architecture, Canada
Mostafavi Sina
TU Delft & Dessau Institute of Architecture, Netherlands
Mullins Michael
Aalborg University, Denmark
Mussi Andréa
IMED, Brazil
Naboni Roberto
CREATE - University of Southern Denmark, Denmark
Nejur Andrei
Université de Montréal, Canada
Newton David
University of Nebraska-Lincoln, United States
Nikolic Dimitrije
Faculty of Technical Sciences, University of Novi Sad, Serbia
Nováková Kateřina
Faculty of architecture CTU Prague, Czechia
Obradovic Ratko
Faculty of Technical Sciences, Serbia

Obradović Marija
University of Belgrade, Serbia
Oungrinis Konstantinos-Alketas
Technical University of Crete, Greece
Pak Burak
KU Leuven (University of Leuven), Belgium
Paraizo Rodrigo
PROURB/FAU/UFRJ, Brazil
Park Hyoung-June
School of Architecture, University of Hawaii at Manoa, United States
Parthenios Panagiotis
Technical University of Crete, Greece
Pektaş Şule Taşlı
Baskent University, Turkey
Pellitteri Giuseppe
Università di Palermo, Dipartimento di Architettura, Italy
Pratschke Anja
University of São Paulo, Brazil
Rakovic Mirko
FTN, Serbia
Romão Luís
School of Architecture, University of Lisbon, Portugal
Rust Romana
ETH Zurich, Switzerland
Sárközi Réka
University of Pécs, Hungary
Savić Srđan
Faculty of Technical Sciences, University of Novi Sad, Serbia
Schnabel Marc Aurel
Faculty of Architecture & Design Innovation, New Zealand
Schneider Sven
Germany
Sedrez Maycon
University of Nottingham Ningbo China, China
Sidjanin Predrag
University EDUCONS, Faculty of Digital Production, Serbia
Simeone Davide
Webuild, Italy
Sopher Hadas
CRENAU/AAU - UMR_CNRS 1563 - ENSA Nantes, France
Sousa Jose Pedro
University of Porto, Faculty of Architecture + DFL/CEAU, Portugal
Soza Pedro
Universidad de Chile, Chile
Stavric Milena
Graz University of Technology, Austria
Stojakovic Vesna
Faculty of Techical Sciences, Serbia
Stojanovic Djordje
University of Melbourne, Australia
Stouffs Rudi
National University of Singapore, Singapore
Stulic Radovan
Faculty of Technical Sciences, Serbia
Symeonidou Ioanna
Department of Architecture, University of Thessaly, Greece
Tepavčević Bojan
University of Novi Sad, Faculty of Technical Sciences, Department of Architecture, Serbia
Trento Armando
BIMTEGRA S.r.l., Italy
Veloso Pedro
Carnegie Mellon University, United States
Vermillion Joshua
University of Nevada Las Vegas, United States

Vizioli Simone
Instituto de Arquitetura e Urbanismo da Universidade de São Paulo, Brazil
Vučić Marko
Faculty of Technical Sciences, University of Novi Sad, Serbia
Weissenböck Renate
Graz University of Technology, Austria
Wiltsche Albert
Graz University of Technology, Austria
Wurzer Gabriel
TU Wien, Austria
Yazar Tuğrul
İstanbul Bilgi University, Turkey
Yazıcı Sevil
Istanbul Technical University, Turkey
Zavoleas Yannis
University of Ioannina, Greece
Zboinska Malgorzata
Chalmers tekniska högskola AB, Sweden
Zupančič Tadeja
University of Ljubljana, Faculty of Architecture, Slovenia

eCAADe

www.ecaade.org

eCAADe (Education and Research in Computer Aided Architectural Design in Europe) is a non-profit making association of institutions and individuals with a common interest in promoting good practice and sharing information to the use of computers in education and research in architecture and related professions. The organization was founded in 1983, and organizes an annual conference, which is hosted by a different member University each year.

CumInCAD

papers.cumincad.org/

CumInCAD is a valuable resource for researchers, educators and others in the field. eCAADe has also collaborated with sibling associations to create the International Journal of Architectural Computing (IJAC).

Sibling Associations

ACADIA
CAADRIA
SIGradi
ASCAAD
CAAD Futures

KEYNOTE SPEAKERS

Branko Kolarević

Dean and Professor, Hillier College of Architecture and Design, New Jersey Institute of Technology (NJIT)

Branko Kolarevic is Dean of the Hillier College of Architecture and Design at NJIT in Newark. He has taught architecture at several universities in North America and Asia and has lectured worldwide on the use of digital technologies in design and production. He has authored, edited or co-edited several books, including "Mass Customization and Design Democratization" (with Jose Duarte), "Building Dynamics: Exploring Architecture of Change" (with Vera Parlac), "Manufacturing Material Effects" (with Kevin Klinger), "Performative Architecture" (with Ali Malkawi) and "Architecture in the Digital Age." He was elected and served as president of several organizations: Association of Collegiate Schools of Architecture (ACSA), Canadian Architectural Certification Board (CACB), and Association for Computer Aided Design in Architecture (ACADIA). He is a recipient of the ACADIA Award for Innovative Research in 2007 and ACADIA Society Award of Excellence in 2015. He holds doctoral and master's degrees in design from Harvard University and a diploma engineer in architecture degree from the University of Belgrade.

Keynote: Mass Customization and Design Democratization

Thanks to parametric design and digital fabrication it is now possible to mass-produce non-standard, lightly differentiated products, from shoes and tableware to furniture and even houses. Variety no longer compromises the efficiency and economy of production. Furthermore, parametric definitions of products' geometry are made accessible via interactive websites to masses, who could then design their own, unique versions of the product. Such "democratization" of design – through mass-customization – raises many interesting questions such as the authorship of design and the functional and aesthetic quality of products (shoes, tableware, furniture, houses...) designed by non-designers. illustrated with numerous examples, this lecture explores social, cultural and design implications of this emerging "design democracy", starting with its technological origins.

Ammar Mirjan

Professorship for Architecture und Digital Fabrication. Gramazio Kohler Research, ETH Zurich

Ammar Mirjan is an architect and a researcher with a background in automation engineering. He received a B.A. degree in Architecture from the Bern University of Applied Sciences and a M.Arch. degree from the Bartlett School of Architecture, University College London. He has worked for architectural offices in New York, Tokyo and London. His particular interest in the relationship between designing and making with robotic systems motivated him to join the professorship of Architecture and Digital Fabrication (Prof. Fabio Gramazio, Prof. Matthias Kohler) at ETH Zurich in 2011. Between 2013 and 2016 he led the research project Aerial Construction and completed his PhD on architectural fabrication processes with flying robots in 2016. His articles have been published in AD, GAM, Springer, gta Verlag and MIT Press, and he has been engaged in various exhibition and installation projects. More recently, Ammar Mirjan focuses on the industrial implementation of Mesh Mould, an innovative technology that combines formwork and reinforcement into a robotically fabricated construction system.

Keynote: Architecture in the Age of Sensory Construction Machines

Recent developments in sensing, computation, and control have led to the creation of new robotic construction systems that have profoundly different capabilities than their human operated predecessors. Such machines depend on the real time gathering of information about their environment, making them not only aware of their own position in space, but also of the forces acting on its joints and its construction tools while physically interacting with material. Therefore, one can understand such a machine as not being detached from its surroundings, like their robotic predecessors, but embedded in it and potentially become part of it. What does the advent of such sensory construction machines mean for the making of architecture, and will it lead to a change the design practice?

Hans Jakob Wagner

Research Associate, Institute for Computational Design and Construction (ICD), University of Stuttgart

Hans Jakob Wagner is a design research technologist working at the intersection of computational design methods, robotic construction processes and advanced wood building systems. As a research associate and PhD candidate at the ICD – University of Stuttgart, he played a key role in award winning projects such as the BUGA Wood Pavilion and the ITECH Research Pavilion 2016-17. He graduated with distinction from the ITECH Master Program in 2017 after receiving a BSc in Architecture at Vienna University of Technology and working at leading architectural firms in Vienna and Paris. He published, taught and presented internationally and is a peer-reviewer for both Automation in Construction and Construction Robotics Journals.

Keynote: Platform Pluralism: Project-Based Robotic Timber Construction

Computational design and robotic fabrication allow a fundamental reinterpretation of structural tectonics in timber construction. As recent demonstrators such as the BUGA Wood Pavilion 2019 show, intricately differentiated, innovative wood structures can be designed and built cost effectively through the integrative use of digital design and manufacturing processes. This allows for highly material-efficient load-bearing structures and an expressive reinterpretation of performance-oriented sustainable building design. Given these promising results, the question of how these technologies can be embedded within a dynamic building culture and agile construction industry become increasingly important to address. With project-based robotic timber construction an organizational framework is introduced that envisions the dynamic production management of unique architectural artefacts and the continuous integrative co-evolution of building- and automation systems through constant reconfiguration of robotic manufacturing platforms. The framework intends to offer a general roadmap towards the sustainable integration of computation and automation into a socially inclusive and constantly reconfigurable building culture through a radical expansion of the interdisciplinary architectural design research agenda.

Ivan Tomović

Associate partner, project director and executive at Werner Sobek AG, Stuttgart, Germany

Ivan Tomovic acquired his diploma in structural engineering at the University of Belgrade, Serbia. After attending the post-diploma studies and working on several projects and competitions in Serbia, Montenegro and Russia, he joined Werner Sobek in 2007, where he worked his path from a project engineer to a partner and a project director. He is also the general manager of

Werner Sobek Moscow branch, leading there some of the largest projects in company's portfolio and managing multidisciplinary design teams of up to 100 architects, engineers and consultants. Besides project work, he is engaged in teaching and research activities at the Moscow Architectural School and at the Institute for Lightweight Structures and Conceptual Design (ILEK) at the University of Stuttgart.

Keynote: Towards a new Building Environment Through Lightweight and Adaptivity

20th century has brought an extensive use of the artificial construction materials on affordable costs. Global mass construction mostly solved the housing and transportation problem for the rapidly increasing world population, but it quickly began to show its dark sides. Towards the turn of the century, it became clear that the life cycle of many of those buildings is coming to an end, producing a large quantity of non-recyclable waste. More and more researchers started to turn attention on the fact that the construction industry became the largest producer of the CO2 and one of the most insatiable energy consumers, thus making a tremendous contribution to the climate and environmental deterioration. Beginning of the 21st century explicitly shows that we must change the way we build – by developing new materials and improving the traditional ones, while using the available digital tools to create sustainable, effective and clean construction technologies. This is the main field of research at ILEK and the permanent leitmotif of Werner Sobek projects and design philosophy.

ROUND TABLE CHAIR

Milena Stavrić

Professorship for Architecture , Graz University of Technology

Milena Stavrić completed the architectural study and since 2004, she has been working at the Institute of Architecture and Media at TU Graz. She was a visiting scholar at Harvard University joining MaP+S group. She lectured at many Universities like Vienna, Mexico City, Istanbul, Belgrade, Hamburg, Novi Sad, Banja Luka. The focus of her work is on architectural geometry, new materials, digital methods and presentation, robotic in architecture, parametrical modeling and digital fabrication.

Round Table Topic:
Configurable design: architecture between digital and physical worlds

TECHNICAL ONLINE WORKSHOPS

GIS TO GRASSHOPPER

Djordje Spasić (Staticus Austria GmbH)

Workshop Description

Workshop will provide an insight into basics of Gismo - a free and open-source GIS plugin for Grasshopper which enables conversion of vector and raster GIS data to AEC data. Students will learn how to generate 3D building, terrain, roads, greenery data based on location coordinates or address. Such 3D geometry along with its metadata, will then be used to perform different analysis types, as amenities search, terrain, solar shading analysis etc. A novel approach of urban greenery evaluation will also be presented.

Biography

Djordje Spasić is an architect with experience from Serbia, Austria and The Netherlands. Ladybug Tools plugin developer. Mainly worked on the modeling of thermal comfort, mechanical comfort, solar hot water systems and photovoltaics. Creator of Gismo - Grasshopper plugin for GIS environmental analysis. Djordje is an avid grasshopper3d.com and Rhino3d forum aide.

URBAN BEAUTY: QUANTIFYING AND PREDICTING CROWD-SOURCED SUBJECTIVE EVALUATION USING MACHINE VISION

Joy Mondal (WEsearch lab)

Workshop Description

Beauty of cityscapes has long been studied anecdotally through accounts of novels and historical notes; and manually through analysis of scale, order, rigidity, etc. This 2-day workshop is designed to be an introduction to the

use of machine vision and machine learning to interrogate how urban fabric explicitly affects the perception of beauty, and in the process, address the age-old question of "How to quantify subjective spatial experience?"
Machine vision algorithm (such as semantic segmentation) will be used to quantify urban features (e.g., road, people, trees, vehicles, sky, building, signage, etc.) of photographs of cityscapes. Subsequently, participants will rate the photographs. The corresponding quantification of the urban features and beauty scores will be analysed to extract spatial beauty principles. Finally, using the same dataset, a neural network will be trained to predict the perceived beauty of new cityscapes. Google Colab shall be used for semantic segmentation and training neural network

Biography

Joy Mondal leads WEsearch lab which offers design computation consultancy to architecture practices in South-east Asia. His research focuses on automating design workflows and predicting subjective spatial assessment with the use of AI. He has released Grasshopper plugins to automate column-beam placement (Eelish) and to generate Piet Mondrian inspired 3D massing (Chingree). Joy is a TEDx fellow, presenting ways of democratising architecture for everyone by using graph theory and shape grammar to automate residential design generation, thereby making design service more affordable. He has tutored multiple international workshops including at Digital FUTURES, ASCAAD 2021, CAADRIA 2021 and SimAUD 2021.

WOODEN KERF-BENT DEVELOPABLE STRIPS

Marko Jovanovic (University of Novi sad)

Workshop Description

The general scope of the research entails wood bending strategies i.e. the use of kerf bending for flexible wood sheet shaping. The main objective of the workshop is to explore additional possibilities pertaining to the application of kerfs in wood bending strategies. Additional possibilities entail the parametrization of the kerf pattern (the size, density and length of the cuts), bending analysis, and its implementation in a pavilion design. Since the elements can be analyzed best through trial and error, the main contribution is seen through data acquisition and physical prototype analysis.

Biographies

Marko Jovanovic is an Assistant Professor at the Faculty of Technical Sciences in Novi Sad. He has been a part of the digital design implementation in architecture through his engagement with the 2016 RiS eCAADe Workshop including performative design and robotic fabrication. The same year, as a member of the Digital Design Center, he participated in the 2016 European Researcher's Night with a pavilion design project including similar fields of interest. Another portrail of the application of digital tools in architectural design is seen during the 2018 Workshop as part of the MoNGeometrija conference. He has one the best application and best student paper award at the RAAD conference for his work including robotic fabrication in architectural design.

Stefan Pejic hold a bachelor's degree in architecture with a keen interesting in scale model fabrication. Also, he is a liason for all matters pertaining to the student-teacher relationship at the Faculty of technical sciences, acting as the president for architecture. He has been a participant of many workshop that include digital design techniques such as "Designing emergency shelters" in Novi Sad and "Shell Puzzle-Parametric Modeling and Digital Production" in Zagreb. He has exhbited his work at the "25 years of continuity for Djordje Tabakovic", as well as the "Laboratory of space 2.0". Currently, he is a student of a specialized master course dealing with digital techniques, design and production in architecture with an interest in kerf-bending.

URBAN AGGREGATOR - THE DISCRETE BATTLE BETWEEN AGGREGATION SYSTEMS FOR MEANINGFUL URBAN SPACES

Zvonko Vugreshek (TU Berlin – CyphyLab)

Workshop Description

The interest comes from putting all discrete aggregation systems to an architectural challenge one against another for an evaluation of the strengths and weaknesses they provide given a standardized architectural or urban design task. The point is not to determine the ultimate best method, as that cannot be evaluated so easily and often it is personal/biased. Continuing from the last point, we are going to limit the selection to 3 systems: Cellular Automata (CA), Wave Function Collapse (WFC) and Graph-Grammar Aggregations (GGA). These systems, as said before, would be put in a sandbox scenario to see their unique properties and characteristics. That could involve various spatial organization problems regarding large-scale urban design but also floor plan layout.

Biography

Zvonko Vugreshek went through his entire education in Macedonia from where he left for Denmark after becoming a Master of Architecture to seek for better job opportunities regarding implementation of new workflows and techniques regarding the general production process in the AEC. Then moved to Germany and switched to Academia after working at large corporations to have more freedom to experiment with the state-of-the-art in optimization, automation and digital fabrication.

AGILE PERFORMANCE-BASED BUILDING DESIGN OPTIMIZATION AND EXPLORATION

Likai Wang (Nanjing University)

Workshop description

For performance-based design, computational design optimization has been widely applied to detailed design improvement. However, it is still rare and challenging to apply it to abstract design idea exploration. For bridging this gap, this workshop introduces a new design tool for optimization-based building design exploration, called EvoMass. EvoMass is an intelligent building massing generation and optimization tool in Rhino-Grasshopper, aiming to offer designers an efficient way to obtain intriguing but also practical building configurations coupling with various building performance objectives at an abstract level. Along with producing high-performing design solutions, EvoMass also provides designers with insights into the performance implications associated with building geometry, which enables them to achieve a performance-informed and -inspired design. In this workshop, participants will learn the operation for design generation and optimization of EvoMass and how it can be applied to building design tasks with challenging performance and design objectives.

Biography

Likai Wang is a Postdoctoral research fellow at the School of Architecture and Urban Planning in Nanjing University (China) and the developer of EvoMass. His research focuses on the application of computational design optimization to performance-based building design, with a special emphasis on parametric design generation and evolutionary design optimization. He has extensive experience in developing generative design algorithms and conducting computational design optimization for various performance-based building design tasks including wind flow, daylighting, and solar radiation. In addition, he teaches and instructs students in the design studio and workshops related to computational design and performance-based design optimization.

COLLABORATIVE AI AGENTS

Chien-hua Huang (China Academy of Art)

Workshop Description

This workshop explores the intersection of game and AI as a novel way to approach architectural participatory generative design. The recent rapid advancement of machine learning and AI in architectural industries is operating with limitation to allow a wider audience or human perception. As architects and designers, allowing a wider spectrum of evaluation will be vital in the design process. Inspired by machine learning (ML) application in Unity3D as game design elements, there are potentials to promote the active participation of architects, artists and even the public in the design generation processes by gamification. In the workshop, participants will work with a given set of reinforcement-learning-based frameworks and package in Unity3D to explore design ideas and potentials of perception-aware human-machine interaction. Eventually, we will approach collective layers of design generation through human and ai collaboration.

Biography

Chien-hua Huang is an architecture computational designer and design researcher based in Vienna, Taipei and Shanghai. His current research focuses on AI-driven material design, machine learning, and participatory approaches in design and construction. He received a master degree of architecture with distinction at Greg Lynn Studio at the University of Applied Arts in Vienna with thesis on machine-learning-driven searching design tool to achieve circular strategy. He is currently teaching at Institute of Intelligence & Systematics, School of Innovation and Design, China Academy of Art, China.

FREEFORMING CORAL-LIKE PLANAR 3D PRINTS

Marko Vučić (University of Novi Sad)

Workshop Description

The main objective of this workshop is to explore the possibility of using desktop 3D printers for fabrication of large scale objects by printing smaller patches. We intend to bend planar 3D printed patches with heat impact in order to reduce 3D printing support consumption. Later the patches will be connected together and form a doubly curved surface. For easier heat forming, coral-like pattern will be used since it creates cuts in different directions which ease double curved bending. The contribution is seen in fabrication of physical prototypes which show the possibility of approximating large scale freeform surfaces out of 2D planar printed patches.

Biography

Marko Vučić is a teaching assistant at the University of Novi Sad, Department of Architecture, Faculty of Technical Sciences. He is a PhD student of Architecture and he holds a Master degree in Architecture. His interests are related to descriptive geometry, graphics, CAD/CAM and their application in architecture and design.

(DESIGN) SMART CONTRACTS (FOR CONFIGURABLE DESIGN)

Theo Dounas (Robert Gordon University), Wassim Jabi (Welsh School of Architecture)

Workshop Description

The scope of the workshop is to introduce the Ethereum Blockchain and Solidity smart contracts as a vehicle for governing, and con-figuring, architectural design. During the two days participants will be introduced to blockchain primitives and learn to develop smart contracts in solidity and their connectors in python and javascript via a hands-on approach. The first day will be devoted to developing the participants' knowledge and as an introduction to the code, while the second day participants will design and develop their own solutions. Learning to use open source tools such as Blender and Topologic.app will be part of the workshop as well. Participants will learn how to set up their own decentralised autonomous organisations to design, develop Dynamic Non Fungible Tokens(NFTs) as autonomous digital twins, connect their design tools with supply chain information or create incentivised mechanisms for architects to optimize their designs.

Biographies

Dr Theo Dounas is an architect and the learning excellence leader at the Scott Sutherland School of Architecture and Built Environment at Robert Gordon University. His research expertise encompasses blockchain, generative and parametric systems with a tight orchestration between design and fabrication. He is currently directing www.archchain.cc, a project that seeks to establish a decentralized Building Information Modeling toolset and mechanisms for the AEC industry.

Dr Wassim Jabi is a Reader at Welsh School of Architecture. Dr. Jabi has published widely on topics ranging from parametric and generative design to the role of light in architecture and building performance simulation. His current research is at the intersection of parametric design, the representation of space, building performance simulation, and robotic fabrication in architecture.

REALTIME RENDERING OF ARCHITECTURE SPACES WITH UNREAL ENGINE 4

Nemanja Jaćimovski (Case-3D)

Workshop description

Unreal Engine 4 workshop for beginners. Working on a pre-made scene using UE4. Focus of the workshop is to make realistic presentations by working on lights, materials and blueprint interactions. Unreal engine gives opportunity to create interactive presentations unlike traditional still renderings. The idea is to educate students to the possibility of using game engines for real time architectural presentation.

Biography

Nemanja Jaćimovski is a project lead in the R&D team working closely with programmers and the art team to develop new products and improve existing ones. As a lead he has learned to set priorities, recognize and solve problems during projects. Also, he always searches for ways to improve workflows and build new tools and scripts. As an architect by profession he has a deep understanding in spatial relations and the ways they can affect the user experience, especially in VR.

WILD STORIES

Erzë Dinarama (Polytechnic University of Milan), Iacopo Neri (IAAC, Institute for Advanced Architecture of Catalonia)

Workshop description

Vjosa River is the largest wild river in Europe. Recently, local and global activists have gathered to ensure that the river keeps running wild. The workshop focuses on the application of advanced computational tools for designers to explore and represent the agency of rivers. The workshop on the one hand aims at exploring how designers can learn from and communicate with the environment by analyzing scientific data coming from ecology, and work in a more-than-human perspective. On the other hand, how this knowledge can be represented and made accessible to the activists and the general public so that the river gains more voice. The aim of the workshop is to strengthen designers' skills to work in a systematic computational workflow related to ecology, from raw data to knowledge, to environmental stories and visualizations.

Participants will learn how to import and work with geospatial data in Rhinoceros 3D, in a programmable and open-ended manner thanks to its visual scripting addon Grasshopper 3D. The output will be a set of cartographic representations that are based on geospatial data and critical thinking.

Biography

Erzë Dinarama and Iacopo Neri are interdisciplinary designers who work at the intersection between architecture, landscape urbanism, and computational design. Erzë and Iacopo use ecology and spatial data as drivers for their projects.

Erzë has practiced in Italy, Kosovo, Germany, and Austria, and has also been involved in teaching activities at the Polytechnic University of Milan, Turin, Piacenza, and at the School of Design in Milan. Additionally, she has been an invited critic at Pratt Institute, Rice University, and IAAC - Institute for Advanced Architecture of Catalonia. Erzë has exhibited at Pecci Museum in Prato and at the Landscape Festival Prague and has been published at the ACADIA conference.
Erzë currently teaches at the Polytechnic University of Milan and Polytechnic University of Turin and works at Carlo Ratti Associati.

Iacopo has been involved in teaching activities at the University of Florence, The Polytechnic University of Milan, and at IAAC - Institute for Advanced Architecture of Catalonia, where he is currently faculty of computational design and part of the Advanced Architectural Group's Computational Design Research Team.
Additionally, Iacopo has been faculty for workshops and lecturer in several international universities among which the New York Institute of Technology and the Ecole des Ponts - ParisTech.

Contents

Agent-based modeling and machine learning in design

Intensive Differences in Spatial Design

Reversing form-finding

Christina Doumpioti[1], *Jeffrey Huang*[2]
[1,2]*EPFL - École Polytechnique Fédérale de Lausanne*
[1,2]*{christina.doumpioti|jeffrey.huang}@epfl.ch*

Drawing from the philosophy of science, `intensive' qualities define differences in degree instead of `extensive' ones that define additive quantities. More relevant to architecture, intensive differences can define transient boundaries such as warmness and coolness, dryness and moisture, light and shadow, or visual accessibility, to name a few.The question that serves as a starting point of this study is whether the attributes mentioned above can become form-giving agents during the design process and, therefore, whether they become fundamental parameters for the conceptualization and configuration of extensive spatial qualities. This question is explored using Generative Adversarial Networks and image-to-image translation. The dataset consists of two types of images; one consists of spatial configurations representing extensive attributes. The second set depicts intensive characteristics of visual accessibility. The study proposes a conceptual model and workflow that reverses form-finding and enables the design of environments through the specification of desired intensive attributes. Furthermore, it discusses the advantage of working with this method in search of architectural environments with embedded spatial experiences.

Keywords: *Intensive Differences, Form-Finding, Isovist Simulation, conditional Generative Adversarial Networks (cGAN)*

INTRODUCTION

Intensive and extensive differences

Intensive and extensive differences create a complementary relationship. DeLanda (2005) has expressed this duality in the built environment as intensive and extensive space. While the former describes additive quantities such as volume, area, or length, the latter describes quantities that cannot be divided or transformed without changing in nature, such as temperature, speed. In architecture, similar distinctions have been described as 'hardware' and 'software' [1], with the former representing the static elements of architecture such as walls, roofs, and floors, and the latter describing 'soft' and temporary factors such as sounds, smells, temperatures, or radio waves.

However, the enhancement of the 'software' necessitates an understanding of the effect of what is geometrically static as architecture and environment are -always- produced simultaneously (Gissen 2009); by altering the form and arrangement, we simultaneously change the intensive qualities of the environment we create.

Intensive conceptualization in Architecture: from the atmospheric to the performative

The research builds on architecture theories and practices that attempt to establish an epistemology of intensive, non-visible, immaterial, but perceptive qualities within the core of architectural design thinking and making.

They do so by engaging with concepts such as climate-based and environmental design sensibilities, vernacular architecture, thermodynamic architecture (Abalos 2015; Garcia-German 2017), performance-oriented architecture (Hensel 2013), meteorologic architecture (Rahm), material energies (Lally 2009 and 2014), field conditions (Banham; Allen), heterogeneous space (Hensel et al. 2009) and atmospheres (Wigley 1998; Böhme 1993; Pallasmaa 2014). The spectrum spans from attempts to enhance performance, such as energy usage and thermal comfort (performative objective), to attempts that enrich sentient experiences of spaces (sentient purpose).

Vernacular architecture has served as an example in constant exchange with its context: air flows, radiation, light, and shadow, are external environmental -and intensive- conditions that vernacular architecture responded to through local material usage, suitable morphology, and urban patterns. From desert climates to alpine contexts, vernacular incorporated microclimatic phenomena as part of local architecture design, consequently modulating activities and events of the local life and social interactions. Moreover, intensive attributes are at the forefront of architectural research on digital simulation and performance-driven environmental optimization within sustainable design strategies in architecture and urban design. Parametric simulations provide immediate feedback on performance objectives, generating variant design outcomes with embedded climatic sensibility.

On the other end of the spectrum, architectural discourse is revolving around the topic of designing 'an architecture of atmospheres' (Wigley 1998); the affective and sensorial experience of space or intervention; the indeterminant quality or spatial 'aura' radiating from objects and environments and perceived by subjects (Böhme 1993). Architects who put atmospheric parameters in the spotlight argue on the importance of architects having 'multisensorial and empathic imagination' as well as the capability to 'feel and imagine the building and its countless relationships' (Pallasmaa 2014).

In-between performative and sentient

For years, Philippe Rahm has exhibited work that communicates this idea of an architecture seamlessly related to the microclimate. His projects often emerge out of heat transfer properties, leading to unusual programmatic distributions, as is the case with the most recent Jade Eco Park project. Likewise, Sean Lally (2009; 2014) regards architecture as a reinvention of the site itself and sees an opportunity to shape energy systems and intensify them as distinct ecosystems. Lally believes that environmental energies can become the materials used to build architecture and calls them 'material energies.' Material energies can lead to new spatial typologies and influence new social experiences (Lally 2014, 201-224). Similar notions can be identified in Banham's writing when comparing structural to power-operated environmental management; according to the author, the latter suggests the spatial experience of vague and non-regular boundaries; zones of intensities (Banham 1984).

IMAGE-TO-IMAGE TRANSLATION

Similar to this study's question, ML Benedikt (1979), a pioneer of isovist research, has inquired whether isovist fields already contain the environment and, therefore, whether one can design environments 'not by the initial specification of real surfaces but by specification of the desired (potential) experience-in-space.'

The hypothesis we formulate that intensive differences can be translated to spatial configurations is tested by setting up a workflow that utilizes Generative Adversarial Networks (GANs), a class of machine learning that enables data generation by using two sets of separate neural networks; the generator and the discriminator. The generator's goal is to create a non-existing image close enough to the actual image from the training set. The discriminator's goal is to classify whether an image is 'fake' (created from the generator) or 'real' (from the training set).

The pix2pix model of image-to-image translation employed here was first introduced by Isola et al. (2017). Examples vary from satellite images turned to map views, edge drawings to colorful objects, and daytime images turned to night-time ones. Using pairs of images (Input and Target), it capitalizes on the capacity of the model to translate an image from one domain to another and vice versa. Making back the connection to Benedikt's aspiration, if the two datasets represent a) 'surfaces' and b) 'experiences' respectively, one can go from A to B or from B to A. The creation of a dataset, therefore, is one of the most critical things.

Relevant research in Architecture

Generative Adversarial Networks and image-to-image translation have been applied in various case studies in the architectural research domain, especially for floor plan explorations. For example, Huang and Zheng (2018) explored its potential for architectural plan recognition and generation based on colored labeled images of the same plans. Similarly, Chaillou [2] investigated the possibility of establishing an apartment building generation pipeline by creating a sequential process from footprint massing to program repartition, furniture layout and ultimately proposing a user interface for interaction. Equally influential have been previous research by Galanos et al. (2019) and Duering et al. (2020), who assessed the potential of Deep Learning (DL) in Computational Environmental Design (CED) workflows to establish microclimatic performance feedback during the early stages of urban design projects. The current study utilizes a related pipeline of exploration to the examples above, differentiating in the dataset preparation and the goal of reverse-engineering the process by going from analysis to formation.

The generation of urban layouts from visuospatial properties has been attempted (Schneider and Koenig 2012) using multi-objective optimization. Compared to the approach explored here, evolutionary optimization is more efficient due to a numerically based association of parameters (contrasted to the visual-based explored here) and applying a fitness function for extracting optimum solutions. On the other hand, the image-to-image setup allows for more flexibility and intuitive results to come out of the process, depending on the initial data preparation stage. Furthermore, while in parametric approaches, the design space is limited to a priori defined parametric configurations, the ML dataset can vary considerably.

WORKFLOW

Visual accessibility is the intensive attribute to trigger the form-finding process. It relates to "the degree to which different parts of the building (..) can be seen from various locations". It is often associated with spatial comprehension, orientation, and consequently perception and the triggering of diverse psychological feelings such as stress or boredom (Montello 2014). Isovist analysis is the means that visual access is being studied. An isovist is the collected 360 degrees spatial extent of all views around a vantage spot, and the area of an isovist 'describes how much one can see from a certain vantage point.'

Occlusivity analysis, which is the focus of this study, 'indicates the number of open edges,' such as walls (Schneider and Koenig 2012) and 'represents how unseen space may be revealed during movement (Benedikt 1979), offering instances of significant visual variation and long-distance views.

For this case study, an open-source model based on [4] has been utilized, developed by City Intelligence Lab [5]; it allows for an integrated workflow of dataset generation, training, and output, within Rhino/Grasshopper, with the implementation of scripts that run as external processes parallel to Grasshopper. The design pipeline consists of three essential parts: creating and preparing the dataset and training the model (Figure 1) and the machine/human design output (Figure 2).

Dataset Generation

The dataset's creation consists of two sub-modules related to the two pairs of data images we feed into the ML training: the first pair of images consists of the architectural configuration and the second pair of the occlusivity analysis. More specifically,

a) a) The first dataset, generated parametrically, is a field configuration. It is comprised of a linear field system. Abstraction was a deliberate act as it allowed both scale and program not to be directly attributed to form. The simplicity of the configuration allowed us to focus on the technical aspects and further understand the machinic training logic.

b) The second dataset is the visual analysis run in Grasshopper and using [6]. Visual access was selected due to serving as an intuitive user input for the

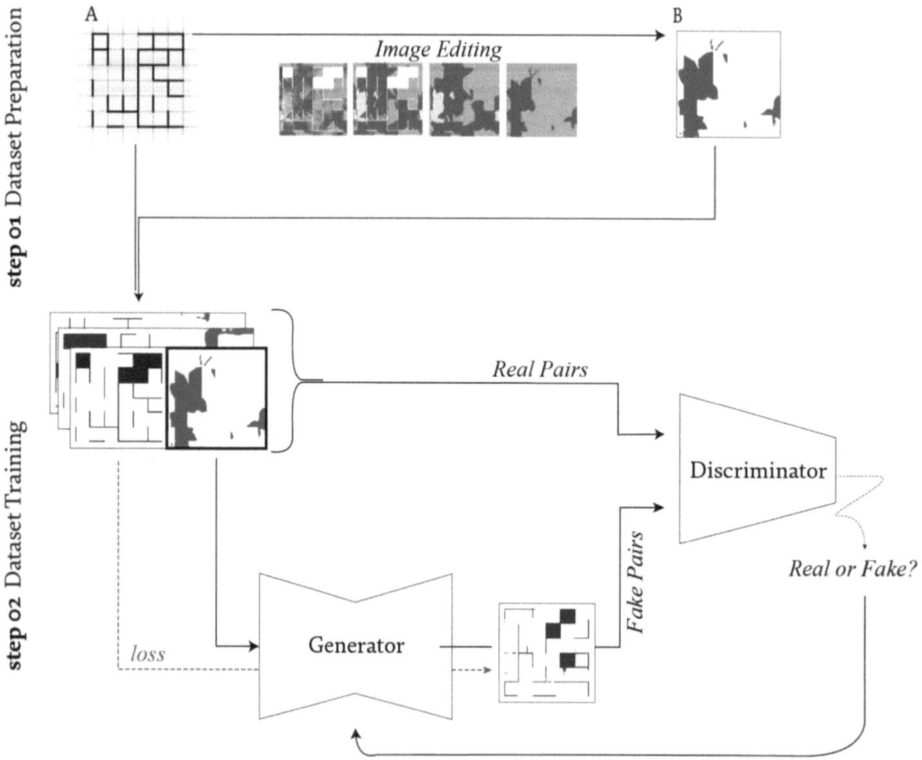

Figure 1
Diagram of workflow: steps 1 and 2

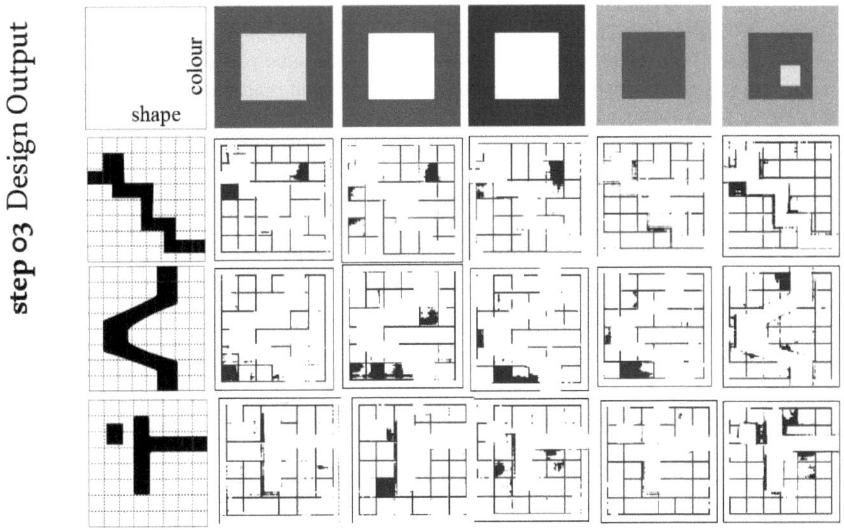

Figure 2
Third step of human/ machine design output

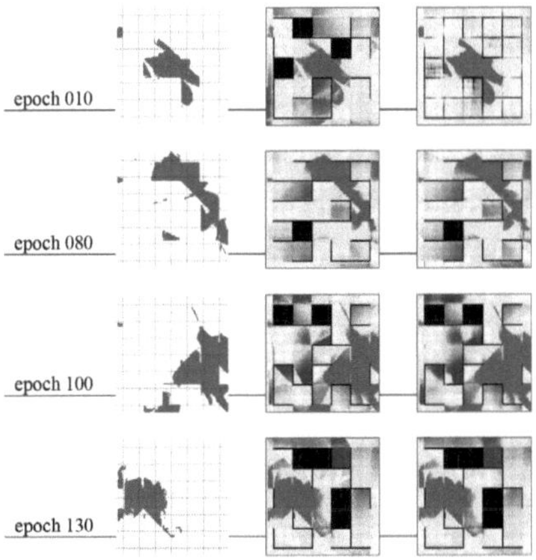

Figure 3
The output of this dataset combines configuration and occlusivity heatmap analysis

latter stage of human/machine interaction and not least due to low computational demands during simulation. An' isovist field' is being created to evaluate all possible vantage points within the configuration, formed by a regular grid of points. Since each point represents a different vantage point within the heterogeneous spatial arrangement, each one has different isovist values depicted through a heatmap.

These two datasets are the input and the target pair of datasets, which will be trained, with (A) corresponding to the colored heatmap and (B) to the configuration. Both datasets are 512 x 512 pixels. The input dataset is further edited within the GH environment, using [7] to simplify information and bring it closer to what a user would draw later in the design implementation step (Figure 1). In one of the final attempts, the target dataset is slightly enhanced with the addition of the visibility analysis (Figure 3).

Training

During the first part of the training process, the generator generates a 'fake' output image that resembles the target image. Then, in each iteration, specific parameters are tuned to find which datasets perform better. Those are the epochs, the color channels (combinations of red, blue, yellow, green), and the number of image samples to be trained.

The discriminator is trained by guessing how realistic the two pairs of input/target and input/-fake seem and, consequently, adjusting its weights. Lastly, the generator's weights are adjusted based on the discriminator's classification [3].

Design implementation

The interaction between the user/designer and algorithmic output is the final step of the workflow. Similar to the target images, the user's input is a sketch idea on the visual access they would like to achieve with their design; the sketch is in the form of a floor plan with a basic color scheme related to the training to differentiate open areas visual connections. Figure 4 shows two different kinds of inputs of sketch design, made either in a CAAD environment (Rhino) by using polylines or in Photoshop by using the brush tools. Those two inputs are compared with the first set of default machinic inputs.

Results and next steps

The method was evaluated using a test scenario to determine how an intuitive idea on occlusivity expressed through drawing or sketching can lead to different spatial configurations. These first outcomes validate the workflow as a form-finding method starting from intensive properties in the early design stages.

Due to the homogeneity of the paired data, the training process has been sufficient even with small amounts (less than 200 images).

The differences among different color combinations are not easily discernible; however, the multicolor combination resulted in clearer configurations.

The comparison between user input and parametric input demonstrated that the output config-

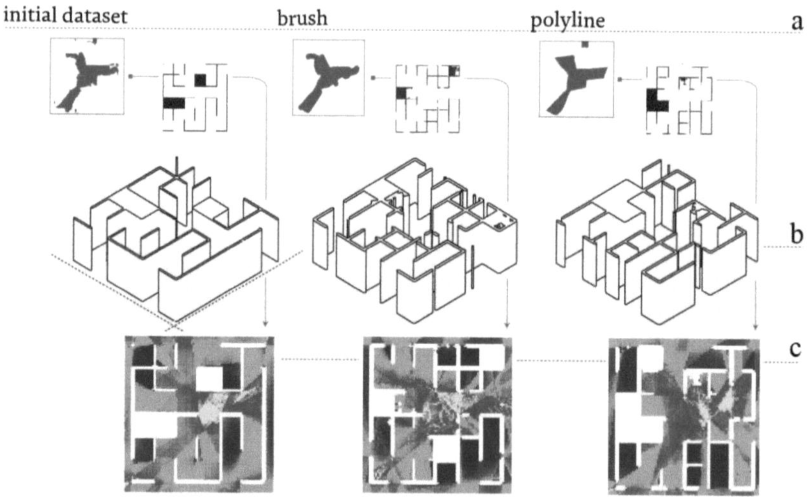

Figure 4
Different media of user input lead to different results

uration changes with subtle changes in the input image. In all three cases, however, the occlusivity heatmap pattern is retained (Figure 4).

During the last test, which combined the configuration with the occlusivity analysis as an input dataset, the networks learned faster the mapping from the observed image.

Further development will expand the information on both the input and target dataset; we strive to introduce more diverse configurations and material behaviors for the former. For the latter, the aim is to combine multiple analyses into one heatmap. Encoding information, therefore, is an integral part of the process that necessitates further investigation.

GENERAL REMARKS

The paper's scope is to provoke a discussion on how intensive attributes can become the starting point of design processes. The focus is on inversing the standard design sequence and make the heatmap of intensities and gradients become the form-giving agent of spatial arrangement and configuration. In this case, both intensive (heatmap) and extensive (static structures) differences become interconnected, with the former defining the latter. Thus, the contribution is twofold; both expanding a conceptual framework into a design workflow while informing the technical aspects of the method used.

Designing with intensive differences can lead to different outcomes depending on the context, the brief, the scale, and the aim. It means that we can design with behaviors and sentient qualities, with microclimatic gradients, or larger scale phenomena such as urban heat islands or air pollution as long as we can encode their information into heatmaps.

Moreover, the workflow can have pedagogical relevance by strengthening design intuition at the early stages of conceptualization as it formulates one way that environmental sensitivity can permeate design education. Its implementation raises awareness of the impact that environmental attributes can have on space physiognomy through abstraction. The ubiquitous effects of climate change make us realize the importance of thinking with dynamic and temporal considerations. Architecture need not be static but conceptualized as a 'graphic record' of 'field conditions' (Allen 2009).

Finally, incorporating Machine Learning in the design process is different from other parametric generative design solutions. The setup of ML models provides flexibility and intuitive results to come out of the process, although they may lack precision. Data preparation is crucial in both cases; in parametric approaches, the design space depends on the predetermined relations between numerical parameters and form. In ML, the dataset can consist of configurations of qualitative values and can be expanded to multiple typologies. It has already been demonstrated (Tamke et al. 2018) that integrating both methods in design workflows can bring together the analytical and the generative and assist in non-anticipated outputs.

REFERENCES

Abalos, I and Sentkiewicz, R (eds) 2015, *Essays on Thermodynamics, Architecture and Beauty*, Actar

Allen, S 2009, 'From Object to field: field conditions in architecture and urbanism', in Hensel, M, Hight, C and Menges, A (eds) 2009, *Space Reader: Heterogeneous space in architecture*, Wiley

Banham, R 1984, *The architecture of the well-tempered environment*, University of Chicago, Chicago

Benedikt, ML 1979, 'To Take Hold of Space: Isovists and Isovist Fields', *Environment and Planning B: Planning and Design*, 6, pp. 47-65

Böhme, G 1993, 'Atmosphere as the Fundamental Concept of a New Aesthetics', *Thesis Eleven*, 36 (10.1177/072551369303600107), pp. 113-126

DeLanda, M 2005, 'Space: Extensive and Intensive, Actual and Virtual', in Buchanan, I and Lambert, G (eds) 2005, *Deleuze and Space*, Edinburgh University Press, pp. 80–87 , pp. 80-87

Duering, S, Chronis, A and Koenig, R 2020 '2020 Optimizing Urban Systems: Integrated optimization of spatial configurations in SimAUD 2020 May 25-27 Vienna, Austria', *SIMAUD*, Vienna

Galanos, T, Chronis, A, Vesely, O, Aichinger, A and Koenig, R 2019 'Best of both worlds – using computational design and deep learning for real-time urban performance evaluation', *OPIARCH - 1st International Con-*

ference on Optimization Driven Architectural Design*, Amman, Jordan
Garci⊠a-Germa⊠n, J (eds) 2017, *Thermodynamic Interactions: An Exploration into Physiological, Material and Territorial Atmospheres*, Actar
Gissen, D 2009, *Subnature: Architecture's Other Environments*, Princeton Architectural Press
Hensel, M (eds) 2013, *Performance-Oriented Architecture: Rethinking Architectural Design and the Built Environment*, Wiley
Hensel, M, Hight, C and Menges, A (eds) 2009, *AD Reader, Space Reader: Heterogeneous space in architecture*, Wiley
Huang, W and Zheng, H 2018 'Architectural Drawings Recognition and Generation through Machine Learning', *ACADIA -Annual Conference of the Association for Computer Aided Design in Architecture*, Mexico City, pp. 156-165
Isola, P, Zhu, J, Zhou, T and Efros, AA 2017 'Image-to-Image Translation with Conditional Adversarial Networks', *IEEE Conference on Computer Vision and Pattern Recognition (CVPR)*, pp. 5967-5976
Lally, S (eds) 2009, *Energies: new material boundaries, Architectural Design*, Wiley, Chichester
Lally, S 2014, *The air from other planets: A brief history of architecture to come*, Lars Mu⊠ller, Zu⊠rich
Montello, D R 2014, 'Spatial Cognition and Architectural Space: Research Perspectives', *Architectural Design*, 84, pp. 74-79
Pallasmaa, J 2014, 'Pallasmaa, J 2014, Empathic Imagination: Formal and Experiential Projection: Empathic Imagination: Formal and Experiential Projection.', *Architectural Design*, 84, p. 80–85
Schneider, S and Koenig, R 2012 'Exploring the Generative Potential of Isovist Fields: The Evolutionary Generation of Urban Layouts based on Isovist Field Properties in Proceedings of the 30th eCAADe Conference - Volume 1, . 12-14 September, pp. 355-363', *Proceedings of eCAADe 2012*, Czech Republic
Tamke, M, Nicholas, P and Zwierzycki, M 2018, 'Machine learning for architectural design: Practices and infrastructure', *International Journal of Architectural Computing*, 16(2)(10.1177/1478077118778580), pp. 123-143
Wigley, M 1998, 'The Architecture of Atmosphere', *Daidalos*, 68, pp. 18-27
[1] http://www.haque.co.uk/papers/hardsp-softsp-ope n-so-arch.PDF
[2] https://devblogs.nvidia.com/archigangenerative-st ack-apartment-buildingdesign/
[3] https://affinelayer.com/pix2pix/
[4] https://github.com/phillipi/pix2pix
[5] https://github.com/city-intelligence-lab/digital-futu res-2020
[6] https://toolbox.decodingspaces.net/
[7] https://www.food4rhino.com/app/aviary

Training Spaces

Fostering machine sensibility for spatial assemblages through wave function collapse and reinforcement learning

Alessandro Mintrone[1]*, Alessio Erioli*[2]
[1,2] *University of Bologna*
[1] *alessandro.mintrone5@gmail.com* [2] *alessio.erioli@unibo.it*

This research explores the integration of Deep Reinforcement Learning (RL) and a Wave Function Collapse (WFC) algorithm for a goal-driven, open-ended generation of architectural spaces. Our approach binds RL to a distributed network of decisions, unfolding through three key steps: the definition of a set of architectural components (tiles) and their connectivity rules, the selection of the tile placement location, which is determined by the WFC, and the choice of which tile to place, which is performed by RL. The act of thinking becomes granular and embedded in an iterative process, distributed among human and non-human cognitions, which constantly negotiate their agency and authorial status. Tools become active agents capable of developing their own sensibility while controlling specific spatial conditions. Establishing an interdependency with the human, that engenders the design patterns and becomes an indispensable prerequisite for the exploration of the generated design space, exceeding human or machinic reach alone.

Keywords: *Reinforcement Learning, Machine Learning, Proximal Policy Optimization, Assemblages, Wave Function Collapse*

INTRODUCTION

As AI simultaneously pervades and restructures our technological ecology, it also reshapes our cognitive processes and habits along with it. Conquering territories of knowledge that were thought to be inviolably human only few years ago, complex non-human cognitions compel us to rethink our model of authorship, acknowledging the implied intricacies, and questioning both our relationship with tools and conception of creativity.

We propose to explore a paradigm for architectural design in which non-human forms of cognitions are embedded into the decision network (Clark 2008). Instead of mere passive devices, we consider those forms active agents able to promote, select, reinforce and inhibit design directions by their own affordances (Leach 2016). These liberated tools, instead of being aimed at parroting human thinking, are acknowledged in their own sensibility and biases; non-human cognitions enabled to claim a broader autonomy and authorship coparticipation, by continuously negotiating both their agency and their authorial status (Picon 2016) (Parisi 2014).

General Adversarial Network (GAN) based applications of AI for the generation of architectural proposals such as Bolojan [1], Chaillou (2020), del Campo (2019, 2020) train algorithms to produce outputs as wholes, mostly in the form of images, be they plans or pictures, out of other images or language. These applications leverage on an idea of conception deliberately declared as a form of intuition, in which AI replace in some measure the human mind in the act of conceiving a fully-fledged outcome. Instead, we employ Reinforcement Learning (RL) to develop a local distributed behavior, which continuously mediates between internal and external conditions, and whose outcome over time is a three-dimensional assemblage, generated by an inherently spatial and material-aware process.

In order to form three-dimensional spatial organizations, RL must be coupled with an iterative generation algorithm such as Wave Function Collapse (WFC), which relies on a discrete representation of both space and connectivity structure [2]. Given a limited set of parts (tiles), their local connection rules, and information about the topological structure of space, the algorithm can unravel a vast array of different spatial conditions. Albeit the WFC design space is ripe with variety, the algorithm nature makes it fragmented and its unaided navigation (i.e. converging towards an established goal by tweaking initial conditions) impossible.

We present a methodology for steering the generation of these assemblages towards specific spatial qualities via a continuously enacted feedback-loop between the human designer and the AI. Coupled with WFC, an Artificial Neural Network (ANN) is trained implementing Proximal Policy Optimization (PPO) (Schulman et al. 2017 [6]). Thus, the system takes responsibility in shaping the global space by learning how to perform local component selection, ostering the development of a cognitive structure capable of pursuing specific and articulated spatial conditions resulting from the iterative assemblage of three-dimensional parts. More specifically, our results show how, selecting quantified spatial descriptors representing both local and global features, it is possible to characterize the assemblage's spatial qualities, enabling the designer's analysis and intervention, while providing continuous feedback to the algorithm.

METHODS

Assemblages

The notion of assemblages we refer to is Manuel DeLanda's expansion of Deleuze's *agencements* (Deleuze and Guattari 1987): arrangements in which both the qualities of parts and their mutual relations play a crucial role in defining the qualities of the whole (DeLanda 2006). DeLanda aims to move beyond the structuralist metaphor of the organism (parts have no existence outside the whole) without returning to the collage model (there are no relations, only individual parts), since both show a limited ability to explain emergence (Johnson 2001). In the assemblage framework, while parts maintain their own individual identity, they might acquire further characterization from their interactions inside the assemblage. Also, they can be detached from an assemblage and plugged in another one where, while maintaining their embedded "properties", they can exhibit different relational "capacities", afforded by the mutated interactions within the new assemblage.

DeLanda's theory is aimed at society at large, and establishes a theoretical framework based on parts and their mutual relations, independent of the application domain and its specific nature. In architecture, focusing on their topological (and not semantic or structural) aspects, assemblages align with a view based on tectonics (the construction from parts, proceeding by addition or growth), rather than hylomorphism (the imposition of a figure over inert matter) or stereometry.

The design of parts, or components, and their connectivity, plays a key role in the design process. In a typical functionalist approach, the elementary component is a finalized unit, its function not supposed to exceed the designated purpose; a column or a beam correspond to single, specific elements. To fully inquire the assemblages' potential, it is necessary to loosen up this specificity, leaving space for genericity and incompleteness: a radical opening to foster context-dependent emerging conditions, as well as differentiation and variety, all based on the constitutive interrelation among parts. As a consequence, the definitions and understanding of architectural semantics and tectonics change: "column" or "beam" rather than elements, identify conditions that can be expressed by one as well as several elements, while each element can determine multiple conditions at once.

The design process we propose unfolds through three key moments in which critical choices are deployed: the definition of a set of tiles, their connectivity rules, and the grid of cells to be populated, the selection of the next location where a tile will be placed, which is determined by the WFC algorithm, and the choice of which tile to place, which is performed by the ANN. While tiles and connectivity design happen outside the simulation, the system affords mutual feedback-loops of influence: tiles and connectivity design shape the assemblage's space of possible configurations, while the assessment of the assemblage qualities reveals the tiles capacities and provides the necessary input to act back on the tiles themselves.

Wave Function Collapse

Wave Function Collapse (WFC) is a constraint solving algorithm, that iteratively places tiles in a predetermined grid of cells, complying with a set of provided adjacency rules, regardless of the tiles content (Figure 1). In particular the algorithm has gained momentum in game design, especially for procedural textures synthesis and world generation, since it spatializes information in a coherent topological structure, generating aperiodic patterns. Our implementation, made in *Unity3D*, is intended both as a platform for the generation and exploration of a large field of three-dimensional assemblages, and as training environment for an ANN, making goal-oriented spatial generation manageable via Machine Learning techniques.

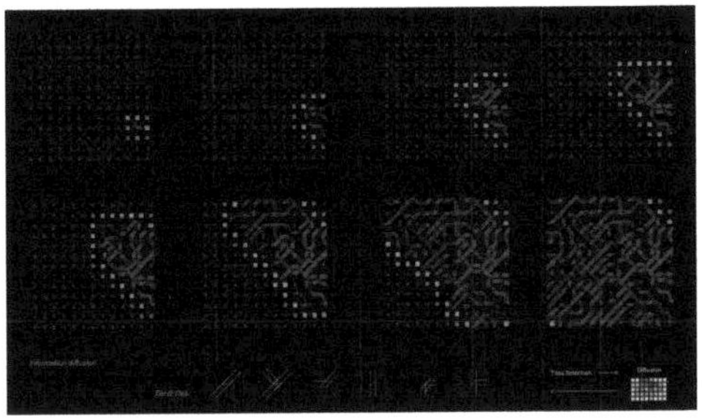

Figure 1
Iterative tile placemente inside the grid.

WFC requires a discretized representation of space, a grid defined by a set of cells along with the topological structure of their connections. The algorithm is not limited by a regular grid or a specific network topology; different grids have been explored, both in two and in three dimensions, ranging from square to hexagonal, up to space-filling polyhedral grids such as cubical, rhombic dodecahedral and truncated octahedral. The initial implementation was performed on a bidimensional square grid in which every cell is connected with its adjacent ring of eight neighbors (four sides and four corners). This setup combines an affordable simplicity in tiles design with a rich, yet manageable, connectivity set, while granting complex enough outcomes and clarity in the assessment phase.

Each cell is initialized to an unobserved state; instead of containing a tile, the state is the superposition of all the probabilities of containing every specific tile (akin to a picture resulting from the semi-transparent overlay of several images). A single iteration consists of three phases: *observation, collapse* and *propagation*. During each observation, a new unobserved cell is selected and collapsed to a defined state containing a particular tile. WFC relies on an entropy function to measure, for every cell, the degree of uncertainty about the possible tiles it may contain. The next cell to collapse is selected choosing the cell with the lowest entropy value; in other words, the point with the lowest level of uncertainty, which contains the lowest number of possible states. This fosters more coherence into the assemblages, making the algorithm less prone to fall into contradiction (i.e., the impossibility to place a tile that satisfies all the connectivity constraints). To quantify uncertainty, we follow the original implementation by Maxim Gumin [2] evaluating the Shannon entropy. Given a discrete random variable x, if $x_i, \ldots, x_n$ are the possible outcomes, and $P(x_i), \ldots, P(x_n)$ their probabilities to occur, the entropy of x is defined as:

$$H(x) = -\sum_{i=1}^{n} P(x_i) \cdot \log P(x_i) \quad (1)$$

Subsequently, during the collapse phase, a tile is placed, randomly selecting among those who satisfy the connectivity constraints. Then, during propagation, the new information gained from the previous collapse is diffused. For each neighbor cell the list of suitable tiles and the entropy values are recursively updated based on the new constraints defined by the placed tile. If no tile satisfies these constraints, the algorithm falls into contradiction and stops, otherwise the process continues with another iteration, until grid completion [3].

Tiles Design and Spatial Configurations

Every tile is provided with three types of information: a set of connection rules determining the allowed adjacencies in every direction, the contained geometry, and, in order to establish all its possible permutations, a symmetry type identifier. A large number of tilesets was tested on both bidimensional and three-dimensional grids. Complexity brews quickly: even a slim tileset grants the emergence of a large collection of articulated and diverse outcomes. This abundance in results largely depends on the careful design of the adjacency constraints; minor changes can mark the difference between a successful system and one prone to contradiction.

The algorithm manifests a tendency towards pattern homogeneity and self-similarity in its spatial outcomes (Figure 2). Though those may be desired qualities, said results still represent a narrow subset of all the spatial configuration the components are inherently able to produce. The random tiles selection mechanism gives each tile the same probability to occur without the possibility to control this choice; as a consequence, the system lacks the capacity to stabilize patterns outside its bias range and/or orient the final outcome. To address this limitation, some authors assign probability "weights" to each tile [4], affecting their chances of being selected. We propose to train an ANN leveraging Deep Reinforcement Learning techniques to perform this choice. The aim is to achieve, by mean of an intelligent, context-aware and open-ended agency, a wider range of configurations with more control on their spatial qualities.

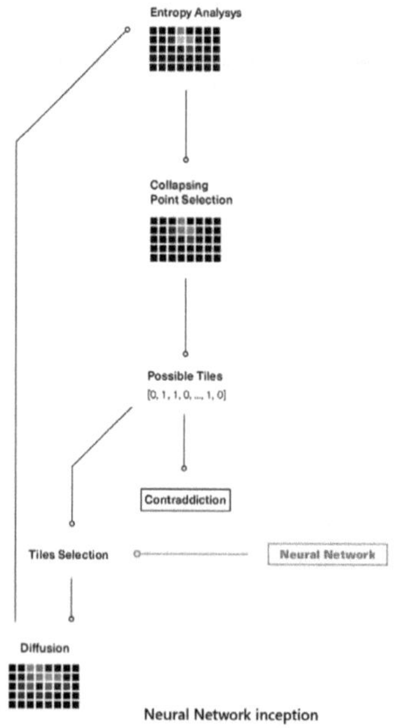

Figure 2
Algorithm structure and AI insertion

Reinforcement Learning

Differently from other kinds of Deep Learning algorithms (Goodfellow 2001), RL is not based on a pre-existing dataset (Figure 3). The ANN instead learns its behavior from the experience accumulated by an agent interacting with an environment, trying to maximize a series of rewards awarded after its actions. In this process, the algorithm itself generates its own set of data from which its behavior is developed. The agent and the environment are part of a mutual feedback-loop. The agent performs actions based on its perception of the environment's current state. These actions modify the environment, changing its state and, by doing so, affecting the agent's subsequent actions.

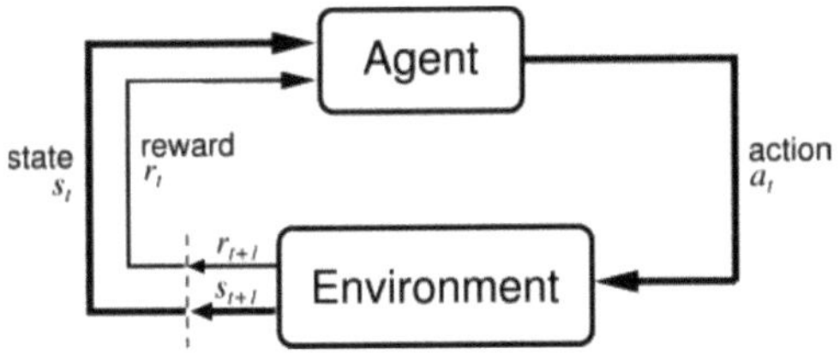

Figure 3
Information flow in RL.

During the training process, the environment provides an additional signal: a positive or negative reward associated to every state that guides the training process. The agent shapes its behavior trying to maximize this reward, learning from how its actions lead to higher or lower values. Therefore, a careful engineering of the reward function is essential to orient and widen the spectrum of agent's behaviors. If defining such function can be straightforward for simple problems, when complexity increases or when facing open-ended problems such as the ones characterizing architecture, translating the desired qualities of the outcome in terms of rewards becomes challenging.

Nonetheless, since the designer is required to set goals instead of hardcoding behaviors inside the algorithm, a task that proves to be hard in terms of human understanding, such as mapping the complex non-linear correlations between local actions and global outcomes, can be externalized to the RL algorithm that trains the ANN and iteratively refines its policy. This method appears more capable of approaching those ill-defined problem whose boundary conditions are difficult to trace, since, instead of learning how to deliver complete, definite solutions, what the algorithm develops is a sensibility, the ability to produce structured yet adaptable proposals, interacting with the environment and navigating different, often conflicting, conditions.

Quantitative Spatial Analysis

A set of six quantified spatial descriptors is defined with a twofold purpose: trying to characterize space by analyzing different qualities at both the global and local scale, and defining the associated reward functions. Translating architectural spatial qualities into quantitative design goals for the ML algorithm, they enable the comparative analysis of the resulting assemblages' features, and set up the data in a computable and intelligible form for the AI.

1. Density. Every tile has an associated local density value, representing the degree to which the cell is filled. Density is defined as the average local density of the observed cells. The associated reward is calculated by defining a *desired density* and then comparing it with the actual one.

$$1 - |\text{desiredDensity} - \text{actualDensity}| \quad (2)$$

2. Spatial distribution. While density is a global parameter, spatial distribution is defined as the coherence of a desired local density distribution with the actual one. The associated reward is calculated by computing at each cell's collapse the difference between the *desired local density* and the *actual local density*. During training the desired distribution is randomly generated by the system via an attractor field. After the training, the designer can provide a custom desired distribution.

$$1 - |\text{desiredFieldValue} - \text{actualFieldValue}| \quad (3)$$

3. Orientation. Principal directions are associated to each tile from a predetermined set, in a range of none to two per tile. Orientation designates the main direction inside the assemblage, if the main direction does not surpass the others at least by a threshold amount, the assemblage is marked as *non-directional*. The corresponding positive reward is awarded if the main direction corresponds to the *de-*

sired main direction.

$$\frac{\text{directionalTiles}}{\text{totalTiles}} > \text{threshold} \quad (4)$$

4-5. Structural and spatial connectivity. The tiles are divided into two categories according to their local density value: *void tiles* and *solid tiles*, which when connected with others from the same category form structural and spatial clusters respectively. When working in a tridimensional space, the information about whether or not each structural cluster is connected to the ground is also retained. Setting a threshold, it is possible to identify, for each structural cluster, tiles clusters that are either disconnected from the ground, or whose size is below the threshold.

$$1 - \frac{\text{tilesUnderThreshold}}{\text{totalTiles}} \quad (5)$$

6. Planar connectivity. This parameter is defined only for a three-dimensional assemblage. A plane representing the element orientation can be assigned to each tile by providing its normal vector. Tiles which plane is horizontal (within a given threshold), are clustered as in connectivity analysis. Given a threshold, planar connectivity and its reward are defined with the same formula used for structural and spatial connectivity.

Training

The implemented machine learning algorithm is PPO (Proximal Policy Optimization), a state-of-the-art deep RL class of algorithms developed by *OpenAI* (Schulman et al. 2017 [6]). This model, unlike previous RL algorithms, is able to operate with continuous inputs and outputs. It selects actions relying on an advantage function that estimates the expected value of each possible choice and updates its policy according to the divergence between its inferences and the actual outcome.

The algorithm is implemented in the *Unity ML-Agents Toolkit*, a library seamlessly integrated in *Unity3D* (Juliani et al. 2020 [5]). The ANN architecture consists of 3 hidden -layers, each containing 256 units. This architecture has proved sufficiently robust when operating in 2D and 3D with different sets of tiles, while maintaining the same structure and hyper-parameters.

Given a starting grid of cells, a training episode is made of as many iterations are needed to complete an assemblage or run into a contradiction. At each iteration, the environment provides information about its current state, and the collected inputs are normalized (remapped in a 0-1 range). Information regarding the allowed tiles in the collapsing cell and the tiles already placed in the adjacent ones is represented in one-hot encoder form. The remaining information is given in a continuous form as normalized scalars, and contains both the desired and actual values of the selected spatial features, along with their relative weights.

Subsequently, the ANN selects, among a list of allowed elements, which tile place inside the collapsing cell. The ANN returns an array of normalized values as a one-hot encoder, representing the probability of each candidate tile to be the overall most valuable choice; sampling from this probability distribution, the tile is selected. After updating the environment and awarding the correspondent reward, the ANN policy is also updated.

For each training, a subset of active spatial qualities is set, a weight is provided for every feature, and the corresponding rewards are scaled so that the maximum total achievable reward during each training episode is 1. Additional reward is awarded for each completed step, up to a maximum of 0.25, encouraging the agent to complete the assemblage without falling into contradiction.

During training, a generalization function modifies the desired values and their relative weight at given intervals. Multiple instances of the assembling algorithm, each one with different values, are run at the same time. These two strategies prevent the ANN from overfitting to a limited set of goal values. The training performance is monitored via TensorBoard, assessing through its generated charts the cumulative reward, as well as the episode length and behavior entropy, averaged over the last 100 episodes.

Resulting Assemblages

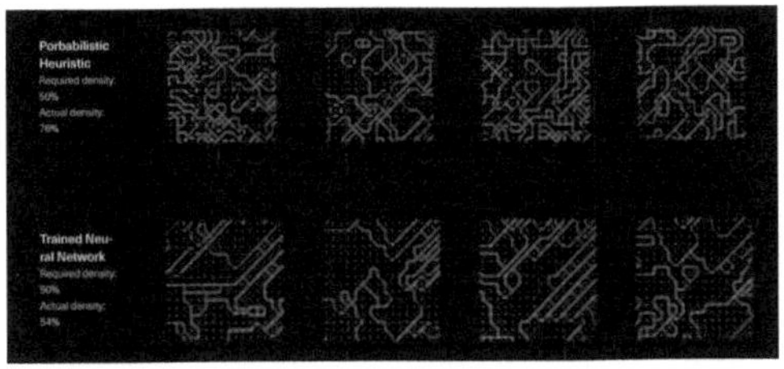

Figure 4
Results: comparison between heuristic guided and AI guided assemblage.

The assemblages realized by the trained ANN are compared against a stochastic baseline that assigns to each tile a different probability in a random choice (Figure 4). In one set of 25 tests, in which the shared goal was to obtain an assemblage with a target density of 50%, the ANN consistently outperformed the baseline (average 54% against 73% of the baseline), while also exhibiting more structured patterns (Figure 5).

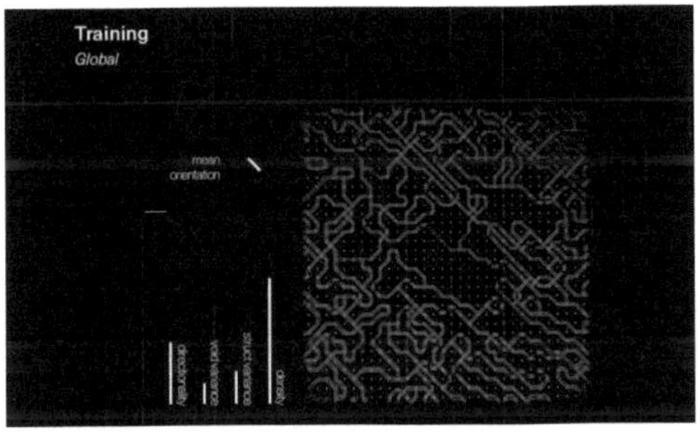

Figure 5
Results: Output of the ANN guided assemblage when trained on all the descriptors at once.

Given a common set of initial tiles, each descriptor consistently led to the appearance of specific patterns in the outcome. Since these patterns emerge as a byproduct of the repetition of certain sequences of actions, they display how strategies developed to maximize the assigned reward also yield related formal qualities. These qualities and their causal correlation with the set goals can be clearly discerned in the case of a single descriptor, while in the case of a larger number of descriptors this correlation is more difficult to discern, hindering the designer's ability to fine tune the training. Despite the inherent difficulties of understanding a system with high dimensionality and interrelated simultaneous parameters, this can be considered a limit of this approach.

The emergent cognitive behavior is not bounded to a defined dimension of the grid, so what is learned in the training environment's limited space can be applied to larger assemblages. This behavior is contingent to the inherent history of the undergone training: repeating the training process, even with the same parameters, can lead to different actions and strategies in the same conditions and with the same reward values. In this sense the descriptors are not intended as objective representations of the assemblage's spatial features, but as stimuli to hone the AI's sensibility.

Mapping and Visualizing

Transitioning from a bidimensional space to a tridimensional one, the increased dimensionality and related number of permutations leads to an inflation of the possible tiles to compute and, consequently, of the number of parameters inputted into the ANN. In order to maintain sufficient design agility and provide a design space that facilitates the individuation of the ANN contribution, after experimenting with sets differentiating in tiles amount, geometry and connectivity, a simple and limited set of tridimensional tiles is adopted: a total of six planar elements, three horizontal, two vertical, and one diagonal (Figure 6). The set was used to produce a database of approximately 10,000 assemblages performed in a 10x10x10 grid containing the placed tiles as well as the coded resulting spatial qualities (Figure 7).

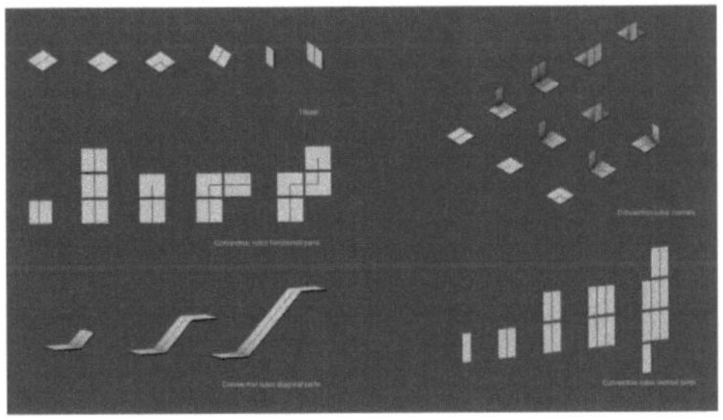

Figure 6
Three-dimensional tileset and connectivity rules.

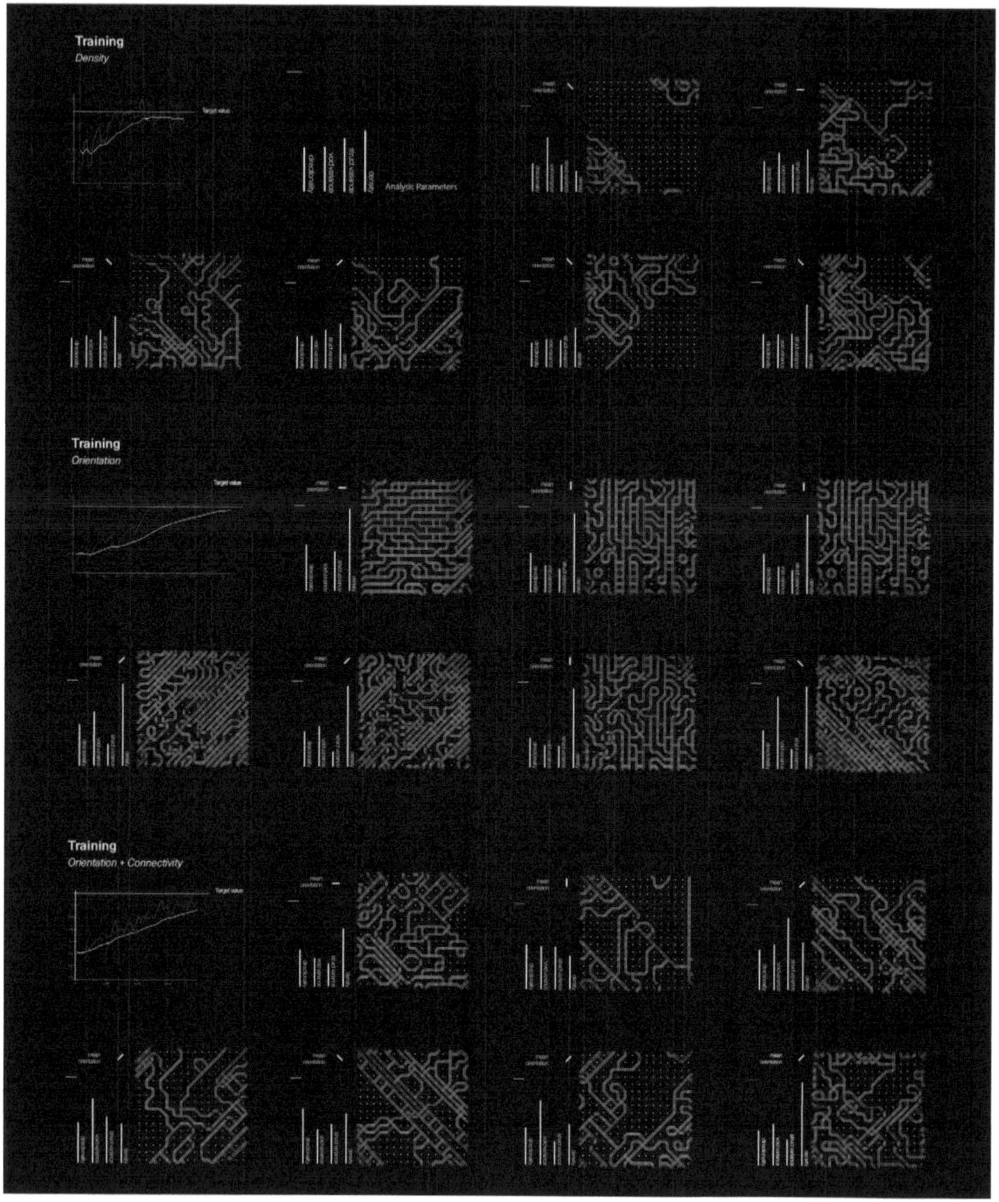

Figure 7
Results: Output of the ANN guided assemblage when trained on density, orientation and a combination of orientation and connectivity.

Figure 8
Multiple visualizations of a resulting assemblage.

Figure 9
Global view on the resulting assemblages

Superabundance of mathematically unique results is a typical consequence of procedural generative processes, and WFC makes no exception. This excess of information defies analysis in human terms. Manual methods are unfeasible for such large amounts, while quantitative analysis on its own fails to account for all the qualitative and perceptual features embedded in the assemblage. Furthermore, the understanding of a three-dimensional intricate spatial assemblage cannot rely on visual inspection alone: making comparisons, and even grasping the spatial structure of a single episode, is a complex cognitive task which can be significatively eased when supported by an externalized representation (Clark 2008). Therefore, an interface, mediating between human and non-human cognitions and intelligible to both is required to help orientation while navigating the algorithm-generated outcomes. A coordinate system is implemented using the previously established quantitative spatial descriptors, making the database addressable for human and machinic inquiries alike. This orientation system, allows the selection of a specific assemblage based on the analyzed spatial qualities: it is coupled with a visualization system that displays the resulting three-dimensional assemblage, an automated selection of multiple viewpoints, and various graphic representation of the parameters set (Figure 8). Quantitative and qualitative features complement each other, enhancing the completeness of the assessment process.

However, the analysis system is still limited by the difficulty of visualizing and examining this high dimensional space in a three-dimensional representation (Figure 9). Dimensionality reduction techniques such as *Self-Organizing Maps* (Harding 2016), although not implemented at the present stage of research, can help this process.

CONCLUSIONS

This research explores a granular and distributed paradigm for cognition and creation of architectural space. Acknowledging the limitations of a self-contained human creativity and challenging the myth of its primacy, the generation process adopted is not anthropocentric, as it puts the human in a more extended cognitive ecology where the algorithmic intelligence of WFC and ANN participate as co-contributors with autonomous agency and authorship.

The current state of our research refers to a notion of architectural space that is deliberately partial to its topological features and includes only visual accounts of phenomenological qualities. Despite such self-imposed restrictions and the limitations that ensue, quantitative and qualitative complexity must be reckoned with early on. The presented method provides a compass to navigate an otherwise scattered design space: the descriptors perform the dual role of connective tissue for the design space and coordinate system for the analysis of multiple outcomes.

Goals and reward functions are indicators of abstract performances formulated by a human. Given a set of tiles and connectivity constraints, each descriptor is entangled with its own emergent patterns and form stable connections with the outcome's properties. Nonetheless, said qualities and their expression exceed the boundaries of this influence, since they are the result of autonomous machinic sensibilities developed during the training. Thanks to the WFC properties these patterns are extendable, with unaltered tileset and training, to larger or multiple grids, therefore suitable for agile design iterations. Even so, combined goals interact in a non-linear fashion, which defies a priori effect prediction and detection of individual contributions. The use of machine learning techniques to deal with high dimensionality (such as self-organizing maps) seems promising, and it is considered as a future implementation to strengthen post-generation analysis.

The interplay among tile design, WFC, and RL produces topologically coherent spatial structures, which are directly computable based on intrinsic measurable properties and their inherent data representation. Our goal is neither a phenomenological use of AI, where ANNs are trained to develop features based on preexisting catalogs, nor the reduction of the architectural outcome to its fitness against some predetermined condition. Instead, we aim at the expansion of the creative architectural horizon by including non-human, autonomous agency and sensibility in the design of spatial arrangements.

REFERENCES

del Campo, M, Carlson, A and Manninger, S 2020, 'Towards Hallucinating Machines - Designing with Computational Vision', *International Journal of Architectural Computing*, Online, pp. 1-16

del Campo, M and Manninger, S 2019 'Imaginary Plans', *Proceedings of the 2019 ACADIA Conference – Ubiquity and Autonomy*, Austin, pp. 412-418

Chaillou, S 2020 'Archigan: Artificial Intelligence X Architecture', *Architectural Intelligence*, Singapore, pp. 117-127

Clark, A 2008, *Supersizing the Mind: Embodiment, Action, and Cognitive Extension*, Oxford University Press, New York

DeLanda, M 2006, *A New Philosophy of Society: Assemblage Theory and Social Complexity, Annotated edition*, Continuum, London

Deleuze, G and Guattari, F 1987, *A Thousand Plateaus*, Minnesota University Press, Minneapolis

Goodfellow, I, Bengio, Y and Courville, A 2016, *Deep Learning*, MIT Press, Cambridge

Harding, J 2016 'Dimensionality Reduction for Parametric Design Exploration', *Advances in Architectural Geometry 2016*, Zurich, pp. 274-287

Johnson, S 2001, *Emergence: The Connected Lives of Ants, Brains, Cities and Software*, Scribner, New York

Juliani, A, Berges, V P, Teng, E, Cohen, A, Harper, J, Elion, C, Goy, C, Gao, Y, Henry, H, Mattar, M and Lange, D 2020, *Unity: A General Platform for Intelligent Agents*, arXiv:1809.02627v2

Leach, N 2016 'Digital Tool Thinking: Object Oriented Ontology versus New Materialism', *ACADIA 2016 POSTHUMAN FRONTIERS: Data, Designers, and Cognitive Machines Projects Catalog of the 36th Annual Conference of the Association for Computer Aided Design in Architecture*, Ann Arbor, p. 344–351

Parisi, L 2014, 'Automated Architecture: Speculative Reason in the Age of the Algorithm', in Mackay, R and Avanessian, A (eds) 2014, *#Accellerate#, the accelerationist reader*, Urbanomic Media Ltd, Falmouth, pp. 401-424

Picon, A 2016, 'Free the Robots!', *Log*, 36, pp. 146-151

Schulman, J, Wolski, F, Dhariwal, P, Radford, A and Kilmov, O 2017, *Proximal Policy Optimization Algorithms*, arXiv:1707.06347v2

[1] https://vimeo.com/425905084

[2] https://github.com/mxgmn/WaveFunctionCollapse

[3] https://robertheaton.com/2018/12/17/wavefunction-collapse-algorithm/

[4] https://github.com/heyx3/EasyWFC

[5] https://arxiv.org/abs/1809.02627

[6] https://arxiv.org/abs/1707.06347

Reinforcement Learning for Sequential Assembly of SL-Blocks

Self-interlocking combinatorial design based on Machine Learning

Bastian Wibranek[1], Yuxi Liu[2], Niklas Funk[3], Boris Belousov[4], Jan Peters[5], Oliver Tessmann[6]
[1]The University of Texas at San Antonio [2,6]Digital Design Unit, TU Darmstadt
[3,4,5]Intelligent Autonomous Systems, TU Darmstadt
[1]bastian.wibranek@utsa.edu [2]yuxi.liu@stud.tu-darmstadt.de
[3,4,5]{niklas|boris|jan}@robot-learning.de [6]tessmann@dg.tu-darmstadt.de

Adaptive reconfigurable structures are seen as the next big step in the evolution of architecture. However, to achieve this vision, new tools are required that enable autonomous configuration of given elements based on a specified design objective. Various approaches have been considered in the past, ranging from rule-based methods to evolutionary optimization. Although successful in applications where search heuristics or informative objective functions can be provided, these methods struggle with long-term planning problems. In this paper, we tackle the problem of sequential assembly of SL-blocks which has the character of a combinatorial optimization problem. We explore the applicability of deep reinforcement learning algorithms that recently showed great success on combinatorial problems in other domains, such as board games and molecular design. We highlight the unique challenges presented by the architectural design setting and compare the performance to evolutionary computation and heuristic search baselines.

Keywords: *Reinforcement Learning, Architectural Assembly, Discrete Design, SL-blocks, Dry Joined*

INTRODUCTION

Reversible building elements offer unique opportunities for the construction industry to reduce its carbon footprint, minimize waste and decrease the use of non-renewable resources. Among these advantages, the use of dry-fitted connections between elements allows for fast assembly and disassembly of structures out of prefabricated modules, thereby unlocking the path towards a circular economy in the construction industry (Durmisevic, 2019).

Today, most reversible connections rely on fixation via screws or other adhesives. On the other hand, topological interlocking (Tessmann and Rossi, 2019) provides an alternative approach to construction, in which stability and mechanical fixation are achieved purely based on the arrangement and connectivity of the building elements.

Construction elements are often fit for a limited set of arrangements and cannot be easily reused. To enable greater flexibility and component reuse for future constructions, concepts such as Combinatorial Design (Sanchez, 2016), Digital Materials (Gershenfeld, et al. 2015), and Programmable Matter (Tibbits and Cheung, 2012) are challenging the current use of preassigned building components, instead putting the emphasis on reusability and recombination of large amounts of repetitive elements. In this paper, we focus on the SL-block proposed by Shih (2016) as the basis for exploring combinatorial design possibilities. SL-blocks enable flexible design while at the same time providing the benefits of self-interlocking assembly and straightforward reassembly (Figure 1).

Although repetitive components that can be connected in many different ways are advantageous for reversible assembly, it introduces new challenges to the design process. The problem of finding an arrangement of interlocking elements in which they assemble into a stable structure is complicated for a human designer. Its complexity grows exponentially with the length of the assembly sequence. Therefore, advanced optimization approaches are required to tackle this sequential combinatorial problem.

Several automated approaches to optimization of interlocking assemblies have been considered in the past. The use of graph representations and heuristic-based search methods were investigated by Wang et al., (2018). However, classical graph search methods are restricted by the branching factor of the problem and quickly reach their limits when faced with large-scale designs as required by architectural applications. Therefore, we are interested in considering machine learning methods that have recently shown success in other challenging combinatorial optimization domains, such as games of Chess and Go (Silver et al., 2017). In general, there is a significant amount of work on applying machine learning to combinatorial problems, as demonstrated in the recent survey by Bengio et al., (2020). In the context of construction, the first steps have been made by Bapst et al., (2019), who applied reinforcement learning to sequential assembly problems, albeit in a 2D setting.

In this paper, reinforcement learning is utilized for the sequential interlocking of dry joined blocks. Different algorithms were tested for rebuilding various curves that serve as a design input. The previous tedious combinatorial task is algorithmically optimized to design complex interlocking structures with modular building blocks.

MODULAR DESIGN AND ASSEMBLY WITH SL-BLOCKS

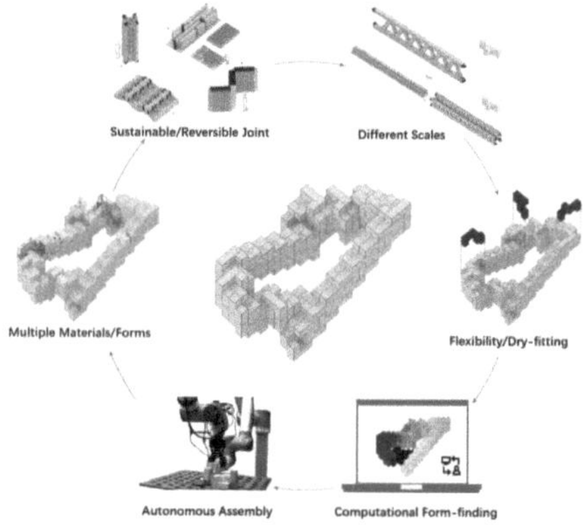

Figure 1
Advantages of SL-block in modular design.

The SL-block is an octocube consisting of one S-shaped and one L-shaped tetracube attaching along their sides (Shih 2016). The specific shape of the SL-block provides the most extensive space of possible combinations compared to other octa cubes (Chou, 2020). The basic relationship of two attaching SL-blocks is called engagement. There are six types of engagements defined as geometric transformations between the host pair and the new pair that is to be added. An SL-Strand is represented as a sequential concatenation of engagements, which specify the assembly process starting with an initial SL-block and adding blocks one by one. (Shih et al. 2019). For example, the string aaaa specifies a string of four engagements lining up to form the configuration presented in Figure 2.

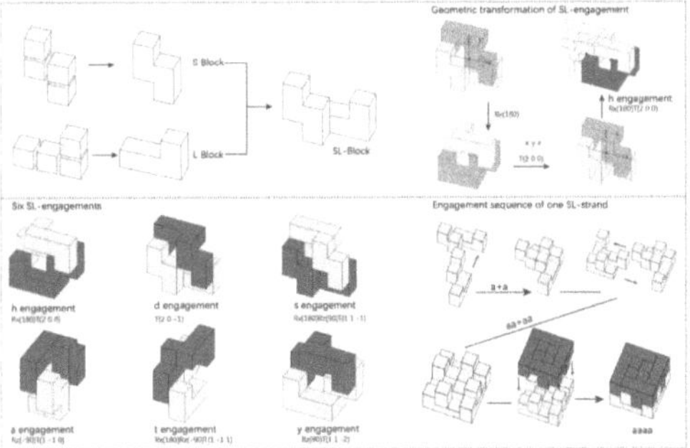

Figure 2
The arrangement of the S and L blocks and their various engagements.

With multiple SL-strands, various interlocking building elements (e.g., column, wall, and slab) can be configured, where only blocks highlighted in black can be removed without breaking the whole structure (Figure 3). Currently, these elements are created by manually defining the engagements, which is a very tedious task.

When designing and constructing with SL-blocks, one significant difficulty is to draw a connection between the discrete engagements and their effect on the overall structure. Since the geometric transformations are defined relative to the previously placed block, from a global point of view, selecting the same engagement may produce a different effect depending on the previous actions.

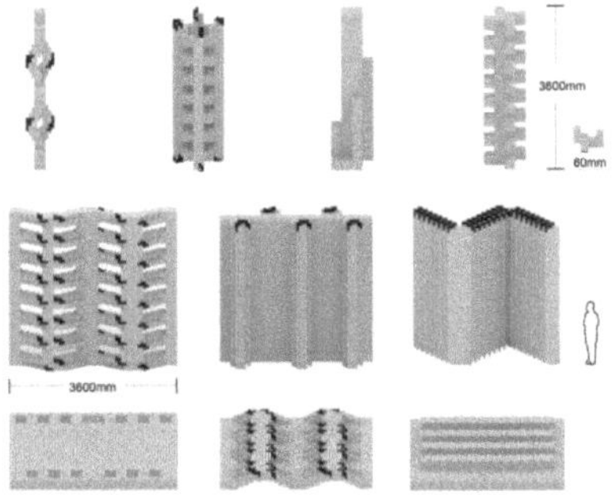

Figure 3
Different building elements from SL-blocks.

To circumvent this complexity, we propose to use curves as an interface to indicate the desired shape of the structure that needs to be assembled with SL-blocks. Parametrized curves take a leading role in design and architecture, being one of the main and delimiting elements of the form. Most iconically, Greg Lynn proposed to use curves for computer-aided design and has recently been transferred into the Digital and Discrete domain (Retsin, 2016).

In order to create an internal connection between the curve and the SL-blocks, our approach needs to transform the given curve into a sequential assembly sequence which is represented by a string of letters where each letter denotes the respective engagement. However, without the help of algorithms, this string generation process must be explored manually. Thus, in this paper, we focus on using different algorithms that can simplify the design process. In particular, we propose reinforcement learning as a promising approach for solving sequential assembly problems that provide a natural interface between the designer and modular building structures.

OPTIMIZATION ALGORITHMS FOR SEQUENTIAL ASSEMBLY

The problem of sequential assembly with SL-blocks falls into the scope of performance-driven architectural design (Shi & Yang, 2013). This approach aims to use numerical optimization to generate a structure based on provided design criteria. There are already several methods available to the community through Grasshopper plugins and external programs, such as evolutionary algorithms, direct search, and model-based methods, as surveyed by Wortmann & Nannicini (2017). However, these approaches do not take into account the sequential nature of the assembly problem. They treat the whole assembly sequence as one evaluation point and compute the fitness of the resulting structure only at the end of the assembly process.

In contrast, reinforcement learning can be viewed as an alternative to black-box optimization, where the agent makes decisions at every step of the assembly and thereby uses the fitness signal (reward function) more efficiently. The advantages of reinforcement learning have been recently demonstrated on extremely challenging combinatorial optimization problems, such as games of Chess, Shogi, and Go (Silver et al., 2017; Schrittwieser et al., 2020). Therefore, we aim to transfer the insights from the domain of reinforcement learning to architectural design since our problem has a similar combinatorial structure.

SEQUENTIAL ASSEMBLY AS A REINFORCEMENT LEARNING PROBLEM

We want to solve the task of realizing a user-defined curve. That is, given a curve, we want to find a sequence of engagements resulting in a chain of SL-blocks that follows the curve. The variations of this task differ in the complexity of the target curve. To formalize this problem in the language of reinforcement learning, we need to define action, observation, and reward.

In a reinforcement learning loop (Figure 4), the agent (Python script) takes an action (put the next block) and the environment (Grasshopper) returns an observation (e.g., positions of parts relative to the curve) and a reward (numerical value reflecting how well the curve is covered by SL-blocks). The agent keeps improving its actions based on observations and rewards with the objective to maximize the total sum of rewards in expectation.

Action in our case is an integer between zero and five, indicating which of the six possible engagements of SL-blocks should be executed next. Note that the action is relative to the previously placed block. Therefore, we need to keep track of the current state of the environment. Conceptually, the state is represented by the poses of all already placed parts and the target curve.

Our observation consists of three parts: i) list of normalized values that encode the distance from each of the 16 voxels of the current SL-Engagement to the curve, ii) flattened transformation matrix describing the pose of the current SL-engagement, and iii) coordinates of three points on the curve in front of the agent. Figure 5 provides a visual illustration of how the observation is constructed. It is essential to provide some local information about the future direction of the curve; therefore, we add three leading points to the observation. Adding more future points to the observation makes the problem of value estimation easier. However, at the same time, it increases the dimensionality of the observation space and causes the agent to overfit to the current curve. On the other hand, providing only one point makes the agent short-sighted, precluding it from taking into account the direction of the curve or obstacles a few steps ahead. In our experiments, we found that providing three points is sufficient to solve the considered tasks. In other scenarios, this parameter may be adjusted for improved performance.

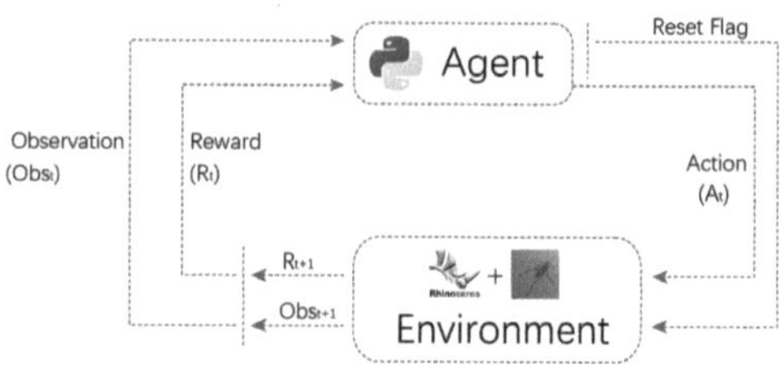

Figure 4
Reinforcement Learning Loop with Rhino/Grasshopper as Environment.

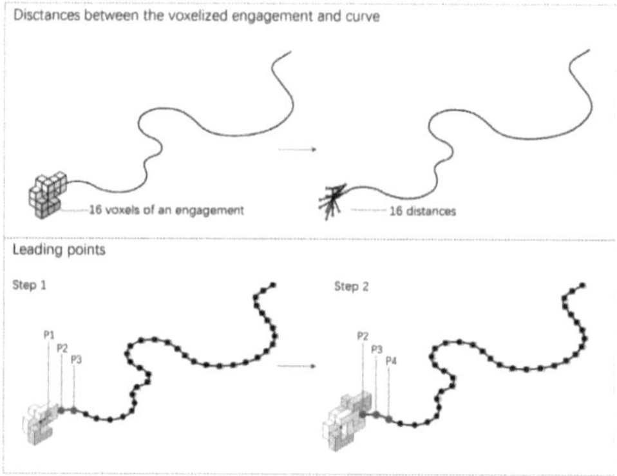

Figure 5
Two major parts of the observation: distances from each of the 16 voxels of the current engagement to the curve (top) and coordinates of 3 leading points (bottom). This additional information allows the agent to anticipate how the curve will evolve in the future.

The reward function and the reset flag are used to encourage the agent to follow the desired curve. In particular, the reward (defined as one minus the smallest distance of the current block to the curve) is maximized when the structure perfectly follows the curve. If the agent deviates too much from the curve, the environment is reset to the initial state, which stops the accumulation of rewards and forces the agent to start anew.

INTERFACE BETWEEN GRASSHOPPER AND REINFORCEMENT LEARNING ALGORITHMS

To solve the above-defined reinforcement learning problem, we employ the stable-baselines3 library (Raffin et al. 2019), which is a de-facto standard for benchmarks in the RL community. We implemented a socket-based interface to use Grasshopper as an RL environment in combination with stable-baselines3, and we made it available for other researchers at https:github.com/b4be1/gh_gym. Among the available algorithms, we chose the two most suitable for our setting and that are known to work well for a wide range of hyperparameters: proximal policy optimization (PPO) and deep Q-learning (DQN). These algorithms represent two major classes of methods: actor-critic and value-based methods. Actor-critic methods learn a policy (actor) and a value function (critic), whereas value-based methods only learn the critic. The Python scripts and the Grasshopper files for running reinforcement learning on sequential assembly of SL-blocks are available at https:github.com/b4be1/rl-for-sequential-assembly. A video presenting our complete approach and describing how to use the interface can be found at https:youtu.be/owHATVWgNk4.

BASELINE: GREEDY SEARCH WITH A HEURISTIC

An alternative approach to optimizing a sequence of SL-Engagements is the heuristic-based search. Here the user provides a search heuristic that guides the agent at every step. The heuristic can be seen as the value function of the reinforcement learning agent, but instead of being learned through interaction with the environment, it is provided by the user.

In our curve following task, it is possible to provide a sufficiently good heuristic. Namely, the distance from the current engagement to a point slightly down the curve provides a strong signal, pulling the agent as a magnet towards placing the next block along the curve. We report the results of running this method as another baseline for evaluating the performance of reinforcement learning. We refer to this method as the greedy algorithm, as it greedily chooses the best action based on the heuristic's value. In this way, the greedy algorithm builds a single solution consisting of a sequence of SL-Engagements that follow the provided curve.

Related Work on Reinforcement Learning for Combinatorial Optimization in Construction

Performance-driven architectural design is a broad field (Shi & Yang, 2013). However, so far, mainly evolutionary algorithms have been explored (Wortmann & Nannicini, 2017; Fang, 2017; Costa et al., 2015). Only recently reinforcement learning started gaining interest in architecture for design (Mandow et al., 2020) and physical construction (Apolinarska et al., 2021). Our approach is conceptually related to that of Mandow et al. (2020) in that we use RL for design optimization; however, they use RL to evaluate designs generated by learned shape grammar, whereas we use RL to generate designs themselves.

Since the problem of sequential assembly belongs to the class of combinatorial optimization problems, research on methods for solving such problems, in general, is highly relevant. In recent years, there has been an increasing interest in applying deep learning techniques to combinatorial optimization problems (Bello et al. 2016, Khalil et al. 2017) as well as in using intelligent algorithms for construction and assembly tasks (Bapst et al. 2019, Thompson et al. 2020, Cho et al. 2020). However, most of the previous works on intelligent construction focused on automating the entire process end to end, i.e., without any means for the user to influence the design process (Bapst et al. 2019, Thompson et al. 2020). While this might result in an overall optimal design, it also clearly limits the interactivity of the approaches. Moreover, in those setups, the design objectives have to be defined rather passively through the reward function. On the contrary, the approach presented here allows the user to directly inform the algorithm by specifying the curve which needs to be built. This approach is more closely related to the setting presented by Janner et al. (2019), in which sequential assembly sequences were generated from image inputs.

RESULTS

This section presents evaluations and comparisons of PPO and DQN to evolutionary optimization and a greedy heuristic search algorithm on the curve following tasks with curves of varying degrees of complexity. Furthermore, evaluation on a task with obstacles is presented to demonstrate the adaptability of the reinforcement learning approach to constraints and additional objectives. Finally, the generated designs are validated in terms of stability and constructability by building a physical model using dry-fitted self-interlocking SL-blocks. The experiments were run on a laptop with Intel-Core-i7-4710HQ-Processor and 16GB-Memory.

EVALUATION OF REINFORCEMENT LEARNING ON THE CURVE FOLLOWING TASK

We compare two reinforcement learning algorithms, PPO and DQN, on the task of sequential assembly along a given curve. Three types of curves are considered: open 2D curve, open 3D curve, and closed 3D curve. For each curve type, we evaluate on two curve lengths: short (requires about 20 SL-Engagements) and long (requires about 40 SL-Engagements). Evaluation takes between 10-30 minutes depending on the difficulty of the curve. Table 1 shows representative samples obtained with PPO and DQN, as well as by the baseline algorithms - the genetic algorithm and the greedy algorithm.

While the genetic algorithm converges faster than reinforcement learning, in 5-10 minutes, it finds a reasonably good solution on 2D curves but fails on open and closed 3D curves (Figure 6). The reason for difficulties with 3D curves must lie in the higher complexity of the problem in 3D space because many more possibilities for placing SL-blocks are available. The algorithm cannot handle such an exponential increase in combinations.

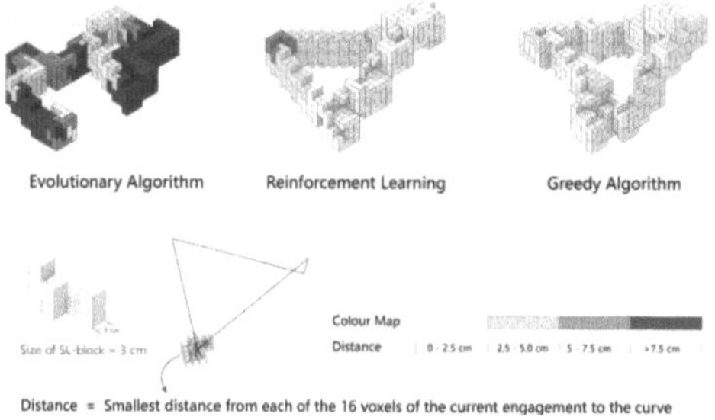

Figure 6
Colormap of the errors during the placement of SL-blocks occurring with the different algorithms on the 3D closed curve. The distances are based on a 3cm voxel-sized SL-block.

Compared to the evolutionary algorithm, the reinforcement learning algorithms succeed in finding sequential interlocking assemblies on curves of different lengths and dimensions, as shown in the middle columns of Table 1. Both presented algorithms, DQN and PPO, obtain similar solutions. The quality of the generated assembly sequences slightly degrades for the most complex problem instances, i.e., the closed 3D curves. This may be caused by insufficient training time since it was limited by 30 minutes to keep the interface interactive, as longer waiting times may be inconvenient to users. Increasing the training duration can improve the results on those complex problem instances. Currently, we only consider the standard RL setting where an agent is evaluated on the same task on which it is trained, i.e., we train an RL agent and evaluate it on the same curve. Ideally, we would like the agent to be able to generalize to novel curves without full retraining. The algorithms capable of such generalization are currently being researched in the fields of multitask and transfer learning, as well as meta-reinforcement-learning. We plan to investigate them in future work.

The rightmost column in Table 1 shows the results obtained by the greedy algorithm. As described earlier, this algorithm exploits an approximately opti-

Table 1
Evaluation results for two reinforcement learning algorithms, PPO and DQN, on the task of sequential assembly along curves. RL is compared to a genetic algorithm and a greedy optimization method with a manually provided heuristic.

	Evolutionary Algorithm		Reinforcement Learning				Greedy Algorithm
Curves	Results_Genetic Algorithm		Results_PPO		Results_DQN		Results
2D short open curve	20 engagements	20 engagements	21 engagements	21 engagements	24 engagements	25 engagements	22 engagements
2D long open curve	36 engagements	36 engagements	35 engagements	30 engagements	42 engagements	41 engagements	38 engagements
3D short open curve	20 engagements	20 engagements	18 engagements	15 engagements	18 engagements	16 engagements	21 engagements
3D long open curve	36 engagements	36 engagements	33 engagements	48 engagements	36 engagements	36 engagements	37 engagements
3D short closed curve	20 engagements	20 engagements	25 engagements	23 engagements	26 engagements	27 engagements	22 engagements
3D long closed curve	36 engagements	36 engagements	32 engagements	32 engagements	39 engagements	42 engagements	38 engagements

mal heuristic for choosing the next action, and therefore its results may be considered as the target for evolutionary and reinforcement learning algorithms. Since the heuristic is provided, the algorithm runs very fast, finding a solution in under 2 minutes. In all cases, the algorithm finds assembly sequences that closely reproduce the specified curves.

ADAPTABILITY OF REINFORCEMENT LEARNING ON A TASK WITH OBSTACLES

An important advantage of reinforcement learning compared to the greedy optimization approach with heuristics is that RL algorithms are learning the value function autonomously. In contrast, for the greedy optimization a human designer needs to specify the heuristic. Although it is straightforward to provide a reasonable heuristic in the simple curve-following task, we are ultimately interested in more abstract tasks, such as optimizing a structure based on generic design criteria, and in that case, finding a robust heuristic may not be possible.

Figure 7 shows a straightforward modification of the curve following task by introducing obstacles. As illustrated, the greedy algorithm is not able to adapt to the task change, whereas RL finds a strategy that is able to solve the problem. In this scenario, following the rigid and predefined heuristic results in a suboptimal solution. To improve the result obtained by the greedy algorithm, the user would be required to manually adapt the heuristic to the novel scenario, which might be a cumbersome process. In contrast, reinforcement learning needs no further adaptations, and the exact same algorithm can be applied to the modified problem.

ARCHITECTURAL VERIFICATION OF THE GENERATED DESIGNS

The proposed interface where an architect specifies a curve and an algorithm finds an assembly sequence can be utilized in different ways as a creative tool in the design process. Here we provide an example of stacking the curves to generate a wall, as shown in Figure 8.

Furthermore, the designs generated by reinforcement learning for closed 3D curves can be used to fabricate and assemble complex cantilevering structures (Figures 9 and 10).

Thus, we confirm that the assembly sequence generated by the considered algorithm is feasible and leads to a physically constructible and stable structure. Therefore, reinforcement learning can support discrete form-finding and assembly based on the design preferences indicated by the architect.

CONCLUSION

Sequential assembly is a challenging combinatorial optimization problem. This paper has explored the applications of deep reinforcement learning to the automated design of open and closed curves based on interlocking dry-fitted SL-blocks. Two types of reinforcement learning methods were evaluated: actor-critic proximal policy optimization and value-based Q-learning. We described how an architectural problem can be translated into an RL problem and how the optimization can be performed using standard open-source Python packages of prominent RL algorithms.

Our results have demonstrated the potential of reinforcement learning, showing that it is able to generate significantly better designs on 3D curves compared to evolutionary algorithms, and we provided a real-world assembly based on the generated design to highlight its stability. For the curve following task considered in this paper, we designed an approximately optimal search heuristic that allowed us to compare the RL results against the greedy search approach. A notable observation here is that reinforcement learning achieves comparable results but

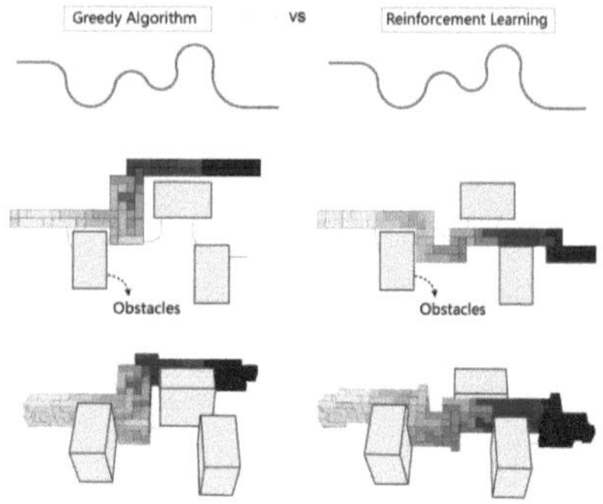

Figure 7
Comparing the assemblies generated by the greedy algorithm and DQN in the setting where three obstacles are added along the curve.

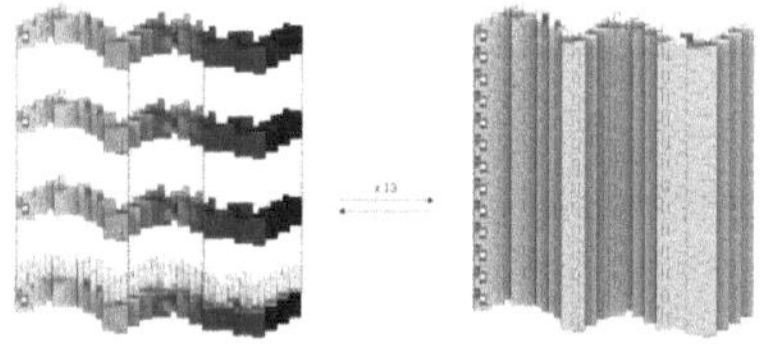

Figure 8
Exploiting the results from the RL algorithms on the 2D curve following the problem to obtain a wall made up of SL-blocks.

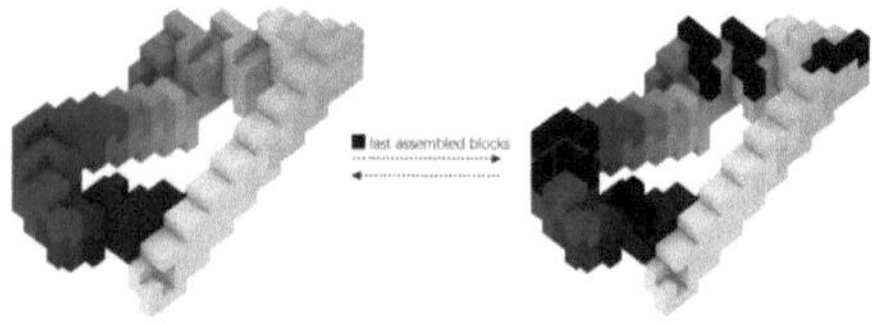

Figure 9
A color gradient shows the assembly sequence of a complex cantilevering structure from light to dark blue (left), and the key pieces for final fixation that are placed last indicated in black (right).

takes a significant amount of time to learn the value function on the order of tens of minutes. The key reason for this is the high number of trial-and-error attempts that RL algorithms require and the fact that Grasshopper is not optimized for such use and is therefore slowing down the pipeline.

We consider the results encouraging and in the future plan to explore the ways to speed up the simulation procedure in Grasshopper and consider more abstract optimization criteria, such as filling a 3D silhouette of a desired shape with SL-blocks, or optimizing based on architectural metrics such as the amount of lighting in an area or energy efficiency of construction.

Figure 10
Cantilevering model made from veneer plywood and 3D-printed SL-blocks.

Figure 11
Proposal for a bridge design made from 8.000 SL-blocks. The blocks in contact with soil could be cast in concrete and the top part fabricated from plywood.

Future research will have to shed light on the fabrication aspects for producing meaningful architectural structures (Figure 11). These investigations should include explorations of various materialities and fabrication techniques. The structural behavior and analysis of such assemblies should be examined for various load cases. The vast amount of assembly steps and the complex combinatorics are currently under investigation to be automated with robots.

RL integration for intricate design with SL-blocks makes it possible to design a dry-assembled structure that can be easily disassembled after usage. The adaptation of machine learning algorithms results in an informed design tool to obtain the assembly sequence of elements. The focus on reversible building elements that are self-interlocking requires architects to rethink certain design aspects without hindering their creative explorations. The presented approach is the first step in embedding the assembly procedure and charging it with various criteria to design with the help of machine intelligence.

ACKNOWLEDGMENTS

This project has received funding from the European Union's Horizon 2020 research and innovation programme under grant agreement No 640554 and from the Forum for Interdisciplinary Research at TU Darmstadt for the project Multimaterial Modular Design Through Robot Learning and Tactile Sensing. The authors acknowledge the support from the Artificial Intelligence in Construction (AICO) grant by Nexplore/Hochtief Collaboration Lab at TU Darmstadt.

REFERENCES

Apolinarska, AA, Pacher, M, Li, H, Cote, N, Pastrana, R, Gramazio, F and Kohler, M 2021, 'Robotic assembly of timber joints using reinforcement learning', *Automation in Construction*, 125, p. 103569

Bapst, V, Sanchez-Gonzalez, A, Doersch, C, Stachenfeld, K, Kohli, P, Battaglia, P and Hamrick, J 2019 'Structured agents for physical construction', *International Conference on Machine Learning*, pp. 464-474

Battaglia, PW, et al. 2018, 'Relational inductive biases, deep learning, and graph networks', *arXiv preprint arXiv:1806.01261*, 1806, pp. 1-40

Bello, I, Pham, H, Le, QV, Norouzi, M and Bengio, S 2016, 'Neural combinatorial optimization with reinforcement learning', *arXiv preprint arXiv:1611.09940*, 1611, pp. 1-15

Bengio, Y, Lodi, A and Prouvost, A 2020, 'Machine learning for combinatorial optimization: a methodological tour d'horizon', *European Journal of Operational Research*, 290, pp. 405-421

CHO, M, JUNGTAEK, K, HYUNSOO, C, LEE, JH and PARK, J 2020 'Combinatorial 3D Shape Generation via Sequential Assembly', *Advances in Neural Information Processing Systems*

Chou, LW 2019, *The Study on SL-Blocks*, National Chiayi University

Costa, A, Nannicini, G, Schroepfer, T and Wortmann, T 2015, 'Black-box optimization of lighting simulation in architectural design', in Cardin, MA, Krob, D, Lui, PC, Tan, YH and Wood, K (eds) 2015, *Complex systems design & management Asia*, Springer, pp. 27-39

Dai, H, Khalil, EB, Zhang, Y, Dilkina, B and Song, L 2017, 'Learning combinatorial optimization algorithms over graphs', *arXiv preprint arXiv:1704.01665*, 1704, pp. 1-24

Durmisevic, E 2019, *Circular economy in construction design strategies for reversible buildings*, Elma Durmisevic

Fang, Y 2017, *Optimization of Daylighting and Energy Performance Using Parametric Design, Simulation Modeling, and Genetic Algorithms*, Ph.D. Thesis, North Carolina State University

Gershenfeld, N, Carney, M, Jenett, B, Calisch, S and Wilson, S 2015, 'Macrofabrication with digital materials: Robotic assembly', *Architectural design*, 85(5), pp. 122-127

Janner, M, Levine, S, Freeman, WT, Tenenbaum, JB, Finn, C and Wu, J 2018, 'Reasoning about physical interactions with object-oriented prediction and planning', *arXiv preprint arXiv:1812.10972*, 1812, pp. 1-12

Sanchez, J 2016 'Combinatorial Design: Non-Parametric Computational Design Strategies', *ACADIA // 2016: POSTHUMAN FRONTIERS: Data, Designers, and Cognitive Machines [Proceedings of the 36th Annual Conference of the Association for Computer Aided Design in Architecture (ACADIA)*

Scarselli, F, Gori, M, Tsoi, AC, Hagenbuchner, M and Monfardini, G 2008, 'The graph neural network model', *IEEE transactions on neural networks*, 20(1), pp. 61-80

Schrittwieser, J, et al. 2020, 'Mastering atari, go, chess and shogi by planning with a learned model', *Nature*, 588(7839), pp. 604-609

Schulman, J, Wolski, F, Dhariwal, P, Radford, A and Klimov, O 2017, 'Proximal policy optimization algorithms', *arXiv preprint arXiv:1707.06347*, 1707, pp. 1-12

Shi, X and Yang, W 2013, 'Performance-driven architectural design and optimization technique from a perspective of architects', *Automation in Construction*, 32, pp. 125-135

Shih, S 2016 'On the Hierarchical Construction of SL Blocks A Generative System that Builds Self-Interlocking Structures', *Advances in Architectural Geometry 2016*

Shih, SG, Yen, CH and Chou, LW 2019 'Extensible Structures of Interlinking SL Strands', *Proceedings of Bridges 2019: Mathematics, Art, Music, Architecture, Education, Culture*, pp. 415-418

Silver, D, et al. 2017, 'Mastering the game of go without human knowledge', *nature*, 550(7676), pp. 354-359

Tessmann, O and Rossi, A 2019, 'Geometry as Interface: Parametric and Combinatorial Topological Interlocking Assemblies', *Journal of Applied Mechanics*, 86(11), pp. 1-12

Thompson, R, Ghalebi, E, DeVries, T and Taylor, GW 2020, 'Building LEGO Using Deep Generative Models of Graphs', *arXiv preprint arXiv:2012.11543*, 2012, pp. 1-12

Tibbits, S and Cheung, K 2012, 'Programmable materials for architectural assembly and automation', *Assembly Automation*, 32(3), pp. 216-225

Wang, Z, Song, P and Pauly, M 2018, 'DESIA: A general framework for designing interlocking assemblies', *ACM Transactions on Graphics (TOG)*, 37(6), pp. 1-14

Wortmann, T and Nannicini, G 2017, 'Introduction to architectural design optimization', in Karakitsiou, A, Migdalas2, A, Rassia, ST and Pardalos4, PM (eds) 2017, *City Networks*, Springer, pp. 259-278

Gridworld Architecture Testbed

Anatolii Kotov[1], *Ilija Vukorep*[2]
[1,2]*BTU Cottbus-Senftenberg*
[1,2]*{anatolii.kotov|ilija.vukorep}@b-tu.de*

Over centuries architects have developed frameworks of representation of the built surroundings in diverse types of drawings or models. With the rise of digital techniques, virtual models slowly replace these representation techniques but are still far from replicating the real world's ambiguity and complexity. This paper wants to address the representational problems of architecture combined with architecture-related AI systems and missing standardized tests for such systems. For this, we suggest a standardized computational testbed that can serve for developing, testing and benchmarking design solutions for abstracted architectural problems with various AI approaches in a game-like environment.Furthermore, this paper will discuss architectural problems' subdivision into atomic subtasks solvable by specific AI systems. Ideally, there is a waste number of possible architectural subtasks that can be applied. The paper presents some examples of possible architectural game strategies that abstractly deal with concepts of walls and borders, zones and connections. Although this paper mentions different Reinforcement Learning techniques, it is not focusing on fine-tuning the AI algorithms. It aims to help achieve automation of specific design workflow phases, then in the longer term to optimize and propose alternative design solutions and improve the architectural community's overall work.

Keywords: *Gridworld Testbed, AI Aided Architecture, Benchmarking AI Algorithms*

STATEMENT OF THE PROBLEM

The ability for abstract thinking is one of the crucial skills of an architect. It means the reduction of detailed information in dependency of the process phase, and this concerns not only the subject of the architectural design but also the architectural process itself. Abstraction helps us to keep in mind the "big" goal of the architectural problem. Following this, we will not start with a staircase core design before we have a house's footprint. Still, broad architectural knowledge is necessary to successfully abstract certain dispositions, like the approximate size and location of a staircase in the house footprint's dependency. Furthermore, architectural design problems involve performing a series of actions where the goal state is not known in advance (Chan, 1990).

For the AI field to apply those action steps, we have to limit the analyzed problems and used tools. In this research, we are dealing with spatial, volume and connectivity scope of problems. We also assume that architects can formulate architecture design problems with a certain degree of simplification that is also beneficial in formulating the goals in specific AI-compatible mathematical definitions.

In the last years, researchers conducted AI-related spatial and architecture related experiments using the voxelized world of Minecraft (López Méndez et al., 2017), and one team developed a competition to generate settlements (Salge et al., 2020). Their experiments showed that the main problem of setting such multi-objective settlement-related goals is the provision of a quantitative analysis of delivered solutions. Although the aim is high, this work shows the applicability of gamelike tools for solving complex architecture problems.

The ability of AI-driven intrinsic motivation to change an environment can be observed in other Salge research work (Salge and Polani, 2013) and serves as a basis for diverse scenarios. Their architectural applicability we will concretize in the chapter Concept of the Gridworld.

COMPARISON OF AI METHODS

In many cases, developing AI tools in architecture will face the problems of data representation (Zwierzycki, 2020), manipulation, and evaluation. The chosen AI method for a given situation is conceptually and methodologically affecting potential design solutions.

There is a certain number of possible AI-systems, like Generative Adversarial Networks (GAN), Deepdream (Christian Szegedy et al., 2014) and latest systems like CycleGAN (Zhu et al., 2017), CLIP (Radford et al., 2021), which are using the embedding representation and/or latent space. In architecture, several experimental examples are using GAN for manipulating floor plans (Chaillou, 2019). Such types of systems are heavily dependent on datasets. The recent trend in the AI-related architecture debate is the formulation of problems towards their optimization possibility using genetic algorithms and swarm intelligence (Vukorep and Kotov, 2021). However, those types of methods do not intrinsically search for a design solution.

A subset of AI is Reinforcement Learning (RL), a method that belongs to unsupervised learning techniques. This approach utilizes a concept of an environment and an agent capable of interaction with the environment via different actions. Using feedback data based on actions, also known as a reward, agents can develop quite complex behaviour. For instance, in the case of positive reward, the agent can associate previously executed actions with a successful result, thus enabling the training process. In the case of a simple game, where a car should reach the finish, the positive reward is given when the cars are going forward on the track and negative when it is going backwards or hitting other cars and/or track borders. However, some games do not have such continuous feedback. Certain games, e.g. chess, do have a positive or negative reward only in the end. This condition is the so-called sparse reward function and in comparison to other types, it may require significantly more iterations and/or complex learning strategies to converge. The exact time of simulation is entirely dependant on the particular game and its goals and can vary from minutes to weeks of real-time computation. Learning strategies can also include the usage of human-generated data.

The representation of problems in the form of games is a common technique in RL. Games, over time, became an essential benchmarking tool within standardized frameworks. One such standardized testbed is the OpenAI framework releasing environments for various purposes known as the gym (Brockman et al., 2016). Currently, it hosts everything from pole balancing games to robotic simulations. The architecture-based standardized testbed presented in this paper is based on this gym and will be shared on a Git-Lab platform.

We have chosen RL as the AI-basis for our architectural gridworld testbeds because of its meta-learning capabilities (Yu et al., 2020) and some achievements that overplay human performance in games such as chess and go (Schrittwieser et al., 2020).

CONCEPT OF THE GRIDWORLD

Testbeds are used for replicable testing of scientific prototypes. Gridworlds are discrete 2D virtual environments with complete or incomplete information for independent software systems solving basic principles. We can find gridworlds in almost all fields where the self-learning agent-based AI technique is applied. As the gridworld is organized as a 2D-matrix, its data representation is machine- and human-readable (figure 1).

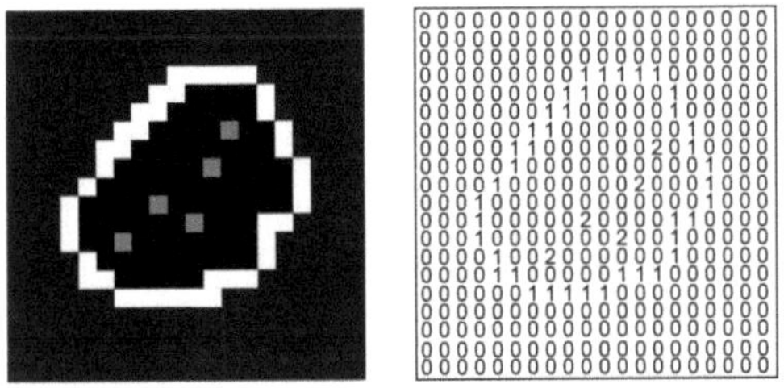

Figure 1
Gridworld state and its internal representation

In standard testbeds, agents are acting in a fixed environment. Contrary to this, we propose to reverse the principle and let the agend manipulate the environment to achieve a goal (figure 2). The success in standard testbeds is measured through the agent's relation to the implanted subjects inside the environment. In our testbed, the success is evaluated through the environment's relation to the implanted subjects or the relationship between different environmental elements. The agent is changing the states of gridworld cells, thereby changing the environment configuration.

The capabilities of agents to manipulate the environment depends from game to game. In simpler games, the agent can create or eliminate environmental elements. In advanced options, the environmental elements can undergo other manipulations like being moved or transformed.

Its grid-like representation has some abstract visual overlappings with architectural or urbanistic drawings, and thus organic data compatibility is one of the main reasons why gridworld testbed might be a helpful tool.

Defining architectural problems that can be solved with such a testbed are various but share one common ground: space. Space is what all "game-levels" or problems have to deal with. AI systems that are solving some spatial and/or functional problems can be tested here, as the first step towards automatic or suggestive floor-layouting or urban development models: defining inside and outside, area zoning, functional relations between zones, environmental analysis in dependencies of the orientation and many more (figure 3).

On an abstract level, those concepts are a testbed for part of architecture intuition providing AI-concepts capable of generalizing mentioned aspects in architecture design. For instance, after succeeding simpler games, it is possible to merge goals into one game that shares the qualities of the previous ones. Thus, increasing the complexity and merging more and more games, it will be possible to achieve a game sophisticated enough to represent more real-world problems.

An essential question in the implementation of AI in such game levels is a trained system's ability to generalize between the tasks, in other words, to transfer the gained experience to changing environments (Cobbe et al., 2019). Although generalization and transfer of experience between RL game levels are possible, further research will deliver significant reliable data that also depends on implemented RL-Algorithms.

SYSTEM DESCRIPTION

Our environment is wrapped in the OpenAI Gym interface, thus enabling a general interface for AI models. For benchmarking, we use the open-source implementation of OpenAI Baselines. The observed data is a tensor, holding different observation parameters, such as the vision of the world and the vision of the current agent position. The default formulated action space is defined as:

- Four actions to encode movements
- One action to switch the current zone type of the environment
- One action to finish the game

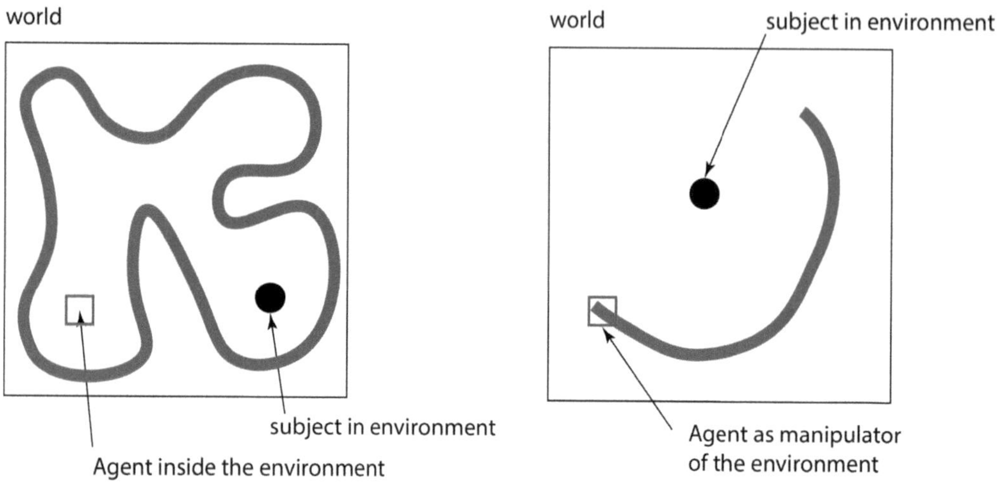

Figure 2
left: concept scheme of a common testbed; right: concept scheme of the architecture testbed

The AI player usually is figuring out the rules based on the reward when the game terminates. This sparse reward makes the problem solving more complex since we don't have continuous functions, which would give agents a hint regarding its performance. Rewards are internally calculated following the rules of each game. These rules and their well-tuned reward calculation provides the system with its intrinsic motivation.

Game problems are formulated by direct game terminal conditions and additional metadata. Some of the games may require metadata and there are several ways of passing them into the testbed. Generally, metadata differ by data type and how they affect the systems' overall generalizing capabilities and AI's required complexity. For instance, metadata can be rules or descriptions and can be transferred via text and further processed by dedicated artificial neural network (ANN) layers. The text-based rule can be: "divide into two equal zones" or "build a border with an inner area of 20% of total". Currently, the system can generate metadata by using a template form.

We can pass various data parameters like the number of objects, amount of resources and similar directly because of its simplicity. However, some data normalization may be required.

Since specific architecture problems can be structured in a graph type of data, it's required for some of the game-goals to pass those data to the agent. Currently, graph data is being represented in a matrix-form, that can give connectivity information and target area of the zones. However, it may be inefficient to pass this data directly to the agent because the agent will be too specific and dependent on the matrix's particular dimensionality. For instance, if you train an agent with *n* room, n will be the max limitation of room count.

Several terminal conditions are possible - terminal action, timesteps or reached goal by some quantification logic. The specific agent termination action has the goal of training the agent to perceive some ideal solving condition. All of the games are currently using timestep limitation to have a good learning process.

We tested the following AI Algorithms on the simple "border around a subject" and "connection between two subjects" games: Deep Q learning(DQN), Advantage Actor Critic(A2C) and Proximal Policy Optimization(PPO). We can see the general

Figure 3
Different schematic concepts of simple games and levels. Further research will show how AI-experience is transferable over the boundaries of the concepts: borders - connections - zones.

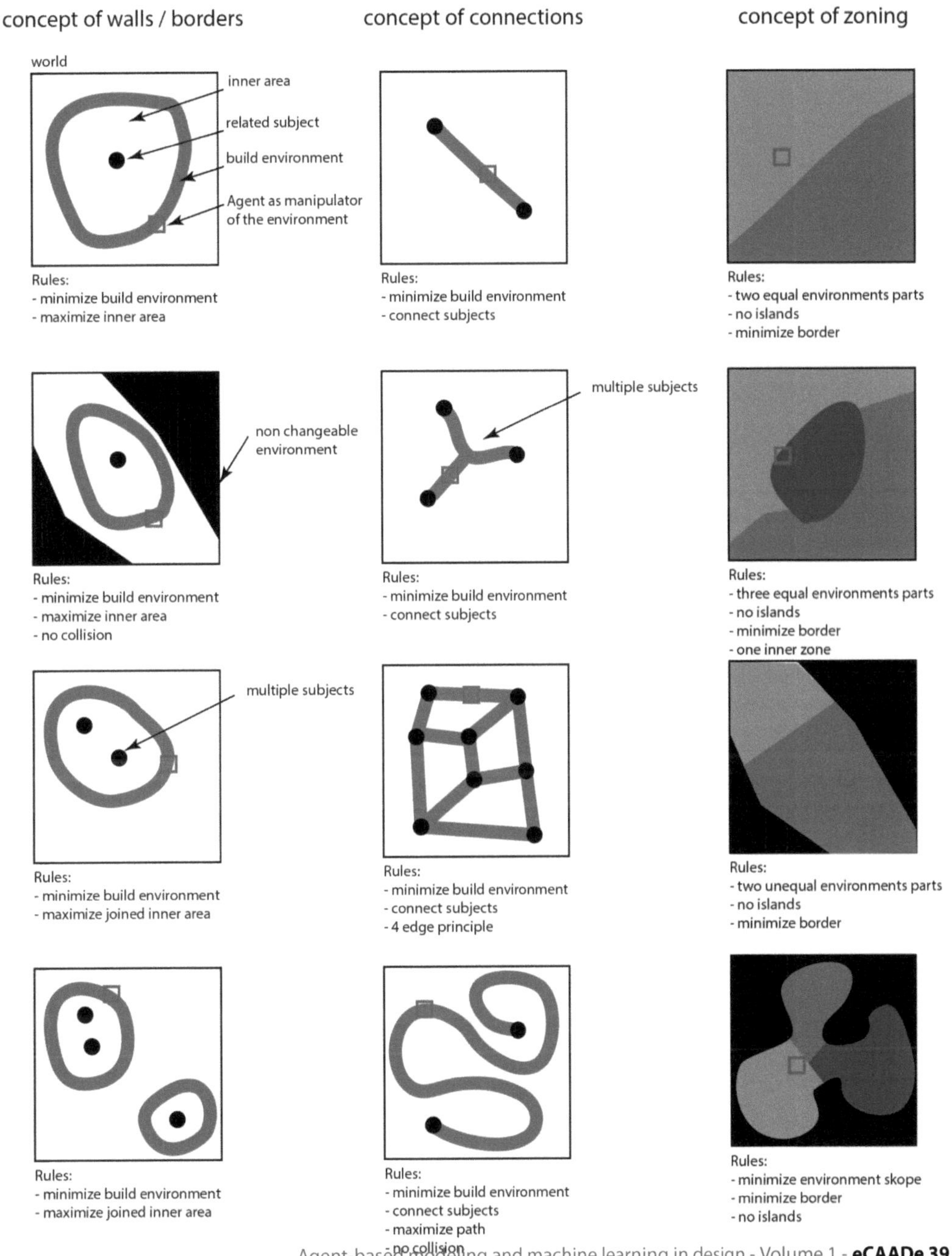

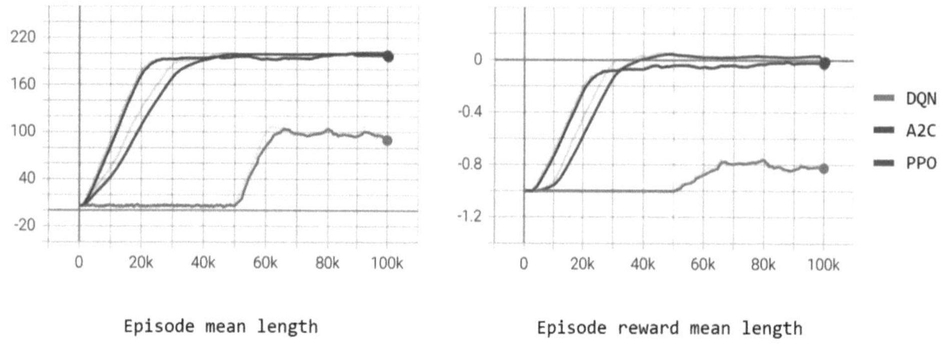

Figure 4
Performance graphs of the "border around a subject" game

behaviour differences between DQN and A2C/PPO. DQN requires significantly more time steps to activate the terminate-button correctly. However, we can reduce those problems with a larger buffer size and other modifications. Through tests, PPO is demonstrating the most stable and increasing performance (figure 4,5).

During development and testing, we found that the proper tuned reward function definition plays a crucial role in the system's overall convergence due to the overall complexity of some games and sparse reward. Sometimes it's more efficient to give a small, but still positive intermediate reward to foster the learning process.

RESULTS & FURTHER WORK

This paper aims to help achieve automation of specific design workflow phases, in the longer term to optimize and propose alternative design solutions

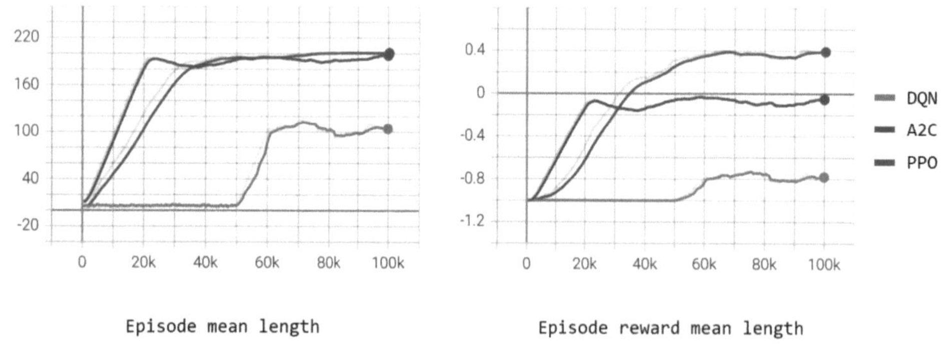

Figure 5
Performance graphs of the "connection between two subjects" game

Figure 6
Gridworld as a part of the programming workflow of architectural software tools

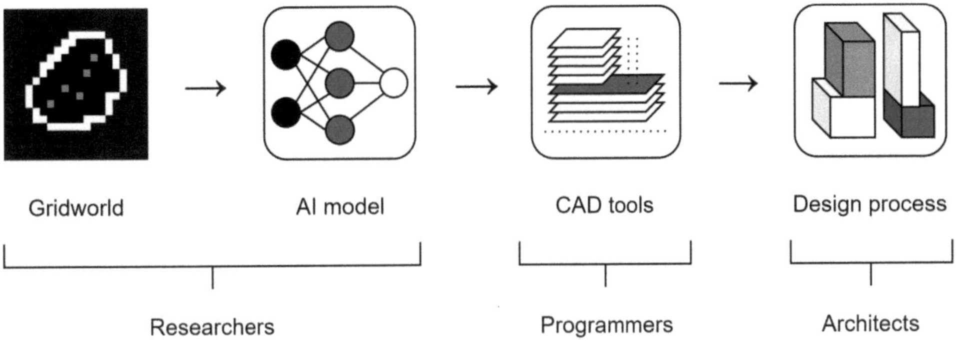

and improve the architectural community's overall work (figure 6). Further modifications of the proposed system will enable creating of the next generation of automated design tools for architects, engineers, and designers with AI system co-authoring in the design process.

The work focuses on developing an AI tool for architecture that primarily tests AI concepts against basic architecture-related tasks. Although we delivered some schemes related to concepts of borders, connections and zones, and two examples of games, the main work in developing concrete games is still to do.

The main difference to conventional gridworld testbeds is the notion of a manipulatable environment and intrinsic motivation to change the environment. This is provided by setting the right rules and the capability of the framework to implement various AI algorithms. The following research steps will deal with crossover-generalization of concepts (borders+connections+zones), incorporating graph-based data, the atomic subdivision of architecture and their game-form implementation, and most importantly, with the scalability from gridworld to real-world cases.

REFERENCES

Brockman, G, Cheung, V, Pettersson, L, Schneider, J, Schulman, J, Tang, J and Zaremba, W 2016, 'OpenAI Gym', *arXiv:1606.01540 [cs]*, /, p. /

Chaillou, S 2019, 'AI + Architecture: Towards a New Approach', *Harvard University*, /, p. /

Chan, CS 1990, 'Cognitive Processes in Architectural Design Problem Solving', *Design Studies - DESIGN STUD*, 11, pp. 60-80

Cobbe, K, Klimov, O, Hesse, C, Kim, T and Schulman, J 2019, 'Quantifying Generalization in Reinforcement Learning', *arXiv:1812.02341 [cs, stat]*, /, p. /

López Méndez, MDC, González Arrieta, A, Queiruga Dios, M, Hernández Encinas, A and Queiruga-Dios, A 2017 'Minecraft as a Tool in the Teaching-Learning Process of the Fundamental Elements of Circulation in Architecture', *International Joint Conference SOCO'16-CISIS'16-ICEUTE'16*, Cham, pp. 728-735

Radford, A, Kim, JW, Hallacy, C, Ramesh, A, Goh, G, Agarwal, S, Sastry, G, Askell, A, Mishkin, P, Clark, J, Krueger, G and Sutskever, I 2021, 'Learning Transferable Visual Models From Natural Language Supervision', *arXiv:2103.00020 [cs]*, /, p. /

Salge, C, Green, MC, Canaan, R, Skwarski, F, Fritsch, R, Brightmoore, A, Ye, S, Cao, C and Togelius, J 2020, 'The AI Settlement Generation Challenge in Minecraft', *KI - Künstliche Intelligenz*, 34(1), pp. 19-31

Salge, C and Polani, D 2013, 'Changing the Environment based on Intrinsic Motivation', *arXiv:1310.3692 [nlin]*, /, p. /

Schrittwieser, J, Antonoglou, I, Hubert, T, Simonyan, K, Sifre, L, Schmitt, S, Guez, A, Lockhart, E, Hassabis, D, Graepel, T, Lillicrap, T and Silver, D 2020, 'Mastering Atari, Go, chess and shogi by planning with a learned model', *Nature*, 588, pp. 604-609

Szegedy, C, Liu, W, Jia, Y, Sermanet, P, Reed, S, Anguelov, D, Erhan, D, Vanhoucke, V and Rabinovich, A 2014, *Going Deeper with Convolutions*, arXiv.org

Vukorep, I and Kotov, A 2021, 'Machine learning in architecture', in As, IA and Basu, PB (eds) 2021, *The Rout-*

ledge Companion to Artificial Intelligence in Architecture, Taylor & Francis, pp. 93-109

Yu, T, Quillen, D, He, Z, Julian, R, Hausman, K, Finn, C and Levine, S 2020 'Meta-World: A Benchmark and Evaluation for Multi-Task and Meta Reinforcement Learning', *Conference on Robot Learning*, pp. 1094-1100

Zhu, J, Park, T, Isola, P and Efros, AA 2017 'Unpaired Image-to-Image Translation Using Cycle-Consistent Adversarial Networks', *2017 IEEE International Conference on Computer Vision (ICCV)*, pp. 2242-2251

Zwierzycki, M 2020 'On AI Adoption Issues in Architectural Design - Identifying the issues based on an extensive literature review.', *Werner, L and Koering, D (eds.), Anthropologic: Architecture and Fabrication in the cognitive age - Proceedings of the 38th eCAADe Conference - Volume 1, TU Berlin, Berlin, Germany, 16-18 September 2020, pp. 515-524*

Comparative Evaluation of Tensor-based Data Representations for Deep Learning Methods in Architecture

Viktor Eisenstadt[1], Hardik Arora[2], Christoph Ziegler[3], Jessica Bielski[4], Christoph Langenhan[5], Klaus-Dieter Althoff[6], Andreas Dengel[7]
[1,2,6,7] German Research Center for Artificial Intelligence (DFKI) [3,4,5] Technical University of Munich
[1,2,6,7] {viktor.eisenstadt|hardik.arora|klaus-dieter.althoff|andreas.dengel}@dfki.de [3,4,5] {c.ziegler|j.bielski|langenhan}@tum.de

This paper presents an extended evaluation of tensor-based representations of graph-based architectural room configurations. This experiment is a continuation of examination of recognition of semantic architectural features by contemporary standard deep learning methods. The main aim of this evaluation is to investigate how the deep learning models trained using the relation tensors as data representation means perform on data not available in the training dataset. Using a straightforward classification task, stepwise modifications of the original training dataset and manually created spatial configurations were fed into the models to measure their prediction quality. We hypothesized that the modifications that influence the class label will not decrease this quality, however, this was not confirmed and most likely the latent non-class defining features make up the class for the model. Under specific circumstances, the prediction quality still remained high for the winning relation tensor type.

Keywords: *Deep Learning, Spatial Configuration, Semantic Building Fingerprint*

INTRODUCTION

Deep learning (DL) is widely used for many research areas of computer science, however, its application to computer-aided architectural design (CAAD) is still not as common as in other domains. Mainly this is caused by missing a common representation of spatial configurations that is fully compatible with contemporary DL methods. While images of floor plans can be an obvious choice, they do not explicitly provide semantic information necessary for decision-making of many DL methods, and more suitable ways to represent architectural data in DL exist.

In the context of research on DL-based autocompletion of room configurations, several data representations in the form other than images were investigated (Eisenstadt et al., 2021). As a result, the data structure "relation map" was developed that uses a specific adjacency matrix-based tensor to represent semantic relations between the rooms in a spatial configuration. Using a specifically configured convolutional neural network (CNN), text-based, numerical layer-based, and one-hot vector-based types of relation map were pre-evaluated using the task of classification based on a set of spatial relation classes. This preliminary evaluation was performed automatically by the DL framework, the winning one-hot vector-based relation map type classified the samples with approx. 98% validation accuracy.

In this paper, a more in-depth subsequent evaluation of these representations is presented that investigates how their corresponding deep learning models evaluate spatial configuration samples not present in the training dataset. It is intended to answer the following research questions:

1. Which of the representation type models classifies structurally unknown and manually created samples correctly in the majority of cases?
2. When classifying data initially known but slightly or heavy modified in relational structure, will the predicted class remain appropriate?

Using a set of data augmentation rules to operate on consistently modified datasets for the evaluation and manually design multiple spatial configurations, it is intended to simulate real-world classification usage. The main goal of this evaluation is to find the relation map type that provides the best classification response to changes in the semantic information available in spatial configurations. Additionally, we aim to find out which modifications are responsible for significant changes in the overall classification rate. The results of the evaluation are required for improvement of the CNN-based approach for retrieval of contextually similar floor plans to support early phases of architectural design (Eisenstadt et al., 2020). In this approach, classification of spatial configurations narrows down the set of relevant retrieval candidates based on classes recognized in the query. The winning type of relation map will also be used in a sequential form in the upcoming segmentation-based floor plan autocompletion approach.

RESEARCH CONTEXT & RELATED WORK

During the currently running research project *metis-II* (2020-2023, supported by the DFG - German Research Foundation), we examine and develop DL-based methods and approaches for support of the early conceptual phases in architectural design. Taking into account the vagueness and uncertainty of architectural design data in the form of graph-based spatial configurations, we investigate how auto-completion of floor plans (comparable to e.g., word and sentence completion on keyboards of modern mobile devices) can be achieved using artificial neural networks. Based on early sketches of the building designs, rooms and the possible relations between them are suggested to the architect to enhance the early ideation process. The auto-completion methods are intended to be a helpful tool for architects during the early conceptual process supporting them in working more efficiently, while being able to focus on the creative aspects/tasks. Providing the architects with the different design continuation options, it is intended to create interaction patterns to assess their own design decisions and explore the possible further developments of the current spatial configuration state.

To represent the spatial configuration in the form compatible with the deep learning methods, but also keep the relevant semantic information entered by the architect, we use a number of *Semantic Building Fingerprint* graphs (SBF), where nodes represent rooms and edges represent relations (connections) between the rooms. The information encoded as an SBF-based graph contains topological as well as non-topological data distributed among several different patterns (see figure 1). For use of these patterns in DL methods, they are transformed into the numerical tensor format "relation map" which represents a modified adjacency matrix of the spatial configuration graph using relations between the rooms of the graph to encode semantic information. The re-

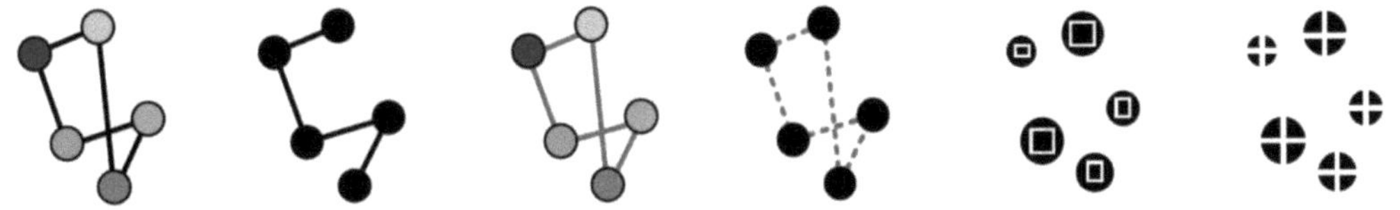

Figure 1
Examples of semantic building fingerprints (SBF). With topology (1-4): semantic spatial graph, through-path-graph, semantic spatial connection graph, spatial distance. Without topology (5, 6): envelope area, center of room.

lation map concept was designed using the idea of reverse compatibility, i.e., the tensor can be transformed back into spatial configuration and displayed as such in the user interface. The early types of relation maps were used for data augmentation (Arora et al., 2020). The further developments of them were preliminary evaluated (see next section), but until now not applied in any approach as they were not extensively tested yet for unexpected classification cases, this testing will be described in this paper.

Currently, deep learning approaches in architecture use raster- or vector-based images of floor plans, mostly due to their availability and as an obvious choice for use in popular DL methods, such as CNNs, for which many applicable and extendable applications examples from other domains already exist. However, as examined during development of approaches for our research project, such entirely pixel- or vector-based color data does not provide the necessary semantic information. For example, for semantic building fingerprint-based auto-completion, the recognition of relational dependencies between the rooms is required that is not possible with image-based data. Nevertheless, successful approaches for purposes other than ours use architectural image data: as examples, search for similar designs (Sharma et al., 2017), modification of the design style (Newton, 2019; Silvestre et al., 2016), or estimation of the layout in 3D (Sun et al., 2019) can be named.

An additional problem, that became evident during the research project, is that even when non-image-based data samples (e.g., as graphs in XML format) are available, a suitable common representation of spatial configurations for DL is missing, as the sufficient amount of data might be available from different sources that do not have common semantic representation requirements and the pure XML-based data is not a numerical tensor format required for the contemporary DL frameworks e.g. TensorFlow or PyTorch. While it is also possible to use specific DL abstraction layers, such as *Deep Graph Library* (Wang et al., 2019), they do not provide architecture-specific DL representations and/or models and they have to be additionally developed nevertheless.

DL REPRESENTATIONS & PRE-EVALUATION

To overcome the deep learning representation problems described above, a number of architecture-specific tensor-based data structures were developed that can be used with standard methods of contemporary DL frameworks. All these representations are based on the common concept of "relation map", an adjacency matrix modified to encode the relevant semantic features detected in the topology of the spatial configuration graph. Each row of such matrix tensors stands for a particular room of the floor plan and its outgoing connections to other rooms. Geometrical parameters of the building design are not considered. Relation maps are inspired by architectural morphospaces (Steadman and Mitchell 2010) and geometry maps (De Miguel et al., 2019), but also by Hickman and Krolik (2009) who used the adjacency matrices to encode general availability of connections in spatial configurations.

The essential semantic entity of a relation map is the *relation code*, that numerically encodes the connection information in a triple **<source room, target room, connection type>** in the cells of the matrix rows using a specific typology in which each room and connection type are assigned to the specific integer numerical value (see Figure 2). For example, in the relation code **562**, the source room type *Living*

(5) is connected to the target room type *Bathroom* (6) by the connection type *Door* (2). Currently, five types of the relation map exist. The *simple relation map* is a 1D tensor and uses relation codes in the form described above. The *zoned relation map* enriches the relation codes with the information about *architectural room zones*, the categorical taxonomy of room types that groups them by their functionality (Langenhan, 2017). For example, the relation code **35162** represents the room type *Kitchen* (3) from the *Habitation* zone (5) connected to the room type *Corridor* (1) from the *Service* zone (6) by a *Door* (2). The zoned connection map was developed to eliminate possible repetition of relation codes. Later, more advanced types *multilayer map*, *one-hot encoded map*, and *textual map* were developed.

The multilayer map (see Figure 2, upper right part) was developed for the situations where the typology of room and connection types is not explicitly available for the given dataset of spatial layouts. To encode relevant semantic information in samples from such datasets, the conversion methods of the multilayer map use the cryptology method of *hashing* of values detected as possible room and relation types. Provided that the data was unified during the creation of the dataset, the hashing will return the same values for the same room and connection types. The subsequent encoding into decimal fraction will result in the 3-element relation code array for source room, target room, and connection type. For example, the connection *Living <- Door -> Bathroom* can be encoded as an array **[0.15383, 0.25237, 0.32474]**. Inspired by the RGB scheme channels, a multi-layered 3D map can then be constructed consisting of the source room layer, target room layer, and the connection type layer. Each layer will use the values from the corresponding array index only.

The one-hot encoded map (see Figure 2, middle part) was designed to properly encode categorical data instead of categorization of pure numerical data, which is used in all previously presented maps. Using the classic one-hot encoding technique for categorical data, the room and connection types are encoded as *one-hot vectors*, the position of **1** in the vector defines the corresponding type. All other positions are filled with **0**. Each vector has as many elements as the overall number of types for the respective information type (i.e., room or connection type). This method avoids summarization of semantic information in the form of source, target, and connection into one numerical value, where the order of the numbers and the position further left or further right in the relation code has a larger or smaller influence on this value. Additionally, the one-hot representation eliminates the risk of assigning categories to numbers which can be interpreted as ranking and/or similarity measure. For example, using the typology numbers of Figure 2, the difference between *Toilet* (7) and *Sleeping* (2) would be greater than between *Living* (5) and *Corridor* (1): **7-2=5** vs. **5-1=4**.

Finally, the textual relation map (see Figure 2, lower part) was developed for adaptation to the changes in the number of room types or edge types in the typology preserving the original shape of the tensor and to solve the problem of sparsity (for example, for spatial configurations with a small number of connections in relation to the number of rooms). The textual relation map is a variation of the simple relation map, that uses sentences to represent connections between rooms as relation codes. An example of such a sentence is **'living connects with sleeping using wall'**. To represent non-existing connections between two rooms the textual placeholder **'no connection'** is used (instead of using 0 like the number- or vector-based maps described above). Given that this map representation is text-based, it can also be used in a different form for multiple DL approaches including sequence learning or text classification.

For the last three representations described above, a preliminary evaluation (Eisenstadt et al., 2021) was performed, that should provide an initial answer on the question if the relation map tensors are able to properly encode the relevant semantic information contained in the spatial configuration graphs, so that the DL models can understand this information and meet the correct deci-

Figure 2
Original floor plan SBF and its conversions into multilayer map, one-hot encoded map, and textual map. For selected numerical encodings of the underlying typology, their corresponding room and connection types are shown.

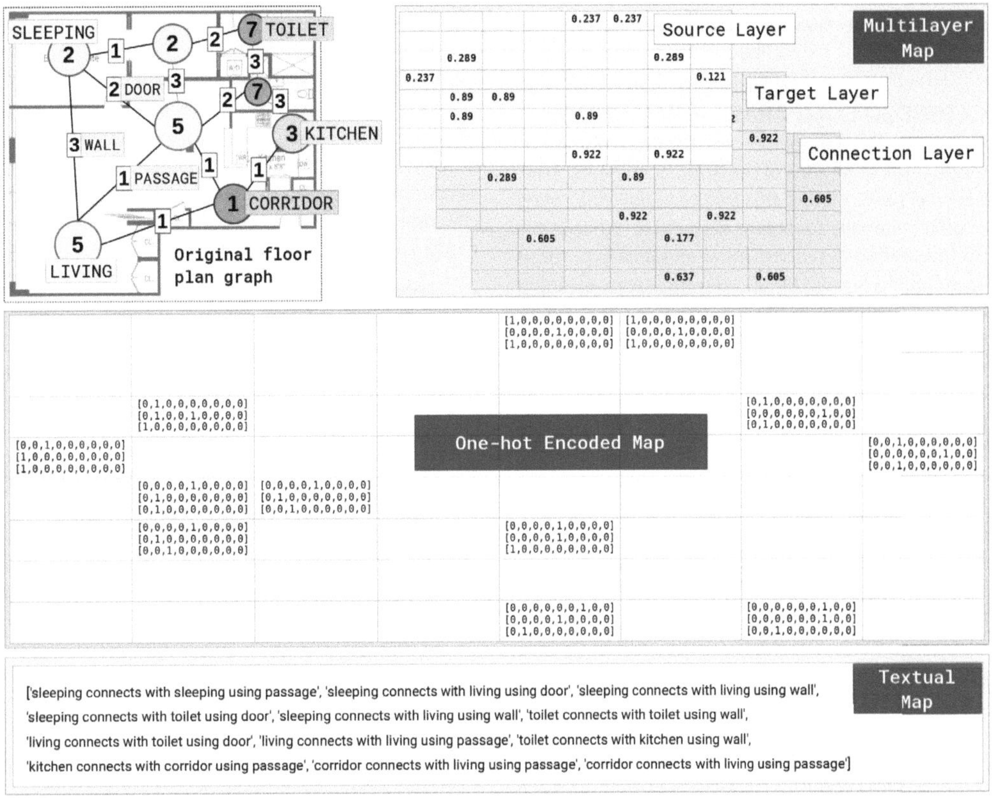

sion, e.g., correctly classify the spatial configuration. An automated experiment using the straightforward classification process was selected as the evaluation method due to the availability of classification and its validation techniques directly in the modern DL frameworks. For training the DL models in the form of CNNs, a dataset of 2544 housing floor plans was used. It was based on the original 200 data samples that were extended using a number of variation and consistency rules. The measurement of training and validation accuracy was performed automatically using the built-in DL framework tools. The results of this pre-evaluation indicated that the DL models are able to process and understand the latent semantic structure of the selected relation map types and the information contained in them. A max. validation accuracy of 98% was achieved for the winning type, the one-hot encoded map. The multilayer map and textual map could achieve a max. of 84% and 83% respectively. *These results are our current benchmarks for validation of the prediction quality of the models.*

While the pre-evaluation provided satisfactory results that confirmed the direction of our research efforts, it was still not clear how the DL models trained on the selected relation map types would react when introduced spatial configurations not available in the training dataset. To answer this question, an extended evaluation that involved again the multilayer, one-hot encoded, and textual map was conducted and will be described in the next section.

EXTENDED COMPARATIVE EVALUATION

The extended comparative evaluation of tensor-based representations of semantic building information was performed to finalize the initial exploration of their suitability for standard DL tasks. While in the pre-evaluation described above an initial hypothesis on suitability should be tested using no means other than the built-in tools of DL frameworks, in this evaluation, the selected relation maps should prove their potential for use in DL-based applications developed in context of the research project. Identically to the pre-evaluation, tests shall show which relation map type provides the best performance.

To answer the question described above, a *double-phase evaluation scenario* was developed which was aimed at extensive testing of class prediction quality of the relation map models. The tests were conducted under different *grades of modification* of the original training dataset and spatial configuration samples not available in the original dataset, but *created manually* using the same format and consistency checking tools. The relation map DL models from the preliminary evaluation were reused without re-training them. The class labels were reused from the pre-evaluation as well: each class indicated the *amount of habitable spaces*, i.e., Sleeping, Living, Children, Working, and Room (generic room label), and if the spatial configuration is open or closed, identified by whether there is a Passage between the kitchen and the living room. An example of such a class label is **"3_closed"**. Overall **10** classes were created.

The background idea of the evaluation was to perform the classification of the manually created spatial configurations first, in order to get an immediate initial estimation on how good the models can classify unknown cases. Based on the result of this initial estimation, i.e. low or high prediction quality, the task would be to investigate what modifications might have caused it and if this result is a random occurrence. That is, either the most likely failure trail should be reconstructed (in case of low quality) and/or the possible fluctuations in the classification rate should be tracked (for both low and high rates).

In order to measure the sufficiency of the classification of unknown and modified samples by the models, it was decided to calculate the percentage of correctly predicted labels using following two specific metrics and then compare them to the benchmarks from the pre-evaluation (see previous section):

- **First result** out of overall 10 possible class labels outputs in order to follow the classic classification accuracy measurement
- **3 first results** in order to assess if the sufficient coverage of correct classification was available nevertheless

The reason to introduce the latter metrics was an existing research application use case. The semantic building graph retrieval method developed for the research project uses a max. of 3 class labels to make up a set of contextually suitable retrieval candidates for the subsequent graph isomorphism process.

In the next sections, the evaluation of manually created cases and the subsequent investigation phase using modified spatial configuration data samples will be described. For each of them, the corresponding measurement of prediction quality using the two metrics described above will be presented.

Phase 1: Evaluation of Manual Graphs

As explained above, the evaluation of manually created spatial configuration graphs should provide an immediate estimation of classification quality of the convolutional neural networks trained using one-hot encoded, multilayer, and textual maps on the same dataset and with the same model configuration. Overall, **12** manual room graphs based on a selection of already existing buildings were created using a specific spatial configurations editing tool *RoomConf Editor* (source code available at: *github.com/cenetp/roomconf-editor*) that allows for creation of graphs in the format *AGraphML*, which provides compatibility for conversion into relation maps. The converters are published under *github.com/metis-caad/roomconf-converter*.

Table 1
Results of prediction quality in % (higher = better) on manually created spatial configuration graphs.

Map type	*First result*	*All 3 results*
One-hot encoded	41.67%	91.67%
Multilayer	16.67%	66.67%
Textual	8.33%	50.0%

These 12 manually created spatial configuration graphs were then converted as well and fed as relation map tensor queries into the corresponding convolutional neural networks of the evaluated map types. Table 1 shows the measured prediction quality in the form of classification rates achieved by each map type in this evaluation phase.

The majority of the results *did not provide a sufficiently high percentage of correct predictions* when comparing them to the benchmarks from the pre-evaluation. Considering the first result only (which was the training and validation accuracy metrics in the pre-evaluation) none of the map models performed as good as in the pre-evaluation. Except for the performance of the one-hot encoded map, other maps did not provide a good performance on the first 3 results as well. That is, in the subsequent investigation phase, it should be examined what modifications might lead to the decrease of prediction quality and if the one-hot encoded map's result on the 3 first samples is not just a randomly achieved high rate.

Table 2
Amounts of data samples for each evaluation step for each evaluation path of the investigation phase.

↓Step / Path ⇢	*SEPARATED*	*SUBSUMED*
1	1672	1672
2 (1+2 Subs.)	3406	3377
3 (1+2+3 Subs.)	2544	4894
4 (1+2+3+4 Subs.)	2057	2356

Phase 2: Investigative Evaluation

Two investigative evaluation paths, *SUBSUMED* and *SEPARATED* (see Figure 3), were introduced to examine findings of the manual graph evaluation. Both paths used a set of **4 dataset modification steps**.

The first modification step was identical for both investigation paths, however, the further application of modifications differed between them:

1. *SUBSUMED*: each subsequent modification step after the first step is performed on the already modified dataset from the previous step
2. *SEPARATED*: each modification step is performed on the original training dataset

All modification steps were defined by the architecture domain experts from the research project *metis-II*. After each modification process performed by a specific *rule-based data augmentation* tool, the new modified dataset was *checked for consistency* by a specific tool developed according to the rules defined by the domain experts during the pre-evaluation. The modified graphs that did not adhere to the consistency rules were left out from the classification process. Following Listings show the modification rules for all 4 steps of the evaluation paths. Table 2 shows the amounts of samples remained for each step after modification and consistency check.

```
Step 1: Modification of access type
  Replace ENTRANCE with DOOR
  IF no ENTRANCE available THEN
   ↪ PASSAGE and DOOR can be
   ↪ interchanged between CORRIDOR
   ↪ and LIVING
  IF CORRIDOR and LIVING are not
   ↪ connected THEN replace random
   ↪ PASSAGE with DOOR (or other way
   ↪ round) except the PASSAGE
   ↪ between KITCHEN and LIVING

Step 2: Replacement of habitable and
 ↪ non-habitable spaces
  The room types ROOM and CHILDREN /
   ↪ WORKING can be interchanged
  IF no ROOM available, THEN one of
   ↪ the following rules applies:
```

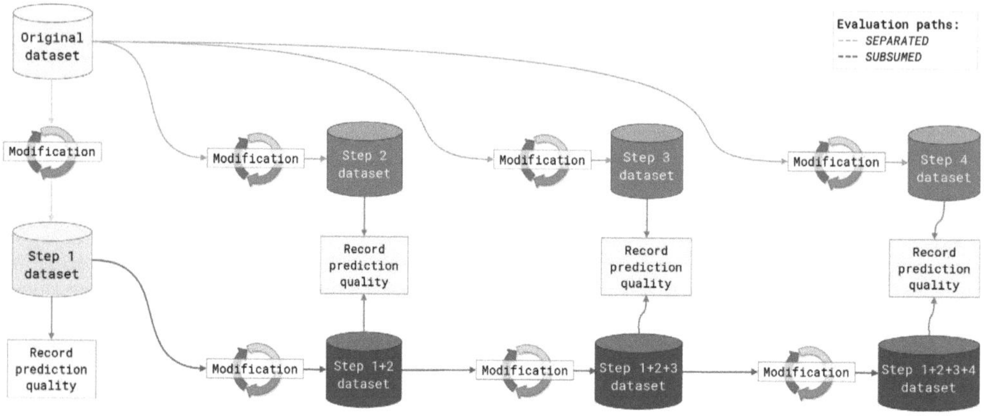

Figure 3
Overview of the investigation phase of the extended comparative evaluation.

```
   BATH or STORAGE are
    ↪ interchangeable with TOILET
    ↪ but not with each other
   CHILDREN and WORKING are
    ↪ interchangeable

Step 3: Adding / removing of non-
 ↪ habitable rooms to keep the
 ↪ current labels intact
  Add one from {CORRIDOR, STORAGE,
   ↪ KITCHEN, TOILET, BATH}; this
   ↪ will not change the amount of
   ↪ habitable rooms
  Randomly, one of {TOILET, KITCHEN,
   ↪ BATH} can be added and connected
   ↪  to CORRIDOR

Step 4: Breaking the label (re-
 ↪ labeling) by adding or removing
 ↪ habitable rooms
  Add one from {ROOM, LIVING, SLEEPING
   ↪ , WORKING, CHILDREN}; this will
   ↪ change the amount of habitable
   ↪ rooms and break the label
  IF there is CORRIDOR THEN add a new
   ↪ ROOM to it with DOOR or PASSAGE
  Randomly, one of {CHILDREN, ROOM,
   ↪ WORKING} can be removed
```

As can be read from the list of modification steps, the modification rules were defined with a specific goal each, increasing the modification strength from step to step. The idea behind this order was the intention to detect when it gets or starts to get better or worse, to identify "good" or "bad" intermediate modifications. The main research question was to find out what provided a bigger influence? "Hard facts" that define the class label from the architectural point of view (openness/closedness, number of habitable spaces) or non-class-defining latent features? Maybe the hard facts are in fact not what defines the class for the DL model? Following two hypotheses were defined for the investigative evaluation:

- *Hypothesis 1:* Prediction quality does not decrease if class-defining features are changed and another class is the result of this modification (Step 4)
- *Hypothesis 2:* Prediction quality should not heavily decrease if "latent features" are changed (Steps 1-3)

Results

The results of the investigative evaluation (see Figures 4 and 5) revealed a general pattern that all maps react similarly to the changes to the data available in the dataset they were trained on. *The stronger the modification the lower is the rate of correctly predicted classes.* The highest influence on the classification

Figure 4
Results from the SEPARATED evaluation path. M stands for the prediction quality on manual graphs, 'all' stands for 'All 3 results' (see Table 1).

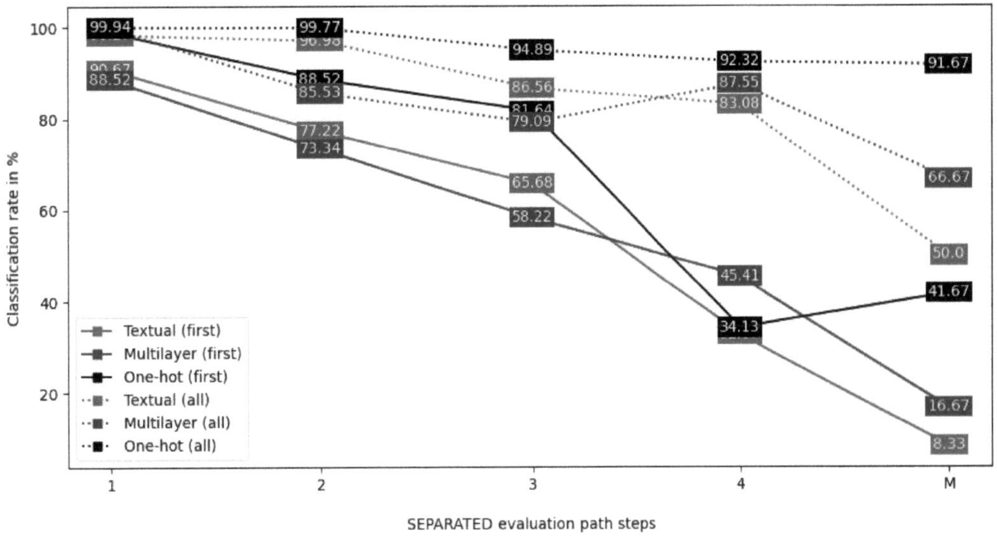

Figure 5
Results from the SUBSUMED evaluation path. Steps 12, 123, and 1234 indicate modifications subsumed from the previous modification step(s).

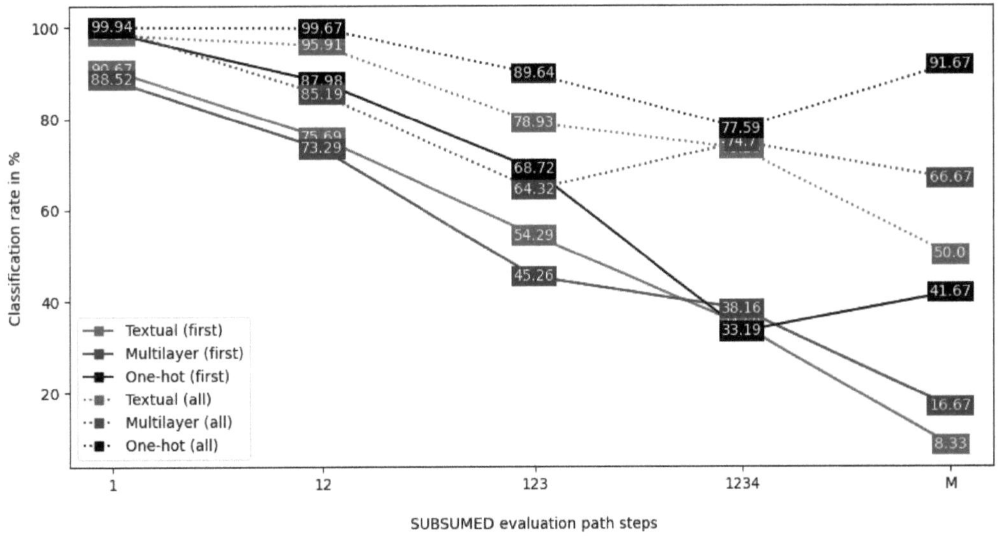

rate has the *breaking of the class label*, which *does not confirm Hypothesis 1*. The CNNs seem to take the latent features into account as well, and most likely even *build their classification decision* on said features and *not on the label-defining* ones.

Moreover, examining the *SUBSUMED* path, it can be concluded that the *application of further latent modifications on already modified data has a stronger and more stable influence on prediction quality*, resulting in mostly stable decrease in prediction quality. For the *SEPARATED* path, this behavior could be detected only partly, as the first 3 steps provide somewhat stable prediction rates, with a strong decline in steps 4 and M (manual graphs). This *partly confirms Hypothesis 2*, as at least for *SEPARATED* path heavy and sudden decreases could not be recorded.

As an exception from the conclusions described above, the performance of one-hot encoded map can be seen. It increased its rate for the manually created samples in the majority of cases. While the number of 12 cannot be seen as a significant comparison number, a *clear tendency towards the stable performance of one-hot encoded map* can be seen when considering all 3 first results. This is a clear answer that the high classification rate of manual graphs for this type of relation map is not random, and the selection of 3 class labels most likely guarantees that the correct label is available among the first 3 results. This can be seen as improvement for the floor plan retrieval application, as the determination of the suitable search context will be more precise based on the results achieved by the investigative evaluation.

CONCLUSION & FUTURE WORK

In this paper, we presented an extended comparative evaluation of deep learning models that use the tensor-based data structure "relation map" for semantic building fingerprint data. Using a classification task, three types of the relation map were evaluated to find out how the map-based DL models react to data not available in the training dataset. The results revealed that the stronger modified data influences the decrease in prediction quality, except for the winning type, the one-hot encoded relation map. Investigating which modifications can be responsible for decline in prediction rate, we came to the conclusion that modification of features that influence the class label is the most likely candidate. For the future, a user study is planned, where the DL models should justify and make transparent their classification decision using different explainable AI methods.

REFERENCES

Arora, H, Langenhan, C, Petzold, F, Eisenstadt, V and Althoff, KD 2020 'METIS-GAN: An approach to generate spatial configurations using deep learning and semantic building models', *ECPPM 2020-2021*

Eisenstadt, V, Arora, H, Ziegler, C, Bielski, J, Langenhan, C, Althoff, KD and Dengel, A 2021 'Exploring optimal ways to represent topological and spatial features of building designs in deep learning methods and applications for architecture', *CAADRIA 2021*

Eisenstadt, V, Langenhan, C, Althoff, KD and Dengel, A 2020 'Improved and Visually Enhanced Case-Based Retrieval of Room Configurations for Assistance in Architectural Design Education', *ICCBR 2020*

Hickman, G. and Krolik, J.L. 2009, 'A graph-theoretic approach to constrained floor plan estimation from radar measurements', *IEEE transactions on signal processing*, 57(5), pp. 1877-1888

Langenhan, C 2017 'Datenmanagement in der Architektur', *TU Munich Doctoral Diss.*

de Miguel, J 2019 'Deep Form Finding-Using Variational Autoencoders for deep form finding of structural typologies', *eCAADeSIGraDi 2019*

Newton, D 2019 'Deep Generative Learning for the Generation and Analysis of Architectural Plans with Small Datasets', *eCAADeSIGraDi 2019*

Sharma, D, Gupta, N, Chattopadhyay, C and Mehta, S 2017 'DANIEL: A deep architecture for automatic analysis and retrieval of building floor plans', *14th IAPR ICDAR*, pp. 420-425

Silvestre, J and Ikeda, Y 2016 'Artificial imagination of architecture with deep convolutional neural network', *CAADRIA 2016*

Steadman, P and Mitchell, LJ 2010, 'Architectural morphospace: mapping worlds of built forms', *Environment and Planning B: Planning and Design*, 37(2), pp. 197-220

Sun, C, Hsiao, CW, Sun, M and Chen, HT 2019 'Horizonnet: Learning room layout with 1d representation and pano stretch data augmentation', *IEEE/CVF Conference on Computer Vision and Pattern Recognition*, pp. 1047-1056

Wang, M, Yu, L, Zheng, D, Gan, Q, Gai, Y and Ye, Z 2019, 'Deep Graph Library: Towards Efficient and Scalable Deep Learning on Graphs', *arXiv:1909.01315*

A Chained Machine Learning Approach to Motivate Retro-Cladding of Residential Buildings

Paul Nicholas[1], Yu Chen[2], Nihit Borpujari[3], Nitsan Bartov[4], Andreas Refsgaard[5]
[1,2,3,4] Royal Danish Academy, School of Architecture [5] Inflation
[1] paul.nicholas@kglakademi.dk [2,3,4] {yuch1949|nibo1955|niba2041}@edu.kglakademi.dk [5] mail@andreasrefsgaard.dk

This paper investigates how a novel approach to visualisation could help address the challenge of motivating residential retrofitting. Emerging retrofitting research and practice emphasises retro-cladding - the upgrading of the exterior facade of a building - using a modular approach. We present a machine-learning based approach aimed to motivate residential retrofitting through the generation of images and cost/benefit information describing climatically specific additions of external insulation and green roof panels to the façade of a Danish type house. Our approach chains a series of different models together, and implements a method for the controlled navigation of the principle generative styleGAN model. The approach is at a prototypical stage that implements a full workflow but does not include numerical evaluation of model predictions. Our paper details our processes and considerations for the generation of new datasets, the specification and chaining of models, and the linking of climatic data to travel through the latent space of a styleGAN model to visualise and provide a simple cost benefit report for retro-cladding specific to the local climates of five different Danish cities.

Keywords: *Retrofitting, Machine Learning, Generative Adversarial Networks, Synthetic Datasets*

INTRODUCTION

Hiding just behind the C40's ambition that all new buildings be net zero by 2030 is a second, larger ambition: that all buildings be net zero by 2050 [1]. Currently, energy use in buildings accounts for almost 40% of all CO2 emissions in the European Union. The long life of buildings means that the majority of today's buildings were built before the current era of low energy regulation. This means that while discussions of low energy architecture often have focus on new commercial buildings, the largest potential for energy reductions are actually found within existing non-commercial buildings. In this context, retrofitting of suburban housing is considered to be one of the most effective strategies for reducing energy consumption and increasing resilience to climate change. Over the next 10 years, it is estimated that retrofitting of existing buildings will account for 70% of total construction work in Denmark, with a majority of this work undertaken on suburban homes. This context is captured in the idea that 'the home of the future is the one that you already live in'.

In this paper we describe a visualisation tool aimed to motivate residential retrofitting. The tool focuses on retro-cladding - upgrading the exterior façade of a building through fitting of new elements - as façades and roofs play a central role in heat transfer and water management. . The tool takes the form of a dashboard that 1) visualises the adapted state of an existing residential building corresponding to average monthly weather, and 2) provides simplified 'what if' analytics that decrease uncertainty about the investment required and benefits achieved, specific to particular Danish cities.

We detail a novel modelling approach, which leverages the generalizability of ML and the possibility to chain together a series of different ML-based models. Our approach is chosen to address a base case for retrofitting in Denmark: the retrofitting of 1960s era residential developer-built housing, known as 'typhuse'. This case replicates the same house throughout Denmark and across different climatic zones. While a wide variety of expert architectural simulation tools and methods are already present in the design workflow for new-build, these tools are not directly transferable to the retrofitting context, where non-expert household level decision-making is a central driver of change. Here, research has identified owner engagement and economic viability are principal barriers, due to uncertainty about the investment required and the potential benefits achieved (Pardo-Bosch et al. 2019, El-Darwish & Gomaa, 2017).

To describe this modelling approach, our paper details our processes and considerations for the generation of new datasets, the specification and chaining of models, and the linking of climatic data to travel through the latent space of a styleGAN model to visualise and provide a simple cost benefit report for retro-cladding specific to the local climates of five different Danish cities.

A MACHINE-LEARNING BASED APPROACH

Our visualisation tool is developed using several different Machine Learning models, including Generative Adversarial Networks (GAN) and neural nets. These models present significant challenges to the architectural design workflow, where modelling, visualization and simulation tools are typically deployed to support one-off design.

Tamke et al. 2018 provides a broad overview of the emerging trajectories of application of Machine Learning for Architectural Design. In the field of image generation, styleGANs have been trained on architectural drawings related to satellite urban plan, building plan, and section as input training data to generate 2d drawings (Zhang 2019). cGANs have been trained on low resolution scans of hand drafted plan drawings, to generate new plan drawings (Challiou 2017 [2], Kvochick 2018). Other contemporary research has explored the image to image translation to shortcut CFD simulation (Galanos et al 2019, Mokhtar et al 2020, Musil et al 2019), using a 2d ground floor plan input to represent building boundaries, and Nicholas et al 2020 describes the use of Pix2Pix to generate image-based predictions of material behaviour as a basis for design and fabrication. We are not aware of other approaches that use machine learning to visualise adaptations to existing buildings.

Generating synthetic datasets

The training of machine learning-based models requires a large data set of images. For architectural applications these cannot be scraped off the internet or accessed in a pre-existing database, but need to be generated from scratch. Similar to the approach taken in some computer vision tasks in which labels are difficult to generate, such as pose estimation (Tjaden 2017), synthetic architectural images can be created from CAD models. In conjunction with automation, this technique can be used to make large high quality datasets relatively quickly (Sun et al 2015). Render quality is an important consideration: Jabbar et al 2017 test Unity 3D (a realtime renderer) and Blender (a photorealistic renderer which is slower), and show that for an image segmentation model, more photorealistic images lead to much improved performance. The self-generation of synthetic datasets has multiple advantages: Zhang 2019 identifies improved control over the features in the images, while Rossi and Nicholas 2020 demonstrate how an image representation can be used abstractly to encode multiple types of information across its different channels.

Generative Adversarial Networks

The basis of our workflow are two GAN models - a form of generative model commonly used to create new images. In GANs the generative model is pitted against an adversary: a discriminative model that learns to determine whether a sample is from the model distribution or the data distribution- (Goodfellow et al, 2014). The advantage of using GANs is that they are flexible and can be trained on anything that can be represented as an image. Because GANs learn a loss that adapts to the data, they can be applied to a multitude of tasks that traditionally would require explicit feature description and very different kinds of loss functions (Isola et al, 2018).This allows for simple and generic inputs to quickly yield a design space that goes beyond the training data.

Navigating Latent Space

During the training process, the model learns underlying patterns from the image dataset and simplifies them into a compressed but high dimensional representation known as the latent space. After the model is trained, points in the latent space are sampled to generate new images. The ability to control the output of a GAN model to achieve a desired image occurs through the sampling and navigation of the latent space. A significant limit is that controlled movement is difficult to achieve as the features in the latent space are normally very entangled. However since their appearance, it has been known that semantically meaningful vector operations can be made in a GAN's latent space. Modes of sampling the latent space can include uploading an image and finding a closest match, taking a random walk, or tracking along particular vectors. Radford et al 2015, for example, demonstrate projection and vector arithmetic in the latent space, as well as interpolation along a vector defined by two points in the latent space. A problem for recent research has been that finding meaningful movements through the latent space has required supervised approaches and human labelling. Recently, new unsupervised methods for finding semantically meaningful controls for movement in latent space have emerged, including Voynov & Babenko 2020 [3] and Härkönen et al 2020. In this research, we use the method developed by Härkönen et al 2020, which applies Principal Components Analysis (PCA) in the activation space of a styleGAN model to identify latent directions without any supervision.

Chaining Machine Learning Models

Our ML modelling pipeline is developed as a sequential model chain. In a chained model, single models encode specific independent operations as discrete modules with an input and output, and self-contained modules can be connected together. Chaining multiple models together sequentially enables a continuous modelling pipeline, with each module specific to a particular aspect of generation/prediction.

The advantage of this approach is that model architectures can be matched specifically to tasks, rather than trying to predict all relevant aspects via a single model. However with more models, the need for more training data is compounded. We circumvent this problem by training multiple models on the same base set of training data (see figure 1). Different combinations of image and labelling are used for the different models - this is further described in the case presented below.

This research moves beyond state of the art in a number of ways. Our model is developed for a specific existing building. Rather than aiming to generate a single image, our approach generates image sequences in which critical aspects of the content of

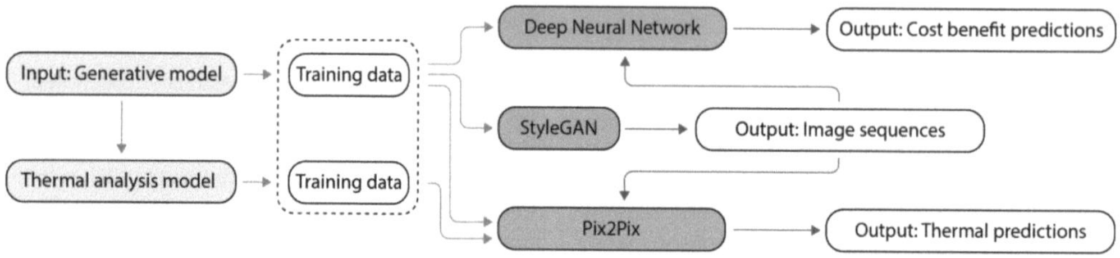

Figure 1
Flow diagram for chained models

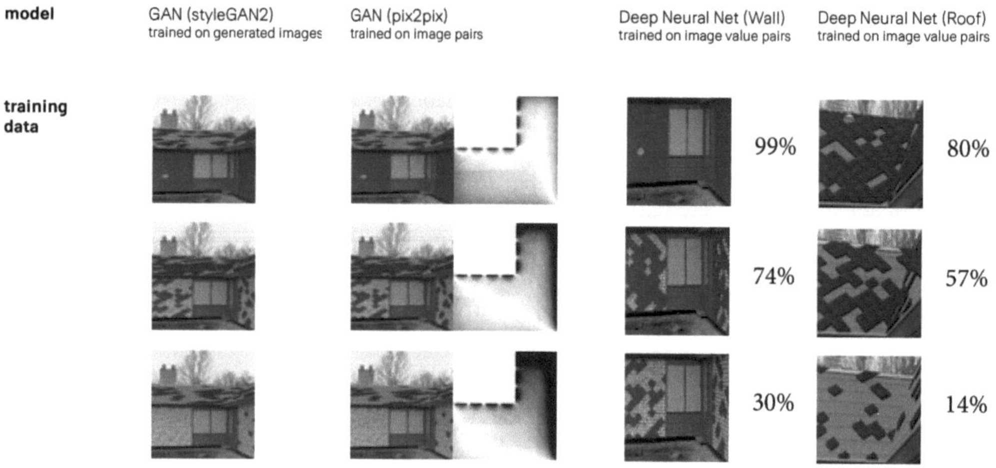

Figure 2
Chained ML models

each image are controlled. We implement a method for controlling movement through the latent space of a GAN model via architecturally relevant parameters, specifically climate related parameters. Model-chaining is used for both image generation and the evaluation of the generated images. Our evaluation approach allows us to search the GAN latent space to find specific series of images. The development and testing of this approach is still in progress.

EXPERIMENT

Our method is developed against a specific case: the Johan Christensen typehus (see figure 3), of which approximately 20,000 were built across Denmark from the mid 1960s.

Figure 3
The Johan Christensen typehus

To generate adapted versions of this house showing

different configurations of wall and roof cladding, we train three different kinds of machine learning-based model (see figure 2). A styleGAN model learns to generate new images of roof and wall panel configurations onto the base façade. A second type of GAN known as a Pix2Pix model learns to generate energy simulations that correspond to the facade and roof cladding configurations generated by the styleGAN. Lastly, two deep neural networks learn to predict numerical values including economic cost and yearly CO_2 absorbed, taking the styleGAN-produced image as input.

Figure 4
Parametric modelling for wall and roof coverage iteration

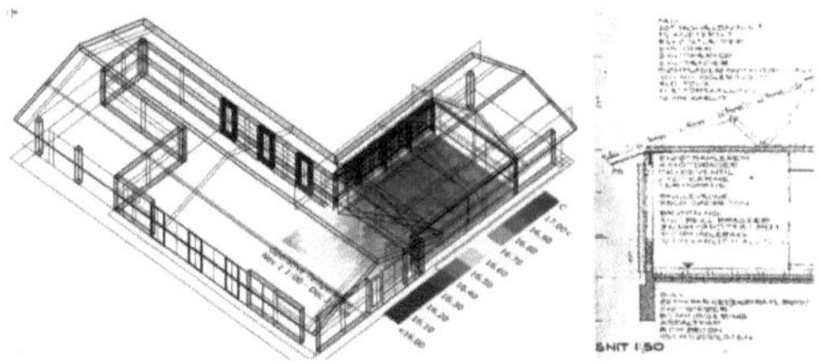

Figure 5
Modelling the baseline thermal context

Figure 6
StyleGAN generated images

Figure 7
Pairing rendered images with thermal simulations

To produce these images, we build a parametric model that generates different percentages of roof and wall coverage (see figure 4). It is important to note that this modelling and visualization approach does not aim to accurately reproduce the actual appearance of the façade and roof claddings. As claddings of differing thickness are visually identical, this variable is instead converted to visually communicate a panelisation of varying coverage. An initially full coverage of diamond panels is randomly reduced on the basis of two variables of "reduction" and "seed". The reduction variable controls the degree of reduction in panel coverage while the seed determines the reduction pattern. By randomly varying the input for the variables a dataset of 780 unique configurations is generated. Each time a configuration is made it triggers the rendering process within the definition and saves a file with the respective panel type and percentage of coverage. A dataset is made from these saved renders, as well as associated values stating the percentage of wall and roof coverage.

As the parametric model is automatically varied, an associated thermal model is also updated (see figure 5). This model is parameterized using geometric and material specifications taken from original drawings of the Johan Christensen house. With each iteration, the percentage of façade coverage is interpreted as a variable thickness material that completely covers the wall surface, excluding openings. In this conversion, 100% equates to 200mm thickness of insulation. In the context of building and construction, the thermal resistance per unit area of a material is defined by its R-value. The material definition within the thermal simulation allows for such specifications. We use an R value of 3 . These parameters are automatically input into the simulation. To produce a generalized simulation result, we simulate all versions with a base thermal context and measure change from a baseline of no added insulation. Simulations are performed on a simulation grid of size 64*64, and results are saved as an image paired with its respective render.

Figure 8
Moving along the principal direction for wall panels

The online machine learning platform Runway was used to train the styleGAN2 model, from a dataset of 780 render images. The styleGAN is able to generate new images that capture many of the visual qualities of the training images, but also introduce new qualities not in the original data - for example, tiles of differing sizes, differing distributions and differing densities (see figure 6). To train the Pix2Pix model, the renders generated for the styleGAN training set are paired with their associated thermal simulations (see figure 7). These images are downsampled to 64*64 and trained using a custom code running on Jupyter Notebooks. From this paired data, the pix2pix model learns to generate new heatmaps of the thermal environment from new rendered images of the building created by the styleGAN.

The final models to be trained are two Deep Neural Networks that predict a value when they are shown an image. Both networks are trained from the same render dataset used to train the styleGAN, but each extracts a different region of interest from this image (see figure 9). The network predicting roof coverage crops the image to the extents of the roof, and then resizes this crop to a 64*64 image. The network predicting wall coverage crops the image to the extents of the facade, and then resizes this crop to a 64*64 image. Both networks are trained using a custom code running on Jupyter Notebooks.

Finding directions in latent space

To control the transformation of specific features within image sequences, we use the GANspace approach developed by Harkonen et al 2020, which finds important latent directions based on Principal Component Analysis (PCA) applied in the latent space. Using this approach, we are able to identify the two distinct directions in the styleGAN model primarily related to wall and roof paneling. A series of four numbers are used to describe the settings for the wall and roof directions that determine the layers activated within the GANspace.

For example, for initiating a point to generate an image within the latent space we input a 'seed' value and define an edit. The edit specifies the principal direction, the first layer of activation, the last of activation, the movement along the principal direction interpreted as a -10 to 10 scale, and a direction. An initial edit is made to move to a set start point, and subsequent edits define incremental movement along the principal direction (see figure 8).

Figure 9
Extracting regions of interests for Deep Neural Networks

The same trajectories can be travelled from any seed point. The choice of a seed is considered a pivotal one that affects the search within the latent space drastically. An exploration of seeds as a departure point quickly reveals the entangled nature of the latent space as a majority of the seeds assessed draw the images away from their type house representation and into increasingly abstract collages of pixels and form, often influenced by the number and intensity of moves made (see figure 10). The challenges of navigation within the latent space is thus compounded by the search for a suitable seed.

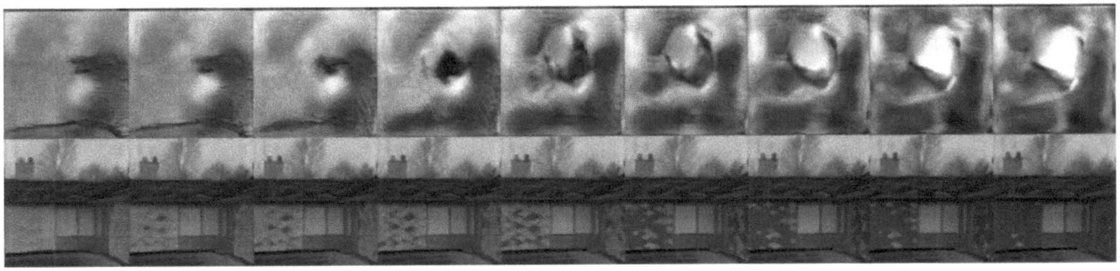

Figure 10
Challenges of navigating latent space

Figure 11
Cities range of yearly weather change

Finding yearly city climates in the latent space

Together with finding a suitable seed, navigation requires travel along the green roof and wall vectors. To relate climate parameters to travel in the latent space, we link progression along the principle directions to Danish city climate contexts. We choose two variables - monthly average rainfall and monthly average temperature - and associate them with the corresponding directions in the latent space that control the wall and roof panel coverage. We have developed this mapping using five city climate contexts that differ from one another in their relative change with regards to temperature and rain. The cities are Copenhagen, Tønder, Thule, Nuuk, and Tórshavn.

The maximum and minimum weather parameters between all cities are used as a bounds to map onto the full range of panel and roof coverage (0-100%) (see figure 11). The bounds for temperature are set by Copenhagen (18 C) and Thule (-24.6 C), and the bounds for rainfall are set by Tórshavn (162mm) and Thule(4mm).

This mapping is used to support location and monthly specific predictions within the visualisation tool, by using values for monthly average rainfall and monthly average temperature to navigate through the latent space.

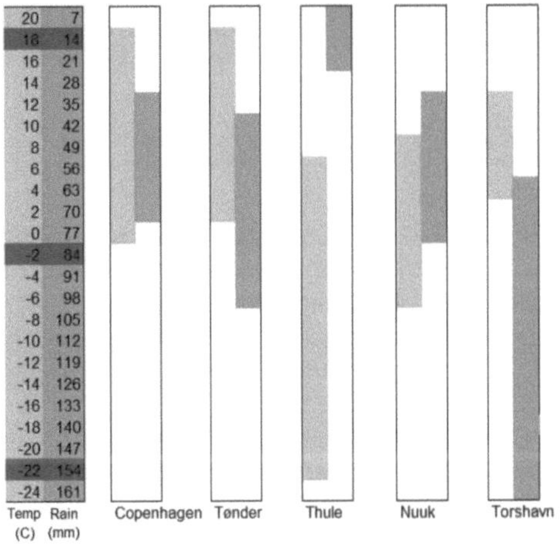

Once the mapping is established, we use it to search for suitable seeds that, when used as a start-point for travel along the two principal directions for roof and wall, result in images that visualise the appropriate coverage for roof and wall throughout the range. As the rates of change differ throughout the latent space, we generate multiple images across the range to find more linear gradients. To make this search, an iterative method is employed that runs through thousands of seed candidates, and assesses every resulting image sequence.

Table 1
Mapping wall and roof coverage to latent space

Copenhagen	Jan	Feb	Mar	Apr	May	Jun	Jul	Aug	Sep	Oct	Nov	Dec
Temperature (C)	0	0	2	7	12	16	18	17	14	9	5	3
Rain (mm)	49	39	32	38	40	47	71	66	62	59	48	49
Wall coverage %	40	40	36	24	13	4	0	2	9	20	29	33
Roof coverage %	23	15	10	15	16	22	40	36	33	31	22	23
Wall position	1	1	2	5	7	9	10	10	8	6	4	3
roof position	5	6	7	6	6	5	2	3	3	4	5	5

Figure 12
Image sequence for Copenhagen from January to December

Figure 13
Image sequence for Nuuk from January to December

Once a seed is found to match the rate of change for a particular city within its range, the weather variables are mapped directly into the moves within the latent space to extract the precise images that depict the change in retrofit that reflect the average monthly weather (see table 1).

This sequence of images are then input into the pix2pix model to generate the respective thermal images (see figure 12 and 13), and the deep neural networks to enable estimated economic costs and environmental benefits. The deep neural networks predict the square meterage of green roof and façade paneling shown in each image. The estimate for green roof is multiplied by a given price per square metre to calculate overall cost, and by 2kg a square meter to estimate the quantity of CO2 that would be absorbed each year. The prediction of wall coverage is converted to a thickness of insulation and multiplied by a per meter cost. The benefit of this additional insulation is communicated visually by the thermal prediction. All calculations use current estimated prices within Denmark.

The entire modeling chain is then run in a simple web browser interface (see figure 14), allowing a non-expert user to choose cities and generate new images corresponding to specific months or periods of the year. New cities can be subsequently found in the model using the approach described above, and added to the web interface through specification of the seed and movement sequence.

DISCUSSION AND CONCLUSION

This research is ongoing. To date, we have developed effective methods for generating large synthetic datasets of architectural images, and associations of renders, simulations and numeric information. We have also been successful in chaining together multiple machine learning models. This approach opens opportunities to connect , add or replace models for calculation, simulation, and representation within a prediction pipeline.

This has demonstrated that the approach of training multiple models, which will subsequently become inputs for one another, on the same data set, can be successful. Our case has particularly demonstrated the generalisability achieved by the Pix2Pix model, which is able to make good predictions from images generated by the styleGAN that are qualitatively different from those it has been trained on. The deep neural networks exhibited less generalisability when input with the same images. A next step is to gain a more precise evaluation of the predictive performance of each model.

The case we have tested is relatively simple, with

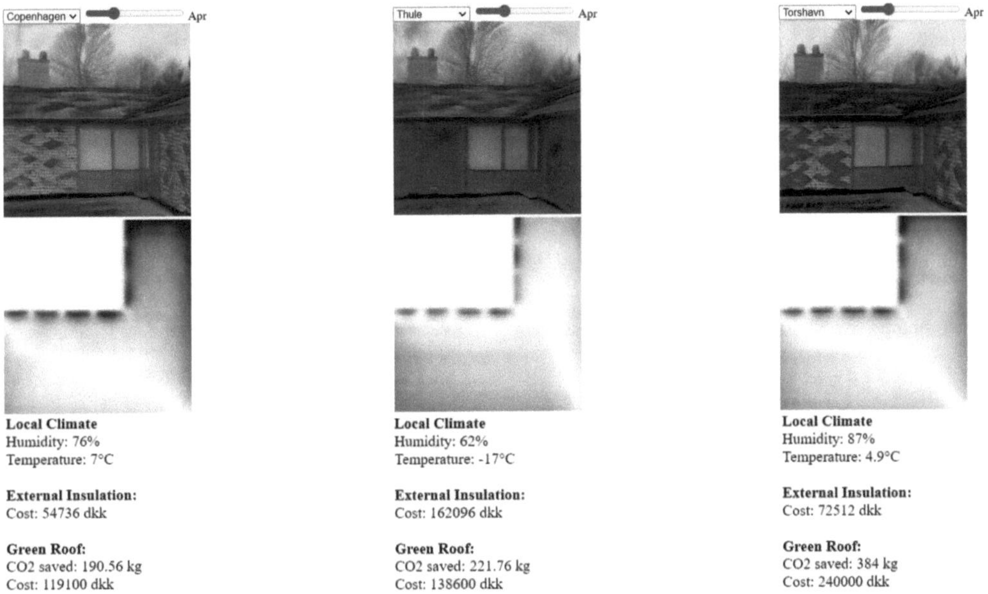

Figure 14
Browser interface

only two dimensions of change. Even so, we have had to choose representations that were not physically accurate but which allowed for learning. As we have self-generated the datasets, we have had full control over these features. The process of extracting these directions using the GANspace approach was also straightforward. However the ability to move along those directions in controllable ways was not straightforward, with the non-linearity of change being a particular and unforeseen problem. Here we have only begun to understand how to architecturally navigate the multiple dimensions and complexities of the trained models.

We believe that modeling workflows of this kind could have an important role to play in suburban retrofitting by leveraging the generalisability of ML, and the ability when working with ML models to frontload effort without needing all of the specifics.

For these types of architectural problem - multiple deployments exhibiting small amounts of variation - they offer a compelling alternative to an exhaustive modelling approach. In the specific context of our case, we don't need to know the cities in advance if we can find them later. Beyond our case, our method could extend as a means to model the adaptation of architectural typologies that are characterised by their mass deployment, versioning and repetition, for example urban squares, pocket parks, playgrounds, transport hubs, kiosks, as well as housing. Next steps in the project will further explore means for searching the GAN latent space for desired and controlled series of images, and performing numerical evaluation on our models.

REFERENCES

El-Darwish, I. and Gomaa, M. 2017, 'Retrofitting strategy for building envelopes to achieve energy efficiency. DOI: 10.1016/j.aej.2017.05.011', *Alexandria Engineering Journal*, 56, pp. 579-589

Galanos, T., Chronis, A., Vesely, O., Aichinger, A. and Koenig, R. 2019 'Best of both worlds – using computational design and deep learning for real-time urban performance evaluation', *1st International Con-*

ference on Optimization Driven Architectural Design
Goodfellow, I.J, Pouget-Abadie, J., Mirza, M., Xu, B., Warde-Farley, D., Ozair, S., Courville, D. and Bengio, y. 2014 'Generative adversarial nets', *NIPS*, p. Pages 2672–2680
Härkönen, E., Hertzmann, A., Lehtinen, J. and Paris, S. 2020 'Discovering Interpretable GAN Controls', *NeurIPS 2020*
Isola, P., Zhu, J., Zhou, T. and Efros, A.A 2017 'Image-to-Image Translation with Conditional Adversarial Networks', *IEEE Conference on Computer Vision and Pattern Recognition (CVPR)*
Jabbar, A., Farrawell, L., Fountain, J. and Chalup, S.K 2017 'Training Deep Neural Networks for Detecting Drinking Glasses Using Synthetic Images', *International Conference on Neural Information Processing*
Kvochick, T. 2018 'Sneaky Spatial Segmentation. Reading Architectural Drawings with Deep Neural Networks and Without Labeling Data', *Proceedings of the 38th Annual Conference of the Association for Computer Aided Design in Architecture (ACADIA)*
Mokhtar, S., Sojka, A. and Davila, C.C. 2020 'Conditional Generative Adversarial Networks for Pedestrian Wind Flow Approximation', *Proceedings of SimAUD 2020*
Musil, J., Knir, J., Vitsas, A. and Gallou, I. 2019 'Towards Sustainable Architecture: 3D Convolutional Neural Networks for Computational Fluid Dynamics Simulation and Reverse Design Workflow', *NeurIPS Workshop on Machine Learning for Creativity and Design 3.0*
Nicholas, P., Rossi, G., Williams, E., Bennett, M. and Schork, T. 2020, 'Integrating real-time multi-resolution scanning and machine learning for Conformal Robotic 3D Printing in Architecture', *International Journal of Architectural Computing*, 18, pp. 371-385
Pardo-Bosch, F., Cervera, C. and Ysa, T. 2019, 'Key aspects of building retrofitting: Strategizing sustainable cities', *Journal of Environmental Management*, 248, p. 109247
Peng, X. and Saenko, K. 2018 'Synthetic to Real Adaptation with Generative Correlation Alignment Networks', *IEEE Winter Conference on Applications of Computer Vision (WACV)*
Radford, A., Metz, L. and Chintala, S. 2016 'Unsupervised Representation Learning with Deep Convolutional Generative Adversarial Networks', *ICLR*
Rossi, G. and Nicholas, P. 2020 'Encoded Images: representational protocols for integrating cGANs in iterative computational design processes', *ACADIA 2020 : Distributed Proximities*
Sun, B., Peng, X. and Saenko, K. 2015 'Generating Large Scale Image Datasets from 3D CAD Models', *CVPR Workshop*
Tamke, M., Nicholas, P. and Zwierzycki, M. 2018 'Machine learning for architectural design: Practices and infrastructure', *International Journal of Architectural Computing*
Tjaden, H., Schwanecke, U. and Schömer, E. 2017 'Real-Time Monocular Pose Estimation of 3D Objects using Temporally Consistent Local Color Histograms', *In Proceedings of the IEEE Conference on Computer Vision and Pattern Recognition*
Zhang, H. 2019, '3D Model Generation on Architectural Plan and Section Training through Machine Learning', *Technologies Special Issue "Computer-Aided Architectural Design"*, 7(4), p. 82

[1] https://www.c40.org/other/net-zero-carbon-buildings-declaration
[2] https://issuu.com/stanislaschaillou/docs/stanislas_chaillou_thesis_
[3] https://arxiv.org/abs/2002.03754

Differences between Architects' and Non-architects' Visual Perception of Originality of Tower Typology

Quantification of subjective evaluation using Deep Learning

Joy Mondal[1]
[1] *Jadavpur University*
[1] *joy.architect@yahoo.com*

The paper presents a computational methodology to quantify the differences in visual perception of originality of the rotating tower typology between architects and non-architects. A parametric definition of the Absolute Tower Building D with twelve variables is used to generate 250 design variants. Subsequently, sixty architects and sixty non-architects were asked to rate the design variants, in comparison to the original design, on a Likert scale of `Plagiarised' to `Original'. With the crowd-sourced evaluation data, two neural networks - one each for architects and non-architects - were trained to predict the originality score of 15,000 design variants. The results indicate that architects are more lenient at seeing design variants as original. The average originality score by architects is 27.74% higher than the average originality score by non-architects. Compared to a non-architect, an architect is 1.93 times likelier to see a design variant as original. In 92.01% of the cases, architects` originality score is higher than non-architects'. The methodology can be used to capture and predict any subjective opinion.

Keywords: *Originality, Visual perception, Crowd-sourced, Subjective evaluation, Deep learning, Neural network*

INTRODUCTION

Architecture is a unique discipline where art and engineering meet subjective demands. Architects offer design solution to their clients (predominantly non-architects), but these two groups may not always have the same aesthetic sensibilities. Different studies have shown that architects and non-architects have different preferences (Gifford et al. 2000, Llinares et al. 2011, Ghomeshi and Jusan 2013). Jeffrey and Reynolds (1999) studied the differences in aesthetic "code" of architects and non-architects, and argued that buildings constructed according to the "code" of architects is less likely to receive popular acclaim. Montanana et al. (2013) focused on the decision-making in purchasing residential properties. They found that non-architects ranked a property perceived as "family home" higher than a property perceived as "light and outward facing". This finding indicates that subjective factors tend to be more relevant to non-architects than objective design goal. Moreover, Brown and Gifford (2001) concluded that typically, architects cannot predict the non-architect's aesthetic evaluation of architecture. Therefore, a potential conflict exists between architects and non-architects, who may have different expectations from a building.

This research investigates the differences between architects and non-architects with regard to the visual perception of originality of design of the tower typology. Throughout the history of architecture, the tower typology has been a symbol of power and wealth, the identity of city skylines, and iconoclastic landmark for human navigation (Moldovan et al. 2014). Within the tower typology, as Vollers (2009) explains, "Twisted geometries with repetition of elements are applied not so much for economic gain as for semiotic connotation". This research uses the design of Absolute Tower D (Lagendijk et al. 2012, see figure 1) as the original design against which architects and non-architects are asked to evaluate the originality of design variants.

The following sections elaborate the background, the research methodology, the use of deep learning for quantification, the results, and the future scope of work.

Figure 1
Absolute Tower D on the right; clicked by Sarbjit Bahga, reproduced under CC license.

BACKGROUND

Originality in Design

The definition of originality in the context of design is rather subjective and open-ended. It is often conflated with innovation, novelty and creativity. The problem in having a universal definition of originality is in the fact that originality in design can be discerned in several ways - in the process, function and form. Originality of a process may be defined as a byproduct of creativity that makes an idea evolve into to a system and then into an artefact (Satir 2015). Originality may be sought in the function of a design which typically manifests itself through transformation of scientific or technical research into a product (Shibayama and Wang 2020). Originality may also be sought in the form of a design. Often times form is explored with structural performance (Adriaenssens et al. 2014) and energy performance (Tian et al. 2015) in mind. Since non-architects are typically not privy to the process of design, their sense of originality in architecture is primarily derived from visual stimuli (Sanatani 2020).

The aim of this research is to compare the visual perception of originality between architects and non-architects. In other words, this research aims to quantify the originality of forms. Evaluating the originality of a given form in the absolute sense would require the evaluator to subliminally conjure all the forms ever seen, and then compare the given form with the conjured forms. Therefore, understanding originality of form in the absolute sense is an exercise of visual comparison with one's experiences. For the purpose of this research, instead of relying on visual comparison with the sub-conscious, forms of design variants will be compared to the form of the original design of the Absolute Tower D.

Machine Learning in Architecture

Artificial intelligence, and in particular machine learning, has become a popular topic in all computational processes across industries. Since the 2010s it has been incorporated in various researches in architectural design as well. Machine intelligence can be utilised to support creativity (Bruno 2019), automate housing layout generation (Chaillou 2019), automate implicit design iteration through discretisation (Koh 2019), transfer 3D style of a geometry to another geometry (Ren and Zheng 2020), appropriate performance simulation (Yousif and Bolojan 2021), and calculate urban space perception (Verma et al. 2018).

Traditional linear programming requires the programmer to explicitly define the rules. Subsequently, output is generated utilising the programmer defined algorithm. Deep learning is a departure from such a system. It is a subset of machine learning that uses deep neural network with multiple hidden layers to statistically appropriate the entire solution space (see figure 2). It does so by training on discrete sample dataset with known input variables (independent variables or features), and known output (dependent variable(s) or label(s)). On completion of training, the neural network is capable of predicting output for any new set of input variables. Thus, by statistically mapping the relationship between the independent and dependent variables, deep learning eliminates the requirement of explicitly defined algorithm. Consequently, deep learning is the ideal way of quantifying crowd-sourced subjective evaluation.

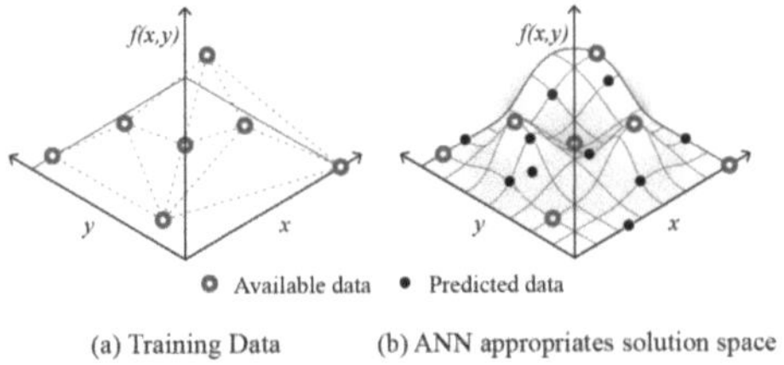

Figure 2
Training and prediction by neural network.

RESEARCH METHODOLOGY

This research uses a computational methodology (see figure 3) that can be used to quantify and predict any kind of subjective evaluation of design. The methodology combines crowd-sourced design evaluation with the statistical power of deep learning. The methodology has four key steps mentioned as following -

- *Defining design variants*: The first step in the process is to collect or generate design variants that can be evaluated. For example, if urban streetscapes are to be evaluated for beauty, images of urban streetscapes need to be collected for evaluation. If a parametric definition is being used for design, design variants need to be generated by varying the parameters (independent variables).
- *Crowd-sourced evaluation*: The second step in the process is to get the design variants evaluated by relevant group(s). The evaluation data is discrete in nature and does not truly represent the solution space (see figure 2a). Therefore, it is not directly used for comparative study.
- *Neural network training*: The third step in the process is to train a deep neural network with the evaluation data (output or dependent variable) and the design parameters (input or independent variable) that define the design variants. Through training, the neural network learns to appropriate the solution space (see figure 2b).
- *Predicting subjective evaluation*: On the completion of training of the neural network with sufficient accuracy, the fourth step is to predict subjective evaluations of a larger new set of design variants. Since neural networks learn the solution space during training, they can predict for new variants by virtue of interpolation (see figure 2b). Finally, the predicted values are used for comparative analysis.

The following sub-sections discuss the four steps in detail and with respect to this research, along with discussing the preliminary analysis of the evaluation data and the limitations in the process of quantification.

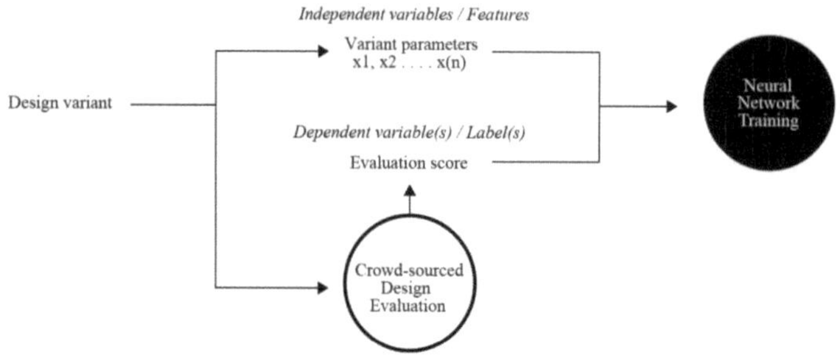

Figure 3
Computational methodology for quantifying and predicting crowd-sourced subjective evaluation.

Step 1: Defining Design Variants

Design variants of Absolute Tower D were defined and generated by a parametric Grasshopper definition of the original design. The original design (Lagendijk et al. 2012) can be parametrically represented by only five parameters - the two radii of the elliptical floor plan, total number of floors, floor to floor height (or total height), total rotation (or floor to floor rotation), and offset and parapet height of balconies. In order to have design variants of similar visual weightage, total number of floors and floor to floor height are not varied to generate design variants. In addition to the three other parameters of the original design, nine additional parameters are added to the parametric definition. These additional parameters change the shape of the floor plan from ellipse to a four-legged star to a square and to a rhombus, control the nature of the rotation of floor plates (linear or bezier), change the state of the balconies (present or absent), and scale the floor plates towards the top and the bottom of the tower. The floor plan is represented by a NURBS curve instead of an ellipse, and the corner point weights of the control polygon and the position of the mid-points of the control polygon are varied to morph the floor plan into the four shapes. The parameters (see table 1) are elaborated as following -

- *(x1) Radius 1 of the floor plan (plan_r1)*: Controls the length of the bounding box of the floor plan. When the floor plan is elliptical, it represents one of the radii of the ellipse.
- *(x2) Radius 2 of floor plan (plan_r2)*: Controls the width of the bounding box of the floor plan. When the floor plan is elliptical, it represents one of the radii of the ellipse.
- *(x3) Floor plan corner point weight (crpt_weight)*: Controls the weightage of the corner points of the control polygon of the floor plan. When all the other parameters are kept constant at the values of the original design, *crpt_weight* = 0.0 yields a rhombus floor plan, *crpt_weight* = 0.5 yields the original design, and *crpt_weight* = 1.0 yields a rectangular floor plan (see first row of figure 4).

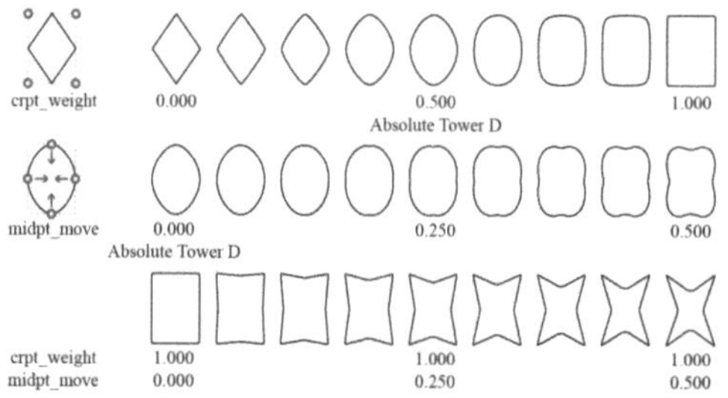

Figure 4
Variation in plan with crpt_weight and midpt_move.

- *(x4) Floor plan mid-point movement (midpt_-move)*: Controls the displacement of the mid-points of the control polygon of the floor plan towards the centre of the floor plan. When all the other parameters are kept constant at the values of the original design, *midpt_move* = 0.0 yields the original design, and *midpt_move* = 1.0 yields a blunt four-legged star floor plan (see second row of figure 4). When all parameters except *crpt_weight* and *midpt_move* are kept constant at the values of the original design, *crpt_weight* =1.0 and *midpt_move* = 0.5 yield a sharp four-legged star floor plan (see third row of figure 4).

- *(x5) Total rotation (tot_rot)*: Controls the total angle of rotation between the bottom and the top floor plates.
- *(x6-x9) Distribution of the rotation values (rotstart_x, rotstart_y, rotend_x, rotend_y)*: The four parameters control the nature of the distribution of the rotation values of floor plates. The distribution is calculated by a bezier S-curve. Therefore, the four parameters are the two anchor points (*rotstart_y* and *rotend_y*) and the two handles (*rotstart_x* and *rotend_x*) of the S-curve. When all of the four parameters have a value of zero, the S-curve takes the shape of a straight line, thereby making the distribution linear in nature.
- *(x10) Presence or absence of balcony (bal_state)*: Controls the presence or absence of balcony projections using a discrete boolean value. When *bal_state* is zero, the balconies are replaced by glazed facade.
- *(x11-x12) Scaling values of the floor plates (scale_top, scale_bottom)*: Controls the amount of scaling in the top three quarters (*scale_top*) and the bottom quarter of the tower (*scale_bottom*). The scaling of the floor plates start from the top of the bottom quarter towards both the directions.

In multivariate studies such as this research, the minimum number of data samples needed to train a neural network can be determined using few industry accepted rules of thumb. Sekaran and Bougie (2016) prescribe the 10x rule which states that the number of data samples should be at least ten times the number of independent variables. To test the correlations of independent variables, Green (1991) recommends a minimum sample size of 50 + 8k, where k is the number of independent variables. To conclusively make predictions, Green (1991) recommends a minimum sample size of 104 + k, where k is the number of independent variables. Given that the number of independent variables is twelve in this research, the rules of thumb recommend a minimum of 120, 146 and 116 data samples respectively. To accommodate additional testing data to measure the accuracy of neural network, this research has used 250 data samples (design variations) for crowd-sourced evaluation.

Table 1
Domains of the parameters (independent variables) of the design variants.

Parameters	Minimum	Maximum	Absolute Tower D
plan_r1	10.00	15.00	13.70
plan_r2	15.00	25.00	18.50
crpt_weight	0.000	1.000	0.500
midpt_move	0.000	0.500	0.000
tot_rot	0	720	208
rotstart_x	0.000	0.750	0.535
rotstart_y	0.000	0.750	0.000
rotend_x	0.000	0.750	0.395
rotend_y	0.000	0.750	0.000
bal_state	0	1	1
scale_top	0.010	1.000	1.000
scale_bottom	0.500	1.000	1.000

Step 2: Crowd-sourced Evaluation

The second step in the process of quantifying subjective evaluations is to evaluate the design variants. To facilitate interpolation of the extreme cases, fifty of the 250 design variants were generated by combining the minimum, maximum and original design values of the independent variables. The rest of the 100 design variants were generated using random values. Similar to the calculation of minimum number of data variants needed for evaluation, the minimum number of participants needed in the process of evaluation also needs to be ascertained. As a rule of thumb, Clark and Watson (1995) recommend ten participants per item on the rating scale, whereas DeVellis (2003) recommends 15 participants per item on the rating scale. This research has used a Likert scale of four items for crowd-sourced evaluation. Thus, following the latter rule of thumb, sixty participants were needed for evaluation. Since this research compares the evaluations of two groups, i.e., architects and non-architects, the 250 design variants are evaluated by sixty architects as well as sixty non-architects. The lowest age amongst the architects was 23. Consequently, all the selected non-architect participants were older than 22.

Since the evaluations are comparative in nature, to acquaint the participants to the extremities of the design variants, all the design variants were shown to each of them before the process of evaluation. The architects and the non-architects were asked to rate the design variants against the following question -

"How would you rate the visual relationship of the displayed designs with respect to the reference design?"

A Likert scale of 'Plagiarised', 'Similar', 'Different', and 'Original' was used for evaluation. The design variants were shown alongside the reference design (original design). To mitigate the effect of decision fatigue (Pignatiello et al. 2018) in the last third of the form, the order of sets of three design variants was randomised. The participants were not informed that the design variants are derived from a universal parametric representation. This information was skipped to understand the visual perception of originality of the design variants as an explicit artefact, without any connection to the process of generation of the design variants. For every design variant i, the originality score is calculated by equation 1 as follows:

$$OS(i) = \frac{\sum_{n=1}^{r} L(i)(n) \cdot W}{r} \quad (1)$$

where,

OS = Originality score
i = Design variant identifier
r = Number of Likert evaluations per design variant
L = Likert evaluation
W = 0.00, if L(i)(n) is 'Plagiarised'
= 0.33, if L(i)(n) is 'Similar'
= 0.67, if L(i)(n) is 'Different'
= 1.00, if L(i)(n) is 'Original'

If all the evaluations of a design variant are 'Plagiarised', the originality score of the design variant becomes 0. If all the evaluations of a design variant are 'Original', the originality score of the design variant becomes 1. In other words, originality score of 0 implies that the particular design variant is visually perceived as 'Plagiarised' by everyone, and originality score of 1 implies that the particular design variant is visually perceived as 'Original' by everyone. Each design variant has two originality scores - one for architects (*Originality score (ar)*) and one for non-architects (*Originality score (non_ar)*). As a result, two tables (one each for architect's and non-architect's originality scores) of data with 250 rows and thirteen columns were compiled to train two neural networks. The rows represent the design variants. The first twelve columns represent the independent variables that define the design variants. These are common for both the tables. The last column stores the respective dependent variable, i.e., the originality scores of the respective design variants by architects in one and by non-architects in the other.

Preliminary Analysis of Evaluation Data

Correlations (see table 2) were generated to understand the relationships between the independent and the dependent variables. The analysis of the correlations reveals that seven out of the ten independent variables are inversely correlated to the dependent variables. Floor plan mid-point movement (*midpt_move*) exhibits highest correlations with the originality scores of architects (r = 0.29) and non-architects (r = 0.22). This independent variable changes the shape of the plan from an ellipse to a four-legged star. It indicates that when visually comparing towers, both architects and non-architects tend to subliminally concentrate more on visual features that horizontally control the overall silhouette of towers. Presence or absence of balcony (bal_state) has the lowest correlations with the originality scores of architects (r = -0.50) and non-architects (r = -0.49). Additionally, it exhibits the lowest absolute difference in correlations ($|\Delta r| = 0.01$) between architects and non-architects. This suggests that when visually comparing towers, both architects and non-architects tend to ignore features that affect local articulation. Total rotation (*tot_rot*) exhibits the highest absolute difference in correlations ($|\Delta r| = 0.20$) between the originality scores of architects ($r = -0.17$) and non-architects ($r = -0.37$). This would appear to indicate that architects tend to be more visually sensitive towards rotation of floor plates. Conversely, non-architects tend to see rotated towers as a visually homogeneous group without much regard to the amount of rotation.

Table 2
Correlations of independent and dependent variables in crowd-sourced data.

Independent Variables	Originality Score (ar)	Originality Score (non_ar)	Absolute Difference
plan_r1	-0.10	-0.07	0.03
plan_r2	0.16	0.21	0.05
crpt_weight	0.03	0.00	0.04
midpt_move	0.29	0.22	0.07
tot_rot	-0.17	-0.37	0.20
rotstart_x	-0.22	-0.17	0.05
rotstart_y	-0.06	-0.11	0.05
rotend_x	0.01	-0.01	0.02
rotend_y	0.08	0.04	0.04
bal_state	-0.50	-0.49	0.01
scale_top	-0.17	-0.06	0.11
scale_bottom	-0.12	-0.02	0.10

Steps 3 & 4: Neural Network Training and Predicting Originality Score

The third step in the process of quantifying subjective evaluations using deep learning is to train a neural network with the evaluation data. On the completion of training of the neural network with sufficient accuracy, the fourth step is to predict subjective evaluations of a larger set of design variants.

Google Colab was used to write, edit and execute the code for steps 3 and 4. Scikit-learn machine learning library was used for greater flexibility and control over the neural network models. Choosing the hyper-parameters of a neural network (e.g., the number of hidden layers, the number of neurons in each layer, activation function, loss function, batch size, and number of epochs) is a complex process, that affects the network's efficiency. Scikit-learn's 'GridSearchCV' class was used to iteratively train the two neural networks with varied hyper-parameters, until best results were attained. The two neural networks were trained on 200 design variants. The effectiveness of the two neural networks was tested on the remaining fifty design variants. The select neural network model for architects can predict originality score of design variants with root mean square error of 0.08, R2 score of 0.81 and accuracy of 91.35%. The select neural network model for non-architects can predict originality score of design variants with root mean square error of 0.07, R2 score of 0.83 and accuracy of 90.04%.

As part of step 4, the two trained neural networks were used to predict the originality scores of 15,000 design variants. The values of the independent variables required to generate the 15,000 design variants were calculated by combining equidistant interpolation of the domains of each independent variable. Finally, the 15,000 originality scores by architects as well as non-architects were tabulated to quantify the differences.

Limitations of Quantification

Each step of the methodology and each aspect of each step of the methodology have intrinsic as well as extrinsic limitations which may affect the quantification of the originality scores. Given the variance in absolute differences between the correlations of independent and dependent variables between architects and non-architects (see table 2), changes in the selection of parameters to be varied and the range in which they are to be varied to generate the design variants will yield different originality scores. The form used in step 2 of the process, i.e., collection of crowd-sourced evaluation has intrinsic limitations. Changing the perspective from which design variants are seen in the form, and changing the medium of seeing the design variants (rendered, diagrammatic, pictures of model, animated, vs mounted on VR set etc.) will affect the visual perception of objects or buildings. Collection of such comparative data sparks questions about the extrinsic influences, e.g., is the visual perception of architecture by non-architects who are either designers or are trained in artistic fields more correlated to architects instead of non-architects not trained in creative fields? Additionally, the data used to train the neural networks is reflective of the socio-cultural bias of the volunteers. This feature of the nature of crowd-sourced data can be utilised to analyse and predict design preferences specific to groups of people (see section "Conclusion").

RESULT AND DISCUSSION

The percentage distribution of the originality scores of 15,000 design variants by architects as well as non-architects are shown in figure 5 through ten bins with bin-width of 0.10. Table 3 shows the numerical summary of the predicted originality scores. To understand the nature of the respective originality scores, figure 5 and table 3 are to be read in conjunction. The nature of the percentage distribution bins indicates two differentiators between architects and non-architects. Firstly, the tallest bins of architects are closer to 'Original' (1.00) than the tallest bins of non-architects. It implies that architects tend to be more lenient than non-architects at seeing design variants as original. This observation is corroborated by the higher mean (0.76) and median (0.83) originality scores by architects compared to the mean (0.59) and median (0.62) originality scores by non-architects. In fact, the mean and median originality scores by architects are between the 'Different' and 'Original' categories in the Likert scale, whereas for non-architects they are between the 'Similar' and 'Different' categories.

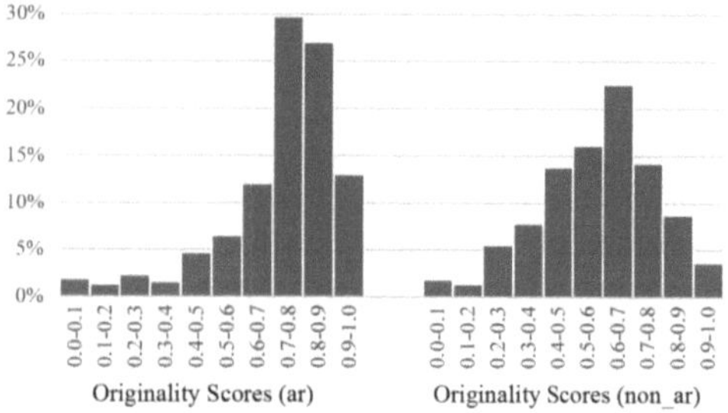

Figure 5
Percentage distribution of predicted originality scores by architects and non-architects.

The second differentiator is that the tallest bins of architects are taller than the tallest bins of non-architects. It implies that architects tend to have a better consensus than non-architects at reading the visual perception of originality. This observation is corroborated by the lower coefficient of variation (0.22) of the originality scores by architects compared to the coefficient of variation (0.39) of the originality scores by non-architects. In fact, in the case of non-architects, the coefficient of variation is higher than the step value (0.33) of the Likert categories. Additionally, the numerical analysis of the originality scores (see table 3) reveals that an architect is 17.14 times likely to see a design variant as 'Original' instead of 'Plagiarised', whereas, for a non-architect, the likelihood drops down to 5.26 times.

Table 3
Numerical summary of the predicted originality scores.

Description	Originality Score (ar)	Originality Score (non_ar)
Mean	0.76	0.59
Median	0.83	0.62
Standard Deviation	0.17	0.23
Coefficient of Variation	0.22	0.39
Original/Plagiarised Ratio	17.14	5.26

Subsequently, the comparative relation between the originality scores by architects and non-architects was ascertained (see table 4). The average originality score by architects (0.76) is 0.16 higher than the average originality score by non-architects (0.59). In other words, the average originality score by architects is 27.74% higher than the average originality score by non-architects. The mean difference of corresponding originality scores by architects and non-architects is 0.18. In other words, on an average, each originality score by architects is 38.94% higher than the corresponding originality score by non-architects. In as many as 92.01% of the 15,000 design variants, architects' originality score is higher than non-architects'. When the data distribution of the originality scores by architects and non-architects is analysed with respect to the Likert scale categories, the finer differences become clear. Compared to an architect, a non-architect is 1.71 times likelier to see a design variant as 'Plagiarised', and 3.14 times likelier to see a design variant as 'Similar' or 'Different'. However, the relationship is inversed at the other end of the spectrum. Compared to a non-architect, an architect is 1.93 times likelier to see a design variant as 'Original'.

All of these observations reiterate that architects tend to be more lenient than non-architects at seeing design variants as original. It may be argued that architects are trained to observe the nuances of visual difference between artefacts. Consequently, what may seem like same artefacts to non-architects will look more varied (comparatively original) to architects. The other takeaway is that architects have a better consensus than non-architects at evaluating the originality of design variants. This phenomenon may be explained by the similar rigour of academics and training of architects compared to a more diverse academic and professional background of non-architects. It is to be noted that the reasons speculated behind the varied observations are rather anecdotal in nature. Anecdotal correlations are often not causal. A psychological and/or neuro-response study is needed to explain the subliminal reasons for the observed variance.

Table 4
Numerical summary of the comparative relation of predicted originality scores.

Description	Value
Mean Originality Score (ar-non_ar)	0.16
Mean Originality Score % ((ar-non_ar) / non_ar)	27.74%
Mean Difference (ar-non_ar)	0.18
Mean Difference % ((ar-non_ar) / non_ar)	38.94%
Originality Score (ar>non_ar)	92.01%
Plagiarised Rating Occurrence (non_ar/ar)	1.71
Similar & Different Ratings Occurrence (non_ar/ar)	3.14
Original Rating Occurrence (ar/non_ar)	1.93

CONCLUSION

Subjective evaluation of the visual perception of originality of the rotating tower typology by architects and non-architects is predicted by training two deep neural networks with crowd-sourced data of 250 data samples. Use of neural network allows the appropriation of the entire solution space by using limited number of training data samples. Predictions of 15,000 design variants are tabulated to quantify the differences of originality scores between architects and non-architects. It is concluded that the average originality score by architects is 27.74% higher than the average originality score by non-architects. Compared to a non-architect, an architect is 1.93 times likelier to see a design variant as original. In fact, in 92.01% of the cases, architects' originality score is higher than non-architects'. Within themselves, architects tend to have a better consensus than non-architects at reading the visual perception of originality. Analysis of the correlations of the independent variables revealed that both architects and non-architects tend to subliminally concentrate more on visual features that horizontally control the overall silhouette of towers (like shape of floor plan).

The methodology of training a neural network on crowd-sourced data marks a departure from the top down evaluative guidelines published by experts to a more inclusive bottom up evaluation by end users. The methodology can be used to quantify subjective evaluation of any kind. Beauty or safety perception of urban streetscapes can be predicted as a part of urban design aid by training a neural network with crowd-sourced ratings of pictures of urban streetscapes. The independent variables for such an exercise can be calculated by applying image segmentation (Mousavirad and Ebrahimpour-Komleh 2017) on the pictures to extract the areas and mutual positions of roads, signage, greenery, sky, vehicles, etc. Subsequently, the trained network can be used to calculate the fitness function of an evolutionary algorithm to optimise design proposals. The socio-cultural bias embedded in crowd-sourced evaluation can be utilised to analyse and predict design preferences specific to groups of people. For example, in the case of predicting beauty or safety perception of urban streetscapes, evaluation data may be categorised by the cities of residence of the participants. Consequently, the same design proposal will have different predicted scores not only depending on its location, but also on the basis of how it is perceived by different age groups, race, gender, etc.

The next objective in research is to apply the same process discussed in this paper to different building typologies. A summation of results of multiple typologies will comprehensively quantify the differences of visual perception of originality of design between architects and non-architects in global terms.

REFERENCES

Adriaenssens, S, Block, P, Veenendaal, D and Williams, C (eds) 2014, *Shell Structures for Architecture: Form Finding and Optimization*, Routledge

Brown, G and Gifford, R 2001, 'Architects predict lay evaluations of large contemporary buildings: Whose conceptual properties?', *Journal of Environmental Psychology*, 21(1), pp. 93-99

Bruno, E 2019, 'Commentary / Integrating AI and Deep Learning within Design Practice Processes: XKool Technology', *Ardeth - INNOVATION as It happens*, 05, pp. 220-226

Chaillou, S 2019, *AI+ Architecture: Towards a New Approach*, Master's Thesis, Harvard University

Clark, LA and Watson, D 1995, 'Constructing validity: Basic issues in objective scale development', *Psychological Assessment*, 7(3), pp. 309-319

DeVellis, RF 2003, *Scale Development: Theory and Applications*, Sage Publications

Ghomeshi, M and Jusan, MM 2013, 'Investigating different aesthetic preferences between architects and non-architects in residential facade designs', *Indoor and Built Environment*, 22(6), pp. 952-964

Gifford, R, Hine, DW, Muller-Clemm, W, Reynolds Jr., DJ and Shaw, KT 2000, 'Decoding modern architecture: A lens model approach for understanding the aesthetic differences of architects and laypersons', *Environment and Behavior*, 32(2), pp. 163-187

Green, SB 1991, 'How Many Subjects Does It Take To Do A Regression Analysis', *Multivariate Behav Res.*, 26(3), pp. 499-510

Jeffrey, D and Reynolds, G 1999, 'Planners, Architects, the Public, and Aesthetics Factor Analysis of Preferences for Infill Developments', *Journal of Architectural and Planning Research*, 16(4), pp. 271-288

Koh, I 2019, 'Discrete Sampling: There is No Object or Field ... Just Statistical Digital Patterns', in Retsin, G (eds) 2019, *Architectural Design 89(2)*, Wiley, pp. 102-109

Lagendijk, B, Pignetti, A and Vacilotto, S 2012, 'Case Study" Absolute World Towers, Mississauga', *CTBUH Journal*, IV, pp. 12-17

Llinares, C, Montanana, A and Navarro, E 2011, 'Differences in Architects and Nonarchitects' Perception of Urban Design: An Application of Kansei Engineering Techniques', *Urban Studies Research*, 1, pp. 1-13

Moldovan, I, Moldovan, SV and Nicoleta-Maria, I 2014 'Iconic Architecture: Skyscrapers', *Proceedings of 5th International Conference Civil Engineering - Science and Practice*, pp. 1461-1468

Montanana, A, Llinares, C and Navarro, E 2013, 'Architects and non-architects: Differences in perception of property design', *Journal of Housing and the Built Environment*, 28(2), pp. 273-291

Mousavirad, SJ and Ebrahimpour-Komleh, H 2017, 'Image Segmentation as an Important Step in Image-Based Digital Technologies in Smart Cities: A New Nature-Based Approach', in Ismail, L and Zhang, L (eds) 2017, *Information Innovation Technology in Smart Cities*, Springer, pp. 75-89

Pignatiello, GA, Martin, RJ and Hickman Jr., RL 2018, 'Decision fatigue: A conceptual analysis', *Journal of Health Psychology*, 25(1), pp. 123-135

Ren, Y and Zheng, H 2020 'The Spire of AI - Voxel-based 3D Neural Style Transfer', *Proceedings of CAADRIA 2020*, pp. 619-628

Safarova, K, Pirko, M, Jurik, V, Pavlica, T and Nemeth, O 2019, 'Differences between young architects' and non-architects' aesthetic evaluation of buildings', *Frontiers of Architectural Research*, 8(2), pp. 229-237

Sanatani, RP 2020 'A Machine-Learning driven Design Assistance Framework for the Affective Analysis of Spatial Enclosures', *Proceedings of CAADRIA 2020*, pp. 741-750

Satir, S 2015, 'Innovation and Originality in Design', *IJIRES*, 2(5), pp. 372-376

Sekaran, U and Bougie, R 2016, *Research Methods For Business*, Wiley

Shibayama, S and Wang, J 2020, 'Measuring originality in science', *Scientometrics*, 122, p. 409–427

Tian, ZC, Chen, WQ, Tang, P, Wang, JG and Shi, X 2015, 'Building Energy Optimization Tools and Their Applicability in Architectural Conceptual Design Stage', *Energy Procedia*, 78, pp. 2572-2577

Verma, D, Jana, A and Ramamritham, K 2018, 'Quantifying Urban Surroundings Using Deep Learning Techniques: A New Proposal', *Urban Science*, 2(3), p. 78

Vollers, K 2009, 'The CAD-Tool 2.0 Morphological Scheme of Non-Orthogonal High-Rises', *CTBUH Journal*, III, pp. 38-49

Yousif, S and Bolojan, D 2021 'Deep-Performance - Incorporating Deep Learning for Automating Building Performance Simulation in Generative Systems', *Proceedings of CAADRIA 2021*, pp. 151-160

Bionics, bioprinting, living materials

Designing a Living Material Through Bio-Digital-Fabrication

Guiding the growth of fungi through a robotic system

Dilan Ozkan[1], Martyn Dade-Robertson[2], Ruth Morrow[3], Meng Zhang[4]
[1,2,3]Newcastle University [4]Northumbria University
[1,2,3]{d.ozkan2|martyn.dade-robertson|ruth.morrow}@newcastle.ac.uk [4]meng.zhang@northumbria.ac.uk

Designing with living materials require designers to look for new methods of fabrication since living cells exhibit their own agency, and are able to sense and respond to environmental stimuli. Therefore, there is an urgent demand to design a framework for fabricating living materials. This paper investigates the digital-fabrication of fungi as a new way of designing and crafting living materials without genetic manipulation. In this research, fungi act as a bio-material probe to generate and test new design strategies that enable a dialogue between digital and biological systems. Conceptual experiments, that use fungi to investigate the proposed bio-digital-fabrication scenarios, are central in this study. The research attempts to generate new information for the design process of an organism in the field of architecture. The project will expand on the latest thinking on the bio-material fabrication by allowing the living material to be engaged in the fabrication process.

Keywords: *Bio-digital-fabrication, Biological interactions, Self-organizing material systems, Robotic growth chamber*

INTRODUCTION

Mushrooms are the fruiting bodies of fungi, formed by a stipe (stalk) that supports a pileus (cap) where the spore production occurs (Watkinson et al. 2016). Mycelium, the root network of fungi, is of general interest as a building material as it can be grown rapidly on various forms of waste creating a bulk building material (Islam et al. 2018). Recently, some architects have been experimenting with mycelium to create structures, which include 'The Growing Pavilion' and 'Hi-Fi Tower' [1], [2]. However, while mycelium is relatively simple, the fruiting bodies (which are composed of cells with the same genetic code as the roots) are morphologically complex with a high degree of cell differentiation and plasticity. Plasticity allows mushrooms to alter their morphology to adapt to changes in their environmental conditions (Skipper et al. 2010). Harnessing this self-assembly system of fruiting bodies for the development of materials offers an interesting contrast to the existing work on mycelium. It also offers some challenges to existing ideas of fabrication since the relationship between genetics, environment and cellular growth is complex.

This study suggests a form of bio-digital fabrication for fungi in which the fruiting body is grown with minimal direct physical intervention (ie typically moulds are used to constrain fungus growth) but is guided through the digital control of the growth conditions of the mushrooms in terms of temperature, humidity, CO_2 level and light exposure. This fabrication process involves both biological and digital sensing, and feedback. The aim is to guide mushroom growth digitally following similar approaches offered by projects such as 'Florarobotica' which focuses on the symbiotic relationships between robots and plants and Zolotovsky's 'guided growth' of cellulose-producing bacteria (Hamann et al. 2017; Zolotovsky 2017). Both these projects, and the work described in this paper, can be considered as biohybrids which combine computational tools and living materials to build manufacturing systems for architectural purposes.

This paper describes a 'robotic growth chamber', which is used to inform the morphology of the oyster mushrooms (Pleurotus ostreatus) through the initial biological experiments (humidity and CO_2). Although the mushrooms obtained as a result of the experiments have no apparent value to architecture, they help to demonstrate a broader concept, indicating a new type of parametric design. The mushrooms are used as a bio-material probe to gain new knowledge and transfer that knowledge for future studies on how to guide the growth of a bio-material with its own morphological tendencies and capacities. The adaptation of the probe method to biomaterials was pioneered by Ramirez-Figueroa to enable direct engagement with the biological systems. She conducted design experiments using organisms to explore ideas, for example, the patterning of bacterial growth (Ramirez-Figueroa 2017). In these contexts, bacteria and mushroom, acting as bio-material probes, are explicitly not for the development of 'useful' materials but for the development of design frameworks which reveal the complexity of biological systems and processes.

METHODS

The design and construction of a robotic growth chamber

The project is based on the design and construction of a growth chamber in which the environmental conditions of the growing mushrooms can be controlled. This in turn alters the developmental pathway of the mushrooms leading to different morphologies.

To make this system, an Arduino UNO, a computer, Arduino sensors (DHT11 air humidity and temperature sensor, SEN0219 infrared CO_2 sensor, V1.0 soil moisture sensor and HC-SP04 ultrasonic distance sensor) as shown in Figure 1 and devices (12V DC fan, humidifier, 450 nm LED blue light source and 75watt heat bulb) have been integrated into a plastic container as shown in Figure 2 [3]. This chamber can be called a robotic chamber since it *senses*, with the Arduino sensors; *thinks*, with the algorithm; and *acts*, through command implementing devices (Ben-Ari and Mondada 2018).

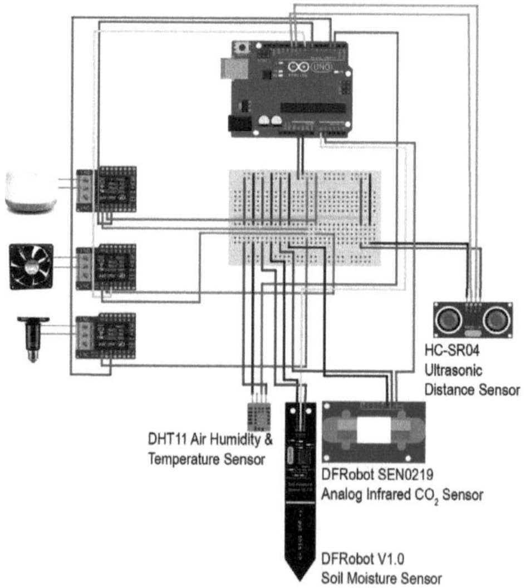

Figure 1
The wire connection of Arduino, sensors, relay modules and command implementing devices

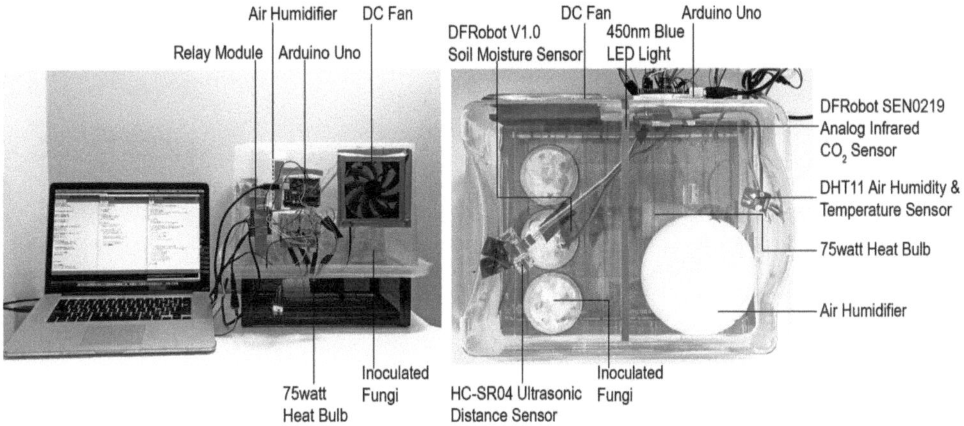

Figure 2
The robotic growth chamber [3]

The system, for the growth chamber, as seen in Figure 3, is relatively straightforward. It works principally with 'on' and 'off' codes which can be set by inputting the numerical value for the condition according to the designer's desires. This in turn modulates the device, which controls that variable by simply turning it on or off.

All the sensors, other than the distance sensor, measure the environmental conditions of the chamber. The distance sensor measures the growth of the mushroom. This, in turn, provides feedback for the control or the environmental controls to create the conditions to inhibit or promote growth.

Experimental design

The scientific method is adopted to explore and test the effects of humidity and CO_2 levels on the morphology of fungal fruiting body. Firstly, a direct comparison of the specific conditions helps to understand the influence of each condition on the organisms' morphology. To achieve that only one variable is changed at a time and all other variables remain constant. The ambient conditions required for fruiting body maturation and mass cultivation for agricultural purposes are summarised in table 1 (Jang et al. 2003, Bellettini et al. 2019, Watkinson et al. 2016). These results have been used to give some scope to make decisions while setting up experiments.

All experiments were conducted in triplicates to help to detect the 'typical' fungal morphology formed each time under a single condition. Each set of mushrooms grown in the experiments started with the same substrates (10g of strawbale, 10g of wood shavings, 10g of coffee grounds), which were sterilised in an autoclave at 121^0C for 15 minutes. This mixture was then seeded with 10g of oyster mushroom spawn from GroCycle, UK under the same conditions (in sealed plastic boxes, in the dark, at ambient temperature). After three weeks, they were exposed to different environmental conditions, for 8 days, controlled by altering one parameter at a time.

Humidity experiment

The variable of humidity in this controlled experiment was measured using a DHT11 air humidity sensor and adjusted with a humidifier. In this way, the ambient conditions could be adjusted to 75%, 85% and 95% air humidity, utilising code which programs the Arduino. The other variables ie CO_2 level at 3000 ppm, light exposure for 4 hours per day at same time of the day and temperature at 22^0C were kept constant in this set of experiments.

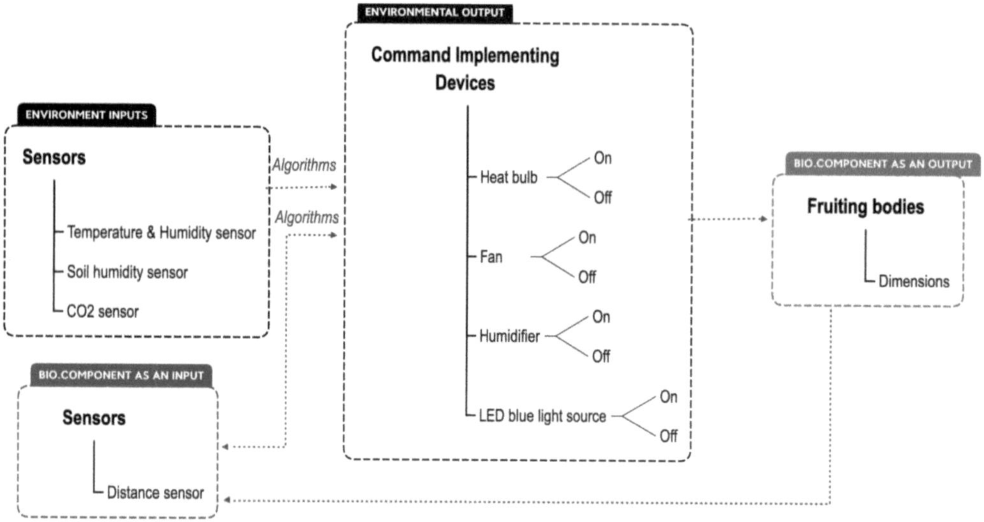

Figure 3
The diagram of relations

CO2 experiment

In this set of the experiments the CO_2 levels were tested at 1000 ppm, 3000 ppm and 5000 ppm. These were achieved by the help of the fan and SEN2019 Analog Infrared CO_2 sensor in the growth chamber. The other variables ie air humidity at 80%, light exposure for 4 hours per day at same time of the day and temperature at 22^0C were kept constant.

Recording results

The experiments were stopped on day 27 as the fruiting bodies tend to start forming by day 21 and wilting often is seen after day 30, as seen in Table 1. The mushroom morphology was documented at this endpoint of day 27 using photography (Fujifilm X-T2 with 80mm lens), microscopy (Dino-Lite digital microscope at 70X magnification) and 3D scanning (EinScan-SE desktop scanner). Photography helped to analyse the overall form and general tendency of mushrooms. Microscopic images captured the details, smaller features and non-measurable characteristics such as the surface texture and colour. The images from photography and microscopy generated the qualitative data for this study. The 3D scanning

	Mycelial growth	**Pinehead Induction** (the transition stage from mycelium to fruiting bodies)	**Fruitification**
Temperature	*5-35 ⁰C*	*18 ⁰C*	*20-25 ⁰C*
Light	*Dark*	*Regular light-dark cycle 500 lx light*	
Humidity	*85-90 % humidity*	*90-95 % humidity*	*80-90 % humidity*
CO_2 level	*2000-2500 ppm*	*1500–2000 ppm*	*1500–2000 ppm*
Duration	*0-14 days*	*14-21 days*	*21-30 days*

Table 1
The ambient conditions required for fruiting body maturation

allowed the form to be translated into a digital model, using Rhinoceros. This helped to measure the angle and dimensions of the caps and stalks more precisely without damaging the organism. It also became possible to overlay the triplicate 3D scans of the mushrooms grown under the same environmental conditions to compare and contrast morphologies through the digital file. It helped to visually represent the average morphology for each condition.

RESULTS

The results evaluate both the performance of the growth chamber and mushroom morphologies in different environmental conditions. The mushroom formations are compared using photographs both in micro and macro scales and digital model comparing measurements of their dimensions.

The performance of the robotic growth chamber

While conducting the experiments, it is noticed that there are factors which complicate the system of the growth chamber. This complication arises from involving a living bio-material and environmental control being multifactorial. Therefore, the system is constantly working and adjusting to reach a desired equilibrium. The cellular respiration of the mushrooms produces CO_2, heat and water, affecting humidity, temperature and CO_2 levels in the chamber. Another complicating factor for the system is the operation of the devices, although aiming to affect one variable it affects the entire system. For instance, running the fan reduces the CO_2 as hoped but also inadvertently affects the humidity level and temperature in the chamber. Thirdly, independently of the devices, there is an innate relationship between the environmental factors such as when temperature drops humidity will rise, which is a feature of closed systems. Although there is this interplay of the mushroom, devices and closed environment, which is quite complex, all the devices work simultaneously to keep the conditions constant. This is achieved by each device having a main action and the result of this being monitored by the sensors to make regular adjustments to maintain desired conditions.

The mushroom morphologies

This robotic growth chamber acts as a proof of concept. It both establishes the conditions for and impacts on the growth and formation of, the mushroom fruiting bodies, with minimal physical contact.

As seen in Figure 4, the copies grown under the same conditions exhibit similar forms, therefore it is possible to state that the morphology of the fruit body is significantly influenced by each condition. Humidity increases the curviness of cap edges and the stalks (see figure 4-a). The texture of stalks gets hairier, gills get shallower, and pinheads swell as humidity increases (see figure 5-a). When observing the cap size there is not a significant trend seen with altering humidity levels (see figure 6). Although the stalk length does suggest linear growth, it does not show as much variation as changing CO_2 levels (see figure 7).

On the other hand, CO_2 mainly affects the size of the caps (see figure 4-b). The caps get bigger with a decrease in CO_2 levels. The stalks get longer with high CO_2 up to a certain level (see figure 5-b). However, after a certain point (approximately over 3500ppm) their length does not increase anymore, and they become leaner (see figure 7). In short, while humidity has more influence on the curvature of the stalk, CO_2 significantly affects the cap size.

CONCLUSION

The initial attempt to influence the growth of mushrooms using the growth chamber points towards a novel form of fabrication. It connects robotic sensing and actuation to the growth and self-assembly processes of a biological system. The robotic growth chamber provides a potential site for communication between designer and organism, where interactions occur through continuous modifications of a range of variables. This interactive and collaborative way of fabricating allows the material to go beyond the role of simply shape filling (Oxman 2010) and accordingly,

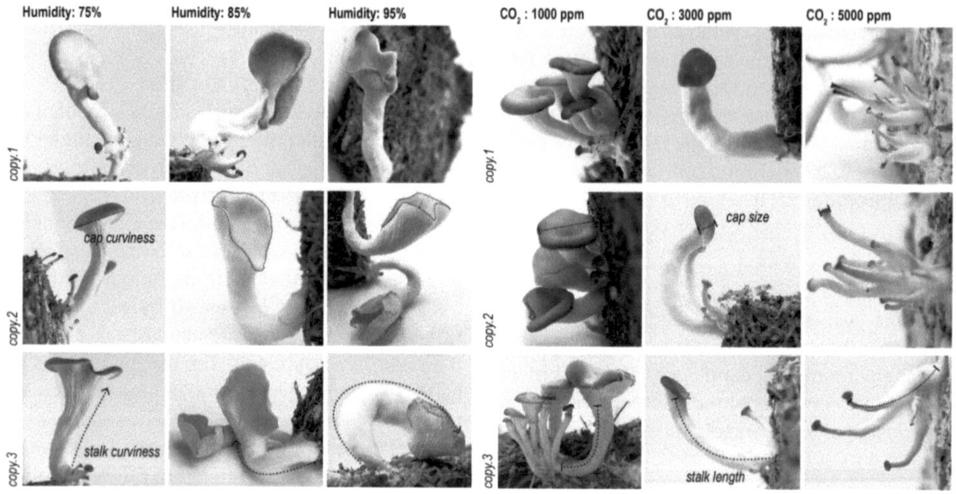

a

b

Figure 4
The effects of humidity and #CO_2# on mushroom morphology

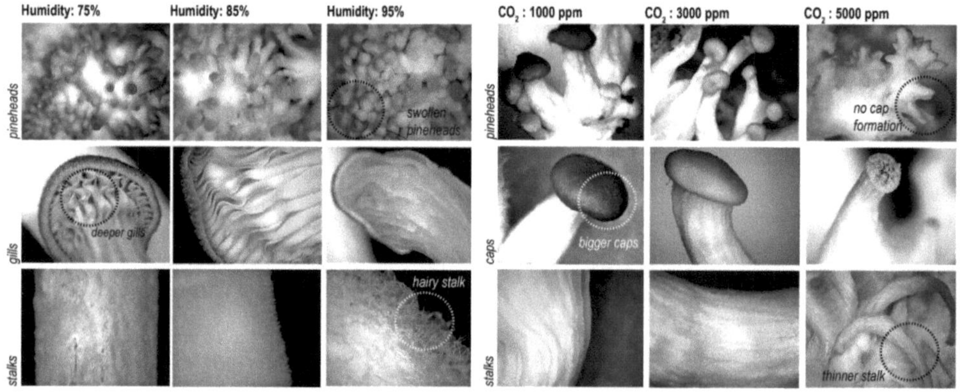

a

b

Figure 5
Microscopic images of different parts of mushrooms

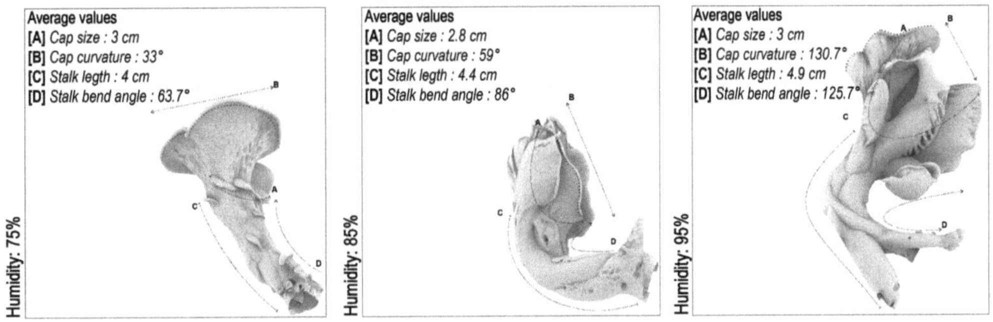

Figure 6
The average sizes and the overlayed mushrooms in the humidity experiment

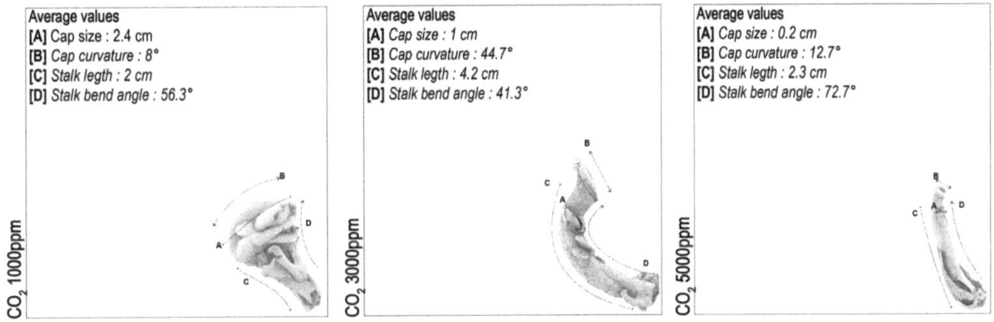

Figure 7
The average sizes and the overlayed mushrooms in the #CO_2# experiment

new relations start to emerge.

This work demonstrates that fungi exhibit parametric properties when a single parameter is changed. However, these experiments were carried out within a limited range. Future research could explore the critical thresholds were changing the variable no longer impacts (or impacts as expected) upon mushroom morphology. A further question might be, what happens if two or more variables are changed in the environment at the same time. Finding that out provides a design opportunity by presenting the parametrisation of a complex growth process leading to a complex 3D form.

Despite the lack of obvious value of the mushrooms within the architectural field, the process of guiding their growth using a digital system is an important demonstration of innovative architectural fabrication. Predicting the effect that altering more than one variable will have on mushroom morphology, and understanding and extrapolating the proportional relationship of the different variables will answer the question of how designers can craft biology through a new type of parametric design approach. It also exhibits a physical manifestation of a 'Creodic' design process. Dade-Robertson translates Waddington's idea of an epigenetic landscape into design framework and defines creodic design as *"...searching for the necessary paths for living cells to fabricate materials and for methods to alter the landscape towards a path which is favorable to the outcomes we want"* (Dade-Robertson 2021). Understanding how to influence the form of a living material helps us to design by using the intrinsic properties of that material.

Observing how fungi form in different growth conditions within this research informs an understanding of the influences of the environment on a range of biological systems and the tools we, as designers, have to inform this process. Furthermore, harnessing both biological and digital computation to generate 3D material forms opens up discussion about the relationship between digital and biological systems as well as the role of the designer in processes which are complex and outside their direct control.

REFERENCES

Bellettini, M. B., Fiorda, F.A., Maives, H.A., Teixeira, G.L., Avila, S., Hornung, P.S., Junior, A.M. and Ribani, R.H. 2019, 'Factors Affecting Mushroom Pleurotus Spp.', *Saudi Journal of Biological Science*, 26 (4)(https://doi.org/10.1016/j.sjbs.2016.12.005), pp. 633-46

Ben-Ari, MR and Mondada, F 2018, *Elements of Robotics*, Springer

Dade-Robertson, M 2021, *Living Construction*, New York: Routledge

Hamann, H, Soorati, MD, Heinrich, MK, Hofstadler, DN, Kuksin, I, Veenstra, F, Wahby, M, Nielsen, SA, Risi, S, Skrzypczak, T, Zahadat, P, Wojtaszek, P, Støy, K, Schmickl, T, Kernbach, S and Ayres, P 2017, 'Flora Robotica - An Architectural System Combining Living Natural Plants and Distributed Robots', *Emerging Technologies*, arXiv:1709.04291, pp. 1-16

Islam, MR, Tudryn, G, Bucinell, R, Schadler, L and Picu, RC 2018, 'Stochastic Continuum Model for Mycelium-Based Bio-Foam', *Materials and Design*, 160, p. 549–56

Jang, KY, Jhune, CS, Park, JS, Cho, SM, Weon, HY, Cheong, JC, Choi, SG and Sung, JM 2003, 'Characterization of Fruitbody Morphology on Various Environmental Conditions in Pleurotus Ostreatus', *Mycobiology*, 31 (3), pp. 145-150

Oxman, N. 2010, *Material-Based Design Computation*, Ph.D. Thesis, Massachusetts Institute of Technology

Ramirez-Figueroa, C 2017, *Biomaterial Probe - Design Engagements with Living Systems*, Ph.D. Thesis, Newcastle University

Skipper, M, Weiss, U and Gray, N 2010, 'Plasticity', *Nature*, 465, p. 703

Watkinson, SC, Boddy, L and Money, P 2016, *The Fungi*, Elsevier

Zolotovsky, K 2017, *Guided Growth: Design and Computation of Biologically Active Materials*, Ph.D. Thesis, Massachusetts Institute of Technology

[1] http://www.thelivingnewyork.com

[2] https://thegrowingpavilion.com

[3] http://bbe.ac.uk/index.php/2020/09/01/guiding-the-growth-of-fungi-through-a-robotic-system/

Multi-Material Fabrication for Biodegradable Structures

Enabling the printing of porous mycelium composite structures

Ariel Cheng Sin Lim[1], *Mette Ramsgaard Thomsen*[2]
[1,2]*Royal Danish Academy, CITA*
[1]*arli2033@edu.kglakademi.dk* [2]*mette.thomsen@kadk.dk*

Our awareness of the earth's depleting resources has directed focus towards biomaterials, which can be extracted sustainably and biodegraded after use. Current fabrication of biomaterial structures is still restricted in strength and geometry, limiting its use in construction. This paper presents a novel two-phase multi-material fabrication process to create mycelium composite structures of higher porosity and complexity with speculated improvements in strength. First, cellulose pulp inoculated with mycelium is extruded. Then, each layer is filled by a secondary supporting material. This material, in the form of a gravel- and sand-slurry, acts as an inhospitable medium steering mycelial growth, additionally improving aeration to produce stronger structures. After an intermediate growth period, the secondary material, reusable in a closed-loop production model, is removed to reveal the fully-grown mycelium structure. The paper reports on each of the three aspects: the fabrication process, material experimentation of primary and secondary substrates, as well as geometry of varying porosity and performance.

Keywords: *biomaterials, mycelium, biodegradable structures, robotic fabrication, additive manufacturing*

INTRODUCTION

The global construction industry is on an unsustainable path of consumption, with raw materials usage expecting to double in 2060 (OECD, 2018). As one of the largest consumers of raw materials and contributors of carbon emission (OECD, 2019), there is an urgent need to reconsider the way we design and construct our built environment. Currently, there is a mismatch between material durability and usage duration. Materials such as concrete can be made extremely durable - albeit accumulating high maintenance costs (Saad, 2016) - such that the end of a building's life depends on its use becoming obsolete rather than the aging of the material. In light of the new ecological age, this is a paradigm worth reconsidering. While materials should be strong and sturdy to be functional, it should not be so that it remains in the environment when it is no longer needed.

Biomaterials are a potential alternative that can be manufactured sustainably and returned to nature after completing its purpose. Mycelium, in particular, is an organic polymeric composite material comprising chitin, cellulose, and proteins. Its self-growing nature constitutes a natural manufacturing process that requires minimal additional energy. As a material, it has yet to reach sufficient mechanical strength (Islam et al., 2017) for construction applications in terms of its load-bearing properties. Industry use of mycelium involves casting of mycelium into brick moulds, and additionally, compression of the bricks to improve performance. However, this limits the geometry achievable, as well as results in varying mechanical properties across the brick due to the unequal access to oxygen which determines the level of mycelium colonisation. While more complex forms can be achieved with 3D printing of mycelium, it is still restricted in geometry due to layer constraints in printing biomaterials.

Adapting solutions from the field of 3D printing, our contribution lies in a two-phase fabrication process that includes the addition of a secondary material serving as a support structure. This removes the geometrical constraints of printing and allows for the fabricable form to be growth-optimised rather than dictated by the printing method. The printing takes place in an open container, the size of which can be decided by the bounding volume of the desired print. After the extrusion of each inoculated pulp layer, the remaining negative space is filled with a secondary material to create a supporting bed for the next layer to be printed on. Our contribution lies in the novel fabrication process for robotically steering the extrusion of mycelium (Figure 1). The method extends the geometrical and fabrication possibilities of biomaterials by removing the limitations of typical bio-printing, improving potential for architectural applications. Furthermore, the increased possibility in complexity and thus porosity allows for the design of forms that are better optimised for the growth of the living organism. The focus of this investigation is to develop a workflow steering three key aspects: fabrication, material, and geometry.

BACKGROUND

On Biomaterials and Mycelium

Abundant in nature with the ability to be fabricated in low-energy processes (Wijk et al., 2015), biomaterials present an opportunity for sustainable construction. Structures such as the Aguahoja from Mediated Matter Group demonstrate the potential of creating bio-composites with high material tunability. By altering the constituent composition, the degree of stiffness, opacity, and decay can be controlled. With biomaterials, the structure can also be returned to nature after it has fulfilled its purpose, creating a bio-based circular design process. Its degradation and susceptibility to changes in the environment defy the current building paradigm where objects are built to last. Rather than viewing its decay as an obstacle, it

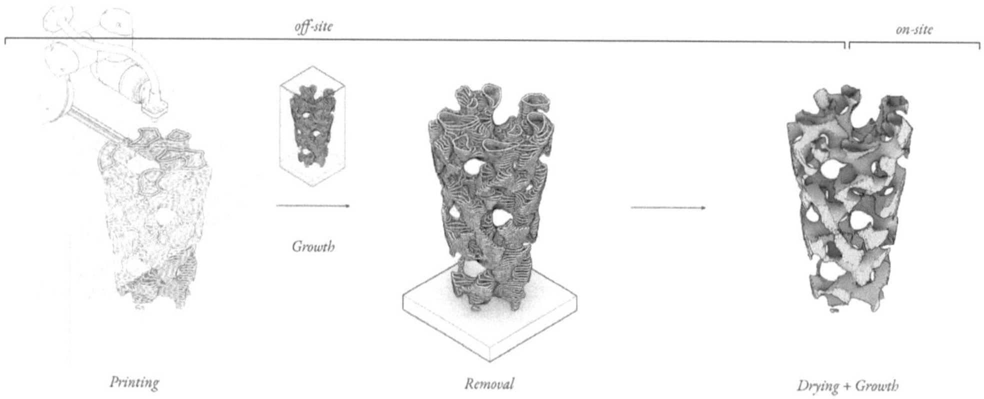

Figure 1
Overall process of printing, growing and drying

could instead give rise to a new design approach that accounts for the different stages across a structure's lifespan.

Mycelium presents interesting alternatives for rethinking material performance and expectancy. As a living organism, it reacts to external stimuli, restructuring its hyphal network to optimise nutrient intake. As a material, it morphs continually to generate varying properties across the mycelial body. It self-replicates to create seemingly endless material in the presence of suitable substrates that can be fully sourced from waste (Jambaro et al., 2014). When subjected to trauma, it is a 'self-healing' material capable of sealing breaks in the structure. Its advantages in sound, fire insulation, and water-proofing (Jones et al., 2018) present interesting application potential. Furthermore, the abundance of fungi species is largely unexplored in their application in construction materials and future research could yield strains and composites of improved performance. The ease of replicability, low cost and environmental sustainability indicate its potential to play a significant role in the future sustainable construction.

Fabrication with Mycelium

Fabrication of mycelium for industrial use is still undergoing development. The main process explored to date is the casting and compression of mycelium bricks (Ross, 2016) - improving strength by maximising its density. An efficient and practical way of using mycelium as a material, this technique is being used to produce insulation panels by firms such as Mogu (Appels et al., 2019). In terms of its use as a construction material, mycelium bricks and panels have been used in temporary structures such as the Hy-Fi tower (Nagy et al., 2015), the Growing Pavilion (Elsacker et al., 2021), and the works of Philip Ross. However, the strength of mycelium composites falls far below concrete even after compression (Islam et al., 2017), which is currently the biggest obstacle in its use in construction. Compressive strength is greatly dependent on the substrate constituents (Vidholdova et al. 2019), and there is potential for stronger composites as new fungal strains and substrate combinations are tested for construction applications. Stronger forms could potentially be generated through design of forms better optimised for the colonisation of mycelium. Extent of mycelium colonisation is strongly related to the access to oxygen (Tang et al., 2003), hence cast bricks in solid volume result in lower colonisation in the overall volume and limit potential strength of the form. By designing for forms with greater surface area, composite strength could be improved as mycelium coverage increases. In nature, termite-constructed fungus nests are also made sufficiently porous to allow for gaseous exchange to keep both termites and fungus alive (Turner, 2005). These natural forms, optimised for fungi growth with a constant width, also demonstrate a high level of complexity that can be achieved with mycelial composites.

Projects such as the Mycotree (Heisel et al., 2018) show the possibility of mycelium being used structurally by designing forms that optimise material properties. Besides casting, more complex geometry can be achieved with 3D printing as demonstrated by several prototypes by Blast Studio and Bio-Digital Matter Lab. These forms greatly improve the aeration of the structure through increased surface area and reduced mycelial wall width. However, the geometrical possibilities are limited by the restrictions of 3D printing: sagging of layers due to excessive self-weight and failed overhangs that exceed the maximum possible angle (Figure 2).

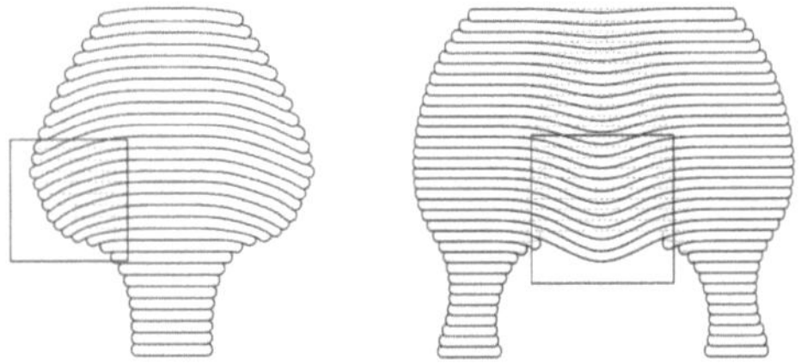

Figure 2
Sagging due to self weight (left), Failing overhang (right)

This research aims to increase the geometrical possibilities of mycelium composites and overcome the limitations of mycelium fabrication to create biodegradable structures with wider architectural applications. The experiments reported in this paper aim to achieve the following goals:

- Fabrication: Minimal waste production, enabling production of complex geometries, promoting growth of mycelium
- Design: Improved myceliation of structure, measurable porosity
- Materials: Locally sourced waste substrate and reusable secondary material

FABRICATION METHOD

A two-phase multi-material fabrication process is explored in this paper to create mycelium composite structures of higher porosity and complexity. These forms not only test the limit of geometrical complexity, but also present an opportunity to better fabricate with mycelium by catering to its biological properties and providing better aeration. To make these intricate structures possible, the proposed method overcomes current printing limitations by introducing a secondary material to serve as structural support. A fabrication set-up is designed to both extrude the primary inoculated pulp which makes up the form, as well as deposit the secondary material that supports and shapes it.

Fabrication Set-up

The printing process takes place within an open container which is sealed post-fabrication with a microfilter lid to minimise exposure to contaminants during the growth process. The overall set-up (Figure 3) designed for this method comprises the extrusion set-up for the inoculated pulp, which is controlled by a collaborative robot affixed with a customized extrusion system, and a deposition set-up which enables the secondary material to be applied in the remaining negative area.

The extrusion set-up comprises a collaborative robot, nozzle, connecting pipe, storage unit to hold the pulp and pulp-pushing device. The latter can take the form of either an air compressor and pneu-

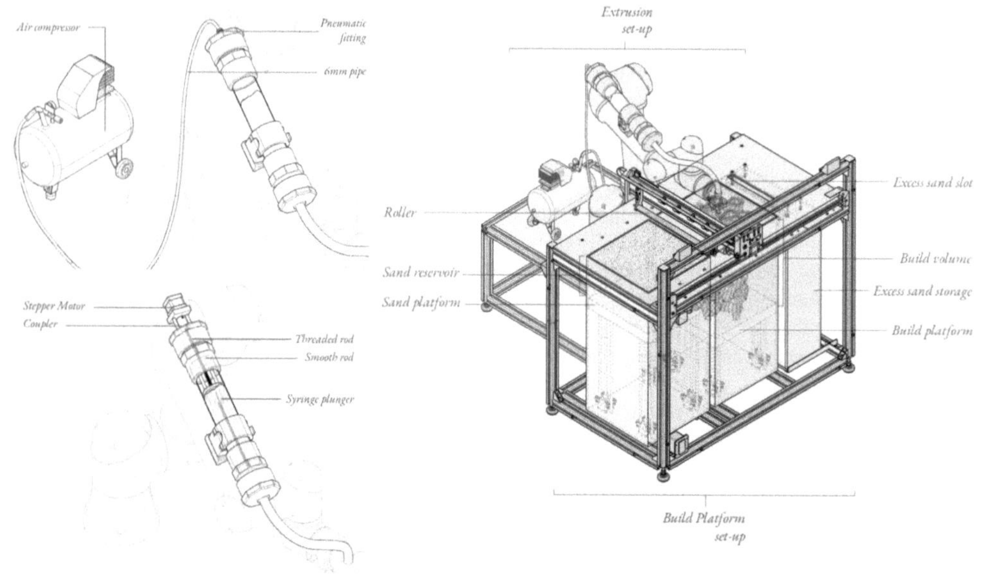

Figure 3
Designed set-up: Pneumatic extrusion set-up (top left), Mechanical extrusion set-up (bottom left) Overall set-up: Extrusion + Deposition (right)

Figure 4
Set-up prototype, using a UR5 robot

matic fitting set-up or a stepper motor and plunger set-up; both systems have been proven to work in projects with similar wet pulp extrusion (Wang et al., 2018). A pneumatic set-up was used for this prototype for its simpler set-up (Figure 4).

The deposition set-up can be partially adapted from a Selective Laser Sintering (SLS) machine (Hussain et al., 2019), where two moving platforms for the secondary material and printed artefact move accordingly each layer. A roller pushes the secondary material from the top of the reservoir to fill in the negative space in the build volume; any excess is pushed through the slot where it can later be reused. An alternative set-up would be the design of an aggregate deposition device (beyond the scope of this paper) to deposit the material at negative areas. This area of research in aggregate deposition is to be further explored beyond this paper. A manual deposition method is used for this set of experiments.

Fabrication Process

The fabrication process, the first step in the overall timeline (Figure 1), can be divided into two phases. In phase one, inoculated pulp is printed with a collaborative robot arm. In phase two, the remaining negative space left over in each layer is filled by a secondary supporting material, completing the layer. This repeats for each layer until the structure is fully printed, and the container is sealed with a microfilter lid as the artefact enters the first growth phase. This technique leverages on the delayed forming process of mycelium, which takes time to colonise the substrate and to create a rigid structure. After a period of about 14 days, the structure, along with the adjacent secondary material (which is reusable in a closed-loop production model) can be removed from the container (Figure 5). At this point, a decision can be made whether to integrate the secondary material into the form as a texture or removed completely. After the removal and exposure to the external environment, the structure undergoes an intermediate growth and drying phase where it begins solidifying into the final form (Figure 6). Any remaining secondary material that has not been integrated into the mycelium starts to fall from the structure from this point in time.

Figure 5
Grown artefact after removal from container

Figure 6
Unveiled artefact after secondary growth and removing of secondary material

EXPERIMENTS

A series of experiments were carried out at different points to test the workability of the fabrication technique and remedy any potential issues, as well as prove the feasibility of shaping mycelium composites with a secondary material during its growth phase. Introduction of contaminants was minimised by sterilising the substrates (prior to inoculation) and secondary material with a pressure cooker, reducing contact time of the biocomposite materials to the external environment, and constant cleaning of the set-up with alcohol. This proved sufficient for the growth of mycelium in this set-up and no visible contamination was observed in the final experiments. This research uses Ganoderma Lucidum (G. lucidum) for its fast-growing nature, structural performance and extensive published use in research. However, this is interchangeable with other species in the application of this technique, especially in a site-specific context in consideration of biodiversity compatibility.

Fabrication Set-up Prototype

The pneumatic extrusion set-up (Figure 4) was built to investigate the steering of the primary substrate using a robot arm. For initial testing purposes, the secondary material deposit was done manually by pouring it into the remaining unprinted space each layer. The variables in this set-up include the size of the print storage box, which restricts the printable extents, as well as nozzle size which affects the resolution of the print. Several iterations of the set-up were visited, each improving upon the main issue arising from clogging of the pulp along the nozzle. The recipe of the extrusion pulp was found to be crucial in the success of the extrusion, and should be thoroughly blended and filtered to ensure minimal clogging. This set-up was used in a series of material experiments with recipes varying primary substrate composition and secondary material type to determine the best mix for growth of the artefact.

Primary Substrate (Extrusion Pulp)

For a suitable extrusion pulp, there are two main criteria to create the primary substrate: suitability for fabrication and support of fungus growth. The main composition was experimented with varying concentrations of mycelium spawn, mycelium feed, binding agent and water. In alignment with the experiment's aim of using biodegradable materials, the mycelium feed would ideally be sourced from a waste stream that can be broken down by the fungus, such as non-recyclable paper including food-soiled paper packaging and wax/plastic-lined paper. For the context of this research, waste paper pulp has been selected for its high cellulose content and ease of availability. Xanthan gum was selected from a range of binding agents for its performance in holding the substrate together and keeping it suitably viscous. The water content in the mixture, a necessity for mycelial growth, had to be sufficient without causing excessive pooling within the container such that the mycelium drowns. However, this can also be mitigated by elevating the print with additional layers of secondary material prior to printing. The final composition used in successful subsequent experiments comprises, by weight: 11% mycelium spawn, 56% paper pulp, 1% xanthan gum and 32% water by weight. This achieved a smooth extrusion process with viscosity low enough to flow through the nozzle yet sufficiently solid for shape retention during and after the printing process. The recipe allowed for sufficient mycelium colonisation of the printed structure (Figure 5) within 14 days.

Secondary Material

The inorganic nature of the secondary material allows it to act as an inhospitable medium steering mycelial growth and supporting the weight of the extrusion pulp. The scale of the secondary material also affects the forming of mycelial skin on the artefact. Larger aggregates are able to provide greater aeration, but reduce the resolution of the final artefact as its removal leaves an imprint on the surface (Figure 5). Hence, the coarseness of the surface can be controlled by varying the diameter of the secondary material. Depending on the application, a decision to retain the secondary material on the structure after the growth phase can also be made. Besides the appearance in texture, this could have implications on the structural performance of the final artefact, possibly improving stiffness and load-bearing properties although this is not explored in this paper.

A series of experiments (Figure 7) were conducted to investigate the impact of choice of secondary materials. Here, sand (0.02-0.05mm) and gravel (4-8mm) were used for their contrasting scales, left adjacent to a mix of inoculated wood chip substrate in an enclosed container with a micro-filter. After 7 days, the contents were removed and left to dry for a day. The results give an insight to the interaction between primary and secondary material during the growth period. A gradient of bonding corresponding to the extent of mycelium colonisation is observed at the boundary between the two materials, as the secondary material gets increasingly difficult to remove without destroying the substrate. Experiments attempting to shape form with the secondary material (Figure 8) by manually extruding orthogonal stripes with a piping bag proved relatively successful. The effect of the secondary material was clearly observable in the grown artefacts, with the sand and gravel creating vastly different textures. It is observed that the sand left a much finer texture along the boundary and could be easily removed with water. Overall, the selection of secondary material results in varying results of surface texture, and possibly, strength of the final artefact.

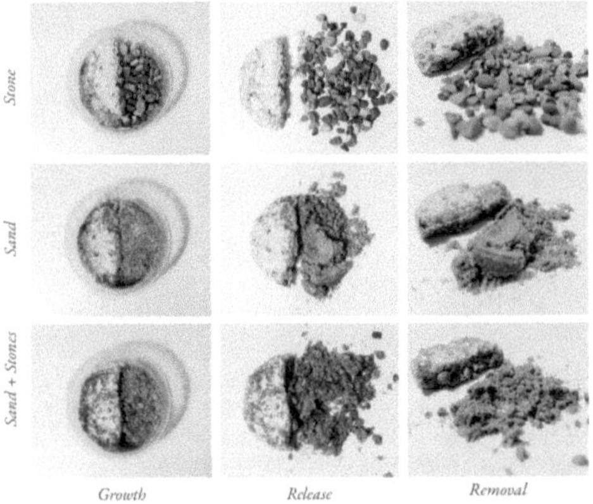

Figure 7
Series of material experiments with sand, gravel and both

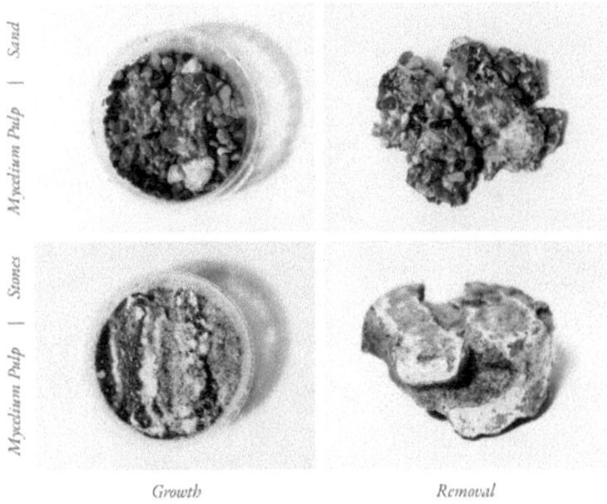

Figure 8
Series of experiments exploring possibility of forming with the secondary material

In order to test the proposed fabrication process, a sufficiently complex form pushing the typical sagging and overhang limits should be attempted. Minimal surfaces are engaged in the design strategy for

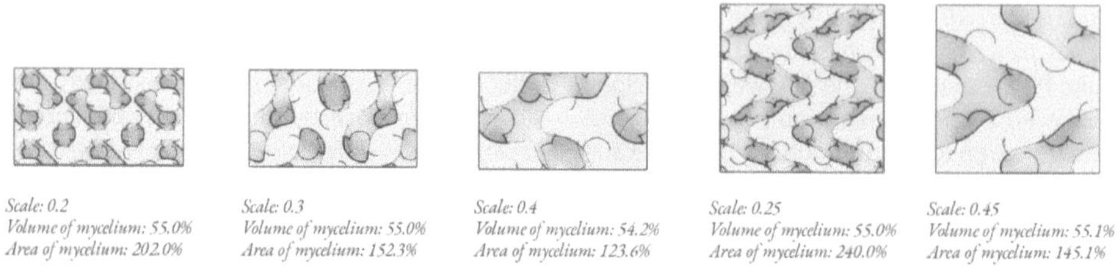

Figure 9
Series of porosity explorations with minimal surfaces

Figure 10
Initial prototypes in mould of dimension 150x90x90mm, varying porosity

Figure 11
Scaled-up prototypes in mould of dimension 150x150x150mm, varying porosity

its ability to generate porosity within a given volume, increasing the surface area for improved aeration for the mycelium. Porosity is compared by taking the difference in volume between the final mininal surface form and the boundary volume (Figure 9). Its overhanging volumes also test the ability of the proposed multi-material fabrication system, while allowing for the removal of secondary material after the growth period due to the interconnected volume. Porosity and thickness of mycelial composite walls can be controlled to produce varying material properties of artefacts. Performance studies of gyroid forms with other materials have proven to have improved deformation (Yang, 2019) which could be transferable to bio-composite forms as well. Results in Figure 10 were prototyped in the Fisherkoch form in a mould of dimensions 150x90x90mm. However, the scale of the print proved to be too small in comparison to the thickness of the extrusion thickness (5mm) hence the details of the form were less discernible. This was remedied in another set of prints scaling up the size of artefacts with a larger cubic mould of width 150mm (Figure 11).

CONCLUSIONS

The experiments demonstrate the potential of a multi-material process of fabricating with mycelium bio-composites. While the fabrication method could be further refined, the prototypes have shed some light on potential pitfalls and areas of improvement such as the relationship between scale of material, extrusion thickness and print dimension that would affect print resolution. We pinpointed a crucial problem linked to the clogging of pulp that emphasised the need for a good water-to-binding agent ratio and sufficient blending of pulp. With a finer pulp, nozzle size can also be reduced to create finer prints. The process of manually depositing the aggregates also highlighted the importance of precision in the secondary material deposition set-up as significant effort had to be exerted to prevent the aggregates from falling and sticking onto the extrusion pulp. Further considerations will also include the integration of secondary material into the primary pulp itself to test the effect on structural performance.

The primary material explorations provide an adequate extrusion pulp for the proposed method, with healthy mycelial growth and retention of shape. Introduction of the secondary material not only opens the possibility of more complex geometry, but also brings in aspects of porosity and aeration that could improve the final structural performance and growth of the mycelial skin. Furthermore, the choice of secondary material adds an interesting design aspect in terms of texture, whether by fusing it with the mycelial skin or removing it to reveal the indents left behind. An extension of this research in the material aspect would include further exploration of growing inorganic material with the living matter, as well as simulating the interaction and evolution of the two contrasting elements.

PERSPECTIVES

Further investigation can be conducted to observe the evolution of the grown structure. By working with minimal surfaces, a clearer relationship between porosity, surface area and wall thickness can be established with more results. The porosity of the artefacts and thickness of composite walls will likely correlate with the rate of degradation, a factor which can be controlled in the design process. This would allow designers to programme the lifespan of the structure, planning the various stages of degradation according to the desired function. Appearance of the skin can be varied by choosing a keep the secondary material and choosing a suitable scale of the aggregates. By keeping the secondary material, the evolution of the artefact also includes the eventual detachment of secondary material. A simulation could be developed to better understand and work with these evolving factors in a biodegradable structure. Depending on the site context, considerations in fungal strain and substrate constituents have to be considered and determined to be compatible with existing biodiversity especially if introduced in a large quantity. The architectural applications of this fabrication process could involve a shifting programme that evolves along with the structure. Overall, this fabrication process expands the possibilities of fabricating with bio-composites in terms of geometry, performance and lifespan.

REFERENCES

Appels, F, Camere, S, Montalti, M, Karana, E, Jansen, K. M. B., Dijksterhuis, J, Krijgsheld, P and Wosten, H 2018, 'Fabrication factors influencing mechanical, moisture- and water-related properties of mycelium-based composites', *Materials & Design*, 161, pp. 64-71

Elsacker, E, Søndergaard, A, Van Wylick, A, Peeters, E and De Laet, L 2021, 'Growing living and multifunctional mycelium composites for large-scale formwork applications using robotic abrasive wire-cutting', *Construction and Building Materials*, 283, pp. 1-16

Goidea, A, Andreen, D and Floudas, D 2020 'Pulp Faction: 3d printed material assemblies through microbial biotransformation', *Fabricate 2020*

Heisel, F, Schlesier, K, Lee, J, Rippmann, M, Saeidi, N, Javadian, A, Hebel, D and Block, P 2017 'Design of a load-bearing mycelium structure through informed structural engineering: The MycoTree at the 2017 Seoul Biennale of Architecture and Urbanism', *World Congress on Sustainable Technologies (WCST-2017)*, Cambridge, UK

Hussain, G, Khan, WA, Ashraf, HA, Ahmad, H, Ahmed, H, Imran, A, Ahmad, I, Rehman, K and Abbas, G 2019, 'Design and development of a lightweight SLS 3D printer with a controlled heating mechanism: Part A', *International Journal of Lightweight Materials and Manufacture*, 2(4), pp. 373-378

Islam, MR, Tudryn, G, Bucinell, R, Schadler, L and Picu, R 2017, 'Morphology and mechanics of fungal mycelium', *Scientific Reports*, 7, pp. 1-12

Jambaro, A, Neri, K and Alvarez, L 2014, 'Utilization of Selected Urban Wastes as Substrate Solutions in the Growth and Yield Performance of Pleurotus sajor-caju Fr. (Singer) (Gray Oyster Mushroom)', *PUP Journal of Science and Technology*, 6, pp. 1-9

Jones, MP, Bhat, T, Kandare, E, Thomas, A, Joseph, P, Dekiwadia, C, Yuen, R, John, S, Ma, J and Wang, C 2018, 'Thermal Degradation and Fire Properties of Fungal Mycelium and Mycelium - Biomass Composite Materials', *Scientific Reports*, 8, pp. 1-10

Muhammad, H, Ceseracciu, L, Canale, C, Heredia-Guerrero, J and Athanassiou, A 2017, 'Advanced Materials From Fungal Mycelium: Fabrication and Tuning of Physical Properties', *Scientific Reports*, 7, pp. 1-11

OECD, . 2019, *Global Material Resources Outlook to 2060: Economic Drivers and Environmental Consequences*, OECD Publishing

Ross, P 2016, 'Method for producing fungus structures', *U.S. Patent and Trademark Office*, U.S. Patent No. 9,410,116, p. -

Saad, L 2016, *Life cycle cost optimization of reinforced concrete structures*, Ph.D. Thesis, Ecole supérieure d'ingénieurs de Beyrouth,

Schmieder, S, Stanley, C, Rzepiela, A, van Swaay, D, Sabotič, J, Nørrelykke, S, deMello, A, Aebi, M and Künzler, M 2019, 'Bidirectional Propagation of Signals and Nutrients in Fungal Networks via Specialized Hyphae', *Current Biology*, 29, pp. 217-228

Tang, Y and Zhong, J 2003, 'Role of oxygen supply in submerged fermentation of Ganoderma lucidum for production of Ganoderma polysaccharide and ganoderic acid', *Enzyme and Microbial Technology*, 32, pp. 478-484

Turner, S 2005, 'Extended Physiology of an Insect-Built Structure', *American Entomologist*, 51, pp. 36-38

Vidholdova, Z, KORMÚTHOVÁ, D, ŽDINSKÝ, J and Lagana, R 2019, 'COMPRESSIVE RESISTANCE OF THE MYCELIUM COMPOSITE', *Annals of WULS, Forestry and Wood Technology*, 107, pp. 31-36

Wang, Q, Sun, J, Yao, Q, Ji, C, Liu, J and Zhu, Q 2018, '3D printing with cellulose materials', *Cellulose*, 25, p. 4275–4301

van Wijk, A and van Wijk, I 2015, *3D printing with biomaterials: Towards a sustainable and circular economy*, IOS Press

Yang, L, Raya, M, Massimiliano, F, Yan, C, Shi, Y and Yang, S 2019, 'Continuous graded Gyroid cellular structures fabricated by selective laser melting: Design, manufacturing and mechanical properties', *Materials & Design*, 162, pp. 394-404

[1] https://www.blast-studio.com/

[2] https://www.researchgate.net/lab/bioDigital-matter-David-Andreen

PH Computation to Growth Prediction

Farahbod Heidari[1], Mohammadjavad Mahdavinejad[2], Liss C. Werner[3], Sima Khayami[4]
[1] Ph.D.Student in Architecture,Department of Architecture,Tarbiat Modares University, Tehran, Iran [2] Professor of Department of Architecture, Tarbiat Modares University, Tehran, Iran [3] Professor of Bio-Inspired Architecture and Sensoric, Institute of Architecture ,Technische Universitat Berlin,Berlin,Germany [4] Master of Architecture, Department of Architecture, Tarbiat Modares University, Tehran, Iran
[1,2,4] {F-Heidari|mahdavinejad|simakhayami}@modares.ac.ir [3] liss.c.werner@tu-berlin.de

Bacterial cellulose is a bio self-assembled organic material with unique features such as great tensile strength, biodegradability, and renewable potential that has made it worthwhile for different fields of industrial development research. Since the past decade, in the field of architecture also, enormous efforts were done to reach the desired guided shape of bacterial cellulose with optimized structural features. However, all these efforts are in their infancy. To reach the adaptive architectural bio-component, we need something beyond static prototyping. Therefore, we investigate the specific type ``Bacterium Glucoacetobacter xylinus(BC)" cellulose growth procedure by syncing the culture medium (cellulose growth environment) to a virtual stimulating environment to introduce the computational architectural design process based on dynamic biological structures. This research presents the smart design process via the syncing of CAD environment and growth environment to create a framework that provides data analysis that the implementation of its outcomes can revolutionize the bio-digital fabrication process.

Keywords: *Bio-fabrication, Bio-based material, Biocomputation, Living Functional Components, Pattern Recognition, AI prediction*

INTRODUCTION

"Bacterial Cellulose is a highly Crystalline Linear biopolymer of glucose, which is produced with a width of less than 100 nm primarily by the bacterium Gluconacetobacter xylinus in both synthetic and non-synthetic mediums through oxidative fermentation"(Jung et al.2007;Falcao et al.2008;Rehm 2009;Klemm et al.2001;Moniri et al.2017). Cellulose is one of the most plentiful biopolymers on earth and exists in cotton, wood, and other plant-based materials, and serves as the dominant reinforcing phase in plant structures. Cellulose is also synthesized by algae, tunicates, and some bacteria (Klemm et al.2006; Henriksson and Berglund, 2007; Iwamoto et al. 2007). Bacterial cellulose has many unique properties, including high purity, high water retention, and a hydrophilic nature, tensile strength, thermal stability, and biodegradability, This Material can be used for a wide range of applications, such as Architectural Component (Derme et al. 2016). The use of biomaterials for large scale architectural and engineering applications is still underdeveloped. Since the past decade, in the field of architecture also, enormous efforts were done to reach the desired guided shape of bacterial cellulose with optimized structural features, the use of bacterial cellulose in industry has advanced our knowledge of its properties and encouraged forward-looking designers to examine the material both as a model for architectural strategies and as a potential fabrication component (Benyus 1997; Vincent 2012). Due to the lack of suitable fabrication methods and digital design tools, cellulose is still disregarded as a building material. Current approaches towards virtual and physical prototyping with non-fuel-based materials also lack the capacity to model and fabricate with continuously varying material properties (Oxman 2011). In order to introduce cellulose as a building material, it is therefore important to develop Bio-Manufacturing methodologies linked to materially informed computational modeling. Bacterial Cellulose structural and functional diversity, underlines their capacity to replace existing synthetic bio-polymers and to provide new methods of bio-fabrication as well as new applications and structures. Current design practice is mostly characterized by the domination of shape over matter, consequently prioritizing virtual shape-defining parameters over physical material and fabrication constraints, leading to a geometric-centric design phase (Oxman 2011; Menges 2007; Mogas 2015). Nevertheless, some recent developments in direct digital manufacturing enable a shift towards a material centric design practice, such as water-based fabrication techniques (Oxman 2011). Additive manufacture (AM) technologies for rapid prototyping employ virtual, computer-aided designed models, and translate them into thin horizontal successive cross-sections to define three-dimensional physical objects (Suchs et al. 1993). Most traditional design methods cannot take advantage of the unique capabilities of AM, because they are established on the manufacturability of traditional manufacturing methods. AM technologies have become an efficient and common means to deliver geometrically precise functional prototypes in relatively short periods of time (Oxman et al. 2012). At the same time, there is a need to expand manufacturing processes towards Bio-Manufacturing based approaches, borrowing techniques from biological science and tissue engineering. Bio-manufacturing for bacterial cellulose is still in its infancy, despite the urgent need for alternatives to Architectural Component Products (Derme et al. 2016).

To produce biological components on an architectural scale, it is first necessary to know how biological materials grow and assemble. Knowing how to grow and the effect of environmental parameters in the growth environment can control biological components and convert them into various forms in the biological fabrication method structure (Heidari et al.2021; Heidari et al.2017). In order to achieve biological fabrication, it is necessary to model the assembly information of biological materials. This modeling in the culture medium of biological materials includes various parameters. Culture medium conditions, materials, and environmental factors are among the critical parameters affecting growth. This study investigated the pH parameter as one of the critical information in growth modeling for biological fabrication and its effect on bacterial cellulose formation. By modeling the culture medium information, the growth of microorganisms can be directly and indirectly controlled, and by connecting the biological modeling environment to the physical environment, various formal components can be made in different scales, including the architectural scale. The proposed method in this research is used in a wide range of different sciences (Figure 1). It can create

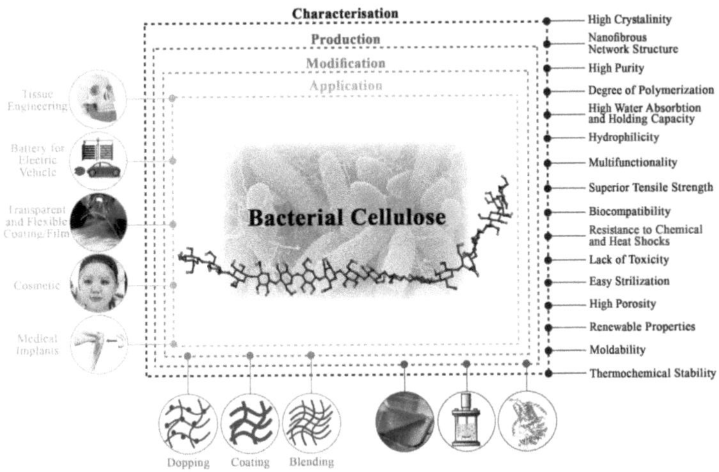

Figure 1
bacterial cellulose:Characterization to application process (adapted from Jang, W. D., et al. 2017)

an essential change in the manufacturing methods and integration of architecture, biology, and computational design, or the same infrastructure of biocomputing and bio-manufacturing in architecture.

FABRICATION INFORMATION MODELLING (FIM)

Recent research in digital fabrication has created the opportunity to integrate tools in the physical environment with various algorithms and solutions in the digital environment. This integration has led to personalization on various scales and mass production of desired products and personalization on a large scale. In general, to design and build based on materials, tools are needed to calculate the geometry and form components based on them. A method that can shape materials at different scales according to the desired geometry and shape, and also it can analyze and predict the properties of the structures composed of them based on the properties of the material particles (Duro Royo et al.2014; Duro Royo 2015). Nevertheless, the challenge faced with is the gap between virtual and physical platforms which restricts integrated feedback across media, and limits invention and imagination of new designs and production processes. (Duro Royo et al.2014; Duro Royo 2015). Researchers in architectural design and advanced manufacturing are working towards the integration of material and fabrication constraints in the design process (Oosterhuis 2004; Oosterhuis et al.2004; Chiu and Yu, 2008). To design and fabricate based on biological materials, there is a need for guided growth of microorganisms with control by modeling information affecting growth, that can build a form based on physical environment information, feedback, and materials towards the architect's ultimate goal. In order to incorporate material constraints, academic institutions and industry are rapidly developing complex multi-material manufacturing hardware, which can present software designers technical challenges in taking full advantage of novel hardware capabilities (Chiu and Yu, 2008; Shapiro et al.2004; Shapiro et al.2011; Duro Royo 2015). These challenges are because of that, although conventional computer-aided design (CAD) tools can enable and support the manipulation of geometric and topologic virtual constructs; but they generally lack the means to embed material data within virtual model constructs mostly since material homogeneity is typically assumed (Biswas et al.2004; Duro Royo et al.2015; Chiu and Yu, 2008; Duro Royo 2015).Current design practice is mostly characterized by the domination of shape over matter, consequently prioritizing virtual shape-defining parameters over physical material and fabrication constraints, leading to a geometric-centric design phase (Oxman 2011; Menges 2007; Mogas 2015). Nevertheless, some recent developments in direct digital manufacturing enable a shift towards a material-centric design practice, such as water-based fabrication techniques (Oxman 2011). Additive manufacture (AM) technologies for rapid prototyping employ virtual computer-aided designed models and translate them into thin horizontal successive cross-sections to define three-dimensional physical objects (Mogas 2015). Most traditional design methods cannot take advantage of the unique capabilities of AM, because they are established on the manufacturability of traditional manufacturing methods. AM technologies have become an efficient and common means to deliver geometrically precise functional prototypes in relatively short periods of time (Oxman et al.2012). At the same time, there is a need to expand manufacturing processes towards Bio-Manufacturing based approaches, borrowing techniques from biological science and tissue engineering. (Derme et al. 2016; Heidari et al.2021)

MATERIALS AND METHODS

Research Structure

The microorganism growth procedure could be described as contribution of the two-independent proceeding "Morphological process" and "Function's adaptability". In order to achieve digital fabrication of these living organisms, it is very important to know the patterns of growth and the internal forces that impact the growth trajectory. Based on the above literature review studies we know that by the environmental conditions change, the behavior of the microorganism will change and eventually lead to a change in the direction of growth and deformation of the final patterns (or change of form in the final products behavior). Thus, in the first step we focused our efforts to explore the behavior of the microorganism in different culture medium and record the feedback in various schedules according to the environmental parameters. The feedbacks of this experiments then be monitored and be used as numerical data which leads us to simulation modeling process in CAD environment (Figure 2). All data were monitored for eight days from 4 containers with different initial PH. Ultrasonic sensors every two days detect growth based on the formation and movement of particles on the surface of culture media, and pH changes are also

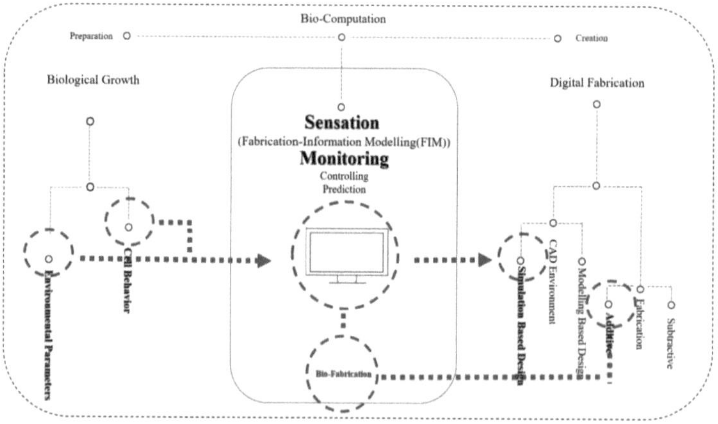

Figure 2
Research Structure

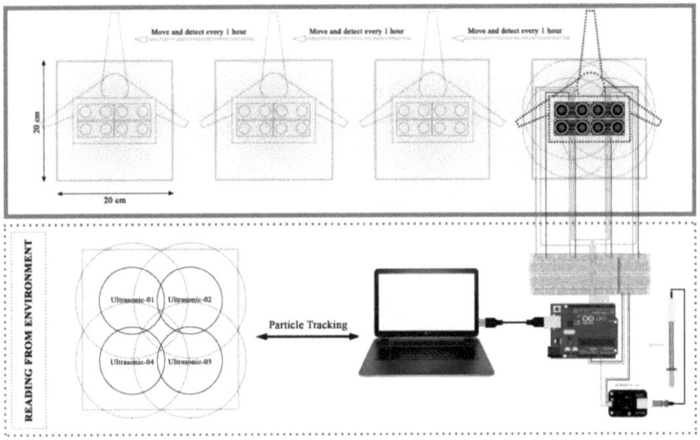

Figure 3
Experiment simulation

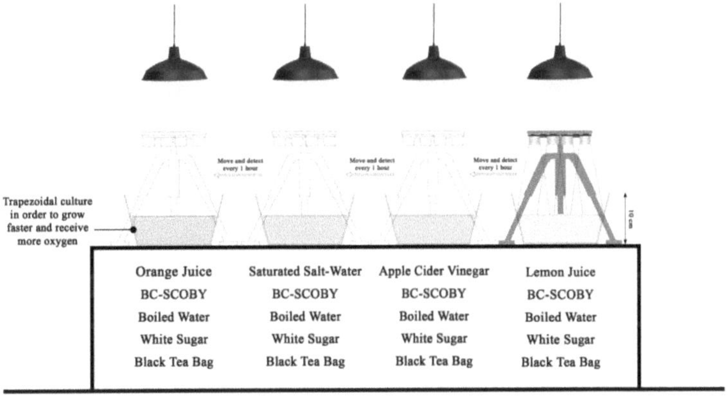

Figure 4
Experiment simulation

recorded. Due to the need to cover the entire surface of the culture medium, these sensors are used in quadrants and are placed on different culture media at certain intervals by a moving base, simultaneously with the recording of pH changes in the environment. Digitally, changes in particle-based cellulose formation have also been recorded.

Computational Part

This Project Focused on Syncing Culture Medium (Cellulose growth environment) To Virtual Stimulating Environment to Create the Computational natural architectural Component. This approach is made up of two main parts: Culture Medium, and Modules. Effective Values Are Sensing by Different modules, such as Ultra Sonic meter, Psychomotor, Thermometer, Infrared that are placed in the cultural medium (Figures 3,4). The feedbacks of environmental sens-

Culture	 Container - 1	 Container - 2	 Container - 3	 Container - 4
Nutrients	Apple Cider Vinegar 200 ml (Fermented apple cider vinegar) BC-SCOBY 1 cup Boiled Water 450 ml White Sugar 5 spoon 2 Black Tea Bag	Orange Juice 200 ml (Natural orange juice concentrate, Sugar and Purified water) BC-SCOBY 1 cup Boiled Water 450 ml White Sugar 5 spoon 2 Black Tea Bag	Lemon Juice 200 ml (Lime juice, Sodium Metabisulfite and Antioxidant 250PPM) BC-SCOBY 1 cup Boiled Water 450 ml White Sugar 5 spoon 2 Black Tea Bag	Saturated Salt-Water 200 ml (Fresh water 200ml, NaCl 72 g) BC-SCOBY 1 cup Boiled Water 450 ml White Sugar 5 spoon 2 Black Tea Bag

	Time	Protein	Humidity	pH	Temperature	Light
Container - 1	0	4.23	24%	4/5	26 °C	200 lux
Container - 2	0	4.23	24%	4/1	26 °C	200 lux
Container - 3	0	4.23	24%	2/4	26 °C	200 lux
Container - 4	0	4.23	24%	8	26 °C	200 lux

Table 1
Nutrients and primitive environmental conditions

ing are Numerically delivered to our Created Local Database. Subsequently, the created algorithm performs data analysis and classification and compares the on-going growth conditions with the desired goal features automatically. As a result of that, the ultrasonic modules monitor our growth scaffold during the growth procedure and collect the growth procedure data for pattern recognition. The classification process aids us in growth pattern recognition that can be used for generative design process. This data managing and data mining process provide an opportunity for us to develop the Bio-Manufacturing in the future. When we have the dataset of the parameters and their effects on bio-material behavior we can analyze them to predict its future characteristics before the physical implementation that results in time waste and also it will open new doors for us to consider the aspect we didn't thought before that.

Biological Part

In This Project to build this culture medium, we used a microbiological ecosystem called Kampuchea scope and contains yeast protozoa and bacterial colonies of xylinus, this ecosystem creates the fermentation process of the culture medium to growth and cellulose Production. In order to implement the proposed method, we have proposed four containers with different materials as cultivation. The main difference between the dishes is based on the culture medium's acidic substance, which in most laboratory cases uses apple cider vinegar. In this study, in addition to this substance, other dishes are composed of Portuguese juice, lemon juice, and saltwater, respectively (Table 1). Because during the growth period, pH changes occur based on chemical interactions in the culture medium and change its amount, this parameter has been measured again at certain defined intervals by a digital pH meter to influence the changes. It should also be examined in the formation of the cellulosic shell of the container.

DATA ANALYSIS

Ultrasonic sensors in the upper part of the medium, with a 15-degree operating radius, scan the environment in real-time (Figures 5-7). Each sensor has a power frequency of 40 kHz and a precision of 2 mm, which covers 1/5 range of the culture surface. Each sensor triggers 20 times per second. Ultrasonic sensors are designed only to detect the first echo. Thus, other echoes may affect when the sensor is triggered again. Therefore, we designed an algorithm that reflects the receiver system. It was able to achieve 5 more pulses in each trig. As a result, every 5 milliseconds we get the numerical value of 5 echoes in the form of an array. We divide the level of the receiving waveforms into four parts. Each segment receives its own unique five-point signal. These batch numerical signals are called by Gh-python remote in the Rhinoceros environment. We have used the "py-serial" library to read port serials. Figure 8 represents the ultrasonic sensors scanning zones and figure represents the real-time simulating process with the advantage of the created point cloud in a parametric CAD environment. The PH meter in each container measures the growth environment PH in real-time and send it to the computer numerically with an Arduino-Uno board kit that is connected with. Temperature and the culture other nutrients are also measuring in a defined period of time in parallel when the point cloud measuring trigger is initiated.

With the help of instant outputs of the built-in device, we can store the parameters that influencing the growth rate and its orientation. We store this received data in datasets Due to vast correlated parameters of nutrient and medium environmental conditions that affect the growth rate. We store each experiment in our dataset. this prepared dataset then will be mine to predict the topmost features with accurate predictive models that affect BC growth. In this way, 80% percent of our data will be trained and testing will be done on the rest 20% data. The mining model will be in three-step: Creating a decision tree, Nave base classification, Linear regression. We work on the output of the mining data and the intelligence growth controller for our future works.

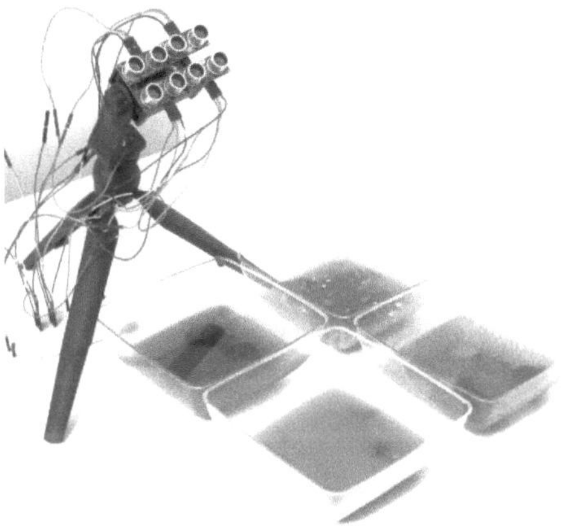

Figure 5
Particle tracking mechanism

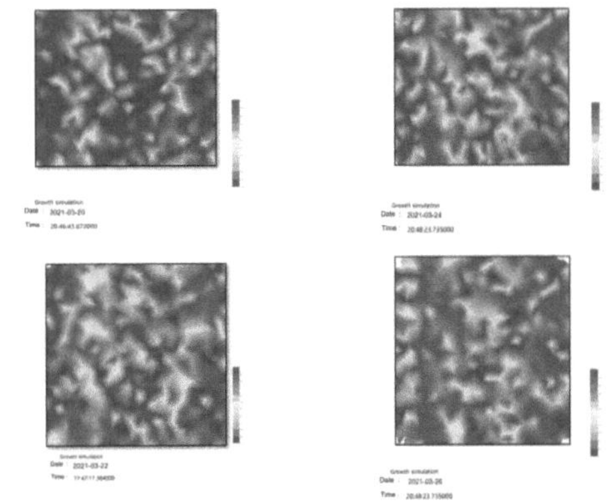

Figure 6
Particle tracking during 8 days

Figure 7
Cellulose formation after 13 days

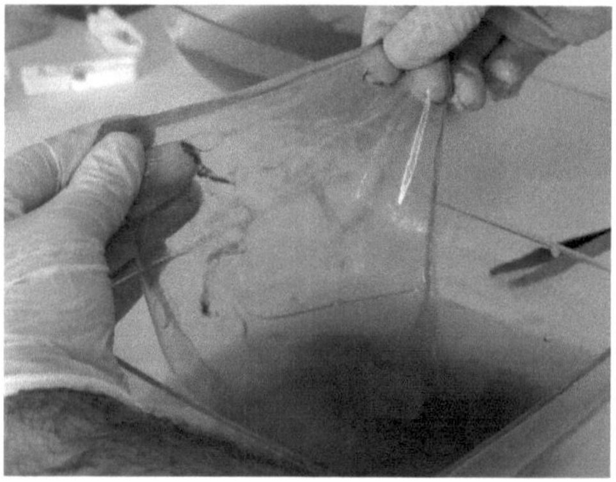

Figure 8
Cellulose result in container 1

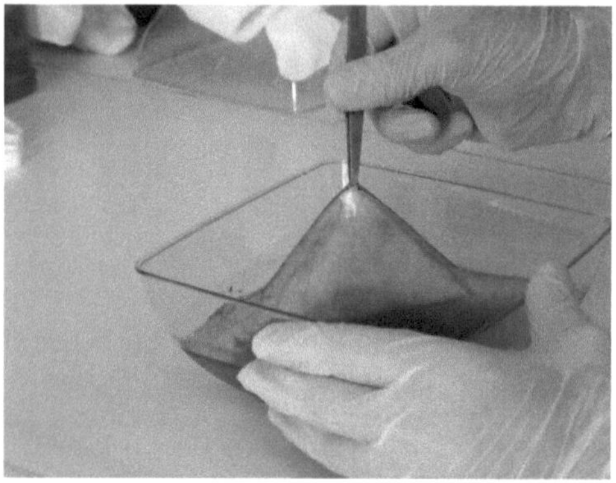

Figure 9
Cellulose result in container 2

CONCLUSION

According to this procedure the bio-monitoring method via ultrasonics can do pattern recognition in cellulose formation process and translate it to leads us to significant outputs process like 1.bio- manufacturing in the 2. material behavior prediction and 3. creation an artificial bio-component via cybernetic design process. This project will be an origin of next generation of bio-computation in design process by bridging the virtual and physical environment to provide real-time data. By controlling the cell growth status, the bio-monitoring tools sends its movements patterns as numerical data to the CAD environment. The recorded data despite being used for real-time growth simulation is stored in a provided database as a value of an experiment number key table. This database mining and data analysis lead us to cell growth pattern recognition. As a result of that, we can simulate the behaviors of the cells under different situations with a trained system thus by the change of the environment parameters in a virtual scene we can predict the output material behaviors. This research outputs will open new doors to us in synthetic biological matter creation that able us to simulate the functionality of the material before the creation and tune it in a way to reach the maximum adaptability after physical formation.

In the future development, we will try to use these results and simulations in the context of the additive manufacturing process by the use of artificial and virtual environment connections and controlling the 3D printer systems during the printing. It would provide an opportunity to predict the needed material characteristics, by the real-time physical environment simulation, and sends the best components requirements amounts to reach the goal material adaptability during the printing process. It also can be implemented in a discrete assembly modeling as a controller. Each step of an assembly process could be simulated to find the best relation topologies for each iteration of the assembly process. This implementation requires the middle processing procedure to translate the growth and continues material attributes to the discrete building blocks and define how the assembly of them can react like it. This effort will shift the digital manufacturing process in different scales and could be an approach for the large-scale assembly production because the iteration and the most of the energy consumption part of the assembly will be done in a simulated environment and the final fitted position will be sent to the building blocks to bind.

REFERENCES

Benyus, J.M 1997, *Biomimicry: Innovation Inspired by Nature*, Harper Perennial, New York

Biswas, A, Shapiro, V and Tsukanov, I 2004, 'Heterogeneous material modeling with distance fields', *Computer Aided Geometric Design*, 21(3), pp. 215-242

Chiu, W.K and Yu, K.M 2008, 'Direct digital manufacturing of three-dimensional functionally graded material objects', *Computer-Aided Design*, 40(12), pp. 1080-1093

Derme, T, Mitterberger, D and Di Tanna, U 2016 'Growth Based Fabrication Techniques for Bacterial Cellulose: Three-Dimensional Grown Membranes and Scaffolding Design for Biological Polymers', *ACADIA 2016*, pp. 488-495

Duro-Royo, J, Mogas-Soldevila, L, Kayser, M and Oxman, N 2015 'Modelling Behaviour for Additive & Distributed Digital Construction', *Proceedings of the DMSC Design Modelling Symposium*, Copenhagen

Duro-Royo, J, Zolotovsky, K, Mogas-Soldevila, L, Varshney, S, Oxman, N, Boyce, M and Ortiz, C 2015, 'MetaMesh: A hierarchical computational model for design and fabrication of biomimetic armored surfaces', *Computer-Aided Design*, 60, pp. 14-27

Falcão, S.C, Coelho, A.R and Evêncio Neto, J 2008, 'Biomechanical evaluation of microbial cellulose (Zoogloea sp.) and expanded polytetrafluoroethylene membranes as implants in repair of produced abdominal wall defects in rats', *Acta Cirurgica Brasileira*, 23(2), pp. 184-191

Heidari, F and Mahdavinejad, M 2017 'High-performance Sonitopia (Sonic Utopia): Hyper intelligent Material-based Architectural Systems for Acoustic Energy Harvesting', *IOP Conference Series: Earth and Environmental Science*, Rome, Italy, p. 012021

Heidari, F, Saleh Tabari, M.H, Mahdavinejad, M.J, Werner, L.C and Roohabadi, M 2021 'Bio-Energy Management from Micro-Algae Bio-Computational Based Reactor', *CAADRIA 2021*, Hong Kong, pp. 401-410

Henriksson, M and Berglund, L 2007, 'Structure and Properties of Cellulose Nanocomposite Films Containing Melamine Formaldehyde', *Applied Polymer Science*, 106(4), pp. 2817-2824

Iwamoto, S, Nakagaito, A.N and Yano, H 2007, 'Nanofibrillation of pulp fibers for the processing of transparent nanocomposites', *Applied Physics A*, 89, p. 461–466

Jang, W.D, Hwang, J.H, Kim, H.U, Ryu, J.Y and Lee, S.Y 2017, 'Bacterial cellulose as an example product for sustainable production and consumption', *Microbial Biotechnology*, 10(5), p. 1181–1185

Jung, J, Khan, T, Park, J and Chang, H 2007, 'Production of bacterial cellulose by Gluconacetobacter hansenii using a novel bioreactor equipped with a spin filter', *Korean Journal of Chemical Engineering*, 24, pp. 265-271

Klemm, D, Schumann, D, Kramer, F, Heßler, N, Hornung, M, Schmauder, H.P and Marsch, S 2006, 'Nanocelluloses as Innovative Polymers in Research and Application', in Klemm, D (eds) 2006, *Polysaccharides II*, Springer, Berlin, Heidelberg, pp. 49-96

Klemm, D, Schumann, D, Udhardt, U and Marsch, S 2001, 'Bacterial synthesized cellulose — artificial blood vessels for microsurgery', *Progress in Polymer Science*, 26(9), pp. 1561-1603

Menges, A 2007 'Computational Morphogenesis: Integral Form Generation and Materialization Processes', *ASCAAD 2007*, Alexandria, Egypt, pp. 725-744

Mogas-Soldevila, L 2015, *Water-based digital design and fabrication : material, product, and architectural explorations in printing chitosan and its composites*, Master's Thesis, MIT

Moniri, M, Boroumand Moghaddam, A, Azizi, S, Abdul Rahim, R, Bin Ariff, A, Zuhainis Saad, W, Navaderi, M and Mohamad, R 2017, 'Production and Status of Bacterial Cellulose in Biomedical Engineering', *Nanomaterials*, 7(9), p. 257

Oosterhuis, K, Bier, H.H, Aalbers, C and Boer, S 2004 'File to Factory and Real Time Behavior in ONL-Architecture', *Proceedings of the 23rd Annual Conference of the Association for Computer Aided Design in Architecture and the 2004 Conference of the AIA Technology in Architectural Practice Knowledge Community*, Cambridge, pp. 294-305

Oxman, N 2011, 'Variable property rapid prototyping', *Virtual and Physical Prototyping*, 6(1), pp. 3-31

Oxman, N, Tsai, E and Firstenberg, M 2012, 'Digital anisotropy: A variable elasticity rapid prototyping platform', *Virtual and Physical Prototyping*, 7(4), pp. 261-274

Rehm, B.H.A (eds) 2009, *Microbial Production of Biopolymers and Polymer Precursors: Applications and Perspectives*, Caister Academic Press, UK

Duro Royo, J 2015, *Towards Fabrication Information Modeling (FIM) : workflow and methods for multi-scale trans-disciplinary informed design*, Master's Thesis,

MIT
Duro Royo, J, Mogas-Soldevila, L and Oxman, N 2014, 'Methods and Apparatus for Integrated Large Scale Robotic Fabrication of Functionally Graded Materials and Structures', *US provisional patent pending (M.I.T. Case No. 17388T)*
Sachs, E, Cima, M, Cornie, J, Brancazio, D, Bredt, J, Curodeau, A, Fan, T, Khanuja, S, Lauder, A, Lee, J and Michaels, S 1993, 'Three-Dimensional Printing: The Physics and Implications of Additive Manufacturing', *CIRP Annals*, 42(1), pp. 257-260
Shapiro, V, Tsukanov, I and Grishin, A 2011, 'Geometric Issues in Computer Aided Design/Computer Aided Engineering Integration', *Computing and Information Science in Engineering*, 11(2), p. 021005 (13 pages)
Vincent, J 2012, *Structural Biomaterials*, Princeton University Press , Princeton, New Jersey
[1] https://patents.google.com/patent/US20050060130

The Design and 4d Printing of Epithelial Cell-Inspired Programmable Surface Geometry

Teng Teng[1], Jenny Sabin[2]
[1,2]Cornell University
[1,2]{tt537|jes557}@cornell.edu

As a design research project, this paper aims to provide a novel surface geometry design and fabrication strategy. As the foundation, this paper discusses and investigates the deformation mechanism and geometric features of cellular epithelial tissues, especially the generation of the newly discovered scutoid shape. Subsequently, we utilize the mechanism to design and fabricate programmable physical surface geometry that can change shape autonomously based on external stimulation. We summarize the work we have conducted thus far into two aspects: First, inspired by the deformation mechanism of epithelial cells we propose a new design strategy for generating complex surface geometry from transformable individual units; Second, we also develop a new 4d printing method, which allows the surface geometry to be programmed on demand and to emulate the generative and bio-inspired design model analogically.

Keywords: *programmable material, 4d printing, bio-inspired design, epithelial cell, scutoid, surface design*

INTRODUCTION

Surface modeling and design in the digital environment has become a significant part of computational design and fabrication planning. Designers can efficiently obtain access to digital surface design toolkits, now readily available through online forums such as "Food4Rhino". Nevertheless, designers and makers still have fewer available methods for fabricating complex surface geometry. The repetitive operation of designing complex surface geometry is inevitable as designers often face more parameters and notation systems to optimize and organize the freeform surface morphology than conventional cubic architectural geometry. Additionally, we propose a bottom-up strategy for coordinating complex surface design that starts with local component-based rules and transformations to inflect a global change in surface curvature . This is in contrast to more traditional optimization methods that frequently privilege a top-down methodology where global surface change is organized into a family of non-standard discrete components post-facto.

The success of the surface design development process heavily depends on the design medium that the designers use. While the digital model helps to visualize the design intent, comparatively, it is reported (Sun. et al, 2014) that the physical model provides designers higher accuracy and acceptance in terms of spatial understanding and usability . Given the higher uncertainty and complex geometric property of freeform surface design, it is necessary to develop a new physical design media and shape-changing interface. This new interface can change surface geometry morphology based on the designer's intent and manual, analog input to facilitate a designer's spatial understanding. Various projects have explored and employed the ability of shape-changing interfaces in the domain of design. However, the biggest challenges of shape-changing design media lie in two aspects: First, most of the precedent works rely on electronic parts to power and control the shape, which limits a designer's degree of interaction while conducting real-time design activities and updates; Second, the possibility of an interactive design process is subject to the limited movement of a shape-changing interface since most such assemblies are implemented through the actuators' linear or rotary motion. Coelho. et al, 2011) In this case, the new shape-changing interface for surface geometry design proposed in this paper needs to satisfy two features: A, The changing shape should not be driven by any electrical actuator; B, the physical interface needs to be easily deformed and programmed to any degree of freedom.

In this paper, combining the two above expectations, we explore two methods as a new design foundation .

Our work focuses on the surface geometry bending mechanism. Specifically, we are inspired by the epithelial tissue's bending mechanism. Epithelial tissue that is constituted with tightly packed epithelial cells envelopes into complex cavities to cover the majority of the surface area of living being's bodies, including skin, organs, and blood vessels. Such features allow epithelial cells to deform and proliferate locally and adapt to different environmental conditions globally. This intriguing feature motivates us, as design researchers, to develop a novel design strategy that generates complex surface structures in both digital and physical surface geometry through the combination of individual units. Scientists (Gómez-Gálvez, et al, 2018) recently discovered that epithelial tissue's deformation capability is contributed to the emergence of scutoid geometry at the micro-scale. And scutoid is an ideal 3d package solution for a highly curved environment.(Mughal, A., et al. 2018) Scutoid, as three-dimensional geometry, bridges two parallel surfaces and is often described as a combination of the frustum and a prismatoid as it has a different number of edge segments on its basal surface and apical surface. One of this paper's targets is implementing the deformation process of epithelial tissue at a material scale and developing physical prototypes to implement the deformation. Then to eventually take the prototype as a design media to facilitate design activities.

By integrating the bio-inspired surface geometry bending mechanism, we aim to use smart material to fabricate the physical surface geometry that can change its shape autonomously based on external stimulation without any electric input element. Such work is implemented through 3 dimensionally printing with shape memory polymer. The long-term development of 3d printing technology has dramatically reduced the application threshold for designers. In recent years, many design practitioners and researchers utilize smart materials' characteristics such as shape memory further to expand the concept of 3D printing into 4D printing (Behl, M, and Lendlein, A, 2007,) . Our work in this paper focuses on taking advantage of the material behavior to execute the surface geometry bending process and how we can adequately fabricate such surface geometry.

RELATED WORK

There are related exploratory works that have been done in both trajectories recently

There is a lot of percent work in different fields that have been done and sets a solid foundation for our investigation. To be specific, in terms of using cell morphology for geometric modeling, Subramanian, et al. (2019) proposed a 3d space tiling method inspired featuring scutoid's geometric feature on its apical and basal surface. From the perspective of bio-inspired surface design, by investigating the biological principles in a micro-scale, Sabin and Jones (2008) investigated code-driven parametric design method, models, and tools to gain new insights into how nature deals with dynamics, environment, and feedback within cell and tissue structures, and in turn utilize those into architectural scale. Although the scutoid was discovered and termed in 2018, a few precedents work that links scutoid/epithelial cell with design and fabrication can still be found. (Tsikoliya, et al.2021) discussed architectural structure molding method that is based on differential growth of epithelial tissue. Inspired by epithelial tissue's deformation and the emergence of scutoid geometry, the authors proposed a continuity folds modeling approach and fabrication planning with concrete for architectural scale experiments. However, the deformability of epithelial cells can only be fully demonstrated over time. Instead, the work they proposed results in a set of static architectural elements, which we consider do not make full use of epithelial cells' deformability. Some other works paid attention to the cellular structure of epithelial cells. Due to scutoid's structural stability, Dhari, et al.(2021) proposes a 3D-printed Scutoids-inspired cellular structure for use in lightweight sandwich structure designs that copes compression loads. The structure was made of aluminum alloy and is reportedly to be able to absorb more energy than a regular compressive structure. The work scientifically demonstrates that, from a structural point of view, the bent epithelial tissue and scutoid shape are highly rational. Yet, the work leaves a blank space on scutoid fabrication with soft material. Teng, Jia and Sabin (2020) claimed a novel masonry shell system embedded with the geometric features of scutoid. Inspired by scutoids having different adjacent cells on different faces, all bricks in the mentioned masonry shell interlocked each other without external joints needed. The work took one step out in terms of using scutoid geometric features as a standing point of surface design.

As we are targeting to implement the deformation process at the material scale, we examined material and methods that can be potentially used to fabricate Epithelial cell-inspired Surface Geometry. Specifically, we evaluated precedent works of three-dimensional printing objects with active material and 4d printing process. In a lot of Tibbits 's work (2012,2014) , the material is pre-programmed and equipped with actuating abilities and reacting ability. It allows the material to self-deform over time when exposed to external stimulation and morphs into the desired 3d shape. Lee, A.Y., et al.(2017) comprehensively summarizes the fabrication method of reversibility of 3D-printed shape-memory materials such as depositing with additives or use multiple materials.

METHOD

Computer Simulation

We firstly investigate the deformation of epithelial cells thorough a scientific literature review. Referring to research in cell and molecular biology, (Gibson, et al. 2006. Lecuit , et al. 2007. Martin, et al. 2009. Kong, et al. (2017), we learned that the global deformation of the epithelial tissue is proceeded by the position rearrangement of individual epithelial cells in the tissue. We then computationally simulate the bending process within the tissues through a generative modeling methodology. The simulations demonstrate the emergence of scutoid geometrical shapes within the epithelial cells. We conclude that the cell rearrangement is achieved through cells revolving and contracting (Figure 1). These morphological transformations create a triangle face on the volume, transiting the extra edge on the apical surface to the basal surface through an extra vertex.

Our previous work (Teng, Jia and Sabin, 2020) has investigated that scutoid's extra edge segments on one of the surfaces merge into vertexes in the intermedia level to equalize the edge segment's number on another surface. We also discovered that epithelial tissue's curvature positively correlates to the length of the boundary between two adjacent epithelial cells as scutoid cells are generated through cells revolving and squeezing. Bending within the Epithelial tissue causes different motion tendencies on epithelial tissues' apical and basal surfaces (Figure 2). When the epithelial tissue is bent, the adjacent cell surfaces will squeeze each other where the curvature

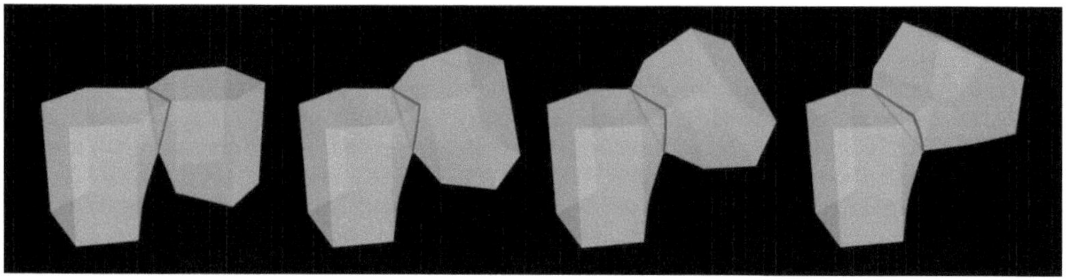

Figure 1
cell rearrangement is achieved through cells revolving and contracting

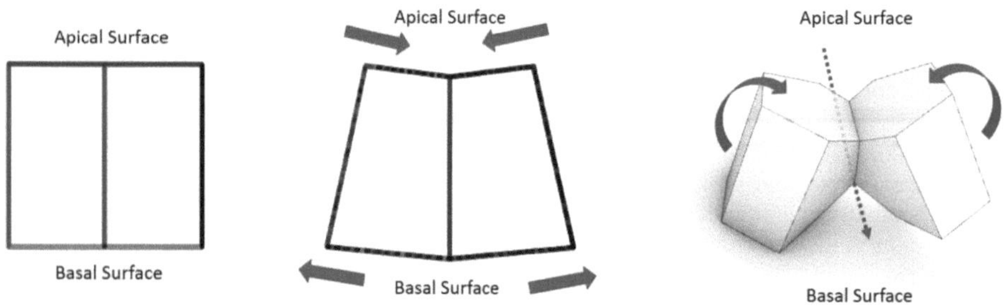

Figure 2
Two adjacent cells bent towards to apical surface. The apical and basal surface of each cell has a different motion tendency. left: a flat tissue constituted by two cells, middle: two cells tissue bent towards to apical surface from the side view. right: two cells tissue bent towards to apical surface in 3D.

is positive and separate where the curvature is negative. The geometric centers of adjacent cells' profiles move towards each other where the curvature is positive. The closer the two cells' geometric centers are, the greater the squeezing between the two cells is, resulting in a longer boundary line. In summary, the greater the curvature of the epithelial tissue, the longer the boundary between two adjacent cells at the curved position. Cells in highly curved global epithelial tissue deform along the apical-basal axis. The deformation process results in cells having different neighbors in their basal and apical surfaces.

Physical Prototype

Based on the above findings and geometric relationships, when designing a physical surface geometry with scutoid components embedded, we look into the dialectical relationhips between global surface geometry and local units. We hypothesized that if we can change the length of the boundaries between any pair of adjacent cells within a given model, we can then change the curvature of global surface geometry. Moreover, when the length of the boundary between any pair of adjacent cells is programmed, the global surface's overall morphology can be precisely controlled. The hypothesis is verified in a later context.

We identified two appropriate materials to be the most suitable deformable material through a series of material experiments: silicon and Shape Memory Polymer, as both materials are reversibly deformable and can translate the cells' behavior to a greater scale. In addition to the findings on the epithelial cells' geometric features that we discuss, the physical prototype and material studies should also follow the cell's geometric constraints. Study (Rupprecht, Jean-Francois, et al. 2017) investigated that cells compete for space under geometric constraints. The cell's three-dimensional morphology and packing within epithelial tissues is significantly impacted by geometric constraints. According to the literature, the geometric constraints include expansion force from the cytoskeleton and adhesion between cell membranes.

Based on these constraints, we further developed a set of programmable surface geometry prototypes to illustrate the global surface geometry deformation at a material scale using 3d printable shape memory polymer filament and silicon. The heat transfer of liquid-crystalline domains causes the shape memory effect. After the 3d printer heats the polymer to the isotropy state, the nozzle starts depositing the filament layers into the specified 3d shape. Polymer is initially programmed at this moment. As the material remains at a high temperature (temperature A), the printed 3d shape stays in its initial state A and remains soft. When the printing is done, and the 3d shape cools down to room temperature, it becomes firm. Following reheating the shape to temperature B, the shape becomes soft again. The designer can deform the printed 3d shape into state B on demand. After cooling down and changing the environmental temperature between temperature A and temperature B, designers obtained one object with two deformable morphologies at two different times. The forming of silicon in this project is fabricated through casting after we 3d print the formwork with PLA.

Aside from the digital simulation mentioned earlier, two types of deformable surface geometry are then designed and built for serving two purposes: First, the physical prototype verifies if scutoid cells will actually emerge at the local unit when the global surface curvature changes. Second, dialectically, the prototype also verifies if the global surface will be bent when the local units deform into scutoid cells. Both types of prototypes share a common design: To analogically translate the expansive force from the cells' cytoskeleton, we developed a set of cell units to be inserted into a constrained frame, which simulates the adhesion between cell membranes. The configuration constitutes a surface geometry while maintaining a dense packing of cells.(Figure 3)

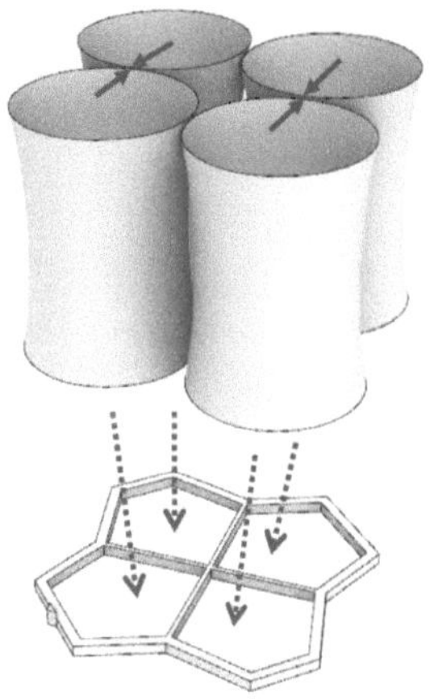

Figure 3
we developed a set of cell units to be inserted into a constrained frame

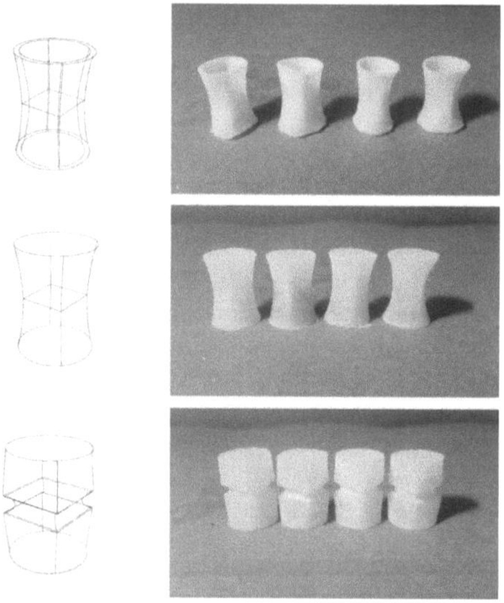

Figure 4
different type of
casted silicon unit

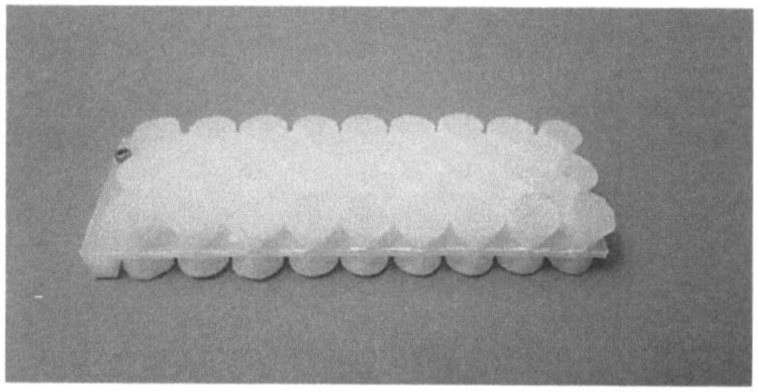

Figure 5
silicon unit inserted
into Shape Memory
Polymer constraint
frame.

The first prototype is generated by inserting cast silicon units into a 3d printed Shape Memory Polymer constraint frame. As active material, the Shape Memory Polymer, which represents the global surface geometry, is deformed according to environmental stimulation, the thermal environment, in this case. We designed and programmed the Shape Memory Polymer frame to stay flat as the initial state at temperature A and to bend towards the apical surface when the temperature reaches at B degree. The silicon units (Figure 5)representing the local units act as a passive deformation material and are tightly packed by the constraint frame. We then set the prototype in temperature A and have it stay flat and still(Figure 6). After gradually raising the temperature to B, the flat surface geometry starts bending towards its apical surface. Meanwhile, the local silicon units exhibited the expected behavior. As the global surface geometry prototype bends towards the apical surface, and all local silicon units revolve around the corresponding horizontal axis, adjacent local units squeeze each other through their boundaries. (Figure 6 and 7) The length of boundaries becomes longer when the globe curvature increases . Such local units' behavior generates the scutoid shapes. This process illustrates how the curvature change of the global surface geometry impacts local cell morphology.

In contrast, the constraint frame for the second surface geometry prototype is made by silicon representing the global surface, and all local cell units are 3d printed with SMP. We firstly 3d printed all SMP local units as regular frustums with its apical and basal surface flat at temperature A. We then programmed each SMP unit individually to deform into a scutoid shape at temperature B. Deforming units into scutoid cells means purposely changing the length of the common boundary between two adjacent units and the triangular face's size that transitions the polyline edge into a vertex to determine the expected curvature of the final global surface geometry at that unit's position. First, the SMP units are tightly packed into a global surface with the constraint frame and the surface prototype is placed in the thermal environment. Next, the SMP cell units actively deform from regular frustums into scutoid shapes with various sizes generated at the common boundary length or connection at the triangulated face. Thus, the prototype deformed from a flat surface geometry into a curved and programmed surface geometry. This prototype illustrates how local units impact global geometry deformation and morphology. (Figure 8)

To conclude with the above observations from the physical prototype experiment, in a surface geometry (epithelial tissue) constituted by smaller units (epithelial cells), the global surface and local unit's morphology influences each other. To activate such

Figure 6
Two cell's tissue bent towards to apical surface, the length of the common boundary between two cells becomes longer when overall curvature increases. Photo taken from side view.

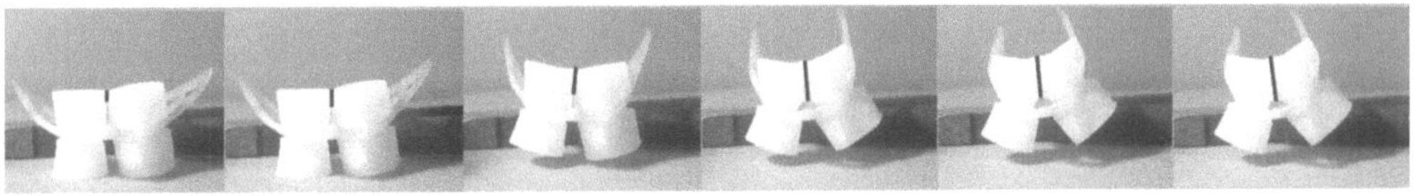

Figure 7
3d printed SMP active constraint frame inserted with silicon unit, when constraint frame bent towards to apical surface, all units deforms into scutoid. Photo taken from front view.

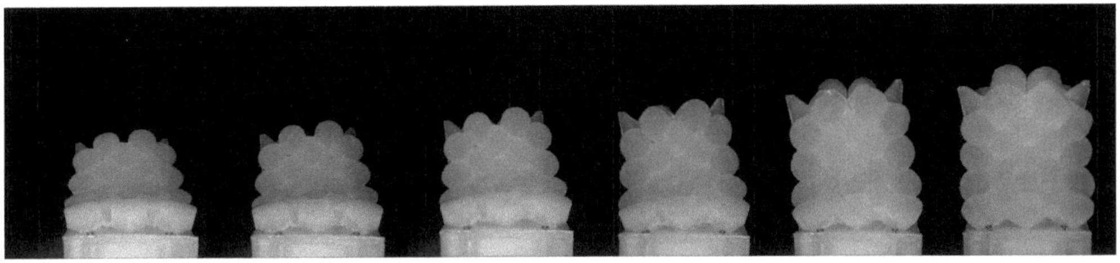

surface geometry, we either program the overall global surface curvature or program the individual units' morphology.

APPLICATION

The work we have completed thus far has illustrated how we combine the geometric features of epithelial cells with smart material additive manufacturing to achieve bioinspired programmable surface geometry. Importantly, this work leverages local transformations at the cell/component level to achieve global changes to surface curvature.

However, such programmable surface geometry is still not an ideal shape-changing interface for design applications. As a physical interface, interaction design and responsivitiy has not been emphasized in this latest set of experiments. As mentioned previously, the purpose of using a physical model in this design research is to demonstrate at the material level, a bottom-up strategy for bio-inspired complex surface design that leverages local component-based rules and transformations to inflect a global change in surface curvature . This construct also benefits the designer through an intuitive methodology that links responsive material interface with complex component-based surface design. We propose two ways that the bioinspired programmable surface geometry can interact with the designer: First, the designer interacts with the surface geometry by programming its target morphology. When a designer deliberates a complex surface design, it is easier for the designer to shape the desired morphology by manually stretching or bending the material assembly than by modifying it in a digital environment.

Second, we designed an embeddable flex sensor to attach to the physical surface geometry (Figure 9). When the designer shapes the surface on demand, the flex sensor, which consists of conductive ink, bends with the physical surface. The bending behavior forms a flexible potentiometer in which resistance changes upon deflection. (Figure 10) Higher curvature on the physical surface results in higher re-

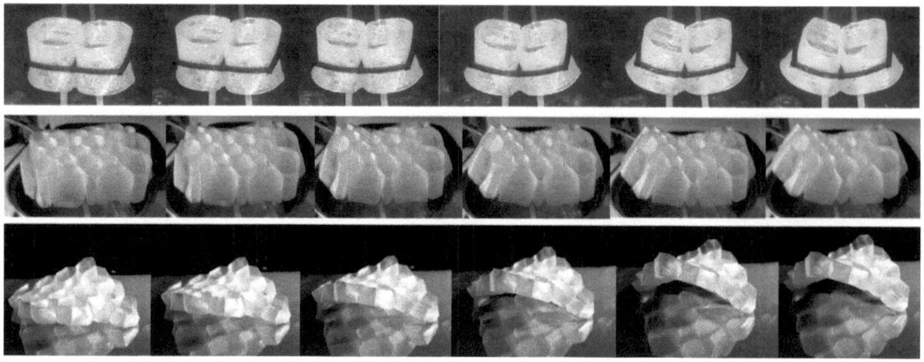

Figure 8
Upper: Two SMP cells tissue bent towards to apical surface. Two cells actively revolving and contracting towards each other results in constraint frame bent. Middle: SMP cells actively deform themselves into scutoids to bend globe surface geometry towards the apical surface. Lower: SMP cells actively deform themselves into scutoids to bend globe surface geometry towards the basal surface.

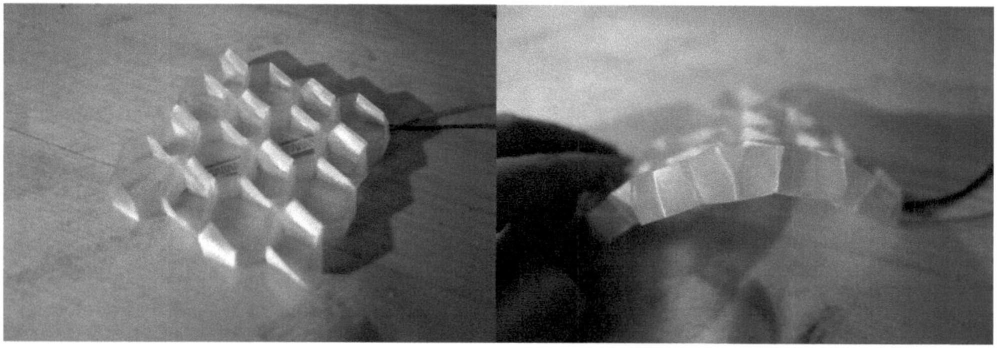

Figure 9
flex sensor attach to the back of physical surface geometry

Figure 10
The designer manually shapes the physical geometry, and the flex sensor captures the curvature data to digitize the surface.

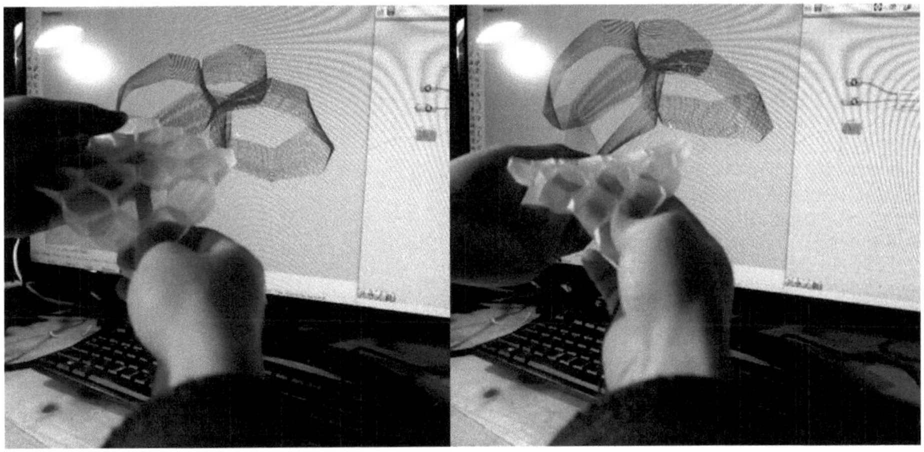

sistance on the flex sensor . A microcontroller (Arduino) connects with the flex sensor and converts the resistance to curvature data in real time , then transmits data to computer modeling software (Rhino and Grasshopper) to digitize the physical surface.

The above two ways create a feedback loop that allows the designer to incorporate his/her design intent directly with the physical surface geometry. Adjustments to the morphology are immediately input as updated data in the digital modeling environment.

CONCLUSION

We have proposed a materially-based bottom-up strategy for coordinating complex surface design that starts with local component-based rules and transformations to inflect a global change in surface curvature . We have summarized the work thus far into two aspects: 1.) Inspired by the deformation mechanism of epithelial cells, we propose a new design strategy for generating complex surface geometry from transformable individual units; 2.) We developed a new 4d printing method, which allows the surface geometry to be programmed on demand and to emulate the generative and bio-inspired design model analogically.

In this paper, we outline the methods developed to prototype a bio-inspired programmable surface geometry as a design interface concept. We have successfully satisfied the two initial requirements that we proposed: 1.) We eliminated the electrical actuator, a commonly used driver in actuating a programmable surface to inflect changes to surface geometry. This is achieved by incorporating responsive 3d printed shape memory polymer and through a design methodology that leverages the deformation mechanism and geometric features of cellular epithelial tissues. We also developed a bottom-up design methodology to work with surface geometry that can be deformed and programmed to any degree of freedom, at local and global levels, by embedding scutoid geometric features. Beyond proposing the programmable surface geometry as a design interface, the work we have completed provides a novel and interactive strategy for designing surface geometry.

REFERENCES

Behl, M, and Lendlein, A, 2007, 'Shape-memory polymers', *Materials today*, 10(4), pp. 20-28

Coelho, M, et al. 2011, 'Shape-changing interfaces', *Personal and Ubiquitous Computing*, 15(2), pp. 161-173

Dhari, R. S. and Patel, N. P. 2021, 'On the crushing behaviour of scutoid-based bioinspired cellular structures', *nternational Journal of Crashworthiness*, 2021, pp. 1-10

Gibson, M. C, et al. 2006, 'The emergence of geometric order in proliferating metazoan epithelia', *Nature*, 442(7106), pp. 1038-1041
Gómez-Gálvez, P, et al. 2018, 'Scutoids are a geometrical solution to three-dimensional packing of epithelia', *Nature communications*, 9(1), pp. 1-14
Kong, D, et al. 2017, 'Forces directing germ-band extension in Drosophila embryos', *Mechanisms of development*, 144, pp. 11-22
Lecuit, T, et al. 2007, 'Cell surface mechanics and the control of cell shape, tissue patterns and morphogenesis', *Nature reviews Molecular cell biology*, 8.8, pp. 633-644
Lee, A. Y., et al. 2017, 'Two-way 4D printing: a review on the reversibility of 3D-printed shape memory materials', *Engineering*, 3.5, pp. 663-674
Martin, A. C, et al. 2009, 'Pulsed contractions of an actin–myosin network drive apical constriction', *Nature*, 457.7228, pp. 495-499
Mughal, A, et al. 2018, 'Demonstration and interpretation of 'scutoid'cells formed in a quasi-2D soap froth', *Philosophical Magazine Letters*, 98.8, pp. 358-364
Rupprecht, J.F, et al. 2017, 'Geometric constraints alter cell arrangements within curved epithelial tissues', *Molecular biology of the cell*, 28(25), pp. 3582-3594
Sabin, J. E., and Jones, P.L. 2008 'Nonlinear systems biology and design: surface design', *ACADIA 2008*
Subramanian, S. G, et al. 2019, 'Delaunay Lofts: A biologically inspired approach for modeling space filling modular structures', *Computers & Graphics*, 82, pp. 73-83
Sun, L, et al. 2014, 'Differences in spatial understanding between physical and virtual models', *Frontiers of Architectural Research*, 3.1, pp. 28-35
Teng, T, Jia, M and Sabin, J. 2020 'Scutoid Brick - The Designing of Epithelial cell inspired-brick in Masonry shell System', *eCAADe 2020*, Berlin, Germany, pp. 563-572
Tibbits, S 2012, 'Design to Self⊠Assembly', *Architectural Design*, 82.2, pp. 68-73
Tibbits, S 2014, '4D printing: multi⊠material shape change', *Architectural Design*, 84.1, pp. 116-121
Tsikoliya, S, et al. 2021, 'Tectonics of Differential Growth. Folds in Additive Fabrication and Moulding for Architectural Design', *Formal Methods in Architecture*, Springer, Cham, pp. 29-35

An Integrated Structural Optimization Method for Bacterial Cellulose-Based Composite Biofilms

Gözde Damla Turhan[1], Guzden Varinlioglu[2], Murat Bengisu[3]
[1,2,3] Izmir University of Economics
[1,2,3] {gozde.turhan|guzden.varinlioglu|murat.bengisu}@iue.edu.tr

Today's technologies offer exciting new horizons to reconfigure the realm of digital design and fabrication with the use of biologically active materials. Some of the recent works have been exploring the potentials of utilizing biological systems either as mathematical models for digital design or as the material itself in digital fabrication. As one of the novel processes of recent design thinking approaches, this paper presents an example for the collaboration with living organisms and a multidisciplinary process in which the overall structure is based on the analysis of biological material properties, mechanical data acquisition and the integration to digital optimization. In this regard, bacterial cellulose-based composite biofilms were grown and tested for their tensile properties, followed by a proposal to integrate mechanical data to digital optimization for catenary forms to better engage with real world applications. The findings have shown that the use of catenary geometry for such biologically active materials that are relatively novel to the structural use has proven effective for different prototypes thanks to their natural and customized material properties such as the ability to self-stand and biodegrade.

Keywords: *Material-based design, Structural optimization, Bacterial cellulose, Catenary geometry*

INTRODUCTION

From the late 19th century on, people have become aware of global warming and its effects. The scientists, researchers and scholars, have put forward the scope of human influence on Earth, entitling it as "Anthropocene" (Zalasiewicz et al. 2011). Marsh's work "Man and nature: or, physical geography as modified by human action" (1864) is possibly the earliest research that discusses anthropogenic global change. In addition, the term was elaborated deeply in the 19th century by Arrhenius (1896), focusing on carbon dioxide emissions and global warming. In the following years, Crutzen revived the concept of Anthropocene in 2002 by defining the current era as the era that is dominated by humans' negative environmental impact regarding the irresponsible use of natural resources.

There are currently many studies and responses which advocate that the solution is the "growth" regarding the ever growing environmental problems of Anthropocene, as one of the concepts of genetics applied to architecture and design (Estevez and

Navarro 2016). There is a wide range of environmentally friendly materials for digital fabrication technologies today, however, as a significant extension to the conventional material list, "biologically active materials" are currently under discussion as one of the potential solutions.

In this regard, bacterial cellulose-based composite biofilms were explored as load-bearing materials for design prototypes. The bacteria cultures were grown and sterilized; composites were formed and mechanically tested for their tensile strength. The results were discussed within the framework of digital optimization of catenary geometries. Various methods and tools from different disciplines were brought together in order to explore the potentials of bacterial cellulose-based composite biofilms as structural materials. The methodology involved the growth of Acetobacter Xylinus (A. xylinus) to form the cellulosic biofilms; the use of jut fabric as reinforcement for the composites; Texture Analyzer (TA-XTplus, Stable Micro System, UK) for tensile tests; and Kangaroo Physics/Grasshopper for digital optimization.

THEORETICAL BACKGROUND

Nature has a survival strategy that sustains life with minimum resources and maximum performance (Oxman 2012). From a biomechanical perspective, maximum diversity is achieved with minimum inventory as one of the results of nature's mechanisms such as growth, evolution, mutation or natural selection (Pearce 1981). Therefore, each biological organism reconfigures itself according to different environmental conditions, as nature relentlessly evolves (Koch, Bhushan and Barthlott, 2009). Developments in biology and material sciences started to be considered as fundamental sources for advanced material design (Thom 1975; Ruse and Hull 1989; Bar-Cohen 2006). In this regard, a new materiality approach has attracted growing interest from designers to develop organic, degradable and renewable materials through biologically inspired processes.

As seen in nature, there are also great examples of what is possible with a particular material in man-made structures such as the Parthenon, the Eiffel Tower or the Golden Gate Bridge. These structures are built by necessarily taking material properties into consideration (Ashby and Johnson 2014). Another earlier example is Frei Otto's experimental setup in his work "Tensile structures: Cables, nets and membranes" (Otto and Glaeser 1972) where minimal surfaces with minimal nets were calculated through mathematical equations within a physical form finding method.

In the past 20 years, as happened in the transition to the Industrial era, how we design and manufacture have changed, besides what we design and manufacture. Form finding processes and material behavior studies have become one of the hot topics again in design studies, which originally date back to the 16th century: Antoni Gaudi's chapel for Colonia Guell and arches for the Casa Mila exemplify the principles of form-finding processes for hanging catenary structures (Huerta 2006). After the 1950s, catenary structures were studied further through physical models in terms of thicknesses and placement of reinforcements although mathematical analysis was missing (Naboni 2016). Unlike the rope with two support points, these hanging structures have complex networks in which they end up with multiple formations. The reason is that the ways of load distribution might differ for each case (Ochsendorf and Block 2014).

Optimization, which has been qualified as an important tool in the form-finding processes over the past decades, is the process of finding the fittest values for the given variables of a particular problem in order to minimise or maximise an objective function (Saremi, Mirjalili and Lewis 2017). Among the common optimization approaches, nature-inspired algorithms are the most prevailing in which the techniques mimic natural problem-solving methods, those used by organisms in nature. Since survival is the main goal for all living organisms, their way of evolving and adapting become algorithmic models for many design optimization tools such as Grasshopper's built-in plug-in Galapagos.

Figure 1
Production of pure bacterial cellulose and bacterial cellulose-jut composite

By prioritizing the material itself and its behavior, and by constructing the foundations onto the new materiality approach, this research dives into the experimental process of digital design and digital fabrication with biologically active materials. Bacterial cellulose, a microbial polysaccharide, have found to be a proper source of knowledge for design applications due to its unique material properties such as its structural integrity, hydrophilic nature and biodegradability (Fernandez 2006). Although the use of bacterial cellulose for design and fabrication is still in its infancy, yet has a potential to be further explored, as seen in previous experiments (Turhan, Varinlioglu and Bengisu 2020).

There are several more motivations to use A. xylinus as a biologically active material. For instance, it is known that it can stay active and can be attached into a 3D network that cellulose fibers create (Derme, Mitterberger and Di Tanna 2016). Since this bacteria is a single cell organism that adapts itself to the changes in the environment such as temperature, humidity or sugar levels, it can be further engineered in order to allocate various functions as desired. Due to its high water content, it can sustain the system for long durations (Backdahl et al. 2006). Another reason for using this bacteria is that it can be rapidly grown into desired form through guidance. This has been very critical to fashion and product designers since they are very much attracted to it due its rapid growth. Moreover, cellulose, in general, as an environmentally friendly material, has a high demand to replace petroleum-based products (Huang et al. 2014).

PRODUCTION, TESTING AND DATA INTEGRATION

Bacterial cellulose production

A. xylinus samples were studied as the most abundant bacteria on earth and one of the prominent producers of cellulose (Vincent 2012). The production process employed an incubation for 7 days to grow the bacterial cellulose (BC) biofilms together with plant cellulose-based jut fabric (Figure 1).

The production of BC took place within 1 L. of water, added with 4 gr. of green tea that was infused for 10 mins. at 100°C, 100 gr. of sucrose and together with the 30 mL. of fermented liquid for acidification at 20 ± 2 °C and 65 ± 5% moisture in static conditions for 7 days. After 7 days of cultivation, the biofilm on the surface of the container was removed. For the pretreatment, the biofilm was placed with an alkalic solution to detach the residue of the growing medium for 8 hours. At the end of the 1st, 2nd and 4th hours, the solution was refreshed. The culture was sterilized at 121°C for 15 minutes with the use of an autoclave machinery, as described in the literature (De Filippis et al. 2018; Domskiene, Sederaviciute and Simonaityte 2019).

Tensile testing

The composite samples were tested via Texture Analyzer (TA-XTplus, Stable Micro System, UK) with the probe Mini Tensile Grip (A/MTG) to measure their tensile characteristics such as strength, strain, stress and conventional deflection under tensile forces. In mechanics, Force (F) is defined as the effort that is applied to the material that creates an internal force, or stress, distributed over the cross section of the material. Tensile Strength, also known as the Ultimate Tensile Strength, is defined as the maximum stress that a material can handle before irreversible deformation (Smith and Hashemi 2006).

Tensile test was conducted for two samples (40mmx80mmx1mm): Sample 1: Pure BC biofilm (S1) and Sample 2: BC-jut composite biofilm (S2). The tests were performed at room temperature, T = 22.0 ± 2.0 °C. The samples were mounted between an upper and a lower clamp and force was applied from the upper clamp with a speed of 0.5 mm/s in tension mode (positive force) (Figure 2). Tensile stress at break (σ) was found by calculating the ratio of the tensile force (F) applied to the samples, to the cross-sectional area (A_o). Elongation at break (ε) was calculated by the ratio of the change in the samples' length to their original length ($\frac{\Delta_L}{L_o}$).

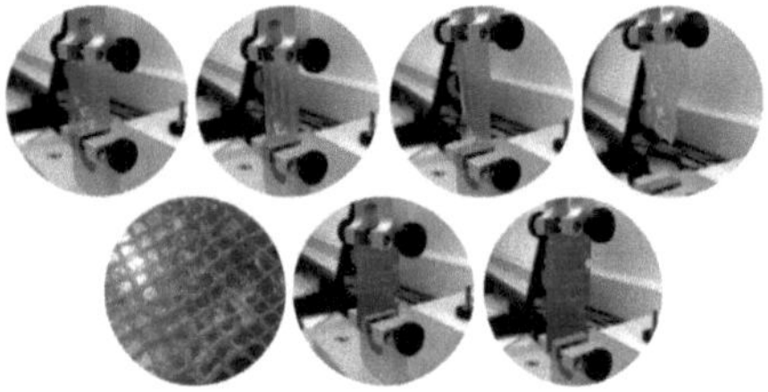

Figure 2
Tensile tests, conducted with Mini Tensile Grip (A/MTG) for S1 and S2

The experiment wlth the S1 showed that the tensile strength (TS) is 48MPa for a BC biofilm. In the literature, TS values for pure BC films have been reported between 5-96 MPa (Cai and Kim 2010). There seems to be a wide range of TS values since the cellulose properties depend on the assembling order that is controlled by the culture medium, the conditions of fermentation and treatment, as well as the conditions of measurement or the moisture amount (Hu et al. 2011). The strain rate (1) has been found to be 2%, and the tensile stress at break (σ) is found to be 2.3kg/1mm (2) in the pure BC biofilm.

$$L - \frac{L_o}{L_o t} \qquad (1)$$

$$\frac{F}{A_0} \qquad (2)$$

The experiment with the S2 indicated that the TS is 324.6 MPa for the BC-jut composite biofilm which is a way higher than pure BC according to the literature findings. It can be derived that the plant cellulose fibers increase the TS strength compared to the pure BC biofilm, although the strain rate does not change with an important difference.

Data Integration to digital structural optimization

Although material behavior is rather linear in Kangaroo physics, it is stated in the literature that the modulus of elasticity, therefore stress, strain and other values that are linked to it, can be introduced into Kangaroo Physics in order to have a more accurate simulation, while it was also observed in the literature that this behavior varies depending on the materials that has the modulus up to 1200 GPa (Cheraud 2020).

In order to integrate the acquired data of tensile tests into the digital structural optimization and form-finding process, Kangaroo Physics' solver component and other complementary components were investigated (Figure 3), and a generic definition was created (Figure 4).

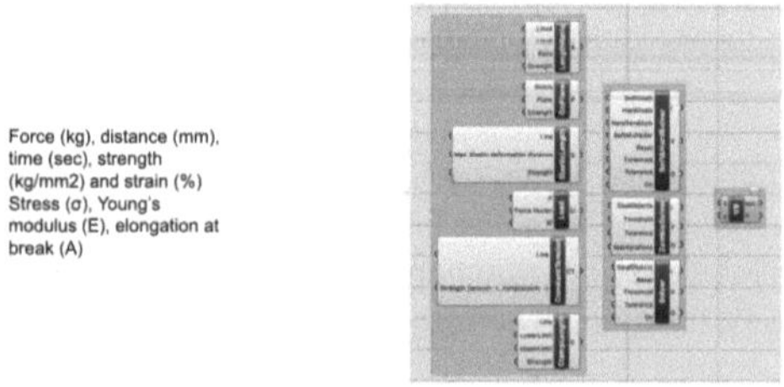

Figure 3
Kangaroo's solver component and other complementary components to integrate tensile test results

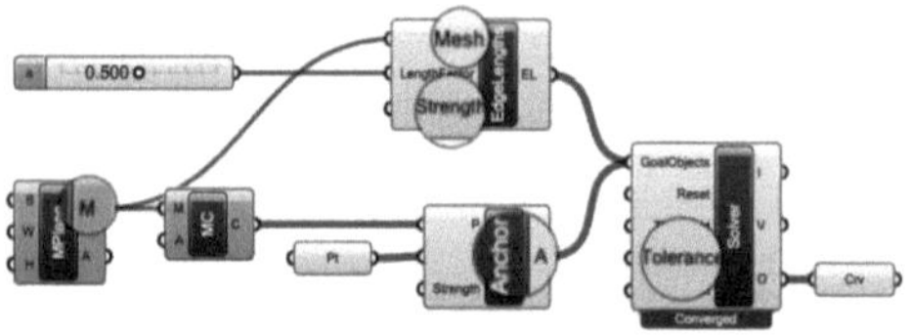

Figure 4
Algorithm for a generic tensioned surface in Grasshopper with Kangaroo Physics

In Kangaroo definition, the input is a mesh that has vertices and edges which become anchors. The output is a set of curves that are assembled within a mesh. There are four inputs on the solver component: "GoalObjects" that refers to the sum of forces; "Reset" is to be connected to a button to reset the simulation; "Tolerance" indicates a threshold for which two points are merged and "On" to be connected to a boolean operator to turn on/off the solver. The algorithm stops when it reaches the threshold value where static position of the geometry is achieved.

In relation to Hook's Law (3), the initial length of the mesh edges gives L_i for each edge. Moreover, "a" is the length factor (4), and strength corresponds to the stiffness of the connection: "k". Again from the Hook's law, stiffness can also be calculated through another equation (5). This equation can be introduced into Kangaroo through mathematical expressions (Figure 5).

$$F = k(L_0 - L_i) \tag{3}$$

$$L_0 = a \cdot L_i \tag{4}$$

$$E \cdot \frac{S}{L_0} = k \tag{5}$$

In order to simulate the point that the yield strength (Pa) is exceeded at, another expression (6) is introduced. Moreover, by reusing the modulus of elasticity equation, another calculation is expressed (7) in order to compare the ratio of force (F) to maximum force (F_e) for validating the simulation. If the ratio of F to F_e is among 0-1, then it indicates that the connection is in elastic behaviour, so the simulation is correct. If this value is higher than 1, then the material is in plastic behaviour, so the simulation is incorrect (Figure 6).

$$R_e = \frac{F_e}{S} \tag{6}$$

$$F = E \cdot S\left(\frac{L}{L_0} - 1\right) \tag{7}$$

CONCLUSION AND DISCUSSION

The results show that the BC-jut composite sample has displayed a higher tensile strength in mechanical tests, compared to the pure BC biofilm due to the reinforcement of its three-dimensional network structure, although tests should be repeated several times more for validation. By incorporating the tools shown earlier in the paper, Kangaroo ran for pure BC and BC-jut composite biofilms, resulting in a value between 0-1 as 0.072594, which indicates an elastic behavior (Figure 7). Although the results prove the simulation, however, there is a challenge in finding the modulus of elasticity for BC and composites since it is a constant value that is predefined in the literature for various types of materials such as metals, plastics, concrete etc. However, for the BC, it varies depending on the assembling order in the culture medium, the conditions of fermentation and treatment, as well as the conditions of measurement or the moisture amount as indicated in the literature (Hu et al. 2011).

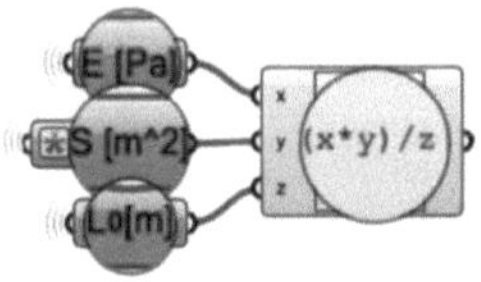

Figure 5
Definition for stiffness calculation

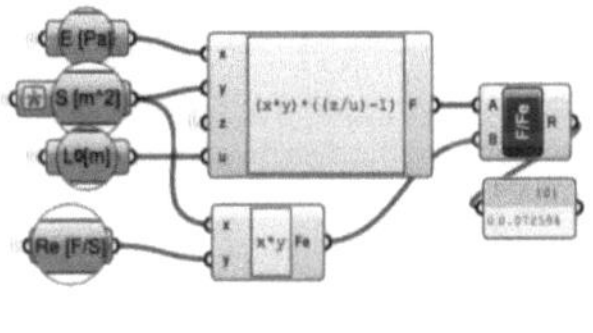

Figure 6
Definition for yield strength calculation

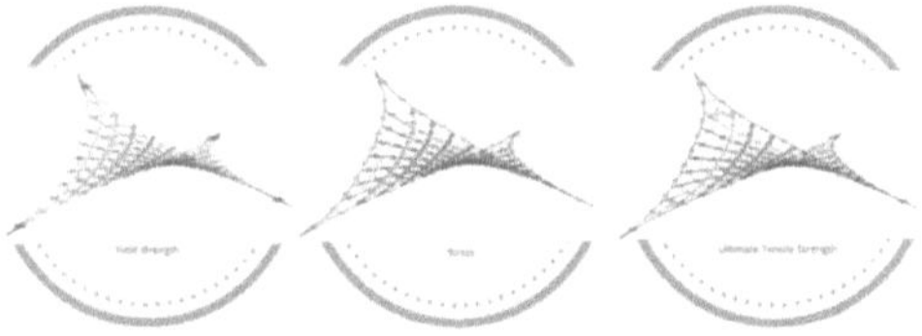

Figure 7
Form finding simulation

Nevertheless, since the result falls in between the literature findings, it can be stated that this integration approach has proven effective that Kangaroo is able to simulate material behaviour with different types of materials, once the mechanical testing is conducted and data to be integrated is derived from the tests. This result has also proved the potential of BC as a load-bearing construction material, if further experimented. It was seen that the mechanical and digital testing of such biologically active materials together leads to an integrated structural optimization with high level of accuracy. Such process might also result in a customized plug-in for a large number of customized biodegradable design prototypes within the context of form finding of complex geometries for real-life design applications.

REFERENCES

Arrhenius, SA 1896, 'On the influence of carbonic acid in the air upon the temperature of the ground', *Lond. Edinb. Dublin Phil. Mag. J. Sci.*, 5, p. 237–275

Ashby, MFA and Johnson, KJ 2014, *Materials and Design: The Art and Science of Material Selection in Product Design*, Elsevier

Backdahl, HB, Helenius, GH, Bodin, AB, Nannmark, UN, Johansson, BRJ, Risberg, BR and Gatenholm, PG 2006, 'Mechanical properties of bacterial cellulose and interactions with smooth muscle cells', *Biomaterials*, 9(27), pp. 2141-2149

Bar-Cohen, YB 2006, *Biomimetics: Biologically inspired technologies*, Taylor & Francis, Florida

Cai, ZC and Kim, JK 2010, 'Bacterial cellulose/poly(ethylene glycol) composite: characterization and first evaluation of biocompatibility', *Cellulose*, 1(17), p. 83–91

Cheraud, FC 2020 'Beyond Design Freedom Providing a Set-up for Material Modelling Within Kangaroo Physics', *Proceedings of eCAADe 2020*, Berlin, pp. 459-468

Crutzen, PJC 2002, 'The "Anthropocene"', *J. Phys.*, 5, pp. 1-5

Derme, TD, Mitterberger, DM and Di Tanna, UDT 2016 'Growth Based Fabrication Techniques for Bacterial Cellulose Three-Dimensional Grown Membranes and Scaffolding Design for Biological Polymers', *Proceedings of ACADIA*, Michigan, pp. 488-495

Domskiene, JD, Sederaviciute, FS and Simonaityte, JS 2019, 'Kombucha bacterial cellulose for sustainable fashion', *International Journal of Clothing Science and Technology*, 31(5), pp. 644-652

Estevez, AE and Navarro, DN 2016 'Biomanufacturing the future: Biodigital Architecture & Genetics', *Proceedings of RESIM*, Leiria, pp. 14-17

Fernandez, JF 2006, *Material Architecture: Emergent Materials for Innovative Buildings and Ecological Construction*, Taylor & Francis

Hu, WH, Liu, SL, Chen, SC and Wang, HW 2011, 'Preparation and prop-erties of photochromic bacterial cellulose nanofibrousmembranes', *Cellulose*, 18(3), p. 655–661

Huang, YH, Zhu, CZ, Yang, JY, Nie, NY, Chen, CC and Sun, DS 2014, 'Recent advances in bacterial cellulose', *Cellulose*, 21, pp. 1-30

Huerta, SH 2006, 'Structural Design in the Work of Gaudi', *Architectural Science Review*, 49(4), pp. 324-339

Koch, KK, Bhushan, BB and Barthlott, WB 2009, 'Multifunctional surface structures of plants: an inspiration for biomimetics', *Prog Mater Sci*, 54(2), pp. 137-178

Naboni, RN 2016 'Form-finding to fabrication of superthin anisotropic gridshell', *SIGraDi 2016, XX Congress of the Iberoamerican Society of Digital Graphics*, Buenos Aires, pp. 418-425

Ochsendorf, JO and Block, PB 2014, *Exploring shell forms. Shell Structures for Architecture: Form Finding and Optimization*, Routledge

Otto, FO and Glaeser, LG 1972, *The work of Frei Otto*, Museum of Modern Art, New York Graphic Society, Greenwich

Oxman, NO 2012, 'Programming Matter', *Architectural Design Special Issue: Material Computation: Higher Integration in Morphogenetic Design*, 82(2), pp. 88-95

Pearce, PP 1981, 'Structure of Nature Is a Strategy for Design', *Leonardo*, 14(2), p. 175–176

Ruse, MR and Hull, DLH 1989, *What the philosophy of biology is: Essays dedicated to David Hull*, Kluwer Academic, Dordrecht; Boston

Saremi, SS, Mirjalili, SM and Lewis, AL 2017, 'Grasshopper Optimisation Algorithm: Theory and application', *Advances in Engineering Software*, 105, pp. 30-47

Smith, WFS and Hashemi, JH 2006, *Foundations of Materials Science and Engineering*, Mcgraws – Hill Book

Turhan, GDT, Varinlioglu, GV and Bengisu, MB 2020 'Dynamic Relaxation Simulations of Bacterial Cellulose-based Tissues', *In Proceedings of eCAADe 2020*, Berlin, pp. 61-66

Vincent, JV 2012, *Structural Biomaterials*, Princeton University Press

Zalasiewicz, JZ, Williams, MW, Haywood, AH and Ellis, ME 2011, 'The Anthropocene: a new epoch of geological time', *Phil. Trans. R. Soc. A*, 369, pp. 835-841

CAAD, creativity and design thinking models

Effect of Immersive VR on Communication Patterns in Architectural Design Critiques

Hadas Sopher[1], John S. Gero[2]
[1]CRENAU/AAU – UMR_CNRS 1563 – School of Architecture Nantes. Design Research Laboratory Hybridlab, University of Montreal [2]University of North Carolina, Charlotte
[1]hadas.sopher@CRENAU.archi.fr [2]john@johngero.com

Immersive Virtual Reality (iVR) systems hold a promise to affect design behavior by allowing users to experience presence, as they are embodied in the digital display. However, the lack of research articulating how embodiment enabling media change design behavior limits integrating iVR systems in design pedagogy with a well-defined framework. This paper presents the preliminary results from a case study of a work in progress comparing the communication patterns of critique sessions in an architecture studio in two kinds of media: iVR and non-immersive desk-crits. We employed protocol analysis methods to track the distribution of conversational turns and the first occurrence of design issues emerging over the different media. Results show that compared to non-immersive critiques, the iVR had a lower number of conversational turns and an increase in the first occurrence generated by students, indicating support in a learner-centered activity. Elucidating the effect of the communication medium on design behavior provides an empirical foundation for its inclusion in a design theory that encapsulates embodied cognition.

Keywords: *Immersive VR, Studio, Design cognition, Critique, Virtual Reality*

INTRODUCTION

The increasing use of immersive virtual reality (iVR) systems in design pedagogy raises a significant need to examine the ways iVRs as communication media support design learning. However, a lack of studies articulating how communication in iVR learning sessions differs from non-immersive sessions limits integrating iVR systems as educational media.

In response, this exploratory case study is used to examine a research question concerning the impact of iVRs on the emerging communication in iVR studio crits, compared to non-immersive media used in conventional studio desk-crits. Explicating how communication media impact design activity provides a basis for integrating iVRs in design pedagogy as educational means to support learning.

Communication at the Design Studio

The studio forms the core environment for learning how to design. Following the situated learning approach, students learn by actively practicing design activities and generating design issues that concern the development of a design artifact (Schön, 1985). In so-called "crits", or "desk-crits", the work done by the student is regularly assessed and discussed with an expert tutor and peers, an activity that supports further design progress by generating new design issues and discussing existing ones, and gaining competence (Oh, Ishizaki, Gross, & Do, 2013; Schön, 1987). Generating new design issues, also known as First Occurrences (FO), is considered an essential indicator of design progress. The ability to generate new ideas testifies to divergent thinking, an activity that includes introducing new issues or design alternatives, and is often linked with creativity and design progress (Dorst & Cross, 2001). The process repeats itself during an entire semester and supports design development from an abstract to a more concrete artifact.

Learning how to design poses no easy challenges. Design activity predominantly occurs over representations such as drawings or models that deliver a particular message (or more) concerning design issues of the artifact (e.g., a building section provides information regarding each floor's height). Representations serve as media for creating, developing, and communicating design issues between the designer and self or other participants, as happens during crits (Kalay, 2004). However, the medium of representation plays a significant role in delivering the message, as it carries a change in properties of the object in mind, such as scale, materials, or motion (McLuhan, 2006). Given that different media deliver different messages, using particular media during design activity may stimulate or hamper subsequent design activities by affecting the creation and interpretation of the message. In addition, design problems are considered to be wicked (Rittel & Webber, 1973). They have no determined solution and leave traces upon subsequent problems, characteristics which may create difficulties in assessing whether the design is satisfactory and hamper design progress, particularly for inexperienced designers such as students. These characteristics may be more challenging in the early design stages when the representations are less concrete.

These difficulties make crit communication an essential component in the learning process. Studies investigating student-tutor communication in design crits found the tutor dominant in the conversation structure by generating more conversational turns (Milovanovic & Gero, 2018), and explicating design issues (Goldschmidt, Hochman, & Dafni, 2010). A study tracking evidence of FO of design issues in design crits found that compared to the student, the teacher generated more FOs concerning the artifact's structure and expected behavior (Gero & Jiang, 2016). Since the studio encourages a learner-centered approach, such hidden hierarchy, often criticized over the years (Dutton, 1987; Wang, 2010; Webster, 2008), puts the success of the educational approach to accomplish this goal into question and indicates the need to support enhanced learner activity during crits.

Immersive Virtual Reality Media of Communication

The use of iVR systems as communication media in design practice and pedagogy has grown significantly. By allowing users to experience a sense of presence in the digital display, iVR systems hold promise to affect design learning by creating a change in crit communication. The common definition states that the two major components, immersion and presence, embedded in virtual reality, assist in allocating the communication between the system and the user. Immersion describes the physical and virtual conditions that comprise the system. Presence refers to the way the display is experienced by users (Slater, 2009). Sanchez-vives and Slater (2005) describe immersion as the extent to which a computational display is able to generate an extensive, inclusive, continuous, and surrounding illusion of reality and its capacity to provide a display, matching the user's movements with the feedback generated in the visual display. Presence is described as the illusion of being in a place, or a situation, as conveyed by an immersive system. Described by Merleau-Ponty

(1962) embodiment stands for the human-world relationship. Since humans inhabit the environment, any choice of behaviour is intertwined with their surroundings. Following Merleau-Ponty (1962), presence is a psychological state of consciousness that leads to forms of behaviour that correspond to what would have occurred if met in similar real settings (Slater, 2009). Differing from other representations that are external to the user, the interaction with iVR media occurs as the users are embodied in the display. A similarity in users' navigation was found in a study comparing design activity in an iVR and a real site during early design stages (Date, 2018).

These unique characteristics enable iVR to support situated learning by allowing the users to simulate a real-life situation and acquire desired behaviors and skills (Slater, 2017). A recent survey depicts the educational advantages of iVR systems in simulating environments and supporting training and interaction (Beck, Morgado, & O'Shea, 2020). In addition, it also identifies gaps requiring further investigation, such as the ways iVRs foster exploration and interaction, essential factors in design activity. A study investigating the current focus of research in iVR shows that few studies focus on the iVRs' capacity to support the performance of desired activities (Hamilton, McKechnie, Edgerton, & Wilson, 2020), while a different study points to the need in providing more rigorous methods to evaluate iVRs' support in situated learning (Mikropoulos & Natsis, 2011). In the studio context, iVR systems were found supportive of important factors in design learning, including increased design activity (Sopher, Kalay, & Fisher-Gewirtzman, 2017), design development and design convergence (Sopher, Fisher-Gewirtzman, & Kalay, 2018; Sopher, Fisher-Gewirtzman, & Kalay, 2019), and spatial comprehension (Zhao et al., 2020), indicating that iVR should be integrated into design syllabi. Multi-user virtual environments were found advantageous for collaboration between learners in terms of presenting their work and generating progress (Fruchter, 2014). Studies tracking collaborative ideation in iVR crits indicate the media's role in shaping crit communication (Boudhraa, Dorta, Milovanovic, & Pierini, 2019; Dorta et al., 2011; Dorta, Kinayoglu, & Boudhraâ, 2016). However, since these studies focused solely on iVR crits, further knowledge is required to articulate how communication in iVR crits differs from non-immersive crits to discuss the implications iVR media may have on design pedagogy and integrate iVRs as educational media in the studio.

ANALYZING CRIT COMMUNICATION USING PROTOCOL ANALYSIS METHODS

Protocol analysis methods are widely used to analyze cognitive processes during a design activity (Cross, Christiaans, & Dorst, 1996). By coding elements in transcribed design conversations, these methods reveal the conversations' structure and identify commonalities and saliences in communication patterns. To identify the medium's role during crit communication, we employed protocol analysis methods (Gero & Mc Neill, 1998; Kan & Gero, 2017). The coding scheme includes the tutor-learner conversational turns and FOs generated by each participant. Measurements based on the distributions of these codes assist in revealing the structure of conversations (Sacks, Schegloff, & Jefferson, 1978). Conversational turns provide information regarding the structure and the contribution of each participant to the conversation (Gero & Kan, 2009). FOs are considered essential indicators of design progress, hence the interest in measuring the number of FOs generated and their distribution over time for each medium. Studies tracking evidence of FOs in design conversations (Gero & Jiang, 2016), or patterns of collaborative ideation (Dorta, Kalay, et al., 2011) articulate how design behaviors are structured, independent from either the design process or supporting media. In this sense, these studies provide a means to assess how iVRs affect design communication during crits. In this study, the first time a design issue is mentioned in a particular crit is considered an FO and is coded as such. Repetitions of this word as the crit progresses are not coded.

CASE STUDY

In this case study, we monitored a third-year architecture studio course taught by Dr. Fisher-Gewirtzman at The Technion, Israel Institute of Technology, that used an iVR system (Figure 1) and non-immersive desk-crits (Figure 2). The iVR system is a room-sized setting containing a 7 x 2.5 meter screen and synchronized sensors that allow for single user navigation in a 3D display of digital design models. The setting affords a shared presence experience for twenty attendees. The desk-crits sessions included various representations communicated in non-immersive media. The brief required the design of a public building, including adaptive reuse of the existing context. Two weekly crits were given during a sixteen-week semester. The tutor and four undergraduates (age 22-25) with previous experience in digital modeling software formed the case that was studied. None of the students had used the iVR system before the course. The tutor had prior teaching experience in the iVR.

Three iVR and their parallel three desk-crit sessions were used as the data source for this study. Figure 3 illustrates the sessions recorded throughout the course. Two pairs of sessions were recorded at each time slot, allowing for tracking temporal differences over time. The crit duration ranged from ten to fifty minutes. The results were normalized to remove differences in the crits' durations.

Figure 1
A design crit taking place at the immersive VR system

Figure 2
A non-immersive desk-crit at the conventional studio

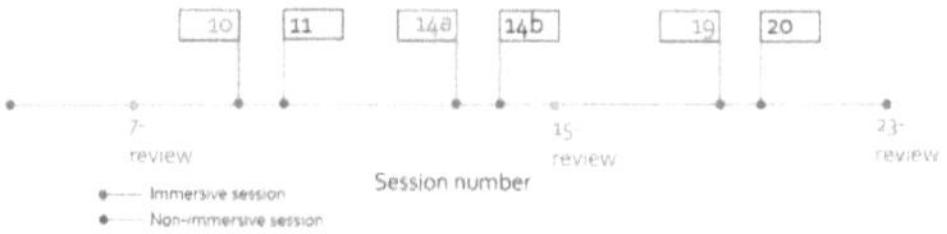

Figure 3
Sessions recorded thoughout the course

RESULTS

Seven and a half hours of crit conversations were recorded, transcribed, and coded using the two coding schemes resulting in 4,152 conversational turns and 5,324 FOs. iVR crits had an average of 6.1 tutor-student conversational turns per minute (SD=1.64), while non-immersive desk-crits had an average of 9.0 turns per minute (SD=2.05). $p<0.001$. These results served as a preliminary basis for further investigation. A second analysis tracked the FOs generated by the crit participants in each medium. A t-test was used to determine if there were significant differences between the two classes of crit (Table 1).

We observed no significant difference between the media in terms of the total number of crit FOs. However, an analysis conducted to separate the FOs generated by each participant revealed statistically significant differences between the two media types. As seen in Table 1, the iVR crits had a higher number of FOs generated by the students, indicating the medium's capacity in supporting this important activity. These results align with previous comparative studies concerning design activity in iVR and non-immersive crits (Sopher et al., 2017; Sopher et al., 2019) and expand them to include new understandings of the characteristics of conversational patterns supported by the media.

Examining the teacher's activity revealed that compared to the students' activity, more FOs were

Figure 4
The distribution of First Occurrence of design issues made during student-teacher interaction in non-immersive crits (left) and immersive crits (right).

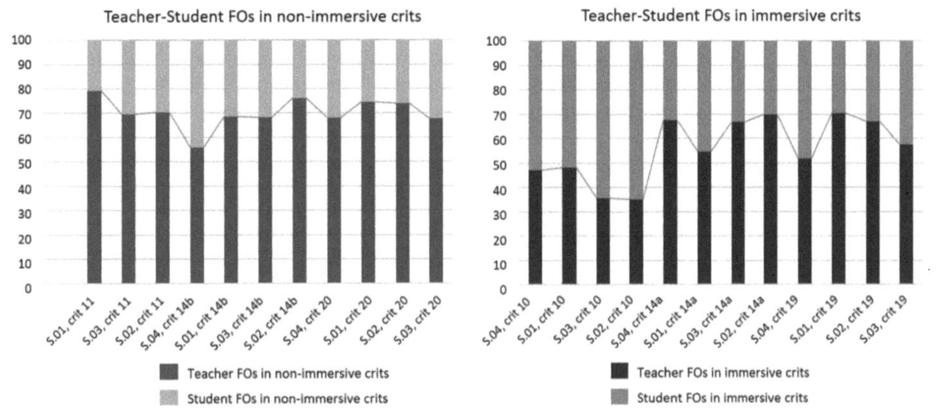

Table 1
The distribution of First Occurrence of design issues in immersive and non-immersive crits

FOs per minute	Communication media	Mean (SD)	P values
Crit FOs (generated by both students and teacher)	Immersive VR	9.9 (2.58)	p>0.1
	Non-immersive	10.1 (2.3)	
Student FOs	Immersive VR	4.3 (1.61)	p<0.1
	Non-immersive	3.1 (1.17)	
Teacher FOs	Immersive VR	5.6 (2.06)	p<0.1
	Non-immersive	7 (1.41)	

Table 2
The percentage of FOs generated by different students in immersive and non-immersive crits

Students	FOs (%) in immersive VR crits	FOs (%) in non-immersive crits
S.01	59	41
S.02	54	46
S.03	65	35
S.04	56	43

generated in both the immersive and the non-immersive media (Table 1). The teacher was dominant in generating FOs regardless of the media involved, providing preliminary evidence of teacher-centered learning taking place during the course. These results align with other studies investigating design activity in non-immersive crits (Goldschmidt et al., 2010; Milovanovic & Gero, 2018).

Despite the teacher's dominance, the iVR was found to encourage learner activity. The percentage of student-teacher FOs generated in each media is shown in Figure 4. Compared to non-immersive crits, we observed increased student FOs in iVR crits and decreased teacher FOs. This finding, if generalizable, has important implications for studio-based design pedagogy, as it implies that it encourages a learner-centered learning approach.

Table 2 presents the percentage of FOs generated by each student over the two media. Revealing each student's activity allows a teacher to personalize the use of a certain medium to support design progress. For example, student S.03 had 65% of FOs generated in iVR, clearly showing that the student has benefited from the medium, in terms of introducing new issues, and should be encouraged to use it when a decrease in activity is identified.

Temporal changes in crit activity

Figure 5 presents the variation in the distribution of FOs at each media throughout the course. A difference is observed in the first pair of sessions (10 and 11), where the iVR session had a higher number of student FOs compared to the following non-immersive session. Of note, the session also had the highest number of all student activity. Since generating FOs faces difficulties, particularly in the early design stages (Dorta, Lesage, Pérez, & Bastien, 2011), these results provide evidence of the support the iVR lends to cope with this educational challenge.

The number of FOs largely decreases (over both media) from the early sessions to mid-course sessions, followed by a marginal decrease until the final sessions, indicating convergence, an expected behaviour as the design progresses. As seen in Figure 5, the teacher's activity complements the students' activity by introducing a high number of FOs when a poor student FOs occurs, indicating the teacher's role in the process. The variations seen in the teacher's activity over the media indicate the need to further investigate the impact iVR systems may have on design teaching.

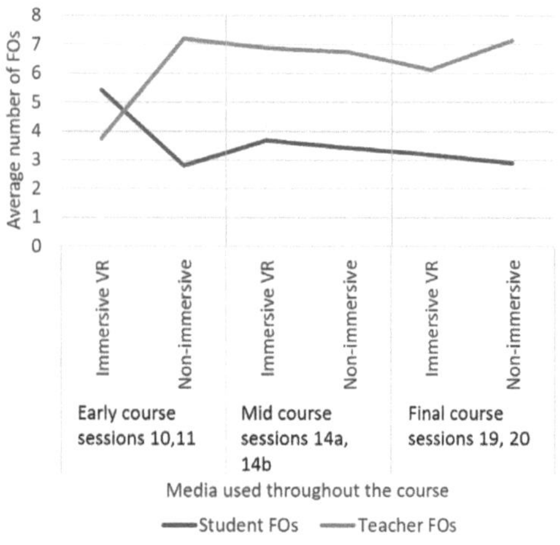

Figure 5
Distribution of the average number of FOs per minute, generated in immersive and non-immersive crits throughout the course

DISCUSSION

This exploratory case study demonstrates how the introduction of computational support, in the form of iVR, to the teaching of architectural design in the studio affects communication during design crits. The results show that compared to non-immersive crits, iVR crits have a lower frequency of conversational turns while being similar in generating FOs, results that indicate the iVR's capacity to support design progress. A significant salience between the media was found in the students' FOs, revealing a higher frequency of FOs generated in iVR crits. These results align with existing studies concerning design learning in iVR media (Boudhraa et al., 2019; Dorta et al., 2016; Sopher, Kalay, and Fisher-Gewirtzman, 2017; Sopher, Fisher-Gewirtzman and Kalay 2018, 2019) and expand them to include the communication patterns emerging in iVR crits. Despite the teacher's dominance in generating FOs in both media, an increase in students' FOs was observed in iVR crits, indicating the medium's role in supporting enhanced learner activity. While similar teacher dominance was previously found in non-immersive crits (Goldschmidt et al., 2010; Gero & Jiang, 2016; Milovanovic & Gero, 2018), this study opens the way to rethink the teacher's profile in different kinds of media. Preliminary evidence found the iVR's capacity to support student activity in early design stages in terms of generating FOs, provides ground for further research under the aim of integrating iVR in future syllabi within a well-defined framework.

CONCLUSIONS

This paper examines the impact of iVR systems on design crits by comparing the communication patterns in iVR and non-immersive crits. The findings show preliminary evidence that iVRs affect design crit activity in terms of conversational structure and ideation patterns. The iVR was found to have a lower frequency of conversational turns and a higher number of FOs generated by students, particularly in the early design stages. An increased frequency of student FOs followed by a decreased teacher FOs indicates the important role the iVR plays in fostering learner-centered communication. No significant differences were found in the emergence of the total number of FOs due to the teacher's complementary behaviour to reduced student activity. Future research will expand this corpus by further detailing the ways iVR systems impact learners' cognitive activities.

This study has several limitations. The small number of subjects limits the ability to draw representative conclusions. The study ameliorates this limitation by focusing on the numerous FOs generated by the participants. An additional limitation is that the analyses related to teaching performance are based on a single teacher. Further investigation is needed to determine how iVRs affect different teacher profiles.

IVR systems stimulate embodied cognition in ways that the non-immersive media do not. This study provides a foundation for integrating iVRs in design pedagogy as the means to enhance a learner-centered approach.

ACKNOWLEDGEMENTS

The authors wish to thank Associate Professor Dafna Fisher-Gewirtzman and the students for their participation. This study is supported by the West Creative Industries grant.

REFERENCES

Beck, D., Morgado, L. and O'Shea, P. 2020, 'Finding the gaps about uses of immersive learning environments: a survey of surveys.', *Journal of Universal Computer Science*, 26, p. 1043–1073

Boudhraa, S., Dorta, T., Milovanovic, J. and Pierini, D. 2019, 'Co-ideation critique unfolded: an exploratory study of a co-design studio 'crit' based on the students' experience', *CoDesign*, 17, pp. 1-20

Cross, N., Christiaans, H. and Dorst, K. (eds) 1996, *Analysing design activity*, Wiley, Chichester

Date, K. 2018, *Immersion in Early Architectural Design in the Age of Computing.*, Ph.D. Thesis, University of California, Berkley

Dorst, K. and Cross, N. 2001, 'Creativity in the design process: co-evolution of problem–solution', *Design Studies*, 22(5), p. 425–437

Dorta, T., Kalay, YE, Lesage, A. and Pérez, E. 2011, 'Design conversations in the interconnected HIS', *International Journal of Design Sciences and Technology*, 18(2), p. 65–80

Dorta, T., Kinayoglu, G. and Boudhraâ, S. 2016, 'A new representational ecosystem for design teaching in the studio', *Design Studies*, 47, pp. 164-186

Dorta, T., Lesage, A., Pérez, E. and Bastien, JMC 2011, 'Signs of Collaborative Ideation and the Hybrid Ideation Space Signs of Collaborative Ideation and the Hybrid Ideation Space', in Taura, T. and Nagai, Y. (eds) 2011, *Design Creativity 2010*, Springer

Dutton, T. 1987, 'Design Studio Pedagogy', *Journal of Architectural Education*, 41(1), pp. 16-25

Fruchter, R 2014 'Transformative 3D immersive collaboration environment in support of AEC global teamwork', *Computing in Civil and Building Engineering - Proceedings of the 2014 International Conference on Computing in Civil and Building Engineering*, p. 1425–1432

Gero, JS and Jiang, H. 2016, 'Exploring the Design Cognition of Concept Design Reviews Using the FBS-based Protocol Analysis', in Adams, RS and Siddiqui, JA (eds) 2016, *Analyzing Design Review Conversations*, Purdue University Press

Gero, JS and Kan, JW 2009 'Learning to collaborate during team designing: some preliminary results from measurement-based tools', *ICORD 09: Proceedings of the 3rd International Conference on Research into Design Engineering*, pp. 560-567

Gero, JS and Mc Neill, T. 1998, 'An approach to the analysis of design protocols', *Design Studies*, 19(1), pp. 21-61

Goldschmidt, G., Hochman, H. and Dafni, I. 2010, 'The design studio "crit": Teacher–student communication', *Artificial Intelligence for Engineering Design, Analysis and Manufacturing*, 24, p. 285–302

Hamilton, D., McKechnie, J., Edgerton, E. and Wilson, C. 2020, 'Immersive virtual reality as a pedagogical tool in education: a systematic literature review of quantitative learning outcomes and experimental design', *Journal of Computers in Education*, 8, pp. 1-32

Kalay, YE 2004, *Architecture's new media: principles, theories, and methods of computer-aided design*, MIT press, Cambridge, Massachusetts

Kan, JWT and Gero, JS (eds) 2017, *Quantitative Methods for Studying Design Protocols*, Springer, Dordrecht

McLuhan, M. 2006, 'The Medium is the Message', in Durham, MG and Kellner, DM (eds) 2006, *Media and cultural studies*, Blackwell Publishing Ltd, Oxford, pp. 100-107

Merleau-Ponty, M. 1962, *Phenomenology of Perception (Landes, Donald A., Trans.).*, Routledge, New York

Mikropoulos, TA and Natsis, A. 2011, 'Educational virtual environments: A ten-year review of empirical research', *Computers & Education*, 56(3), p. 769–780

Milovanovic, J. and Gero, JS 2018 'Exploration of cognitive design behaviour during design critiques', *Proceedings of International Design Conference, DESIGN*, p. Vol. 5, pp. 2099–2110

Oh, Y., Ishizaki, S., Gross, MD and Do, E.YLD. 2013, 'A theoretical framework of design critiquing in architec-

ture studios', *Design Studies*, 34(3), p. 302–325
Rittel, HWJ and Webber, MM 1973, 'Dilemmas in a general theory of planning', *Policy Sciences*, 4(2), pp. 155-169
Sacks, H, Schegloff, EA and Jefferson, G 1978, 'A Simplest Systematics for the Organization of Turn Taking for Conversation', in Schenkein, J (eds) 1978, *Studies in the Organization of Conversational Interaction*, Academic Press, pp. 7-55
Sanchez-vives, MV and Slater, M 2005, 'From Presence Towards Consciousness', *Nature Reviews Neuroscience*, 6(10), p. 332–339
Schön, DA 1985, *The design studio⊠: an exploration of its traditions and potentials*, RIBA Publications, London
Schön, DA 1987, *Educating the Reflective Practitioner. Toward a new design for teaching and learning in the professions*, Jossey-Bass, San Francisco
Slater, M. 2009, 'Place illusion and plausibility can lead to realistic behaviour in immersive virtual environments', *Philosophical Transactions of the Royal Society B: Biological Sciences*, 364, p. 3549–3557
Slater, M. 2017, 'Implicit Learning Through Embodiment in Immersive Virtual Reality', in Liu, D., Dede, C., Huang, R. and Richards, J. (eds) 2017, *Virtual, augmented, and mixed realities in education*, Springer, Singapore, pp. 19-33
Sopher, H., Fisher-Gewirtzman, D. and Fisher-Gewirtzman, YE 2018 'Use of Immersive Virtual Environment in the Design Studio.', *Proceedings of the 36th eCAADe Conference*, Lodz, p. Vol 2, 853–862
Sopher, H., Fisher-Gewirtzman, D. and Kalay, YE 2019, 'Going immersive in a community of learners? Assessment of design processes in a multi⊠setting architecture studio.', *British Journal of Educational Technology*, 50(5)(10.1111/bjet.12857), p. 2109–2128
Sopher, H., Kalay, YE and Fisher-Gewirtzman, D. 2017 'Why Immersive? - Using an Immersive Virtual Environment in Architectural Education.', *Proceedings of the 35th eCAADe Conference*, Rome, p. 313–322
Wang, T. 2010, 'A new paradigm for design studio education', *International Journal of Art and Design Education*, 29(2), p. 173–183
Webster, H. 2008, 'Architectural Education after Schön: Cracks, Blurs, Boundaries and Beyond', *Journal for Education in the Built Environment*, 3(2), pp. 63-74
Zhao, J., Sensibaugh, T., Bodenheime, B., McNamara, TP, Nazareth, A., Newcombe, N., Minear, M. and Klippel, A. 2020, 'Desktop versus immersive virtual environments: effects on spatial learning', *Spatial Cognition and Computation*, 20(4), pp. 328-363

Understanding Design Justice in a Bottom-up Housing through Digital Actor-Network Mapping

The case of solidary mobile housing in Brussels

Rosaura Noemy Hernandez Romero[1], *Burak Pak*[2]
[1,2]*KU Leuven Faculty of Architecture Campus Sint-Lucas Brussels*
[1,2]*{rosauranoemy.hernandezromero|burak.pak}@kuleuven.be*

This paper is a study of an ongoing housing project in Brussels (SMH) which involves bottom-up spatial occupation and `making' by activists, activist architects, social workers and citizens. The particular focus of this paper is on the critical spatial agency of the citizens, activist-architects and artefacts for enabling architectural design justice (ADJ) in the SMH. Building on the Actor-Network Theory of Latour (2005) we developed an analytic method called Actor Link Mapping and Analysis (ALMA) which involves data collection from a wide range of network actors, the generation of a variety of digital network maps, making computational analysis, followed by workshops and interviews to discuss the findings. ALMA was used to recognize potential assets which are essential for design justice practices and networks. The analysis revealed the limits to community control of design processes and practices as well as limits to the conceptual links surrounding socio-spatial equality, thus limits to design justice in the SMH project. Our research also revealed a plethora of new roles and agencies in bottom-up housing production which were essential to understanding the dynamics and power distribution among the different actors.

Keywords: *Network Mapping, Network Analysis, Housing, Co-creation, Design Justice, Actor-Network Theory*

1. INTRODUCTION

This study is a part of the PhD research of the first author advised by the second author which focuses on extending Costanza-Chock's (2020) theory of Design Justice to Architectural design, resulting in a framework to understand and act on real-world cases in Brussels. Design Justice (DJ) aims to ensure a more equitable distribution of benefits and burdens of design processes and products (Costanza-Chock 2020). Architectural Design Justice (ADJ) is a particular form of DJ, focusing on enabling DJ through various altered and participatory architectural design and co-creation frameworks.

In order to transform architectural design into a more equitable and just practice, novel roles and methods are needed. An essential element of our study's analytical part was the digital mapping of the co-creation processes and actors involved in projects aiming at ADJ to understand how they collaborate and alter the traditional roles in architectural design. To achieve this, we developed a method based on the Actor-Network Theory (ANT) of Latour (2005).

ANT is a theoretical approach to interpret the social phenomena, where the social and the physical world are constantly influencing each other in a network of relationships. ANT is a way of mapping the materials and how these participate in our everyday routines. The novel method we developed was named Actor Link Mapping and Analysis (ALMA), a network mapping method based on ANT that recognizes human and non-human actors equally (including processes, artefacts and environments), to analyze the performance of a network. It is focused on recognizing the agency of non-human actors in the creation of networked design practice. It is a mapping method for analyzing co-creation in a measurable way.

This paper will use the ALMA method to study a housing case in Brussels; Solidary Mobile Housing Project (SMH), and its intensive bottom-up co-creation with a wide range of actors. The SMH project is embedded in the peculiarities of Brussels, an alternative rebellious city, which harbors numerous solidarity network practices, diverse in culture, and with an expansive universe of spatial activism responding to socio-spatial injustices. The co-creative housing project shows the capacities of a bottom-up design project to reach a high level of participation and, therefore, project a just and long-lasting spatial agency over the future built-environment.

This paper's particular focus is on the critical spatial agency (Awan et al., 2020) of all actors involved; with a particular interest in revealing the role(s) of citizens, activist-architects, concepts and artefacts for enabling architectural design justice. Based on the data collected from the actors, a variety of ALMA maps are generated to study and reveal how spatial agency is constructed in the social processes of bottom-up spatial production. Recognizing the importance of artefacts people interact with and how they fundamentally shape the dynamic itself (Robinson & Baum, 2019) the research questions to be tackled by this study are:

- What is the critical spatial agency of the actors, particularly, citizens, activist-architects, and artefacts for enabling architectural design justice in the SMH project?
- What are the potentials of the ALMA method to understand and enable the above?

Our paper will start with a literature review on Design Justice, Actor-Network Theory and its links to Network Theory (Section 2). Then we will introduce the SMH housing case and present our analysis (Section 3). In conclusion, we will discuss a plethora of roles beyond the traditional ones implemented and adopted (Section 4). We will end this section with a critical reflection of the method and the roles employed, which is interesting for spatial practitioners and participatory design researchers.

2. BACKGROUND

Design Justice is an approach that aims to ensure a more equitable distribution of the benefits and burdens of design, and enable meaningful participation in design decisions and recognition of community-based, indigenous, and diasporic design traditions, knowledge and practices (Costanza-Chock 2020). In this sense, Architectural Design Justice looks to explore possibilities on how the benefits and burdens of the design process and the product can be distributed among the various groups affected by an architectural project. When considered a form of Critical Spatial Practice, ADJ aims to challenge the status quo of design practices by going to the root question: *'Who gets to design?'*. More importantly, similar to critical spatial practice, ADJ takes an activist stance by proposing a switch to the control of the design process, with the question *'How do we move to community control of design processes and practices?'*(Miessen, 2016).

Awan et al. (2020) explain the agency of space in

their book 'Spatial agency: Other ways of Doing Architecture' and give various examples of alternative practices emerging. The idea of expanding the word Spatial to cover more than just architecture allows for the agency of space to move beyond the known parameters of Architecture.

In this context, Networked ADJ Practices can be defined as interdisciplinary collectives of autonomous practices uniting around a shared vision and a common platform, leveraging their skill sets to create a more unique value proposition (Morgan & Roach, 2011, p.7). The networked spatial practitioner or 'crossbencher' of today acts as a public intellectual who mediates and articulates a medium for spatial design, uses networked intelligence, and sets the spatial agency in the projects to arrive at continuous co-creative processes (Wigley, 2007, p.47). The use of the term 'networked' in this context is not limited to the technological understanding of networks but refers to the collective performance of spatial practitioners interlinked with a wide range of actors, spaces, spatial intervention ideas, processes, and instruments (Latour, 2005).

Actor-Network Theory for Understanding ADJ Networks

ANT focuses on the relationships between the actors in the network and the importance of the inclusion of non-humans such as; spaces, processes, nature, and objects. It highlights the perspective of the interconnectivity and agency of everything at the same level. For doing research, this approach is helpful because it allows for a holistic view and understanding of the dynamics and relations between actors and the importance of ambiguity in design to enable different interactions between the actors. This perspective also allows for the investigation of power dynamics that can be hidden in the physical urban environment and can only be seen through the tracing of each network. The agency of objects can also be a potent tool used to empower less powerful actors in the network and create an inclusive dialogue that facilitates the co-development of spaces. These objects can be seen as interfaces or communication tools translating between different actors by allowing multi-languages of interactions.

ANT is compatible with Network Science and computational methods to study networks. According to the Network Theory, networks consist of nodes and links, connections that conform to various organisational topologies that affect the nature of the relationships they embody and how they may be analyzed and understood (Burke and Tierney, 2009). Through qualitative evaluations and systematic means using indicators such as Degree Centrality, Betweenness Centrality, and Closeness Centrality, in addition to Network Centralization, Network Integration and Peripheral Players, we can identify key value creators and informal knowledge (O'Malley and Marsden, 2008, p.224)(Orgnet, 2018). Centrality measures are used to identify powerful and important actors in a network (Analytic Technologies, 2008).

3. UNDERSTANDING DESIGN JUSTICE THROUGH ACTOR-NETWORK MAPPING

SMH is practice-based research project and a joint initiative by eight people in precarious housing conditions, the non-profit organization Samenlevingsopbouw Brussel, the Faculty of Architecture of KU Leuven, people from the Brussels-Capital Region (BCR), and the Brussels Center for Social Welfare (CAW). The bottom-up project is funded by the BCR's Research Institution INNOVIRIS, under the Co-create program and by the BCR's Minister responsible for Housing, Céline Frémault. BC Architects bvba office and the non-profit organizations Atelier Groot Eiland, Casablanco and Sociale Innovatie Fabriek also contributed to the project's design, its technical implementation and skill-building, and support activities aiming at upscaling its potential.

Since 2017 the SMH network has been working on developing, testing and fine-tuning a resilient model for the co-creation of solidarity living in mobile homes on vacant lots in the BCR. The SMH partners experimented with research-driven design and co-creation of mobile housing in waiting spaces while ensuring the safeguarding of the solidarity character of temporary use for and with citizens in need. In this project, they aimed to develop an innovative, mobile and modular type of housing for the most vulnerable users, where collectivity and solidarity between the network actors are central to accomplish adaptability and flexibility. The project created small-scale solidarity networks in interaction with the immediate environment (the street, the neighborhood, the city) and involved vulnerable people in the temporary use of urban Waiting Spaces. Currently, eight housing units of the SMH project are being built in Jette, Brussels.

Figure 1
the Solidary Mobile Housing Project: ALMA visual survey, and Co-creation workshops.

ALMA: ACTOR LINK MAPPING AND ANALYSIS METHOD

We developed a mixed-method for collecting, mapping and verifying information on the network (Figure 1). ALMA involves a triangulation of various methods to increase rigour and reliability:

- Participatory data collection via visual surveys
- Network construction and mapping by using *Graph Commons*
- Visual and computational network analysis
- Workshops and interviews with network members for social construction and verification of the findings
- Content analysis of written reports by 18 network actors and testimonies of the future inhabitants using *Infranodus*.
- Synthesis

Data Collection: A visual survey was conducted to collect information from the human network actors, including the future inhabitants under social workers' guidance. This survey was designed as an easy to understand and inclusive tool which involved the identification of actor names, organizations, perceived roles and intensity of involvement (weight).

Mapping and Analysis of the co-creation process: We used the *Graph Commons* software (Arikan, 2021) to generate Actor Network maps including non-human actors. We visualized them using Force Atlas 2 Layout Algorithm based on the nodes and link weights collected (Figure 2). This analysis revealed the central and peripheral actors. Central actors were deeply integrated into the network, linked with human actors, participated in and facilitated numerous activities and methods to enable the project. Among those were researcher-architects (Aurelie) as well as social workers (Geraldine). The most exciting finding is the identification of centrality and central roles played by a future inhabitant (Jeremy), revealing the extent to end-user empowerment as a critical indicator of ADJ.

Network mapping helped us to identify the peripheral players, nodes at the edges of the network, whose involvement in the project was limited. This exercise revealed the end-users with limited participation. Some of these users were not sufficiently included and got disconnected from the project, and other ones joined later as replacements, showing the limits to ADJ in the project. Through this, we identified some of the methods and tools with low-impact, which were not so sufficient in enabling the engagement of network actors. These findings helped us to understand the co-creation process and evaluate the success of the methods and tools for empowerment. From a constructive perspective, peripheral nodes can be understood as potential edge actors to focus on to be integrated, resulting in the expansion of the network.

We took our analysis beyond visual graphs and used a computational method to identify two main types of centrality (degree and betweenness). Each of these methods analyzes the network actors' position and power from a different perspective (Wasserman and Faust, 1994). Centrality measures are indi-

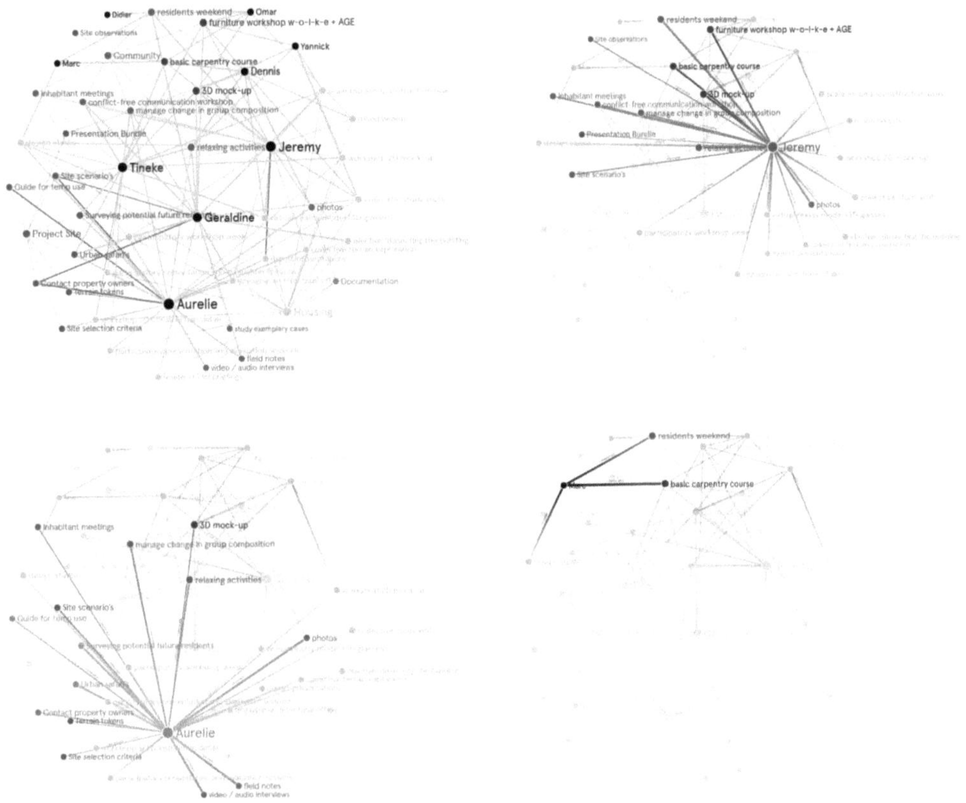

Figure 2
Actor-Network maps including non-human actors Using Force Atlas 2 Layout Algorithm based on the nodes and link weights collected.

cators of collaboration and cooperation, connectivity, and communication that are objectives of creating network structures.

We found that node-degree distribution follows a power law similar to real-world networks to which the Pareto principle applies (Figure 3). This principle stipulates that 'the vital few', 20% is responsible for 80% of the activities, and 'the trivial many', the 80% for only 20% of the outcomes. Through the Pareto analysis of the betweenness centrality of the actors, we quantified the top 20% of actors that were human, including a successful activity (residents' weekend). Integrating descriptive statistics such as the median, mode and the mean enabled us to rank the centralist of the actors. The method was also quite successful in identifying the peripheral actors.

Content analysis of the network actor reports: Following the ANT approach, we have considered declarative concepts in reports as participants of a network. We have collected a corpus of 18161 words written by eighteen network actors of the SMH project. This corpus also included transcribed verbal testimonies of the future inhabitants. Infranodus (2021) was employed for networked content analysis to research key concepts and generate insight. This tool made it possible to analyze the corpus text as a network to show the most relevant topics, their relations, and the structural gaps in-between to enable understanding and bridging the identified gaps (Figure 4). Reflecting the conceptual links made through text by the network actors, this analysis revealed the structural gaps between the topical clusters. This analysis also helped to identify the diversity of the discourse. The structural gaps in the graph indicated the *'parts of the discourse where the connections are lacking'* (Paranyushkin, 2019) therefore highlighting the areas to be improved and potential for new ideas. These results included suggestions to bridge the gaps which were aimed at by the project but not established sufficiently. Examples of these gaps were between the a) Brussels planning policy and the site-building process b) Brussels regional planning policy social housing and solidarity c) Brussels planning policy, the inclusion of people, and the time dimension. The identification of these also called for new roles for achieving these goals. It was interesting to see that the gaps in the text echoed the gaps in the realization of the project. The limitation of this analysis was that the body of text mainly represented the facilitating actors' declarative statements whereas the future inhabitants' statements were limited to individual testimonies, thus underrepresented.

Workshops and interviews: We have combined network mapping and analysis with structured interviews and two workshops for allowing negotiation and deliberation of the perceived links. These revealed the key intellectual assets; groups and individuals that can then become priorities for retention and efforts to spread their knowledge. It was important to recognize that co-design processes emerged from the interactions and dialogues of different actors, different forms of knowledge through different

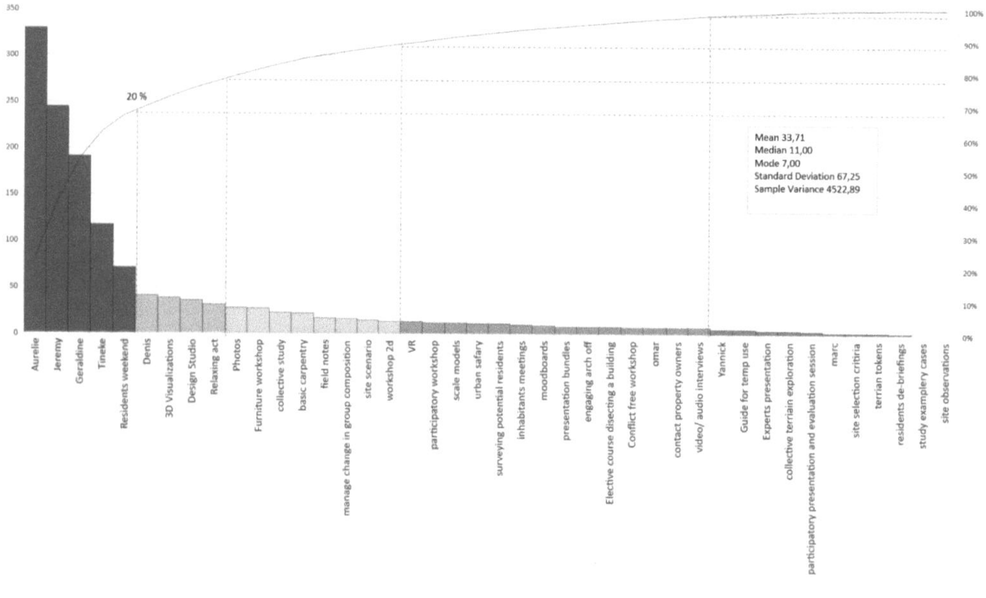

Figure 3 Betweenness Centrality Histogram Pareto Analysis to identify actor centrality in an algorithmic manner

Figure 4
Analysis of a corpus of 18161 words written by 18 network actors of the SMH project, including the transcribed verbal testimonies of the future inhabitants. This analysis revealed the structural gaps between the topical clusters where the connections are lacking and helped to identify the diversity of the project discourse.

communication platforms and interfaces.

Synthesis: Integrating the findings of network mapping, analysis with interviews and workshops helped us to identify various roles and their engagement intensity. **Human actor roles were identified by tracing and mapping the network through the following steps:**

- A paper-based survey with the partners to identify the roles they acknowledged in the project (rating engagement intensity).
- Field observation, analysing meeting minutes and e-mails between the partners, informal interviews to evaluate current collaboration patterns: this inquiry focuses on both reason for and frequency of interactions with a certain role.
- Generating detailed quantitative and visual summary of the informal network; this "roles map" provides an assessment of the quality and number of linkages between people and the collectively identified roles and spotlights people who generate critical insights (Krebs, 1996).
- Periodically resurveying the project partners and end-users to determine the attempts to improve communications flow and protect critical human assets. Creating longitudinal snapshots of the organization in relation to the projects created and monitoring the affordances of networked spatial design.
- Combining qualitative and quantitative network indicators (e.g. Degree Centrality, Betweenness Centrality, and Closeness Centrality, Network Centralisation, Network Reach, Network Integration, Boundary Spanners, Peripheral Players) to uncover knowledge communities, interactions organised by the community of knowl-

edge, tracking design idea and innovation flow between the actors.
- Focus group workshops with key network actors for consulting the results, improvement directions and actions to be taken through the 'roles network map'.

In the case of SMH the architectural design justice goal was to make a positive impact on the life of homeless people by co-creating transitional housing. Architectural design justice guides the partners to value the process in which the homeless people as the end-users become part of the project to ensure a more equitable distribution of the benefits and burdens of the project. It then requires meaningful participation, and recognition of the skills and knowledge from the partners, and the end-users of the spaces. The roles then emerge from this mentality of mediating, facilitating, interacting, learning, teaching, connecting, and guiding within this network. Three sectors were involved in the SMH project; social, academic, and architectural practices. The ALMA analysis revealed the following roles: **Process Manager**, **Team Caretaker**, **Project Coordinator**, **Design Studio teacher**, **Participatory Action Researcher**, **Practising Architect**, **Construction worker**, **Problem mediator**, **Interpreter**, **Interface with municipality**, **Interaction Designer**, **Skills Development Guide**, **Student, Facilitator**, **Neighbourhood Connector**, **Personal Development Guide**, **Network Connector**.

Many of the emerged roles rotated throughout the project and played by those who were able to take on the task. The responsibility to take on these tasks also grew according to the amount of time and dedication each actor made towards the project. The more the actor was involved in the project, the more roles the actor played. This also showed the importance each actor gave to solidarity beyond their individual gain. Some roles were not interchangeable since they required previous knowledge, like the practicing architect or construction worker, but most of the roles were roles that could be learned within the project.

4. CONCLUSIONS

Network analysis and mapping are potential ways to track the progress of the project in terms of design justice. These helped us to take necessary actions to improve the involvement of certain actors, leading to positive feedback loops. We found that interconnections between the human actors, participatory processes and co-creative tools can reveal their impact potential. The ALMA method helped to detect potential assets which are essential for ADJ practices and networks. Particularly, centrality measures were useful to identify powerful and important actors in a network. The analysis presented revealed the limits to community control of design processes and practices as well as limits to the conceptual links surrounding socio-spatial equality, thus limits to ADJ in the project.

In addition, our research revealed a plethora of new roles and agencies in bottom-up housing production. Actor Roles were essential to understand the dynamics and power distribution among the different actors. Therefore it was equally important to recognize that roles have an impact on the co-design processes that emerge from the dialogue and knowledge exchanges. From the results of the Network Analysis, we were able to capture the relations between the actors. These results were then used to develop the co-creation process itself, thus the spatial interventions. In this manner, the spatial interventions became a product of the network relationships and empowerment as well as the social-spatial product of Networked Spatial Practices. We believe that the revealed Actor Roles can inspire new agendas and agencies to be considered from a co-creative perspective and expand our understanding of housing as a collective practice. These can contribute to "changing how design practice is understood, developed and deployed." in other words "Design Futuring" as described by Fry (2009).

Employing ANT as a philosophical lens brought attention to the importance of design concepts and designed objects, and how aiming at maintaining ambiguity in the design can give a variety of "action possibilities" with the object. These enable and encourage actors to form new connections with the object, giving the actors to create their own unique relationship experience. Design concepts in networked practices should be flexible in order to provide room for diverse forms of co-creation and empowerment, and they should be assembled to communicate various narratives in one form (Aydemir et al., 2017). The findings of our study paralleled with former research on the inclusion of vulnerable social groups making them quite useful from a diversity engagement perspective (O'malley and Marsden, 2008, p.224).

We found that the power-law for the node degree distribution had serious implications for networked participatory design practices. The number of human and non-human actors involved in the design process exponentially increases the number of links and centrality of the key actors. This creates a potential load imbalance and puts too much stress on certain actors and activities (the vital few versus the trivial many). Therefore for co-creative bottom-up practices involving networks, it is quintessential to carefully design and monitor the number of actors to avoid burn-outs and overload for non-human actors.

Our analysis was limited to two snapshots in time. It will be repeated to monitor the changes in the roles and engagement intensity. This will help us understand the following stages in time with multiple phases and the involvement of a network of actors. Our study focused on the beginning phases of a building project: "design-before-use". However, the ALMA method can be extended to "design-in-use", layering and linking socio-spatial observations and appropriations. Such a map would deliver insights into the "social space" constructed. In the future, the ALMA method can be developed and tested further to understand and facilitate design justice by providing analyses of the power relations within the project. This can be accomplished by studying the interconnections to the participatory processes and co-creative tools, and understanding which links help create an inclusive and empowering environment for the participants. The ALMA method's strength is its potential to build causal relationships combining network analysis, workshops and interviews which enable the social deliberation and construction of knowledge. More experimentation on how to capture and analyze collective intelligence is needed to understand how projects can converge toward socio-culturally diverse and qualitative, equitable, common and resilient goals through networked practices.

This study provoked the question of **'who gets to design'** and the roles of human and non-human networks in design. Design within a network can easily become a decentralised practice. We are witnessing a wave of social and spatial innovations, where citizens and civil society are starting to claim their right to design. The SMH project is one of these innovative ventures which employed open co-design processes which reframed design as a distributed activity, also known as diffuse design, performed by everybody. This contrasts with expert design performed by those who have been trained as designers (Manzini, 2015). Design is power, but only those that have power get to decide which design is valorised. Once design is professionalized it becomes harder to create an inclusive vision of design as a universal human activity, which goes against the realities of the political economy of design (Costanza-Chock 2020). In order to enable systematically disadvantaged groups to get involved in design, there is a need for the agents to act in a critical manner. Designers should develop new ways to include the citizens and empower them to interact, experiment, share their narratives through architecture and (re-)create their living spaces with financial means, and knowledge capabilities.

The beneficial and unique characteristic of a networked practice is that the network actors can play a consortium of roles that are gathered depending on the skills needed to guide the project to its fruition according to the goals set by the client and building regulations. In financial profit-oriented practices, these goals are directed by financial gains directly or indirectly produced by the built project. In these standard architectural projects, several roles can be recognised: client, investor, architect, constructor, specialists, inspectors, and governmental officials. The decision structure in this case is determined by the financial provider and the local government. The difference between profit-driven projects based on a conventional top-down actor structure and a bottom-up project like SMH is that the goal is not advancing financial gains but to procure social impact and empowerment. This implicates a change in mentality that takes place towards solidarity, instead of individualized profit. In solidarity projects like SMH, the networked collaboration practice naturally arrives at a more democratic distribution of decision power among the consortium of project partners. A social-driven consortium is made up of actors interested in making a social impact, and therefore includes other types of professions such as; social workers, researchers, students, educators adding to professional roles, and allows for alternative roles to emerge. The collective intelligence of the networked practice is harvested and transferred through the novel and emergent roles (described in Section 3) following the collective goals set by the consortium.

Acknowledgements: this study was funded by a research project supported by the INNOVIRIS Brussels Research Agency: "Proof of Concept for the Solidary Mobile Housing Co-Creation Model and the Realized Housing Prototype (PoC SMH)" supervised by Burak Pak and Yves Schoonjans. This study is also funded by KU Leuven 3E181038 PhD Research Fund "Networked Spatial Practices" researcher: Rosie Romero supervised by Burak Pak. We would like to thank Aurelie de Smet, Geraldine Bruyneel, Tineke van Heesvelde and the inhabitants.

REFERENCES

Awan, N, Schneider, T and Till, J 2011, *Spatial agency: Other ways of doing architecture.*, Routledge, London

Aydemir, A, Pak, B and Scheerlinck, KS 2017 'The Role of Representations in Architectural Design Learning', *Architectural Research Addressing Societal Challenges: Proceedings of the EAAE ARCC*, Lisbon, pp. 1107-1113

Burke, A and Tierney, T 2009, *"Introduction": Network practices: new strategies in architecture and design*, Princeton Architectural Press, New York

Costanza-Chock, S 2020, *Design Justice: Community-Led Practices to Build the Worlds We Need*, The MIT Press

Fry, T 2009, *Design Futuring*, University of New South Wales Press, Sydney

Latour, B 2005, *Reassembling the Social: an Introduction to Actor-Network-Theory*, Oxford Univ. Press, Oxford

Manzini, E 2015, *Design, when everybody designs: An introduction to design for social innovation.*, MIT press

Miessen, M 2016, *Crossbenching*, Sternberg Press, Berlin

O'malley, AJ and Marsden, PV 2008, 'The analysis of social networks', *Health Serv Outcomes Res Method*, 8(224), p. 222–269

Pak, B and Aydemir, Z 2016 'Understanding the Verbal Concepts Appropriated by the Students in the Architectural Design Studio', *eCAADe 2016*, Oulu, p. 387

Paranyushkin, DP 2019 'InfraNodus: Generating Insight Using Text Network Analysis', *WWW '19: The World Wide Web Conference*, p. 3584–3589

Roach, C and Morgan, J 2010, *Networked Practices*, Lulu.com, USA

Robinson, RNS and Baum, T 2019, 'Work(ing) artefacts: Tools of the trade, totems or trophies?', *Sage Journals*, 73 issue: 2, pp. 165-189

De Smet, A, Pak, B and Schoonjans, Y 2019, 'Solidary Mobile Housing Live Project', in Boie, G, Boutsen, D, Fens, R, De Maeyer, G, Houttekier, B and Schamelhout, J (eds) 2019, *WTC Tower Teachings, reports from one and a half years of nomadic architecture education in Brussels*, KU Leuven Faculty of Architecture, Brussels, pp. 122-129

De Smet, A, Pak, B, Schoonjans, Y, Bruyneel, G and Vanlerberghe, K 2019, 'Wonen in de tussentijd als springplank naar een stabielere huisvestingssituatie', in Vandromme, T, Vermeir, V, Winters, S and Hubeau, B (eds) 2019, *Sociale huisvesting in Vlaanderen. Blikken naar de toekomst*, Oud-Tunhout / 's-Hertogenbosch: Gompel&Svacina, pp. 73-90

Wasserman, S and Faust, K 1994, *Structural analysis in the social sciences. Social network analysis: Methods and applications*, Cambridge University Press

Wigley, M and Burke, A 2007, *"Redefining network paradigms": new strategies in architecture and design*, Princeton Architectural Press, NY

[1] https://infranodus.com/

[2] https://graphcommons.com/

[3] http://www.orgnet.com/

[4] http://www.analytictech.com/networks/centrali.ht m

Towards Abductive Reasoning-Based Computational Design Tools

Using Machine Learning as a way to explore the combined design spaces of multiple parametric models

Adam Sebestyen[1], Johanna Rock[2], Urs Leonhard Hirschberg[3]
[1,3]Institute of Architecture and Media, Graz Universitya of Technology [2]Signal Processing and Speech Communication Laboratory, Graz University of Technology
[1,2,3]{Sebestyen|johanna.rock|hirschberg}@tugraz.at

Abductive Reasoning - reasoning based on experience - is important for design. This research tries to lay the groundwork for using Variational Autoencoders (VAE) - currently one of the most established deep learning architectures for generative modelling, a subfield of Machine Learning (ML) - as a way to support abductive reasoning in early design stages. While our research is still in its early stages, the first results look promising. In this paper we explain the current state of our research, its premises and methods, and discuss the results achieved thus far. We also explain the motivation behind our work and the potential we see in using VAE in this way and why we believe our approach could represent a paradigmatic shift in the way parametric models can be used in design.

Keywords: *Machine Learning, Parametric Design, Variational Autoencoders, Generative Modeling, Abductive Reasoning*

INTRODUCTION

Architectural Design is famously a "wicked problem", that is it involves too many conflicting criteria as to be solved analytically. This is one of the reasons why purely analytical approaches to design are insufficient. That experience plays an important role in design, has long been recognized, for example in the research on case-based reasoning in design (Maher et al, 1995). Nevertheless, to this day digital design tools, including CAD software, offer no means to reason from past experience. They tend to be at their best when they are used to tackle technical and engineering problems or to support detailing, in other words: during advanced design stages. In conceptual early design stages, however, most designers find them less helpful. This is often attributed to the rigidity of CAD models. In response to this problem, a growing number of architects opt to create their own custom tools, mostly through scripting or visual programming (Cudzik and Radziszewski, 2018). With their help it becomes possible to quickly try out different variations. The problem, and the reason why such models aren't used more widely, is that they are difficult to create. Setting up a useful parametric design model is in itself a design-challenge (Hovestadt et al., 2020, p 362). Therefore, most practices don't make use of parametric models in their early design stage workflows. This is a pity, as the early design stages are the time when testing variations would be most useful as it is also the time when the most consequential design decisions are made (As et al., 2018). The research described in this paper tries to achieve two things: to make it easier to benefit from past experience in design and at the same time to generate models that introduce the variability and flexibility of parametric models into early design stages. It is based on recent advances in Artificial Intelligence (AI) and Machine Learning (ML), which promise to open up novel and hands-on ways to support abductive reasoning - reasoning from experience.

Abductive reasoning and Machine Learning

Abductive reasoning - as opposed to inductive or deductive reasoning (logical and scientific reasoning) - is the reasoning based on experiences. Many have pointed out that it is essential for design. Cross goes so far as to argue that it is because of the process of abductive reasoning that "designing (is) one of the highest forms of human intelligence" (Cross, 2011, p 12). Cross mentions "...designers' reliance on what they regarded as 'intuition', and on the importance of an 'intuitive' approach." (Cross, 2011, p13). He states: "The concept of 'intuition' is a convenient, shorthand word for what really happens in design thinking. The more useful concept that has been used by design researchers in explaining the reasoning processes of designers is that design thinking is abductive." (Cross, 2011, p14). Similarly, Steinfeld argues that the lack of support for abductive reasoning is the reason why digital design tools are often limited for design use. "CAD software (has) been fashioned to support modes of reasoning only of secondary importance to design activity" (Steinfeld, 2017, p 590). According to Steinfeld, CAD software compels us to reason like a user rather than a designer: "Because a computer cannot see the way we see, they cannot help us to reason the way we wish to reason." (Steinfeld, 2017, p591). Steinfeld proposes that recent advances in the field of Artificial Intelligence may change this. He states that "Machine Learning (ML) is abductive in nature" due to pattern recognition by learning from previously seen data ("past experiences"). "As a model of computation that facilitates abductive reasoning" ML is more aligned with the process of human design thinking (Steinfeld, 2017, p592). Thus, through the implementation of ML, a viable design thinking tool based on abductive reasoning could be developed. This is what we are investigating in this research project. Currently our investigations are at a proof of concept stage and we deliberately focus on simple geometries and purely formal explorations. Issues of performance simulation and optimization that have been recognized as important topics in early design stage parametric explorations are not discussed in this paper. As these topics can also be addressed in an ML based approach (Sebestyen and Tyc 2020), we plan to incorporate them in the future.

Variational Autoencoders (VAE) and parametric design

Our approach is based on Variational Autoencoders (VAE), a well established deep learning algorithm for generative modelling. In a VAE, a neural network is trained to compress and afterwards recreate the input data of a large training set (Foster, 2019, pp 61-96). A good training set consists of thousands of related examples. In our research we use parametric models to create those very large training set. Parametric models are often described as having a so-called 'design space': the set of all possible parametric variations and its resulting geometries. The nature and variability of this design space is defined by the number and kind of parameters of the model. When a VAE is trained with a wide variety of instances of a parametric model, the result is what is referred to as the 'latent space'. Properly trained, the VAE can recreate the design space of the parametric model. In fact, one can navigate the latent space very much like the design space of a parametric model. A parametric model has a number of parameters, a latent space is characterized by its number of dimensions.

Parameters and dimensionalities bear some similarities, but due to the nature of the process (the encoding in a neural network will always retain some fuzziness) the mapping is never 1:1. The training of a neural network will not be able to replicate the exact parametrization of the training set. But depending on the dimensionality chosen and on the nature of the training set, the design space of the parametric model and the latent space of the VAE can be remarkably similar. Of course the recreation of a parametric model in a latent space would be somewhat pointless. However, the application of VAE algorithms becomes interesting the moment it is trained with a number of different parametric models. Now, the resulting latent space will actually contain solutions that weren't part of any predefined design spaces. It will still resemble a parametric model in the way it can be used to try out variations. But this variability will go beyond the variability of the individual models used as part of the training set. In other words, depending on the training set, VAEs can enable rather sophisticated design space explorations without the overhead of first having to define a complex parametric model. It thus potentially enables adaptation and re-use of previous designs as well as their fluid variation and exploration. This paper documents our first successful experiments with this approach.

Scope of this paper

This paper aims to contribute to ongoing AI research in the field of architecture and design by addressing the potential role of ML for understanding and manipulating 3D geometries. In particular, we use the Variational Autoencoder (VAE) to learn the makeup of 3D objects and use the learned representation to create new geometries. We focus on four main objectives:

1. We explore the capabilities of a Deep Neural Network (DNN) to detect and extract patterns in 3D design data. We show that one model can learn the object manifold of multiple object types and successfully recreate geometries from all learned distributions.
2. We show that semantic object information is contained in the learned object manifold and how this representation can be used to manipulate geometry through morphing the shapes inside the solution space of all possible combinations of geometrical components and transformations in order to create novel outputs.
3. We work exclusively with 3D data, i.e. a binary voxel grid, during the entire process. This ensures the incorporation of information along all three spatial dimensions in contrast to 2D images, i.e. pixels.
4. We present a viable workflow for creating vast amounts of data needed for training DNNs by utilizing classical parametric design tools.

RELATED WORK

Imdat As et al. (2018) recognize the need for an abductive reasoning tool during the early stage of design. They focus their tool on architectural functions rather than 3D shape creation. They implement neural networks based on graph theory to represent architectural assemblies. "We trained and used deep neural networks to evaluate existing designs encoded as graphs, extract significant building blocks as subgraphs and merge them into new compositions" (As et al., 2018, p 306). They further apply their methods to Generative Adversarial Networks (GANs) to generate new graphs representing novel architecture. However, the dataset the authors use is very small, consisting of only 15 Building Information Modeling (BIM) format design samples. Ren and Zeng (2020) aim to develop a workflow for 3D style transfer usable for architectural design. Similar to our project their focus lies on geometrical outputs represented as voxels. They outline a detailed workflow of all their steps and implement a case study where they apply their workflow to the redesign of the spire of Notre Dame De Paris. However, their method of 3D neural style transfer is based on existing 2D style transfer algorithms. Instead of performing a single 3D style transfer on the entire geometry the authors cut their geometry into multiple 2D horizontal sections and perform 2D style transfer on all those individual images, before recombining the newly created 2D outputs into a final 3D form. We speculate that such an approach of mixing 2D and 3D ML applications will not allow for the neural network to grasp the entirety of a 3-dimensional object. Özel (2020) focuses his work on the implementation of ML in the creation of concept sketches for the purpose of novel shape creation. He further points out the limitation of current design tools as being "linear and subservient to the architect's creativity and disciplinary zeitgeist" (Özel, 2020, p 104). His approach focuses on neural networks which solely process 2D pixel images. Generation of final 3D objects emerge through classical computational design methods by converting the ML 2D output into 3D geometry. Chaillou (2020) proposes ArchiGAN a GAN network that can produce floorplans in different scales: building footprint massing, program reparation, and furniture layout. By nesting these three tasks one after another with human interaction in between, he proposes a human AI workflow tandem. His work focuses solely on the creation of floorplans not taking vertical assemblies into account. The author also points out the limitation of producing 2D pixel images. Del Campo et al (2020) contemplate the meaning of the architectural "style" and about the possible implication the method of Natural Style Transferee (NST) could bring to the architectural discourse. The authors compare methods and applications of NST to the ones of GANs introducing two style transfer based architectural projects. Like Steinfeld (2017) they reference Google's Deep Dream Project [1] recognizing the potential for computers to create or as the authors put it "hallucinate" new forms of architecture. This could potentially lead to the "discovery of novel architectural opportunities dormant in its historical core matter and uncovered through the hallucinations of machines" (Del Campo et al. 2020, p 183). Wu et al (2017) focus on the task of 3D voxel object generation through the implementation of a 3D-GAN. Instead of rearranging subcomponents from different existing models their approach taps into a probabilistic latent space to generate new objects. In a similar manner to our project they explore the method of latent space manipulation. Smith et al (2017) extend the 3D-GAN training objective for improved and more robust training and Smith et al (2019) explore different geometric structures for representing 3D objects, namely voxels, point clouds and different mesh representations. Yang et al (2018) propose a special architecture for an Autoencoder that is able to reconstruct point cloud objects.

METHODOLOGY

Selecting a suitable ML architecture

Foster (2019, pp 1-30) explains the process of generative modeling regarding ML: "A generative model describes how a dataset is generated in terms of a probabilistic model. By sampling from this model, we are able to generate new data" (Foster, 2019, p1). This is done through the principle of representation learning: A high dimensional dataset - in our case 3D geometrical shapes - will be compressed into a more manageable low dimensional representation. This lower representation is called the 'latent space': "The power of representation learning is that it actually learns which features are most important for it to describe the given observation and how to generate these features from raw data...by tweaking the values of features in the latent space we can produce novel representations" (Foster, 2019, pp 25,26). Although there exist multiple ML approaches for generative modeling, we use a VAE (Kingma and Welling, 2014) for 3D shape creation: according to Foster, VAEs are one of the most established ML architectures for generative modeling. Further, the VAE mechanism is capable of providing semantically meaningful latent space representations, which allows manual latent space vector manipulation and therefore the creation of new geometries by the designer. An Autoencoder (AE) is a neural network composed of two parts: The encoder and the decoder. The encoder compresses a high dimensional input (3D object) into a lower dimensional latent space vector. The decoder reverses this process by decompressing the latent space vector back into the original higher dimensional representation (3D object reconstruction) (Forster, 2019). The VAE is an extension of this concept. It incorporates a regularization of the latent space, and thus enforces a meaningful representation of semantic features within that space. This enables us to generate new objects, with smooth transitions according to the underlying latent space vector manipulation, e.g. morphing between two shapes. This regularization is implemented by replacing the point encoding (AE) with a Gaussian encoding (VAE). Thus, the semantic representation in the latent space is regularized, such that it resembles a multivariate Gaussian distribution. During training, the latent vector is sampled from that latent distribution and decompressed by the decoder. This extension ensures that similar latent vectors produce similar outputs and thus enforce a semantically meaningful representation in the latent space and enable non-random object generation with realistic object characteristics.

Experiment Setup

Our experiment is a two-stage process: First, we generate multiple data sets of geometrical objects. This is done through classical parametric design. Each data set comprises objects from a combination of one basic object type (e.g. 'cube') and one geometric transformation (e.g. 'squeezed') which is applied to that basic object type. Each basic object type and each transformation is described by a specific set of parameters. Each sample in the data set is generated according to the same logic but with different, and randomly chosen, values for its parameters. Thus, objects in one set were generated through the same parametric script and therefore inherit the same rules of geometric modeling. Second, we feed the training data into the custom built VAE and begin the training process using gradient-based optimization. Through back propagation, the VAE learns how to compress the geometry into the latent space and how to correctly decompress the latent space back into a 3D representation (Kingma and Welling, 2014). After training is finished, we uncouple the encoder, remaining just with the latent space, and the decoder. In our experiment we aim to manipulate the latent space and observe if the decoded 3D geometry morphs its shape in a coherent, smooth and comprehensible way. We aim to combine different shapes in order to create new geometries. Through arithmetic operation within the latent space, we want to extract certain object characteristics, and apply them to different shapes. Thus, we aim to perform simple and semantic arithmetic for generating new geometries.

Data

There are six training sets consisting of 15000 geometries each: three datasets being based on a sphere and the remaining on a cube. Each object in any of the datasets is deformed by randomly scaling in the X,Y, and Z directions. Four of those datasets are further modified by applying one of two geometrical operations to the objects. One geometrical operation squeezes or expands the geometry at its midsection (in the horizontal plane) often producing shapes roughly resembling a sand clock. The second geometrical operation performs a Boolean Difference between the geometry and a cylinder lying in the horizontal plane producing a round cutout. The magnitude of the squeeze and the size of the subtracted cylinder are random in a given range. The dataset consists of:

1. deformed spheres with midsection squeeze/expansion
2. deformed cubes with midsection squeeze/expansion
3. deformed spheres with cylindrical cutout
4. deformed cubes with cylindrical cutouts
5. deformed cubes without further manipulation (basic shape)
6. deformed spheres without further manipulation (basic shape)

All datasets are parametrically created with SideFX's 'Houdini' [2]. The software is automated to produce random variables (for scale in X,Y,Z, and if necessary for the squeeze or cutout factor) and apply those as the input parameters of the geometries. Afterwards the objects are fitted inside a normalized volume to ensure all shapes occupy the same spatial domain. In the next step the geometries are voxelized based on a 32 x 32 x 32 grid inscribed in the bounding volume. Finally, each voxelized geometry is exported as a CSV file and afterwards combined into a hdf5 file using a custom python convertor script. Before training, each dataset is labeled according to which basic shape it was based on ('sphere' or 'cube') and what additional geometrical operation was applied to it ('squeeze', 'cutout', 'none'). Figure 1 shows four example geometries. We deliberately chose a small amount of very basic parametric models, however we expect that a succsefull ML algorithm could be sucsefully extended to to more convoluted geometries.

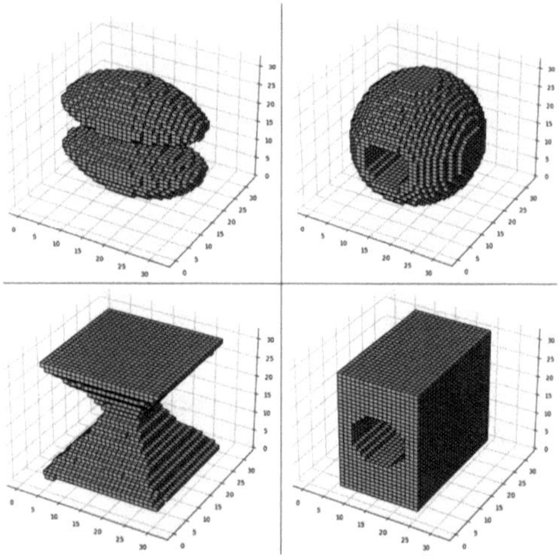

Figure 1
A selection of four shapes generated for training the VAE network

VAE setup and training

The VAE architecture we used in our experiments is shown in Figure 2. The encoder and decoder are symmetric and consist of multiple layers with 3D convolutions/deconvolutions and LeakyReLU activation functions. Binary 3D voxel grids with size 32 x 32 x 32 (= 32768 data points) are used as inputs and outputs; they contain the 3D object representation. The encoder and the decoder consist of four layers each and they are connected by a fully connected layer, i.e. the latent space. During training, the encoding (latent vector) is sampled from the latent mean and variance. This encoding is the basis for reconstructing the input through the decoder. During sample generation, the latent vector is sampled, or manually manipulated, before reconstruction. Through manipulating the latent space, specific characteristics can be incorporated in the newly created 3D output shape. We split all data sets in training, validation and test sets. We use the training sets for learning the network weights, the validation sets for early stopping and a performance estimate, and the test sets for the evaluation itself. For network training, we use the Adam optimizer (Foster, 2019) and a weighted Binary Cross Entropy Loss between input and reconstructed output. The weight is set to 2.5 in order to compensate for the imbalance of occupied and unoccupied voxels in the 3D data. We optimize for 50 epochs with a batch size of 64 samples. The VAE was trained with all six datasets at the same time. This enables the model to learn a multi-object manifold including common characteristics between multiple object types and their relations. We believe that this holistic training approach is essential for the VAE to find truly novel shapes, since training on the individual data sets would merely produce geometries form the same solution space as the corresponding parametric script. However, by using all data sets jointly during training, we can find a ruleset that encompasses the rules of all scripts.

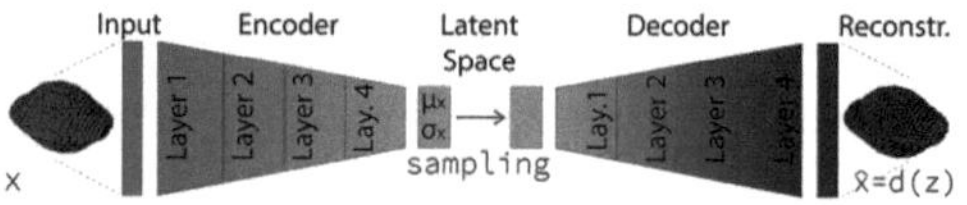

Figure 2
Block diagrammatic representation of the Variational Autoencoder as used in this work

EVALUATION

Validating VAE reconstruction capabilities

We train multiple VAE architectures with differing latent space dimensions and hyper-parameters. We select the best variants with latent space sizes of 4, 10, and 40 for the evaluation of this work. To ensure that the VAE has successfully learned to encode the 3D shapes into the latent space and to decode that representation back into a 3D shape with sufficient quality, we evaluate the reconstruction capability, i.e. the accuracy. The accuracy is calculated by encoding and subsequently decoding the test set geometry. The accuracy of correctly reconstructed voxels is computed sample-wise and averaged over all test set sample geometries. The best performing VAE with a latent space size of 4 haa a reconstruction accuracy of 98.9%. For the model with latent space sizes 10 and 40 these are 99.8 % and 99.9 %, respectively. Figure 3 shows original geometries and the reconstructed geometries using the latent space of size 4 and 10.

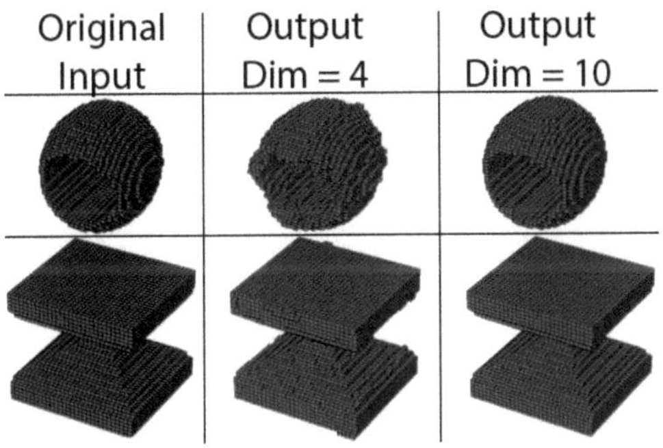

Figure 3
Validation of the VAEs capability to encode and decode geometry: Original geometries (red) and reconstructed geometries with latent space sizes 4 & 10 (blue)

Combining geometries by averaging within the latent space

Our aim is to average two latent space vectors in order to obtain a new latent space vector, which yields a new geometry hybrid not found in the original data sets. A pair of geometries is manually chosen from the test set and decoded into the latent space. The statistical mean of these two vectors is used with the decoder network to create the new geometry. All three models are able to reconstruct a reasonable shape, however the lower reconstruction accuracy for the small latent space model leads to slightly less clean outputs. Figure 4 shows the original geometry pair and their newly created combination using the latent space of size 40.

Combining geometries by morphing within a reduced latent space using PCA dimensionality reduction

Principal Component Analysis (PCA) is a popular method for dimensionality reduction of high dimensional data points (Géron, 2019, p213-243). This is achieved by finding linear combinations of the original features, that best describe the data. By selecting only the most descriptive of these new features, the dimension can be reduced. The data points are projected to the new (smaller) subspace, such that the approximation loss is as small as possible. We project our latent space using PCA onto a 2 dimensional hyperplane, thus the reduced latent space is represented by only two variables. We select two starting geometries, encode them into the latent space and further project that onto the reduced latent space. Then, we morph each of the two variables of the reduced latent space between the values of the two starting geometries. The newly created vectors in the reduced latent space are transformed back into latent space and decoded by the model to produce the new 3D geometries. The result is a 2D grid which produces multiple mixtures and thus novel geometry of 2 chosen geometrical shapes. However, latent space information is partially lost during the PCA approximation. Thus, this method only seems applicable to smaller latent space models. Figure 5 shows the grid arrangement of morphing between two geometries using the latent space of size 4.

Manipulating single and multiple latent space variables

Although the process of morphing between two existing geometries produces novel ones, we believe that the true potential of the VAE based shape creation lies in more precise control of the latent space manipulation. We are interested to see if the learned relationship of how the data is mapped into latent space resembles geometrical properties of the 3D shapes and whether the latent space representation

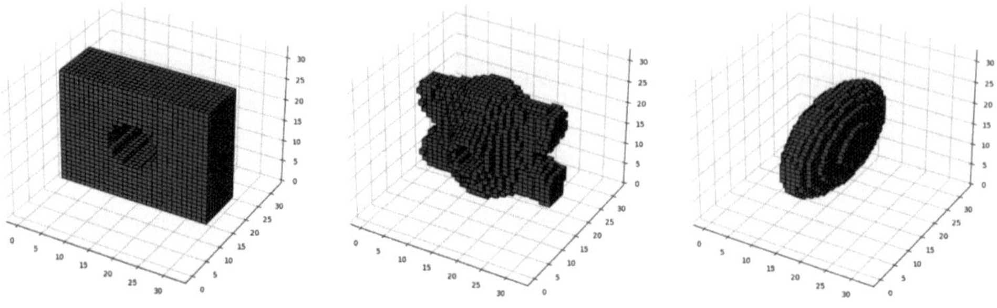

Figure 4
Morphing between two geometries: Starting objects (red) and reconstruction of their statistical mean in the latent space (green)

is intuitive and logical to a human designer. In this experiment, we select a geometry from the test set and encode it into latent space. Then, we gradually manipulate a single variable in the latent space and observe the changes in geometry. As expected, changing a single variable for the model of latent space size 4 produces more significant changes in geometry than manipulating a single latent variable of the model with latent space size 40. If a designer would prefer a novel geometry closely resembling the original one a high latent space VAE would be recommended and for significant geometrical changes a low latent space model is beneficial. A latent space of size 10 provides us a good balance of producing novel geometry still resembling some visual character to the original shape. Figure 6 shows the reconstruction output, when gradually manipulating a single variable in latent space from the minimum to the maximum value from the training set. For this specific object, the manipulated variable controls the porosity of the cube's midsection. Decreasing its value leads to a dissolving of geometry while increasing its value leads to a denser voxel agglomeration. As an extension to this experiment, we gradually change two latent space variables at the same time. This produces extreme changes in the output, which most likely results from the change being uncorrelated. Visually observing the reconstructions, we find that the VAE model assigns geometrical properties to latent space variables in a (to us humans) unintuitive, and for larger latent space models seemingly arbitrary, way. Meaning, that although this approach can provide a tool for the discovery of novel geometry, there is a surprise element to the newly produced outputs.

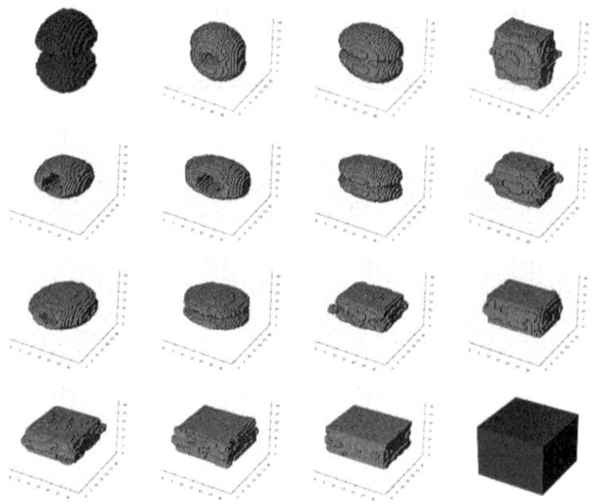

Figure 5
Morphing two objects through dimensionality reduction using PCA: Two starting geometries (red) and novel geometries (yellow) along the two principal components of the compressed latent space

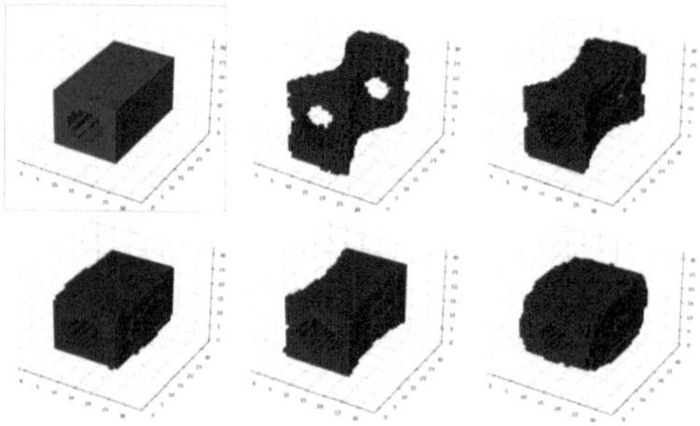

Figure 6
Morphing one object through the manipulation of a single latent space variable of the starting geometry (red) results in novel geometries (purple)

Figure 7
Semantic operations using latent space arithmetic: 'Squeezed Cube' - 'Regular Cube' + 'Regular Sphere' = 'Squeezed Sphere'

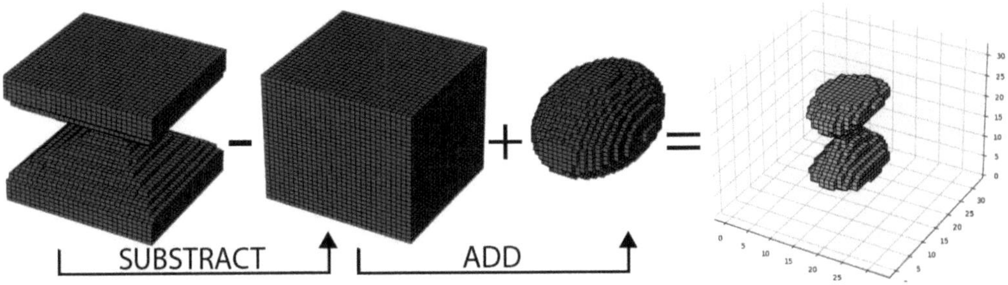

Semantic operations using latent space arithmetic

"One of the advantages of using representation learning is that we can perform operations within the more manageable latent space that affect high-level properties of the image" or in our case the voxel representation (Foster, 2019, p 44). Foster further explains: "One benefit of mapping images into a lower-dimensional space is that we can perform arithmetic on vectors in the latent space" (Foster, 2019, p 113). In the previous experiments we generated new geometry by linearly combining or manually manipulating single or multiple variables inside the latent space. In this experiment, we aim to extend these arithmetic operations for latent space manipulation in order to perform targeted semantic operations. In principle, we want to extract semantic concepts and apply these concepts to other shapes generating new ones. Since the latent space represents the semantics of all learned objects, we perform basic arithmetic operations on the latent space in order to extract, i.e. subtraction, these semantics and to apply them to other representations, i.e. addition. Such a semantic operation could be: 'cube with hole' - 'cube' + 'sphere' = 'sphere with hole'. Note, that the operation directly corresponds to latent space vector arithmetic. Figure 7 shows such a semantic operation, producing a squeezed sphere by first extracting the concept of a squeeze-transformation ('squeezed cube' - 'cube') and applying this concept to another object (+ 'sphere').

CONCLUSION

We successfully trained a VAE with geometries generated from multiple parametric design scripts. Based on a data set comprising multiple object types, we are able to produce novel geometries that do not belong to the target space of a single parametric design script. Thus we created inter object geometry hybrids. Producing those using parametric design models would require more complex logic which does not scale well to a multitude of diverse geometries. We compared multiple models with different latent space complexities and highlighted differences in (1) their reconstruction performance and (2) their suitability for a targeted creation of new geometries. We showed how the latent space can be manipulated: by combining different objects, by changing specific variables, and even by semantic arithmetic operations in the latent space. All these manipulations led to new geometries, whereas the influence over the new geometry by the designer differs. The use of ML models in the design process raises the question whether a future designer, working with an established ML workflow, spends more time designing training data rather than the final object itself. This paper is a starting point for a ML tool which gives the designer the possibility to combine different pieces of work produced through parametric design, and thus control and discover new, more complex geometry from the combined solution space of the entire data set. In future work, we want to use a more diverse and complex set of parametric scripts in order to create novel and convoluted geometries.

We also want to consider other geometrical representations, such as meshes and point clouds, which would reduce the computational complexity and enable us to work with larger shapes and more details. Furthermore, we are interested in using other generative models, such as GANs.

REFERENCES

As, I, Pal, S and Basu, P 2018, 'Artificial intelligence in architecture: Generating conceptual design via deep learning', *International Journal of Architectural Computing*, 16, pp. 306-327

del Campo, M, Manninger, S and Carlson, A 2020, 'A Question of Style', in Yuan, PF, Xie, M, Leach, N, Yao, J and Wang, X (eds) 2020, *Architectural Intelligence: Selected Papers from the 1st International Conference on Computational Design and Robotic Fabrication (CDRF 2019)*, Springer, Singapore, pp. 171-188

Chaillou, S 2020, 'ArchiGAN: Artificial Intelligence x Architecture', in Yuan, PF, Xie, M, Leach, N, Yao, J and Wang, X (eds) 2020, *Architectural Intelligence: Selected Papers from the 1st International Conference on Computational Design and Robotic Fabrication (CDRF 2019)*, Springer, Singapore, pp. 117-127

Cross, N 2011, *Design Thinking: Understanding How Designers Think and Work*, Berg Publishers, Oxford ; New York

Cudzik, J and Radziszewski, K 2018 'Artificial Intelligence Aided Architectural Design', *Proceedings of eCAADE 2018*, Lodz, pp. 77-84

Foster, D 2019, *Generative Deep Learning: Teaching Machines to Paint, Write, Compose, and Play*, O'Reilly Media, Sebastopol, CA

Géron, A 2019, *Hands-On Machine Learning with Scikit-Learn, Keras, and TensorFlow: Concepts, Tools, and Techniques to Build Intelligent Systems, 2nd Edition*, O

Hovestadt, L, Hirschberg, U and Fritz, O 2020, *Atlas of Digital Architecture*, Birkhäuser

Kingma, DP and Welling, M 2014 'Auto-Encoding Variational Bayes', *ICLR*

Maher, ML, Balachandran, MB and Zhang, DM 1995, *Case-Based Reasoning in Design*, Lawrence Erlbaum Ass, Publishers, Mahwah, NJ

Ren, Y and Zeng, H 2020 'The Spire of AI - Voxel-based 3D Neural Style Transfer', *Proceedings of eCAADE 2020*, Bangkok, pp. 619-628

Sebestyen, A and Tyc, J 2020 'Machine Learning Methods in Energy Simulations for Architects and Designers - The implementation of supervised machine learning in the context of the computational design process', *Proceedings of eCAADe 2020*, Berlin, pp. 613-622

Smith, EJ, Fujimoto, S, Romero, A and Meger, D 2019 'GEOMetrics: Exploiting Geometric Structure for Graph-Encoded Objects', *Proceedings of the 36th International Conference on Machine Learning*, Long Beach, CA, pp. 5566-5876

Smith, EJ and Meger, D 2017 'Improved Adversarial Systems for 3D ObjectGeneration and Reconstruction', *1st Conference on Robot Learning (CoRL 2017*, Mountain View, USA

Steinfeld, K 2017 'Dreams May Come', *ACADIA 2017: DISCIPLINES + DISRUPTION*, Cambridge, MA, pp. 590-599

Wu, J, Zhang, C, Xue, T, Freeman, WT and Tenenbaum, JB 2017 'Learning a Probabilistic Latent Space of Object Shapes via 3D Generative-Adversarial Modeling', *NIPS 2016*, Barcelona

Yang, Y, Feng, C, Shen, Y and Tian, D 2018 'FoldingNet: Point Cloud Auto-Encoder via Deep Grid Deformation', *Proceedings of the IEEE Conference on Computer Vision and Pattern Recognition (CVPR)*, pp. 206-215

Özel, G 2020, 'Interdisciplinary AI: A Machine Learning System for Streamlining External Aesthetic and Cultural Influences in Architecture', in Yuan, PF, Xie, M, Leach, N, Yao, J and Wang, X (eds) 2020, *Architectural Intelligence: Selected Papers from the 1st International Conference on Computational Design and Robotic Fabrication (CDRF 2019)*, Springer, Singapore, pp. 103-116

[1] http://ai.googleblog.com/2015/06/inceptionism-going-deeper-into-neural.html
[2] https://www.sidefx.com/

Techno-Anthropological Inquiry into VDC Impact on Expert Collaboration in the AEC Industry

Interdisciplinary interactions through Virtual Design and Construction (VDC)

Kristine Slotina[1], Michael U. Hensel[2], Eilif Hjelseth[3]
[1]Norwegian University of Science and Technology (NTNU) and Nordic – Office of Architecture [2]Dep. Digital Architecture and Planning, Faculty of Architecture and Planning, Vienna University of Technology [3]Norwegian University of Science and Technology (NTNU)
[1]krisslot@stud.ntnu.no [2]hensel@iemar.tuwien.ac.at [3]eilif.hjelseth@ntnu.no

In the architecture, engineering and construction industry (AEC) the transfer of knowledge and information through sharing, cooperation and collaboration serves to manage the inherent complexity of projects. Inter- and transdisciplinary teams including architects, engineers, consultants, contractors, suppliers and building owners, require shared design processes and understanding. Virtual Design and Construction (VDC) is part of how architectural information and knowledge is transferred through integrated processes. As part of an ongoing research this conference paper employs a Techno-Anthropological perspective to map existing research on the subject, to identify research gaps and to suggest further research. Given the ongoing changes the AEC industry is undergoing, we believe that Techno-Anthropology can contribute to systematic analysis and understanding of human-technology interactions. This research examines how VDC impacts upon the output of processes and how it affects the way interdisciplinary teams in AEC industry conceptualize and configure outputs.

Keywords: *Techno-Anthropology, Virtual Design and Construction (VDC), Building Information Modelling (BIM), knowledge transfer, collaboration, configurability*

INTRODUCTION

Building projects require collaboration between expert groups in the AEC industry. If important items that are known to one expert are not identified by others, it can lead to problems in the design process and the delivery of a building project (Andrule Slotina, Kristine, 2014). The successful transfer of knowledge requires experts to immerse themselves in the thinking processes of the other experts (Puonti, 2004) and requires that knowledge is transferred through sharing, cooperation and collaboration (Blau 2011). The newest framework to facilitate the processes of sharing, cooperation and collaboration as well as information and knowledge transfer is VDC with one of its main technologies - Building Information Modelling (BIM). VDC is a communication framework for AEC industry experts that uses BIM technology.

Drawing upon previously conducted field studies and an ongoing PhD study with a focus on the impact of VDC implementation in architectural building projects, this conference paper employs a Techno-Anthropological inquiry to examine the existing research done on the subject in order to identify the research gap and further research questions.

This research takes critical distance from the everyday work of architects and looks at it from a broader Techno-Anthropological perspective. As Børsen and Botin (2013) pointed out, the nature of a Techno-Anthropological investigation is threefold: (a) to get a sense of existing and/or different expert cultures and how they are shaped by technology; (b) to analyze and understand the nature of the technologies in use; and (c), to identify any transitional, transformational and hybrid spaces that may be created as a result of such an engagement (see figure 1). In this case the existing expert cultures in AEC industry and the nature of BIM technology within VDC framework.

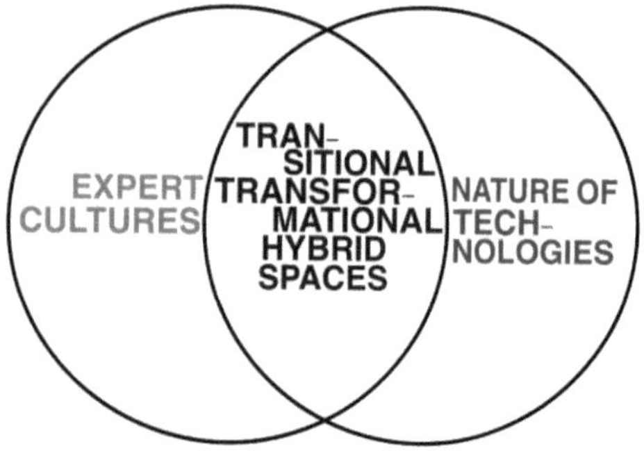

Figure 1 Techno-Anthropology

This paper aims to recognize the research gap and identify whether and how VDC impacts on expert collaboration in the AEC sector, as well as whether it could affect the way architects conceptualize and configure outputs.

CURRENT STATE OF THE ART

Two main thematic strands of literature are related to this topic and require closer examination. The first strand concerns expertise and expert cultures in architecture and its related fields, while the second strand concerns information systems, and more specifically BIM technology within VDC framework.

Expert cultures in Architecture

The work of Puonti (2004), Brown & Duguid (2001), Haldin-Herrgard (2000), Blau (2011) is drawing from the fields of organizational sociology, learning in organizations and information technology. The strength of these studies is that they bring to the fore the social context of knowledge acquisition and differentiate between explicit and tacit knowledge. Tacit knowledge being the individual experiences and talents that is difficult to code and transfer to another person and the explicit knowledge being the managed and shared knowledge through reports, documentation, lectures etc. (Haldin-Herrgard, 2000). This difference is useful for understanding the knowledge exchange processes. Knowledge includes information, skills, explanations and understandings someone possesses. To transfer knowledge successfully it requires to immerse oneself into the thinking processes of the other (Puonti, 2004) and requires that knowledge is transferred through sharing, cooperation, and collaboration (concepts from Blau 2011). Consideration of the social context of knowledge acquisition is relevant for this paper because the exchange of information and knowledge is the basis for the collaboration processes.

Furthermore, there exists a growing amount of research on the expert cultures that are specific to the disciplines of architecture and engineering (Schön,

1984; Murphy, 2005; Tanggaard, 2013; Gade et al., 2019; Van der Linden, Dong and Heylighen, 2019). One line of research is based on the understanding that architects imagine and create buildings as a result of the collaborative processes with clients, consultants and contractors, while considering the social and physical surroundings as part of their everyday work (Murphy, 2005). Tanggaard (2013) stated that "creativity is an everyday phenomenon resulting in continual processes of 'making world' (p.20)". While Schön (1984) suggests that designing is the making of representation of things to be built.

The creative part of architecture affects the communication between experts in the AEC industry. Most architects communicate not only through written or spoken word, but also through drawings. Most of the time architectural talking/drawing communication cannot be separated, because talking and drawing on their own only represent partial meaning. Schön (1984) calls this type of talking and drawing the *language of designing*.

The paper architect often draws while talking. This form of operating can be described as the material part of creativity. We believe that "the paper" has partially been replaced / supplemented by the new technologies like Building Information Modelling. Without the materials that surround them, the architects' performance and creativity cannot be fully explored (Tanggaard 2013).

Creativity is an important aspect of an architect's expertise, but not the only one. Being recognized and acknowledged by clients and the architectural community is important too because expertise is confirmed by this community. The challenge for architects and those involved in the designing, building and construction processes is in merging the two worlds - the technical and artistic to create a building to the satisfaction of all.

Information Systems related to Architecture and VDC

Technology has been described as being something external to humans and society. However, the increase of technology in today's society draws attention to how much people are in fact entangled with it and that today's humans are part of a technological civilization (Bauchspies, Croissant and Restivo, 2005). In the mid-1960s, computer-aided design (CAD) technology emerged, later bringing along BIM technology and framework to facilitate Virtual Design and Construction.

For years, the main problem in the construction industry has been poor quality of information sharing and communication amongst the design teams (Crotty, 2012). The BIM technology promises to solve these issues by adding information to the building information models and enabling the information and communication flow freely between different design groups (Crotty, 2012).

Al Hattab and Hamzeh (2018) stated that "using BIM as production tool does not explicitly improve workflow or achieve the full potential unless fundamental conditions are present, namely collaboration and changes in traditional mindsets". Frameworks like VDC are attempting to improve the effectiveness of the technological turn in the construction industry. The main principles of VDC are to use multi-disciplinary virtual models that are computer enabled descriptions of the projects and integrate those to support explicitly the objectives of the project and the client (Kunz and Fischer, 2020).

Summary of a current State of the Art

All elements of a successful construction project including the VDC framework are a part of a larger picture. VDC is not designed to help architects communicate their expertise better or to explicitly improve collaboration between AEC industry experts but might indirectly improve it or lead towards it. VDC is there to structure and abstract the necessary information out of data, knowledge out of information and a useful application/utility out of knowledge to be able to achieve the explicit objectives of the individual project.

Glick (2013) positions knowledge in between data and information on the one hand and utility on the other, and points out an increasing gap between the two over time. (See Figure 2) It requires abstraction to gain knowledge from information. Abstraction serves the purpose of generalization so that insights can be used for broader sense making of the information produced.

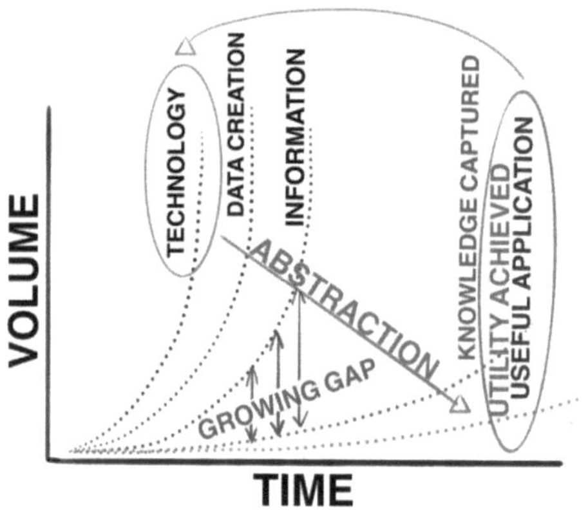

Figure 2
Intepretation of Glick (2013)

As more and more technology get created not because of the 'human needs' but because of the technological development itself, modern technology over-speeds the 'human needs' as the human culture begins to lag behind the technological development and blurs the technological means and human objectives (Børsen and Botin, 2013). We suggest that technology creation therefore is not only part of the utility achieved, but also becomes an entity of itself with its own evolution.

While VDC framework contributes to the effectiveness of the technological turn in the construction industry and contributes to the abstraction of the knowledge and therefore bridges 'the growing gap', it also contributes to more information, data generation and technology development.

METHODS

For the research discussed in this paper three main methods were deployed:

(1) initial field observation on VDC course at NTNU (January 2021), (2) extensive literature review, (3) visualisation of bibliometric networks for the purpose of analysis and initial research gap identification.

This paper reflects upon the necessity to do further research on the implications of the VDC implementation and how that effects the sharing, collaboration and communication processes within an architectural project using Techno-Anthropological methods. Techno-Anthropology is a new direction in Science Technology studies that draws from humanities and engineering, science research (Jensen, 2013). Methods that support techno-anthropological investigations place value on understanding the nature of communities, tools and cultural practices and making sense of the life-worlds of people. Typically, this requires that researchers immerse themself in the community, engage in conversations and observe the interactions. The first step of anthropological research is the formulation of a theoretical problem (Bernard, 2011). To achieve that one needs to emerge oneself in the communities one intends to research.

As the first step in this process, the NTNU VDC course / community of practice (Hjelseth & Fisher, 2021) was observed. That enabled a better overview of the Virtual Design and Construction Framework principles and the current state of the art.

Furthermore, a quantitative method was used by way of visualisation of bibliometric networks through the VOS viewer software (Eck, N. J. and Waltman, L., 2010). This was done with the aim to identify the main subject areas that are being researched, as well as scientific articles related to VDC framework implementation. As the results on 'Virtual Design and Construction' term was relatively low, additional analysis was done on 'Building Information Modeling' (BIM) being the main technology used in VDC Framework. This conference paper uses the definition of Building Information Modeling being the technology used in the VDC framework. Kunz and Fischer (2020) describes that "Building Information Modelling (BIM) focuses on the building physical elements of the VDC", whilst the VDC framework brings in performance, organisational and process interactions to address the management issues.

Based on the bibliometric analysis and the research done in 2014 (Andrule Slotina, Kristine, 2014) a manual and more detailed literature review was undertaken, as well as a manual review of the relevant previous eCAADe conference papers and presentations were examined to gain an overview of the conference scope. The manual search used terms like 'Virtual Design and Construction', 'Building Information Modeling', 'Knowledge exchange in architecture', 'Knowledge transfer in architecture', 'Collaboration processes in architecture' and 'integrated processes in architecture'.

RESULTS

VDC courses at NTNU act as Community of Practice

Norwegian University of Science and Technology (NTNU) has in collaboration with Stanford Center for Professional Development completed a one-year VDC-certification course (2019-2020) with 200 students from the entire AEC industry. The course was organized with one mentor for a class of 20 students. The 10 mentors, who all where AEC industry experts, established a community to share practice. Both students and mentors were from all areas of a construction project - contractors, clients, engineers, the public sector, private sector etc. All these discipline experts come together to learn to use VDC framework for implementation in their expertise area. The outcome of this course has been better than ordinary courses with 20 students from one company (Hjelseth & Fischer, 2021). These results has been explained by the Community of Practice theories (Wenger, McDermott and Snyder, 2002). Implementing solutions in their own practices is a significant aspect in this type of course. Knowing that you are part of a "community" increases confidence to do changes in practice (Hjelseth & Fischer, 2021). Hjelseth & Fischer (2021) suggests that getting feedback from mentors and fellow students reduces the risk of failure and increases the impact to the changes in the established practice. Architect profession had relatively low representation in comparison to the rest of the industry. Limited awareness of the architect's role in VDC might be one explanation. By attending the course, the first insights of the community were made.

Kunz and Fischer (2020) explains that "VDC framework includes explicit target and measured client/business objectives, Product design as a Building Information Model (BIM), Organisation design and Process models of the tasks to do design, construction, commissioning and operations. [..] These iterative Plan, Do, Check tasks take place in the multidisciplinary Integrated Concurrent Engineering (ICE) collaboration process." (Kunz and Fischer, 2020)

VOS viewer - Web of Science analysis

After the observation period at the NTNU, a VOS viewer analysis was made to visualise the bibliometric networks and identify the initial gaps in research done on VDC framework implementation. The first term that was searched for and visualized was:

"Virtual Design and Construction, -2021" VOS viewer analysis. Limited research was found on the term Virtual Design and Construction. There were only 53 research results found in all time Web of Science data. The bibliometric network analysis is using the abstracts of the research found (filtering out terms appearing less than three times) and illustrating the most common text found in these abstracts. Even the term 'Virtual Design and Construction' itself did not pass criteria 'for the term to be repeated more than three times' and was filtered out. The closest terms to the 'Virtual Design and Construction' that passed the criteria was 'VDC Practice' and 'VDC task'.

53 research results done on the subject is relatively low for identifying research clusters, therefore a further analysis was done. In the NTNU course observations it was recognised that digital support is the basis for the VDC framework. BIM technology is what supports this need. As this research is using Techno-Anthropological perspective to inquire in the expert cultures and the nature of technologies re-

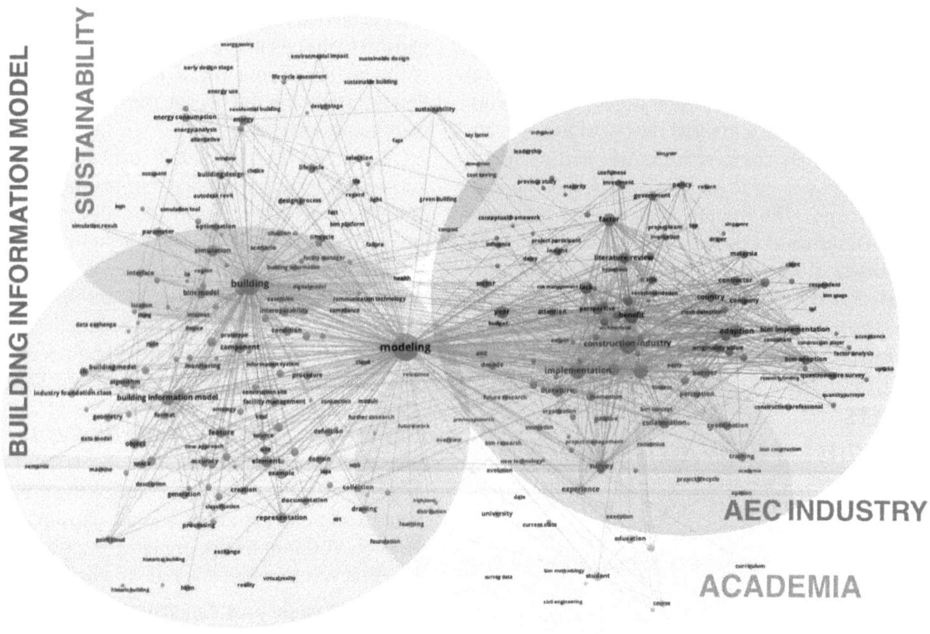

Figure 3
Map for a term 'Building Information Modeling' most common terms

lated to VDC framework, further analysis was done on the term 'Building Information Modeling' as the technology used in Virtual Design and Construction Framework.

"Building Information Modelling, 2013-2021" VOS viewer analysis. The visualisation was created from 1181 results found from 2013 to 2021. The year 2013 was chosen as that is the year Andrule Slotina, Kristine (2014) did the last extensive literature review on the same topic MSc Thesis research. The bibliometric network in the figure 3 is illustrating the most common keywords found in the abstracts.

The bibliometric network was further analysed by mapping the four clusters that arose during the analysis - 'Building information model', 'Sustainability', 'AEC industry' and 'Academia'. AEC industry and Academia clusters displayed the most overlap. Building information cluster shared overlaps with all other clusters. Sustainability cluster was most remote. AEC industry cluster was intertwined with Academia cluster through collaboration, integration, development processes. One might expect integrated processes like VDC, expertise or HCI (human-computer-interaction) studies to be present here. Neither seem to be present in the bibliometric analysis of Building Information Modeling.

Review of selected papers

As described in the Methods section a more manual and detailed analysis was done. The selected papers points to similar research gap as intended research and/or are relevant in the context of this research.

eCAADe. There were two papers in the previous eCAADe conferences addressing the BIM implementation in the architectural offices and the affects it has (Abdelhameed (2006) & Hermund (2009)). Abdelhameed (2006) suggests that CAD systems do not have a significant role on the initial shapes that are designed with traditional methods. Abdelhameed (2006) also claims that the CAD systems can in fact help the form creation, though they are not created for that purpose at the moment. Hermund (2009) expands further by suggesting that compulsory implementation of Building Information Modeling in the architectural practices, more linear and systematic working methods are promoted and therefore creative loops reduced. Hermund (2009) recommends to consider carefully the BIM method implementation. He challenges the AEC industry to explore other alternatives to keep the architectural value/quality: "to create meaningful and beautiful spaces for real people." Both authors suggest AEC industry to explore the processes further, but do not mention integrated frameworks like VDC.

Gade, P. N. et al. (2019) 'A holistic analysis of a BIM-mediated building design process using activity theory'. This paper is included as it has a holistic review of the BIM-mediated building processes. It recognizes the limited research done on an in-depth and holistic analysis of how BIM is used in the design processand attempts to provide that. Gade, P. N. et al. (2019) also indicate that "other studies have already contributed to improving the understanding of how BIM is used in practice, each focusing on individual aspects of using BIM, for example, representation (Bouchlaghem et al., 2005), collaboration (Kerosuo, Mäki and Korpela, 2013) (Kokkonen and Alin, 2016) (Poirier, Forgues and Staub-French, 2016), interaction (Oxman, 2006) and decision-making (Schade, Olofsson and Schreyer, 2011)".

Li, X. et al. (2017) 'Mapping the knowledge domains of Building Information Modelling (BIM): A bibliometric approach'. Li et al. (2017) in their article mapped the different knowledge domains related to Building Information Modelling (BIM). It illustrates the quantitative approach to summarize the BIM knowledge by using bibliometric techniques. Through these analyses they identify knowledge domains and hidden connections within BIM discipline in a period from 2004 to 2015 (Li et al., 2017). Li et al. (2017) ended up with 60 key research topics and ten knowledge clusters: "architectural design studio, building information, lean construction, different discipline, augmented reality, unified building model, point cloud, multi-standpoint framework, CEM curriculum, and existing building". Similarly, as this paper's bibliometric analysis, it shows the lack of humanistic approach of analysis of HCI.

Shen et al., (2010) 'Systems integration and collaboration in architecture, engineering, construction, and facilities management: A review'. Shen et al., (2010) suggests nine topics they believe will be the most active topics of the next 10 years. Some of those are relevant even today. They discuss the FIATECH (Fully Integrated and Automated TECHnology) organization and the ECTP - the European Construction Technology Platform project where the whole construction sector has been tried to be mobilized. These integrated processes resemble the VDC framework. The article presents a possibility to investigate further the integrated processes that are similar to VDC.

DISCUSSION

The architecture, engineering, and construction (AEC) industry necessitates and evolves in part through new ways of collaboration. Although these changes may be compulsory/mandatory/necessary (Hermund, 2009), they might also feel unwelcome or unwanted. Architecture is a discipline that involves the merging of the artistic and technological world. Architects aim to become more technologically advanced, especially by means of computational methods and tools, whilst also being conservative of "the self-protecting mystique of design" (Schön, 1984). This means that some architects may tend towards preserving their talents by keeping an aura of secrecy and mystery in the work. As Hermund (2009) describes implementation of BIM methods can provoke distress among the architects as it reduces the creative loops by introducing more linear and systematic approach to design thinking.

The creative aspect of architecture is often the most intriguing for people who research architectural studies. Creativity is a fascinating topic and therefore has been researched at length. Tanggaard (2013) provides a helpful suggestion for architectural creativity that relates to the material world around architecture. Creativity is present within every individual, but when researching creativity in architecture the material basis needs to be taken into consideration together with the socio-material aspects of creativity. With that she seems to imply that creativity should be connected to everyday life, and that materials form an important part in supporting creativity as design. Tanggaard (2013) highlights also that designs are not realized without being materialized on paper or computer in the same way that an architectural drawing does not become a house without building materials.

Architects communicate by using the language of designing (Schön, 1984), thus they are readily able to communicate in a more visual manner than other AEC industry-related disciplines. This suggests that VDC implementation, along with 3D modelling, BIM and ICE meetings using 3D model as a communication tool is already an everyday workflow for the architectural discipline. By having Integrated Concurrent Engineering (ICE) and ICE meetings as a base for VDC framework, one can assume that this could take away the creative loops Hermund (2009) describes, and cause distress as the design issues are being solved there and then without an ability for the architectural team to use their traditional language of designing and limiting their creative processes.

BIM technology changes the way architects conceptualize and configure design (Abdelhameed, 2006), Hermund (2009) (Shen et al., 2010). However, BIM technology is only a part of VDC framework. VDC is a more wholistic approach that incorporates numerous workflows, methods and is more systematic and structured than BIM technology on its own. As the bibliometric analysis shows, Li et al. (2017) and Shen et al. (2010), there is insufficient research done on the ways VDC affects the ways inter- and transdisciplinary teams in AEC industry conceptualize and configure outputs. Most of the research done on Virtual Design and Construction is concentrated on the benefits and value of VDC and the methodologies within the framework. BIM-specific research is more extensive, and some individual research also examines the impact of BIM on the architectural design processes. This has mostly been done from the architectural perspective and rarely from a more wholistic perspective. Gade et al., (2019) is one of the first that attempts to provide in depth wholistic analysis through the lens of Activity Theory.

Overall, the results of initial data collection in the context of a VDC community, literature review, and bibliometric networks analysis show the lack of research on VDC's impact upon the architectural processes in AEC industry and how the architectural discipline is reconfiguring.

The research gap that can be identified is 'the impact on expert collaboration in the Architecture, Engineering and Construction (AEC) industry through VDC, and how this affects the processes of interdisciplinary team interaction through Virtual Design and Construction (VDC) framework'. This could lead to the following further research questions (1) What is the content of information that architectural and engineering experts communicate through integrated processes like VDC? (2) How is both information and the knowledge resulting from it produced and how is that different from the information / knowledge produced by other ways AEC experts communicate? (3) How does VDC impact interdisciplinary teams in AEC to conceptualize and configure outputs?

Tanggaard (2013) suggests that there "is a close relationship between continuity and renewal, meaning that materials, tools, things, institutions, normative practices and 'ways of doing' already in the world are taken as starting points for new creations". In this context Tanggaard (2013) implies that these components - also referred to as socio-material aspects - do not only form creativity, but also themselves represent "a substantial component of creativity". This can be extended to the following questions: (4) How is creativity and the socio-material aspects of creativity part of interdisciplinary team information formed through integrated processes like Virtual Design and construction (VDC)? (5) Are these digital methods becoming part of the socio-material aspects used by AEC experts?

Further research activities will include (1) focused ethnography to create ethnographic descriptions (2) participant observations to collect data of the expert's every-day lives with and without VDC implementation, (3) structured and semi-structured interviews to both gain the trustworthy relationship with the participants and to compare and reflect upon the observations, (4) surveys to have a comparison data to the qualitative analysis, and (5) further literature reviews / bibliometric network analysis to look at other aspects of VDC.

CONCLUSIONS

The research discussed in this paper employed a techno-anthropological approach for the purpose of examining the impact of VDC on expert collaboration in the AEC sector. From a research method perspective this entailed (1) data collection in the context of a VDC community, (2) extensive literature review, (3) and visualisation of bibliometric networks for the purpose of analysis and initial gap identification. The gap that was identified is *'the impact on expert collaboration in the Architecture, Engineering and Construction (AEC) industry through VDC, and how this affects the processes of interdisciplinary team interaction through Virtual Design and Construction (VDC) framework'*.

The conference paper also recognizes that VDC would indeed significantly impact expert collaboration in the AEC sector, as well as it could affect the way architects conceptualize and configure outputs. VDC is a framework that has digitalisation as basis and combines technologies known to the AEC industry (f.ex. Building Information Modeling) and systemizes those by using multi-disciplinary Integrated Concurrent Engineering (ICE) collaboration process. It is noted that BIM technology on its own affect the way interdisciplinary AEC teams collaborate and work together, therefore implementing the VDC will reconfigure the collaboration processes and the outputs AEC industry will create in future.

This insight will lead to further research with focus on transformations on the interdisciplinary / trans-disciplinary knowledge space through integrated digitalisation processes like VDC.

REFERENCES

Abdelhameed, W 2006 'How Does the Digital Environment Change What Architects Do in the Initial Phases of the Design Process?', *Communicating Space(s) [24th eCAADe Conference Proceedings / ISBN 0-9541183-5-9] Volos (Greece) 6-9 September 2006, pp. 532-539*

Bauchspies, WK, Croissant, J and Restivo, S 2005, *Science, Technology, and Society: A Sociological Approach*, Wiley-Blackwell, Malden, MA

Bernard, HR 2011, *Research methods in anthropology qualitative and quantitative approaches*, AltaMira, Blue Ridge Summit, PA, USA

Blau, I 2011, 'E-Collaboration Within, Between, and Without Institutions: Towards Better Functioning of Online Groups Through Networks', *International Journal of e-Collaboration*, 7(4), pp. 22-36

Bouchlaghem, D, Shang, H, Whyte, J and Ganah, A 2005, 'Visualisation in architecture, engineering and construction (AEC)', *Automation in Construction*, 14(3), pp. 287-295

Brown, JS and Duguid, P 2001, 'Knowledge and Organization: A Social-Practice Perspective', *Organization Science*, 12(2), pp. 198-213

Børsen, T and Botin, L 2013, *What is Techno-Anthropology?*, Aalborg University Press, Denmark

Crotty, R 2012, *The Impact of Building Information Modelling: Transforming Construction*, Routledge, New York, NY, 10001

Eck, NJ and Waltman, L 2010 'VOSViewer: Visualizing Scientific Landscapes', *Software*

Fischer, M 2021 'VDC Course', *Lecture*, NTNU

Gade, PN, Gade, AN, Otrel-Cass, K and Svidt, K 2019, 'A holistic analysis of a BIM-mediated building design process using activity theory', *Construction Manage-*

ment and Economics, 37(6), pp. 336-350
Glick, J 2013, 'Chapter 8 - Ontologies and Databases – Knowledge Engineering for Materials Informatics', in Rajan, K (eds) 2013, *Informatics for Materials Science and Engineering*, Butterworth-Heinemann, Oxford, pp. 147-187
Al Hattab, M and Hamzeh, F 2018, 'Simulating the dynamics of social agents and information flows in BIM-based design', *Automation in Construction*, 92, pp. 1-22
Hermund, A 2009 'Building Information Modeling in the Architectural Design Phases: And why Compulsory BIM can Provoke Distress among Architects', *Computation: The New Realm of Architectural Design [27th eCAADe Conference Proceedings / ISBN 978-0-9541183-8-9] Istanbul (Turkey) 16-19 September 2009, pp. 75-82*
Haldin Herrgard, T 2000, 'Difficulties in diffusion of tacit knowledge in organizations', *Journal of Intellectual Capital*, 1(4), pp. 357-365
Hjelseth, E. and Fisher, M. 2021 'Experiences from large scale VDC-education in Norway', *ECCPM2020-21*, Moscow, p. CRC Press, https://ecppm.ispras.ru/
Jensen, TE 2013, 'Techno Anthropology: A new move in science and technology studies', *STS Encounters - DASTS working paper series*, 5(1), pp. 1-22
Kerosuo, H, Mäki, T and Korpela, J 2013 'Knotworking - A novel BIM-based collaboration practice in building design projects', *5th International Conference on Construction Engineering and Project Management ICCEPM*
Kokkonen, A and Alin, P 2016, 'Practitioners deconstructing and reconstructing practices when responding to the implementation of BIM', *Construction Management and Economics*, 34(7-8), pp. 578-591
Kunz, J and Fischer, M 2020, 'Virtual design and construction', *Construction Management and Economics*, 38(4), pp. 355-363
Li, X, Wu, P, Shen, GQ, Wang, X and Teng, Y 2017, 'Mapping the knowledge domains of Building Information Modeling (BIM): A bibliometric approach', *Automation in Construction*, 84, pp. 195-206
Van der Linden, V, Dong, H and Heylighen, A 2019, 'Tracing architects' fragile knowing about users in the socio-material environment of design practice', *Design Studies*, 63, pp. 65-91
Murphy, KM 2005, 'Collaborative imagining: The interactive use of gestures, talk, and graphic representation in architectural practice', *Semiotica*, 2005(156), pp. 113-145
Oxman, R 2006, 'Theory and design in the first digital age', *Design Studies*, 27(3), pp. 229-265
Poirier, E, Forgues, D and Staub-French, S 2016, 'Collaboration through innovation: implications for expertise in the AEC sector', *Construction Management and Economics*, 34(11), pp. 769-789
Puonti, A 2004, *Learning to Work Together : Collaboration Between Authorities in Economic-Crime Investigation*, Ph.D. Thesis, University of Helsinki, Faculty of Education, Department of Education
Schade, J, Olofsson, T and Schreyer, M 2011, 'Decision making in a model based design process', *Construction Management and Economics*, 29(4), pp. 371-382
Schön, DA 1984, 'The Architectural Studio as an Exemplar of Education for Reflection-in-Action', *Journal of Architectural Education*, 38(1), pp. 2-9
Shen, W, Hao, Q, Mak, H, Neelamkavil, J, Xie, H, Dickinson, J, Thomas, R, Pardasani, A and Xue, H 2010, 'Systems integration and collaboration in architecture, engineering, construction, and facilities management: A review', *Advanced Engineering Informatics*, 24(2), pp. 196-207
Andrule Slotina, K 2014, *Exchanging knowledge in the BIM environment: How different experts produce and transmit architectural information*, Ph.D. Thesis, Aaborg University
Tanggaard, L 2013, 'The sociomateriality of creativity in everyday life:', *Culture \& Psychology*, 19, pp. 20-32
Wenger, E., McDermott, R.A. and Snyder, W. 2002, *Cultivating Communities of Practice: A Guide to Managing Knowledge*, Harvard Business Press

Floating Modular Houses as Solution for Rising Sea Levels

A case study in Kiribati island

Jovana Stanković[1], Sonja Krasić[2], Petar Mitković[3], Marko Nikolić[4], Nastasija Kocić[5], Mihailo Mitković[6]
[1,2,3,4,5,6]Faculty of Civil Engineering and Architecture, University of Niš, Serbia
[1,4,5]{jovana__stankovic|marko.nk|nadja93.al}@hotmail.com [2,6]{krasic.sonja|mihailo.mitkovicgaf}@gmail.com [3]dekan@gaf.ni.ac.rs

Many island states, due to rising sea levels, have a problem with losing inhabitant homes. One of those countries is Kiribati island. Nowadays, this problem is solved by applying floating architecture, so life on the land is transferred to the water surface. Building settlements of this type is very complex. This paper proposes a unique concept for architectural and urban design using computational intelligence methods and the principles of regular tessellation. It is necessary to define the architectural program, ie. input data for the design process based on the general and special needs of users in terms of the functional organization of space. Each data will be represented by a module of unique dimensions, and the connections between the data by parameters, which result in a functional Bubble diagram of a modular floating house. By setting the requirements for the minimal perimeter and maximum area, the most optimal design of each of geometric shapes of regular tessellation will be chosen and evaluated by objective and subjective parameters of the design quality to find out which one is the most suitable for the modular floating house and then sustainable floating settlement.

Keywords: *floating architecture, regular tessellation, parametric design, architectural optimization, Kiribati island*

INTRODUCTION

Global warming is a characteristic of the modern world. According to the Panel on Climate Change (IPCC 2018) [1], population growth, economic activity, lifestyle, energy use, land use templates, technology and 21st-century climate policy initiate almost all greenhouse gas emissions and lead to catastrophic changes in nature, which are seen and felt every day. According to the research of the author team Slater et al. (2021), in the period from 1994 to 2017, 28 trillion tons of ice melted, which affected the rise of the average global sea level by 3.5 cm and this trend will continue.

Small island developing states are particularly vulnerable to rising sea levels due to low altitudes (Balesh 2015). These problems of the modern world have encouraged architects and urban planners to reject the paradigm of building on the ground, broaden their horizons and adopt the principle - to start associating with water and not always consider it an enemy. At the beginning of the 21st century, a new typology of architecture called aquatecture developed, as architecture shaped in the aquatic environment (Piatek 2016), so that the change of context led to changes in the understanding of architecture.

Floating structures, as a type of aquatecture facilities (Piatek 2016), stand out due to the possession of special mooring systems, which allow free vertical movement by providing synchronization with water level fluctuations, adaptation to natural conditions and thus, impose as an effective solution to sea level rise challenges (Simović et al 2019, El-Shihy and Ezquiaga 2019, Endangsih 2020). The floating house is an innovation, which is currently recommended for housing needs (Endangsih 2020) in terms of energy independence, sustainable development and environmentally friendly solutions. The advantage of the application of these facilities is the possibility of a modular system design and construction, which is conducive to low cost and construction time.

PARAMETRIC DESIGN THINKING MODEL AND OPTIMIZATION FOR FLOATING HOUSES

The modular floating house is an optimal solution to the consequences of rising sea levels whereby, its multiplication can result in a system of modular floating houses, ie. a sustainable floating settlement. Designing a settlement of this type is not easy, so it is necessary to find a unique concept/algorithm by which this can be achieved and thus optimize the process of architectural and urban design (Cubukcuoglu et al 2016, Caetano et al 2020).

Designing modular measures in architecture and urbanism requires the application of auxiliary design modular grids. An auxiliary grid is a guarantee against arbitrariness. The auxiliary grid satisfies the spirit. An auxiliary grid is a tool, not a recipe. Its choice and its expressive modalities are an inseparable part of architectural creation (Corbusier and Claudius-Petit 1977). The geometry of the auxiliary design modular grid can be identified with the geometry of two-dimensional plane tessellation because they are based on the multiplication of basic geometric shapes without overlaps and gaps using isometric operations of translation, rotation, axis and symmetry of sliding reflection (Chang 2018). If the two-dimensional plane of tessellation is identified with the water surface, tessellation polygons with three-dimensional models of floating objects for residential, public and commercial purposes, a modular floating house and a later settlement can be designed, but the definition of connections between modules is missing. ie whether tessellation polygons have common edges and what isometric operations enable them, in order to create a compact whole with maximum utilization of the water surface. These connections can be materialized into parameters based on the general and special needs of space users in terms of the purpose of space, number and layout and communication connectivity of functional units, ie. defined design process program (Zawidzki and Szklarski 2020).

The design process, which is based on algorithmic thinking, ie. the one that uses rules and parameters as constraints, is called parametric design. In the process of parametric design, after the rules and parameters are changed, an unlimited number of alternative solutions can be generated in parallel (Oxman and Gu 2015). By applying parametric design thinking, architectural optimization and generating plans in software Rhinoceros and Grasshopper, an orderly formation can be created (Cubukcuoglu et al 2016), i.e. the universal concept of architectural and urban design and iterations choose the shape with the maximum area and minimum perimeter (Egor et al 2020). A polygon that possesses the ability to tessellation can obviously have infinitely different shapes, but by imposing serious limitations on the composition and task of classification and enumeration, tessellation is reduced to something that can be managed. Based on the parameters of evaluating the quality of the solution (parameter of nature and urbanity; functional; constructions and materialization; social and psychological needs of users; financial profitability), an optimal geometric shape can be selected and an architectural and urban design solution developed. Finally, the application of mathematics will avoid empty modularity.

A CASE STUDY KIRIBATI ISLAND

One of the states facing the consequences of rising sea levels is Kiribati, located in the central part of the Pacific Ocean with the highest absolute elevation of the terrain currently 2 meters (Qu et al. 2020). The population of Kiribati has a problem with territorial loss, health, infrastructure and economy, which will ultimately result in the disappearance of the indigenous people and state. According to The Pacific-Australia Climate Change Science and Adaptation Planning Program (PACCSAP 2011-2015) [2], the sea level can increase to 87 cm by 2090 and about 50% of the island's surface will be underwater, which implies that a long-term solution to the problem in the shortest possible time with a smaller financial budget is necessary for the state's survival. According to El-Shihy and Ezquiaga (2019), Donner and Webber (2014), immigration to an artificial island is imposed as a solution with moderate to high financial resources, high durability, longer lifespan, moderate to longer construction time, positive impact on the environment and total impact of 72.5%. Therefore, the advantages of this proposal are the retention of coral reefs, the culture and identity of the people, and the disadvantages cost and time of implementation, which are the main parameters of valorization of solutions in small island developing states such as Kiribati. This state imposes itself as a good example of a case study, where the problem can be solved by applying a floating architecture.

The subject of research in this paper will be the parametric design of modular floating houses and their system (floating settlement) with limitation to the design network of regular (Platonic) tessellation in order to find out which geometric shape of the module base (equilateral triangle, square or hexagon) will suit to the state of Kiribati and its population. In this way, a universal architectural and urban solution (concept/pattern) can be offered to all island and coastal states, which are facing the consequences of climate change.

Research methodology

This research has the following methodology:

Stage 1: Architectural program as a list of input data for research. The program in the architectural design represents a clearly defined need and conditions for a certain new architectural space. By their nature, needs can be general and special, where the human needs as a biological and social being are general, and special needs represent needs for a certain type of built space.

The general needs of the population in Kiribati are not fully met. As one of the countries with the lowest standard of living and high birth rate, only 20% of the population has access to the sewage system, and 64% of them do not have a bathroom in their homes (Balesh 2015). Uncontrolled discharge of wastewater leads to pollution of groundwater, which is the main source of drinking water on the islands of Kiribati.

Limited available resources and technical-technological development have resulted in emphasizing the functionality and simplicity of the shape and volume of buildings (Whincup 2010). The foundations of the buildings are in the form of raised rectangular platforms, while the volume is represented by large oblique planes covered with local materials. A large percentage of residential buildings is open-ended, ie. covered space that is accessible from all sides. It is used only for sleeping, and other activities are performed outdoors. Although nature is their natural habitat, the population must be modernized.

Agriculture is the main activity of the population. Almost every household grows fruit and vegetables for its needs, keeps animals, and 70% of the population is engaged in fishing. According to The 2015

Population and housing census [3], fishing and local crops are the primary food source of almost every household in accordance with the standard of living.

Taking social needs into account, *mwaneaba* is extremely important for the inhabitants of Kiribati, as a place of tradition, rituals and significant social events. *Mwaneaba* is the largest single cultural artifact in Kiribati and its size signals community significance (Whincup 2010).

Therefore, the functional units that must be provided by the program in the new floating settlement are functional residential zones (basic housing unit for a minimum of 4 people with a flexible structure in terms of expanding household members and contact with the natural environment, gardens and animal storage areas in their immediate vicinity nearby) and functional public areas (areas for gathering the population-*mwaneaba*, pools for fishing, walkways, large areas of greenery). As a special part of the program, the necessity of appropriate technologies in terms of energy independence and ecological construction can be singled out. *Note: The floating island must have a connection to the mainland due to other public facilities.*

Stage 2: Defining a basic floating object module with a unique area. Dimensioning of prefabricated buildings requires coordination of measures in order to achieve simplicity, efficiency and economy of construction, but also speed in the design process. With the aim of realizing the above, the modular grid of architectural and urban design is being identified. Therefore, each of the functional zones of the basic housing unit (modular floating house), ie. the entrance, auxiliary, main and open areas zones are represented by a module of unique dimensions, area and volume. This would mean that the basic floating object module must be of such dimensions that each of the rooms of the corresponding zone can be accommodated in its predetermined boundary size. By studying all the rooms of functional zones on the basis of the area occupied by the furniture element, the area for access and performance of activities, as a single area of the basic floating object module is defined as an area of 10 square meters. Within the modular floating house, the following modules can be distinguished: entrance zone (free space), main zone (dining room and living room, bedroom), auxiliary zone (kitchen and bathroom) and open areas (animal shelter, vegetable garden). It can be noticed that the communicative zone is omitted because its area is redistributed to the premises of other zones and in that way their area is increased.

Stage 3: Defining connections between functional zones of a modular floating house in the form of tessellation geometry parameters in parametric design software. The basic housing unit of a four-member household [3] (modular floating house) contains 7 basic modules: one module of the entrance zone (free space), 3 modules of the main zone (two modules with a bedroom, one module with a dining room and a living room), one module of the auxiliary zone kitchen and bathroom) and two modules of open areas (one vegetable garden and one animal shelter). The way of grouping the basic modules of functional zones will depend primarily on the purpose of space, the complementarity of functions and the tessellation grid, which will cause grouping around the center area, corridor or surface assembly without a clear constitutive motive. Mutual relations of individual zones from the program, ie. modules for residential purpose, which should be adhered to in the process of designing a modular house, are defined in the form of tessellation geometry parameters in parametric design software (Rhinoceros and Grasshopper) (see figure 1):

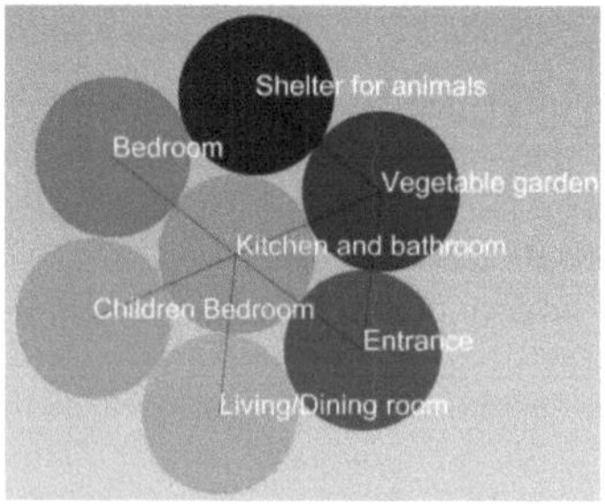

Figure 1
Bubble diagram of functional layout for floating modular house (Space Syntax)

Figure 2
Regular (Platonic) tessellation: (a) equilateral triangle; (b) square; (c) hexagon

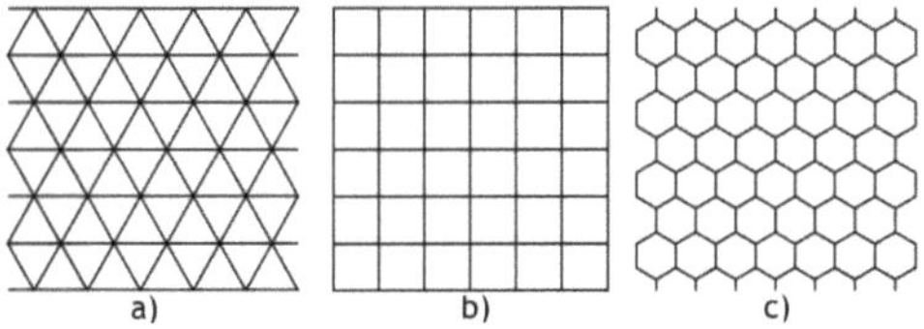

Figure 3
Triangle modular floating house: (a) Functional layout, (b) Floor plan design

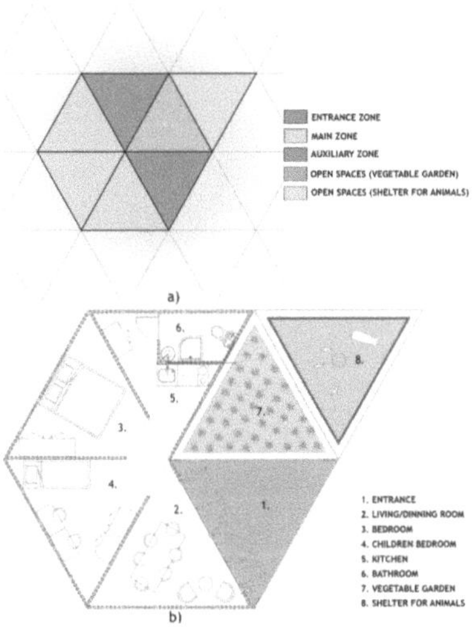

Figure 4
Square modular floating house: (a) Functional layout, (b) Floor plan design

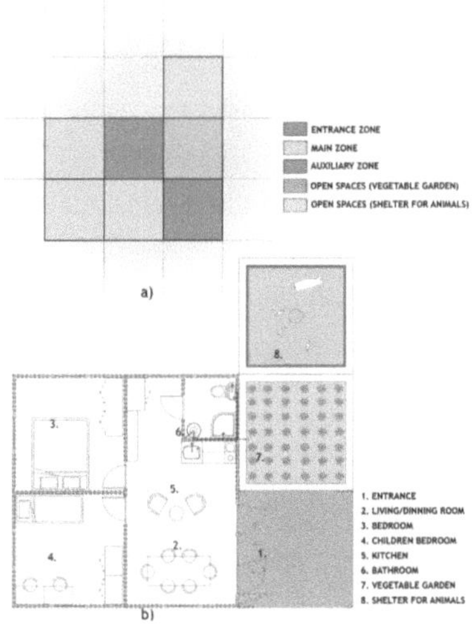

- the position of the auxiliary zone is of exceptional importance due to the application of self sufficient technologies;
- main zone modules must be connected to the auxiliary zone (*edge to edge*);
- the zone of open areas is connected to the entrance zone (*edge to edge*);
- modules of open areas zone, ie the vegetable garden and the animal shelter must be next to each other (*edge to edge*);
- the vegetable garden, as a module of the open areas zone, must not be covered;
- the vegetable garden, as a module of the open area zone, must be positioned next to the auxiliary zone module due to watering with technical water (*edge to edge*);
- the animal shelter, as a module of the open area zone, must have a special rainwater collection system and
- the entrance zone module does not have to be covered by a full structure.

Stage 4: Setting conditions / constraints: Design with the minimum perimeter of a modular floating house. Based on the scheme presented using the Bubble diagram, it can be concluded that the auxiliary zone module and the vegetable garden, as a module of open areas zone, have the most common edges with other modules. Therefore, the positioning of the polygons of these modules is the initial step in the design process. Then, the parameters can be used to make an algorithm of the modular floating house on the water surface for each of the geometric shapes of regular tessellation (see figure 2) and by evaluating many combinations, an adequate way of grouping residential modules within an auxiliary modular grid of regular tessellation can be chosen. On the end, the condition is set: the design with the minimum perimeter of the modular floating house (see figure 3-5).
Stage 5: Defining connections between functional zones in the form of tessellation geometry parameters in software for parametric design of floating settlements. The space that unites modular

floating houses into a sustainable settlement on the water surface is the public space. The modules that are planned for public purpose are pools for fish farming, walkways, greenery and a space for gathering residents- mwaneaba. The number of modular floating houses is limited to 12 (about 50 inhabitants). The large shape of the floating settlement means the application of symmetry. Tessellation planning of a floating settlement is facilitated by the following geometry parameters and isometric operations (see figure 6):

- the space for gathering residents (*mwaneaba*) occupies a central position (center of symmetry);
- walkways rely on the space for gathering residents (*edge to edge*);
- greenery and walkways are alternately placed (*edge to edge*);
- pools for fish farming are connected to walkways (*edge to edge*);
- the module of the entrance zone of the modular floating house is connected to the walkways, as modules of public purpose (*edge to edge*);
- the animal shelter, as a module of the open area zone of the modular floating house, must be positioned towards the open sea (*there are no common edges with the modules that are planned for public purpose*);
- at least one module must be omitted between individual modular floating houses and modules for a public purpose (*modular floating houses do not have a common edge, all functional zones of a modular floating house, except the entrance and vegetable garden, do not have a common edge with public modules*) due to the insolation of each of the houses and the privacy of the residents.

Stage 6: Setting conditions / constraints: Design with the minimum perimeter of a floating settlement. Based on the scheme presented using the Bubble diagram, it can be concluded that mwaneaba must be positioned in the center of the settlement, and then connected to the modular floating houses by modules of walkways and greenery. The parameters can be used to create an algorithm of settlement on the water surface for each of the geometric shapes of the regular tessellation and by evaluating many combinations, an adequate way of grouping modular floating houses with the minimum perimeter and modules of public use within an auxiliary modular grid of regular tessellation can be chosen. On the

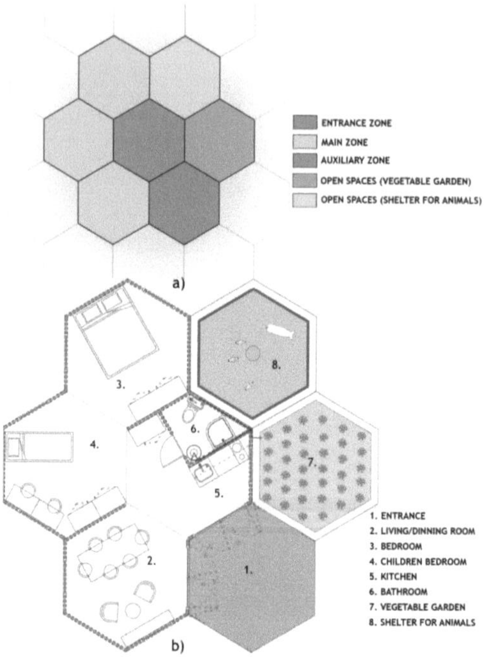

Figure 5
Hexagon modular floating house: (a) Functional layout, (b) Floor plan design

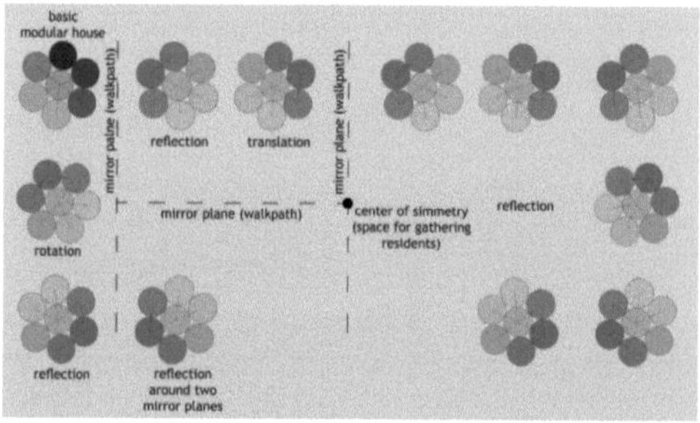

Figure 6
Bubble diagram and applied tessellation operations for floating settlement

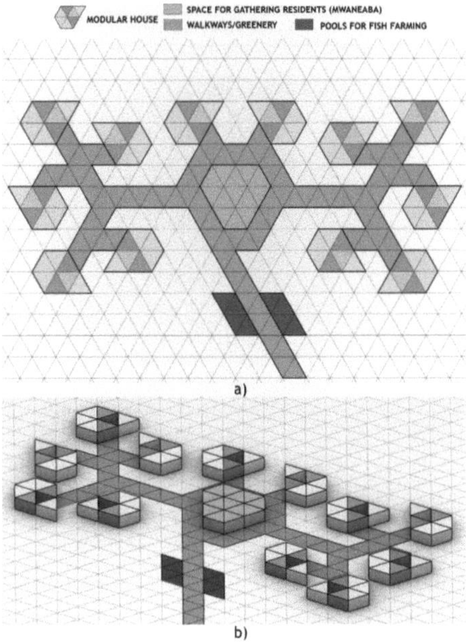

Figure 7
Triangle modular floating settlement: (a) 2D model, (b) 3D model

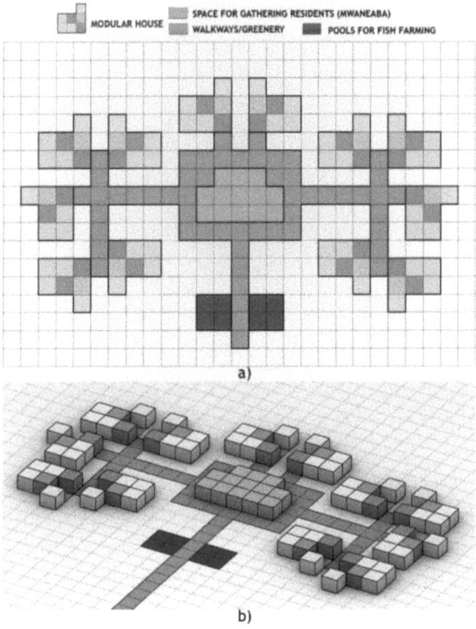

Figure 8
Square modular floating settlement: (a) 2D model, (b) 3D model

end, the condition is set: the design with the minimum perimeter of the floating settlement (see figure 7-9).

RESULTS AND DISCUSSION

Each geometric shape will be evaluated on the basis of realized parameters of urbanity and nature, functional (purpose of space, layout and number of functional zones, a communicational connection of zones), construction and materialization, psychological and social needs of space users and financial profitability (see table 1).

Based on the research results, it can be concluded that the triangle is unsuitable for all parameters, due to insufficient surface utilization.

A square is a geometric shape that is very favourable in terms of function, constructive stability, social and psychological needs, flexibility in designing and creating ordered formations. However, the position of the rainwater harvesting system does not give good results, as well as the position of the vegetable garden due to insufficient insolation of the whole structure. The author team of Czapiewska et al. 2013 [4] uses a pentagon and a square in the urban design of settlements because they consider the circular formation to be the most stable structure, and with their combination, it is possible to achieve that.

El-Shihy and Ezquiaga (2019) in their research present two models of a floating module in the form of hexagons and squares, emphasizing them as a perfect combination for solving the consequences of sea-level rise (the case of Abu-Qir) because the square module allows linear expansion and formation of the traffic network while the hexagonal module enables a strategy of dynamic expansion of the island. In this research, however, the hexagon proved to be a suitable geometric shape of the module, because it meets all the parameters and is a polygon that can make the most of the area with the smallest perimeter. The auxiliary zone with the rainwater collection system has an ideal position because it is possible to collect rainwater from all roof planes evenly. Another advantage of the hexagon is the possibility

Floating modular house										Floating modular settlement						
Shape	Length of polygon side a (m)	A (m^2)	p (m)	Urbanity and nature parameter	Function parameter	Construction and materialization parameter	Psychological and social needs of space users	Financial profitability		A (m^2)	p (m)	Urbanity and nature parameter	Function parameter	Construction and materialization parameter	Psychological and social needs of space users	Financial profitability
	4.8	70	33.6	L	VL	VL	VL	L		1930	686	VL	M	L	M	VL
	3.2	70	38.4	M	VH	M	VH	M		1590	678	M	VH	H	VH	M
	2	70	36	VH	H	VH	VH	VH		1490	580	VH	VH	H	VH	VH

H: High, VH: Very High;M: Moderate; L: Low; VL: Very Low.

Table 1
Evaluation design matrix for equilateral triangle, square and hexagon modular floating house/settlement

of dynamic organic (bio-inspired shape) expansion of the floating house and settlement in case of expansion of families and households. Lister and Muk-Pavic (2015) offered a hexagonal community of six triangular modules to solve the Kiribati problem and presented an artificial island by its tessellation.

We can conclude that the hexagon with an area of 10 square meters on the side of the 2 m polygons is suitable for the geometric shape of the Kiribati floating house module. By multiplying this shape an ordered formation is formed, ie. a floating settlement with the smallest perimeter and the largest area. This data is extremely important for the population of Kiribati because the perimeter of the modular house multiplied by the height of the building gives the area of the module panel, which is, financially, the most profitable here due to the smaller area. The research team Donner and Webber (2014) in their study points out that the construction of an artificial island is a solution to the problem of Kiribati and its popula-

Figure 9
Hexagon modular floating settlement: (a) 2D model, (b) 3D model

Figure 10
Concept design

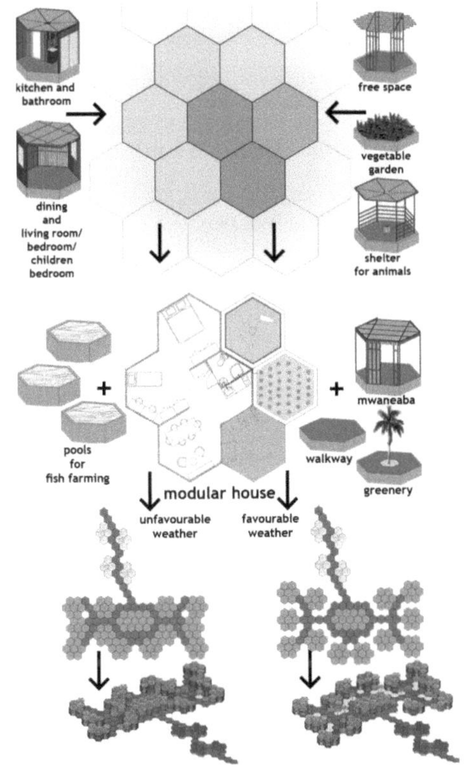

Figure 11
Architectural visualization

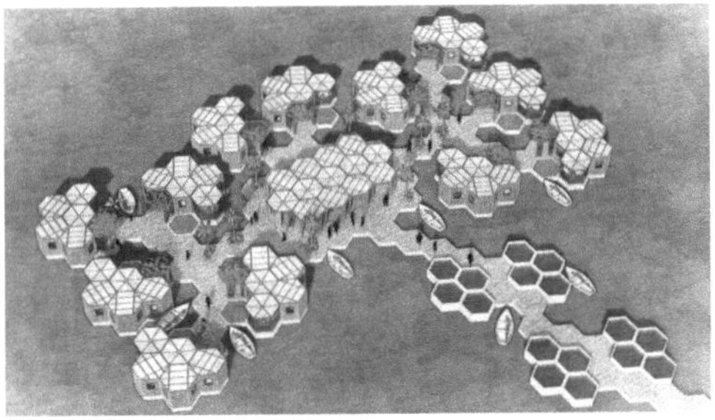

tion, where the speed of implementation and financial profitability are cited as defects. This study eliminates these defects by applying a modular hexagonal design and expands the understanding of previous studies. This solution is also suitable in terms of the mobility of the floating house because the hexagonal floating settlement can have a combination of houses both when the weather is favourable or unfavourable. All this is made possible by the application of parametric design so that it can be used in the education of students and other architects for the design of floating houses and settlements on the water.

At the end of the research, the elaboration of the concept and visualization can be further developed (Figure 10,11).

FUTURE RESEARCH

Parametric design is a good tool for forming settlements with different types of houses so that the final design would be less symmetrical. This paper presents one type of modular floating house for a family of 4 members because according to statistical data [1] it is the minimum number of members of one household in the state of Kiribati. Future research would focus on the development of floating houses for several household members and a study to check the suitability of the same geometric shape due to the larger number of different floating houses in the settlement.

CONCLUSION

Floating architecture is the architecture of the modern age. With its potential, it can help solve global problems such as the consequences of rising sea levels with which the island and coastal states are facing. Defining the parameters, as a connection between the necessary functional zones, will facilitate and speed up the design process. By applying the hexagon module, isometric operations of the tessellation procedure and parametric design, a modular house can be designed, and after that, a floating settlement as well. This concept can serve as a universal architectural and urban solution.

REFERENCES

Balesh, R 2015, 'Submerging Islands: Tuvalu and Kiribati as Case Studies Illustrating the Need for a Climate Refugee Treaty', *Earth Jurisprudence & Envtl. Just. J.*,

5, p. 78
Caetano, I, Santos, L and Leitão, A 2020, 'Computational design in architecture: Defining parametric, generative, and algorithmic design', *Frontiers of Architectural Research*, 9(2), pp. 287-300
Chang, W 2018, 'Application of tessellation in architectural geometry design', in Bennacer, R (eds) 2018, *3S Web of Conferences*, EDP Sciences
Corbusier, L and Claudius-Petit, E 1977, *Vers une architecture*, Poitiers: Arthaud.
Cubukcuoglu, C, Chatzikonstantinou, I, Tasgetiren, MF, Sariyildiz, IS and Pan, QK 2016, 'A multi-objective harmony search algorithm for sustainable design of floating settlements', *Algorithms*, 9(3), p. 51
Donner, SD and Webber, S 2014, 'Obstacles to climate change adaptation decisions: a case study of sea-level rise and coastal protection measures in Kiribati', *Sustainability Science*, 9(3), pp. 331-345
Egor, G, Sven, S, Martin, D and Reinhard, K 2020, 'Computer-aided approach to public buildings floor plan generation. Magnetizing Floor Plan Generator.', *Procedia Manufacturing*, 44, pp. 132-139
El-Shihy, AA and Ezquiaga, JM 2019, 'Architectural design concept and guidelines for floating structures for tackling sea level rise impacts on Abu-Qir', *Alexandria Engineering Journal*, 58(2), pp. 507-518
Endangsih, T 2020 'Floating Houses Technology as Alternative Living on The Water', *In IOP Conference Series: Materials Science and Engineering*, p. (Vol. 797, No. 1, p. 012020)
Kizilova, S 2019, 'Form and functional features of modular floating structures', *In E3S Web of Conferences*, Vol. 91, p. 05013
Lister, N and Muk-Pavic, E 2015, 'Sustainable artificial island concept for the Republic of Kiribati', *Ocean Engineering*, 98, pp. 78-87
Oxman, R and Gu, N 2015 'Theories and Models of Parametric Design Thinking', *Proceedings of eCAADe 2015*, Vienna, pp. 477-482
Piątek, Ł 2016, 'Displacing architecture? From floating houses to ocean habitats: Expanding the building typology.', in Słyk, J and Bezerra, L (eds) 2016, *Education for research, research for creativity.*, Wydział Architektury Politechniki Warszawskiej, Warsaw, pp. 273-280
Qu, V, Wang, Y and Zhang, H 2020 'Global Sea Level Forecast Based on Markov Model', *2nd International Conference on Electronic Science and Automation Control (ESAC 2020)*, pp. 211-217
Simovic, M, Krasic, S and Nikolic, M 2020, 'Floating Solutions: The New Meaning of Mobility', in Wang, CM, Lim, SH and Tay, ZY (eds) 2020, *WCFS2019*, Springer, pp. 411–426
Slater, T 2021, 'Earth's ice imbalance', *The Cryosphere*, 15(1), pp. 233-246
Whincup, T 2010, 'TE MWANEABA NI KIRIBATI: The Traditional Meeting House of Kiribati:', *Shima*, 4(1), pp. 113-130
Zawidzki, M and Szklarski, J 2020, 'Multi-objective optimization of the floor plan of a single story family house considering position and orientation', *Advances in Engineering Software*, 141, p. 102766
[1] https://www.ipcc.ch/2018/
[2] https://www.pacificclimatechangescience.org/wp-content/uploads/2013/06/11_PACCSAP-Kiribati-11pp_WEB.pdf
[3] https://spccfpstore1.blob.core.windows.net/digitallibrary-docs/files/f7/f7cfec2ebf832f6234b03342eb99c4e3.pdf?sv=2015-12-11&sr=b&sig=tUQxUNGlawFJmi2WrlUqewyLjx%2BkVPZSifS1VchAqM%3D&se=2021-08-25T15%3A27%3A06Z&sp=r&rscc=public%2C%20max-age%3D864000%2C%20max-stale%3D86400&rsct=application%2Fpdf&rscd=inline%3B%20filename%3D%22Kiribati_2015_Population_Census_Report_Vol_1.pdf%22
[4] https://www.blue21.nl/wp-content/uploads/2020/03/Seasteading-Implementation-Plan.pdf

Collaborative, participative or responsive design

Augmented Reality for Experience-centered Spatial Design

A quantitative assessment method for architectural space

Muchen Yan[1], Martin Tamke[2]
[1,2]CITA - Royal Danish Academy – Architecture, Design, Conservation
[1]muya2051@edu.kglakademi.dk [2]martin.tamke@kglakademi.dk

While interaction and product design are using data-driven methods on a daily basis, not only similar data but also methods for making use of such data for designing architectural space is missing. The spatial design feedback loop is broken, as we lack quantitative assessment systems that reveal experience and interaction from the user's perspective. This paper describes the first of its kind development of a spatial assessment and design methodology utilizing Augmented Reality headsets, aiming to fill the gaps in the spatial design iteration loop.

Keywords: *Augmented Reality, Behaviour Tracking, Feedback Loop, Occupancy Observation, Mixed Reality*

INTRODUCTION

When designing, architects use their tacit knowledge with intuitions accumulated over years. However, compared to other design fields, such as interaction design, there is not much measurable feedback to tell architects if their design is well perceived by users.

Other design disciplines use a more defined iterative design process – for example, a product goes through loops of Design - Prototype - Assess (Gossain and Anderson, 1990). User's interaction data with prototypes are collected and analyzed for design optimization. However, this iteration loop is broken in spatial design (Figure 1). The optimization of spatial design normally goes through phases of Design - Visualize - Assess. Compared to product or UX design (Thompson et al., 2020), the user's feedback in spatial design is often ambiguous, retrospective or limited to verbal expressions, due to the lack of an empirical measuring and assessing method, and also the lack of a spatial feeling and presence in 2D visualization (Hermund et al., 2017).

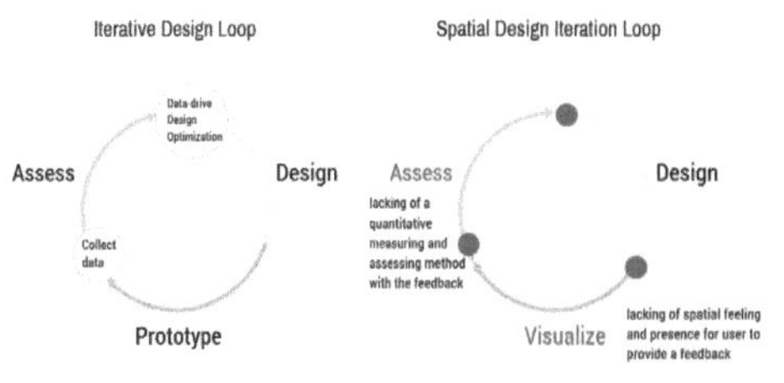

Figure 1
Left: Iterative Design Feedback Loop. Right: Spatial Design Feedback Loop.

The current state of the art research investigates the use of Virtual Reality headsets in simulating the entire architectural space and observing users' responses through tracking of eye-gaze, movement of people and EEG monitoring (Shemesh et al., 2017), in order to improve the space. We find that VR is however of limited use in the assessment of architectural design, as the required user's immersion is limited by the quality of the synthetic 3D environment and the user's inability to experience space in bodily movement (Heydarian et al. 2015). Augmented Reality headsets on the other hand are by nature immersive (Carmigniani and Furht 2011). We find that these have the potential to collect more intuitive reactions of the users towards the proposed design, as it modifies the world that users are physically moving in. Understanding that a majority of architecture projects takes place in existing urban spaces or the interior, AR bears the potential for novel design-related dialogue and data collection.

This paper presents the development of a spatial assessment and design methodology utilizing the embedded tracking functions of Augmented Reality headsets to collect occupants' feedback. Combined with technologies in space scanning, point cloud processing and data visualization, we aim to develop and test a workflow to fill the gaps in the feedback loop, enabling architects to engage users and speculate occupancy in an early stage of design.

FRAMEWORK

The proposed method is developed to facilitate spatial design optimization, ideally in the native software environment for designers in order to allow for ease of use. Draft design is to be placed in space as holograms, and users will be asked to navigate and complete certain tasks in the augmented environment. Behaviour data including circulation, attention and view recording are to be collected and visualized to help designers identifying the problems in the navigation experience and verifying the efficacy of design decisions. Those outcomes can then inform the next design iteration(Figure 2). The following experiments describe the motivation and development of the framework and the observations in terms of design feedback.

Workflow

Hardware: Faro scanner, Microsoft Hololens2

Software: Faro *Scene*, Rhino, grasshopper(plugin: *Fologram*, *Volvox*)

The physical environment is to be scanned and represented as point clouds, which will be the base for behaviour mapping but will not be visible in AR.

To align the point clouds to HoloLens's internal spatial mapping, the site is to be scanned by both Faro scanner and Hololens2. Scan result from

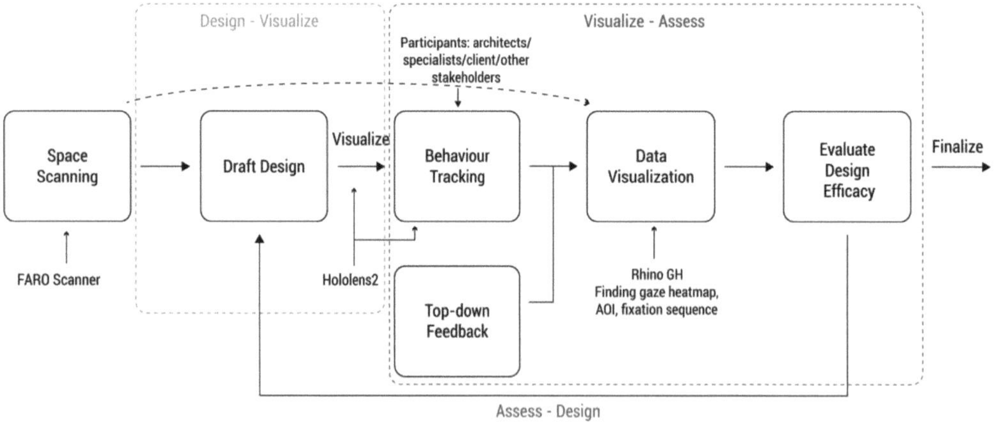

Figure 2
Refined feedback loop workflow

Hololens2 is exported as mesh in Rhino with Fologram Grasshopper plugin. Scan results from FARO are registered and colourized with FARO Scene and imported into Rhino as point clouds, aligned to the mesh scan from Hololens2 as the base for tracking visualization.

The design intervention is modelled in 3D software and visualized in Hololens2 through Fologram Plugin in Rhino. The test subjects are to be equipped with Hololens2 and to navigate the space freely or with certain tasks. Hololens2 is connected to Rhino with the *Fologram* plugin in grasshopper so participants' positions and gaze directions were recorded and stored. The tracking marks the headset's position points and orientation vectors every 20ms. The position points are visualized with small spheres of gradient colours to indicate the sequence of movement.

A more detailed understanding of users attention to the space around them could be achieved with eye-gaze tracking. This is supported by Hololens2, however, that data can only be extracted through software (eg. Unity with MTRK) (Microsoft 2019) outside the design environment. However, the following studies show that the orientation vector from tracking devices in Fologram, with appropriate calibrations, can indicate the gaze direction accurately enough for application on an architectural scale. Therefore we find it is justified to minimize the complexity of the workflow and use a calibrated orientation vector only.

For lighter data processing, environment point clouds are voxelized with the *Volvox* plugin in Grasshopper, and the first intersection of the gaze vectors with the voxel mesh or with the hologram breps are found to indicate where gaze falls. Based on the distance between intersection points and mesh vertices, We then developed a heat mapping method that visualizes where users' attention falls, with coloured dots evenly distributed as an overlay on the environment model and virtual objects. In this way, both the stimulus and the level of attention can be clearly seen. Depending on the task, gaze information is also visualized into areas of interest and fixation sequence, which will be detailed in the Museum study.

METHOD & EVALUATION CRITERIA

Three studies were conducted to test the framework against design use cases on a technological level. The development of the framework and toolset has taken place with an agile method, meaning that the findings of each iteration inform the next use case. These use cases have been chosen by an increasing degree of complexity for both the AR technology, as well as the developed framework:

- Interior design - small and large scale
- Outdoor space
- Renovation project

Parallel to the tracking data a video of the users movements in space was recorded within the AR device. This served as ground truth for the evaluation of the tracking quality.

STUDY 1 - INTERIOR DESIGN

Study 1 aims to test the scanning capacities of different scanning devices and developing a method of converting tracking data to clear visual feedback. To test spaces of different scales, a 25sqm classroom and a 1240sqm auditorium were chosen as sites. Holograms of varying sizes were placed on different heights to test the spatial mapping and visualization capacity of Hololens2.

Outcome and reflection

The scanning distance of Hololens2 is limited to around 4.5m, therefore additional scanning devices are required to obtain the environment model. For the experiments in this paper, a FARO scanner is used to obtain point clouds of the existing environment. Holograms of varying sizes and locations are displayed correctly, even when the distance to the user is further than the scanning limit.

The coloured dots are overlaid on the scanning result of the physical environment (Figure 3) and virtual objects (Figure 4) which clearly shows where

Figure 3
Gaze Heatmap overlaid on (voxelized) environment scan

the gaze stayed longer and where details are overlooked. The result corresponds to the video recorded in Hololens2, so this method can be a valid indication of attention-tracking.

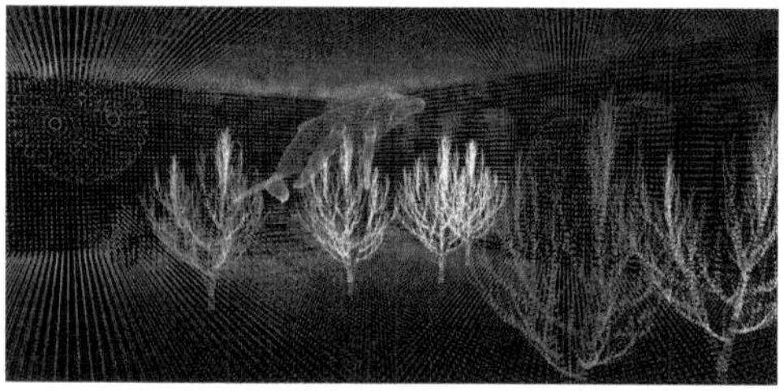

Figure 4
Gaze heatmap on both (voxelized) environment scan and virtual objects (base model hidden).

STUDY 2 - OUTDOOR SPACE

Study 2 focuses on observing the impacts of virtual interventions on people's spatial behaviour and testing the workflow for evaluating design efficacy. The site was chosen on an open square, and a series of virtual walls were set up as a draft exhibition design example. The virtual walls were designed with a proposed visiting circulation path and modelled with timber texture. With data recorded in Hololens2, the case study observes if the designed walls can direct people to follow the proposed path and find the exit without signs, and where are the problems in navigation.

Outcome and reflection

The virtual wall setup with timber material and shadow was displayed in AR (Figure 5 left). The hologram walls show a strong sense of presence as people are following the interventions instead of walking through the holograms. The heat map from recorded data is overlaid on the virtual wall, and in this study, was made into animation in the movement sequence. The pattern of space perceiving can be understood from the heatmap and animation, as the movement speed and time of focusing is shown with the animation. However, in the analysis of design efficacy, it is unclear about the cause of the gazing. The questionnaire can be cross-referenced to give indications on the causes.

With the method described in chapter2.1, the heatmap visualizes the visual attention on the virtual walls (Figure 5 right) and series of gradient-coloured dots indicates visiting paths. It is clear that areas at the intersections receive a lot of attention and witness back and forth in moving. This method of collecting and visualizing circulation and gaze data provides a quick overview of visitors' navigation experience and helps to identify areas that attract more attention. However, for a more specific design efficacy analysis, the cause of the gazing is unclear. A retrospective questionnaire can be employed for cross-referencing where qualitative information is needed.

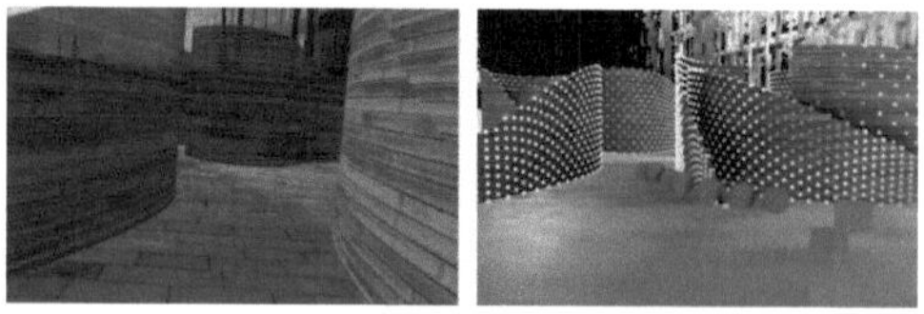

Figure 5
Left: view recorded from Hololens2.
Right: Gaze heatmap overlay

Figure 6
Heatmap on Exterior Hologram setup

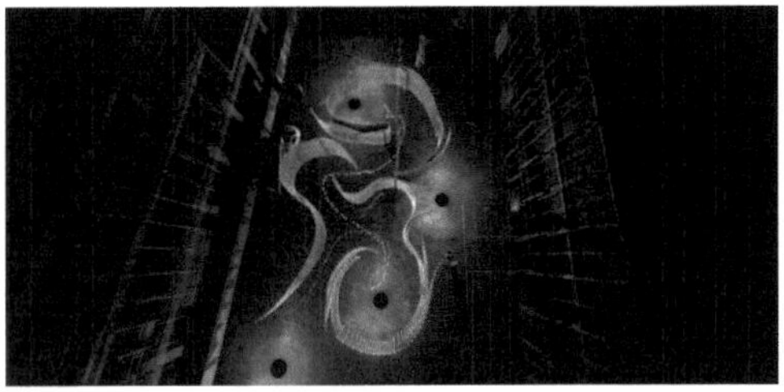

STUDY 3 - MUSEUM STUDY

The study takes place in the Ny Carlsberg Glyptotek for the ongoing renovation of this listed exhibition space in Copenhagen, Denmark. In this study, the current gallery setup was modified by the virtual hologram setups: a proposed juxtaposition of modern and classic Danish Art was designed, by repositioning some existing artworks and adding contemporary artworks in an augmented environment (Figure 7).

Table 1
Participates profile

Participate	Age	Gender	Education Background	Experience with AR
A	18	Male	Highschool	No
B	22	Male	BA - Music	No
C	25	Female	MA - Strategic Design	No
D	24	Female	MA - Architecture	Yes

Visitor's behaviour data under both existing environment and augmented setups were tracked, visualized and analyzed for further design reference using methods described in Chapter 2.1. Tests were conducted under COVID restriction by 4 participants, with different academic backgrounds, ageing from 18 to 25 (Table 1). Without instructions on time limits, participants were asked to visit the gallery freely for as much time as they would like.

Additionally, since most AR visualizations are adding elements to space, we also attempted to visually subtract objects by using holograms to cover existing objects (Figure 8). In Figure 8 (left), by overlaying the floor and wall material, the red separation wall appears to be transparent. In Figure 8 (right), the mint walls and paintings on top are holograms, which shows effective covering on the red existing walls and paintings below. This demonstrates expanded possibilities of modifying the built environment with augmented reality. Interactive feedback methods were also tested: scans of the painting are extracted and duplicated so that the user can drag the hologram of the paintings to their preferred positions. Also, the hand tracking data is used to generate pipes when the user is using the gesture of drawing in air, which allows on the spot mark-ups.

Outcomes and reflections

The recorded positions and directions are processed into heatmap with the method described in the framework. In addition, as a widely used parameter in eye-tracking analysis (Massaro et al. 2012), Area of interest(AOI) was found for areas where more than 5 points are within distance of 30cm, which indicates that the gaze stays for more than 1s. The fixation sequence is then labelled to show what is prioritized by a participant when they perceive the space (Krajbich et al. 2011).

Table 2
information derived from tracking data

Part	Test 1:Time spent in the room (min)	Number of Areas of Interest	Max Fixation Time(min)	Test 2:Time spent in the room (min)	Number of Areas of Interest	Max Fixation Time(min)
A	02:00	15	0:05	01:10	4	0:10
B	07:58	16	0:20	06:32	n/a	n/a
C	09:30	23	0:31	05:10	10	0:15
D	03:20	14	0:10	02:04	6	0:12

We first compared the navigation pattern of each test subject in the existing environment. We can see that despite that almost everyone roughly follows a clockwise sequence, there are huge differences in the preferred pieces and visiting time. We could not draw a conclusion of a common visiting pattern with this small sample size, but we could observe each individual's perception pattern and roughly identify their interest points. Based on that, we can further extract information about the numbers of stimuli (Area of interest), fixation time on each stimulus, areas that receive the maximum fixation time, etc (Table 2). Those

Figure 7
Existing exhibition (left) Augmented exhibition (right)

Figure 8
'Removing' the separation wall in AR (left). Covering existing walls and displace paintings in AR (right).

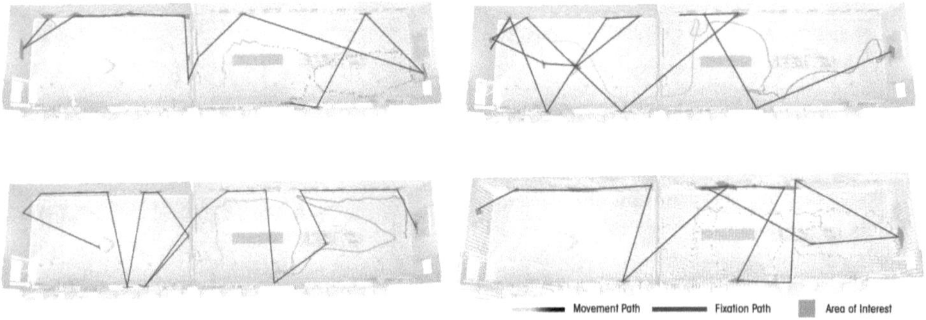

Figure 9
Participate A (left up) : Participate BRight up Left bottom: Participate C Right bottom: Participate D)

data, if collected on a larger scale, can be used to

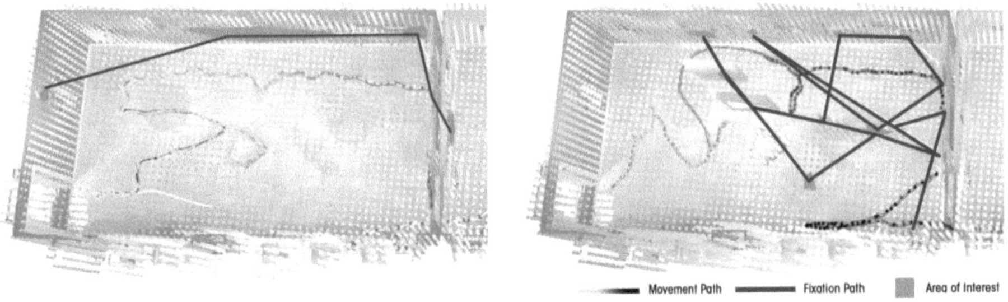

Figure 10
Left: Movement, gaze heatmap, AOI and fixation sequence with existing gallery room. Right: Movement, gaze heatmap, AOI and fixation sequence with augmented gallery room.

speculate visitors' preferences and visiting habits

When comparing the visualized feedback of augmented and non-augmented exhibition spaces, we find significant changes in circulation and focus patterns. Figure10 shows the behaviour data of participate D before and after adding digital setups. The digital setup seems to attract more attention and the paintings close to the entrance were overlooked and the attention goes to the contemporary artworks first.

However, because of the novelty and interactive nature of AR and hologram, the comparison cannot be valid evidence for evaluating two design set, but more as an observation on how people react to hybrid exhibitions. We could reduce the bias in future experiments by comparing designs that are both displayed as holograms. The other participants show varying levels of willingness for interacting with holograms: Participate B went direct to move and rearrange the holograms, while Participate A and C were more conservative in displacing the setups. We realized our method is limited in recording close interactions like these, which could be expanded in further investigations.

CONCLUSION

The methodology and workflow of spatial design assessment presented in this study show that AR devices can provide a foundation for spatial behaviour studies and a refined design feedback loop. It expands the use case of AR headset to a combination of design, visualization and assessment tool. The movement, areas of interest and fixation sequence has the potential to provide insights to design problems that are overlooked in retrospective evaluations, and therefore architects can better engage users who are not professionally trained in the design phase. This method best fits in experience-centred or site-specific design such as exhibition design, wayfinding design or urban renovation design.

However, the study is limited to a small sample number. Bearing that people's spatial behaviour is heavily influenced by collective behaviours and social interactions(Yehuda, 2012), we are looking into possibilities of studies with larger sample size and social interactions. A limiting factor for the approach is the availability of AR technology. This is currently geared towards individual experiences, as in design meetings. However AR technology might become more common place, as in a speculative setting of a future exhibition, where any user would wear an AR device for the purpose of displaying additional information. This collection of user data would enable a dynamic analysis of users' interest pattern and a coupled tailored visiting experience for each individual. If the method is combined with machine-learning recognition, it has the potential to recognize the specific occupancy interaction behaviour and enable architectural practices to inform their designs on specific occupant centric parameters (Jørgensen et al. 2020). For larger behavioural studies tracking technologies, such as beacon-based or camera-based tracking, seem more suitable(Jørgensen et al. 2020), though one would not get specific data from a user's gazing.

REFERENCES

Carmigniani, J and Furht, B 2011, *Augmented Reality: An Overview*, Springer New York, New York

Gossain, S and Anderson, B 1990 'An Iterative-Design Model for Reusable Object-Oriented Software', *Proceedings of the European Conference on Object-Oriented Programming on Object-Oriented Programming Systems, Languages, and Applications*, New York, NY, USA, pp. 12-27

Hermund, AK, Klint, L and Bundgård, TS 2019 'Neurological feedback from perception of architecture in virtual reality: A methodology study', *ASA 2019 - Revisiting the Role of Architecture for Surviving Development: Proceedings of the 53rd International Conference of the Architectural Science Association (ANZAScA)*

Heydarian, A, Pantazis, E, Gerber, D and Becerik-Gerber, B 2015 'Use of Immersive Virtual Environments to Understand Human-Building Interactions and Improve Building Design', *HCI International 2015 - Posters*, pp. 180-184

Jørgensen, J, Tamke, M and Poulsgaard, K 2020 'Occupancy-informed: Introducing a method or flexible behavioural mapping in architecture using machine vision', *Proceedings of eCAADe 2020*, Berlin, pp. 251-258

Krajbich, I, Armel, C and Rangel, A 2011, 'Erratum: Visual fixations and the computation and comparison of value in simple choice', *Nature Neuroscience*, 14(9), pp. 1217-1217

Massaro, DAS 2012, 'When Art Moves the Eyes: A Behavioral and Eye-Tracking Study', *PLOS ONE*, 7(5), pp. 1-16

Shemesh, A, Talmon, R, Karp, O, Amir, I, Bar, M and Grobman, J 2016 'Affective response to architecture – investigating human reaction to spaces with different geometry', *Architectural Science Review, Vol. 60*

Thompson, D, Clayton, A, Conroy, S and Tite, M 2020, 'Analysis of the Experience-Based Design Feedback Data on a National Scale', *Journal of Patient Experience*, 7, p. 237437352096925

Yehuda, S 2012 'An Event-Based Model to Simulate Human Behaviour inBuilt Environments', *Proceedings of the 30th eCAADe Conference*

[1] https://docs.microsoft.com/en-us/windows/mixed-reality/design/eye-tracking

Reappraising Configuration and its Potential for Collaborative Objects

Alexander Grasser[1], Alexandra Parger[2]
[1,2] Institute of Architecture and Media, Graz University of Technology
[1] contact@alexandergrasser.com [2] alexandra.parger@gmail.com

This year's conference theme `Towards a new configurable architecture`, provides a good starting point for reappraising and reapplying previous concepts of `Configuration' in architectural design. The concept reappears often, but was particularly powerful whenever new computational tools and architectural concepts emerged and revealed strong synergies. In the 1960ties there was such a moment when configuration's pluralistic properties embraced architectural concepts of structuralism and early computing. Therefore this paper looks back at previous concepts of configuration to identify capacities that could inform current synergies of computational tools, such as open platforms, and architectural concepts of the second digital turn in architecture. The way we communicate, access, and exchange information recently accelerated towards realtime sharing of data, bits & pieces, and experiences. Open platforms that enable user-generated content and collective production of value are becoming more common in design. This paper discusses ways in which this collective content production can enable a computational and human-centric architecture, by reappraising previous concepts of configuration such as: open configurations, latent structures and variable infills.

Keywords: *Collaborative Objects, Open Configurations , Latent Structures, Vaiable Infill, Realtime Platform, Participation*

Ars Combinatoria

In general, a configuration is defined as: *the particular arrangement or pattern of a group of related parts.[1]* It derives from the Latin word "configurare": *'shape after a pattern' from: con 'with, together' + figurare 'to form, shape' [2]* - that was introduced in the 16th century to denote the relative position of celestial objects, therefore describing it's form based on relations and patterns of collaborative objects.

Today configuration is commonly used in the context of computing, as software and hardware are embedded in a standardized and open structure/framework/network, that enables the exchange and adaptation of compatible components, here configuration is a process to: *arrange or order (a computer system or an element of it) so as to fit it for a designated task.[2]* This fundamental requirement for universal compatibility of parts and their relations to other parts in computational systems leads to a design method where: *"Configuration is a special type of design activity, with the key feature that the artifact being designed is assembled from a set of predefined components that can only be connected together in certain ways." (Mittel, Fraymann 1989)*

It is not by chance that the concept of configuration is a recurring method in architectural design as its *modus operandi* of ordering, arranging, versioning as well as its capacity for individualization and customization, reveals fundamental tectonic design principles. *"No idea in the theory of architecture is more seductive than that architecture is an ars combinatoria - a combinatorial art: the idea that the whole field of architectural possibility might be made transparent by identifying a set of basic elements and a set of rules for combining them so that the application of one to the other would generate the architectural forms which exist, and open up possibilities that might exist and be consistent with those that do." (Hillier 2015)* From, the classical order and its specific components of greek columns, to descriptive sets of rules and parts of Vitruv, to catalogs of parts and patterns of Durand, to the universal system of the Modulor by Le Corbusier, to a period of modular and metabolistic design, and to recent concepts of digital architecture such as parametricism or discrete architecture, - all have in common, a general tendency to embrace the configurational and combinatorial methods of using parts and rules or patterns to aggregate architectural form.

Therefore it is valuable to look back at previous concepts of configuration in architecture and reappraise their capacity for reapplying and reevaluating them for computational design.

REAPPRAISING CONFIGURATION IN STRUCTURALISM

In the 1960ties, a critique of modernism led to two main new tendencies in architectural discourse, one towards postmodernism, and one that followed structuralist ideas and cybernetic systems that: *"saw the computer as a partner for democratic forms of conversation - developing computer languages and programs that offered a more participatory approach to the urban fields." (Gethmann 2017)* Furthermore the concept of configuration, simultaneously reemerged in the fields of architecture and computing, influencing each other, and leading to early concepts of computer-aided architectural design. The work of the Architecture Machine Group of Nicholas Negroponte at the Massachusetts Institute of Technology - MIT, as well as their collaboration with Yona Friedman, can be considered a milestone. The projects: SEEK (Blocksworld), Architecture- by - yourself *(Weinzapfel, Negroponte 1976)*, the Flatwriter and YONA, are well-documented highlights of those synergies*(Vardouli 2013)*.

Concerning the structuralist project, the work of the Austrian architect Bernhard Hafner, highlights configuration as a design method. Bernhard Hafner can be considered one of the founders of structuralist architecture in Austria since his exhibition "Struktureller Städebau", in 1966 at the Forum Stadtpark, received extensive international recognition. Today some of the exhibited models, such as from his project "Linear City" are part of the collection at the FRAC Centre in Orléans. Moreover, Hafner moved to Los Angeles for a professorship at UCLA School of Architecture and Urban Planning from 1967-74. There his projects 'Comparative Simulation of Alternative Urban Prototypes', as well as it's application on a competition in Vienna, mark a milestone where computational tools and behavioral simulation were used for urban design.*(Gethmann 2017)* So on the one hand Hafner applied configuration as a tectonic method in structuralist architecture, and on the other hand, utilized configuration as an organizational method for behavioral modeling. However, the act of configuring - of arranging and ordering parts - in architecture and computation anticipated further developments of computer-aided design tools, and therefore these projects have high capacities to be revisited, reappraised, and to get reapplied.

Therefore this paper will synthesize Hafner's theory on structuralism in architecture, by highlighting three main concepts that have the capacity to inform current computational design: open configurations, latent structures, and variable infill.

Figure 1
Bernhard Hafner, 'Mehrdeutige Zuordnung', in: Hafner, Bernhard 2002,Architektur und sozialer Raum:Aufsätze und Gespräche über Architektur und die Stadt, Löcker, Vienna, p.325

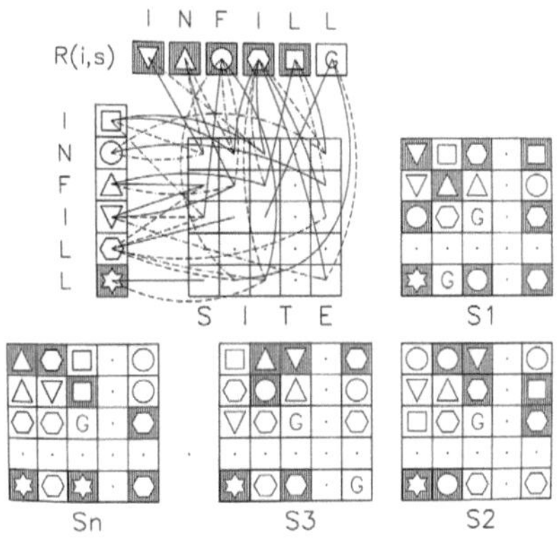

Open Configurations

Bernhard Hafner defines Structuralist architecture as follows: *"architectural objects configured in assembled form." (Hafner 2002)* Configuration was an essential method to design Structuralist architecture*(Hertzberger 2015)*, where units, parts, and polyvalent parts *(Hertzberger 2014)* that are compatible with each other, were configured, ordered, and set in relation to each other to assemble buildings as open form. Bernhard Hafner describes this as: *"The configured form of structural architecture is not - deterministic. It is aesthetically, spatially, and functionally pluralistic. Structural architecture is time-dependent, social, and democratic. It is contextual."(Hafner 2002)* Applying his theory on an urban scale, means, to first design infrastructure and then over time and according to social demand, develop the plots of land, according to different uses. Similarly, on a building scale, the infrastructure and construction are the main concerns, since the use or the function of a specific space is regarded as a temporary occupation, which might change frequently. Furthermore, its non-deterministic open form allows for further growth or degrowth, and flexible adaptations if needed.

This suggests that Structuralist architecture stands for a configuration that is non-deterministic because it is open and free in its assembly and therefore unfinished. These open structures offer a robust framework for inviting the context, the community, and its users to contribute and add value to the open configuration, similar to qualities that Mario Carpo assigned to digital platforms, like Wikipedia, *"This is why we are - slowly - getting used to technical objects of all kinds that are never finished nor ever stable; which are designed for permanent evolution and variations, and seem to live forever in trial mode, always waiting for the next patch or fix - to some extent working most of the time, but never entirely or fully predictably. (Carpo 2013)*

By reappraising the concept of an open configuration of structuralism, and enabling versioning and flexible adaptations, as we see it in computational open platforms, which allow user-generated content, open configuration as a design method can enable a resilient architecture as a collective project.

Latent Structures

Considering that a property of a configuration is to be built following specific rules or patterns, these set of regulations can be based on part to part relationships, as well as follow specific instructions, or social interactions. Bernhard Hafner calls this "Latent Structures": *"In the social space of society, they gen-*

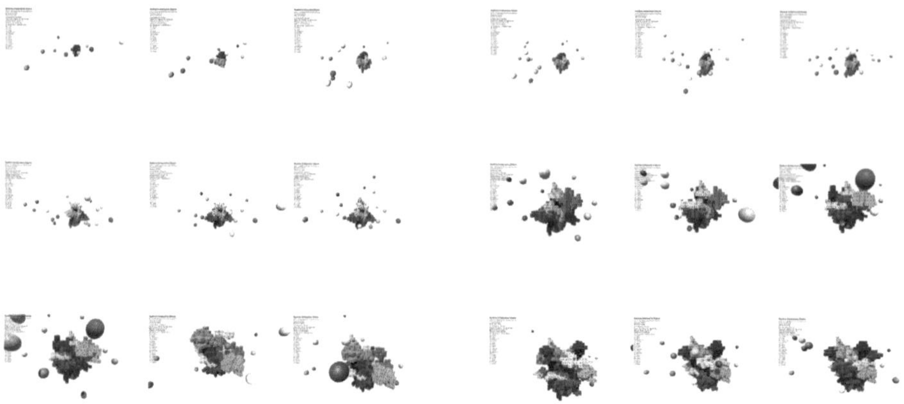

Figure 2
Open
Configuration, at
the Realtime
Architecture
Platform

erate a socio-economic order that is manifested in behavioral patterns."(Hafner 2002) . Although, one has to be careful when applying a specific pattern or set of rules that follow traditional methods of ordering objects such as composition. If composition rules follow a certain ratio, like the golden ratio, for example, it is considered a close system, as it is a top-down logic, resulting in a deterministic form. This leads to a closed-form that loses its ability to be further reconfigured. Whereas non-deterministic latent structures provide a framework that can follow individual sets of rules and customized patterns of an assembly logic, which follow a bottom-up logic of local design decisions, enabling an architecture of tangible complexity *(Grasser, Parger, Hirschberg 2020)*. Therefore the planning of open structures could enable community engagement where: *" the completion of collective form overtime does not lie with the single authorship. It can and should have a plurality of authors because of the diversity that promotes freedom; completion through freedom and diversity within limits."(Hafner 2002)*

In the current discourse of the discrete, similar bottom-up logic can be identified as Mollie Claypool writes: *"In a Discrete ecology the meaning and value of the relationships between different agents emerges through their appearance rather than a top-down approach, as an accumulation of self-similar parts into heterogeneous assemblies, over time. This suggests a new understanding of the ecology between things, where the relationship between individuals, society, and nature should not be fixed or predetermined through top-down universalism. (Claypool 2020)*

Provided that, we can assume that parts that can be configured belong to a shared network of latent structures that follow an individual set of rules. In this sense, the word "configurare" meaning "shape after pattern" introduces the activity of configuring, regarding those patterns and relations as a bottom-up latent structure of social value, and their capacity for shared authorship.

Variable Infill

Furthermore, these open structures can likewise have the potential for mass individualization and customization on an urban scale and an architectural scale. In other words, the concept of variable infill can be adapted to a city, a building, a house, a room etc. Non-deterministic open configurations, based on latent structures, can be adapted over time with the variable infill, as Hafner writes: *"Each representation of structural architecture shows only one possibility among many: the one that corresponds to a certain choice of architectures from the infill program and air*

Figure 3
Variable Infill

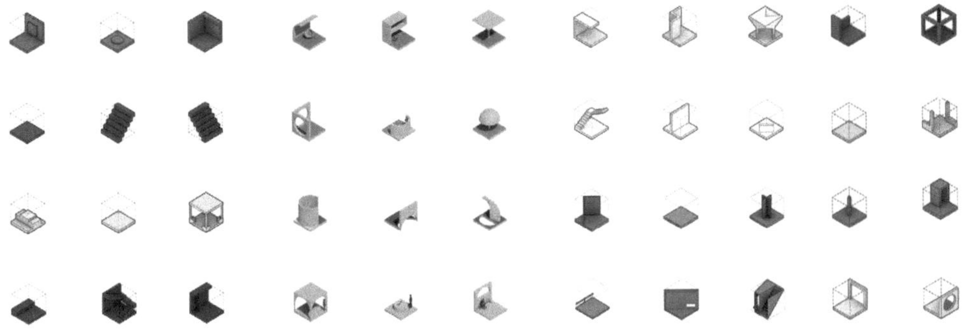

spaces. The network is a potential, which allows different solutions of filling. It allows and ensures architectural diversity. (Hafner 2002) Each part in the structure can get individually informed, updated, adapted, and reconfigured, as they are embedded in a system of compatible units or parts. Here a rationalized kit of parts or all unique parts can be placed in a network of configured compatible parts. *(Figure 1)* This concept of variable infill was explored in structuralism as: Variation through Participation - in projects of Eilfried Huth *'Variety as Principle'(Zach 1996)*, John Habraken *'Support and Infill'(Habraken 1999)*, or Lucien Kroll *'An Architecture of Complexity(Kroll 1986)*.

As it is an open system, where the input and infill can be manifold, "Variation through Participation" also applies to digital architecture, as in digital architecture, open structures and systems, allow for user-generated variability as Mario Carpo suggests: *"All that is digital is variable, and all that is digitally variable is potentially open to interaction, communality and participation." (Carpo 2013)* Any computational logic, digital process or parametric rule set in an open system allows for a diverse input, where the users of the space can pick and choose configurations and make individual design decisions within the limits of the proposed algorithm. Therefore a more human-centric computational architecture is possible as Daniel Köhler explains: *"It is no longer the performance or mode of an algorithm that drives change but its participatory capacities. (Koehler 2020)* As a consequence of opening up the design process, Mollie Claypool regards the role of the architect as following: *"The role of the architect becomes one of facilitation of a framework of production, linking the digital tools for design and fabrication in a way that makes them accessible." (Claypool 2020)*

That said, the introduced special design activity of configuration, meaning working with a set of parts in an open computational framework, allows for mass-customization and architectural variation. It can be seen that the use of digital configurators has had an essential influence on opening architectural systems and providing a more participatory building process as well as individualized architectural infills.

CASE STUDY, REALTIME COLLABORATIVE OBJECTS

At last, following previous research on open architectures, realtime architectural platforms, and collaborative objects, a case study project is introduced. It is proposing a custom open realtime platform, developed by the authors. Based on the concept of "Collaborative Objects" it enables realtime participatory engagement in spatially distributed teams. Further-

Figure 4
Latent Structures

more, it is reappraising and implementing previous concepts of: open configurations, latent structures, and variable infill.

Realtime Open Configurations. The platform represents a persistent virtual environment that invites for an open configuration of multiple authors.*(Figure 2)* During realtime design session at the platform, participants place their parts and are actively contributing to the digital configuration. It is an open design process as all online users share the same context and can contribute to the open configuration at any time, therefore it's non-deterministic. Change and improvement play an important role in the sessions, as users need to react in realtime to local design decisions. Furthermore pervasive collaboration *(Grasser, Parger, Hirschberg 2020)* and communication within the group are embraced, as different spatial configurations of parts can be discussed and improved. The assembled structure is a network of relationships between collaborative objects in space and time. As a result there is no static form, more a 'work in progress' or 'beta version' of an collective architectural project.

Realtime Latent Structures. Hereby a fundamentally digital architecture of discrete parts gets informed by personalized design value and computational design strategies. The open configuration at the realtime platform is based on individual kits of parts, and individual patterns that embed certain combinatorial assembly logic, revealing multiple latent structures of multiple authors. *(Figure 4)* The platform's framework allows for local design decisions of part to part relations, as well as provokes communication and negotiation on a global scale, resulting in a multi-subjective collaborative whole.

Realtime Variable Infill. Furthermore, the collaborative objects, the shared parts, embrace the concept of variable infill. They embed individual visions of spatial appropriation, and mass customization ensuring an architectural variation through participation. *(Figure 3)* In this sense, this platform is providing a human-centric computational framework for the stacked building components of the many. These open architectures represent a fuzzy form of user-generated architectural content of tangible complexity. *(Figure 5)*

Conclusion

Reappraising previous concepts of configuration can be valuable, since: the inherent logic of arranging and ordering parts in an open configuration, the embedded behavioral patterns in latent structures, and the capacity to enable variation through participation via variable infills; amplifies and accelerates synergies in tectonic and computational applications, providing a framework for a computationally enhanced and human-centric collective architecture that is adaptable, resilient and open.

Credits

The Realtime Architecture Platform, developed by Alexander Grasser and Alexandra Parger was applied with a group of students as part of the W6 - Introductory Workshops 2020 at the B- Pro, The Bartlett School of Architecture.

W6 Instructors: Alexander Grasser, Alexandra Parger

W6 Students: Grigoriadou Despoina, Pagar Saee, Yue Chen, Wang Hoanan, Liu Yuexi, Quan Zikun, Guo Zhihan, Pan Huiyin, Lui Yuqi, Duan Yaxin, Du Yang, Feng Jing, Wang Aijia, Zhang Huan, Zhan Beiyuan, Wang Yunhao, Bayraktaroglu Yelay

REFERENCES

Carpo, Mario 2013, 'Digital indeterminism: the new digital commons and the dissolution of architectural authorship', in Lorenzo-Eiroa, Pablo (eds) 2013, *Architecture in Formation: On the nature of information in digital architecture*, Routledge, New York, pp. 48 - 52

Claypool, Mollie 2020, 'Architecture Goes Digitla: The Discrete', in Fankhänel, Teresa and Lepik, Andres (eds) 2020, *The Architecture Machine: The Role of Computers in Architecture*, Birkhäuser Verlag GmbH, Basel, pp. 60-68

Gethmann, Daniel 2017, 'Integrated planning and the design of urban agglomeration: Bernhard Hafner', *arq: Architectural Research Quarterly*, Volume 21, pp. 10 - 20

Grasser, Alexander 2019 'Towards an Architecture of Collaborative Objects', *Proceedings of eCAADe 2019*, Porto, pp. 325-332

Grasser, Alexander, Parger, Alexandra and Hirschberg, Urs 2020 'Pervasive Collaboration and Tangible Complexity in Realtime Architecture', *Proceedings of eCAADe 2020*, Berlin, pp. 393-400

Habraken, N. J. 1999, *Supports: An alternative to mass housing*, Routledge

Hafner, Bernhard 2002, *Architektur und sozialer Raum: Aufsätze und Gespräche über Architektur und die Stadt*, Löcker, Vienna

Hertzberger, Herman 2014, 'Polyvalence: The Competence of Form and Space with Regard to Different Interpretations', *Architectural Design*, Volume 84, Issue 5, pp. 106 - 113

Hertzberger, Herman 2015, *Architecture and structuralism: The ordering of space*, nai010 publishers, Rotterdam

Hillier, Bill 2015, *Space is the machine: A configurational theory of architecture*, Space Syntax, London

Koehler, Daniel 2020, 'Introduction to Issue 01: Mereologies', *Prospectives*, Issue 1: Mereologies, pp. 5-10

Koehler, Daniel 2020b, 'From Partitioning to Partaking, or Why Mereologies Matter', *Prospectives*, Issue 1: Mereologies, pp. 11 -33

Kroll, Lucien 1986, *The architecture of complexity*, Batsford, London

Mittel, Sanja and Fraymann, Felix 1989, 'Towards a generic model of configuraton tasks', *IJCAI'89: Proceedings of the 11th international joint conference on Artificial intelligence*, Volume 2, p. 1395–1401

Sanchez, Jose 2021, *Architecture for the commons: Participatory systems in the age of platforms*, Routledge, Taylor & Francis Group, London

Vardouli, Theodora 2013 'Performed by and Performative for: Rethinking Computationally-mediated User Participation in Design', *Proceedings of eCAADe 2013*, Delft, pp. 243-252

Weinzapfel, Guy and Negroponte, Nicholas 1976 'Architecture-by-yourself: an experiment with computer graphics for house design', *In Proceedings of SIGGRAPH*, p. 74–78

Zach, Juliane 1996, *Varietät als Prinzip: Eilfried Huth*, Gebr. Mann Verlag, Berlin

[1] https://www.etymonline.com/word/configuration

[2] https://dictionary.cambridge.org/dictionary/english /configuration

[3] https://www.frac-centre.fr/_en/art-and-architecture -collection/rub/rubauthors-316.html?authID=231

Figure 5
Collaborative
Whole

Drawing-to-Factory Process

Using freehand drawing to drive robotic assembly of brick walls

Pedro Azambuja Varela[1], José Pedro Sousa[2], Joana Silva Dias[3]
[1,2]Faculty of Architecture, University of Porto + DFL/CEAU/FAUP [3]INESC TEC
[1,2]{pvarela|jsousa}@arq.up.pt [3]joana.s.dias@inesctec.pt

The developments of digital technology applied to architecture in the recent decades has allowed for direct communication from the studio to fabrication. However, this process is typically dependent on complicated computational processes, enlarging the distance from the benefits of the traditional drawing approaches employed by architects. This research intends to explore possibilities of reenacting the drawing as a means of computational generative design which feeds automated systems of construction. By using a Cobot directed by an algorithm which reads a simple drawn curve on paper, an automated brick wall is built, as demonstrated in two exhibitions. This mixed approach allows for technology in architectural design and construction to be more accessible to a wider audience, while blurring the boundaries between concept and materialization.

Keywords: *robotic assembly, human-robot collaboration, non-standard structures, digital fabrication, computational design, interactive fabrication*

INTRODUCTION

Digital fabrication has been a growing field in architecture in the last two decades. Its operative logic lies in the direct connection between digital models and a computer driven machine, which is commonly referred as *file-to-factory* process (Kolarevic 2004). This digital continuity information and materialization has introduced a high precision in the process as well as enabled formal and material possibilities beyond the capacities of traditional processes. Nonetheless, digital fabrication requires the ability to develop a consistent digital model and extract the necessary information to drive a specific materialization process.

In this context, this paper presents a research work on robotic assembly that tries to envision and set up a different scenario for design and fabrication. Using drawings instead of models as the initial input, this strategy aims at achieving a more flexible, interactive and user-friendly process, called here as drawing-to-factory processes. A review of similar works provides hints to develop an in-house system to build brick walls from drawn curves. The setup is described and the main algorithmic challenges explained, giving way to the description of the results gathered by the demonstrations of this experiment.

COMPARATIVE WORKS

The series of experiments entitled Spatial Aggregations developed by Gramazio & Kohler (Willmann 2012) are demonstrative of constructive systems dependent not only on robotic fabrication, but also on human interaction. Long constructive elements, such as wood beams or plastic tubes are cut to measure and positioned in space by the robot, to have a human perform the fixation of the newly cut element to the ones already assembled in the main structure. This sort of collaborative work allows for the successful maximization of possibilities by joining the mechanical accuracy of the robot to the cognitive intelligence of human beings.

Augmenting the linear predetermined actions of a machine such as a robot may be achieved through the live collaboration with human interactors, or may come with added capabilities to the machine itself. Following the implementation of electronics and mechatronics in production lines, the 4th Industrial Revolution caters for processes which exhibit intelligence. Through the inclusion of sensing abilities, or the power to collect and process information, cyber physical systems are able to take decisions in the midst of the fabrication process (Menges 2015), achieving the totality of the intended structure from a smaller subset of information, as information is mainly based in the intention rather than complete and exhaustive instructions.

The direct interplay between augmented realities and brick construction has been the subject of experimentation either in human empowered assembly of structures driven by digital design (Sousa et al., 2015) where digital projection drives human fabrication, or in the direct generation of brick designs using chalked curves on the floor (Helm et al., 2014) or hand gestures in AR (Johns, 2013) which are subsequently robotically fabricated. The potential of directly interacting with the built environment in order to directly inform construction is furthermore argued by Johns (2013) to foster a design with a human scale, while taking advantage of the strength and accuracy of machines (Johns, 2013).

PROJECT

Goal

This investigation looks for establishing a direct connection between freehand line drawing information and digital fabrication that would not require the manipulation of digital models. This paper thus presents the drawing-to-factory strategy, and describes a practical experiment developed on the assembly of brick wall structures using a collaborative robot (CoBot).

Development

The framework for this project considers: a surface for design input, a design algorithm embodying a tectonic concept for assembly structures, an image capture system and the collaborative robot.

The definition of the tectonic concept plays an essential role in the process given that it rules an infinite space for design possibilities to take place.

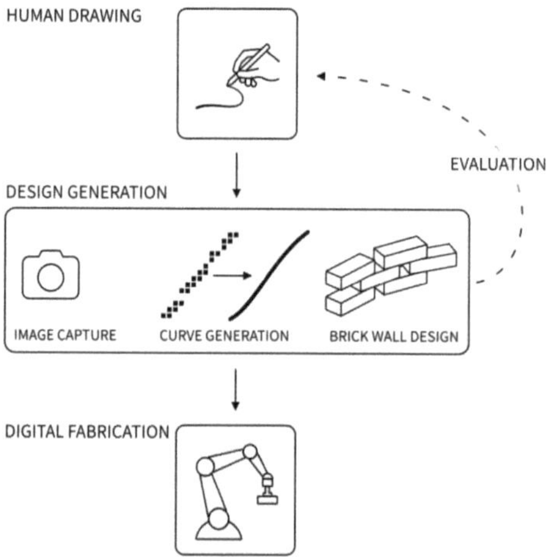

Figure 1
Sequence of the drawing to factory process.

Methodology. The experiment, having the final goal of a brick wall automatically built using a drawn curve as a design, is dependent on the following key elements: the design, the construction agent and the building material. The strategy (Fig. 1) is based on the reading of the intended design, drawn on paper, in order to create an automated brick wall design: as the algorithm gains access to the image of the curve, it processes the pixel information as to infer a NURBS curve which will serve as the basis for a tried and tested brick wall generation algorithm. With the final design of the wall created and the full set of coordinates of every construction element, the robot code is run in a fully automated way. This way, it is expected that the brick wall is built on top of the traced curve, closing the flow from design to construction.

Figure 2
a) Camera module;
b) Vacuum gripper;
c) Drawing in sheet of paper

Setup. The setup of the experiment is built around a table where the drafting paper and the robot, and the portico with the camera are located. The robot is a CoBot (Fig. 2) equipped with a vacuum gripper (b), assisted with a vision sensing system in the form of a digital camera (a) pointed downwards to the drafting paper (c), and connected to the controller. In this sheet of paper the designer will draw a curve with a thick marker, the only human interaction in the complete design to construction process. Beside the robot there is an additional base where the bricks are piled up in known positions to the algorithm. Made of a composite MDF board (FINSA Finlight), these bricks dimensions, 150x67x45mm, are scaled to the overall scale of the experiment, where the robot would also be of industrial scale.

Algorithm. The computer processing of this experiment revolves around the Grasshopper programming interface of Rhinoceros 3D software (Fig. 3). The image acquisition system comprises a Raspberry Pi (version 3B+) and Raspberry Pi camera module v2. An application software (for Windows), which communicates with the Raspberry Pi, was used to capture the images of the drawings. This application provides a video streaming of the camera and allows image capturing. The latter is manually performed by the user by pressing a button. The captured image is stored in a predefined folder of the computer and automatically loaded by the Image Sampler in Grasshopper.

The image processing part of the algorithm is the initial computational task and has the objective of producing a NURBS curve from the input bitmap image. Illustrated in Fig. 4, a grid of points is laid on the bitmap in order to read the image brightness in each point. The points with a darker value than the calibrated benchmark are selected, as they give information about the coordinates of the ink on the paper (b). The previous grid is taken into account, filtering each square. Adjacent squares are joined in geometric entities supporting multiple joined squares, whose boundary is then converted to a NURBS curve for more efficient subsequent operations (c). These closed curves are then enlarged by a known positive offset (d), joined by a boolean union operator (effectively transforming all these independent curves into one large shape encompassing all the points) (e), smoothed into a NURBS curve (f) and then shrunk by the same known (negative) offset (g). At this moment we are left with a closed NURBS curve which

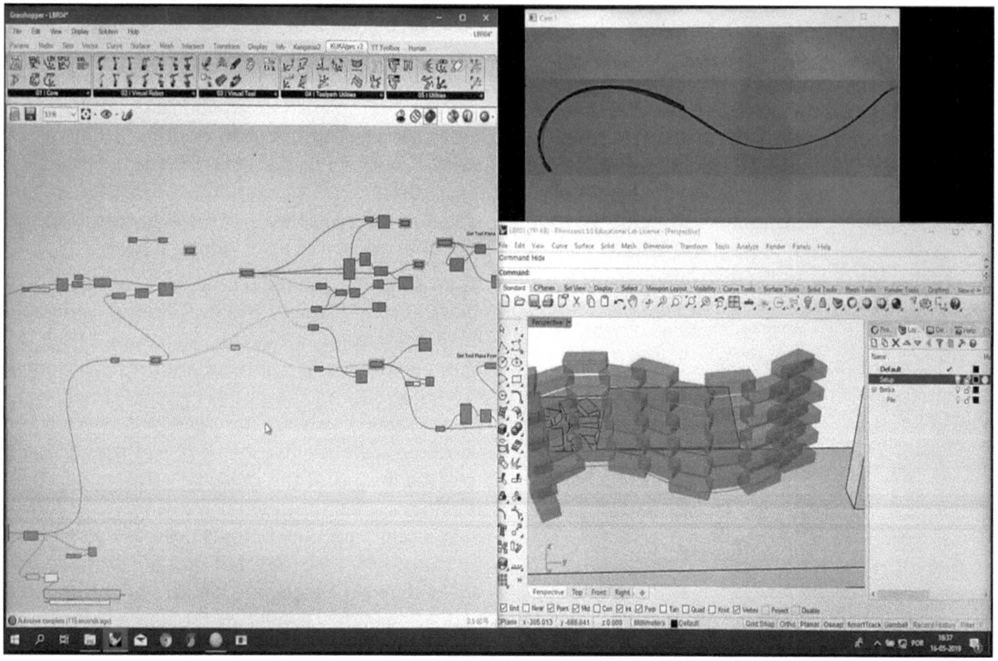

Figure 3
Computer interface showing the visual programming, image capture of the curve, and 3D preview of the brick wall.

is a close approximation of the boundary curve of the inked stroke (h). Since we are not taking stroke varying thickness into account and need a widthless curve in order to generate the brick wall, we need a final step in the algorithm that infers the generating curve which produced the ink stroke. A dense number of equal spaced points is generated in the closed curve (i). These points are averaged by distance, leaving a spinal cord, despite lacking the ends. For these, a line (fitted between all the points) sorts all the points, and the first and last of these is extracted (j). These endpoints, together with the averaged points sorted along the previous line, are the vertices of the intended polyline (k) which may be smoothed into a curved curve (l).

For the generation of the brick wall design, a tried and tested algorithm was used (Sousa et al., 2015), where contours of the vertically extruded curve are populated with bricks whose rotation follows that of the contour curves (l). The placement of bricks in an alternating pattern (n) generates the brick wall, closely following the original drawn curve (o).

The robot programming routine follows that of a typical pick and place strategy, with specific adjustments. This type of routine instructs the robot to move from a pick location, activate its gripper, and move to the place position (Fig. 5), where the gripper is deactivated. The place positions correspond to planes in the bottom face of every final positioned brick, oriented to their longer dimensions. The pick positions correspond to piles of bricks with their position being constant and predetermined. The total pick positions have its number equal to the total of bricks used in the structure. In each movement from and towards the built structure, the robot is not allowed to move below a safe Z height so as not to collide with the wall.

Figure 4
Sequence of algorithm operations to infer a curve (k) from a raster image (a), leading to the generation of a brick wall design (n)

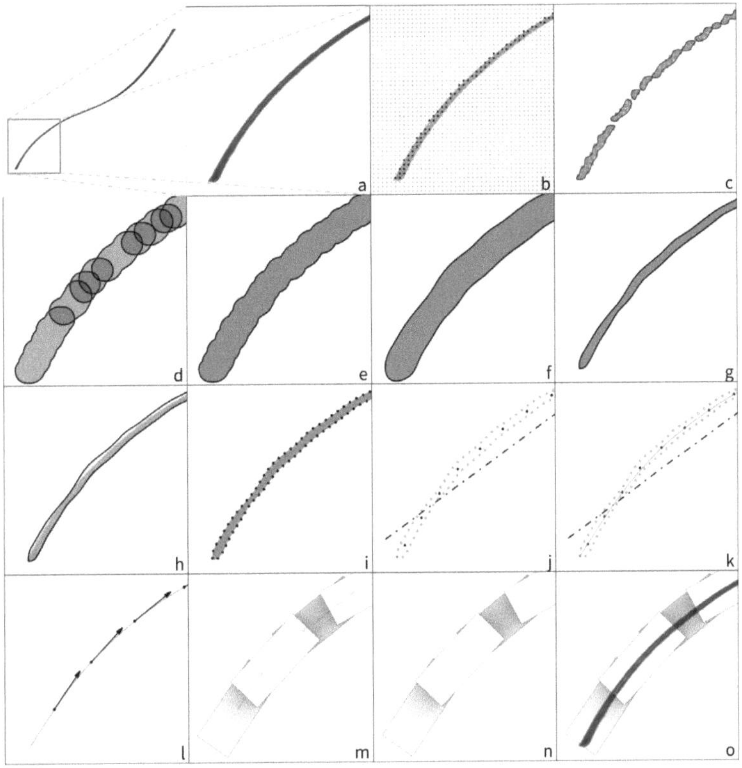

Figure 5
Close up showing vacuum gripper placing wood brick

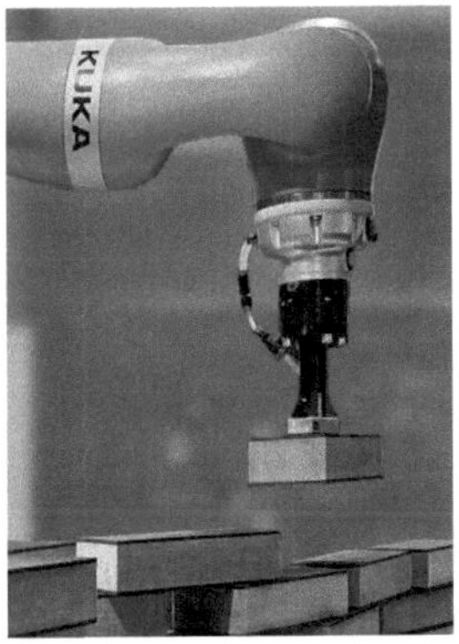

Demonstration

This experience was exhibited and tested with the public in two construction trade shows (Fig. 6 and 7) where the same equipment was used, yielding the same results. A visitor was invited to design a brick wall by means of drawing a curve in a piece of paper fixed to the construction table, in front of the CoBot. After sketching the curve with a thick black marker, the automatic process was initiated: the image of the curve was captured by the camera, immediately showing in the screen the proposed brick wall. After the acceptance of the design by the visitor, the robot program was run, effectively building the full wall in a matter of minutes. If there was no one waiting to design the next wall, the robot was run in a similar program in reverse, so that the brick wall was disassembled back to the original brick piles. During the exhibition days, the robot built several brick walls, none of them designed by the research team.

Figure 6
Demonstration event #1, showing a nearly built wall offset from the drawn curve in order to show achieved accuracy

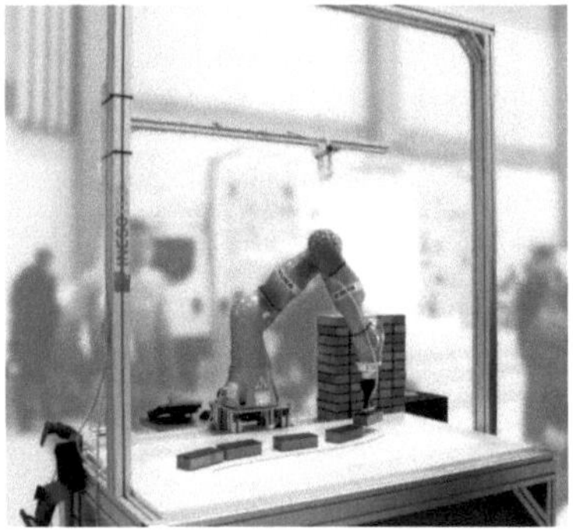

Figure 7
Demonstration event #2, here showing the initial stages of the construction

CONCLUSION

The relevance of this research work is double. On the one hand, it makes technology in architectural design and construction more accessible and meaningful to a wider audience allowing to use traditional representation to directly drive the fabrication process. On the other hand, it allows for an intuitive and instant gesture to drive a more flexible materialization of design ideas. Hand drawing is rescued to take advantage of all the precision and flexible possibilities of digital fabrication, blurring the boundaries between concept and materialization. This experience also points towards the paradigm of Industry 4.0 by enhancing modes of collaboration between human and robots (Schwab 2016).

ACKNOWLEDGEMENT

This research has the financial support of FCT, within the project UID/AUR/00145/2019.

REFERENCES

Das, A 2020 'Designing with a Robot - Interactive methods for brick wall design using computer vision', *Proceedings of the 38th eCAADe Conference - Volume 2, TU Berlin, Berlin, Germany, 16-18 September 2020, pp. 605-612*

Helm, V, Willmann, J, Gramazio, F and Kohler, M 2014 'In-Situ Robotic Fabrication: Advanced Digital Manufacturing Beyond the Laboratory', *Springer Tracts in Advanced Robotics*, pp. 63-83

Johns, RL 2013 'Augmented Reality and the Fabrication of Gestural Form', *Rob Arch 2012*, pp. 248-255

Kolarevic, B 2004, *Architecture in the Digital Age: Design and Manufacturing*, Taylor \& Francis

Menges, A 2015, 'The New Cyber-Physical Making in Architecture: Computational Construction', *Architectural Design*, 85(5), pp. 28-33

Moorman, AL 2016 'RoboSense: Context-Dependent Robotic Design Protocols and Tools', *Proceedings of the 36th ACADIA ISBN 978-0-692-77095-5] 174-183*

Sousa, JP, Varela, PA and Martins, PF 2015 'Between manual and robotic approaches to brick construction in architecture', *Real Time-Proceedings of the 33rd eCAADe Conference*, pp. 361-370

Willmann, J, Gramazio, F, Kohler, M and Langenberg, S 2013 'Digital by Material - Envisioning an extended performative materiality in the digital age of architecture', *Rob Arch 2012*, pp. 12-27

From Physiology to Architecture

The methodology for interactive architecture behavior design

Jie Liu[1]
[1] *Tsinghua University*
[1] *ljsusie@sina.com*

Interactive architectural design is a booming topic in current architectural research, which requires thinking about how to realize buildings provide various spatial services according to users' needs. In the human-building interaction (HBI) design, the architectural behavior design plays as one of the most relevant and essential parts of architectural space design. HBI design requires the establishment of a standard behavioral language system for architecture and people. Therefore, this paper proposes that the design of architectural behavior can mimic human behavior at the physiological level, thus making it easier for people to understand the behavior of architecture. The paper systematically analyzes the design methods and design routes to build muscular and glandular systems for architecture through some case studies.

Keywords: *interactive architecture, human-building interaction, design methodology*

1. INTRODUCTION

With the continuous development of cutting-edge technologies, architecture is trying to break through the original static state and evolving into a new dynamic interactive state. Interaction in architecture deals with the meaningful exchange of information and physical acts between building and person(Achten, 2019). It is not just the automatically adjust the room temperature or change the louver according to the sunlight angle; the building could present a much more meaningful spatial atmosphere according to users' potential spatial requests, like adjusting the spatial layout, telling a spatial story and beyond that. Thus, architects are attempting to design some building behaviors to interact with users continuously, which helps the architecture look more intelligent and interesting.

However, due to insufficient imagination or deficient design experience, how to ensure people understand the meaning of information expressed by architecture becomes the most challenging question that needs to be solved by architects. Researchers have proposed many architectural behavior design methods to help architects better systematically design meaningful interaction behaviors. M.Fox explained the mechanism of interactive architecture from the perspective of cybernetics and explained possible methods and goals of architectural behavior design through some cases(Michael Fox, 2016; M. Fox & Kemp, 2009). H. Achten introduced method structure of interaction design which contained analysis, concept generation, simulation and assessment four steps(Achten & Kopřiva, 2010). He also provided 20 personality traits as the metaphor of interactive architecture to help architects understand how to design(Achten, 2013, 2014). J. Kim suggested selecting metaphors for interactive architecture such as devices, robots, friends to help the designer specify the building behavior characteristics within human-building interaction design(Kim, Maher, Gero, & Sauda, 2018).

After all, as we re-examine the essence of human-building interaction design, we found that creating the same mutually understandable language system between people and buildings is the key point to ensure the accurate transmission of information to each other. Suppose the behavior of buildings expressing information is the same as the way people express information. In that case, people will more easily get buildings' language based on their existing cognitive knowledge.

A similar concept has already been proved in Human-Robot Interaction (HRI) design. C. Breazeal confirmed that robots which mimic the facial movements of infants are more likely to be understood by users when they expressed emotional messages(Breazeal & Scassellati, 1998). G Hoffman tested robots imitating human appearance does not significantly promote users' understanding of robot behavior but imitating human body movements can increase the robot's attention-grabbing power and promote people's understanding and acceptance of the robot(Hoffman & Ju, 2014). J.R Cauchard discovered that by changing the speed, altitude, and other information of the drone, people could feel the different character traits of it, and this trait is related to the behavior of people when they are in different mental states(Cauchard, Zhai, Spadafora, & Landay, 2016).

Although the related design field has confirmed that imitation of human behavior can improve the user's understanding of the information conveyed by items, vividly mimicking human behavior remains a challenge. In this scenario, we believe that we may develop a systematic methodology for behavior design by dissecting human behavior from a physiological perspective and analyzing the causes and underlying logic of behavior formation.

2. ANALYSIS OF HUMAN BEHAVIOR

Firstly, we need to understand how human behavior is produced and expressed at the physiological level. In Merriam-Webster dictionary, behavior is defined as 'anything that an organism does involve action and response to stimulation. From a physiological perspective, behavior arises from Action Potential. It means that when a cell receives an external stimulus, the cell membrane is deformed, resulting in a transient and specific waveform of transmembrane potential pulsations(Kandel, 1991). The potential is then transmitted along with the cell, through nerve cell conduction, to the muscle cell or gland, triggering muscle contraction or gland secretion, resulting in action or response (Figure1).

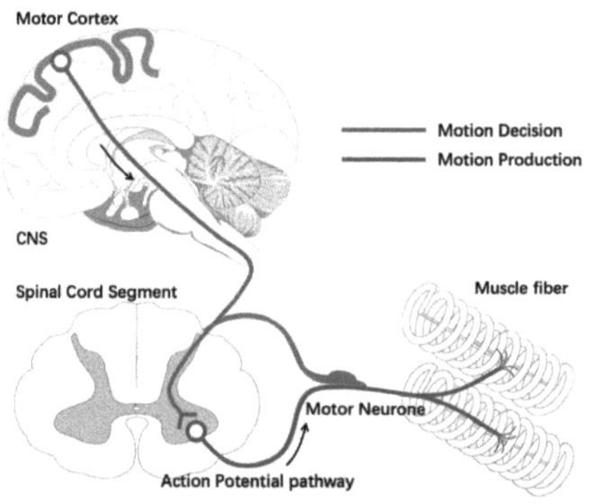

Figure 1
Physiological processes of human behavior generation

The skeletal muscular system plays the most critical role in producing outwardly visible behavioral movements among all muscles. According to the state of functional partitioning of motor control in the precentral gyrus of the brain, it could be found that the amount of cortex devoted to a given body region is proportional to the number of muscles and motor units in that region(Kenneth, 2017). The amount of cerebral tissue significantly more dedicated to the hands, face, and tongue reflects the importance of fine motor control in the use of hands, facial expression, and speech(Kenneth, 2017). Since hands are positioned by the arms and legs, and they all belong to limbs, we can divide the most important motor muscles into three types. Limb muscles control the body movements, facial muscles that control facial expressions, and tongue muscles that control speech. This classification principle can be vividly reflected by Motor Homunculus (Kenneth, 2017)(Figure2).

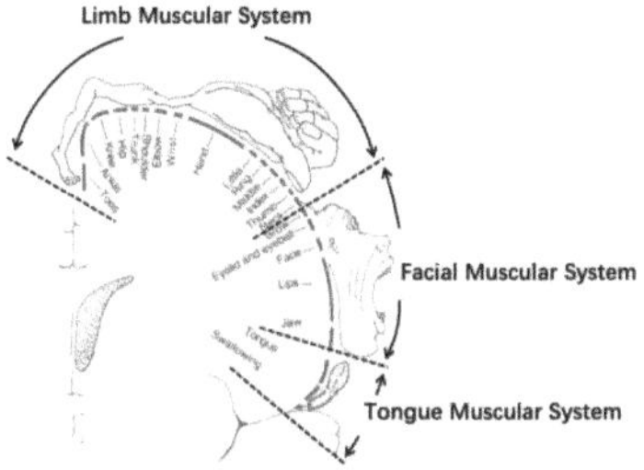

Figure 2
Classification of muscle composition can be reflected by Motor Homunculus

Unlike the muscular system that controls behavioral actions so visibly, the glandular system subliminally changes people's behavior. The glands can be categorized into endocrine glands and exocrine glands based on whether glandular secretions are emitted from the body. The endocrine glands are the glands without excretory ducts that release their secretions internally into the bloodstream, lymphatics, or intercellular spaces(Schuenke, Schulte, & Schumacher, 2011). The exocrine glands are the glands that release their secretion externally to the skin or mucosa, either directly or through excretory ducts(Schuenke et al., 2011). Typically, the endocrine cells control the body temperature and emotions, and exocrine cells control the body odor and humidity. These different muscle cells and glands, as terminal response tissues, form different behavioral characteristics depending on their variable combinations. For example, a person's expression of nervousness would simultaneously include small tremors caused by contraction of limb and facial muscles, flushing caused by endocrine cells, and sweating caused by exocrine cells. These different actions ultimately form the behavior language in which people express their personal inner feelings.

3. BEHAVIOR SYSTEM DESIGN FOR ARCHITECTURE

Due to the wide use of metaphors in design, the generative mechanisms of human behavior can be applied to architectural behavior design in the same way. The behavior of the building could be similarly divided into architectural muscle contraction and architectural glandular secretion (Table1).

3.1. Architectural Muscle Contraction

The building muscles refer to the building components and equipment that form the space. We can consider the supporting structure system as the skeleton of the building, while other visible interfaces such as floors, walls, doors, windows, and other components are the building's muscles. Since the muscles can contract and deform, these building components should also have the ability to transform, generating different actions and behaviors.

The muscular system of architecture also comprises three types of muscles: limb muscles, facial muscles, and tongue muscles .

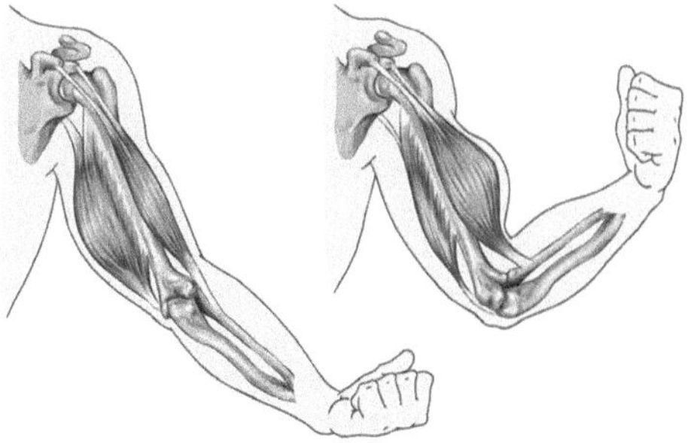

Figure 3
Limb muscles construct three-dimensional transformation

Limb muscles. The limb muscles are usually large in size and number, attached around the bones (Figure3). By controlling the state of the muscles, it can allow people to form actions such as bending, lifting legs, grabbing objects, and other obvious behav-

Physiology category	Muscular system			Glandular system	
	Limb muscles	Facial muscles	Tongue muscles	Endocrine glands	Exocrine glands
Definition	Numerous muscles that serve primarily for movement of the body and manipulation of objects	A complex array of muscles that insert in the dermis and subcutaneous tissues, which tense the skin and produce expressions as a pleasant smile, a threatening scowl.	The tongue is a very agile organ which presents complex movements controlled by intrinsic and extrinsic muscles, plays the most important articulator of speech.	Glands without excretory ducts that release their secretions internally into the bloodstream, lymphatics, or intercellular spaces.	Glands which release their secretion externally to the skin or mucosa, either directly or through excretory ducts.
Function	Balance body, organize movement, present gesture	Add subtle shades of meaning to our spoken words.	Produce diverse sounds.	Control the body temperature and emotions.	Control the body odor and humidity.
Characteristics	Large in size and numbers, organized into distanced compartments separated from each other.	Small in size, large in numbers and small area with multiple muscles tightly bound together.	Small in size and numbers, determine people's ability to speak by delicate control of several tiny muscles.	Internal hormonal regulation of the body, the secretion cannot be touched by the people, but its effects can be observed, such as color and temperature.	Internal chemicals excreted from the body which could be smelled or touched by others, such as sweat.
Definition in HBI	Some spatial constituents of the building which act as envelope elements around the load-bearing structure, with the ability to form spatial transformations.	The numerous small components of the building interface which could change the shape in the two-dimensional plane with a very limited range, and do not affect the overall form of the space.	The components which can produce ambient sound and language so that the building can intuitively communicate with individuals.	Devices which regulating light and temperature adjustment within the building.	The collection of equipment which change the molecular composition of the built environment by releasing gases or liquids.
Equivalent examples in HBI	Bendable wall, integration of the building components which can be split and combined into furniture	The surfaces of the walls, ceilings, floors, windows and so on.	Building components which could vibrate or embedded with audio equipment, such as speakers.	The lighting system and heating system.	The air conditioning system and odor system

Table 1
The behavior systems comparison between human and architecture

iors. For architecture, the limb muscular system of the building refers to some spatial constituents of the building, which act as envelope elements around the load-bearing structure. The architectural limb muscular system owns the ability to form a spatial transformation, such as the bendable wall, transforming from a two-dimensional shape to a three-dimensional form or integrating the building components that can be split and combined into furniture.

The deformation of the building's limb muscular system usually requires mechanical structural systems (such as hydraulic rods, hinge structure, and so on) to support the change of the building's spatial form. For example, when we design the reception pavilion in Xiahuayuan Village, we chose hydraulic rods as the architectural limb muscular system, helping the pavilion realize spatial morphological changes (Figure4). Two hydraulic rods (muscles) were installed on the frames (skeletons) of each wall. The hydraulic rods contract and extend according to the building's 'brain' commands, driving the walls to rotate and open, thus achieving various form change possibilities.

In addition to traditional mechanical components, the formation of architectural muscular systems can also be achieved through smart materials and pioneer technologies. *Alloplastic Architecture*, an interactive architectural installation designed by Behnaz Farahi Bouzanjani, adopted shape memory alloys (SMA) as the muscular system of the installation(Farahi Bouzanjani, Leach, Huang, & Fox, 2013) (Figure5). The deformation of the wall is controlled by changing the length of the SMA springs at each construction node so that the wall could change its movement following the Kinect's capture of the human limb position. Thus, the wall could maintain the same posture and form as the human.

Figure 4
Xiahuayuan Village Reception Interactive Pavilion adopted the limb muscular system to realize the deformation of the walls

Facial muscles. Facial muscles are usually small in size and large in number, and by controlling the state of the muscles, people can produce rich expressions such as blinking, smiling, and raising eyebrows (Figure6). The magnitude of these expression-controlling muscles' movements is much smaller than the limb muscles and is more like a two-dimensional dynamic deformation. The facial muscular system of architecture refers to the numerous small components of the building interface which could change the shape in the two-dimensional plane with a minimal range and do not affect the overall form of the space. By combining morphological changes of building components in different positions, a rich pattern of information is formed, equivalent to the expression system of architecture.

Figure 5
Alloplastic Architecture took Shape Memory Alloys as the muscular system of the installation

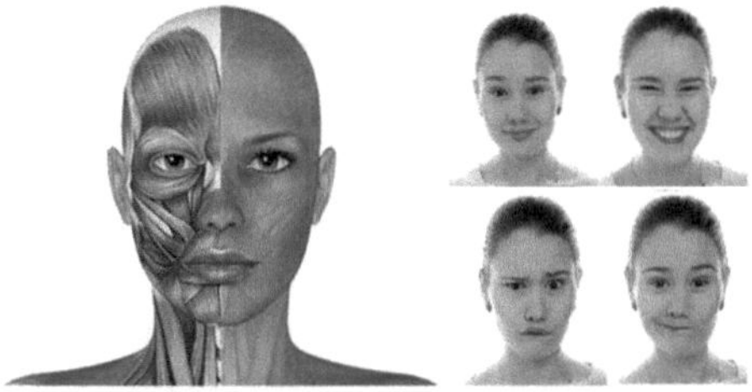

Figure 6
The facial muscles construct rich expressions

Figure 7
Interactive Building Façade installation embedded facial muscular system to present varies expressions

We practiced the design strategy of the facial muscular system through an installation design named interactive building façade to explore the possible ways of forming architectural language through facial expressions (Figure7). The system consists of 96 folding units that can be expanded and deformed. By changing the rotation angle and shrinkage ratio of the mechanical structure separately, each unit drives the folded skin on the surface to extend and contract according to the users' hand positions. Although the unit's deformation is not huge and does not change the shape of the wall and space, the façade system has various appearances and expressions with different extension and contraction action combinations. Therefore, a dialogue between architectural installation and human behavior is created by changing the permeability of the wall skin.

Tongue muscles. Although small in size and number, the tongue muscles determine people's ability to speak by delicate control of several tiny muscles (Figure8). Through the shape change and contraction frequency of tongue muscles, people can produce different tones and produce different syllables, thus allowing people to communicate verbally to express their thoughts and feelings effectively. The tongue muscular system of the building refers to the components which can produce ambient sound and language so that the building can intuitively communicate with individuals. The architectural tongue muscular system can either imitate the principle of tongue muscle generation with building components vibration to create characteristic sounds or embed audio equipment such as speakers to talk to the users directly.

For example, in Triennale di Milano 2016, we designed an interactive installation Swarm Nest to imitate speech behavior via components vibration. Multiple motors fitted with eccentric vibrating blocks were placed in the installation as the tongue muscular system. By controlling the speed of the different motors depending on the position of the visitors, the tone and the volume of the beeping sound can be diversely changed, thus allowing the installation to convey different types of sound messages (Figure9).

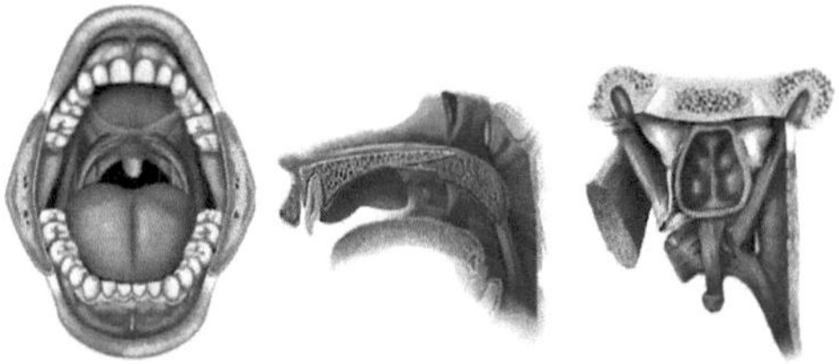

Figure 8
The tiny tongue muscles enable people to speak

Figure 9
Swarm Nest utilized vibrating motors as the oral muscular system

Figure 10
Flipped Space communicated with users through speakers

In another interactive installation work, Flipped Space, we equipped two speakers in the installation as the tongue muscular system (Figure10). Through speech recognition, intelligent Q&A system, and speech synthesis technologies, the installation could communicate with the user like a person, enabling it to understand individuals' needs clearly and efficiently for the architectural space.

3.2. Architectural Glandular Secretion

The glands of the architecture refer to the integration of various equipment units that help the building function properly, such as lighting, HVAC, etc. Unlike the building muscular system emphasizes the morphological changes of building components, the building glandular system emphasizes the environmental regulation by building equipment. Instead of secreting hormones, the architectural glands, which means the building's equipment secreting energy regulatory factors, can adjust the amount and type of supplied energy when stimulated, enabling architecture to convey the intangible approach's behavioral information.

The glandular system of the building could also be classified into the endocrine glandular system and the exocrine glandular system according to the principle of whether any substances are discharged from the building or not.

Endocrine glandular system. The endocrine glandular system of a building refers to devices regulating light and temperature adjustment within the building. What is secreted by the endocrine system (such as electric current) cannot be touched by the user, but the users can observe its effects. Take the lighting system as an example. The lights receive the signal from the central processor and change the intensity of the current in the light system so that the brightness and color of the lights can be modified.

In the interactive installation Flipped space, we chose tri-color LED lights as the endocrine gland system of the architectural space. By varying the current intensity of the three LED colors (red, blue, and green), the LEDs in the installation can display different colors and brightness levels depending on the user's state, thus conveying an intuitive visual message to the user (Figure11). As color psychology already proved, color has an important impact on people's psychological perception and emotional interference. People would map different psychological feelings for different colors. For example, people consider red as excited and blue as calm. Therefore, the architecture may adjust light environment colors based on people's emotions to effectively create an empathetic environmental atmosphere.

Figure 11
Flipped Space chose tri-color LED lights as the endocrine gland system

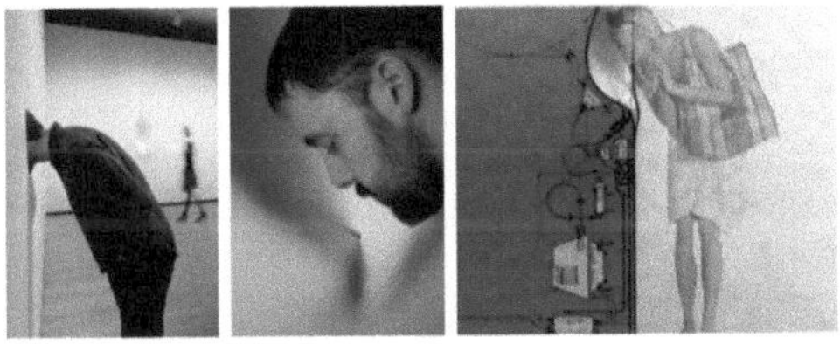

Figure 12
The Art of the Scent incorporated an exocrine gland system

Exocrine glandular system. The exocrine glandular system of a building refers to the collection of equipment that changes the built environment's molecular composition by releasing gases or liquids, such as the air conditioning, humidity adjusting, and odor system. Users could easily perceive the behavioral information produced by this system through the senses of touch, smell, and taste.

For example, the air conditioning system changes the temperature state by releasing warm or cold air into the building space, allowing people to feel the building behavior changes through their skin. The odor system changes the composition and distribution of the odor molecules in the building space, allowing people to perceive the architectural behavior through their noses. *The Art of the Scent*, designed by Diller Scofidio + Renfro, presented at the Museum of Arts and Design in New York in 2012, could be considered as an example that incorporates an exocrine gland system in the installation (Figure12). When the visitor approaches the recessed wall, the exocrine gland system of installation begins to operate, releasing air-carrying aroma molecules that form the installation's odor message[1]. The architectural exocrine gland system helps the building create a tactile and olfactory-based user spatial experience, allowing people to interact with the architectural space from multiple dimensions.

4. THE 'WHAT-HOW' PRINCIPLE FOR INTERACTIVE BEHAVIOR DESIGN

Through the previous narrative, the paper introduces the characteristics of multiple architectural behavior systems. The different combinations of architectural limb muscles' contraction and relaxation potentiate the significant three-dimensional morphological changes of the space. The differences of architectural facial muscles enrich the diversities of the building interface appearance. The changes of architectural vocal muscles enable a colorful ambient acoustic environment. The architectural endocrine cells help adjust the light and thermal setting of the building, and the exocrine cells enrich the smell and humidity of the space.

Once we understand how interactive architecture generates various behaviors, we can further develop the methods to design architectural behaviors by thinking about how humans communicate. This process requires the 'what-how' design principle. The 'what' principle focuses on what kind of behavior an interactive architectural space should have, and the 'how' principle focuses on how to design a space to have such behavior. To clarify the behavior design methodology, we would take an interactive apartment unit as an example. The apartment was designed with multiple hydraulic rods-controlled ceiling system as the limb muscular system, the deformable walls by inflatable materials as facial muscular system, speakers at the head of the bed as tongue muscular system, adjustable light, and heating system as an endocrine glandular system, and air conditioner with scent player as an exocrine glandular system (Figure 13).

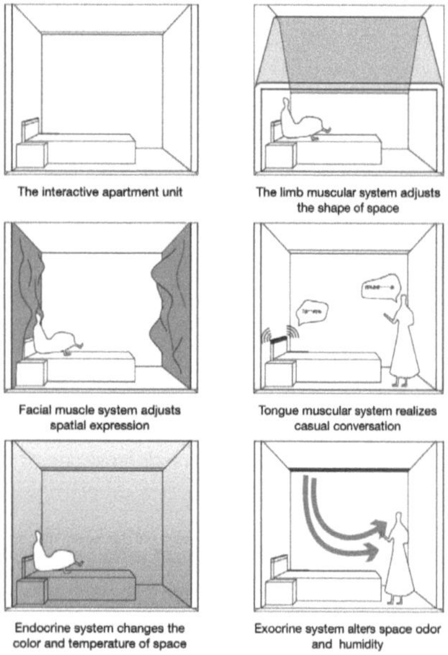

Figure 13
The interactive apartment unit can build behavioral systems on multiple levels

4.1. The 'what' principle

First, we need to analyze the types of behaviors that architectural spaces may have under specific scenarios and personality traits. For example, we can consider the apartment as a hospitable cohabitant and analyze its behavioral design in a homecoming scenario.

In a typical positive relationship, if the cohabitant hears someone coming home from outside, it produces the following three sequential behaviors in chronological order.

Checking for the returning people. From a security standpoint and in terms of its affable personality, if someone returns, it will first look in the direction of the door and ask who is returning.

Expressing welcome to the returned people. If only the apartment owner comes back, the cohabitant smiles and happily says welcome home casually. And suppose the cohabitant finds that the owner brings a guest to the apartment. In that case, it will first express the feeling of surprise, then identify the guest's relationship with the owner and show welcomes to the guest by smiling, waving hands, and hugging warmly.

Caring for the returned people. When the apartment with a hospitable character, it prioritizes interactive behavior with the guest over the host. It would ask the guest about his or her various environment preferences first, change the home environment according to the guest's preferences instead of the owner's preferences, and chat with the guest. And if there's only the owner in the home, it would adjust the apartment environment according to the owner's habits and exchange daily news with the owner.

The above example is just a behavior pattern of a particular character's personality in one specific scenario (if the set personality is different, the behavior pattern will change). In this behavioral pattern, various behavioral actions are included, such as checking for returning people, smiling, waving, hugging, adjusting the environment, communicating, and so on. Moreover, even the same type of behavior can be different in response to different people. For example, the magnitude and duration of smiles that people show to strangers and familiar people varies.

After analyzing the behaviors which could be generated in the apartment, it evolves to the 'how' principle.

4.2. The 'how' principle

How to realize the apartment act with specific behavioral characteristics and emotional states is the second question that needs to be solved in the behavioral design of architectural spaces. A more detailed behavioral generation analysis from a physiological perspective needs to be further developed at this stage.

First, we need to sort out the physiological systems associated with the different behaviors. Some behavior actions only need one behavior system, like hugging is achieved through limb muscles, and smiling is achieved through facial muscles. However, most behavior actions require different behavior systems collaboration. For example, checking for returning people involved both limb and facial muscles, adjusting environment behavior may relate to both endocrine and exocrine glandular system, and communicating behavior achieved by tongue and facial muscles. Also, different behaviors can be triggered and activated by each other. For example, when a person smiles, it is often accompanied by giggles and hormonal changes. Giggles can be expressed through the sounds formed by the tongue muscular system. Although we cannot directly observe hormonal changes, they can still be detected by some external appearances. For example, in the happy mood, the human faces turn in red at the cheeks and temples and a little blue around the chin(Benitez-Quiroz, Srinivasan, & Martinez, 2018), and the bodies would emit specific chemo signals which contribute to the transmission of positive emotions(de Groot et al., 2015). Based on the potential behaviors mentioned in the 'what' principle, the logic of architectural behavior design in this specific homecoming scenario can be constructed as Table2.

Table 2
Possible interactive architectural behavior design under the 'what-how' principle

Behaviors			Muscular system			Glandular system	
			Limb muscles	Facial muscles	Tongue muscles	Endocrine glands	Exocrine glands
Checking for the returning people		Physiological behavior	Body tilted toward the doorway.	Puzzled expressions involve raised eyebrows and wide-eyed for a certain time.	Changing the position of the tongue muscles to form specific language, such as ' who's back?'.	–	–
		Equivalent behavior in HBI	The ceiling of the doorway becomes lower and the whole ceiling of the space slopes towards the doorway.	The upper part of the wall unit inflates, increases in volume, and remains stationary for a certain time.	Play the sound "Who's back" through the speaker.	–	–
Expressing welcome to the returned people	Smiling	Physiological behavior	–	Facial muscles show an upward trend with the muscles of the cheeks and orbits contract and the muscles around the chin stretch.	Greeting through language, such as ' welcome home' for the owner, 'nice to meet you' for the guest.	Red at the cheeks and temples and a little blue around the chin.	Emit specific chemo signals.
		Equivalent behavior in HBI	–	The upper and middle part of the wall units become smaller, and lower part of the wall units are inflated, showing the dynamic effect of the units moving upwards.	Different voices are played by the speaker depending on the target audience, such as ' welcome home' for the owner, 'nice to meet you' for the guest.	Lighting environment with the slightly red upper wall and slightly blue lower wall.	Air conditioning system with scent players to emit a specific flavor of air.
	Surprising	Physiological behavior	–	The eyebrows are stretched out and raised, the eyes are wide open, the mouth is slightly open.	–	–	–
		Equivalent behavior in HBI	–	The upper and lower part of the wall units inflates, increase in volume, and the middle part of the wall remains stationary.	–	–	–
	Waving hands	Physiological behavior	Swinging the forearm or hand back and forth at a certain angle and amplitude.	–	Changing the position of the tongue muscles to form specific language, such as 'hello', 'welcome',etc.	–	–
		Equivalent behavior in HBI	Rhythmically controling the ceiling up and down in a certain degree.	–	Play the sound 'hello'or 'welcome' through the speaker.	–	–
	Hugging	Physiological behavior	The limbs are close together and encircle the individual to form a small space.	–	–	–	–
		Equivalent behavior in HBI	Partly lowering the height of the ceiling to form a small space.	–	–	–	–
Caring for the returned people	Adjusting the environment	Physiological behavior	–	–	Producing specific words, like communicating with the person about the current state adjustment of the environment until the person is satisfied.	Change in body temperature and face color through hormonal regulation.	Regulates body surface micro-environment and smell by emitting substances to the external environment.
		Equivalent behavior in HBI	–	–	Broadcast the status of environmental adjustment and ask if the current environment is satisfactory with designed language via speakers.	The temperature of the space is adjusted by regulating the heating system, and the brightness and chromaticity of the space is changed by the lighting system.	The air conditioner regulates the ambient temperature, the humidifier regulates the ambient humidity and changes the smell of the space through the scent player.
	Communicating	Physiological behavior	–	The eyes are focused on the person communicating, and the mouth opens and closes rhythmically.	Producing specific words, such as communicating with owner about the day's events and asking the guest some questions about the personal preferences.	–	–
		Equivalent behavior in HBI	–	The wall faced by the person changes the volume of the unit according to the rhythm of the sound.	Through the speaker to ask the owner about his/her day according to his/her schedule, or randomly ask questions and talk to the guest based on the stored corpus.	–	–

Through the 'what-how' design principle, architects can systematically identify what kind of behavior architecture should have and understand how to construct architectural behavior through human-building interaction design.

5. CONCLUSION

The design of the building's behavioral system directly affects users' experience of the space. Unlike the interaction design of other smart products, the human-building interaction design is much more complicated and sophisticated. This paper details the method of constituting the architectural behavioral system from a physiological perspective through a metaphorical approach. The interactive architectural behavior design needs to go through two steps. The first step is to select what type of human behavior the building should imitate. The second step is to analyze how these behaviors could be expressed through different architectural behavior systems. This approach to design interactive architectural behavior maybe not the best method for interactive architectural behavior design, but an easier way to help architects quickly figure out the possible design points and approaches.

However, there are limited suitable completed interactive architecture projects to demonstrate the methodological theory presented in the paper. The next step of the research will be to evaluate the effectiveness of this methodology through user experiments. On the one hand, we would like to test whether the adoption of this methodological theory could help architects accelerate the behavioral design process of interactive architecture. On the other hand, we would like to examine whether the spaces designed by this method are more conducive to the experiencers' understanding of the intent and language expressed by the architecture.

REFERENCES

Achten, H 2013 'Buildings with an Attitude', *31st eCAADe Conference*, pp. 477-485

Achten, H 2014 'The Psychology of Buildings-Computational cognitive strategies for interactive buildings', *the 32nd eCAADe Conference*, pp. 621-627

Achten, H 2019, 'Interaction narratives for responsive architecture', *Buildings*, 9(3), p. 66

Achten, H and Kopřiva, M 2010 'A design methodological framework for interactive architecture', *Proceedings of the 28th eCAADe Conference*, pp. 169-177

Benitez-Quiroz, CF, Srinivasan, R and Martinez, AM 2018 'Facial color is an efficient mechanism to visually transmit emotion', *Proceedings of the National Academy of Sciences*, pp. 3581-3586

Farahi Bouzanjani, B, Leach, N, Huang, A and Fox, M 2013 'Alloplastic Architecture: The Design of an Interactive Tensegrity Structure', *ACADIA 13: Adaptive Architecture [Proceedings of the 33rd Annual Conference of the Association for Computer Aided Design in Architecture (ACADIA)*

Breazeal, C and Scassellati, B 1998, 'Infant-like social interactions between a robot and a human caretaker', *Behavior*, 8, pp. 1-43

Cauchard, J. R, Zhai, K. Y, Spadafora, M and Landay, J. A 2016 'Emotion encoding in human- drone interaction.', *11th ACM/IEEE International Conference on Human-Robot Interaction*

Fox, M 2016, *Interactive architecture: adaptive world*, Chronicle Books

Fox, M and Kemp, M 2009, *Interactive Architecture*, Princeton Architectural Press

de Groot, J. H, Rowson, M. J, Bulsing, P. J, Blonk, C. G, Wilkinson, J. E and Semin, G. R 2015, 'A sniff of happiness', *Psychological science*, 26(6), pp. 684-700

Hoffman, G and Ju, W 2014, 'Designing robots with movement in mind', *Journal of Human-Robot Interaction*, 3(1), pp. 91-122

Kandel, ER 1991, 'Nerve cells and behavior', *Principles of neural science*, 2, pp. 24-25

Kenneth, S.S 2017, *Anatomy & physiology: The unity of form and function*, McGraw-Hill

Kim, J, Maher, ML, Gero, J and Sauda, E 2018 'Metaphor-A tool for designing the next generation of human-building interaction', *Computing for a better tomorrow-Proceedings of the 36th eCAADe Conference*, pp. 19-21

Schuenke, M, Schulte, E and Schumacher, U 2011, *General Anatomy and Musculoskeletal System (THIEME Atlas of Anatomy)*, Thieme

[1] https://dsrny.com/project/art-of-scent?index=false &tags=installation&section=projects

The Development of Design Support System for Public Participation of Community Public Space Design Using Mixed Reality

Yuze Dan[1], Zhenjiang Shen[2], Yumin Lin[3], Yiyun Zhu[4], Jianqiang Xiao[5]
[1,2,3,5]Kanazawa University [4]Chongqing College of Electronic Engineering
[1]danyuze@outlook.com [2]shenzhe@se.kanazawa-u.ac.jp [3]linyuming9@foxmail.com [4]yyun401@163.com [5]kxiao@csl.ec.t.kanazawa-u.ac.jp

Public participation has been continuously encouraged in community planning and design. However, lacking effective participatory tools, the professional design documents are complicated for the public to understand, let alone express their design intentions. The advancement of computer graphics brings possibilities to suppress this barrier, especially for the emergence of Mixed Reality (MR). In this research, we used MR technology to develop a design support tool for public participation. We implemented this system successfully by creating interactive interfaces, developing design functions, implementing design data, and establishing interactive visualizations. To examine its effectiveness, we did a participatory design experiment. We invited twelve participants to view the 3D design proposal and then make adjustments based on their respective preferences using the MR design support system. This experiment demonstrated that this system could achieve intuitive on-site 3D visualization for the public to understand professional design proposals and real-time design interactions to present their design intentions.

Keywords: *Public participation, Design support system, Mixed Reality, Interactive visualization, Community design*

INTRODUCTION

With the rapid urban development in recent years, community public space has begun to play a more important role, carrying on the more prosperous daily life (Houa and Grohmannb 2018). The public has always been invited to participate in the planning and design of the community public space. However, there are still some mismatches between the demands of the public and the design proposal from the professionals. As the diversity of knowledge context and the lack of practical tools, the public hardly understands the professional design documents accurately and scarcely expresses his or her design intention clearly.

The rapid development of computer graphics provides the possibilities to bridge the gap between the public and professionals in community planning and design. Especially for the emergence of Mixed Reality (MR), MR is the merging spectrum of real and virtual worlds to produce new environments and visualizations where physical and virtual objects coexist and interact in real-time, which provides considerable potentials to implement the new tool to realize on-site visualization and even real-time interaction of design object (Milgram and Kishino,1994).

Since 1990, scholars began to use MR technology to develop design support tools for public participation in planning and design fields. Feiner et al. (1995) firstly applied MR technology to implement a design support system called "Architect Anatomy" to provide the public an "X-ray vision" to visualize digital design elements overlaying on the physical place.

Subsequently, to achieve interaction and add design functions, tangible design tabletop began to be developed as the primary form of MR design support system to facilitate public participation. Typically, URP or Luminous Table could provide the public with real-time design sketches inputting on the table surface (Underkoffler and Ishii, 1999; Ishii et al., 2002). Whereas, they were limited to the usage of physical models had to be prepared in advance and could not be adjusted in real-time. So the following MR design tabletop began to try the virtual 3D models. For example, Sketchand+ and Benchwork utilized a digitizer tablet as the input interface to create 3D house models for interactive visualization (Seichter, 2003; Seichter, 2004). Then the interaction mode of the MR design tabletop had been upgraded further. ARTHUR firstly offered wand and gesture interaction for users creating, viewing, and editing 3D models from the first-person perspective (Broll et al., 2004; Schieck et al., 2005; Wang, 2013). Nevertheless, these MR design tabletops always were blamed for never immersed design objects into their real environment (Schubert et al., 2015).

Therefore, the on-site MR design support system MR Tent was developed, which brought the laboratory technologies to design sites and provided the public an interactive approach to input sketches (Sareika and Schmalstieg, 2007; Maquil et al., 2009). However, MR Tent involved tedious on-site installations and was limited at a single viewpoint (Schubert et al., 2015).

The subsequent MR design support systems began to explore the use of mobile devices, especially smartphones (Oksman et al., 2014). The early MR design support system on smartphones mainly focused on providing the public on-site virtualization for 3D objects and alternative design elements (Allen et al., 2011). Then, Skov et al. (2013) developed ArchiLens on the smartphone, which could offer real-time adjustment functions for the public to control the position, appearance, shape, and size of 3D design objects on-site. However, the 2D screen display based on the smartphone could hardly provide the public with an intuitive visual understanding (Wang et al., 2018). Similarly, the narrow tangible interaction interface based on the smartphone could barely support the public to make effective design representation (Chi et al., 2013).

With recent technology improvements, more advanced wearable MR devices have emerged. In particular, Microsoft HoloLens (Microsoft, Redmond, WA) is equipped with unique features like 3D visual display, special interaction mode, and spatial depth perception, bringing the possibilities for improving further the MR design support system for public participation.

Therefore, the purpose of this research is to develop an MR design support system on Microsoft HoloLens to facilitate public participation in community public space design. This system intends to realize 3D on-site visualization assisting the public in understanding the professional design proposal. Besides, it plans to provide real-time interaction possibility for the public to express their design intentions.

METHODS

MR design support system development

Concept design. As shown in Figure 1, the MR design support system was planned to operate in a WiFi environment. Design data (including 3D models and 2D

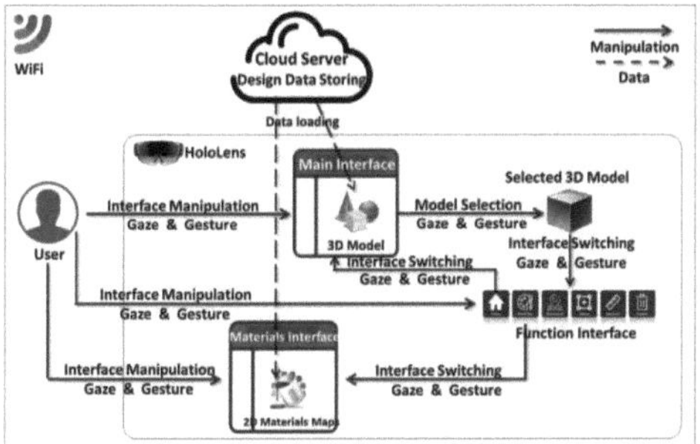

Figure 1
Concept design of MR design support system

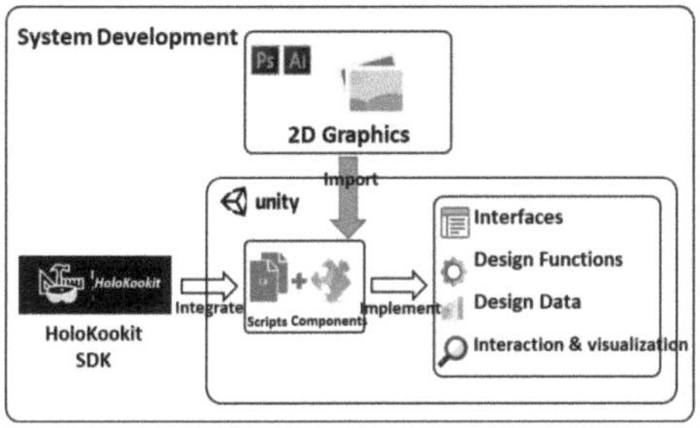

Figure 2
Development process of MR design support system

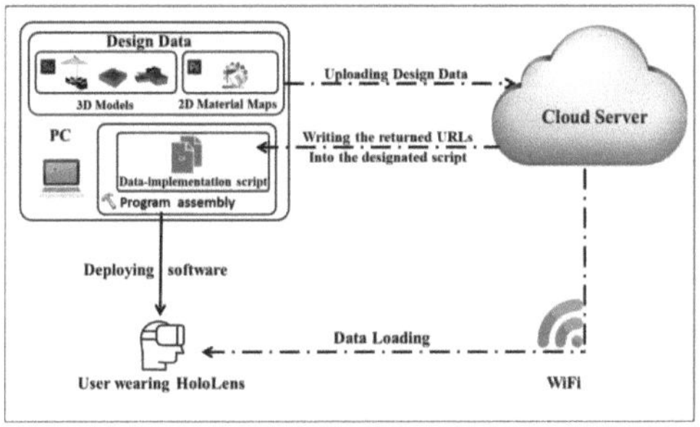

Figure 3
Data workflow

material maps) were intended to store in a cloud server. We designed three interactive interfaces for this MR design support system, the main interface for loading 3D models, a materials interface for loading corresponding 2D material maps, a function interface for providing some essential design functions. These design functions mainly include model adjustment (moving, rotating, scaling), model placement, model materials selection, model deletion, and spatial distance measurement. Additionally, the unique interaction mode depending on gaze and gesture was ready to be inducted for users' control.

Development process. As shown in Figure 2, we used Unity 3D as the core platform to develop the MR design support system. Further, we referenced some prefab development components from the HoloToolkit Software Development Kit (SDK). Specifically, we mainly referenced the input component for inducting gaze and gesture inputting, spatial mapping component for establishing physical interaction between the virtual object and natural world, and the object control component for providing 3D models adjustment. Additionally, we imported 2D graphics for the next interface creation. All coding was performed by the included compiler of Unity 3D in C sharp language. Specifically, this MR application software development involves four critical processes: creating interactive interfaces, developing design functions, implementing design data, and establishing interactivity and visualizations.

Data workflow. According to our concept, design data were intended to be loaded from a cloud server (Figure 3). Design data mainly contained 3D models and 2D material maps. The former was created in model-making software like SketchUp, and the latter was made in graphics-editing software like Adobe Photoshop. The edited design data were uploaded into the cloud server to acquire the corresponding URLs. The returned URLs were written into the matching data loading script to implement design data.

Testing and evaluation

To test the effectiveness of this MR design support system for public participation, we organized a participatory design experiment with twelve participants at a typical community public space.

Experimental case. In the research, we selected a typical design scene of community public space as the experimental case (Figure 4). This community public space is located at Kakuma Machi of Kanazawa City in Japan, which was preliminarily planned to add some greens and street furniture according to the public's demands and the professionals' suggestion (Figure 5). Thus, we prepared corresponding 3D models and 2D material maps for the planned greens and street furniture and uploaded them into the designated cloud server.

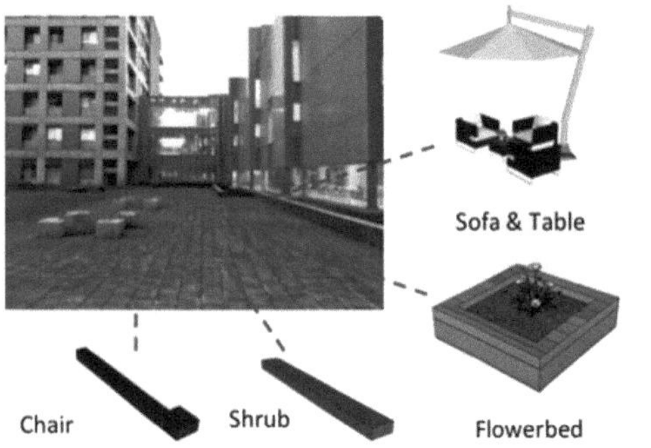

Figure 4
Experimental scene

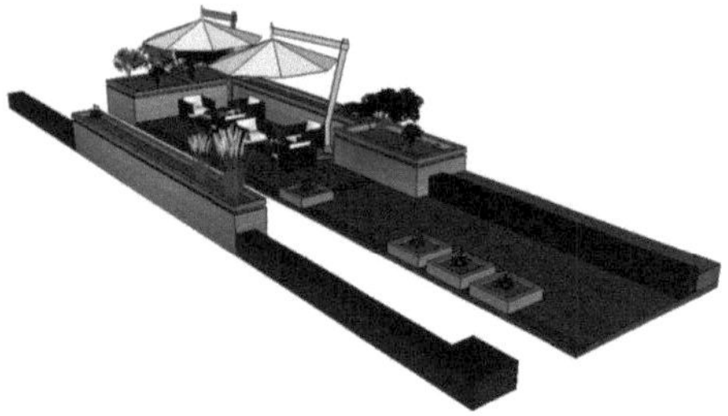

Figure 5
Preliminary design proposal

Participants. The twelve participants contained six males and six females. All of them were non-experts from the local community. Their familiarity with participatory community design and MR technology would be collected through the subsequent questionnaire survey.

Experimental procedures. After a brief usage instruction of this MR design support system, each participant began his or her participatory design experience (Figure 6). Specifically, each participant firstly visualized and understood the professional design proposal at the actual design site with this MR design support system. Then each participant expressed his or her design intention through changing design objects or adjusting design parameters (position, size, and materials) with this MR design support system.

Subsequently, we made a questionnaire survey with each participant to evaluate the effectiveness of this MR design support system in facilitating public participation. The following main questions were asked, all ranked on a five-point Likert scale⊠

1.Are you familiar with participatory community design? (1: Not at all, 2: Slightly, 3: Moderately, 4: Very, 5: Extremely)

2.Are you familiar with MR technology? (1: Not at all, 2: Slightly, 3: Moderately, 4: Very, 5: Extremely)

3.Do you agree MR design support system makes the professional design proposal understandable? (1: Strongly disagree, 2: disagree, 3: Neither agree nor disagree, 4: Agree, 5: Strongly agree)

4.Do you believe this design support system is helpful to express your design intention? (1: Strongly disagree, 2: disagree, 3: Neither agree nor disagree, 4: Agree, 5: Strongly agree)

The results of the questionnaire survey were described in terms of means and standard deviation. In addition, we used correlation analysis with significance at the 5% level to explain further the results based on the familiarity with participatory design and MR technology of participants.

RESULTS AND ANALYSIS

Descriptive statistics

Figure 7 displays the scores (mean and standard deviation) for the central questions of the questionnaire survey. Specifically, about the familiarity of participatory community design, most respondents barely involved in related design activities, thus not understanding it well and giving relatively low scores (mean ± standard deviation: 2.00±0.74). Regarding the familiarity of MR, most participants knew little about this cutting-edge technology and gave rather negative scores (mean ± standard deviation: 2.25±1.05). At the same time, Figure 7 presents the relatively high ratings (mean ± standard deviation: 4.33±0.78 and 4.42±0.79) for respondents un-

Figure 6
The 3D on-site interactive visualization using the MR design support system

derstanding the professional design proposal and expressing design appeals, respectively. That suggested a positive effect for this MR design support system to facilitate public participation in community public space design.

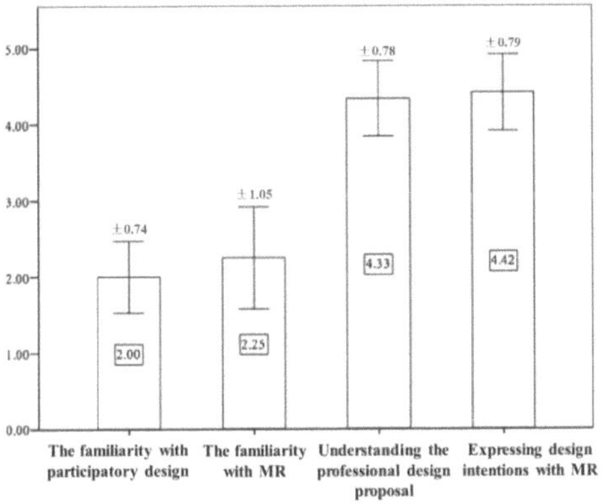

Figure 7
The mean and standard deviation of the scores for the main questions of the questionnaire survey

Correlation analysis

Since most scores for the main questions of the questionnaire survey were in skewed distribution (Table 1), we adopted to calculate the Spearman's rank correlation coefficient to verify their correlation.

Table 2 revealed a strong positive correlation (correlation coefficient and P-value: 0.791 and 0.002) between the familiarity of participatory community design and understanding the professional design proposal with the MR design support system. Similarly, from table 2, we could find a strong positive correlation (correlation coefficient and P-value: 0.733 and 0.007) between the familiarity of MR and expressing design intentions with the MR design support system.

However, there was no identified correlation (correlation coefficient and P-value: -0.111 and 0.012) between the familiarity of MR and understanding the professional design proposal with the MR design support system(Table 2). Also, we could not find a significant correlation (correlation coefficient and P-value: 0.000 and 1) between the familiarity of participatory community design and expressing design intentions with the MR design support system (Table 2).

DISCUSSION

Understanding the professional design proposal with this MR design support system

From Figure 8, we can see most participants believed the MR design support system could make the professional design proposal more understandable. Six respondents scored five points, and four respondents gave four points. However, two participants with low familiarity with participatory community design just scored three points. Also, we can found a significant increasing trend for the scores for understanding the professional design proposal with the increase of familiarity with participatory community design, which explained the correlation analysis results further (Figure 8).

Table 1
The skewness of the scores for the main questions of questionnaire survey

		The familiarity with participatory design	The familiarity with MR	Understanding the professional design proposal with MR	Expressing design intention with MR
Skewness	Statistic	-0.000	0.522	-0.719	-0.988
	Std. Error	0.637	0.637	0.637	0.637

Table 2
Spearman's rank correlation analysis

		Understanding the professional design proposal with MR	Expressing design intention with MR
The familiarity with participatory design	Correlation Coefficient	0.791	0.000
	P-value	0.002	1.000
The familiarity with MR	Correlation Coefficient	-0.111	0.733
	P-value	0.12	0.007

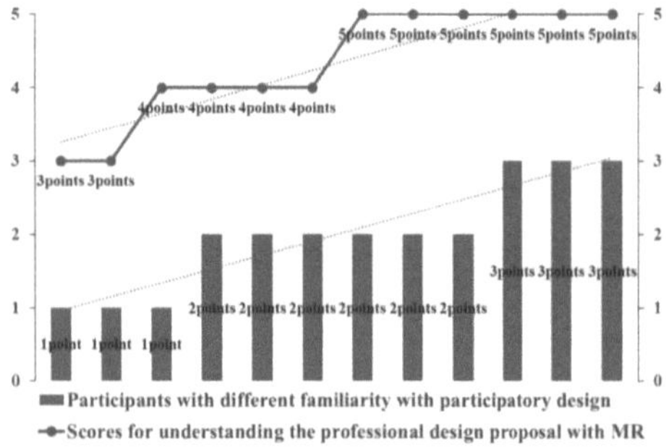

Figure 8
The scores distribution for understanding the professional design proposal using the MR design support system based on the familiarity with participatory community design of participants

Specifically, the MR design support system could bring the digital design model to the community scene for on-site visualization. Further, this visualization displayed the stereoscopic form and accurate size for the design proposal model. Also, this visualization presented the real spatial depth and relationship between the virtual objects and the real environment. Additionally, with the portability of this system, the participants could select view freely to understand the vivid design blueprint intuitively instead of tenebrous design documents. However, a few participants who were never involved in related participatory design activities could not experience the significant benefits from MR.

Expressing the design intention with this MR design support system

According to Figure 9, we could see most respondents agreed the MR design support system was helpful for users to express their design intention. Seven participants scored five points, and three participants gave four points. However, two respondents with low familiarity with MR technology just gave three points. Also, we can found the scores for expressing the design intention with this MR design support system rise sharply with the increase of familiarity with MR technology, which also further proved the correlation analysis results (Figure 9).

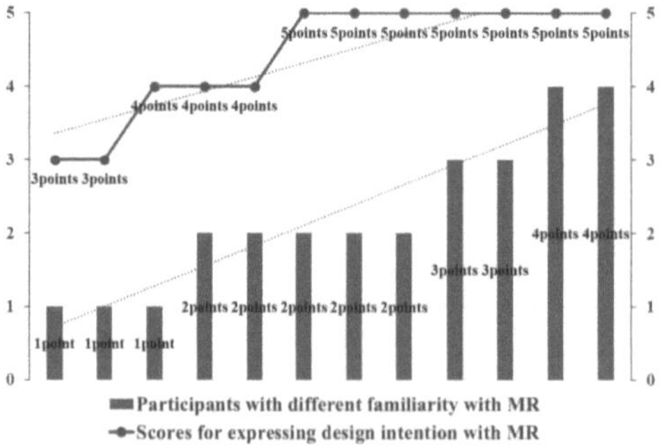

Figure 9
The scores distribution for expressing the design intention using the MR design support system based on the familiarity with MR of participants

In this regard, this MR design support system provided a convenient approach for participants interacting with the MR environments and conveying design intention. First, the design data were prepared according to the preliminary design proposal in advance, which contributed to the participants making quick design judgments instead of complicated and tedious design deductions. Furthermore, the control of this MR design support system was relatively simple. Just through a brief usage training, most participants could select the suitable design objects and set the appropriate form, position, materials using convenient gesture and gaze control. Nevertheless, a few respondents with low familiarity with MR technology could not grasp the basic usage skills of this system in such a short time, thus not completing design intention expression smoothly.

Limitations

However, there still are some limitations to our research. First, this system's narrow field of view (FOV) made it difficult for the participants to visualize the whole design proposal in the real community environment. Second, there are some chromatic aberrations and sawtooth for 3D design objects under the strong sunlight sometimes. These two limitations might affect the participants' perception and understanding of the professional design proposal. Third, this MR design support system sometimes operated slowly with laggy control when referring the complicated design models. Fourth, design data used in the experiment were prepared beforehand, which might have limited the design imagination of the participants. The latter two limitations might affect the participants to express their design intentions.

CONCLUSION

In this research, we developed an MR design support system to facilitate public participation in community public space design. Through a participatory design experiment with twelve participants, we have demonstrated it could achieve 3D interactive on-site visualization of virtual design objects. The results validated the effectiveness of this system to support public participation.

To be more specific, this MR design support system could realize 3D visualization of design objects on-site. It could contribute to the public experiencing and understanding the life-like details, exact scale, and accurate spatial perception of the design proposal in the real community environment intuitively, avoiding abstract design imagination and deduction based on conventional professional design documents. Meanwhile, the MR design support system could support real-time interaction between users and virtual design objects. It provided a convenient entrance for the public to adjust the design objects directly by gesture and gaze, instead of conveying design intention using indirect language, drawing, and texts.

Future works will be optimizing the MR design support system for more clear display, more stable operation, more prosperous functions and applying it to the actual community planning projects to promote public participation.

REFERENCES

Allen, M, Regenbrecht, H and Abbott, M 2011 'Smartphone augmented reality for public participation in urban planning', *Proceedings of the 23rd Australian Computer- Human Interaction Conference*, Canberra, pp. 11-20

Broll, W, Lindt, I, Ohlenburg, J, Wittkamper, M, Yuan, C, Novotny, T, Schieck, AF, Mottram, C and Strothmann, A 2004, 'ARTHUR: A Collaborative Augmented Environment for Architectural Design and Urban Planning', *Journal of Virtual Reality and Broadcasting*, 1, pp. 102-109

Chi, HL, Kang, SC and Wang, X 2013, 'Research Trends and opportunities of augmented reality applications in architecture, engineering', *Automation in Construction*, 33, pp. 116-122

Feiner, S, Webster, A, Krueger, T, MacIntyre, B and Keller, T 1995, 'Architectural anatomy', *Presence: Teleoperators and Virtual Environments*, 4, pp. 318-325

Hou, J and Grohmann, D 2018, 'Integrating Community Gardens into Urban Parks: Lessons in Planning, Design and Partnership from Seattle', *Urban Forestry & Urban Greening*, 33, pp. 46-55

Ishii, H, Ben-Joseph, L, Underkoffler, J, Yeung, L, Chak, D, Kanji, J and Piper, B 2002 'Augmented Urban Planning Workbench: Overlaying Drawings, Physical Models and Digital Simulation', *Proceedings of the 1st International Symposium on Mixed and Augmented Reality (ISMAR '02)*, Darmstadt, pp. 203-214

Maquil, V, Sareika, M, Schmalstieg, M and Wagner, D 2009 'MR Tent: A Place for Co- Constructing Mixed Realities in Urban Planning', *Proceedings of Graphics Interface 2009 (GI'09)*, Kelowna, pp. 211-214

Milgram, P and Kishino, F 1994, 'A taxonomy of mixed reality visual displays', *IEICE Transactions on Information and Systems*, 12, pp. 1321-1329

Olsson, T, Kärkkäinen, T, Lagerstam, E and Ventä-Olkkonen, L 2012, 'User evaluation of mobile augmented reality scenarios', *Journal of Ambient Intelligence and Smart Environments*, 4, pp. 29-47

Sareika, M and Schmalstieg, D 2007 'Urban sketcher: Mixed reality on site for urban planning and architecture', *Proceedings of the 2007 6th IEEE and ACM International Symposium on Mixed and Augmented Reality (ISMAR '07)*, Nara, pp. 27-30

Schieck, AF, Penn, A, Mottram, C, Strothmann, A, Ohlenburg, J, Broll, W, Attfield, S and Aish, F 2005, 'Interactive Space Generation through Play Exploring Form Creation and the Role of Simulation on the Design Table', *International Journal of Architectural Computing*, 3, pp. 3-25

Schubert, G, Schattel, D, To⊠nnis, M, Klinker, G and Petzold, F 2015, 'Tangible mixed reality on-site: interactive augmented visualizations from architectural working models in urban design', in Celani,, G, Sperling, DM and Franco, JMS (eds) 2015, *The Next City - New Technologies and the Future of the Built Environment*, Springer, Berlin, pp. 55- 74

Seichter, H 2003 'Sketchand+ a Collaborative Augmented Reality Sketching Application', *Proceedings of the 8th International Conference on Computer-Aided Architectural Design Research in Asia (CAADRIA 2003)*, Bangkok, pp. 209-222

Seichter, H 2004 'Benchworks - Augmented Reality Urban Design', *Proceedings of the 9th International Conference on Computer-Aided Architectural Design Research in Asia (CAADRIA 2004)*, Seoul, pp. 193-202

Skov, MB, Kjeldskov, J, Paay, J, Husted, N, Nørskov, J and Pedersen, K 2013, 'Designing on-site: Facilitating participatory contextual architecture with mobile phones', *Pervasive and Mobile Computing*, 9, pp. 216-227

Underkoffler, J and Ishii, H 1999 'Urp: A Luminous-Tangible Workbench for Urban Planning and Design', *Proceedings of the SIGCHI conference on Human Factors in Computing Systems (CHI '99)*, Pittsburgh, pp. 386-393

Wang, X 2009, 'Augmented Reality in Architecture and Design: Potentials and Challenges for Application', *International Journal of Architectural Computing*, 7, pp. 309-326

Wang, W, Wu, X, Chen, G and Chen, Z 2018, 'Holo3DGIS: Leveraging Microsoft HoloLens in 3D Geographic Information', *ISPRS International Journal of Geo-Information*, 7(2), p. 60

Augmented Bodies

Interactive wearables for local-global synergies

Ioanna Symeonidou[1]
[1]*Assistant Professor, University of Thessaly, Greece*
[1]*symeonidou@uth.gr*

The paper documents the research and design of an interactive dance performance which was devised as a collective project of an interdisciplinary team comprising of architects, digital designers, musicians and dancers. The project employed methodologies of research by design and utilized a range of digital technologies for 3D body scanning, digital design, 3D printing of the wearables incorporating sensors of different types that would translate the data from the motion tracking into music and interactive video projections. The design process employed ad hoc methodologies, as there was constant feedback across designers, musicians, engineers and dancers. The design of the wearables was done on a 3D avatar, obtained through 3D scanning of the dancer's body. The wearables were designed with algorithmic tools and optimized in order to accommodate the necessary space for the sensors and microcontrollers. During the interactive dance performance the sounds are perceived to be coming from the body.

Keywords: *motion capture, arduino microcontrollers, 3D scanning, 3D printing, digital fashion, cross-disciplinary design*

INTRODUCTION TO INTERACTIVE ARTS WITH DIGITAL MEDIA

Interactivity within the arts is not a new concept, while the ever-growing use of digital media for artistic projects not only facilitates design collaborations, but also gives rise to an emerging field of algorithmic arts which applies both to musical composition, design studies and choreography. More specifically, algorithmic music which has been around for some decades already, seems to share a lot of compositional strategies with architectural design. At the same time, creative programming is gaining ground among artists and coding afficionados. Algorithmic composition however, apart from the immense possibilities of complex structures with emergent results, displays a huge potential with regards to interactivity. In 2007 New Interfaces for Musical Expression (NIME) Conference an overview of interactive music applications was presented during the lecture titled "The acoustic, the digital and the body: A survey on musical instruments", where more than 200 musicians, composers, engineers, designers, artists participated in a survey that attempted to map activities related to interactive musical instruments or compositions in flexible audio programming environments such as SuperCollider, Pure Data, ChucK, Max/MSP, CSound (Magnusson & Mendieta, 2007). Among the remarks of this survey was the fact that playing digital instruments for the majority of the participants appeared to be less of an embodied practice, when compared to acoustic instrument where the embodiment is of major importance. However, the use of fine-tuned wearable sensors and the appropriate mapping between gesture and sound could strongly influence the degree of embodiment. Nowadays digital technology permits real-time audible feedback, therefore an artist can easily gain an intuitive understanding of the response of a digital instrument and even receive haptic feedback when sensors are combined with actuators.

Within the dance and choreography discipline, interactive performances mainly employ motion capture, and process the collected data to create visual or musical environments. Motion capture is believed to originate from the experiments carried out by the physiologist Etienne-Jules Marey and the photographer Eadweard Muybridge who pioneered chronophotography in the 1880s (Jensenius, 2013). However digital motion capture that can generate real-time data has opened up new possibilities within digitally interconnected artistic environments. A big variety of sensors and a series of simple motor-based actuators are readily available and easy to program with Arduino microcontrollers, making interactivity accessible to artists of different disciplines. More specifically, for dance performances, motion capture has become a new powerful tool in the hands of dancers and choreographers.

Motion capture in dance performances can be achieved with either optical or inertial systems (Solberg & Jensenius, 2016), each of which display their different characteristics and modus operandi. Optical would include a setup with multiple infrared cameras to record the position of reflective markers on the body of the dancers, while inertial sensor devices mainly accelerometers, gyroscopes can either record or send the data via wireless networks. Accelerometers measure the 3d orientation and linear acceleration, while gyroscopes measure the rotational velocity. For the project presented here, motion capture was achieved with a variety of inertial sensors, that will be presented in the following sections.

Figure 1
The three dancers with the 3D printed prosthetics

CROSS-DISCIPLINARY ARTISTIC COLLABORATION

Precedents in interactive music and dance performances, wearable computing and data-driven animations

There are several precedents of interactive dance performances and motion capture (R. Aylward et al., 2006; Ryan Aylward & Paradiso, 2006; Dixon, 2007; Erdem et al., 2020; Jessop, 2015; Johnston, 2015; Lindborg, 2018; Martin et al., 2020; Raheb et al., 2018; Vincs & McCormick, 2010). The CyberShoe (Paradiso et al., 1999) was one of the early models that employed sensors (accelerometers and gyroscopes) and RF communication protocols for capturing data from dancer's feet. The creators of the CyberShoe had written software applications to map the data from the shoes onto a simple musical structure and tested the process during an artistic performance at MIT.

Since the CyberShoe and until today wearable computing has also seen great developments, though not all relate to artistic projects. Wearable computing mainly includes devices that monitor health, such as smart watches or fitness trackers, smart clothes that include thermometer and heart rate monitors, smart glasses and head mounted displays that augment our vision with new layers of information. However we are currently witnessing an ever growing use of wearable computers for artistic projects, from wearables that control sound (Birringer & Danjoux, 2013) to electronic textiles (Buechley et al., 2008; Liang et al., 2019; Stewart, 2019) to fashion tech applications (Bruggeman et al., 2019) and even living musical instruments like the Serendiptichord (Murray-Browne et al., 2013) and SONIFICA by MONAD and Anouk Wipprecht (Goldemberg, 2017).

There is also a great wealth of precedents of interactive video projections during dance performances. From Cunningham's influential BIPED which premiered in Berkeley California in 1999, to contemporary performances like the cyberPRINT project (Bermudez et al., 2000), Collapse, which involved 3D projection of scientific data with motion capture-based interaction and visualized T-LiDAR data sets and interaction between performers and visualizations (Neff et al., 2010) and the works of Troika Ranch (Kepner, 1997) that are known for merging dance with digital media and giving control to the performer, which led to the development of award-winning software Isadora®, a flexible graphic programming environment that provides interactive control over digital media (Coniglio, 2005, 2006).

The innovation of the performance "Trajectory of an Idea" presented in this paper lies in the combination and cross-fertilization of all the above. While wearable computing was employed for gathering the data to be processed by the musical composition algorithm, at the same time the motion capture data and physical forces from the dancer's interaction where real-time visualized through video animations that interpreted the data and created interactive visuals.

Figure 2
Dancers with cybernetic arms experimenting with musical output. Each arm device is 3D printed and contains a 9-DOF inertial sensor, a rotary potentiometer, an Arduino microcontroller and an RF modem

Prosthetics, digital fashion technology, and cybernetic aesthetics

Having gained valuable feedback though observation of the performer's body movements during the performance, it was necessary to create a series of wearable devices that would incorporate the necessary electronics and fit on the dancer's body without obstructing the movement, while adhering to the performance's cybernetic aesthetic, seeking inspiration in science fiction, prosthetics and cyborgs.

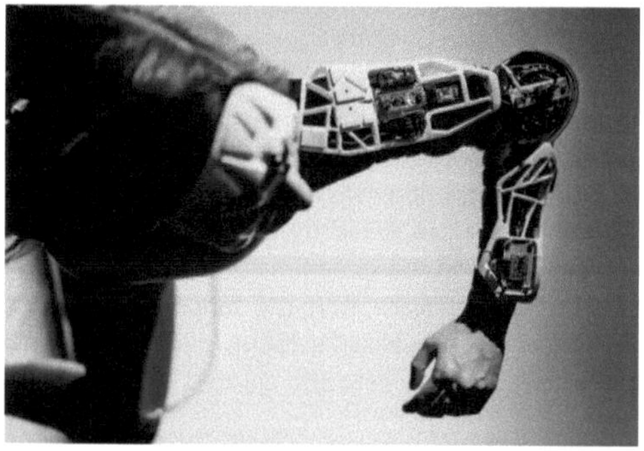

Figure 3
The cybernetic arm

Stelarc, a provocative yet prophetic artist, is the personification of post-humanism, he has always explored prosthetics and amplifications of the human body, As McLuhan explained "In the electric age, when our central nervous system is technologically extended to whole of mankind and to incorporate the whole of mankind in us, we necessarily participate, in depth, in the consequences of our every action" (McLuhan, 1964). For Stelarc technology is symbiotic with the human body, creating a new synthesis of a hybrid human with augmented capabilities (Goodall, 2005). Stelarc in his performances used electrodes that transmitted the electromyographic signals, and created a soundscape while in Exoskeleton: Ciborg Frictions (1999) he employed prosthetic legs of hexapod robot structure. More recently fashion tech Anouk Wipprecht has created fururistic cyborg body augmentations like the Smoke Dress and Spider that react when some walks in her personal space (Wipprecht, 2014). Cyberpunk aesthetics is an ever-growing trend in performances and digital art (Psarra, 2014). Cyberpunk is integrated with other critical theoretical tenets, such as posthumanism, the Anthropocene, animality, and empire (McFarlane et al., 2019).

More recent precedents of cybernetic interactive wearables like the work of Pauline van Dongen, Iris van Herpen, Bart Hess, have been important sources of inspiration, with regards to interactivity as well as style (Hemmings, 2019; Smelik, A.M. & Smelik, Anneke, 2017). Computational couture and 3D printing wearables (Bitonti, 2017; Casas, 2017; Doubrovski et al., 2017; Koerner, 2017; Rosenkrantz & Louis⊠Rosenberg, 2017). As Neil Leach explains "both architecture and 3D-printed body architecture fall under the category of design, and should not be distinguished in terms of scale" (Leach & Farahi, 2017).

The digital workflow of the design process

During the initial stages of the performance preparation the first working prototypes of the wearables were created on an orthopedic device for the arm, where inertial sensors and Arduino microcontroller were mounted, together with RF modem and a battery. The dance performer would wear this hinged elbow brace during the initial rehearsals. The movement repertoire and the musical output counter informed each other. During each act the music composer tested different mapping algorithms, to associate different data values to different musical outcomes, which included changes in the tonal structure, volume, blending of different musical layers, as well as more complex operations that would utilize prerecorded material from physical instruments together with electronic sound. Both wireless communication and ethernet was used. More specifically, the data gathered from the sensors would be sent through an RF modem to an Arduino microprocessor and then transferred as Open Sound Control (OSC) protocol through ethernet to the router. A local area network (LAN) of exclusive use for the performance would then send OSC packets over User Datagram

Figure 4
Real-time processing of the sensor data with SuperColide, MaxMSP and Isadora

Protocol (UDP). The arrays of data received would be processed to generate the music, the video animations and the lights of the performance. The music was created real-time through SuperColider based on different methodologies. The data from the sensors would affect the balance of different musical layers, therefore adding depth, polyphony, volume or dissonance. Music composition also involved granular techniques for compositing multiphonic sounds, with sensor data affecting the granular synthesis parameters. For the interactive visuals and video animations, the data was first preprocessed by MaxMSP, for filtering or other mathematical operations and subsequently processed in Isadora.

The design process involved the constant feedback across designers, musicians, engineers and dancers. An initial mapping of the movements on stage helped to devise a strategy regarding the type of sensors that the performers would be wearing and the type of data that were to be gathered (coordinates, acceleration, gravity, rotation, flexion, tension). The aim was to test different methodologies of translating the data obtained from the sensors into artistically useful material (Jensenius, 2018).

Figure 5
The Arduino microcontroller and the RF modem

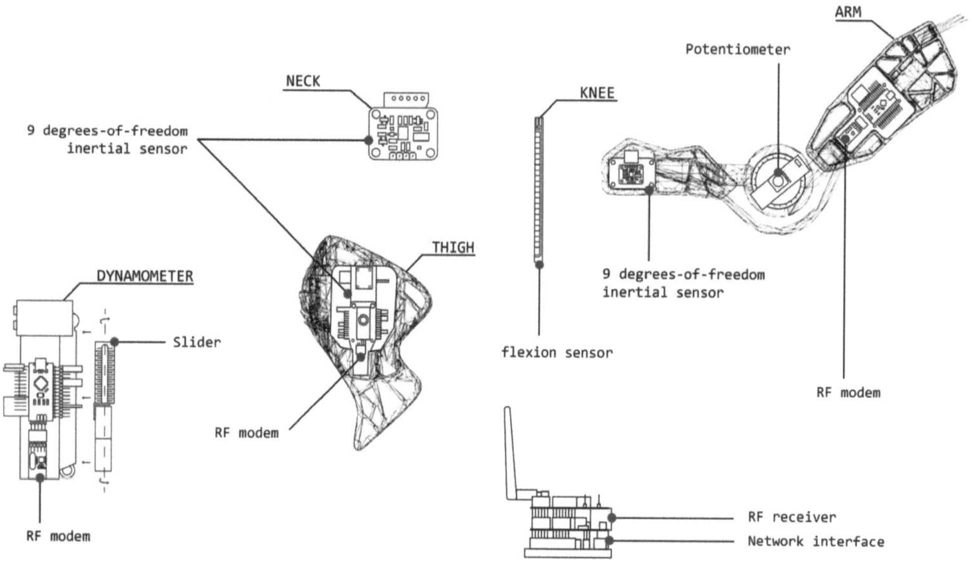

Figure 6
Wearables with sensors and microcontrollers: The neck piece, the thigh piece, the dynamometer, the knee flex sensor, the arm device and the RF receiver

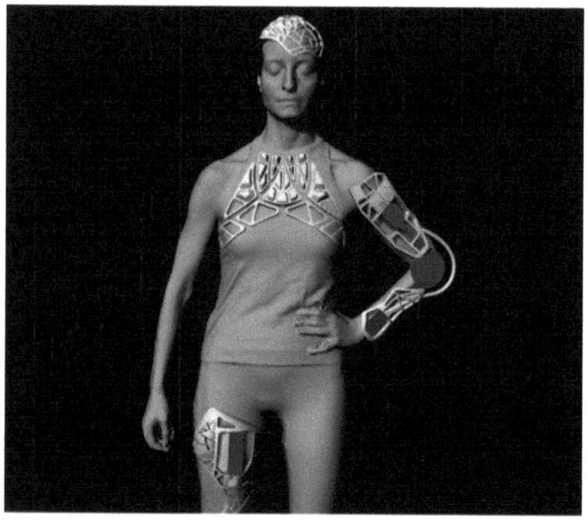

Figure 7
The digital avatar with the wearable devices

In order to obtain a digital avatar of the dancer's body with relatively high geometric precision, 3D scanning was employed. A Portable White Light technology 3D Scanner was used (see figure). The mesh was then imported in Rhino3D to be used as a base for the design of the wearables. It was important to ensure that the wearables would fit exactly on the body of the dancer, especially the parts on the thigh, that would carry the intertial motion sensor, the RF modem and the battery, and the chest piece; during the choreography the body contracts and expands, therefore causing different muscle movements that should not be conditioned by the wearables.

The headpiece and masks were modeled on a generic 3D face model, as they were to be worn by several different performers and the exact fitting was not such a strong design constraint. The half masks of the performance aimed to adhere to the overall cyberpunk aesthetic which was further augmented by the interactive video projections. For the design of the components to be 3D printed, it was important to consider the hidden spaces for the batteries, the cavities for the microcontrollers and sensors and the location of the RF modem, that had to be as visible as possible not to impede the signal communication with the RF receiver. The internal part of the wearables contained numerous cables that connected all of the components together and in some cases were carried to other sensors located on the dancer's body, through a cyborg style transparent tube that would connect different parts of the body to a unique RF modem on each dancer that would collect and send all the data from the sensors.

THE PERFORMANCE

During the performance, data from more than 12 different sensors was sent as RF signal to the RF receivers. These sensors included two 9-DOF inertial sensors and two rotary potentiometers on the arms, one inertial sensor on the neck, two flex sensors on the knees, and an inertial motion sensor on the thigh. Complementary to the wearable devices a dynamometer with RF modem and a set of scales with pressure sensors provided with constantly changing data sets. Careful calibration before each performance was necessary, to avoid technical failures during the show.

Essentially, the piece uses motion data, such as the accelerations or inclinations of various body parts, filters them, and applies them to algorithmic logic that is specifically tuned for each composition. Sometimes it makes the interaction obvious, to draw the viewer's attention to the interactivity of the composition, whereas in other parts the motion influences the composition as a whole, contributing to macroscopic or statistical parameters. A major priority was not to marginalize the performance's artistic and aesthetic value in favor of technique. Yet we wanted sensors and microcontrollers to be visible on the body adhering to the cybernetic aesthetics. Similarly, for the interactive video animation, the design strategy was on one hand to reveal the internal logic by explicitly printing the numerical data of the forces' values on the screen, and on the other hand to conceal the technical parameters and algorithmic logic behind the animation and generate an seamless data transfer within an atmosphere were all chore-

Figure 8
Choreographic action - reaction with real-time sonar and visual output

ographic events, music and projections blend, they are generated organically without any obvious cue on what is influencing what. Densities, modulations, deviations from various attractor states: each part constitutes a different interaction experiment, also involving, for example, whether the sounds are perceived to be coming from the body or are part of its environment. Within this cross-disciplinary project, the design intent was to use the technology as a means, and not as a subject itself: often, the interactive parts constitute one stem that combines with a more elaborate, time-based composition, in order to achieve the desired result. In other words, technology is used where it outperforms the human: as an augmentation, not as a replacement.

Figure 9
Interactive grid distortion based on motion capture

On the conceptual level, the individual parts are made up of metaphorical imagery (Lakoff & Johnson, 2003). The full performance is made up of five segments, each representing a stage in the life of an idea, whereas the other forms of the performance lose the long-term structure and focus more on the individual scenes. The piece introduces the audience to an intracellular construction zone, with a "mitochondrial modality in a tuning operation"; it will investigate growth and interconnection through statistics and a "compositional tug-of-war", will consider multilevel concepts as containers that may - metaphorically - fill up, empty, or overflow, while also engaging with purely mental imagery, like "the Cartesian Self as a distant landscape", or classical dynamics and elements borrowed from chaos theory. Eventually, it will contemplate the body and the mind as machines, trains of thought, individuality, and collectiveness. The augmented body becomes an instrument and choreography interactively creates the music composition.

ACKNOWLEDGEMENTS

The performance "Trajectory of an Idea" was conceived by Die Wolke art group and was financially supported by the Greek Ministry of Culture and Sports. The contributors of the original performance were the following. Choreography/performance: Drosia Triantaki, Performance: Areti Michou, Marianna Leptokaropoulou, Music/Interactive programming: Dani Joss, Interactive videos: Aliki Iosafat, Electronics: Giannis Perisoratis, Wearables/3D print design: Ioanna Symeonidou, Costumes/Fitting: Maria Louvari, Additional sound design: Paradigm Weave - Alfonso De Grandis, Recording musicians: Lazaros Pliambas (percussion), Dimitris Dalezis (trumpet), Iraklis Iosifidis (double bass), Giannis Kyratsos (vocals), Michalis Karanikos (trombone), 3D scanning: Digital Manufacturing and Materials Characterization Laboratory, International Hellenic University.

Performances took place on 24, 25 May, 8, 9 June 2019 at Vitruvian Thing in Thessaloniki, 31 May 2019 at Olvio theatre in Athens, October 2020 at ISO ses-

Figure 10
The final scene of the performance

sions during Dimitria festival in Thessaloniki (online), 2021 as a solo version at MOMus State Museum of Contemporary Art in Thessaloniki, Greece. More information and videos can be found on the official performance webpage [1] and on Die Wolke Art Group vimeo channel [2].

REFERENCES

Aylward, R, Lovell, S and Paradiso, J 2006 'A compact, wireless, wearable sensor network for interactive dance ensembles', *Proceedings of the International Workshop on Wearable and Implantable Body Sensor Networks (BSN'06)*

Aylward, R and Paradiso, J 2006 'Sensemble: A Wireless, Compact, Multi-User Sensor System for Interactive Dance.', *Proceedings of the 2006 International Conference on New Interfaces for Musical Expression (NIME06), Paris, France*

Bermudez, J, Agutter, J, Lilly, B, Syroid, N, Westenskow, D, Foresti, S and Sharir, Y 2000 'Cyberprint: Toward an Architecture of Being', *ACADIA Quarterly, vol. 19, no. 3, pp. 8-12*, p. 5

Birringer, J and Danjoux, M 2013, 'The Sound of Movement Wearables: Performing UKIYO', *Leonardo*, 46(3), pp. 232-240

Bitonti, F 2017, 'Micromechanical Assemblies and the Human Body', *Architectural Design*, 87, pp. 64-69

Bruggeman, D, Mahy, J, Tap, R, Wubs, B, Feijs, L, Os, Kv, Kenning, G, Toussaint, L and Wensveen, S 2019, *Unfolding Fashion Tech: Pioneers of Bright Futures*, Onomatopee Projects, Eindhoven

Casas, N 2017, 'Interactions: Dialogues on Body, Protections and Derivatives', *Architectural Design*, 87(6), pp. 34-39

Coniglio, M 2006, 'Materials vs Content in Digitally Mediated Performance', in Broadhurst, S and Machon, J (eds) 2006, *Performance and Technology: Practices of Virtual Embodiment and Interactivity*, Palgrave Macmillan UK, London, pp. 78-84

Coniglio, M 2005, 'The importance of being interactive', in Carver, G and Beardon, C (eds) 2005, *New Visions In Performance*, Routledge

Doubrovski, Z, Stokhuijzen, D and Aberle, N 2017 'Fabricating the Foliage Dress: Computational Design in Couture', *Proceedings of SCF '18 ACM*, Cambridge, MA, USA, p. 3

Erdem, C, Schia, KH and Jensenius, AR 2019 'Vrengt: A Shared Body-Machine Instrument for Music-Dance Performance', *arXiv:2010.03779 [cs, eess]*
Goldemberg, E 2017, 'The Sonic Spectacle of the Enhanced Body', *Architectural Design*, 87(6), pp. 120-125
Goodall, J 2005, 'The will to evolve', in Smith, M and Clarke, J (eds) 2005, *Stelarc: the monograph*, MIT Press, Cambridge, Mass.
Hemmings, J 2019, 'Iris van Herpen: Transforming Fashion', *Fashion Theory*, 24(2), pp. 287-291
Jensenius, A 2013, 'Some Video Abstraction Techniques for Displaying Body Movement in Analysis and Performance', *Leonardo, The MIT Press*, 46(No. 1), pp. 53-60
Jensenius, AR 2018, 'Methods for Studying Music-Related Body Motion', in Bader, R (eds) 2018, *Springer Handbook of Systematic Musicology*, Springer, Berlin, Heidelberg, pp. 805-818
Jessop, E 2015, 'Capturing the Body Live: A Framework for Technological Recognition and Extension of Physical Expression in Performance', *Leonardo*, 48(1), pp. 32-38
Johnston, A 2015, 'Conversational Interaction in Interactive Dance Works', *Leonardo*, 48(3), pp. 296-297
Kepner, LS 1997, 'Dance and digital media: Troika Ranch and the art of technology', *Digital Creativity*, 8(1), pp. 11-19
Koerner, J 2017, 'Digitally Crafted Couture', *Architectural Design*, 87(6), pp. 40-47
Lakoff, G and Johnson, M 2003, *Metaphors We Live By*, University of Chicago Press, Chicago, Ill
Leach, N and Farahi, B (eds) 2017, *3D-Printed Body Architecture*, Wiley
Liang, A, Stewart, R and Bryan-Kinns, N 2019, 'Design of Textile Knitted Stretch Sensors for Dance Movement Sensing', *Proceedings*, 32, p. 14
Lindborg, P 2018, 'Interactive Sonification of Weather Data for The Locust Wrath, a Multimedia Dance Performance', *Leonardo*, 51(5), pp. 466-474
Magnusson, T and Mendieta, EH 2007 'The acoustic, the digital and the body: a survey on musical instruments', *Proceedings of the 7th international conference on New interfaces for musical expression*, New York, NY, USA, pp. 94-99
Martin, CP, Jensenius, AR and Torresen, J 2018 'Composing an Ensemble Standstill Work for Myo and Bela', *Proceedings of the International Conference on New Interfaces for Musical Expression*, pp. 196-197
McFarlane, A, Schmeink, L and Murphy, G (eds) 2019, *The Routledge Companion to Cyberpunk Culture*, Routledge
McLuhan, M 1964, *Understanding Media:*, Routledge, London
Murray-Browne, T, Mainstone, D, Bryan-Kinns, N and Plumbley, MD 2013, 'The Serendiptichord: Reflections on the Collaborative Design Process between Artist and Researcher', *Leonardo*, 46(1), pp. 86-87
Neff, M, Sumner, D, Bawden, GW, Bromberg, E, Crutchfield, JP, Davidson, D, Gilbride, S, Kellogg, LH and Kreylos, O 2010, 'Blending Art and Science: Collapse (suddenly falling down)', *Leonardo*, 43(3), pp. 274-281
Paradiso, J, Hu, E and Hsiao, Ky 1999 'The CyberShoe: A Wireless Multisensor Interface for a Dancers Feet', *Proceedings of International Dance and Technology 99*, Tempe, AZ
Psarra, A 2014, *Ciberpunk y arte de los nuevos medios: performance y arte digital*, Ph.D. Thesis, Universidad Complutense de Madrid
Raheb, KE, Tsampounaris, G, Katifori, A and Ioannidis, Y 2018 'Choreomorphy: a whole-body interaction experience for dance improvisation and visual experimentation', *Proceedings of the 2018 International Conference on Advanced Visual Interfaces*, New York, NY, USA, pp. 1-9
Rosenkrantz, J and Louis Rosenberg, J 2017, 'Dress/Code Democratising Design Through Computation and Digital Fabrication', *Architectural Design*, 87(6), pp. 48-57
Smelik, A 2017, 'Cybercouture: The Fashionable Technology of Pauline van Dongen, Iris van Herpen and Bart Hess', in Smelik, A (eds) 2017, *Smelik, Anneke (ed.), Delft Blue to Denim Blue. Contemporary Dutch Fashion*, London : I.B. Tauris, pp. 252-269
Solberg, R and Jensenius, A 2016 'OPTICAL OR INERTIAL? EVALUATION OF TWO MOTION CAPTURE SYSTEMS FOR STUDIES OF DANCING TO ELECTRONIC DANCE MUSIC', *Proceedings SMC 2016*, Hamburg, Germany
Stewart, R 2019, 'Cords and Chords: Exploring the Role of E-Textiles in Computational Audio', *Frontiers in ICT*, 6, pp. 1-12
Vincs, K and McCormick, J 2010, 'Touching Space: Using Motion Capture and Stereo Projection to Create a "Virtual Haptics" of Dance', *Leonardo*, 43(4), pp. 359-366
Wipprecht, A 2014, *The Technosensual Body*, transcript-Verlag
[1] https://die-wolke.org/trajectory
[2] https://vimeo.com/diewolkeartgroup

Computational design

Web-Based Collaborative Method for the Design and Fabrication of Gridshells

Marko Vučić[1], *Bojan Tepavčević*[2]
[1,2]*University of Novi Sad, Faculty of Technical Sciences, Department of Architecture*
[1,2]*{vucic.marko|tepavcevicb}@uns.ac.rs*

Abstract: Advancements in computational design and fabrication along with development of web-based platforms for 3D modeling instigated new approaches for the development of collaborative tools in architecture and building industry. This paper presents a collaborative method to design and fabrication of geodesic D-strips gridshells which can be used for mass customization of lightweight wooden shell pavilions. Collaborative design-to-fabrication method is presented in 2 phases: digital form-finding process with custom designed online parametric tool for creating funicular D-stripe gridshells and using Microsoft Hololens for making physical prototype in mixed reality environment. As a proof of concept design and manufacturing of geodesic D-strips gridshell models are realized within online and onsite workshop as a part of model making course class for the students without previous 3D modeling experience.

Keywords: *Collaborative Design, Geodesic D-strip models, Mixed reality, Gridshells*

INTRODUCTION

Advancements in computational design and fabrication along with development of web-based platforms for 3D modeling instigated new approaches for the development of collaborative tools in architecture and building industry (Leung et al. 2019, Canadinc et al. 2020). Due to the growing need for fast and more efficient job productivity, it is necessary to speed up the process of communication between collaborators. Hence there is a growing need for some things to be done remotely, for communication to be facilitated, and for the quality of work not to be degraded. Some projects (Yan 2017) via web platforms try to connect users, such as architects, civil engineers, clients, etc. and give them a common approach to the same problem in order to solve it more efficiently. However, such projects require a certain user experience in order to be involved in the use of the platform itself. Some other platforms are designed for less experienced users such as students to be able to parametrically model complex structures (Janssen and Mohanty 2016), but also require knowledge of the logic of visual programming. Gridshells are lightweight structures whose shape is complex and defined by the influence of forces. Therefore, modelling such constructions in a digital environment requires prior experience and knowledge of digital form-finding techniques. The production process of gridshells also requires a certain skillset.

The aim of this research was developing a tool

for users without previous 3D and parametric skills for digital form finding and manufacturing to fabricate geodesic D-strips gridshells. This paper presents a collaborative method to design and fabrication of geodesic D-strips gridshells which can be used for mass customization of lightweight wooden shell pavilions. Also this method is intended for students which have zero experience in any method modelling of complex structures, but want to exploit it in the field of fabrication.

Collaborative design-to-fabrication method presented in this work consists of 2 phases: digital form-finding process with custom designed online parametric tool for creating funicular D-stripe grid shells (GDS Tool) and using Microsoft Hololens for making physical prototype in mixed reality environment.

For the development of GDS tool, ShapeDiver platform for integrating Rhino files and Grasshopper definitions was used. Inside the grasshopper definition Kangaroo physics solver was implemented bringing the digital form-finding through dynamic relaxation of spring particle systems into the web environment. Along with parameters for the design variation for D-strips, GDS Tool provides mesh input parameters for generation of initial shell layout with openings and delivers as an output 3D preview of final shape along with CAD files for manufacturing process.

For the production process (Holo-Make), a mixed reality-based collaboration tool Fologram and Microsoft HoloLens was used. Holo-Make processes provide fabrication within mixed reality environments enabling unskilled users to assemble complex bending structures with minimal errors (Gwyllim et al. 2018).

As a proof of concept design and manufacturing of geodesic D-strips gridshell models are realized within 2 hours online and 5 hours onsite workshop as a part of model making course class for the students without previous 3D modeling experience. Workshop results and applied collaborative methods for the design and fabrication of gridshells are presented in this paper.

FORM-FINDING OF GRIDSHELLS IN WEB ENVIRONMENT

A gridshell is a lightweight structure, which derives its strength from double curvature. Geodesic gridshells use geodesic curves on the surface for creating gridshell networks. One of the most important geometric properties of geodesic curves is straightness property for planar unfolding. Straightness property of geodesic curves enables fabrication of inexpensive gridshells with flat straight boards.

Designing and creating wooden gridshells is often associated with experiments involving physical form-finding following the tradition of Frei Otto as well as digital form-finding (Pone et al. 2019, Lidel 2015). There are many digital form-finding methods such as force density method, thrust network analysis, dynamic relaxation, particle-spring method which can be used for shell form-finding as well as gridshells and all of them have a purpose of finding the force equilibrium in structures (Adriaenssens et al. 2014). All previously mentioned methods are time consuming and requires previous engineering knowledge and skills. However, GDS collaborative tool enables intuitive and interactive play with digital form-finding process in an online environment.

GDS tool is based on creating cloud application based on ShapeDiver platform. With simple embedding iframe link into any web page, ShapeDiver provide an online interface to web servers that compute Grasshopper files in the cloud.

In order to create tool that will enable efficient form exploration for the users that doesn't have previous knowledge of structural optimization, geometry and 3D, we define set of parameters and inputs that will enable simple and flexible design of gridshell based on geodesic D-strips.

GDS collaborative tool have 3 types of user interface components: upload buttons for importing geometry, range sliders for changing shape parameters and export button for automatic generation of fabrication files (Figure 1).

Upload buttons enables importing 2 types of data: mesh for creation of Gridshell floor layout and

Figure 1
User interface of the GDS tool

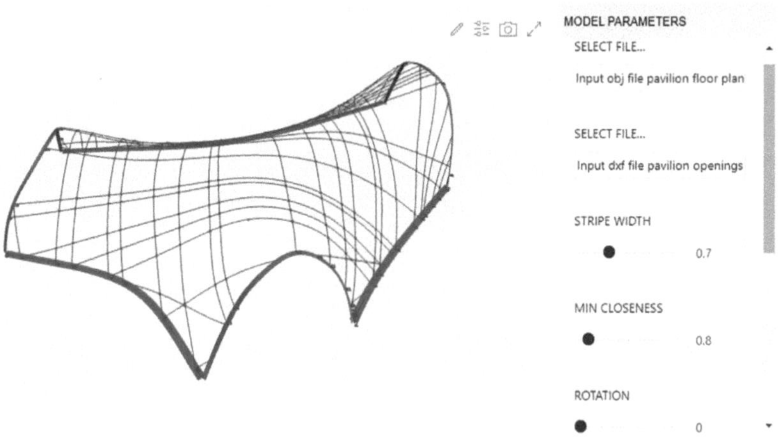

curves for positioning openings/entrances in gridshell. Gridshell floor layout is automatically generated with Catmull-Clark subdivision algorithm applied to horizontal low poly mesh given as geometry input. Gridshell entrance openings are defined with closed curves that intersect mesh. Closed curves as an input data are used for testing whether edge nodes of the mesh used for generating the gridshell layout inside the curves. If edge nodes of the mesh is located outside the region of closed curves they remains fixed in the process of relaxing networks of springs. This method enables simple generation of various Gridshell forms with openings as it is shown on Figure 2.

Second type of GDS Tool interface, range sliders, are used for controlling height of geodesic shell, strip density, and geodesic network regularity, geodesic width and rotation angle of gridshell network. Parameters of each slider are tuned for design and fabrication of 40x60 cm gridshell model size. Apart from design and fabrication constraints, domain range for each slider is also determined with the limit of 10 seconds of computation time. Export button enables exporting final gridshell design and production file for laser cutting. GDS tool presented in this work (Figure 2) can be accessed on the following link: www.ddc-make.com/gridshell-pavilion-3d-configurator

Users input data with a minimal knowledge of the Rhinoceros 3D software environment, while having unlimited possibilities in designing the structures in floor plan. In this way, users are able to prepare an object that is elongated, circular, curved, winding, etc., as well as the quantity and size of openings (Figure 3).

When the input data prepared in this way is entered, the dynamic relaxation is applied on a plane mesh that is under gravitational load where the corner edges are fixed. Structure is then converting into gridshell network where the user defines input parameters such as number of curves, minimum and maximal space between curves, randomness of grid, etc. The user therefore goes through the whole process by setting the input data as the basic model, parametrically influencing it by moving the slider until the desired gridshell is derived, and also automatically gets the output data in the form of prepared drawings for cutting and fabrication, as well as the mixed reality model which will be used in assembly phase.

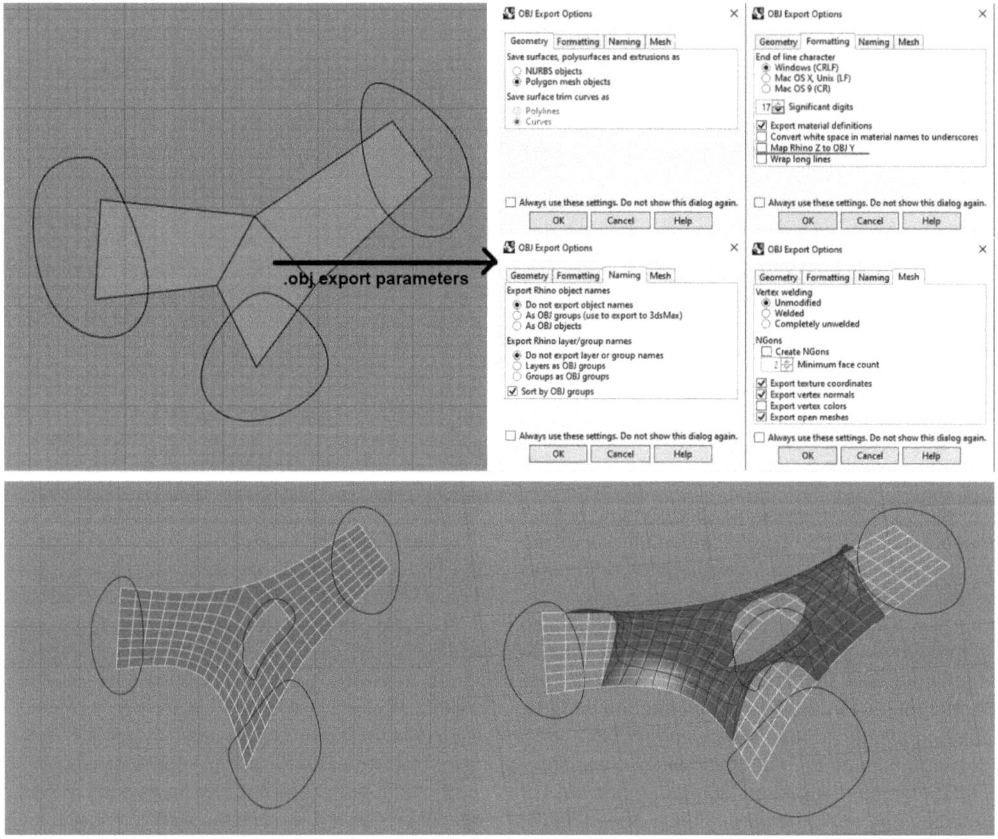

Figure 2
Input geometry and relaxation of the mesh in plane

MIXED REALITY FOR PHYSICAL PROTOTYPING

Augmented and mixed realities have been in use in architecture for a long time in the field of architectural presentation (Wang and Schnabel 2008). The advent of headsets like Microsoft Hololens provides a remarkable tool for moving from traditional visualization of 3D objects on a 2D screen, to fully experimental 3D visualizations embedded in the real world (Hocket and Ingleby 2016, Karthika 2017). With special reference to the application of Fologram, this relatively new technology quickly found its application in the field of in situ construction of complex shapes whose production by traditional methods would require much more time and effort (Jahn 2019). In addition to the construction tool, this tool finds application in the field of supervision and quality control of performed works by generating clouds of points of the derived state and comparison for the digital model (Jahn et al. 2019).

Second phase of our collaborative method utilize mixed reality for making the physical models of the structures. In accordance with the remote workflow the production process with the mixed reality is

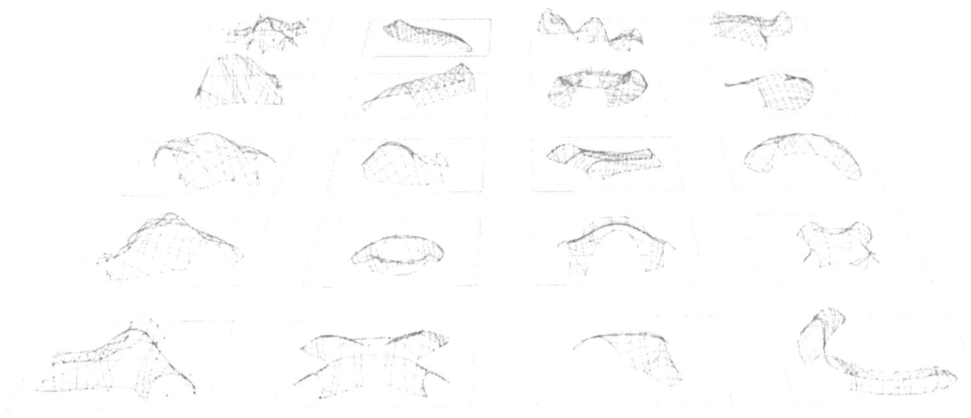

Figure 3
The variety of conducted gridshell models

taken into consideration. In that manner instructions for assembling the gridshells are presented in digital mixed reality environment and user only requires a mixed reality tool, in our case the Hololens headset. For this purpose Hololens application named Fologram is used to create mixed reality 3D environment in order to ease the fabrication of complex gridshells. 3D wireframe model of gridshell structure is created in Rhinoceros and its add-on Fologram sends it to Hololens which also have Fologram application. In the application 3D model can be manipulated in such a manner that can be moved, rotated, scaled, aligned with QR coded markers, etc. After it is adjusted to the desired position and scale it can guide further assembly. For this purpose the model is updating from step to step by adding strips and in that manner the assembly of the physical model can follow developing of the digital model in mixed reality.

Since there were 20 student groups with 1 structure each it is decided that prototypes will be fabricated in scale of 1:100. In the web configurator mentioned in previous chapter students also had the possibility to generate 2D cutting template of the elements. That included unrolled straight D-strips with circular marks on the intersection positions on them and unrolled curved strips that form the openings on the structures. General assembling strategy for all groups was aligning a few major strips which can form a rough shape of the structure and then add strip by strip until whole structure is assembled. Strategy for strips connecting is tested in two ways. One part used paper clamps to hold the strips in place (allowing rotation) without adding glue until they were convinced the strips are at right position (D'Amico 2014) (Figure 4a), and second part used glue from the beginning. Through the whole process of assembling one member of group constantly visually inspects how each strip should form in the context of the whole structure (Figure 4b).

DISCUSSION

After the workshop is obtained, the results are presented trough 20 physical models where all of the applied groups finished each model (Figure 5). The first part of the workshop where the main topic was utilization of web based configurator resulted in the big variety of generated 3D models as well as precisely prepared 2D drawings for the laser cutting, (Figure 6).

All groups succeeded to implement their models and keep the track of the assembly of gridshell physical model. The fabrication part of the workshop delivered some issues with maintaining the desired shape of gridshell model owing to bad decisions about method of connecting and gluing the strips. There was not any particular assembly strategy im-

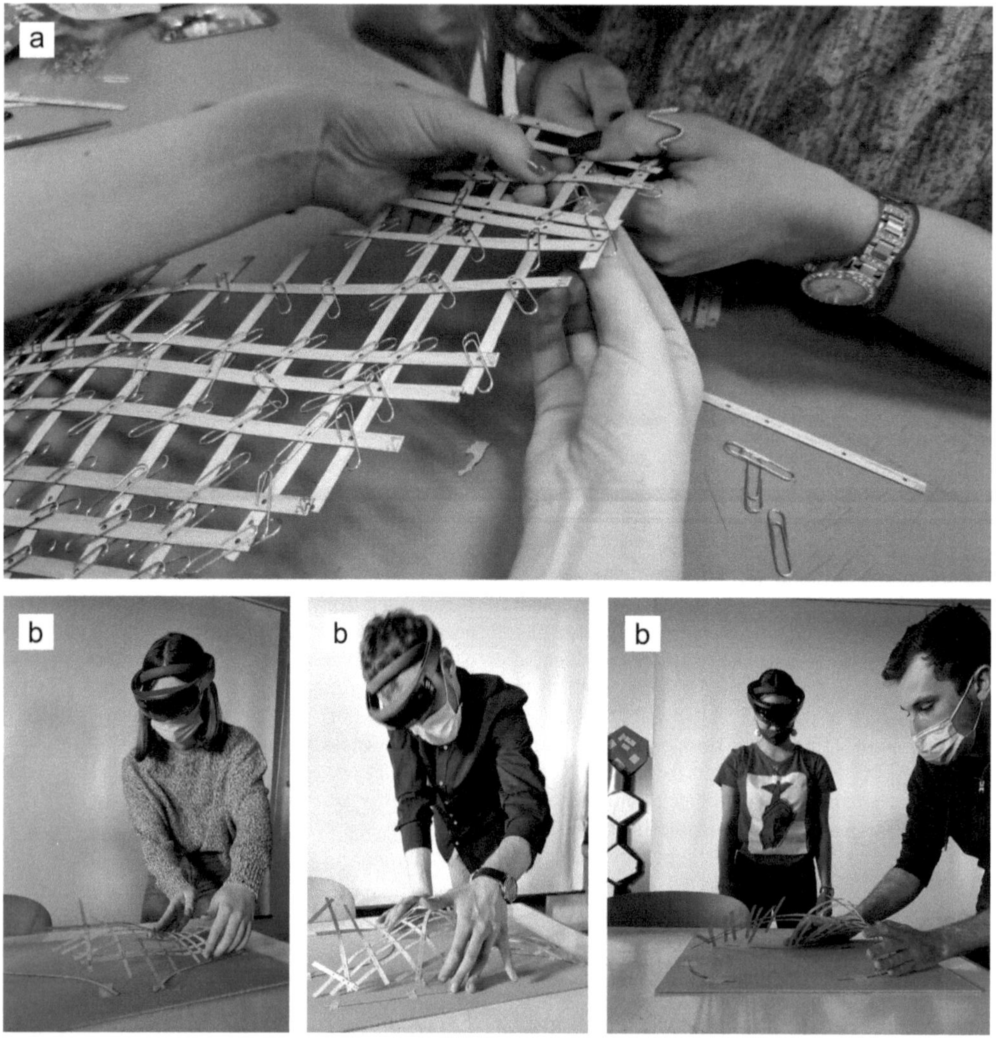

Figure 4
a) Process of connecting the strips with paperclips and b) visual inspection of assembly with Hololens headset and holografic projection

posed to the students, but were given some advices which were taken from the experience on projects from previous years. Some student groups accepted advices and assembled the model with dry connectors first and some other groups started glued assembly from the beginning. First part of the groups, which used paperclips for dry connections, was allowed afterward to assimilate the whole shape according to the holographic projection since paperclips were allowing rotation between strips. The

Figure 5
Physical prototypes as the result of workshop

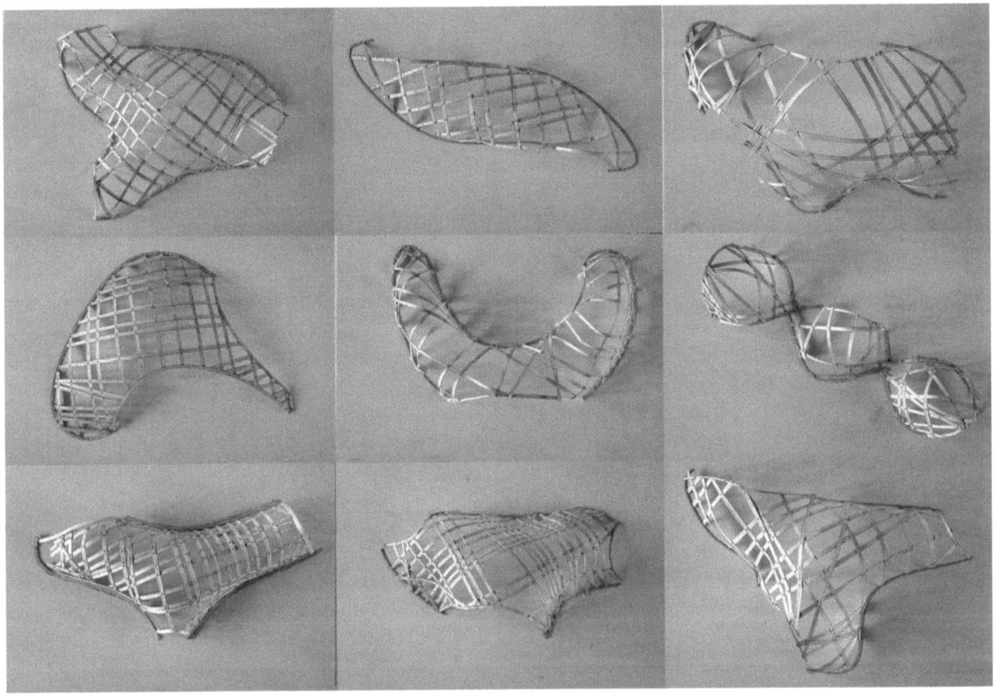

Figure 6
Output model for the fabrication

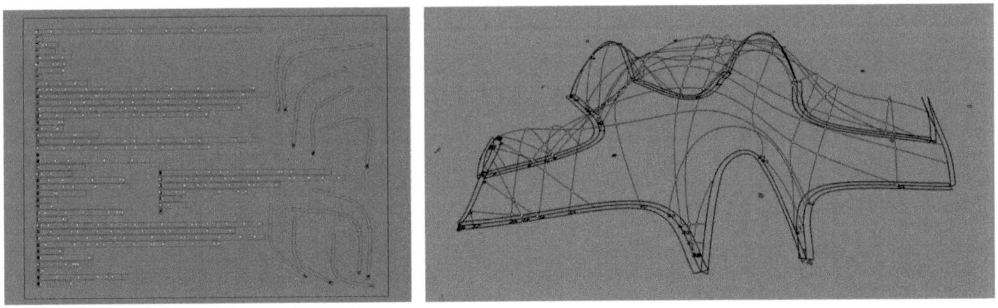

groups that glued the strips from the beginning of the work relied on the choice of tapes from which to start assembling and on the assumption that the tapes that are glued do not have torsion. If the strip is twisted, its torsion need to be fixed with another strip, otherwise the assembly can be corrupted. It follows that groups with more regular and simpler forms of structures in this way could get a good result, while groups with more complex structures had assembly mistakes. Four physical models were needed extra time for fixing the fabrication problems after the workshop period. However, all models were finished which implies that both methods gave good results, yet the latter had some difficulties. Those problems are mainly the result of the lack of experience in the field of fabrication since the participants were students that attend Scale modeling course for the first time. With second approach there were certain inaccuracies when comparing the physical and digital models in mixed reality environment. These errors were mainly manifested through the height of the structure because the second groups did not have the opportunity to bring the structure to the desired height by lateral pressure as the first groups could. Also the selection of material could be reconsidered for some future work. Veneer sheet used in this workshop is heterogeneous material with non-uniform direction of fiber provision which lead to some unpredicted cracking of the strips despite cutting them in the same direction as fibers. This problem can be detected on the opening edges where strips that define them are not geodesic curves and therefore cannot unfold to the straight strip.

There was also a limit on the number of MR tools i.e. Hololens (we had only one device), and there were 20 student groups. Students were able to partially assemble structures analogously (by following the marking holes on the strips), but so that everyone could follow the assembly of their models in digital environment had the ability to use the Fologram application on their mobile devices. The Hololens device was available to them from time to time to compare their models in a more precise environment. Certain differences were observed when using different MR tools. Accuracy was not the same with Hololens and mobile devices. Hololens was quite precise and, most importantly, reliable by detecting position markers very quickly and accurately and automatically adjusting the scale according to the markers. In the mobile application, these two parameters varied in quality. Mobile applications did not allow for a large range of motion in space resulting in the removing of a digital object from view. If the device is moved frequently, a new 3D mapping of the environment and search for markers is started, which was much slower than with the Hololens. Also when re-searching the marker it happened that the scale was broken and in order to fix it, the application had to be restarted. There was also a small difference between iOS and Android operating systems, so there were more mentioned problems on the Android operating system.

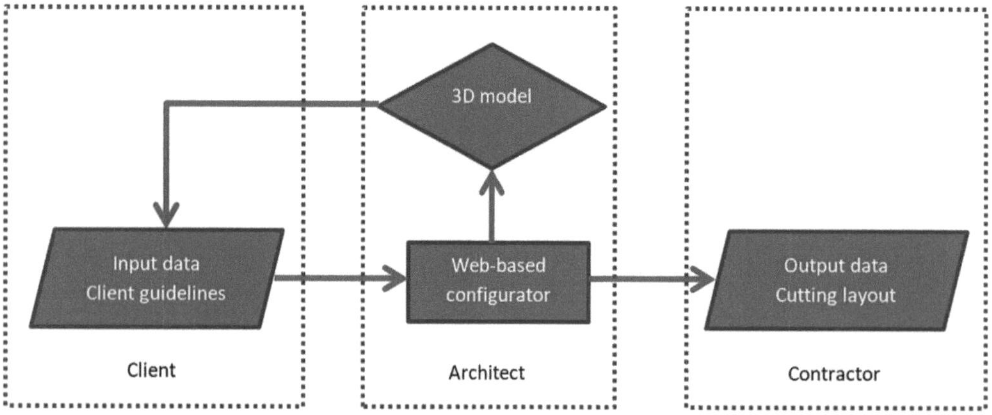

Figure 7
Diagram of collaboration between Client, Architect and Contractor

Taking into consideration the restricted time for the workshop conducting which were 2 hours for the first part and 5 hours for the second part (laser cutting of the material not included) it can be evaluated as successful since all groups finished their projects without any previous experience with fabrication of complex self-supportive D-strip gridshells.

This paper presents a method of collaboration in a web environment between a client, an architect and a contractor. The web application included in the first phase the input data provided by the client, the elaboration of the structure by the architect, as well as the return and re-examination and refinement between these two parties. When a satisfactory solution is reached through the same web application, the necessary drawings for the CAM creation of the elements that will be used to fabricate the structure are created and forwarded to contractor (Figure 7). In our scenario, the client was a professor, the students were architects, and the contractor was a laboratory technician who cut the elements for assembly. However, this method can also be applied in practical work in a non-teaching environment when the parties involved in the process are unable to make physical contact (as was often the case in the recent covid-19 epidemiological situation).

CONCLUSION

Collaborative design-to-fabrication method for creating wooden gridshells is presented in this paper. This research shows that collaborative web based 3D tools developed for digital form finding, can be used for extending intuition for the design of gridshell through virtual simulation of material behaviour and getting the feel and experience for shaping self-supporting structures. Over the course of 2 hour online lecture, students without previous experience in design and construction of self-supporting structures learned how to use, interact, play with GDS tool and create their own design solutions. Apart from collaborative design, this research has shown that mixed reality can be used as a powerful collaborative tool in assembly process. Future research will be directed towards making full scale prototype as well as designing web-based tools for other kinds of complex active bending forms.

REFERENCES

Adriaenssens, S, Block, P, Veenendaal, D and Williams, C (eds) 2014, *Shell structures for architecture: Form finding and optimization*, Routledge

D Amico, B, Kermani, A and Zhang, H 2014, 'Form finding and structural analysis of actively bent timber grid shells', *Engineering Structures*, 81, p. 195–207

Canadinc, ST, Wang, B, Pi, Y and Yan, W 2020 'Multi-User and Web-based Parametric Modeling with Multiple Visual Programming Tools', *Proceedings of the 38th eCAADe Conference*, pp. 19-28

Gwyllim, J, Cameron, N and Matthew, B 2018 'Recalibration: On Imprecision and Infidelity', *Proceedings of the 38th ACADIA Conference*, pp. 88-97

Hockett, P and Ingleby, T 2016 'Augmented reality with HoloLens: Experiential architectures embedded in the real world', *arXiv:1610.04281*

Jahn, G, Newnham, C, van den Berg, N, Iraheta, M and Wells, J 2019 'Holographic Construction', *Design Modelling Symposium Berlin*, pp. 314-324

Jahn, G, Wit, AJ and Pazzi, J 2019 'BENT', *ACADIA 19:UBIQUITY AND AUTONOMY [Proceedings of the 39th Annual Conference of the Association for Computer Aided Design in Architecture*, pp. 438-447

Janssen, P, Li, R and Mohanty, A 2016 'Mobius: a parametric modeller for the web', *Proceedings of the 21st International Conference on Computer-Aided Architectural Design Research in Asia (CAADRIA 2016)*, pp. 157-166

Karthika, S, Praveena, P and GokilaMani, M 2017, 'Hololens', *International Journal of Computer Science and Mobile Computing*, 6(2), pp. 41-50

Leung, E, Butler, A, Asher, R, Gardner, N and Haeusler, M 2019 'Redback BIM Developing a Browser-based Modeling Application Software Taxonomy', *Proceedings of the 24th CAADRIA Conference*, pp. 775-784

Liddell, I 2015, 'Frei Otto and the development of gridshells', *Case Studies in Structural Engineering*, 4, pp. 39-49

Pone, S, Colabella, S, D Amico, B, Fiore, A, Lancia, D and Parenti, B 2013 'Timber Post-formed Gridshell: Digital Form-finding / drawing and building tool', *Beyond the Limits of Man (IASS) Symposium*

Soriano, E 2017, 'Low-tech geodesic gridshell: Almond pavilion', *ArchiDOCT*, 4(2), p. 29–38

Wang, X and Schnabel, MA (eds) 2008, *Mixed reality in architecture, design, and construction*, Springer Science & Business Media
Yan, W 2017 'WP-BIM: Web-based Parametric BIM Towards Online Collaborative Design and Optimization', *Proceedings of the 35th eCAADe Conference*, pp. 527-534

Computational Design and Robotic Fabrication Based on 3D Graphic Statics

Xiao Zhang[1], Xiang Wang[2], Zhongsheng Yu[3], Chao Yuan[4], Jingjing Jiang[5], Qingfeng Yang[6], Bian Lin[7]
[1,4,5]Tsinghua University [2]Tongji University [3]Fab-Union [6]Shanghai Jiao Tong University [7]Shanghai MAOMU Architects
[1]z-x20@mails.tsinghua.edu.cn [2]18310021@tongji.edu.cn [3,6]{zhsh.yu|qingfeng_yang}@outlook.com [4]1037303749@qq.com
[5,7]{jjj18645123619|linbianarch}@163.com

Graphic statics vividly shows the topological relationship between the ``form" represented by the structure itself and the ``force" generated by its action through graphic method, which has become an important tool for architects to carry out structural innovative design in the past century. In the 21st century, with the development of computer technology, graphic statics has developed from the dual relationship between 2D thrust network and closed force polygon to the dual relationship between 3D thrust network and space closed force polyhedron. In this paper, the design method of graphic statics based on 3D graphic statics is applied to a stainless chair and an ice pavilion design. Researchers used different digital fabrication methods to manufacture the chair and the pavilion according to its material attribute.

Keywords: *3D Graphic Statics, Computational Design, Ice Structure, Robotic Fabrication*

1. BACKGROUND

As an important tool in structural design methodology, graphic statics has been widely used in a large number of innovative projects in the field of structural design and researches in recent centuries(Block and Van Mele et al. 2017) . With the popularity of contemporary computational design methods and the extensive application of computer algorithm aided design, the emergence of related design plug-ins has also brought many form finding design methods based on graphic statics (Zhao, Ma and Qiao, et al. 2019) The traditional graphic statics is based on the polygon rule of force. By understanding the spatial balance force system as the "form" diagram showing the transmission of force in the structure and the "force" diagram formed by the balance between force systems, the solution of structural balance problem can be transformed into the construction of closed polygon in the "force" diagram, and the internal force calculation of three-dimensional balance in the structure. At the same time, for designers, the basic problem of structural design is more intuitively transformed from the solution of abstract balance equation to the active control process of structural internal force.

However, the traditional graphic statics is limited to the basic theory of the dual relationship of shape and force, and can only be applied to the form finding design of two-dimensional truss, cable structure, shell structure and so on. In 2016, Masoud Akbazardeh of in ETH, Switzerland, extended the graphic statics theory of two-dimensional to three-dimensional, based on the relationship between 3D thrust network and space closed force polyhedron by Maxwell and Rankine in the 19th century(Maxwell and Rankine,1876). As the name suggests, three-dimensional graphic statics expands the dimension of form involved in traditional graphic statics, and extends the application scope of graphic statics from equilibrium structure which can only be defined by two-dimensional abstract to complex three-dimensional equilibrium structure(Akbarzadeh M, 2016).

Based on the basic theory of three-dimensional graphic statics, this paper discusses the graphic statics design method and its application possibility based on the dual properties of three-dimensional polyhedron from two cases. From the perspective of digital fabrication technology, it finally shows its great application potential in the exploration of material performance-based design represented by ice and snow construction.

2. THE GENERAL PRINCIPLE OF THREE-DIMENSIONAL GRAPHIC STATICS

2.1 Force Polygon Rule in Two-Dimensional Graph Statics

In the traditional graphic statics theory, the two-dimensional equilibrium force system can be transformed into a continuous closed force polygon by the method of vector translation, so it is also called "polygon rule of force".

As shown in Figure 1-A, five coplanar external forces F1-F5 constitute an equilibrium force system, that is, the resultant force of the five forces is zero. Figure 1-A is the "form" diagram of the balanced force system, in which five external forces are represented by FN, the external forces intersect at a point P, and the plane space is divided into five subspaces represented by clockwise A to E. According to the vector representation of the force, the five components of the balanced force system can be connected end to end by translation, thus forming a closed continuous polygon. Figure 1-B is also called the "force" diagram of the equilibrium force system. In the "force" diagram, the point P of the original resultant force in the plane is transformed into a closed force polygon. The duality between these figures is also called the reciprocal relationship between the "form" diagram and the "force" diagram.

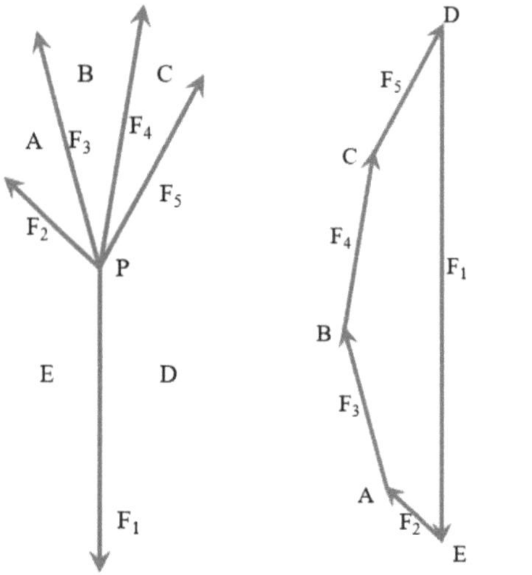

Figure 1
The general principle of two-dimansional graphic statics: Force Polygon Rule

2.2 Force Polyhedron Rule in Three-Dimensional Graphic Statics

In three-dimensional graphic statics study, more general dual properties of the spatial equilibrium force system are considered. Among them, the three-dimensional equilibrium force system is no longer transformed into a plane force system by projection method, but is matched with the three-dimensional closed force polyhedron according to the duality theory proposed by Maxwell and Rankine, so as to establish the duality relationship between "force" and "form" diagram in graphic statics in a higher dimension.

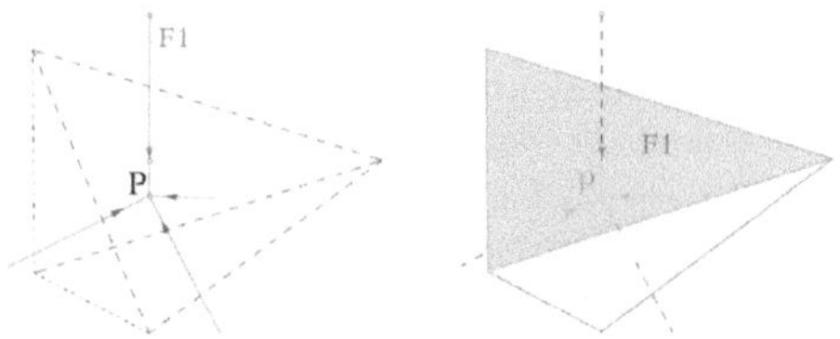

Figure 2
The general principle of three-dimansional graphic statics: Force Polyhedron Rule

As shown in Figure 2, the four external forces in space get equilibrium at point P. In the dual "force" diagram, the intersection point is represented as a closed force tetrahedron, and the four forces in the shape diagram are represented as four corresponding planes in the "force" diagram. The direction of the plane is perpendicular to the direction of the force vector in the "form" diagram, and its area is equal to the size of the force in the equilibrium state in the "form" diagram.

3. "EXPERIMENTAL CHAIR" DESIGN OF SPATIAL STRUCTURE BASED ON THE METHOD OF THREE-DIMENSIONAL GRAPHIC STATICS

The abstract relationship between force and form in three-dimensional graphic statics often makes it difficult to be directly used in structural innovative design. This section discusses the basic design method of three-dimensional graphic statics combined with the design process of an assignment - "experimental chair" in a teaching course.

3.1 Splitting Mode and Structural Morphology of Force Polyhedron

Different from the two-dimensional graphic statics, the design process of three-dimensional graphic statics often starts directly from the framework of three-dimensional force diagram. Therefore, the construction mode of initial force polyhedron often determines the basic form in structural design (Figure.3 shows the geometric structure characteristics of various initial polyhedrons and the dual force diagram).

Therefore, in order to find the form of spatial structure by using 3D graphic statics method, it is necessary to establish the initial force polyhedron combination according to the assumption of structural stress characteristics. In the force model design of this case, the four fulcrums of the chair leg are used as the anchor supports. In order to simplify the model, the chair back is also used as the anchor supports. The applied load is decomposed into vertical downward pressure on the chair surface and horizontal lateral thrust on the chair back. Based on this, a simple force polyhedron cluster is constructed, and the force model of the chair is preliminarily established (Figure.4).

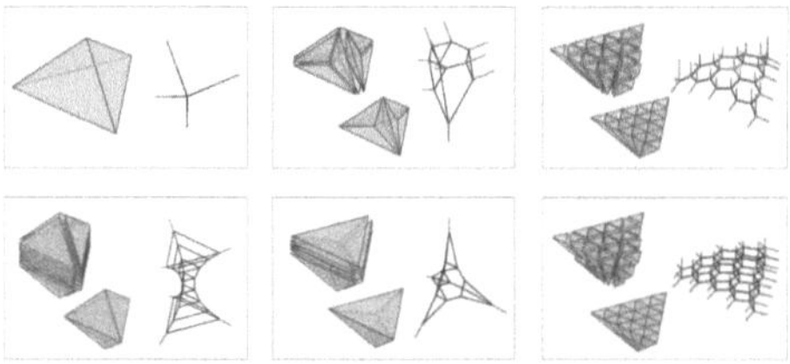

Figure 3
The basic prototype analysis of the form diagram based on the force polyhedron diagram

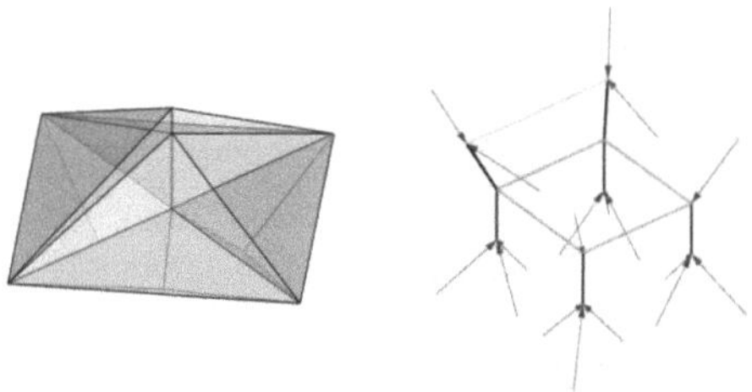

Figure 4
Initial force polyhedron combination mode in the case of "experimental chair"

3.2 Subdivision and Form Optimization of Force Polyhedron

The construction of initial force polyhedron represents the basic assumption of pure compression force transmission path of basic structure in preliminary design. At the same time, in the force diagram, a force polyhedron is divided according to some rules. Under the condition that the force polyhedron is still closed, the decomposed small polyhedron cluster can be regarded as the equivalent of force decomposition under the condition that the global force in the equilibrium force system remains unchanged. Therefore, the method of polyhedron subdivision is also an important method in the structural design and form optimization.

In this example, the designer starts from the chair surface, and changes the topological relationship of the structure by dividing one force polyhedron and adding the a new polyhedron. Frst, the chair surface is regarded as four support points and subdivided to form a balanced plane force system; secondly, the force polyhedron is added downward to change the global force, so that it becomes a three-dimensional balanced force system with the final force transmitted to the four support points of the chair legs; finally, the internal force is calculated and the part structure is partitioned into a dual ideal force polyhedrons (Figure. 5).

Figure 5
Research on force polyhedron subdivision and optimization design in the case of "experimental chair"

3.3 Relationship between structural performance and form finding strategy by three-dimensional graphic statics

In graphic statics, the process of defining the initial configuration and confirming the final equilibrium of a structure is divided into two parts: the basic configuration of the force diagram, and the secondary optimization of the geometric relationship between the shape diagram and the force diagram. Therefore, in the operation process of form and force, the designer can start from the form operation of any diagram, adjust and limit the target form, and finally make the form diagram and force diagram "vertical" through the overall application of optimization method, so as to find the global force system after the final equilibrium.

In the design study of graphic statics principle under specific boundary conditions, the topological structure of optimal force transmission is given by graphic operation and splitting combination method, which is suitable for a large number of structural design problems with special requirements such as material properties and processing properties. For example, in this case, the material selection is 0.5mm ultra-thin steel plate, and its hollow structure makes its surface stress performance far weaker than the structure performance along the crease direction. Therefore, in the early design process of the structure, the relevant force transmission path (Figure. 6 is the finite element calculation model of the structure, which shows the corrugated area formed by the stress distribution along the crease) and the basic geometric form of the structure are considered, so that the material and structural form can be used more efficiently.

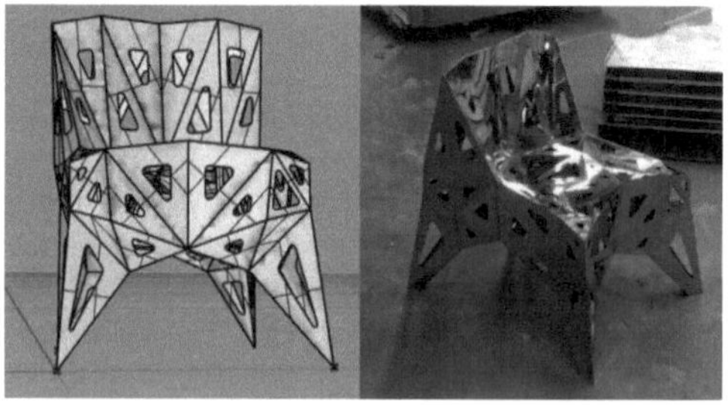

Figure 6
Structural finite element analysis verification and final construction effect of "experimental chair"

4. THE COMPUTATIONAL DESIGN AND DIGITAL FABRICATION OF COMPLEX ICE STRUCTURE DRIVEN BY 3D GRAPHIC STATICS

Ice is a kind of hard and fragile material, which can bear large pressure, and has poor bending and shear resistance. Therefore, it is the most reasonable way to find the form of ice masonry structure by graphic statics. The principle of graphic statics is to make the relationship between force and form match each other, and the form matching the solution of graphic statics only transmits the force along the axial direction of the member, so each member is not subject to bending moment. This kind of stress characteristic is very suitable for "ice" material. Due to the precise structure of the whole pavilion, the connection between the ice blocks needs to be very smooth, and only water is used as the adhesive, so the researchers use the KUKA robot to cut the ice blocks to ensure the accuracy.

4.1 Form finding process

Considering that ice is a kind of hard and fragile material, in order to avoid the danger in the installation process, the research team plans to design a pavilion whose bottom part is big and top part is small. To this end, the team takes the regular tetrahedron as the prototype (Figure 7-B), and subdivides the polyhedral geometry with a triangular plane upward to increase the number of members at its core (Figure 7-A). The subdivision is divided into two levels. The first level is the subdivision of the "core" of the structure. The author takes the center of the regular tetrahedron as the starting point and connects the four vertices to divide the regular tetrahedron into four groups. The second layer is the subdivision of the "branch" of the structure, which is subdivided into two groups of tetrahedral combinations to shape the geometric form of the branch triangular pyramid (Fig. 7-C). At the same time, considering the processing time and other factors, the final number of members selected by the team is 10.

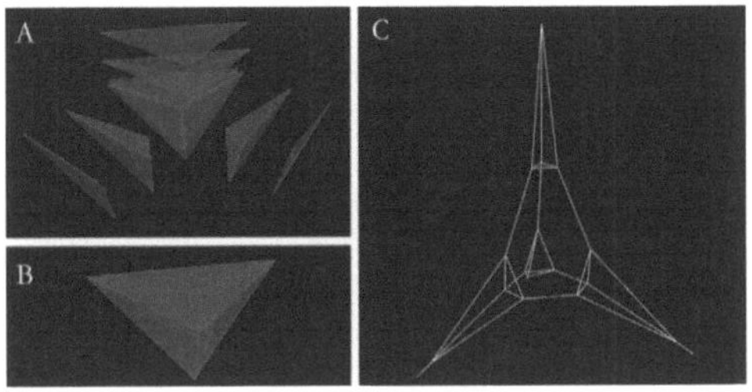

Figure 7
Ice pavilion form finding process

4.2 Geometric optimization

In order to optimize the geometric wireframe obtained by form finding into ice blocks that can be processed and assembled, the research team needs to carry out geometric optimization work. There are two methods to optimize. Method 1: each rod is used as the path to form a cylinder. Method 2: each rod is used as the contour of the ice polyhedron to form the final ice geometry directly. Researchers firstly built a 1:10 model of method 1. Even through high-precision 3D printing, each ice block had a large cumulative error in the splicing process. Therefore, in order to reduce the number of processed ice blocks and the cumulative error, the group decided to adopt method 2, cutting with the basic geometry of polyhedral pyramid, and appropriately reducing the overall size of the structure in order to meet the radius requirements of the robotic arm for each unit (Figure. 8).

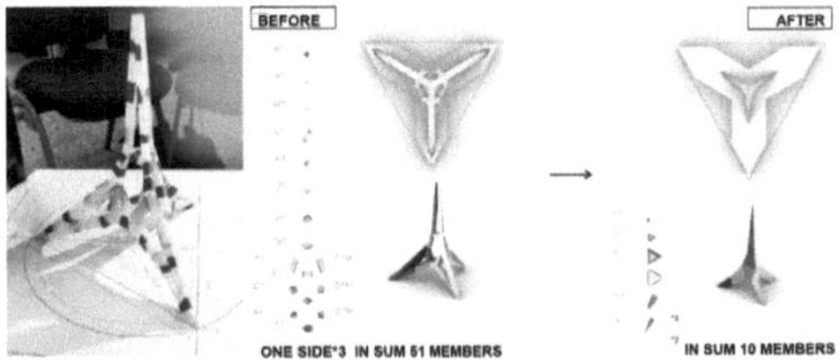

Figure 8
Geometric optimization process of the ice pavilion

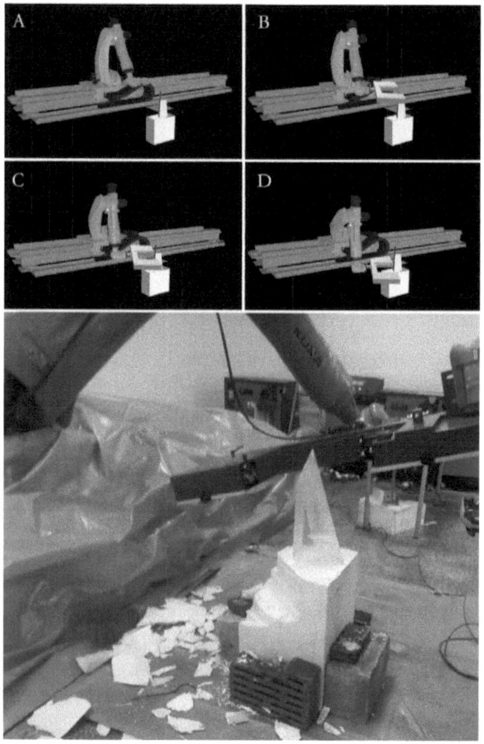

Figure 9
Robotic fabrication process on one single piece of ice block

4.3 Robotic fabrication

The research team firstly carried out the "bounding box" operation on the ice block to be cut, so as to generate the cuboid that can include the heteromorphic polyhedron, and asked the workers to have a rough cut on the ice first, and then cut it with the robotic arm wire saw. The research team used the FUrobot plug-in to customize the corresponding tool path for KUKA robot. Its operation mode is similar to the "sweep 2 rails" in the rhino command. After extracting the two boundaries of the required cutting surface, the points are evenly divided, and the tool end of the manipulator moves along this path. At the same time, the wire saw is turned on to complete the ice cutting (Figure.9).

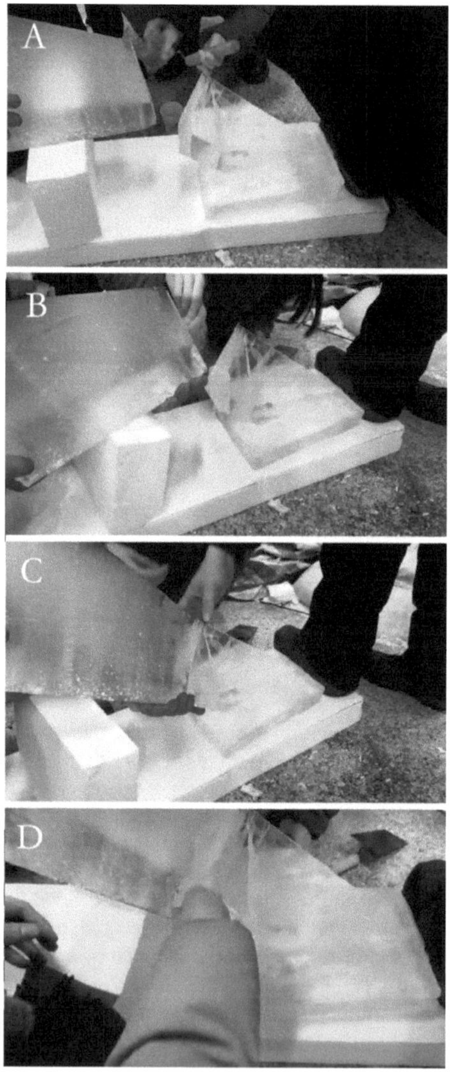

Figure 10
Ice blocks pasting process

Figure 11
Final effect of the ice pavilion

4.4 Onsite construction

In the process of onsite construction, the research team carried out the reference line laying on the three ice platforms of 450mm high and 700mm*1650mm plane size, and used foam board as scaffolding to form the support of the core ice block. Secondly, the team "pasted" the three landing branches of the whole structure. In this work, the surfaces of the two connected ice blocks need to be smoothed, and then hot water is used to evenly smear a small amount on the surface of the ice block, and then the two geometric bodies are quickly aligned and glued, and then a small amount of ice and snow mixture is used to reinforce the glued gap, and finally it got frozen (figure. 10).After completing the paste and installation of the ice, the foam plastic is removed and the image of the final structure (Figure.11) is formed.

5.CONCLUSION AND FUTURE RESEARCHES

The successful design and building experiments of the ice pavilion and experimental chair, its robotic fabrication, full-scale assembly demonstrated the feasibility to use three-dimensional graphic statics method to make structural design. The research method of the generation process of this structural concept will lead a further detailed research on the digital simulation of the material behavior of the ice block under the pressure, as well as a full-automated robotic fabrication.

ACKNOWLEDGEMENTS

This research is funded by the National Social Science Fund of China (Grant No.17ZDA019).

REFERENCES

Akbarzadeh, Masoud 2016, *Three-dimensional Graphical Statics using Polyhedral Reciprocal Diagrams*, Ph.D. Thesis, ETH

J. Clerk, Maxwell F.R.S. 1864, 'On reciprocal figures and diagrams of forces', *Philosophical Magazine and Journal of Science*, 7(81), pp. 250-261

Jie, Zhao, Sijia, Ma, Wentao, Qiao and Shiyu, Zhang 2019, 'Study on form design method of plane truss based on graphical statics', *Building Science*, 35, pp. 53-58

William John Macquorn, Rankine 1876, *A Manual Of Applied Mechanics (English)*, R. Griffin, London

Philippen, Block, Tom, Van Mele and Rippmann, Matthias 2017, 'Exploring Form and Forces: Graphic Statics in the Digital Age', *Architectural Journal*, 11, pp. 14-19

Limits to Applied ML in Planning and Architecture

Understanding and defining extents and capabilities

Sam Conrad Joyce[1], *Ibrahim Nazim*[2]
[1,2]*Singapore University of Technology and Design*
[1,2]*{sam_joyce|nazim_ibrahim}@sutd.edu.sg*

There has been an exponential increase in Machine Learning (ML) research in design. Specifically, with Deep Learning becoming more accessible, frameworks like Generative Adversarial Networks (GANs), which are able to synthesise novel images are being used in the classification and generation of designs in architecture. While much of these explorations successfully demonstrate the `magic' and potential of these techniques, their limits remain unclear, with only a few, but crucial, discussions on underlying fundamental limits and sensitivities of ML. This is a gap in our understanding of these tools especially within the complex context of planning and architecture. This paper seeks to discuss what limits ML in design as it exists today, by examining the state-of-the-art and mechanics of ML models relevant to design tasks. Aiming to help researchers to focus on productive uses of ML and avoid areas of over-promise.

Keywords: *Machine Learning, Artificial Intelligence, Creativity*

INTRODUCTION

At the current epoch, it seems an undeniable fact that AI will have a significant impact on human activity. Whilst the resultant effect has been hypothesised to range from the ubiquitous and benign (Jack Ma) to the potentially catastrophic (Elon Musk, Bill Gates), there are clear indicators that this technology will impact many industries and ways of life (Frey and Osbourne 2017). Whilst this report indicates that creative design-related roles are some of the least likely to succumb to automation, discussions around current practice paints a different picture. Thom Maine, head of Morphosis architects, said that "I can have an office instead of 80 people there'll be eight of us.. ..I'm producing 100 variations more [with AI] than I could do with 10 times the amount of people" [10], and "There are going to be less and less people needed for the pure technical mechanical stuff" [2], with more and more published work showing the breadth and depth of applied AI already infiltrating the practice.

However, technology is not omnipotent. ML techniques, which have progressed the field of AI the most in the last decade, are reliant on a set of fundamental concepts and paradigms and are inherently limited by them. Deep Learning algorithms, which have enabled GAN and style transfer (Newton 2019), simultaneously defines certain fundamental limits of the system as well (Heaven 2019, Olenik 2019), much like Turing's famous NP-completeness defines the limits of computing upon which ML is dependent.

The aim of this paper is to trace this limit, which

in some places is concrete and well defined by the mechanics of ML and in other places is ambiguous and linked to human issues of perceptual, qualitative, and experiential issues of architecture. Drawing this boundary is inherently limited to human perception and prediction based on current ML techniques and whilst it extrapolates and hypothesises about future capabilities, it cannot predict revolutionary new approaches or hardware. However, the aim of drawing such a boundary is intended to be useful so that designers may know where we may be able to rely on AI for support, and where this might be out of its reach, and where humans and AI might find the appropriate/comfortable/productive mix of capabilities.

During this consideration of limits, we start with clearer aspects of design; Level of detail and scale, Representation, Input data and Resolved-ness, and work up to more ephemeral considerations such as Creativity, Autonomy and Design quality. We will consider these aspects in relation to the perceived potential to change architectural design and consider what limitations are present due to processing power, algorithmic capability, and human/design issues. By considering important aspects of design representation/encoding, and the type of interaction with the user.

SCALE LIMITS

Architectural design works across multiple scales and levels of detail, from whole urban blocks to interiors and construction details. Within a specific scale, design can be represented at various levels of detail, typically increasing as the design gets closer to realisation. A floor plan can be represented as simple as a layout diagram or can be detailed to include furniture and finishes. Similarly, a 3D model of a building might be as simple as a massing model or detailed as a Building Information Model 'B.I.M.'(Figure 1).

Currently, deep learning models mostly use array-based tensors which work well with 2D data, so it has become a standard to use images such as floor plans to train and generate architectural representations (Figure 2). At this basic level, we encounter our first issue, if we want to represent a wider area then we need a bigger picture, if we want more details we also need more pixels. Currently, much of ML is done on images that are less than 300x300 in size to reduce memory size and increase processing speed. Algorithms like StyleGAN2 (Karras et al. 2019) use 'Progressive Growing' to allow for improvement in details, but these are not globally aware and instead are simply experts in enhancing local detail without considering global effects. This can result in issues such as nonsymmetric representations, for example, earrings or eye shapes on both sides not matching in generated images of faces (Tolosana et al. 2020).

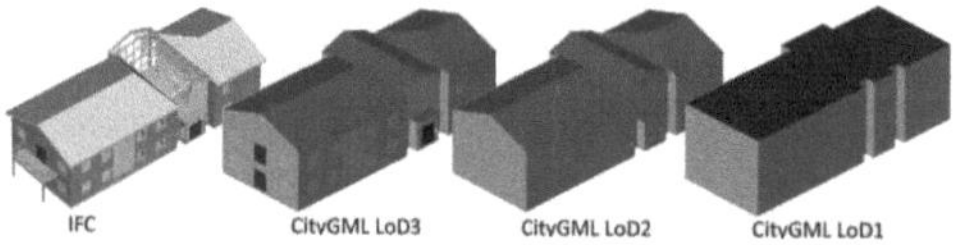

Figure 1
3D models ofdifferent levels ofdetails (LOD)(source: simplebim.com)

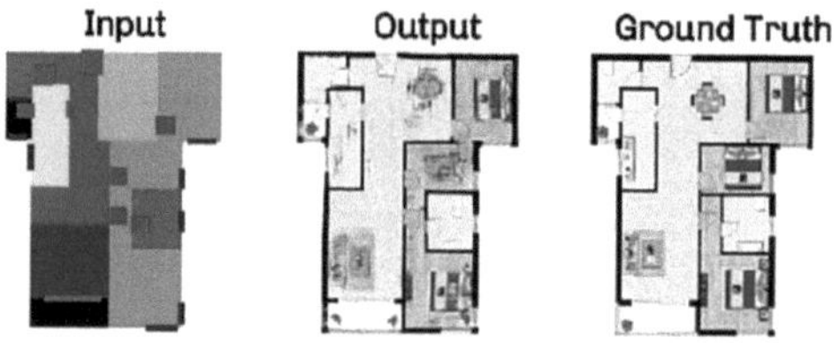

Figure 2
Floor plans generated from labelled images (Huang and Zheng 2018)

However, problems are exponential when extending these capabilities to 3D (Ahmed et al. 2019). Current deep learning techniques all require 3D data to be translated into tensor/array-based data structures, with voxel-based encoding being the most widely used. These are the 3D equivalents of a pixel, representing a point over a regular 3D grid, encoded as a binary value (0 or 1) for material or not. While possible, accurately representing architectural and building geometry comes at a high resource expense due to scale. As Galileo understood, if you increase the linear dimension you increase the volume cubically. Thus for an image, if you go from 100px to 500px on each side you go from a total of 10,000px to 25,000px, 2.5 times larger, whereas for a volume you go from

1million px, already a lot, to 125million, 125 times larger. As it stands currently, we are only able to represent crude geometric models and are not able to integrate data-rich models such as BIM. Thus with this representation even with compression, storage and processing become non-trivial. A small residential site of 20x20x10m would use 2.8 trillion pixels even with a course pixel size of 1cm.

Arguably this issue can be solved by higher computing power and intelligent uses thereof, however, compute power according to Moore's law doubles every two years (Moore 1998) , thus assuming current state of the art models operate on 1000px square images we would still need 40 years of doubling to scale up even to the residential site discussed.

REPRESENTATIONAL LIMITS

Additionally, unlike pixels in images, 3D data has no direct representation or a consistent universal format, and therefore exists in many forms; point clouds, polygons, meshes, B-splines, constructive-solid-geometry etc. as well as combined formats as in DXF, Revit and IFC models (Figure 3). All of these are effectively object lists or hierarchical-tree data structures, devised as they are more compact and aligned with how buildings have been represented (drawing lines) or constructed (floors, walls). However, these structures do not readily capture important ML features such as neighbouring relationships. Just as humans need software to process 3D models into images to comprehend and compare the actual design, existing ML would need this converted into tensors or similar to understand. In terms of ML image recognition and generation, this essentially has to do with correlating pieces of data that are spatially and thus logically close together. However, in the case of relational/hierarchical type data structures, this is non-trivial, with few current ML algorithms developed to operate on them (Nauata 2020). Exacerbated by the fact that many other applications are satisfied with tensor/image/voxel type representations, such as video tracking, image recognition, oncology and fin-tec.

However, there are encouraging developments in recent advanced models such as GPT-3 [7] and Image-GPT [1] which are trained on text and tree-based data structures like websites (Brown et al 2020). Whilst these are not practical to fully train by one individual they have shown commendable capability to operate at higher levels of abstract and structured representation such as making whole websites [16] or generating images based on text inputs (Ramesh et al. 2021). Equally, we are seeing some progress in turning the focus away from tensor/array/grid type representations, Nauata et al. (2020) demonstrate a graph centric approach that has been used since the dawn of computational representation of space both interior and exterior (Hillier 1996).

Figure 3
Different representations of 3D forms: Mesh, Point cloud (Fujimura 2018), Voxels [19] and Hamiltonian cycles (Soler, Retsin and Garcia 2017)

LEVELS OF INPUT DATA

Most developments in ML research in recent years has been model-centric, focussing primarily on making better models and algorithms training on common public datasets [9] . This has its benefits, by many researchers using a small number of known data sets, issues and improvements in algorithms can be easily benchmarked and shared (Phillips et al. 2000), helping to progress the field faster. However, these are typically well-curated and large data-sets usually consisting of 10 thousand to 10 million images. Whilst expanding the potential and accuracy this also has a wider positive pressure on researchers to devise algorithms that work best for problems with large amounts of data.

In architecture, the current ability to build equally large data sets represents a major challenge. There are fewer buildings or even photos of them than people's faces. For example, for some typologies such as opera-houses, there may be less than 1000 in the whole world, many are unlikely to have a CAD representation. Even for general buildings with a digital model representation, there would be different layers and representations based on when and by who they were made. The first 3D Revit model was only made in 2000. Thus, training sets are smaller, and a lot more varied than is typically used.

An alternative approach might be to generate data based on mapping and sensors. Open Street Map and Microsoft ML have been broadly effective in getting basic 2D building outlines [18]. Other sources like LIDAR and photogrammetry may be able to get 3D shapes of buildings, but capturing the inside and floor plans, let alone construction details of buildings, at the data scales required to train existing quality Deep Learning is a much larger challenge. Even if possible, this kind of training will only enable a model to learn general configurations and thus categorise and generate 'typical buildings', of which there are many. While some problems in Architecture can be considered as general problems this excludes much of the work that architects do on exceptional buildings.

However, there are new algorithms specifically aimed to operate on small(er) data sets(Ronneberger et al. 2015, Koch et al. 2015). And this trend is likely to continue as even in conventional fields large data sets are proving to be controversial due to privacy [12], so there is pressure to be able to do this. But it is unclear how well they can generalise and operate with smaller data [13]. One encouraging approach is in ML that is first trained generally with wide amounts of data and then trained again on a specific problem. This increases complexity and again moves the skills away from the individual model, but this is how GPT-3 functions and has shown to be very effective (Brown et al. 2020). Arguably this is also how architects are trained, by looking at many classes and ranges of buildings, but when working on a specific building they focus on a specific location, scale, and typology.

LEVEL OF RESOLVED-NESS

Architecture is an iterative process that starts from conceptual design ideas and explorations and develops to a more detailed and refined design. At every stage, the designer seeks to resolve functional, practical as well as aesthetic issues concerned at that stage so that the design reaches a level of resolved-ness before it moves on to the next. This process requires a general understanding of design and functionality as well as specific requirements of the given context and a mechanism for dynamic modification and refinement.

In image-based learning, such dynamic refinement has been used to generate realistic-looking photographs of humans [14]. As explained earlier some of the success there are based on reprocessing low-resolution generated images to 'shore them up' to make them more rational. However again this is a very localised process and doesn't understand the real purpose or context.

Figure 4
Example GAN image output from thisrentaldoesnotexist.com [6]

If we consider a similar output from an architectural example[6] using style GAN but less well refined, we see in Figure 4 fundamental issues such as non-functional chairs, chairs that clip through tables, kitchen cupboards with no depth, very narrow beds or simply nonsensical wall arrangements. These are a product of the ML simply reproducing an image in the style of those inputs, but not knowing the way that the space is supposed to function. This is a critical issue in architecture for two reasons, firstly and ultimately linked to Plato's The Allegory of the cave (Plato 2000), the image of the room is all that the ML sees and knows as so it is not inherently a 3D space to the ML. So, any image reproduced does not understand what is physically possible in a 3D space, as the ML is simply trying to make a passable image in 2D. Whilst more data and better training would reduce this we are still left with a critical issue that the ML cannot comprehend that the design/output needs to be functional. Ultimately ML is an expert of imitation, but this is no guarantee of functionality. Unlike approaches like Evolutionary Optimisation (Machairas et al 2014) there is no explicit measure of a generated solutions performance with most ML techniques. They are concerned not with the solution being right or wrong but more about appearing right or wrong.

This might be solved in one of two ways, the first is to reinforce functional solutions in the generation of solutions, or alternatively to provide a layer to only select those identified to be functional. This would require explicit analysis to realise. The second is for the quality of the imitations to be sufficiently good as to minimise these errors happening in the first place. The latter solution pre-supposes that there is not only enough data to train but also enough angles/sections/plans etc or full 3D data is input so that the needs would be reproduced. Even then the output would be confined to the technology of the day. This is clear in Figure 5 for example, that if trained on just Baroque buildings then the resultant structure is less space-efficient because it requires more support material. However, if we instead used real metrics we would require advanced, potentially 3D, representation so that the training results can be analysed.

Beyond the details of this discussion, there is a further consideration about how functional the output should be of such systems. In fact, early architectural sketches and indeed whole conceptual design process may be antithetical to direct functional needs. Because by posing designs unhindered (initially) by functional needs this provides more expressive/creative freedom but also perhaps it poses challenges to other members of the team (structural engineers, etc.) to realise the things that hereto have not been done. This follows into the next aspect of creativity.

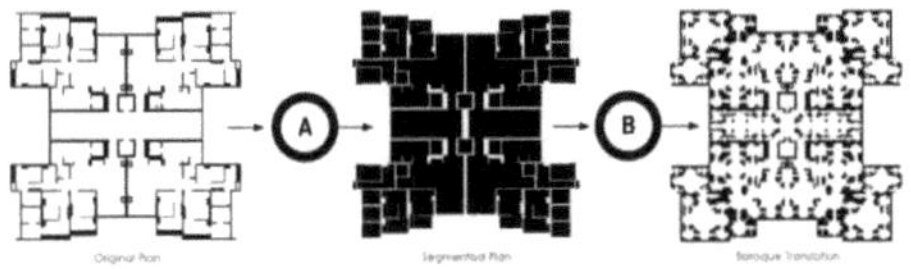

Figure 5
Sample floor plan as interpreted in the Baroque style (Chaillou 2020)

LEVEL OF CREATIVITY

As discussed in the section above Deep Learning models produce novel results, and this is intrinsically linked to human ideas of creativity. However, within a computational framework, there are degrees of creativity. Being a subjective quality there is no universal measure, paradoxically the easier it is to measure change the less novel the change, as truly novel changes operate by radical ideas never considered before, thus unlikely to be measured also.

A case in point is Brown and Mueller's Work (2019) on Parametric variation, here 'Novelty' is reduced to a normalised vector of the input 'slider' values of the parametric model. In parametric models, this limited number of inputs makes the novelty/change tractable, with a study showing most parametric models in a corpus of 2002 contained between 1-11 parameters (Davis 2013). Whilst optimisation techniques might refer to each unique slider input vector as a new design, in reality, most designs are only minor relative changes and are more 'evolution' than 'revolution', it is the underlying parametric code that enables but also tethers the output to quite similar results. Systems such as 'Meta-Parametric Design' (Joyce and Ibrahim 2017, Harding et al 2013) can be used to modify the components and typology of a parametric model in addition to sliders. However ultimately, this and other generative design approaches still have their own limitations as described by Davis [8].

Simple levels of variability don't directly translate to creativity. In many optimisation methods, number of possible design states can be considered as the amount of data and thus possible design information in the model. This may be described by Shannon's Entropy, with enough data required to convey information, a large building (information) cannot be described by very few lines (data). Thus, data is not information, and also information is not creativity. As Brown and Muller identified, the amount of change is influenced by relative change showing that a design's level of change is in relation to what already exists (Gero 2002). Current Deep learning models are trained on historical data to statistically extract the features of a known solution space. This space essentially encodes the design 'experience' of the ML and also focuses the output of any generative ML. The ML is therefore bounded by the limits of that space and inherently limited to produce similar things that can exist within it. Whereas when we speak of novel and original ideas, we tend to describe things that depart from the existing in some significant way.

Change is a challenge for ML, a GAN trained on buildings will not spontaneously produce coherent images of chairs. Even ML that has been explicitly built to change something is still bound to the input. For example, with style transfer (Figure 6) we see that it is possible to transfer an image to a different artistic style, sometimes with radical changes if the style is very abstract. However, even then this requires the input of an existing style, it can only transfer those that already exist or alternately blend between styles, which although novel is still ultimately derivative.

Figure 6
Photograph of Germany in the style of 4 different iconic paintings The Shipwreck of the Minotaur, The Starry Night (left top and bottom), The Scream, Seated Nude(right top and bottom) [15]

However, this mechanism inherent in ML (training) raises questions about the share of creativity between algorithm and human. The user stops being the direct author and instead become more of an 'inspirational curator', feeding a model to define the kind of output produced. To use an art analogy, the user becomes Peggy Guggenheim like a curator who influences the output but doesn't make it directly.

Lauded architects like Wolf Prix and Thom Mayne are already using this approach to generate alternatives (DigitalFUTURES 2020). Prix inputting all of the images of existing outputs from Coop Himmelb(l)au office, to produce a range of images of possible future forms for his own inspiration. Whereas Thom Mayne is showing its use in a more constrained way as a generator of similar alternatives produced from a single handmade work (Figure 7).

These lauded office leaders are also discussing this impact on their practice. Mayne directly saying a few options were hand modelled in 5 days whereas now 100-200 options can be generated in 8/24 hours. A very real sign that automation will have an impact within even the creative domain, especially in the case of practices with one central figure, who's capabilities may be augmented by this technology and not need as many assistants.

Others are celebrating the aesthetic of ML. An example is Matias Del Campo's winning entry 24 Highschool in Shenzhen (Del Campo 2021). Where images produced using an AttnGAN which converted text related to the aspirations of the building such as "A building with four walls and tomorrow inside Self discipline and social commitment" into an image that was translated into a floorplan or projected onto facades. Perhaps this is not surprising, human creativity has often been born out of impoverishment or limitations. In this case, the ML style becomes a strength as it drives current uniqueness and a link to new technology. However, this is perhaps better termed an artistic medium in which humans manipulate creativity. Maybe the creativity is not from the ML but the user in the same way that it would not be the drips but Jackson Pollock being creative despite the drip mechanism making most of the detailed marks.

The current computer-generated art may or may not represent something more long-lived than a single fad. ML will need to be creative enough to stop people getting bored from of it. Much like the representational limitation on novel designs that comes from simple parametric variation, many of the output from GANs or Deep Dream [5] show limited not universal variability. Indeed, whilst Deep Dream images were of intense interest when they came out in 2015, these images don't excite people as much now, perhaps because these alien scenes have little relation to wider human aesthetics or issues.

This is fundamentally linked to important issues of what architecture is. If we consider it as a purely technical practice, simply creating liveable habitation then creativity may be considered as capability to solve problems in unique ways or adapt to new situations/sites but possibly this is better characterised as 'innovative'. However, architects see themselves as part of culture. In this context we go back to the issue of artistic creativity, here producing the same design even if it is one's own work is unacceptable, copy or self-similar reproduction is in some way not creative. ML is able to produce a huge number of options thus able to sidestep this issue however ultimately it would need self and perhaps even cultural reflection/feedback to truly represent a creative agent.

Figure 7
Top: Examples of closely similar generated designs by Morphosis, Bottom: GAN generated images from Coop Himmelb(l)au, produced by training on images of their previous work (DigitalFutures 2020).

LEVEL OF AUTONOMY

Architecture is primarily for humans and driven by human needs. The role of the designer is essentially to understand those needs and articulate them through space and form. The complexity of planning and architecture arises from the evolving and ill-defined nature of these needs (Rittel and Webber 1973). And therefore, requires the active input and involvement of a human to both describe the needs as well as interpret if a design solution addresses them. And therefore, it is unlikely to realistically have AI design agents that are completely autonomous unless they too also become the target users of the building, or AI gains enough power to build a human theory of mind and be empathetic to human needs.

Assuming human in the loop at least to be the client or target user, then the question is, in which tasks can they be autonomous and in which capacity can they freely operate without the active engagement of a human. This can also point to the design tasks that are most replaceable by an AI, and in turn which tasks might be secure.

With traditional computational design, design approaches, rules, requirements, and conventions are encoded as rigid logic and parameters within the models and the automation happens in the exploration of these parameters. This ensures that generated designs are predictable; in that they follow the design logic set up by the designer. Coupled with meaningful evaluation parameters, these methods have proven to be useful in practice but are ultimately deterministic and rely on significant human programming input. Thus, due to the human needs these automated systems are either geared towards generic or highly specialised (single building) automation.

However, with current Deep Learning the outcomes are almost the opposite. Depending on the inputs, results are often unpredictable, in-precise, and with inexplicable generation rationale (a 'black box'), but are able to produce outputs which are reasonably flexible and fast once trained. Depending on input data, they can implicitly encode design conventions, but cannot be expected to be 100% compliant due to their statical nature. However, they are more likely to produce something adaptive in previously unseen/-trained edge cases and robust enough to try to respond even if proposing a solution is challenging. Although the quality of that solution is likely questionable.

As a result, it is hard to expect that a design produced by ML will be used without some human checking. We can expect to have more conventional post-processing of ML output to rationalise image input into lines/BIM families etc. or throw out malformed designs. And with this, some further common sense and algorithmic refinement may be possible, in the same way as noise reduction or image sharpening is done on other media now. Ultimately a human will have to check them, to ensure that output is sensible and for the prior mentioned appraisal in terms of human and perhaps functional aspects if that can't be analysed automatically. Although ML will most likely be able to guess/estimate this if it is possible to capture the data as a training set. Arguably the most significant utility in ML in design will be its ability to automate or co-opt the actual spatial design. Extending automation beyond existing rules-based systems used for defining door schedules, panellisation planning etc. into subjective but fundamentally rational design activities like furniture and room layout.

The exciting challenge will be in relation to interfaces between ML and users. Ultimately the effectiveness of any ML beyond basic generative capability will be contingent on its ability to understand and thus provide for human spatial needs. Practically this will be in the form of responding to human input to change a design. Due to trained ML's fast response, there is potential for systems to engage in repeat interchanges, unlike typical analysis reliant Multi-Objective Optimisation (MOO) methods where options are generated over a long time and a solution is chosen in one-shot. ML based interfaces could be more multidirectional. As demonstrated by Chaillou (2020), they can be designed to allow for fast sketching and modification by a user in response to the ML generated design, or have autocomplete/-fill type functionality as shown in Image GPT. Sites like 'Picbreeder' [11] show interfaces for interactive generative design, Ibrahim and Joyce (2019) demonstrates a similar approach on Meta-parametric models. Where a generative tree of options can be interactively navigated, which is similar to how human generated options are explored (Fujimura 2018) or in a GitHub type parametric model versioning system (Cristie and Joyce 2019, Mohiuddin et al. 2017).

Beyond direct high-bandwidth brain-machine connections envisioned by Elon Musk's 'Nuralink' this lack of intellectual expediency in the to-and-fro of design might be one of the biggest barriers to quality design production in ML, as currently a relatively general ML requires significant interaction to tune its output to fit a designer's/user's needs. But examples of link between images and text such as Dall-e [3] and Clip [4] point to more expedient high-level guidance of ML output.

LEVEL OF DESIGN QUALITY

The previous section considered the use of ML for inspirational means and the sections before considered ML as a useful functional helper. What we may consider as 'good/great' architecture often goes beyond fulfilling basic functional requirements or even pure aesthetics and style. Most of a singular building is driven by the high-level needs of the client. At the same time, buildings as a whole can be an expression and self-reflection of the values and ethos of the designer(s). Much of these ideas may not be explicit or captured formally. Currently, ML does not have a past, nor any 'ambitions' beyond what is programmed to them. However, in some respects, larger General AI is arguably beginning to share some aspects of humans. For example, GPT-3 uses a large corpus of data including all of Wikipedia which only representing 6% of the data it uses. After initial training, estimated to cost $4.6M in compute alone (Li 2020), it can then learn quickly with limited input, able to extend existing texts, mimic different authors' styles, and even write in other languages. It is a 'pattern machine' able to abstract existing text patterns using its 175Billion parameters. In this way the model may be said to be aggregating 'experience', humans gain learn linearly over time, but ML can learn in a highly parallel way to shorten that time but at the cost of using up power.

Whilst the experience (training data sets) flavour ML output in a similar way that a designer might produce architecture as a product of who they worked with or what buildings they saw, we still see a lack of self-motivated activity. Perhaps unless an ML becomes active in pursuing and also preferential and

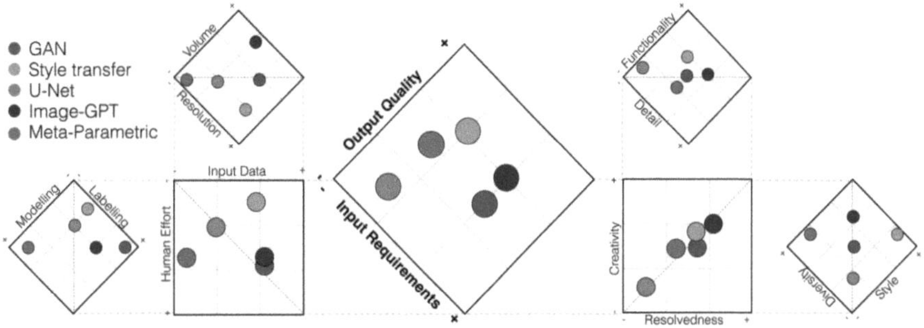

Figure 8
Mapping of ML tools based on the different issues which contribute to their input requirements and output quality

critical about its input data then there is not any sense of "Self" or "Self-actualisation". Limiting its output and scope from a designer to instructed assistant.

If instead, we focus more on the 'tool' nature of ML we also come up against limits. Currently, ML appears to be more effective when trained on lots of data, and with high levels of complexity. Assuming there are no shortcuts, then we enter a limitation related to being able to afford and ultimately own ML tools. Whilst high-quality models might be very useful, as GPT-3 shows they are not cheap, nor are they easy to understand or work with. Tools like Lobe.ai[17] show human usable GUI interfaces for these systems and, with correct automatic tuning, ML may be relatively easy for non-technical people to use and train. However even then there is still much work to do in the realms of 'Explainable AI' to help users understand what is going on in the black box, trust is less of an issue assuming that all designs are vetted by a human which is a reasonable assumption still for buildings.

A commercial issue also exists especially with General AI, that the high cost means that they are likely to be controlled by larger software companies. If they become more useful there is a danger our ability as designers will be limited by access to them, which may be controlled by the commercial interests of those able to afford them and few architecture firms are likely to be able to do so. AEC has already has been affected by similar issues in relation to data exchange with Revit which was restricted by creators Autodesk. Whereas the previous text-based .dxf (also by Autodesk) was truly open. Perhaps what we are seeing is the difference between low-level TensorFlow tools (early stage) and high-level GPT-3 tools (late-stage). The industry navigation of this issue may prove to be an important one especially if architecture wants to maintain its autonomy.

CONCLUSION

In some ways, this paper echoes Rittel and Webber's (1973) 'Wicked Problems' , which highlighted the limits of solving planning problems with a conventional design process. However, at the cost of under-representing the beneficial power inherent in design. This paper suffers similarly in emphasising the 'wickedness' of applying ML to design while not highlighting its strengths. However, we believe that ML is not at a loss for supporters with abundant explorations in applying individual ML tools in design. However, there is a lack of studies that evaluate and cross-compare different ML tools for their limits and applicability in design. Such studies can help to map the world of ML and determine the most project appropriate tools for the level of intervention or output detail required. In figure 8, we present our attempt at organising and mapping some of these tools against issues discussed in the paper. We hope this may provide a starting point for others, to expand on and this paper, like Rittel and Webber's, helps those who are working with these tools focus their talents on solving the real challenges and avoid the pitfalls of this powerful computing paradigm.

REFERENCES

Ahmed, E, Saint, A, Shabayek, AER, Cherenkova, K, Das, R, Gusev, G, Aouada, D and Ottersten, B 2019 'A Survey on Deep Learning Advances on Different 3D Data Representations', *arXiv:1808.01462 [cs]*

Brown, TB, Mann, B, Ryder, N, Subbiah, M, Kaplan, J, Dhariwal, P, Neelakantan, A and ., et al 2020 'Language Models Are Few-Shot Learners', *arXiv:2005.14165 [cs]*

Brown, NC and Mueller, CT 2019, 'Quantifying Diversity in Parametric Design: A Comparison of Possible Metrics', *AI EDAM*, 33, pp. 40-53

Del Campo, M 2021 'ARCHITECTURE, LANGUAGE AND AI:Language, Attentional Generative Adversarial Networks (AttnGAN) and Architecture Design', *Proc. CAADRIA 2021*

Chaillou, S 2020, 'ArchiGAN: Artificial Intelligence x Architecture', in Yuan, PF, Xie, M, Leach, N, Yao, J and Wang, X (eds) 2020, *Architectural Intelligence: Selected Papers from CDRF 2019*, Springer, Singapore

Cristie, V and Joyce, SC 2019 'GHShot', *Proc. eCAADe/SIGraDi 2019*

Daniel, D 2013, *Modelled on Software Engineering: Flexible Parametric Models in the Practice of Architecture*, Ph.D. Thesis, RMIT

Frey, CB and Osborne, MA 2017, 'The Future of Employment: How Susceptible Are Jobs to Computerisation?', *Technological Forecasting and Social Change*, 114, pp. 254-280

Fujimura, R 2018, *The Form Of Knowledge, The Prototype Of Architectural Thinking And Its Application*, Toto

Gero, JS 2002 'Computational Models of Creative Designing Based on Situated Cognition', *Proc. 4th Conf. on Creativity & Cognition*

Harding, J, Joyce, S, Shepherd, P and Williams, C 2013, 'Thinking Topologically at Early Stage Parametric Design', *Advances in Architectural Geometry 2012*, 2012, pp. 67-76

Heaven, D 2019, 'Why Deep-Learning AIs Are so Easy to Fool', *Nature*, 574, pp. 163-166

Ibrahim, N and Joyce, S.C 2019 'User Directed Meta Parametric Design for Option Exploration', *Proc. ACADIA 2019.*

Joyce, S.C and Ibrahim, N 2017 'Exploring the Evolution of Meta Parametric Models', *Proceedings of ACADIA 2017*

Karras, T, Laine, S and Aila, T 2019 'A Style-Based Generator Architecture for Generative Adversarial Networks', *Proc. IEEE/CVF Conf. Comp. Vision and Pattern Recogn.*

Koch, G, Zemel, R and Salakhutdinov, R 2015 'Siamese Neural Networks for One-shot Image Recognition', *Proc. of 32nd Int. Conf. on Mach. Learning*

Machairas, V, Tsangrassoulis, A and Axarli, K 2014, 'Algorithms for Optimization of Building Design: A Review', *Renewable and Stust. Energy Rev.*, 31, pp. 101-112

Mohiuddin, A, Woodbury, R, Ashtari, N, Cichy, M and Mueller, V 2017 'A Design Gallery System: Prototype and Evaluation', *Proc. ACADIA 2017*

Nauata, N, Chang, KH, Cheng, CY, Mori, G and Furukawa, Y 2020 'House-GAN: Relational Generative Adversarial Networks for Graph-Constrained House Layout Generation', *arXiv:2003.06988 [cs]*

Newton, D 2019, 'Generative Deep Learning in Architectural Design', *Technology|Architecture + Design*, 3, pp. 177-189

Oleinik, A 2019, 'What Are Neural Networks Not Good at? On Artificial Creativity', *Big Data & Soc.*, 6, pp. 1-13

Phillips, P.J, Moon, H, Rizvi, S and Rauss, P Oct./2000, 'The FERET Evaluation Methodology for Face-Recognition Algorithms', *IEEE Trans. on Patt. Analysis and Mach. Int.*, 22, pp. 1090-1104

Ramesh, A, Pavlov, M, Goh, G, Gray, S, Voss, C, Radford, A, Chen, M and Sutskever, I 2021, 'Zero-Shot Text-to-Image Generation', *arXiv: [cs]*, 2102.12092, pp. 1-20

Rittel, HWJ and Webber, M 1973, 'Dilemmas in a General Theory of Planning', *Policy Sciences*, 4, p. 155–169

Ronneberger, O, Fischer, P and Brox, T 2015, 'U-Net: Convolutional Networks for Biomedical Image Segmentation', *arXiv: [cs]*, 1505.04597, pp. 234-241

Soler, V, G, Retsin and Garcia, M J 2017 'A Generalized Approach to NonLayered Fused Filament Fabrication', *Proc. ACADIA 2017*

Tolosana, R, Vera-Rodriguez, R, Fierrez, J, Morales, A and Ortega-Garcia, J 2020, 'Deepfakes and beyond: A Survey of face manipulation and fake detection', *Inf. Fusion*, 64, pp. 131-148

[1] https://openai.com/blog/image-gpt/
[2] https://www.archdaily.com/938693
[3] https://openai.com/blog/clip/
[4] https://openai.com/blog/dall-e/
[5] http://ai.googleblog.com/2015/06/inceptionism-going-deeper-into-neural.html
[6] https://thisrentaldoesnotexist.com/
[7] https://lambdalabs.com/blog/demystifying-gpt-3/
[8] https://www.danieldavis.com/generative-design-doomed-to-fail/
[9] https://youtu.be/06-AZXmwHjo
[10] https://youtu.be/OlvYzmWuMsU
[11] http://picbreeder.org/
[12] https://www.ft.com/content/7d3e0d6a-87a0-11e9-a028-86cea8523dc2
[13] https://www.technologyreview.com/2020/10/16/1010566
[14] https://thispersondoesnotexist.com/
[15] https://github.com/cysmith/neural-style-tf
[16] https://www.technologyreview.com/2020/07/20/1005454
[17] https://lobe.ai/
[18] https://www.nytimes.com/interactive/2018/10/12/us/map-of-every-building-in-the-united-states.html
[19] http://transnatural.org/wp-content/uploads/2011/09/EZCT_Booklet-Screen.pdf

Yarn-Level Modeling of Non-Uniform Knitted Fabric for Digital Analysis of Textile Characteristics

From a bitmap to the yarn-level model

Maria Anishchenko[1], *Ingrid Paoletti*[2]
[1,2] *Politecnico di Milano, Department of Architecture, Built Environment and Construction Engineering*
[1,2] *{Maria.Anishchenko|Ingrid.Paoletti}@polimi.it*

Modern CNC weft knitting machines are capable to produce textiles with complex non-uniform structures and shapes in a single operation with minimum human intervention. The type of knit structure and the settings of the knitting machine significantly influence the fabric characteristics and its role in architectural comfort. However, there is still no open-access tool for fast and efficient analysis of textiles with consideration of their knit structure, especially if they are knitted non-uniformly. Moreover, the existing methodologies of digital modeling of the knit structure are not linked to the actual production of textiles on flat-bed knitting machines. This paper presents a tool that ``reads" a bitmap image that can be as well imported into a knitting machine software and generates a yarn-level geometry of the knitted textiles, that can be further integrated into the behavior analysis software within the rhino-grasshopper environment. This methodology helps to preview and analyze knitted textiles before production and can help to optimize the programming of bespoke knitted textiles for large-scale architectural applications.

Keywords: *knitting, computational knitting, digital simulation, textile characteristics, textiles for architecture*

INTRODUCTION

Textiles are widely used in architecture both for interior and exterior applications. They are used in active-bending, air-supported structures, recently they were proven to be as well a feasible solution for the creation of resource-efficient formwork (Brennan Ba et al., 2013) and for complex bespoke concrete geometries (Popescu et al., 2018). Besides exterior applications, textiles are widely used in interior design. The use of fabrics in the interior space influences its acoustics, creates solar screens and light reflectors, helps to define a space, and increases the comfort level.

Textile environments should satisfy the aspects of safety and architectural comfort. Both can be controlled on the levels of fiber composition and the way of textile production (Anishchenko, 2020). The look and characteristics of the textiles depend on their structure and choice of yarns. On the level of fiber engineering, there is constant research of resistance to fire, ultraviolet rays, moisture, and other aspects that should be considered for construction. The way of fabric production, density, and thickness of the material play as well a significant role in the perception of architectural textiles and their role in architectural comfort. All these characteristics influence the way we perceive the fabrics and their capacity to distribute light and air, their insulation characteristics, and structural resistance.

Knitted textiles in large-scale applications are mostly used in the same way as woven materials and in most cases, their complete potential is not revealed. The main benefit of the knitted textiles with respect to woven ones is the possibility to create a non-uniform composition and complex shapes minimizing the need for cutting and connecting separate pieces. Moreover, the knitted textiles are naturally much more flexible and elastic because their structure benefits easy elongation without the deformation of fibers (Cooke, 2011). It increases the lifespan and the recovery properties of a material.

Knitting has advantages at the production stage due to the possibility to program every single loop of textile individually, respecting the limitations of a knitting machine. It enables a high variety of patterns and yarns composition to be combined in a single piece of fabric, to obtain an optimized bespoke fabric structure. The requirements to the particular areas of a piece of textile can be defined on the design stage, for example, to detect where an open structure is needed to provide more natural light, or more dense and bulky to absorb sound. However, there is no actual link between the analysis of required characteristics and the production of the textiles. As well there is no open-access database of textile structures that could help to choose an optimal knit pattern and especially combine different ones together.

The software for the CNC-knitting machines is relatively easy to use to design and produce flat uniform textiles. Production of more complicated structures with a specific shape or with non-uniform compositions requires a lot more experience. Moreover, it is generally impossible to preview the complex structures within the software. The built-in visualization system within some knitting machine software, for example, M1Plus by Stoll, renders well simple two-dimensional patterns but fails to render more complicated structures and shapes. The topic of rendering and predicting the behavior of knitted fabrics is under the research for animation design. Though there is ongoing research that explains the physics of the knitted textiles, there is no actual way to link the digital simulation to the actual production and to predict the physical characteristics of textiles.

The methodology described in this paper aims to facilitate the preview and production of bespoke knitted textiles. In the further chapters is presented a script based on Rhinoceros-Grasshopper-Python environment that creates a lightweight three-dimensional model of a knit structure taking as an input a bitmap image that can be as well used to produce textile on a knitting machine. The main aim of this tool is to create a direct link between real textile production on flatbed knitting machines and its simulation in the digital environment. As an output, the script generates geometry representing the knitted textile depending on the user request: points, lines, curves, or surfaces for further integration of the model into the existing behavior simulation plug-ins.

The suggested tool is designed as a first step of the methodology of automatic generation of the code for the knitting machines for the production of bespoke non-uniform performative fabrics. This research aim is to facilitate the overall process of the design of textiles from the choice of optimal textile structure to real production.

STATE OF THE ART

Knitting in general is a widely researched field. But being mostly used in the fashion industry, where the production tips are normally kept in secret, this research doesn't get much spread in the open-access networks (Underwood, 2009). In recent years knitting has attracted the attention of people from different fields: product design, aerospace, automotive, marine, geotextiles, medicine, protective clothing industries. Moreover, there is an interest in knitting from the computer animation field to digitalize the behavior of knitted textiles. The use of knitting in architecture is a relatively new topic. Among the innovative applications of the knitted textiles are stay-in-place concrete formworks (Popescu et al., 2018), knitted textiles with non-homogeneous structures for the bending-active structures (Deleuran et al., 2015), integration of conductive fibers into the knitted textiles for the interactive environments (Ahlquist, 2016).

The State-of-the-Art relative to this paper can be divided into 3 major categories: production of non-uniform knitted fabrics, digital analysis of knitted textile on a macro mesh level, and digital analysis on micro yarn contact level.

Knitting of non-uniform textiles is quickly getting popularity within the fashion field, especially by sports brands for the production of garments and shoes to engineer zones for temperature regulation, sweat, movement, support, etc. The choice of a fabric structure is based on physical tests and the experience of knitting engineers. Programming and knitting three-dimensionally shaped seamless non-uniform garments still require more time in respect to the production of uniform flat fabric. This time is not always compensated by the reduction of the number of operations of cutting and sewing, thus the seamless production is not necessarily economically valuable. It may be different for the production of large-scale bespoke textiles for architectural applications, where each programmed piece should be produced only once or in a very limited amount of copies and each additional prototype may increase significantly the costs. Thus, large-scale bespoke applications require more precise programming and simulations to avoid the trial-and-error method and wasteful full-scale prototyping stage.

Normally to analyse fabric on a macro level a piece of textile is presented as a mesh in which all the edges are springs that tend to contract. This gives a relatively realistic image of the tensile behaviour on a large scale. This way it is possible to see in a fast manner the behaviour of a textile piece but without consideration of its structure and the behaviour on a yarn level.

Tamke et al. (2016) have proposed a methodology of import of bitmap images with predefined shape and structure divided into zones depending on structural requirements in the knitting machine code. The projects of Hybrid Tower and Isotropia canopy (Thomsen et al., 2019) for Biennale 2018 use bespoke CNC-knitted textiles with complex structures. Working with bending-active systems, they perform as well the analysis of the textiles on macro-scale within the rhino-grasshopper environment, using software like Kangaroo, Kiwi3D, SOFiSTiK ((La Magna et al., 2018)). They detect the areas with different structural requirements and export the data as a bitmap for direct import in the knitting machine software. The choice of the most suitable knit pattern is done through a series of physical experiments including 3d scanning.

A research group from CIRTex college from Shenkar in Israel (Karmon et al., 2018) works on automatization of the creation of knitted patterns based on the prediction of fabric deformation which helps to achieve more precision between design and production stages. It is done on a mesh level by defining various elasticity characteristics to areas of fabric with different knit patterns.

The modeling of knitted textiles on the yarn level is mostly researched for animation purposes, where it is important to obtain a realistic image, but not unveil the performative characteristics of the fabric. In 2008 Kaldor et al. have suggested an efficient methodology of analyzing the knitted textiles on yarn level considering yarn-yarn friction and sliding, pulls, frayed edges, or detailed fracture between all the points in the model, which creates a reliable, but however very heavy computational model. Yuksel et al. (2012) suggested a 'stitch mesh' methodology with a finer mesh representing the layout of stitches in the garment. It helped to significantly decrease the time of calculations.

Cirio et al., (2014, 2017) propose an efficient representation of loops geometry and kinematics, capturing the essential deformation modes. The design force models reproduce macroscopic characteristics of knitted fabrics. McKee et al., 2017 and Liu et al., 2018 use finite element analysis to check the behavior of textiles on a yarn-level scale. Sperl et al. (2020) have proposed a method of animating yarn-level cloth effects using a thin-shell solver. They use a large number of yarn-level simulations to build a model of the potential energy density of the cloth and then use this energy density function to compute forces in a thin shell simulator.

While the macro-scale simulation observes the overall behavior of fabrics without consideration of fabric structure, the micro-scale yarn-level contacts analysis provides a way more realistic model, though with much higher requirements for the time of calculation and the computational capacities of a machine. Thus, the existing methodologies of modeling knitted textiles are not suitable for analyses of textiles on a large scale with consideration of the textile structure. As well, the current yarn-level simulations are not linked to the real production of knitted textiles and to physical simulation analysis software.

METHODOLOGY

The aim of this research is to create a methodology of digitalizing the knitting texture on yarn-level in a fast and computationally light manner using the logic of a CNC-knitting machine for further integration in performance analysis software.

This paper suggests a methodology of modeling the knitted textiles following the operational logic of a knitting machine to obtain the connection between the digitalization and actual production of textiles. This allows to facilitate the preview of the final result and to use the resulted three-dimensional model for further analysis. However, the paper doesn't specify the compatibility of the model with some particular plug-ins for physical analysis. Instead, it suggests a tool that can generate as an output various types of geometries from points to surfaces that would represent the required knit structure.

To enable yarn-level modeling of non-uniform knit structures it is important to understand how a knitting machine works. Initially designed to create plain fabrics, the interface of a knitting software reminds a raster 2D graphic editor where every "pixel" contains instructions about which actions should perform each pair of needles located on the parallel beds. These instructions can be given manually by designing directly inside the knitting machine software, otherwise, they can be also imported as a bitmap. During the import, it is possible to choose manually the correspondence between each color of the image to the commands of the software or upload the saved settings which will automatically assign the predefined commands to each color.

The following chapters explain the basic principles of the work of a knitting machine and suggest a script that is repeating in a simplified manner the needle actions in a digital environment. As an input, it takes a bitmap image where each color corresponds to a set of instructions. In the further stages, the resulted geometry is integrated into the Kangaroo2 plug-in for the application of the forces to see the behavior of the fabric. The same model can be as well integrated into other plugins for further physical analysis within the grasshopper environment.

WORKING PRINCIPLE OF A WEFT KNITTING MACHINE

The modern knitting machines consist of 2 needle beds - two parallel platforms on which are located the hook needles (Figure 1). The distance between them is set by the gauge of the machine and influences the space between the loops and their size. The needles on different beds are located perpendicular to each other permitting the transfer of loops from one side to another. Items located on opposite beds in front of each other will be further called "corresponding needles" or "needle pairs". The beds can move horizontally relative to each other to change the position of the needles on different beds respectively.

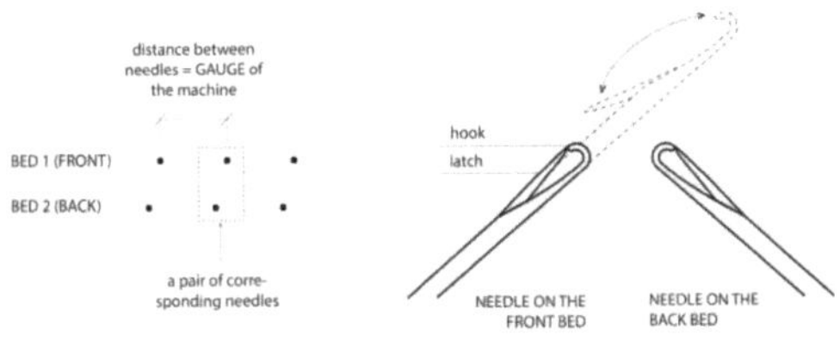

Figure 1
On the left: a representation scheme of 2 needle beds. On the right: graphical scheme of the needles

Any manipulation with needles and yarn is called a stitch. Any movement of exiting stitch to another needle - a transfer. Simple knitting patterns can be done with the use of one needle bed. The second bed serves to create more complicated patterns that would include the use of both beds in parallel and the transfer of the loops from one needle to another.

There are 3 basic operations with yarn that each needle can do: loop, tuck, or float. The essential base for all the patterns is a loop or a plain stitch. A new loop is formed when a yarn is drawn through a previously existing loop. Alternative stitches are tuck and float. For the tuck stitch, the needle creates a new loop but does not draw it through the previously existing one: it keeps both stitches on the same needle. The tuck can be also done on an empty needle. For the float, the loop is skipped, and the needle keeps the previous loop.

All these operations can be done both on front and back needle beds. In a knitting machine code, the operations that each needle needs to perform are described consistently. By default, the carriage starts moving from the right side of the needle bed and the direction alternates every row. During every single run in one direction, the carriage does needle actions with yarn or actions without yarn - transfers. Operations with transfers always require more time since the carriage should pass at least 2 times. Within one pair of corresponding needles, the needle actions can be performed consequently on both needles in one single carriage run if they use the same yarn, or separately in two or more runs if the yarns are different or special instructions were given. The order of these actions is defined for each pair of needles.

Transfer means moving an existing loop from one needle to another. It can be done only between the corresponding needles of opposite beds. To do that an empty needle from one bed passes through a loop on a corresponding needle of another bed to pick it up. During one carriage move, the transfer can be done only in one direction (for instance from front to back). Thus, for the rows where are present transfers in both directions, the carriage should do 2 passes. In case if the transfer should be done between two needles of the same needle bed, the loop should be first transferred to the opposite bed and then be transferred back to the original one after the rack was moved.

DIGITAL MODELING OF KNITTED TEXTILES

The script to digitalize the structure of knitted textile on the yarn level is programmed within the Grasshopper for Rhinoceros and consists of three major parts: Reading of a bitmap, generation of loops geometry, and application of forces. Following the logic of the knitting machine that was described above, the suggested script requires as input two sets of data: a bitmap image, in which every pixel corresponds to the needle actions on one needle pair, and a table of correspondence where are described the commands that should be performed for each "pixel" depending on its color.

Reading the bitmap

At the first stage, the image, imported as a bitmap file, is read by the Aviary1 plug-in for Grasshopper that works with raster images. This script extracts the width and the height of the image, and the RGB color of each pixel. In the next step, the Python script confronts the data from each pixel of the image to the data in an imported table, where each RGB is transformed into a special code described below and the meanings are stored in a "matrix". Matrix is a grafted list, that contains a series of sub-lists corresponding to the rows from the bottom to the top of the bitmap, which contain the codes with the needle actions.

The nine-digit code assigned to each pixel has its own meaning and corresponds to the needle actions that should be performed to the current needle pair. The first two digits represent the needle actions with yarn on the front bed. The first digit, which can be L, T, or F corresponds to "loop", "tuck", or "float" respectively. 0 instead means that no action should be performed. The second digit says which yarn should be used for this operation. The next couple of digits has the same meaning but corresponds to the actions on the back bed. The last 5 digits correspond to the transfer operations. The 5th digit may have meanings 0, F, or B (no transfer, transfer to the front, transfer to the back). The last 2 pairs instead inform if the front or rear racks should be moved to a side, moving the loops to the neighboring needles.

Generation of the loops geometry

The second part of the script generates the geometry of the stitches. As an input, it takes the "matrix" with a code for each stitch, and the initial positions of the needle beds in respect to each other. As an output, the script generates four types of geometry: points, lines approximating the segments of the yarn, splines, and pipe surfaces. Generation of the pipe surface takes a significant part of the time of calculation of the script and can significantly slow down the overall process for calculation of large pieces of fabric. For this reason, the output can be limited to the generation of points and lines to speed up the calculation process.

As a base for the knit geometry is used a hexagonal grid as suggested in (Cirio et al. 2017). The hexagonal grid allows to represent in a simplified way the geometry of loops and keep all the points of the hexagons as the nodes. To represent the two beds of a knitting machine, two parallel grids of the same size are generated. They can be moved with respect to each other. All the points of both grids are divided in a three levels tree structure corresponding to the row, the column numbers, and the point index inside of the hexagon. The sizes of the grids depend on the size of the bitmap (Figure 2).

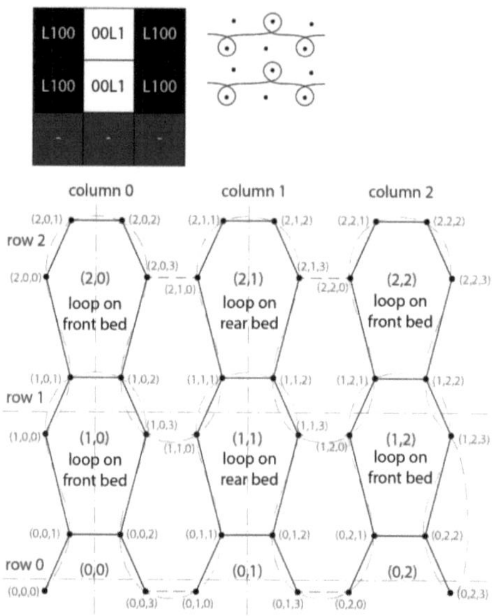

Figure 2
Transformation of a part of the input matrix to the hexagonal grid, where each node has a code corresponding to three-level data tree and each hexagon has a type code

Depending on the number of yarns introduced in the matrix, the script creates one or more lists which, contain consequent sub-lists of the points that yarn is passing to form stitches. Each sub-list contains several points corresponding to the type of the stitch: 8 points for loop, 4 points for tuck, and 2 for float (Figure 3).

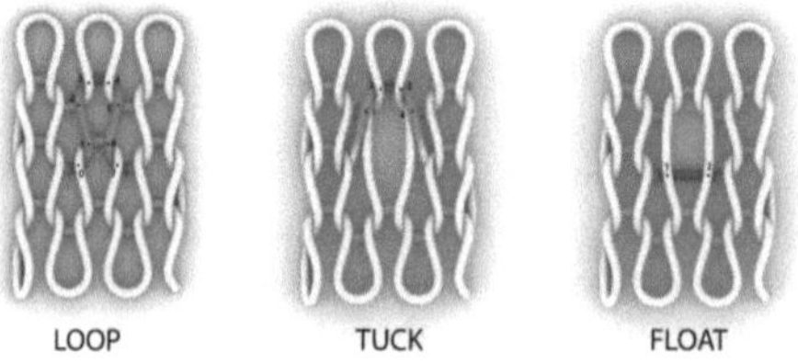

Figure 3
Loop, tuck and float stitches generated on the front bed

After each stitch, the lists representing the occupancy of each needle are updated, saving information about how many loops are contained by each needle. The loop erases all the previous information

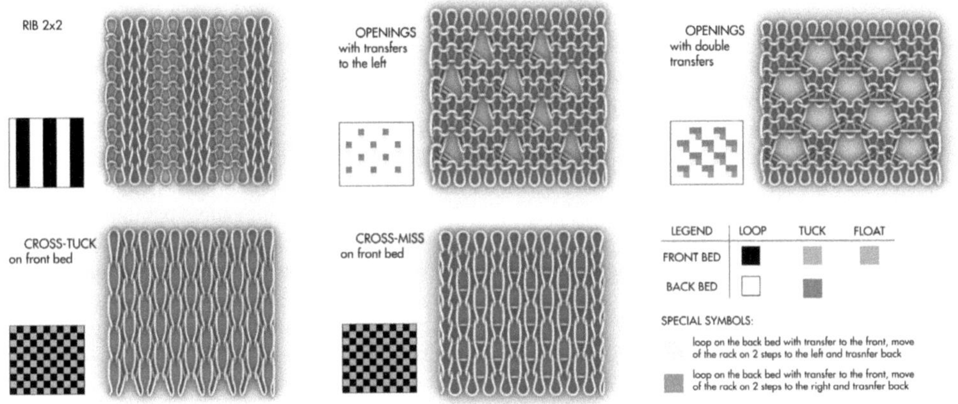

Figure 4
Various knit structures knitted with one yarn. on the left of each pattern is the bitmap imported as input and on the right is the output mesh

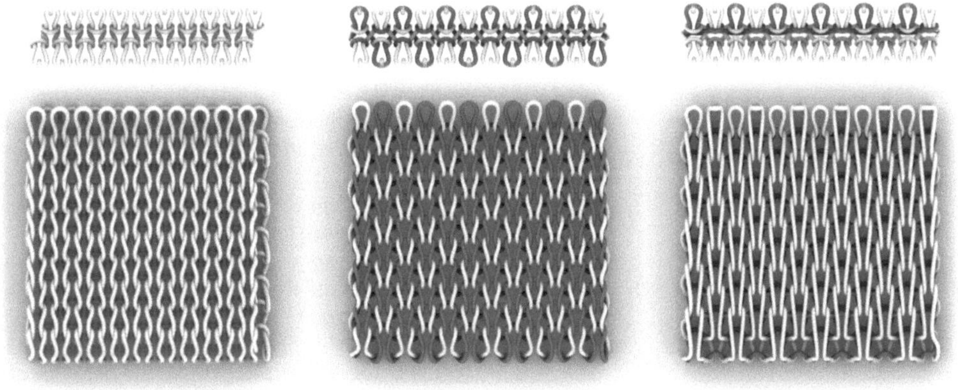

Figure 5
From the left to the right: double jersey knitted with one yarn with the back rack moved on half a gauge to the right; interlock fabric knitted with two yarns; interlock with alternating loops and floats knitted with two yarns

and sets the occupancy to 1. The tuck stitch adds an additional loop, keeping the previous ones and the float doesn't change the number of loops on the needle, so the previous number remains. This information is updated as well after the transfers. Before each float or tuck, the script is also checking if there are any loops on the needle and if yes, elongates them, moving the points to the next row.

As a result, the script generates one or several lists of points corresponding to the number of yarns used in the code. After the end of the calculation, single continuous curves or pipe surfaces representing the yarns are generated. The thickness of the pipe surface may be modified to represent different types of yarns. Figure 4 shows various knit structures with 1 yarn generated with the described script. It includes textile structures knitted on one and two needle beds, some of them with the use of transfers. Figure 5 demonstrates patterns knitted on both beds with the use of all of the needles with one and two yarns.

With the increase in the size of the textile, the

computational effort obviously grows. Since the script is calculating the positions of points that form the yarn shape one after another independently, the change of time to calculate the position of points and preview the springs or spline is relatively linear with respect to the number of loops. Instead, the calculation effort to preview the pipe surface grows significantly with the increase in complexity and fails when the fabric is too big. The graph in figure 6 demonstrates the almost linear dependency of the time in seconds needed for the calculation of the number of loops in the fabric.

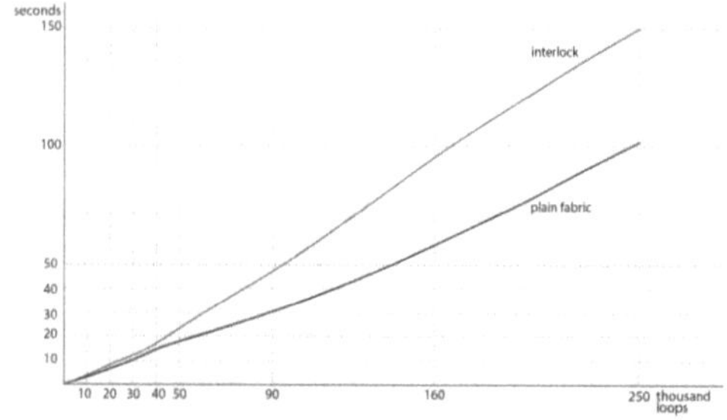

Figure 6
The graph demonstrating the dependency of time in seconds needed for the calculation depending on the number of loops.

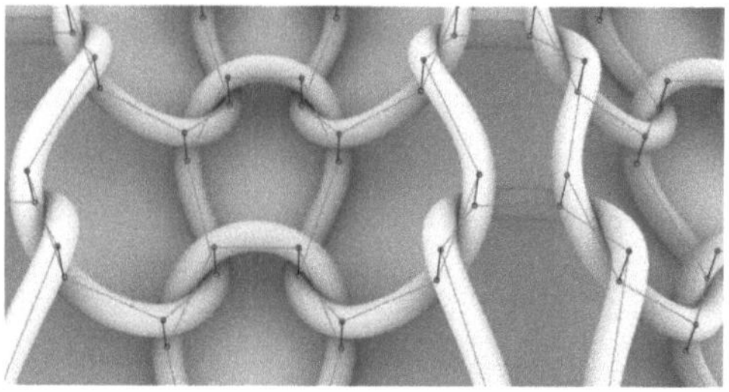

Figure 7
Green lines connect the continuous list of points that approximate the pieces of yarn. Black lines connect the corresponding points at the nodes

At the stage of loops modeling the script produces well recognizable knit structures, which can be already used to preview an approximate look of the textile before the production. However, since the physical forces acting both internally and externally are not considered yet, the further step of the calculations is required to obtain a more realistic model.

Application of forces

The application of forces is done through the Kangaroo2 plug-in for Grasshopper. To launch the simulation the collection of points and two sets of lines connecting them are required as input. The first are the lines that connect the neighboring points in the flattened list of points produced by the loop generation script and the second are the lines connecting the corresponding points (Figure 7).

The first group of lines represents the pieces of yarns that should maintain their length. Though in reality, it is not a line, but a curve segment that should keep the original length, inserting the lines in the calculation as springs provides a big economy in time. The yarn within the knit structure tends to straighten and obtain the initial shape, so the neighboring segments of the yarn tend to maintain an angle of 180 degrees between each other.

The second set of lines represents the contact points of the yarn. These lines should maintain the minimum length equal to a double radius of the yarn and stay perpendicular to the plane of the local area of fabric. For the current experiment, to see how the textile will behave in a relaxed horizontal position thus aligning the springs to the axis z. To switch to the simulation of knitted fabric placed in a not horizontal position, it is necessary to instead set an angle between the connection points and the plane of the nearby loops close to perpendicular.

To simulate gravity, the Kangaroo2 gives a minimum weight to all the points of the lines to keep the internal forces dominant with respect to the gravity force. The anchors are set to all the points located on the border of the piece to see the behavior of a slightly stretched fabric.

The current script still needs to be calibrated to achieve precision with the use of different yarns. However, the deformation of the fabrics after the application of forces demonstrates quite reliable results. For example, plain fabrics tend to deform the stitches in a diagonal direction; in cross-miss fabrics, the loops tend to become more round to occupy all the available space while the yarn tends to straighten. The analysis performed with Kangaroo demonstrates very similar behaviour to the plain and cross-miss fabric knitted with a hairy Polyester fibre

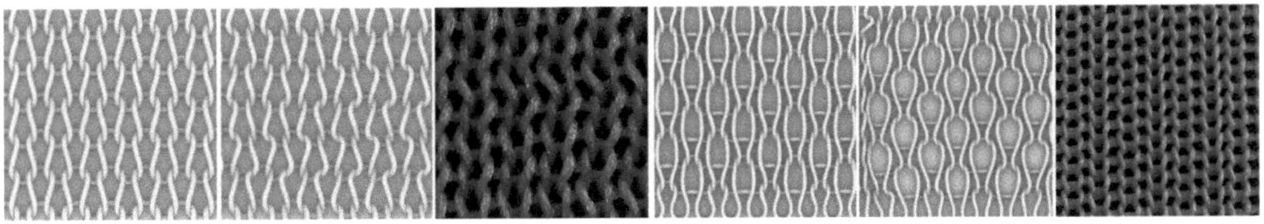

Figure 8
From the left to the right: single jersey before the deformation; single jersey after deformation; the picture of a physically produced sample. Cross-miss before the deformation; cross-miss after deformation; the picture of a physically produced sample

which slows down the sliding effect (Figure 8).

Since the yarn is approximated with springs and points, the simulation of the fabric behavior in the Kangaroo2 requires only slightly more computational effort to calculate additional forces with respect to the classical methodology where a mesh is represented as a rectangular grid of springs.

CONCLUSION

The methodology and script presented in this paper suggest a way of modeling a simplified knitted textiles structure produced on a CNC knitting machine. It proposes an intermediate way between the simulation of knitted fabric on mesh and yarn-contacts levels, approximating the yarn with lines to minimize the time of calculation. For this reason, it provides a less realistic model in respect to existing yarn-yarn level simulations but provides a way of representation of the fabric textile with respect to its structure for the macro-scale simulations.

One of the main advantages is that the script permits the preview of non-uniform knit patterns within the rhino-grasshopper environment and provides discretized geometry that can be directly introduced into the other plugins within the same environment for further analysis. For example, the output surface can be introduced into the Ladybug plugin to detect the light penetration characteristics, or to the Pachyderm plugin to analyze the acoustic characteristics. The reliability of this analysis is still to be performed by comparison of the computational models and the real-life physical tests.

The proposed methodology has several ways of further development. The first one is the calibration of the methodology by the series of physical experiments to detect better the forces acting internally and externally of the textiles. As well, it is important to understand the influence of the type of fibres used for the production. Understanding the influence of the fibre type is crucial for the further understanding of the fabric behaviour.

Another important aspect to develop is the possibility to generate the structure of three-dimensionally knitted textiles. The methodologies of knitting fabrics of particular shapes were carefully described by (Popescu et al., 2017) and (Hodgins et al., 2016) who have proposed converting a 3d mesh into knitting instructions. Another approach of simplifying the process of programming the 3d textiles was proposed by (Kaspar et al., 2019), who have designed an interactive system for simple garment composition and surface patterning. Within the framework suggested in this paper, the three-dimensionality can be obtained on the phase of application of physical forces by detecting the springs of the long loops that should contract.

The direction in which this current research will develop is the design of a complementary tool that will store the information obtained by physical and digital simulations of various knit patterns, save them in a database, and advise the optimal choice of the knit structure depending on the required characteristics for bespoke projects.

Digitalization and prediction of the behavior of knitted textiles have great potential for the fashion, engineering, and construction industries. However, there are still many open gaps in the field that do not reveal the complete potential of CNC knitting.

ACKNOLEDGEMENTS

The production of the samples for the proof of the reliability of the script was kindly supported by the

Block Research Group at the ETH Zurich, who have provided a possibility to do the experimentation phase on the Steiger knitting machine.

REFERENCES

Ahlquist, S 2016, 'Sensory material architectures: Concepts and methodologies for spatial tectonics and tactile responsivity in knitted textile hybrid structures', *International Journal of Architectural Computing*, 14(1), pp. 63-82

Anishchenko, M 2020, 'Bespoke knitted textiles for large-scale architectural projects', in Paoletti, I and Nastri, M (eds) 2020, *SpringerBriefs in Applied Sciences and Technology*, Springer, pp. 75-82

Cirio, G, Lopez-Moreno, J and Otaduy, MA 2015 'Efficient simulation of knitted cloth using persistent contacts', *SCA '15 Proceedings of the 14th ACM SIGGRAPH / Eurographics Symposium on Computer Animation*, Los Angeles, California, pp. 55-61

Cirio, G, Lopez-moreno, J and Otaduy, MA 2017, 'Yarn-Level Cloth Simulation with Sliding Persistent Contacts', *IEEE Transactions on Visualization and Computer Graphics*, 23(2), pp. 1-11

Cooke, B 2011, 'The physical properties of weft knitted structures', in Au, KF (eds) 2011, *Advances in knitting technology*, Woodhead Publishing Limited

Deleuran, A, Schmeck, M, Quinn, G, Gengnagel, C, Tamke, M and Thomsen, MR 2015 'The Tower : Modelling , Analysis and Construction of Bending Active Tensile Membrane Hybrid Structures', *Proceedings of the International Association for Shell and Spatial Structures*

Hodgins, J, McCann, J, Grow, A, Albaugh, L, Mankoff, J, Matusik, W and Narayanan, V 2016, 'A compiler for 3D machine knitting', *ACM Transactions on Graphics*, 35(4), pp. 1-11

Kaldor, JM, James, DL and Marschner, S 2008, 'Simulating knitted cloth at the yarn level', *ACM Transactions on Graphics*, 27(3), p. 1

Karmon, A, Sterman, Y, Shaked, T, Nir, S and Sheffer, E 2018 'KNITIT: A Computational Tool for Design, Simulation, and Fabrication of Multiple Structured Knits', *ACM SYMPOSIUM ON COMPUTATIONAL FABRICATION*, Cambridge, MA, USA

Liu, D, Shakibajahromi, B, Dlon, G, Breen, D, Kontsos, A, Seiki, S, Lab, HT, Breen, D and Kontsos, A 2018, 'Genevieve Dion A Computational Approach to Model Interfacial Effects on the Mechanical Behavior of Knitted Textiles', *Journal of Applied Mechanics, Transactions of the ASME*, 85(4), pp. 1-12

La Magna, R, Fragkia, V, Langst, P, Lienhard, J, Noel, R, Baranovskaya, Y, Tamke, M and Thomsen, MR 2018 'Isoropia : an Encompassing Approach for the Design , Analysis and Form-Finding of Bending-Active Textile Hybrids', *Proceedings of the IASS Symposium 2018 Creativity in Structural Design*, Boston, USA, pp. 1-8

McKee, PJ, Sokolow, AC, Yu, JH, Long, LL and Wetzel, ED 2017, 'Finite element simulation of ballistic impact on single jersey knit fabric', *Composite Structures*, 162, pp. 98-107

Mozafary, V, Payvandy, P and Rezaeian, M 2018, 'A novel approach for simulation of curling behavior of knitted fabric based on mass spring model', *Journal of the Textile Institute*, 109(12), pp. 1620-1641

Popescu, M, Reiter, L, Block, P, Flatt, R, Liew, A and Van Mele, T 2018, 'Building in Concrete with an Ultra-lightweight Knitted Stay-in-place Formwork: Prototype of a Concrete Shell Bridge', *Structures*, 14, pp. 322-332

Popescu, M, Rippmann, M, Van Mele, T and Block, P 2017 'Automated Generation of Knit Patterns for Non-developable Surfaces', *Design Modelling Symposium Paris 2017. Humanizing Digital Reality*, pp. 271-284

Tamke, M, Baranovskaya, Y, Deleuran, A and Monteiro, F 2016 'Bespoke Materials For Bespoke Textile Architecture', *Proceedings of the International Association for Shell and Spatial Structures*, Tokyo

Thomsen, MR, Baranovskaya, Y, Monteiro, F, Lienhard, J, La Magna, R and Tamke, M 2019 'Systems for transformative textile structures in CNC knitted fabrics – Isoropia', *Proceedings of the Tensinet Symposium 2019*, pp. 95-110

Underwood, J 2009, *The Design of 3D Shape Knitted Preforms*, Ph.D. Thesis, RMIT University

[1] https://arxiv.org/abs/1904.05681

Reconfigurable Domes

Computational design of dry-fit blocks for modular vaulting

Selina Bitting[1]*, Shervin Azadi*[2]*, Pirouz Nourian*[3]
[1,2,3]*Delft University of Technology*
[1]*s.bitting@student.tudelft.nl* [2,3]*{s.azadi-1|p.nourian}@tudelft.nl*

In contrast to the contemporary aesthetic account, Muqarnas are geometrically complex variations of Squinches used for structural integration of rectilinear geometries and curved geometries. Inspired by the historical functionality of Muqarnas, we present a generalized computational workflow for generating dry-fit stacking modules from two-dimensional patterns in order to construct a dome. Similar to Muqarnas these blocks are modular in nature, complex in geometry, and compression-only in their structural behavior. We demonstrate the design of such structures based on the exemplary Penrose pattern and showcase the variations & potentials of this method in comparison to conventional approaches.

Keywords: *Muqarnas, Generative Design, Modular Design, Unreinforced Masonry Architecture, Penrose Tiling, Workflow Design*

INTRODUCTION

Muqaranas (Tabbaa 1985) are an archetype of the middle-eastern architectural vernacular, often recognized by their intricate design. They are created using various modules, and are difficult to replicate without specific knowledge and materials due to their intricacy as well as the relevant construction techniques. Muqarnas originated as a structural method for transitioning from a rectilinear space to a dome, as a geometrically more complex squinch (Koliji 2012). This method of using modules to transition between different types of geometries is the inspiration behind the proposed generative method as it takes into consideration the force flows through the topological connections of said modules (Chassagnoux 1970). Additionally, the different techniques used to understand and replicate traditional muqarnas are essential to the generalization of the construction method into a computational process.

Traditionally, muqarnas use a pattern which specifies the juxtaposition of modules in the horizontal plane. By reading the pattern, it is apparent which modules are located where in order to create the overall dome or squinch (Yaghan 2001, [4]). This relationship between pattern and block is replicated in the computational process which results in a dry-fit, pre-cast set of interlocking blocks that are held together via gravity; thus resulting in a compression-only structure. In order to translate the muqarnas into such a method, two vital elements are required: a 2D pattern and a specification of how the blocks relate to the pattern.

The generative method (see Algorithm 1 in Figure 1) begins with the creation of a Penrose pattern

Algorithm 1: Computational Muqarnas Procedure

```
ComputationalMuqarnas ():
    Tessellate a polygon of a given diameter with Penrose pattern
    Mark the vertex to be identified as an apex point in the pattern
    Find the centroids of all geometries belonging to the tessellation
    Organize all geometries radially from the apex point
    Enumerate all geometries by distance from the apex point and
      sequence within said group
    Traverse the tessellation (pattern) and identify ordered pairs
    Extrude each geometry of the pair according to its typology
    Displace the pair of extrusions to the corresponding height for
      their location in the pattern
```

Figure 1
Computational Muqarnas Procedure

[2], then navigates the pattern, and later extrudes the modules. The Penrose pattern is exemplary, but any other 2D pattern can be utilized instead (Castera 2003). This specified relationship between the pattern and the block results in a system of overlapping, stacked modules with an overall design that is indicative of traditional muqarnas (Sakkal 1988), but is general in its implementation. The modules are simple enough in design to be constructed with neither particular knowledge about materiality nor additional equipment.

In order to evaluate the different potential methods for creating the modules, three main criteria are identified as priorities for the design to accomplish. The first is to limit the number of distinct modules to a maximum of 20, and the second is to obtain the maximum amount of variation using these modules. This variation should result in an interesting pattern that has a similar aesthetic to the original muqarnas. The final criteria is that the method of construction be simple enough for a person to build it themselves, which therefore rules out structural systems in which one block is held in place by neighboring blocks, as one example, to instead favor stacking methods.

The motivation behind the proposed computational method presented in this paper is to explore and validate the feasibility of procedural design of muqarnas-like discrete blocks for low-tech modular construction of vaults/domes by means of dry-stacking. The remainder of the paper presents an exemplary implementation of a reproducible method for generating the 3D geometry of the blocks based on a Penrose tiling (a 2D tessellation) of the floor plan of the dome to be muqarnas-vaulted, based on the following meta-procedure:

BACKGROUND

Domes present a number of challenges to modularization in that while they are constructed out of standard bricks or stone blocks, successfully doing so requires expert knowledge of how to achieve strength and stability through ad hoc placement of bricks. Therefore a dome structure is either constructed by a highly skilled mason or imitated through some other material such as steel. Incorporating the structural performance in a computational method allows the block geometries to account for the flow of forces in the dome and to design a stacking system that accomplishes a similar form that is easy to construct. By doing so the process can be expanded to shapes that are not just circular domes but can also replicate transitional spaces such as squinches.

In contrast to conventional bricklaying methods, existing dry-fit systems incorporate structural evaluation in their design to confirm their validity, rather than gluing blocks together or using a mortar between them. Two such examples are the Armadillo Vault constructed by the Block Research Group (BRG) of ETH Zurich [5] and Block Moulds [6]. The Armadillo Vault is a complex example whereas Block Moulds is a more practical implementation of a dry fit system. However, both exemplify the spectrum of dry-fit systems and how simple or complex constructions can become relatively easy to construct and possible to disassemble.

In an effort to create structural muqarnas, referred to as "genuine" muqarnas by Yaghan in his paper "Self-Supporting Genuine Muqarnas Units", the first option is to use a radial method of creating blocks. Figure 2 shows the radial slicing in both plan and section, which leads to a basic block as shown in the same figure. The next step is to carve or add to the inner face of this block in order to make a pattern reminiscent of traditional muqarnas. However, due to the varying radii as slices are made along with the dome, this method results in far too many modules and thus fails the first of the design criteria. This method is based on a simplification of the method used by Yaghan which is an early example of generating genuine muqarnas computationally.

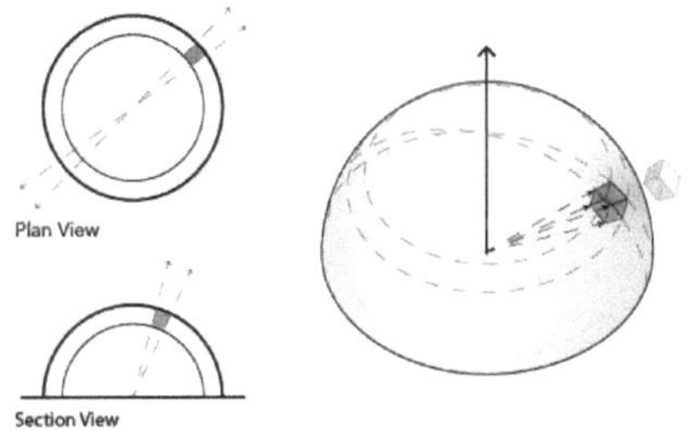

Figure 2
Diagram of the radial approach.

The second option is to use a stacking method derived a careful study of the vaulted dome of the "Masjed-e Jameh mosque" (Friday mosque) in Isfahan, Iran. The repeating shapes of the stone are simple and serve a structural purpose. These shapes are created using multiple simple, rectangular bricks. The main downfalls of this precedent are that it functions at a very large scale and that the system is not compression-only. A projected 2-Dimensional (2D) pattern of the Friday mosque dome demonstrates how each block sits over the top of a gap, showing that this design results in areas of tension. This indicates that it is not optimized for a structure comprised of only masonry.

A different approach to generating muqarnas is presented in Alaçam (Alaçam and Güzelci 2016) where the outline of the space is used to develop a plan projection. The pattern is generated by subdividing this outline into triangles. Afterwards, a surface is produced corresponding to the plan. This is a different approach which does not result in 3D blocks, and would therefore require additional steps to transition from a surface to modules.

The 2D pattern of the stacking approach resulted in a realization that virtually any pattern on the 2D plane can be navigated to generate block forms. In investigating the viability of this approach, a third option emerged. This option is to traverse patterns with different logics to generate geometries in a generalized workflow. The Penrose Pattern emerges as a promising pattern to couple with this pattern-navigating its 5-fold symmetry and lack of repetition. However, the entire pattern consists of only two types of triangles: kites and darts (Gardner 1989). This inherent modularity of the pattern meets the design criteria for modularity and variability, so the final criteria of structural self-sufficiency is all that remains for this method to fulfill all three design criteria.

Simple orthogonal extrusions of the triangles confirms that the variability is preserved in the 3-Dimensional (3D) form, however the structural criteria remains unfulfilled. This method is therefore accepted as the most promising approach, and the next challenge is to navigate the pattern in a way that produces a free-standing form which fulfils the structural design criteria.

FRAMEWORK

Traditionally, muqarnas are superficial rather than integrated structural elements of a building commonly made of wood or stucco. The blocks are then essentially "glued" to the building via additional stucco or nails (Yaghan 2007) according to a 2D plan projection, which is the same process as with their structural counterparts. The computational method focuses on this particular element to expand and generalize the process in order to generate any number of patterns or tessellations into domes, or possible vaults.

Within the scope of this paper, we assume that the final form is a dome-like structure, with the outer ring as the main support and the apex in the center. Consequently, the symmetry of the Penrose Pattern becomes an advantage for this input condition.

METHODOLOGY

In this section we will present the details of the computational workflow in the following order: construction of the Penrose pattern, sorting the modules to model the topological structure of the pattern, identification of the rings in the topological structure, navigation of the pattern, and finally construction of the 3D mesh of each one of the modules. The inherent modularity and variability of the Penrose Pattern prove it to be favorable, as it provides a limited set of modules while preserving the variety in the designs. Each structural module is constructed out of two triangular tiles in the Penrose pattern to ensure stackability. The pattern is navigated from the outermost edges to the centroid in order to create pairs of triangles. This logic allows modules to overlap, and therefore support each other structurally.

Step One: Pattern Generation

The initial step is to dynamically generate a Penrose Pattern. Given a diameter, the number of subdivisions, and the number of sides to the initial polygon, an initial set of acute triangles are created (see figure 3)

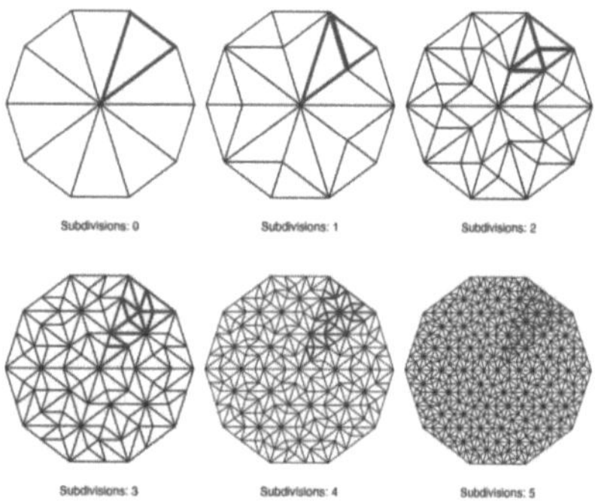

Figure 3
Generated Penrose pattern subdivision method illustrated.

$$\phi = \frac{1+\sqrt{5}}{2} \tag{1}$$

The algorithm which performs this function is largely based on a python script previously written by Josh Preshing [1]. Within his implementation, triangles have two options for color: red and blue. Red indicates an acute triangle and blue indicates an obtuse triangle. The algorithm also stores the triangle corners as complex numbers, which contain the information of the (x, y) coordinates for each of the corners A, B, and C. These coordinates are stored as python complex numbers, meaning that the imaginary value of A corresponds to it's x coordinate, and the real value corresponds to it's y coordinate. The following shows the tuple with all subsequent information:

$$(\text{color}, A, B, C) \tag{2}$$

For the creation of a dome, the number of subdivisions is set equal to 5, the diameter is equal to 6.6 meters, and the number of sides is equal to 10. The algorithm stores the triangles as complex numbers in creating the acute triangles, to then perform the subdivision algorithm with those triangles using an algorithm which subdivides an input triangle by the golden ratio ϕ, and then appends the relevant data, *(color, A, B, C)*, of the newly generated triangles to the results and outputs the list of all the newly subdivided triangles.

Algorithm 2, figure 4, begins with creating a polyline that connects the three corners of the triangle. Then the centroid of the triangle is found using to following equation [3]:

$$O_x = \frac{A_x + B_x + C_x}{3} O_y = \frac{A_y + B_y + C_y}{3} \tag{3}$$

This centroid is essential to understanding the location of the triangle in relation to the center of the overall pattern. The distance to the center of the pattern provides a method of constructing a triangulation between the centroid of the pattern, the centroid of the triangle, and the horizontal seam in the

Figure 4
Triangle Data Algorithm

Input	Data Type	Input Name: Notes
triangles	List of Tuples	The subdivided triangles, in this case subdivided by the golden ratio as input for this algorithm

Output	Data Type	Output Name: Notes
singleTri	List of polygons	Within the list are polylines or meshes related to the generated pattern triangles. In this case, polylines.
tri_info	List of floats	This list of lists contains the distance from the triangle centroid to the pattern centroid, the arcsine and the cosine thereof

Problem: Draw the triangles resulting from the subdivision, then find the centroids of the shapes in order to obtain distance and radial data to later sort and locate the shapes.

Algorithm 2: Triangle Data Algorithm

```
TriangleData (triangles):
    foreach color, A, B, C in triangles do
        Apt ← map x,y,z to 3D plane
        Bpt ← map x,y,z to 3D plane
        Cpt ← map x,y,z to 3D plane
        Dpt ← calculate centroid of the triangle and map x,y,z to
          3D plane
        DSa ← arcsine of the centroids
        DCa ← arcosine of the centroids
        singleTri ← construct polyline geometry
        tri_info ← append relevant locating data to the list
    return singleTri , tri_info
```

pattern (as can be seen in figure 5), to then locate the triangles in relation to one another. The arcsin and arccos provide the information needed to sort triangles radially counterclockwise starting at the seam in the pattern, which is performed in the following step of the code.

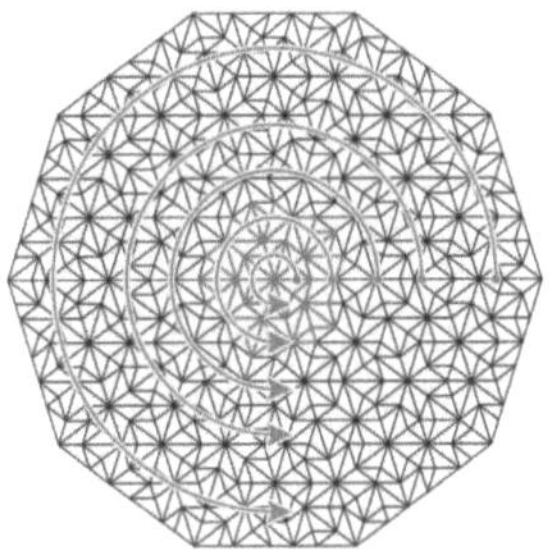

Figure 5
Diagram of the triangle sorting.

Input	Data Type	Input Name: Notes
aw	Integer	Weighted number conveying the importance of the angular location, , in the implementation 1 was used
dw	Float	Weighted number conveying the importance of the distance from the pattern centroid, in the implementation 10^8 was used
Output	**Data Type**	**Output Name: Notes**
order_values	Weighted Sorting List	This list contains a weighted value which locates the triangle in a relative radial system rather than a standard Cartesian system.

Algorithm 3: Triangle Sorting Algorithm

```
TriangleData (s, d, n):
    foreach ti in tri_info do
        sdeg ← convert arcsine to degrees
        cdeg ← convert arcosine to degrees
        if 90 ≥ sdeg ≥ 0and 0 ≥ cdeg ≥ 0 then
            deg = sdeg
        else if 90 ≥ sdeg ≥ 0  and  180 ≥ cdeg ≥ 90 then
            deg = cdeg
        else if 90 ≥ sdeg ≥ 0  and  180 ≥ cdeg ≥ 90 then
            deg = cdeg
        else if 0 ≥ sdeg ≥ −90  and  90 ≥ cdeg ≥ 0 then
            deg = 360 - cdeg
        else if 0 ≥ sdeg ≥ −90  and  90 ≥ cdeg ≥ 0 then
            deg = 360 + sdeg
        order_value = aw · deg + dw · ti[0]
        order_values ← append order_value to a list
    return order_values
```

Figure 6
Triangle Sorting Algorithm

Figure 7
Pattern Navigation Algorithm

Input	Data Type	Input Name: Notes
l	Integer	This number indicates which level or ring the geometry in list tris is located at
$tris$	Geometry	A list of the triangle geometries ordered by location
Output	**Data Type**	**Output Name: Notes**
all_pairs	Ordered List	This list contains the triangle geometries paired together to form the resultant pairs of shapes from the pattern navigation

Problem: Sort the arcsine and cosine data according to what quarter of the circle they lie in

Algorithm 4: Pattern Navigation Algorithm

```
TriangleData (s, d, n):
    tris_leveled ← initiate an empty list
    this_level ← initiate an empty list
    foreach i, t in enumerate(tris) do
        this_level ← append t
        if levels[i]!=levels[(i + 1)%len(tris)] then
            tris_leveled ← append this_level
            this_level ← set equal to an empty list
    order ← list of pairs which are the manually determined pattern
    all_pairs ← initiate an empty list
    foreach o in order do
        first_pairs ← index o[0] in tris_leveled
        second_pairs ← index o[1] in tris_leveled
        this_pairs ← zip the first_pairs and second_pairs data
          together
        all_pairs ← append the this_pairs value
    return all_pairs
```

Step Two: Triangle Sorting

The values of the distances along with the arcsin and arccos are the inputs to algorithm 3, figure 6, which gives priority to the sorting method. In this algorithm, distance has higher importance than angle $(dw > aw)$, which allows the sorting of the individual triangles to be from the center of the pattern to the outside, as well as counterclockwise from the horizontal seam on the right (figure 5).

For the organization portion, the algorithm uses the information previously appended to *tri_info* in order to locate the points radially. These values are converted to degrees, and then ranges are defined in order to determine in what quadrant of the circle the triangle is located. To elaborate, the domains of arcsin and arccos are shown below, and illustrated in figure 8:

$$\text{arcsin}\,\{x\} \Rightarrow \left[\frac{\pi}{2}, \frac{-\pi}{2}\right] \quad (4)$$

$$\text{arccos}\,\{x\} \Rightarrow [0, \pi] \quad (5)$$

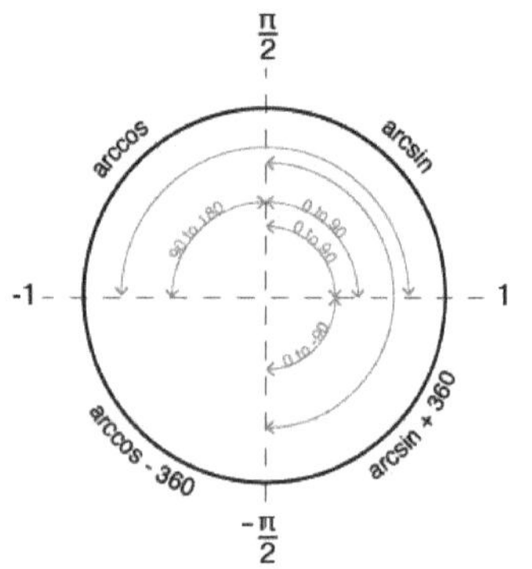

Figure 8
Diagram showing the sorting of calculated values into circle quadrants.

Associated with arcsin is the y-coordinate, and associated with the x coordinate is arccos. Therefore all four quadrants of a circle are included by evaluating them together. Referring to figure 8 can help to visualize the sorting code.

Next, the deg values are defined according to which quadrant each triangle is, and thereafter each triangle is sorted throughout the entire pattern according to degrees and distance from the center.

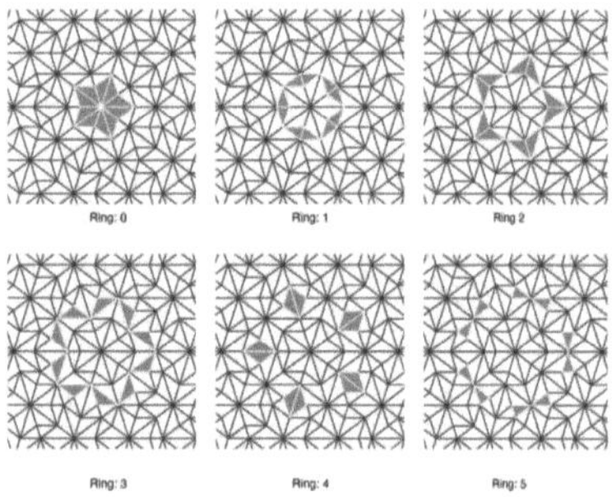

Figure 9
Grouping triangles into rings.

Step Three: Pattern Rings

Triangles equidistant from the center are located within the same ring, see figure 9. All triangles are first sorted by indexing each triangle. Then the distance of the triangle prior and the current triangle to the centroid are compared to determine if they are in the same ring, in which case the index increases by 1.

Step Four: Pattern Navigation

The method developed for the pattern navigation is to select a pair of adjacent triangles and then define one of those triangles as an angled piece and the other as a flat piece (algorithm in figure 7). This process is performed manually through trial and error, as not all combinations allow the pairs to overlap in a way which reaches the center of the pattern. Ideally this process begins at the outer edge and works toward the center until all shapes are incorporated in a sequence.

A single module is comprised of a flat piece and an angled piece. The flat piece is the largest part of the module, best described as an orthogonal extrusion of the triangle. The angled piece is the part of the module which is extruded to a point. The point in question is the corner of the triangle closest to the centroid of the pattern. The next pair of triangles form the following module, wherein the current angled piece becomes defined as the flat piece for the next module and the next adjacent triangle is the angled piece of the module, and so on and so forth until the centermost triangles have been included in the extrusion process to make modules. In this way, flat pieces sit overtop angled pieces, to form a system of modules that stack and distribute their load downwards to the next module. The method is elaborated upon in step six, where the modules are extruded.

The first section of the algorithm iterates through the rings such that each ring is given an index, and the triangles within the ring are indexed as well. The second section, for *o* in *order*, takes each pair in the manually determined pattern navigation and identifies those triangles in the list *tris_leveled*. The next step is to take the first and second triangles and combine them together so that a triangle with index 0 of level 0 is paired with the triangle of index 0 of level 1, and so on. The result is pairs of triangles that step their way from the centroid out. Figure 10 shows one of these 'strings' beginning at the outside of the pattern and working its way inwards. Figure 11 shows the adjacent 'strings' as well for context.

Figure 10
Plan showing a singular string of triangle pairs progressing towards pattern centroid.

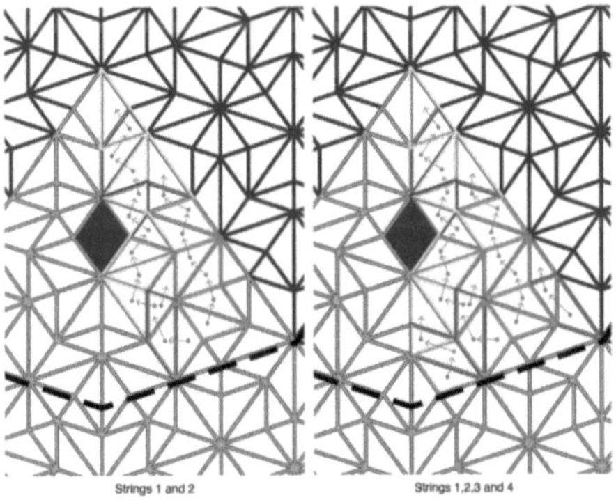

Figure 11
Plan showing adjacent, shorter strings.

Step Five: Adjustments for Triangle Displacement

The 'strings' within the paired triangles have different quantities of modules. The steps in the process which displace and extrude the modules rely on an initial displacement of the triangles to their relevant distances from the top of the dome. This can be seen in figure 10 where some strings extend from the outside to the very center of the pattern. However, there is, for example, a string that ends approximately three rings from the top. This translates to:

$$z = 3 \cdot bH \tag{6}$$

Therefore the values are manually redefined so that the associated index (i) of the strings accounts for the distance from the top of the dome. This updated value is instead stored as a new value, *z*, so that the original *i* is not lost. The modules are then vertically displaced according to this value.

Step Six: Module Extrusion

Each module, as explained before, consists of an angled and a flat piece. A for loop iterates through the list of pairs to perform basic extrusions on the triangles based on whether they are the angle or flat piece. Regardless of the type of piece associated with the triangle, the initial step is to retrieve the vertices of the triangles.

Angled Piece. For the angled piece, the next step is to sort the vertices and determine which vertex is closest to the center of the pattern, now referred to as the origin. The input for the *getCorners* function is the polyline of the angled piece, and the output is *(cornerPoints[0],cornerPoints[1], minPoint)* where *minPoint* indicates the vertex closest to the origin.

This output provides the two inputs, *(cornerPoints[0],cornerPoints[1])*, for the *duplicatePoints* function. This function displaces the vertices vertically by the block height *(bH)*. This provides the final data needed to construct a vertical polyline rectangle to be extruded toward the vertex closest to the origin. This extrusion is performed in a loop that iterates over the pairs of triangles. This concludes the process for creating the angled portion of the module, visualized in the top sequence of images in figure 12.

Flat Piece. A similar yet simpler process constructs the flat pieces of the modules. For the flat piece an arbitrary curve is used as the input for the *ExtrudeCurveStraight* function to produce an orthogonal extru-

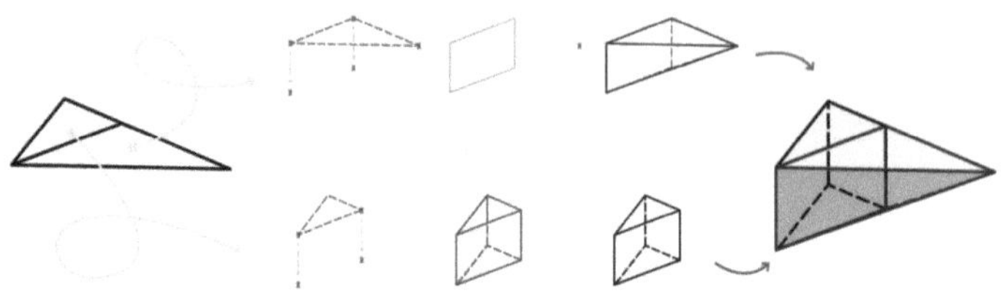

Figure 12
Diagram showing the steps performed by the algorithm to extrude the module geometries.

sion. The initial step is to retrieve an arbitrary corner using the function *getOneCorner*. Then, the function *duplicatePoint* makes a duplicate point displaced by block height *bH*. This results in the orthogonal line to guide the extrusion of the flat piece. The resultant flat portion of the module is shown in the bottom sequence of images in figure 12.

Displacement of the Modules. The displacement of the modules is performed in the negative z-direction, due to the overall methodology first addressing geometries near the pattern centroid and progressing outwards.

The flat and angled pieces are displaced individually by the same distance. The adjusted levels list is used in order to define the magnitude of the displacement, and all geometries are moved accordingly. The method of stacking can be seen in figure 13 in order to clarify how the 2D plan translates to a 3D form

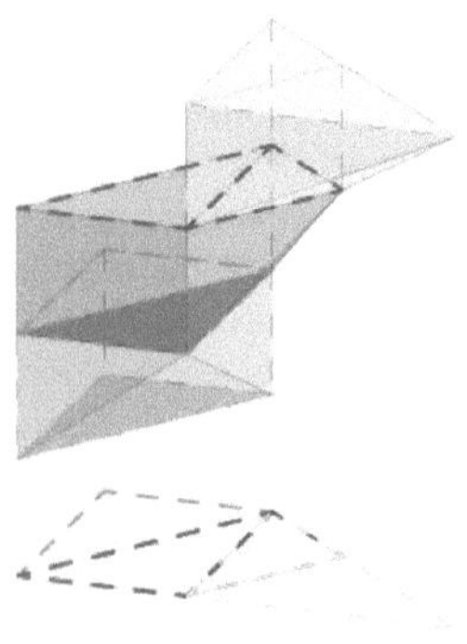

Figure 13
Diagram showing three stacked modules, and their original geometries projected below.

DISCUSSION & FUTURE WORK

An overarching element which the methodology lacks is compatibility with a variety of inputs. The process as exists at this stage, the inputs limit the variety of results, which could otherwise expand in scope to explore a variety of patterns and block shapes. The traversal scheme, currently manual, is essentially represented with tree graphs. Thus, one future direction is to utilize graph traversal methods, particularly breadth first search, to pair triangles of the Penrose pattern and generate modules.

Although the results show modules which can be stacked and result in a free-standing dome, there is no structural evaluation incorporated within the methodology. This is an essential step to be incorporated in the future iterations of the methodology as it represents a major hurdle to translating the generated scheme into a physical construction. Two options for enhancing this portion of the methodology are the dynamic relaxation method [7] and the force density method (Schek 1974), both of which are form-finding methods which take the tessellated pattern as a network and relax it under a set of forces until it reaches equilibrium. Incorporating this step also allows the modules to be reshaped in order to approximate a relaxed form which accommodates for the material properties and structurally feasibility, ultimately optimising the form.

Figure 14 is our proposed meta-procedure for topologically generalizing the proposed method so that it can work on input shapes that are not necessarily as symmetrical as the presented polygon.

Figure 14
Road-map of Computational Muqarnas Procedure

Algorithm 5: Road-map of Computational Muqarnas Procedure

ComputationalMuqarnas (**InputPolygon**):
- Tessellate the floor plan of the space to be covered by muqarnas blocks as a mesh
- Mark the [singular] vertices to be transformed into apex points in the discrete muqarnas vault
- Find the faces incident to these vertices
- Construct a dual graph encoding the connectivity between the face of this mesh
- Run a graph traversal method to find a path from every apex vertex towards the nearest boundary edge.
- For every edge of the found paths on the dual graph, choose the corresponding faces and extrude them into prisms
- Optimize the shape of the dual graph by means of the Force Density Method and extract the resultant heights of nodes from the method
- Move and duplicate a copy of the prisms above themselves into stepped distances in accordance with the heights found above
- Coalesce every such pair of consecutive prisms into one 3D block
- Scoop out excess mass out of the blocks from below.

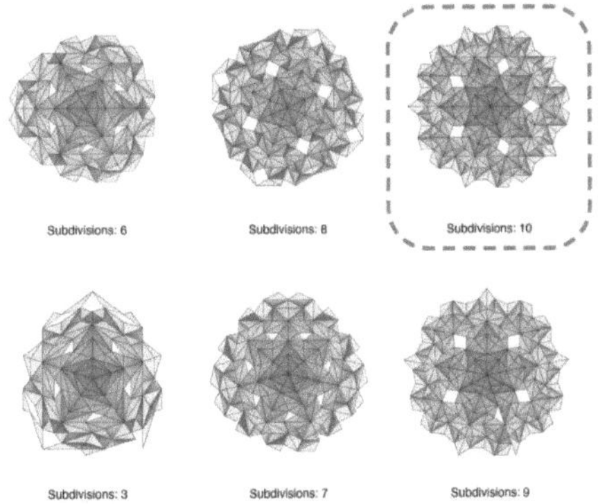

Figure 15
Views from below of different generated domes.

The resultant blocks of this process will simplify and optimize block construction methods. Dry stacking modules allow for total demountability which is in congruence with the intentions and goals of the circular construction practices. Circular spaces or transitions between rectilinear and circular spaces can be generated with this modular method to provide the easy to construct dry-fit blocks. Additionally, a further generalization of the method has the potential to produce re-configurable vaulting systems (Alaçam et al. 2017). As this methodology was initially developed in the context of the MSc EARTHY Studio at TU Delft (Nourian et al. 2020), these blocks were originally intended to be made of cast earth blocks. Within that educational context, the main task was to develop a low-tech construction process for the domes of a heritage complex dedicated to Syrian heritage. Throughout the course it was determined that exploring the intersect of muqarnas and computation would be aligned with the intention behind the heritage complex. In designing the process which resulted in this paper, it was further realized that this process had the potential to be generalized and reformulated to qualify for other contexts based on the variety of spatial quality that it can potentially spawn and not just cultural significance. Nevertheless, the methodology stays true to its origin as it is still compatible with using local material for manufacturing the simple blocks that are not only circular as they are dry-fit, but also are aligned with the skill level of the local workforces as their assembly process is based on simply stacking them.

CONCLUSION

As opposed to traditional muqarnas modules which are attached to the building superficially for decoration, these computationally generated modules are produced for simplifying the construction process of a masonry vault by making it easy for people without sophisticated masonry skills to make complex form active shells out of a few types of easily mass-produced blocks. The proposed method relies upon prescribed pattern navigation which relates to the pattern navigation utilized in traditional muqarnas. The method and the forms generated by it are therefore derivations of the traditional designs rather than imitations, which was the original intention. A variety of designs are achieved, shown in figure 15, and show great promise should the methodology be further developed.

REFERENCES

Alaçam, S and Güzelci, O 2016 'Computational Interpretations of 2D Muqarnas Projections in 3D Form Finding', *no source given*

Alaçam, S, Güzelci, OZ, Gürer, E and Bacınoğlu, SZ 2017, 'Reconnoitring computational potentials of the vault-like forms: Thinking aloud on muqarnas tectonics', *International Journal of Architectural Computing*, 15(4), pp. 285-303

Castera, JM 2003 'Play with infinity', *Meeting Alhambra, ISAMA-BRIDGES Conference Proceedings*, pp. 189-196

Chassagnoux, A 1970, 'Persian vaulted architecture: morphology and equilibrium of vaults under static and dynamic loads', *WIT Transactions on The Built Environment*, 16

Gardner, M 1989, *Penrose Tiles to Trapdoor Ciphers ...and the Return of Dr.Matrix*, The Mathematical Association of America, Washington, DC

Koliji, H 2012, 'Revisiting the squinch: From squaring the circle to circling the square', *Nexus Network Journal*, 14(2), pp. 291-305

Nourian, P, Azadi, S, Hoogenboom, H and Sariyildiz, S 2020, 'EARTHY, Computational Generative Design for Earth and Masonry Architecture', *RUMOER*, pp. 47-53

Sakkal, M 1988, 'An introduction to Muqarnas domes Geometry', *Structural Topology 1988 núm 14*

Schek, H.J. 1974, 'The Force Density Method for Form Finding and Computation of General Networks', *Computer Methods in Applied Mechanics and Engineering*, 3, pp. 115-134

Tabbaa, Y 1985, 'The Muqarnas Dome: Its Origin and Meaning', *Muqarnas*, 3, pp. 61-74

Yaghan, M 2001, 'The Muqarnas Pre-designed Erecting Units: Analysis, Definition of the Generic Set of Units, and a System of Unit-Creation as a New Evolutionary Step', *Architectural Science Review*, 44, pp. 297-318

Yaghan, DMA 2007, 'Self-Supporting Genuine Muqarnas Units', *Architectural Science Review*, 48(3), pp. 245-255

[1] https://preshing.com/20110831/penrose-tiling-explained/

[2] https://www.maths.ox.ac.uk/node/865

[3] www.mathopenref.com/pageurl.html

[4] http://www.shiro1000.jp/muqarnas/default-.htm

[5] https://block.arch.ethz.ch/brg/

[6] https://www.blockmoulds.com/

[7] https://github.com/Pirouz-Nourian/VectoRelax_Vectorized_Dynamic_Relaxation/tree/v1.3

A Function-Based Design Approach for Early Planning Phases for Healthcare Buildings

Petra von Both[1], Simon Sommer[2]
[1]Karlsruher Institute for Technology KIT [2]a|sh - sander.hofrichter architekten GmbH
[1]petra.both@kit.edu [2]simon.sommer@a-sh.de

This contribution introduces a methodology for early planning phases, which is based on a stakeholder oriented analysis of process-related user functions and supports the elaboration of a structural and formal building concept. Also a so-called FunctionsTool is presented, that supports the user oriented development, structuring and grouping of user functions and leeds to a qualified allocation of the functions and their spatial-temporal interdependencies. This tool and also other existing methodical and digital approaches have been evaluated for the complex application-context of hospital planning. So, on a methodological level, a further concept could be drawn up as well as recommendations for the further development of the digital FunctionsTool.

Keywords: *design methodology, stakeholder- and function-based design, webbased tool, hospital planning, early planing phase*

1 INTRODUCTION

Digitization is permeating more and more processes in the construction industry. The Building Information Modeling (BIM) method in particular is seen as having great potential for optimization in terms of planning quality and efficiency. However, with regard to the current component oriented BIM planning practice as well as the available tools, deficits become apparent from a planning methodological point of view: Existing BIM tools are so far mostly focussing on the modeling of concrete building elements, which in part can also be "assembled" from predefined catalogs with BIM objects. Catalog based tools with predefined content, however, often lead to a premature and partly unreflective use of predefined building elements and qualities (efficiency before quality). (von Both 2017).

Assisting methods and tools,supporting a user oriented cooperative specification of the demands and first considerations about structural and building concepts in the early planning phases, do not yet exist on the market. Especially there is a gap on the more abstract functional and conceptual level, which can deliberately widen the solution space and thus enable a more solution open design approach. Here only a few exceptions (for example, the dRofus tool for developing spatial and functional programs) can be found. From this, an urgent need for action can be derived on the part of research (methodology) as well as on the part of application software for the development of cooperative assisting tools and models to support the demand planning and early functional or conceptual planning processes (von Both 2017).

2 THE 'FUNCTION BASED METHODOLOGY' - A GENERALIZED METHODICAL FRAMEWORK FOR A USER AND FUNCTION BASED DESIGN

The 'Function based Methodology' (FbM) describes a methodical procedure model for the early phases of a user- and function-based design. It thus provides an overarching methodological framework and offers specific methods and tools for the individual steps (von Both 2019).

The first step is the development of a holistic target system that makes the impact of planning activities assessable with regard to the entire life cycle of the building - considering also its interactions with the superordinate systems and stakeholders (ReBB 2009) . Relating methods and tools are presented in (von Both 2009, HoSc 2019, EbBR 2010, ReBB 2009).

From the objectives of this superordinate system, the purpose and utility of buildings and thus the specific object-related objectives and functional requirements (including functional performance) of the planning subject can be deduced as cooperative and participatory as possible. Here, it is important to analyse also the value systems, consumer behaviour and development strategies of the clients and also later building users (ReEB 2013). An important mean for the identification of value systems and consumer behavior are also socio scientific approaches of life world studies like the sinus milieu data (von Both, 2006).

Basing on these targets, use related functional requirements of buildings can be determined and taken into account - also with regard to possible organizational, logistic and process-related options (von Both 2019). In this way these interdependencies can be reflected and the topological structure can be transferred into process- and space-efficient spatial structures (von Both 2006) that fullfill the needs of the

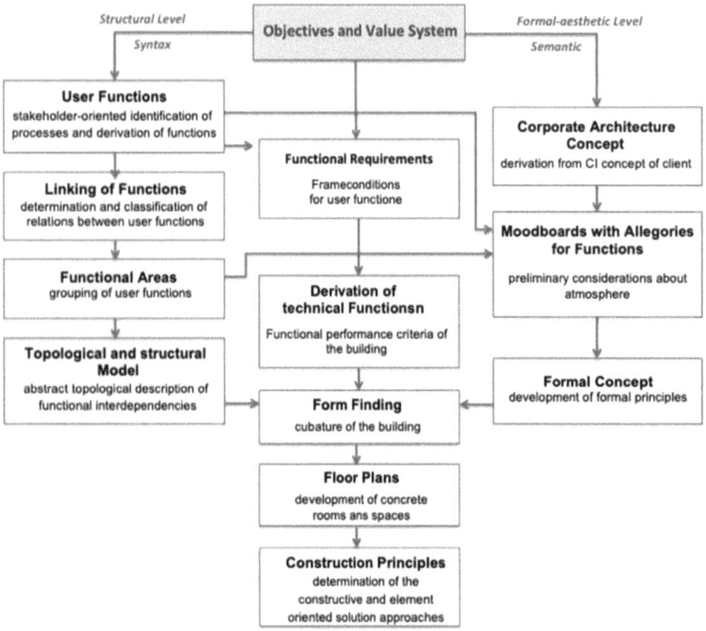

Figure 1
Process-logic of the FbM

specific target group.

The following process model supports the design process on two levels (see figure 1): At the structural level (process shown on the left in figure 1), the development of spatiofunctional topologies and spatial structures takes place, basing on the capturing and organization of the relevant user processes and their interdependencies.

To avoid a pure technocratic procedure, the methodology also offers support on the formal-aesthetic level with the semantic conception and the development of the formal concept and CA Concept (shown on the right).

These steps are carried out in close coordination with the functional requirements for the user functions, which are developed from the projects objectives and the necessary technical functions of the building, derived from them.

On the structural level, the process starts with a stakeholder and user analysis, using methods like stakeholder analysis or stakeholder expectation management (see e.g. Anderl 2016) and the analysis of the activities and proceses of the identified users and their transfer into solution neutral descriptions of user functions.

This process can be supported by a so called "structure matrix' - an adjacency matrix, which helps the architect - in close cooperation and exchange with the client and users - to analyse, qualitatively specify and formalize process related user functions for the different stakeholders (see figure 3). This should be developed in interaction with the functional requirements in the target system (see von Both 2006, Anderl 2016). The analysis and overlay of daily and annual routines of the different users can reveal first relevant correlations. Here, it is very important to specify the functions qualitatively, because it has different spatial consequences.

The next step is the analysis and survey of qualified functional correlations. The quality of the relations in the matrix is configurable and can thus be adapted to the respective project context.

The use related functional relationships can be described, for example, spatiotemporally or in relation to the flow of materials or persons (logistics) and can be mapped in the adjacency matrix (see Figure 3). With regard to sustainability and space-efficiency, the challenge is to identify possibilities for (temporal) spatial overlaps and mixed-use spaces.

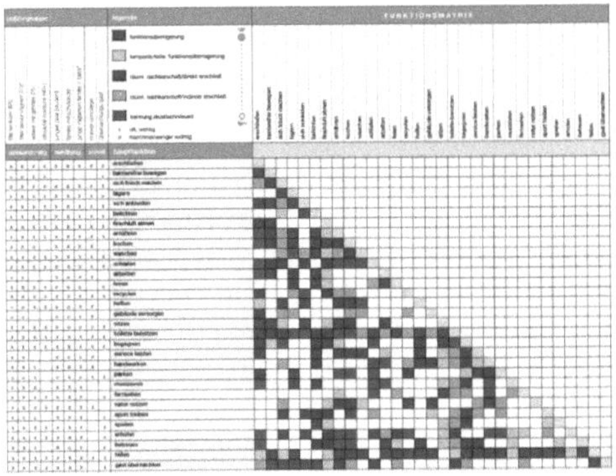

Figure 2
Structure-Matrix for the Analysis of Functional Correlations; student example of a mixed-used housing project, Noel Rabuffetti, 2017

Additional preconditions for the structural formation process in the sense of a systemic approach are considerations about the required technical and physical conditions as well as emissions of the functions with regard to lighting, air conditioning, acoustics and other aspects. An assessment of functional output and required or permitted input of the system dimensions serves as complementary base for the mapping and structuring.

As a first step toward the following space formation, first arrangements of functional groups and areas and for the spatial positioning of functions in the building can be made in a reflected way, based on these identified relations and functional conditions. Here, the functional mapping supports the identification of overlay and flexibility options, which can later be realized, for example, e.g. via so-called cluster flats, a combination of minimized apartments and shared living area and kitchen or via so called joker rooms, which could be assigned to different housing units temporarily.

The planner is, thus, actively encouraged to think about area and space related optimization potentials and can transfer the topological structure of functions into a space efficient floor plan concept. Sustainability assessment systems here also speak about functional equivalence.

To avoid a pure technocratic approach, the building conception in the early design stages also takes place on a semantic level, in which the designer deals with corporate architecture and the adaequate architectural language and the semantic statement the building (Baumberger 2015) as well as the question of the required atmosphere of the functional areas as a basis for later form finding and spatial design. Here the analysed value systems of the customer and target group specific requirements concerning space and architecture perception help to develop a specific customer and user oriented architectural statement and semantic (Flade 2020). So, in parallel to the identification and grouping of functions, the elaboration of suitable formal design principles and atmospheric concepts for the identified functions takes place. Working with mood boards, ideographs and symbols for the functions and functional areas supports an abstract and thus more experimental approach, which has been seen to be able to expand the range of solutions consciously.

The merging of structural and semantic level leads to the reflexive conception of the cubature of the building. Input workshops about form finding methods (YoSK 2016) can enhance the quality of results noticeable. Under consideration of the cubature and the functional topology, now the floor plans can be elaborated. A feedback loop with the stakeholder oriented processes and time schedules can help to evaluate the logistic quality of the floor plans (see figure 3).

Supported by morphological matrices also first ideas about constructive principles can be elaborated. Also on level of the building elements the elaborated strategies for the flexibilisation of space shall be implemented by appropriate constructive solutions flexibly configurable wall elements or furniture.

2.1 FunctionsTool

For the steps of stakeholder related identification and structuring of functions (see FbM in figure 1), a web-based tool has been developed that is also able to support a cooperative approach together with the customers and users.

The so called 'FunctionsTool' supports a user oriented development, structuring and grouping of user functions and allows a qualified representation of the functions and their spatiotemporal interdependencies. The tool automatically generates a structural bubble diagramm - an abstract topological graph schema - from the entries and qualified relations in the adjacency matrix.

Varied predefined qualities of functions relations leed to different length of the relations edges and different forces of attraction of the functions (nodes). Also differentiations of the relations quality in colour allow an easier comprehension and facilitate the pre-structuring and grouping of functions as base for the next step, the spatial location of functional areas and the geometric room generation. In addition of the functions name, graphics and ideographs can be stored and represented in the structur nodes.

Figure 3 shows a screenshot of the functionsTool with a students' design project (Hodulak, 2019).

So, the functional and topological structure of the building can be presented and edited in a transparent and ergonomic way by direct visual feedback, so that also non professional customers and users can be involved in the process. This facilitates a reflected spatial allocation of functional areas and the generation of performant layouts.

3 SPECIFIC APPLICATION AND EVALUATION IN HOSPITAL PLANNING

As part of a master's thesis (Sommer 2019), existing specific methods and digital tools for structural hospital planning in early planning phases - including the FunctionsTool - were examined and evaluated during the design process. The master's thesis deals with the method based design of a hospital, whereby special attention was paid to process related, logis-

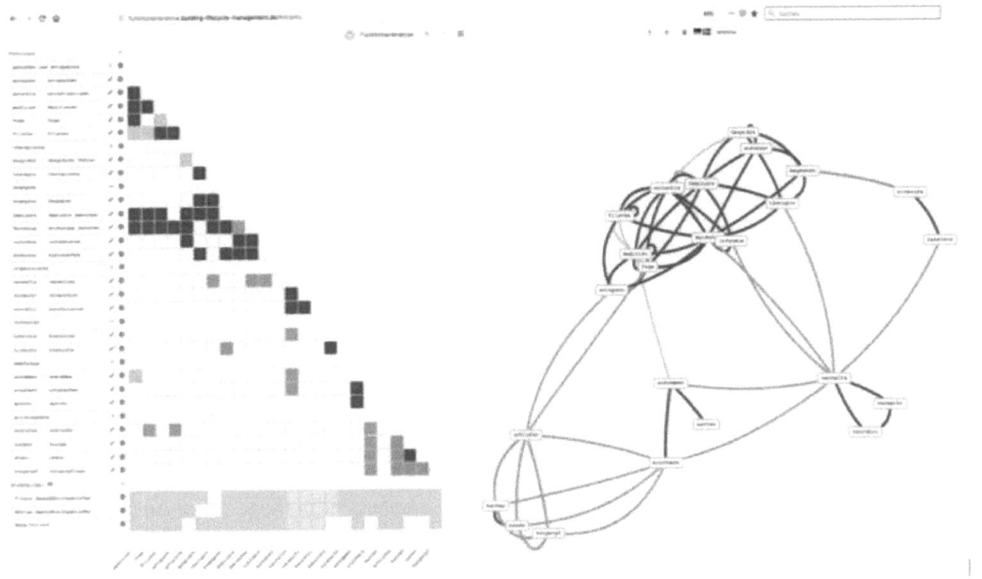

Figure 3
Screenshot of the 'FunctionsTool' with structure matrix and the automatically generated bubble diagram, students project, Conway C and Djokic 2018

tical and business management aspects with regard to to the specific framework conditions in the field of hospital planning.

In addition, there are project-specific requirements. Different treatment focuses and deviating, everchangingmedical processes require specific assessments, flexible planning and transparent handlingof the parameters used.

3.1 Special requirements and processes in hospital planning

The requirements in a hospital are complex and dependencies can usually only be described multicausally. It makes sense, both for experienced planners and for communication with the customer or later user, to have a structural representation of the specific functional and process related dependencies as a basis for joint discussions and user-oriented decisions. ShShort path lengths are a decisive factor for economic efficiency and treatment quality in a hospital. The routes of logistics, staff and patients overlap and in some cases require different connections. It is imperative that these be evaluated on a project specific basis, as there are strong deviations here depending on the treatment strategy and range of services (Stockhorst et al. 2019). However, so called "treatment paths" can be extracted that describe regularities in certain process chains and condition affinities.

In principle, these affinities can be considered at different scale levels. In the classic process of project development of a new hospital, first the targeted clinical performance data are translated into a space and function programme and an operational organisation concept is developed together with the customer. If necessary, this can be brought together in the form of a dependency matrix, similar to the Structure Matrix of the described "Functions Tool". These can be translated into a layout plan, on which the detailed planning for individual rooms is based.

In general, the planning conditions for the specific area of hospital planning can also be adapted and transferred to other building tasks. The hospital essentially serves as an example, as functional dependencies can be clearly described here and are thus well suited as parameters for a tool application.

3.2 Investigate existing digital methods and tools for their suitability for use in hospital planning

First, existing digital tools, especially in the field of generative design, were examined for their suitability in cooperative hospital planning, which can fulfil the specific requirements described above.

The focus was on the generation of area layouts in hospital construction, as this is where there is aparticularly high degree of planning optimisation potential. The basic organisation and dependenciesof functions can be described qualitatively and transferred into functionalities of planning tools. Asimilar matrix as shown in Figure 2 should serve as a basis for further processing.

The field of application for generative design in the area of hospital planning has only been dealt withsporadically. One approach, but only in outline, is the work of Joel Simon. He wanted to optimisehospital floor plans by means of a logarithm based on various parameters. These were mainly pathlengths, but also dependencies between rooms. This resulted in polygons whose areas already corresponded to the target sizes of the rooms. However, he himself came to the conclusion that hisresults were less rational and not directly usable in practice. (see figure 4) (Simon, 2017).

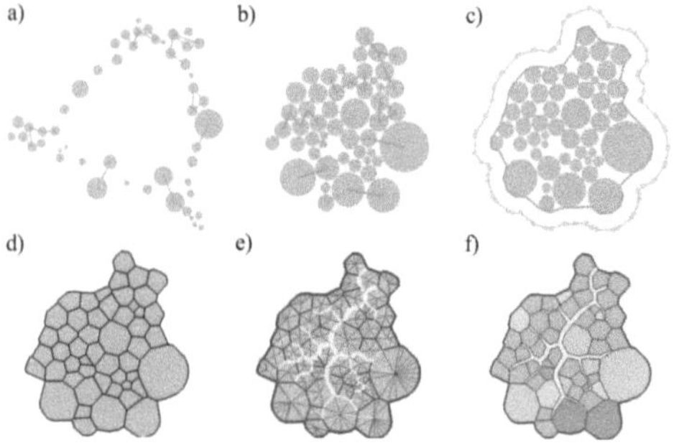

Figure 4
The complete mapping process (Simon, 2017) [3]

Another example is the Early Design Configurator (EDC) of the EU project STREAMER. It generates and presents layouts for hospitals in the design phase. The input parameters for generating layouts are outlines of the building, the already specified room book and design rules. The room floor plans of the planned building are generated automatically with an evolutionary algorithm whose objective function includes the requirements and restrictions of the room book and design rules. But the focus of the structural optimization is on the energy optimisation of the buildings and the operation of an OpenBIM strategy (IFC). However, the process described does not aim to support the process of the collaborative specification and linkage of the functions and functional areas but on the automated generation of finished planned building models, to incorporate the information from the design phase as a Building Information Model into the life cycle of the building. (Geiger et al. 2018)

So it was necessary to look beyond the field of hospital construction for possible applications and tools for function-based planning to find more examples that can be optionally adapted or modified - among others the FunctionsTool.

An initial examination of the FunctionsTool with regard to its use in this specific context showed that it reaches its limits in such complex projects with multi layered functional interrelationships at the level of the entire building, as the multitude of functions can no longer be clearly mapped and handled. The function grouping offered in the tool allows a hierarchisation of the functional structures (e.g. into individual departments and functional areas), but does not allow individual subfunctions of the functional areas to be networked beyond the area or department boundaries. The complex process flows existing in hospital operations can thus not yet be fully mapped in their structure.

In addition, the FunctionsTool - in contrast to the Excel-based predecessor of the object matrix - is not flexibly configurable with regard to the types of relationships. The suggestions provided in the tool, which tended to come from the residential and business sectors, were unfortunately not consistent useful.

Software development in particular is researching and developing in the area of generative design. The aim is to generate different design variants, compare them with each other and select the best design in the course of an optimisation process based on various parameters. Pirouz Nourian developed a plug-in called space syntax for Grasshopper and Rhino applications. Here, arrangements can be generated based on the dependencies of subsequent studies. However, a differentiation of dependencies can hardly be mapped here (see figure 5) (Sommer, 2019; Nourian, 2013 [2]) and the tool seems not to be able to support the involvement of the customer.

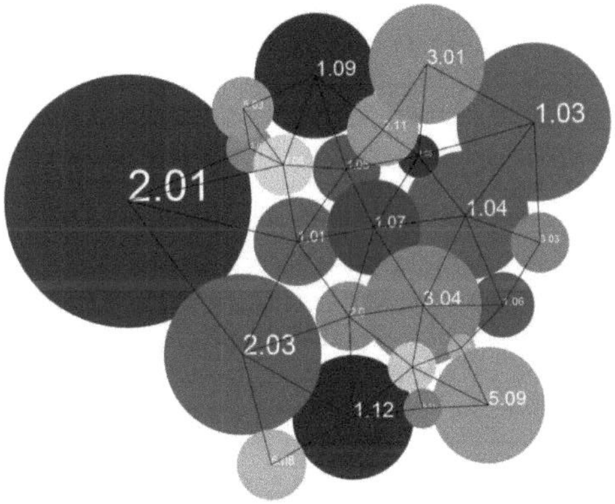

Figure 5
Testing Space Syntax Add-In for Grashopper (Sommer, 2019)

Autodesk also publicises the state of the art in operations, among other things, by using generative methods in the planning of their new office and research centre in Toronto. 10,000 floor plan variations are computer generated and evaluated before selection is made. [1]. What the latter example has over the others is to bring the structure into a spatial-functional context. But also this approach seems not tob e able to support a collaborative process and iteration cycles including the users.

One aim of the master's thesis was, among other things, to find out which decision rules and parameters have to be added to the FunctionsTool, or what a new planning tool has to do in order to be helpful for the application in the hospital. None of the tools shown so far can be easily applied directely to the special requirements of hospitals in the early planning phase.

As a conclusion, it can be said that for the use-case of hospital planning neither in the specific field nor on a generalized level suitable tools exist, which support both the identification of functions and their linkage as well as the transfer into topological structures and layout concepts - especially in the sense of an assisting tool for cooperative planning and involvement of the customer.

Although the underlying methodological approach of the FunctionsTool (FbM) provides suitable support for the important early processes, it requires further development and adaptation to handle the necessary complexity in hospital planning. Also integrated concepts for supporting the the next planning steps - the spatial positioning of the functional areas - has to be developed.

3.3 Further methodical development basing on the 'Schmigalla'-method

So the next step was to look about existing theoretical methods. However, methods for the parameter based arrangement of individual areas that have some relationship to each other appeared long before the era of computer aided design. One of these methods was developed by Hans Schmigalla in the 1970s. Actually, originating from the planning of factory layouts, the triangular grid method was used to create layouts functionally and parameter based (Schmigalla 1995). After this, a methodological approach was developed in the course of a master's thesis, which not only aimed at sorting and structuring areas, but which can be used as a decision supporting method in the development of the building structure and provides an evaluation of the resulting floor plans at hand.

Thus, this method can be seen as a follow-up and supplement to the above described FunctionsTool and supports the superordinate planning process in the process steps of spatial localization of the tolopogical structure in feedback with the building cubature (form finding) as well as the development of concrete spatial floor plans and layouts.

Linguistic variables, which describe the dependencies of the functional areas on each otherother (e.g. coming from the object matrix of the FbM), are coded with colors and brought together in a table as shown in figure 2. These dependencies are converted into a numerical value, taking into account empirical values (Blöchle, 2014), so that a basis corresponding to Schmigalla's method is available, a numerically describable affinity matrix. A triangular grid is defined for the placement of the functions in space (fig. 6, left). The order of arrangement and position results from the affinity of the function to the already placed functions (fig. 6, right). The result of the calculations is shown in the abstract surface layout as a compact arrangement of the areas in figure 6.

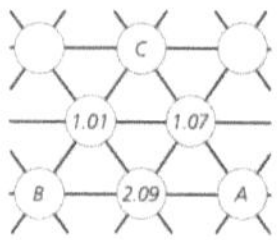

	affinity for 1.05	position A		position B		position C	
		dist.	logistical effort	dist.	logistical effort	dist.	logistical effort
1.01	0,47	2	0,94	1	0,47	1	0,47
1.07	0,72	1	0,72	2	1,44	1	0,72
2.09	0,23	1	0,23	1	0,23	2	0,46
total	1,42	1,33	1,89	1,33	2,14	1,33	1,65

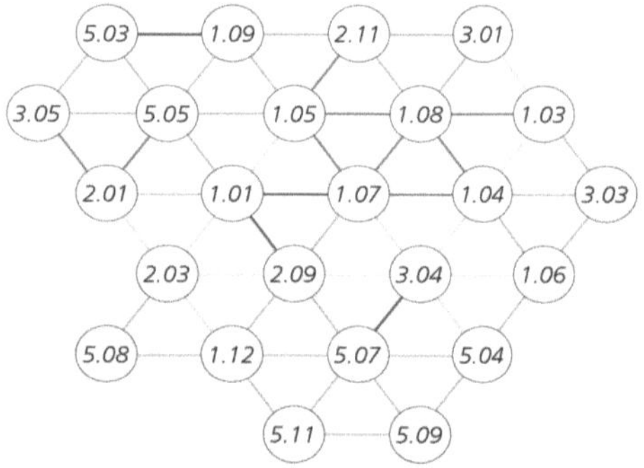

Figure 6
left: triangular grid with the possible positions, right: determination of position, down: result of the first calculation (Sommer, 2019)

This is where the method of Schmigalla ends. In the following, it was supplemented by an affinity (object) matrix as a target value with a distance matrix as an actual value in order to carry out an evaluation. The product of attraction and distance value can be described as the logistic effort in a simplified way.

From the application, it appears that the method worked well. Only individual placements are rated as critical. Almost all affinities are included in the abstract surface layout, which thus depicts a sensible order of the functional locations. Not taken into account here are the sizes of the individual areas and the distances within the structure that change as a result. In addition, no spatially differentiated statement can be made from the ideal order.

3.4 Application and evaluation of the method

The method was applied and further developed in the context of the master student design of a hospital. For this purpose, the method was refined and supplemented in some decision rules in further test runs. The grid was transferred to a previously designed layout, several floors were considered, and fixed points such as entrances and lifts were located. Vertical movements were put in relation to horizontal movements by means of effort studies, and waiting and travel times were also modelled (Blöchle, 2014). In addition, the functions were assigned an extension in the grid according to their actual size in the space programme. Natural lighting requirements were also part of the consideration when placing the functions. Limit values for assessment were adjusted and evaluated according to the new parameters. The evaluation was also carried out in parallel with the placement, so that problem areas could be identified and avoided more quickly. With this basis, a functionally sensible and assessable arrangement within any basic geometry could be achieved within a short time.

CONCLUSION AND GOALS FOR FURTHER DEVELOPMENT

The extended Schmigalla Method has proven to be a good complement to the object matrix and FunctionsTool of the superordinated Function Based Method (FBM) as it builds on the identified and interlinked user functions and transfers them into a spatial context. However, within the scope of the master thesis, only basic methodical concepts could be developed and evaluated, so that the authors see an urgent need for further development.

The following conclusions can be drawn for the further developments of methods and digital tools for the early design stages of hospital projects - especially for the further implementation of the FbM.

The development of the topological structure should not only be unicritically oriented towards logistics. As mentioned in section 2.1, an additional consideration of the flows of system variables (emissions and immissions) could be a useful supplement, for example, to be able to match existing acoustic emissions of certain functions with allowed immissions or to be able to take into account lighting requirements. Thus, also the qualified system flows can influence the attraction forces of the functional bubbles and finally the topology of functional areas.

In order to be able to map the method with regard to the qualification of the logistic performance, the relations have, on the one hand, to be editable and thus adaptable to the specific application (building typology). In addition, the relations should not only be qualitatively describable (as an enumeration or previously defined list of possible values) as it is the case in the FunctionsTool (as well as in the other available approaches of section 3.2), but should be flexibly quantifiable and scalable. By quantified values also the aggregation of different relation types would allow a better multi-criterial structuring.

To allow a better handling of complex functions structures, a better concept for cross-level hierarchization and linking is needed as well as considerations about the structural representation of functions groups (e.g. semantic net instead of hierarchy tree):

The method developed in the master thesis included the step of locating the functions in their spatial context in order to better evaluate and optimize the topology model found. For the superordinated 'Function based Methodology', this means allowing iteration cycles between the two steps (see. Figure 1) 'development of the abstract topology model' and the steps 'formfinding / building cubature' and the development of spatial floor plans.

With regard to the tool level, it became apparent that digital support for the architectural design would also be useful for the downstream process of locating the developed abstract topological models and comparing them with the formal form finding concept and the special cubature and orientation of the building. In this respect, it would be worth considering to what extent it could be useful to include this process in the FunctionsTool in order to be able to compare the abstract bubble diagram with the spatial conditions and thus to include an initial localization and a comparison with studies on form-finding and cubature as a subsequent step.

REFERENCES

Anderl, N 2016, *Tools for Project Management, Workshops and Consulting: A Must-Have Compendium of Essential Tools and Techniques*, Publicis

Baumberger, Ch and Schlaberg, C (eds) 2015, *Neue Arbeiten zur Architketursemiotik, Reihe: Zeitschrift für Semiotik / Architektur, Zeichen, Bedeutung*, Stauffenburg Verlag

Blöchle, D 2014, *Evaluation von Krankenhauslayouts unter Zuhilfenahme der Fuzzy-Logik*, Ph.D. Thesis, KIT

von Both, P 2006, *A systemic project model for a cooperative design of complex one of a kind buildings*, Ph.D. Thesis, KIT (University of Karlsruhe)

von Both, P 2019 'A stakeholder- and function-based planning method for space-efficient buildings', *Con-*

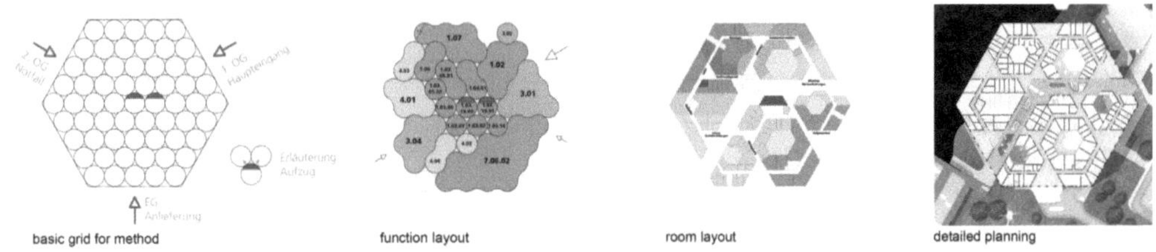

Figure 7
developing a floorplan (Sommer, 2019)

ference Proceedings of the SBE 19 Graz - Sustainable Built Environment D-A-CH Conference 2019 - Transition Towards a Net Zero Carbon Built Environment

von Both, P and Kohler, N 2005 'An integrated system for the cooperative development and management of project objectives and building requirements', *Proceedings of the 2nd Int. SCRI Research Symposium*, Salford, Greater Manchester, UK

von Both, P 2017, 'Integrale Planung und BIM', in Westphal, T and Hermann, E (eds) 2017, *Detail resaerch: Methoden und Strategien für den Planungsprozess | Beispiele aus der Praxis*, Edition Detail

Ebertshäuser, S, von Both, P and Rexroth, K 2010 'The SIAS tool - systemic benchmarking as a base for the development of strategies for energy efficient cities', *Conference Proceedings of the SB10 Finland*, Helsinki, Finland

Flade, A 2020, *Kompendium der Architekturpsychologie: Zur Gestaltung gebauter Umwelten*, Springer Verlag

Geiger, A, Benner, J and Häfele, K.-H. 2018 'Building Information Modeling in der Konzeptionephase der Planung', *Proceedings of the IBPSA BauSIM 2019 Conference*, Karlsruhe, p. DOI 10.5445/IR/1000085743

Hodulak, M and Schramm, U 2019, *Nutzerorientierte Bedarfsplanung: Prozessqualität für nachhaltige Gebäude*, Springer Vieweg

Rexroth, K and von Both, P 2016, 'Planungsprozessmodelle: Synthese und Übertragbarkeit für den Anwendungskontext energieeffiziente Stadt', in Koch, M and McKenna, R (eds) 2016, *Wettbewerb Energieeffiziente Stadt : Band 3: Methoden und Modelle*, LIT Verlag, Berlin

Rexroth, K, Brüggemann, Th and von Both, P 2009 'Methodology of target and requirements management for complex systems concerning the applicationfield of an energy-efficient city', *Proceeding of the Real Corp 2009 Conference*, pp. p. 353-359

Rexroth, K, Ebertshäuser, S and von Both, P 2013, 'Potentiale sozialwissenschaftlicher Ansätze zur Lebensweltuntersuchung für die Erklärung des Energieverhaltens von Haushalten', in Koch, M and Wagner, H.J. (eds) 2013, *Wettbewerb Energieeffiziente Stadt : Vol 1: Gebäude und Haushalte*, LIT Verlag, Berlin

Schmigalla, H 1995, *Fabrikplanung. Begriffe und Zusammenhänge*, Hanser Verlag

Sommer, S 2019, *hospital planning methods in the early planning phases*, Master's Thesis, KIT

Stockhorst, H, Hofrichter, L, Franke, A, Bartenbach, A, Bergmann-Drees, S and Bleckmann, M 2019, *Krankenhausbau. Architektur und Planung, bauliche Umsetzung, Projekt- und Betriebsorganisation*, Medizinisch Wissenschaftliche Verlagsgesellschaft, Berlin

Yormakka, K, Schürer, O and Kuhlmann, D 2016, *Methoden der Formfindung*, Birkhäuser Verlag

[1] https://damassets.autodesk.net/content/dam/autodesk/www/solutions/generative-design/autodesk-aec-generative-design-ebook.pdf

[2] https://www.youtube.com/watch?v=SgTiGKkDD0U

[3] https://www.joelsimon.net/evo_floorplans.html

[4] https://blm.ieb.kit.edu/1615.php

[5] www.sinus-institut.de/en/

[6] https://blm.ieb.kit.edu/943_1598.php

GoDesign

A modular generative design framework for mass-customization and optimization in architectural design

Shervin Azadi[1], *Pirouz Nourian*[2]
[1,2]*Delft University of Technology*
[1,2]*{s.azadi-1|p.nourian}@tudelft.nl*

We present a modular generative design framework for design processes in the built environment that provides for the unification of participatory design and optimization to achieve mass-customization and evidence-based design. The paper articulates this framework mathematically as three meta procedures framing the typical design problems as multi-dimensional, multi-criteria, multi-actor, and multi-value decision-making problems: 1) space-planning, 2) configuring, and 3) shaping; structured as to the abstraction hierarchy of the chain of decisions in design processes. These formulations allow for applying various problem-solving approaches ranging from mathematical derivation & artificial intelligence to gamified play & score mechanisms and grammatical exploration. The paper presents a general schema of the framework; elaborates on the mathematical formulation of its meta procedures; presents a spectrum of approaches for navigating solution spaces; discusses the specifics of spatial simulations for ex-ante evaluation of design alternatives. The ultimate contribution of this paper is laying the foundation of comprehensive Spatial Decision Support Systems (SDSS) for built environment design processes.

Keywords: *Generative Design, Spatial Configuration, Serious Gaming, Mass Customization, Decision Problems*

INTRODUCTION

This paper presents a 'participatory generative design framework' emblematically called 'Go Design' after the game of Go. This framework is designed to enable Mass-Customization and application of Multi-Criteria Decision Analysis for supporting multi-actor decision-making processes such as those aimed at reaching consensus among stakeholders on goals and design requirements, objective decision-making processes such as finding the best configuration respective to environmental factors (e.g. light, energy), and finally subjective processes such as choosing styles, materials, and colors of the final structure. The focus of this paper is on the mathematical formulation of the spatial configuration problem, given exemplary inputs for user preferences to establish the generality of the framework as to different optimization/decision-making approaches and various participatory processes. Thus, the details of implementation and the participatory processes are beyond the scope of this paper. Effectively, the proposed framework reformulates architectural design as a chain of systematic decision-making problems in terms of given inputs and desired outputs rather than ad-hoc drawing and representation challenges.

We present a mathematical categorization and formulation of archetypical design problems, that provides for adequate utilization of a variety of computational methodologies. This categorization sets out a spectrum of decision-making problems ranging from the most abstract to the most concrete: 1) [space] planning in the context of Graph Theory, 2) configuring in the context of Algebraic Topology, and 3) shaping in the context of Computational Geometry. This categorization distinguishes the priorities of decision-making and specifies the widely-spoken notion of early-stage design decisions. By revisiting such typical architectural design problems from 'drawing' problems to 'decision' problems, they fall naturally within the purview of "The Sciences of the Artificial" (Simon, 2008), as defined by Herbert A. Simon. As such, this framework is a tribute to the initiative of several pioneers of computational design, namely the eloquent quest of Yona Fridman's "Towards a Scientific Architecture" (Friedman, 1980).

BACKGROUND

It has been argued that design and planning problems are "wicked problems"(Rittel, 1973); evading formulation, benchmarking, objective definitions of goals, etc. Inspired by (cf. (Voordijk, 2009)) we provide four lenses for revisiting such compound complexities by suggesting that the multi-dimensional and multi-criteria complexity of decision-making in design is attributable to the physical nature of the design task, while the multi-actor and multi-value complexities of decision-making are attributable to the concerning human factors in design (see Figure 1). Multi-dimensional complexity corresponds to the complex spatial (geometrical, topological, and graph-theoretical) relations that need to be orchestrated between spaces and elements. Multi-criteria complexity is concerned with balancing static and dynamic/operational qualities that a design is required to provide, such as light, solar energy, etc. The multi-actor complexities stem from the difference in the goals of stakeholders. Finally, the multi-value complexity originates from the uncertainties and ambiguities inherent to human perception and communication, which can be traced in self-contradictory preferences, bounded-rationality, miscommunication of goals, and individual-communal good dilemmas as discussed in Game Theory (q.v. (Cunningham, 2018)).

Given this decision-making approach, we naturally aim to structure the decisions to maximize the customizability for the actors while maintaining the explainability of the process. In doing so, we generalize this framework to incorporate an arbitrary number of spatial quality criteria, some of which might be related to human factors. In addition, we proffer a mechanism for integrating Multi-Criteria Decision Analysis (abbr. MCDA, q.v. (Ogrodnik, 2019) & (Huang, 2011)).

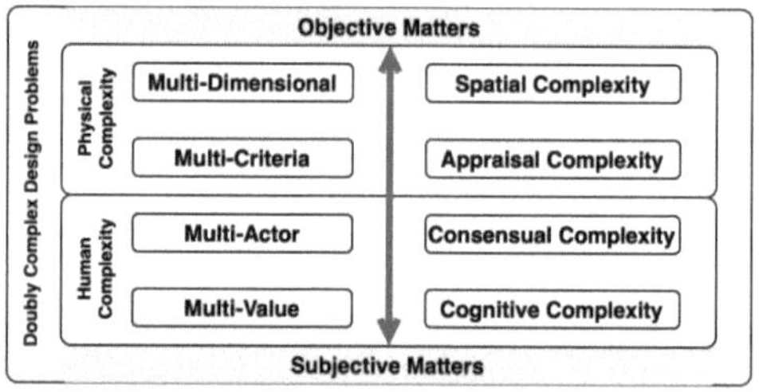

Figure 1
Variety of complexities involved

Explicitly discretizing the decision space facilitates analyzing the computational space and time complexity of procedures, enabling the simulation of spatial quality aspects related to accessibility, visibility, etc. Discretization of a design space not only facilitates the computational processes for providing play & score 'design games' (q.v. (Sanoff,1978) & (Bots, 2003)) but also inherently supports ultimate modularization of buildings as products, thus reducing the costs of production (q.v. (U|lrich,1995), (Salvador, 2002), (Salvador, 2007), and (Rocha, 2015)).

However, the mathematical formulation of design and planning problems is a challenge that precedes the use of computation and explainable Artificial Intelligence. A rigorous mathematical framework for design processes can create the methodical foundation necessary for developing Artificial Intelligence that can incorporate objective environmental factors and multi-actor user preferences in the process of design/planning. Within such frameworks, it is necessary to include a set of objectives for the design tasks that can describe the user preferences and environmental necessities, a model for spatial relations and qualities, and an assessment module that can assess the spatial relations and configurations based on the user preferences and environmental factors.

FRAMEWORK

We propose to organize the order and priority of design decision-making processes from abstract to concrete through three significant procedures: Planning, Configuring, and Shaping as a meta-level procedures with precise inputs, outputs, and problems. **Planning** is the first procedure in which stakeholders will collectively specify the relations and criteria of spaces. Planning involves multi-value, multi-actor, and multi-criteria complexities and aims to reach a graph theoretical description of spatial specifications, spatial relations, and collective design goals. **Configuring** is a procedure focused on generating a configuration of spaces from the specified criteria and relations in the previous step. Configuring is primarily concerned with the multi-dimensional and multi-criteria complexities and aims to explore different spatial configurations and represent them as graph mappings that describe 'discrete dimensionless [topological] design' (Steadman,1983). **Shaping** is the latest step that focuses on concretizing the geometry of the last procedure's topological design. Shaping involves multi-dimensional and multi-value complexities of design as it determines the aesthetic styling of design.

The precise formulation of the data structures passed between these procedures is crucial as they function as interfaces between the procedures. To ensure the modularity and generality of the framework, we propose a mathematical formulation of these data structures. The same logical transition from abstract to concrete that is present in the order of steps is also evident in the data structures passed between steps as they are formalized using different branches of mathematics from graph theory to topology to geometry.

Table 1
Meta-procedures in the proposed framework

Process	Product	Scope	Complexities
Planning	Network	Graph Theory	multi-value multi-actor multi-criteria
Configuring	Configuration	Algebraic Topology	multi-dimensional multi-criteria
Shaping	Shape	Geometry	multi-dimensional multi-value

Avoiding the black box approach and explicating the design process in utmost clarity to the actors fundamentally supports human participation. This vertical inclusion of stakeholders will enable them to customize the design not only to match their personal goals but also to adhere to the societal context that the design is situated in.

Generally, this framework utilizes feed-forward mechanisms in the micro-level when decisions are numerous, and they need objective adherence to preset spatial constraints and criteria, and feedback mechanisms at the macro-level when human insight is required in societal and cultural connotations of spatial constraints and criteria, or when subjective opinions are to be addressed in customization.

Framework: Planning

Ensuring actors' participation with customization capabilities requires strategies for targeting social, economic, and environmental sustainability goals. Formulating, communicating, and justifying such strategies and decisions for/together with multiple stakeholders is challenging from a scientific point of view, mainly due to the multi-actor and multi-value complexities. Overcoming this challenge requires including the inhabitants [and contextual stakehold-

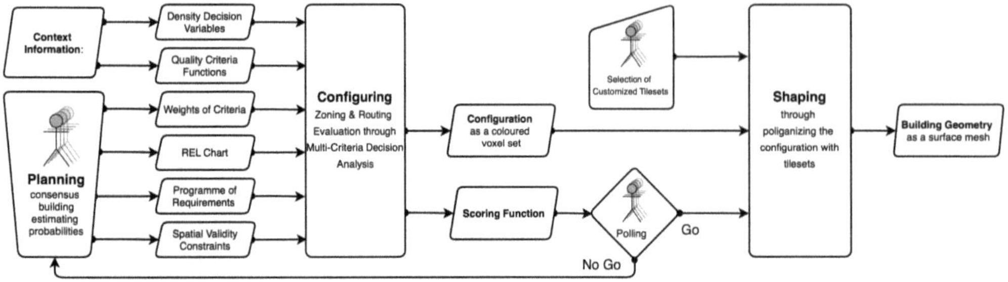

Figure 2
Main flowchart of the framework

ers] in the decision-making process (inclusion) as well as explaining and justifying the decisions (transparency). Thus, the planning phase frames an interactive approach for collaboratively setting out the spatial specifications and relations.

Table 2
Framework of Planning Procedure

Input	Data Type	Input Name: Notes
$\mathbf{c}$	$[c_k]_{m\times 1}$, $c_k \in \mathbb{N}$	List of indices of spatial quality criteria
$\mathbf{s}$	$[s_i]_{n\times 1}$, $s_i \in \mathbb{N}$	List of indices of spaces
Output	**Data Type**	**Output Name: Notes**
$\mathbf{P}$	List of Lists	static properties of spaces in terms of area, minimum ceiling height, label colour, space-specific local constraints (such as contiguity, [star] convexity, rectilinearity, single-layered vs multilayered, fixed locations, etc.) indexed w.r.t. an ordered set.
g_b	List, $b \in \{0, 1, \dots, r\}$	List of global constraints to be staisified by the configurator such as adjacency, compactness/cohesion, rectilinearity, non-overlapping spaces, adjacency to fixed elements, reachability, etcetera.
$\mathbf{G}$	$[G_{i,j}]_{n\times n}$, $G_{i,j} \in [0,1]$	desired closeness between s_i and s_j
$\mathbf{W}$	$[W_{i,k}]_{n\times m}$, $W_{i,k} \in [0,1]$	weights of spatial criteria for spaces, such that $W_{i,k} \in [0,1]$ shows the relative importance of criterion c_k for space s_i

Problem: Given the list of spaces $\mathbf{s}$ and spatial quality criteria $\mathbf{c}$, the actors are asked to reach a consensus on space properties $\mathbf{P}$, the desired closeness ratings $\mathbf{G}$, and spatial quality criteria's weights $\mathbf{W}$.

By abstracting and discretizing the design space, we mathematically formulate the planning phase as a multi-actor and multi-criteria decision-making problem. Within this formulation, the actors/stakeholders to negotiate, reach a consensus, and graph theoretical objects will represent the final decision. These objects consist of the relation of spaces with each other as a uni-partite graph and the relation of spaces with criteria as a bipartite graph. This phase's gamification provides for reaching consensus on the user-preferences (Bots, 2003) and provides transparent and inclusive decision-making processes for the planning phase.

Framework: Configuring

Given the contextual information, the main objective of configuring is to find a configuration as a colouring of a discretized design space (building envelope) that satisfies the local and global spatial validity constraints, the desired spatial relations, the spatial quality criteria, and their corresponding weights that have been determined in the planning phase. The resultant configuration will be represented by a graph mapping or graph colouring that assigns a colour/label to each of the envelope's volumetric cells. As such, configuring is formulated as a feed-forward process since the contextual information and spatial criteria are provided at the beginning of the phase. The buildable envelope can either be empty or contain already existing buildings.

Figure 3
Z-Order Indexing of Voxels, Visualization of the density matrix, and Configuration

Within this procedure, contextual information layers correspond directly to the set of criteria in the planning procedure. The weights of importance given by the actors will indicate how the MCDA will evaluate the allocation of different voxels based on their value in the quality criteria functions. Within this framework, each information layer is a quantity that has a value in each position of discrete space. Thus it can be formalized as a field: $f_k : [0,1]^{o \times n} \mapsto [0,1]^o k \in \{0, 1, \dot{s}, m\}$ and thus they can be called spatial quality criteria functions. As such, we can distinguish two categories of quality criteria based on their computational nature: Firstly, Accessibility-Related Quality Criteria, which must be computed based on geodesics and geodesic distances on [approximate/discrete] 2D manifolds. Secondly, Visibility-Related Quality Criteria must be computed based on straight-lines of sight and Euclidean distances on [approximate/discrete] 3D manifolds (e.g., direct sunlight, sky view, noise, etcetera). It is important to note that field formulation of quality criteria allows for including any quality criteria function as long as they are computable.

Furthermore, as the configuring procedure is often iterative, fields can be categorized into three categories based on how they should be re-evaluated given an existing configuration: firstly the **Static** fields representing quantities that their value in space are entirely independent of the configuration, such as height, distance to the facade, etcetera; and secondly, the **Dynamic** fields representing quantities that theoretically can be evaluated in the absence of configuration, yet the configuration affects their evaluation (e.g., direct sunlight, sky view, etc.; and finally, the **Dynamic & Dependant** fields representing quantities that their evaluation is only possible when a configuration exists (e.g., closeness to the entrance, closeness to the lobby, etc.)

As indicated in Table 1, the configuring procedure does not include human complexities such as multi-actor and multi-value aspects. This ensures the generality of the framework and allows for both optimization and participatory decision-making formulations of such configuring procedures. However, given the typical challenges in formalizing societal, cultural, and other human-related criteria, an optimization formulation of this step could be excessively simplistic and reductionist. Thus, we advocate for a participatory decision-making formulation that allows for explorative approaches and utilization of various Multi-Criteria Decision Analysis methodologies.

Table 3
Framework of Configuring Procedure

Input	Data Type	Input Name: Notes
$\mathbf{v}$	$[v_l]_{o \times 1}$	Array of volumetric cells (voxels) that comprise the rasterized envelope.
$\mathbf{X}$	$[X_{l,i}]_{o \times n}$	Array of denisties of volumetric cells (voxels) indexed with l per space colour/lable indexed with i, optional input, necessary when working with an existing configuration.
f_k	$f_k : [0,1]^{o \times n} \mapsto [0,1]^o$ $k \in \{0, 1, \ldots, m\}$	Quality Criteria functions mapping the set of coloured density matrix $\mathbf{X}$ to a vector of evaluated criteria whose compoents are mapped in range of $[0,1]$; this mapping transforms objectives to unitless criteria that are individually understandable for the human actors.
$\mathbf{P}$	List of Lists	static properties of spaces
g_b	List, $b \in \{0, 1, \ldots, r\}$	List of global constraints to be staisified by the configurator
$\mathbf{G}$	$[G_{i,j}]_{n \times n}$	desired closeness between s_i and s_j
$\mathbf{W}$	$[W_{i,k}]_{n \times m}$	weights of spatial criteria for spaces
Output	**Data Type**	**Output Name: Notes**
$\mathbf{X}$	$[X_{l,i}]_{o \times n}$	Matrix of denisties of volumetric cells (voxels) indexed with l per space colour/lable indexed with i; representing the configuration of spaces in the discrete (voxelated) design space. At the output, this matrix only contains discrete values from the set $\{0, 1\}$.
$\mathbf{\Sigma}$	$[\Sigma_{i,k}]_{n \times m}$	The scoring function that aggregates the compliance of each configured space with respect to the set goals $\mathbf{P}, \mathbf{G}, \mathbf{W}$

Problem: Given the discrete envelope as a set of voxels $\mathbf{v}$, the quality criteria functions f_k, the space properties $\mathbf{P}$, the desired closeness ratings $\mathbf{G}$, and spatial quality criteria's weights $\mathbf{W}$, it is desired to find a configuration $\mathbf{X}$ satisfying the local constraints as listed in $\mathbf{P}$ and the global constraints g_b.

Nevertheless, the proposed procedure is so general that, if desired, it can frame the problem of configuring as a generalized Topology Optimization procedure similar to those exploited in structural design, mechanical engineering, and fluid dynamics. For this reason, the decision variable matrix $\mathbf{X}_{o \times n}$ can contain continuous density variables inside the configurator so that the functions remain differentiable and that the gradients required for the updating scheme of topology optimization algorithms can be computed. However, once the decision is taken and fixated at the front-end of the process, the continuous densities will be mapped to the set $\{0,1\}$. Furthermore, as indicated in the main flowchart (Figure 2), this step's resultant configuration is subject to polling amongst actors to ensure the ultimate consistency with unquantifiable values and criteria.

A generic formulation of such configuring procedures is proposed in Table 3. Such configuring procedures can be implemented as a **Configurator** (industrially known as Configure, Price & Quote systems, q.v. (Jordan, 2020)) as a Decision-Support System that is capable of facilitating Play & Score processes, which can be possibly multi-player or single-player. To assess the different aspects of the resultant configuration, we propose a set of MCDA aggregators capable of reporting the quality of a configuration concerning the set of spaces, the set of criteria, the set of actors, or one single score for the configuration as a whole.

Framework: Shaping

In the shaping procedure, the previous step's configuration will be polygonized to create the geometrical representation of the configuration. Two main approaches can be distinguished in such procedures: discrete & continuous. In the discrete approach, a tileset is used to specify the geometry, which inherently facilitates modular construction. In the continuous approach, a level set is generated based on the difference in the voxel colors. The continuous approach offers a more robust process though it limits the customizability of the architecture of the resultant mesh. In its utmost generality, however, the continuous approach can significantly increase manufacturing costs -only if continuous density variables are to be permitted. It must be noted that given a voxelated domain and discrete densities from the set $\{0,1\}$ even a continuous iso-surface will be a mesh that can be post rationalized as a modular surface. The discrete approach, on the other hand, allows the actors to customize the tilesets and consequently personalize the final design; while still benefiting from the economy of scale in that they will be using a set of few tiles (to be precise, between 8 to 256 tile geometries, irrespective of their other attributes). This entails that the whole building is not only customizable to a high level of detail, it is also going to be affordable because of the possibility of mass-production of such tiles as construction components.

Table 4
Framework of Shaping Procedure

Input	Data Type	Input Name: Notes
$\mathbf{v}$	$[v_l]_{o\times 1}$	Array of voxels
$\mathbf{X}$	$[X_{l,i}]_{o\times n}$	Matrix of denisties of volumetric cells (voxels) indexed with l per space colour/lable indexed with i; representing the configuration of spaces in the discrete (voxelated) design space.
Output	**Data Type**	**Output Name: Notes**
$\mathbf{M}$	Surface Mesh	A surface mesh representing the geometry of the configuration, whose attributes may include indicies referring to the materials of choice, codes for the construction details, etcetera.
Problem: Given the configuration $\mathbf{X}$ on an array of voxels $\mathbf{v}$, it is desired to find the mesh that interior-exterior bounds the spatial regions in the configuration		

METHODOLOGY

The same way a structured collection of techniques is referred to as a technology, a structured collection of methods is referred to as a methodology. As indicated earlier, each of the three procedures focuses on different aspects of the design process and has different complexities. In this section, we elaborate on the suitable methods for each procedure. In the following section, we present a spectrum of methods from domains ranging from the digital game industry and Procedural Content Generation (a.k.a. Scene Synthesis) to Engineering Optimization methods and Artificial Intelligence, all of which can be utilized within our proposed framework.

Methodology: Planning

An exemplary mathematical definition of a multi-actor game for reaching consensus on the user preferences on shared/communal spaces based on abstractions of Game Theory and Graph Theory is proposed by (Bai, 2020). This can be extended by the opinion pooling method suggested by (Batty,2013)or consensus Building suggested by (Sanoff,2000) to model different decision factors and their dynamics with Network Models.

Methodology: Configuration

As indicated in Configuring Framework Section the configuring phase provides a problem formulation that allows for applying a spectrum of existing methods such as Engineering Optimization, MCDA, and gamification. However, the feed-forward nature of such procedures requires a new category of simulation and approximate evaluation tools capable of taking highly abstract inputs.

Starting from the most automated (and yet explainable) approach, this formulation provides the structure for application of Topology Optimization (TO) (Bendsoe, 2013) as the configuration is represented by a discrete density matrix **X**, and a reciprocal analogous of the strain energy (compliance) in a conventional TO is the spatial quality criteria functions f (see Table 3). This formulation is thus suitable for gradient-based mathematical programming. The caveat here is that in this framework we formulate the quality criteria as benefits to be maximized for better human understanding as it is common in RL framework which they formulate as rewards, however in TO approach it is more common to formulate objective functions as cost to be minimized.

Furthermore, given the spatial validity constraints g_b, a family of Combinatorial Optimization methods is also applicable similar to the approach of (Hua, 2019), and(Peng, 2016) which apply Integer Programming in multiple scales to layout and routing problems in discrete spaces; or as in (Wu, 2018) which applies Mixed-Integer Quadratic Programming(MIQP) to discrete interior design problems. Also, Reinforcement Learning (RL) methods are compatible with this formulation since we can define the configuring procedure as a Markov Decision Process (MDP) given that **X** represents the state space, spatial constraints can be embedded in the definition of agents' actions, and spatial quality criteria function f can provide the rewards for the learning agents. An example of such application is "Academy Spatial Agents" (Veloso, 2020) where spatial agents utilize DDQN to make decisions in a discrete space.

Moreover, the search process can be gamified to establish a play & score environment as well. Within such an approach, grammatical itemization can be used as the generative mechanism of playing (as applied in [ref. removed for annonymity]) and MCDA methods (as reviewed in (Huang, 2011) for scoring the configuration alternatives. Finally, there are also potentials for hybrid approaches such as combining a Multi-Agent System (q.v. (Veloso, 2018)) approach with local MCDA evaluators that guide their decisions about configuration in a discrete environment ([ref. removed for anonymity]).

Methodology: Shaping

As stated in Shaping Framework Section, polygonization of the configuration can be performed through a continuous or discrete approach. An exciting example of the continuous approach is the Marching Cubes algorithm applied in (Nourian, 2014). The discrete approach can be deterministic as proposed by (Savov, 2020) where geometric tiles are placed if a particular combination is present in the configuration, or they can follow a stochastic approach such as Wave Function Collapse Algorithm in which the tile selection for each location is modelled as a probability function that changes based on the selection of tiles in the neighbouring locations (Gumin, 2021). There have also been efforts to combine these approaches and generalize from a regular grid to non-regular grids. (Stalberg, 2015)

APPLICATION & RESULTS

The 'Go Design' framework has been partially implemented in the form of an open-source python package named topoGenesis to maximize its accessibility and reproducibility. We have developed a python library called topoGenesis (Azadi, 2020) The proposed

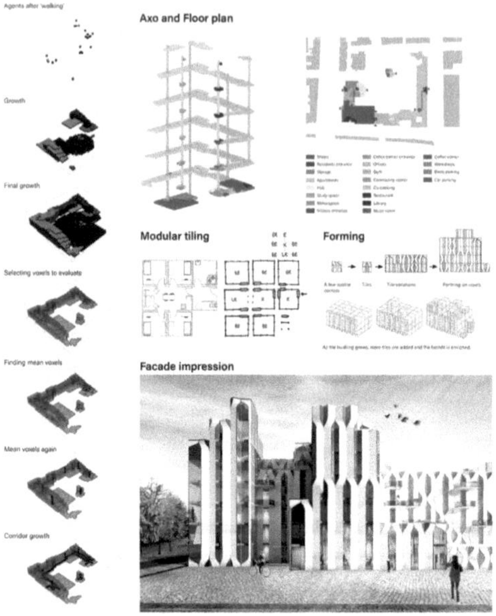

Figure 4
Examples of application of GoDesign framework in student projects: BSc [1]

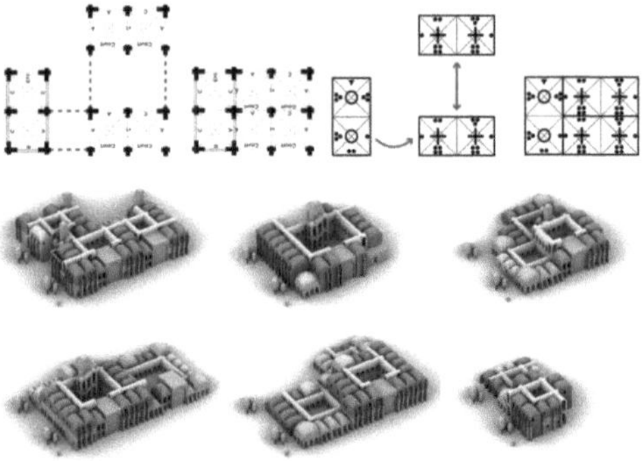

Figure 5
Examples of application of GoDesign framework in student projects: MSc [2][3]

workflow and this tool-set have been applied in educational design studios at TU Delft. In the BSc Spatial Computing design studio, students are asked to develop systems that allow future inhabitants to customize the configuration while satisfying environmental constraints such as direct sunlight, sky view factor, noise, etc. (see Figure 4). Their site is located in Agniesebuurt near the central station of Rotterdam. Students were asked to design a mixed-use complex in a specified parcel. They were instructed to identify future inhabitants and develop a gamified process for the planning phase to specify the inhabitants' preferences as to the aforementioned spatial quality criteria. Next, students were instructed to utilize a Multi-Agent System in the configuring process; embed spatial constraints in the agents' behaviors to avoid complex mathematical formulation of the constraints; utilize MCDA to aggregate each voxel's total value concerning different spatial quality criteria functions; and finally, synthesize a configuration based on the relative advantage of allocating each space to a particular voxel [1].

In the MSc EARTHY design studio (Nourian, 2020) the framework has been utilized for temporary accommodation of displaced communities in Al Zaatari Refugee Camp in Jordan. Students were asked to develop systems/games that allow inhabitants to customize the configuration of their collective habitats while satisfying structural and low-tech constructability constraints of adobe buildings. Their system is required to produce assembly plans of a set of modules to construct the buildings (see Figure 5) Students have developed combinatorial games for exploring configurations as modular permutations. In this project, students have taken a participatory grammatical approach to provide maximum control over the configuration for the future inhabitants [2],[3].

In the EARTHY studio, as the structural constraints are the main feasibility constraints of the design process, successful projects have adopted a modular approach based on different structural elements (e.g. dome, vault, arch, etc) as the basis of their configuration system. With this approach, they not only managed to gamify the decision-making process for inhabitants but also eliminated the need for post-design structural analysis of the structures to increase the independence of the inhabitants in configuring and constructing the buildings [2],[3]. On the other hand, in the Spatial Computing studio, the structural constraints were not as limiting as in the case of EARTHY. Thus successful projects focused more on spatial quality criteria such as daylight, accessibility, visibility, noise, etc., and developed a gamified decision support system that allows the stakeholders to set their preferences and see the effect of their preferences on the design. [1]

CONCLUSION & DISCUSSION

Generality

As the primary feature of this framework is to offer a **general formulation** of the design problem that does not only provide the structure required for the application of optimization and AI methods but also makes the design process more transparent by providing interfaces for participants to be part of the design process, inject their preferences and customize the design. This is particularly important as it provides for argumentation on spatial decisions in an evidence-based approach. As a result, spatial decisions can be traced back to the context conditions, quality criteria, and stakeholder preferences. Also, the framework in general, and the planning phase in particular, can support various forms of multi-actor decision-making mechanisms (participatory design) to ensure customization of the design in various steps. Beyond the decision-making perspective, this framework structures the design space as a countable set of solutions while maintaining topological and geometrical diversity.

Furthermore, the configuring meta-procedure offers a generalized formulation of quality criteria functions that encompasses any criteria that could be expressible as a function of space (field). Besides, the modularity of these quality critera functions allows for including an arbitray set of multiple criteria. Similiarly, various types of local and global spatial validity constraints can be included in such proecdures.

The combined implementation of configuring and shaping meta-procedures is compatible with both modular and integral construction techniques. Finally, the inherent process-modularity of the framework provides for partially adopting it or combining it with other frameworks.

Limitations

As explained in the Framework Section, this framework mathematically prioritizes abstract decisions over concrete ones. This prioritization structures the solution space and facilitates the formalization of objectives and constraints in the process. Consequently, specific solutions will be harder to reach. Mainly, designs that are geometrically simpler but topologically complicated are less likely to be generated. Furthermore, the mathematical nature of the framework requires the quantifiability of spatial criteria prior to their integration in the framework. However, there are ongoing research projects to assess its potentials in integrating non-quantifiable quality criteria such as the heritage value of attributes of existing structures in case of renovation projects.

Future Work

Primarily, this framework provides a foundation for the mathematical formulation of spatial quality criteria f and spatial constraints g. As the built environment is present in many aspects of human life, it influences and is influenced by many physical and societal aspects of human life. Consequently, a spectrum of different qualities needs to be modeled, formalized and added to the system. As such, the mainline of future work within this framework will be about developing various specialized evaluation procedures.

The configuring procedure provides the potential for applying MCDA and optimization methods, a couple of examples of which have been mentioned in the manuscript. However, there is yet much more room for exploring the applicability and suitability of a wide range of compatible methods for solving benchmarked problems. This is particularly important in order to situate the framework in the AEC industry, thus further investigation into the compatibility of the framework with existing conventional workflows is required to consolidate more test cases.

Finally, this framework offers an explicit formulation of spatial design problems that is compatible with many modern Machine Learning methods, not only for automating decision making by means of Generative Adversarial Networks (GANs), Deep Q-Networks (DQN), etc, but also, more importantly, for growing a body of evidence-based knowledge of 'quality' and its complex relations to our design decisions.

REFERENCES

Azadi, S and Nourian, P 2020, *topoGenesis*, Zenodo, DOI: 10.5281/zenodo.4006514

Bai, N, Azadi, S, Nourian, P and Roders, AP 2020 'Decision-Making as a Social Choice Game', *eCAADe 2020*, Berlin, p. 16

Batty, M 2013, *The New Science of Cities*, MIT Press

Bendsoe, MP and Sigmund, O 2013, *Topology optimization: theory, methods, and applications*, Springer Science \& Business Media

Bots, PWG and Hermans, LM 2003 'Developing 'playable metagames' for participatory stakeholder analysis', *34th Conference of the International Simulation and Gaming Association (ISAGA)*, pp. 647-657

Cunningham, S and Hermans, L 2018, *Actor and Strategy Models: Practical Applications and Step-wise Approaches*, John Wiley \& Sons, Inc., Hoboken, NJ, USA

Friedman, Y 1980, *Toward a Scientific Architecture | The MIT Press*, MIT Press

Hua, H, Hovestadt, L, Tang, P and Li, B 2019, 'Integer Programming for Urban Design', *European Journal of Operational Research*, 274(3), pp. 1125-1137

Huang, IB, Keisler, J and Linkov, I 2011, 'Multi-criteria decision analysis in environmental sciences: Ten years of applications and trends', *Science of The Total Environment*, 409(19), pp. 3578-3594

Jordan, M, Auth, G, Jokisch, O and Kühl, JU 2020, 'Knowledge-based systems for the Configure Price Quote (CPQ) process – A case study in the IT solution business', *Online Journal of Applied Knowledge Management*, 8(2), pp. 17-30

Nourian, P, Azadi, S and Hoogenboom, H 2020, 'EARTHY: Computational Generative Design for Earth and Masonry Architecture', *BOUT RUMOER: Periodical for the Building Technologist*, 74, pp. 47-53

Ogrodnik, K 2019, 'Multi-Criteria Analysis of Design Solutions in Architecture and Engineering: Review of Applications and a Case Study', *Buildings*, 9(12), p. 244

Peng, CH, Yang, YL, Bao, F, Fink, D, Yan, DM, Wonka, P and Mitra, NJ 2016, 'Computational Network Design from Functional Specifications', *ACM Transactions on Graphics*, 35(4), pp. 1-12

Rittel, HWJ and Webber, MM 1973, 'Dilemmas in a General Theory of Planning', *Policy Sciences*, 4, p. 15

Rocha, C, Formoso, C and Tzortzopoulos, P 2015, 'Adopting Product Modularity in House Building to Support Mass Customisation', *Sustainability*, 7, pp. 4919-4937

Salvador, F 2007, 'Toward a Product System Modularity Construct: Literature Review and Reconceptualization', *IEEE Transactions on Engineering Management*, 54(2), pp. 219-240

Salvador, F, Forza, C and Rungtusanatham, M 2002, 'Modularity, product variety, production volume, and component sourcing: theorizing beyond generic prescriptions', *Journal of Operations Management*, 20(5), pp. 549-575

Sanoff, H 1978, *Design Games*, Create Space Independent Publishing Platform

Savov, A, Winkler, R and Tessmann, O 2019 'Encoding Architectural Designs as Iso-surface Tilesets for Participatory Sculpting of Massing Models', *Design Modelling Symposium Berlin 2019*, pp. 199-213

Simon, HA 2008, *The Sciences of the Artificial*, MIT Press, Cambridge, Mass.

Steadman, P 1983, *Architectural Morphology: An Introduction to the Geometry of Building Plans*, Pion

Stålberg, O 2016, 'Voxel House: Breaking Down the Voxel House Demo by Oskar Stålberg', *Vertex*, 3 , pp. 170-176

Ulrich, K 1995, 'The role of product architecture in the manufacturing firm', *Research Policy*, 24(3), pp. 419-440

Veloso, P and Krishnamurti, R 2020, 'An Academy of Spatial Agents', *eCAADe 2020*, -, p. 10

Veloso, P, Rhee, J and Krishnamurti, R 2008, 'Multi-Agent Space Planning', *International Conference on Computer Aided Architectural Design Futures*, 18, p. 24

Voordijk, H 2009, 'Construction management and economics: the epistemology of a multidisciplinary design science', *Construction Management and Economics*, 27(8), pp. 713-720

Wu, W, Fan, L, Liu, L and Wonka, P 2018, 'MIQP-Based Layout Design for Building Interiors', *Computer Graphics Forum*, 37(2), p. 11

[1] https://github.com/Pirouz-Nourian/Spatial_Computing_Design_Studio20

[2] https://github.com/Pirouz-Nourian/earthy_20

[3] https://github.com/Pirouz-Nourian/earthy_19

A new Relation Matrix as a Fruitful Meta-Design Tool

How to overcome typological limits

Ugo Maria Coraglia[1]*, Zhelun Zhu*[2]*, Antonio Fioravanti*[3]*,*
Davide Simeone[4]*, Stefano Cursi*[5]
[1,4,5]*www.aec-agency.com* [2,3]*Sapienza University of Rome*
[1,4,5]*{um.coraglia|d.simeone|s.cursi}@aec-agency.com* [2,3]*{zhelun.zhu|antonio.fioravanti}@uniroma1.it*

The use of meta-design tools to support the early stages of the design process is widely proven in literature. Among these tools, the adjacency matrix and the bubble diagram provided the various professionals involved - not only in the AEC sector - with some useful information mainly regarding the connection types between spaces and the sizing of their dimensions. With the evolution of design and the change of architectural aims (e.g. sustainability, refurbishment), it is not fruitful, especially related to complex buildings (e.g. hospital, airport), to manage spaces and their connections through the traditional Adjacency Matrix and its dual (Bubble Diagram). These tools, used as they were originally designed, do not consider other characteristics but basic topological ones and are still linked to 2D geometry. For this reason, this research aims to increase the unexplored design potential of these tools considering huge advances in building object representation and links with knowledge. The first research steps led to a 3D analysis capable of providing knowledge on the connections and adjacencies between spaces and its environments located on different floors. Therefore, we decided to define further goals, breaking limits of the ``adjacency" concept for a more extendable and general concept of ``relation" between spaces and environments.

Keywords: *Relation Matrix, Meta-design, Architectural design theory, Tool*

STATE OF ART AND PROBLEMS

The design and construction of buildings - complex by their nature given the presence of multiple disciplinary domains - has always required a high expenditure of money, energy, resources, activities, and land usege. In the last decade (Monsù Scolaro, 2017) the approach of the experts has tried to favour a philosophy that foresees, if possible, the preservation and reuse of existing buildings and the redevelopment of those in a state of neglect.

An important aspect related to this type of approach that convinced professionals is that relating to sustainability. In fact, by not carrying out demolitions and relative displacements of waste materials, the use of new resources is avoided, unless radical transformations are necessary. Some British research institutes have found that the amount of CO2 produced per m^2 to build a new building is 4,5 times greater than the amount emitted for the renovation of an existing building. In fact, in regard to the production cycle and the transport phases inherent in a new construction, the data collected refer to 475 kg of CO2/m2 produced compared to only 104 kg of CO2/m2 emitted during a renovation. All this has been estimated in countries such as Great Britain by the stable demographic, social and economic structure, with a reduced seismic risk (VV.AA., 2008).

The challenge of improving and renovating existing buildings (e.g. hospitals, barracks, residences, etc.) has also fascinated internationally renowned architects, with remarkable results, such as Lina Bo Bardi in São Paulo for the transformation of a metal barrel factory (Vainer, 2013), MVRDV in Amsterdam for the conversion of silos [1], and Coop Himmelb(l)au in the redevelopment of three gasometers carried out in Vienna [2]. In the latter case, a building object of a purely industrial nature and of monumental dimensions has been transformed into a construction for residential purposes.

The building renovation design is often faced with the challenge of bringing the relationship between man and the building object back to a more human dimension and taking into consideration an architectural promenade, gradually closer, to appreciate the elements of beauty and richness of space at various distances and sizes (Baker, 1989).

However, the processes that characterize the renovation or reuse of buildings frequently have more similar approaches to the interventions of "fixing" and "repairing", mainly consisting of the following four operating methods (Figure 1):

- Change - change of intended use;
- Upgrade - improvement or expansion, A $\rightarrow$ A+;
- Downgrade - reduction or demolition, A $\rightarrow$ A-;
- Mix - combination of the previous three, A $\rightarrow$ A+ and / or A- and / or B.

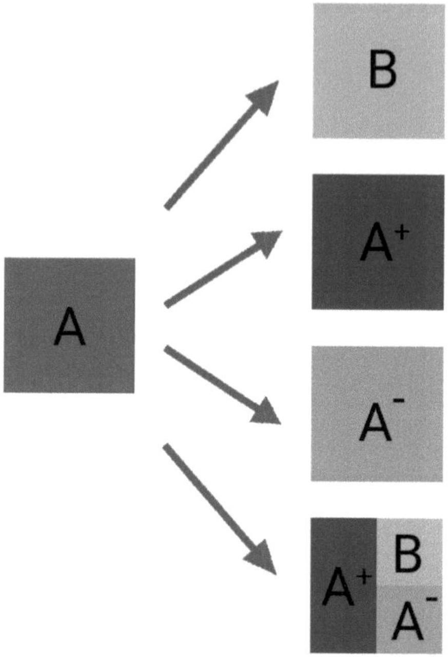

Figure 1
Existing building restructuring or re-use process characterizing solutions

The meaning of Upgrade and Downgrade, in this case, does not refer to the mere dimensional aspects but rather extends to the technological-performance aspects characterizing the building object under consideration and the functions performed within it.

In the integrated approach to the design and creative process of making architecture, a not negligible part - especially at the beginning of the current "Evo Informatico" - is due to the methodologies and technologies of ICT (Information and Communication Technologies), which allow to expand the design possibilities, providing tools as well as analysis, verification and optimization also for the production of new creative design solutions (e.g. architectural, distributive).

The world of CAAD (Computer Aided Architectural Design) is therefore not relegated to a marginal role in design but becomes the "characterization"

Figure 2
Adjacency matrix – Classic symbols

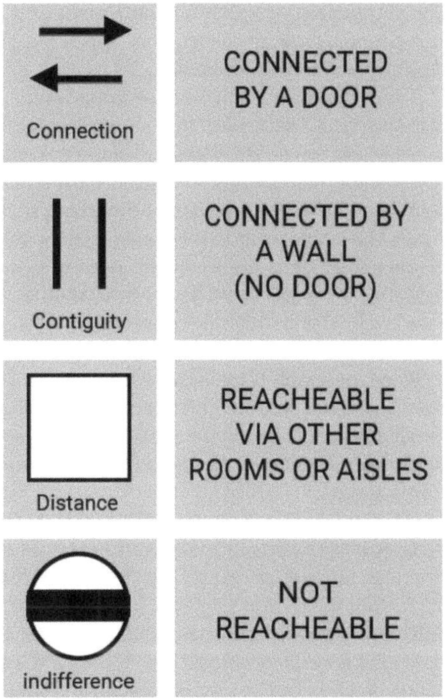

of a new scenario of possibilities, open to design in the broadest sense: Design theory. Fifty years have passed since the minting of this acronym which has dramatically expanded its branches and possibilities. It is known in fact how the development of ICT is so rapid that a single year of it equals ten years of the evolution of other sectors.

Some building construction "hybridizations" with ICT and other disciplines, carried out years ago, encountered objective computational or methodological difficulties, or insufficient understanding of design theory and were therefore abandoned. Now, however, they can be resumed and integrated into a design process that is more appropriate to current times. The reflection on these research focuses on the theoretical study of the design process and how the latter can become "autonomous" (Gerber, 2017).

The "automated" design solutions that were produced in the early years of the CAAD were so embryonic that they could not be considered an effective support for the designer's work. They were simplistic solutions that could be easily obtained with traditional methods.

One of the first results of these hybridizations occurred by associating the related geometry, Topology, with the bodies that represented the concept of "Room", generating and spreading the terms "Environmental Unit", "Space Unit", etc (White, 1986).

The basic idea was to associate the "vertices", representing the housing units, with the "edges", representing the connections between them, and consequently to verify objectively, automatically and in real time the compliance with predefined design constraints that they were limited to "connection", "contiguity", "distance" and "indifference" (Figure 2), such as to generate a matrix relating to the aforementioned adjacencies. This matrix was symmetrical with respect to the main diagonal, since the relationship, for example the "communication" one, could not specify whether this was bidirectional or unidirectional (Cocomello, 1980).

The relationships between the entities were formalized through algorithms which, processed computer-based, could immediately verify the correspondence to the two simple design constraints mentioned above. The approach proved to be sufficiently valid to verify these relationships in the presence of a project of extreme complexity where not all connections were visually perceptible while in simple projects, with few Environmental units, it was not very useful as these relationships were immediately perceptible (Coraglia, 2018a).

METHODOLOGY

The aim of this research is to introduce innovations in the adjacency matrix that will allow it and its automated processing to increase its validity to make to turn it into a better design tool. On the one hand they will concern new Environmental units and on the other new types of connections, also in the 3 dimensions, and related hierarchies.

The early stages led to propose as innovation an adjacency type relationship that is not only that in the plane, but also in the space and along the edges of the Environmental Units. This aspect is particularly useful because in the presence of disturbing sound sources one is able to understand immediately which Environmental Units are involved. And by switching to the BIM model, it can be checked whether the shared walls and/or floors are adequate as a soundproofing power for the disturbance suffered.

Since the graph is spatial, and there are no flatness constraints, you can hierarchize the Environmental units and explode the subsets of them without worrying about any intersections or apparent link inconsistencies.

On entities with a higher intelligence/abstraction layer, it will be possible to activate further generative rules, to produce new solutions based on rules, and to skim the design solutions, introducing other constraints. For example, spatial contiguities for the opening of temporary compartments during the execution of works can be used in construction site designs, as well as defining the optimized electrical diagrams for the length of the cables and optical fibres by resorting to the logical overlap affine geometry - Cartesian geometry. Always at a "layer" of intelligence, the logical links between the various Environmental units can be controlled.

Many of these checks and layouts can take place in the preliminary design phase, operating only on its typology, even before operating on an accurate design model. Hence the qualitative leap made on this new adjacency matrix results useful for the creative phase of the design.

The Adjacency Matrix relations in the case of a building recovery and/or renovation design are all known from the beginning. From this point on, the designer begins his creative work and focused on the details to be confirmed, modified or canceled. In the design of new buildings, the relations are only partially known because they are defined by the building program, by the parametric performance specifications and by the first design hypotheses. The other relations are, however, all to be invented, the result of the designer's skills and the relations that are refined during the course of the design itself. For this reason, as regards the aspect strictly related to adjacency, it was decided to "enhance" the types of relations between the Environmental units. The "enhancement", indeed, is to be understood both from the numerical point of view (increasing the entities, e.g. the external unit, etc.), and from the qualitative point of view (the adjacency relations in a vertical as well as horizontal way).

The symbol used to date - the two vertical bars || - and valid for any type of contiguity, it is no longer sufficient and is integrated with a new symbology that allows the professional to immediately receive much more information. In this regard, the symbology proposed in this research, based on the problems that may occur during the renovation and reuse works, takes into consideration not only the planimetric contiguity [||] but also the diagonal [//] and vertical [=] (see Figure 3). By diagonal contiguity we mean a "contiguity of edge" both planimetric and between different floors. The contiguity refers to the "Mix" type in the "State of the art" paragraph, in particular those works that may have to be carried out in parallel with the usual work activities characterizing part of the building object in question.

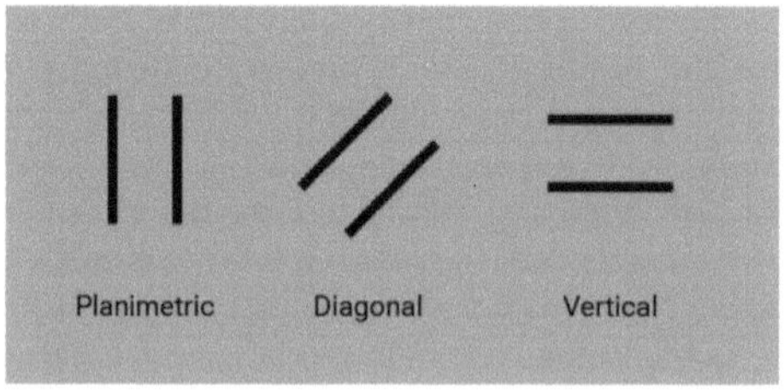

Figure 3
"Simplified" contiguity

Figure 4
Diagonally adjacent rooms , horizontally (1) and vertically (2)

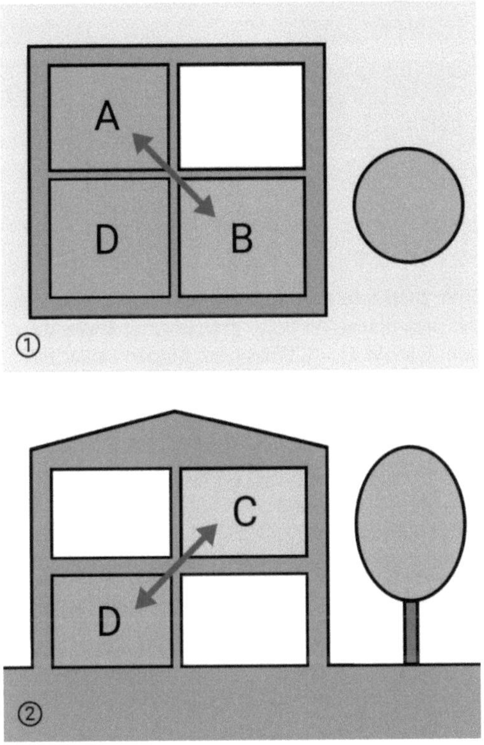

Figure 5
"Directional" contiguity

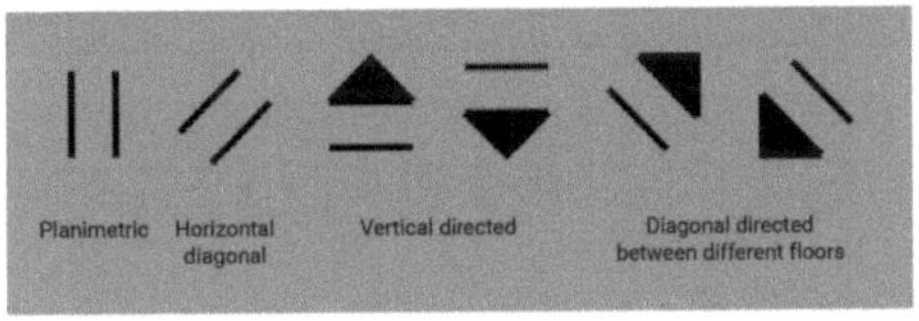

In fact, many times, especially within complex structures, such as hospitals, offices, etc., renovations activities can have a negative impact, for example due to noise and vibration, on the daily routines carried out within the areas of the building still in operation (Coraglia, 2018b). These negative impacts, which until now have only been considered for direct adjacency, communication or contiguity, through a shared wall, could also have repercussions on adjacent rooms diagonally, both horizontally and vertically (see Figure 4). Given that the renovations within complex structures may concern a multitude of rooms and floors, it is considered more correct to proceed further, detailing the first series of new adjacency symbols, henceforth defined as "simplified" contiguity, through a further specification of the two symbols just proposed. This additional new series of symbols, which has been defined as "directional", requires that the contiguity between different floors, upwards or downwards, both vertically and diagonally, be taken into consideration, as shown in Figure 5.

This specification, made necessary precisely by the analysis of negative impacts due to noise and vibrations, for example, allows the professional to immediately have a more detailed view of the problems that could be triggered through the implementation of certain renovation works. Further levels of specification have already been analysed but they have proved to have a negative impact on the understanding of the matrix that derives from it, which instead must remain fast and easy to read. For further degrees of specification, in fact, it is more correct to directly analyse the floor plans or the 3D model of the building in question.

In addition to what has been illustrated up to this point, to further expand the range of information obtainable through the consultation of the New Adjacency Matrix, it was decided to introduce some concepts that serve for evaluating the quality of a room, also introducing the qualitative relationship that this has with the other rooms, especially with the exterior.

The first concept we introduced is that of Luminosity, already expressed by E.T. White (1986) as the presence or absence of daylight according to the Low, Medium, and High classification. In our research, however, we decided to manage this information by classifying the window orientation characterizing the room itself, using a scheme that provides for the absence of a window [X = 0] or a specific value for each orientation [N = 1, W = 2, E = 3 and S = 4]. Switching to a classification with 4 parameters, instead of 3, allows you to further specify and differentiate the environments.

NB: in this paper, the orientation of the apartment and the windows has been simplified to only 4 cardinal points (N, E, S and W) but in Dynamo the algorithm has been programmed to obtain values from the BIM model with an accuracy of 1 degree.

Furthermore, as far as renovations are concerned, this data is useful both when you decided to open a new window and when it is assumed that two or more rooms join together.

The first situation gave the opportunity to introduce the Heat Dispersion coefficient, which takes into account the negative impact of the orientation of the window due to the lower radiation of the facades facing north in the northern hemisphere and south in the southern hemisphere [X = 0, N = −0.20, W = −0.10, E = −0.15, S = 0]. [3]

Given the numerous cases of the restructuring activity, the system proposed in this research takes into consideration the following 4 cases, useful for design purposes, which however have general validity:

1. 1 Room with (or without) 1 Window, this case serves as a basis for evaluating the quality of the room;
2. 1 Room with 2 Windows, in addition to providing an evaluation for a room characterized by 2 windows, allows us to evaluate the quality of a room whose renovation includes the addition of a window;
3. 2 Rooms with 1Window, in addition to providing the assessment of a large room, comparable to two rooms, characterized by a single window, allows us to evaluate the quality of a renovation that involves the union of 2 rooms, of which only one of these characterized by the presence of a window;
4. 2 Rooms with 2 Windows, in addition to providing the assessment of a large room, comparable to 2 rooms, characterized by the presence of 2 windows, allows us to evaluate the quality of a renovation that involves the union of 2 rooms, both characterized by the presence of a window.

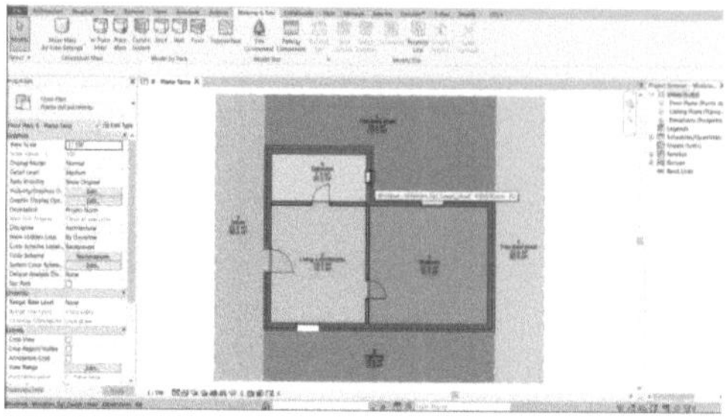

Figure 6
Revit model of a simplified apartment typology with 4 different external situation (N and E = tree-lined street, S = highway, W = street)

From case 2, foreseeing the presence of 2 windows, the parameters "Air flow" [flows from parallel directions (N-S, W-E) = 1, flows from perpendicular directions (N-E, S-E, S-W, N-W) = 0,5, absent = 0] and the "Light variation" [no window = -0.25, light from N = 0, light from E and W = 0,5, light from S = 1] have been introduced.

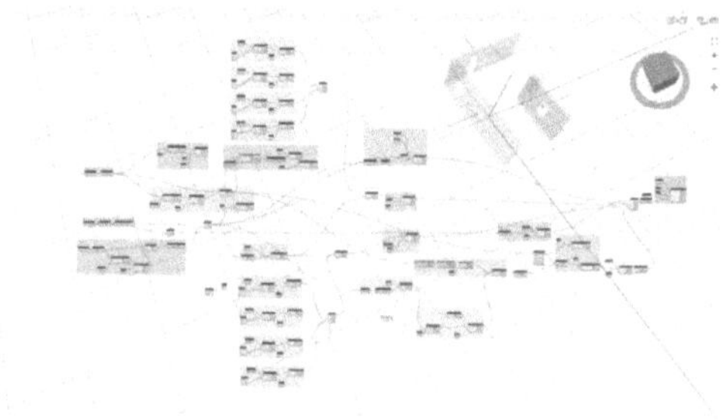

Figure 7
Dynamo workflow: from BIM model to Excel, useful data collection for the automatic evaluation of the room quality

Room ID	Window Orientation 1	Window Orientation 2	Window Orientation 3	Free Wall 1	Free Wall 2	Free Wall 3	POV rate 1	POV rate 2	POV rate 3	Connect. wall 1	Connect. wall 2	Connect. wall 3
Room 01	N	nf	nf	E	S	nf	4	4	-2	W	nf	nf
Room 02	S	nf	nf	W	nf	nf	-2	2	nf	N	E	nf
Room 03	E	nf	nf	W	N	nf	4	2	4	S	nf	nf

Table 1
Data collected by Dynamo (NB: nf = not found)

In the initial phase of a new project or immediately after carrying out an inspection for a refurbishment, using a BIM modeling software (such as the Autodesk Revit model shown in figure 6) it is possible to set up and enrich the model with information.

1Room 1Window				
Room	W01	Total value	POV W01	Total according to POV
Room 02	S	4	-2	2
Room 03	E	3	4	7
Room 01	N	1	4	5

Table 2
Room quality evaluation - Classification drawn up according to the Window Orientation (third column) and POV (fifth column)

This step is necessary to ensure that, using the Dynamo plug-in and through the setting of specific algorithms (see Figures 7 and Table 1), it is possible to automatically obtain the room quality evaluation, as

Table 3
Ranking of the best design solutions related to add a new window and sorted by Total value

1Room 2Windows																	
Room	WO1	WO2	OV1	OV2	Subtotal 1	Light Variation		Subtotal 2	Air flow	Heat loss		Area plus	Total value	POV WO1	POV WO2	Total according to POV
Room 02	S	W	2	4	6	1	0,5	7,5	0,5	0	-0,1	0	7,9	-2	2	8,3
Room 01	N	S	1	4	5	0	1	6	1	-0,25	0	0	6,75	4	-2	9,5
Room 03	E	W	3	2	5	0,5	0,5	6	1	-0,15	-0,1	0	6,75	4	2	13,5
Room 01	N	E	1	3	4	0	0,5	4,5	0,5	-0,25	-0,15	0	4,6	4	4	12,7
Room 03	E	N	3	1	4	0,5	0	4,5	0,5	-0,15	-0,25	0	4,6	4	4	12,7

illustrated in Table 2.

Furthermore, another aspect that has been taken into consideration to define the room quality even more in detail is the point of view (POV) that characterizes an existing window or the one that could be had in the case of a refurbishment that plans to equip the room for a further window. In Table 1, the data collected by Dynamo are organised in 4 blocks, Window orientation, Free wall (external walls without windows) , POV rate and Connected wall (related to wall connected to the rest of the apartment). Moreover, in Table 2, the last 2 columns on the right show the evaluation of the POV and the new total value of the room in accordance with the POV value.

For this reason, the following classification has been drawn up which makes it possible to simplify the evaluation of the relations of the external spaces with the room under consideration and make it compatible and collaborative with the other evaluations proposed so far:

- +5 Park, Heritage;
- +4 Square, Tree-lined street;
- +3 Courtyard;
- +2 Street;
- +1 Chiostrine, Alley;
- 0 Parking;
- -1 High density road;
- -2 Highway, Train station.

Thus, the ability to set the parameters within the BIM model and manage them through Dynamo has allowed us to expand the information that can automatically be provided to the designer. It is known that there are more accurate calculation systems that are suitable for calculating some of the information treated so far (e.g. sunshine of a facade, quality of air exchange) but each of them would be ineffective at this preliminary design stage because it would require a multitude of data not accessible at this phase.

Through the data collected by Dynamo, in addition to being able to automatically assign a value to each room, our algorithm is able to provide a ranking of the best possible interventions in reference to both the opening of a new window inside a room (see Table 3) and considering the union of two contiguous environments (see Table 4).

In both cases, the algorithm provides a ranking based on the Total values obtained by taking into consideration the parameters of Window Orientation, Light Variation, Air Flow, Heat Loss and Surface Increment (Area plus is a coefficient of 0.5 but can be 0 if there is no fusion between 2 environments).

Our simplification, of course, is open to be constantly updated with new parameters or to consider new levels of depth. The classification of the view from a window, in fact, could be implemented through the additional evaluation of the "Distance" parameter. This parameter would allow to evaluate differently, for example, the presence of a railway station, this in fact if placed in the distance - like skyline - could acquire an improvement coefficient instead of the negative one (-2) assigned to date.

CONCLUSIONS

This article, which is part of the still utopian concept of autonomous design, heir to automated de-

Table 4
Ranking of the best design solutions related to the merger of 2 rooms and sorted by Total value

2Rooms 2Windows																	
Room	Room	WO1	WO2	OV1	OV2	Subtotal 1	Light Variation		Avg. Light	Air flow	Heat loss		Area plus	Total value	POV WO1	POV WO2	Total according to POV
Room 02	Room 03	S	E	4	3	3,5	1	0,5	0,75	0,5	0	-0,15	0,5	5,1	-2	4	7,6
Room 01	Room 02	N	S	1	4	2,5	0	1	0,5	1	-0,25	0	0,5	4,25	4	-2	6,75

sign, aims to contribute to it through a piece, that of the automatic control of topological relationships redesigned in a more design perspective. In view of the new spatial relationships introduced and the new types of Environmental Units included in the Adjacency Matrix, the usual limitations imposed by this type of representation have been overcome, such as: the creation of a planar topology, the relationships exclusively between the Environmental and the adjacency relations only on the contact surfaces between the Environmental units. In this way, the generation of design solutions enriched by new relationships or constraints, which highlight additional information more useful for the design, allows to highlight the most appropriate subset of objectives required by the large number of automatically produced solutions.

This improvement of the assisted design tool is consequently placed within a wider field of man-machine co-design, trying to increase more and more the possibilities offered by the automated design, in view of the autonomous one, also facing a specific topic such as that of the management and control of adjacencies. In this way, the consequences and opportunities that came to light through the improvements of this representation can allow the designer to get rid of the repetitive and stressful controls inherent in the relationships between spaces and to focus, instead, on the most creative and exciting aspects of the design theme seen in its entirety.

Certainly, the process that will lead to automation is still very long and in some cases, for a sort of survival instinct or, perhaps, just for a kind of romanticism, some aspects related to emotions have been still left to the judgment and common sense of the designer. For this reason, the algorithm has been set up to provide rankings by ordering them by Total values and not by values recalibrated according to the POV. In other words, it was preferred to assign the responsibility of tipping the scales in cases of equal values after the POV evaluation.

In this case, the rooms were taken into consideration without considering the function attributed to them. Obviously, the evaluation of the function would involve an additional level of in-depth analysis. In fact, for example, more than one window is rarely designed inside a bathroom or kitchen and in this case we should set the algorithm to exclude these environments or take them into consideration for refurbishment activities that involve a change of window position.

REFERENCES

Baker, GH 1989, *Le Corbusier - an analysis of form*, Van Nostrand Reinold (Intl.) Co Ltd., London (UK)

Cocomello, C and Paoluzzi, A (eds) 1980, *Planarità e Dualità nei Problemi di Progettazione Assistita*, Tipografia ESA, Rome (Italy)

Coraglia, UM, Wurzer, G and Fioravanti, A 2018a 'ORe – A simulation model for Organising Refurbishments', *Proceedings of the 36th International Conference of eCAADe*, Lodz (Poland), pp. 605-610

Coraglia, UM, Wurzer, G and Fioravanti, A 2018b 'Noise Solver for Refurbishment Construction Site Design', *Proceedings of the 22nd International Conference of SIGraDi*, São Carlos (Brazil), pp. 517-522

Gerber, D 2017 'Interactive Design of Shell Structures Using Multi Agent Systems: Design Exploration of Reciprocal Frames Based on Environmental and Structural Performance', *Proceedings of CAAD Futures 2017*, Istanbul (Turkey), pp. 601-616

Monsù Scolaro, A (eds) 2017, *Progettare con l'esistente. Riuso di edifici, componenti e materiali per un processo edilizio circolare*, FrancoAngeli Edizioni, Milano (Italy)

Vainer, A (eds) 2013, *Cidadela da Liberdade*, Lina Bo Bardi e o SESC Pompéia, Sao Paulo (Brazil)

VV, AA 2008, *New Tricks with Old Bricks*, The Empty Homes Agency Ltd., London (UK)

White, ET 1986, *Space Adjacency Analysis, Diagramming Information for Architectural Design*, Architectural Media.

[1] https://www.mvrdv.nl/projects/163/silodam

[2] https://www.coophimmelblau.at/architercture/projects/apartment-building-gasometer-b

[3] http://store.uni.com/catalogo/uni-ts-11300-1-2014/

Design Methods for Variable Density, Multi-Directional Composite Timber Slab Systems for Multi-Storey Construction

Orozco Luis[1], Anna Krtschil[2], Hans-Jakob Wagner[3], Bechert Simon[4], Felix Amtsberg[5], Lior Skoury[6], Jan Knippers[7], Achim Menges[8]
[1,3,5,6,8]Institute for Computational Design and Construction, University of Stuttgart, Germany [2,4,7]Institute of Building Structures and Structural Design, University of Stuttgart, Germany
[1,3,5,8]{luis.orozco|hans.jakob.wagner|felix.amtsberg|achim.menges}@icd.uni-stuttgart.de [2,4,7]{anna.krtschil|simon.bechert|info}@itke.uni-stuttgart.de [6]liorsk947@gmail.com

This paper presents an agent-based method for the design of complex timber structures. This method features a multi-level agent simulation, that relies on a feedback loop between agent systems and structural simulations that update the agent environment. Such an approach can usefully be applied for the design of variable density timber slab systems, where material arrangements based on structural, fabrication, and architectural boundary conditions are necessary. Such arrangements can lead to multi-directional spanning slabs that can accept pointwise supports in unique layouts. We discuss the implementation of such a method on the basis of the structural design of a pavilion-scale multi-storey testing setup. The presented method enables a more versatile approach to the design of multi-storey timber buildings, which should increase their applicability to a diverse range of building typologies.

Keywords: *Agent-Based Modelling, Robotic Timber Construction, Computational Design, Multi-Storey Timber Buildings*

AIM

This paper presents an Agent Based Modelling (ABM) method for the design of slabs in multi-storey timber buildings. This method leverages ABM to organise the components and assemblies that make up the building's structure. The agent-based model features a changing environment within which a multi-level agent simulation is run. This environment is based on the results of structural simulations. The multi-level simulation has separate agent systems for each type of building component to be arranged: columns, slab plates, and reinforcement within the slab plate. Each level of agent systems is dependent on the results of the level above itself.

CONTEXT

Urban populations have grown, and it will continue to do so for the foreseeable future (World urbanization prospects 2019). A growing population needs not only residential, but civil, public, and commercial buildings. Due to their limited space, cities will need to densify. Urban densification means that individual buildings will need to contain multiple uses, and to be taller.

There are a variety of reasons why urban densification should happen in timber as opposed to steel or concrete, the two most proliferous construction materials of today (Foster and Reynolds 2018). Among them are timber's physical properties and its environmental credentials. Timber offers a tremendous strength-to-weight ratio advantage, especially over concrete (Foster and Ramage 2017). Concrete is the most polluting building material in the world, with approximately 8% of global CO2 emissions coming from the more than 4 billion tonnes of cement that are produced annually (Lehne and Preston 2018). This contrasts timber's ability to capture atmospheric carbon while its constituent trees are being grown, and the role building in timber plays in storing that carbon (Churkina et al. 2020).

Timber buildings are getting taller than they have been for decades (Kuzmanovska et al. 2018). The increased capacity for height increases both the capacity for density and its attractiveness for urban construction. However, multi-storey timber buildings do not currently exhibit the variety of typologies needed to support the rich variety of urban building uses. This can be linked in large part to the way that timber buildings are currently built; their construction methods and building systems. Timber construction manuals, such as those published by DETAIL (Fischer et al. 2019; Kaufmann et al. 2018), show mostly schools or apartments, but no larger public buildings. Surveys of the current state-of-the-art for timber focus on room modules (Huß et al. 2019), when they do not focus on panelised construction (Hugues et al. 2004). The height and width restrictions of room modules makes them unsuited for the construction of office or communal spaces. The nature of load bearing wall panels is to support unidirectional spanning floor panels, limiting how open and how flexible spaces can be. If the urbanisation of the planet is to be addressed in timber, how we build in timber will need to be further developed.

STATE OF THE ART

Agent-based models (ABMs) are by now a well-known topic both within and beyond architecture. They are well defined (Macal and North 2010), and have been around architecture for a long time (Krause 1997). There have been many uses of ABMs in architecture.

ABMs consist of an Environment, the Agents that inhabit that Environment, and the Behaviours those agents exhibit with respect to each other and to the Environment, as codified in engineering standards (VDI/VDE 2653). Macal (2016) states: "in ABMs, the fundamental modelling construct is the agent and its behaviours, behaviours that affect the agents' own action, the actions of other agents, and the environment" (p. 145). How you define the agents, behaviours, and environment depends on how you conceptualise what is being simulated. Schwinn (2021) categorises ABMs in architecture based on what the agents in the model represent. This includes: agents as people and stakeholders; agents as physical builders; agents as virtual builders; and agents as building elements. Conceptualising agents as building elements has been useful for the successful subdivision of and material arrangement in other timber projects, such as segmented shells (Groenewolt et al. 2018).

With the agents conceptualised, one can then simulate the desired system by either modulating the types of agents or the behaviours of those agents (Levitis et al. 2009). Agents can have one or more behaviours, and these in turn can act on multiple time frames. In some cases, a discrete-event based simulation, in which the agents' interactions occur and behaviours change at semantically significant instants is desirable (Theodoropoulos et al. 2018). Usually implemented as a queue of events, this approach is especially useful when agents exist in hierarchical arrangements, and their behaviours must be executed accordingly. The more common discrete time-based agent simulations, where "the outputs of a system at time t [affect] the inputs of that system at time t+1" (Carmichael and Hadžikadić 2019, p.10), is useful when agents react spatially to the state of the entire agent system. An example of a behaviour that benefits from discrete time simulations such is Lloyd's Algorithm, which can be used to more evenly distribute collections of cartesian agents (Lloyd 1982).

Unlike some ABMs, which harness emergence for design exploration and explorative modelling, the method presented in this paper harnesses the self-organisation of complex systems (De Wolf and Holvoet 2004). Self-organisation can be related to the agent environment as well as to other agents. Though it is possible to conceive of the environment as an agent itself, as Minar does (1996, p. 7), this is not necessary. It is possible to define the environment as the variable field of forces the agents find their positions in. Such an environmental definition has been successful in aiding the additive aggregation of reinforcement on complex surfaces that adapt over time (Vasey et al. 2015).

RELEVANCE

Timber construction lends itself to the prefabrication of building components. As with all prefabricated components, these must be mass-manufacturable and transportable. Unlike prefabricated concrete elements, timber ones are limited by their unidirectionality and limited span. A building system with hollow slabs and long bi- or multi-axial fields would address these limits. Hollow slabs reduce material use, increasing material efficiency and reducing the embodied energy of a building. Hollow slabs have the added building physics advantage of reducing impact sound transmission when their hollow cavity is filled with insulation or other infill (Krötsch and Huß 2018). However, both trusses for long spans and box beams for shorter spans, the two types of hollow systems in timber, only function well when they span unidirectionally.

Wood's anisotropic structure gives it strength parallel to the grain similar to that of reinforced concrete (Ramage et al. 2017), but considerably less so against the grain. It is generally difficult to have hollow timber systems that span in multiple directions because this anisotropy. This limitation can be addressed by arranging material in the location and orientation where it is structurally needed. The structural simulation of a slab would elucidate the forces therein and inform where and how material should be arranged to resist them. The integration of such structural simulations within the design process of a building would help avoid the pitfalls of the "digital chain" method of architectural design prevalent in today's professional practices (Dohmen and Rüdenauer 2007). Such a method could be said to be of a mind with the "extended digital chain," within which design, analysis, and optimisation cycles are merged (Tamke and Thomsen 2018; Thomsen 2019). A direct digital feedback loop to structural simulations would allow for a digital optimization cycle, and further extend ideas of integrated co-design (Wagner et al. 2020a).

Unlike in-situ cast concrete, timber floor slabs must be subdivided for prefabrication and shipping. The distribution of stresses in the slab depends on how the slab is subdivided. Multi-directional spanning slabs out of timber would require slab to slab joints that transfer loads and moments to overcome the limits of their subdivided slab sizes. These joints will also need to connect wood fibres in different orientations, which is known to affect the strength of glued connections. Joints such as these are a contemporary topic of study (Zöllig et al. 2016; Claus 2020).

Complex local and global arrangements need to account for fabricability, both off-site and in-situ. Robotic timber construction, as defined by Willmann, Knauss et al. (2016), is a promising method for the additive manufacturing of batch size 1 construction assemblies in architecture. Constraints like material size, transportation envelope, and machine payload, among others, need to be understood as part of the arrangement of subdivided panels and their internal elements. Previous experimental research showed how robotic on-site fabrication can be integrated in the design of slab systems (Wagner et al. 2020b).

Efficiently arranging material based either on general principles or other domain-specific knowledge would be nearly impossible. ABM methods can be leveraged to produce efficacious arrangements of complex systems based on conflicting parameters that would not have been otherwise possible. ABM techniques have been used to harness geometric complexity in the subdivision of timber structures before (Schwinn and Menges 2015; Alvarez et al. 2019). Their applicability to multi-storey timber buildings is worth investigation.

By understanding fabrication constraints and how they affect the discretization of a timber building system it is possible to allow for the free placement of columns within the limit of the slab's maximum spanning distance. This free placement of vertical supports will lead a move away from restrictive, small structural grids. We believe that shifting from a grid- to a network-based logic will allow for a more versatile approach to the design of timber buildings and allow the material system to be applicable to a wider variety of typologies. Further investigation into the architectural effects of a network-based structural approach will be necessary.

SETTING

The research shown in this paper was conducted under the umbrella of the Cluster of Excellence on Integrative Computational Design and Construction for Architecture (IntCDC), addressing the co-design-based development of methods, processes, and systems for multi-storey timber buildings. The case study project was developed with support from the students of the master's program "Integrative Technologies and Architectural Design Research" (ITECH), under the guidance of the authors.

The research framework of this project proposes a variable density timber building system as an approach to encourage the wider adoption of timber for different building uses and types. (Figure 1) The slab of this building system changes material density according to the occurring forces. Within this slab there are high peaks of shear and moment where the columns meet the slab, and there is therefore additional material there to reinforce against it. To deal with bending moment, the top and bottom of the hollow slab are made of solid timber. Shear webs are intelligently arranged between the top and bottom plates so that they may work together as one multi-directional spanning slab. Their placement is informed by both the moment and shear forces occurring in the slab. The points of highest moment depend on the columns' locations. The high shear areas depend on both the subdivision of the slab into plates and the location of the columns. A central part of the development of the building system was the development of the strategies necessary for its cyber-physical fabrication.

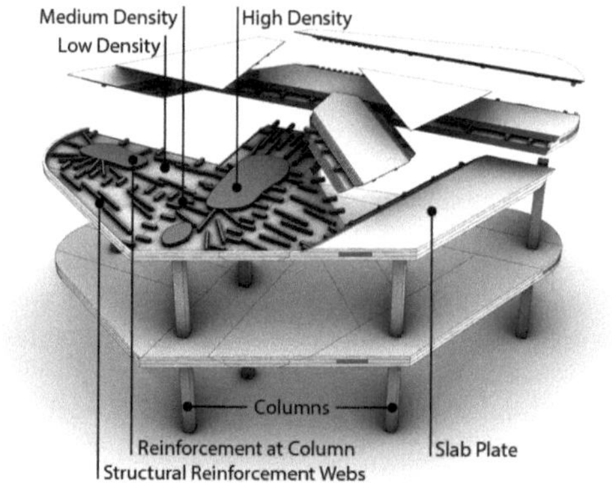

Figure 1
Variable Density Building System and its Components

SCOPE

The multi-level agent simulation at the core of the ABM method presented in this paper is best thought of as sequential arrangement of dependent agent systems, unlike a "nested" or otherwise conventionally hierarchical approach to ABM, where each agent is itself an agent system composed of "sub-agents"

(Minar et al. 1996). Each level of agent systems corresponds to a different kind of building element, not to a different storey in the building. At least conceptually, each storey in a multi-storey building could have its own agent systems at each level of the multi-level simulation. In this example, we will be simulating but a single floor level, while still utilising all levels in the multi-level agent simulation.

This paper presents and describes a method excluding a greater generalised methodology or a precise, benchmarked implementation. The necessary comparative studies are alluded to in the Discussion section of this paper.

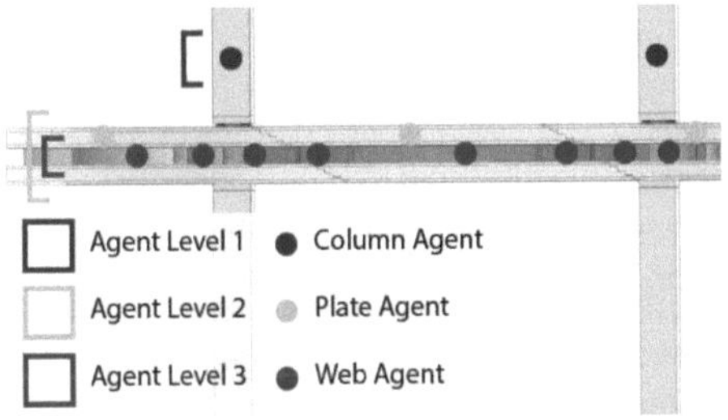

Figure 2
Multi-level Simulation Levels and their Agents

The discussion about the implementation of the ABM shown in this paper will focus on the lower two levels of the multi-level simulation: the arrangement of slab plates and their reinforcement. (Figure 2) It will not focus on the arrangement of columns. This is a separate process that is more closely tied to the architectural design of the building than its structural resolution. This process will need to directly consider architectural parameters, such as building use, making it a less suitable candidate for automation. Unlike the arrangement of plates and their reinforcements, it would be better handled with direct input from designers. To show the multi-level agent simulation, this paper will use a single pre-set configuration of columns, within a predefined slab boundary.

This paper will also show how the output from structural simulation is set as the agent environment, and how that environment is updated. The details of the structural simulations themselves are out of scope and will be examined in a future publication.

METHODS

Overview

The general method presented in this paper contains an iterative feedback loop between structural simulations and the agent systems at the different levels of a multi-level agent simulation. One or more agent systems, perhaps even of different varieties, can inhabit each level of the multi-level simulation. The agent systems at one level are run to convergence. The new state of dynamic equilibrium is given as an input to a structural simulation, which is then run. The results of the structural simulation update the agent environment for a subsequent level of agent systems. This is repeated until all agent systems have converged; that is to say, all the diverse building elements that make up a building system are satisfactorily arranged.

The different agent systems in this multi-level agent simulation are themselves defined by the type of building component their agents are simulating. These are Columns, Slab Plates, and Structural Reinforcement Webs, respectively. The behaviours exhibited by the different kinds of agents are specific to them and will be explained further in this paper.

An iterative loop between agent simulation and structural simulation was chosen instead of integrating the structural simulation within each iteration of the agent simulation. This allows for checking the converged results of each agent simulation for structural performance, as well as fabricability. The iterative loop also reduces the time it takes for each step of the agent simulation to compute.

Implementation

The ABM method is enacted in the design of a small, pavilion-scale multi-storey demonstrator. It was done so using Rhino 3D's Grasshopper [1], with the agent simulation, its constituent classes, and its iterative solver implemented in C#. Finite element analysis was performed SOFiSTiK [2]. The connection to the structural simualtion is beyond the scope of this paper.

The testing setup for the ABM method is so named because it allowed variations on the method to be tested and compared. It was designed around specific structural and architectural boundary conditions. The primary features are a) two-way spanning fields, b) a network arrangement of columns, and c) ample cantilevers and open corners. The columns are up to 7.5 m apart, they have varying relations to each other, and the cantilevers not only are up to 2 m long, but meet at corners smaller than 90, greater than 90, and much greater than 90 degrees.

The agent environment is a two-dimensional force field. Its attributes are a) a boundary shape, as a polyline, b) a 2D mesh approximating the surface defined by the boundary shape, c) a principal moment vector for each vertex of the mesh, and d) a scalar shear value for each vertex of the mesh. The mesh, the moment vectors, and the shear values will adapt over time, corresponding to a monolithic isotropic slab or a segmented anisotropic slab depending on the stage of the process. The ABM method begins with the initial definition of the environment using a single building outline. A low-resolution mesh surface is approximated to this boundary curve. The top level of the multi-level simulation arranges columns within the slab bounds. The columns so placed, along with the slab boundary, are the inputs for the first structural simulation. The first structural simulation produces a map of primary and secondary moment vectors and their scalar values. The moment maps are brought together to create a single principal moment field. (Figure 3) The previously flat, homogenous environment is updated with the newly produced moment field, giving it local directions in preparation for the second-level agent simulation.

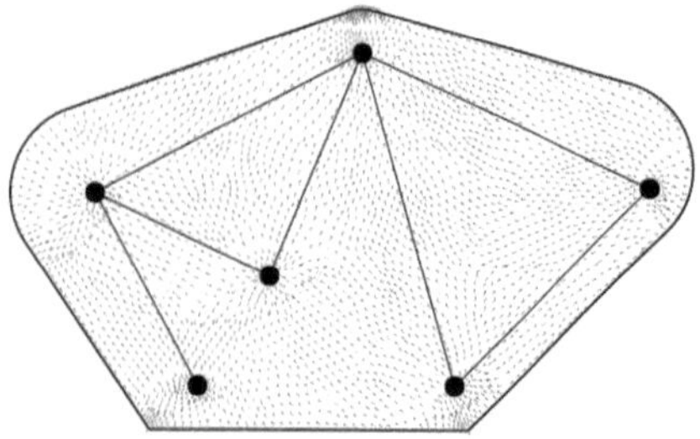

Figure 3
Principal Moment Field with adjusted Delaunay Mesh Edges

The second-level agent simulation subdivides the slab into slab plates. This simulation is discrete-event based, where agents add their behaviours as events to a queue to be executed. The column agents from the previous simulation remain in the field. The agents in this simulation are the segmented slab plates. Their primary attributes are a) their position in cartesian space, b) their primary direction as a unitized 2D vector, and c) their boundary shape as a polyline. Their positions are instantiated as the midpoints of the edges of Delaunay mesh based on the column points. Their primary direction is set as the direction of their respective mesh edge. The agent behaviours produce the boundary shape, which is instantiated without a value.

The first behaviour reduces the number of plates by removing any whose principal direction is beyond a given angle threshold from the principal moment at the nearest environment vertex. The second behaviour adjusts the location of the panel. A) If the agent is close enough to the edge of the slab perpendicular to its primary direction, it aligns itself to it. B) If a single panel could span the entire floor boundary, the agent centres itself. C) If it cannot span but is too close to the edge of slab in its primary direction, it will shift away from the edge. Finally, the initial shape of the subdivided plates is set by creating a rectangle whose length and width are defined by fabrication and construction constraints. (Figure 4) The third and final behaviour of the plate agents eliminates intersections between subdivided plates by hierarchically cutting their outlines down to size. The order by which agents pass their third behaviour into the event queue is set by the greatest moment length within by their boundary. The first plate is left as is. The subsequent plates check for intersections with all previous plates, and are trimmed accordingly, defining their final shape. Any leftover space within the environment boundary has a new agent instantiated at its area centroid. This agent adds its behaviours to the event queue, thereby establishing its closest moment direction, creating an initial shape of maximum fabricable size, and trimming itself using the bound-

Figure 4
Panel Position
Adjustment
Behaviours

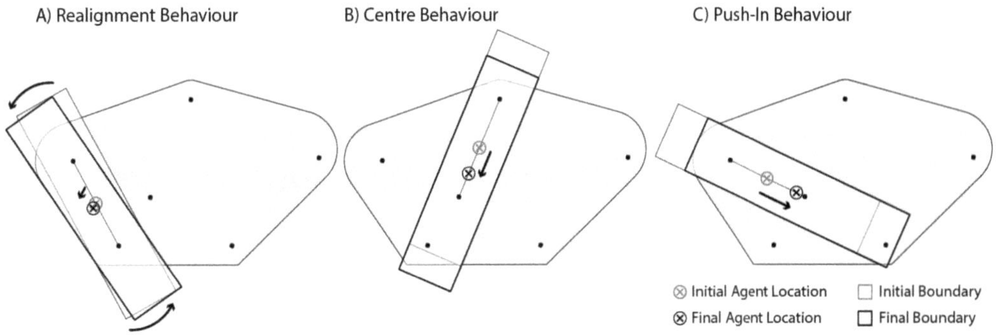

aries of all agents that came before it in the plate hierarchy.

The boundary shapes of all the plate agents are given as input to the second structural simulation. The mesh, the moment vectors, and the shear values of the Environemnt are replaced by the output of this structural simulation. Varying the density of the slab requires a higher resolution mesh than the definition of plate boundaries. High density areas around where the columns meet the slab are defined by smoothed and rebuilt curves that trace a threshold in the shear value map for greater fabricability. (Figure 5)

Figure 5
Shear Map and
subdivided Slab
Plates

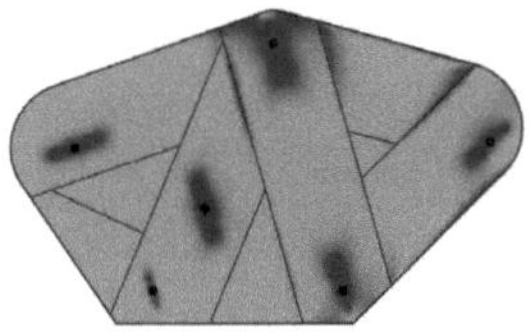

The third-level agent simulation places reinforcement within the slab. High-density areas around the columns and plate-to-plate joint widths reduce the available area for Structural Reinforcement Webs. The attributes of these Cartesian "web" agents are a) their cartesian position, b) their spanning direction as a unitized 2D vector, and c) their length, in mm. The designer sets a number of agents to populate the slab. This number is proportionally distributed into separate agent systems, one for each subdivided panel, based on its area. To begin, web agents are randomly populated with more agents in higher shear areas. Their first behaviour aims to distribute them more evenly, following a Lloyd's algorithm weighted to have more movement in areas with less shear, and less movement in areas with more shear. This algorithm is run until either the smallest distance between two points crosses a threshold, or a maximum number of iterations is reached. The second behaviour generates the linear webs. The agents set their spanning direction from the principal moment vector closest to their position. The initial length of the webs is set globally by the designer and verified by the fourth structural simulation. In future, specific lengths for each web could be set with a feedback loop to the fourth structural simulation, perhaps using reinforcement learning or genetic algorithms. The third behaviour checks for fabricability by resolving webs that intersect or are too close to each other. If the position of two webs is within a set tolerance, a new web agent is instantiated at the midpoint between them, and they are removed from the simulation. The new agent performs the second behaviour again, but with its length set as the distance between the two previous webs' furthest endpoints, up to given threshold.

The design method concludes with the addition of connection elements at the boundaries between adjacent plates, and a third and final structural simulation. Parameters and variables throughout the entire method can be altered until the results of the third structural simulation are satisfactory. The agents and their semantic data, including weight, gripping location, materiality, etc. can then be prepared for robotic prefabricated assembly.

DISCUSSION, AND OUTLOOK

The method presented in this paper will be validated in the near future by the construction of a small prototype in whose design it was implemented.

To further define the "agents as building components" approach to ABMs in architecture, and to make a multi-level agent simulation such as the one shown in this paper more applicable, a robust systematisation of building components and how they relate to each other is necessary.

The method outlined in this paper (cf. Figure 6) allows for the complex arrangement of building components that could not have been possible by hand, nor by single-objective optimisation techniques. Not only does the optimisation of a single element, be it the shape of a panel or the rotation of a web, have the potential to negatively impact the performance of all other such components around it, but there is no single nor set of parameters to optimise. There are, however, multiple ways of organising complex systems, including: ABMs without a changing environment, agent distribution using only changing global information (without local agent behaviour), or reinforcement learning. The viability of other computational arrangement would be worth investigating.

Past experiments in machine learning have demonstrated that minimising the domain-specific knowledge embedded in a system often leads to better solutions in the long run (Sutton 2019). This is a strong indication that methods such as reinforcement learning may produce more performative outcomes. A future study comparing other possible design methods would help determine the efficacy of the current method, which combines both local agent behaviour and global information through the changing agent environment.

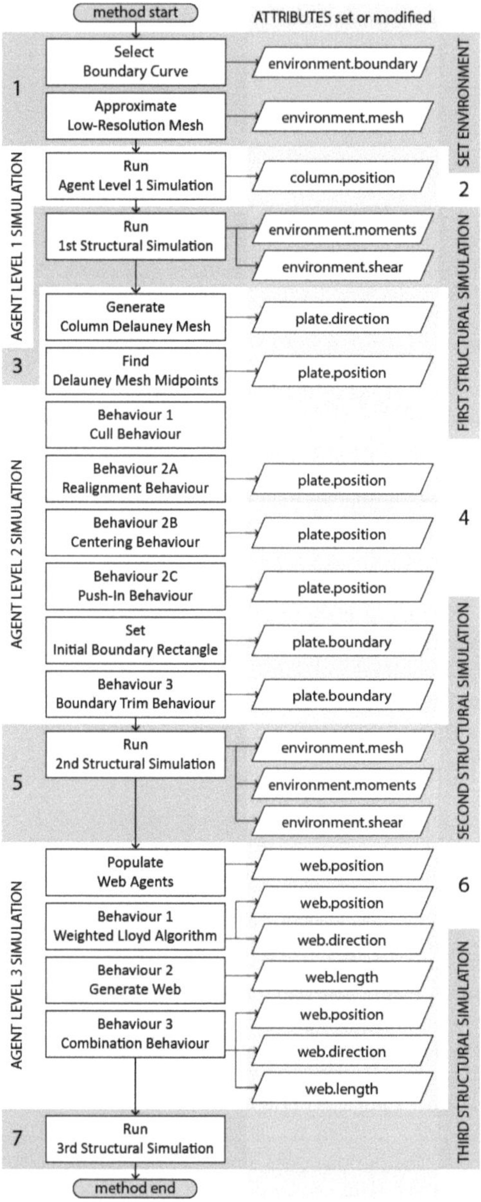

Figure 6
Method and Agent Attributes

In this paper had each agent system converges before the next begins its simulation. It would be worth investigating whether it would be possible to run all types of agents in a single concurrent agent system. Simultaneous simulation would not only affect the relations of the agents, but how structural simulations are incorporated into the agent system.

A future paper should take a further look at how columns could be arranged into a non-orthogonal network with a method that accounts for structural considerations and architectural intention, such as space planning and building services, while allowing direct input from a designer. The linking of structural analysis models to an agent-based model was a key facilitator in this paper's method. This symbiotic relationship should be investigated from the structural perspective.

Finally, this paper's case study took direct feedback from structural considerations, while curated feedback was taken from fabrication considerations. A future application of a similar system would do best to take both direct and curated feedback from both fabrication and statics. It would also benefit from taking direct and curated feedback from other disciplines, such as building physics, and life cycle analysis.

ACKNOWLEDGEMENTS

The research has been partially supported by the Deutsche Forschungsgemeinschaft (DFG, German Research Foundation) under Germany's Excellence Strategy - EXC 2120/1 - 390831618.

The authors would like to express their gratitude towards their fellow investigators: Cristobal Tapia and Dr. Simon Aicher of the Materials Testing Institute, and Theresa Müller and Prof. Philip Leistner of the Institute for Acoustics and Building Physics. The authors would like to thank all the students were involved in the master's program "Integrative Technologies and Architectural Design Research" (ITECH) at the University of Stuttgart within which the presented method was developed: Kiril Bejoulev, TzuYing Chen, Ryan Daley, Takwa ElGamal, Grant Galloway, August Lehrecke, Daniel Locatelli, Madie Rasanani, Parisa Shafiee, Anand Shah, Lior Skoury, Cody Tucker, Xiliu Yang, Max Zorn, Ingo Haller, Francesca Maisto, Nils Opgenorth, Ekin Sahin, Lorin Samija, Lena Strobel, Håkon Toth, Simon Treml, Julian Trummer, with support from Omar Abdelhady, Yousef Elshafie, Pai-Yi Huang, Xinyou Kou, Jiaxin Li, Simon Reuter, Alice Roy. Special thanks to Research Associate Daniel Sonntag.

All image credits (C) ICD/ITKE University of Stuttgart

REFERENCES

Alvarez, M, Wagner, HJ, Groenewolt, A, Krieg, OD, Lyjanek, O, Sonntag, D, Bechert, S, Aldinger, L, Menges, A and Knippers, J 2019 'The Buga Wood Pavilion: Integrative Interdisciplinary Advancements of Digital Timber Architecture', *Ubiquity and autonomy: Paper proceedings of the 39th annual conference of the Association for Computer Aided Design in Architecture : ACADIA 2019, October 24-26, 2019*, the University of Texas at Austin, United States, pp. 490-499

Carmichael, T and Hadžikadić, M 2019, 'The Fundamentals of Complex Adaptive Systems', in Carmichael, T, Collins, AJ and Hadžikadić, M (eds) 2019, *Complex Adaptive Systems*, Springer, Cham, pp. 1-16

Churkina, G, Organschi, A, Reyer, CPO, Ruff, A, Vinke, K, Liu, Z, Reck, BK, Graedel, TE and Schellnhuber, HJ 2020, 'Buildings as a global carbon sink', *Nature Sustainability*, 3(4), pp. 269-276

Claus, M 2020, November 25, *Geklebte Verbindungen von Brettsperrholz-Platten in der Nebentragrichtung unter Verwendung von CNC/robotisch gefrästen Anschlussleisten aus Furnierschichtholz*, Master's Thesis, Materialprüfungsanstalt, Universität Stuttgart

Dohmen, P and Rüdenauer, K 2007, 'Digital Chains in Modern Architecture', in Kieferle, JB (eds) 2007, *Predicting the future*, Kanne Graph. Betrieb, Ginsheim-Gustavsburg, pp. 801-804

Fischer, O, Lang, W, Winter, S and Dotzler, C (eds) 2019, *Hybridbau: Holzaussenwände*, Detail Business Information GmbH, München

Foster, RM and Ramage, MH 2017, 'Briefing: Super tall timber – Oakwood Tower', *Proceedings of the Institution of Civil Engineers - Construction Materials*, 170(3), pp. 118-122

Foster, RM and Reynolds, TPS 2018, 'Lightweighting with Timber: An Opportunity for More Sustainable Urban Densification', *Journal of Architectural Engineering*, 24(1), p. 02518001

Groenewolt, A, Schwinn, T, Nguyen, L and Menges, A 2018, 'An interactive agent-based framework

for materialization-informed architectural design', *Swarm Intelligence*, 12(2), pp. 155-186
Hugues, T, Steiger, L and Weber, J 2004, *Timber Construction: Details, Products, Case Studies*, Birkhäuser; Edition Detail, Basel; Munich
Huß, W, Kaufmann, M and Merz, K 2019, *Building in Timber - Room Modules*, Detail, Munich
Kaufmann, H, Krötsch, S and Winter, S 2018, *Manual of multi-storey timber construction*, Detail Business Information, Munich
Krause, J 1997 'Agent Generated Architecture', *ACADIA 97: Representation & Design*, Cincinnati, OH, United States, pp. 63-70
Krötsch, S and Huß, W 2018, 'Structural components and elements', in Kaufmann, H, Krötsch, S and Winter, S (eds) 2018, *Manual of multi-storey timber construction*, Detail Business Information, Munich, pp. 50-69
Kuzmanovska, I, Gasparri, E, Tapias Monné, D and Aitchison, M 2018 'Tall Timber Buildings: Emerging trends and typologies', *2018 World Conference on Timber Engineering*, Seoul, Korea, Republic of
Lehne, J and Preston, F 2018, *Making Concrete Change: Innovation in Low-carbon Cement and Concrete*, Chatham House, The Royal Institute of International Affairs, Cambridge, UK
Levitis, DA, Lidicker, WZ and Freund, G 2009, 'Behavioural biologists don't agree on what constitutes behaviour', *Animal behaviour*, 78(1), pp. 103-110
Lloyd, S 1982, 'Least squares quantization in PCM', *IEEE Transactions on Information Theory*, 28(2), pp. 129-137
Macal, CM 2016, 'Everything you need to know about agent-based modelling and simulation', *Journal of Simulation*, 10(2), pp. 144-156
Macal, CM and North, MJ 2010, 'Tutorial on agent-based modelling and simulation', *Journal of Simulation*, 4(3), pp. 151-162
Minar, N, Burkhart, R, Langton, C and Askenazi, M 1996, *The Swarm Simulation System: A Toolkit for Building Multi-Agent Simulations*, Swarm [Santa Fe Institute], Santa Fe
Ramage, MH, Burridge, H, Busse-Wicher, M, Fereday, G, Reynolds, T, Shah, DU, Wu, G, Yu, L, Fleming, P, Densley-Tingley, D, Allwood, J, Dupree, P, Linden, PF and Scherman, O 2017, 'The wood from the trees: The use of timber in construction', *Renewable and Sustainable Energy Reviews*, 68, pp. 333-359
Schwinn, T 2021, February 25, *A Systematic Approach for Developing Agent-based Architectural Design Models of Segmented Shells: Towards Autonomously Learned Goal-oriented Agent Behaviors: [PhD Presentation]*, Ph.D. Thesis, Institute for Computational Design and Construction, University of Stuttgart
Schwinn, T and Menges, A 2015, 'Fabrication Agency: Landesgartenschau Exhibition Hall', *Architectural Design*, 85(5), pp. 92-99
Sutton, R 2019 'The Bitter Lesson', *Incomplete Ideas*, Department of Computer Science, University of Alberta, Edmonton, Alberta, p. http://www.incompleteideas.net/IncIdeas/BitterLesson.html
Tamke, M and Thomsen, MR 2018, 'Complex Modelling', *International Journal of Architectural Computing*, 16(2), pp. 87-90
Theodoropoulos, GK, Minson, R, Ewald, R and Lees, M 2018, 'Simulation Engines for Multi-Agent Systems', in Uhrmacher, A and Weyns, D (eds) 2018, *Multi-agent systems: Simulation and applications*, CRC Press, Boca Raton, FL, United States, pp. 77-105
Thomsen, MR 2019, 'Complex Modelling: Questioning the Infrastructures of Information Modelling', in Beesley, P, Bonnemaison, S and Hastings, S (eds) 2019, *Living Architecture Systems Group white papers, 2019*, Riverside Architectural Press, Toronto, pp. 265-280
United, Nations 2019, *World urbanization prospects: 2018 : highlights*, United Nations, New York
Vasey, L, Baharlou, E, D"orstelmann, M, Koslowski, V, Prado, M, Schieber, G, Menges, A and Knippers, J 2015, 'Behavioral Design and Adaptive Robotic Fabrication of a Fiber Composite Compression Shell with Pneumatic Formwork', in Combs, L and Perry, C (eds) 2015, *Computational ecologies: Proceedings of the 35th Annual Conference of the Association for Computer Aided Design in Architecture (ACADIA)*, University of Cincinnati, Cincinnati OH, pp. 297-309
VDI, VDE May 2018, *Multi-agent systems in industrial automation: Fundamentals (VDI/VDE 2653)*, Verein Deutsche Ingenieure, Verband der Elektrotechnik Elektronik Informationstechnik
Wagner, HJ, Alvarez, M, Gronewolt, A and Menges, A 2020, 'Towards digital automation flexibility in large-scale timber construction: integrative robotic prefabrication and co-design of the BUGA Wood Pavilion', *Construction Robotics*, 4(3-4), pp. 187-204
Wagner, HJ, Chai, H, Guo, Z, Menges, A and Yuan, PF 2020 'Towards an On-site Fabrication System for Bespoke, Unlimited and Monolithic Timber Slabs', *IEEE/RSJ International Conference on Intelligent Robots and Systems (IROS)*, Las Vegas, NV, USA
Willmann, J, Knauss, M, Bonwetsch, T, Apolinarska, AA, Gramazio, F and Kohler, M 2016, 'Robotic timber construction — Expanding additive fabrication to new dimensions', *Automation in Construction*, 61, pp. 16-23
De Wolf, T and Holvoet, T 2004 'Emergence and Self-Organisation: a statement of similarities and differences', *Proc. of the 2nd International Workshop on Engineering Self*, Leuven, Belgium, pp. 96-110
Zöllig, S, Frangi, A, Franke, S and Muster, M 2016 'Timber Structures 3.0: New Technology for Multi-Axial, Slim, High Performance Timber Structures', *World Conference of Timber Engineering 2016*, Vienna, Austria
[1] www.rhino3d.com
[2] www.sofistik.de

Digital design for sustainable buildings

Protection by Generative Design

Designing for full-culm bamboo durability using sunlight-hours modelling in Ladybug

John Osmond Naylor[1]
[1] *University of Newcastle upon Tyne*
[1] *j.naylor73@newcastle.ac.uk*

High yield cultivated construction materials such as bamboo could reduce our overconsumption of concrete and sand. Full-culm bamboo has low natural durability which in construction makes it imperative that the design affords protection from rain and sunlight. This paper presents and advocates a generative design workflow for full-culm bamboo using widely applicable architectural design software. A series of trials were carried out to modify the geometry of a planar truss and gablet roof with input parameters tested to determine the optimal roof surface area which could provide full solar protection at three different sites. This algorithmic process tested both straight and curved poles. Depending on the site, when compared to a symmetrical uniform 45 degree overhang, less or greater roof surface area is required in order to provide full solar protection. The use of curved poles and an asymmetrical truss could maintain full protection yet reduce the roof surface area further.

Keywords: *Full-culm bamboo, Generative design approach, Ladybug, Architectural design, Digital materiality*

INTRODUCTION

By 2050, some 50% of the world's population will live in the tropics (State of the Tropics, 2020). Tropical Low-to Middle-Income Countries (LMIC's) have a shortage of housing which lacks structural quality and durability (UN-Habitat, 2016) yet have a latent opportunity to utilise locally sourced bamboo (Lobovikov, Paudel, Piazza, Ren, & Wu, 2007). Our global construction industry has a decisive role to play in climate-change mitigation with annual cement production accounting for around 8% of anthropogenic carbon dioxide emissions (Lehne & Preston, 2018). Replacing conventional materials with bio-based materials that store carbon can be one solution to help us reduce our overconsumption of concrete and sand (Pomponi, Hart, Arehart, & D'Amico, 2020; UNEP, 2019; van der Lugt, 2017). In many regions of the world, timber will most likely never be able to provide the sustainable alternative we need. Given the speed of growth and quantity required, extraction could have a deleterious effect on ecosystems (Pomponi et al., 2020). Therefore we need to develop the use of high yield cultivated construction materials such as bamboo (van der Lugt, 2017). Bamboo can absorb carbon dioxide and stabilise slopes to tackle the effects of deforestation (Tardio, Mickovski, Stokes, & Devkota, 2017).

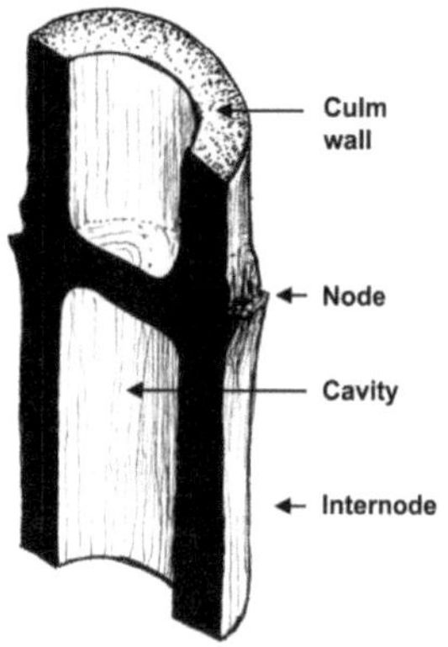

Figure 1
Sketch section and terminology of a bamboo culm through the node. Sketch by author.

It can be a challenge however to incorporate bamboo into contemporary design and construction practices. This is due to the natural variability of bamboo between the over 1200 species of bamboo, individual plants, and individual culms. Within culms there is a non-regular distribution of node locations, a tapered diameter of the bamboo culm, and a reduced width of the culm wall over the length of the culm. Even within the same species, mechanical properties can differ since bamboo grown in drier areas and on slopes may have a higher fibre density and increased strength properties (Liese & Tang, 2015b). One response to this has been to standardise the material through the manufacture of Engineered Bamboo Products (EPBs) (Sharma, Gatoo, Bock, Mulligan, & Ramage, 2015). However, the greater challenge is to use the raw form of bamboo, *full-culm bamboo*. In doing so, we can ensure that the most affordable and sustainable form of bamboo is enfranchised (Harries, Sharma, & Richard, 2012). Another challenge for architects when designing with bamboo, and the focus of this paper, is the low natural durability of bamboo (Kaminski, Lawrence, Trujillo, & King, 2016). Bamboo is more prone to decay than timber. Bamboo does not develop reaction wood, and though there are minor amounts of resins, waxes and tannins, none of these have enough toxicity to provide any natural durability (Kumar, Shukla, Dev, & Dobriyal, 1994). Bamboo is hollow (Figure 1) and with typically thin walls, this means that a small amount of decay can have a significant effect on the bamboo (Janssen, 2000). There are abiotic factors which can affect bamboo in a structure (Liese & Tang, 2015a). If bamboo is exposed to the sun and rain and in contact with soil the lifespan of the bamboo in the structure can be only 1-3 years (Janssen, 2000). Changes in temperature and humidity may produce steep moisture gradients between surface and inner layers, and direct exposure to sun causes unbalanced and repeated swelling and shrinkage (Liese & Tang, 2015a) (Figure 2).

Figure 2
Full-culm bamboo poles cracked and showing signs of mould due to exposure of excess moisture and bleaching due to sunlight exposure. Photograph taken by author in 2020.

UV and visible light radiation also causes photodegradation which breaks down bonds of the lignocellulosic polymer causing the bamboo surface to turn grey and coarse (Liese & Tang, 2015a). Such processes have contributed to a societal attitude of bamboo as a temporary *"poor man's timber"*. When bamboo is exposed or inappropriately applied in a structure and degrades, bamboo will often be blamed for the action of the architect. As Janssen writes, *"No chemical treatment will be good enough to solve the problems caused by incorrect design"*. (Janssen, 2000). This is a rallying call for architects to make sure that fundamental to any design process for bamboo, the bamboo is protected from rain and UV light. This is a concept known as *protection by design*. The title of this paper refers to this phrase. Large roof overhangs provide protection to bamboo members from wind driven rain (Figure 3), with a rule of thumb of 45 degrees (Kaminski, Lawrence, & Trujillo, 2016a). The angle of wind driven rain is largely consistent worldwide, however the sun angle is not.

Figure 3
A large roof overhang provides protection to the structural full-culm bamboo members. ZERI Pavilion, Simon Velez, 1999. Sketch by author based on the ZERI Pavilion image from the book, Grow your own house: Simón Vélez and bamboo architecture (Vélez et al., 2000).

In some locations and orientations the overhang of 45 degrees will always be required to protect against wind driven rain but this may not provide enough solar protection particularly if a site is further away from the equator. A design decision can be to cover the bamboo behind adobe or cement mortar such as bahareque construction techniques (Kaminski, Lawrence, et al., 2016a). However for cost, aesthetic or biophilic reasons the designer may decide to make the full-culm bamboo visible. There are impressive examples of buildings with structural full-culm bamboo visible externally such as the Amairis Factory in Puerto Caldas, Colombia, by Ruta 4 [4], or the ZERI Pavilion, by Simon Velez in Manizales, Colombia (Figure 3). Conversely, where rainfall is low and characteristic of a dry steppe climate or subtropical ridges, this overhang can be surplus to needs. Large overhangs can also reduce the occupiable footprint of a building if the necessary extension of the roof requires an encroachment into a neighbouring site. Large overhangs can also be aesthetically cumbersome and also prone to wind uplift. Whenever bamboo is exposed, the design should afford the bamboo protection to maintain its structural and aesthetic properties.

Computational design processes and full-culm bamboo

Generative Design refers to a design approach that uses algorithms to generate designs (Caetano, Santos, & Leitão, 2020). Such processes save time and allow the testing of various iterations in order to find a more optimal design solution (Jabi, 2013). The process of *form-finding* emerges from analysis with the output exclusively determined by function (Laiserin, 2008). In the case of this paper, generative design tools applied to the architectural design process are designed to deliver an optimal design output which provides full protection from sun and rain with minimal material usage and minimal cost on a site by site basis. A wider challenge of computational design tools with their great accuracies and full-culm bamboo is the difficulty in accurately modelling an anisotropic material with natural variability (Crolla, 2017; Qi et al., 2021). In 2005, Willis and Woodward suggested design parameters such as material flaws, grain directions and inconsistent densities will make it difficult to achieve a direct correlation between digital data and a constructed building, but note this gap between the building and the model will continue to narrow (Willis & Woodward, 2005). Far from trying to bridge this gap, mainstream architectural design practice operates on *"reduced matter-models designed to behave like pristine, controlled numerical milieu"* (Kwinter, 1996, p. 70). Using a generative design approach to design with full-culm bamboo is situated in a wider discourse within architectural design crystalised by two terms. *Digital materiality* as coined by Fabio Gramazio and Matthias Kohler (Gramazio & Kohler, 2008), and *digital materiallurgy* coined by Adam Fure in 2011 (Fure, 2011). Kohler and Gramazio use the term *digital materiality* to suggest a departure from the design of purely form, but a design that is informed by the constructive organisations and methods of implementation (Willmann, Gramazio, Kohler, & Langenberg, 2013). Instead of realising a design or an image, a comprehensive design and building process is conceived. Constructive principles can be determined that define the production of architectural components as interrelated production steps (Willmann et al., 2013). *Digital materiallurgy* (a play on the ancient craft of metallurgy) builds on this and suggests to intentionally cede limited design control to the material's innate ability to produce and to take advantage of unexpected formal and material complexity (Fure, 2011). Such an attitude can be the pivot point around which we use computational tools with materials with natural variability, where contrary to materials waiting to be formed a *"productive slack between materials and digital form"* emerges (Fure, 2011). Examples of these two terms in use can be seen in the ongoing movement to incorporate bamboo into a design process which utilises computational design tools. This happens on a spectrum of scales from mapping the pole, to looking to model the variable nature of bamboo as part of the building system. Before I highlight some examples and in order to better situate the design process I detail in this paper, I have listed what I believe to be two ways in which bamboo is used in a computational design process (Figure 4). The first is where an inventory of pre-selected bamboo is mapped in order to establish parameters for the design, and the second is where an algorithm determines the specification of bamboo required. In other words a specification as an input (Type 1), or a specification as an output (Type 2). I have split Type 1 into A and B, where B looks to compensate for the variability of bamboo by designing additive components.

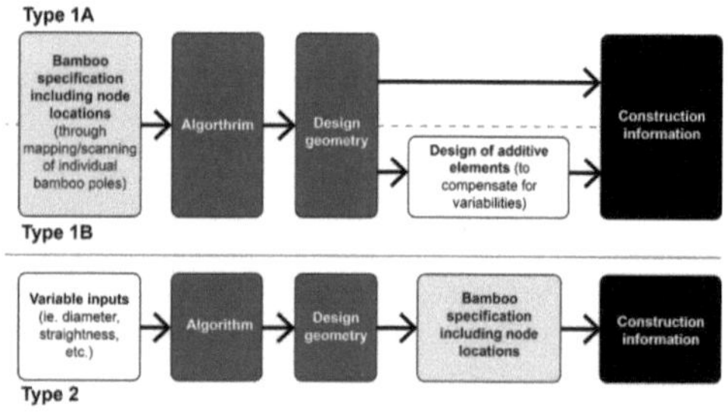

Figure 4
Conceptual representation of a categorisation of how computational design processes address the natural variability of full-culm bamboo in the design process.

An example of Type 1A is the paper *BIM Bamboo*. Here the conceptual details of a framework are presented which use digital modelling and robotic fabrication to enfranchise bamboo poles by mapping them locally (each individual pole) and designing for each distinct characteristic, as opposed to negating the natural variability (Lorenzo, Lee, Oliva-Salinas, & Ontiveros-Hernandez, 2017). An example of Type 1B is the paper *Working with Uncertainties: An Adaptive Fabrication Workflow for Bamboo Structures* which uses vision augmentation research to respond to the deviations between bamboo as built- and designed form in real-time so as to compensate for cumulative deviations caused by material uncertainties (Qi et al., 2021). An example of looking to implement global variabilities of bamboo into a design process, Type 2, is the ZCB Pavilion by the Chinese University of Hong Kong built in October 2015 in Kowloon Bay, Hong Kong (Crolla, 2017). This was an event space for the Zero Carbon Building (ZCB) with a forty-yard span (Crolla, 2018). A physical scale model built from bamboo was brought into Rhinoceros 3D and Grasshopper using the Kangaroo plug in. Bending forces present in the physical model were abstracted into vector forces and applied on a discretised curve network. The digital setup would find its force equilibrium in comparable emerging geometries (Crolla, 2017). Unlike those processes I classify as Type 1, the ZCB Pavilion workflow produced a digital emulation model which embodied variability, not an accurate model of individually digitised culms with their local variances that would be replicated. Using the gablet roof type as the basis of this study, the goal of this paper is to advocate both awareness for protection by design for bamboo structures and demonstrate the applicability and efficiencies of computational design tools when working with bamboo. This paper is not about mapping the eccentricities of bamboo in order to organise their role in a building system. The design process in this paper is situated between Type 1 and 2. The algorithm builds immaterial geometry as a representative roof form in order to test the shading performance against cylindrical geometry which represents the bamboo poles which would be visible externally. This model can be used as both a quantification tool to suggest the curvature of the bamboo that should be used, but the model also allows the input of material parameters. These inputs attempt to standardise pole parameters through allowing the ability to adapt to curvatures and pole diameters in a global manner. The question of building future tolerances into the construction information would occur after the steps identified in Figure 4.

Tools

The software used in this study are widely used in the architecture profession. Firstly Rhinoceros 3D (Version 7) which is a three-dimensional computer graphics and computer-aided design software [2]. Secondly, Grasshopper [1] which is a graphical algorithm editor integrated with Rhinoceros 3D. Grasshopper is used to build generative algorithms. Ladybug [3] is an open source environmental plugin for Grasshopper. Ladybug allows the designer to explore the direct relationship between site specific environmental data through the importation of standard EnergyPlus Weather (EPW) files, and the generation of graphical data outputs which can also act as inputs into the geometry building process (Sadeghipour Roudsari & Pak, 2013). Galapagos is an evolutionary solver embedded within Grasshopper. It is a heuristic solver, which are used when there are a large number of variables to consider and an exact solution cannot be found so a best fitness to the problem is sought.

METHODOLOGY

Constructing the roof geometry in the algorithm

This process starts by drawing a closed quadrilateral shape in Rhinoceros which should have sides no larger than 6m and this *'closed curve'* is assigned in Grasshopper. This allows the roof geometry to be built over any quadrilateral site. The first edge of this quadrilateral will define the location of the planar truss and the truss will be constructed perpendicular to the base plane. The design of the planar truss is based on a design in Building with Bamboo, by Gernot Minke (Minke, 2016). This truss is suggested to be no more than a span of 8m. The choice of a planar truss for roof construction has many advantages for buildability. A planar truss can be built flat on the ground then raised and pivoted into place. This provides a safer work environment due to less working at height.

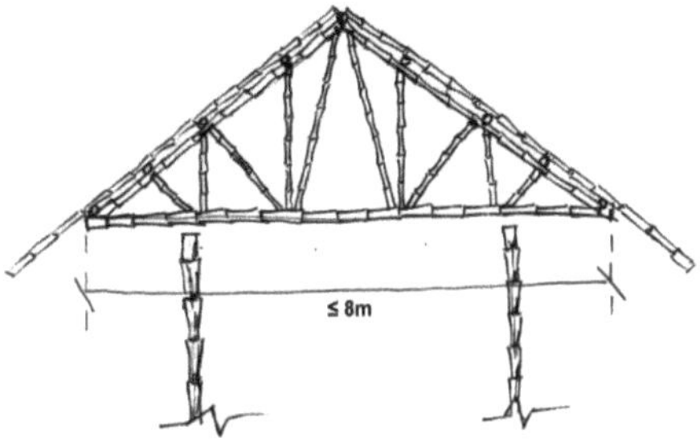

Figure 5
Planar truss spanning up to 8m (Minke, 2016, p. 51). Sketch by author based on truss design referenced from Building with Bamboo by Gernot Minke, 2016.

The truss (Figure 5) is modelled, within the algorithm generating secondary members. Producing the geometry for the individual poles in the truss will allow for drawings to be produced which show bamboo elements to cut with node and bolt locations. This truss defines the transverse section of the roof geometry, where this truss will be replicated and arrayed along the length of the building. The roof type used as the basis of this study (Figure 6), is known in the UK as a Dutch gable roof or gablet roof. For straightforwardness this is the terminology I use in this paper. There are examples of this roof design present in Kerala (Heston, 1996), and Indonesia, known as a Javanese *kampung roof* (Samodra, 2009). A conceptual representation for this process is shown in (Figure 8).

Input parameters

The algorithm which generated the gablet roof geometry was built with a series of variable input parameters (Figure 6): (1) The peak height of the roof truss in meters; (2) The position of the ridge line as a percentage of the width of the building; (3) The height of the gable as a percentage of the height of the roof truss (Input parameter 1); (4) The width of the roof in meters; (5) The depth of the roof overhang in meters which is mirrored on the opposite edge; (6)

The height of the arc segment as a percentage out of straightness which defines the curved rafters; and the additional length of the overhang (each opposite edge can be independently input). (7A) is the extension in meters of the straight rafters in Trial 1, and (7B) is the extension of the arc of the curved rafters used in Trial 2 and 3. Within the input parameter 7A and 7B, minimum values can be set to ensure that the 45 degree guideline roof overhang is maintained, if required. Input parameter 2 allows the truss to become asymmetrical to assist in finding the optimal roof geometry and surface area.

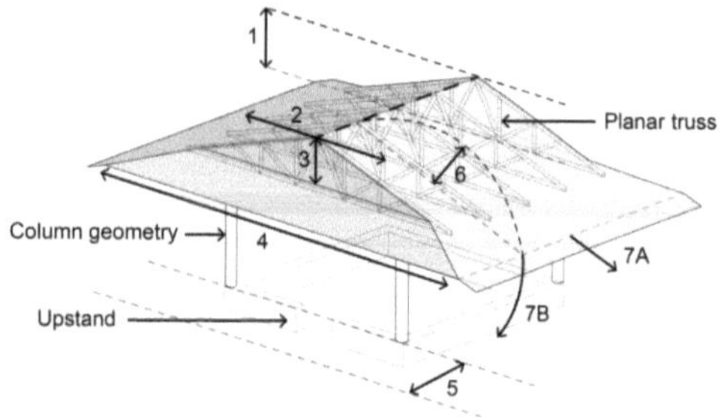

Figure 6
Parameters of the gablet roof design which are input into the algorithm in order to define the gablet roof geometry.

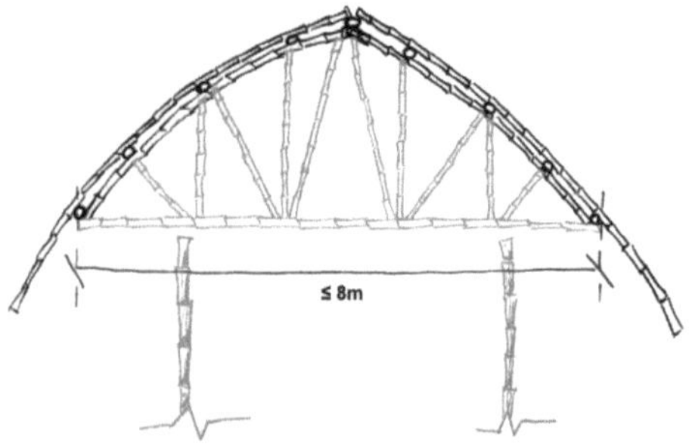

Figure 7
Planar truss design from Figure 5 spanning up to 8m (Minke, 2016, p. 51), with rafters replaced with curved members. Sketch by author, referencing truss design from Building with Bamboo by Gernot Minke, 2016.

Considering the curvature of bamboo culms

Bamboo has a natural arch in growth yet straight poles are often used. This can render the majority of the available bamboo stock an unused latent asset, pushing up the price of available poles and creating an architecture which seeks to find bamboo which fits the design, rather than designing for the natural state of bamboo. The use of curved poles can both perform an aesthetic and performative role. It could be the case that we want to use a species of bamboo which is generally more curved than another. In Trial 1, the algorithm negates any curvature of the bamboo, assuming that the bamboo that would be used in construction would be less than 1% out of straightness (Kaminski, Lawrence, & Trujillo, 2016b). Using curved poles as rafters (Figure 7) is later implemented in the algorithm and in Trial 2 and 3, this is compared to the results of the Trial 1 environmental analysis. Trial 2, generates curved rafters with a 5% out of straightness and Trial 3, connects the input parameters for the rafter curvature to the Evolutionary Solver in order to let the algorithm suggest the optimal curvature of rafters we should use in order to reduce the surface area of the roof.

Selected climates and optimisation methodology

In order to run the solar hours study in Grasshopper we need a series of input geometry and components which are provided in Grasshopper through the Ladybug plug-in (Ladybug Tools LLC, 2020). The geometry to be exposed to the solar study (the bamboo columns), the geometry which will provide the shade, known as the *Context* (the roof), and the locations of the Sun we wish to test which are available through the Ladybug component *'Ladybug_-SunPath'*. This generates a 3D sun path in the Rhinoceros 3D window and with the sun path oriented east to west as default. In all tests in this study the building is positioned north/south, however this can be easily changed by rotating the sun path as necessary. A file path container and the *'ImportEPW'* component is used to link this algorithm to an EPW file. Three sites were chosen to reflect a variety of geographies in which bamboo could be locally sourced and utilised. These were Kunming, China, which is north of the tropics, Bengaluru, India, situated between the Tropic of Cancer and the Equator, and La Libertad, Ecuador, which will be exposed to equatorial sunlight but is characterised by a local steppe climate with little rainfall throughout the year and proximity to local bamboo resources. For Kunming and Bengaluru, the 45 degree guideline roof overhang is set as a minimum value in input 7 given the protection required for rainfall and the script looks to validate or add to this in order to provide full protection from UV light. In La Libertad, given the steppe climate and lack of rainfall, the goal here is to optimise and potentially reduce the roof overhang therefore there is no minimum value set for input 7. EPW weather files were used for each of these three locations. Hourly sun locations for each of these sites were taken from 10:00 to 16:00 for each solstice (21st June and 21st December), which is when the sun would be at extreme angles. This information as well as the input geometries were input into the *'SunlightHoursAnalysis'* component which ran the calculation and output the combined hours of sunlight for both periods and dates.

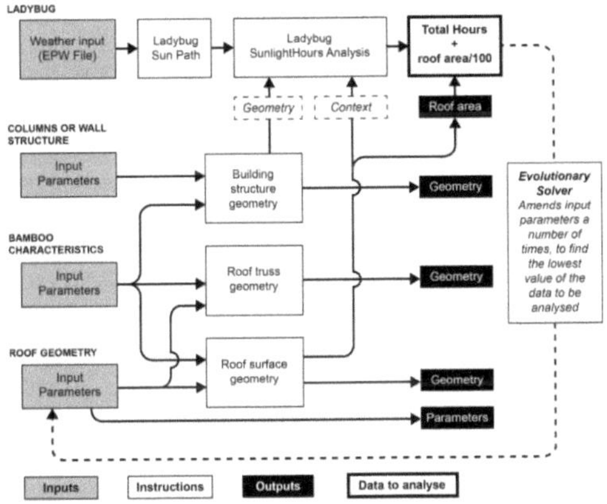

Figure 8
Conceptual representation of the generative design process in this paper, based on Laiserin (2008) and (Tedeschi, 2014).

The optimisation methodology involved the Galapagos evolutionary solver running for 100 steps, with 50 iterations per step, with an additional 50 iterations in the first step. Therefore 5,050 total iterations. The objective function is the minimum value for: one hundredth the value for the roof area plus the hours of direct sunlight on the bamboo poles. The set of variables which define the gablet roof geometry and the objective function are each defined by a range, a start and an end value. The variable sliders which were input as part of the *'genome'* to find this objective function differed in each of the 3 trials. These are referenced individually for each of the three trials in this study.

Baseline geometry: Roof with 45 degree overhang. As a baseline roof geometry to compare the studies to, a gablet roof is modelled which maintains a uniform overhang on all sides of the building of 45 degrees.

Trial 1: Optimised roof using straight poles. For Trial 1, all members in the truss and roof rafters are straight. In this trial, input parameter 6 and 7B (Figure 6) are not used.

Trial 2: Optimised roof with percentage straightness as an input. The goal of Trial 2 and Trial 3 is to compare a roof design with curved rafters to the roof design with straight poles in Trial 1. In Trial 2 the user can input the % out of straightness value that is required. This can be determined from the available material. In this case 5% has been used.

Trial 3: Optimised roof with percentage straightness as an output. It could be the case that we want to find the optimal roof area prior to selecting the bamboo poles we will use in construction. Therefore in Trial 3, the inputs which define the straightness of the bamboo poles used as rafters were input into the Evolutionary Solver to find the most optimal curvature of pole to use.

RESULTS AND ANALYSIS

The resultant geometry is shown in Figure 9 and the resultant values are shown in Table 1. It is interesting to note that in Kunming where the uniform 45 degree overhang was tested, there were still parts of the columns that received hours of direct solar exposure. In order to provide full shade in Kunming, the roof was required to be larger than the uniform baseline roof geometry. In Bengaluru the algorithm validated the required 45 degree overhang as providing enough solar protection. In La Libertad, where the dry climate meant we could overlook the 45 degree guideline roof overhang, the roof was found to

Roof type	Location (EPW file used)	% out of straightness of rafters (%) (Input 6)		Truss height (m) (Input 1)	Roof surface area (sqm)	Change in roof area compared to baseline roof area (sqm)	Max. daily hours of solar exposure to full-culm bamboo columns (hours)
		West	East				
Baseline – Uniform 45 degree roof overhang	Kunming	N/A		1m	114.14	N/A	< 6
	Bengaluru	N/A		1m	114.14	N/A	0
	La Libertad*	N/A		1m	114.14	N/A	0
Trial 1 - Straight rafters	Kunming	N/A		1m	141.25	+24%	0
	Bengaluru	N/A		1m	112.80	-1%	0
	La Libertad*	N/A		1m	88.03	-23%	0
Trial 2 - Rafter curvature as an input	Kunming	5		1m	141.91	+24%	0
	Bengaluru	5		1m	112.88	-1%	0
	La Libertad*	5		1m	89.12	-22%	0
Trial 3 - Optimal rafter curvature as an output	Kunming	1	4	1m	141.60	+24%	0
	Bengaluru	1	2	1m	111.69	-2%	0
	La Libertad*	2	1	1m	87.49	-23%	0

Table 1
Baseline roof information and results of all trials. For clarity, the values of input parameters 2, 3, 4, 5 and 7, as referenced in Figure 6, are not shown. (*the 45 degree guideline roof overhang was not applied and there is no minimum value set for input 7).

be significantly less area yet provide full solar protection to the columns. By implementing curved poles into the algorithm this showed in some cases there could be marginal reduction in the roof surface area whilst still ensuring full solar protection. In all cases an asymmetric truss was found to be optimal with the height at the minimum value of 1m. In Trial 3 which looked to find the most optimal curvature of bamboo pole, the optimal curvature was between 1 and 4 out of 100. Given the many inputs, the evolutionary solver may need more than 100 steps for an improved fitness to be found. A next step could be to run the solver by fixing certain values such as the 1m truss height and the curvature of the bamboo poles at 1% to 4% to reduce the possible combinations of inputs in future tests. The roof structure and joinery is also something which needs to be considered and I have not covered it here given the scope of this paper. In this paper a centre line model was used as the basis of the truss, however this can be taken further to ensure the node, bolt and cut locations are all taken into account when placing secondary members. These can be easily added to the algorithm.

CONCLUSION

Architects should be aware of the low natural durability of bamboo and align their design tools more closely for bamboo to ensure durability. This paper demonstrates one such process. Results also showed that using curved poles instead of straight poles can reduce the surface area of the roof and the material quantity required. Contrary to negating the curvature of bamboo, if a design process following a generative design approach can use the curvature of bamboo as an opportunity this can potentially provide cost savings. If this design was more than a bespoke dwelling, and was a mass building programme, scaling this material reduction over many projects could see substantial cost savings. A next step could be to embed rainfall data to decide whether the minimum 45 degree overhang is required or not as part of the algorithm. The performance of bamboo structures and the societal attitude to bamboo can be greatly improved through the design decisions of architects. At least, this is an awareness of the need to protect exposed bamboo from the sun and rain. At best, architects should follow a design process which balances the formal and functional requirements of a design with the material considerations of using high yield

Figure 9
Screenshot front elevations and axonometric views of output geometry visualisation from Rhinoceros interface, following the Sunlight Hours Analysis in Grasshopper and Ladybug.

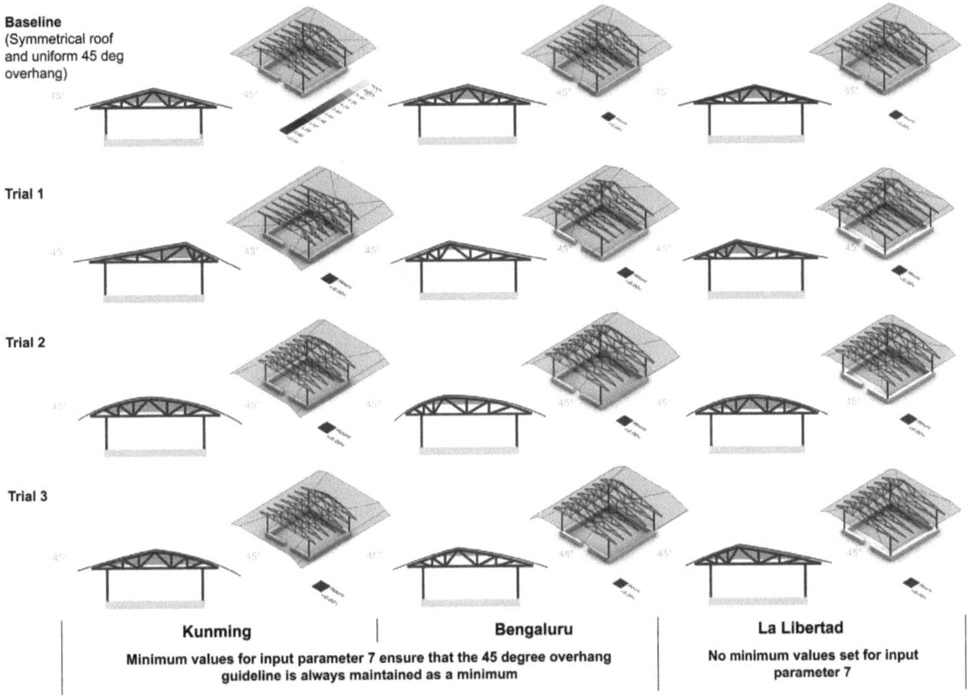

cultivated materials such as bamboo. We need to align our tools and processes to consider materials which will provide ecological restoration, particularly in tropical LMIC's in which bamboo is available. If this happens we can see a construction industry as one of the biggest catalysts to improved ecosystems and climate change, instead of the present reverse condition.

REFERENCES

Caetano, I, Santos, L and Leitão, A 2020, 'Computational design in architecture: Defining parametric, generative, and algorithmic design', *Frontiers of Architectural Research*, 9(2), pp. 287-300

Crolla, K 2017, 'Building indeterminacy modelling – the 'ZCB Bamboo Pavilion' as a case study on nonstandard construction from natural materials', *Visualization in Engineering*, 5(1), pp. 1-12

Crolla, K 2018, 'Bending Bamboo Rules: Beyond Century-Old Typologies', *Journal of Architectural Education*, 72(1), pp. 135-145

Fure, A 2011 'Digital Materiallurgy: On the productive force of deep codes and vital matter', *ACADIA 2011*, University of Calgary, pp. 90-97

Gramazio, F and Kohler, M 2008, *Digital materiality in architecture*, Lars Muller / Springer distributor, Baden / London

Harries, K, Sharma, S and Richard, M 2012, 'Structural Use of Full Culm Bamboo: The Path to Standardization', *International Journal of Architecture, Engineering and Construction*, 1(2), pp. 66-75

Heston, M B 1996, 'The Nexus of Divine and Earthly Rule: Padmanābhapuram Palace and Traditions of Architecture and Kingship in South Asia', *Ars Orientalis*, 26, pp. 81-106

Jabi, W 2013, *Parametric design for architecture*, Laurence King Publishing, London

Janssen, JJA 2000, *Designing and Building with Bamboo*, INBAR
Kaminski, S, Lawrence, A and Trujillo, D 2016a, *Engineered Bahareque Technical Report*, INBAR
Kaminski, S, Lawrence, A and Trujillo, D 2016b, 'Structural use of bamboo: Part 1: Introduction to bamboo', *The Structural Engineer*, 94(8), pp. 40-43
Kaminski, S, Lawrence, A, Trujillo, D and King, C 2016, 'Structural use of bamboo: Part 2: Durability and preservation', *The Structural Engineer*, 94(10), pp. 38-43
Kumar, S, Shukla, KS, Dev, T and Dobriyal, PB 1994, *Bamboo preservation techniques: A review*, INBAR
Kwinter, S 1996, 'Flying the bullet, or when did the future begin?', in Kwinter, S (eds) 1996, *Rem Koolhaas: Conversations with students*, Rice University, Princeton Architectural Press, pp. 67-94
Laiserin, J 2008 'Digital Environments for Early Design: Form-Making versus Form-Finding', *First International Conference on Critical Digital: What Matters(s)?*, Cambridge, USA, pp. 235-242
Lehne, J and Preston, F 2018, *Making Concrete Change: Innovation in Low-carbon Cement and Concrete*, Chatham House Report: The Royal Institute of International Affairs, London
Liese, W and Tang, TKH 2015a, 'Preservation and Drying of Bamboo', in Akinlabi, ET, Anane-Fenin, K and Akwada, DR (eds) 2015a, *Bamboo: The Multipurpose Plant*, Springer, pp. 257-297
Liese, W and Tang, TKH 2015b, 'Properties of the Bamboo Culm', in Akinlabi, ET, Anane-Fenin, K and Akwada, DR (eds) 2015b, *Bamboo: The Multipurpose Plant*, Springer, pp. 227-256
Lobovikov, M, Paudel, S, Piazza, M, Ren, H and Wu, J 2007, *World bamboo resources - A thematic study prepared in the framework of the Global Forest Resources Assessment 2005*, FAO, Rome
Lorenzo, R, Lee, C, Oliva-Salinas, JG and Ontiveros-Hernandez, MJ 2017, 'BIM Bamboo: a digital design framework for bamboo culms', *Proceedings of the Institution of Civil Engineers - Structures and Buildings*, 170(4), pp. 295-302
van der Lugt, P 2017, 'Engineered Bamboo Products - A Sustainable Choice?', in Hebel, DE and Heisel, F (eds) 2017, *Cultivated Building Materials: Industrialized Natural Resources for Architecture and Construction*, Birkhäuser, Basel, pp. 86-95
Minke, G 2016, *Building with Bamboo*, Birkhäuser
Pomponi, F, Hart, J, Arehart, JH and D'Amico, B 2020, 'Buildings as a Global Carbon Sink? A Reality Check on Feasibility Limits', *One Earth*, 3(2), pp. 157-161
Qi, Y, Zhong, R, Kaiser, B, Nguyen, L, Wagner, HJ, Verl, A and Menges, A 2021, 'Working with Uncertainties: An Adaptive Fabrication Workflow for Bamboo Structures', in Yuan, PF, Yao, J, Yan, C, Wang, X and Leach, N (eds) 2021, *Proceedings of the 2020 DigitalFUTURES*, Springer Singapore, pp. 265-279
Sadeghipour Roudsari, M and Pak, M 2013 'Ladybug: A parametric environmental plugin for grasshopper to help designers create an environmentally-conscious design', *Proceedings of BS 2013: 13th Conference of the International Building Performance Simulation Association*, pp. 3128-3135
Samodra, FXT 2009, 'Analysis Of Solar Geometry Influences To The Roof Of The Roof Architecture In The Tropical Region', *REGOL - Journal of Architecture and Environment*, 8, pp. 35-48
Sharma, B, Gatoo, A, Bock, M, Mulligan, H and Ramage, M 2015, 'Engineered bamboo: state of the art', *Proceedings of the Institution of Civil Engineers - Construction Materials*, 168(2), pp. 57-67
Tardio, G, Mickovski, SB, Stokes, A and Devkota, S 2017, 'Bamboo structures as a resilient erosion control measure', *Proceedings of the Institution of Civil Engineers - Forensic Engineering*, 170(2), pp. 72-83
Tedeschi, A 2014, *AAD Algorithms-Aided Design: Parametric Strategies using Grasshopper*, Le Penseur
State of the Tropics, Report 2020, *State of the Tropics 2020 Report*, James Cook University, Townsville, Australia
UN-Habitat, Report 2016, *Slum Almanac 2015/2016: Tracking Improvement in the Lives of Slum Dwellers*, UN-Habitat, Nairobi
UNEP, Report 2019, *Sand and Sustainability: Finding new solutions for environmental governance of global sand resources*, UNEP, Geneva, Switzerland
Vélez, S, Vegesack, Av and Kries, M 2000, *Grow your own house: Simón Vélez and bamboo architecture*, Vitra Design Museum, Weil am Rhein, Germany
Willis, D and Woodward, T 2005, 'Diminishing Dificulty: Mass Customization and the Digital Production of Architecture', *Harvard Design Magazine*, 23, pp. 71-83
Willmann, J, Gramazio, F, Kohler, M and Langenberg, S 2013 'Digital by Material', *Rob | Arch 2012*, Vienna, Austria, pp. 12-27
[1] https://www.grasshopper3d.com/
[2] https://www.rhino3d.com/
[3] https://www.ladybug.tools/ladybug.html
[4] https://www.dezeen.com/2020/07/28/amairis-clothing-factory-ruta-4-colombia/

Investigating Computational Methods and Strategies to Reduce Construction and Demolition Waste in Preliminary Design

Omar Majzoub[1], M. Hank Haeusler[2]
[1,2] UNSW / Computational Design
[1,2] {o.majzoub|m.haeusler}@unsw.edu.au

The waste produced in construction and demolition presents social, economic, and environmental challenges on a global scale. Research suggests that effective decision-making mechanisms are needed during preliminary design stages to minimise the production of waste. In early research, we presented a beta version of a waste reduction tool which is now in need of a User Experience (UX) and Interaction Experience (IX) strategy to meet our research aims of (a) supporting architects in making informed decisions and (b) offer general as well a specific design optimisation to reduce waste. Thus in our research, we arrived at a point that required an investigation into computational methods and strategies to meet these aims. While optimisation and decision-making in architecture are often achieved through generative design strategies, we aim to investigate and discuss alternatives. Thus we propose the hypothesis of employing augmented intelligence. The paper presents work in augmented intelligence undertaken outside the architecture discipline and presents our literature review with a discussion and conclusion.

Keywords: *Waste reduction, computational methods and strategies, sustainable development goals, augmented intelligence, position paper*

INTRODUCTION

In earlier research (Haeusler et al., 2021b), we argued that the problem of material waste is often framed as an end-user responsibility. From fashion garments to manufactured objects and food, consumers are encouraged to reduce, recycle, re-use, up-cycle, and repair. In the architecture, engineering, and construction (AEC) industry, waste is typically understood as an economic problem dealt with primarily in the construction and demolition phase of a building's life cycle. Alternatively, the published research project (Ibid.) reconceptualises construction and demolition waste (CDW) as a data and informational problem in the design process that can be addressed at far early stages when key spatial and material design decisions often 'lock-in' waste outcomes. This follows the logic of Zero Waste that calls for the consideration of waste at the source through responsible production practices that aim to minimise inefficiencies in the use of materials, energy, and human resources. Architectural designers however are not accustomed to accounting for waste in early-stage design processes and there is a limited range of accessible and integrated tools suitable to the task. Accordingly, our earlier research developed a proof-of-concept computational design decision support tool for use by architectural designers to estimate and raise awareness of CDW in early-stage design. This resituates waste as a data problem with material dimensions and properties associated with 3D spatial geometries and Building Information Model data. Through computational prediction, waste production is materialised as a significant interdependent variable in a design system. Developing a novel computational method to highlight waste production in early-stage design aims to encourage architects and designers to better account for the implications of their design decisions and to challenge the systems of consumption and production that generate CDW. This earlier research (Ibid.), and the research presented in this paper, further contribute to wider epistemological questions about when and what kind of information is useful to architectural design decision-making.

BACKGROUND AND MOTIVATION

Background on waste. The waste produced in construction and demolition presents social, economic, and environmental challenges. Rapid growth in construction activities in Australia in recent years has led to increased generation of Construction and Demolition Waste (CDW) (Shooshtarian et. al, 2019). Ibid. argues that, according to the latest statistics from Australian National Waste Report 2018 [1], about 20.4 Mt of CDW was generated across Australia during 2017-2018. That equates to 30.5% of the total waste generated, of which 33% is disposed of in landfills. Since 2016-17, construction waste has increased, according to the Australian Bureau of Statistics by 22% [2] and, with the existing rate of migration and population growth (APH, 2018), it is expected that CDW generation will continue to grow steadily in the coming years. Worldbank's 2018 report [3] projects that rapid urbanisation, population growth, and economic development will increase overall global waste by 70% over the next 30 years - to a staggering 3.40 billion tonnes of waste generated annually. Globally, CDW contributes 30% of total annual waste generation (Jun et al., 2011) and 16.8% in Australia [2].

- **Social.** Worldbank's Research [3] suggests that it does make economic sense to invest in sustainable waste management. Uncollected and poorly disposed waste have significant health and environmental impacts, of which the cost of addressing is many times higher than the cost of developing and operating simple, adequate waste management systems.
- **Economic.** The concept of waste needs to be considered as inefficiency in the production process. The construction industry spent AUS$2 billion on waste services in 2016-17 [2]. The economic cost of waste also imposes costs on existing and potential future generations as outlined by the Australian Productivity Commission [4].
- **Environmental.** Risk of contamination to groundwater systems, in particular, if landfill sites are located in proximity to urbanised areas [4]. Natural resources are limited and there is evidence that due to rapid urbanisation materials will become scarce, hence one cannot afford to waste them.

Thus, it is imminent that waste production consequently results in high social, economic and environmental costs.

Waste reduction challenges in the AEC sector. Akinade et al. (2018) argue the literature reveals that the largest percentage of CDW is caused at pre-construction stages and those design decisions have a high impact on CDW generation (Ajayi et al., 2016a, Ajayi et al., 2016b, Faniran and Caban, 1998). Effective decision-making mechanisms are therefore needed during the design stages to minimise their impact. Osmani (2013) refers to waste generated at this point as "Design Waste". Yet while there are opportunities to reduce CDW at the design stage, the existing tools do not help designers (Osmani et al.,

2008) as they are detached from the design process (Akinade et al. 2018). While several studies (Ajayi et al., 2015a, Liu et al., 2011, Porwal and Hewage, 2011) have identified that Building Information Modelling (BIM) has the potential to design out waste, none has provided clear instructions on how to use BIM for this purpose. Akinade et al. (2018) research - using focus group interviews conducted in the UK's AEC sector - revealed that a "computer-aided simulation scenario and visualisation of waste performance" tool a number-one priority. This view is confirmed by the results of other studies (Bilal et al., 2016). Although the research listed above suggests the design stage plays a crucial role, architects do not see waste management as a priority in their design process (Osmani et al., 2006, 2008). We discuss BIM or generative design used in CDW management in our previous publications (Haeusler et al., 2021b).

RESEARCH AIMS AND QUESTION

Based on the aforementioned review of the conceptualisation of waste, current approaches to waste reduction in the AEC industry and existing CDW tools, our research (WITHHOLD, 2021a, 2021b) has developed a beta-version tool, which developed a novel computational method that connects databases and communicates CDW information to architects to support more informed design decision-making that is mindful of CDW potential as it connects to material and formal decisions during the early-stage design. While the beta-version tool has provided the research team with a proof concept of an equation that brings into relation: (i) HTML-scraped construction materials with dimensions and environmental, physical, and economical properties, with (ii) BIM data, scraped out of a Revit model, outlining the composition and characteristics of families, (iii) and schematic spatial and geometric information of rooms as variables from which one can computationally predict waste quantities - the following question remains: *How to receive the information of waste production and respond upon this knowledge?* Ultimately our waste reduction tool will provide a result based on the above-listed equation with the main aim of reducing waste. Thus one can assume that optimisation towards waste production appears a logical step forward. In order to achieve an optimised outcome, our overall research aim is to apply knowledge gained through literature review and design research to:

- **AIM 1.** Developing visualisation models and tools, to support architects to make informed decisions during the pre-construction stages to raise awareness of waste generation and resourcefulness design.
- **AIM 2.** Provide architects with general design optimisation advice to reduce CDW in their design in general and with specific advice to reduce waste of materials with high embodied carbon - or ones that are non-biodegradable or toxic -and, thus, should not end up on landfill sites.

Specific for this paper we investigate the main question of whether: *The waste reduction tool will be integrated into the concept design process as a generative design tool or as a part of an augmented intelligence strategy in which Artificial Intelligence and humans collaborate to achieve the desired outcome?* Based on the overall research aims we argue for an approach of 'augmented intelligence' in which the human and machine collaboratively work together vs. a generative design approach that provides the designer with a result.

GENERATIVE DESIGN OR AUGMENTED INTELLIGENCE?

In his article *'Generative Design is Doomed to Fail'*, Davis [5] explains his concerns with generative design methods approaching the topic from a technical and a human perspective. Davis (Ibid.) refers to the generative design as a three-step process: (i) a set of goals of the project is set by designers, (ii) solutions options are generated by algorithms and (iii) the best option(s) are chosen by designers. This notion of generative design and algorithms is rooted in research done by John Frazer from the mid-1960s with his seminal work 'An Evolutionary Architecture' (1995), Bentley and Wakefield's 'Conceptual evolutionary design by a generative algorithm' (1997), and Cotes 'Programming Architecture' (2000). It stands to reason that his thinking was also influenced by more recent research published in the field by Kocabay (2017a, 2017b); Makki et al. (2015, 2018); or Wortmann et al. (2016, 2019) - all work that influences our thinking towards the direction our research will take as well.

Back to Davis [5], he outlines six points to support his argument. First, the generative design process involves the complex and time-consuming creation of algorithms that generate lots of similar-looking design options limiting the ability to explore the full range of design outcomes. In the second, third, and fourth points, Davis discusses the issue of generating too many options that cannot be identified as good or bad by the algorithm(s). With the quality of the solutions being questioned, the large quantity of design solutions whose performance is difficult, if not impossible, to quantify, actually complicates the decision-making task for designers. This may lead to longer and unexpected working times and may increase the tendency to have more errors. In the fifth point, the generative design process undermines and doesn't take into consideration the iterative nature of the design process where the first option is never the final one. Additionally, in real-world practice, circumstances continuously change leading to design variations and revisions that generative design tools do not accommodate for. Regarding the sixth point, Davis explains that no other creative industry works this way.

At the end of the article, Davis [5] concludes that the main focus has so far been on understanding the technology rather than understanding the design process in the digital world. The interface of technology and its integration within this process is the challenge, not the development of the technology itself. For Davis, the future of the architectural profession will see a new relationship between intelligent machines and designers, one that will be based on partnership and collaboration. The algorithms will take advantage of human intelligence to enable humans to work more efficiently to achieve well-defined tasks. [6] According to Peter Rowe (1982), the process of design is one guided by heuristic reasoning which is an approach to problem-solving. It involves provisional solutions based on the interpretation of a problem, generation of a potential solution, representing the problem, and assessing the solution. As humans, we tend to simplify and drop things when dealing with complex and large amounts of data. While artificial intelligence is superior at tasks that require pattern recognition and is hard-wired for big data [7], humans still have the upper hand in emotional and moral intelligence. Humans can understand the data context of many issues. A simple observation may completely alter the outcome of the machine trained and assigned to perform a narrow and well-specified task (Carpo, 2018, Botelho and Bigelow, 2019, Brynjolfsson and McAfee, 2011, Hurwitz, 2019).

Based on what has been presented so far, we can conclude and argue that the focus of our investigation to meet the above-listed aims needs to be on developing an augmented intelligence rather than a generative design tool that fits within the digital architectural design process in an actual practice setting. The following section presents a literature review of emerging applications of augmented intelligence outside the profession of architecture - in the disciplines of medicine, movie production and video creation, linguistics, and advanced-driver assistance systems. This literature review aims to put forward the hypothesis that augmented intelligence will 'better' support architects to make informed decisions during the pre-construction stages to raise awareness of waste generation and resourcefulness design - AIM 1 of this research. We further put forward the preposition that AIM 2 - Provide architects with general design optimisation advice to reduce CDW in their design in general and with specific advice to reduce waste - could be 'better' achieved via augmented intelligence vs a generative approach.

AN OVERVIEW OF AUGMENTED INTELLIGENCE OUTSIDE THE DISCIPLINE OF ARCHITECTURE

Emerging outside the architectural profession new applications of artificial intelligence that augment human intelligence are developed, tested, and put into practice. Understanding the relationship between AI and the other disciplinary tasks, the critical questions that justify their implementation, and the framework of these applications can prove to be beneficial to conceptualize augmented intelligence to achieve the above-listed aims. Hence, we undertook a systematic literature review that explores these applications. Initially, while looking for sources in the Scopus database, interrogative words were each used as a keyword combined with the term 'Artificial Intelligence' + 'Augmented Intelligence' + 'Human' to investigate what the most common question asked might be when implementing AI. We used interrogative words as a 'shot in the dark' approach to unpacking the use, usefulness, or in-use of augmented or artificial intelligence in our first literature search. Only the combination of Augmented Intelligence with the interrogative words 'Which', 'When' and 'How' recommended the same number of documents; the oldest to be published in 2012, while all others gave back a null result; refer to the table in Fig. 1. This result was considered while reviewing the chosen sources referred to in tables in Fig. 2-5. We extracted the different quotes that point to the relation between AI and a disciplinary task. These were then classified based on the answer they respond with to any of the 10 different interrogative words; (table not included in this paper). The different sources along with the classified quotes reveal the importance of 'When' in the process does Augmented Intelligence need to be implemented. Additionally, the literature review also concludes with the need to have a clear framework, protocol, and user interface, hence the significance of 'How' to achieve augmented intelligence. This section gives an overview of some of the Augmented Intelligence applications implemented.

Figure 1
Search Result in Scopus using Keywords 'Augmented Intelligence' + 'An Interrogative Word'

Keywords		Scopus Database Search Result (2012-2021)
Artificial Intelligence +	+ What	0
Human+	+ Which	237
Augmented Intelligence	+ When	237
	+ Where	0
	+ Who	0
	+ Whom	0
	+ Whose	0
	+ Why	0
	+ Whether	0
	+ How	237

Medicine

Figure 2
Sources used for the Literature Review in Augmented Intelligence Models in Medicine.

Discipline	Common Keywords	Research Platform - Database	Source Type and Number
Medicine	Augmented Intelligence Collaborative Intelligence Artificial Intelligence Machine Learning Trends Medicine Health Care	Scopus	9 Journal Articles
		Web of Science	3 Journal Reviews 1 Editorial Material 2 Proceeding Papers
		Other Resources - UNSW Library Search Engine and Web Search	3 Journal Articles
			Total: 18 Sources

The American Medical Association among many others in the medical industry currently endorses the term Augmented Intelligence instead of focusing on AI versus human intelligence (Arieno et al., 2019). The majority of these tools have been developed in fields that are visual-based like radiology and pathology (Sheikh, Fann, 2019). Other fields of AI implementation in medicine include complex medical data analysis (Xu et al., 2019), critical care monitoring (Görges, Ansermino, 2020, Stewart et al., 2018), and data literature (Mehta, Devarakonda, 2018, Xu et al., 2019). In radiology, AI has been implemented on medical images to perform a variety of tasks at different phases in the medical treatment process ranging from detection to diagnosis, to prognosis, and patient management. Radiomics refer to converting images into mineable data (Sheth and Giger, 2019). The significance of using AI in this process is that it can process and analyse a considerably higher amount of useful data than a human eye can see in an image (Siegersma et al., 2019). The research and application of AI in imaging have been implemented in a variety of medical specialties including breast cancer (Arieno et al., 2019, Harvey et al., 2019, Korkinof et al., 2018, Sheth, Giger, 2019), cardiovascular diseases (Siegersma et al., 2019), dental medicine (Joda et al., 2020), pulmonary diseases (Cai, Zhu, 2019), brain tumour (Bhanumurthy, Anne, 2014), each relying on different types of imaging techniques.

Movie Production and Video Creation

Movie and Video Production and Creation	Artificial Intelligence	Scopus	1 Journal Article
	Machine Learning		3 Conference Papers
	Deep Learning	Web of Science	3 Journal Articles
	Natural Language Processing		
	Video Editing / Video / Movie	Other Resources - UNSW Library Search Engine and Web Search	1 Conference Proceeding
	Film/Movie Production		11 Web Pages
			Total: 19 Sources

Figure 3
Sources used for the Literature Review in Augmented Intelligence Models in Movie and Video Production.

Investments of AI in audio-visual related applications can be seen in two main domains: movie production and video creation and editing. For movie production, the process can be complex and costly. It involves many different tasks like planning and rehearsing, involvement of high-pay actors, filming and shooting, communication, and creative editing to name but a few (Akser et al., 2017). One significant role that AI can play in this process is advising whether or not to produce the movie. [8] The implementation of AI to forecast box-office has been targeted and applied by different researchers. While some have looked into pre-release predictive models analysing features related to production, distribution, and advertising (Anantha Natarajan et al., 2019, Quader et al., 2017), others have looked into using such features to bring prediction forward to the pre-production phase (Ghiassi et al., 2015).

The use of screenplays or scripts to predict movie success is also an area of research and application harnessing rich predictive material and showing promising results (Wehrmann et al., 2016). An example of that is ScriptBook, an AI company that analyses movie scripts to predict target audience, box-office revenue, and audience. [8,9] Applying AI on scripts has also been used to predict emotions to forecast movie success (Kim et al., 2018). Besides the use of AI in predicting movie success, AI has been implemented in video creation and editing showing promising results both in and out of the movie production industry. Video editing is a complex task that takes much more time than video shooting would. It is believed that the incorporation of AI would change the rules of this task and speed it up to previously unexpected levels. [10] Certain applications of AI have incorporated text such as transcript or dialogue and scene description to create and edit videos. An AI-based program called Simon Says Assemble auto-transcribes videos so editors can more effectively arrange and edit the transcript before easily creating a video based on their edit. [11] A joint research project between Adobe and Stanford yielded an application that can collaboratively work with humans to create and edit dialogue-driven scenes (Leake et al., 2017). Another research project at Ulster University looks into using AI to generate multi-modal 3D animations from scene descriptions enabling humans to easily visualise draft scene views to better take decisions (Akser, 2017).

Linguistics

Linguistics	Artificial Intelligence	Scopus	1 Journal Review
	Machine Learning		2 Journal Articles
	Natural Language Processing	Web of Science	1 Journal Review
	Linguistics		2 Journal Articles
	English		
	Syntax and Semantics		
		Other Resources - UNSW Library Search Engine and Web Search	1 Conference Proceeding
			6 Web Pages
			Total: 13 Sources

Figure 4
Sources used for the Literature Review in Augmented Intelligence Models in Linguistics.

Natural Language Processing (NLP) represents a range of computational techniques that enable computers to process natural language and it is used in both, speech processing and word processing (Zhang and Bi, 2018). Focusing on the use of NLP in word processing, one of the successful applications that can be looked at is Grammarly which offers automated suggestions to correct detected errors and improve English writing such as grammar, clarity, conciseness, etc. Grammarly is trained on a large database of text known as corpus and learns from both, wrong and correct examples to work at different levels ranging from single characters to full texts. [12,13]

Advanced Driver-Assistance Systems

Advanced Driver-Assistance Systems	Augmented Intelligence Collaborative Intelligence Artificial Intelligence Machine Learning Driving Assistance	Scopus	3 Conference Papers
		Web of Science	2 Proceeding Papers 2 Journal Articles
		Other Resources - UNSW Library Search Engine and Web Search	1 Conference Paper
			Total: 8 Sources

Figure 5
Sources used for the Literature Review in Augmented Intelligence Models in Advanced Driver-Assistance Systems.

To maximise the detection and minimise the reaction times to risks associated with driving, Advanced Driver-Assistance Systems (ADAS) developed by car manufacturers is currently one of the main research topics in the automotive field (Moujahid et al., 2018). Most ADAS are either purely or partially vision-based, each implementing some form of camera system that have become essential sensors in the industry (Horgan et al., 2015). ADAS can be classified into three categories based on the level of control given to the AI-driven system: alert, semi-automated, and automated. Examples of alert-based ADAS are (i) longitudinal control-based such as Object Detection or Collision Avoidance Systems-Alert, Traffic Sign Recognition, and Cross-Traffic Alert, (ii) lateral control-based such as Lane Departure Warning, and (iii) Driver Monitoring Systems also known as Driving Vigilance Systems. As for semi-automated ADAS, High Beam Assist, Adaptive Cruise Control, and Automatic Emergency Braking are used for longitudinal control, whereas Lane Keeping is used for lateral control. An example of automated ADAS where both the system and the driver collaborate is Highway Driving Assist (Horgan et al., 2015, Moujahid et al., 2018).

DISCUSSION AND CONCLUSION

Discussion. At the outset of this paper, we introduced our work towards a waste reduction tool intending to support architects to make informed decisions during the pre-construction stages to raise awareness of waste generation and resourcefulness design and provide them with general design optimisation advice in general and/or specific. While we do not aim to ignore research and progress in generative design overall we want to develop the tool as an augmented intelligence tool rather than a generative design tool. Consequently, we sourced and reviewed 31 journal articles, papers, and to a smaller extent web sources to understand work in the field and to back up our hypothesis that augmented intelligence will 'better' support architects and us in meeting our two research aims. Reviewing the above-listed papers and the case studies presented, it becomes clear that a common and significant reason for their success is having a clear interaction protocol with well-defined objectives. Additionally, unlike the case in generative design, comprehensibility is key in augmented intelligence. This is accomplished through validation, single and easy to understand solution outputs that can accommodate for human manual input, classification and a brief explanation of flagged errors and proposed solutions, and through appropriate selection of message communication modes. Examples of validation are the predictive information as in the case of medical imaging where results are easily assessed against a set of benchmarks (Sheth and Giger, 2019, Arieno et al., 2019), ICU monitoring for physiologic deterioration through the use of biological indicators as predictors (Görges and Ansermino, 2020), and movie success and box-office forecasting in which a percentage of the dataset is used to compare and validate the results (Ghiassi et al., 2015). For the single and easy to understand and manually edit solution output, we can see that in the video creation and editing tools mentioned above; Simon Says Assemble [14], Adobe/Stanford Dialogue Driven Scenes Tool (Leake et al., 2017), and SceneMaker (Akser et al., 2017). As for the classification and a brief explanation of errors and proposed solutions, this is successfully integrated into Grammarly [15], while a good example of clear and appropriate selection of message communication modes are the different alert systems integrated into vehicles in a way that aims to provide maximum safety and quickest response possible, and minimal distraction (Izquierdo et al., 2017).

Conclusion and next steps. In the end, a series of observations and questions can be raised to help establish a roadmap for the development of the tool in the future: (i) What decisions are to be supported by AI? And, when do these decisions need to happen during the concept design phase? (ii) Based on the previous two questions, how can the tasks in the existing design process be re-arranged and on what basis are these assigned to AI or human? (iii) Considered a companion, how can AI be improved as collaboration happens? And, what human feedback is required for that purpose? (iv) How can the user interface be designed to present the above issues? And, how can it facilitate ease of communication, flexibility, thoroughness, and comprehensibility of feedback? Tamke et al. (2018) refers to two emergent practices that integrate machine learning in architecture; analysis of design space and optimising choice of parametrically generated solutions and short-circuit simulations targeting ill-defined problems, constant change, lack of resources and time, and lack of performance data. So, we can already start to speculate what a future tool might look like. Similar to the Adobe/Stanford tool, we can imagine one which offers an initial optimised floor plan (general solution) based on set criteria integrating manufacturers' and suppliers' data - product material, size, location, embodied energy, etc. - and a benchmark number representing the optimal solution. This then allows the architects to add their input and amend the presented option by drawing or modelling while considering the automatically updating benchmark number driven by instant simulation. As is the case with semi-automated ADAS, the system can automatically take action and amend the option to avoid violating embedded rules visually learned from precedent projects for example. Also, as is the case with Grammarly, the system can highlight and classify potential issues in the model without taking action. But the question in mind is if that is the case, will a mandatory action be required at some point and when in this case? Again, many questions can be raised and an important one is when would this collaboration eventually end.

While the research offered valuable insights into the field of augmented intelligence and we clearly see an opportunity for further investigations we yet do not have definite answers. We consider augmented intelligence as a new approach for architecture which we aim to study in future research with using the above-listed observation and questions as a starting point.

REFERENCES

Ajayi, S.O., Oyedele, L.O., Akinade, O.O., Bilal, M., Owolabi, H.A., Alaka, H.A. and Kadiri, K.O. 2016a, 'Competency-based measures for designing out construction waste: task and contextual attributes', *Engineering Construction Architectural Management*, 23(4), pp. 464-490

Ajayi, S.O., Oyedele, L.O., Akinade, O.O., Bilal, M., Owolabi, H.A., Alaka, H.A. and Kadiri, K.O. 2016b, 'Reducing waste to landfill: a need for cultural change in the UK construction industry', *Journal or Biological Engineering*, 5, pp. 185-193

Ajayi, S.O., Oyedele, L.O., Bilal, M., Akinade, O.O., Alaka, H.A., Owolabi, H.A. and Kadiri, K.O. 2015a, 'Waste effectiveness of the construction industry: Understanding the impediments and requisites for improvements', *Journal of Resources, Conservation and Recycling*, 102, pp. 101-112

Akinade, O.O., Oyedele, L.O., Ajayi, S.O., Bilal, M., Alaka, H.A., Owolabi, H.A. and Arawomo, O.O. 2018, 'Designing out construction waste using BIM technology: Stakeholders' expectations for industry deployment', *Journal of Cleaner Production*, 180, pp. 375-385

Akser, MA, Bridges, BB, Campo, GC, Cheddad, AC, Curran, KC, Fitzpatrick, LF, Hamilton, LH, Harding, JH, Leath, TL, Lunney, TL, Lunney, FL, Ma, MM, Macrae, JM, Maguire, TM, McCaughey, AM, McClory, EM, McClory, VM, Mc Kevitt, PMK, Melvin, AM, Moore, PM,

Mulholland, EM, Muñoz, KM, O'Hanlon, GO and Roman, LR 2017 'SceneMaker: Creative Technology for Digital StoryTelling', *Proceedings of The 5th International Conference on ArtsIT, Interactivity and Game Creation 2016*
Arieno, AA, Chan, AC and Destounis, SVD 2019, 'A review of the role of augmented intelligence in breast imaging: From automated breast density assessment to risk stratification', *American Journal of Roentgenology*, 212, pp. 259-270
Bentley, P.J. and Wakefield, J.P. 1997, 'Conceptual evolutionary design by a genetic algorithm', *Engineering design and automation*, 3, pp. 119-132
Bhanumurthy, YB and Anne, KA 2014 'An automated detection and segmentation of tumor in brain MRI using artificial intelligence', *Proceedings of 2014 IEEE International Conference on Computational Intelligence and Computing Research*
Bilal, M., Oyedele, L.O., Akinade, O.O., Ajayi, S.O., Alaka, H.A., Owolabi, H.A., Qadir, J., Pasha, M. and Bello, S.A. 2016, 'Big data architecture for construction waste analytics (CWA): a conceptual framework', *Journal or Biological Engineering*, 6, pp. 144-156
Brynjolfsson, EB and McAfee, AM 2011, *Race Against the Machine: How the Digital Revolution is Accelerating Innovation, Driving Productivity, and Irreversibly Transforming Employment and the Economy*, Digital Frontier Press
Cai, JC and Zhu, HZ 2019 'Lung image segmentation by generative adversarial networks', *Proceedings of SPIE 2019*
Carpo, MC 2018, 'Excessive Resolution: Artificial Intelligence and Machine Learning in Architectural Design', *Architectural Record*, 2020, p. 135, 136
Coates, P. 2000, *Programming Architecture*, Routledge, Taylor and Francis Group, London and New York
Faniran, O. 1998, 'Minimizing waste on construction project sites', *Engineering Construction*, 5, pp. 182-188
Frazer, J 1995, *An Evolutionary Architecture*, Architectural Association , London
Ghiassi, MG, Lio, DL and Moon, BM 2015, 'Pre-production forecasting of movie revenues with a dynamic artificial neural network', *Expert Systems with Applications*, 42, pp. 3176-3193
Görges, MG and Ansermino, JMA 2020, 'Augmented intelligence in pediatric anesthesia and pediatric critical care', *Curr Opin Anaesthesiol*, 33, pp. 404-410
Haeusler, MH, Gardner, N, Butler, A, Sepasgozar, S and Pan, S 2021a 'Wasted ... Again - Or how to understand waste as a data problem and aiming to address the reduction of waste as a computational challenge', *CAADRIA 2021*, Hong Kong, pp. 371-380
Haeusler, MH, Gardner, N, Yu, D, Oh, C and Huang, B 2021b, '(Computationally) designing out waste: Developing a computational design workflow for minimising construction and demolition waste in early-stage architectural design', *IJAC*, 19(3), p. TBC
Harvey, HH, Karpati, EK, Khara, GK, Korkinof, DK, Ng, AN, Austin, CA, Rijken, TR and Kecskemethy, PK 2019, 'The Role of Deep Learning in Breast Screening', *Current Breast Cancer Reports*, 11, pp. 17-22
Horgan, JH, Hughes, CH, McDonald, JM and Yogamani, SY 2015 'Vision-Based Driver Assistance Systems: Survey, Taxonomy and Advances', *Proceedings of 2015 IEEE 18th International Conference on Intelligent Transportation Systems*
Hurwitz, JH 2019, *Augmented Intelligence The Business Power of Human-Machine Collaboration*, Auerbach Publishers, Incorporated
Izquierdo-Reyes, JIR, Curiel-Ramirez, LACR, Ramirez-Mendoza, RARM and Bustamante-Bello, MRBB 2017, 'A Logic Architecture for 360 ADAS-Alerts for Hazards Detection Based in Driver Actions', *MATEC web of conferences*, 124, pp. 4011-4017
Joda, TJ, Bornstein, MMB, Jung, REJ, Ferrari, MF, Waltimo, TW and Zitzmann, NUZ 2020, 'Recent Trends and Future Direction of Dental Research in the Digital Era', *International journal of environmental research and public health*, 17, pp. 1-8
Jun, L, Quizhen, W and Qingguo, M 2011, 'The effects of project uncertainty and risk management in IS development project performance: a vendor perspective', *International Journal of Project Management*, 29, pp. 923-933
Kim, DMK, Lee, SHL and Cheong, YGC 2018 'Predicting Emotion in Movie Scripts Using Deep Learning', *Proceedings of 2018 IEEE International Conference on Big Data and Smart Computing (BigComp)*, pp. 530-532
Kocabay, S. and Alacam, S. 2017a 'A Multi-Objective Genetic Algorithm Framework for Earlier Phases of Architectural Design', *22nd CAADRIA 2017*, Suzhou, China, pp. 293-302
Kocabay, S. and Alacam, S. 2017b 'Algorithm Driven Design Comparison of Single-Objective and Multi-Objective Genetic Algorithms in the Context of Housing Design', *CAAD Futures 2017*, Istanbul, Turkey, pp. 492-508
Leake, ML, Davis, AD, Truong, AT and Agrawala, MA 2017, 'Computational video editing for dialogue-driven scenes', *ACM transactions on graphics*, 36, pp. 1-14
Liu, Z., Osmani, M., Demian, P. and Baldwin, A. 2011 'The

potential use of BIM to aid construction waste minimisation', *Proceedings of the CIB W78-W102 2011: International Conference.*, Sophia Antipolis, France , pp. 16-28
Makki, M., Farzaneh, A. and Navarro, D. 2015 'The Evolutionary Adaptation of Urban Tissues through Computational Analysis', *eCAADe 2015*, Vienna, Austria, pp. 563- 571
Makki, M. and Showkatbakhsh, M. 2018 'Control of Morphological Variation Through Population Based Fitness Criteria', *CAADRIA 2018*, Beijing, China, pp. 153-162
Mehta, NM and Devarakonda, MVD 2018, 'Machine learning, natural language programming, and electronic health records: The next step in the artificial intelligence journey?', *Journal of Allergy and Clinical Immunology*, 141, pp. 2019-2021.e1
Moujahid, AM, ElAraki Tantaoui, MET, Hina, MFH, Soukane, AS, Ortalda, AO, ElKhadimi, AE and Ramdane-Cherif, ARC 2018 'Machine Learning Techniques in ADAS: A Review', *Proceedings of 2018 International Conference on Advances in Computing and Communication Engineering (ICACCE)*
Osmani, M. 2013, 'Design waste mapping: a project life cycle approach', *ICE-Waste Resource Management*, 166, pp. 114-127
Osmani, M., Glass, J. and Price, A.D.F. 2006, 'Architect and contractor attitudes to waste minimisation', *Waste and Resource Management,*, 159(2), pp. 65-72
Osmani, M., Glass, J. and Price, A.D.F. 2008, 'Architects' perspectives on construction waste reduction by design', *Waste Management*, 28, pp. 1147-1158
Porwal, A. and Hewage, K.N. 2011, 'Building Information modelling–based analysis to minimize waste rate of structural reinforcement', *Journal of Construction, Engineering, Management*, 138, pp. 943-954
Rowe, PR 1982, 'A Priori Knowledge and Heuristic Reasoning in Architectural Design', *JAE*, 36, pp. 18-23
Sheikh, AYS and Fann, JIF 2019, 'Artificial Intelligence: Can Information be Transformed into Intelligence in Surgical Education?', *Thoracic Surgery Clinics*, 29, pp. 339-350
Sheth, DS and Giger, MLG 2019, 'Artificial intelligence in the interpretation of breast cancer on MRI', *J Magn Reson Imaging*, 51, pp. 1310-1324
Shooshtarian, S, Maqsood, T, Khalfan, M, Wong, P and Yang, R 2019 'Construction and Demolition Waste Management in Australia: Review of Differences in Jurisdictional Regulatory Frameworks', *CIB World Building Congress 2019*, Hong Kong SAR, Chian, pp. 1-11
Siegersma, KRS, Leiner, TL, Chew, DPC, Appelman, YA, Hofstra, LH and Verjans, JWV 2019, 'Artificial intelligence in cardiovascular imaging : state of the art and implications for the imaging cardiologist', *Neth Heart J*, 27, pp. 403-413
Stewart, JS, Sprivulis, PS and Dwivedi, GD 2018, 'Artificial intelligence and machine learning in emergency medicine', *Emergency Medicine Australasia*, 30, pp. 870-874
Tamke, M, Nicholas, P and Zwierzycki, M 2018, 'Machine learning for architectural design: Practices and infrastructure', *International Journal of Architectural Computing*, 16(2), pp. 123-143
Wehrmann, JW, Barros, RCB, Simões, GSS, Paula, TSP and Ruiz, DDR 2016 '(Deep) Learning from Frames', *Proceedings of 5th Brazilian Conference on Intelligent Systems (BRACIS) 2016*
Wortmann, T. 2019, 'Genetic evolution vs. function approximation: Benchmarking algorithms for architectural design optimization', *Journal of Computational Design and Engineering*, 6, pp. 414-428
Wortmann, T. and Nannicini, G. 2016 'Black-Box Optimisation Methods for Architectural Design', *CAADRIA 2016*, Melbourne, Australia, pp. 177-186
Xu, JX, Yang, PY, Xue, SX, Sharma, BS, Sanchez-Martin, MSM, Wang, FW, Beaty, KAB, Dehan, ED and Parikh, BP 2019, 'Translating cancer genomics into precision medicine with artificial intelligence: applications, challenges and future perspectives', *Human Genetics*, 138, pp. 109-124
Zhang, ZZ and Bi, XB 2018, 'Research and Experiment of Intelligent Natural Language Processing Algorithms', *Wireless Personal Communications*, 102, pp. 2927-2939
[1] www.environment.gov.au
[2] www.abs.gov.au
[3] www.worldbank.org
[4] www.pc.gov.au
[5] www.danieldavis.com/
[6] www.danieldavis.com
[7] https://searchdatamanagement.techtarget.com
[8] https://futurism.com
[9] https://medium.com
[10] https://artlist.io
[11] www.forbes.com
[12] https://bdtechtalks.com
[13] www.grammarly.com
[14] www.simonsays.ai
[15] www.grammarly.com/

A Research On Building Cluster Morphology Formation Based On Wind Environmental Performance And Deep Reinforcement Learning

Yanan Song[1], Philip F. Yuan[2]
[1,2]Collage of Architecture and Urban Planning, Tongji University
[1,2]{yannasong|philipyuan007}@tongji.edu.cn

Nowadays, numerous researchers emphasize the significance of the environmen-tal performance-driven generative methodology. However, due to the complex coupling mechanism of environmental regulation factors, the existing optimiza-tion engines and applications are time-consuming and cumbersome. In this re-search, we propose a novel design methodology based on Deep Reinforcement Learning (DRL). This paper is divided into 3 sections, including theoretical framework, design strategy, and practical application. It first introduces an over-view of basic principles, illustrating the potential advantages of DRL in perfor-mance data-driven design. Based on this, the paper proposes a DRL-based gener-ative method. We point out a more specific discussion about the application and workflow of core DRL elements in architectural design. Finally, taking a grid-form urban space composed by multitude high-rise building blocks as an exam-ple, we present a application through a DRL agent to conduct numerous active wind environmental performance-based design tests. It is an interactive and gen-erative design method, owning multiple advantages of timeliness, convenience, and intelligence.

Keywords: *Deep Reinforcement Learning, Environmental Performance Design, Generative Design, Building Cluster Formation*

INTRODUCTION

In the urbanization process, the high-rise architectural cluster results in the high-density urban space which aggravated the deterioration of urban ventilation, heat island effect, air pollution, and so on (Ng, Yuan et al. 2011). As of today, wind data-driven performance optimization has become a challenging topic and future direction of architecture discipline, with popular applications in the following two methods. The first one is a physical technique called the "white box" method, which is used to model hydrodynamic behavior of buildings based on CFD simulation soft-ware for repetitive calculation of the Navier-Stokes equations (Foucquier, Robert et al. 2013). However, the regulation of building environmental performance optimization is a complex task (Duriez, Brunton et al. 2017). Because of the characteristics of non-linearity, time dependence, and high dimensionality in processing data, it is high-sensitive to the change of design parameters, which is hard to meet the needs of design decision-making and rapid deduction in the conceptual stage.

The second modeling method presents a statistical or deep learning formulation (Brunton and Noack 2015) named "black box" or "data-driven model" (Foucquier, Robert et al. 2013). This approach is mainly used in the aim to collect a relevant environmental database and derive a predictive model from it. In the past ten years, considerable progress has been made in high-performance computing science and sensing technologies, spawning a variety of optimization (Kitchin 2014) and control methods (Brunton, Noack et al. 2020). As of today, this black box method for environmental performance design is supported by abundant research. Therefore, looking for a suitable deep learning algorithm, which achieves a good compromise between accuracy and computational cost (Roman, Bre et al. 2020), has become an efficient approach for complex construction environment engineering problems solution. (Nguyen, Reiter et al. 2014).

In recent years, the combination of deep learning (DL) with reinforcement learning (RL), called deep reinforcement learning (DRL), has provided a new powerful tool. This new algorithm can use high-dimensional space for feature extraction and has great potential in computational or experimental fluid dynamics applications. DRL managed to perform tasks with unprecedented efficiency in many fluid engineering domains (Garnier, Viquerat et al. 2019), including complex flow controlling (Guéniat, Mathelin et al. 2016), shape optimizing (Lampton, Niksch et al. 2008, Viquerat, Rabault et al. 2019), fluid dynamics visualizing (Kim, Azevedo et al. 2019), to name just as a few. However, despite great potential, the relevant research applying DRL in the architecture discipline is still in a blue ocean.

This paper presents a DRL-based environmental performance formation method of building clusters. The paper consists of three sections: theoretical research, policy proposals, and partial application. To begin, it outlines the fundamental principle of DRL and offers an overview of its applications for aerodynamics simulation (Lillicrap, Hunt et al. 2015, Schmidhuber 2015). Then, this paper introduces this DRL-based environmental performance metamorphism method in fourfold detail phase, including environment preparation, actions execution, reward obtaining, and decision-making.

Motivated by our previous observation of the advantage and potential of DRL methodology, this paper presents an architectural high-rise cluster morphology generation method based on DRL. We use DRL algorithms to optimize the morphology of gridded urban. Consistent with these (Garnier, Viquerat et al. 2019, Viquerat, Rabault et al. 2019) prior studies, near-end strategy optimization strategies (Schulman, Wolski et al. 2017), multilayer neural network and proximal policy optimization algorithms (PPO) are combined with the traditional architecture of DRL. As research on the methodological considerations of this DRL generative design paradigm, the research unitizes its experimental grid and units, saving simulation experiment time and computing power. It is an interactive generation design method that transcends human intelligence, and undoubtedly helps the conversational relationship between architecture and the environment return from the passive response of an active system to the morphogenesis-driven dynamic response.

METHODOLOGY

Deep Reinforcement Learning

This chapter briefly introduces the related concepts of deep learning (Goodfellow, Bengio et al. 2016), reinforcement learning (Sutton and Barto 2018), and deep reinforcement learning (Li 2017).

Reinforcement Learning (RL). Reinforcement learning is an important branch of machine learning. Different from supervised learning (which learns from the preprocessed labeled training dataset for inferring and generalizing), and unsupervised learning (which implies the extraction of implicit features from the database without a ground-truth label, for dimensionality reduction, quantization, and clustering), RL is the third learning paradigm alongside above, implying goal-directed interactions of an agent with its environment. RL algorithm is a mathematical framework, whose complete, interactive, goal-oriented agent determines a given state through a trade-off between "trial" and "development" with an uncertain environment, and tries the best action to maximize its long-term cumulative reward in the environment. The classical Markovian decision process (MDP) of RL algorithms (Bellman 1957, Howard 1960) includes four main elements, shown as follows in Table1.

Table 1
Four main elements of MDP <A, S, R, P>

A	/	A is the set of executable actions of the agent, $a_t \in A$ denotes the action taken by agent at time t.
S	/	S is the set of all environmental states, $s_t \in S$ denotes the state that agent is in at time t.
R	$S \times A \rightarrow R$	Real number R is the reward function, $r_t \sim \rho(s_t, a_t)$ represents the immediate reward value obtained by the agent in the state s_t with performing action a_t .
P	$S \times A \times S \rightarrow [0,1]$	$P(s'\|s,a)$ is the probability of getting to state s' from state s following action a

Deep Learning (DL). Deep learning (DL) with a multilayered architecture can process original databases from higher abstract levels (Goodfellow, Bengio et al. 2016) for easy decision making, and streamline the solution for non-linear and complex functions modeling. There are numerous successive hidden neural network layers between the input and output of DL, which are equipped with non-linear activation functions. Besides, DL capability of weight update and loss function optimization provides a suitable platform for the backpropagation algorithm. In practical applications, DL is able to achieve higher speed and accuracy on more complex tasks as compared with traditional algorithm. Now DL has formed some generally accepted network architectures. These architectures include the widely used convolutional neural network (CNN), artificial neural network (ANN), deep neural network (DNN), and recurrent neural network (RNN), which are in different concepts and categories. With the help of these algorithm networks, DL has offered numerous innovations in mathematical tools in fluid mechanics application (Kutz 2017), including model reduction operations(Wang, Xiao et al. 2018), visualization expression (Chu and Thuerey 2017, Rabault, Kolaas et al. 2017, Um, Hu et al. 2018), digital twin(Han and Zhang 2020, Willard, Jia et al. 2020).

Deep Reinforcement Learning (DRL). The real development of deep reinforcement learning (DRL) is attributed to the invention of neural networks and in hand with an ever-increasing amount of computing power. The invention of AlphoGo (Silver, Huang et al. 2016) demonstrates the superhuman potential of DRL. Leveraging the advantage of the generalization ability of deep learning neural networks to continuously approximate the value function (Lillic-rap, Hunt et al. 2015), DRL has brought unprecedented influence in propagating the state and action results of reinforcement learning to a larger action space. DRL can be roughly organized into twofold classes: one is the Model-Based algorithm, which is mainly based on dynamic programming value iteration and strategy iteration; the other is the Model-Free algorithm, including policy gradient algorithm and Q Learning. For the sake of brevity, more detailed discussions are referred to related works (Bertsekas, Bertsekas et al. 1995, Sutton and Barto 1998, Littman 2015, Li 2017) on this topic.

This research focuses on the Proximal Policy Optimization method (PPO), which is used to perform active flow control in a continuous simulation environment. PPO (Schulman, Wolski et al. 2017) is a policy gradient method, belonging to reinforcement learning family. . The PPO agent is a Tensorforce-based open-source implementation, proposed by OpenAI in 2017. This method was selected for the considered application for the following two reasons: (1) PPO constraints its policy change in a small range, for high-dimensional continuous control tasks and stable learning. So (2) the PPO requires less complex mathematically and little to no meta parameter tuning, so it is faster and more suitable for continuous control problems, just like active flow control. The objective function of PPO is optimized as:

$$\mathbb{E}_{L^{CLIP}(\theta)} = \hat{E}_t[\min(\alpha)] \quad (1)$$

$$\alpha = r_t(\theta)\hat{A}_t, clip\Big(r_t(\theta), (1-\varepsilon, 1+\varepsilon)\hat{A}_t\Big) \quad (2)$$

θ is the policy parameter; $\hat{E}_t$ demotes the empirical expectation over timesteps; r_t is the ratio of the probability under the new and old policies; $\hat{A}_t$ is the estimated advantage at time t; ε is a hyperparameter, which is used to assist in setting the update range of the strategy; the clip is a truncation function, which limits the value of the parameter $r_t(\theta)$ into the range of $[1-\varepsilon, 1+\varepsilon]$. This formula is cited from *(Abbeel and Schulman 2016).*

In this paper, we propose an interaction framework between DRL and the experimental environment, in order to generate a reasonable result of building cluster morphology within a limited step. The so-called "a reasonable result" in this paper should be explained to maximize the environmental performance index R_t (Reward function R_t) of the tested agent O_t by changing the simulate action A_t (Here A_t is the active control of the height of the dynamic grid unit, which is stimulated by the agent of DRL) of building group morphology.

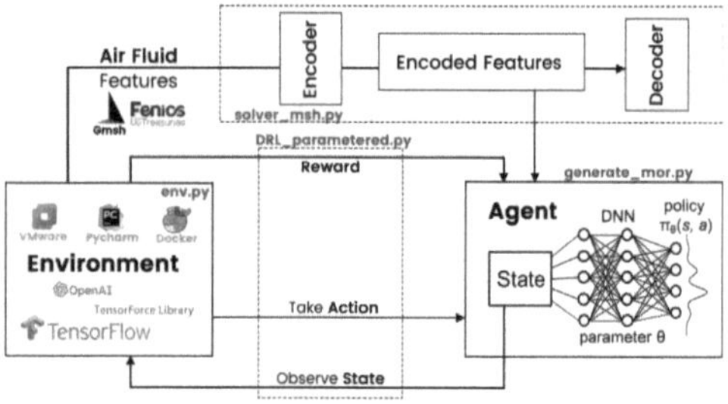

Figure 1
Generic structure of deep reinforcement learning

Simulation environment

In the current urbanization process, because of its intensive and comprehensive nature, high-density cities are favored and popularized. However, high-rise building monoliths have a strong shading and turbulence effect on natural ventilation due to their huge volume, while the discrete layout of the building complex has a greater impact on the local ventilation performance and pollutant dispersion in urban public spaces. Wind environmental performance can be optimized by adjusting the building height staggering, building density, and plan dispersion of building group morphology in the initial design stage.

The development of high-performance computing tools sensing technologies has prompted the transformation of design methodology, from geometric-based parameter design (Lynn 1993) into the performance-based simulation (BPS) (Yezioro, Dong et al. 2008, Hensen and Lamberts 2012) and generation (Mahdavi 1999, Hensen and Lamberts 2012), based on environmental database, and formed the integration trend of architectural geometric with performance design pattern (Nguyen, Reiter et al. 2014) under the logic of digital thinking. When trained with numerous fluid data, the DRL algorithm can perform a mathematical methodology for real-time analysis and simulation predictions (Nguyen, Reiter et al. 2014, Roman, Bre et al. 2020), whose results inform smarter design decisions and creative deliberations in the conceptual design

Table 2
Reinforcement learning agent basics

Policy	Policy can be regard as a mapping rule, between action A and perceived environment $\pi(a\|s)$.	*Stochastic Policy:* $\sum \pi(a\|s) = 1$; *Deterministic Policy:* $\pi(s): S \rightarrow A$
Reward Signal	Reward signal defines the learning target R_t.	$\boldsymbol{s_0, a_0, r_1, s_1, a_1, r_2, \dots, s_{n-1}, a_{n-1}, r_n, s_n}$ *s_0 is State, a_0 is action, r_1 is reward, and s_n is terminal state* $\boldsymbol{G_t = \sum_{n=0}^{N} \gamma^n r_{t+n}, 0 < \gamma < 1,}$ *G_t is the long-term return expectation; γ is the discount factor for long-term returns.*
Value function	Value function is a prediction of the expected future reward, measuring how good each state is.	$\boldsymbol{V_\pi(s) = E_\pi[G_t\|S_t = s] = E_\pi\left[\sum_{k=0}^{\infty} R_{t+k+1} \|S_t = s\right]}$ *$V_\pi(s)$ is the long-term expected return of policy π in state s.* $\boldsymbol{Q_\pi(s,a) = E_\pi[G_t\|S_t = s, A_t = a]}$ *$Q_\pi(s,a)$ is a long-term expected return with action a in the state s of policy π*
Model	Model is a simulation of the real environment.	Model-free & Model-based

phases.

To perform required interactive simulation numerical computations, the domain and geometries of CFD mesh is generated by FeniCs and Gmsh in this DRL environment. FeniCs (Alnæs, Blechta et al. 2015), a finite element mesh solver composed of a set of multiple interactive components, computes numerical simulations by Navier-Stokes (NS) equations for computational fluid dynamics. And Gmsh (Geuzaine and Remacle 2009), an open-source 3D finite element mesh generator with geometry, mesh, solver, and post-processing, is used to perform lightweight and user-friendly execution domain and geometric mesh generation. Our DRL training experiment is with reference to (Martilli and Santiago 2007, Santiago, Martilli et al. 2007, Toparlar, Blocken et al. 2017).

$$\rho\frac{\partial\vec{v}}{\partial t}+\rho(\vec{v}\cdot\nabla)\cdot\vec{v}=-\nabla P+\vec{\gamma}\rho+\mu\nabla^{2}\vec{v} \quad (3)$$

Formulae (2) is a typical Navier-Stokes equation, where g is the gravity acceleration, ρ is the density and μ is the viscosity.

The DRL-based CFD simulation approach here is a branch of fluid mechanics which uses Navier-Strokes equation for numerical analysis. Air flows here are allowed to be considered at a low Reynolds of 200. It is suitable for quick conceptual decision making as well as fast-trained future benchmarking within a limited computational budget and resources.

APPLICATION

In recent years, DRL has become a rapidly growing field of artificial intelligence. Following the developments in algorithm iteration updating, the computational logic of RL, DL, and DRL approaches have classified into forwarding derivation (predicting state evolution over time), and reverse solution (backward derivation for parameter optimization of physical systems based on physical phenomena). We can combine the environmental performance-based generation model into the optimization loop of the DRL algorithm.

DRL has become a fundamental mode of problem-solving in reproduce the dynamics of airflow in aviation and machinery, here are some related papers.

Table 3
Deep reinforcement learning for fluid mechanics

	Algorithm	References
Flow Control	QL	(Guéniat, Mathelin et al. 2016)
	DQN	(Gazzola, Tchieu et al. 2015, Novati, Verma et al. 2016, Novati, Verma et al. 2017)
	ADQN	(Verma, Novati et al. 2018)
	TRPO	(Ma, Tian et al. 2018)
	PPO	(Rabault, Kuchta et al. 2018, Viquerat, Rabault et al. 2019, Rabault, Ren et al. 2020, Tang, Rabault et al. 2020)
Homogeneity optimization	QL	(Colabrese, Gustavsson et al. 2017, Gustavsson, Biferale et al. 2017, Tsang, Tong et al. 2020)
	PSO	(Mason, Mannion et al. 2016, Samma, Lim et al. 2016)
	CNN	(Wiewel, Kim et al. 2020)
	PDE	(Holl, Koltun et al. 2020)
Shape Optimization	PPO	(Rabault, Ren et al. 2020, Viquerat, Rabault et al. 2021)
	DATCOM	(Yan, Zhu et al. 2019)
	MD	(Teboul, Kokkinos et al. 2011)
	DNN	(Chen, Cakal et al. 2020, Um, Holl et al. 2020)
Fluid Simulation	CNNs	(Eckert, Um et al. 2019, Ummenhofer, Prantl et al. 2019, Kohl, Um et al. 2020)
	GAN	(Xie, Franz et al. 2018, Kim, Azevedo et al. 2019)
Chaotic Systems	DDPG	(Gadaleta and Dangelmayr 1999, Bucci, Semeraro et al. 2019)
	TDGAR	(Lin and Jou 1999)

EXPERIMENT

The training process of environmental performance DRL-based urban morphology generation consists of four phases: the configuration initialization phase, the execution phase, the reward obtainment phase, and the decision-making phase. The specific training process of our DRL algorithm is organized as follows.

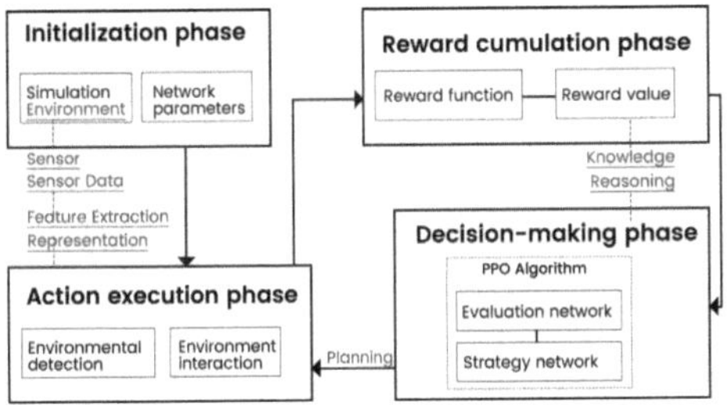

Figure 2
Training process of DRL algorithm

Initialization phase

In the initial stage, we first configure the DRL training environment and perform mesh generation of the domain and geometries for aerodynamics simulation, parameters of which all depend on basic flow physics, including Navier-Strokes equation and evaluation index of aerodynamics performance in urban space. Here, several external libraries are required for the correct installation of matching versions, including TensorFlow, Tensorforce, Fenics, Gmsh modules, and the reproduction software stack. Proximal policy optimization (PPO) is introduced in, performing active flow control in a 3D simulation environment.

This CFD-DRL program is concerned with the rapid derivation of large-scale volume models in the conceptual design phase, assisting designers with rapid deduction and better environmental performance-based design decisions. In order to simplify the architecture of the training model and control the mathematical calculation variables, abstract unit grids are carried out for a brief representation of the architectural form type and spatial layout orientation. Following the similarity principle of CFD simulation (see Equation 2), all quantities are dimensionless parameters. Different from the popular multi-agent system, in this research, the entire network grids are treated as a single-agent system with certain changing rules. We simulate the morphology of building groups and organize environment interactions by setting the action behavior of the dynamic grid agent, by controlling the Z-axis height of dynamic grid units in different locations

This research preset120 dynamic grids as the morphogenesis domain, among which 64 units in the central area are seen as the main areas of the test. Each grid is of typical dimension 1. The dynamic grids are immersed in a rectangular computational space, of length L = 30, width W = 18, and height H =12. The origin of the coordinate system is at the center of the dynamic grid, which deviates from the center of the test area and is located about two-thirds away from the air inlet of the test section in the Y direction.

The airflow around dynamic grid cubes is assessed and discretely calculated via finite element at moderate Reynolds numbers using FeniCs (Alnæs, Blechta et al. 2015). To perform computations, unstructured grids of rectangular space and geometries of dynamic grids are performed by Gmsh (Geuzaine and Remacle 2009). We input a constant velocity v=$v_i \cdot e_x$. Free-slip boundary conditions are set on the top and bottom of the domain, at the same time non-traction conditions are on outflow contour.

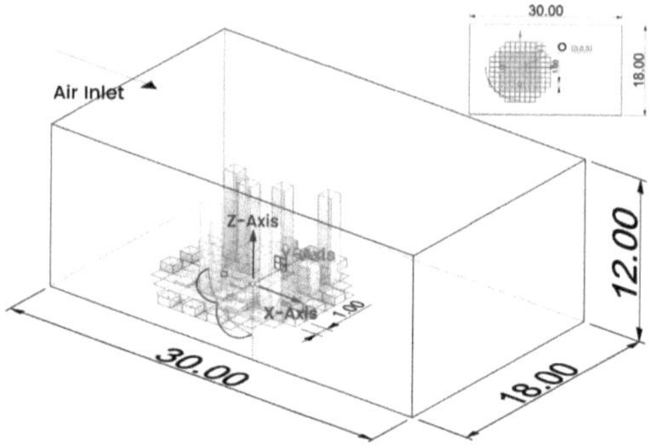

Figure 3
Rectangular computational domain

It is worth mentioning that all parameters of DRL in this paper are in a low configuration level, for fast training and proof-of-concept demonstration, and they can be easily increased in future research for more accurate simulation results, including the matrix of grid heights, mesh density, Reynolds number.

Execution phase

The urban wind environment remains in a high dimensional state of continuous change. A huge amount of aerodynamics data requires numerous computing time and arithmetic costs, meaning that analytical solutions, and real-time predictive simulations out of reach. Therefore, to minimize the complexity of their actions, we preset the minimum lifting distance of dynamic grids in the Z-axis direction, to transform the continuous space form of agents into a finite set of discrete points. The specific parameter settings are as follows. The coordinate of a grid vertex is $A_n \leq ft(x_n, y_n, z_n right)$; the length and width of single grid cells are l, and its height is h. In this paper, L=1, and$x_1 = n_1 \cdot L = n_1; y_1 = m_1 \cdot L = m_1;$ $H = 0.1 \cdot \mu$, where m and n are integers, and μ is a positive integer.

In this study, the observed wind environment information should include as following: (1) spatial formation index of the dynamic cell grid, formed by various plane layout patterns and random heights of its 64 lift-up tested grids; (2) urban morphology index, including building density and staggered windward side; (3) evaluation index of wind environment performance, including wind speed V_s and wind load force f_d. All these indexes should be measured in the same simulation state.

The response of the environment to the action is a coupled discrete vector, lifting up and down. Agent's all behavior determinations are affected by the following twofold factors: (1) The height of all measured grid cells is less than 1/2 of the simulation domain; (2) The layout of test girds often meets spacing control requirements. It is tough for us to find an appropriate rule for the real project plan layout management, because of its complex generation index. Therefore, in order to simplify the ideal model and control variables, the layout generation methodology adopted in this paper is to set the surrounding open space interval distance. Reflected to dynamic grid system, the rule can be expressed as follows: Among the ω grids ($\omega \in 1,2,3$) centered on building A_n, there shall be no grids with a height greater than zero.

Reward obtainment phase

Our DRL agent configures a set of scientific standards for the evaluation of ur-ban wind environmental performance. It is the 1.5-meter pedestrian-height wind in-dex that is selected as the main evaluation standard for an urban environment (Zheng 2018). The performance-based strategies used in most published works are only simplistic (and probably suboptimal), so there is a need to develop efficient control methods with a multitude, complex and active control parameters. In this paper, the following evaluations are selected: average wind speed $\overline{v}$Wind comfort deviation ΔWind speed dispersionσ, and probability of uncomfortable wind speed ζ. All above are seen the reward function for the DRL algorithm to constrain the building form:

$$f_{\overline{v}}(x_1, x_2, \ldots, x_n) \in (a, b) \quad (4)$$

$$\min f_{\Delta,,}(x_1, x_2, \ldots, x_n) \quad (5)$$

where $x = \{x_1, x_2, \ldots, x_n\}^T$ is an n-dimensional design variable of the formation of the building cluster. In our research, a=1.5, b=5, and v_i=3. $f_i(x)$, {i=1,2,3,...,m} is the objective function of the relevant parameter i.

Constraints can eventually prohibit undesired behaviors from the network (in a non-mathematical sense), with the adding penalties of the reward function (Rabault, Kuchta et al. 2018). By limitation of reward barrier in the action space, the agent will learn to avoid the associated behavior. Here, the goal of constraints is to satisfy the pre-set morphology index, including floor area ratio, building density, and staggering index. Here $G_i(x)$ is a constraint function. To that end, one can simply add here

$$X = \{x | x \in R^n, a_j < G_i(x) < \beta\} \quad (6)$$

$$i = 1, 2, \ldots, m; j = 1, 2, \ldots, p \quad (7)$$

Decision-making phase

DRL models are the attempt to learn the correct strategies through the feedback signal obtained by interacting with the environment and describe the learning goal by maximizing the expected cumulative reward. Each DRL training experiment consists of a set of learning episodes. Considering the time budget and arithmetic cost of computing, this research sets 20000 episodes. The DRL code training material of this project mainly includes the following files:

(1) **Morpholgoy_0** folder, which concludes four basic documents of the initial shape at the beginning of each episode; (2) **Fenics_solver.py** is the CFD solver file based on Fenics; (3) **Paramrtered_-DRL.py** is used to adjust the training parameters of the DRL algorithm; (4) **Environment_UMG.py** is used to modify the reward computation of DRL training; (5) **Constraints.py** is used to satisfy the preset morphology index, including both staggering index training graph (left) and windward area index; (6) **Bake.py** is used to baking mathematical data of building groups into 3D models in Rhinoceros platform.

```
def solve_flow(*args, **kwargs):
    mesh_file/output/final_time/cfl/xmin/xmax......
    v_in/mu/rho/x_shape/y_shape......

    class Obstacle(SubDomain):
        def inside(self, x, on_boundary):
    def epsilon(u):
    def sigma(u, p):
    def compute_drag_lift(u, p, mu, normal, gamma):
        return (fX, fY)
    dt/timestep/T= final_time/num_steps = math.floor(T/dt)
    shape= 'on_boundary && x[0]>(-'+str(x_shape)+') && x[0]<'+
str(x_shape)+' && x[1]>(-'+str(y_shape)+') && x[1]<('+str(
y_shape)+')'
    global n_call/u_0
    for m in range(num_steps):......
    return drag, lift, True
```

Figure 4
The structure of code 'Fencis_solver.py'

```
import rhinoscriptsyntax/math/re
interval = int(interval_h)
inList = [[0 for j in range(sizeX)] for i in range(sizeY)]
trans_heights = []
def check(x, y):
    if inList[x][y] != 3:
def IsCanDoIt():
result = IsCanDoIt()

inList = []
for i in heights:
    inList.append(float(i))
avg = sum(inList) / len(inList)
avg_height = round(avg, 3)
sum = 0.000
for i in inList:
    sum += pow((i-avg), 2)
O = pow((sum / len(inList)), 1 / 2)
O_height = round(O, 3)
print('avg:',avg_height)
```

Figure 5
The structure of code 'Constraints.py'

RESULT

This training experiment performs on a local computer engine. The computer is configured as a Windows 10 professional system, with an Inter(R) Core(TM) i7-8700 CPU and memory of 16GB. Our DRL agent controls 64 dynamic grids lifting up-down in the computational domain, while the rest 56 grids are all set to H=0, trying to simulate the morphology of the high-rise building groups located in an open site. In this experiment, the interval distance of building grids is limited among [1.3], while the density of building groups is set among [0.5,0.7]. The convergence results of this DRL-based method show that at the initial training stage, the agent has not been fully trained, whose random probability is still high, where multiple building blocks are still in close proximity (see the left-top picture of Fig.7). However, after numerous "trial and error" iterative training, the agent gradually transforms from exploration to exploitation (see the left-middle picture of Fig.7), the success rate of which increases rapidly (see the left-down picture of Fig.7).

In the end, we make a cyber-physical experiment for the training result validation. We choose the CPWT wind tunnel developed by our team earlier (Lin 2019), to simu-late the DRL-based generation results in the convergence stage and the final stage. It is shown that as the iterations continue to converge, the sensing data gradually be-come stable, and the magnitude of wind speed values converge within the range of better environmental performance evaluation indexes. The results of physical wind tunnel experiment again validate the effectiveness of this DRL generation method (see the right picture of Fig.7).

CONCLUSIONS

In this research, We use the DRL-based algorithm to conduct numerous generative design tests for environmental performance morphology generation. This design method demonstrated its multiple advantages of timeliness, convenience, and intelligence. It is an interactive generation design method that transcends human intelligence, and undoubtedly helps the conversational relationship between architecture and the environment return from the passive response of an active system to the morphogenesis-driven dynamic response.

This work is the potential of considerable importance for both Fluid Mechanics and DRL-based architectural design methodology. After the publication of our research papers, we would like to release the source code of this project as open-source on Github. In the future, we will package, and deploy the training environment in a separate unit via Docker container, for multiple calls of virtualization and reproducibility.

REFERENCES

Anh-Tuan, Nguyen, Sigrid, Reiter and Philippe, Rigo 2014, 'A review on simulation-based optimization methods applied to building performance analysis', *Applied Energy*, 113, pp. 1043-1058

Aurélie, Foucquier, Sylvain, Robert and Frédéric, Suard 2013, 'State of the art in building modelling and energy performances prediction: A review', *Renewable and Sustainable Energy Reviews*, 23, pp. 272-288

Byungsoo, Kim, Vinicius C, Azevedo and Nils, Thuerey 2019 'Deep fluids: A generative network for parameterized fluid simulations', *Computer Graphics Forum*, pp. 59-70
Nadia D, Roman, Facundo, Bre, Victor D, Fachinotti and Roberto, Lamberts 2020, 'Application and characterization of metamodels based on artificial neural networks for building performance simulation: A systematic review', *Energy and Buildings*, 217, p. 109972
Edwar, Ng, Chao, Yuan, Liang, Chen, Chao, Ren and Jimmy CH, Fung 2011, 'Improving the wind environment in high-density cities by understanding urban morphology and surface roughness: a study in Hong Kong', *Landscape and Urban planning*, 101, pp. 59-74
Garnier, Paul, Viquerat, Jonathan, Rabault, Jean, Larcher, Aurélien, Kuhnle, Alexander and Hachem, Elie 2019, 'A review on deep reinforcement learning for fluid mechanics', *arXiv preprint arXiv:1908.04127*, ., p. .
Goodfellow, Ian, Bengio, Yoshua, Courville, Aaron and Bengio, Yoshua 2016, *Deep learning*, MIT press Cambridge
Guéniat, Florimond, Mathelin, Lionel and Hussaini, M Yousuff 2016, 'A statistical learning strategy for closed-loop control of fluid flows', *Theoretical and Computational Fluid Dynamics*, 30(6), pp. 497-510
Howard, Ronald A 1960, 'Dynamic programming and markov processes', ., ., p. .
Jürgen, Schmidhuber 2015, 'Deep learning in neural networks: An overview', *Neural networks*, 61, pp. 85-117
Kim, Byungsoo, Azevedo, Vinicius C, Thuerey, Nils, Kim, Theodore, Gross, Markus and Solenthaler, Barbara 2019 'Deep fluids: A generative network for parameterized fluid simulations', *Computer Graphics Forum*, pp. 59-70

```
import os/glob/math/time/PIL/matplotlib/numpy  # Generic imports
from shapes_utils/meshes_utils/fenics_solver import *

class env():   # Define environment class for rl
    # Static variable
    episode_nb =-1 / control_nb = 0
    # Initialize morphology
    shape = Shape()
    def __init__(self, ......):
        # Saving model periodically
        env.saving_model_period = saving_model_period
        env.shape.read_csv(self.reset_dir+'/Morpho_0.csv')
        env.shape.generate(centering=False)
        # Initialize arrays
        self.drag/self.lift/self.reward/...= np.array([])
    def reset(self):
        env.episode_nb += 1   # Console output
        if (env.episode_nb%100 == 0): time.sleep(10)
        env.control_nb  = 0                          # Reset control number
        next_state = self.fill_next_state(True, 0)  # Fill next state
        return(next_state)
    def execute(self, action=None):
        # Console output actions to numpy array
        deformation = np.array(action).reshape(...)
        for i in range(self.nb_pts_to_move):
            ......
        env.shape.modify_shape_from_field(......)   # Modify shape
        try:......
        except Exception as exc:
        # Generate image & Save png and csv files
        env.shape.generate_image(csv/png/)
        os.system('mv '+env.shape.name+'_'+str(env.shape.index)+'.... '+self.comp_dir+'/save/.../.')
        self.compute_reward(meshed)
        return(next_state, terminal, self.reward[-1])  #Return

    def compute_reward(self, meshed):
        if (meshed):
            try:name = self.comp_dir+'/'+env.morpho.name+'_'+str(env.morpho.index)+'.xml'
                drag, lift, solved = solve_flow(......)
                os.system('mv '+str(env.shape.index)+'.png '+self.comp_dir+'save/sol/.')

            if (solved):......   # If solver was successful
            else:                # If solver was not successful
        # Save drag, lift, reward and penalization
        self.drag/lift/reward/penal = np.append(self.drag/lift/reward/penal,
drag/lift/reward/penal)
    def fill_next_state(self, meshed, index):......
        return next_state
```

Figure 6
The structure of code 'Environment_UMG.py'. The source code of this project will be released as Open Source on Github later

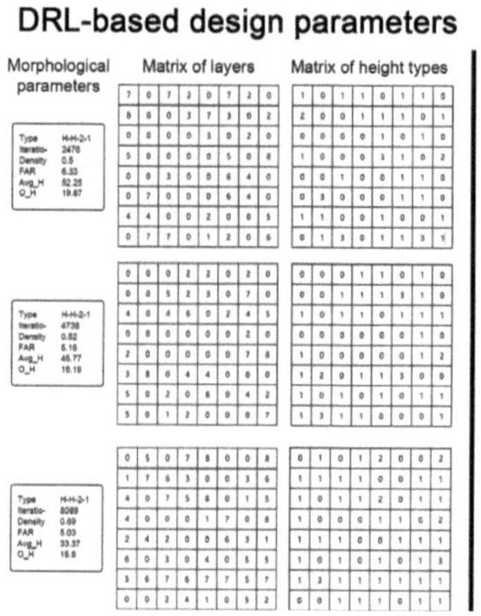

Physical validation experiment parameters

类型编号	建筑密度 (D)	容积率 (FAR)	测点1风速值	测点2风速值	测点3风速值	测点4风速值	迎风面积指数 (λ f)	错落度 (C)	高度均值 (H_avg)	风速平均值 V_a	舒适风速偏差均值	风速离散值Vde	不舒适风速概率Puc
L-H-1-1	0.28	7.55	1.28	1.35	4.5	3.29	0.13	63.86	23.7	3.12	1.92	1.86	0.63
L-H-1-1	0.23	5.02	1.04	3.08	2.88	2.12	0.08	30.93	15.75	2.28	1.08	0.45	0.13
L-H-1-1	0.19	5.02	1.24	2.45	3.37	2.17	0.1	52.98	15.75	2.74	1.54	0.86	0.38
L-H-1-1	0.27	5	1.14	2.12	2.45	3.08	0.1	47.43	15.7	2.36	1.16	0.34	0.25
L-H-1-1	0.3	5.38	1.43	2.45	4.41	2.12	0.14	52.8	16.88	2.58	1.38	0.83	0.25
M-H-1-1	0.39	5.39	0.78	3.15	4.5	3.51	0.11	47.46	16.93	2.77	1.57	1.16	0.50
M-H-1-1	0.47	5.72	1.47	1.87	2.82	2.75	0.09	33.28	17.96	2.28	1.08	0.39	0.13
M-H-1-1	0.38	5.06	1.6	3.29	2.34	2.95	0.09	28.55	15.9	2.35	1.15	1.04	0.38
M-H-1-1	0.34	5.37	0.73	2.69	4.68	2.82	0.13	47.66	16.88	2.58	1.38	1.27	0.25
M-H-1-1	0.36	7.42	1.28	1.51	2.69	3.02	0.09	33.19	23.31	1.93	0.73	1.04	0.25
M-H-1-1	0.31	5.55	1.1	1.31	3.59	2.28	0.14	48.89	17.42	2.23	1.03	1.64	0.25
M-H-1-1	0.34	5.53	1.21	0.98	2.34	2.28	0.11	34.26	17.37	2.00	0.80	0.31	0.00
M-H-1-1	0.34	5.75	0.92	2.02	4.15	2.34	0.11	42.96	18.06	2.57	1.37	1.21	0.38
M-H-1-1	0.5	6.72	0.98	1.51	3.51	2.07	0.09	31.44	21.1	1.66	0.46	0.75	0.13
M-H-1-1	0.33	6.5	0.73	2.82	4.77	2.63	0.11	38.51	20.41	2.37	1.17	1.57	0.13
H-H-2-1	0.5	6.33	2.12	1.04	3.37	2.17	0.14	52.25	19.87	1.81	0.61	0.66	0.13
H-H-2-1	0.52	5.16	1.24	2.88	3.66	2.45	0.08	45.77	16.19	2.28	1.08	0.72	0.13
H-H-2-1	0.69	5.03	1.47	1.82	3.22	2.88	0.08	33.37	15.8	2.18	0.98	0.92	0.25
H-H-2-1	0.59	5	1.43	2.82	3.66	2.82	0.09	38.49	15.7	2.23	1.03	0.66	0.13
H-H-2-1	0.66	5.11	1.1	0.78	3.82	2.45	0.08	36.7	16.04	2.19	0.99	1.45	0.38
L-M-1-1	0.23	3.31	2.69	4.07	2.82	2.51	0.07	26.86	10.4	3.08	1.88	0.27	0.50
L-M-1-1	0.11	2.78	1.64	4.68	1.43	2.69	0.07	28.76	8.73	2.88	1.68	0.95	0.50
L-M-1-1	0.28	2.78	3.29	4.86	3.59	2.07	0.06	29.64	8.73	3.14	1.94	0.81	0.50
L-M-1-1	0.25	2.39	2.63	4.96	2.57	1.92	0.05	23.31	7.51	2.86	1.66	0.80	0.38
L-M-1-1	0.27	2.94	2.57	4.77	3.37	2.51	0.07	26.05	9.22	3.43	2.23	0.59	0.63
M-M-2-1	0.44	3.08	1.41	2.95	2.75	2.88	0.05	20.79	9.66	2.40	1.20	0.29	0.00
M-M-2-1	0.39	3.67	1.43	3.22	3.02	2.88	0.07	29.41	11.53	2.43	1.23	0.48	0.25
M-M-2-1	0.47	2.88	1.31	2.63	3.51	2.39	0.04	15.84	9.03	2.59	1.39	0.51	0.25
M-M-2-1	0.42	2.53	0.66	2.07	4.41	3.02	0.03	12.36	7.95	2.74	1.54	1.02	0.50
M-M-2-1	0.44	2.91	1.01	3.02	3.66	2.23	0.06	24.84	9.13	2.44	1.24	0.55	0.25
H-M-2-1	0.58	2.73	0.89	2.51	2.45	3.08	0.03	9.89	8.59	2.16	0.96	0.59	0.13
H-M-2-1	0.5	4.66	1.92	3.15	3.66	2.34	0.09	38.23	14.62	2.20	1.00	1.25	0.38
H-M-2-1	0.53	3.5	0.83	3.44	3.15	3.15	0.05	23.15	10.99	2.54	1.34	0.85	0.50
H-M-2-1	0.56	3.41	1.24	3.37	3.59	2.63	0.05	21.42	10.7	2.65	1.45	0.63	0.38
H-M-2-1	0.56	3.78	1.24	2.82	2.39	3.08	0.06	19.22	11.87	2.43	1.23	0.25	0.13

Figure 7
DRL-based generation results (left) & its corresponding physical wind tunnel experiment results (right)

Kutz, J Nathan 2017, 'Deep learning in fluid dynamics', *Journal of Fluid Mechanics*, 814, pp. 1-4

Steven L, Brunton and Bernd R, Noack 2015, 'Closed-loop turbulence control: Progress and challenges', *Applied Mechanics Reviews*, 67, p. 5

Steven L, Brunton, Bernd R, Noack and Petros, Koumoutsakos 2020, 'Machine learning for fluid mechanics', *Annual Review of Fluid Mechanics*, 52, pp. 477-508

Lampton, Amanda, Niksch, Adam and Valasek, John 2008 'Morphing airfoils with four morphing parameters', *AIAA Guidance, Navigation and Control Conference and Exhibit*, pp. 72-82

Lin, Yuqiong 2019, *An Architectural Cluster Morphology Generation Method Based on Physical Wind Tunnel and Neural Network Algorithm*, Master's Thesis, Tongji University

Timothy P, Lillicrap, Jonathan J, Hunt, Alexander, Pritzel and Nicolas, Heess 2015, 'Continuous control with deep reinforcement learning', *arXiv preprint arXiv:1509.02971*, ., p. .

Paul, Garnier, Jonathan, Viquerat, Jean, Rabault, Aurélien, Larcher, Alexander, Kuhnle and Elie, Hachem 2019, 'A review on deep reinforcement learning for fluid mechanics', *arXiv preprint arXiv:1908.04127*, ., p. .

Rob, Kitchin 2014, 'The real-time city? Big data and smart urbanism', *GeoJournal*, 79, pp. 1-14

Schulman, John, Wolski, Filip, Dhariwal, Prafulla, Radford, Alec and Klimov, Oleg 2017, 'Proximal policy optimization algorithms', *arXiv preprint arXiv:1707.06347*, ., p. .

Sutton, Richard S and Barto, Andrew G 2018, *Reinforcement learning: An introduction*, MIT press

Teboul, Olivier, Kokkinos, Iasonas, Simon, Loic, Koutsourakis, Panagiotis and Paragios, Nikos 2011 'Shape grammar parsing via reinforcement learning', *CVPR 2011*, pp. 2273-2280

Thomas, Duriez, Steven L, Brunton and Bernd R, Noack 2017, *Machine learning control-taming nonlinear dynamics and turbulence*, Springer

Viquerat, Jonathan, Rabault, Jean, Kuhnle, Alexander, Ghraieb, Hassan, Larcher, Aurélien and Hachem, Elie 2019, 'Direct shape optimization through deep reinforcement learning', *arXiv preprint arXiv:1908.09885*, ., p. .

Viquerat, Jonathan, Rabault, Jean, Kuhnle, Alexander, Ghraieb, Hassan, Larcher, Aurélien and Hachem, Elie 2021, 'Direct shape optimization through deep reinforcement learning', *Journal of Computational Physics*, 428, p. 110080

Wang, Zheng, Xiao, Dunhui, Fang, Fangxin, Govindan, Rajesh, Pain, Christopher C and Guo, Yike 2018, 'Model identification of reduced order fluid dynamics systems using deep learning', *International Journal for Numerical Methods in Fluids*, 86, pp. 255-268

Yan, Xinghui, Zhu, Jihong, Kuang, Minchi and Wang, Xiangyang 2019, 'Aerodynamic shape optimization using a novel optimizer based on machine learning techniques', *Aerospace Science and Technology*, 86, pp. 826-835

Augmented Accuracy

A human-machine integrated adaptive fabrication workflow for bamboo construction utilizing computer vision

Yue Qi[1], Ruqing Zhong[2], Benjamin Kaiser[3], Yasaman Tahouni[4], Hans-Jakob Wagner[5], Alexander Verl[6], Achim Menges[7]
[1,2,4,5,7]Institute for Computational Design and Construction, University of Stuttgart
[3,6]Institute for Control Engineering of Machine Tools and Manufacturing Units, University of Stuttgart
[1,2]{dbddqy|zrq.zhongruqing}@gmail.com [3]benjamin.kaiser@isw.uni-stuttgart.de [4,5]{yasaman.tahouni|hans.jakob.wagner}@icd.uni-stuttgart.de

Despite being sustainable, strong and lightweight, naturally grown bamboo poles are currently used in restricted building typologies. This is due to the large tolerances in the built structures, which is caused by the variations in the dimensions and geometry of natural material as well as the manual, uninformed and imprecise assembly methods. In previous work, we introduced an adaptive fabrication method for bamboo structures that can monitor the fabrication process and compensate for deviations between built and designed form. As a proof of concept, the method is suitable for small scale bamboo structures in 2D- or simple 3D configuration. This paper extends the previous method by integrating the adaptation strategies into a cohesive fabrication and assembly workflow for large scale complex bamboo structures. To enable that, a more effective sensor localization method, adaptation algorithm, connection and assembly system, as well as web-based user interface are developed. The effectiveness of the proposed methods is demonstrated through the fabrication of a pavilion scale branching bamboo structure that complies with intended geometric boundary conditions. Even though the material has substantial geometrical variations, the final structure shows small geometric deviations and a successful interface with the prefabricated roof elements. Our work shows how vernacular materials and processes can be digitally augmented in order to reliably produce building structures, hence enabling their usage in modern applications to a larger extent.

Keywords: *Adaptive Digital Fabrication, Construction Uncertainties, Computer Vision, Bamboo Structures, HMI*

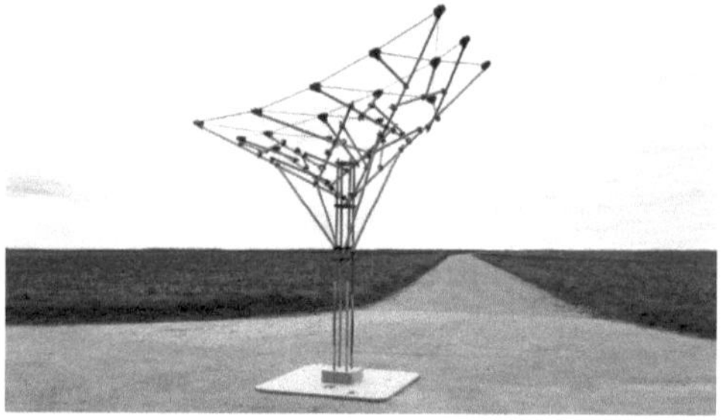

Figure 1
Final demonstrator

INTRODUCTION
Research Context
Bio-based material in construction. According to the projections of the United Nations, there will be 2.3 billion new urban dwellers by 2050 (United Nations 2018). The demographic increase will bring huge demand for the construction of new housing, commercial buildings and supporting infrastructure, which obviously entails a growing demand for construction material and energy resources. As claimed by the global status report for buildings and construction (United Nations 2019), in 2018, the buildings and construction sector accounted for the largest amount of both global energy consumption (36%) and energy-related CO_2 emission (39%), 11% of which came from manufacturing widely-used building materials and products such as steel, cement and glass. In contrast, utilizing bio-based materials in construction has a positive impact on the environment. Recent research shows that bio-based construction materials with good carbon storage capacity can help alleviate the emission of CO_2 and be part of a solution for the global warming issue (Churkina et al. 2020). Among the natural materials, wood and bamboo are especially suitable for building construction due to their favorable mechanical properties.

Computational design and robotic fabrication with naturally grown material. Both being naturally grown materials, developments in computational design and robotic fabrication are focusing more on wood rather than bamboo, since engineered wood technologies are more advanced. Some performative wood architectures (Willmann et al. 2016; Yuan et al. 2016; Wagner et al. 2020) have been enabled based on engineered wood and high-tech machinery. Nevertheless, high energy and resource consumption for material standardization are required in such construction methods. Besides, the machines are not applicable in remote areas. Natural bamboo already has performative material properties before machinery. However, due to its intrinsic geometric variations, the usage of raw bamboo in the current construction industry is hindered. With the development of new technologies, recent researchers are getting more and more interested in this material, experimental digital methods are explored for the construction process (dbt 2020), sensing technologies and tailor-made connection components are utilized to deal with the material individuality (Amtsberg and Raspall 2018).

Cyber-physical construction and HMI (Human Machine Interface). Although natural materials are sustainable for the environment and have plentiful processing possibilities, many of the construction and assembly tasks still rely on the agility and cognitive abilities of humans, which makes fully automated workflow hardly implementable in the foreseeable future. In the scenario of human machine collaboration, cyber-physical systems can help manage the collaborative building tasks by utilizing sensor networks, iterative data processing, and feedback loops (Vasey and Menges 2020). In such systems, computational processes and information flow are usually complicated, hence not easily leverageable by average users who have limited knowledge about the system. User interfaces can serve as a platform for bi-directional flow of information, meanwhile helping users intuitively understand processes and properly perform tasks. "The Hive" (Vasey et al. 2016), enables the collaboration between untrained workers and industrial robots for fabricating a computationally designed structure with interconnected devices and an effective user interface. Another project "CROW" (ICD 2018; Kyjanek et al. 2019) presents fluid human computer interaction by utilizing a head-mounted display and a mixed reality based user interface. "Fologram" (Jahn et al. 2018) proposed a software platform that can enable a flexible and interactive fabrication process with mixed-reality instructions. A woven steel structure was constructed in the CAADRIA 2018 Workshop using this AR-platform. "Augmented Bricklaying" (Mitterberger et al. 2020) explored an object-aware AR-guided assembly system, which includes tracking and visual guiding, for in situ assembly of complex brickwork.

In the fabrication process of natural bamboo structures where construction uncertainties are easy to appear and adaptation needs to be performed, an intuitive user interface can enable the workers to assemble complex structures in a short time frame without knowing details of the digital tools.

Previous Work

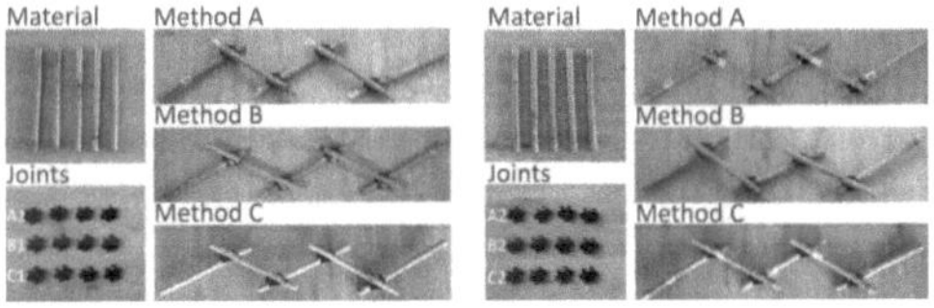

Figure 2
Bamboo structure in 2D arrangement fabricated with an adaptive workflow. Two groups of materials are experimented. Method A is in-progress survey, Method B is pre-scan, Method C is manual measurement

This paper presents further development of work presented at CDRF 2020 (Qi et al. 2021). In our previous work, a cyber-physical adaptive fabrication system was implemented for bamboo structures, which monitored the as-built structures with a computer vision system and responded to deviations by adaptively generating updated instructions during the fabrication process. The fabrication system was tested to build 2 basic demonstrators. As the main intention was to validate the effectiveness of adaptive fabrication strategies, the demonstrators were designed to have only 5 elements in 2D- or simple 3D arrangement (Fig. 2). However, the workflow was not directly transferable to larger and more complex structures, due to following limitations:

Applicable scale of the sensor localization method. As the camera had to be localized with a reference object (a circle grid pattern), it could only be placed where the whole reference object was visible. As a result, the camera had limited workspace, which made it difficult to survey large structures.

Effectiveness of the adaptation algorithm. While solving the adaptation problem, we noticed that the genetic algorithm used in the previous experiments usually took minutes to converge. Besides, lacking the ability to solve constrained problems, the genetic algorithm could not cope with potential connection related constraints.

Effectiveness of the connection strategy. Custom connection parts had to be produced with 3D printing or CNC machining, because the geometry of these parts was unique and needed to define the correct pose (position and orientation) to assemble the new bamboo element. Such a production process was necessary in every single iteration of the fabrication loop, making the whole workflow fragmented and expensive.

Lack of designed user-interface. To complete the task, the user had to run C++ programs, Python scripts, as well as Grasshopper scripts. Furthermore, the user had to produce parts with the method of 3D printing or CNC machining. Such operations are not suitable for average construction workers.

Facing aforementioned limitations, this research focuses on developing a cohesive fabrication and construction assembly workflow, which can be used to build bamboo structures with increased scale and complexity. The major improvements are:

- Sensor localization method inside workspaces of construction scale.
- Algorithm for efficiently solving constrained adaptation problems.
- Connection and assembly strategy without the need of tailor-made parts.
- User interface that can guide human workers through the whole fabrication and assembly process.

ADAPTIVE FABRICATION WORKFLOW

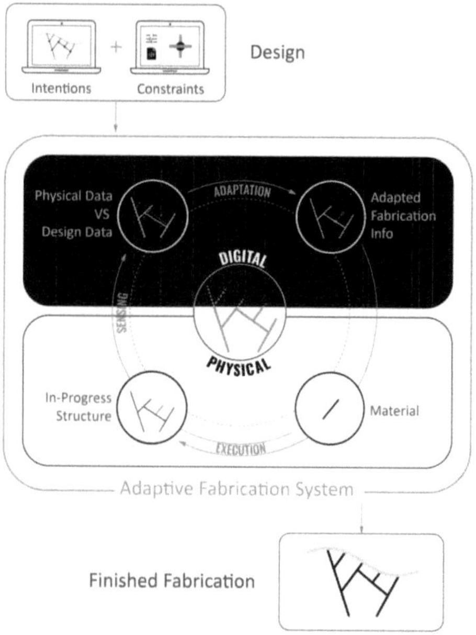

Figure 3
Adaptive fabrication workflow for bamboo structure

The fabrication task is to manually assemble bamboo structures that achieve not only a designed global form, but also a precise enough boundary to interface with other prefabricated building layers. As is shown in Fig. 3, the fabrication process contains multiple iterations of adding a new bamboo pole onto the existing structure, accomplishing predefined design intentions while satisfying necessary fabrication related constraints. In each iteration, the in-progress structure and the next bamboo element to be added are scanned with an RGBD camera. Combining the data of measured physically built form and the digitally designed form, the pose to add the next bamboo element can be adjusted to adapt to the current fabrication status and compensate for the existing deviation. Finally, the adapted result is transferred into visual guidance, enabling the user to correctly position the bamboo element during the assembly. After a bamboo element is connected onto the existing structure, a new iteration begins. The loop repeats until the fabrication task is completed.

Sensor Localization

Distributed fiducial markers are used to localize the camera. With an increasing number of markers, the workspace of the camera can be significantly extended. The ArUco Library (Garrido-Jurado et al. 2016; Romero-Ramirez et al. 2018) is used for the generation and detection of fiducial markers. The markers can be installed around or on the structure in arbitrary poses. In order to describe their poses in one consistent global coordinate frame, a one-time calibration has to be performed before fabrication starts. For the calibration step, the user has to collect images from different perspectives, and each image has to contain at least 2 markers. A C++ program is then responsible for the detection of markers, estimation and refinement of their poses. Let $\mathbf{a}_j$, $\mathbf{b}_i$ and $\mathbf{c}_k$ be the j-th camera pose, i-th marker pose and k-th marker corner (described in the marker coordinate system), assuming there are n markers in m views, the following nonlinear optimization problem has to be solved:

$$\min_{\mathbf{a}_j,\mathbf{b}_i} \sum_{i=1}^{n}\sum_{j=1}^{m}\sum_{k=1}^{4} v_{ij}||Q(\mathbf{a}_j,\mathbf{b}_i,\mathbf{c}_k)-\mathbf{x}_{ijk}||^2, \quad (1)$$

where $Q(\mathbf{a}_j,\mathbf{b}_i,\mathbf{c}_k)$ signifies the function which projects 3D coordinates of the marker corner to its 2D position on image, $\mathbf{x}_{ijk}$ signifies the corresponding perceived 2D coordinates, $\mathbf{v}_{ij}$ is a binary variable with the value 0 if the i-th marker is not on the image, with the value 1 elsewise. The optimization problem is solved with Ceres-Solver (Agarwal et al. 2018).

Figure 4
Setup of fiducial markers and calibration process

Figure 5
Calibration result of fiducial markers

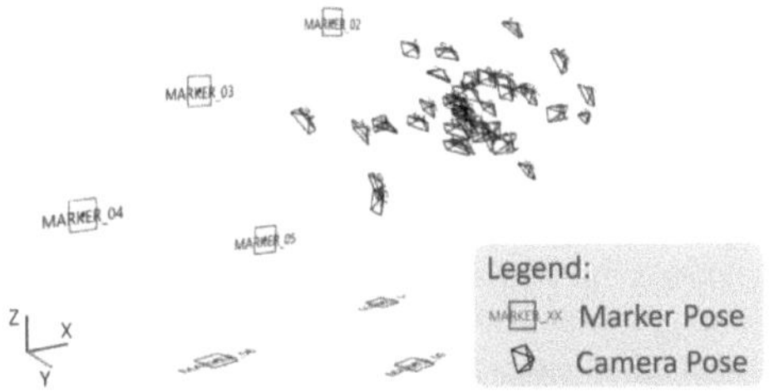

After the calibration, all the corner positions can be described in one consistent global coordinate frame. They can be used in the Perspective-n-Point (PnP) algorithm for the camera localization. In practice, at least 2 markers are used to ensure the localization accuracy.

Fig. 4 shows the setup for testing the fiducial marker based sensor localization method. Seven ArUco markers are measured in 37 images from different perspectives. Fig. 5 shows the result map of markers, as well as the camera poses. The accuracy of the map is checked by comparing corner distances in the digital model with the physical measurement. In this specific test, the two measured corners have a distance of approximately 400 mm and the error is below 1 mm. The accuracy of the camera poses is not measured in this research since the ground truth is not available. According to existing literature (Muñoz-Salinas et al. 2018), millimeter level accuracy can be achieved.

The localized sensor is then used for the scanning of the material and the existing structure. The result is the geometrical information of bamboo segments around connection areas. The detailed method for obtaining that information can be referred to from the previous publication (Qi et al. 2021).

Adaptation of Bamboo Poses

The adaptation process (Fig. 6) generates the most suitable pose to assemble the next bamboo pole based on the sensory results of the previously assembled elements. This can be seen as an optimization problem of achieving the design intentions to the greatest extent, while keeping the connection with the existing structure feasible. Therefore, the objective function depends on the design intentions, whereas the constraints depend on the achievable angles and distances between elements. Let $\mathbf{p}_0$ be the target point at the boundary, which is intended to be reached, $\mathbf{p}$ and $\mathbf{v}$ be the starting point and vector of the bamboo segment, $\mathbf{R}$ and $\mathbf{t}$ be the rotation matrix and translation vector of the pose. The cost function is formulated as follows:

$$\min_{\mathbf{R},\mathbf{t}} D(\mathbf{p_0}, \mathbf{Rp}+\mathbf{t}, \mathbf{Rv}) + \lambda_1\theta(\mathbf{R}) + \lambda_2||\mathbf{t}||. \quad (2)$$

The first distance term evaluates how well the boundary condition is fulfilled, and the following two regularization terms suggest the preference for small adjustment around the intended pose over a large one. The manually tuned coefficients λ_1 and λ_2 are used to weight the rotational and translational magnitudes. $D(\mathbf{p}_i, \mathbf{p}.\mathbf{v})$ is the distance function from point to the axis, which is formulated as:

$$D(\mathbf{p}_i, \mathbf{p}.\mathbf{v}) = \frac{||(\mathbf{p}_i - \mathbf{p}) \times \mathbf{v}||}{||\mathbf{v}||}. \quad (3)$$

And the rotated angle $\theta(\mathbf{R})$ is given by:

$$\theta(\mathbf{R}) = \arccos\left(\frac{tr(\mathbf{R}) - 1}{2}\right), \quad (4)$$

The formulation of constraints will be introduced together with the connection strategy. The problem is solved with the method of sequential quadratic programming. The optimization module from library SciPy (Virtanen et al. 2020) is utilized.

Figure 6
Adaptation

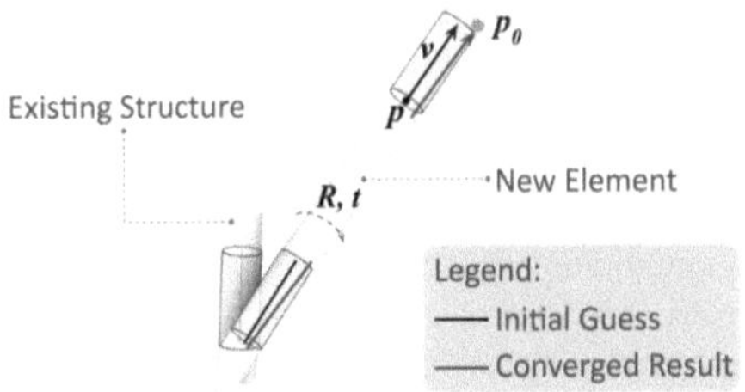

Connection and Assembly Process

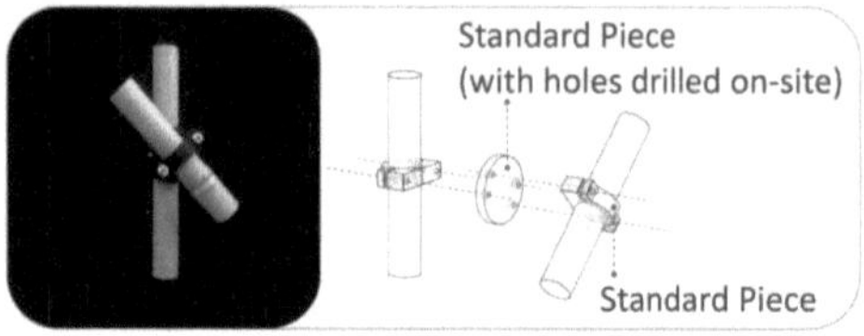

Figure 7
Clamping node prototype

Connection. As is illustrated in Fig. 7, the two poles are connected via clamps and a circular middle piece. In this way, the distance between them is fixed. The angle between two poles can also be fixed with the 4 holes on the circular element. Thus, the angle can be customized by only the placement of the drilled holes, rather than producing a completely new part in the fabrication loop, which is costly and inefficient. With the distance and angle fixed, the positioning of the elements can still be adjusted by sliding the new pole along the existing one, or rotating around it. Determined by the characteristics of the joint, the following constraints have to be considered while optimizing the poses of the poles to be added:

$$d(\mathbf{T}(\mathbf{l}), \mathbf{m}) = d_0 \quad (5)$$

$$\theta^l \leq \theta(\mathbf{T}(\mathbf{l}), \mathbf{m}) \leq \theta^u, \quad (6)$$

where **l** signifies the cylinder segment of the next bamboo element to be assembled, **m** signifies the cylinder segment on the existing structure. **T** signifies the six degrees of freedom transformation, which essentially defines the assembly pose of segment **l**. d_0 is the required distance between two bamboo elements, whereas θ^l and θ^u signify the lower- and upper bound of the required angle.

Assembly process. A quasi-mixed reality style visual augmentation system (Fig. 8) is developed to provide instructions for the assembly of 3D intricate bamboo structures. The axis of the bamboo pole is combined onto the video stream, which gives the user an intuition about the correct pose to connect the next element.

Moreover, with the sensory data from the RGBD camera, a numerical error metric can be provided to measure how well the pose of the physical building element fits the digitally adaptively generated one, so that the physical element can be adjusted back and forth until a good fit is reported. To avoid excessive computation, we implemented a depth monitoring process without estimating the actual pose of the building element, which can run at a high frame rate. Let d_k and $\hat{d_k}$ be the actual depth value of the k-th sample point read from the sensor and the corresponding depth value calculated through the camera projection model, and n be the number of points, the calculation (Fig. 9) is as follows:

$$\frac{1}{n}\sum_{k=1}^{n}\left|d_k - \hat{d_k}\right|, \quad (7)$$

The 2D coordinates of the projected points on the image only need to be calculated once (the camera has to stay stationary), the model consumes little computational power.

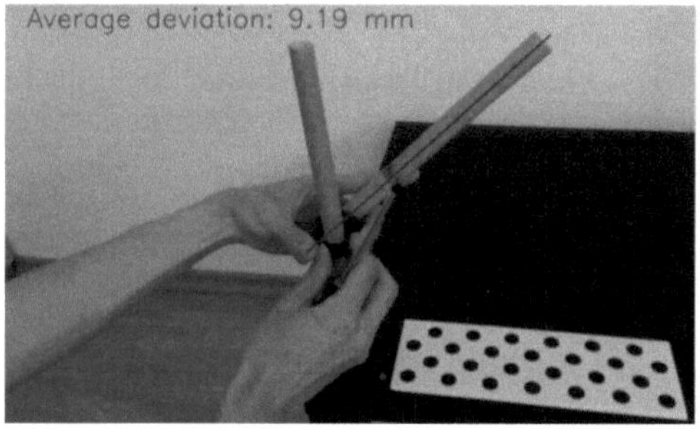

Figure 8
Quasi-mixed reality style visual augmentation system

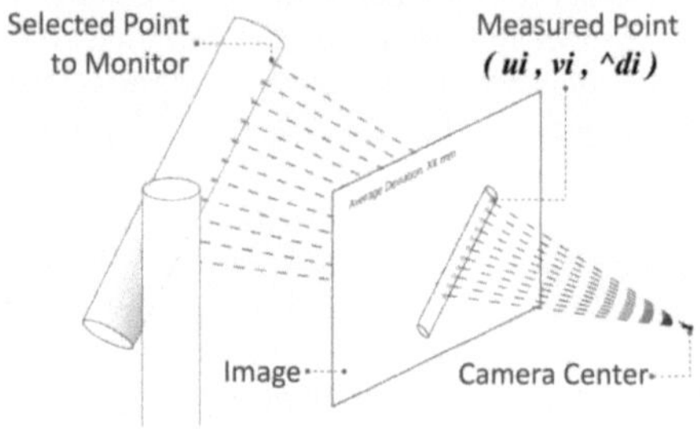

Figure 9
Calculation of the error metric

Figure 10
(a) Design intention. One part of the whole design is used for final demo (b) Fabrication process (c) User interface

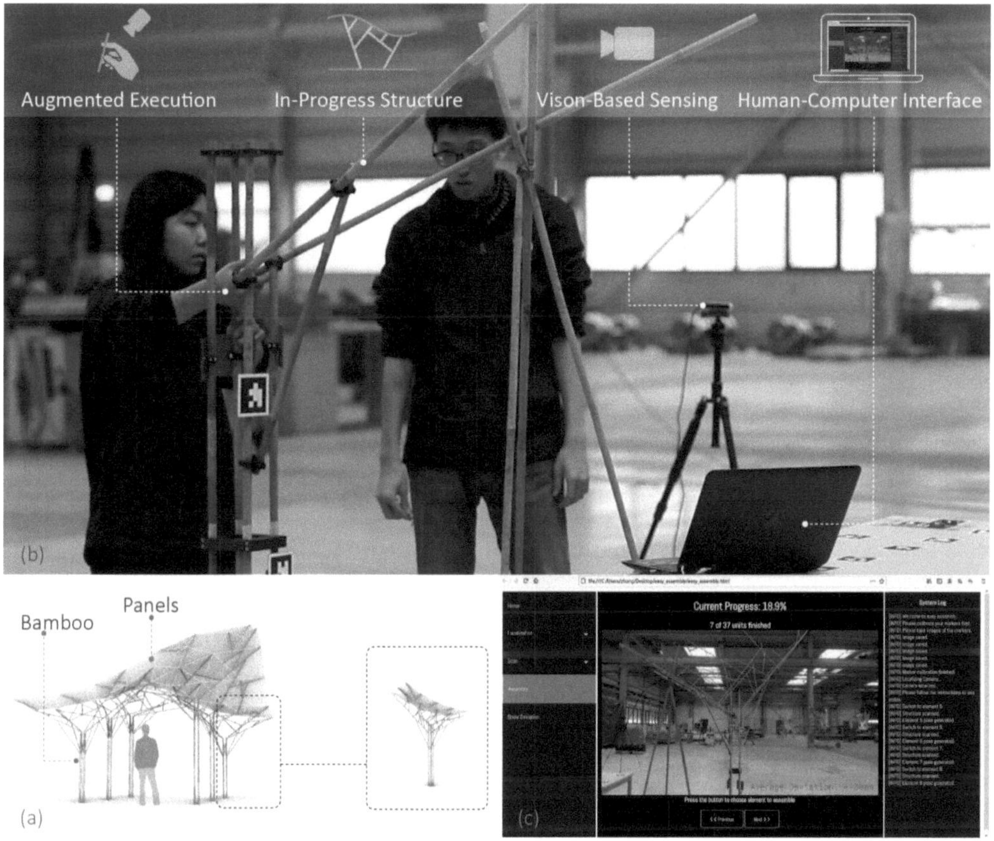

User Interface

To make the workflow usable and accessible to the builders, a graphical web interface is developed. It allows the users to access all the computational tools, and can be accessed from various devices, such as laptops, smartphones and tablets. The graphic design follows a concise style, consisting of a left side menu bar, a main window and a system logger. Different functionalities such as camera localization, in-progress structure surveying and assembly assistance can be selected from the menu. The main window displays the video stream from the sensor and the fabrication progress. The logger prints out system messages and keeps records of conducted fabrication actions.

LARGE-SCALE DEMONSTRATOR

With the aforementioned methods, we are able to work with a larger scale bamboo structure in complex 3D configurations, while also enabling a predictable interface between the bamboo structure and prefabricated roof components. To achieve that, the intention of reaching defined target points is set to higher priority compared to the intention of accomplishing the general form. The built form is a part of a branching tree-like substructure for a curved roof. It is 2.5 m tall at its highest point, covering 2 m^2 of area (Fig. 10(a)). The intended built form consists of 37 bamboo elements with different lengths, and 50 joints at different angles. The roof consists of 18 uniquely prefabricated roof panels, and they have to be installed with custom made connection parts.

The demonstrator is fabricated in an indoor environment over the course of seven days, and the assembly of the bamboo structure took approximately 12 hours. Fig. 10(b) and Fig. 10(c) document the fabrication process, which is a realization of the proposed workflow. The finished structure (without roof) is scanned (Fig. 11(a)) and compared with the design intention. Even though the material has substantial geometrical variations, 85% of the measured points around the interface area have deviations less than 30 mm, and 68% among them less than 15 mm. This demonstrates the capability of the adaptive fabrication process to manage cumulative deviations that stem from the natural construction material. Fig. 11(b) and Fig. 11(c) document the final built structure with the roof plates installed.

DISCUSSION AND OUTLOOK

Previous experiments (Qi et al. 2021) have validated the effectiveness of the proposed adaptive strategy for the fabrication of bamboo structures. In this article, we showcase how such a strategy can be integrated into the construction workflow of a pavilion-scale demonstrator to achieve a reasonable result. As such fabrication processes can be implemented with a low budget sensor, it opens up novel possibilities of low cost digitally augmented bamboo construction in remote areas. The feasibility of the current solution in an outdoor environment still has to be studied, as RGB-D sensors are expected to be less performative in such environments. The accuracy could be further improved by using an industrial grade sensor, which the authors recommend for large scale mission critical applications, as this would drastically further improve the achievable tolerances.

There exists a limitation in the aspect of connection. All the nodes are considered to connect only two bamboo poles, which critically affects the spatial pole arrangement. Because in the built structure, the joints may take considerable bending moments. More performative structural typologies such as space frames can be achieved if the workflow is extended to cope with more complicated connection strategies.

The user interface is still under improvement. Additional functionalities like camera positioning guidance and existing structure assessment are planned, but not developed yet. It is also a good direction to have the user interface based on head-mounted mixed reality devices. In this way, interactive holographic instructions can be created to further improve the user experience.

IMPACT

Based on this research, we summarize two main trajectories of applications of the presented adaptive fabrication system. One focuses on sustainable materials like bamboo, the other looking at the general cyber-physical fabrication framework:

As the workflow that applied on the fabrication of bamboo structure indicates promising results, one can envision the vernacular materials and fabrication processes being augmented to produce comparable results as their modern counterparts. In this way, the usage of these sustainable materials in modern applications can be largely extended.

From a more general point of view, the concept of adaptive fabrication is not limited to any specific material system or fabrication method. The presented research can be seen as a case study of cyber-physical fabrication processes, which have the potential to be deployed to collaborative, flexible, as well as non-standard fabrications (Vasey and Menges 2020). The proposed system framework in this project can be a step towards robust fabrication under various sources of uncertainties. In this regard, one of the future directions is to extend this system to in-situ fabrication under unstructured environments, collect-

Figure 11
(a) Scan result of the finished structure
(b) Structure detail
(c)Final structure

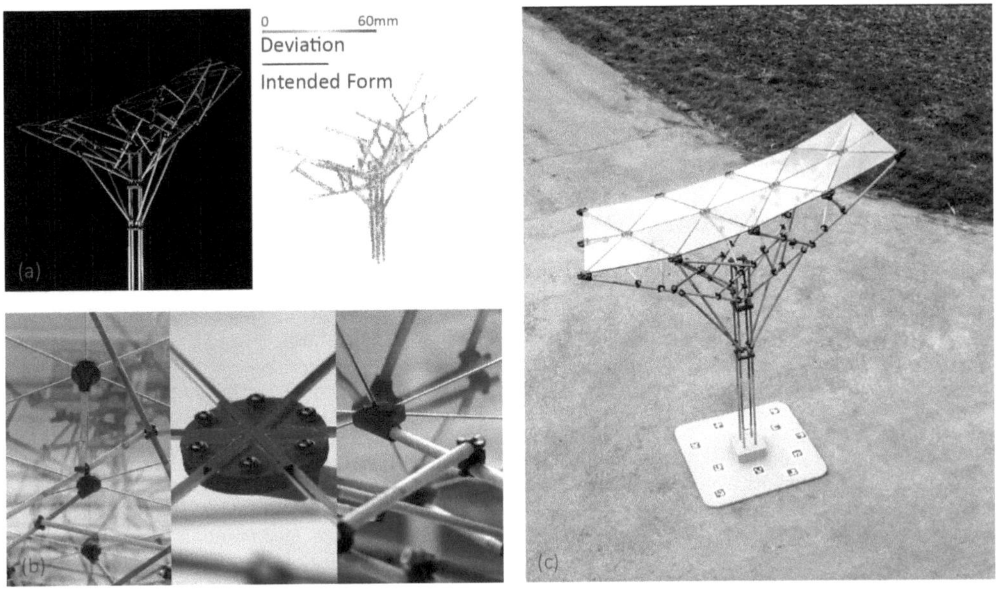

ing data from different sensors, enabling the networked collaboration of multiple agents, such as robots, domain-specific machines and human workers, at the same time, ensuring a predictable and reliable result.

ACKNOWLEDGMENT

The presented work was conducted within the ITECH master thesis program at the University of Stuttgart, Germany. We would like to thank the following for their support and feedback during the course of research: the Integrative Technologies and Architectural Design Research (ITECH) program, researchers at the Institute for Computational Design and Construction (ICD) and Institute for Building Structures and Structural Design (ITKE), researchers at Institute for Control Engineering of Machine Tools and Manufacturing Units (ISW). This work was partially supported by the State of Baden-Wuerttemberg, the European Regional Development Fund and by the German Research Foundation under Germany's Excellence Strategy - EXC 2120/1 - 390831618. The work received further support through the DFG Excellence Cluster IntCDC's Master Thesis Grant of 2020.

REFERENCES

Agarwal, S, Mierle, K and Other Contributors, - 2018, *Ceres Solver (Version 1.14) [Open Source Code]*, Available at: http://ceres-solver.org

Amtsberg, F and Raspall, F 2018 'Bamboo3', *Proceedings of the 23rd International Conference of the Association for Computer-Aided Architectural Design Research in Asia (CAADRIA)*, Tsinghua University, Beijing, China, pp. 245-254

Churkina, G, Organschi, A, Reyer, CPO, Ruff, A, Vinke, K, Liu, Z, Reck, BK, Graedel, TE and Schellnhuber, HJ 2020, 'Buildings as a global carbon sink', *Nature Sustainability*, 3, pp. 269-276

dbt, Digital Building Technologies 2020, *Digital Bamboo*, ETH, Available at: https://dbt.arch.ethz.ch/project/digital-bamboo/

Garrido-Jurado, S, Muñoz-Salinas, R, Madrid-Cuevas, FJ and Medina-Carnicer, R 2016, 'Generation of fiducial marker dictionaries using Mixed Integer Linear Programming', *Pattern Recognition*, 51, pp. 481-491

ICD, Institute for Computational Design and Construction 2018, *CROW: Collaborative Robotic Workbench*, University of Stuttgart, Available at: https://www.icd.uni-stuttgart.de/research/research-projects/crow-collaborative-robotic-workbench/

Jahn, G, Newnham, C, Berg, N and Beanland, M 2018 'Making in Mixed Reality', *Proceedings of the 38th Annual Conference of the Association for Computer Aided Design in Architecture (ACADIA)*, Mexico City, Mexico, pp. 88-97

Kyjanek, O, Bahar, BA, Vasey, L, Wannemacher, B and Menges, A 2019 'Implementation of an augmented reality AR workflow for human-robot collaboration in timber prefabrication', *Proceedings of the 36th International Symposium on Automation and Robotics in Construction (ISARC)*, Banff, Canada, pp. 1223-1230

Mitterberger, D, Dörfler, K, Sandy, T, Salveridou, F, Hutter, M, Gramazio, F and Kohler, M 2020, 'Augmented bricklaying - Human–machine interaction for in situ assembly of complex brickwork using object-aware augmented reality', *Construction Robotics*, 4, pp. 151-161

Muñoz-Salinas, R, Marín-Jimenez, MJ, Yeguas-Bolivar, E and Medina-Carnicer, R 2018, 'Mapping and localization from planar markers', *Pattern Recognition*, 73, pp. 158-171

United Nations, - 2018, *2018 Revision of World Urbanization Prospects*, United Nations, Available at: https://www.un.org/development/desa/publications/2018-revision-of-world-urbanization-prospects.html

United Nations, - 2019, *2019 Global Status Report for Buildings and Construction Sector*, United Nations, Available at: https://www.unep.org/resources/publication/2019-global-status-report-buildings-and-construction-sector

Qi, Y, Zhong, R, Kaiser, B, Nguyen, L, Wagner, HJ, Verl, A and Menges, A 2021 'Working with Uncertainties: An Adaptive Fabrication Workflow for Bamboo Structures', *Proceedings of the 2020 DigitalFUTURES (CDRF 2020)*, Shanghai, China, pp. 265-279

Romero-Ramirez, FJ, Muñoz-Salinas, R and Medina-Carnicer, R 2018, 'Speeded up detection of squared fiducial markers', *Image and Vision Computing*, 76, pp. 38-47

Vasey, L, Grossman, T, Kerrick, H and Nagy, D 2016 'The hive: a human and robot collaborative building process', *ACM SIGGRAPH 2016 Talks*, New York, United States, pp. 1-2

Vasey, L and Menges, A 2020, 'Potentials of cyber-physical systems in architecture and construction', in Sawhney, A, Riley, M and Irizarry, J (eds) 2020, *Construction 4.0: An Innovation Platform for the Built Environment*, Routledge, pp. 91-112

Virtanen, P, Gommers, R, Oliphant, TE, Haberland, M, Reddy, T, Cournapeau, D, Burovski, E, Peterson, P, Weckesser, W, Bright, J, van der Walt, SJ, Brett, M, Wilson, J, Millman, KJ, Mayorov, N, Nelson, ARJ, Jones, E, Kern, R, Larson, E, Carey, CJ, Polat, İ, Feng, Y, Moore, EW, VanderPlas, J, Laxalde, D, Perktold, J, Cimrman, R, Henriksen, I, Quintero, EA, Harris, CR, Archibald, AM, Ribeiro, AH, Pedregosa, F, van Mulbregt, P and SciPy 1.0 Contributors, - 2020, 'SciPy 1.0: fundamental algorithms for scientific computing in Python', *Nature Methods*, 17, pp. 261-272

Wagner, HJ, Alvarez, M, Groenewolt, A and Menges, A 2020, 'Towards digital automation flexibility in large-scale timber construction: integrative robotic prefabrication and co-design of the BUGA Wood Pavilion', *Construction Robotics*, 4, pp. 187-204

Willmann, J, Knauss, M, Bonwetsch, T, Apolinarska, AA, Gramazio, F and Kohler, M 2016, 'Robotic timber construction — Expanding additive fabrication to new dimensions', *Automation in Construction*, 61, pp. 16-23

Yuan, PF, Chai, H, Yan, C and Zhou, J 2016 'Robotic Fabrication of Structural Performance-based Timber Grid- shell in Large-Scale Building Scenario', *Proceedings of the 36th Annual Conference of the Association for Computer Aided Design in Architecture (ACADIA)*, Ann Arbor, pp. 196-205

The Use of Natural Materials in Additive Manufacturing of Buildings Components

Towards a more sustainable architecture

Tatiana Campos[1], *Paulo J. S. Cruz*[2], *Bruno Figueiredo*[3]
[1,2,3] *University of Minho, Architecture School, Lab2PT - Landscapes, Heritage and Territory Laboratory*
[1] *tatianavcampos@outlook.com* [2,3] *{pcruz|bfigueiredo}@arquitetura.uminho.pt*

The demand for sustainable building materials is currently a major concern of society. It is known that the traditional construction industry requires a high consumption of inorganic materials, which is associated with the excessive production of waste. Thus, this article intends to demonstrate the possibility of using the Additive Manufacturing (AM) technique Paste Extrusion Modeling (PEM) in the production of reusable, biodegradable and recyclable construction systems, using a combination of different natural materials that have created multiple pastes with different additives.Cellulose is a natural material - biodegradable, recyclable and low cost - and its implementation aims to change some aspects of the current state of the construction sector and can have a real impact on the exploration of innovative solutions and more sustainable alternative building systems. The integration of AM techniques, PEM method, supported by computational modelling tools, will allow the definition of a building system and its components. Depending on the material used - natural materials or biomaterials - the constraints and limitations of AM will be considered.

Keywords: *Cellulose, Natural Fibers, Additive Manufacturing, Sustainable Construction*

INTRODUCTION

With the constant development of man and the search for new answers to society's need for survival, the impact of these actions led to the need to introduce new concepts, such as sustainability. This concept is being used in the most diverse sectors, namely in the discipline under study, contemporary architecture. As construction is the main contributor to global energy consumption and responsible for high amounts of CO2 emissions, sustainable architecture has risen thus determining the way buildings and cities are being constructed today. Architects stop designing a project, with a concept, form and function and are challenged to create integrated solutions that take into account green or environmental architecture. "While the use of glass and steel results in a clear delimitation between the building and nature, whereas before there was pride in industrialization, today nature is a partner in the study of construction, which is conducted mainly with the conscious choice of materials. It is not surprising that wood has had a renaissance in the last decade of the twentieth century, as a building and cladding material." (Gossel & Leuthauser, 2001)

The search for new emerging solutions aims to halt the continuous expansion of architecture with the use of non-renewable energies. Designing the form and developing the design of a building cannot continue to be defined in isolation. This agreement must be progressively worked on, from construction techniques to materials. It is necessary to develop a sustainable balance between the way of thinking about a building, obtaining raw materials and construction techniques.

The appearance of the internet and the constant development of digital technologies make it possible to include complex forms in architecture, which in the past would have been only design proposals by the observer, stated as organic. However, more than innovation in data processing, it is the high refinement in the representation of a sketch that determines the success of new concepts of space (Gossel & Leuthauser, 2001). This exhibition would only be possible with the three-dimensional representation elaborated using computational modeling systems. According to Gossel & Leuthauser, the progress now made in Computer Aided Design (CAD), the support of calculation work during the design and construction, not only resulted in an incredible extension of the representation methods but also in the possibility of obtaining complex blanks for computerized production (2001). The use of additive manufacturing to explore new techniques of architectural construction aims to solve the problem described above. Therefore, this study aims to investigate the need to search for sustainable emerging solutions through the exploration of materials in common use or natural materials - natural biopolymers abundant in nature - and to develop new forms of construction. It intends to combine the most diversified raw materials and generate mixtures capable of responding to additive manufacturing (AM), using techniques such as Paste Extrusion Modeling (PEM) mediated through the use of computational design tools.

RESEARCH CONTEXT

Additive manufacturing is the term used to define the process of joining materials to make parts from 3D model data, usually layer upon layer, as opposed to subtractive manufacturing and formative manufacturing methodologies (ISO/ASTM 52900:2015). The uses of AM techniques work as viable alternatives to conventional manufacturing processes, in which models are produced using moulds, or by subtracting the material until obtaining the final prototype. According to the normative guideline ISO/ASTM 52900:2015, AM processes can be easily divided into multiple categories such as: (a) binder jetting (BJT), (b) direct energy deposition (DED), (c) material extrusion (MEX), (d) material jetting (MJT), (e) powder bed fusion (PBF), (f) sheet lamination (SHL) and (g) vat photopolymerization (VPP). This normative was developed taking into account small-scale and series production, so it was necessary to adapt it for the creation and production of large-scale objects and buildings.

3D printing by Paste Extrusion Modeling (PEM) is a widely used approach to rapid prototyping. PEM is rapidly becoming an accessible means for 3D printing very diverse materials (Rael & San Fratello, 2018). The PEM process - through the use of specialized equipment - has the ability to create a physical object through the continuous overlapping of layers. This process is usually performed on a flat surface (XY axis), with layers overlapping vertically (Z axis), according to the 3D digital model created. Over the last ten years, clay extrusion has become very popular, due to the low cost of the machines, the low cost of the material itself, and the durability of the clay (Rael & San Fratello, 2018). With the evolution of

AM techniques, the materials have also progressed, mainly due to the search for more sustainable materials.

The use of PEM technique allows complete manipulation through the use of computational tools that allow the generation of design solutions in accordance to a set of specific formal relations. It also allows control over the manufacturing process, resulting in complex design construction systems. The constant evolution of the manufacturing process and the ability to manipulate objects has led to the discovery of new materials that are strongly influenced by the need of obtaining more sustainable, reusable and biodegradable mixtures.

There are countless scientific investigations developed with the objective of promoting alternative solutions to common materials. In an attempt to reduce the pollution inherent in the excessive consumption of inorganic resources, the solutions presented use natural biopolymers as a research motto - starch cellulose, among others - and can function as a substitute material for construction techniques.

Researchers such as Rael & San Fratello (2018) have produced architectural components and decorative elements using various materials such as clay, coffee grounds, recycled paper, bioplastics, sand, salt and others. According to these authors, the discovery of new materials occurred from simple processes such as adding water to clay powder, creating a mouldable paste that could be transformed into a brick, or using sand that could be transformed into glass after melting.

Menashe et al. (2020) reinforce the idea of the possibility of a pulp architecture, built from wood pulp. Similarly, the present investigation focuses on the search for new renewable materials - Nano-Fibrillated Cellulose (NFC) - and demonstrating the process of obtaining the material, proving that its performance significantly contributes to a better future. Cellulose, the most abundant renewable biopolymer in the world, when properly processed can demonstrate potential benefits for application in architecture, such as strength, hardness and biodegradation. In the ongoing investigation, these researchers introduce the idea of 'Cellulosic Architecture' and suggest its implementation for the generation of architectural components.

In an attempt to demonstrate that a new era of materials, Chiudjea e Nicholas (2020), explain that the use of natural biopolymers may contribute to the change in the material crisis, caused by the excessive consumption of resources. The research presents new experiments on cellulose-based materials and describes how to control the relationship between the manufacturing process and the material's performance during AM. It also explores an emerging alternative to AM with cellulose, reporting on the design and manufacture of porous and biodegradable panels through the use of the most abundant biopolymer in nature.

At Singapore University of Technology and Design, Dritsas et al. (2020) show another AM solution using cellulose as a base material, for the production of sustainable architectural components. Biological polymers produced by plants and animals are in the realm of billions of tones annually. Their ongoing investigation was developed along a set of rules as a way to generate a sustainable manufacture. A sustainable, biological and renewable composite material was then developed FLAM composed of natural biopolymers, cellulose and chitin. To demonstrate the potential of FLAM, the researchers developed a column, an architectural scale with 1 meter in diameter and 5 meters in height.

Sustainability in AM is a domain that only recently came to the foreground (Dritsas et al., 2020). AM has become a dominant paradigm during the past few decades, presenting itself as the future of contemporary architectural construction. The search for new ways to build, as observed by the aforementioned investigations, aims to show that it is possible to change the current economic system and introduce new, sustainable, recyclable and biodegradable materials.

MATERIALS

Wood is one of the most important raw material in the evolution of man, erstwhile and today. Cellulose - the most abundant polymer in nature - is a natural, biodegradable and recyclable material and the main component of wood. Although wood is the most common raw material used to obtain cellulose, many other plant fibers as well as nonplant fibers are also used (Sisko & Pfaffli, 1995). The most important group of these are the nonwood plant (or vegetable) fibers. The process for obtaining cellulose - cellulose pulp for the paper industry - consists of comminating the raw material (wood) and then separating the lignin. Once the components have been separated, the cellulose is submitted to a set of chemical processes transforming it into micronized cellulose (Figure 1) - the material used to develop this scientific investigation. Starch is also a natural material produced by plants, and since it is found in high percentages in nonwood plants or plant (vegetable) fibers, such as potatoes, it is a carbohydrate found in the human diet and is a common local resource.

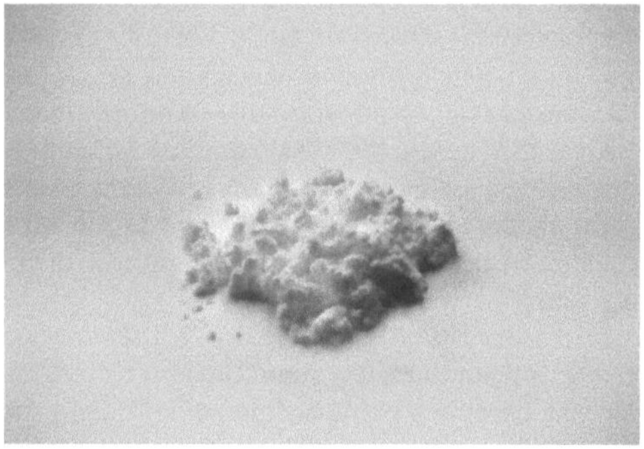

Figure 1
Micronized cellulose. (2021)

The possibility of combining these two natural materials aims to achieve high-performance mixtures that can be used in AM of architectural components. The subsequent addition of natural fibers from nonwood plants or vegetable fibers aims to enhance the behaviour and workability of the previous combination. The use of recipes based on cellulosic materials for AM it's not a straightforward process, since these natural biopolymers shrink during drying stage due to the evaporation of water, causing physical defects, which will be listed in the next section of this paper. The addition of natural fibers has the function of attenuating or eliminating the possible physical defects described. The natural fibers used for this investigation are based on local products, such as fruit and vegetable peels, wood fibers or beverage lees, such as coffee.

METHODOLOGY

Manufacturing

The recipe for cellulose-based composite materials used within the manufacture process was as follows: mix 300grams of water with 40grams of starch powder; boil the mixture until a viscous paste is obtained; add 60 grams of micronized cellulose and 50 grams of glycerine to the viscous paste; add 50grams of nonplant fibers (or vegetable fibers) to the mixture.

60gr cellulose + 300gr starch (300grams of water is mixed with 40grams of starch powder) + 50gr glycerine + 50gr additives

The exploitation of recipes for cellulose-based composite materials, was strongly influenced by the resources and equipment available in the laboratory. In order to test the feasibility of the mixtures and to perform a comparison term between them, five different recipes were developed, as shown in Table 1.

Table 1
Mixtures used in the development of research. (2021)

MIXTURE	BASE	BIOPOLYMER	BIOPLASTICIZER	SOLVENT	ADITIVES
C.1	CELLULOSE	STARCH	GLYCERIN	WATER	-
C.2	CELLULOSE	STARCH	GLYCERIN	WATER	SAWDUST
C.3	CELLULOSE	STARCH	GLYCERIN	WATER	COFFEE
C.4	CELLULOSE	STARCH	GLYCERIN	WATER	KIWI PEEL
C.5	CELLULOSE	STARCH	GLYCERIN	WATER	POTATO PEEL

Each mixture was subjected to the same set of tests, which allowed to draw up a comparative table between them. In a first phase of study, a set of prototypes were produced (see Figure 2), whose main research motto was to find the maximum degree of curvature supported by each mixture when used in 3D printing. In a second phase, an attempt was made to develop an object - study specimens - on which it was possible to observe different comparative parameters, namely resistance, retraction, water loss, delamination, change in shade, final texture and behaviour of the natural fibers.

Figure 2
Additive manufacture of the test specimens with the mixture C.4 - Cellulose, starch and kiwi peels. (2021)

Digital Fabrication

With the constant development of Computer-Aided Design (CAD) tools, Nick Dunn (2012) reinforces the idea that the use of digital design processes is growing at an exponential level, influencing the manufacture of contemporary architecture and the generation of its components. The growing proliferation of three-dimensional modelling software and computers, has helped numerous sectors, architecture, engineering and construction to grant new concepts and projects with levels of complexity such as those supported by traditional construction methods. The emergence of 3D modelling and fabrication allowed the definition of algorithmic designs, based on mathematical rules, defining highly customisable parametric systems and complex geometries, offering new creation standards for the production of architectural components. In addition, the application of CAD technologies as part of the production of physical models and prototypes is becoming increasingly widespread through processes such as CAD/-CAM (Computer-Aided Manufacture), Computer Numerical Control (CNC) milling, and rapid prototyping (Dunn, 2012).

The AM technology used was a 3D printer - Lutum 4.0 (Figure 3) - composed by three servomotors that control the movement of the extruder through the X, Y and Z axis. Each mixture tested was filled into corresponding cartridges and connected to the extrusion nozzle of the machine. For the correct extrusion of the mixtures, air pressure according to the viscosity of the material, in conjunction with the movement of the stepper motor. For the work developed, two extrusion nozzles were used with diameters of 3 mm and 6 mm, varying according to the grain size of the fiber introduced in the recipes.

By using computational modelling software - Rhinoceros and Grasshopper - it was tried to optimize the AM process by defining a continuous printing trajectory that verifies the successive movement of the extrusion nozzle. This printing technique is implemented during the generation of the G-code - in grasshopper (Figure 4), with the parameters of the equipment used - thus guaranteeing the reduction of the visible deformations of the objects caused by the paste retrained at the seams of each layer. Through a continuous spiral movement, it was increased the uniformity of the extrude layers.

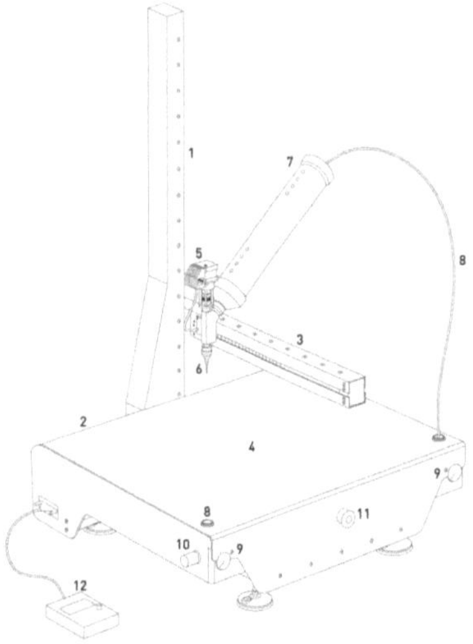

Figure 3
Lutum 4.0. (1) Z-axis (2) Y-axis (3) X-axis (4) Printbed (5) Extruder (6) Nozzle Extruder (7) Cartridge (8) Air pressure tube (9) Barometer (10) Control air pressure (11) Stop Button (12) Control box

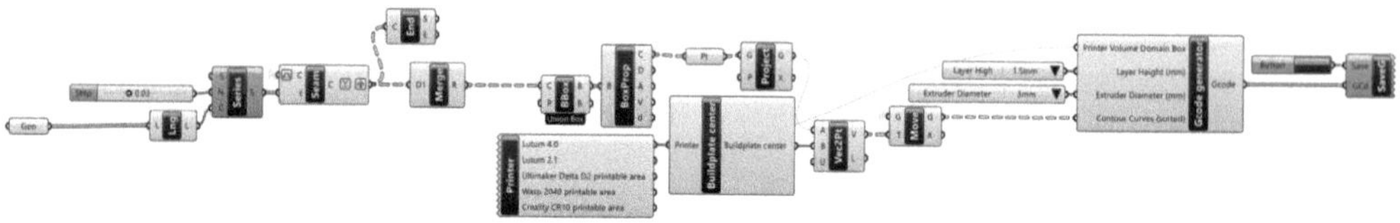

Figure 4
G-code obtained in Grasshopper, defined for the available equipment. Possibility of manipulating the final result of the pieces. (2021)

Results and Analysis

All predicted mixtures provided properties for their use in AM, such as plasticity and viscosity. The variation of ingredients within the recipe, such as the addition of different natural fibers, affected the manufacturing parameters, namely adjustments: in the airflow for each recipe, which was strongly influenced by the plasticity exhibited by the paste; in the speed of movement of the spindle, which was caused by the viscosity of the mixture; and in the diameter of the extrusion nozzle, which resulted from the granulometry of the natural fibers.

For the use of each mixture, it was necessary to check beforehand which parameters to use according to the observed properties, in order to guarantee the quality and behaviour of each produced object at the drying stage. Changing the production mode of the models, using the continuous printing trajectory technique, significantly changed the final behaviour of the object after drying.

Analysing the results obtained for each mixture, it was demonstrated that the workability was slightly below the target value, regardless of the validation of the printing parameters. In order to validate the maximum supported degree of curvature for each mixture, a set of test pieces were developed, varying the curvature of the vertical wall from 10º to 50º (Table 2).

MIXTURE	0º	10º	20º	30º	40º	50º
C.1	✓	✓	✓	✓	✗	✗
C.2	✓	✓	✓	✓	✗	✗
C.3	✓	✓	✓	✓	✗	✗
C.4	✓	✓	✓	✓	✗	✗
C.5	✓	✓	✓	✓	✗	✗

Table 2
Demonstration of the maximum degree of inclination supported for each mixture. (2021)

Once the prototypes were made, it was found that the use of mixtures based on cellulosic materials conditioned to low degrees of inclination, proving that all mixtures responded well up to inclinations of 30º (Figure 5). The introduction of natural fibers (additives) had no effect on the workability of the mixtures, the behaviour of mixture C.1 being equal to that of the others.

Figure 5
Observation of the maximum degree of inclination supported by the mixture C.5. (2021)

The drying process of the specimens is conditioned by the type of paste used and subsequently by the viscosity present. Since the mixtures used here are derived from cellulosic materials and water, when it is evaporated it will cause contractions in the volume of the pieces. The fabrication of specimens for each mixture - Test 2 - aimed to analyse this condition and verify the degree of deformation, retraction, delamination and lost water volume. All the specimens under study were placed at controlled temperatures between 35ºC and 50ºC. Due to the volume of the specimens, the drying stage took 24 hours. Each specimen produced was measured and weighed before and after drying.

When considering the results obtained (e.g. Figure 6), it was found that the granulometric dimension of the natural fibers, which are later added to the recipes, significantly influenced the retraction of the produced objects. According to Table 3, it is proved that the initial weight of the specimens varies according to the percentage of water present in the recipes, after drying, the final weight is similar between the different mixtures. The shrinkage index is higher in mixtures with a larger particle size of natural fibers, namely in mixture C.4 and C5. On the other hand, the delamination caused by the evaporation of water was lower in mixtures with greater retraction, since the aggregation between layers is higher than in the other recipes. The use of sawdust (mixture C.2.) and coffee grounds (mixture C.3) attenuated the delamination process - despite being powdered fibers - if compared to the process observed in mixture C.1. The introduction of these powdered fibers reduces the viscosity of the mixture and consequently lowers the percentage of water present. The same happens in mixtures C.4 and C.5.

The final appearance of the tone and texture are caused by the addition of natural fibers to the mixture. If they were not added, all objects produced would have the white cellulose colour. The texture varies depending to the grain size of the fibers added. In general, all mixtures have properties for AM, with the C.1 mixture being the most fragile. The research showed the degradation time was longer for mixtures that contained kiwi peels and faster for potato peels that decomposed rapidly due to the proliferation of bacteria, leading to the appearance of fungi and a bad odour.

Figure 6
Observation of test pieces produced using mixture C.4, without drying. (2021)

Looking at Figure 7, we can clearly see the color change caused by the addition of natural fibers. It is also possible to observe that deformation and discouragement was greater in the mixture C.1(cellulose) compared to C.2 (cellulose and sawdust) and C.3 (cellulose and coffee grounds).

Figure 7
Observation of the final finishing of the pieces. Left specimens_mix C.1. Central specimens_mix C.2 . Right specimens_mix C.3. (2021)

Table 3
Demonstration of the variants obtained after performing the test 2. Analysis of the test specimens for each mixture. (2021)

MIXTURE	SPECIMEN	INICIAL WIDTH (mm)		INICIAL HEIGHT(mm)		FINAL WIDTH (mm)		FINAL HEIGHT (mm)		INICIAL WEIGHT (grams)		FINAL WEIGHT (grams)		PERCENTAGE OF LOST WATER		RETRACTION INDEX	
	C.1.1	52,30		96,81		49,25		71,06		82,80		20,50		62,30%		28,80%	
C.1	C.1.2	51,60	52,00	97,13	96,40	50,43	49,49	74,20	71,25	84,50	84,10	20,90	20,63	63,60%	**63,47%**	24,10%	**27,65%**
	C.1.3	52,10		95,25		48,80		68,50		85,00		20,50		64,50%		30,05%	
	C.2.1	51,20		98,20		49,70		75,70		80,80		22,80		58,00%		24,00%	
C.2	C.2.2	51,50	51,57	99,00	98,67	49,60	49,88	76,80	76,23	85,50	83,83	23,40	23,23	62,10%	**60,60%**	24,10%	**24,12%**
	C.2.3	52,00		98,80		50,35		76,20		85,20		23,50		61,70%		24,25%	
	C.3.1	55,39		102,38		53,40		81,30		121,00		32,00		89,00%		23,07%	
C.3	C.3.2	55,40	55,29	101,60	102,26	52,63	52,78	78,80	79,11	115,80	116,07	30,40	30,53	85,40%	**85,53%**	25,57%	**25,66%**
	C.3.3	55,08		102,80		52,30		77,24		111,40		29,20		82,20%		28,34%	
	C.4.1	51,90		99,90		48,90		52,40		121,00		25,00		96,00%		50,50%	
C.4	C.4.2	51,40	51,60	100,70	100,77	49,90	49,53	48,90	50,10	115,80	116,07	24,10	24,50	91,70%	**91,57%**	53,30%	**52,73%**
	C.4.3	51,50		101,70		49,80		49,00		111,40		24,40		87,00%		54,40%	
	C.5.1	49,10		98,00		47,60		65,70		70,00		24,70		45,30%		33,80%	
C.5	C.5.2	52,50	51,47	97,70	98,47	51,00	49,60	69,40	68,03	95,60	87,53	26,40	26,00	69,20%	**61,53%**	29,80%	**32,30%**
	C.5.3	52,80		99,70		50,20		69,00		97,00		26,90		70,10%		33,30%	

DESIGN EXPERIMENT

Modular Column

The model presented was conceived with the purpose of demonstrating the use of the mixtures obtained previously, through the combination of natural materials. Each exposed component was developed using computational modelling tools and later, produced using the AM method, PEM. Therefore, the purpose of the prototype was to develop a modular system that could easily constitute a column, an acoustic or solar blocker (Figure 8).

For the geometric definition of the shape of the components, an algorithmic design was developed, based on a set of mathematical rules, which aimed to define a parametric linear path, thus making it possible to increase the level of complexity of the final geometry obtained. The defined path allowed to define an underlying computational logic, letting the variation of the geometry, as well as the amount of information desired according to the standards designed by the user. The customization of each component includes the variation in height and the radius of the shape; the number of points and the amplitude of each undulation on the outer wall of the element; the number of divisions of the inner walls that allow the union between the outer wall and the inner wall of the object; and finally, the height of the contour intended for the layers, which is essential for additive manufacturing, as can be seen in figure 9.

Each component consists of: (1) an outer wall that has a regular central undulation and an edge at both ends, giving a complex geometry; (2) a simple interior wall strictly structural; and finally (3) an internal structure creating a link between the finishing walls of the object and giving it rigidity (compare with Figure 10, 11). The internal structure is defined according to a set of points obtained by the mathematical division of both base geometries, and subsequently joined together according to a regular triangular mesh. This is projected along the desired total height for the component, assuming the divergences present in the undulation defined for the outer wall.

Figure 8
Proposal of a columnade to be produced trough AM. (2021)

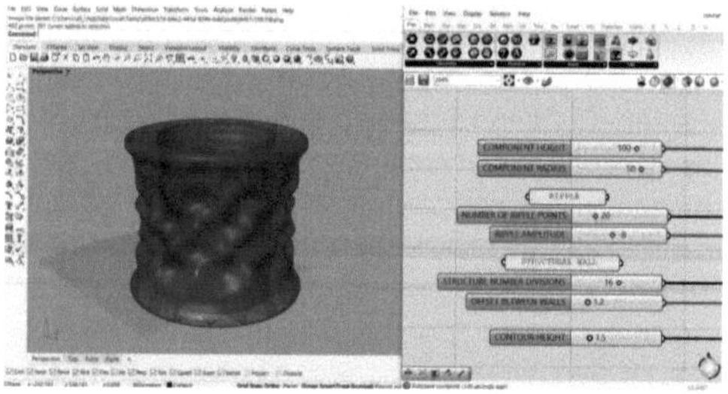

Figure 9
Rhinoceros - Grasshopper work interface. Component customization. (2021)

Figure 10
Raw manufactured pieces (without drying). Left piece produced with mix C.2; Center piece produced with mix C.3; Right piece produced with mix C.1. (2021)

The optimization of the digital model included the definition of a continuous printing path, eliminating possible deformations in the final shape after drying. Given the use of composite mixtures based on cellulosic materials, water is the main element that provides fluidity and viscosity, necessary for the PEM process, and when subjected to high temperatures, this ingredient is expelled from the object through evaporation, considerably increasing the shrinkage and deformation of the objects, often caused by the

Figure 11
Final pieces manufactured using the Paste Extrusion Modeling technique. Left piece produced with mix C.2. Right column: Upper piece produced with mix C.3; Central piece produced with mix C.1; Lower piece produced with mix C.5. (2021)

Figure 12
Definition of variable points for the position of the seam between layers. (2021)

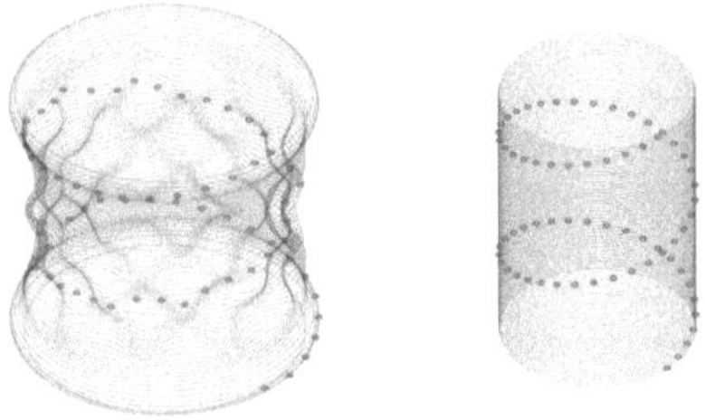

continuous overlapping of paste in the seam of the layers. As a way of eliminating these defects, a set of variable points was defined in the generation of G-code, according to a parametric mathematical reason, eliminating the overlap of the layer seam, as shown in figure 12.

In short, the evaluation of the behaviour of the components was extremely positive when subjected to the drying phase. The presence of the internal structure allowed the delamination between layers to be smaller and the previous definition of the printing path ensured that the visible deformation in the objects initially produced - with overlapping seam - considerably less. The introduction of fibers in cellulosic mixtures gave an optical variety to the components produced, as well as greater aggregation between layers and stiffness.

Although the elements are simple geometries, it was possible to verify that the mixtures are able to give shape to construction systems for application in architecture, as well as presenting themselves as ecological and reusable solutions.

CONCLUSION

The research allows to conclude that the use of cellulosic materials in conjunction with AM techniques has the potential to develop constructive systems, sustainable, ecological and reusable. It was found, by the analysis of the results obtained, that cellulose-based mixtures have great potential for use in AM, they also have major disadvantages that must be considered from the logical thinking of the piece to the act of printing. Any defined object or system must take into account the maximum degree of curvature that the material will support and the fluidity of the mixture in question. All mixtures have different printing properties because the recipes being different from each other.

The use of additives or natural fibers in the recipes determines the degree of fluidity of the mixture as well as the final result of the desired object. The higher the percentage of fibrous elements in the mixture, the lower the percentage of water in the recipe. This factor was crucial because it determined a set of final parameters that the C.1 mixture - without additives - could not answer. Drying is the critical stage of all mixtures because the recipe is based on cellulosic materials and water, which, when evaporated, the material retracts and in turn creates a set of defects in the piece. The lower the percentage of water present, the lower the observed defects, such as delamination between layers. This effect is essentially due to the shrinkage of the layers by evaporation of the water. Drying of pieces must always take place in environments with controlled temperatures between 30ºC and 55ºC and air circulation must be continuous.

This investigation is a work in progress with the future goal of printing with biopolymers on a macro scale trough robotic fabrication. It is intended to develop a constructive system with a higher performance, resorting to the use of computational modelling tools for the generation of form. The prototype must be developed according to a set of parametric and highly customisable rules, from the combination of materials to the AM of the components.

ACKNOWLEDGMENTS

This work was financed by the Project Lab2PT - Landscapes, Heritage and Territory laboratory - UIDB/04509/2020 through FCT - Fundação para a Ciência e a Tecnologia and the FCT Doctoral Grant with the reference SFRH/BD/144794/2019. We thank to RAIZ - Institute Research of Florest and Paper, for their support and partnership in this re-search, namely through the supply of cellulose. We are grateful to the Institute of Design of Guimarães for hosting and supporting the Advanced Ceramics R&D Lab on the use of their facilities and equipment.

REFERENCES

Ban, S., Miyake, R., Luna, I. and Gould, L.A. (eds) 2019, *Shigeru Ban: Paper in Architecture*, Rizzoli International Publications, New York

Chiujdea, RS and Nicholas, P 2020 'Design and 3D Printing Methodologies for Cellulose-based Composites Materials', *Proceedings of eCAADe 2020*, Berlin, pp. 547 - 554

Dritsas, S, Vijay, Y, Halim, S, Teo, R, Sanandiya, N and Fernandez, JG 2020 'Cellulosic Biocomposites for Sustainable Manufacturing', *Fabricate 2020*, pp. 74 - 81

Goidea, A, Floudas, D and Andréen, D 2020 'Pulp Faction: 3D printing material assemblies through microbial biotransformation', *Fabricate 2020*, pp. 42 - 49

Gossel, P and Leuthauser, G 2001, *Arquitetura no Século XX*, Taschen

Latka, JF 2017, *Architecture and the built environment - Paper in architecture: Reserah by design, engineering and prototyping*, Master's Thesis, Delft University of Technology of Architecture and the Built Environment and Department of Architctural Engineering + Technology

Menashe, O, Peters, B and Sain, M 2020 'Cellulosic Architecture', *Proceedings of eCAADe 2020*, Berlin, pp. 593 - 600

Rael, R and Fratello, VS 2017, *Printing Architecture: Innovative recipes for 3D printing*, Princeton Architectural Press, New York

Sisko, M and Pfaffli, I 1995, *Fibers Atlas: Identification of papermaking Fibers*, Springer-Verlag , Berlin Heidelberg

[1] https://www.iso.org/obp/ui/#iso:std:iso-astm:52900:dis:ed-2:v1:en

Towards a Digital Workflow for Designing Bistable Kinetic Façades

Elena Vazquez[1], Berfin Evrim[2], Jose Duarte[3]
[1,2,3]Penn State University
[1,2,3]{emv10|bpe5045|jxp400}@psu.edu

New engineered materials present an excellent opportunity for architects and researchers to reimagine traditionally static building components as dynamic and shape-changing. Bistable materials show two zero energy states and can transition between them with the input of a small force. These engineered materials have yet to be explored for large-scale architectural applications. This study presents a digital workflow for designing a kinetic shading system for facades with bistable laminates. The workflow includes an FEA model that predicts the curved shape of bistable laminates and a digital simulation model that predicts the natural light performance of the resulting kinetic screens. We describe the workflow and demonstrate its use with a case study of a manually operated bistable facade. The study forms part of a larger research agenda to develop kinetic architectural systems using bistable and smart materials.

Keywords: *Compliant mechanisms, bistable laminates, kinetic facades, snap-through, dynamic shadings, carbon fiber laminates*

INTRODUCTION

The emergence of new materials provides architects and researchers with the opportunity to design dynamic, shape-changing building components and responsive buildings (Addington & Schodek, 2005). Among such new materials, bistable materials have interesting properties that make them particularly suitable for this purpose. They have two zero energy states and can transition between them with the input of a small force. What makes them promising for shape-changing applications is the low energy required to transition between states and their large deflections (Emam & Inman, 2015). Current applications include soft robotics, smart actuators, and aerospace applications. These engineered materials, however, have yet to be explored for large-scale architectural applications. A limitation in applying these materials to architectural design is the lack of methodological approaches for designing with them.

This study presents a digital workflow for designing kinetic shading systems for facades with bistable laminates. The workflow includes an FEA model that predicts the shape of the curved shape of bistable laminates and a digital simulation model that predicts the performance of the resulting kinetic screens in terms of natural lighting. The FEA model predicts the curved shapes of the laminates in both stable states, which can then be used in a larger model of the shading system to predict the designs' daylight performance. These two complementary digital models support a workflow where designers can develop and test new shapes at two different scales, engaging in a creative loop. We demonstrate the use of the digital workflow through a case study. The study contributes to the literature on using bistable laminates for shape-morphing applications by presenting a digital workflow for designing kinetic facades with snap-through elements at both the material scale and at the building scale.

BACKGROUND

Bistability is a phenomenon that can be seen in everyday life with light switches and snap bracelets. The literature on bistable laminates has highlighted several applications related to energy harvesting and shape-morphing structures (Emam & Inman, 2015). Shape morphing applications of bistable laminates include aircraft technology (Thill et al., 2008) and wind turbines (Lachenal et al., 2013). Another area of application of bistable structures which has received enormous attention in recent years is energy harvesting from ambient vibrations (Harne & Wang, 2013). This study uses bistable systems in a novel way for a shape morphing application, a manually operated kinetic shading system.

So far, little attention has been paid to bistable systems from an architectural point of view. These materials, however, present several features that make them promising for architectural applications, namely the large deflections that they show with relatively low input energy. Recent studies for building applications only include snap-through beams, which are limited to linear bistable elements. For instance, Song et al., 2018 developed a snap-through façade using bistable beams coupled with a shading membrane. The authors use a snapping beam with two stable states to prototype a dynamic façade mechanism. Moreover, Vander Werf (2009) presented a study of a bistable mechanism programmed to open and close an aperture according to thermal loads and lighting, aiming to provide shade and thermal comfort inside buildings. This study relies on bistable laminates, which can act as the membrane itself, unlike linear systems that actuate a secondary membrane. In other words, the bistable laminates are the skin of the kinetic system providing shading to the interior of buildings.

Bistable laminates have yet to be thoroughly explored for building design. Several studies have addressed the development of compliant mechanisms-characterized by gaining motion through elastic deformation-for kinetic applications in architecture. Compliant mechanisms change shape due to material flexibility (Howell et al., 2013). Bistable laminates also present material flexibility that enables shape-morphing capabilities. However, a key difference is their ability to maintain two distinct zero energy states, which is not a condition of compliant mechanisms; that is, one can design a compliant mechanism using a bistable principle, but not all compliant mechanisms are necessarily bistable. Researchers have developed kinetic façade systems using compliant mechanisms rather than complex hinges due to the simplicity of the approach and to avoid traditional mechanical mechanisms, which can be costly and hard to maintain.

An example of a compliant mechanism that does not rely on bistability can be seen in the work of Mesa et al. (2020), who developed woven compliant mechanisms for architectural surfaces. These are actuated by pulling the fabrics from the sides, acquiring different porosity levels depending on whether they are actuated on one axis at a time or two. Another example is the work of Lienhard et al. (2011), who developed a hinge-less mechanism called Flectofin, inspired by plant kinetics. The mechanism is made of a fiber-reinforced polymer, which can present sizeable elastic deformation. Compliant mechanisms are common in the natural world; therefore, researchers have used a biomimetic approach to translate the principles of plant movements into compliant kinetic systems (Poppinga et al., 2016). These studies show how the careful tailoring of material geometry and flexibility can yield simple and inexpensive mechanisms with extensive shape-morphing capabilities. The research presented in this paper also relied on innovative geometries to develop bistable kinetic

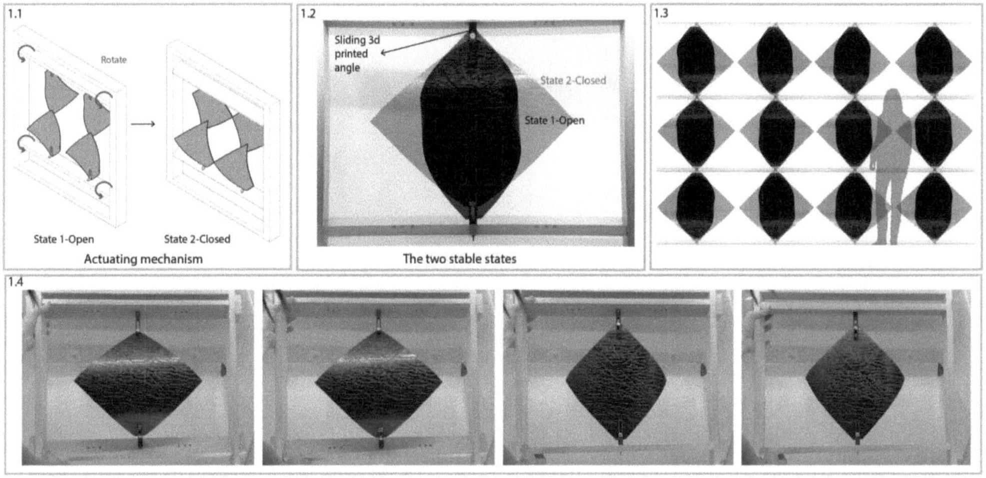

Figure 1
Frame mechanism design (1.1), a picture of the prototype frame (1.2), an example of a design solution showing open and closed kinetic shades (1.3), screen capture of actuation sequence (1.4).

shading systems for façades.

The proposed bistable kinetic facades also expand the work on smart materials for architectural applications, particularly studies on kinetic systems for façade design (Poppinga et al., 2018; Vazquez et al., 2019). New engineered materials allow designers to rethink traditionally static building components as dynamic and efficient (Fiorito et al., 2016). Smart engineered materials can replace complex mechanisms for kinetic architectures, creating responsive environments. Some strategies include kinetic facades made with wood laminates with differential swelling reactions to moisture (Wood et al., 2016) and thermobimetals that curl under the sun due to differential thermal expansion (Sung, 2016).

The brief literature review just described revealed opportunities for advancing existing work on kinetic architectural skins. Mainly, this paper expands on the current use of bistable shape-morphing systems in architecture by proposing a workflow for designing compliant bistable laminates for kinetic shading design, relying on two simulation models. The following section describes the design of a manually actuated kinetic shading device used as a case study and then introduces the digital workflow. Afterward, we detail the implementation of the workflow.

METHODS

The case study: Designing a bistable kinetic shade

This study adopted a case-study methodology, where the goal is to design a bistable kinetic shade using carbon fiber laminates. The bistable laminates are fabricated using the method described in (Lele et al., 2019), which involves cutting carbon fiber prepregs, layering them, and then curing them in the oven. Readers can refer to a more detailed description of the fabrication process in Vazquez & Duarte (2021). The shading device is designed to control daylight in a small office space with a rectangular footprint of 11′ by 18′ with a large window opening of 9′ by 4′ facing southeast. The user manually actuates the shading device. It relies on a frame that rotates and applies pressure on the laminates, forcing them to change from one state to another. Figure 1.1 describes the actuation mechanism, showing the rotating frame with the two states. Figure 1.2 is a photo of the 18″ by 20″ frame with an overlay of two stable

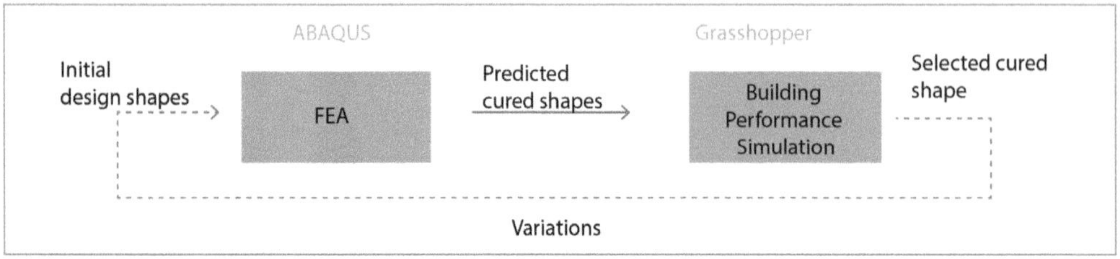

Figure 2
The digital workflow

states that shows the sliding 3d printed angle that accommodates the shape-change of the bistable laminates. These frames are the units that are combined to form the shading system, as seen in Figure 1.3. Figure 1.4 shows clips from a video depicting the actuation system. The shading system is to be placed behind the window in an office space.

The digital workflow

The proposed digital workflow, shown in Figure 2, comprises the following steps. A set of initial shapes or flat base surfaces are introduced into the FEA model. The FEA model predicts the curved shapes of the input forms, which can be used to construct a digital model at the architectural scale. The cured shapes are then incorporated in a parametric model of the entire shading system, and building performance simulation (BPS) is used to predict its performance. The BPS model can thus be used to select the most promising shapes in terms of performance. These shapes can inform subsequent design loops to try out different variations of the shape(s), using the FEA model to obtain the cured forms. Our study used ABAQUS to develop the FEA model and Grasshopper for Rhinoceros to develop the BPS model. However, this digital workflow is not software-dependent because other software can be used to create both models and carry out the study.

The digital workflow deals with two scales, the smaller scale of simulating the material behavior and the larger scale of simulating building performance. There has been extensive research on modeling bistable laminates. FEA models can predict both the curved state of bistable composites and the energy required to transition from one stable state to another (Tawfik et al., 2007). This paper focuses on the former because the systems considered at this stage of the study are actuated manually, which means that it was not necessary to calculate the force of the actuator. Automated actuation will be sought in subsequent stages of the research. In the following section, we detail the implementation of the digital workflow.

RESULTS

The first step in the digital workflow is to define a set of initial shapes to feed the FEA model and predict their cured state. To validate the model, we fabricated some of the chosen initial shapes to compare their cured shapes with the cured shapes predicted by the FEA model. Figure 3.1 shows the set of selected initial shapes, including squares, rectangles, and octagons, and combined two layers of unidirectional carbon fiber prepregs and woven carbon fiber. This set also included different fiber angle configurations, such as 0-90 degrees and 45-135 degrees, and different stacking configurations for the unidirectional carbon fiber layers. Figure 3.1 shows the different fiber configurations and stacking order of the initial set. Note that samples A, B, and D follow the same logic of having a single continuous longitudinal piece and two additional pieces placed on each side of this continuous piece. The resulting samples have surfaces in which the plane of principal curvature changes direction, as shown in Figure 3.2. The geometric configuration responds to the frame mechanism that actuates the samples, forcing the bistable

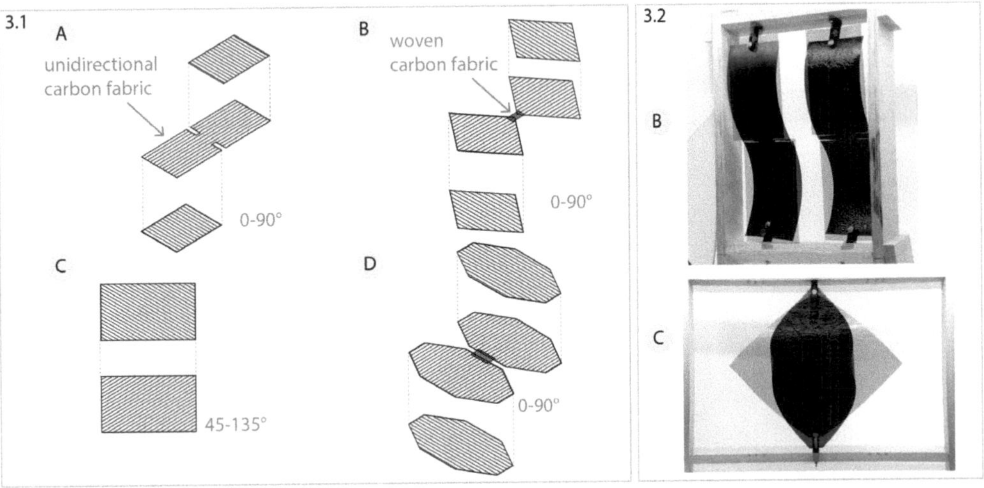

Figure 3
Initial set of bistable designs (3.1), fabricated bistable laminates (3.2)

laminates to change shape when the rotating frame applies pressure.

As mentioned above, the FEA model was developed using ABAQUS to simulate the curvature that results from a composite layup of unidirectional carbon fiber heated uniformly and then allowed to cool down. The differential thermal stresses from the curing process induce the bistable behavior of the laminates. The model used ABAQUS thick shell element SR4, which is deemed best for the model's convergence (Zhang et al., 2013). The development of the model can be roughly summarized in the following steps: 1) Defining the base geometry of the shell, the orthotropic material properties, and the composite layup, as shown in Figure 4.2; 2) Setting the boundary condition by fixing the middle of the samples; and 3) Setting a predefined field of temperature to simulate the uniform heating of the samples followed by the cooling down of the samples. The properties used in this model are based on a similar carbon fiber prepreg material reported in the literature (Lele et al., 2019).

Figure 4.1 shows how layers were composed in ABAQUS (composite layups). Figure 4.2 compares the curvatures obtained with the FEA model with the ones obtained by 3D scanning the fabricated samples. Figure 4.3 compares meshes obtained with the FEA model with the 3d scanned meshes of samples B, C, and D. Overall, the model successfully predicts the cured state of the bistable sheets and, therefore, its accuracy is considered appropriate for the design purpose of this study.

The next step in the digital workflow is to simulate the performance of the cured shapes obtained from the FEA model. In the case study, we are interested in simulating daylight performance since the kinetic shades are intended to regulate daylight entering the building. A daylight model was therefore developed in DIVA for Grasshopper. The shading system was placed behind the office space window that is shown in Figure 5.1. All four cured shapes were tested in their 'open' and 'closed' positions. We conducted an annual daylight study to test the difference in performance between two states when all the elements are either in the 'open' and 'closed' positions. The goal was to identify which shading system presented more distinct daylight performance between their two states.

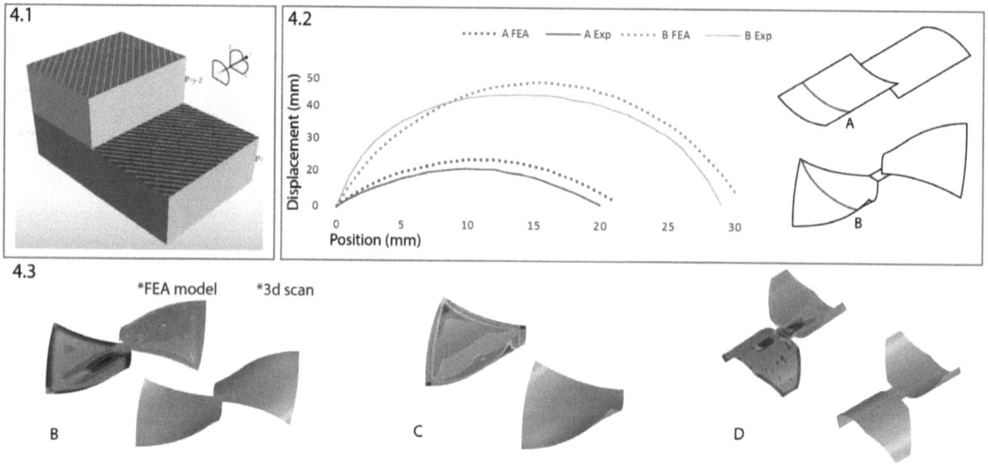

Figure 4
Composite layup in ABAQUS (4.1), Comparing FEA and experimental curvatures (4.2), comparison between obtained meshes and 3d scanned samples (4.3)

The results are summarized in Figures 5.2 and 5.3. Prototype A does not present distinct daylight performance between its open and closed position. It might work better by rotating the laminates so they are not parallel to the glazed window, although the current actuation mechanisms will not work under that condition. Prototype B and prototype C present distinct performance between their open and closed states and, therefore, are considered promising for our design purposes. Finally, prototype D is similar to prototype A in that the difference in performance between open and closed is not significant. Note that we are only evaluating the different designs in terms of daylight. Other performance and aesthetic considerations might also be considered in deciding which prototype to develop further.

The daylight study concludes one loop in the digital workflow. The next loop would select the most promising prototype and explore design variations using the FEA model. We concluded that prototypes B and C were more advantageous with the daylight study in terms of daylight performance. Subsequently, we could use additional FEA models to explore different composite layups (changing the number of layers), other material thicknesses, or variations in the shape of the composites. These subsequent explorations are not addressed in this paper, but there are no fixed iterations in the design process. The back and forth between the two digital models is up to the designer and researcher.

CONCLUSION

This study set out to develop a digital workflow for designing bistable kinetic shades. We demonstrated the implementation of the workflow with a case study, the design of a bistable kinetic shading system for an office space. The paper provides a new strategy for designing with bistable elements through a detailed recount of the design process aided by two digital models at different scales, the FEA, and the daylight simulation models. The study also contributes to the emerging language of designing kinetic architectural systems and compliant mechanisms that do not require complex mechanical systems.

A limitation of the study is that we validated only the FEA model with experimental data. The daylight model was not validated yet. Thus, it can only serve in this particular implementation as a reference in the design process and should not be the only criteria for selecting designs. However, since the study

Figure 5
Simulation settings (5.1), Daylight performance results (5.2 and 5.3)

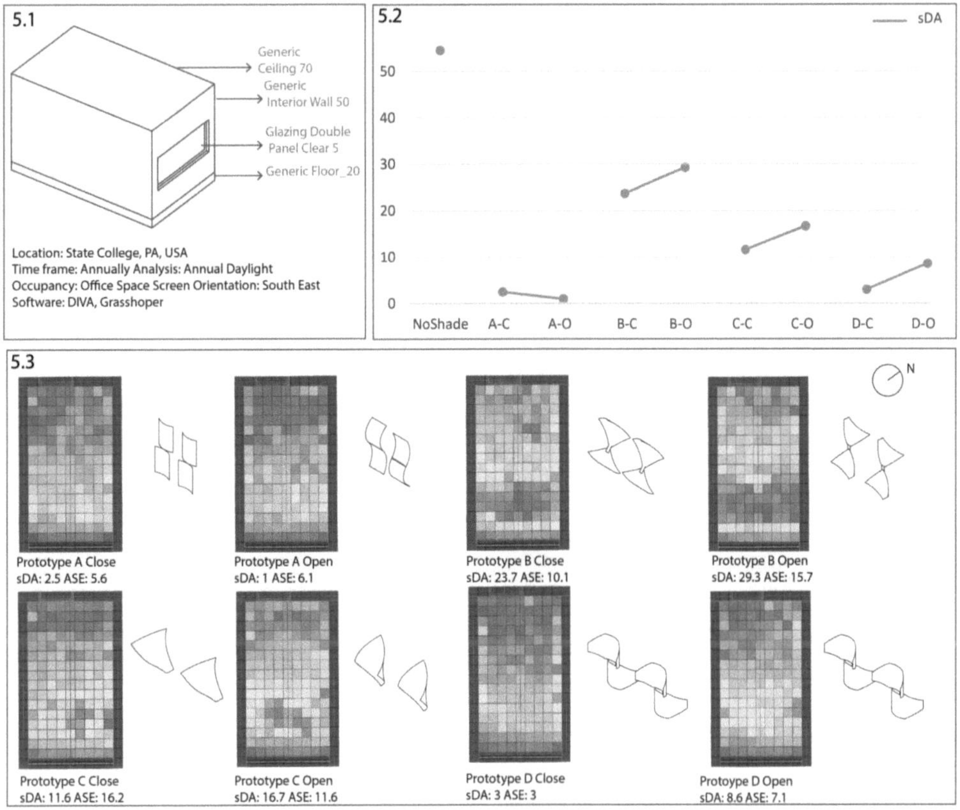

proposes a design workflow, the daylight model can help identify the more promising designs. Another limitation is that we only tested the digital workflow with daylight as the only performance criteria. Future steps of the study will aim to validate the daylight model and test the workflow implementation with other performance criteria.

This paper is part of a larger research agenda to develop a kinetic shading system using bistable and smart materials. In this study, the actuation mechanism is thought out to be manual. However, our ultimate goal is to actuate the system using shape-changing smart materials. Finally, the paper contributes to an emerging body of research aimed at implementing compliant and smart mechanisms to produce responsive and more efficient buildings.

ACKNOWLEDGEMENTS

The authors thank Vishrut Deshapande for his help with developing the ABAQUS FEA model.

REFERENCES

Addington, M and Schodek, D 2012, *Smart Materials and Technologies in Architecture: For the Architecture and Design Professions*, Routledge, Oxford

Emam, SA and Inman, DJ 2015, 'A review on Bistable Composite Laminates for Morphing and Energy Harvesting', *Applied Mechanics Reviews*, 67(6)

Fiorito, F, Sauchelli, M, Arroyo, D, Pesenti, M, Imperadori, M, Masera, G and Ranzi, G 2016, 'Shape morphing solar shadings: A review', *Renewable and Sustainable Energy Reviews*, 55, pp. 863-884

Harne, RL and Wang, K 2013, 'A review of the recent research on vibration energy harvesting via bistable systems', *Smart materials and structures*, 22(2), p. 023001

Howell, LL, Magleby, SP, Olsen, BM and Wiley, J (eds) 2013, *Handbook of compliant mechanisms.*, John Wiley \& Sons, Incorporated,

Lachenal, X, Daynes, S and Weaver, PM 2013, 'Review of morphing concepts and materials for wind turbine blade applications', *Wind energy*, 6(2), pp. 283-307

Lele, A, Deshpande, V, Myers, O and Li, S 2019, 'Snap-through and stiffness adaptation of a multi-stable Kirigami composite module', *Composites Science and Technology*, 182(May)

Lienhard, J, Schleicher, S, Poppinga, S, Masselter, T, Milwich, M, Speck, T and Knippers, J 2011, 'Flectofin: A hingeless flapping mechanism inspired by nature', *Bioinspiration and Biomimetics*, 6(4)

Mesa, O, Mhatre, S and Bechthold, M 2020 'Woven Compliant Composites', *Proceedings of eCAADe 38*, pp. 79-88

Poppinga, S, Korner, A, Sachse, R, Born, L, Westermeier, A, Hesse, L, Knippers, J, Bischoff, M, Gresser, GT and Speck, T 2016, *Compliant mechanisms in plants and architecture*, Springer

Poppinga, S, Zollfrank, C, Prucker, O, Ruhe, J, Menges, A, Cheng, T and Speck, T 2018, 'Toward a New Generation of Smart Biomimetic Actuators for Architecture', *Advanced Materials*, 30(19), pp. 1-10

Song, JY, Heo, S and Shim, J 2018, 'Snapping Facades: Exploring Elastic Instability for the Building Envelope', *Technology Architecture and Design*, 2(1), pp. 45-54

Thill, CL, Etches, J, Bond, I, Potter, K and Weaver, P 2008, 'Morphing skins', *The aeronautical journal*, 112(1129), pp. 117-139

Vazquez, E and Duarte, JP 2021, 'Snap-through carbon fiber laminates: Exploring geometry and fiber arrangements for bistable kinetic building shadings', *manuscript submitted for publication*

Vazquez, E, Randall, C and Duarte, JP 2019, 'Shape-changing architectural skins: a review on materials, design and fabrication strategies and performance analysis', *Journal of Facade Design and Engineering*, 7(2), pp. 91-102

Vander Werf, B 2009, *Elastic Systems for Compliant Shading Enclosures*, Ph.D. Thesis, University of Arizona

Wood, D, Correa, D, Krieg, OD and Menges, A 2016, 'Material computation-4D timber construction: Towards building-scale hygroscopic actuated, self-constructing timber surfaces', *International Journal of Architectural Computing*, 14(1), pp. 49-62

Zhang, Z, Wu, H, He, X, Wu, H, Bao, Y and Chai, G 2013, 'The bistable behaviors of carbon-fiber/epoxy anti-symmetric composite shells', *Composites Part B: Engineering*, 47, pp. 190-199

Digital representation and visualization

DAttE - Detection of Attic Extensions

Workflow to analyze the potentials of roofs in an urban environment

Wolfgang E. Lorenz[1], *Arnold Faller*[2], *Gabriel Wurzer*[3]
[1,2,3] *TU Wien*
[1,2,3] *{wolfgang.lorenz|arnold.faller|gabriel.wurzer}@tuwien.ac.at*

European cities like Vienna are characterized by strong growth and, as a result, by high demand for living space. Extending the attic is one way of meeting this demand. However, there is a lack of data to know which roofs are already expanded and to what extent. The city is interested in the data in two ways: firstly, in relation to the distribution of potentials (a possible change in population density, for example, has an impact on infrastructure and parking space) and, secondly, in relation to the material composition (city as a material resource). This paper provides a workflow to fill this gap of knowledge. The new methods of detecting attic extensions are described and a case study is given at the end to show workability.

Keywords: *point clouds, thermal detection, drone detection, participation*

MOTIVATION

The city of Vienna has, on the whole, a good 3D database of its built environment, however, information about roof extensions is incomplete (In Vienna, attic extensions are not subject to any official registration, which is why there are no exact dates, only estimates; Gruber et al. 2018). On the one hand, this is because of insufficient digital data about submissions of roof extensions (up to a certain year this data is only available in analog form and not connected to the digital 3D city model). On the other hand, regarding rooftops, LOD2 (level of detail 2, which is the level of detail for all buildings of the city) is too imprecise and LOD3 (level of detail 3) data is only available for a few selected parts of Vienna. The goal of this paper is to fill this gap and to provide a framework through which the data can be improved (see Figure 1). There are two main reasons why knowledge about attic extensions is of interest (not only for the city government but also for investors and construction companies): (1) it influences the likelihood of demolition/new construction (the absence or existence of an attic extension gives information about reserve spaces and the probability of possible expansion hence investments), and (2) it improves the knowledge about the city's material resources (regulations on earthquake safety, building physics, and other specifications affect the materials used, which makes such material compositions clearly distinguishable from other constructions).

Attic extensions of the classic so-called "Gründerzeit" houses (epoch in Vienna from 1840 to 1918) serve as an example. These buildings are proven construction volumes that the city administration would like to preserve (apart from tried and tested floor plans, they offer a pleasing external appearance, or

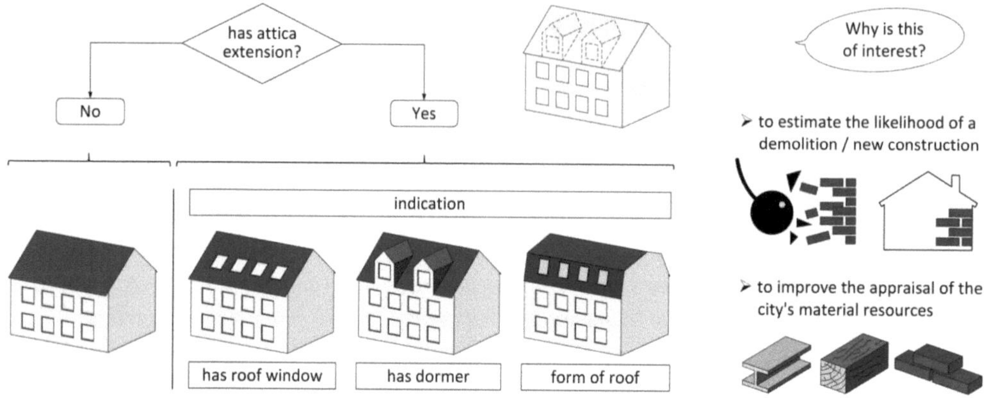

Figure 1
Problem: How to identify attic extensions in order to estimate the likelihood of a demolition / new construction and to improve the appraisal of the city's material resources

are even protected as a historic ensemble). Entirely in line with the wish of the city, the presence of an attic extension reduces the likelihood of a demolition (if at all allowed) not least because such extension usually goes hand in hand with a holistic renovation (from bottom to top). In short, an existing attic extension together with other indices (year of erection, utilization, ownership structure [single owner or community of owners], historic building preservation) gives a good indication about the likelihood of demolition/new construction or possible addition (if allowed by law). Concerning the materials, the outer wall of such a "Gründerzeit" house is typically made of brick, the uninsulated attic of a brick-covered wooden construction, while the floor of the basement mostly simple consists of solid clay. With an attic extension, finally, insulation, steel, and concrete are incorporated. Important for the selection of materials are static requirements, load transfer, but also earthquake protection. In contrast to that, modern buildings consist of stacked stories with flat roofs, made of concrete with thermal insulation composite systems (with more concrete, but far less steel and wooden components).

This paper follows on from a broader project to improve data on cities in terms of material resources (M-DAB: digitize, analyze and sustainably manage the material resources of a city; see Wurzer G et al., 2020). One starting point of M-DAB was to think of buildings within a city as resources that can be reused instead of being disposed of (calculating the exact material resource recovery and forecast their future availability) [1]. This especially is important on the way to a decarbonized future. Since material compositions of existing buildings are (up to now) not digitally available in any database, other methods for material evaluation have to be used. Kleemann et al. (2016) propose an aggregated method that uses (1) existing documents of buildings that are analyzed for the materials used to construct and modify the building, and (2) statistical data that derives from on-site inspection, measurements, and selective sampling before the deconstruction/demolition of the building. Based on this data the material composition of pre-existing buildings can be derived from: the building period (1800-1918, 1919-1945, 1946-1980, 1981-2000, 2001-2015), the utilization (residential, commercial, industrial, and other buildings), and from other information (with/without attic extension, renovated or not). Since the relationship between building data and material composition depends on statistical data, improving the knowledge about the location of attic extensions would lead to a better overall dataset on material resources in the city.

BACKGROUND

Vienna is one of the fastest-growing metropolises in Europe. Seen from the vantage point of limited and valuable space, densification is an option to meet this demand. This includes attic extensions (mainly on "Gründerzeit" buildings) which have the advantage to create new living spaces in more densely built-up inner-city districts; this implies that infrastructure already exists while at the same time no green space has to be destroyed. In 2004 the annual potential was estimated to be 400 attic extensions per year, which lead to a remaining total potential of approximately 9,300 extensions (with 2-3 apartments per unit) (Gruber et al.). Since these are only estimates, a more accurate data set would improve planning security and forecast for the entire city.

The geometric (outer) form of a roof – for example, dormers and other shapes that stand out of the pitched roof – can give a first indication of the degree of an attic extension. (Improved) feature extraction algorithms are already used for roof detection (Yeh 2021). Vienna provides an open-source generalized roof model (level of detail 2, LOD2) of all buildings inside the city borders. The data derives from a semi-automatically process and reflects only prototypical roof shapes but no detailed shapes. However, a solely geometric investigation excludes other possible indications of usage, such as roof windows. Apart from that, the available LOD2 data set is too imprecise and can therefore not be used as the only source. A more detailed roof model (level of detail 3, LOD3) that, eg include details such as dormers, would better indicate attic extensions. However, the city administration of Vienna determines such data only project-related (on the basis of aerial photo evaluations) [2].

Photogrammetry

In the field of architectural building survey different methods are used, which differ both in terms of their precision and their speed: (1) the (classical) hand measurement is time-consuming and its accuracy depends on the care of the person measuring; (2) the tacheometry together with specific measurement software produce precise plan drawings, but is time-consuming when applied to complex buildings; (3) laser scanning generates very quickly point clouds, while the post-process of combining the data of various locations into a 3D representation is time-consuming and complex; (4) photogrammetry, finally, produces with the help of suitable software point clouds, preserving the textures as well (Donath 2008, Willibald 2011, Kals 2019). In most cases, a combination of these methods can be useful, depending on the aim of the architectural building survey, as well as, a combination of UAV (Unmanned Aerial Vehicle) and hand-held photos (Kals 2019).

In our test case, we concentrate on photogrammetry, which is a well-established possibility to obtain digital 3D data of existing buildings. In simple terms, an algorithm determines distinctive points on every image, out of which the camera position and the position of the images in relation to one another are calculated. This underlines the importance of sufficiently large overlaps of the images and, following from that, the importance of defining the flight route at the beginning of the recordings. After determining the rough point cloud follows the generation of a dense point cloud. Finally, a triangulation-algorithm combines the points to editable geometries. Various software systems are available to convert 2D images, taken from different positions, into a point cloud and finally in geometry (the Poisson or Delauney algorithm are possibilities to obtain a polygon mesh representation out of point clouds). During this research, for the process of photogrammetry, two different programs were used: 1) Autodesk ReCap Photo, and 2) Meshroom (AliceVision 2018), which is more or less a GUI for AliceVision (an open-source framework for photogrammetry, developed as a collaboration of several universities together with VFX-Studio Mikros Image in France). Caching is one advantage of Meshroom allowing to pause working on projects at any time in order to be continued later. A disadvantage, however, is that it is slower compared to other software (Hofmann 2018). With Autodesk ReCap Photo, in contrast, overlapping photos are uploaded to Autodesk ReCap Photo. Thereafter a point cloud and a 3D model in various formats are available.

Photogrammetry enables a broad range of applications: eg in combination with VR and AR, it allows users to "walk through" (historical) existing buildings without being on-site, but it also enables to present different configurations of furnishing to a customer (e.g. in event management). For our framework, close-up photogrammetry (Luhmann 2018) with multiple image recordings and digital evaluation is the choice.

Thermographic Inspection

Infrared thermography (IRT) is an investigative technique that displays surface temperature distribution. Since the equipment gets cheaper, IRT areas of application increase rapidly; eg in medicine (monitoring body temperature; see Lahiri et al. 2012), in the industry (detection of motor failures; see López-Pérez et al. 2017), for military purposes (Akula et al. 2011), and in agriculture and food industry (reaching from assessing the seedling viability to the evaluation of the maturity of fruits and vegetables; see Vadivambal et al. 2011). With buildings, thermography not only detects heat losses but also enables methods to measure the insulation values of the building envelope (calculation of the heat transfer coefficient (U-Value) via IRT; see Nardi et al. 2018).

Thermography on buildings is well established to discover different temperatures and subsequently detect thermal bridges (temperature distribution on the component surface as a heat/cold map). According to Entrop et al. (2017), however, there are three modes in which energy can be transmitted: (1) reflection, where the energy comes from the same side of the record; (2) transmission, where the energy is recorded on the opposite side of delivering; and (3) internal, where the energy is generated within an object and recorded externally. With attic extensions, thermal bridging is hardly avoidable (around openings and in the case of materials with less thermal insulation) and is therefore an indication of the expansion stage. The degree of difference between the inside of a building under investigation and the outside air depends on the model of the camera used. Other influencing factors are wind, rain, and direct sunlight. Since solar irradiation affects the result, it is recommended that an inspection should be carried out before sunrise.

The combination of infrared (IR) thermal sensing and Unmanned Aerial Vehicles (UAVs) technologies improve accessibility (and speed). It is only with UAV made possible to examine the top floors and the roof or at least it is made easier to reach these parts of the building. However, regulations (distance to airports, restriction in inhabited areas) limit its use.

Online participation

The participation of the citizens via digital services allows recording and collecting information about a large area in greater detail. With Smartphones and wireless internet, data is permanently available and can be added or adjusted just-in-time. Private associations, as well as public institutions, operate such digital platforms for various purposes. As an example, various cities run the open-source platform "decidim" [3] in order to push for democratic governance. City governments want to encourage their citizens to participate politically and use the collective intelligence to introduce, discuss and implement proposals. The so-called "Leerstandsmelder" (vacant reporter), established in a couple of German and Austrian cities, in turn, allows registered users to report, comment, and update the vacancy of buildings, apartments, bars, and shops (since 2010). Digital platforms, provided by municipalities, also empower their citizens to quickly report sources of danger or malfunctions/problems in the urban space (reaching from broken street lights to potholes). This speeds up identification compared to conventional routine controls by the authorities. For example, with the app called "Sag's Wien" (since 2017) the City of Vienna runs an online service that enables direct communication between citizens and the city administration with just a few clicks [4]. The citizen sends his/her concern as a message via text and optionally with up to three images. Registration is not required. Location can either be located automatically via GPS or by entering an address. For more examples of intended uses and comparisons between various apps see Höffken (2013).

METHOD

All building geometries in Vienna, including rooftops, are available as LOD2 data and freely provided by the government (Stadt Wien, 2020) (The detailed roof model LOD3 shows the exact roof shapes but is not generated for the whole city). The data gives an initial indication of the degree of attic extension (whereby conclusions are drawn from the principal shapes). In order to improve the available geometry, aerial photos and drone flights are used, taking 3D scans and photogrammetric recording (Shariq & Hughes, 2020) (using algorithms to detect and interpret e.g. dormers and skylights). Thermal recordings provide additional information on whether or not (parts of) rooftops are inhabited or not. The improved data is then made available in a web-based open-source 3D environment (see Figure 2).

Digital citizen participation has the potential to improve urban planning (Burak Pak, 1016) and is a common method to quickly get information about public space (eg Brovelli et al., 2016). (Web-based) apps are one possibility, with which, for example, citizens can add data to buildings. This dramatically improves the knowledge about the building stock, especially when homeowners add details about parts of the building (including wall constructions or habitation).

A concept of roof detection from geometry

The first step is to examine the digital data provided by the City of Vienna. To allow automatic detection of the degree of attic extension, every single (geometric) element has to be examined regarding its position within the building. The LOD2 data of the building geometries basically includes three different elements, which consist of several polygon networks: 1) the roof, 2) the building structure (the main floors), and 3) (for most cases) the base area. The affiliation to a single building (-complex) is defined by their allocation on one and the same layer. Since this paper is about a workflow for recognizing the degree of attic extensions (and not about the development of an all-in-one program), the first step has been analyzed with the aid of a little script written in Grasshopper® (for Rhino® [McNeel & Associates, 2015)). It allows to separately examine a single layer (i.e. a building (-complex)). On this layer, the color of the element (polygon network) provides an initial indication of the elements' affiliation. Eg the roof has the color RGB (153,38,0), while the main building structure and the base area are of grayscale (RGB (173,173,173)). A distinction between the base area and the structure is then made according to their height. Since within building complexes, eaves heights can change, it follows an (automatic) detection and subsequently a separation of building parts.

In a next step, the outlines of the roof areas are extracted to define the heights of the eaves of each building (of each layer respectively). That allows recognizing connected areas, which provides further information about the interrelation between building structure and attic. In our approach of developing a framework to detect the degree of attic extension, the focus, for the moment, lies on buildings of the

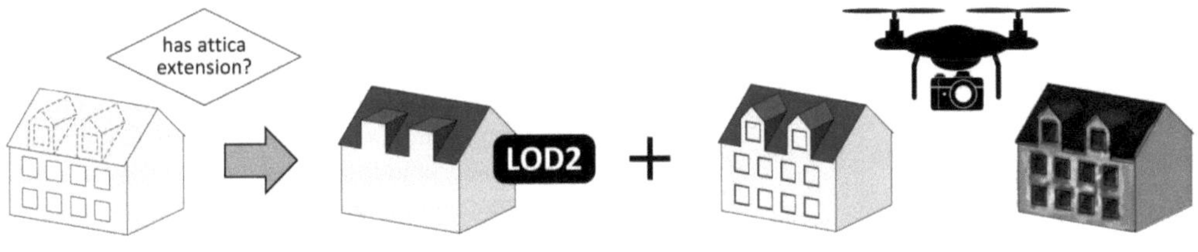

Figure 2
Improving the data by adding photogrammetric and thermographic information using a drone

Gründerzeit. This is because they are well suited for attic extension (they offer large empty attics with suitable roof inclination) – another reason lies in the fact that, on the one side, there already exist many examples of such extensions, and, on the other side, there is still a lot of potential. In the next step, the normals of each individual surface provide further information about the geometry. The algorithm looks, at this stage of development, for roof inclinations between 30 and 60 degrees. This is because 45 degrees is the maximally allowed slope (Viennese building regulations) if the building height is fully used; but it is also in the range of the typical slope of roofs of the Gründerzeit (35-45 degrees).

Photogrammetry

With photogrammetry, the quality of data and thus the information content about the shape (of roofs) is improved; moreover, it is a possible method of getting the basic shape if no LOD2 model is available. At first, point clouds are generated from photographs taken from different locations and perspectives. Then follows a triangulation to get a 3-dimensional mesh representation. Since mainly roof surfaces are in the focus of our project, drone flights along a predefined flight route are suited for taking overlapping images. It turned out that a circular route around the object is best (compare Kals 2019). In the next step, those images are eg uploaded to Autodesk ReCap Photo and converted into a georeferenced point cloud and mesh. The data can now be manipulated with certain tools in order to narrow down the extraction to a relevant section, eg by removing unnecessary points or triangles. After the preparatory step (see Figure 3, top), both, the 3D model and the point cloud are exported and can be post-processed in other programs. Since the obj file format is a simple data format that represents 3D shapes alone as vertices and texture vertices, it is used by many 3D graphics applications, including Rhino. That's why this format is particularly suitable for transferring the data. It is recommended to reduce the number of triangles before the detection process of attic extensions starts (for the building complex shown in Figure 3 (top) the number of triangles eg exceeds 45.000). The reduction can be performed either directly in Autodesk ReCap Photo or afterward in Rhino. At the moment we use a self-written script in Grasshopper® (for Rhino® [McNeel & Associates, 2015)) that translates the resulting shapes (from photogrammetry) into a form similar to the LOD2 data (see Figure 3, bottom). This allows us to use the same algorithm for the separation of building parts and the detection of roofs as described before ("A concept of roof detection from geometry"). Nevertheless, the correct choice of triangle reduction and the detailed translation workflow are the subject of future research.

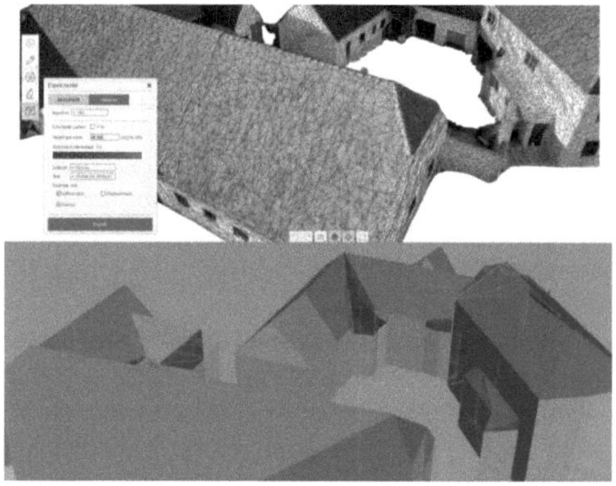

Figure 3
Top: Autodesk Recap Photo (Point cloud, triangulation);
Bottom: Identification of attic extensions.

Additional information through thermography

The previously described analysis of LOD2 building structures and the photogrammetric recordings, respectively, give a first cautious estimate about the degree of attic extension. However, dormers, cross dormers, extended dormers, and the like alone are not exclusive or unmistakable factors for the identification of attic extensions. Roof windows, for example, are completely excluded, although they provide another indication of the use. One possibility of detecting such an indicator lies in the analysis of satellite images, where roof windows stand out as reflective or dark surfaces (in contrast to the surrounding roof surfaces that are covered with eg red tiles). However, there nevertheless exist restrictions due to possible (color) variants of the roof and the risk of confusion with solar panels and photovoltaic systems. The latter also holds true for the analysis by means of thermographic recordings, since such surfaces usually emit more heat than their surroundings. Nonetheless, thermography provides important additional information. With a conventional thermal image, window frames distinguish from their surroundings due to greater thermal weakness. This applies both to the window glass (double or triple glazed) and to the well-insulated roof structure. In order to analyze roof surfaces with this method, the recordings are made with drones. By doing so a large area can be reached in a relatively short time. The obvious disadvantage lies in no-fly zones of densely populated areas and above people, but also in the interpretation of the results. The latter includes the definition of the color ranges. The assignment of the thermographic images and thus the temperature profile to the respective roof surface, in turn, is simply done by georeferencing the images. If the roof surface of a building does not display a uniform heat emission, but rather different distributions, then size, and relation to the total surface are further indicators for the degree of attic extension.

Web-based application

With FLÄVIZ (a tool to visualize alternatives of land-use planning), two of the authors have already presented an application that is based on LOD2 data of the building stock, provided by the City of Vienna (Lorenz WE et al 2020). More specifically, it is a web-based application developed in Java Three.js using TDSLoader (3DSMax). Three.js is a JavaScript library that uses WebGL to display 3D graphics in web browsers, while the TDSLoader is a NodeJS wrapper for the TDSLoaderlibrary to convert 3D graphics to Three.js. With the here presented workflow the buildings in question and their roof faces are loaded separately to the model as 3DS-files. An advantage of this procedure lies in a possible combination of the post-processed data set (Rhino/Grasshopper) and the original data set (LOD2 model or data from photogrammetry), which allows adding the terrain model as well.

CASE STUDY

The workflow specified above – from analysis of LOD2/photogrammetry data to the involvement of homeowners – is verified in a case study. Since it is primarily about the workflow and the basic conception of the methods, partly manual data acquisition is used.

LOD2 data analysis

A specific test dataset, provided on the webpage of the City of Vienna, is used for the first phase of analyzing the LOD2 data [5]. This data is available, among other formats, as dxf file, which is at first loaded into Rhino® and subsequently analyzed by an algorithm implemented in Grasshopper®. Further adaption (analyzation and rework) of the LOD2 data is necessary eg to define the geometry of the outer form of an attic. Basically, the data is available as polygon networks that define an outer surface without representing a 3-dimensional shape. Moreover, sometimes they represent a bigger building complex. In order to give the most accurate picture of the roofscape, it is necessary to detect and define single connected roof surfaces first. Accordingly, the original dataset is subdivided into smaller contiguous units. The normal vector on those surfaces yield two different groups: 1) flat roofs, and 2) pitched roofs (or less steeply inclined roofs and their combinations). In the first case, an attic extension is primarily indicated by setbacks of one or two roof stories (number depends on the regulations that limit the roof height to either 7.5 meters or with special indication to 4.5 meters). In the City of Vienna, such setback shapes mainly appear on modern buildings from the 1970ies onwards. However, our initial focus lies in the detection of the degree of attic extensions on top of Gründerzeit buildings which were originally unused. Those attics belong to the second category of less steeply inclined and pitched roofs. It is the course of the outline of the eave that provides an initial indication of the degree of extension. For example, with dormers, the height of the outer roofline not only changes according to the roof ridge but also along the eave (a special case concerns dormers that are set back or dormers in combination with widely projecting roofs; they are indicated as closed polygons inside the outer borderline of the roof).

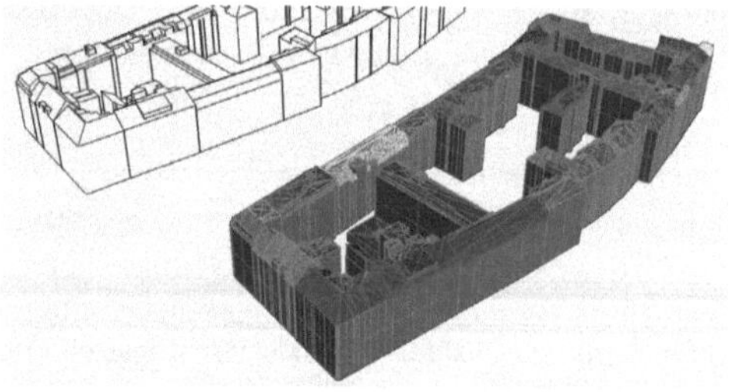

Figure 4
Analysis of the test data: The degree of the possible attic extension ranges from red (with a ratio between the actual volume and the maximum possible of about 0.5) over orange tones to green (with a ratio above 0.9).

The lowest point of the outer roofline, which means the lowest eave point, also defines the lower fictive roof termination of smaller contiguous building units (it is a xy-parallel through the lowest z-value of the roof polygon network). In this way, even pent roofs – which are otherwise only represented as a sloping surface in the LOD2 data – are indicated as 3-dimensional shapes (see Figure 4). The ratio between the so determined volumes and the maximum possible – defined by an extra fully utilized story with a flat roof – gives a first indication of the degree of attic extension. A solely pitched roof with a continuous eave would result in 0.5. The analyzed data so far show ratios around 0.6 for pitched roofs with dormers. An initial conclusion about the attic extension can be drawn based on these results together with the calculation of the face normal vectors of all roof fragments. However, examinations so far have also shown that the representation of the data as polygon networks and their interpretation or further adaption respectively (by dismantling them into smaller units) can cause uncertainty or even errors. Eg dormers that start at the roof ridge are interpreted as separate areas and therefore may lead to higher base areas in relation to the surrounding (the actual roof surface). This is another topic for future research.

Thermography

In our test case, the thermographic and photogrammetric recordings are carried out together during a predefined flight route. This avoids, on the one hand, flying in thermographic mode while on the other hand, both data sets are made available at all. An important difference between the two recordings concerns their resolution, with an image size of 640x360 pixels for thermal images and 4056x2280 pixels for photographs (72dpi each). Especially, the low resolution in the first case causes difficulty for detailed recognition of (roof) windows. Moreover, external weather conditions heavily influence the results. Even unheated attics can show high temperatures in the afternoon of a cold but very sunny February day due to the reflection of the solar radiation, depending on their orientation. Future research will therefore focus on the improvement of the quality of the results and on how to transfer the data onto the Rhino model.

Figure 5
Web-based representation of the information about attic extensions

Web-based representation

The web-based platform developed for FLÄVIZ is now used to visualize the data (Lorenz WE et al. 2020). Within the application, shapes can simply be exchanged by replacing the 3DS files; this applies to both, the building volumes with their roofs and the terrain model (see Figure 5). Since all buildings are pre-manipulated in Grasshopper (or Rhino, respectively), there exists also the possibility of setting them on different layers. As a result, information can be added to single blocks separately in the Three.js model, including the estimated degree of attic extension and physical address. It also enables the assignment of messages that are entered by users. The additional attributes are the subject of future work.

CONCLUSION

In this paper, the authors presented a workflow to detect the degree of attic extensions. This workflow consists of 1) an interpretation of LOD2 data of the building stock, provided by the City of Vienna, 2) photogrammetric recordings of the roof areas with drones (as additional information and if no LOD2 model is available), and 3) thermographic recordings, again shot with drones. The workflow's aim is to provide a basis for a more in-depth study in the future. In the course of this study, two scripts were written in Grasshopper® (for Rhino®) to capture and interpret the data, and to translate photogrammetry data into LOD2 equivalents, respectively.

Due to population growth, mainly as a result of an influx from outside, there exists a constant need for additional living space in Vienna. This demand can be met either through inner densification or through new constructions in the periphery. The first case includes, among others, attic extensions. Many extensions that have already taken place have not been recorded, nor are the location of further potentials known (attics that can still be expanded). However, it is important for the city to know the potential in order to implement the necessary infrastructure or to provide target support.

The City of Vienna provides the whole building structure as LOD2 data. These data contain polygon networks from which roof surfaces can be extracted because of their unique color. The difficulty lies in the recognition of single buildings and in the translation of the 2-dimensional roof surfaces into 3-dimensional volumes that describe the attic. The authors developed a Grasshopper® script that provides an initial approach to translate LOD2 data into attic volume and that illustrates the difficulties encountered by such a translation. Despite some unsolved challenges, it could be shown that two parameters give a first indication of the degree of expansion: 1) the ratio between the actual volume and the maximum possible extension, and 2) the size of partial roof surfaces together with their vector normals. However, due to fuzziness (level of detail and inaccuracy in data interpretation), this initial assessment requires further consideration. The improvement of data, especially the level of detail of roof surfaces, can be achieved by photogrammetric recordings with drones. With this, the difficulty lies, on the one side, in the flight permission in densely populated areas and, on the other side, in the extraction of the roof surfaces. Concerning the latter, the algorithm used to interpret the LOD2 data can be applied with slight modifications. In both cases, surface normals and adjacencies recognize interconnected roof surfaces. In more detail, the script interprets the triangulated individual areas resulting from the point clouds. Although a first conclusion about the usage can be made due to the shape, including eg dormers, still uncertainty exists. Thermographic recordings with drones can improve this data. First investigations revealed that the usability of such data depends heavily on several factors: 1) the equipment available (including the resolution and the distance of the trajectory to the object), and 2) the day and time of year of the recording.

Future work concerns the improvement of the script for capturing the most accurate data possible from the LOD2 data and from the photogrammetric recordings respectively. Another aspect that will be looked at more closely concerns the thermographic recordings and how to transfer their result onto the model. The final information about attic extension will then be made available to the public via a webpage in order to be supplemented by reports coming from the population.

REFERENCES

Akula, A, Ghosh, R and Sardana, Hk 2011 'Thermal Imaging And Its Application In Defence Systems', *AIP Conference Proceedings, Volume: 1391*, Kerala, (India), pp. 333-335

AliceVision, - 2018, *Meshroom: A 3D reconstruction software*, https://github.com/alicevision/meshroom (Copyright 2020. This work is licensed under a CC-BY-SA 4.0)
McNeel & Associates, R 2015, *Rhinoceros 3D, Version 5.0*, Robert McNeel & Associates, Seattle, WA
Brovelli, MA, Minghini, M and Zamboni, G 2016, 'Public participation in GIS via mobile applications', *ISPRS Journal of Photogrammetry and Remote Sensing*, 114, pp. 306-315
Donath, D 2008, *Bauaufnahme und Planung im Bestand*, Vieweg+Teubner |GWV Fachverlage GmbH, Wiesbaden
Entrop, AG and Vasenev, A 2017, 'Infrared drones in the construction industry: designing a protocol for building thermography procedures', *Energy Procedia*, 132, pp. 63-68
Gruber, E, Gutmann, R, Huber, M and Oberhuemer, L 2018, *Leistbaren Wohnraum schaffen – Stadt weiter bauen: Potenziale der Nachverdichtung in einer wachsenden Stadt: Herausforderungen und Bausteine einer sozialverträglichen Umsetzung*, AK Wien, Kammer für Arbeiter und Angestellte für Wien, Wien
Günthner, W and Borrmann, A (eds) 2011), *Digitale Baustelleinnovativer Planen, effizienter Ausführen: Werkzeuge und Methoden für das Bauen im 21. Jahrhundert*, Springer-Verlag, Berlin, Heidelberg
Hofmann, G 2018, 'Meshroom – Open-Source-Photogrammetrie auf einen Klick', *Digital Production*, 06, pp. 68-71
Höffken, S and Streich, B 2013, 'Mobile Participation: Citizen Engagement in Urban Planning via Smartphones', in Silva, CN (eds) 2013, *Citizen E-Participation in Urban Governance: Crowdsourcing and Collaborative Creativity*, IGI Global, Hershey-New York, pp. 199-225
Kals, H 2019, *Bauaufnahme Und Echtzeitvisualisierung Historischer Gebäude: Angewandte Photogrammetrie Und Virtual Reality Am Beispiel Von Schloß Waldenfels*, Master's Thesis, TU Wien, Digital Architecture and Planning
Kleemann, F, Lederer, J, Aschenbrenner, P, Rechberger, H and Fellner, J 2016, 'A method for determining buildings' material composition prior to demolition', *Building Research & Information*, 44(1), pp. 51-62
Lahiri, BB, Bagavathiappan, S, Jayakumar, T and Philip, J 2012, 'Medical applications of infrared thermography: A review', *Infrared Physics & Technology*, 55(4), pp. 221-235
Lorenz, WE and Wurzer, G 2020 'FLÄVIZ in the rezoning process: A Web Application to visualize alternatives of land-use planning', *Proceedings of CAADRIA 2020, RE: Anthropocene, Design in the Age of Humans*, Bangkok, Thailand (virtual), pp. 813-822
Luhmann, T 2018, *Nahbereichsphotogrammetrie, Grundlagen-Methoden-Beispiele*, Wichmann-Verlag, Berlin
López-Pérez, D and Antonino-Daviu, J 2017, 'Application of Infrared Thermography to Failure Detection in Industrial Induction Motors: Case Stories', *IEEE Transactions on Industry Applications*, 53(3), pp. 1901-1908
Nardi, I, Lucchi, E, de Rubeis, T and Ambrosini, D 2018, 'Quantification of heat energy losses through the building envelope: A state-of-the-art analysis with critical and comprehensive review on infrared thermography', *Building and Environment*, 146, pp. 190-205
Shariq, MH and Hughes, BR 2020, 'Revolutionising building inspection techniques to meet large-scale energy demands: A review of the state-of-the-art', *Renewable and Sustainable Energy Reviews*, 130(109979), p. -
Vadivambal, R and Jayas, DS 2011, 'Applications of Thermal Imaging in Agriculture and Food Industry—A Review', *Food and Bioprocess Technology*, 4, p. 186–199
Stadt Wien, - 2020, *Generalisiertes Dachmodell (LOD2) Wien, Creative Commons Namensnennung 4.0 International*, https://data.wien.gv.at
Wurzer, G, Lorenz, WE, Forster, J, Bindreiter, S, Lederer, J, Gassner, A, Mitteregger, M, Kotroczo, E, Pöllauer, P and Fellner, J 2020 'M-DAB - Towards re-using material resources of the city', *Proceedings 38th eCAADe, Berlin: Anthropologic - Architecture and Fabrication in the cognitive age*, Berlin, pp. 127-132
Yeh, C-C, Chang, Y-L, Alkhaleefah, M, Hsu, P-H, Eng, W, Koo, V-C, Huang, B and Chang, L 2021, 'YOLOv3-Based Matching Approach for Roof Region Detection from Drone Images', *Remote Sens*, 13(127), pp. 1-23
[1] https://projekte.ffg.at/projekt/3307471
[2] https://www.wien.gv.at/stadtentwicklung/stadtvermessung/geodaten/dachmodell/
[3] https://decidim.org/
[4] https://www.data.gv.at/loesungen/sags-wien/
[5] https://www.wien.gv.at/stadtentwicklung/stadtvermessung/geodaten/dachmodell/daten-lod2.html
[6] https://www.pro-meidling.at/bkl/bkl.html

Virtual Online Living Spaces

The perfect home in the imperfect dream society of digital space

Bartosz Sliwecki[1]
[1]*Bialystok University of Technology*
[1]*b.sliwecki@pb.edu.pl*

Cheap VR technologies have fed the online community a boasting dose of bored individuals that crave rapid, on demand, interactive entertainment, which is freely available on platforms such as VR CHAT. Up to today, VR platforms primarily exist as an extra layered multimedia entertainment platform with fairly shallow character development and scene use. Through the use of such platforms, a general assessment of key traits was formed based on the population status of the most visited worlds by the general public throughout a typical week. Six key traits were used as a baseline view in order to better understand the relations between each world and how the individual differences could have influenced the final result. the traits were design quality, complexity, lighting conditions, function, scale, and asset amount. The final results proved that pre-pandemic online populace chose worlds of fairly mid ranged traits almost all across the board, with the exception of lighting conditions and representative function. Gathered information will form a basic understanding of the desires of the virtual human counterpart, and from a clearer view of the trends in virtual architecture design for online living spaces.

Keywords: *virtual architecture, digital design, virtual reality, computer aided architectural design, online societies*

Overview

Through analysis and elongated use, a general idea has been depicted of the newly emerging online societies of virtual reality. Their unique way of interaction within worlds, socializing and experiencing long stretches of time spent entirely in VR have started to create online living spaces that greatly resemble those of the tangible reality. With thousands of different worlds players could choose from, key traits have been established as those suitable for online worthy homesteads. Being called "worlds", these spaces bear distinct traits that influence their popularity with the daily online VR-goers, and the complexity of these dependencies will be discussed and analyzed in the following text. It is the evolution and development of worlds that match these specific standards that will allow for the growth of the online VR communities. User-created spaces have the same eligibility of being heavily used as those created by field professionals, just as long as they meet distinct criteria (Kieferle,

Woessner 2001). Within the next decade, technological development will allow for purist use, in which uninterrupted operation will be possible.

Evolving standards and heightened expectations of urban inhabitants have been on the rapid rise in the passing decade. The desire for cheap luxury and quick effects has driven the market into supplying the middle class citizens with affordable richness of almost every kind. Whether it is reproductions of world class art, cheap but fancy furniture or the ability to rent out almost anything along the lenient budget lines, humans have become familiarized with the ability to possess items at the click of a few buttons. The market has foreseen this and homesteads are steadily becoming smaller and smaller, as our needs become more compact and online based. With the increase of average living space per capita and the decrease of average household size (Eurostat 2017, p.6), occupants tend to choose to live by themselves in their own "four corners" in dense urban centers with living areas much smaller than those of a typical family home. For example, in 2011 over 51.1% of all households in Paris were occupied by a single person, in which roughly over 55% were a one or two room apartment (Eurostat 2017, p.7) (NETELYNX 2007). Lack of constant human-human interaction and the general decrease of personal space could mean for us humans that it would only be natural that the way we spend our free time goes toward online based activities. With the lack of natural private space such as gardens, yards or even balconies in some cases, the availability of limitless space in the online realm is too good to pass by for many young people.

In general, virtual reality is a consortium of numerous activities that happen only within the frames of computer software, much of which is now online based. To be able to go into VR, the user must acquire a head mounted device, or HMD, that displays content and allows us to semi-anatomically participate in the given realm. Along with the headset, a capable computer with the appropriate software is needed for a pleasurable and seamless gameplay. The current market for VR entertainment generally favors three mainstream uses: video games, live stream events and video entertainment (Goldman Sachs 2016, p.6). The first is generally the mainstream media depiction of VR, with amazing graphics, top tier game design and immersive gameplay, while the other two are where most of the user generated development is made; especially of that in live events. Generally speaking, the ability to develop homemade virtual reality scenarios and games has been made available to any computer user in the world. Free online tutorials, courses and templates are accessible through downloads and customization, which in turn allows for the mass creation of homemade content, especially that of digital architectural design. This tends to cause deviations in level design quality, in which, for example, a shooting range built by an amateur has weapons made in the triple-A quality standard. Visible differences in style, quality and sometimes even scale lead to the unintentional blockage of total immersion (Lee et al. 2017). Without immersion, playability is limited to a shallow engagement, which in turn leads to short play time and minuscule amount of players. Sometimes, even owning a VR headset is not required for development though does help in making the software user friendly. This means that there is a distinct society of mass user made content, where worlds are available for free or for a small sum, in which players can interact with one another, create more worlds, and even have the ability to participate in events that they normally would not attend, or at least not at the given circumstances of age and origin. If viewed without a filter of doubt and concern, these online communities are really a scaled representation of our real world life, in which we build homes, invite friends for free, and interact with them in the normal fashion.

One of the leading online VR platforms is "VR CHAT", a free to play, peer to peer software in which users can talk, move, interact and create worlds with the ability to share between one another. Users log into their account, choose an avatar and land in a sort of common room with random players from around the world. The worlds are made by both professional and amateur graphic designers from around the world, with generally available software and reasonably flexible sets of rules. Similar rules apply to the avatars, as even school children are known to have created their anatomical mates of different scale, proportion and style. With game design software such as Unity, players are given game ready templates that they can use to create both scenes and avatars for the general population to use. It is this part of the VR world that allows for further investigation for a deeper understanding of the relationship between the user - interaction - setting (Kolarevic, Branko 2000).

Some YouTubers whose main focus is making videos about VR and even VR Chat in general have spent long stretches of time purely in VR. One person in particular spent 168 hours, or a full week, in VR in one long stretch of time. He showered, ate, slept and played in VR the whole time with a constant live stream of his progress while staying at home (Disrupt 2019). This just goes to show that it is possible to live fully in VR, but at the current moment would present a lot of difficulties, especially that of meal preparation, facing physiological needs and getting used to having a bulky headset on the whole time. Also, some headsets have a limited battery or wire attached, and so traveling across a large apartment would require users to switch between headsets, which could break the immersion.

In order to comprehend the relationship between different traits of architectural design and population of virtual online worlds, a set of six key traits was established for a base of 20 different worlds currently available via the VR CHAT platform. Each of these worlds is known to be widely popular among the virtual reality community and consists of forms similar to those of the real world architecture. Chosen traits are based on several important factors that play a key role in the architectural design of real world buildings, and so would only be suitable to use for the virtual world. While some sites were quite easily categorized, certain ones with conflicting or clearly mixed traits were placed into the category of the closest possible accuracy. The classification was conducted by the author based on the experience and time spent in VR and especially in VR Chat. The traits are design quality (table 1), complexity (table 2), lighting (table 3), function (table 4), scale (table 5), and asset amount (table 6). Each of these traits has been defined as follows:

Table 1
Assigned grades A, B and C were based on the world authors skill and experience that was visible in the created content of that world.

No. 1 - DESIGN QUALITY	
GRADE	**DESCRIPTION**
Professional (grade A)	High quality textures, high quality models, consequent style in the entire scene, advanced interactions, basic or advanced scripting, appropriate special effects
Adept (grade B)	Mixed quality textures, range of high, medium and low quality models, consequent style for most elements, simple interactions, basic scripting, simple special effects
Beginner (grade C)	Low quality textures, oversimplified models / low quality models, no consequence in style, none or very few interactions, none or very poor special effects

Table 2
Complexity scale based on the amount of rooms, separated areas and portals

No. 2 - COMPLEXITY	
COMPLEXITY	**EXAMPLES**
Low	Single room, simple flat area, able to see other "end", no separated rooms / areas via door or portal
Medium	Stair cases, multi room, fairly modulated, several corridors, doors to closed off rooms, portals
High	Extensive room layouts, multi-story buildings, intricate designs of hallways, passage ways, numerous entrances

Table 3
Lighting conditions were based on time of day as well as type of lighting

No. 3 - LIGHTING	
TYPE	**DESCRIPTION**
Day / Natural	Sunlight, realistic daytime lighting conditions, time of day from morning to evening hours, bright
Day / Fictional	Non Realistic sunlight, bright scenery with no visible light source, fictional / animated style world
Evening / Artificial Realistic	Evening hours, golden hour, realistic lights in addition to low sun light, depicts real world light use
Evening / Fictional	Evening hours with non-realistic lighting, ambience without reasonable source, scene lights without source
Night / Artificial Realistic	Night time, moonlight, visible stars, additional lighting around scene from realistic sources, depicts real world lights
Night / Fictional	Night time, dark setting, lighting looks realistic but fictional, sci-fi styled lighting, fantasy scenarios

No. 4 - FUNCTION	
FUNCTION	**DESCRIPTION**
Night Life	pubs, clubs, dance halls, nightlife representation,
Residential	homes, parts of homes, lofts, relaxed areas, interiors
Urban	cities, suburbs, exteriors of residential areas, fictional areas representing urban centers
Public	Open areas, interior, large convention centers, spaces resembling movie theatres, not associated with nightlife
Fictional	Space, non-existing function, not fitting to other types
Games	Oriented around a game themed setting, main function is to conduct multiplayer games, not related to sports or hobbies

Table 4
Functionality was assigned based on the closest representation in real world

No. 5 - SCALE	
SCALE	**DESCRIPTION**
XS	Single room, dimension of approximately up to 5 x 5m
S	Small space, dimensions of approximately up to 10 x 10m, or ranging from 25m2 to 100m2
M	Average area, floor plan of roughly between 100m2 to even 200m2, typical of a multi roomed area
L	Large open areas of varying complexity, resemble entire sites, exterior and interior scenery, large interiors
XL	Almost open world maps, with extremes in terms of size and complexity, unable to quantify floor space

Table 5
Scale based on the approximate dimensions of a given world

No. 6 – ASSET AMMOUNT	
ASSET AMOUNT	**DESCRIPTION**
Low	Scarce or non-existing items, mostly empty spaces, limited interactions
Medium	Average placement of objects, with tendency to stay on the lower amount, modern hotel like object scarcity
High	Areas packed with numerous objects of both passive and interactive nature, each fragment of space has at least a few objects laying around

Table 6
Complexity scale based on the amount of rooms, separated areas and portals

To better clarify some of the terminology used in the above classification, it should be noted that the presented traits represent the worlds in a very generalized fashion. While complexity may group worlds into three categories, their unique solutions would require much more focus and analytics in order to fully comprehend their designs. For the sake of progress and rational summary, their traits were generalized to a fairly simple extent.

The concept of assets is that of small objects that are used to fill in and decorate a scene. Both with interactivity and passive "stationary" status, their presence is decided upon by the digital architect and the possible desires to have players use those objects for social interaction and general communication (Cannavo et al. 2020). The latter might mean markers that draw in 3D space and allow for users that do not have a microphone to communicate with other players in a make shift fashion. Stationary objects would consist of furniture, wall decoration, virtual foliage, and other objects that would be littered throughout the created architectural space.

PRE-COVID VR WORLDS

Having placed the chosen worlds into appropriate categories, a deeper understanding started to emerge regarding the population-trait relationship. It is important to note that the populace of the worlds can change drastically in the future, as new worlds with disruptive qualities might migrate a lot of traffic into an entirely new fashion of virtual spaces. Disruptive worlds are those that play to the current trends of social media and provoke users to use their new ideas. By creating a trend, worlds that lack an updated inventory would eventually fall off the top ranks and be forgotten all together. The trending worlds would then spawn a new generation of design practices that would appeal to the ongoing fan base and last until the next disruptive world would arise.

Worlds created by the VR CHAT team were also included in this list due to the fact that players choose them even though they are the default areas that players spawn in at the beginning of the game. The world "VR CHAT Home" is the default home for every user, and so it won't take part in the analysis as a choosable world, but will still portray a baseline view in a neutral status. The world "VR CHAT Hub" is technically a default world that has direct access from the VR CHAT Home, but is a separate world, just like any other, and therefore will participate in the analysis.

Population status of worlds was based on the highest occurrence during a seven day period from the 10th of Februrary 2020 to the 16th of February 2020, being checked every 8 hours for updated numbers. Although technically the pandemic had started to erupt at that point, nationwide lockdowns were not in effect yet. It should be mentioned that each world has instances of which players can further choose from, as having hundreds of players gathered in a single area would prove to be chaotic and extremely slow. These instances have population caps of anywhere between 10 to 40 people at once. With such a system, the playability is granted flawless gameplay with minimal lag and glitching. This means that a random world of a global population of 160 may consist of over 10 instances with a population cap of 16 people. The following chart depicts the most popular worlds and their assigned traits (table 7).

The last position marked as nr 21 "VR CHAT Home" is the neutral world into which every player is placed in upon logging in. Through observation, this room is attended for only a few minutes at a time and is treated as a transitional room. The updates on the population show that the numbers fluctuate quite aggressively which would suggest a large ingoing - outgoing traffic. As mentioned before, the population column shows the most visited moment for a given world, and so the time and date for each world is not aligned to one another.

Additionally to the population and trait status, a simple demographics query was conducted between 100 random users in those worlds at random times. The query would have players answer about their age, country of current stay, work / student status, field of work if applied, gender, and the type of VR gear they were currently using. While a number of 100 people may seem insignificant in a 7 day trial, it proved remarkably difficult at times to get an honest answer form the users. Most players would state their age as improbably high, or with a non-numerical answer such as "old enough" when being politely asked. Others would run away or not answer at all once hearing the set of questions. This may be caused by the fact that the players' behavior is commonly erratic and spontaneous with minimal responsibility as an anonymous avatar in an online realm. Therefor a more serious approach generated squeamish answers, and resulted in being made fun of by asking such questions. Those who did answer truthfully did not try to make fun of the query, and so their answers mostly matched the way that they behaved. For example, tone of voice for males resembled the stated age, and the gender statement also could be verified by tonal response. A seemingly particular group of users avoided contact more than anyone else, and that would be youngsters in the ages between 6 and 10. Their reaction to hearing the set of questions would mostly silence them and have them either move away, block the authors avatar (and voice) or switch worlds. This may be due to the fact that kids are being taught not to trust online strangers and for this reason, the actual demography of the VR worlds may be inaccurate for the younger ages. The following chart depicts the gathered age data, as well as the approximate correction in the number of young players (marked by the dotted red line).

Gathered results show that a vast majority of online VR Chat players are people between the ages of 15 and 21, with an estimated correction of the amount of young players in relation to the general population (figure 1). From those one hundred people, with an average age of just over 18 years old, 86% were male and 14% were female, 64% were in the either student age or were currently studying, 16% were unemployed, with the rest 20% working full time. The vast majority of players in VR Chat were from the United States, with 56% stating so, while the United Kingdom had 13%, Canada 10%, and Germany 8%. The rest of the players ranged from countries like South Korea, Japan, Belgium, Australia, New Zealand, Italy as well as singularities from other countries all across the globe. The young player base is a result of targeted marketing that favors teenagers and young adults from whom many of which virtual reality and online socializing is almost natural.

NR.	WORLD NAME	GRADE	POPULATION	SIZE	FUNCTION	COMPLEXITY	LIGHTING	ASSETS
1	MMD Dance World	C	102	S	Fictional	Low	Night / Fictional	Low
2	VR CHAT Hub	A	181	M	Fictional	Medium	Night / Artificial	Low
3	MERoom	B	611	M	Residential	High	Night / Artificial	Medium
4	Murder 2	B	332	L	Game	High	Night / Fictional	Medium
5	The Great Pug	B	265	XL	Night Life	High	Night / Artificial	High
6	Japan Shrine	A	252	XL	Urban	Medium	Day / Natural	Medium
7	Midnight Rooftop	A	772	M	Residential	Medium	Night / Artificial	High
8	Summer Solitude	A	227	M	Residential	Medium	Evening / Artificial	High
9	Void Club	A	96	XL	Night Life	High	Night / Fictional	Low
10	The room of the sleep	B	121	S	Residential	Low	Night / Artificial	Medium
11	The room of the rain	B	318	XS	Residential	Low	Night / Artificial	Medium
12	The Black Cat	B	490	L	Night Life	Medium	Night / Artificial	Medium
13	Root's home movies and animes	B	249	M	Public	Medium	Night / Artificial	Medium
14	Rest and Sleep	A	130	M	Residential	Medium	Night / Fictional	Medium
15	Sala Pak Jai	C	189	XS	Urban	Low	Day / Natural	Low
16	The Black Barn	B	108	M	Residential	Medium	Evening / Artificial	High
17	Yayoi Summer Nights	B	101	M	Urban	Low	Night / Artificial	Medium
18	Furries Convention	A	98	XL	Public	High	Night / Artificial	High
19	Drinking Night	B	76	L	Night Life	High	Night / Fictional	Medium
20	Hwabon Night	C	268	M	Urban	Medium	Night / Artificial	Low
21*	VR CHAT Home	A	1264	S	Fictional	Low	Day / Fictional	Low

Table 7
Worlds listed above were not sorted in any fashion, as their data will be analyzed further on

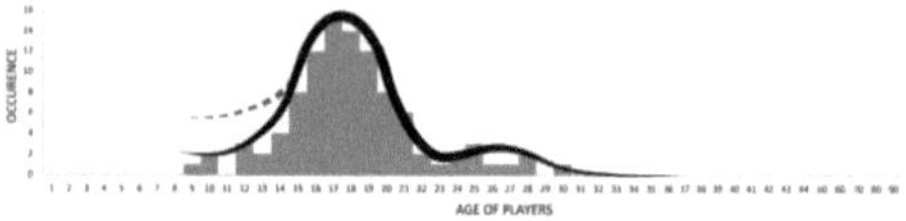

Figure 1
Demography of VR CHAT most frequently visited worlds with the addition of a curve and an estimated correction in young ages.

VR Chat worlds were then pinned up against each other in the six trait categories with the population status as the main quantification element. The following graphs show how the different traits begin to form a public favorite based on the amount of people residing there (figure 2). Color coding was applied locally to each individual comparison and is not to be mistaken as to the relation when viewed between different charts.

SUMMARY

Comparison results present a vivid insight into the most desirable traits of the virtual realms, as the use of the populace as a value proved to be an accurate value system for reason of choice. It seems, that the current trends for the VR market tend to favor worlds of a good or even professional build quality, with a room area of average proportions, with rooms and floors of a medium complexity and asset amount, with night time lighting assisted by realistic artificial lights and a function greatly resembling that of a modern urban homestead. The mentioned results may be influenced in a greater or lesser scale by a few important aspects entangled with the use of VR and the platform itself. First, users generally

Figure 2
Collected data from the virtual world populace and the assembled traits

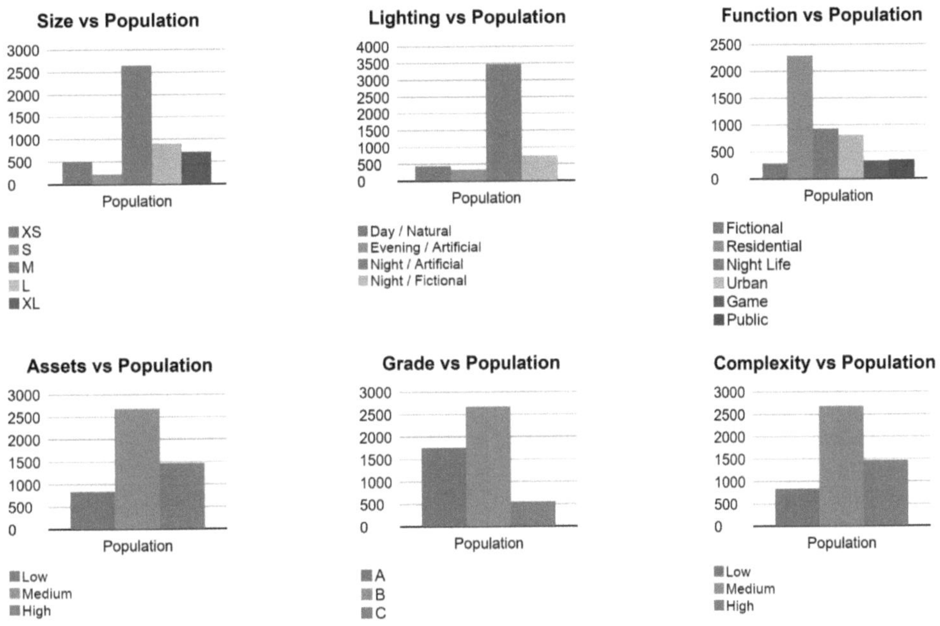

play from their homes, as it is common knowledge that recreational multimedia is generally enjoyed at the comfort of one's own four corners. With the use of such technology at home, it may be so that the reason of choice of the residential function worlds might just mirror that of the natural surroundings of the given player. Basically, being home makes users want to stay at home, with comfort and light recreation unconsciously being the target activity (Anders 1999). Second, VR CHAT is an intelligent system with its own algorithms for promoting certain worlds or styles. Players who visit their interactive menu are placed in front of suggestions from the main system, in which the most popular world is chosen. Since humans have always been attracted to large gatherings of other peers, it's no surprise that a simple reason for choosing a certain world is the fact that it's the most populated. The main advertised goal of this VR platform is interaction, fun and virtual socializing, and so it would only make sense that users want to go to worlds with numerous other players and meet new people.

This comparison showed that a median attribute is favored by the general public, as almost all of the charts suggest a non-aggressive quality of a given world. As players are free to roam around the numerous worlds, their conception of a median is quickly defined after visiting several different ones. By having to interact in extremely large worlds and extremely small ones, those that represent real world scenarios seem to be the most fitting for virtual human to human interactions (Lefebvre 1991). Very small worlds generate an audible chaos in vocal and visual communication as players seem to yell over one another in order to be heard, and preform different acts of grabbing attention when feeling outshouted. On the other side of the scale, extremely large worlds require players to travel long distances in order to socialize with other players. Perhaps if the player limit was greatly increased in such worlds their popularity would become greater. What is most surprising is that there is a fairly large amount of people who choose low to medium quality worlds, as their designs are sometimes oversimplified with visible scaling errors and inconsistent content quality. Through extensive interviews, players noted that they choose low quality worlds because they have below average computers that might not perform well in more extravagant and realistic worlds (Astheimer 1994). In reality, a lot of the low quality worlds are actually heavier to render as their creators did not take much care into optimization, and those high quality worlds are mostly easily rendered as their textures and models are optimized for performance (Smit et al. 2010). Players are also given an option to hide custom avatars to improve gameplay with the reduction of render times.

Architects that will work purely in the digital world will have a task of constantly upgrading knowledge of trends in the digital world, just like those of the tangible world. The difference here would be that buildings could be updated very easily with little effort, unlike that of real world architecture that requires time, effort and considerable funds (Zupanic, Juvanic 2009). Digital designers are also considered as digital builders, as their designs are built by them generally in a considerable amount prior to launching it on the VR platforms. Here, the engineers that build these spaces are left out, as the design suffices as the final site for the given world. With this, architects will not only need to know how to design a virtual building, but also how to create most of the content within, as it is usually fashioned in accordance to a style of the building and/or world.

Keeping disruptive creation in mind, the current trends tend to favor the mentioned traits and it will require more research to figure out what the next favored trends will look like. As for now, the virtual world seems to be on the rapid incline, especially with the upcoming releases of cheaper and more mobile VR HMD headsets in the upcoming months. Trends will come and go, but one thing is for certain, as humanity we are at the verge of a new way of living; the way of VR living.

REFERENCES

Anders, PA 1999, *Envisioning Cyberspace: Designing 3D Electronic Spaces*, McGraw-Hill Professional

Astheimer, PA, Dai, FD, Gobel, MG, Kruse, RK, Muller, SM and Zachmann, GZ 1994, 'Realism in Virtual Reality', *Artificial Life and Virtual Reality*, 1, pp. 189-208

Cannavo, AC, Pace, FP, Salaroglio, FS and Lamberti, FL 2020, 'A visual editing tool supporting the production of 3D interactive graphics assets for public exhibitions', *International journal of human-computer studies*, 141, p. 102450

Kieferle, JK and Wossner, UW 2001 'Showing the invisible - Seven rules for a new approach of using immersive virtual reality in architecture', *19th eCAADe Conference Proceedings*, Helsinki, pp. 376-381

Kolarevic, BK 2000 'Digital Architectures', *ACADIA 2000: Eternity, Infinity and Virtuality*, Washington D.C., pp. 251-256

Lee, JL, Kim, MK and Mik, JM 2017, 'A Study on Immersion and VR Sickness in Walking Interaction for Immersive Virtual Reality Applications', *Symmetry*, 9, pp. 1-17

Lefebvre, HL 1991, *The production of Space*, Wiley

Smit, FS, van Liere, RvL, Beck, SB and Froehlich, BF 2010, 'A shared-scene-graph image-warping architecture for VR: Low latency versus image quality', *Computers & graphics*, 34, pp. 3-16

Zupanic, TZ and Juvancic, MJ 2009 'Virtual Space Design: A Flexible Learning Model. Respecting Fragile Places in Virtual and Physical Realities', *Session 04: CAAD Curriculum 1 - eCAADe 27*

[1] https://ec.europa.eu/eurostat/statistics-explained/pdfscache/41898.pdf

[2] https://www.map-france.com/Paris-75000/housing-Paris.html

[3] https://www.goldmansachs.com/insights/pages/technology-driving-innovation-folder/virtual-and-augmented-reality/report.pdf

[4] https://www.youtube.com/watch?v=BGRY14znFxY

This Is How We Do It

Observing architects sketch to inform effective recognition of semantic building information

Christoph Ziegler[1], Jessica Bielski[2], Christoph Langenhan[3]
[1,2,3] Technical University of Munich
[1,2,3] {c.ziegler|jessica.bielski|langenhan}@tum.de

Sketching is an effective means for architects to develop design thoughts and to communicate ideas. It is a promising method for an interaction with CAAD systems that integrates naturally in the process of early conceptual design. A challenge for the realisation of sketched-based interaction, is for the computer to recognise what the designer is drawing. To inform the development of effective methods for the recognition of semantic building information in schematic layout sketches, we seek for a better understanding of how designers encode this information in their sketches. We therefore piloted a remote user study with trained architects (n=7). The results show variance in the use of symbols and in the drawing technique. However, we also observe commonalities in the approach. Participants always draw the perimeter first and then subdivide the enclosed space. We identified three techniques for subdivision: cut lines, open shapes, closed shapes. Also we identified four different types of information in participants' sketches and observed that certain types of objects are prevalent in all sketches. We discuss consequences of our observations for sketch recognition systems and considerations for the design of a follow-up study.

Keywords: *sketching, sketch-based interaction, user study, recognition, semantic building information, BIM*

INTRODUCTION

Sketching is a craft which supports the development of ideas in early architectural design phases. By making them tangible, sketching allows vague design thoughts to be reviewed and revised (Schön and Wiggins 1992; Buxton 2007). Sketching is a common and effective tool to communicate ideas to colleagues and clients (Laseau 2000). Therefore, sketch-based interaction is a promising method for an intuitive interaction with a CAAD system that integrates naturally into the design process (Leclercq and Juchmes 2002). Early attempts to enable sketch-based interaction with information systems date back more than half a century (Sutherland 1964). A remaining challenge, however, is for computers to recognize information in a sketch that is relevant for a given application (Johnson 2009).

Architects read information that characterises a

building from plans or sketches. But the meaning that results from the composition of individual graphic elements of a building plan is not directly accessible to the computer. Data models for building semantics, such as the semantic fingerprint by Langenhan (2017), are an attempt to bring semantic information such as room type, circulation and adjacency into a computer-friendly representation. Semantic building models are being investigated as a basis for the realisation of use cases, like the retrieval of reference designs from design data bases (Ahmed et al. 2014; Sharma et al. 2016; Eisenstadt et al. 2020), the automatic generation of design variants (Arora et al. 2020) or the automatic completion of partial designs (Eisenstadt et al. 2021).

But how can sketches of architects be mapped to the internal representation of these systems? We believe that a proper understanding of what semantic building information architects communicate in their sketches and how that information is encoded is a crucial prerequisite for the development of effective automatic recognition tools. We think that these aspects have not been explored conclusively so far. With an initial pilot study, this work aims to help shape the outline for research towards this goal. We are interested not only in how the information is represented in the final drawing, but also in metrics for the identification of information units in the drawing which can be observed by technical means. Do, for example, patterns emerge in the temporal sequence in which graphic elements are added to the sketch or in the drawing technique, which may for example manifest in characteristic patterns of pen pressure or pen speed.

The next section overviews existing works on recognition of semantic building information in CAD rendered and free-hand sketched floor plans and discusses their limitations. We then introduce the design of our pilot user study and present our observations. Based on this, we discuss what conclusions can be drawn from our observations and determine the focus, questions and considerations for the design of a follow-up study. Finally, we summarise this work and its main findings.

RELATED WORK

Sketches and the act of sketching are of interest to researchers from various disciplines. Psychologists and cognitive scientists investigated the role of sketching in the mental processes involved in design. From these works we learn for example about how designers use sketching as a medium for self-discourse (Schön and Wiggins 1992), which types of arguments designers use when reflecting ideas through the sketch (Goldschmidt 1994) or which elements in the sketch play a role in the argumentation (Suwa and Tversky 1997). Goel (1995) has described how the sketch, due to its imprecise nature, can be used as a source for self-inspiration. An understanding of what is going on in the designers' minds during the design process provides a basis for shaping the dialogue between the CAAD system and the designer. Other works, for example Bailey (2000) and Do and Gross (2008), have specifically investigated the requirements for this dialogue between man and machine so that CAAD systems can be integrated naturally into the design process and support designers effectively. However, in order for the designer to communicate with the computer via the sketch, the computer must first be able to recognise what has been drawn. Based on the recognition, the computer may draw conclusions and support the designer appropriately.

The challenge for computers to recognise graphic elements in building plans and interpret semantic relationships between the elements has been addressed by a number of works with varying focus. Some are dedicated to the recognition of rooms (Macé 2010) and the respective room type (Ahmed 2011; Ahmed 2012). Semantic relations are often encoded in symbols, such as connection between spaces (door vs. passage). The recognition of such symbols in CAD plans is specifically addressed by Ah-Soon et al. (1996) and Yang et al. (2008). Heras et al. (2014) provide an approach for dealing with varying use of symbols, e.g. between different CAD programs. Sharma et al. (2016) present a way to recognise furniture in rooms based on symbols and the adjacency of rooms. Other works are dedicated to the conversion of 2D CAD plans into BIM models (Domínguez-Martín 2014; Gimenez 2015; Lu 2017).

However, none of the mentioned approaches works flawlessly. And yet, computer-generated building plans have a more regular expression compared to sketches. The imprecise nature of freehand sketches makes automatic recognition particularly challenging (Johnson et al. 2009). Systems for generating CAD plans from hand drawings by Lladós et al. (1997) and Aoki et al. (1996) require that certain rules are followed during sketching to control imperfection. The system by Cutler et al. (2010) generates 3D models from hand sketches, but requires the graphical elements to be coloured according to a predefined colour scheme. Weber et al. (2010) develop a visual query language to input semantic information (rooms, zones, direct/indirect connections) into a reference design retrieval system. All these systems impose strict rules on the designers. It is questionable whether these systems integrate naturally into the design process given the rules they impose on designers.

An alternative approach to managing imperfection of sketches is to understand it better. In her investigation of diagrammatic architectural sketches, Do (1998) found regularities in the use of symbols from which she concluded that automatic recognition of symbols in sketches could provide a basis for computers to deduce the design context in order to automatically offer appropriate assistance to designers, for example with lighting simulations. Achten (1999) has investigated which graphic elements building plans are composed of. Based on this, Achten and Jessurun (2003) discuss how a system for automatic recognition of graphic elements in sketches could be realised. Achten (2005) extends this to a theoretical real-time system. It takes into account the order in which strokes are added to a drawing. However, the recognition of the stroke sequence is not based on an empirical model but on assumptions, such as that graphic elements are composed of consecutive strokes, i.e. that they are always drawn from beginning to end. Moreover, the effectiveness of the method has not been evaluated. Juchmes and Lleclerq (2005) introduce a software architecture for a system that interprets freehand sketches. They describe how different software components that are specialised in the recognition of different aspects in the sketch collaborate and negotiate the recognition result. However they do neither describe what these aspects are and how they are characterised and nir how the individual recognition components work.

Knowledge of regularities of how graphic elements and corresponding building semantics develop in sketches over time could help to recognise them. For example, if we knew that designers pause (lift pen) between sketching walls or other objects, this information could be used for object segmentation. There are approaches to describing the development of designs. Prats et al. (2009) developed a method to describe transitions between shapes in design. Abdelmohsen and Do (2007) propose a method to describe the transition of individual strokes in architectural floor plan sketches over different design variants. Both approaches focus on describing the change in form across variants. The authors are not concerned with a quantitative relationship between the time elapsing during the design process and the shape. Both do also not consider semantic aspects of the variants but focus on the transition of pure geometry.

PILOT STUDY

We want to better understand how architects encode semantic building information in schematic layout sketches. Besides the pure form of the representation, can patterns be found in the temporal sequence of how graphic elements are added to the drawing that can be used for recognition? What other parameters could play a role? A pilot study in which participants draw on paper shall provide us with first qualitative clues to answer these questions. In addition, the observations shall show factors we should focus on in a follow-up study and help us to optimise the study design.

We recruited seven participants, from the chair of Architectural Informatics at the University of Munich, via email. All of them are trained architects who were educated at different schools. Among the participants are six researchers in the field of architectural informatics and one practising architect. The study was conducted in a remote setup via video conferencing due to contact restrictions during the COVID-19 pandemic. Participants received setup instructions before the study, which directed them to have their usual sketching tools (including paper, tracing paper, pen) ready. A webcam was to be pointed at the paper sheet during the study (see Figure 1).

Figure 1
Picture from the study set-up guide showing how the built-in camera of a laptop can be used for the video recording in the study. Left: Laptop with webcam as well as drawing utensils, Right: Camera image of the webcam.

The design task was formulated with the aim of allowing the participants to quickly grasp the boundary conditions and requirements. The design task was formulated with the aim that the requirements and boundary conditions could be grasped quickly. At the same time, however, it should be so challenging that the participants do not immediately have the solution in mind. They should make as realistic use as possible of the sketch as a design tool and approach the solution through the creation of several design variants. The subject of the task was student housing in a shared apartment or for young families in a new single-storey building in the Olympic Village in Munich. Together with the 1972 Olympic venues, the Olympic Village is part of a protected architectural ensemble. The well-known surroundings were chosen so that the participants could quickly familiarise themselves with the architectural context. The participants were asked to develop schematic layouts for two flats, each with a kitchen and living room as well as two to three bedrooms, on a given perimeter of 6.5 metres wide and a total of 16 metres long.

At the beginning of the video conference, the participants were asked whether they agreed to the recording of sound and video. After the setup was checked to make sure that the drawing could be seen well in the video, the task was sent to the participants. Participants were asked to comment on their actions and what they were drawing, if this did not interfere with their creative process. This was primarily to ensure that the drawings would be correctly interpreted in the later evaluation. There was no fixed time limit for the solution. After 20 minutes at the latest, the participants were asked to stop drawing and the study was debriefed. Participants were asked to send pictures of their sketches. Including welcome, setup test and corrections, study task and debrief sessions took between 30 and 45 minutes.

For the evaluation, two of the authors met in seven sessions (one per participant) via video chat and watched the recordings together. In doing so, we noted observations on the following topics in a collaboratively editable online spreadsheet: a) What semantic building information is encoded in the sketches? We focus on representations of Langenhan's (2017) semantic building fingerprints. b) How is the semantic building information encoded? c) What other information is coded in the sketches? d) How is the other information coded? In addition, we noted observations on the general approach to solving the task. We developed criteria c) and d) early during the analysis because we found that some graphic elements were relatively prevalent, but did not contribute to the building semantics. A better understanding of what other information occurs in sketches could help in the recognition process to filter out irrelevant information. From the notes we summarise the similarities and differences in the way the participants draw.

RESULTS

The participants (P) used different tools to solve the task. Only P1 and P2 used tracing paper. Some participants drew only with pencil (P4, P6) or only with

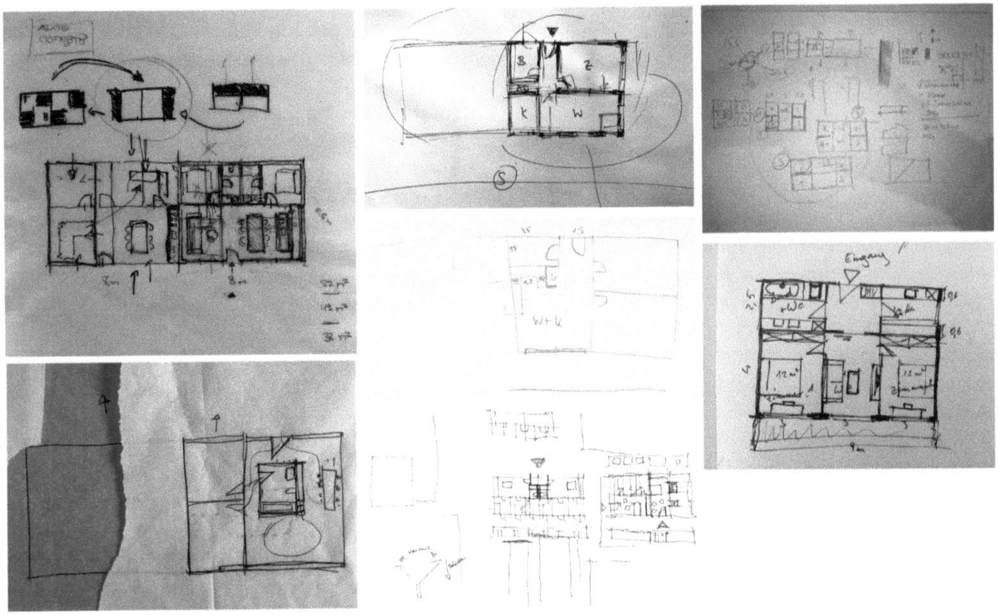

Figure 2
Some of the sketches of the seven participants. Left column (top to bottom): P1 and P2, mid column: P3, P4, P5, right column: P6, P7

a fine liner (P3, P5, P7). Others changed pens. P1, for example, used pencil and fineliner and P2 used a pink highlighter in addition to the fineliner. Only P1 and P2 used tracing paper. P3 would have liked tracing paper, but did not have any at hand. Some participants used a scale ruler to draw a scale perimeter for the flats (P1, P2, P7). P7 also used the scale ruler to draw a grid in the perimeter. All participants drew several variations. P1 drew several layout variants in the same perimeter with fine pencil lines and traced the final layout with a fineliner. P2 used different layers of tracing paper for the variants. P3, P4 and P7 used different sheets of paper for the variants. P5 and P6 drew variants on one sheet of paper. Figure 2 shows an example sketch of each participant.

Except for P1 and P2, all participants used the webcam built into the laptop for the recording. In these cases, the screen of the laptop was directed at the sketch and the task description presented there was no longer visible to the participants. With the exception of P1 and P2, the participants therefore first noted down the requirements in the form of a room programme. All participants began the drawing of the layout with the perimeter in which the layout was to be created. P3, P4, P5 and P6 additionally indicated the development around the perimeter with open (P4, P5, P6) or closed (P3, P6) rectangles. Based on the building context, these participants later justified layout decisions, for example shading (P3), and view axes (P5). P5 first developed some diagrams before drawing the actual layout, including an almost pictographic representation of the parcel and its dimensions, a bubble diagram in which he identifies the living room as the central space, and a sample of different grid patterns. P1 developed a diagram towards the end of the session suggesting which patterns could be used to develop further variations of the layout.

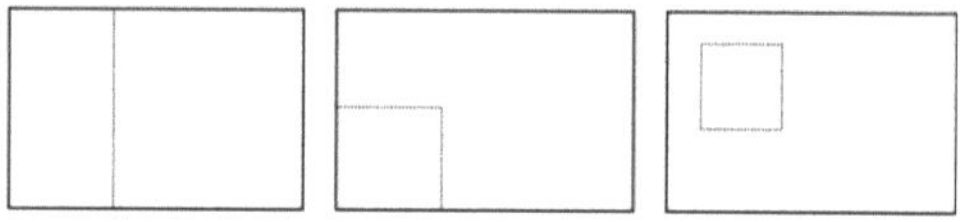

Figure 3
Schematic representation of the observed techniques for subdividing space. Left: subdivision by cut lines, mid: subdivision by open shapes, right: Subdivision by closed shapes.

All participants start the layout development by subdividing the space. We observe three techniques: subdivision by lines, subdivision by open shapes, subdivision by closed shapes (see Figure 3). In most cases, the positioning of graphic elements for subdivision is based on previously developed grids. The grid lines are either drawn with fine lines dividing the space in the perimeter or indicated with short orthogonal strokes at the edge of the perimeter. P2 draws a closed shape on a layer of tracing paper and moves it to determine the position of the space within the perimeter. P1, P2, P3 and P7 flesh out the walls by tracing the room perimeters. The participants develop the layouts to varying degrees of detail. P5, for example, does without doors altogether. P3, P4 and P7 draw windows. All participants draw furniture, but to a different extent. While P6 only hints at a kitchenette by rectangles, rooms in P7's sketch are fully furnished and the representation is comparatively rich in detail. Room types can be inferred from all the sketches.

Table 1
Information observed in sketches with information type. "object": a physical thing, "simulation" of the interplay of the building with the environment and its users, "explanation": to support the explanation for the study observers, "edit operation"

Information	Type	In sketches of
Perimeter	object	all participants
Rooms	object	all participants
Entrance	object	all participants
Furniture	object	all participants
Room type	object	all participants
Room connection type (door, passage, wall, etc.)	object	all participants
Change	edit operation	P1, P2, P3, P5, P6
Neighboring buildings	object	P3, P4, P5, P6
Highlight	explanation	P1, P2, P3, P5
Windows	object	P3, P4, P7
Circulation axis	simulation	P2, P3, P5
Dimensions	object	P1, P4, P7
Delete	edit operation	P1, P4
View axis	simulation	P2

Participants do not only depict physical objects in the drawings. Beyond this level of information, which we call "object", we have identified three further types of information: "simulation", "explanation" and "edit operation". Some participants simulate in the sketch the interplay of the building with its surroundings or its users ("simulation"). For example, we find circulation axes in the sketches of P2, P3 and P5. P3 also draws view axes to the surrounding buildings. Some participants added lines to the sketch to support the explanation of the design to the study observers ("explanation"), e.g. by encircling certain regions (P1, P2, P3, P6). In addition, we observe drawing elements that are intended to change what has already been drawn ("edit operation"). These can be mapped to the editing functions typical for computer programmes "delete" and "change". "Delete" was observed for P1 (crossing a symbol) and for P4 (scribbling over a symbol). "Change" was observed for P1, P2, P3, P5 and P6. By adding lines to the left or right of the wall line, they move the position of the wall in the respective direction. P2 also used the tracing paper to "copy" parts of a sketch. But there is no fragment in the sketch recording the copy action, so we do not mention it in Table 1. Table 1 summarises the information found in the sketches.

The participants use different notations. We see walls, for example, in the form of single lines, double lines, filled double lines and multiple fast lines (see Table 2). P5 and P6 use multiple techniques. We also see differences in the use of symbols. Symbols for the same thing can differ. For example, doors are represented as arcs, open triangles or short lines orthogonal to walls (see Table 3). But the same symbol can also mean different things. For example, arrows can indicate an entrance (P1) or a visual axis (P3). Participants encode the room type in different ways. P3, P4, P6 and P7 put explicit labels in the rooms, with P7 writing out the label and P3, P4, and P6 using abbreviations. For the other participants, the room type is implicit derived from the furniture.

Table 2
Representation of walls in participants sketches

Wall		
Example	*Description*	*Occurrence*
	single line	P4, P5, P6
	double line	P1, P2
	double line filled	P7
	multiple lines	P3, P5, P6

Table 3
Door symbols in participants sketches

Door			
Example			
Description	Arc	Open triangle	Orthogonal line
Occurrence	P1, P3, P4, P5	P2, P7	P6

DISCUSSION

As intended, the design assignment was quickly grasped by all participants. As intended, the task was not too easy to solve, but encouraged participants to iterate over multiple design variants, like in a real design problem solution scenario. The time required for the execution can be reduced. Some participants were not fully set up at the beginning of the study. For a future remote study, we should ensure that participants read the instructions before starting the study. Noting down the building requirements for participants without a second display took time. In the setup instructions, participants should be advised to use a second monitor or to print out the task description. For a future in-depth study, we will recruit practising architects. To avoid biases in the way of sketching, we will look for different experience levels and that the participants work for different offices with different focuses and have been trained at different schools. In this pilot, we have only examined qualitative data. In order to be able to make quantitative statements, such as how often certain symbols are used compared to others, we will have to recruit more participants.

We have seen that certain information is expressed by all participants in the drawing. These are perimeter, entrance, rooms, room type, room connection type, furniture. All of them are information describing the semantics of the built substance ("object"). The participants make different use of other information levels ("explanation", "edit operation", "simulation"). Different ways of expressing the information prevail among the participants. The fact that there are different symbols for one and the same thing makes recognition more complicated. And it can be assumed that in a larger field of participants, even more symbols would have been added. A different challenge is that some symbols showed to have multiple meanings, such as arrows. In order to recognise their meaning, the computer would have to be able to grasp their context of use. On the other hand, we have also identified patterns in the participants' approach. For example, the perimeter is always drawn first and the enclosed space is divided using a set of three techniques. It will be interesting to see if a follow-up study can confirm these observations and how this regularity can be used for recognition. Eventually, all subsequently drawn room boundaries have been based on this initial division of the space.

In the related work section we have mentioned works that propose rules for drawing to deal with imprecise and varying representations (Lladós et al.1997; Aoki et al. 1996; Cutler and Nasman 2010; Weber et al. 2010). These rules are based on assumptions about how architects sketch. An empirical elicitation in a future study could show which type of representation is most common. Based on this consensus, rules for sketch-based interaction can be developed. As with other types of gestures (Vatavu 2019), users will have to learn these sketch gestures. It will be interesting to see how this affects aspects of the designer's user experience, such as the flow state during the design process (Dorta 2008). If sketching at certain information levels was banned or the use of certain graphical thinking methods (e.g. drawing bubble diagrams) was forbidden in favour of recognition, what would be the impact? Can designated areas for free graphical thinking on the drawing canvas solve this issue or do they create new ones?

In a follow-up study, we want to be able to quantify parameters that describe sketching more effectively. Participants should therefore use a digital drawing tool. For example, this allows us to record when the pencil is applied and lifted in order to segment individual strokes and determine the order in which strokes are drawn (Johnson et al. 2009). Additionally the contact pressure of the pen can be measured. The subdivision of the perimeter was usually done with fine lines. Boundaries of rooms were drawn with stronger lines, which might have correlated with higher pressure of the pen. The participants made different use of tools in the study. With the digital drawing device, participants should also be able to switch tools, either through a graphical user interface by choosing for example colour or line width from a menu or by physically switching pens. This way the use of tools can be tracked and evaluated more effectively.

CONCLUSION

We conducted a pilot study in a remote setup via video conference in which we observed participants developing a schematic layout sketch for a given design task. Our design task encouraged participants to sketch during design problem solving. The video recordings provided clues to our questions. We have seen differences among the participants' sketches:

- Different types of information in the sketches which we classified as "object", "explanation", "simulation", "edit operation"
- Different use of sketching tools
- Different symbols for the same thing
- Symbols with multiple meanings

And we have seen commonalities among participants sketches:

- All participants start with sketching the perimeter
- All participants continue with subdividing the space within the perimeter using one or more of three techniques for subdivision: by line, by open shape, by closed shape
- "Object" information that is prevalent in all participants' sketches: perimeter, rooms, entrance, furniture, room type, room connection type

We discussed that a strategy for dealing with variance in the representations could be to prescribe consensus-based rules for sketching and discussed resulting issues for the designers' user experience. We are planning a follow-up study with a larger number of participants in order to enable quantitative statements, for example, regarding the use of symbols. We want to recrute practising architects to have a subject sample that is representative for a potential user group of such a CAAD system. In order to mind biases in sketching style and use of symbols participants should have different experience levels, work for different offices and have been educated at different schools, potentially with different educational focus (for example artistic and technical). The follow-up study is to be carried out with a digital input device that enables free-hand drawing. This will allow us to describe the sketching process more precisely with quantitative parameters. This could, for example, enable the observation of patterns in the stroke sequence or in the contact pressure of the pen and help us and ultimately the computer to understand a little better how architects sketch.

ACKNOWLEDGEMENT

The research that led to the presented results has received funding from the German Research Foundation (DFG). We like to thank all participants in the study for their time, their dedication in solving the design task and their valuable feedback.

REFERENCES

Abdelmohsen, S and Do, EY-L 2007 'Tracking design development through decomposing sketching processes', *International Association of Societies of Design Research*

Achten, H 1999, *Generic representations: An approach for modelling procedural and declarative knowledge of building types in architectural design*, Ph.D. Thesis,

Eindhoven University of Technology
Achten, H 2005 'Resolving some Ambiguities in Real-time Design Drawing Recognition by means of a Decision Tree for Agents', *Computer Aided Architectural Design Futures*, pp. 311-320
Achten, H and Jessurun, J 2003 'Learning From Mah Jong - Towards a Multi-Agent System that can Recognize Graphic Units', *Proceedings of the 10th International Conference on Computer Aided Architectural Design Futures*, pp. 115-124
Ah-Soon, C and Tombre, K 1998 'Network-based recognition of architectural symbols', *Joint IAPR International Workshops on Statistical Techniques in Pattern Recognition (SPR) and Structural and Syntactic Pattern Recognition (SSPR)*, pp. 252-261
Ahmed, S, Liwicki, M, Weber, M and Dengel, A 2011 'Improved automatic analysis of architectural floor plans', *International conference on document analysis and recognition*, pp. 864-869
Ahmed, S, Liwicki, M, Weber, M and Dengel, A 2012 'Automatic room detection and room labeling from architectural floor plans', *10th IAPR international workshop on document analysis systems*, pp. 339-343
Aoki, Y, Shio, A, Arai, H and Odaka, K 1996 'A prototype system for interpreting hand-sketched floor plans', *Proceedings of 13th International Conference on Pattern Recognition*, pp. 747-751
Arora, H, Langenhan, C, Petzold,, F, Eisenstadt,, V and Althoff, K-D 2020 'METIS-GAN: An approach to generate spatial configurations using deep learning and semantic building models', *ECPPM-European Conference on Product and Process Modeling*
Bailey, R 2000 'The Intelligent Sketch: Developing a conceptual model for a digital design assistant', *22nd Annual Conference of the Association for Computer-Aided Design in Architecture*, pp. 137-145
Buxton, WAS 2007, *Sketching User Experiences: Getting the Design Right and the Right Design*, Focal Press
Cutler, B and Nasman, B 2016, 'Interpreting physical sketches as architectural models', in Ceccato, C, Hesselgren, L, Pauly, M, Pottmann, H and Wallner, J (eds) 2016, *Advances in Architectural Geometry*, Ambra, Berlin, pp. 15-36
Do, EY-L 1998, *The right tool at the right time – Investigation of freehand drawing as an interface to knowledge based design tools*, Ph.D. Thesis, Georgia Institute of Technology
Do, EY-L and Gross, MD 2001, 'Thinking with diagrams in architectural design', *Artificial Intelligence Review*, 15(1), pp. 135-149
Domínguez-Martín, B 2016, *Methods to process low-level CAD plans and creative Building Information Models (BIM)*, Ph.D. Thesis, Universidad de Jaén
Dorta, T 2008, 'Design flow and ideation', *International Journal of Architectural Computing*, 6(3), pp. 299-316
Eisenstadt, V, Arora, H, Ziegler, C, Langenhan, C and Althoff, K-D 2021 'Exploring Optimal Ways to Represent Topological and Spatial Features of Building Designs in Deep Learning Methods and Applications for Architecture', *26th International Conference of the Association for Computer-Aided Architectural Design Research in Asia Online and Global*
Eisenstadt, V, Langenhan, C, Althoff, K-D and Dengel, A 2020 'Improved and Visually Enhanced Case-Based Retrieval of Room Configurations for Assistance in Architectural Design Education', *International Conference on Case-Based Reasoning*, pp. 213-228
Gimenez, L, Robert, S, Suard, F and Zreik, K 2015 'Cost-effective reconstruction of BIM from 2D scanned plan: experiments on existing buildings', *Sustainable Places*, pp. 61-69
Goel, V 1995, *Sketches of Thought*, MIT Press, Cambridge, Massachusetts
Goldschmidt, G 1994, 'On visual design thinking: the vis kids of architecture', *Design Studies*, 15(2), pp. 158-174
de las Heras, L-P, Ahmed, S, Liwicki, M, Valveny, E and Sánchez, G 2014, 'Statistical segmentation and structural recognition for floor plan interpretation', *International Journal on Document Analysis and Recognition (IJDAR)*, 17(3), pp. 221-237
Johnson, G, Gross, MD, Hong, J and Do, EY-L 2009, *Computational Support for Sketching in Design*, Now Foundations and Trends
Juchmes, R, Leclercq, P and Azar, S 2005, 'A freehand-sketch environment for architectural design supported by a multi-agent system', *Computers and Graphics*, 29(6), pp. 905-915
Langenhan, C 2017, *Data Management in Architecture – Investigating the organisation of design information in IT infrastructures and identifying potential uses in knowledge-based systems.*, Ph.D. Thesis, Technical University of Munich
Laseau, P 2000, *Graphic Thinking for Architects & Designers*, Wiley
Leclercq, P and Juchmes, R 2002, 'The absent interface in design engineering', *Artificial Intelligence for Engineering Design, Analysis and Manufacturing: AI EDAM*, 16(3), pp. 219-227
Lladós, J, López-Krahe, J and Martí, E 1997, 'A system to understand hand-drawn floor plans using subgraph

isomorphism and Hough transform', *Machine Vision and Applications*, 10(3), pp. 150-158
Lu, Q and Lee, S 2017 'A semi-automatic approach to detect structural components from CAD drawings for constructing as-is BIM objects', *ASCE International Workshop on Computing in Civil Engineering*, pp. 84-91
Macé, S, Locteau, H, Valveny, E and Tabbone, S 2010 'A system to detect rooms in architectural floor plan images', *9th IAPR International Workshop on Document Analysis Systems*, pp. 167-174
Prats, M, Lim, S, Jowers, I, Garner, SW and Chase, S 2009, 'Transforming shape in design: observations from studies of sketching', *Design Studies*, 30(5), pp. 503-520
Schön, D and Wiggins, G 1992, 'Kinds of seeing and their functions in designing', *Design Studies*, 13(2), pp. 135-156
Sharma, D, Chattopadhyay, C and Harit, G 2016 'A unified framework for semantic matching of architectural floorplans', *23rd International Conference on Pattern Recognition (ICPR)*, pp. 2422-2427
Sheraz, A, Weber, M, Liwicki, M, Langenhan, C, Dengel, A and Petzold, F 2014, 'Automatic analysis and sketch-based retrieval of architectural floor plans', *Pattern Recognition Letters*, 35, pp. 91-100
Sutherland, IE 1964, 'Sketchpad a man-machine graphical communication system 2.5 (1964): R-3.', *Simulation*, 2(5), pp. 3-20
Suwa, M and Tversky, B 1997, 'What do architects and students perceive in their design sketches? A protocol analysis', *Design Studies*, 18(4), pp. 385-403
Vatavu, R-D 2019 'The dissimilarity-consensus approach to agreement analysis in gesture elicitation studies', *CHI Conference on Human Factors in Computing Systems*, pp. 1-13
Weber, M, Liwicki, M and Dengel, A 2010 'a.Scatch – a sketch-based retrieval for architectural floor plans', *12th International Conference on Frontiers in Handwriting Recognition*, pp. 289-294
Yang, X, Zhao, W and Pan, L 2008 'Graphical symbol recognition in architectural plans with an improved Ant-Tree based clustering algorithm', *IEEE International Joint Conference on Neural Networks (IEEE World Congress on Computational Intelligence)*, pp. 390-397

What is Architectural Digital Sketch?

A systematic inventory

Dalibor Dzurilla[1], Henri Achten[2]
[1,2]Faculty of Architecture, Czech Technical University, Prague
[1,2]{dzuridal|achten}@fa.cvut.cz

The traditional sketch using pencil and paper is an indispensable medium for architects. Digital technology both imitates and extends the possibilities of the sketch into a new form, the Architectural Digital Sketch. In this paper, we present a descriptive framework from the theoretical perspective of technology parameters. This framework covers traditional and digital sketch. We investigated several representative tools for sketching employing the framework, such as traditional sketch, Wacom SmartPen, iPad Pro, Foldable Notebook Lenovo ThinkPad X1 and Hyve3D. We demonstrate how the framework gives a unified approach to such widely varied tools.

Keywords: *digital sketching, architectural sketch, visual communication*

INTRODUCTION

The architectural digital sketch (ADS), in a sense, is an extension of the traditional sketch, however, with the potential to greatly exceed the possibilities of the traditional sketch. Many aspects from the traditional sketch will be passed on to the ADS. To understand the whole scope of this development, we need a framework that encompasses both traditional and digital sketch. Only then we can distinguish between real differences and more superficial ones. The focus of our research is on the sketch as a communication tool between the architect and client. In this paper, we look at a first comprehensive framework to capture the phenomenon of (digital) sketching. We will discuss several sketching systems utilising this framework, followed by an overview of how to proceed from here.

In the first stage of the research, we investigated contemporary digital sketching tools. Digital technology in architecture is used throughout the whole building process and helps create outputs (2D, 3D), which are valuable forms for clear communication (Kitchens & Shiratuddin, 2007). We have extensive experience from our practice, where we focus on educating architects in presentation skills in terms of comprehensibility for the client plus in terms of sustainability for architects such as time, finance and ease of implementation of these solutions [1]. This provides us with two advantages compared to the traditional academic research approach. First, it gives us a good understanding of architects' needs in their practice, and second, we can closely observe the learning curve and perceived benefits of old and new media for the architect. Throughout our training experience, we have also seen the impact tools have on the communication between architect and client. This aspect bears more investigation since it is not studied in great detail.

From our experience, we can observe that architects feel increasing pressure of all kinds of information in the design process, interactions, decisions, and issue factors. Most architects work on multiple projects at the same time. As Lee (2001) states, modern IT technologies allow the architect to coordinate designs, manage core information, and ensure information flow (Lee, 2001). Despite the advances made in technology, increasing amounts of information that must be managed challenges architects. Additionally, the time required to complete projects has decreased. ICT has the potential to speed up time and understandability during the building process. (Penttilä, 2006). In the communication with the client, we can see that presentation makes up half of the work (Visuin, 2012). Thus, it should be simple, straightforward, fast, non-destructive, semi-automated, organised, original and bear the author's mark from the architect. At the same time, it should be emotional and understandable for the client.

Since the sketch is so well embedded in the architects' practice, it is still a sustainable and effective communication tool, which can save time and mental capacity of the architect. Also, it can bring trust and a quicker decision-making process between client and architect. That is why it makes sense to pay attention to the effective architectural digital sketch, which is part of the sustainable architecture presentation. Since effective communication relies on using the right media (Ean, 2011), we need to understand these media very well.

With the introduction of new technologies, there are two main risks. (1) The first is that in any initial stage, a new technology imitates the old way. Thus, many digital sketching tools build on the metaphor of paper and pencil, using strokes as the main way to build up a sketch. Continuation from traditional sketch techniques is fine by itself since it leverages the architects' experience and skill level when transiting to new technology. It is, however, also very limiting because it does not take full advantage of all new possibilities, many of which are still indeed unimaginable. (2) The second risk is that people get carried away with the possibilities of new technologies without considering what they really need. This means that they may get side-tracked into developments that are not quite that helpful or effective in their work processes. We feel that it is necessary to have a theoretical framework that can capture all these phenomena. Such a framework also helps to more systematically look at possible future developments.

In our research, we focus on the communication between architect and client through the perspective of sketches. Sketches and digital sketches have seen a lot of research. However, most of it is focussed on the creator of the sketch (e.g.Purcell & Gero 1998; Do et al. 2000; Menezes & Lawson 2006), or on the development of sketch tools - again with the focus on the creator (e.g. Gross 1996; Richens 1999; Juchmes et al. 2004) or comparative work between the two (Bilda & Demirkan 2003). However, the communication between architect and client is being explored in papers (e.g. Norouzi et al. 2014; Ean 2011; Siva & London 2011; Taleb et al. 2017) through the informational communication management or information factors, while communication through sketches or digital sketches has not seen much research.

Definition of Terms

Traditional Architectural Sketch. According to [2], the word sketch stems from the Greek **σχέδιος - schedios**, "done extempore." It is usually produred quickly, using freehand methods, that is not intended as a finished work. It is a preliminary sketch of the idea. It is an architectural draft image output describing a certain problem, detail or part of a design visually at a certain stage.

In the architectural design process, representations are used by necessity. Sketches allow the architect to quickly focus on a limited set of key elements in what otherwise would be a very complex problem to solve. Because of their speed and ease to make, sketches support the need for some degree of plasticity of form and the ability to manipulate elements to develop the design. Drawings and physical models offer these possibilities as well. (Alberto, 1982)

Figure 1
Example of architectural digital sketch from iPad + Concepts App. Dalibor Dzurilla, 2020

Architectural Digital Sketch (ADS). ADS can be classified as a form of human communication, namely the computer-mediated communication form (CMC) (Norouzi et al. 2014). The main purpose of using CMC is to streamline and improve communication (Gabriel & Maher 2002). ADS also offers the quick and fast ideation in the design process, using digital tools throughout (thus it should not be confused with *modelling* which is a different activity). The big advantages of ADS are that it is paperless, offers quick editability of sketched content (duplicating, scaling, redrawing), makes it possible to start sketching on the data rather than on a blank canvas and allows distant communication (see Figure 1). Disadvantages include higher entry price, a steeper learning curve for the sketching software, the limited size of the screen, faster hardware obsolescence, and faster software development that requires keeping up to date with the software and interface.

Architect & Client relationship. A lot of understanding between architect and client is built during the meetings (together or through online means), where both parties can immediately discuss and settle issues about the design. The sketch helps establish this mutual understanding, where the client can see or even participate in the construction of the sketch. With the ADS, the possibilities of engagement and explanation become wider than with the traditional sketch.

The most important person in the architect-client relationship is the client. They require accurate information about the building design, and they are the one person who will have a close relationship with the architect (Tessema 2008). In this relationship, there is a client as a contracting authority. And the architect as a supplier of the design. This relationship is defined as a business and should have specific rules according to building regulations law. However, it is usually not specified how much the architect and client should meet during the building construction process. It is clear that it is a question of proper manners and the intent to avoid misunderstandings when in the meeting big decisions come to play. In order to obtain relevant information, the architect is responsible for creating a venue for discussion with their clients (Tessema 2008).

The biggest issues, according to Norouzi (2014), in the communication between these two entities is *"Habitus Shock"*, where the client is confused by the process of the building, and the architect often forget on zero experience of the client and his knowledge about that. The education of the client is a fundamental component of the successful client-architect relationship (Siva & London 2011). The Australian Institute of Architects and Palea, Ciobanu, & Kilyeni (2012) has recommended that the following traits should be possessed by an architect: The ability (a) to communicate effectively, (b) to coordinate and manage complex projects, and (c) to negotiate with a client to resolve issues (Norouzi et al. 2014).

In this context, it is clear that the sketch is a very useful technique how to communicate actual changes on blueprints or drawings. Architect as a contractor should always deliver as clear as a possible explanation to questions of the client. The sketch helps to simplify for the client important issues and thus is a suitable (one of many) techniques in the design process.

Framework for traditional and architectural digital sketch

If we want to understand the potential of ADS, we need a framework that systematically describes both the ADS and traditional sketch.

		Traditional sketch	Architectural Digital Sketch
MEDIUM	Transmitting element	Pen, brush, pencil, crayon	Stylus, mouse, 3D Controller
	Receiving element	Paper canvas, sheet material	PC, tablet, touchscreen, Smart paper
PROCESS ING	Editing	Eraser, craft knife, stump	Tools for erasing, Rotate, Scale, Duplicate, Reshape
	Storage	= Receiving element	Hard-Disk, Flash Media, Cloud
	Transfer	Mail, fax, or email of scanned images	Internet transfer TCP/IP, storage sending, Bluetooth
	Processor	Does not have this component	Synthetic processor of the Tool Algorithms for the display of strokes, Processing of an image, Manipulation of image

Table 1
Difference between traditional architectural sketch and Architectural Digital Sketch

Any sketching system relies on the hand manipulation of a tool that makes some kind of marks on a surface. This means that on the most abstract level, we can distinguish between a *transmitting element* (that which makes the marks) and a *receiving element* (that on which the marks are made). These two components are the *Medium* part (A) of any sketching system.

The second part we call *Processing* (B). When the marks are applied, all kinds of operations can be employed on the marks and the receiving element. First of all, the marks can be *edited*. When the sketch is regarded as finished, it has to be *stored* in some form. If the sketch is used for communication, it has to be *transferred* between parties of the communication process. Finally, in particular relevant for the architectural digital sketch, all aspects mentioned here can be *processed* in some way.

Thus, we define as sketching system as having two parts:

(A) Medium, and (B) Processing:

Component (A) Medium has the following parts:

- (1) Transmitting element: The tool or device that registers the sketching actions.
- (2) Receiving element: The part that receives sketching actions.

Component (B) Processing has the following parts:

- (1) Editing. The tools by which created elements of the sketch can be changed.
- (2) Storage. In the traditional sketch, this is the same as the Receiving element.
- (3) Transfer. The transfer of the stored sketch and other communications between Computing Platforms and/or between Storage.
- (4) Processor. The algorithms that work on the stored elements of the sketch.

The above theoretical framework (see Table 1) allows us to comprehensively document both traditional and architectural digital sketch from perspective technology .

EXAMPLES OF TRADITIONAL AND ADS TOOLS

There is a huge number of commercial and academic applications available for traditional and architectural digital sketching. In this paper, we highlight

Table 2
Traditional sketch inventory

		Traditional sketch	Notes
MEDIUM	Transmitting element	Pencil	Other drawing tools such as pen, marker, stump(historically) …
	Receiving element	Sketchbook + Tracing Paper	Rulers/ Printed maps/ Stencils, template rulers,
PROCESS ING	Editing	Eraser	Scissors, craft knife, Glue,
	Storage	= Receiving element	
	Transfer	Give a Xerox copy of the sketch to the client.	Mail, Scan, Photo,
	Processor	Does not have this component	

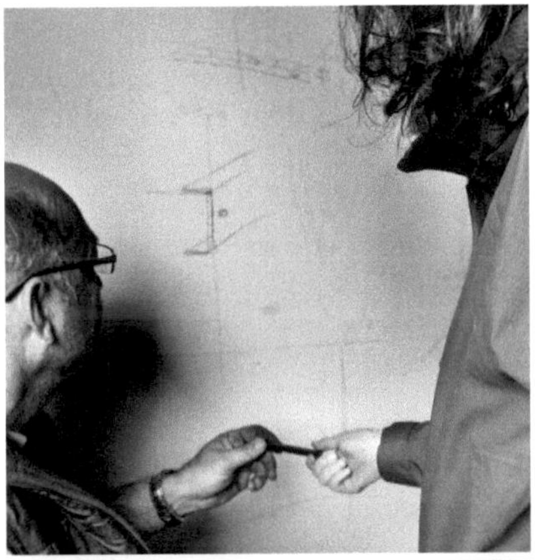

Figure 2
Author's photo from the building site.Visual discussion between architect and the client. Sketching details on the wall. (2018)

Figure 3
Physical sketch immediately converted to digital recording. It can be transmitted directly to the client. As a live stream, timelapse video or a picture. Youtube channel Tech Yi Chie (2016). Link: https://cutt.ly/Bamboo-Slate

a few selected of them to demonstrate the feasibility of the framework. We do not have the space to offer a comprehensive overview in this paper (we are building a comprehensive catalogue that should contain a substantial amount of examples). To start in the current overview, it is clear that the traditional sketch should be part of the examples. The second example represents the class of tools that use a traditional transmitter on a digital receiver. The third example represents completely digital transmitters and receivers. The fourth example represents innovative carriers of digital receivers. Finally, the fifth example goes beyond the traditional paradigm of paper and pen (digital or not) and shows a truly innovative and different use of digital sketching in 3D and VR.

1. Traditional sketch

The traditional sketch is intended as a visual record for the architect and redrawing of queries when discussing with a client (see Figure 2).

The traditional sketch builds on lifelong experience of writing and drawing with pencil on paper. Thus, starting with the sketch has (a) a very shallow learning curve (mastering the sketch obviously is a different story); (b) it is possible to sketch on any surface (and size) that is available; (c) sketchbook and pencil are a very light and portable solution, and easy to replace. Finally, (d) the sketch allows the architect to build a personal style.

The traditional sketch also faces some limitations: (a) It's not possible to draw in dark spots or in rainy environments; (b) physical sketch or note is hard to share instantly; (c) if we want to verify, update, or substantiate something under the drawing, we must first

		Wacom Bamboo Slate (2016)	Notes about effectiveness
MEDIUM	Transmitting element	Smart Pen	- Pen must be charged. - Turning construction causes the pen to turn off. - Thickness of the pen not for everyone.
	Receiving element	Own Sketchbook + Bamboo Pad	+ Possibility to physically sketch as user is used to and the pad receive the strokes and transfer them into the digital environment live or after the sketch is done.
PROCESS ING	Editing	InkSpace App	+ Layers. Progress bar. Further editability in Photoshop. Or other software. + Post-editing is quite limitless.
	Storage	InkSpace App + Cloud	+ Instant saving. Up to 100 drawings or layers. Then need to be transferred from the device.
	Transfer	Bluetooth, Wi-fi	Instant digitalizing sketched content
	Processor	Yes. Two separated.	Bamboo pad + iPad parameters

Table 3
Wacom Bamboo Slate Inventory.

print it out. We cannot react dynamically at the construction site, for example, to new facts or updated data or new map materials; (d) the sketch is not scalable or editable with further devices; (e) organisation of plenty of sketches from different projects in one sketchbook might be chaotic, and some information can be lost; (f) It's hard to sketch in scale (see Table 2).

2. Pencil and paper + digital receiver

Pencil and paper + digital receiver is a physical pad with the ability to scan the strokes and instantly transfer them into the digital form (see Figure 3) (e.g. LiveScribe Pen; InkLink; Wacom Bamboo Folio; Moleskine; SmartPens; etc...).

From the point of view of the effectiveness of communication during the construction process, there are new potentials that expand the physical sketches. They eliminate the disadvantages of physical sketching and cleverly combine physical and digital. (a) An architect can still use his or her style for sketching with no interface, but the sketch is instantly digitalized. When transferred into the computer/tablet it can even be streamed directly to the client's computer for example during a virtual meeting. (b) If there is a need to draw over existing material, then this still has to be printed out before the consultation or talk. (c) The device is very transportable, usable. The battery can hold a long time, and storage can have up to 100 drawings (see Table 3).

3. iPad + Drawing apps

The iPad + Apps (e.g. Morpholio Trace, Concepts App, Procreate, Photoshop CC, etc.) is a miniature computer characterised by offering a large display for all interactions. The display has the ability to receive the user's sketch strokes, thus becoming a substitution for physical paper (see Figure 4).

Figure 4
iPad Pro + Apple Pencil as a digital sketching tool for communication with the client. In-person or remotely. (Author's photo, 2018)

Table 4
iPad Pro inventory

		iPad Pro 2020	Notes about effectiveness
MEDIUM	Transmitting element	Apple Pencil 2nd generation	+Very fast, accurate, light. - Needs to be charged. 15 sec = 30 minutes of usage
	Receiving element	iPad Pro tablet	Glass display 10-12". Drawing foil recommended for better feeling of drawing. Aluminium body. Weight between 500-643g Battery Life up to 9 hours + Silent. - Fragile. Case recommended.
PROCESS ING	Editing	Hundreds of apps	+ User friendly interfaces. In general. + Quick Learning curve - One app per one task
	Storage	Internal + Cloud	Instant saving. No need to assist.
	Transfer	Bluetooth, Wi-fi	Instant digitalizing sketched content
	Processor	Yes + Machine Learning	Processes become better with more repetitions. E.g. Sharpness of photos.

Most sketching applications with iPad build on the traditional sketching paradigm. Since the price tag for an iPad is quite high, it is usually not taken as a mere "digitization" of the sketchbook, but needs a clear idea of the architect how to implement it into the design process if he or she wants to get benefit from it.

With an iPad it is clear that the working surface will always be the same; (a) the pencil needs to be paired and charged to work; (b) there is a short delay between the transmitting tool and the stroke's appearance on the receiver, which can still feel a bit unnatural. As advantages, we can see (a) a wider array of possibilities with the digital pencil (e.g. colours, stroke styles, switching tool operations); (d) The receiver is a very successful design, representative and durable except for the display, which is covered with glass. The surface is fragile and can be scratched. Sketching on glass is also not a standard feeling. This is why many users apply an additional foil that gives back the sense of working on paper (see Table 4).

4. Foldable computer

Foldable laptops (example: Lenovo Think Pad X1 Fold) aim to counter the disadvantages of bulky and heavy laptops that feature 180° rotational displays. The Lenovo Think Pad X1 Fold is an example of foldable laptops, that have a continuous flexible bending display (see Figure 5). They have as advantage (a) great transportability and also good protection; (b)The device is not so heavy to hold in one hand and sketch with the other; (c) Its cover is from leather which makes it appear more representative; (d) However, the operating system is the weak part of this tool (see Table 5).

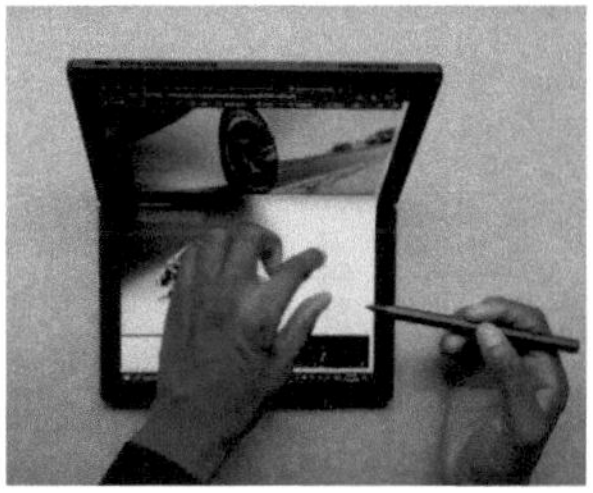

Figure 5
Foldable notebook with fully running Windows 10. Lenovo Think Pad X1 Fold. MKBHD youtube review (2021) Link: https://cutt.ly/foldable

		Lenovo Think Pad X1 Fold (2021)	Notes about effectiveness
MEDIUM	Transmitting element	Stylus – no branded	+ Light + Integrated into the body of the PC
	Receiving element	Lenovo ThinkPad Display	+ Glass display 13" Foldable + Safe, Transportable, Representative + Multifunctional by adding physical keyboard above it.
PROCESS ING	Editing Tools	Apps/ Software based on Windows 10 (W10).	- In general, heavy apps, where user must learn how to use it. Often, they are not optimized for touching gestures. - W10 is disadvantage in case of digital sketching. Mainly due to its complexity. it is a robust system that needs a lot of power. W10 is not representational interface. User must go into folders and find all files… For instance, each iPad app looks like gallery. + Later in 2021 should be released Windows10X which will be more suitable for tablet experience.
	Storage	Internal + Cloud	Instant saving. No need to assist.
	Transfer	Bluetooth, Wi-fi	Instant digitalizing sketched content
	Processor	Yes + Machine Learning	Processes become better with more repetitions. E.g. Sharpness of photos.

Table 5
Lenovo Think Pad X1 Fold. Representative of foldable devices inventory

Figure 6
Hyve3D-sketching demo. Image from website [3].

5. Hyve 3D

Hyve3D (Hybrid Virtual Environment 3DTM) is an innovative ideation technology researched from 2006 at the University of Montreal by Tomás Dorta (see Figure 6). It brings sketches into 3D space with the collaborative intention to work remotely and quickly communicate by sketching in the design's creative phases. Hyve3D uses a smartphone or tablet as a sort of 3-D mouse to a connected screen or headset, which shows a first-person view of a 3-D interface (which can be either the Hyve3D, an Oculus Rift game or even a 3-D operating system) (Dorta et al. 2016).

Hyve3D is revolutionary in the approach to the concept of the Media section. (a) Its Transmitter is not

Table 6
HYVE 3D - Hybrid Virtual Environment inventory. Representative of an experimental approach to the communication by ADS .

		Hyve3D Parameters	Notes about effectiveness
MEDIUM	Transmitting element	Tablet-iPad + Apple pencil or finger	Very natural to move sketching planes and views. Also substitute the complication of the mouse cursor in 3D environment.
	Receiving element	Virtual Environment (Created by Xbox Kinect + Epson Projectors + Reflective Sphere for projection + Curved projecting canvas)	This environment can be projected anywhere. (in Client's TV, Computer, or VR set) Removing boundaries of physical presence.
PROCESS ING	Editing Tools	Duplication, Erase, Mirror,	Basic edits with sketched lines. They are rasterized points. More people at a time = remote immersive editing.
	Storage	Internal + Cloud	Instant saving.
	Transfer	Bluetooth, Wi-fi	Instant digitalizing sketched content. Transferring real-time to all participants.
	Processor	Transmitting element processor + Receiving element processor parts.	3 processors take care on fluency of transferring the 3D space + 3D sketch. More people at a time = remote immersive editing.

a pencil or mouse cursor, but it is an iPad with a 3D virtual reality controller; (b) the Receiver is a projection through a spherical hemisphere onto a curved screen that creates a powerfully immersive experience. At the same time, in the Processing section, we can pick up (c) the possibility of collaborative remote and co-located sketching; (d) Each of the users can move where they want in the given model; (e) Architect can sketch on any surface; (f) Client can observe from any point of view; (g) Sketching takes place on a 1: 1 scale (see Table 6).

Hyve3D shows the potential of bringing in additional techniques to the sketching process. Although it can be moved rather easily, it is not a simple portable solution. In any case, Hyve3D shows us how to break free from the established ideas of digital sketches and pushes the boundaries of sketching efficiency in terms of technical and ergonomic solutions.

	Elements	Parameters	Potentials in Effective Communication
MEDIUM	Transmitting element	Smart Pen Pencil like. Or another approach free from the assumption that it looks like a pencil.	Ideally choose different weight and feel for any person. Durable in outdoor conditions Easy to hold longer time. Lighter More accurate No lag between stroke and the line No need to charge or charge quickly
	Receiving element	Display feeling	The closest to the paper feeling as possible Advanced haptics / Ultra haptics possible Maybe foldable displays to save space and increase transportability and compactness
		Device It can also be free from the physical essence and become a mere virtual affair.	Thin, Light, Durable, Weatherproof, Transportable, Long stamina Quick charge if need to charge.
PROCESSING	Editing	Applications	Easy workflow Easy interface. Quick to learn Possible to cooperate with the client even on distance, simultaneously. (Apps needs to be examined further in separate paper)
		Operating system	Convert to touch experience
	Storage	Internal + Cloud	Here looks like we have everything what we need. Maybe more fluent sharing.
	Transfer	Bluetooth, Wi-fi	Here is also category very equal in all devices. And today it's standard with quite good coverage of current and future needs.
	Processor	Small. Powerful. No energy demanding.	Machine learning, effective in energy consumption. Merging several complicated processes manageable by one processor is desirable.

Table 7
Final conclusion and merging parameters into the framework.

CONCLUSION

Thanks to the framework, we can describe the parameters of traditional and digital sketching tools (see Table 7). This also opens up a reference frame in which we can study in more detail what potentials brings particular elements to the effectiveness of the communication process.

Table of technical aspects in categories of the framework and potentials for effective communication in the building process.

The Processing part adds a lot of functionality to the sketch that up to now has not been possible. Definitely, the most important finding in this categorization is the need for real-time interaction and real-time sharing of the process with the client. This is game-changing in removing the "Habitus Shock" mentioned earlier. The client's strong involvement in the process causes an educational effect that brings more understanding to the building process. It also has the potential to remove misunderstandings and dissatisfactions of the client during the building process.

Portability, storage and durability are important for these devices. Otherwise, they are not used on-site, and the client is not involved. Less power consumption for more complex operations with a 3D model will help to more integrate these portable devices into the communication process, even on-site.

The paradigm of pencil and paper is very powerful, but it also holds inherent limitations that hold back potential innovations. We need to keep an open mind and stay aware that the ADS does not by necessity must imitate sketch by pencil and paper. For example with the Hyve3D solution, we can see where this is the case.

The next steps in the research will be a structured comparison of various ADS tools with architects in practice. Obviously, the traditional sketch will be taken into account to see the differences. The developed framework presented here gives us the right set of parameters to describe the differences between the tools. Additional steps include the description of the communication process, which requires extension of the current framework.

ACKNOWLEDGEMENTS

This research was kindly supported by two grants: SGS20/076/OHK1/1T/15 and SGS21/068/OHK1/1T/15 by Faculty of Architecture, Czech Technical University in Prague.

REFERENCES

Alberto, D. 1982, *Architectural Representation: Spatial Comprehension and Assessment Through Visualization Technique*, Master's Thesis, MIT

Bilda, Z. and Demirkan, H. 2003, 'An Insight on Designers' Sketching Activities in Traditional versus Digital Media', *Design Studies*, 24(1), pp. 27-50

Do, E.L., Gross, M., Neiman, B. and Zimring, C. 2000, 'Intentions in and relations among design drawings', *Design Studies*, 21(5), pp. 483-503

Dorta, T., Kinayoglu, G. and Boudhraâ, S. 2016, 'A new representational ecosystem for design teaching in the studio', *Design Studies*, 47, pp. 164-186

Ean, L. 2011, 'Computer-mediated communication and organisational communication: The use of new communication technology in the workplace', *The Journal of the South East Asia Research Centre for Communication and Humanities*, 3, pp. 1-12

Gabriel, G. and Maher, M. 2002, 'Coding and modelling communication in architectural collaborative design', *Automation in Construction*, 11(2), pp. 199-211

Gross, M. 1996, 'The Electronic Cocktail Napkin - a computational environment for working with design diagrams', *Design Studies*, 17(1), p. 53–69

Juchmes, R., Leclercq, P. and Azar, S. 2004, 'A Multi-Agent System for the interpretation of architectural sketches', *Eurographics Workshop on Sketch-Based Interfaces and Modeling*, 1, pp. 53-60

Kitchens, K. and Shiratuddin, M.F. 2007 'Interactive home design in a Virtual Environment', *7th International Conference on Construction Applications of Virtual Reality*, Pennsylvania, pp. 10-19

Lee, S. 2001, 'Challenges in building design and the construction industry: The future of design and construction in the Internet Age', *The Human Society and the Internet Internet-Related Socio-Economic Issues*, 1, pp. 225-236

Menezes, A. and Lawson, B. 2006, 'How designers perceive sketches', *Design Studies*, 27(5), p. 571–585

Norouzi, N., Shabak, M., Embi, M. and Khan, T. 2014, 'The architect, the client and effective communication in architectural design practice', *Procedia - Social and Behavioral Sciences*, 172, pp. 635-642
Palea, A., Ciobanu, G. and Kilyeni, A. 2012, 'Educational skills in training landscape architecture students: Developing communication skills', *Procedia - Social and Behavioral Sciences*, 46, pp. 4672-4677
Penttilä, H. 2006 'Managing the changes within the architectural practice - The effects of Information and Communication Technology (ICT)', *Communicating Spaces(s): Proceedings of the 24th Conference on Education in Computer Aided Architectural Design in Europe*, Volos (Greece), pp. 252-260
Purcell, A. and Gero, J. 1998, 'Drawings and the design process', *Design Studies*, 19(4), pp. 389-430
Richens, P. 1999 'The Piranesi system for interactive rendering', *Computers in Building: Proceedings of the CAADfutures'99 Conference*, Atlanta (Georgia), pp. 381-398
Siva, J. and London, K. 2011, 'Investigating the role of client learning for successful architect - client relationships on private single dwelling projects', *Architectural Engineering and Design Management*, 7(3), p. 177–189
Taleb, H., Ismail, S., Wahab, M. and Rani, W. 2017 'Communication management between architects and clients', *The 2nd international conference on applied science and technology 2017 (Icast'17)*, Kedah (Malaysia), p. 020136
Tessema, Y. 2008, *BIM for improved building design communication between architects and clients in the schematic design phase*, Master's Thesis, Texas Tech University
[1] https://visuin.cz/about
[2] https://en.wikipedia.org/wiki/Sketch_(drawing)
[3] http://www.hyve3d.com/

Multimodal Virtual Experience for Design Schools in the Immersive Web

George Guida[1], Runjia Tian[2], Yuebin Dong[3]
[1,2,3] Harvard Graduate School of Design
[1,2,3] {gguida|runjia_tian|yuebin_dong}@gsd.harvard.edu

The COVID-19 pandemic has made most schools, universities, and gathering spaces fully virtual. Commonly used communication platforms such as Zoom, Skype, and Microsoft Teams are limited in recreating physical interactions and offer mostly static interfaces with limited occasions for spontaneous encounters. This project creates a space that seeks to address this issue, first through the digitization of familiar physical spaces, and then through their augmentation via WebXR technologies[1]. A gamification strategy is adopted, where users can virtually learn, collaborate and socialize through personalized avatars within a dynamic and multi-sensorial digital environment. In this paper, we present a completed prototype that is currently being tested at the Harvard Graduate School of Design. The school of architecture has been digitized and experientially augmented thanks to an asymmetrical system that offers rich modalities of interaction through different platforms. The project builds upon the wide experiential potential of digital platforms, otherwise not possible in reality, and implements a customized multi-modal user interface (Reeves et al. 2004).

Keywords: *WebXR, Virtual Reality, Human Computer Interaction, Gamification, User Interface*

1 INTRODUCTION

During the ongoing Covid-19 pandemic, many social, educational, and work-related activities have shifted from physical to virtual spaces. Compared with traditional in-person modalities, online platforms shorten time and distance traveled, save the cost of physical space and equipment, and create alternative spaces to socialize, learn and communicate. Because of various quarantine and travel restriction policies across different countries and regions, the current extraordinary circumstances have drastically increased their demand. Online video conferencing infrastructures were introduced and enhanced to facilitate everyday activities from home, yet these carry several shortcomings. Applications typically include real-time text-based or video-based communication software, cloud synchronization services, and file version control systems. These environments typically offer static interfaces, limiting the effectiveness of communication and creativity between users. Within the context of design education, reciprocal peer learning plays a critical component (Sampson and Cohen, 2001) that encounters limitations when applied to video-conferencing-style education. Human interaction modalities can at times insufficient, providing few possibilities for spontaneous encounters.

Experiencing both the advantages and disadvantages of these online systems, while motivated by gamification strategies, we present Gund.IO, a platform that digitizes familiar physical spaces for users to learn, collaborate and socialize within a dynamic and multi-sensorial space. The platform provides an audio-visually immersive, 3D virtual environment where users can collaborate and learn both individually and collectively for education, production, and leisure. Similar to common software for online education, this web-based platform has the functions of voice and video communication, file upload, storage management, and live presentation of 2D and 3D content. By responding directly to the academic, social, and creative needs of students and professors within the architectural domain, the platform permits the speculation of future applications. By taking advantage of a digital 3D environment, human interaction is improved by augmenting physical spaces. The WebXR framework implemented on this platform enables users on both traditional PC and VR devices.

Gund.IO contains a digital 3D model of real physical learning and working spaces, including the interior and exterior of a building, where users can walk or fly around. To date, we have used a detailed model of George Gund Hall, the main architecture school of the Harvard Graduate School of Design (figure 1). The idea to expand the platform to include more parts of the campus and more schools within the university is under discussion. The digitization of this physical site finds particular importance during the current pandemic, offering a familiar space to those who have previously been on campus and a digital introduction to this space for those who have not yet been. Gund Hall is ideal for prototyping because of its emphasis on the collective and reliance on multi-modal communication within the design studio culture. Students working at their desks over the multiple stories can interact with one another through a connected open-plan space under a stepping, clear-span roof. Within the web browser, users are provided with the option to create individual 3D spaces for hosting their work in a space uncluttered by the current prearranged desk layouts. They can encounter other peers and professors, as well as navigate through shared rooms for lectures, seminars, exhibitions, and activities reliant on sound proximity. In addition to 2D media such as images or video content, this interface allows users to upload and arrange personalized or dynamic 3D objects.

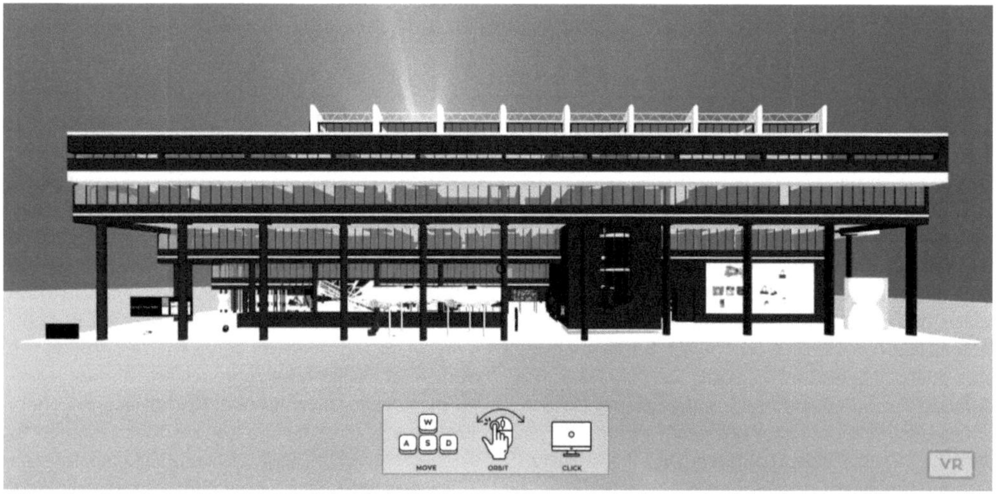

Figure 1
Gund.IO Virtual
Environment

Intended to create an immersive experience within a seamless user interface, this platform includes emerging VR technologies through the use of WebXR, allowing users to operate the platform on VR devices. This is combined with the accessibility and affordability of non-VR devices operated by users via mouses and keyboards. This paper presents a prototype of a user interface that is designed to simulate and digitally augment the academic experience of in-person learning and working at a time when universities and schools are closed or have restricted access. It intends to enhance the existing remote teaching and learning models, providing unique digital modalities within a centralized virtual environment.

2 BACKGROUND

2.1 Telepresence Technologies

Telepresence technologies (Draper et al. 1998) such as video conferencing are used for organizing virtual conferences via video communication. As early as 1998, Nishimura et al proposed the use of a gamification strategy in a video conferencing system called FreeWalk. Within this, videos were mapped onto 3D polygons to effectively display the user's faces (Nishimura et al. 1998). Current video conferencing software, for example, Zoom, Slack, Microsoft Teams, Skype, or Cisco WebEx generally offer homogeneous and static modes of interactions, limiting user participation. More recently, the advancement of Virtual Reality (VR) technologies brought telepresence into three dimensions.

2.2 User Embodiment in Collaborative Virtual Spaces

As early as 1999, researchers proposed the concept of virtual space as a complement to the traditional notion that architecture space must be a materialized entity (Gavin 1999). Dublon et al. developed DoppelLab, a cross-reality virtual space that shows inhabitant movement and data exchanges in a building in real-time. Benford et al. identified presence, identity, history of activity, gesture, facial expression, physical properties, multiple media, distributed bodies, and 12 other features to be the key issues relevant to user embodiment in collaborative virtual environments (Benford et al. 1995). 2.5 D virtual spaces such as Kumospace [2] use similar technologies for user embodiment.

Collaborative virtual space is also gaining increasing application in the domain of architecture design. Coroado et al. proposed a VR tool that allows communication between various stakeholders in virtual space during the architecture design process (Coroado et al. 2015). Coppens et al proposed to use a virtual reality environment for parametric design (Coppens et al. 2019). We leverage this list of features proposed by Benford to be the basic design guidelines for our system. We also leverage gamification strategies relating to architecture and design practices that can be seen in games such as Common Hood [6], which provides a space to interactively build and virtually fabricate digital spaces.

2.3 Design Education in Virtual Spaces

Online education became inevitable in the COVID-19 pandemic. According to the United States Census Bureau, Nearly 93% of Households With School-Age Children Report Some Form of Distance Learning During COVID-19 [8]. Design education in virtual spaces has been investigated in previous research. Ehsan and Chase discussed using virtual worlds as collaborative environments for innovation in architecture design projects (Ehsan and Chase 2009). Clark and Maher investigated the role of place in a virtual design studio, where students learn, and communicate virtually in an immersive 3D virtual world (Clark and Maher 2005). They concluded that a sense of place can be achieved in a virtual learning environment and "identity and presence play major roles in establishing the context for learning in a (virtual) place" (Clark and Maher 2005). More recently, Chase and Scopes used the 'Cyborgogy' pedagogical model for teaching design students in a 3D immersive virtual environment and suggested that increased contact between students has a positive impact on learning outcomes (Chase and Scopes 2012).

2.4 Immersive Web

Immersive Web is a working group of W3C that promotes the use of virtual and augmented realities in the open Web [3]. Web-based immersive technologies provide several solutions including platform-specific sensing, computer vision and custom sensing, geospatial content, visual search, content discovery, immersive-first web browsers, multi-user experience and precise localization, re-localization, and persistence (MacIntyre and Smith 2018). These technologies have experienced greater development since the beginning of the pandemic, as seen in the current developments of Mozilla Hub [4], and Facebook Horizon beta [5].

3 METHODOLOGY

Gund.IO is built on an asymmetrical system that offers rich modalities of interaction that accommodate various platforms. The project relies on a WebXR API for the Front End and makes use of WebRTC, a peer-to-peer framework for real-time audio communication between various users. We deployed a nodeJS server on Glitch [2], a peer-to-peer framework for real-time audio communication between various users and user data management.

3.1 System Architecture

The system is implemented within A-Frame, a web framework for building virtual reality experiences [7]. This permits use across multiple platforms, including VR Head-Mounted Displays (HMD) as well as Desktop Web browser. We implemented a WebXR system with an asymmetrical architecture that allows user collaboration across multiple mediums, therefore Desktop users can interact smoothly with VR HMD users. The server backend is hosted on a Glitch server where users can access user-specific information that is associated from the moment the user enters an A-Frame virtual "room". Upon entry, a unique user ID is generated, which is used to retrieve user attributes such as uploaded objects, materials, and associated usernames.

3.2 Peer-To-Peer Audio Communication

We use WebRTC, a open-source project providing real time communication (RTC) in web browser and mobile applications. (Loreto and Romano, 2014). Because of its flexibility and ease of implementation, WebRTC is used constantly in Web Conferences (Cola and Valean, 2014). Combined with WebXR, WebRTC could create sophisticated social XR experiences in

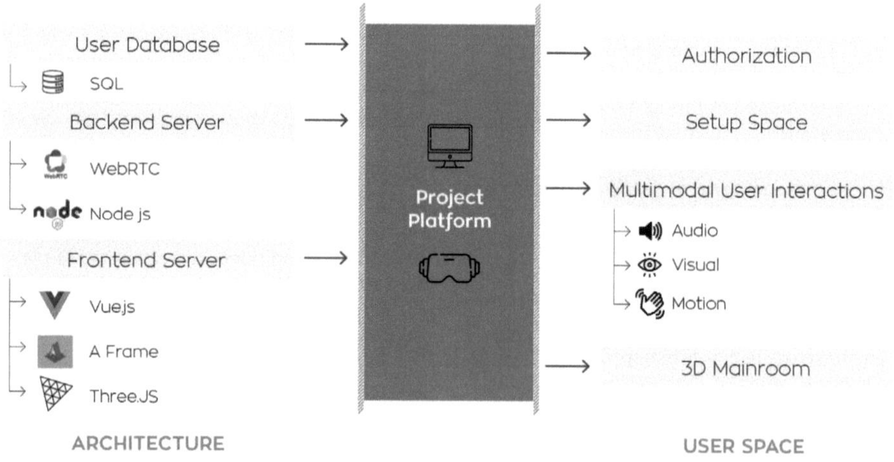

Figure 2
Asymmetric System Architecture

the Web that are similar to the sense of place of public spaces (Gunkel et al. 2017). Therefore, WebRTC is used in Gund.IO to create real-time multi-user social experiences.

3.3 Front End System

The front end of the system is accessible due to the flexibility of WebXR. It is supported on Desktop Web Browsers, VR HMD as well as smartphones that support WebXR. The front end is designed as an extension of reality, in that spatially it simulates the original spaces of George Gund Hall as closely as possible while permitting the augmentation of this digital space with digital media and motion graphics.

3.4 Exhibiting Digital Work

We first crowd-sourced multiple architecture student projects from the students and faculty of the Graduate School of Design and created a customizable exhibition of 2D and 3D content. Sophisticated design projects could also be visualized and experienced in a first-person perspectives and therefore could serve well to augment studio pin-ups or presentations in post-COVID periods.

3.5 Back End System

The backend is hosted on Glitch using WebSocket. The role of the backend is to keep track of room and user id upon the instantiation of the scene in WebXR. Therefore, it completes most of the user-variant tasks such as assigning different material or name tags to users with unique IDs. This complements the peer-to-peer architecture of WebRTC to allow for more user-customizable content creation. The backend also stores user-specific digital assets that the user wishes to carry around and place within the space. Possible use cases include student-professor desk crits, group discussions, or studio workshops. It is common in architecture school to display and discuss studio works to each other. Therefore, we created a space where users can upload, and customize the content they would like to display within the mainroom (figure 5).

4 OUTCOMES AND DISCUSSIONS

Gund.IO's digital replication of Gund Hall does not directly replicate, yet augments the academic university environment through this new multi-user web-virtual experience. Following several iterations and user testing, a seamless user interface combined with curated multimodal user interactions was implemented.

4.1 User Interface

The user interface is envisioned as a seamless display in which the embedded content itself acts as the interface. A simple display in the center of the browser acts as the only exception, containing the 3 navigation settings necessary for users to understand how to navigate within this virtual space. This seamless interface provides full screen real estate to the platform, allowing greater attention and cognitive effort to the unobstructed content.

4.2 Multimodal User Interactions

Through the augmentation of reality, multimodal virtual environments enable a deeper and richer experience (Hecht et al. 2006). This project seeks to develop 3 main types of interaction modalities: vision, audio, and a motion system.

4.2.1 Vision

Vision functions as the principal form of interaction within the 3D mainroom. Visual experiences begin with the virtual reconstruction of this centralized architecture school building. Housed within a spherical sky map and infinite white ground plane, a uniform light provides a clear and unobstructed gamified environment. This use of the spaces or surrounding context remains open-ended, challenging the physical functions of each space, yet facilitating novel educational uses.

These then move onto the embedded 2D, 3D, and dynamic digital content. 2D content varies from announcement boards and school event image posters to rendered or graphic image content generated by students or professors, all of which remain static and visible from one side only. 3D content can

Figure 3
Arrival Mainroom Portico

however be viewed from all directions, including virtual installations or objects (i.e. tables, speakers, interactive objects etc).

Besides modalities that exist in the physical world, we explored modes of interaction that could not exist in real life. Manipulated 3D scanned objects can create a representation of objects that exist in a reality that can then be manipulated and customized in a digital environment. Our gamification strategy allows dynamic animated objects that do not exist in real life. These can include animated virtual drawings, algorithmic art, or dynamic mesh geometries. With the rise of interactive and dynamic media created this year due to the pandemic, users have been able to interactively discuss projects at different scales and personalized viewpoints.

4.2.2 Audio

The addition of several audio modalities provides a greater immersive environment and sense of presence. Our audio system simulates the physical experience based on proximity. This has facilitated group discussions, private conversations, and even spontaneous interactions during virtual guided tours of the building. Additional features include interactive ambient sounds of the academic environment, and a music station that can be activated and deactivated by clicking the cursor onto oversize speakers (figure 4).

4.2.3 Motion System

Virtual avatars are used to metaphorically represent the human body. Initial prototypes contained an integrated physics system for motion simulations. Following focus-group studies, we understood that the removal of this created a more engaging user experience. Therefore, users are now able to point with the mouse and 'fly' across the model and additionally through the embedded geometry. Locomotion checkpoints to accelerate users' motion were inte-

Figure 4
Interactive Spaces: presentation rooms, social music areas, 3D dynamic installations

grated to give alternative modes of navigation within the space.

4.3 File Management
Finally, we created an interface for a file management system that permits users to upload and store personalized content. Users can upload, name, resize and delete 2D images and 3D models. All files are then displayed in 3D preview mode, which has an orbit camera mode through which users can drag and move the files to arrange them intuitively (figure 5). Given the coordinates in the main building, the interface can copy the files to the corresponding individual workspace or collective presentation and exhibition space while maintaining the relative spatial arrangement set in the preview mode.

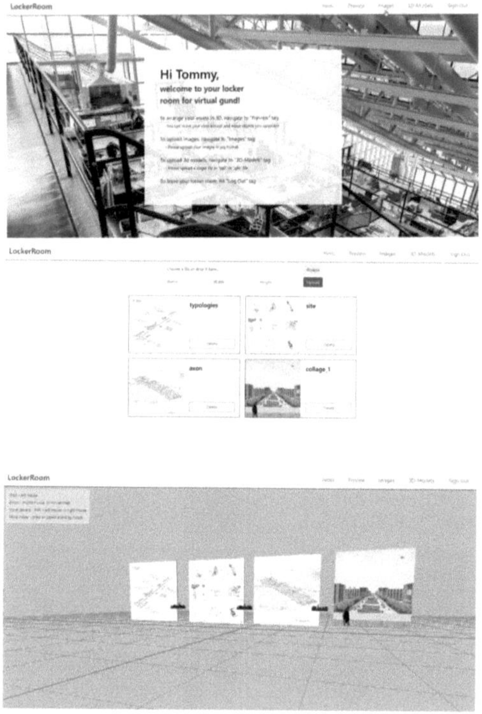

Figure 5
Media Upload Page

5 CONCLUSION
This project presents an immersive 3D environment established for users to virtually learn, collaborate, and socialize within a multi-sensorial academic environment. This gamified prototype finds relevance in light of the current pandemic where so many institutions are currently virtual, lacking the appropriate platforms to create a centralized hub for social, educational, and psychological needs. The use of WebXR technologies provides an intuitive environment that does not intend to replicate the physical architecture school yet capitalizes on the digital space to create open-ended uses and multi-sensorial experiences.

Future Work
Gund.IO has recently launched a prototype at the Harvard Graduate School of Design and is undergoing several iterations. Current work includes the development of private break-out meeting rooms, improved upload, and placement of 2D, 3D, and video content, the development of personalized avatars and chat systems.

With presentations, pin-ups, and exhibition spaces at the core of an architecture school, we are prioritizing a personalized content upload framework. With a current separation of the file management interface and the mainroom interface, it can be challenging for users to upload content to precise spatial coordinates. Future iterations should aggregate both web pages, including the file management functions to allow users to arrange objects directly in the main space.

The platform may be expanded to include the wider community, for example, other schools within the university or additional user groups. With a larger capacity and virtual environment, users could begin gaining similar benefits to in-person campus life and collectively share richer experiences during major events such as open houses or graduation ceremonies. This platform could be modified in the future to include other functions such as offices, event spaces, or museums by altering the 3D environment once the system architecture is proven to be stable.

Figure 6
Collaborative
Review Spaces

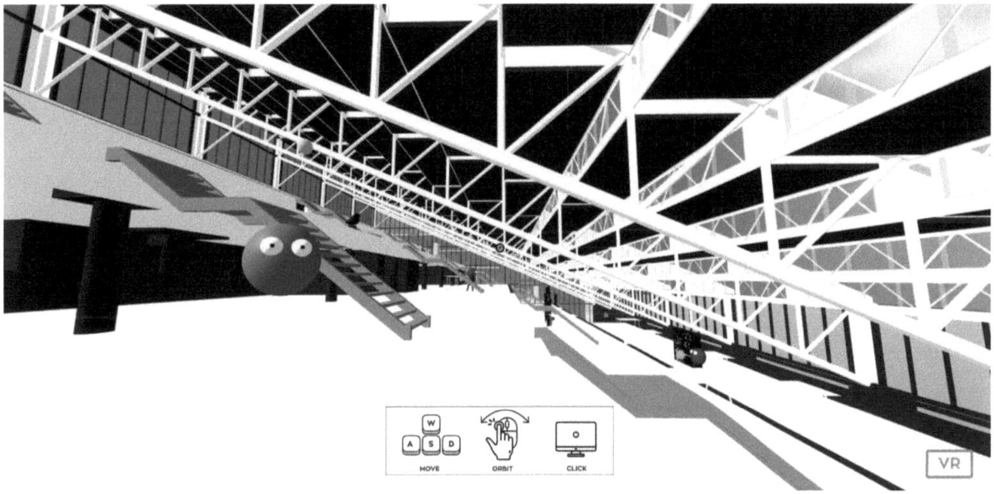

Finally, as we gradually move into a transition period of hybrid or in-person learning models, establishing a feedback loop between the physical and the virtual can establish a new set of relations, extending the physical notion of place within this educational context. The integration of real-time, mobile, and distributed sensing could further enhance the current multi-modal experiences.

ACKNOWLEDGMENTS

We would like to thank Allen Sayegh, Gabriella Perry, Stefano Andreani, Katarina Richter-Lunn, and the Responsive Environments and Artifacts Lab (REAL) for the discussions and support provided during the development of this project. This project was partially funded by the Harvard Master in Design Studies Research and Development Award.

REFERENCES

Benford, S, Bowers, J, Fahlén, LE, Greenhalgh, C and Snowdon, D 1995 'User embodiment in collaborative virtual environments', *Proceedings of the SIGCHI conference on Human factors in computing systems*, pp. 242-249

Chase, S and Scopes, L 2012 'Cybergogy as a framework for teaching design students in virtual worlds', *Digital Physicality – Proceedings of the 30th International Conference on Education and Research in Computer Aided Architectural Design in Europe*, pp. 125-134

Clark, S and Maher, ML 2005 'Learning and designing in a virtual place: Investigating the role of place in a virtual design studio', *Digital Design: the quest for new paradigms – Proceedings of the 23rd International Conference on Education and Research in Computer Aided Architectural Design in Europe*, pp. 303-310

Coppens, A, Mens, T and Gallas, MA 2019 'Parametric modelling within immersive environments: building a bridge between existing tools and virtual reality headsets', *Computing for a better tomorrow - Proceedings of the 23rd International Conference on Education and Research in Computer Aided Architectural Design in Europe*, pp. 711-716

Coroado, L, Pedro, T, D'Alpuim, J, Eloy, S and Dias, M 2015 'VIARMODES: Visualization and Interaction in Immersive Virtual Reality for Architectural Design Process', *Real Time: Extending the Reach of Computation Proceedings of the 33rd International Conference on Education and Research in Computer Aided Architectural Design in Europe*, pp. 125-134

Draper, JV, Kaber, DB and Usher, JM 1998, 'Telepresence', *Human factors*, 40(3), pp. 354-375

Dublon, G, Pardue, LS, Mayton, B, Swartz, N, Joliat, N, Hurst, P and Paradiso, JA 2011 'Doppellab: Tools for exploring and harnessing multimodal sensor network data', *SENSORS, 2011 IEEE*, pp. 1612-1615
Ehsani, E and Chase, S 2009 'Using virtual worlds as collaborative environments for innovation and design: lessons learned and observations from case studies in architectural projects', *Computation: The New Realm of Architectural Design - Proceedings of the 27th International Conference on Education and Research in Computer Aided Architectural Design in Europe*, pp. 523-532
Garvin, L 1999 'Architecture of the Virtual Place', *Architectural Computing from Turing to 2000 – Proceedings of the 17th International Conference on Education and Research in Computer Aided Architectural Design in Europe*, pp. 418-423
Hecht, D, Reiner, M and Halevy, G 2006, 'Multimodal virtual environments: response times, attention, and presence', *Presence: Teleoperators and virtual environments*, 15(5), pp. 515-523
Loreto, S and Romano, SP 2014, *Real-time communication with WebRTC: peer-to-peer in the browser*, " O'Reilly Media, Inc."
MacIntyre, B and Smith, TF 2018 'Thoughts on the Future of WebXR and the Immersive Web', *2018 IEEE International Symposium on Mixed and Augmented Reality Adjunct (ISMAR-Adjunct)*, pp. 338-342
Nishimura, T, Nakanishi, H, Yoshida, C and Ishida, T 1998 'Applying videogame technologies to video conferencing systems', *Proceedings of the 1998 ACM symposium on Applied Computing*, pp. 471-476
Reeves, LM, Lai, J, Larson, JA, Oviatt, S, Balaji, T, Buisine, S, Collings, P, Cohen, P, Kraal, B and Martin and others, JC 2004, 'Guidelines for multimodal user interface design', *Communications of the ACM*, 47(1), pp. 57-59
Sampson, J and Cohen, R 2001, 'Designing peer learning', *Peer Learning in Higher Education. Sterling, VA: Stylus Publishing*, , pp. 21-34
[1] https://www.w3.org/TR/webxr/
[2] https://www.kumospace.com/
[3] https://www.w3.org/immersive-web/
[4] https://hubs.mozilla.com/
[5] https://www.oculus.com/facebook-horizon/
[6] https://www.common-hood.com/
[7] https://aframe.io/
[8] https://www.census.gov/library/stories/2020/08/sc
hooling-during-the-covid-19-pandemic.html

Mass customization in design

Eelish 2.0: Grasshopper Plugin for Automated Grid-Driven Column-Beam Placement on Orthogonal Floor Plans

Formalising manual workflow into an algorithm through empirical analysis

Joy Mondal[1]
[1] *WEsearch lab*
[1] *joy@wesearchlab.com*

The implicitly parametric if-else logic of determining column-beam locations is applied manually on virtually every orthogonal design, thereby inflating workhours and cost through unnecessary repetition of labour. This paper presents the development of a generative algorithm (developed as Grasshopper plugin Eelish 2.0) that automates the placement of column centre points and beam centre lines on orthogonal floor plans. The manual process of column-beam placement is formalised as the algorithm through empirical analysis of layouts drawn by architects. The placement is executed iteratively from the largest room to the smallest room. It is guided by local and/or global orthogonal grids that are generated using walls of other rooms and beams of rooms calculated till the previous iteration. The placements are controlled by the maximum and minimum allowed spans of slabs, and four modes of grid generations. The generated layouts have a qualitative `Satisfactory' or better approval rating of 82.4% by architects and 88.4% by structural engineers.

Keywords: *Column, Beam, Orthogonal, Floor Plan, Automated, Grid*

INTRODUCTION

Architects typically invest substantial amount of workhours to determine the location of columns and beams on floor plans of framed structures before the fuzzy layouts are sent to the structural consultant for calculation of column, beam and slab dimensions and specifications. In the case of orthogonal designs, the process of column-beam placement usually comprises of two sequential steps. Firstly, columns are placed on plan by manual execution of a set of soft if-else logic that is guided by informal rules of thumb (Benzu 2011) and tacit knowledge. The placement of columns in turn determines the placement of beams (Herr and Fischer 2013). Different toolkits and software have been developed over time to rapidly model column and beam layouts. But these solutions require explicit modelling overlaid on and guided by floor plans. The software do not prompt automatic suggestion of column-beam placement. Consequently, the soft if-else logic is repeatedly applied manually from scratch on virtually every orthogonal design. The need of the hour is to develop an algorithm which automatically applies the inherently parametric soft if-else logic of column-beam placement on conceptual plans.

This paper presents the development of such an algorithm. The algorithm places column centre points and beam centre lines on orthogonal floor plans of convex and/or concave rooms. The placement is guided by local and/or global orthogonal grids generated using walls as centre lines. The algorithm is conceived by formalising the sequential workflow of the manually executed column-beam placement layouts. The algorithm was investigated using custom C# scripts on Grasshopper and has been subsequently developed as a Grasshopper plugin named Eelish 2.0. The following sections elaborate the objectives, the empirical analysis of the manual process, its formalisation into an algorithm, the components of Eelish 2.0, and the review of the generated layouts.

BACKGROUND

Related Work

Structural consultants typically calculate the dimensions and specifications of columns, beams and slabs of the layouts made by architects according to the local structural codes. Based on the quantitative and tacit knowledge of decades of calculations, structural engineers have derived rules of thumb for run-of-the-mill buildings of regular orthogonal geometry (Rajapakse 2016). Software (such as STAAD) is typically used for calculations of either designs of irregular geometries, or challenging long spans; or for projects of elevated importance, or budget. Such structural calculations have been attempted to be automated by using evolutionary algorithm (Nimtawat and Nanakorn 2009), adjacency graph (Shaw et al. 2008), and parametric rules of thumb (Sacks et al. 2000). These research typically need to be explicitly given a column-beam placement layout, which is subsequently used as the canvas for executing the calculations.

Architects, on the other hand, have tried to adapt the notations used by structural engineers for better collaboration. Herr and Fischer (2014) have developed a toolkit to model column-beam layouts for reinforced cement concrete structures. To generate layouts, users need to learn and manually overlay notational graphs on plans, making the process semi-automatic. Mondal (2018) has formalised the manual process of repeated sub-division of a room to place column-beam on convex orthogonal plans. The research does not address concave rooms. However, this research borrows the idea of using the rigour of empirical analysis to formalise a manual process that has clear objectives, but ill-articulated process.

To automate column-beam placement, the author has previously released a Grasshopper plugin named Eelish (Mondal 2021) that places column centre points and beam centre lines on orthogonal floor plans with the aim of maximising regular ceiling division. Since the focus of Eelish is not on responding to the wall conditions of neighbouring rooms, the layouts exhibit a high percentage (>33%) of internal slab corners that are common to only two slabs (Table 4). Such slab corners are shall be referred as beam notches (Figure 1b). Eelish 2.0 is developed as a successor and alternative to Eelish to minimise beam notches by guiding column-beam placement using grids generated from the walls of the floor plan.

Column-beam Placement

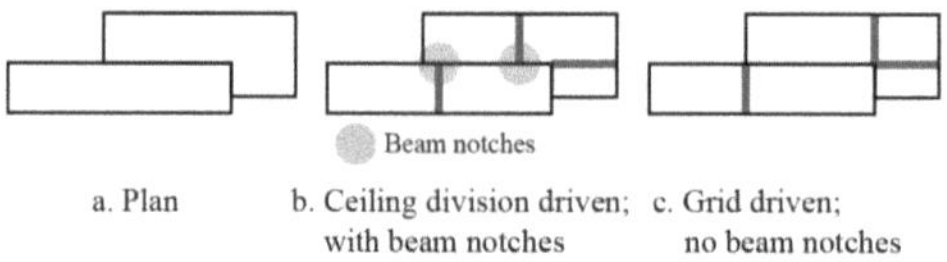

Figure 1
Ceiling division driven vs grid division driven column-beam placement viz a viz beam notches.

Column-beam placements on orthogonal plans can be broadly categorised into two types (Figure 1) as follows:

1. *Ceiling division driven*: Typically lays down equidistant beams and columns in rooms to achieve regular ceiling divisions (Figure 1b). Such layouts exhibit notches at least 33% of the beam intersections (Table 4).
2. *Grid driven*: Typically uses one global grid system or a combination of a few smaller grid systems to overlay column-beam on plan (Figure

1c). Since grids are dependent on the position of walls of neighbouring rooms, such layouts exhibit reduced notches compared to ceiling division driven layouts.

Eelish (Mondal 2021) formalises the column-beam placement process of the former kind, while Eelish 2.0 formalises the placement of the latter kind. Because of reduced notches, grid driven placements are structurally stronger. Such layouts are ideal for buildings with false ceilings that can hide the irregular ceiling division.

Objectives and Variables

The objectives of the algorithm are twofold as following:

1. To place columns and beams such that all the slabs are within predefined maximum and minimum allowed spans, and
2. To minimise beam notches, or in other words, maximise column-beam placement using grid(s).

The column-beam placement is controlled by three primary inputs or variables mentioned as following:

1. The floor plan,
2. Maximum allowed span of slab (*MaxS*), and
3. Minimum allowed span of slab (*MinS*).

All the notations used in this paper are described in Table 1.

EMPIRICAL ANALYSIS OF THE MANUAL PROCESS

The manual process of column-beam placement is documented and empirically analysed to extract and formalise the soft if-else logic into an algorithm.

Data for Analysis

Ten architects, each having professional experience of at least five years, were asked to place columns and beams on four orthogonal plans. Two plans had a combination of convex and concave rooms. The other two plans had only convex rooms and only concave rooms, respectively. The architects were asked to make the layouts while satisfying the objectives mentioned in the sub-section "Objectives and Variables". Each architect was given three sets of *MaxS* and *MinS* (3.0m and 1.5m, 4.5m and 2.2m, and 6.0m and 3.0 m). Thus, each architect made twelve layouts, amounting to a total of 120 layouts in the analysis. All the steps involved in making the 120 layouts, i.e., the placement of any column centre point or beam centre line, were digitally documented.

Observations

Subsequently, the 120 layouts and the steps to make the layouts were analysed to extract takeaways for conceiving the algorithm. The observations are as following -

- In 85.8% of the layouts, placement started from the largest room,
- In 44.1% of the layouts, placement concluded at the smallest room,
- When convex and concave rooms have the same area, in 81.7% of the cases, convex rooms were addressed before concave rooms,
- In the case of concave rooms, in 50.8% of the instances, the rooms were sub-divided into convex parts before proceeding with the placement,
- In 67.4% of the instances of working on a room in a plan, beams were added aligned to the walls of adjoining rooms (Figure 2a),
- In 93.2% of the instances of working on a room in a plan, beams from adjoining rooms that were added in previous steps were extended to the room (Figure 2b), and
- 9.2% of the layouts did not conform to the objectives.

Takeaways for Algorithm

The observations are used as a guide to develop the algorithm of column-beam placement. The takeaways for the algorithm are discussed in the following sub-sections.

Order of Rooms. The findings demonstrate that more importance is given to larger spaces compared to smaller spaces. Therefore, the algorithm shall undertake the placement iteratively from the largest to the smallest room. Convex rooms are given precedence over concave rooms of the same area, possibly due to higher isoperimetric quotient of convex rooms (Croft et al. 1991).

Table 1
Notations used in this paper.

Notation	Description
B(prev)	Beam centre lines added till the previous iteration of the loop
B(room)	Beam centre lines of *R(n)*
B(sel)	Mode of calculating *C(beam)*; 0 = intersection with beams of neighbouring rooms, 1 = intersection with beams of all rooms
C(beam)	Columns added along *R(edge_x)* and *R(edge_y)* to continue eligible *B(prev)* through *R(n)*; see *B(sel)*
C(crnr)	Corners of *R(n)*, *R(bound)* and *R(rec)* projected as columns on *R(edge_x)* and *R(edge_y)*
C(edge)	Additional columns on *R(edge_x)* and *R(edge_y)* if any intra-distance between *C(crnr)*, *C(beam)* and *C(wall)* is < *MaxS*
C(in)	Columns inside *R(n)*
C(prev)	Columns added till the previous iteration of the loop
C(room)	Columns of *R(n)*; *C(room)* = [*C(crnr)* + *C(beam)* + *C(wall)* + *C(edge)* + *C(in)*] coincident on and inside *R(n)*
C(wall)	Columns added along *R(edge_x)* and *R(edge_y)* to add beams aligned to eligible walls of other rooms; see *W(sel)*
MaxS	Maximum allowed span of slab
MinS	Minimum allowed span of slab
R(bound)	The bounding rectangle of *R(n)*; *R(bound)* = *R(n)* for convex rooms
R(edge_x)	The lower edge of the two edges of *R(bound)* that are parallel to x-axis
R(edge_y)	The edge on the right of the two edges of *R(bound)* that are parallel to y-axis
R(n)	The room in the current iteration of the loop
R(rec)	Largest rectangle that can be inscribed in *R(n)*; *R(rec)* = *R(n)* for convex rooms
W(sel)	Mode of calculating *C(wall)*; 0 = intersection with walls of neighbouring rooms, 1 = intersection with walls of all rooms

Types of Beams. Beams may be added across a room in three different ways. Firstly, beams may be added aligned to the walls of adjoining rooms (Figure 2a). Secondly, beams may be added as extensions of beams of adjoining rooms (Figure 2b). Thirdly, in the absence of adjoining room, i.e., absence of grid, beams may be added as equidistant divisions of the room (Figure 2c).

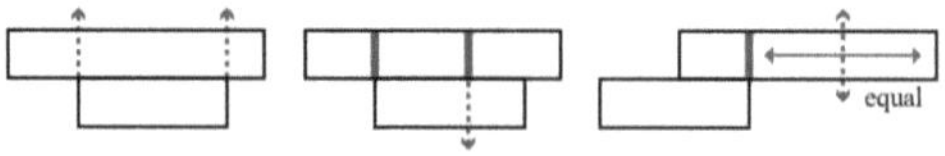

Figure 2
Types of beam grids across a room.

Wall aligned Beams vs Beam extension Beams. There may be rooms with potential beams of the first and the second kind that are at a mutual distance lesser than *MinS* (Figure 3a). In such cases, selecting the potential beam of the second kind reduces the number of beam notches (Figure 3b). Therefore, adding new beams aligned to beams in adjoining rooms is more important than aligning new beams to the walls of the adjoining rooms.

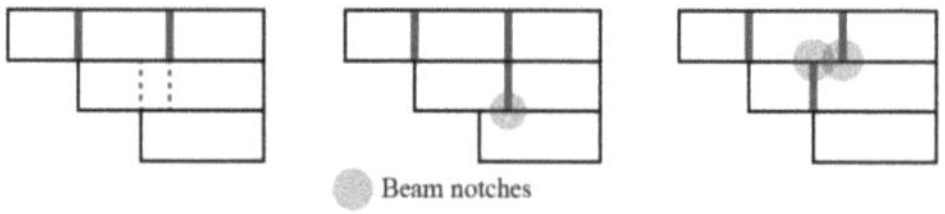

Figure 3
Beam grid vs wall grid viz a viz beam notches.

Additional Variables. The addition of beams across a room can be calculated either with reference to neighbouring rooms, or with reference to all rooms. Therefore, two additional inputs or variables are to be used in column-beam placement as following -

1. Mode of calculating potential beams as extension of previously added beams (*B(sel)*); 0 = intersection with beams of neighbouring rooms, 1 = intersection with beams of all rooms; and
2. Mode of calculating potential beams in alignment to walls of other rooms (*W(sel)*); 0 = intersection with walls of neighbouring rooms, 1 = intersection with walls of all rooms.

AUTOMATED COLUMN-BEAM PLACEMENT

The column-beam placement is controlled by five inputs or variables as mentioned in sub-sections "Objectives and Variables" and "Additional Variables".

Based on the findings of the empirical analysis, the algorithm undertakes the placement iteratively from the largest to the smallest room. In each iteration, the algorithm separately calculates column placements along the length and the width of the selected room (*R(n)*). Different column types calculated through different geometrical features of the plan are assigned decreasing levels of importance that are inversely proportionate to the column types' contribution in adding beam notches. The different column types in decreasing order of importance are as following -

1. Columns at corners of room (*C(crnr)*),
2. Columns as beam extensions (*C(beam)*),
3. Columns aligned to walls of other rooms (*C(wall)*),
4. Additional edge columns (*C(edge)*), and
5. Columns inside room (*C(in)*).

Therefore, if columns are at a distance lesser than *MinS*, the column in the lower level of importance is deleted. Subsequently, room bound orthogonal grid of the columns is added as beam centre lines (Herr and Fischer 2013). On conclusion of all the iterations, columns are added at convex corners of the floor plan perimeter if they do not have a column assigned from the loop. Lastly, beam centre lines are added at segments of the floor plan perimeter which do not have beam centre lines assigned from the loop. Table 2 tabulates the pseudo code of Eelish 2.0. Table 3 tabulates the functions used in the pseudo code. The following sub-sections describe the process of column-beam placement in a room. Steps 2.4 to 2.12 are elaborated by taking one of the edges as example.

Steps 2.1-2.3: Largest inscribable and bounding rectangles, and edges for column placement. For the room in the current iteration of the loop (*R(n)*), largest inscribable rectangle in the room (*R(rec)*) and bounding rectangle of the room (*R(bound)*) are calculated (Figure 4b). In the case of a convex room, *R(n)* = *R(rec)* = *R(bound)*. Prioritising the column-beam placement in *R(rec)* of a concave room minimises the number of slabs with span lesser than *MinS* (Mondal 2021). Additionally, such an approach pushes the smaller irregular slabs to the geometrical and visual periphery of the room. The reader may refer Mondal (2021) for details on how to calculate *R(rec)*.

The lower edge of the two edges of *R(bound)* that are parallel to x-axis (*R(edge_x)*), and the edge on the right of the two edges of *R(bound)* that are parallel to y-axis (*R(edge_y)*) are used to calculate column placements along the length and the width of *R(n)* (Figure 4c).

Step 2.4: Corner columns. In the next step, corner columns (*C(crnr)*) are calculated. Firstly, the corners of *R(rec)* and *R(bound)* (Figure 4d), and the corners of *R(n)* are respectively projected on *R(edge_x)* and *R(edge_y)* as two different sets of points. Subsequently, the points in the second set that are at a distance lesser than *MinS* from the points in the first set are deleted (Figure 4e). This distance check ensures that slabs spans are more than *MinS*. The points in first set and the remaining points in second set constitute *C(crnr)* (Figure 4f). In the case of a convex room, the end points of *R(edge_x)* and *R(edge_y)* constitute *C(crnr)* following step 2.4.

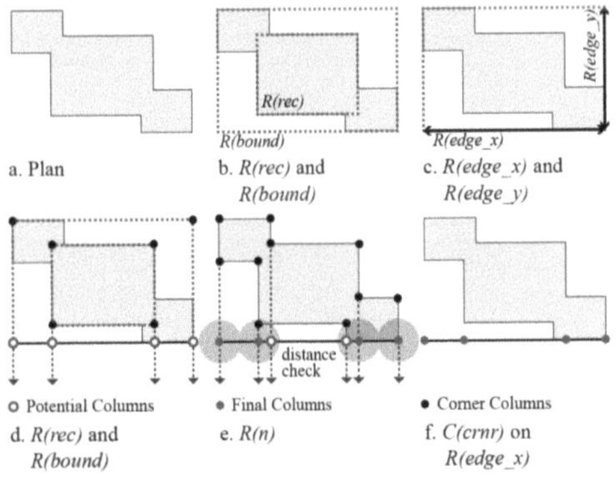

Figure 4
Steps 2.1 to 2.3 in a concave room; step 2.4 on R(edge_x).

Steps 2.5-2.11: Beam extension Columns and Wall aligned Columns. To add columns as extension of beams of other rooms (*C(beam)*), and columns aligned to walls of other rooms (*C(wall)*); end points of beams in rooms till the previous iteration (*B(prev)*), and corners of other rooms are projected on *R(edge_x)* and *R(edge_y)*, respectively for *C(beam)* and *C(wall)*.

Step no.	Step
Input:	Floor plan, *MaxS*, *MinS*, *B(sel)* and *W(sel)* from user
1	Sort the rooms in descending order of area
	// Convex room given priority over concave room of same area
	// All distance checks and projections are to be executed orthogonally
2	**For** each room *R(n)* in the sorted list:
2.1	*// Find largest inscribable rectangle in room; for convex rooms, R(n) = R(rec) = R(bound)*
	R(rec) = largest_rec (*R(n)*)
2.2	*R(bound)* = Bounding rectangle of *R(n)*
2.3	*// Length and width edges for calculation*
	R(edge_x) = The lower edge of the two edges of *R(bound)* that are parallel to x-axis
	R(edge_y) = The edge on the right of the two edges of *R(bound)* that are parallel to y-axis
2.4	*// Corner points of R(n) take highest priority for column placement*
	C(crnr) = Corners of *R(rec)* and *R(bound)* projected on *R(edge_x)* and *R(edge_y)*
	C(crnr) = *C(crnr)* + Projected corners of *R(n)* on *R(edge_x)* and *R(edge_y)* that are at >*MinS* from *C(crnr)*
2.5	*// Potential beam additions as extensions of beams of other rooms*
	If {*B(sel)* = 0} **then**
2.5.1	*C(beam)* = End points of *B(prev)* of neighbouring rooms of *R(n)* projected on *R(edge_x)* and *R(edge_y)*
	Else
2.5.2	*C(beam)* = End points of *B(prev)* of all rooms projected on *R(edge_x)* and *R(edge_y)*
	Delete columns from *C(beam)* that are at <*MinS* from *C(crnr)* of neighbouring rooms projected on *R(edge_x)* and *R(edge_y)*, and from end points of *B(prev)* of neighbouring rooms projected on *R(edge_x)* and *R(edge_y)*
	End If
2.6	Delete columns from *C(beam)* that are at <*MinS* from *C(crnr)*
2.7	*// Delete columns in C(beam) that are too close to each other*
	C(beam) = intra_list_dist_check (sorted along *R(bound)* [*C(beam)*], *MinS*, *R(edge_x)*, *R(edge_y)*)
2.8	*// Potential beam additions aligned to walls of others rooms*
	If {*W(sel)* = 0} **then**
2.8.1	*C(wall)* = Corners of neighbouring rooms of *R(n)* projected on *R(edge_x)* and *R(edge_y)*
	Else
2.8.2	*C(wall)* = Corners of all rooms except *R(n)* projected on *R(edge)*
	Delete columns from *C(wall)* that are at <*MinS* from *C(crnr)* of neighbouring rooms projected on *R(edge_x)* and *R(edge_y)*, and from end points of *B(prev)* of neighbouring rooms projected on *R(edge_x)* and *R(edge_y)*
	End If
2.9	*// Continuing new beam aligned to previously added beam more important than alignment to neighbouring wall*
	Delete columns from *C(wall)* that are at <*MinS* from *C(crnr)* and *C(beam)*
2.10	*// Columns from C(wall) that are centrally placed between previously calculated columns*
	C(wall) = pick_central (sorted along *R(bound)* [*C(wall)*], sorted along *R(bound)* [*C(crnr)* + *C(beam)*], *MaxS*, *R(edge_x)*, *R(edge_y)*)
2.11	*// Delete columns in C(wall) that are too close to each other*
	C(wall) = intra_list_dist_check (sorted along *R(bound)* [*C(wall)*], *MinS*, *R(edge_x)*, *R(edge_y)*)
2.12	*// Add additional columns on R(bound) edges if distance between previously calculated columns is >MaxS*
	C(edge) = intra_list_col_add (sorted along *R(bound)* [*C(crnr)* + *C(beam)* + *C(wall)*], *MaxS*)
2.13	*// Beams as orthogonal grid of columns*
	Temp(room) = Project *C(crnr)*, *C(beam)*, *C(wall)* and *C(edge)* on the sides of *R(bound)* opposite to *R(edge_x)* and *R(edge_y)*
	B(room) = *R(bound)* bound orthogonal grid of columns in *Temp(room)*, *C(crnr)*, *C(beam)*, *C(wall)* and *C(edge)*
	Trim parts of *B(room)* outside *R(n)*
	Add segments of *R(n)* as beam centre lines (if absent) to *B(room)*
2.14	*// Columns inside room*
	C(in) = Points of self-intersection of *B(room)* inside *R(bound)*
2.15	*C(room)* = [*C(crnr)* + *C(beam)* + *C(wall)* + *C(edge)* + *C(in)* + *Temp(room)*] coincident on and inside *R(n)*
	Delete columns from *C(room)* that are at <*MinS* from *C(prev)*
2.16	*// Final column centres of R(n)*
	C(prev) = *C(prev)* + *C(room)*
2.17	*// Final beam centre lines of R(n)*
	B(prev) = *B(prev)* + *B(room)*
3	**Next**
4	Add convex corners of floor plan perimeter as columns (if absent) to *C(prev)*
5	Add segments of floor plan perimeter as beam centre lines (if absent) to *B(prev)*
Output:	*C(prev)* as column placements
	B(prev) as beam centre line placements

Table 2
Pseudo code of column-beam placement as used in Eelish 2.0; refer Table 3 for pseudo code of functions.

Table 3
Pseudo code of functions as used in Eelish 2.0.

```
Functions
intra_list_dist_check (Column(list), dist_check, edge_x, edge_y)
For n=0 to 1; n++
    If {n = 0} then Column(list_temp) = Points in Column(list)
coincident on edge_x
    Else Column(list_temp) = Points in Column(list) coincident on
edge_y
    End If
    For each column couple C(i) and C(i+1) in Column(list_temp)
        If {i = 0 or Column(list_temp).Count – 1} then Skip
        Else If {distance(C(i),C(i+1)) < dist_check} then
            If {distance(C(i-1),C(i)) < distance(C(i+1),C(i+2))}
then Delete C(i) from Column(list_temp)
            Else Delete C(i+1) from Column(list_temp)
            End If
        End If
    i = i - 1
    Next
    Column_new(list).Add(Column(list_temp))
Next
Return Column_new(list)
---
pick_central (Column_topick(list), Column_forcheck(list), dist_check,
edge_x, edge_y)
Temp(list) = intra_list_col_add(Column_forcheck(list), dist_check, edge_x,
edge_y)
For each point P in Temp(list)
    If {P is coincident on edge_x} then Column_new(list).Add(Closest
point to P from Column_topick(list) that are coincident on edge_x)
    Else Column_new(list).Add(Closest point to P from
Column_topick(list) that are coincident on edge_y)
    End If
Next
Remove duplicate columns from Column_new(list)
Return Column_new(list)
---
intra_list_col_add (Column(list), dist_check)
For each column couple C(i) and C(i+1) in Column(list)
    If {distance(C(i),C(i+1)) < dist_check} then
        Divide line between C(i) and C(i+1) into Ceiling
(distance(C(i),C(i+1)) / dist_check) parts
        Column_new(list).Add(Points of division)
    End If
Next
Return Column_new(list)
```

Depending on the input values of *B(sel)* and *W(sel)* (see Table 1), neighbouring rooms or all rooms are used to calculate *C(beam)* and *C(wall)*, respectively. In case *B(sel)* and/or *W(sel)* is 1, *C(beam)* and/or *C(wall)* that are at a distance lesser than *MinS*, from corners and beam end points of neighbouring rooms projected on *R(edge_x)* and *R(edge_y)*, are deleted (Figure 5b). These distance checks reduce beam notches. Thereafter, *C(beam)* that are at a distance lesser than *MinS* from *C(crnr)* of *R(n)* (Figure 5b), and *C(wall)* that are at a distance lesser than *MinS* from *C(crnr)* of *R(n)* (Figure 5c) and *C(beam)*, are deleted.

Thirdly, *C(wall)* columns that divide the portions between the combined list of *C(crnr)* and *C(beam)* appropriately, i.e., between *MaxS* and *MinS*, need to be picked. If any two columns in the combined list of *C(crnr)* and *C(beam)* are at a mutual distance more than *MaxS*, these portions are divided into smaller parts calculated by using ceiling function on the division of length of the portions(s) by *MaxS* (Figure 5d). Subsequently, for each point of division of the longer portions, the closest *C(wall)* column is retained, while the other columns in *C(wall)* are deleted (Figure 5d).

Finally, if any two columns in *C(beam)* and *C(wall)*, respectively, are at a mutual distance lesser than *MinS*, the column that is at a lesser distance to its other neighbouring column is deleted (Figure 5e). The last three distance checks ensure that slab spans are between *MaxS* and *MinS*.

Step 2.12: Additional edge columns. *C(crnr)*, *C(beam)* and *C(wall)* may still leave portions on *R(edge_x)* and *R(edge_y)* that may be larger in length than *MaxS*. These portions are divided into smaller parts calculated by using ceiling function on the division of length of the portions(s) by *MaxS*. The points of division of these portions constitute additional edge columns (*C(edge)*) (Figure 5f).

Step 2.13: Beams of room. An *R(bound)* bound orthogonal grid of the four kinds of columns along edges of *R(bound)* and their projections to the respective opposite edges becomes potential beams of *R(n)* (*B(room)*) (Figure 5g). Since in the case of concave rooms, *R(bound)* goes beyond *R(n)*, portions of *B(room)* outside *R(n)* are split and deleted (Figure 5h).

Steps 2.14-2.15: Final columns of room. The points of self-intersection of *B(room)* that are inside *R(bound)* yield the inside columns of the room (*C(in)*) (Figure 5g). Columns of all five types, i.e., *C(crnr)* , *C(beam)*, *C(wall)*, *C(edge)* and *C(in)*, that are coincident on or inside *R(n)* constitute potential columns of the room (*C(room)*). Additionally, columns in *C(room)* that are at a distance lesser than *MinS* from columns of rooms till the previous iteration (*C(prev)*) are deleted (Figure 5h).

Steps 2.16-2.17: Conclusion of a loop. Lastly, final columns of the room (*C(room)*) are added to *C(prev)*.

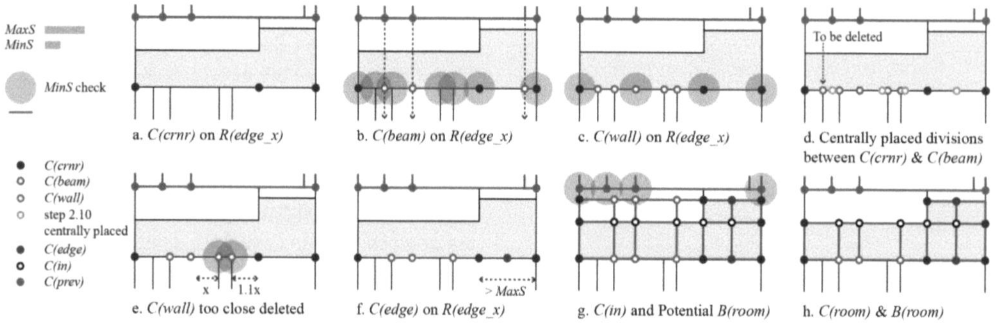

Figure 5
Steps 2.5 to 2.12 on R(edge_x) in a concave room, steps 2.13 to 2.15 in the same room; B(sel)=1, W(sel)=0.

Beams of the room (*B(room)*) are also added to the list of beams in rooms till the previous iteration (*B(prev)*).

EELISH 2.0 GRASSHOPPER PLUGIN

The algorithm discussed in this paper has been developed as a Grasshopper plugin named Eelish 2.0. It uses two components (Figure 6) to generate the column-beam placements. To reduce the barrier to entry of using Eelish 2.0, the components are designed to have five simple inputs as discussed in the preceding sections. The two components are briefly discussed as following -

- *Closed Curve Generator*: Converts any curve network (of closed and/or open and/or overlapping curves) into watertight closed curves. It is used for preparing floor plan curves for column-beam placement. The algorithm of this component is beyond the scope of this paper.

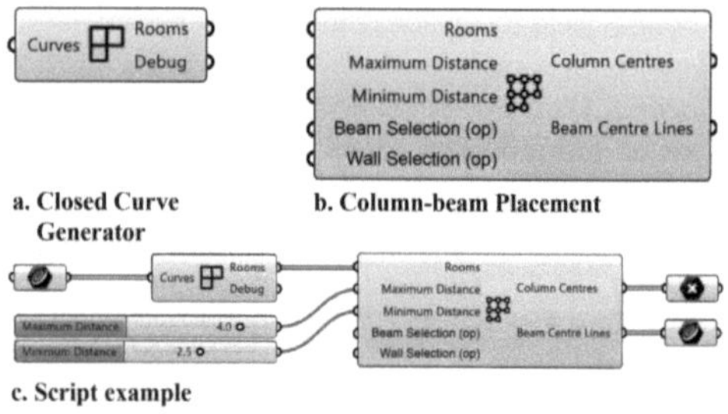

Figure 6
Eelish 2.0 plugin components and example script.

- *Column-beam Placement*: Executes the algorithm discussed in this paper. It uses the closed curves generated in the former component as the input for floor plan (called 'Rooms'), along with values for *MaxS*, *MinS*, CanS, *B(sel)* and *W(sel)*. If the values of *B(sel)* and/or *W(sel)* are not specified by the user, they are considered to be 0. The outputs of this component are the column centres as 'points' and beam centre lines as 'curves'.

RESULT AND DISCUSSION

To quantify the effectiveness of Eelish 2.0 in minimising beam notches, column-beam layouts of 100 different floor plans were generated. Eelish was used to generate one layout per floor plan, while Eelish 2.0 was used to generate four layouts per floor plan (by varying *B(sel)* and *W(sel)*). Figure 7 shows the five column-beam placements of one such floor plan. It is observed that when *MaxS* is more than the average span of rooms, both Eelish and Eelish 2.0 produce layouts with same number of beam notches. However, when *MaxS* is lower than the average span of rooms, Eelish 2.0 reduces beam notches by as much as 39.9% (*B(sel)* = 1, *W(sel)* = 1).

Figure 8 shows column-beam placements generated by Eelish 2.0 on four floor plans with varying *MaxS* and *MinS* (*B(sel)* = 1, *W(sel)* = 1). Even though the layouts made by Eelish 2.0 satisfy the two objectives as mentioned in the sub-section "Objectives and Variables", they were qualitatively reviewed by architects and structural engineers to ascertain Eelish 2.0's suitability in practical project workflows.

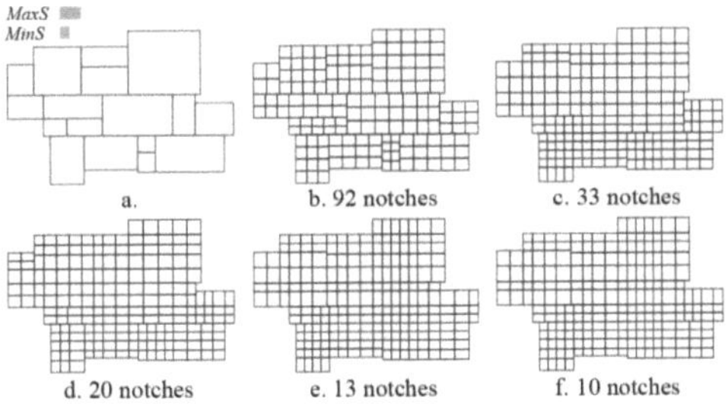

Figure 7
Column-beam placements by Eelish and Eelish 2.0: a. Plan, b. Eelish - 92 notches, c. Eelish 2.0 (B(sel)=0, W(sel)=0) - 33 notches, d. Eelish 2.0 (B(sel)=1, W(sel)=0) - 20 notches, e. Eelish 2.0 (B(sel)=0, W(sel)=1) - 13 notches, and e. Eelish 2.0 (B(sel)=1, W(sel)=1) - 10 notches.

Qualitative Review

Thirty column-beam placement layouts generated by Eelish 2.0 (including the ones shown in Figure 8) were shown to thirty architects and thirty structural engineers for a qualitative review of the usability of the layouts. All the architects and the structural engineers had a minimum of five years of professional experience. The group of architects did not include anyone from the group of architects involved in the empirical analysis of the manual process. The participants were informed about *MaxS* and *MinS* of the layouts.

The architects and the structural engineers were asked to rate the suitablity of the layouts as a deliverable to structural engineer and as a deliverable from architect, respectively. A Likert scale of 'Highly Satisfactory', 'Satisfactory', 'Neutral', 'Unsatisfactory', and 'Highly Unsatisfactory' was used for rating. The descriptions of the scale were allotted 5, 4, 3, 2, and 1 as values, respectively, for statistical calculations. Table 4 shows the summary of the qualitative review of the layouts. 82.4% of the reviews by architects and 88.2% of the reviews by structural engineers categorised the layouts as 'Satisfactory' or better. 7.2% of the reviews by architects and 5.0% of the reviews by structural engineers categorised the layouts as 'Unsatisfactory' or worse. The layouts have a mean approval of 3.78/5.00 by architects and 3.89/5.00 by structural engineers.

Implications

Majority of the buildings that are designed and/or constructed outside the avant-garde practices are orthogonal (Steadman 2006). Consequently, Eelish 2.0 has the potential of impacting the design delivery workflow by emancipating architects from the uninventive manual repetition of column-beam placement. From the performative perspective, with additional data on site specific cost per unit of columns, beams and slabs, the column-beam placement layout incurring minimum cost may be calculated by optimising values of *MaxS*, *MinS*, *B(sel)* and *W(sel)*. The compounding effect of the time and cost savings shall enable redirection of resources towards more creative endeavours and/or towards making design services less expensive. As a solution to the problem of design services' exclusivity to the affluent, Eelish 2.0 is conceived as an important cog in the wheel of an automated (and consequently cheap) alternative of design delivery to the majority of the world population that cannot afford architects. Alongside Eelish 2.0, other automated solutions for generating floor plans, furniture layouts, and mechanical, electrical and plumbing layouts will need to be developed as part of the wheel.

Table 4
Qualitative rating of usability of 30 column-beam placement layouts (generated by Eelish 2.0) by 30 architects and 30 structural engineers.

Likert Description	Architects	Engineers
Highly Satisfactory (5)	5.2% (47)	7.3% (66)
Satisfactory (4)	77.2% (695)	80.9% (728)
Neutral (3)	10.3% (93)	6.8% (61)
Unsatisfactory (2)	4.7% (42)	3.8% (34)
Highly Unsatisfactory (1)	2.6% (23)	1.2% (11)
Total Reviews	900	900
Mean Approval (out of 5)	3.78	3.89
Standard Deviation	0.61	0.59
Coefficient of Variation	16.1%	15.1%

CONCLUSION

Eelish 2.0 automates column-beam placement, thereby going beyond existing drafting solutions that require explicit modelling. The use of grid guided by hierarchical selection of column types reduces beam notches compared to column-beam placements guided by equidistant ceiling division. Usage of all walls and beams in the floor plan to

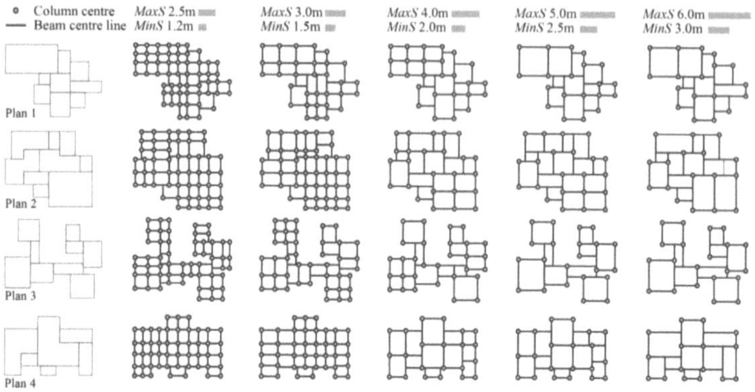

Figure 8
Column-beam placements by Eelish 2.0 on different floor plans; B(sel)=1, W(sel)=1.

derive grids (*B(sel)* = 1, *W(sel)* = 1) minimises beam notches the most. The layouts generated by Eelish 2.0 satisfy the objectives of column beam placement. They have a qualitative 'Satisfactory' or better approval rating of 82.4% by architects and 88.2% by structural engineers. These can act as starting baseline for local modifications. The algorithm is to be expanded to address the intricacies of one way and two way slabs, include columns and beams at predetermined locations (if needed), and include ways to modify the sequence of rooms for iteration. Subsequently, the algorithm shall be released as a free plugin on the AutoCAD platform to facilitate last-mile access of the technology. It is imperative that we automate column-beam placement of orthogonal designs to emancipate architects from uninventive repetition and enable them in redirecting project resources by drastically reducing workhours of the process.

REFERENCES

Benzu, J 2011 'Thumb rules for designing a Column layout', *Civil Engineering Projects*, Available at: http://www.civilprojectsonline.com/building-construction/thumb-rules-for-designing-a-column-layout-building-construction/

Croft, HT, Falconer, KJ and Guy, RK 1991, *Unsolved Problems in Geometry*, Springer-Verlag, New York, United States

Herr, C and Fischer, T 2013 'Generative Column and Beam Layout for Reinforced Concrete Structures in China', *Proceedings of CAAD Futures 2013*, Shanghai, China, pp. 84-95

Herr, C and Fischer, T 2014 'A Notation to Aid Column and Beam Layout Design for Reinforced Concrete Construction in China', *Proceedings of CAADRIA 2014*, Kyoto, Japan, pp. 399-408

Mondal, J 2018 'Automated Column and Beam Placement on Single-storeyed Convex Orthogonal Floor Plans', *Proceedings of Neo-International Conference on Habitable Environments*, Delhi NCR, India, pp. 129-134

Mondal, J 2021 'Eelish: Grasshopper Plugin for Automated Column-Beam Placement on Orthogonal Floor Plans to Achieve Maximum Regular Ceiling Division', *SimAUD 2021*

Nimtawat, A and Nanakorn, P 2009, 'Automated Layout Design of Beam-slab Floors Using a Genetic Algorithm', *Computers & Structures*, 87(21), pp. 1308-1330

Rajapakse, RA 2016, *Construction Engineering Design Calculations and Rules of Thumb*, Butterworth-Heinemann, Cambridge, United States

Sacks, R, Warszawskiu, A and Kirsch, U 2000, 'Structural Design in an Automated Building System', *Automation in Construction*, 10(1), pp. 181-197

Shaw, D, Miles, J and Gray, A 2008, 'Determining the Structural Layout of Orthogonal Framed Buildings', *Computers & Structures*, 86(19), pp. 1856-1864

Steadman, P 2006, 'Why Are Most Buildings Rectangular?', *Architectural Research Quarterly*, 10(2), pp. 119-130

Customization System for Ergonomic Benches

DOMINO_ a parametric design configurator

Mara Capone[1], Emanuela Lanzara[2], Laura Marsillo[3]
[1,2,3] UNINA University of Naples Federico II
[1,2,3] {mara.capone|emanuela.lanzara|laura.marsillo}@unina.it

The principle of customization is based on the concept of modularity, which consists in the repetition of a module without changing size or shape of the single element. Therefore, this concept expands with introduction of smaller sub-modules to obtain the so called ``complex modularity''. According to this research framework our paper focuses on a customization system for designing an ergonomic bench that can be adaptable to different people (kids, adults, elders) and different use, sitting, semi-sitting and lying position. Our goal is to design a parametric ``configurator'', able to modify modules shape in relation to ergonomics specific needs and to combine them in relation to a specific context.

Keywords: *complex modularity, ergonomic bench, parametric configurator*

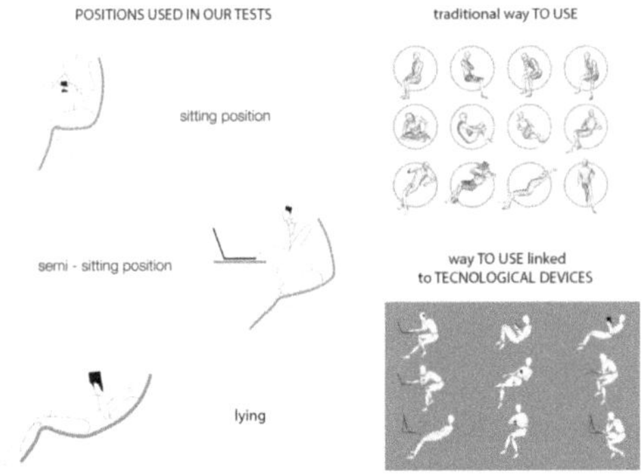

Figure 1
ergonomic postures for our tests

INTRODUCTION

The spread of computational design and digital fabrication techniques open new perspectives in product design process. The possibility to manufacture a custom product, changing some design parameters, involve user in design process. We can identify different levels of customization, starting from basic systems, that allow to combine standard components to define a personalized distribution, to more complex systems that allow to modify each element and interact with shape generation.

The principle of customization is based on the concept of modularity, which consists in the repetition of a module without changing size or shape of the single element. Therefore, this concept expands with introduction of smaller sub-modules to obtain the so called "complex modularity"(Salingaros 2001). Advances in these design systems derive from "dimensional customization" based on variability of elements in relation to specific needs, using a VPL interface (Celani 2020).

According to this research framework our paper focuses on a customization system for designing an ergonomic bench that can be adaptable to different people (kids, adults, elders) and different use, sitting, semi-sitting and lying position.

The goal is to design a parametric "configurator", able to modify modules shape in relation to ergonomics specific needs and to combine them in relation to a specific context. The process is based on the single section design, the construction of the module and the aggregation rules. The anthropometrics data are the parameters that we used to modify and to control the single sections shape. Starting from different sections we can generate the different modules that can be aggregated together using a straight or curve rail.

The main challenge is how optimizing the transition zones between two different modules.

PARAMETRIC BENCH FRAMEWORK

In our research we have grouped parametric benches in two main groups:

- ergonomic system: configuration can be defined in relation to users need an context by designer;
- kinetic Systems: configuration can be modified dynamically by usersIn this paper we are going to deal the firs group

There are a lot of samples of parametric bench most of them are based on use of section that can be parametrically modified. In this case the main goal of the generative process is to design a sculptural object characterized by free form shape, the result of a process aimed to obtain an organic furniture.We are interested in design projects in witch final shape is a

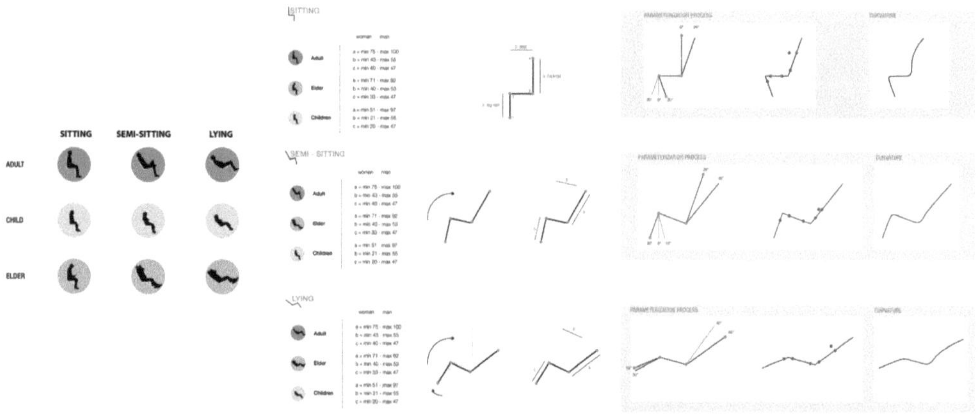

Figure 2
Ergonomic features for section definition. Images by Angela Cicala thesis - Master of Science in Design for the Built Environment - Naples Federico II

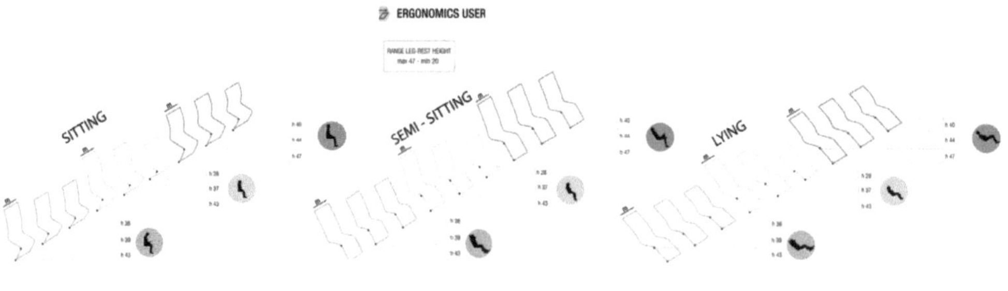

Figure 3
Modules definition. Images by Angela Cicala thesis - Master of Science in Design for the Built Environment - Naples Federico II

Figure 4
Complex modularity. Parametric bench configuration: cluster 4

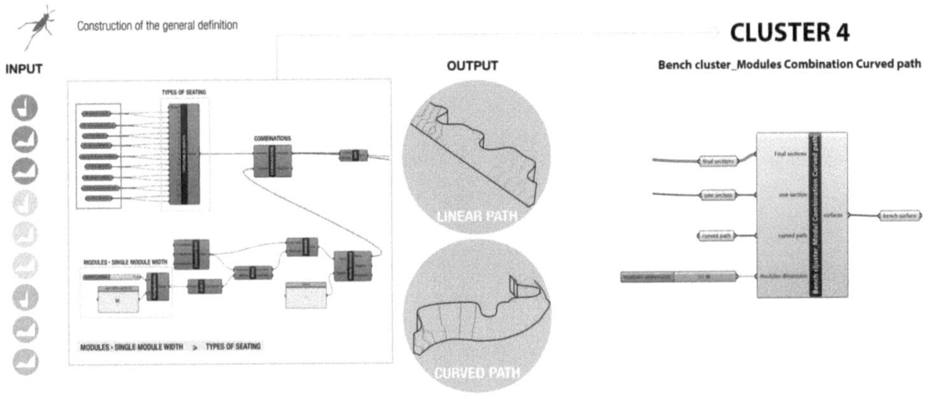

process based on anthropometry studies and on different way to use an urban bench. Each person needs different bench in relation to different uses. The goal is to define a CONFIGURATOR able to assist design process for ergonomic bench.

"One goal of modern ergonomics is to promote posture variability, as we now know being constrained to one posture, even if comfortable, can be detrimental to the health of certain structures in the body". According to Peter Johnson's research, Associate Professor of Environmental and Occupational Health Sciences at Washington University, we have analyzed different postures and we have evaluated the interaction with technology. We have defined a tool based on three different ergonomic posture (sitting, semi sitting, lying) that can be changed in relation to different people (kids, adults, elders). The open process can be improved by others ergonomic solutions parametrically controlled in some specific ranges.Each module can be composed using different submodules. Our tool testing is based on:

- bench submodules: three ergonomic postures (sitting, semi sitting, lying) that can change in relation to users (kids, adults, elders)
- a flexible sub module (in our case is a green module but could be a technological module too)

COMPLEX MODULARITY

We are testing a parametric design process based on complex modularity concept. We have developed a case study to test the tool. The main steps to define our tool are:

- Ergonomic parameters to use
- Bench module definition - different typologies
- Flexible modules definition - different typologies

Figure 5
DOMINO - algorithm configurator

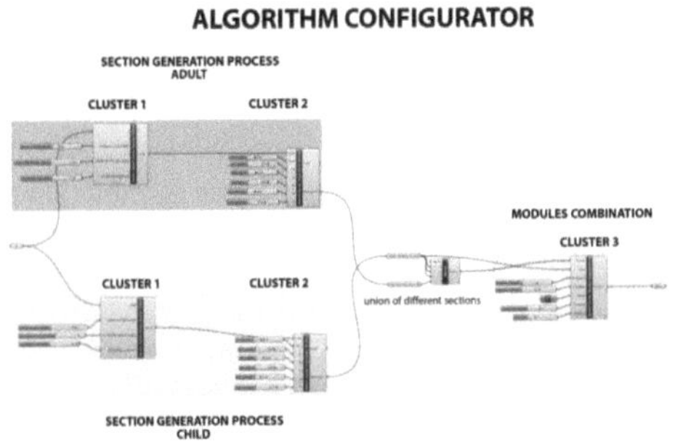

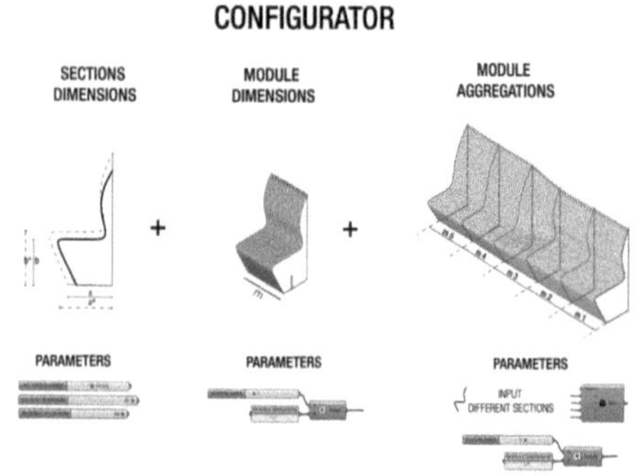

Figure 6
Configurator

CONFIGURATOR

DOMINO allows to combine the submodules and to design the transition element geometry.

The configurator is composed of 5 clusters:

- Cluster 2_bench cluster_ergonomic section
- Cluster 3_bench cluster_modules combination
- Cluster 4_bench cluster_modules combination curved path
- Cluster 5_ transition elements geometry control

Let's see specifically the purpose of each of them.

Cluster 1 allows to generate the linear section of each seat in relation to use flexibility (sitting, semi sitting, lying) and the range fixed in relation to users (kids, adults, elders).

The input parameters that make up this cluster are:

- leg height range: scales the seat according tothe range in relation to the height of the userslegs
- leg rest rotation: allows to modify the rotation angle between the seat and the legs, in order to have a better comfort in the seat;
- backrest rotation: modifies the inclination of the backrest of the chair.

These first three parameters make it possible to manage a sitting seat, while if we insert more as sitting rotation parameters, it is possible to pass from a sitting to a semi-sitting seat. For the passage to the reclined one we have defined the following input parameters:

- leg rest adjustment: it is possible to modify the inclination of the footrest;
- sitting and backrest rotation: it is possible to modify the combined inclination between sitting and backrest.

The output that we can generate is the linear section (line) of the seat.

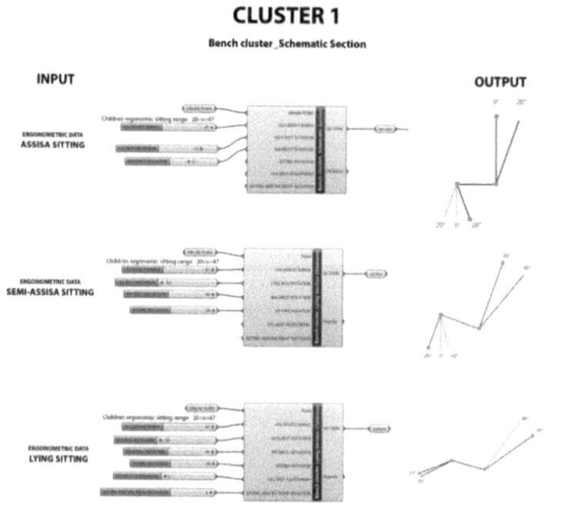

Figure 7
Cluster 1: linear section definition.

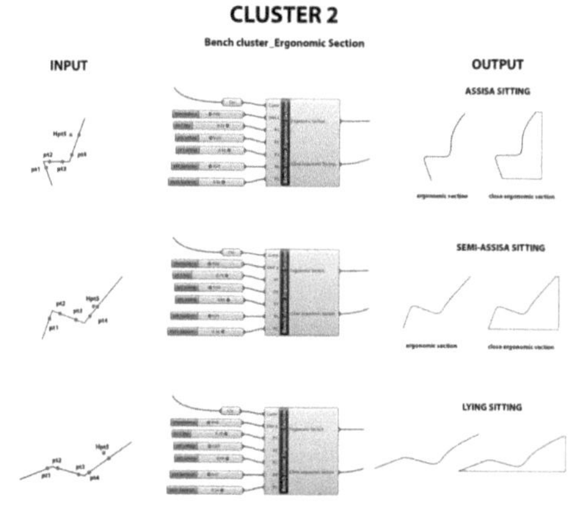

Figure 8
Cluster 2: ergonomic section generation

Figure 9
Transition zone between different modules: optimization process. Images by Angela Cicala thesis - Master of Science in Design for the Built Environment - Naples Federico II

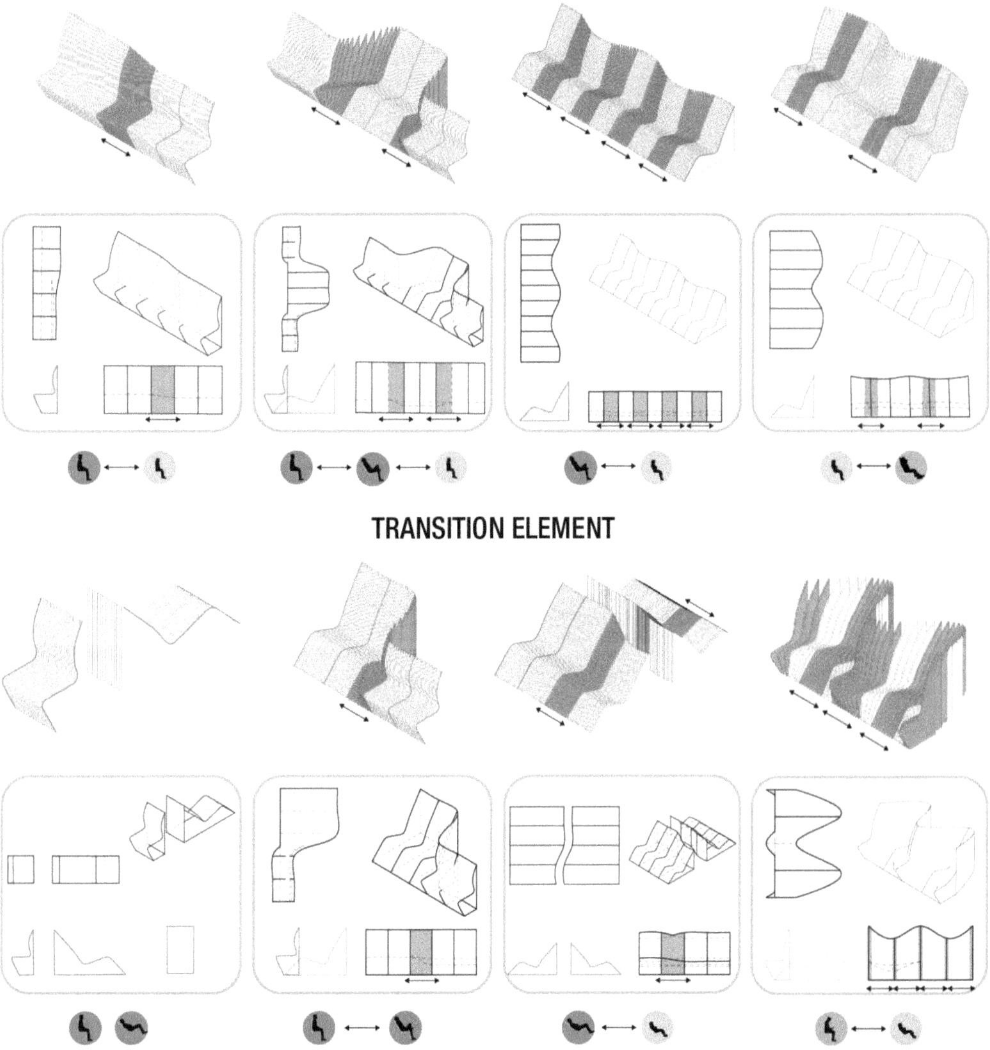

Cluster 2 allows to generate an ergonomic section through the use of curved nurbs passing through control points belonging to the linear section.The output we get are two curves, one represents the ergonomic section and the other represents the closed profile of the section that will allow us to generate the surface for the bench.

Cluster 3 combines the different modules generated by the different possible sections obtained with cluster 1 and 2 in relation to the type of seat and user. It allows us to modify the number of modules that make up the bench and their size, and also allows us to modify the thickness and distance of the panels that will make up the bench itself.

Cluster 4 allows us to aggregate the sections that make up the modules according to a linear or curved path.

Cluster 5 allows to generate and to control the geometry of transition element.

TRANSITION ZONE

Optimizing the transition zones between different "modules" is one of our research topic.

We can configure the transition element geometry as submodule that is generated in relation to modules combination. The size and the geometry of transition element depends on the two modules that we have to connect. The main goal of our tool is the shape control of this submodule. The input parameters to menage geometry of the transition element are the size of submodules and the algorithm used for surface generation. The aim is to generate pleasant and ergonomic shape that can be usable for free uses.

As we can see the size depends on the type of the two benches modules that we have to connect. The size is obviously zero for connection between two equal element, very small for connection between two modules of the same typology (kids, adults, elders sitting, semi sitting or lying) and the size becomes very large when we have to connect a very different modules such as an adult lying with an adult sit module.

Using a curved track along which the modules are aggregated, puts a number of arrangements more than the simple linear aggregation.

Starting from the important fact that the individual sections must be positioned normal to the tangent of the curve at a specific point, a condition necessary to obtain a surface with a constant and linear seating surface.Another fundamental prerequisite, which allows you to modify the shape of the section in relation to different needs are the control points that generate the nurbs curve, which not only allow you to modify the single section but, by increasing the degree of the curve, this allows you to have a greater continuity of the generated surface and in parallel allows you to act in a punctual manner on the parts that represent the transition elements between two different sections

Our parametric tool is based on the main G continuity levels that can be defined:

- G0 or Positional continuity.Two curves having a common endpoint, with no further condition, are positionally continuous. This is the less smooth type of joint, as the only condition to satisfy is the common endpoint, no matter what the flow of the two curves around the joint may be
- * G1 or Tangency continuity.Two curves having a common point and tangent vectors lying along the same direction are said to have tangency continuity. The two curves may seem to have the same direction at the joint, but the way they change their direction may still be very different (the rate of this change of direction is called curvature).
- G2 or Curvature continuity.Two curves having a common point, tangent vectors lying along the same direction, and having the same curvature (which is, the same rate of change of the direction) are said to have curvature continuity. The directions at the joint seem to change with the same "speed".
- Smooth curvature continuity.Two curves having G3 continuity are said to have Smooth curvature

Figure 10
Complex modularity: tests for submodules combination. Images by Angela Cicala thesis - Master of Science in Design for the Built Environment - Naples Federico II

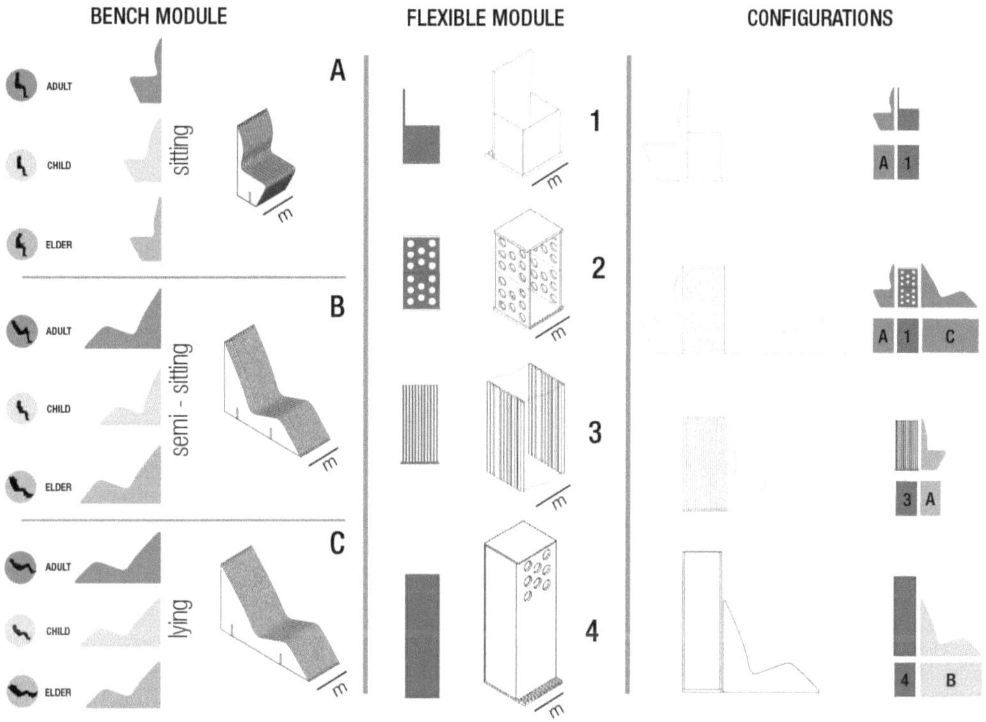

continuity at a joint if there is tangency continuity between the two curvature plots.

A further development is to be able to act in the dimensional control of the transition element, where it is possible to vary the latter in relation to certain requirements (functional, aesthetic, etc.) without having to maintain the size of the basic module. So it is possible to have control of a sub-module that is fully flexible and editable in response to certain inputs, making this complex modularity even more variable.

The control of this complex modularity allows the modules and sub-modules that make up the bench to communicate with other modular support elements.These additional modules, that we can define functional modules, allow to implement the basic function of the bench or the function "sitting".

They can be designed as green modules, technological, and other, modifiable according to users needs.

The control and management of this process is also useful for the implementation and maintenance of these elements, since it is possible to replace modules or individual parts that make it up, without having to act on the entire bench.

CONCLUSION AND FUTURE WORKS

We are working to define a design tool for kinetic ergonomic benches configuration. Our research aims to test how parametric tools can increase the Furniture Design Process.

Our work is based on geometry knowledge, the

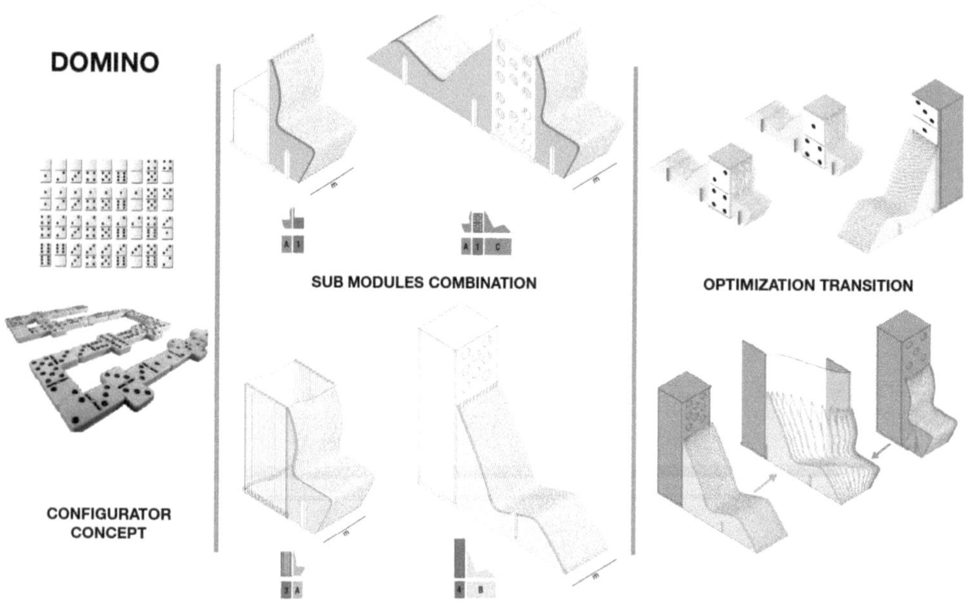

Figure 11
Configuration process: from concept to samples test. Images by Angela Cicala thesis - Master of Science in Design for the Built Environment - Naples Federico II

research for an optimized solution is based on continuity curves condition and surface geometric continuity. The goal is to menage the shape generation process to obtain a design surface comfortable for ergonomic and visual smoothness, light reflection, and airflow.

REFERENCES

Agirbas, A. 2020 'A Teaching Methodology for Parametric Design: A Case Study with Parametric Bench', *Sigradi 2020_ Transformative Design*

Binbin, S. and Huang, S. 2019 'Realizing product serialization by Grasshopper parametric design', *IOP Conf. Series: Materials Science and Engineering*

Leite, R. M. and Celani, G. 2020 'Dimensional mass customization of a flexible furniture system', *Proceeding of SIGraDi 2020_Transformative Design.*, Escuela de Arquitectura y Diseño de la Universidad Pontificia Bolivariana, Medellín (Colombia)

Salingaros, N. A. and Tejada, D. M. 2001, 'Modularity and the Number of Design Choices', *Nexus Network Journal*, 3, p. 99–109.

Shalaw, H.H. and Husein, A.H. 2020, 'The Influence of Parametric Design Tools on Increasing Creativity in the Furniture Design Process', *EAJSE. Eurasian Journal of Science & Engineering*, 6, pp. 199-211

van Stralen, M. 2018 'Mass Customization: a critical perspective on parametric design, digital fabrication and design democratization.', *Proceeding of SIGraDI 2018 TECHNOPOLITICAS XXII*, São Carlos. Brazil

Xin, S. 2020, 'Parametric Model for Kitchen Product Based on Cubic T-Bézier Curves with Symmetry.', *Simmetry*, 12, pp. 1-25

Zvonareva, P. P., Filipskaya, I. V. and Yangulova, I. 2020 'A new approach to the design of street furniture in Krasnoyarsk', *IOP Conf. Series: Materials Science and Engineering 944. Siberian Industrial Days International Forum*

Integrating Sociological Survey and Algorithmic Modelling for Low-Cost Housing

Igor Lacroix[1], Gonçalo Furtado Lopes[2], José Pedro Sousa[3]
[1,2,3] Faculty of Architecture, University of Porto + DFL/CEAU/FAUP
[1,2,3] {ilacroix|glopes|jsousa}@arq.up.pt

This paper presents a study developed in the scope of an ongoing research about the creation of an architectural design system of low-cost housing in Portugal's context. Its goal is to present the survey, analysis and digitization work of a research carried out in the 1960s by Portuguese architect Nuno Portas, with the help of architect Alexandre Alves Costa. The method was to convert mathematical information contained in Portas` and Alves Costa's report from Lisbon's National Laboratory of Civil Engineering (LNEC) into an algorithmic model with Rhinoceros® and Grasshopper® software. Besides revealing for the first time a comprehensive study of this pioneering work, this paper will set the foundations to propose the adaptation of its process into low-cost housing design. The result presented here is an algorithm for selecting the best architectural type from a database of housing floor plans, analyzed by a questionnaire regarding the inhabitants' needs and satisfactions.

Keywords: *sociological survey, algorithmic modelling, low-cost housing, Nuno Portas, Alexandre Alves Costa*

INTRODUCTION

In Portugal, there was a pioneering research about the creation of architectural design from information about users or inhabitants' needs, which tested the application of sociological and technological theories in architectural practice at a time of transformation of the country's society. This paper addresses this specific research as a starting point to create a low-cost housing model.

The work presented here is the first result of an ongoing research about recognizing a specific Portuguese architectural knowledge and turning it into a housing design and building process, and it perceives Portuguese architecture from an European perspective and broad historical context. The first research stage was the analysis of Portuguese architectural theory with special focus on architect Nuno Portas' work. Portas developed a vast and important work for modern Portuguese architecture, and proofed to be a forerunner in realizing a systematic approach to architectural design. Alongside with other collaborators, architect Alexandre Alves Costa played a central role in the research about a computational process for architectural typology analysis, in the 1960s.

Based in Lisbon, the National Laboratory of Civil Engineering (LNEC) hosted and supported the process. Created in 1946, the research center came from two different institutions: the Laboratory of Testing and Study of Materials, an institution with a solid experimental side in activity since 1898, and the Centre for Civil Engineering Studies, a scientific research unit created in 1942, known as Centre for Applied Mechanics Studies at this original moment. The founder and leader was engineer Manuel Rocha, one of the greatest names in 20th century Portuguese engineering and one of the first Directors of the Laboratory.

Within a context of debate on scientific methodology applied to architecture, emerged with the *Congrès Internationaux d'Architecture Moderne* (CIAM), and developed in the 1960s with the theorization on design methods, Portas and Alves Costa investigated on a system for integrating sociological data into architectural practice. One aspect of the research was the connection with digital technology, proofed by their research report for LNEC. However, since Christopher Alexander (1971) and John Christopher Jones (1977) changed their positions regarding design methods research, still in the 1970s, LNEC and the Portuguese group focused their attention on other research subjects.

Portas' and Alves Costa's research could have followed a technological trend from its historical moment, during the 1960s, when LNEC installed their first computer and there was still an expectation that it would be an instrument of transformation of production processes. The idea is to study and update this research in order to integrate its results as a first architectural design step.

This article is divided in five sections. The first one is a brief biography of both architects analyzed here. The second one is a historical background, about the period between the 1960s and the 1970s, which lists some of the possible references Portas and Alves Costa had in international and local contexts. The third section describes the LNEC Report that both architects did together, divided in two parts. The forth section is about the digitization work and discussion about its process and the fifth section is the paper conclusion.

Biographical notes

Since the characters in this paper may be unknown to most of today's international audience, it is pertinent to present some biographical notes on Nuno Portas and Alexandre Alves Costa to better frame their importance in the Portuguese context and the specificity of their work.

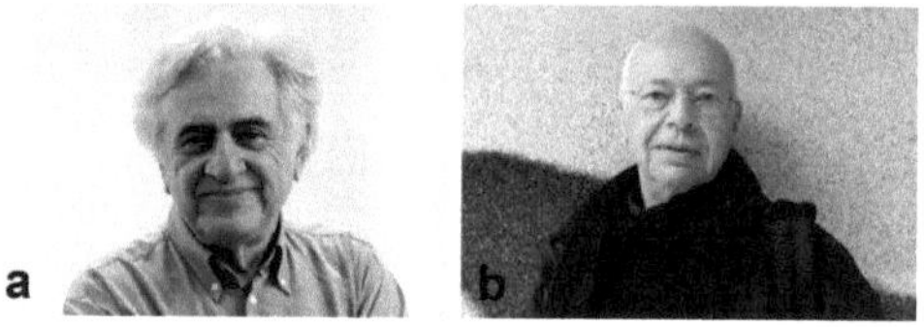

Figure 1
Nuno Portas and Alexandre Alves Costa – Source: Egidio Santos photo and Alexandre Alves Costa archive, respectively.

Nuno Portas (Vila Viçosa, 1934) (Fig. 1a) attended Lisbon's Superior School of Fine Arts (ESBAL) even though he defended his "theoretical" thesis at Porto's Superior School of Fine Arts (ESBAP), in 1959. In terms of research, he coordinated the Research Centre for Architecture, Housing and Urbanism at LNEC, where he joined in 1962 and remained until 1974. In terms of practical activity, Portas integrated Nuno Teotónio Pereira's workshop and, in 1974, they won the Valmor Prize for the building of Jesus' Heart Church in Lisbon. In political-urban terms, he participated in the three provisional post-revolution governments, elaborating the housing policy of Local Ambulatory Support Service (SAAL), a social housing program that responded to the lack of housing in post-dictatorship period, and later participating in urban policies in Portugal. In 2005, he won Sir Patrick Abercrombie Prize for urbanism by the *Union Internationale des Architectes* (UIA), previously won by Jan Gehl, Giancarlo de Carlo and Lucio Costa. It is important to notice that Portas became an official LNEC researcher, even if he was a figure coming from architecture, an area without great reputation in terms of "scientific" research, at a time when he was already a leading professor as well as a critic in specialized publications.

Alexandre Alves Costa (Porto, 1939) (Fig. 1b) attended the Architecture course at ESBAP, after which he trained at LNEC with Nuno Portas, having obtained his degree in 1966. In the 1960s, besides being involved in architectural studies, he became actively involved in the political fight against the fascist dictatorship. Since 1970, Alves Costa has been working in architecture as a liberal professional. He collaborated, among others, with architects Álvaro Siza Vieira, Camilo Cortesão, José Luís Gomes, José Manuel Soares, António Côrte-Real, and Sérgio Fernandez. In the period after April 25, 1974, he was part of the Coordinating Commission of SAAL/Norte, responsible for the Planning and Design Support sector. During Porto 2001 European Capital of Culture, Alves Costa was one of the four winners of the ideas competition for the renovation of downtown Porto. He was a candidate for the Jean Tschumi Prize in 2005. Among the prizes he won, the International Association of Art Critics/Ministry of Culture Grand Prize, 2008, also awarded to Sérgio Fernandez, for the modern and quality work developed by both architects.

HISTORICAL BACKGROUND

The international scene

From an European perspective, it is important to recognize the effervescent historical moment of the 1960s, when the architectural production in Europe embraced, on the one hand, social conscience in dealing with post-war challenges, and, on the other hand, the technological advances of that time.

At *Centre National de la Recherche Scientifique* and *Centre Scientifique et Technique du Bâtiment*, Paul Chombart de Lauwe (1959) presented and developed the research field of housing sociology that consequently influenced other disciplines such as architecture and urbanism.

The University of Cambridge with the Center for Land Use and Built Form Studies (LUBFS), then led by Leslie Martin and Lionel March, launched a precursor algorithmic modelling program for urban planning studies in Cambridge, UK. The computer made it possible to parameterize planning studies based on several parameters, such as sunlight, local legislation, and maximum height of the buildings (Bullock, Dickens and Steadman 1972).

Christopher Alexander (1964) developed a thesis on the application of patterns of use of the building and realized schemes, investigating a diagrammatic thinking for architectural design. In another research direction, Peter Eisenman (1963) investigated an architectural conceptual system, from the same influence coming from LUBFS, but considering a more subjective approach, different from Alexander.

John Christopher Jones (1970), when analyzing the ergonomics of engineering work, focused on design methods research and therefore advanced a whole area of knowledge that persists today with technological developments, such as Artificial Intelligence (AI).

In the housing field, several examples of social housing buildings would consolidate themselves as architectural references. In Italy, there are many examples of minimum housing for the working classes, mainly in the context of *Istituto Nazionale delle Assicurazioni* housing program, known as INA-Casa, for the reconstruction of Italian cities after the Second World War. In Rome, the Tuscolano Quarter, built between 1950 and 1954, features buildings designed by Italian architect Adalberto Libera, with concrete structures and built over *pilotis* (Guccione et al. 2002).

In the Iberian context, the colonization villages in Spain presented housing solution for the country's rural populations, through architecture that referred to Spanish traditions, which date back to Arabic origins. The work of Spanish architect José Luis Fernández del Amo, one of the main authors who stood out in this context until the 1970's, sought to integrate the arts with architecture in a performance linked to Christianity and the idea of family (Centellas Soler 2010).

The Portuguese context

From a local point of view, and according to Jorge Figueira's PhD thesis (2009), Portas contributed to modern Portuguese architecture by creating and developing a social housing design method, which associated the processing of sociological data from the inhabitants themselves to assist in the proper design of the houses, and the interaction with regulatory institutions. Portas did this in a historical moment of increased debate about bringing change to architectural practice, towards a more scientific approach.

The method considered Chombart de Lauwe's sociological theories, and linked architectural design to information that the inhabitants would provide, in order to improve their service by enabling the personalization of spatial solutions (Portas 1959). The method suggests the design process as a function of socioeconomic and material parameters that would result in the most adequate housing solution for the conditions presented by the inhabitants. One year later, Chombart de Lauwe contributed himself to Portuguese journal "*Arquitectura*" with the proposition of a procedure that recognizes the importance of inhabitants' inquiry as a method for housing design (Chombart de Lauwe 1960).

Already at LNEC, Portas tested his method during the 1960s, and his report from 1964 presented minimum standards for affordable housing designs, introducing a research topic that led to many other results (Portas 1964). In this work, the architect presented the evolving concept of "minimum" in the family. "The challenge of social evolution" (Portas 1969b: 11) is perhaps the main definition of what the term evolution means to him, in the sense of social changes and how housing could respond and adapt to them. Portas was in search of a spatial resolution that would guarantee minimum conditions for its inhabitants, keeping the focus on the attended populations. His work seems to stand out precisely because it considers the human being in the first place, by integrating sociology into the process of architectural design. The argument is that sociological data could "[...] determine, in turn, for a given economic and technical construction constraint where the available methods of cost minimization have been entered, a minimum cost per cell, thus socially acceptable, which can finally be used in the programming of investments [...]" (Portas 1964: 9).

Also at LNEC, the important contribution of the then trainee architect Alexandre Alves Costa that also played a role later in Porto during the existence of SAAL housing program. Alves Costa's internship report attests the intention to use a computational approach for the processing of sociological information influenced by previously mentioned report from 1964. In this way, the architect would be able to rationalize typological studies of affordable housing floor plans (Portas and Alves Costa 1966).

Portas developed a concept regarding this investigation: the metadesign. For him (Portas 1969a), this concept considers the available technologies in its time, mainly influenced by Christopher Alexander's experiments and LUBFS research group, with the intention to improve relationships between architecture and urbanism, in a way of treating architecture by its urbanistic features with the concern of city development as a cohesive system.

Finally, published as evolutive housing design system, in 1971, together with Francisco da Silva Dias, Portas understood how to apply the inquiry method into architecture, in a progressive manner and introducing the time factor in order to compose an economic distribution of income from the families with the building evolution of the houses (Portas and Silva Dias 1971).

This systematization process influenced several works from the political transition period that Portugal faced with the end of Salazar's dictatorship, in 1974. Portas created SAAL and even though it existed for only two years, between 1974 and 1976, it resulted in housing buildings with the inhabitants' participation in the process of designing their own houses (Bandeirinha et al. 2014). Alves Costa applied the experimented method in Contumil Neighborhood's architectural design (Fig. 2), through the inquiry to inhabitants removed from their original places. The Malagueira dwellings in Évora by Álvaro Siza Vieira present similarities to evolutive housing, and José Pinto Duarte (2001) analyzed them through shape grammar.

From this understanding, this paper approaches sociological survey through algorithmic modelling in order to codify a digital process of obtaining socio-

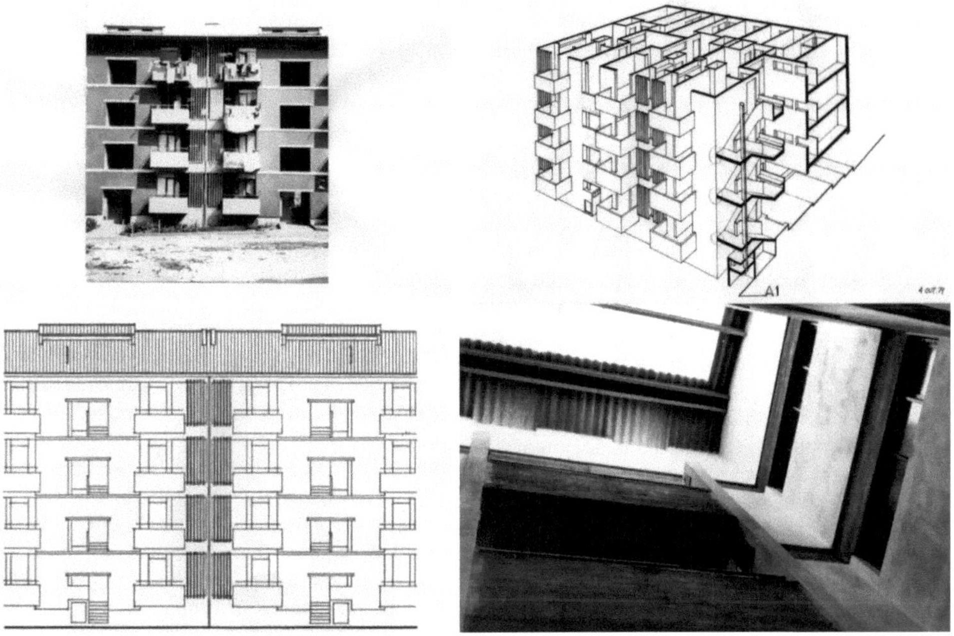

Figure 2
Contumil Neighborhood building photographs and architectural design – Source: Alexandre Alves Costa archive

logical information and turning it into a process of selecting architectural type from a list of preselected designs from around the world. To do so it is necessary to take a deeper review of Portas' and Alves Costa's attempt to create a computational process for architectural analysis.

THE LNEC REPORT

This document is important, because Portas scientifically proofed his method through the experiment developed by Alves Costa. The experiment was a turning point towards evolutive housing theory, because it directly related inhabitant's needs through a computational process. In this way, it could validate the rationalization process the architect would have to accomplish for best attending the population contemplated by social housing programs.

The document is an example of scientific research that can lead to further investigation. Since this pioneering move to explore computational methods applied to architecture, in Portugal during the 1960s, many things have changed from the cultural and technological point of view. However, despite the immensely greater computational power and the ubiquitous presence of the digital in our everyday life, the problem of affordable housing remains as one of the most important challenges.

In this context, the authors propose to review Porta's design principles from the perspective of contemporary digital design, analysis and fabrication technologies. Within such framework, it would be interesting to think and digitally develop the concept of a low-cost housing system that integrates the sociological inquiry as a main driver. This work would thus inquire the possibility to extend Portas' theory to face the social challenges and technological opportunities of the present time. Following, there is an overview of the two parts of the report.

The first part

The first part of the LNEC Report is divided in four sections: Introduction, Questionnaire, Information Processing and Applications, and it also contains an annex.

Introduction. "Inform, program, rationalize" is the method introduced in the first paragraphs of LNEC Report (Table 1). "Inform" through sociological inquiries about what the inhabitants expect, require, wish, for their own houses, thinking on the interaction with governmental social housing programs. The sociological inquiry gather 259 binary, yes or no, questions. Demand levels classify the questions by strictly necessary, necessary, and desirable, which attribute weights for inquiry evaluation.

"Program" through a computational system that selects the best architectural type based on the answers of the sociological inquiry. Alves Costa correlated two databases, one from sociological information, another from 117 housing floor plans, and depending on inhabitants' responses, the process would choose those types that would better fit their needs. Alves Costa applied this process in different examples in order to test the program.

"Rationalize" through an architectural design directly informed by the solutions the program gave previously. In this way, the architect would have his work scientifically proofed and would not have to rely on intuition. Alves Costa rationalized six schemes that would better synthesize architectural solutions into well-defined types.

Questionnaire. The questionnaire describes the characteristics required for the housing cell, or assigns a qualification code to a chosen group of minimum housing types, in other words it assigns meaning to a geometry by means of parameters. A computational system, though not computerized, to integrate sociological data into the analysis of architectural designs.

The idea was that it would integrate a system for measuring the inhabitants' satisfactions about selected dwellings developed at the time, for example, INA-Casa in Italy, HLM in France, ICESA in Portugal. The goal was "[...] to have a prospecting process of type solutions" (Portas and Alves Costa 1966: 6) through a process of comparative analysis. "The prepared questionnaire is limited in principle to the analysis of the housing cell [...]" (Portas and Alves Costa 1966: 7) so it is clear the research purpose to convert dwelling description into questions that would classify the typology and, consequently, make possible to program the information into an accessible database for analysis.

In summary, the questionnaire is "[...] a dimensioning and functional organization analysis of the interior space to verify its probability of satisfying recognized and generalized family needs in the present situation and more predictable evolution." (Portas and Alves Costa 1966: 8) . Four groups divides the questions: typological classification; functional analysis; inter-relationships, communication and functional separation; and exterior relationship.

Information Processing. This section provides comprehensive explanation of Boole's algebra and its application for the construction of matrices. Explains the intersection and addition of matrices and how

Table 1 Synthesis of analysis and rationalization method

Inform	Questionnaire (sociological data)	>	Studied designs (architectural data)	>	Logical relations (socio-functional)
Program	Binary questions (yes, no) and demand classification for architectural data analysis			>	Approximate results
Rationalize	Improve previous results accordingly to architectural design			>	Typologies and schemes

Table 1
Synthesis table

each question from the questionnaire provides a multiple choice answer: negative, positive and neutral, basic binary code, mathematically understood respectively as 0, 1, and 2 in the case of neutral answer that attributes differential characteristics for each type, to be distinguishable in case of two or more similar types (Fig. 3). Even if the original questionnaire contains 259 questions, the authors considered only 224 questions for typology analysis, because the last 35 questions were improbable to achieve information since their description is about exterior characteristics of the dwellings.

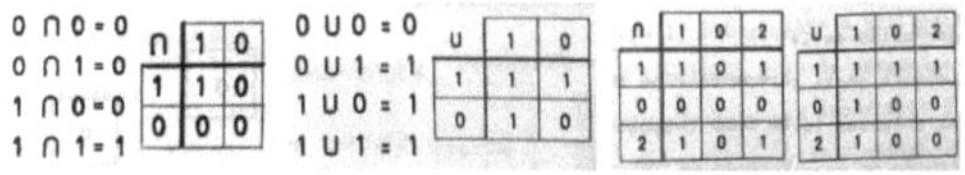

Figure 3
Matrix intersection, matrix addition and neutral answer calculation, respectively – Source: LNEC Report.

Applications. This section presents a common architectural design process that transform an initial and broader proposition into a better-defined solution, adequate to various constraints, such as functional interior composition and relationship between areas. Where Alves Costa presented the tests that made possible the architectural rationalization of the most adequate types, in view of the gathered database, through graphs and schemes that facilitate the visualization of housing floor plan (Fig. 4).

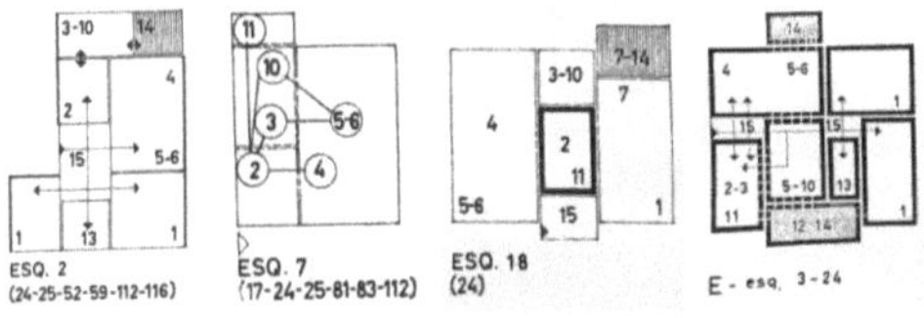

Figure 4
Typology analysis and schemes by Alves Costa – Source: LNEC Report.

Annex. The annex of LNEC Report First Part contains the matrix (Fig. 5), or logical relationship framework, and some additional information for further understanding of the matrix.

The second part

The second part of the report presents a series of schemes, drawn by Alexandre Alves Costa, to better visualize functional relationships within the housing cell (Fig. 6). The intention was the development of design method through analytical graphics that could facilitate architectural analysis following the concepts already described in the first part. Four groups analyzes the spatial relationships: compatibility between functions, grouping of functions into unit spaces, organization of functions by groups, and inter-relationships between functional communication and separation.

Sixteen functions complete the housing cell: 1 - sleeping area; 2 - food preparing; 3 - ordinary dining; 4 - special dining; 5 - general living area; 6 - living area for guests; 7 - recreational area for children; 8 - study room for young people; 9 - work place for adults; 10a - cloth ironing; 10b - cloth sewing; 11 - cloth washing; 12 - cloth drying; 13 - personal hygiene space; 14 - exterior living space; 15a - separation or communication zone between interior and exterior; 15b - separation or communication zone within interior; 16a - clothing internal storage; 16b - general internal storage.

DIGITIZATION WORK

In previous research stage of theoretical analysis regarding evolutive housing theory, it was observed the possibility of converting the laboratory study carried out by Alves Costa, not only into a method of analysis of architectural types, but also into a design tool that integrates fundamental sociological data for the planning and performance of the constructive solution.

In this sense, the second research stage was to digitize the work done by Portas and Alves Costa and convert it into a table for query and choice of the most appropriate type using tools of today, such as Rhinoceros® and Grasshopper® software. The table matched from an online form answered by the hypothetical client.

The first step was turning the questionnaire into a Google Form® for public interaction, so the transcription of 224 questions into Google Sheets® and sequential creation of 224 questions with multiple choices answers, following the three standards proposed in the report, yes, no, and not applied for the

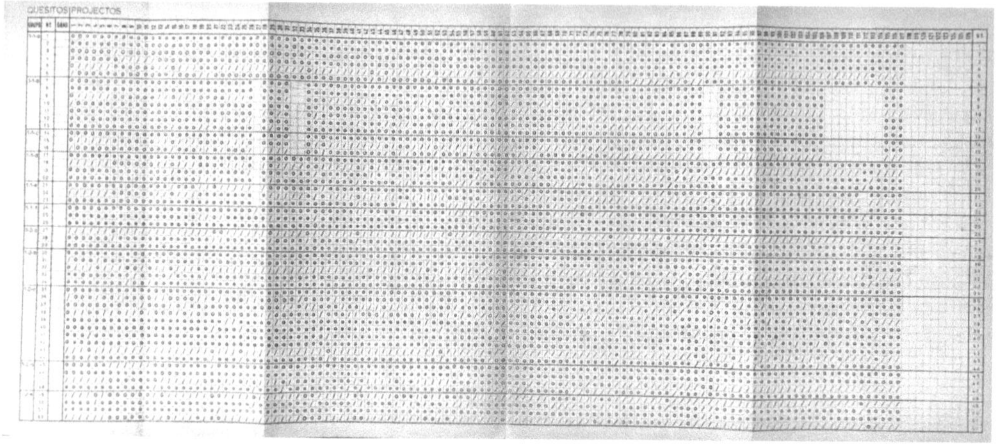

Figure 5
Handmade matrix with binary information of each type according to questionnaire – Source: LNEC Report.

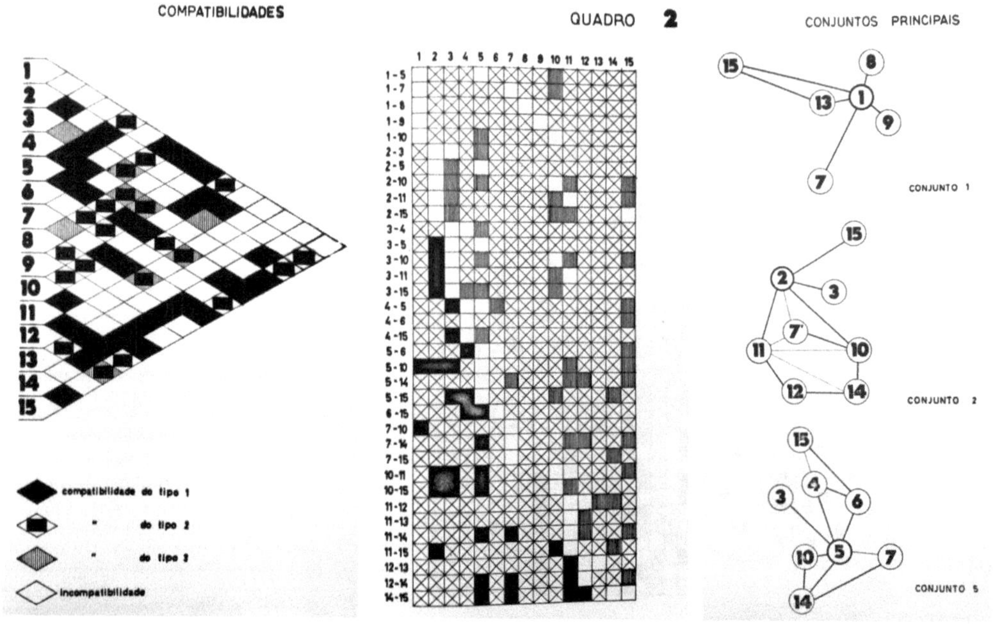

Figure 6
Schemes and graphs by Alves Costa – Source: LNEC Report.

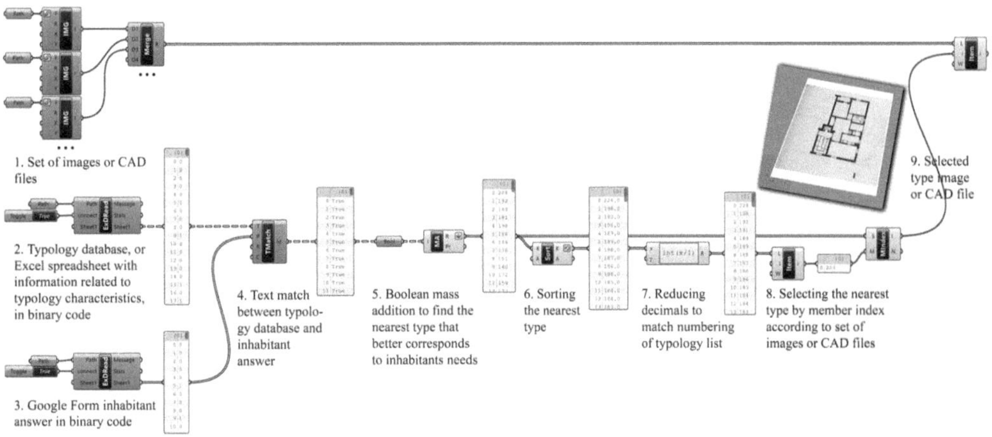

Figure 7
Grasshopper® algorithmic model for selecting architectural type according to questionnaire answer.

neutral answer, with the add-on Form Maker®. Once answered, the form gives a Google Sheet® for every public interaction, and with this information, one can match the typology database.

The second step was turning the handmade matrix into an Excel® spreadsheet, the most difficult task, because it was carefully filled with binary code accordingly with the original information process, containing the database for typology analysis, or the code that describes all 117 types from different sources and countries.

The third step was to create a matching system in Grasshopper® to evaluate and choose the best types accordingly to inhabitant's desires (Fig. 7). This is a work in progress, because to digitize 117 architectural designs is a big task, but the idea is to provide the architect with a floor plan already in vector mode for sequential rationalization process.

The algorithm results in the selection of the most adequate type. From there the design rationalization process through designer's preferences and eventual type optimization, for example, to create a model to inform a digitally fabricated building system.

Evaluation of the digitization work

Nuno Portas experimented with computational methods applied to architecture, and this process resulted in an architectural practice with SAAL program that helped, for example, promote architect Álvaro Siza Vieira's career internationally. Alexandre Alves Costa developed the prototype of a computational system that used a sociological method to contribute to systematize the approach with clients / users. The laboratorial test conducted it into an analysis system, but not converted into a design system. Therefore, the challenge here was to convert it directly to an algorithmic model for application in architectural design, in order to facilitate the practice of evolutive housing nowadays.

Portas and Alves Costa were two characters that met at LNEC and that made it possible to approach design conception from information data. The hypothesis is that it is possible to convert their analytical system into an automated stage of architectural design, in order to meet a socioeconomic demand.

The belief is that it is possible to improve their method by constantly updating and modifying its database according to other inhabitants' functional and behavioral needs. Of course, there is much work until the end user could use this preliminary result, nonetheless, this digitization process was essential, because it involved first the comprehension of an architectural theory and historical context, and second the conversion of data never before computerized.

Studies of CAAD nature should relate to architecture as a priority, and, in this case, to the interdisciplinary approach that the discipline could take to benefit society. One of the most difficult stages of SAAL program was the assistance of inhabitants, because of their quantity, together with the specificity and complexity of their demands. Therefore, this study tackles the emergency of society's needs in order to respond to them efficiently, by digitizing an existing architectural knowledge.

CONCLUSION

One contribution of this paper is the continuation of Portas' and Alves Costa's research that was set aside, due to the moment of political transformation in which Portugal found itself in the 1970s. In other words, it recognizes a pre-existing orientation and, six decades later, intends to review and improve it with current digital technologies.

This approach proved to facilitate a difficult stage of interaction with the client, which is to prepare the form for automatic completion of the algorithm that will choose the best types for each case. In Portugal's context, this could convince, in the sense of the maintenance of the cultural heritage left by both characters presented here.

Considering this design principle, the next research goal is to convert it into an initial stage of low-cost housing design with the intention to organize a digital fabrication process from this analyzed local expertise. In order to achieve that, a model to generate geometrical and constructive information is essential.

ACKNOWLEDGMENTS

We would like to thank Professor Alexandre Alves Costa for sharing with us the original documents of the LNEC Report, and for the interview that cleared many questions about his work. This research has the financial support of FCT, within the project UID/AUR/00145/2019.

REFERENCES

Alexander, C 1964, *Notes on the synthesis of form*, Oxford University Press, London

Alexander, C 1971, 'The state of the art in design methods', *DMG Newsletter*, 5(3), pp. 3-7

Bandeirinha, JA (eds) 2014, *O processo SAAL: arquitectura e participação, 1974-1976*, Serralves, Porto

Bullock, N, Dickens, P and Steadman, P 1972, 'The use of models in planning and the architectural design process', in Martin, L and Martin, L (eds) 1972, *Urban space and structures*, Cambridge University Press, Cambridge, UK

Duarte, JP 2001, *Customizing mass housing: a discursive grammar for Siza's Malagueira houses*, Ph.D. Thesis, Massachussets Institute of Technology

Eisenman, P 1963, *The formal basis of modern architecture*, Ph.D. Thesis, Cambridge University

Figueira, J 2009, *A periferia perfeita: pós-modernidade na arquitectura portuguesa, anos 60 - anos 80*, Ph.D. Thesis, Faculty of Architecture of the University of Porto

Guccione, M (eds) 2002, *Guida ai quartieri romani INA Casa*, Gangemi Editore, Rome

Jones, JC (1970) 1992, *Design Methods*, John Wiley & Sons, New York and Chichester

Jones, JC 1977, 'How my thoughts about design methods have changed during the years', *Design Methods and Theories*, 11(1), pp. 48-62

Chombart de Lauwe, P 1959, *Famille et habitacion - 1. Sciences humaines et conception de l'habitation*, Centre National de la Recherche Scientifique, Paris

Chombart de Lauwe, P 1960, 'Sociologia da habitação: métodos e perspectivas de investigação', *Arquitectura*, 68(7), pp. 41-50

Portas, N (1959) 2004, *A habitação social: proposta para metodologia da sua arquitectura*, FAUP, Porto

Portas, N (1969a) 2007, *A cidade como arquitectura*, Livros Horizonte, Lisbon

Portas, N 1964, *Estudo das funções e da exigência de áreas da habitação. Necessidades familiares e áreas da habitação. Análise de exigências por funções, da habitação. Volumes I, II*, LNEC, Lisbon

Portas, N 1969b, *Funções e exigências de áreas da habitação*, LNEC, Lisbon

Portas, N and Costa, AA 1966, *Racionalização de soluções de habitação. Partes I, II*, LNEC, Lisbon

Portas, N and Silva Dias, F 1971, *Habitação evolutiva. Princípios e critérios de projecto*, LNEC, Lisbon

Centellas Soler, M 2010, *Los pueblos de colonización de Fernández del Amo: arte, arquitectura y urbanismo*, Fundación Caja de Arquitectos, Barcelona

Rob-LCA

An assessment method to support environmental sensitive material selection in robotic fabrication

Adrian Krężlik[1], Orkan Zeynel Güzelci[2], José Pedro Sousa[3]
[1,2,3] University of Porto, Faculty of Architecture + DFL/CEAU
[1] adrian.krezlik@gmail.com [2,3] {oguzelci|jsousa}@arq.up.pt

Facing the current environmental crises, architecture must embrace sustainable modes of design and production. This requires the careful selection of the materials by assessing their lifecycle performance, which is not yet an easy and stable practice. In this context, this paper presents an assessment model called Rob-LCA to evaluate environmental-sensitive material selection for robotic fabrication. The model takes the data related to design and material as an input, it gives the Environmental Impact Indicator based on calculations. Then, designers evaluate and compare the fabrication processes, whether the environmental impact of the materials is satisfactory for the designed object. As a contribution, the proposed model complements information of the environmental impact of the A3, and A5 phases of the typical LCA method, adapting the customization and construction abilities of the robotic fabrication. In this study, the Rob-LCA was tested with the CorkCrete Arch prototype for a compound building system developed by Digital Fabrication Laboratory (DFL). By considering its multi-material panel, the production life cycles of cork and expanded polystyrene were assessed. Initial findings of the test of the model show that the proposed model might open a new path for sustainable manufacturing. This work presents thus a contribution to frame and align the use of digital design and fabrication processes with the current demands for environmental sustainability.

Keywords: *Robotic Fabrication, Life Cycle Assessment, Environmental Impact Assessment, Sustainable Production, New European Bauhaus*

INTRODUCTION

Being responsible for 38% of the world's CO2 emissions, the Architecture, Engineering and Construction (AEC) sector is under fire with the world demanding an urgent change in their modes of action. In this transformation, architects can play a central role if they assume their responsibility and tune designs toward sustainability. To measure the environmental impact of the buildings two methodologies have been adopted: Life Cycle Assessment (LCA) to assess the not-site specific impact, and Environmental Impact Assessment (EIA) to focus on in situ operations

(Crawley and Aho, 1999). The actual focus on reducing energy consumption in the operation phase should be complemented with extensive research on the embodied energy and environmental cost of materials that are strictly related to manufacturing and construction processes. According to Thormark's (2002) study on energy-efficient buildings in Sweden, embodied energy might represent up to 40% of total energy consumed in the building operation in its 50-year life span. Along with the New European Bauhaus outlines [1], the Directive on Circular Economy [2] indicates principles for regenerative development that serve as a reference for design.

The framework of our study is on the pre-operational phase of a building, namely the material fabrication and construction stages. This study considers one-off and batch production processes only. In this context, we introduce an assessment model called *Rob-LCA* to evaluate environmental-sensitive material selection for robotic fabrication. Out of the available fabrication techniques at the Digital Fabrication Laboratory (DFL) at the Faculty of Architecture of the University of Porto (FAUP), the authors decided to choose robotic fabrication since it can be employed for large-scale fabrication, the production of mock-ups, and with different building techniques and components that could be used in real-life architecture. The equipment used and analyzed for the fabrication is a KUKA industrial robot - KR120 HA r2700.

It is thus the first step to develop a calculator based on the proposed assessment model. The formulation of the model is based on processes performed during the development of the *CorkCrete Arch* prototype (Sousa et al. 2016) to obtain three components, namely: panels based on expanded Insulation Cork Board (ICB), molds based on Expanded Polystyrene (EPS), and Glass-Reinforced Concrete (GRC) sprayed panels produced by using the EPS molds. All the prefabricated parts were used as a proof of concept, for material tests, and concluded in spatial structures.

RELATED CONCEPTS AND STUDIES

Life Cycle Assessment

Life Cycle Assessment (LCA) is a method to evaluate the impact associated with a product over its lifetime and could be applied to numerous disciplines including architecture and design. According to the European Norm (EN15804), LCA is divided into four phases: (A1-A3) sourcing, material production, and manufacturing; (A4-A5) transport and construction; (B) use; (C) demolition and disassembly; (D) disposal. In commercial use, the norm is widely translated into the Environmental Product Declaration (EPD). As an independent, third-party, certification system, EPD allows comparing the impact of products and their lifecycle. To compare products of the same function but produced by different materials or from different manufacturers a functional unit (FU) was introduced. FU measures a material unit by its function. For instance, it can be seen in the insulation with a U-value of $0.2W/m^2K$ or a beam that can support 300kg. Regardless of its size or thickness, the performance is the indicator. LCA measures a seven principles domain of impact, energy consumption according to its source, hazardous materials, and water consumption to list the most important for AEC. According to Fernandes et al. (2019), Global Warming Potential (GWP) and Embodied Energy (EE) are typically associated with buildings and built environments. Keeping this in mind, our model will focus on these two dimensions.

Sustainable Manufacturing

In the previous studies that focus on the relationship between LCA and digital fabrication, sustainable manufacturing stands out as an important concept. Energy consumption is one of the key factors that affect the sustainability of the manufacturing process. Galadeta et al. (2019) mentioned the necessity to assess and optimize the energy efficiency of the manufacturing equipment during the process. Considering the industrial robot as a tool, the issue of energy consumption of robots has been discussed since the early 2010s. The factors that affect the energy consumption of the robot comprise its technology, speed, acceleration, operating, and programming strategy, among others. By changing these factors and parameters, a variety of tests have been conducted and important findings have been published related to the energy consumption of robots (Bryan et al. 2010; Chemnitz et al. 2011; Meike and Ribickis, 2011).

Today, evaluating the sustainability of the manufacturing process according to the amount of energy consumed by the tool or equipment is considered as a reductive approach. In particular, in the late 2010s, the issue of how digital fabrication tools improve the sustainability of manufacturing was generally discussed (Agusti-Juan and Habert, 2017; Agusti-Juan et al. 2017). Studies on sustainable manufacturing have tested different digital fabrication techniques and materials in pairs, and these processes were also compared with the conventional ones and evaluated with the LCA method. In these studies, 3D printed eyeglasses (Cerdas et al. 2017) and robotically fabricated walls (Agusti-Juan et al. 2017; de Soto et al. 2018) with a certain level of complexity were some examples. As a common result of these studies, it has been observed that the use of robots makes certain activities possible that are time-consuming and impossible for human labor. As another finding, the increase in the complexity or uniqueness of the product or structure to be produced does not increase the global warming potential of the process. As a result of the analysis of the sustainability of the processes with the LCA method, it is observed that there is a large amount of environmental impact caused by the manufacturing phase of the material. The environmental impact in the digital fabrication process is relatively low compared to the material manufacturing process (Agusti-Juan and Habert, 2017).

LCA can be applied to material fabrication processes that use computer numerical control machines such as robotic arms. This study proposes a framework that focuses only on the stages where the robotic fabrication alternated a mass-production process to estimate its share in the materials' environmental impact. The scheme presented in Figure 1 describes the typical mass-production process (in green) and its complement where robotic fabrication is present (in red).

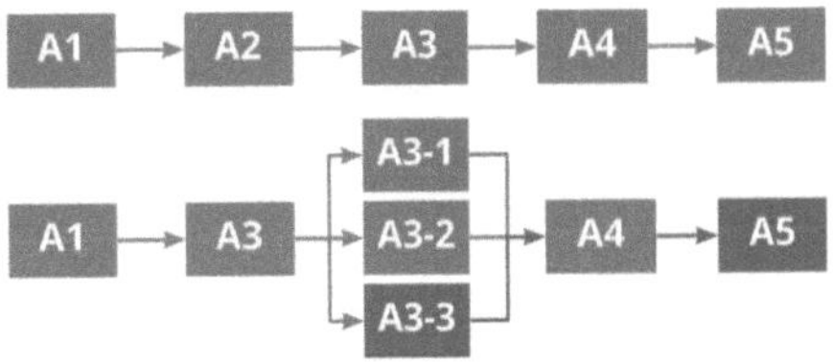

Figure 1
Enriching the typical LCA framework

As shown in Table 1, the proposed method complements the phases A3 (customization in factory), and A5 which looks for digital, robotic-assisted, or robotic-driven construction. Step A3 is supplemented with information on the alternated model of the production process of a material, integrated with CAD, and executed with robotic fabrication. Steps B-D are not evaluated in this process. The proposed model aims to enrich decision-making processes on material selection and performance of KRL-code by informing designers on the environmental impact of the fabrication processes.

MODEL

This study proposes a model called *Rob-LCA* as an answer for the New European Bauhaus [1] and the increasing use of robotic fabrication. *Rob-LCA* integrates the selected aspects: (i) potential of robotic fabrication, (ii) European Norm (EN15804) on The Life Cycle Assessment (LCA), (iii) manufacturing characteristics of diverse locations, (iv) material recycling potential. The methodology follows the agile strategy of product development and therefore the aspect selection and the process itself are evaluated constantly. The proposed model includes input, operation, output, and evaluation parts. The workflow of the proposed model is illustrated in Figure 2.

	Typical Lifecycle	Lifecycle with Robotic Fabrication	Notes
A1	Extraction of raw materials and production of pre-products		Based on information from the manufacturer
A2	Transport to the factory		
A3	Manufacturing	A3-1. Pre-product manufacturing (ex. panels)	Fabrication of standardized panels in the factory (mass or continuous production)
		A3-2. Transport to Digital Fabrication site	Transport from the factory/shop/etc. to the Fab Lab
		A3-3. Digital Fabrication	All the steps that are necessary for digital fabrication: milling, wire cutting, producing molds, use of non-robotic electric tools for the pre-preparation process.
A4	Transport to the construction site		Transport of cut panels/ elements/ components to the assembly location
A5	Construction installation process		On-site assembly, with or without robot
B	Use, maintenance, repair, replacement, refurbishment, operational energy use, operational water use		Since the tested model is a temporary structure the operation phase does not require additional resources
C	De-constructions, demolition, transport, waste-processing, disposal		Not quantified in this study since it focuses on the fabrication process, although recycling and reuse plays an important role comparing the life cycle of biodegradable and not biodegradable materials.
D	Re-use, recovery, recycling potential		

Table 1
Comparison of typical and proposed LCA frameworks

Model Set-Up

Input. The inputs of the *Rob-LCA* are divided into two categories as design data and parameters. In the scope of this paper, while design data refers to general data on a panel design and geometry, provided by the designer; parameters include numeric data specific to location and materials production process and availability (Figure 2).

Design Data:

- *Fabrication material:* 3D model of the raw material block from which a panel would be fabricated, including fabrication position
- *Design:* 3D Grasshopper model of the intended panel design
- *Robot settings:* robot's manufacturer settings such as speed, energy consumption for operation, waiting, and rest.
- *End effector settings:* setting of the end effector corresponding to a fabrication process such as position, shape, size, orientation, energy consumption (for electrical effectors)

Parameters:

- *Local data:* information on fabrication place and

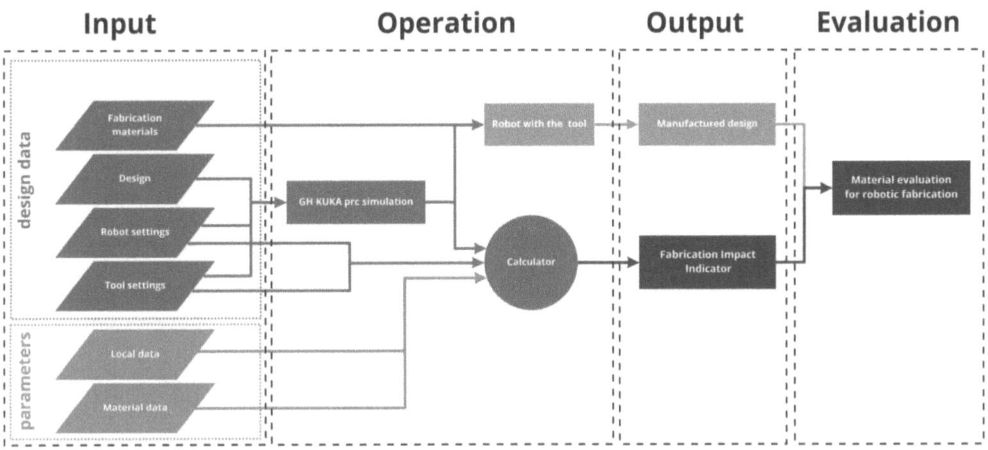

Figure 2
Framework of the proposed model

regional electricity mix (indicator for the source of energy-based various fuels used to generate electricity)
- *Material Data:* information on the material used for fabrication based on Environmental Product Declaration (EPD) of the manufacturer, if not available regional or national data

Operation.
- *KUKA|prc:* KUKA|prc is a parametric modeling environment that enables to program and simulate KUKA robots in the Rhinoceros/Grasshopper environment without the need for any other software. KUKA|prc translates design decision and fabrication intents, combining data on the robot's (with an end effector) movements and settings to generate KRL-code.
- *Robot with an end effector:* KUKA robot fabricating (milling, hot wire cutting) the panel.
- *Calculator:* the tool proposed in this paper that evaluates the environmental impact indicator, which is based on the impact of the material and fabrication processes.

Output.
- *Manufactured design:* the final product of the fabrication process
- *Environmental Impact Indicator:* indicator explaining the environmental impact of the fabrication processes, material's accuracy for the fabrication process, and recycling potential.

Evaluation.
- *Material evaluation for robotic fabrication:* the evaluation of the process, done by the designer to decide whether materials, tools, and tool settings, time, environmental impact are satisfactory for the designed object.

TESTING THE CALCULATOR FOR SELECTED MATERIALS

The calculator is a Grasshopper prototype of the proposed model. To build a prototype of a calculator a specific set of input data, operation and output are defined (Figure 3). The calculation does not include information on the initial material tests and experiments. It looks only at the production of a panel using a ready and tested definition. The output of the calculator completes the fabrication process with output data.

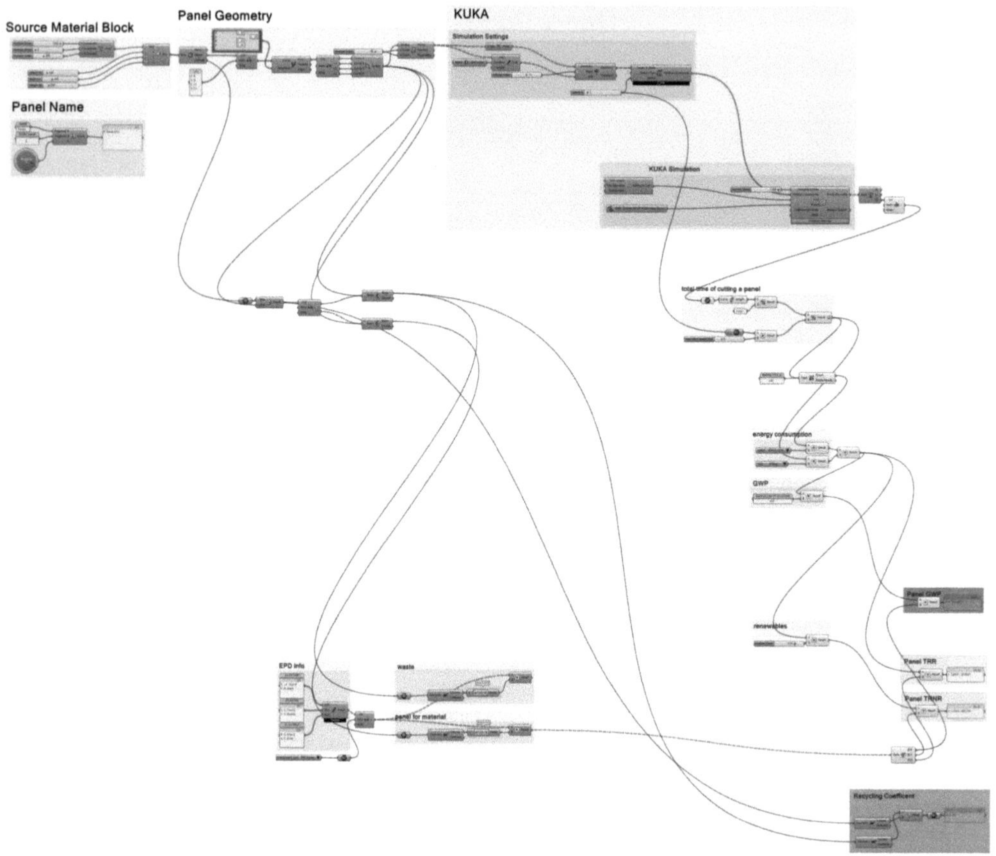

Figure 3
Grasshopper definition of the calculator

In this section, we presented a direct application of the calculator to a robotic fabrication case. The case is a small-scale prototype called *CorkCrete Arch* designed and fabricated by the DFL, and which was described by Sousa, Martins, and Varela (2016). This structure was made of two materials -ICB and GRC-, with the panels of the later produced out of EPS formworks. The two materials are used together with the intention to combine both sustainability and structural performance. *CorkCrete Arch* was designed to be assembled and disassembled, which allowed to be exhibited in different sites and venues (Sousa et al., 2016). To keep the sustainability of the materials in mind, we performed the first test of the calculator based on ICB and EPS materials used in the prototype (Figure 4). The information on the LCA of ICB and EPS comes from the producer itself and was verified by a third-party assessor and published in the Environmental Product Declaration (EPD) [3,4] (Pargana, 2012).

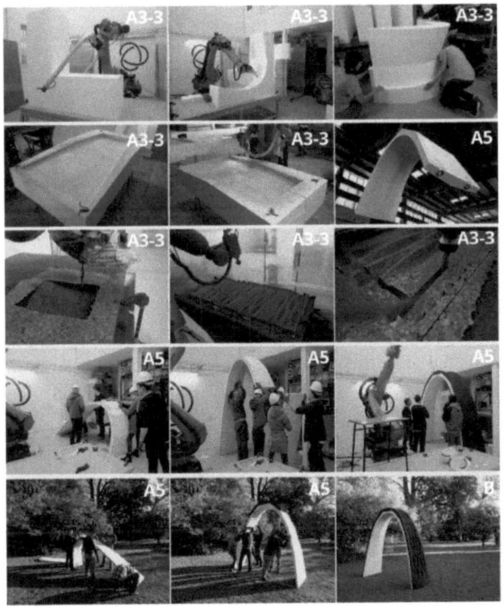

Figure 4
Photos from the steps of the life cycle (fabrication, construction, and use) (Figure reproduced from Sousa et al., 2016)

According to the project leaders (Sousa et al., 2016), the robotic fabrication process of stage A3 of the ICB blocks, which were supplied by Amorim Cork Insulation, explored a sequence of subtractive milling operations (Figure 4). The blocks, 1000x500 mm, of different thicknesses, ranging from 80 mm to 140 mm (to minimize waste material) were milled with the KUKA KR120 HA r2700 by a wide tool with an end shaped as a paraboloid of revolution. The molds of the GRC panels were produced from combinations of 1000x500x500mm high-density EPS blocks, cut with a 1000 mm wide hot-wire bow, featuring a 0.25 mm thick wire.

Based on the framework and Grasshopper definition commented before (Figures 2, 3), the diagram shows the functioning principles of the calculator (Figure 5). Design data are related to the actual panel design, robot type, and its characteristics, fabrication process, and tool. Parameters data are based on the Portuguese energy mix and the material EPD. These input data are distributed into three flows: KUKA|prc, Embodied Material Environmental Impact, and Embodied Energy Material Impact to calculate final indicators. As an output, three values are received Recycling Index, which informs on the amount of material that could be used for recycling, Panel Energy Consumption, which shows how much renewable and nonrenewable energy was necessary to produce such panel from stage A1, and Panel Environmental Impact indicating how much Greenhouse Gas (GHG) are emitted in the production process (Figure 5).

For the initial test presented in Figure 5, two materials, two techniques, and two end effectors (robotic milling for ICB and robotic hot wire cutting for EPS) are included (Figure 4). However, changing such inputs of the model does not change the workflow given in Figure 2 and Figure 5. Instead, it changes values at any stage of calculation including output values. Since the aim of this study is to develop the model *Rob-LCA*, this study is not focused on comparing conventional fabrication processes with robotic fabrication. In the development phase of the *Rob-LCA*, the model does not support the material selection of the previously fabricated *CorkCrete Arch*. However, our documentation (design data, material

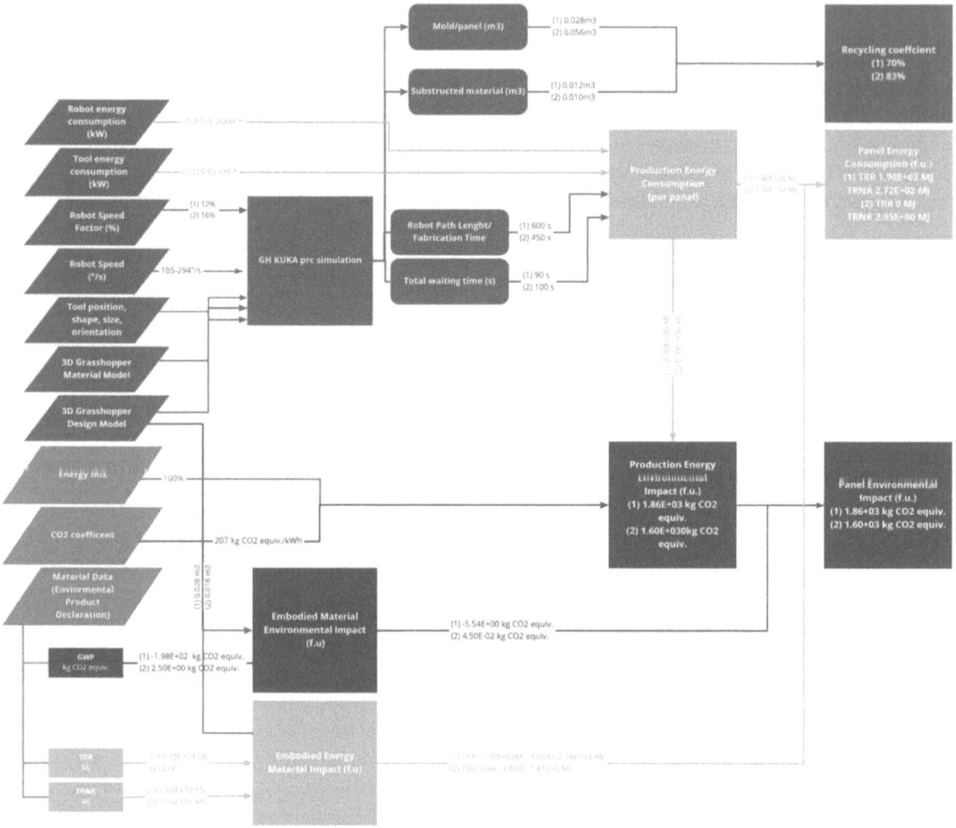

Figure 5
Stage A3-3 of fabrication of (1) ICB panels and (2) EPS moulds

data, robot, tool settings, transportation, assembly, use, etc.) about the life cycle of the *CorkCrete Arch* helped to test the calculator.

Calculator Prototype

The calculator prototype in Grasshopper combines information supported by the designer and KUKA|prc plug-in. Following the principles of agile software development, it is the first iteration of a tool that would be tested in the upcoming fabrication process, all elements of the method would be assessed: input, operation, and output to verify whether all the elements were taken into consideration, the relevance of each of inputs or intuitive use. It is a prototype for future development that could transform into a Grasshopper plug-in.

The calculator is complementing an existing process. Hence, for the first prototype of the calculator, not all data were accessible, such as waiting time or actual robot energy consumption; some approximations were made to verify whether the first iteration is missing inputs or other elements.

The calculator does not recommend a material but enables and facilitates assessing its environmental impact and comparing it with others. The material selection process is much more complex and does not only depend on the environmental impact of materials but also on the availability of material, availability of tools, skills, and experience of the designer. The calculator informs the designer on the environmental impact of the process itself and encourages focusing on the material and manufacturing information. Two materials of the same type (e.g. cork) could have a different environmental impact depending on the manufacturing technique, the quality of material that might reflect in fabrication processes.

CONCLUSION AND FUTURE WORKS

This paper presents an assessment model to evaluate environmental-sensitive material selection for robotic fabrication. The main reason to focus on robotic fabrication is that robotic fabrication is the most complex of digital fabrication techniques and the most automated, and it can produce shapes and forms using materials that are not available to other techniques. Such a fabrication method is flexible to different techniques and materials.

The purpose of the calculator is not to speed up the process but to make it more informed by giving suggestions to the designer about the environmental impact of the materials and fabrication techniques. The aim of the calculator aligns with the strategies used in EPD which is to compare different materials not to give thresholds. In our proposal, it is equivalent to compare various fabrication techniques and materials at the same time. The model can be applied to other prototypes fabricated with robots (single or multiple materials having EPD). The model does not have to be applied to built prototypes and can be used starting from pre-fabrication phases (conceptual) of design.

The future work includes developing a plug-in or an add-on that can be integrated with both CAD and robot operating software. The proposed calculator equips the designer with detailed data on fabrication with selected material and allows comparison between different materials and fabrication techniques. Such a tool encourages the industry to evaluate their products, produce EPD, and integrate databases that could be used in BIM and fabrication processes. So far the database is scattered, poorly digitized, and hard to navigate. Integration for each country or region to create a transparent, easy to compare database of materials is a substantial challenge. Another database, comparing different fabrication techniques from the point of view of their impact on the environment could be established, it might include both panel fabrication (stage A3) and assembly of pieces (stage A5).

Although embodied energy and carbon of the presented materials play a minor role in the environmental impact of a panel, it doesn't mean that it should be marginalized, once the production process is more efficient embodied energy and carbon should diminish due to changes of materials. The fabrication process should be optimized and planned carefully to measure the impact of the prototypes. Energy-efficient KRL-codes and the use of renewable energy to power the robot are crucial to diminish GHG emissions and energy consumption.

ACKNOWLEDGEMENT

This research has the financial support of FCT, within the project UID/AUR/00145/2019. The current research activities of Orkan Zeynel Güzelci are supported by The Scientific and Technological Research Council of Turkey (Grant no: 1059B191900560).

REFERENCES

Agustí-Juan, I and Habert, G 2017, 'Environmental design guidelines for digital fabrication', *Journal of Cleaner Production*, 142, pp. 2780-2791

Agustí-Juan, I, Müller, F, Wangler, T and Habert, G 2017, 'Potential benefits of digital fabrication for complex structures: Environmental assessment of a robotically fabricated concrete wall', *Journal of Cleaner Production*, 154, pp. 330-340

Bragança, L and Mateus, R 2012, *Life-cycle analysis of buildings: environmental impact of building elements*,

Associação iiSBE Portugal
Bryan, C, Grenwalt, M and Stienecker, A 2010 'Energy consumption reduction in industrial robots', *Proceedings of ASEE North Central Sectional Conference*, Pittsburgh, PA, pp. 3C1-3C4
Cerdas, F, Juraschek, M, Thiede, S and Herrmann, C 2017, 'Life cycle assessment of 3D printed products in a distributed manufacturing system', *Journal of Industrial Ecology*, 21 (S1), pp. S80-S93
Chemnitz, M, Schreck, G and Krüger, J 2011 'Analyzing energy consumption of industrial robots', *ETFA2011*, Toulouse, France, pp. 1-4
Crawley, D and Aho, I 1999, 'Building environmental assessment methods: applications and development trends', *Building Research & Information*, 27 (4-5), pp. 300-308
Fernandes, J, Peixoto, M, Mateus, R and Gervásio, H 2019, 'Life cycle analysis of environmental impacts of earthen materials in the Portuguese context: Rammed earth and compressed earth blocks', *Journal of Cleaner Production*, 241, p. 118286
Gadaleta, M, Pellicciari, M and Berselli, G 2019, 'Optimization of the energy consumption of industrial robots for automatic code generation', *Robotics and Computer-Integrated Manufacturing*, 57, pp. 452-464
Meike, D and Ribickis, L 2011 'Analysis of the energy efficient usage methods of medium and high payload industrial robots in the automobile industry', *10th International Symposium - Topical Problems in the Field of Electrical and Power Engineering*, Pärnu, Estonia, pp. 62-66
Pargana, NGSC 2012, *Environmental impacts of the life cycle of thermal insulation materials of buildings*, Master's Thesis, Tecnico Lisboa
de Soto, BG, Agustí-Juan, I, Hunhevicz, J, Joss, S, Graser, K, Habert, G and Adey, BT 2018, 'Productivity of digital fabrication in construction: Cost and time analysis of a robotically built wall', *Automation in Construction*, 92, pp. 297-311
Sousa, JP, Martins, P and Varela, PA 2016 'The CorkCrete Arch Project', *Proceedings of 21st International Conference of the Association for Computer-Aided Architectural Design Research in Asia CAADRIA 2016*, Hong Kong, p. 735–744.
Thormark, C 2002, 'A low energy building in a life cycle—its embodied energy, energy need for operation and recycling potential', *Building and Environment*, 37 (4), pp. 429-435
[1] https://op.europa.eu/en/publication-detail/-/publication/9903b325-6388-11ea-b735-01aa75ed71a1/language-en
[2] https://op.europa.eu/en/publication-detail/-/publication/319e1d6f-18cd-11eb-b57e-01aa75ed71a1
[3] https://www.environdec.com/all-about-epds
[4] https://daphabitat.pt/en_US/home/

Computer-Aided Fabrication Technologies as Computational Design Mediators

Ayça Sönmez[1]*, Arzu Gönenç Sorguç*[2]
[1,2]*Middle East Technical University*
[1,2]*{sonmez.ayca|arzug}@metu.edu.tr*

The developments in recent technologies through Industry 4.0 lead to the integration of digital design and manufacturing processes. Albeit manufacturing continues to increase its importance as design input, it is generally considered at the last stages of the design process. This misconception results in a gap between digital design and fabrication, leading to differences between the initial design and the fabricated outcome in the context of architectural tectonics. Here, we present an artificial intelligence (AI)-based approach that aims to provide a basis to bridge the gap between computation and fabrication. We considered a case study of a 3D model in two stages. In the first stage, an intuitive and top-down design process is adopted, and in the second stage, an AI-based exploration is conducted with three cases derived from the same 3D model. The outcomes of the two stages provided a dataset including different design parameters to be used in a decision tree classifier algorithm which selects the manufacturing method for a given 3D model. Our results show that generative design simulations based on manufacturing constraints can provide a significant variety of manufacturable design alternatives, and minimizes the difference between design alternatives. Using our proposed approach, the time spent in form-finding and fabrication can be reduced significantly. Additionally, the implementation of decision tree classifier learning algorithm shows that AI can serve designers to make accurate predictions for manufacturing method.

Keywords: *Generative Design, Computer-Aided Fabrication, Arcihtecture 4.0, Artificial Intelligence, Digital Tectonics*

INTRODUCTION

The advents of 3rd industrial revolution changed how architects design and fabricate, with new concepts such as computational design, file-to-factory and mass customization. Although these concepts are well-embraced in the field of architecture, "file-to-factory" is mostly an iterative process, and if fabrication is left to the final stages of design process, these iterations can lead to modifications and even a complete change of the initial design. With the advents of Industry 4.0 adapting file to factory becomes more important as design and manufacturing processes start to be integrated. Therefore, architects should recognize fabrication related constraints and potentials in the very initial phases of design processes and in form-finding explorations. With the recent improvements in AI and intelligent manufacturing, design processes can learn from manufacturing data to provide several manufacturable design instances, which can help connecting design and fabrication processes, and preventing tectonic change of the initial model.

This paper aims to provide an exploration of the gap between digital and physical processes, by a bottom-up design approach with generating and evaluating design alternatives through AI based environments. Through this exploration it is aimed to show the importance of a holistic design process, which can be trained by manufacturing constraints.

Background

In order to understand the problem and provide a solution, related research is surveyed in three main headings, which are the technologies that can overcome this problem, impacts on architectural tectonics with accuracy and precision, and lastly, a holistic design process.

Technologies and Implementation. The technologies that can provide an integrated design-manufacturing process are examined in three main headings: Generative design, Cyber-physical systems (CPS) and Machine learning (ML), which are interlocked with each other. CPSs and ML are used in several steps in used in manufacturing (Monostori et al., 2016; Lee et al., 2015) such as design, process planning and modeling, quality control and robotics. (Monostori et al., 1996) Additionally, ML can be placed between design and fabrication data, and between fabrication data and fabrication processes. (Ramsgaard Thomsen et al., 2020) In between design and fabrication data, algorithms can provide the simulation of fabrication, or form-finding, and in the second placement it enables machine to learn from the fabrication process and give feedback. While these applications can be implemented to robotic fabrication easily, it might not be applicable when a sensor-based environment is not available. In this sense, generative design becomes an applicable approach in initial design phases, since it can produce a large variety of design alternatives under manufacturing constraints prior to fabrication, and it is seen to be efficient in time and material use. (Wu et al., 2019; Akella, 2018) Another advantage of such approach is that it can be achieved and run through a network with cloud computing, without the use of advanced scripting or computer power.

Architectural Tectonics. Initial design change between computation and fabrication can be considered as a tectonic change. Therefore, architectural tectonics is becoming a main concern of this research. It is mainly impacted by algorithm and fabrication. Usually, the translation between these two stages of design creates accuracy and precision problems. The impact of fabrication is seen to be mainly dependent on the fabrication techniques or principles that are used (Dunn, 2012; Iwamoto, 2013). The effect of algorithm, on the other hand, provides a freedom in design complexity and form-finding. However, the transition between algorithm and fabrication creates a challenge of bringing digital designs into the physical world. This challenge creates in-between concepts such as digital tectonics (Leach, 2009) and digital materiality, since computationally designed forms have physically solved details, and if the physical details are not solved in the computational stages, this challenge can result in accuracy and precision problems. These problems can be due to manufacturing tolerances (Loh, 2015), but also from neglecting physical aspects of design. Knowing the manufacturing assets or designing for manufacturing can provide advantages to the designer such as efficient time use and reduced cost (Selvaraj et al, 2009), increased precision, or turning manufacturing limitations to improve several aspects of design (Gosselin et al., 2016) To conclude, with manufacturing constraints, initial design starts to compromise, and neglecting the fabrication technique or machine tolerances can result in change of design.

Holistic Design Process. Design problems are usually multi-dimensional and include the design of the process in addition to the end product. Therefore, it can be claimed that it is not possible to design without thinking of material aspects. However, sometimes, the computational design freedom can mislead the designer that anything in the cyber space can be constructed physically, which is due to the separation of cyber and physical making.

To overcome these issues, fabrication can be defined as an initial design input. When it is considered at the last stage with a top-down approach, fabrication process is iterated several times and intermediary steps in the process cause data and material loss. On the other hand, a bottom-up approach can provide a more holistic method in design process as design alternatives include fabrication concerns, and manufacturability of design alternatives can be increased with eliminating intermediary steps. Additionally, all of the design process can be achieved in a single digital ecosystem such as BIM environments to prevent data loss during data conversion processes.

Since selecting the manufacturing method is important in initial design phase, the use of decision support algorithms can help designers in this manner. As manufacturing data is usually multi-faceted, which includes both qualitative and quantitative data, decision tree classifiers are beneficial in such tasks (Priyanka & Kumar, 2020) Decision tree classifiers are used in manufacturing method selection including historical case-based approaches and rapid prototyping methods (Evans et al., 2013; Park & Tran, 2017) They can be studied further in architectural fabrication for suggesting a manufacturing method for the designer to evaluate.

RESEARCH METHOD

This research is comprised of two phases. In the first one, a top-down approach is adopted by fabricating a predesigned form with four fabrication techniques. The outcomes of this phase are fabricated models, and fabrication limitations which led us to a dataset including several parameters for selection of the manufacturing method.

In the second phase we used Autodesk's Fusion 360's generative design space to obtain design alternatives for the same form with three cases and obtained mass volume relations, as well as an assessment for design instances. We created a dataset similar to the first one to train a decision tree classifier algorithm with open-source programming through scikit.learn and used the data from the first phase for comparison.

CASE STUDIES, RESULTS AND DISCUSSION

The objectives, results and the discussion of the results for each phase are presented in detail as follows. In this two-phase experiment, we obtained fabrication limitations, parameters in selection of the manufacturing method, mass-volume relations, and datasets to train the decision tree classifier.

Phase I: Explorations on a Predesigned Form

In the first phase, a top-down and intuitive approach is employed to observe fabrication limitations and tectonic changes. In this phase, the 3D model is designed as a modular wall structure without any material or fabrication constraints. Then it is fabricated with four different manufacturing methods and materials which are tessellating-2D laser cutting with cardboard, 3D printing with ABS plastic, sectioning-2D laser cutting with MDF, and 2.5 axis CNC milling with Styrofoam. The objectives, details of each technique in terms of materials and file formats, and outcomes of this phase are demonstrated in Figure 1. After the fabrication phase, 1 each random assembly units are selected for the decision tree classifier dataset as a base for the real-life case.

For each fabrication technique, limitations are listed as below:

Tessellating: It is the most accurate design alternative compared to the initial design due to being an assembly. However, stability problems are encountered due to improper detailing.

3D Printing: The fabrication process is iterated

several times due to the model being too slender, and the final outcome became very bulky in the end due to modifications.

Sectioning: This design alternative could not be fabricated due to stability issues caused by improper detailing. It had to be eliminated without further explorations because the nesting and assembling processes were done by hand, which caused a significant loss in time and material.

CNC Milling (2.5 axis): It was the most practical method compared to the others. However, the double curvature and the voids of the initial design are lost.

There are three main points derived from the first phase of this study. Firstly, when fabrication is not considered, initial design changes and can even become completely different in terms of tectonics. Secondly, not considering fabrication details can cause structural stability problems, which can even lead designer to quit some design alternatives, which leads to the last point: The number of design alternatives are limited, and not all of them are constructable.

Phase II: AI-Based Explorations

In the second phase of the explorations, an AI-based generative design approach is applied into the same 3D model from the first phase. The aim of this phase is to eliminate iterative actions in form-finding by setting manufacturing inputs at the initial stages of design, and to increase the number of design alternatives through generative design process running in a cloud network. This phase consists of a setup formed by design space, constraints and loads, manufacturing assets, and generative design objectives.

Design space: The design space includes preserve geometries that are kept in outcome generation, obstacle geometries for defining voids, and a starting shape for topology optimization process, or keeping the initial design. The intended design space came out with errors, which can be due to the iteration limits of the program that is used in this study. Therefore, the study is extended into three cases.

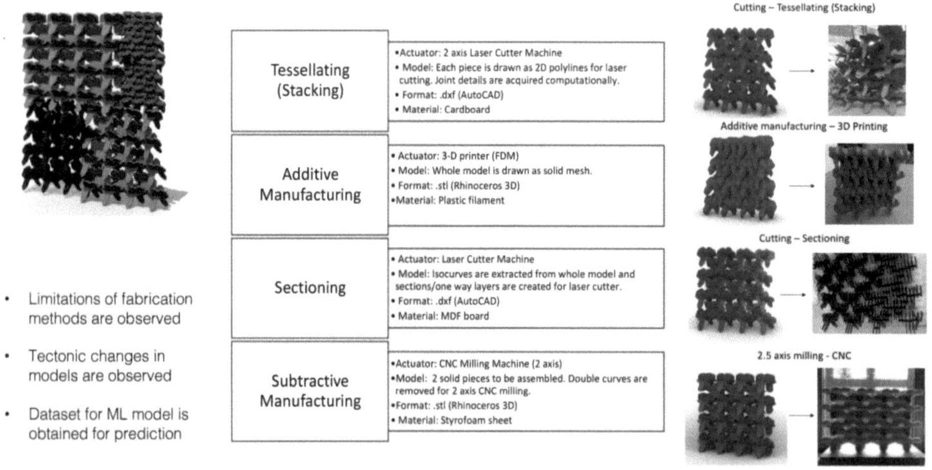

Figure 1
Objectives, fabrication methods and outcomes of Phase I

Figure 2
Intended design space and extended cases

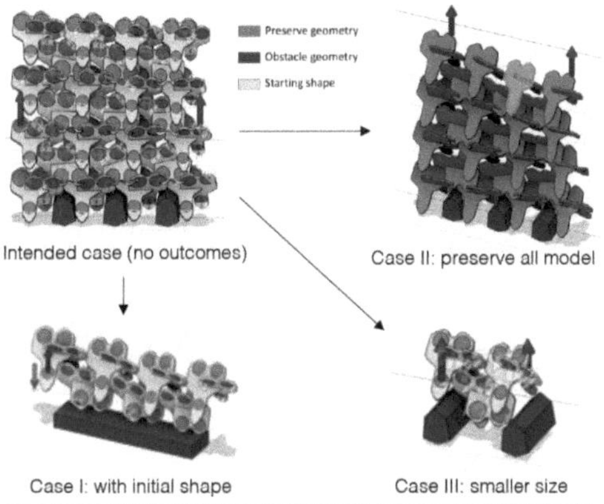

Table 1
Manufacturing assets

Manufacturing	
Tools	**Setup**
Unrestricted	Unrestricted
3D Printing	Overhead angle: 45 degrees Minimum mat. Thickness: 2 mm
2.5 axis milling	Tool diameter: 3 mm Tool direction: Y (Including reverse sides)
Cutting	Tool direction: Y
3 axis milling:	Tool diameter: 3 mm Shoulder length: 4 cm (default) Head diameter: 6 cm (default) Tool direction: X+ Y (+-) Z+ (Including reverse sides)
5 axis milling:	Tool diameter: 3 mm Shoulder length: 4 cm (default) Head diameter: 6 cm (default) Tool direction: Unrestricted

Materials
ABS Plastic
MDF
Aluminum (AlSi10Mg)
Expanded Polystyrene Foam
Thermoplastic Resin

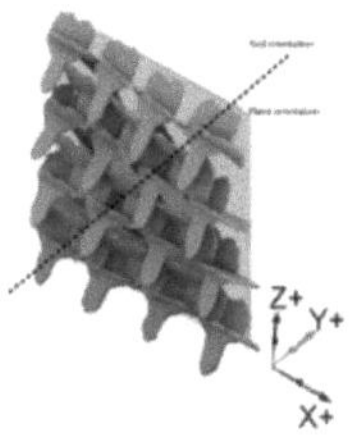

Tool orientation (CNC)

Manufacturing assets: Manufacturing methods and materials are listed as presented in Table 1. Unrestricted means there is no defined fabrication method and the algorithm is free in outcome generation. Additionally, we used 2.5, 3 and 5 axis milling, 2 axis cutting and 3D printing. For materials; ABS Plastic, MDF and Styrofoam are selected since they are used in the first phase. Additionally, aluminum is added to explore with metals, and thermoplastic resin is added to explore with an elastic material.

Structural inputs: Structural constraints are placed at the boundaries of the preserve geometry, and the forces are set opposite to the gravity as the main concern is independent from a stress-strain analysis.

Generative design objectives: Based on the program defaults, the generative design objective is set as minimizing mass with a factor of safety limit of 2.

The generative design process is completed with 3217 iterations, and 135 different design alternatives are obtained from three cases. Some cases have failed outcomes, which can be dependent to program's iteration limits. Additionally, while some outcomes are completed successfully, there are incomplete outcomes that are overfitting, which are converging generative design objectives with few iterations and stop producing details. To compare the three cases in a broader frame, they share some common objectives, but their scale and main objectives differ. The time to obtain design alternatives change from 1 hour to 1 day.

The common objectives of the three cases are listed as below:

- To observe manufacturing and material's effects on initial design and architectural tectonics
- To investigate mass-volume relations per manufacturing methods and materials
- To obtain a dataset for decision tree classifier

Each case is presented in detail with their objectives, outcomes and mass-volume graphs.

Case I: Partial Model with Starting Shape. The first case is a partial configuration of the intended design space. The aim is to observe the design alternatives and mass-volume relations when a starting shape is included in the generative design space. Figure 3 shows the objectives and the outcomes of this case.

In this design space configuration, 15 design alternatives could not be generated, which can be due to iteration limits of the program that is used. The remaining 35 outcomes are generated successfully, without overfitting.

The mass-volume / material graph shows that the lowest mass and volume is in XPS and the highest is in aluminum. This shows that, mass is increasing with the material density as expected, independently from any manufacturing method. Volume, on the other hand, seems directly to be dependent to the manufacturing method. When two extreme cases of materials (aluminum and XPS) are examined closely with design alternatives, it is seen that, as manufacturing method becomes more restrictive, such as cutting or milling, void properties of initial design is lost. Thus, the volume increases. Also, detail generation varies dependent to material.

Case II: Full Model as Preserve Geometry. Case II includes the full model as preserve geometry instead of a starting shape. The objectives are similar to the first case, but here, the goal is to observe design changes when all of the model is preserved. Figure 4 shows the objectives and the outcomes of this case.

Except the scale, outcomes are similar to the first case, as preserve geometry acts like a starting shape. Differing from the first case, here, some instances are incomplete by converging objectives with low iterations, which can mean it is overfitting, and cannot generate further details.

Additionally, the outcomes show that the level of detail decreases when all of the model is preserved, which can be due to structural concerns. Mass-volume graphs are similar to the first case in distribution and alignment, but on a closer look the highest mass and volume is seen in aluminum 3D printing which can be due to overfitting.

Case III: A Few Units from Intended Case. In the last case, four modules of the intended case are studied. The objectives are the same with Case I and II, but the aim is to observe the level of detail. Figure 5 shows the objectives and the outcomes of this case.

This case has the most precise design alternatives as outcomes. Mass-volume graphs are similar to the first two cases as the manufacturing method becomes restrictive voids are lost. Yet, detail precision seems to be highest, and even in restrictive methods such as cutting, it was able to create some voids. This case shows that as the scale gets smaller, the algorithm can focus more on detail generation.

For analyzing the outcomes of the three cases, we grouped the outcomes according to their visual similarity. When considered together with the mass-volume graphs, it is observed that visual similarity and volume are directly dependent to the manufacturing method, whereas mass is correlated with the material selection. Additionally, it is seen that the generative design algorithm can work more on the details if the model is comprised of few modules. The outcomes can be assessed per different criteria for deciding on the design instance. Table 2 shows an example of this instance assessment.

In Table 2, it can be observed that each criterion changes the initial design prior to fabrication. For example, if accuracy is the main concern, 3D printing and 5 axis milling can be used with any material of choice. But when we consider availability or economic constraints, it is more feasible to manufacture it through materials like MDF and XPS and with cutting or milling. In order to keep accuracy and detail level, it can be fabricated as assemblies. But if the ease of fabrication is the main concern, assembly logic can be given up. To consider material waste, subtractive methods can be eliminated.

The variations of these design alternatives show that when a design goal is defined, the initial design starts to compromise with fabrication constraints. Therefore, it can be said that the dialogue between computation and fabrication has a potential to reconfigure the design. Knowing this prior to fabrica-

Figure 3
Outcome matrix of Case I

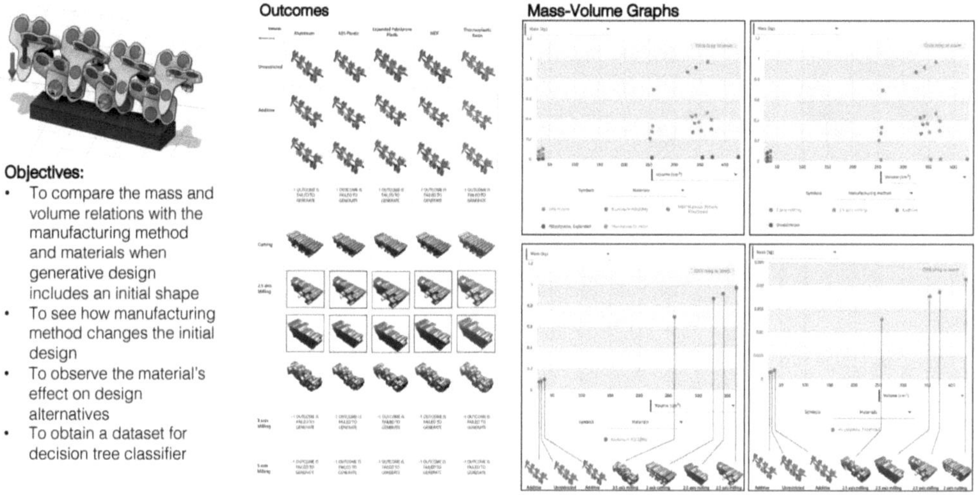

Figure 4
Outcome matrix of Case II

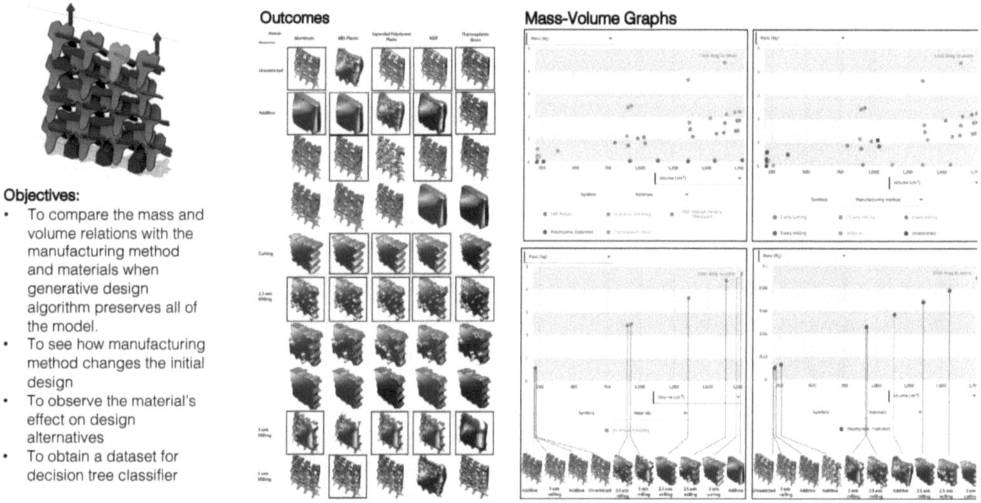

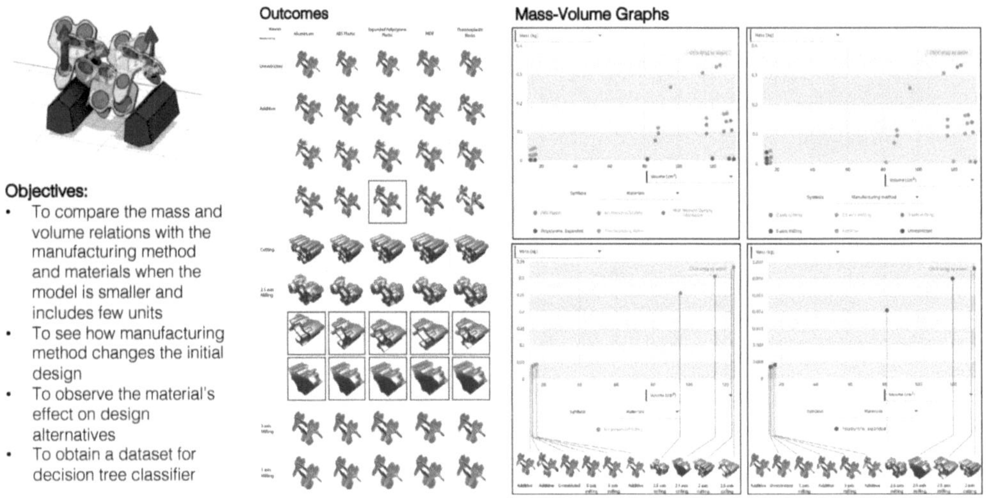

Figure 5
Outcome matrix of Case III

Table 2
Instance assessment

Intended design instance	Initial experiments	Instance per design and fabrication constrains							
		Accuracy	Manufacturing Availability	Material Availability	Ease of Fabrication	Cost	Manufacturing Time	Detail Precision	Material Waste
		ABS Plastic 3D Printing (as assembly unit)	MDF 2.5 axis milling (as assembly unit)	ABS Plastic 3D Printing (as assembly unit)	ABS Plastic 3D Printing	MDF 2 axis cutting (as assembly unit)	MDF 2 axis cutting	Aluminum 5 axis milling (as assembly unit)	ABS Plastic 3D Printing
		Aluminum 3D Printing	ABS Plastic 3D Printing (as assembly unit)	MDF 3 axis milling (as assembly unit)	XPS 2.5 axis milling	XPS 2 axis cutting (as assembly unit)	XPS 2.5 axis milling	ABS Plastic 3D Printing (as assembly unit)	Aluminum 3D Printing (as assembly unit)
		MDF 5 axis milling (as assembly unit)	MDF 2 axis cutting (as assembly unit)	XPS 2.5 axis milling (as assembly unit)	XPS 5 axis milling	MDF 2 axis cutting	XPS 2 axis cutting	Thermoplastic Resin 3D Printing (as assembly unit)	Aluminum 3D Printing (as assembly unit)

tion can make the end product less surprising. If the initial study were to be designed from the start, the design stages would include form-finding with generative systems, instance assessment by evaluation of design criteria and alternatives, and finally checking the model in terms of computer model aspects like file format for fabrication. With this flow, a second form-finding phase between design and fabrication can be eliminated. Thus, initial design changes can be prevented.

Implementation of AI to Decision Making. Design alternatives that are obtained through Fusion 360 are used to construct a dataset to train a decision tree classifier algorithm through scikit.learn. The dataset which is fitted to the ML model comprises of 10 different parameters, which gives an idea about material characteristics, and model complexity. Model parameters are given in Table 3.

Table 3
Parameters in decision tree classifier dataset

MFR Method (Label Parameter)	Above listed manufacturing methods are noted for each 3D model. It is the label parameter for classifier algorithm.
Material density (g/cm^3)	Density of selected material
Young's Modulus (GPa)	Elasticity of selected material
Volume (cm^3)	Volume of the selected design instance
Mass (kg)	Mass of the selected design instance
Planarity (bool)	Set as true (1) if the 3D model is planar
Model depth (cm)	Measured as the depth of the bounding box of the 3D model
Edge quantity (ea)	Mesh edge quantity as joint curves
Reverse sides (bool)	Set as true (1) if the model has reverse sides
Multi-axis (bool)	Set as true (1) if the model allows multi-axis machining

Table 4
Comparison of ML predictions and real life cases

Status	Outcome 1	Outcome 2	Outcome 3	Outcome 4
Data from 1st phase	Additive	2.5 axis milling	Cutting	Cutting
Prediction	5 axis milling	2.5 axis milling	Cutting	Cutting

The aim here is to provide an AI-based tool to help the designer to select the suitable manufacturing method based on 3D model surface and manufacturing data. Failed outcomes, and the ones that are labeled as "unrestricted" are excluded from the dataset which resulted in a dataset formed from 120 different design alternatives.

The machine learning model is evaluated through classification accuracy metrics by training the ML model through a stratified 5 fold cross validation, where the train-test process is iterated 5 times with shuffling and splitting the data into different combinations of 4 training and 1 testing clusters. The mean accuracy is obtained as 88%. Additionally, Table 4 presents the comparison of real-life cases from Phase I and ML-predicted outcomes, which shows the algorithm predicted 75% of the outcomes correct.

The importance of the comparison shown in Table 4 is that it shows while the algorithm is successful in predicting more restrictive methods such as cutting or 2.5 axis milling, as the model and manufacturing method gets more complex, it selected a different method than the initial study. This can mean the dataset needs to be more elaborated, but it can also mean that the model prepared for 3D printing is actually more suitable for 5 axis milling. Since it is a bit challenging to obtain structured data in this field, the data obtained is limited, and we cannot make any generalization. However, this experiment shows that AI can provide suggestions for manufacturing method in the initial design phases.

CONCLUSION

To conclude, in this paper, it is aimed to explore the gap between computational design and fabrication processes, and to present a design approach, which can learn from the manufacturing constraints, and provide suggestions to the designer. The problem is examined with two phases of experiments.

The first set of study which is referred as intuitive shows the problems when manufacturing considerations are not included in the design phase. This case clearly shows how fabrication techniques and principles in terms of 3D model parameters effecting the proper choice of fabrication process and thus, how intended model is evolving and under the control of fabrication rather than the designer.

In the second, AI-based phase, the process included generative design approach to claim design alternatives, and it is observed a decrease in time that is spent in iterative cycles in design process through generative design algorithm running on a cloud network. Moreover, a decision tree classifier ML model is employed in order to make predictions for manufacturing method for future 3D models based on generative design outputs.

To conclude, compared to the top-down approach, AI-powered bottom-up approach showed that when manufacturing is taken as an initial input for design explorations, a large number of manufacturable design alternatives can be assessed before fabrication, which minimizes the difference between initial design and its instances. With this approach, the time spent in form-finding, and fabrication is reduced considerably. Also, our proposed approach shows that with cloud computing, a digital workflow can be achieved without the use of advanced scripting or computer power. Additionally, although the cases given in this study are not including all possible fabrication methods and/or possible materials, it is seen that by learning from design alternatives, artificial intelligence can serve designers to provide accurate predictions for manufacturing method.

The main limitation of this research is the challenge of finding structured data to train the decision tree classifier. For future research, the generative design study can be repeated with an extended dataset to achieve a more sophisticated decision support algorithm. Secondly, forming is excluded from the scope of this research, and it can be examined as a separate case study.

REFERENCES

Akella, R 2018, 'What Generative Design Is and Why It's the Future of Manufacturing', *New Equipment Digest*

Dunn, N 2012, *Digital Fabrication in Architecture*, Laurence King Publishing

Evans, L, Lohse, N and Summers, M 2013, 'A Fuzzy-Decision-Tree Approach for Manufacturing Technology Selection Exploiting Experience-Based Information', *Expert Systems with Applications*, 40(16), pp. 6412-6426

Gosselin, C, Duballet, R, Roux, P, Gaudillière, N, Dirrenberger, J and Morel, P 2016, 'Large-Scale 3D Printing of Ultra-High Performance Concrete – a New Processing Route for Architects and Builders', *Materials & Design*, 100, pp. 102-109

Iwamoto, L 2013, *Digital Fabrications: Architectural and Material Techniques*, Princeton Architectural Press

Leach, N 2009, 'Digital Morphogenesis', *Architectural Design*, 79(1), pp. 32-37

Lee, J, Bagheri, B and Kao, HA 2015, 'A Cyber-Physical Systems Architecture for Industry 4.0-Based Manufacturing Systems', *Manufacturing Letters*, 3, pp. 18-23

Loh, P 2015 'Articulated Timber Ground, Making Pavilion As Pedagogy', *Conference of the Association for Computer Aided Architectural Design Research in Asia*, Hong Kong

Monostori, L, Kádár, B, Bauernhansl, T, Kondoh, S, Kumara, S, Reinhart, G, Sauer, O, Schuh, G, Sihn, W and Ueda, K 2016, 'Cyber-Physical Systems in Manufacturing', *CIRP Annals*, 65(2), pp. 621-641

Monostori, L, Markus, A, Brussel, HV and Westkämpfer, E 1996, 'Machine Learning Approaches to Manufacturing', *CIRP Annals*, 45(2), pp. 675-712

Park, HS and Tran, NH 2017 'A Decision Support System for Selecting Additive Manufacturing Technologies', *Proceedings of the 2017 International Conference on Information System and Data Mining*, pp. 151-155

Priyanka, NA and Kumar, D 2020, 'Decision Tree Classifier: A Detailed Survey', *International Journal of Information and Decision Sciences*, 12(3), pp. 246-269

Selvaraj, P, Radhakrishnan, P and Adithan, M 2009, 'An Integrated Approach to Design for Manufacturing and Assembly based on Reduction of Product Development Time and Cost', *The International Journal of Advanced Manufacturing Technology*, 42, pp. 13-29

Ramsgaard Thomsen, M, Nicholas, P, Tamke, M, Gatz, S, Sinke, Y and Rossi, G 2020, 'Towards Machine Learning for Architectural Fabrication in the Age of Industry 4.0', *International Journal of Architectural Computing*, p. 1478077120948000

Wu, J, Qian, X and Wang, MY 2019, 'Advances in Generative Design', *Comput. Aided Des*, 116(102733)

Performance based design

EvoMass + GH_Wind

An agile wind-driven building massing design optimization framework

Yuhui Shen[1], Likai Wang[2], Ran Zhang[3], Ziyu Tong[4], Guohua Ji[5]
[1,2,4,5]Nanjing University [3]Southeast University
[1]mg1936020@smail.nju.edu.cn [2,3]{wang.likai|ran.zhang.liverpool}@outlook.com [4,5]{tzy|jgh}@nju.edu.cn

The complex interactive relationship between wind flow and building design poses a great challenge in architectural design. Recent research has been conducted to combine Computational Fluid Dynamics (CFD) and computational design optimization to solve the problem. However, due to the time-consuming simulation process and the assertion-oriented computational optimization application, such CFD-based design optimization frameworks are not easy to integrate with architects' early-stage design exploration. To address these issues, this paper proposes an agile wind-driven building massing design optimization framework incorporating EvoMass and GH_Wind in the Rhino-Grasshopper environment. EvoMass is an integrated evolutionary building massing design tool, and GH_Wind is a simulation tool embedded with a Fast Fluid Dynamics (FFD) solver. Combining these two tools allows for fast wind-driven design optimization, thereby enabling architects to apply it to early-stage design exploration. To demonstrate its efficacy, a case study is presented to illustrate how the proposed design optimization framework can provide architects with useful design information and, thereby, facilitate more performance-informed design for early-stage architectural design.

Keywords: *building massing design, performance-based design, design exploration, wind-driven design, Fast Fluid Dynamics, design optimization*

INTRODUCTION

Performance-based design optimization is becoming a popular application of computational design in architecture, which combines parametric modeling, building performance simulation, and computational optimization. Recent research has demonstrated that performance-based design optimization can be an efficient and powerful tool assisting architects in build massing design and provide pertinent performance-oriented information useful to future design and construction. While performance factors such as daylighting, solar irradiation, and energy consumption have been widely investigated in relevant research (Negendahl & Nielsen, 2015; Likai Wang, Janssen, Chen, Tong, & Ji, 2019; Yi & Malkawi, 2012), studies focused on wind-related factors are relatively rare. It is because conducting a wind-driven design optimization is challenging and demanding both for researchers and practitioners. However, considering wind-related performance into architectural design can be of great significance in environmental-friendly and sustainable architectural design, which highlights an urgent need of developing applicable computational design optimization methods and tools both for research and design practice (Kabošová, Katunský, & Kmet, 2020; Kormaníková, Achten, Kopřiva, & Kmeť, 2018; Likai Wang, Tan, & Ji, 2016).

For wind-driven design optimization, the popular simulation method, Computational Fluid Dynamics (CFD) simulation, is too time-consuming to be applied in practice. Moreover, the current practice of performance-based design optimization cannot provide results with sufficient information feedback for architects' early-stage design exploration and synthesis. As Østergård stated, the existing black-box algorithms either produce the best result only or provide incomplete variations in a limited time (Østergård, Jensen, & Maagaard, 2016). Besides, the linear and assertion-oriented nature of computational optimization often separates performance-based design optimization from architects' early-stage design exploration. It is because current techniques and design tools are typically offered to measure the actual building performance or polish the design's predetermined shape instead of providing information or inspiration for architects' design ideation and concept development.

Considering these limitations, this paper proposes an agile wind-driven building-massing design optimization framework for early-stage architectural design. The framework integrates with an evolutionary building massing design tool - EvoMass (Likai Wang, Chen, Janssen, & Ji, 2020b), and a Fast Fluid Dynamics (FFD) simulation solver - GH_Wind (Waibel, Bystricky, Kubilay, Evins, & Carmeliet, 2017). On the one hand, EvoMass is an integrated design tool enabling rapid building massing design prototyping and design optimization. It is designed to allow architects to leverage performance-based design optimization as a means for design exploration and information extraction. On the other hand, GH_Wind is a fast but less accurate wind-related performance simulation tool. With the use of EvoMass and GH_Wind, it is possible to achieve a wind-driven optimization process that can be completed within a reasonable timeframe, while the optimization results also show clear and rich performance implications in relation to building massing design. Incorporating these advantages makes the framework support a rapid wind-driven design exploration that allows the architects to inspect various possible directions at the outset of design, thereby making design optimization an integral part of architects' design ideation and synthesis.

To place this study into context, we first discuss the progress that has been made in the related fields before elaborating the details of the proposed design optimization framework. Afterward, a case study for wind-related design optimization and the corresponding result is presented in order to demonstrate the efficacy of the proposed optimization framework in early-stage architectural design. We conclude the paper by discussing the implications for architectural design and pointing out the limitations.

Background

Over the past decade, wind-related performance has been gaining attention from researchers, and studies have been carried out to investigate the interactive relationship between building design and wind-related performance such as wind pressure and pedestrian wind comfort by using computational design optimization frameworks. Technically, CFD simulation is still prevalent in wind-related design optimization research due to its accuracy. However, the time-consuming simulation process of CFD makes such wind-driven design optimization unlikely to be used in the practice. To speed up the optimization process, FFD is becoming increasingly popular (Chronis, Turner, & Tsigkari, 2011).

FFD can be understood as a simplified CFD simulation with a faster solving speed but less accuracy.

The utility of FFD in wind-driven design optimization has been verified by a number of studies since its introduction (Chronis et al., 2011; Waibel et al., 2017; Zhang, Waibel, & Wortmann, 2020). The fast simulation speed makes FFD very suitable for early-stage design exploration as a part of the computational design optimization framework, and the conclusions drawn from the optimization with FFD are sufficient for architects to identify promising design directions.

While using FFD can potentially provide valuable information for architects' decision-making, it is still challenging to integrate such simulation-based design optimization into early-stage architectural design exploration. For the early design stages, most existing design tools offer an asserted-oriented calculation solver and system of the simulation data, rather than continuous guidance from initial parametric modeling. In order to address this challenge, some researchers have proposed design tools that can be used for design exploration, such as Urban-SOLve (Nault, Waibel, Carmeliet, & Andersen, 2018) for urban design problems and EvoMass (Likai Wang et al., 2020b) for building massing design problems. These tools primarily provide design optimization frameworks that can be easily customized and adapted to different design settings and are aimed to allow the architect to extract information from the optimization result as opposed to merely providing them with a specific solution, thereby enabling a performance-informed and performance-aware design.

This study continues the research on EvoMass regarding the issue in relation to optimization-based design exploration. Due to technical limitations, previous studies focused only on performance factors such as daylighting and solar irradiation. Thus, the recent implementation of GH_Wind enabling FFD simulation in Rhino-Grasshopper provides us with an opportunity to synergize the strengths of FFD and EvoMass for solving complex wind-related design problems, and investigate how such wind-driven design optimization can be incorporated into early-stage architectural design exploration.

METHOD

In order to overcome the existing limitations, this paper presents an agile wind-driven building massing design optimization framework based on EvoMass and GH_Wind. The design optimization framework allows early-stage design exploration on various design directions, thereby, providing rapid and valuable design feedback to the architect and helping them become more performance-informed and -aware in their decision-making and design synthesis. This section elaborates on the details of the proposed design optimization framework and presents a case study to demonstrate how the proposed design optimization framework can be incorporated into early-stage architectural design exploration.

Design Optimization Framework

The proposed design optimization framework comprises design generation, performance simulation analysis, and computational optimization based on EvoMass and GH_Wind (figure 1). On the one hand, EvoMass is applied to generate building massing design variants and evolve the design population for performance improvement with its embedded evolutionary algorithm, Steady-State Island Evolutionary Algorithm (SSIEA) (L. Wang, Janssen, & Ji, 2020).

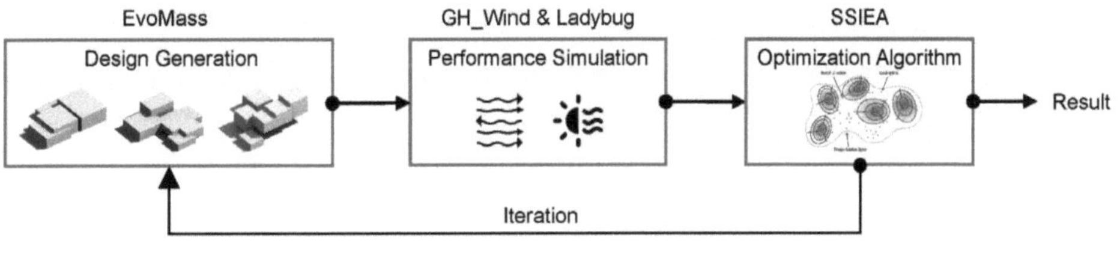

Figure 1
The design optimization framework incorporating EvoMass and GH_Wind.

On the other hand, GH_Wind is used to evaluate the wind-related performance of the design variant generated by EvoMass. The proposed design optimization framework can also be extended with other simulation tools to address architectural design's additional performance concerns. For example, in this study, we also combine the Ladybug tool into the optimization framework for sunlight-hour simluation as shown in the figure 1.

EvoMass is a design tool that can be tailored to different building massing design settings. It is aimed to enable architects to achieve a rapid optimization-based design exploration and to facilitate them to extract information from the optimization result. Herein, the priority of the development of EvoMass is not to directly provide architects with a solution but to use optimization results as a medium of design reflection and exploration. In addition, EvoMass can be customized for various design purposes. Using EvoMass allows for design exploration guided by different design directions, which also helps the architect understand the trade-offs and compromises characterizing the design problem and overcome design fixation and preconception.

Design Generation

For the massing generation, we used an additive algorithm in EvoMass to generate different building massing design variants (Likai Wang et al., 2020a). The additive algorithm creates the building massing by accumulating several mass elements (figure 2). The additive algorithm can be configurated and customized according to different control parameters. In addition, the varying combinations of multiple mass elements result in a wide variety of building massing designs with distinct topological configurations, thereby resulting in great design diversity and variability. The design diversity broadens the design solution space and allows the optimization process to explore a wide spectrum of design alternatives. In contrast, the conventional parametric models often limit the optimization to subtle design variations of a specific and predetermined type of design solutions.

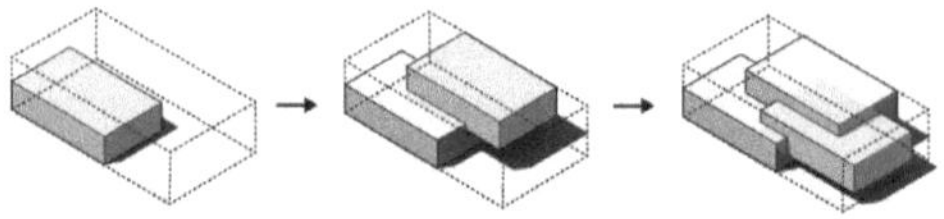

Figure 2
The generation process of the additive algorithm

There are three major constraints in the additive algorithm that allow the users to control the features in the generated design. These constraints serve as hyper-parameters of the additive algorithm, which will remain constant throughout the optimization process. The first constraint is the maximal volume that defines the spatial boundary of the generated design. The maximal volume is determined by the number of column grids (bays) in the X and Y directions as well as the number of floors in the Z direction (The dotted bound volume displayed in figure 2). Users can use this constraint to customize the building typology of the generated design such as high-rise towers or slab-type buildings. The second constraint is the number of mass elements that compose the generated design, which alters the topological configuration and complexity of the generated design. Larger numbers of mass elements tend to create building massing with complex interlocking volumes. The last constraint is the size constraint which determines the dimensions of each mass element by its ranges of column grids and floors. Using these three constraints, the additive algorithm can be customized to generate massing design variants with distinct architectural features. Additionally, the additive algorithm also allows users to specify the target gross area of the generated design, which can ensure the generated design can meet the functional requirement in architectural design.

Performance Simulation

For the wind-related performance simulation, GH_-Wind is applied to the proposed optimization framework. GH_Wind is implemented in the Rhino-Grasshopper environment, thus making it ready to be connected to EvoMass. GH_Wind allows users to define several parameters including the wind speed, step size, dimension of the simulation space. In addition, GH_Wind comes with a component that automatically discretizes input building volumes and transforms them into voxels. Although FFD is not as accurate as CFD, it can still generally differentiate the high-performing design variants from the bad ones. Since early-stage design exploration is more focused on identifying a promising design direction than offering a specific design solution, a degree of inaccuracy is acceptable. Lastly, due to the fact that computational design optimization typically involves hundreds or thousands of design generations and simulations, parameters need to be adjusted to achieve a feasible compromise between simulation time and accuracy when using FFD in design optimization.

Exploratory Design Optimization

To support the optimization-based design exploration, EvoMass provides users with SSIEA to obtain optimization results containing high-performing solutions with rich design diversity. On the one hand, SSIEA adopts an island-based approach to subdivide the design population into several 'niche' subpopulations, and each subpopulation is guided to focus on a different region in the design solution space (figure 3). As a result, the separation of design subpopulations allows for an "implicit" clustering during the optimization process. Therefore, SSIEA can prevent the optimization from convergent into a single region in the design solution space, thereby, decreasing the possibility for optimization results in yielding similar and homogeneous design variants. The design diversity in the optimization result helps to clarify the architectural implications related to the performance factors and enhances the information feedback.

On the other hand, SSIEA applies the steady-state replacement strategy to speed up the evolution of the design population. In contrast to the conventional generational replacement strategy, the steady-stage replacement strategy is designed to replace a small portion of individuals in the design population every generation. This allows the newly-found elite design individuals can affect the whole design population more promptly. On the contrary, using the generational replacement strategy only allows the elite design individuals to influence the design population after all other design individuals in the current generation are evaluated, which can significantly slow down the optimization speed. Accordingly, the use of the steady-state strategy can speed up the design optimization process by increasing the evolutionary pressure, thereby ensuring the optimization can exploit desirable high-performing solutions even when the computational resources allocated to each subpopulation are relatively limited. As a result, using the steady-state replacement strategy prevents SSIEA from making a significant compromise on search efficiency for design diversity.

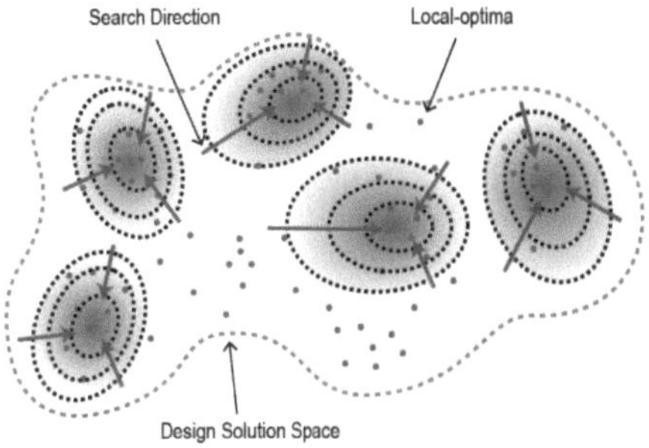

Figure 3
The search mechanism of SSIEA

Case Study

To demonstrate the efficacy of the optimization framework, a hypothetical case study is presented. The case study describes a building design in Nanjing, Jiangsu Province, China. The urban area of Nanjing commonly suffers from unpleasant winters due to the cold winds from the north and the lack of sunlight caused by the dense urban fabric. Hence, it is crucial to mitigate these two negative effects in building design to create a comfortable and pleasant urban environment. In this regard, several design parameters of building massing can affect the wind speed and sunlight in its building plot and the peripheral area, such as the projected area and the porosity with respect to the windward direction and the surrounding mask effect. Considering these, we conducted an optimization-based design explo-

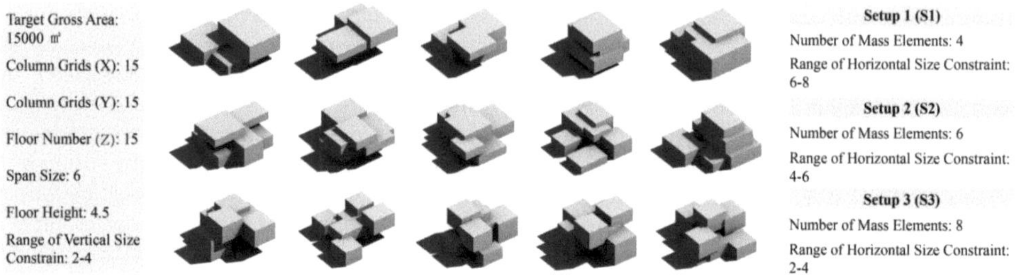

Figure 4
The parameter setups and the corresponding random sampling design variants

ration to investigate how building massing design with different formal traits can affect pedestrian wind comfort and sunlight accessibility in winters.

We focused the case study on the performance implications of building massing design respectively characterized by a smaller number of large mass elements or a larger number of small mass elements. For each set of design, we differentiated the formal features by the parameter setup including the number of mass elements and its size constraint (figure 4). Figure 4 displays the random sampling design variants generated using these three parameter setups. It can be noticed that the design variants in S1 tend to be bulky, whereas those in S2 and S3 become more flexible in terms of the topological configuration. In addition to the above-mentioned parameters, the three sets of design all had the maximal volume with 15*15 column grid units in the X (East-west) and Y (South-north) directions with a 6-meter sized span. In the Z direction, there were 8 floors of 4.5 meters in height each. Lastly, 15000 square meters were set as the target gross area.

For the performance evaluation, both pedestrian level wind speed and sunlight hours were chosen as the main performance indicator (figure 5). To measure the pedestrian level wind comfort, an average wind speed in a predefined area surrounding the target building is used. As high wind speed causes unpleasant human comfort in winters, the goal was to minimize the average wind speed. Based on the meteorological data of Nanjing, the wind direction was set blowing from north to south with an initial wind speed of 3.6 m/s. For the sunlight hours, the average sunlight hours on the winter solstice were used as the performance indicator. To increase sunlight accessibility, the objective was set to maximize the average number of sunlight hours in a peripheral area. The sunlight hour metric was calculated by using GH_Ladybug. Moreover, the gross area of the building was used as an additional penalty function in the fitness evaluation to ensure the optimization result can have desirable architectural feasibility.

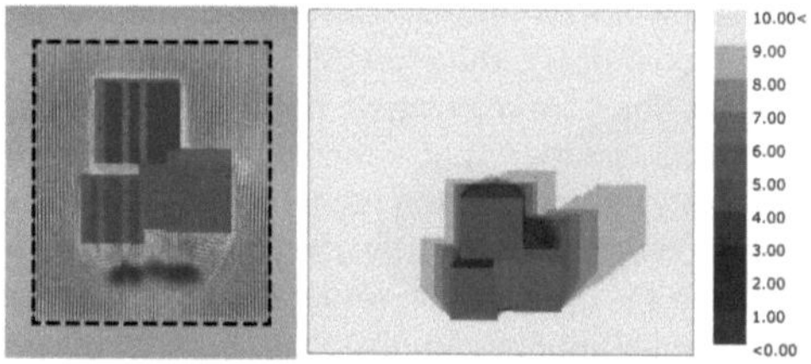

Figure 5
An example of wind-flow simulation and sunlight-hour simulation

The above performance metrics were formulated into a single-objective design optimization problem. While it is possible to use multi-objective optimization (MOO) to incorporate with these objectives, using MOO often results in compromise on search efficiency, and there can be also too many options that are difficult to analyze. In contrast, using SSIEA can achieve a good balance between design diversity and fitness improvement. For the setting of SSIEA, five subpopulations were applied, each with 30 individuals. Considering that each FFD still lasts for approximately 5 minutes based on our parameter setup, the optimization process went through 1050 iterations, with 30 successive generations after the initial generation. Each optimization process lasted around 4 days based on an i7 desktop computer.

RESULT

To analyze the result of the case study, we used the elite design variant in each of the subpopulations as the results of the conducted optimization processes. Figure 6 summarizes the results of the case study. Statistically, the elite design variants from S1 stand out compared with those from S2 and S3 regarding the average fitness. If we a closer look at fitness evaluation item-wise, we can find that the elite design variants in S1 generally have a lower average wind speed than those of S2 and S3. In contrast, it should be stressed that the average wind speed of S2 is only marginally higher than that of S1. On the contrary, the elite design variants from S3 can achieve a more desirable average sunlight accessibility than S1 and S2, although the advantage is less insignificant. The result implies that there is a trade-off between achieving favorable pedestrian wind comfort and sufficient sunlight accessibility in the given design setting.

In terms of the formal features, the design variants in S1 tend to lay more mass elements on the ground as seen in figure 5, which can lower the height of the overall building volume so as to decrease its surrounding mask effect, which increases the sunlight accessibility for its adjacent area. In contrast, S2 and S3 can achieve a more compacted building volume that further reduces the surrounding mask effect by taking advantage of more flexible topological configurations. However, its compacted building volume, in turn, weakens its ability in blocking the wind flow through the targeted area.

Figure 7 shows how the elite design variant affects the pedestrian wind flow. For S1, due to the fact that the building massing has a large projected area in the windward direction and elongates along the east-west direction, it results in a large wind shadow area. In contrast, the smaller mass elements in S2 and S3 can allow more wind to flow through the gap between those mass elements, which increases the average wind speed and reduces the wind shadow area. While the design variants generated by S2 and S3 are not desirable in winters, these design variants may produce better wind flow than those generated by S1 in summers because the sparse building volume at

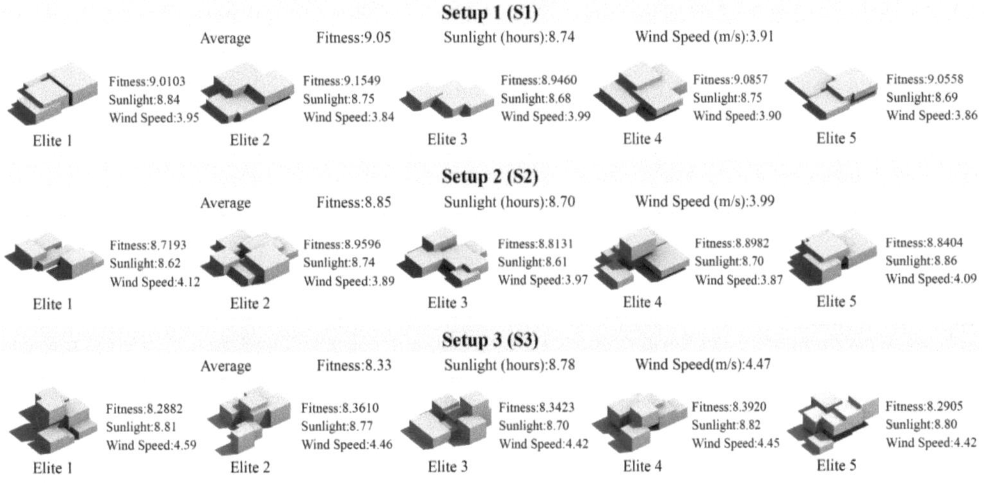

Figure 6
The result of the conducted optimization processes (elite design variants and performance indicators)

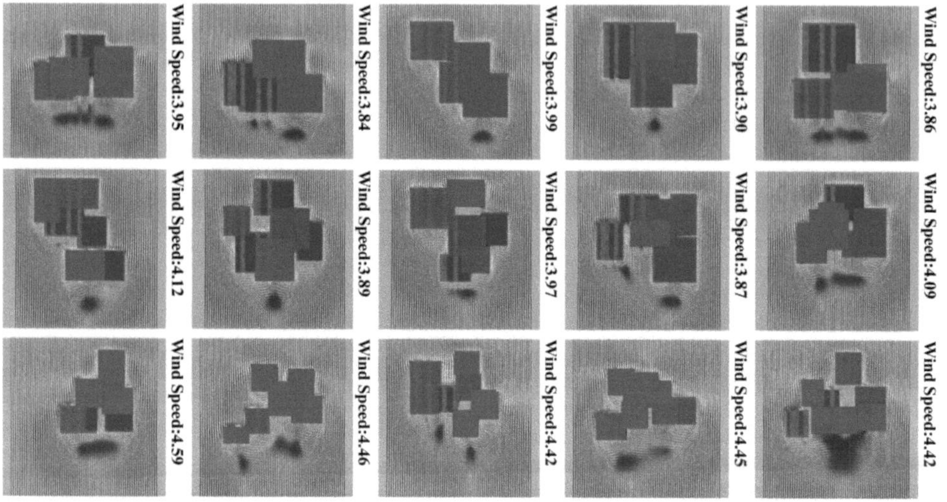

Figure 7
Wind-speed analysis based on the elite design variants

the ground floor can allow more wind flow through the building and increase the wind speed.

Figure 8 demonstrates the relationship between elite design variants and sunlight accessibility. As indicated in figure 5, the differences in sunlight hours among these design variants are relatively insignificant. However, the shaded area remarkably differs from one another. For S1, the large mass elements produce a larger area with severely poor sunlight accessibility (dark blue area) compared to those of S2 and S3. On the contrary, the elite design variants tend to be more compacted and have a smaller footprint. This tendency results in a smaller shaded area even though some of these design variants can produce a long shadow as shown in figure 8 bottom row. However, since the absolute size of the shadow is smaller, these long shadows, indeed, have an insignificant effect on the overall sunlight accessibility. Lastly, as shown in figure 5, the flexible topological configuration of S3 and S2 enables the elite design variants to have some mass elements hidden in the shadow cast by mass elements on the south, thereby reducing the overall surrounding mask effect. This tendency is also in agreement with the passive design strategy of solar envelopes.

As a summary of the case study, the result of the optimization provides valuable information about the design problem in regards to wind-related performance and sunlight accessibility. The three assigned building massing design generative setups enable the optimization process to explore three distinct design solution spaces. The three parallel optimization processes allow for a thorough and systematic investigation of the trade-offs and compromises among different building massing design alternatives in terms of the two performance factors. Furthermore, it is noteworthy that using the proposed optimization framework is not primarily aimed to offer architects a direct solution for the design task. Instead, the architect is recommended to extrapolate the design tendency reflected by the optimization result and conceive novel design schemes that can challenge the "computed optimal" provided by the optimization.

Figure 8
Sunlight-hour analysis based on the elite design variants

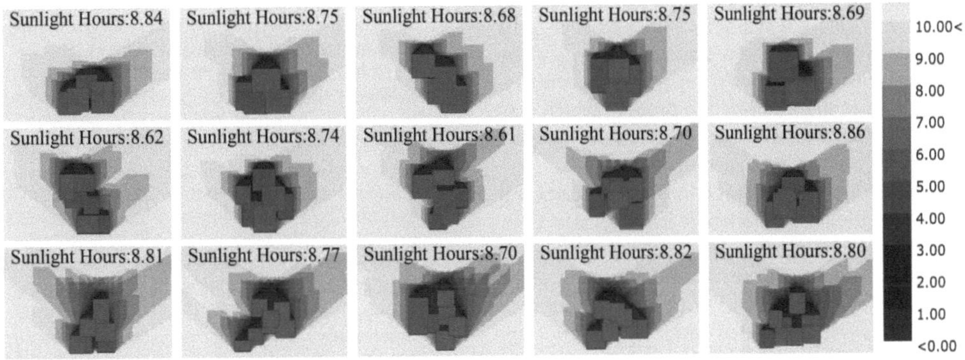

DISCUSSION AND CONCLUSION

This study demonstrates the efficacy of the proposed wind-driven design optimization framework using EvoMass and GH_Wind. By speeding up the optimization process by using a less accurate simulation, the proposed wind-driven design optimization can be more practical for use in early-stage architectural design tasks. Even though FFD only provides a coarse simulation on wind flow, it can differentiate the wind-related performance of different design variants, thereby allowing the optimization process to screen out promising design candidates for architects. Additionally, the application of EvoMass enables architects to conduct a fast investigation towards different directions at the outset of design, and the optimization result provides essential information about the performance implication with respect to different design directions. Considering the frequent data-poor situations encountered by architects during the early design stages, the revealed information offers them an opportunity to promptly understand the design problem. Last but not the least, the proposed optimization framework also has the advantage of easy to use. Without the requirement of parametric modeling, architects can establish the framework in a plug-and-play fashion on the Rhino-Grasshopper platform, and the framework can be readily extended to include more performance evaluation by incorporating other simulation or evaluation tools.

As the first attempt at combining EvoMass and GH_Wind, this study also bears certain limitations worth mentioning. First, in the case study, we did not consider urban environments in the wind flow simulation. As including surrounding urban environments will require expanding the computational domain, this can significantly prolong the simulation and make optimization more time-consuming. Second, the case study only considered one season. The optimization result implies that while using larger mass elements can be more advantageous in winters, it is reasonable to assume that they may have counter-effects in summers, for example, the large mass elements cause a greater resistance to wind flow. Thus, including the design problem in relation to summers in optimization can provide architects with a broader view and a more comprehensive understanding of the design problem. Lastly, the building skin was not considered in this study. However, it has been demonstrated to have a significant impact on the building massing design (H. Zhang, Wang, & Ji, 2021), thus incorporating it into the framework can make the result with greater practical value. Meanwhile, while using four days to complete one design optimization process using FFD is much shorter than those using CFD, it is still not ideal for practice. As a result, parallel computing or cloud computing can be used in future research to further accelerate the running speed of the optimization process, which may also allow for larger numbers of iteration to ensure the accuracy of the optimization result.

To conclude, as displayed in the case study and the result, the incorporation of EvoMass and GH_-Wind allows for a more engaging and pertinent application of wind-driven design optimization in early-stage architectural design. In contrast to the conventional assertion-oriented design optimization approach, the proposed wind-driven design optimization can produce more informative results and help architects in design ideation and overcoming design fixation. As a result, the application of the proposed optimization framework not only allows the architect to achieve a more performance-informed and -aware design process but also makes the wind-related performance more readily a driving force in architectural design.

REFERENCES

Chronis, A, Turner, A and Tsigkari, M 2011 'Generative Fluid Dynamics: Integration of Fast Fluid Dynamics and Genetic Algorithms for wind loading optimization of a free form surface', *Proceedings of the 2011 Symposium on Simulation for Architecture and Urban Design*, pp. 29-36

Kabošová, L., Katunský, D. and Kmet, S. 2020, 'Wind-based parametric design in the changing climate', *Applied Sciences (Switzerland)*, 10(23), p. 1–18

Kormaníková, L, Achten, H, Kopřiva, M and Kmet, S 2018, 'Parametric wind design', *Frontiers of Architectural Research*, 7(3), pp. 383-394

Nault, E, Waibel, C, Carmeliet, J and Andersen, M 2018, 'Development and test application of the UrbanSOLve decision-support prototype for early-stage neighborhood design', *Building and Environment*, 137, pp. 58-72

Negendahl, K. and Nielsen, T. R. 2015, 'Building energy optimization in the early design stages: A simplified method', *Energy and Buildings*, 105, p. 88–99

Waibel, C., Bystricky, L., Kubilay, A., Evins, R. and Carmeliet, J. 2017 'Validation of Grasshopper-based Fast Fluid Dynamics for Air Flow around Buildings in Early Design Stage', *Building Simulation 2017*, August 7-9, San Francisco, California, USA, p. 1–10

Wang, L, Chen, KW, Janssen, P and Ji, G 2020a 'ALGORITHMIC GENERATION OF ARCHITECTURAL MASSING MODELS FOR BUILDING DESIGN OPTIMISATION Parametric Modelling Using Subtractive and Additive Form Generation Principles', *RE: Anthropocene, Design in the Age of Humans - Proceedings of the 25th CAADRIA Conference*, Bangkok, Thailand, p. 385–394

Wang, L, Chen, KW, Janssen, P and Ji, G 2020b 'ENABLING OPTIMISATION-BASED EXPLORATION FOR BUILDING MASSING DESIGN - A Coding-free Evolutionary Building Massing Design Toolkit in Rhino-Grasshopper', *RE: Anthropocene, Design in the Age of Humans - Proceedings of the 25th CAADRIA Conference*, Bankok, Thailand, pp. 255-264

Wang, L, Janssen, P, Chen, KW, Tong, Z and Ji, G 2019, 'Subtractive building massing for performance-based architectural design exploration: A case study of daylighting optimization', *Sustainability*, 11(24), p. 6965

Wang, L, Janssen, P and Ji, G 2020, 'SSIEA: a hybrid evolutionary algorithm for supporting conceptual architectural design', *Artificial intelligence for engineering design analysis and manufacturing*, 34, pp. 1-19

Wang, L, Tan, Z and Ji, G 2016, 'TOWARD THE WIND-RELATED BUILDING PERFORMATIVE DESIGN A wind-related building performance optimization design system integrating Fluent and Rhinoceros based on iSIGHT', *Proceedings of CAADRIA 2016*, 1, pp. 109-218,11

Yi, Y. K. and Malkawi, A. M 2012, 'Site-specific optimal energy form generation based on hierarchical geometry relation', *Automation in Construction*, 26, p. 77–91

Zhang, R, Waibel, C and Wortmann, T 2020, 'Aerodynamic Shape Optimization for High-Rise Conceptual Design-Integrating and validating parametric design,(fast) fluid dynamics, structural analysis and optimization', *Proceedings of the 38th eCAADe Conference*, 1, pp. pp. 37-45

Zhang, H, Wang, L and Ji, G 2021 'The Synergy of building massing and facade - An Evo-Devo approach for performance-based design optimization combining facade design with building massing', *Proceedings of the 26th CAADRIA Conference - Volume 1*, Hong Kong, pp. 451-460

Østergård, T, Jensen, RL and Maagaard, SE 2016, 'Building simulations supporting decision making in early design–A review', *Renewable and Sustainable Energy Reviews*, 61, pp. 187-201

Design and Fabrication of Formwork for Shell Structures Based on 3D-printing Technology

Xiao Zhang[1], Chao Yuan[2], Liu Yang[3], Peiran Yu[4], Yiwen Ma[5], Song Qiu[6], Zhe Guo[7], Philip F. Yuan[8]
[1,2,3,4,5,6]Tsinghua University [7]Hefei University of Technology [8]Tongji University
[1,2,3]{z-x20|yuanc19|yl-19}@mails.tsinghua.edu.cn [4]lastonsf@163.com
[5]359069158@qq.com [6]qiusongtty@sina.com [7]guogal@hotmail.com
[8]philipyuan007}@tongji.edu.cn

Shell structure is a kind of structure using a small amount of materials to obtain a large-span multi-functional space. However, lots of formwork and scaffold materials are often wasted in the construction process. This paper focuses on the shell structure construction using robotic 3D printing PLA (an environmental friendly material) technology as the background. The author explores the possibility of 3D printing technology in shell construction from small scale models in different construction method, and gradually optimizes the shell template shape suitable for PLA material in full-scale construction. Finally, the research team chose the bending-active 3D printing type and completed the construction of three full-scale concrete shell molds. Under the guidance of professor Philippe Block, the research team finished the final 3D printing mold with optimized slicing and bending logic and successfully used it as the template mold to carry the tiles which proved the feasibility of this construction method.

Keywords: *Shell structure , Formwork , Geometric analysis, Form-finding, 3d printing*

1. BACKGROUND

Shell structure is a good choice to cover large spans with less material, its light architectural form also conforms to the aesthetics of structural mechanics(Méndez Echenagucia et al., 2018). The manufacturing process of the shell first requires physical form-finding, and then the geometry form will be fitted by the template in the process of construction, the shell is finally finished by concrete ,brick or wood. And then the scaffolding and template are removed. However, this traditional form-finding method wastes scaffolding materials and requires a lot of time during the construction process. At the same time, in order to carry out the construction activities in a more environmentally friendly way, this paper focuses on the shell structure construction using 3D printing PLA technology as the background. PLA is a kind of printing material which can be made by recycling plastic.

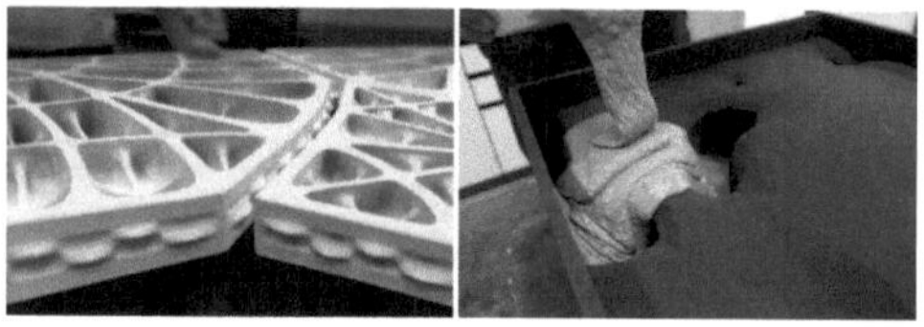

Figure 1
Left: 3d printed unreinforced, structural floor (Philippe Block et al., 2016), Right: 3D-printed formwork for UHPFRC material (Andrei Jipa et al., 2016)

1.1 3D Printing Formwork Techniques Searching

In recent years, with the efforts of Block Research Group in ETH, the shell construction method through 3D printing technology has gradually matured. Their researches can be roughly divided into two directions: the first direction is direct printing of building materials (Philippe Block et al., 2016). Although the formwork is omitted in this construction process, the high price of the equipment and the limitation of the processing size (4 * 2 * 1meters) at the present stage result in that it can only be used for the construction of the floor level (Fig 1. Left). The second type is 3d printing shell structure formwork (Andrei Jipa et al., 2016). This construction method is delicate and can form a beautiful texture on the concrete shell surface, but the construction process itself does not make full use of material properties of the mold itself, and printing the template layer by layer will consume a lot of time (Fig 1. right). Therefore, the first aim of this paper is to 3d print the shell mold by the way of robotic 3d printing, and make full use of the material properties of the mold itself in the process of shell structure construction.

Figure 2
Left: Enhancement at the section on shell principle stress lines in Gatti Wool Mill (Pier Luigi Nervi ,1951), Right: principle stress lines found by researchers with Millipede plug-in.

1.2 Material Efficiency Optimization Searching

Material efficiency is becoming a critical design driver in the construction industry. When the flexible material is used as a formwork, it needs to bear a certain load without deformation, so it is necessary to structurally strengthen itself. How to apply proper amount of material in necessary part and also waste less material to decrease formwork self-weight is also very important. Traditional shell Material Efficiency Optimization methods can be divided into three categories:

- Size Optimization (Mijar et al. 1998). There are a number of different topology optimization algorithms, including Solid Isotropic Microstructure with Penalization (SIMP), Evolutionary Structural Optimization (ESO). Researches found the shape optimized are often complex and some morphological transitions exceed the set limit (less than 45°deflection in Z direction) of the FDM 3d printing.
- Enhancement at the section on shell geometry structural lines. Taking the Roman Gymnasium as an example, it is converted into a spatial structure by setting the beam to the geometric line position of the shell. However, this reinforcement method is not based on finite element analysis which means not every part of the material is useful and it is more like a global strengthen strategy.
- Enhancement of the principle structural stress lines of the shell structure. This analysis requires a combination of finite element analysis to simulate the transfer of force flow through computer simulations and to strengthen the casing at these locations(Adriaenssens et al., 2014). This reinforcement technique is also related to topology optimization and is suitable for Irregularly shaped shell reinforcement(Tam, 2015). Researchers used Millipede plug-in with Rhino and found the principle stress lines according to the load and support situation of Gatti Wool Mill designed by Pier Luigi Nervi in 1951. Through this

experiment, the research team found it useful for principle stress lines enhancement on shell structure by planner construction (Fig.2).

2. INTRODUCTION

This paper presents the research, design , structural performance simulation and construction of a full scale thin 3d printed bending-active formwork for shell structures (Fig.3). In the small-scale model, the research team carried out the research on the unit type, bending-active type and integrated printing type, and used topology optimization method in the test process to minimize the use of 3D printing materials. In this paper, author will discuss the possibility of 3d printing shell and topology optimization design of shell structure from small scale model. Finally, through three full-scale printing experiments, author will present the 1:1 prototype construction optimization process, and summarize the design method of 3d printing bending-active shell formwork.

The idea of using 3d printing to optimize material distribution on a shell structure was firstly proposed by an industrial design research partner. The reason for this study is that a helmet design company hopes the research team to produce a mountaineering helmet by 3d printing. The first approach the research team tried was global printing. In order to reduce the self-weight of the helmet and also make it have the mechanical properties of resisting deformation, the research team used a 3d voronoi polygon to fill the shell first, and then increased the density of the helmet at some part based on the collision experiment, and completed the global 3d printing. However, it is impossible for this global 3d printing method to move to the architectural scale, because there is no such huge printing equipment. Therefore, the research team tried to use discrete and expanded methods to construct the shell template. In the second test, the author found that the accumulated error of the discrete 3d printing shell formwork units in the assembly process was large, and finally chose to use the expanded 3d printing formwork construction method.

In the process of applying the deployable 3d printing formwork to the construction of large-scale pavilion, the research team conducted three experiments on the printing method and slicing logic. The first 3D printing mold can't bear the concrete due to the surface texture during the printing process. The second 3D printing mold can only carry a small amount of concrete due to the initial bending logic. In the third experiment, the research team optimized the element geometry based on the bending-active construction method, and finally completed the shell mold construction, and successfully built a full-scale brick shell.

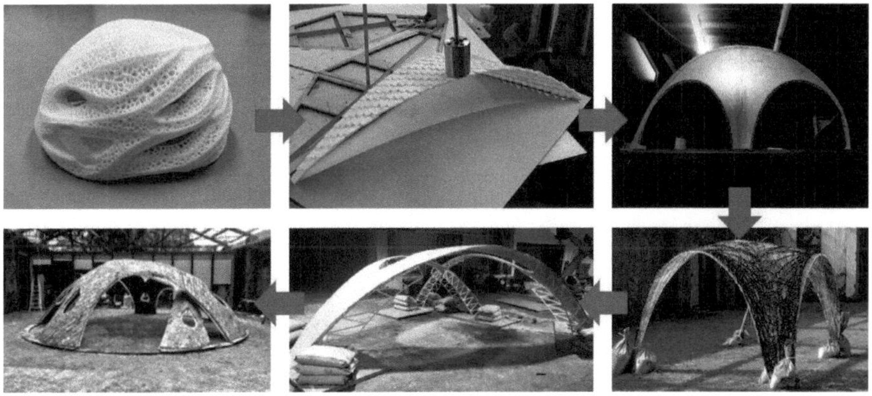

Figure 3
Work flow

3. 3D PRINTING EXPERIMENT OF SHELL STRUCTURE IN SMALL SCALE

3.1 Shell structure design based on volumetric modeling method

Volumetric modeling is an efficient modeling method. In NURBS modeling, geometries are often described by parametric curves, while in volumetric modeling, points, lines can be transformed into independent fields, and a certain volume is formed by wrapping the equipotential surface. The advantage of this modeling method lies in the fast operation speed, which can break through the geometric limitations of the model: the lines in the model are directly divided into points, and the volumetric model is formed by the point cloud.

In this paper, the 3D printing shell structure design of helmet is filled by the 3d voronoi polygon at first, and the curves group on the surface is formed by the voronoi polygon intersected with the helmet B-rep. Secondly, the polygon lines group is divided into uniform point clouds according to the distance. On this basis, based on the stress diagram provided by the helmet manufacturer according to the impact test, the author arranged the densified point cloud in the collision concentration area in the helmet geometry. Finally, the author combines the two groups of point clouds and used the "Dendro" plug-in based on grasshopper platform to turn the points into a closed mesh which can be 3d printed(Fig.4).

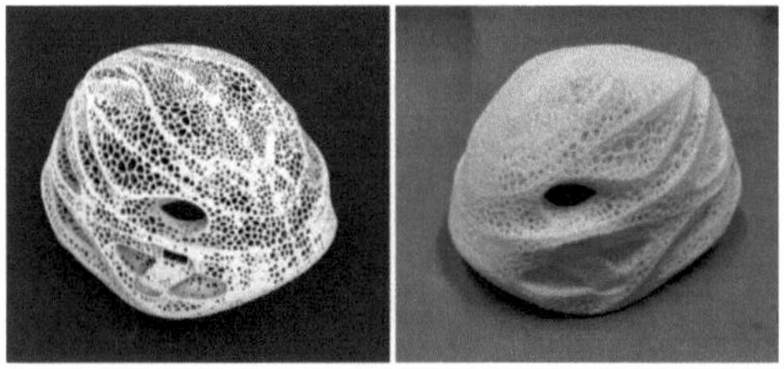

Figure 4
Volumetric modeling design for shell structure based on 3d printing technology

The author found that the point cloud strengthening strategy based on stress analysis is a more efficient formwork design method than shape optimization like ESO. Moreover, this method can ensure the integrity of the shell structure, and the material distribution is more uniform, which is more conducive to the plane processing. At the same time, it is easier to be used as a formwork or mold to carry concrete or bricks then. But this design method is not conducive to be split, integrated printing is more suitable for industrial design, formwork design for architecture scale must consider the split logic.

3.2 Shell structure design based on unit modeling method

Through the study of the construction process of a shell structure, the author found that the construction process is actually a three-dimensional jigsaw puzzle of the bricks in a certain order. The formwork plays the role of supporting the covering like concrete or bricks, while the scaffold plays the role of positioning and supporting. If the unit of the template itself has the function of positioning, and has a certain compression capacity after the construction, then the use of scaffolding materials can be saved in the process of shell construction. Similarly, the unit mold is also very conducive to storage and transportation.

According to the geometric structure line of the shell, the structural lines can be divided equally by dislocation. At the same time, the odd and even rows of bricks are moved in the normal direction of the shell surface to make them staggered. On this basis, the author makes Boolean operations on the shell elements to form 102 different bricks, which are 3d printed. Although the research team has completed the final assembly(Fig.5), but in the process, the research team found that the cumulative error is large. This may be due to the small size of each block unit and the low printing accuracy, which leads to the shape deformation at the printing turning point of each brick. However, if high-precision 3d printing equipment is used in the construction, the processing time of each block will be extended.

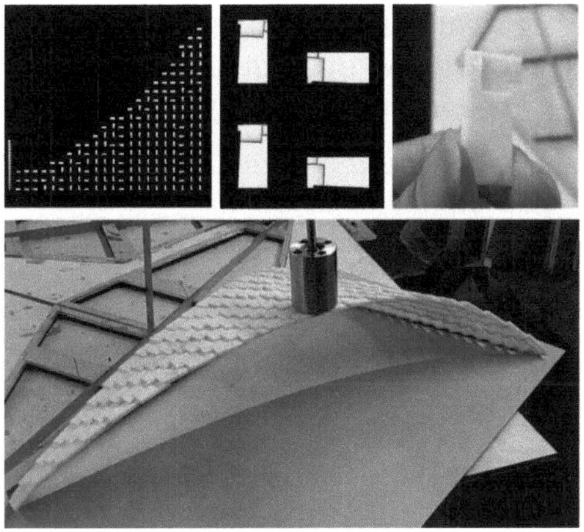

Figure 5
Up: mold design of unit brick of the shell; down: assembly and manufacturing result

Through experiments, the author found that the unit structure is more suitable for the construction of the shell itself. If we want to use 3d printing materials to make shell formwork, we need to reduce the manual splicing part to achieve the accuracy of form finding process. At the same time, if the customized unit construction method is used to complete the shell unit, the casting method may be more economical, and 3D printing is more suitable for the final block mold.

3.3 Shell structure design based on bending-active modeling method

A shell structure is often a hyperboloid like shape, just like the clothes on the body, but the clothes on our body can be divided into several pieces of developable cloth, so that they can be made on a plan easily. If the shell formwork be constructed in this way, the fabrication work would be easier. The research team hopes that the double curved shell surface can be fitted into a combination of several developable surfaces. By unrolling and 3d printing the single curved formwork piece and bending it, the built formwork can be fitted into a shape geometrically similar to the hyperboloid shell, and the bended shape can resist some weight.

3.3.1 Developability optimization by UV curves. The author splits the double curved shell geometry according to the central line symmetry axis and unroll it in two parts. On this basis, the author further solved the principle stress lines of the shell with Millipede in Grasshopper, and then projected it on the developed surface. But the problem is that the stress lines generated is random, so it is difficult to generate the 3d print path directly with "one stroke". Generally speaking, the path that should be drawn in one stroke is regular polygon mesh, so that the vertices of each element can be sorted, and the path can be generated by circular algorithm for FDM 3d printing machine. So the author gets the path which can be printed continuously by the robotic arm point by point, and uses the FDM printing method to complete the mold manufacturing and bending assembly (Fig. 6). The author bent the printed template to form a double curved shell, but also found a problem was found that there are still too many work of hand bonding. So, the author puts forward the idea of unfolding according to the contour of the surface.

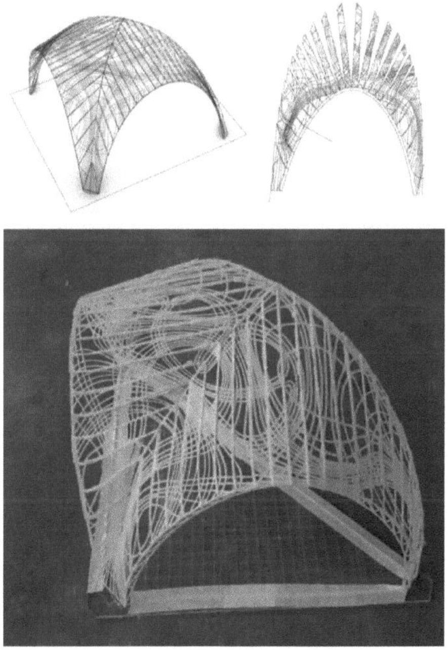

Figure 6
Up: Shell geometry developed based on UV curves; down: final bended form

3.3.2 Developability optimization by profile. Before unrolling, it is necessary to extract the long edge contour of the shell as the "path", and make the short edge straight as the "section line" to complete the fitting of the double curved surface, and then unroll the rebuilt single surface through the algorithm (Fig.7). For the shell in Figure 7, the author further subdivides the shell to make it more similar to the initial shape, which is suitable for printing template. In this way, a single surface can be fitted by the combination of triangular planes.

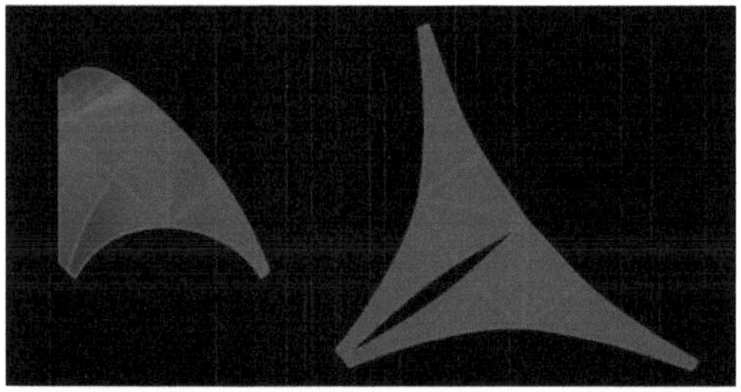

Figure 7
Unrolled formwork according to shell profile

Figure 8
Left: 3d printing shell path; right: plane printed shell formwork and space bended geometry

On this basis, the author projects the principle stress lines onto the planar formwork. As shown in Figure 8, the upper layer is the principle stress line layer, and the first layer is the base. The one stroke path of the base is easy to generate, but there are many singular points in the principle stress line path, which can only be edited manually. The author 3d printed the formwork and bent it into shape (Fig. 8). This process requires very little manual bonding process, has a high degree of mechanization, and the shell formed by bending has a certain bearing capacity, so the author decided to deepen the large model production.

4. 3D PRINTING EXPERIMENT OF SHELL STRUCTURE IN FULL SCALE

4.1 Pre-bending double layer 3d printing method

In order to strengthen the bended formwork to bear certain load, the principle stress lines extracted by Karamba are printed together with the formwork. However, the printed formwork with principle stress lines is very distorted in the bending process. Some areas on the surface would appear unnatural bending phenomenon, therefore, the bending must be simulated to make the most reasonable routing choice. First of all, author simulated the bending of the plane formwork through abaques, pushing the boundaries of the two ends. However, the simulation results do not form the preset surface.

Therefore, the research team set the target displacement for each point on the edge, control the speed and path of each point to simulate the new bended state. The results show that the distribution of stress line formwork is very unfavorable to the bending process. The area where the stress lines intersect will form a harder part than surrounding area, which makes it difficult for the formwork to bend, and even if the edge is locked on the target contour, the whole formwork is still not compliant (Fig.9).

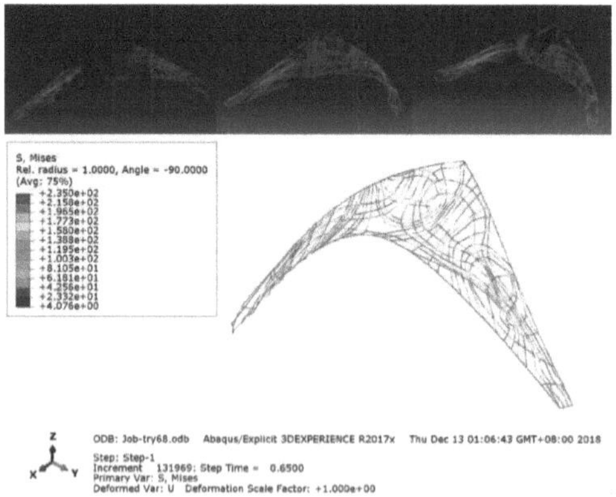

Figure 9
Up: Bending test of shell formwork by Abaqus; down: uneven distribution of internal members of formwork

In order to find the most suitable uniform mesh for bending, the author decided to use three kinds of line distribution simulation to find the most suitable shape for bending: 1. Cross lines uniform grid, 2. Horizontally along the bending direction of the template, 3. The line with constant length in the bending process. After simulation, we find that the third kind of routing can get the closest effect to the target surface (Fig.10). Therefore, in the process of full-scale printing, the short line with constant length is printed on the bottom layer as the base.

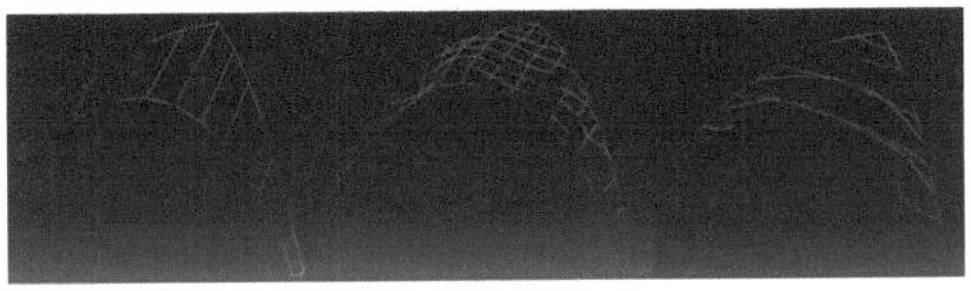

Figure 10
With the help of bending simulation, the most favorable mesh for bending is compared and selected

The first task of the research team is to 3d print the base layer, a layer of parallel grid lines on the plane with PLA to assist bending, and then 3d print the stress lines of the whole shell after bending to strengthen shell structure performance. The fabrication of scaffolding needs to first draw the datum curve on the plane with the KUKA robotic arm, and then draw the position of the height positioning block at the same time, install the pre-cut height limit block on the bottom plate, and finally fix the 3d printed planner formwork on the bottom plate with tie on the height positioning block. The stress line material of space printing is modified plastics mixed with adhesive reinforcement agent. Because of the small contact area of the upper and lower overlapping surfaces of the extruded plastics in the second printing, in order to prevent the separation between layers, a special path must be used for printing. After many experiments, the author needs to raise the mechanical arm to 5cm above the reference plane for printing.

The projection of the first prototype is an isosceles right triangle of 2.6 m * 2.6 m, the height of which is 2.1 m and the thickness of which is 1.5 cm (Fig.11). In the printing process, there are three kinds of lines: 1. The surface structure line perpendicular to the parallel grid, which is not suitable for plane printing in bending simulation, but can increase the integrity of the datum surface in the secondary printing, so that it is more stable in the force. 2. Frame strengthening line. According to the conclusion of bending simulation, the main stress of the shell is concentrated in the edge, so the edge needs to be further strengthened. 3. Stress line of shell element, the shell element is not only subjected to gravity, but also to the pressure of the other half of the shell, so the stress line of this part of the element is different from the overall stress line, and it also needs to be strengthened. The three groups of lines are printed three times in order, and are overlapped and woven to form a self-supporting shell. However, after the shell mold was made, the author found that its surface texture fluctuated too much, which was not conducive to the installation of concrete gauze. Therefore, this template 3D printing method needs to be improved.

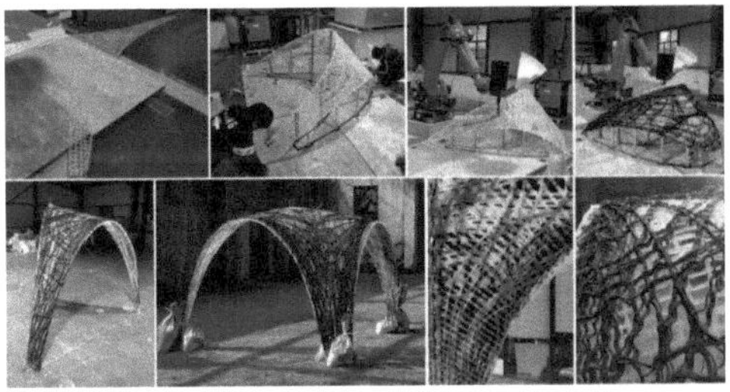

Figure 11
Process and surface texture of full-scale prototype shell

4.2 Y-shape block 3d printing method

o show the feasibility of the building technique in a complicated design case of a shell structure, a more complex form is designed with the same methodology. In the second printing experiment, the author has made two improvements: 1. The principle stress lines on the shell should be evenly distributed, otherwise the bended shape will be greatly affected. 2. The geometry of the shell itself needs to be more complex to have universal significance. In the first printing process, there will be many problems in the second printing. For example, the extruded material is very hot, which will lead to uneven thermal expansion and deformation of the shell. At the same time, the author changed segmentation logic. Each block starts from the singular point of the shell grid, extends a distance to each strip direction as the central block (similar to Y-shape), and then each strip can be unrolled to make more parts more flexible.

The intercrossed geometry is then optimized into a combination of series of lofted developable surfaces. To improve the building process, several side trusses are added to support the structure and to help for the positioning of the shell surface. With such guides, the 3d printed formwork can be easily assembled to reach the geometry and make it as a pure geometric problem. In the final building process, 10mm Glass Fibre Reinforced Concrete (GRC) is casted on-site on the formwork with only supports on the curved edges to test the load-bearing capacity. Finally, the 80 kg 3d-printed formwork took the 400 kg dead load successfully. However, the author finds that the logic of Y-shaped block leads to the appearance of plane part in the bended shell, and the middle of Y-shaped block can hardly be bent, which does not conform to the characteristics of hyperboloid geometry (Fig.12). Therefore, the author conducted the third experiment.

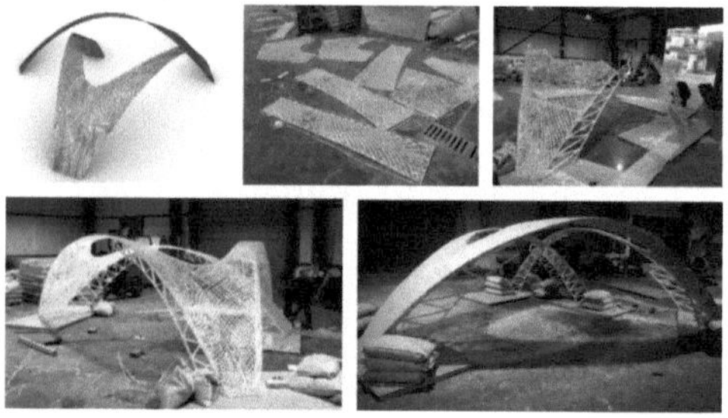

Figure 12
The experiment and assembly process of y-shape block 3d printing and casted result by GRC material

4.3 Shape optimization for f bending active 3d printing formwork

As the geometric rule in the design process relies on the Y-shaped surface geometry, it is required in the early stage of design to define the geometry firstly as a linear system. In the final design of the prototype tile-vaulted shell with a 7 m * 7 m * 2 m space as well as a circular tension ring with 6 mm steel as the support.

The shell geometry is mainly a double-curved surface. In the developable optimization process, the midlines of the surface and the boundary curves are firstly selected. By moving the midlines a little bit higher in the Z-direction, one can change the geometry into some strips lofting the midline curves and the corresponding curves (Fig. 13).

With this geometry, all the surfaces can be defined as developable. As the bending moments concentrate mostly on the foot areas of the structure, it makes this part of formwork hard to bend. Under the suggestion of Prof. Dr. Philippe Block, the research team. The contour of the bottom of the shell is changed into an extended curve to make it fit the double curved surface better in the bending process. But in the bending process, there will still be a large stress concentration in the middle of the formwork, which will lead to a breaking easily in the bending process. The research team decided to reduce the material at the stress concentration position of the formwork. After physical experiments, the research team found that the opening in the middle of the formwork along the folding gap will facilitate the bending process. At the same time, the circular opening contour makes the stress evenly distributed to all positions, which is not easy to cause stress concentration. The method of finite element simulation (Fig. 14) is beneficial to the further verification of the team's conjecture.

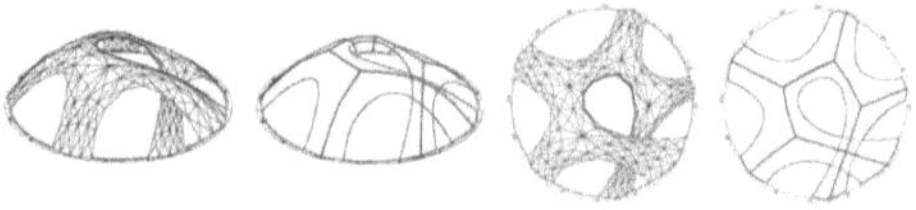

Figure 13
Shape optimization to developable surface

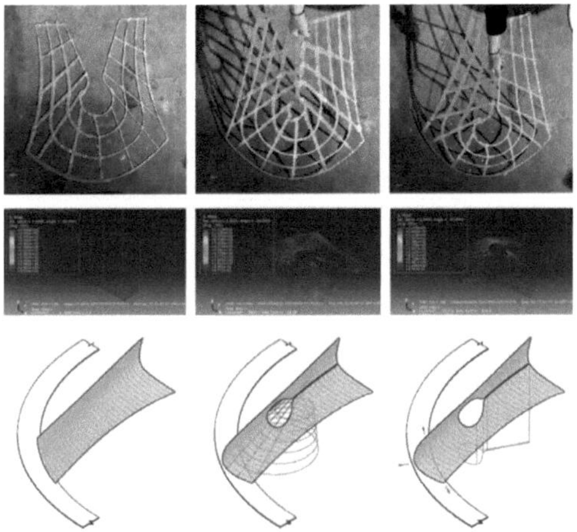

Figure 14
Shape optimization and FEA analysis for better bending performance

In the process of research, the results of finite element analysis are used to interfere with the density of printing template. Finally, the 3d printing path of the shell formwork is formed by the upper and lower contours equally divided and connected by dislocation. This kind of path planning can be done efficiently without connecting irregular principle stress lines manually. Finally, the research team bent the 3D printing formwork, supported a small amount of stick supporting at the bottom of the formwork, and covered the upper layer of the formwork with a layer of gauze, so that it can carry bricks. Subsequently, the research team used a layer of 1cm thick bricks to lay staggered joints layer by layer to prevent stress concentration at the joints. After two weeks of incremental construction, the team completed the construction of the permanent shell pavilion (Fig 15).

Figure 15
Bended 3d print formwork and the final permanent shell pavilion

5. CONCLUSION

This paper presents a particular research process of the design method based on 3d printing technology for shell structure. From the helmet to the shell pavilion in architecture scale, the research team proposed a lot of possibilities in different experiments. Although some of the experiments did not get used in large scale, they may inspire other international research teams to conduct more in-depth research. The final pavilion of the process is generated through a multiphased design-to-fabrication joint workshop organized by theMIT, ETHZ and Tongji University where a systematic design method, geometric consideration, structural behavior as well as the bending simulation are discussed and tested. Furthermore, software tools such as the Millipede, Karamba, Dendro, COMPAS framework, RhinoVAULT, FURobot are selected to work together in the whole design process. Although the research team built the bending active formwork for a brick shell finally, the final global shell structure form is still different from the form found shape in the design process. Whether the bending active form can server the mechanical property against gravity should be further studied. Part of this paper is revised from some published papers such as the introduction of this methodology in the documented book of this workshop (Fab-Union. ,2019) and a conference paper discussing the design of this tile-vaulted pavilion in IASS2019 (Yuan, P. F.,&Philippe, B. ,2019). Therefore, the authors would like to mention again all the participants in this ETH/MIT/Tongji joint workshop 'Robotic Force Printing' project.

ACKNOWLEDGEMENTS

Prof. Philippe Block, Prof. Philip F. Yuan, Dr. Ing. Xiang Wang, Kam-Ming Mark Tam, Gene Ting-Chun Kao, Zain Karsan, Alex Beaudouin, Ce Li, Ben Hoyle, Molly Mason, Weizhe Gao, Weiran Zhu, Zhe Guo, Dalma Foldesi, Hyerin Lee, Jung In Seo, Anna Vasileiou, Youyuan Luo, D, Xiao Zhang, Liming Zhang and Hua Chai.

This research is funded by the National Social Science Fund of China (Grant No.17ZDA019)

REFERENCES

Andrei, Jipa, Mathias, Bernhard, Mania, Meibodi and Dillenburger, Benjamin 2016 '3D-Printed Stay-in-Place Formwork for Topologically Optimized Concrete Slabs', *TxA Emerging Design + Technology*, San Antonio, Texas, USA, p. Volume: 3

Benjamin, Felbrich, Nikolas, Frueh, Marshall, Prado and Saman, Saffarian 2017 'Multi-Machine Fabrication: An Integrative Design Process Utilising an Autonomous UAV and Industrial Robots for the Fabrication of Long Span Composite Structures', *ACADIA 2017*, Cambridge, pp. 248-259

Philippen, Block, Matthias, Rippmann and Tom, Van Mele 2017, 'Compressive Assemblies: Bottom‐Up Performance for a New Form of Construction', *Architectural Design*, 87, pp. 104-109

Sigrid, Adriaenssens, Philippe, Block, Diederik, Veenendaal and Chris, Williams 2014, *Shell structures for architecture: form finding and optimization*, Routledge, London and New York

Tam, Mark 2015, *Principal stress line computation for discrete topology design*, Ph.D. Thesis, MIT

Tomas, Mendez Echenagucia, Dave, Pigram, Andrew, Liew, Tom, Van Mele and Philippe, Block 2018 'Full-scale prototype of a cable-net and fabric formed concrete thin-shell roof', *Proceedings of IASS 2018(25)*, Boston, p. 20

Xiang, Wang, Kam-Ming Mark, Tam, Alexandre, Beaudouin-Mackay, Benjamin, Hoyle, Molly, Mason, Zhe, Guo, Weizhe, Gao, Ce, Li, Weiran, Zhu, Zain, Karsan, Kao, Gene Ting-Chun, Liming, Zhang, Hua, Chai, Philip F., Yuan and Philippe, Block 2020, '3d-Printed Bending-Active Formwork for Shell Structures', in Philip F., Yuan, Mike, Xie, Neil, Leach, Jiawei, Yao and Xiang, Wang (eds) 2020, *Materializing Intelligence*, Springer, German , pp. 295-313

Performance-Driven Design of a Reciprocal Frame Canopy

Timber structure of the FutureTree

Aleksandra Anna Apolinarska[1], *Mathias Kuhn*[2], *Fabio Gramazio*[3], *Matthias Kohler*[4]
[1,3,4] *ETH Zürich, Switzerland* [2] *Basler & Hofmann AG, Switzerland*
[1,3,4] *{apolinarska|gramazio|kohler}@arch.ethz.ch* [2] *mathias.kuhn@baslerhofmann.ch*

This paper presents the design process of a recently built, 107 m2 free-form timber frame canopy. The structure is an irregular, funnel-shaped reciprocal frame resting on a central concrete column, and has been fabricated using a robot-based assembly process. The project addresses several known design and fabrication challenges: modelling of free-form reciprocal frames, complex interrelations between their geometry and structural behaviour, as well as develops custom software tools to represent different models and interface design and structural analysis environments. The performance-driven design is exemplified by studies on the relationship between geometric parameters of the reciprocal frame and the resulting force-flow and flexural stiffness of the structure. The final design is obtained by differentiating geometry and stiffness to reduce deflection and tensile stresses while observing fabrication constraints. The project demonstrates the application of computational design to create customized, performance-driven and robotically fabricated structures, and its successful realization validates the methods under real-life planning and construction conditions.

Keywords: *Integrated computational design , Performance-based design , Reciprocal frames , Timber structures, Robotic fabrication*

INTRODUCTION

The principle of a reciprocal frame, where the supporting and supported elements form a circular relationship, has been known for centuries (e.g through the works of de Honnecourt, da Vinci, Serlio or Wallis). In the early 20th century, the Zollinger system based on this principle was widely used in Europe in roof structures of houses, barns and churches (Erler 2013). It can also be found in a number of large-scale projects (e.g. main train station in Kassel, thermal baths in Bad Sulza, Germany) built in the past decades.

Reciprocal frames are structures that can achieve flexural stiffness regardless of the stiffness of the joints, and can span much further than the lengths of the individual elements. On small scales, this makes them interesting for pre-fabrication and robotic assembly, especially for construction of non-standard structures (Apolinarska et al. 2016). Being aesthetically compelling, with many possible patterns and overall forms, modelling a free-form reciprocal frame can be challenging and has been a popular topic in academia (Song et al. 2013; Tamke et al. 2010), and as a pavilion motif (Melvin 2005; Evolute 2013) in recent years. The interplay of geometry and structural behaviour in reciprocal frames is particularly interesting. Their flexural stiffness depends on where the supported elements lie on the supporting elements. In reciprocal frames derived from a grid (a structure where elements meet at polyvalent nodes) this property can be described as the *node opening* (also called *knot expansion*, see Figure 1). Previous work by e.g. (Kohlhammer et al. 2017; Douthe and Baverel 2009) investigated the impact of the node opening on flexural stiffness, but considered a uniform node opening for all nodes. In contrast to the precedent work, in the FutureTree project this parameter is varied individually for each node to achieve areas with higher and lower stiffness. The resulting differentiation of the frame's pattern provides both an improved structural behaviour and an intriguing visual effect.

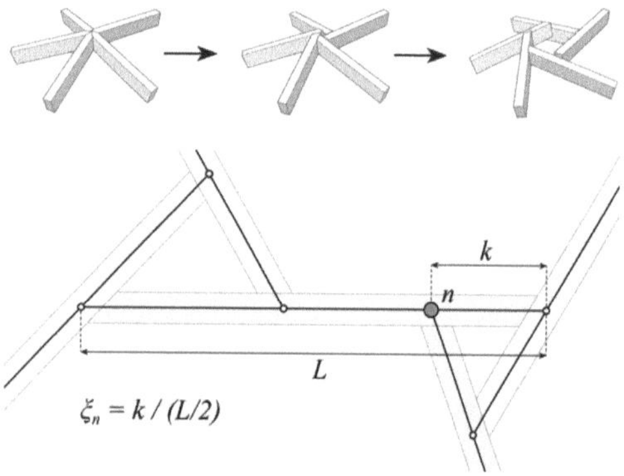

Figure 1
Transformation of a grid into a reciprocal frame (top) by introducing the node opening ξ for each node n (definition, bottom).

In order to study the relationships between geometry and structural behaviour, it is indispensable to translate between design and structural models, usually created in different software and consisting of different entities, data structures and semantic information. For example, frame structures are usually calculated using an abstracted *point+line* (or *node+member*) finite element model. Obtaining this model from solid geometry typically used to represent the architectural design can be non-obvious and project-specific, esp. with regard to how connections between elements are defined. Off-the-shelf interface plugins (e.g. JumpingFrog, RhinoInside) are not designed to solve this automatically, therefore establishing such a translation requires a joint effort of engineers and architects, who co-develop the necessary code based directly on the software's APIs, as in the presented work.

ABOUT THE FUTURETREE PROJECT

The FutureTree is a funnel-shaped canopy spanning over a 107 m2 quadrilateral courtyard of an office building of Basler & Hoffman, in Esslingen near Zürich, Switzerland (Figure 2). The structure consist of a reciprocal timber frame anchored to the building on two sides, with one corner cantilevering (Figure 3, left), and in the centre it is resting on a concrete column built with a novel *Eggshell* technology (Burger et al. 2020), with its eight ribs smoothly following the shape of the timber frame. The frame is made of 380 timber elements with cross-sections of 65 × 140 mm forming the reciprocal structure, framed by four ring beams with cross-sections of 140 × 280 mm. All joints in the frame are butt T-joints connected using a pair of full-threaded screws, arranged in a V-shape. Since the structure is permanently weather-exposed, and the moisture can be trapped in the tight-fitting joints, all timber elements are made of acetylated radiata pine wood (Accoya). The filigree structure is additionally stabilized by eight tension cables to help reduce tensile stresses within the joints and deformation.

The timber structure has been prefabricated in five segments to fit the standard transportation size limits (Figure 3, middle). With the exception of the ring beams, each timber element of the reciprocal frame was manufactured and placed just-in-time by

Figure 2
The FutureTree
(Esslingen ZH,
Switzerland)

Figure 3
Situation and context (left). Segmentation of the timber structure and other components of the structure (middle). Just-in-time robotic fabrication of parts and assembly (right).

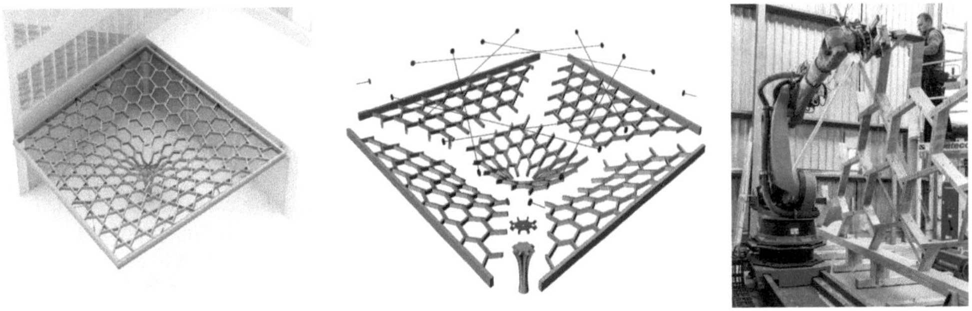

an industrial robot, and manually screwed together, as in (Thoma et al. 2019). The custom fabrication workcell set up by the contractor (ERNE AG Holzbau) consisted of a KUKA KR 240 robot mounted on a linear axis (Figure 3, right) and equipped with exchangeable end-effectors: a gripper, a spindle for pre-drilling of the screw holes and a circular saw for cutting the elements at various angles.

With the aim to transfer and validate research in a real-life planning and construction scenario, the project has been developed in close collaboration between academic and industrial partners. In the

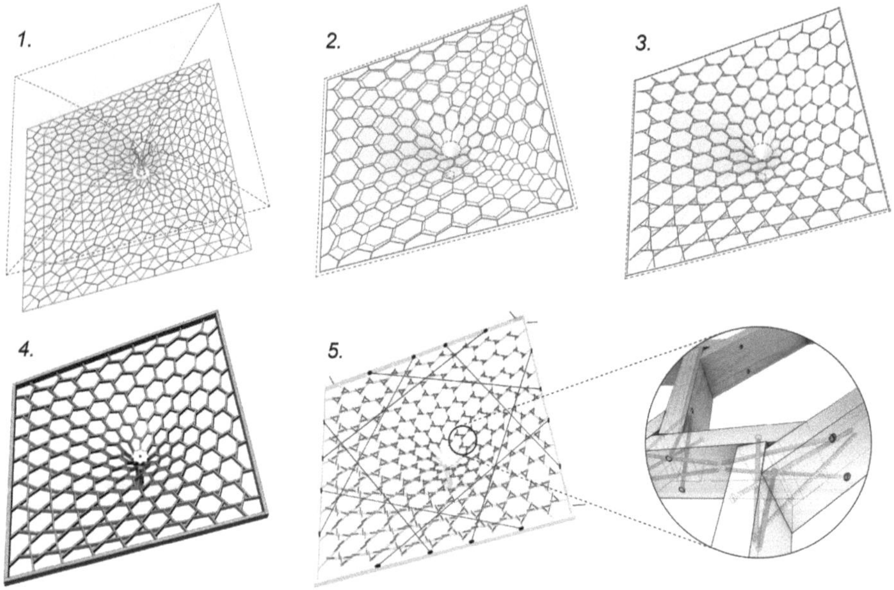

Figure 4
Geometric modelling of the FutureTree reciprocal frame: 1. triangulated grid (orange), its dual (red), and the guide surface, 2. projected (red) and relaxed (blue) hex grid on guide surface, 3. transformation of the hex grid (blue) into a reciprocal scheme (dark blue), 4. solid geometry model, 5. detailing: screw connections, cables and anchors.

subsequent sections, the following aspects of the design development process are discussed: 1) the geometric modelling of the reciprocal frame structure, 2) the structural design studies evaluating the relationship between geometry and structural performance, as well as 3) custom software tools and interfaces.

GEOMETRIC MODELLING

To contain the complexity of the structure, the geometric modelling process is split into smaller steps, each dedicated to a specific concern. Each of the following steps (Figure 4) produces a model that serves as an input (setout) for the subsequent one(s):

1. *Topology.* First, a triangulated 2D scheme (orange) is drawn to set the resolution of the structure. Its dual graph - a hexagonal grid (red) - defines the actual topology.
2. *3D setout.* The hexagonal grid is projected onto a funnel-shaped guide surface. The shape of the guide surface has a higher-level impact on the force-flow in the structure, and a good initial guess can be found early on. Next, the distribution of the edges in the grid is improved by e.g. equalizing lengths and angles (blue).
3. *Reciprocal frame.* The improved grid is transformed into a reciprocal frame by *opening* the nodes (dark blue), done by sliding each line segment's end points along the corresponding neighbouring edge, as in (Apolinarska 2018) (pp. 81-89). This method is simple and fast, although does not solve globally like e.g. (Song et al. 2013). In this iterative process, points' coordinates are updated in small increments, until each reaches its individually set target distance. Here, the node opening ξ is expressed as the proportion of this distance k to the half of the current length L of an element (Figure 1, bottom). Note that the beams tend to get longer with the increasing ξ. Also, on a curved surface,

the connections between elements are likely to become eccentric (centrelines not intersecting). To keep overall shape, an additional constraint pulls an average of the beams' end points at each node towards the guide surface, as well as prevents it from moving too far away from the original node's position.

4. *Solid 3D model.* Cross-section dimensions and orientations of each timber element are specified to create a solid geometry model. Each element's z-axis is aligned to an average normal vector of the guide surface at points closest to the centerline's endpoints.
5. *Detailing.* Connection details such as V-shaped screw pairs, anchoring elements and cables are modelled. Collisions between screws can occur in nodes with a very small ξ and in the area close to the central column, where the timber elements are shorter. Starting with default screw angles and lengths, any detected collisions are resolved by locally modifying these parameters within a permissible range resulting from forces in the affected connections. For fabricability, it also has to be assured that a screw can be inserted at all, i.e. its entering point is not obscured by another timber element, and that there is enough room for the length of the screw and the screwdriver. This problem can occur in areas with a large node opening, and can be resolved by either reducing the node opening or slight local adjustment of the affected timber element.

STRUCTURAL DESIGN

Since the structural behaviour of such reciprocal frames relies heavily on their geometry, this relationship was investigated through series of studies, including the overall shape (e.g. curvature of the guide surface) and the node opening parameter of the reciprocal frame. The latter is discussed below in more detail, with the following assumptions. The structure has eight rigid support points at the interface to the column, and two anchoring each of the two ring beams connected to the building. T-joint connections were modelled using a simplified representation of the screws (Figure 5, red lines) to directly calculate the forces transferred by the screws. This allows to take the stiffness of the connection into account. This approach is conservative since the stiffness is a function of the actual load, i.e. different in the case of tension or compression. The considered load case is a self-weight (C24 timber) combined with an applied vertical load of 10 N/m' of each beams' length, corresponding to a snow load. These are simplified assumptions sufficient for an early design exploration to find an approximately optimal solution.

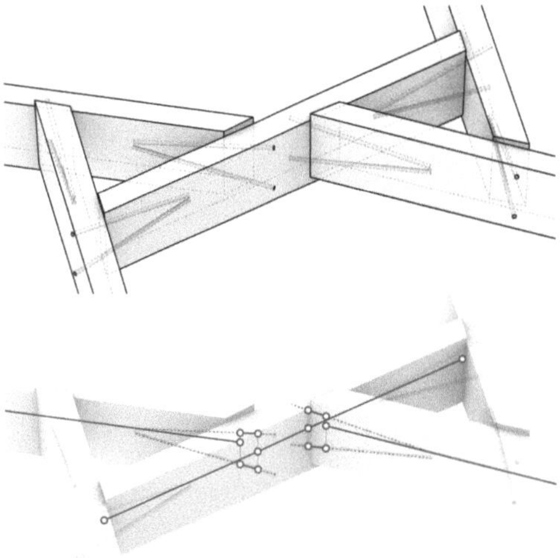

Figure 5
Design model (top) and the derived point+line model (bottom).

The study focuses on forces and displacement at the joints (as opposed to forces in the timber elements), as these are the critical parts of the structure, i.e. the dimensioning of the structure (cross-section sizes) are predominantly driven by the requirements of the connections. It is known that the stiffness of the reciprocal frame of this type increases with the node opening. This is readily exemplified in Figure 6, showing that the displacement of the cantilevering corner is much smaller at ξ=100% than at ξ=40%. Unfortunately, stiffer structures often experience stress peaks locally. Here, the major concern are

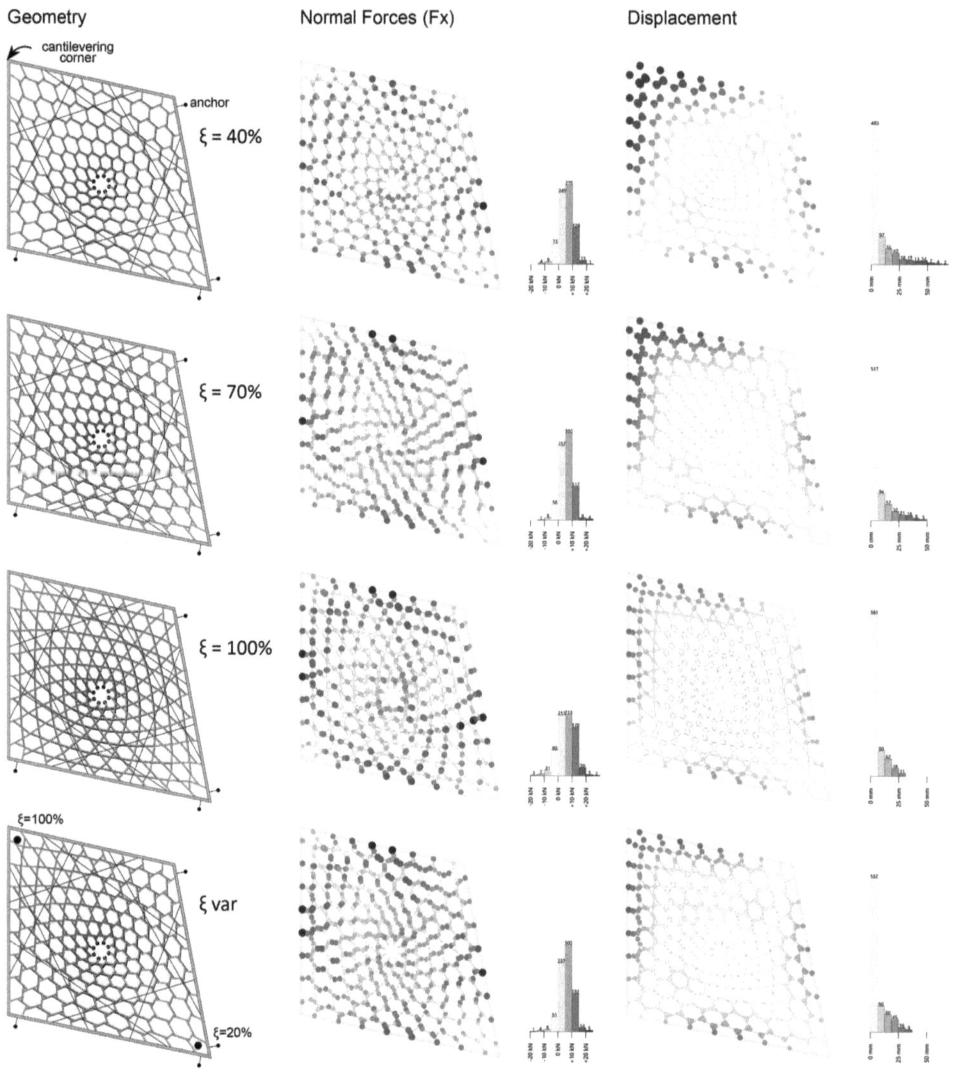

Figure 6
Impact of node opening ξ on normal forces and displacement at the joints.

joints with excessive tension (Fx<0, blue) - a pulling force that is difficult to take up by screws. To negotiate the two conflicting objectives, the node opening is differentiated throughout the structure. The winning solution (bottom row) presents a good compromise, with a gradual transition between the maximum node opening at the cantilevering corner and the minimum at the opposite corner.

IMPLEMENTATION & INTEGRATION

The generation and evaluation of many design variations described above was facilitated by custom-made tools written in Python, using SDK of Rhino as the backbone for 3D modelling, Grasshopper as the main user interface, and API of Autodesk Robot Structural Analysis (RSA) to streamline structural calculations (Figure 7). The overall workflow is as follows:

1. Generate the design model based on given parameters
2. Derive an abstracted structural (point+line) model
3. Build and calculate the structure in RSA
4. Retrieve, evaluate and visualize the results

As such, this workflow is directional, i.e. with no conditional loops, and the satisfactory solution is obtained through search by explicitly varying parameters at different stages of the process (e.g. of the global funnel shape, or of the node opening for all or individual elements).

The geometric design is built using custom object classes to represent different elements (beams, joints, assembly) of the reciprocal frame and the connectivity between them, following the approach described in (Apolinarska 2018, pp. 75-81). For example, the *Beam* class objects are defined by the centreline, the cross-section (its z-direction, width and height) as well as by the elements to which it connects to (incl. which side) and from which the cutting planes at the ends are derived and thus always up-to-date. It combines abstract and solid geometry models, semantic information and other metadata and is designed to store or generate every distinct piece of information only once where possible. Semantically, in the discussed reciprocal frames, the connectivity relationships form a circular graph, i.e. they lack hierarchy, which is a relatively unique setting in structures.

Next, the abstract point+line model is derived, i.e. each centreline (blue line in Figure 5) is subdivided into line segments as members. New members are created to represent connections (red lines: screw members, orange: rigid links) and new nodes are added at the ends or intersections of members. Additional structural setup data (e.g. support points and releases, material properties, loads) is added. This generic model can be used as a basis input for multiple FEA software (e.g. RSA, RSTAB, Sofistik). In terms of implementation, it was sufficient and lightweight to use Python dictionaries to structure the data of nodes and members (instead of instances of custom classes), which are additionally linked to the corresponding objects in the design model.

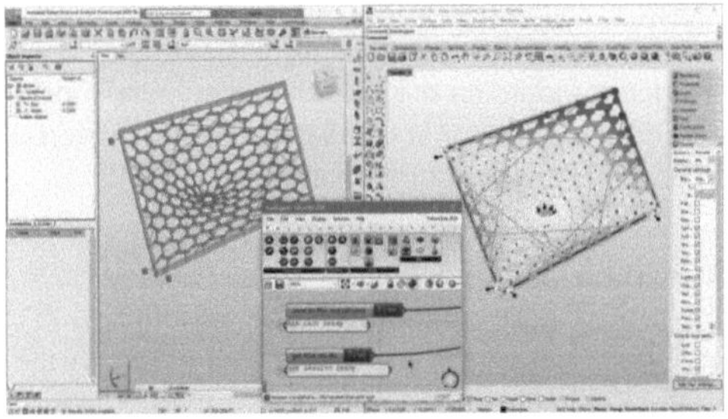

Figure 7
Interface between Rhino/Grasshopper and Autodesk Robot Structural Analysis.

Since every analysis software uses their own data structures and object classes, exposed via its API, the next step is to build the actual structural model for calculation from the abstract one. Some project settings (e.g. cross-section definitions, object groups, load case combinations) are pre-defined in an RSA file used as a template and assigned correspondingly in the abstract model. In the presented work, a COM interface controlled directly from a Python component in Grasshopper was created to start the RSA app, build the model, set up and trigger the calculation, as well as retrieve the results to make them available in the Grasshopper UI. The raw results (e.g. stresses in bars, forces and displacement in the nodes) are then relinked with the design model, evaluated (e.g. compared with maximum allowed values) and displayed as a visual feedback to the user.

CONCLUSIONS & OUTLOOK

The FutureTree demonstrates that computational and performance-driven design methods, still often considered experimental and academic, can be readily applied in an industrial setting, given an early and intense cross-disciplinary collaboration. The practice of pair or side-by-side programming between the authors - an architect and an engineer - significantly helped to establish the right strategy, data structures, coordinate the inputs and outputs between discipline-specific modules, and boosted mutual understanding of the problems and objectives. As a consequence, the project development process that conventionally would be based on separation of disciplines and responsibilities naturally evolved into a deeply integrated process. Looking forward, such workflows would be significantly easier to practice if an open standard for the abstracted structural model would be available that could be used as a universal input model for structural analysis.

ACKNOWLEDGEMENTS

The project was funded by Basler & Hofmann AG, Esslingen, Switzerland and partially supported by the SNSF NCCR Digital Fabrication. We would like to thank partners involved in the planning and realization of the timber canopy of the FutureTree: D. Courtin, S. Hak and F. Baumayer (Basler & Hofmann AG), T. Wehrle, A. Thoma, S. Schleith, O. Ackermann (ERNE AG Holzbau), F. Tschümperlin (SJB Kempter Fitze), as well as the designers and researchers of the *Eggshell* column E. Lloret and J.Burger (Gramazio Kohler Research, ETH Zürich). All figures: (C) Gramazio Kohler Research, ETH Zürich, except: Figure 3 right (C) ERNE AG Holzbau.

REFERENCES

Apolinarska, AA 2018, *Complex Timber Structures from Simple Elements: Computational Design of Novel Bar Structures for Robotic Fabrication and Assembly*, Ph.D. Thesis, ETH Zurich

Apolinarska, AA, Bärtschi, R, Furrer, R, Gramazio, F and Kohler, M 2016 'Mastering the Sequential Roof: Computational Methods for Integrating Design, Structural Analysis, and Robotic Fabrication', *Advances in Architectural Geometry 2016*, CH

Burger, J, Lloret-Fritschi, E, Taha, N, Scotto, F, Demoulin, T, Mata-Falcón, J, Gramazio, F, Kohler, M and Flatt, RJ 2020 'Design and Fabrication of a Non-standard, Structural Concrete Column Using Eggshell: Ultra-Thin, 3D Printed Formwork', *Second RILEM International Conference on Concrete and Digital Fabrication*, Cham, pp. 1104-1115

Douthe, C and Baverel, O 2009, 'Design of nexorades or reciprocal frame systems with the dynamic relaxation method', *Computers & Structures*, 87(21), pp. 1296-1307

Erler, K 2013, *Kuppeln und Bogendächer aus Holz: von arabischen Kuppeln bis zum Zollinger-Dach*, Fraunhofer IRB-Verl, Stuttgart

Evolute, ? 2013, 'Designing KREOD', *?*, ?(online: www.evolute.at/download/130129_designing_-KREOD_web.pdf, Accessed: 29.05.2021), p. ?

Kohlhammer, T, Apolinarska, AA, Gramazio, F and Kohler, M 2017, 'Design and structural analysis of complex timber structures with glued T-joint connections for robotic assembly', *International Journal of Space Structures*, 32(3-4), pp. 199-215

Melvin, J 2005, 'Serpentine Gallery Pavilion 2005', *Architectural Design*, 75(6), pp. 102-106

Song, P, Fu, CW, Goswami, P, Zheng, J, Mitra, NJ and Cohen-Or, D 2013, 'Reciprocal frame structures made easy', *ACM Transactions on Graphics*, 32(4), pp. 94:1-94:13

Tamke, M, Riiber, J, Jungjohann, H and Thomsen, MR 2010 'Lamella Flock', *Advances in Architectural Geometry 2010*, Vienna, pp. 37-48

Thoma, A, Adel, A, Helmreich, M, Wehrle, T, Gramazio, F and Kohler, M 2019 'Robotic Fabrication of Bespoke Timber Frame Modules', *Robotic Fabrication in Architecture, Art and Design 2018*, Cham, pp. 447-458

Iris Diaphragm Mechanism Application for Daylighting Control

Aleksandar Krnjaić[1]*, Marko Jovanović*[2]
[1,2]*Department of Architecture, Faculty of Technical Sciences, University of Novi Sad, Novi Sad, Serbia*
[1]*aleksandar.krnjaic023@gmail.com* [2]*markojovanovic@uns.ac.rs*

Daylight is an important factor in interior design. The benefits can be seen in reduced need for heating and artificial lighting, while the caveats are visual hindrance, glare, thermal discomfort and increased energy for cooling. The industry standard way of controlling daylighting is with roller blinds, venetian blinds, curtains, static and automated façades which do not allow sufficient control over daylight. The aim of this paper is to explore the potential of using circular modules with the iris diaphragm mechanism as a system for controlling the daylight amount, similar to the approach used on Arab World Institute. Circular module that are proposed in the paper consists of an outer casing, inner rotational and stationary rings and blades. A parametric iris model is generated and optimized to conform to the criteria of having the smallest casing, thinnest blades and the least amount of blades to decrease fabrication and assembly time. The circular module is applied in three layouts on a rectangular opening to calculate the efficiency in daylighting control. Obtained results show significant increase in systems flexibility and performance compared to the closest implementation in the south façade of the Arab World Institute.

Keywords: *iris diaphragm, daylight, shading system, daylight control*

1. INTRODUCTION

One of the most important aspects to consider when designing a living and working environment is daylight and its effects on users. Having a sufficient amount of daylight is essential for providing a comfortable indoor environment. Moreover, daylight has numerous positive effects on health (Boubekri, 2008). In order to provide an adequate amount of light, contemporary architecture uses more and more glass surfaces, most prominently seen with the introduction of glass curtain walls. However, excessive amounts of daylight can have negative effects such as glare (Hopkinson, 1972; Osterhaus, 2005; Jakubiec and Reinhart, 2012), visual discomfort and overheating (Altan et. al., 2008; Tillson et. al., 2012; Nebia and Tabet Aoul, 2017) which also increases cooling loads and energy consumption (Tzempelikos and Athienitis, 2007). In order to mitigate these negative effects of daylighting, various shading systems are used. These systems are generally divided into three categories:

1. Static shading systems (Fig 1a)

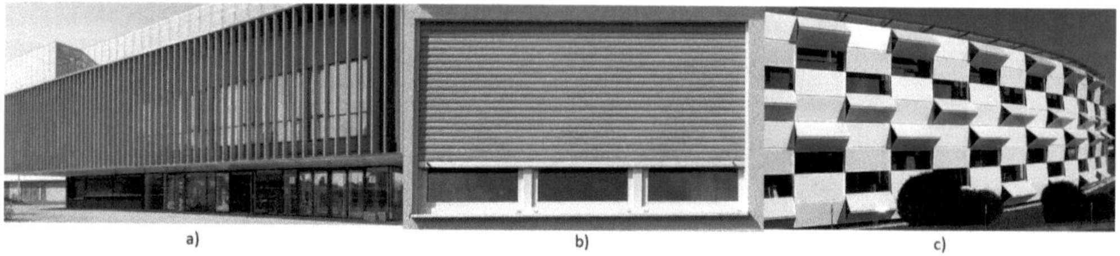

Figure 1
a) Static shading system: brise soleil [2]; b) Manually operated shading systems: roller blinds [3]; c) Automated shading systems on Kiefer Technic Showroom / Ernst Giselbrecht + Partner, 2007. [4]

2. Manually operated shading systems (Fig 1b) and
3. Automated shading systems (Fig 1c)

Static shading systems like Islamic, wooden lattice-screen - mashrabiya (Samuels, 2011; Ashour, 2018) and brise-soleil (Kamal, 2013) work by predicting the angle of the sun throughout the year to provide shade in the summer and allow daylight inside during winter. Even though these systems are beneficial in mitigating negative effects of daylighting in the summer, they do not allow the control of the daylighting amount that passes or is blocked.

Manually operated shading systems give users the most control over setting up their preferred daylight amount in the room. But research has shown that users tend not to use them until they already feel discomfort or do not use them at all (O'Brien et. al., 2013). Systems that fall into these criteria are Venetian blinds (Foster and Oreszczyn, 2001; Kuhn, 2006), roller blinds (Ip et. al., 2013) and shutters (Hamdani et. al.,2016). When observing how this system type operates, it is noticeable that even with a certain control portrayal, the control is still limited. Both roller and Venetian blinds allow users to control daylight linearly across the opening. In the case of roller blinds, the control is from top to the bottom of the window and in case of Venetian blinds and shutters, it is through the horizontal strips that open and close. These systems do not allow for specific part of the opening to be segmented from the rest and stay opened or closed. This approach limits the usability and controllability of these systems. With technology progression, user control was completely substituted with automated systems that have the ability to track or predict the sunpath through sensor information and adjust the daylighting system according to indoor climate in real time.

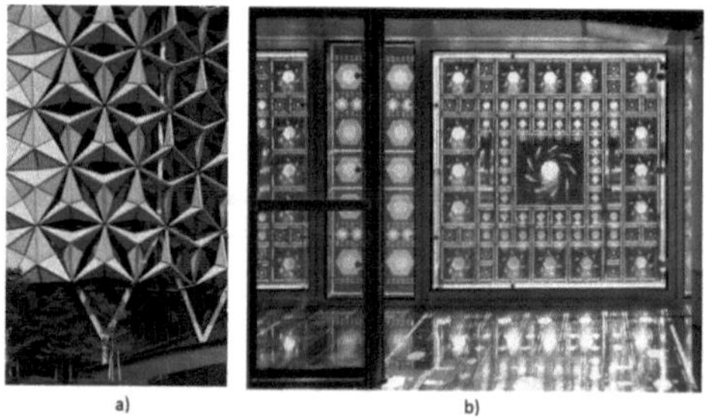

Figure 2
a) Façade of the Al Bahr towers in the UAE, Adreas Architects, 2012.[5]; b) Façade of the Arab World Institute in Paris, Jean Nouvel, 1987.[6]

Automated shading systems are usually part of a façade in combination with glass curtain walls (Hraska, 2018). They strive to create a set temperature in the room but disregard occupants needs (Bakker et.al., 2014; Meerbeek et. al., 2014). An example of such a system can be seen on Al Bahr towers in the UAE (Fig 2a). The system consists of a honeycomb like pattern inspired by mashrabiya and umbrella like elements that open and close, therefore controlling the amount of light inside the object. It is estimated that this system reduces energy consumption by 50% compared to the conventional high-rise building. (Schumacher et. al., 2019). Although the system is impressive it was very expensive to build and its operation is not considered sustainable. Moreover, when employees were asked about their work environment, usually, around half of them said that it was unpleasant due to overheating and distraction from the system itself (Attia, 2018). Another fully automated system can be found on the south façade of Jean Nouvel's Arab World Institute in Paris. The system also takes inspiration from the mashrabiya but this time controls daylight with photocells and 30 000 camera like iris diaphragms (Fig 2b).

This system allows 10-30% of the light in and is controlled by motors every hour to adjust according to the sun (Alenei et. al., 2018). This type of setup makes the system very expensive to fabricate and high maintenance. That's why many of the diaphragms do not work anymore alongside the photocells (Murray and Murray, 2009). This coupled with expensive operation, which has the ability to let in only 10-30% of light makes this system limited to use in its current form.

As aforementioned all of the systems have their benefits and drawbacks, but most of the drawbacks focus on the control of daylighting, or lack thereof. Static systems do not have detailed control, while manually and automatically operated shading systems have limited daylighting control. Manipulating which parts of the opening let the light to pass and at what intensity seems to be the one factor that connects and at the same time limits all the shading systems mentioned so far. Therefore, the existence of a more complete and hence more controllable daylighting system is still a very important factor.

The type of a system that implements an iris diaphragm is relatively unexplored in the field of architecture, apart from Arab World Institute, while in the field of photography it has been used for decades as a system for controlling the intrusion of light on the camera sensor. Per definition - "The iris of the aperture is an adjustable diaphragm of thin opaque plates that can be rotated by a ring so that the diameter of the central aperture changes, usually to regulate the aperture of the lens" (Merriam-Webster, 2021). The straight-forward application of this system on the south façade of the Arab World Institute building neglects the full potential of this system. The shutter can be fully opened and closed, while in the given example it is only partial. Such application limits the system and reduces the ability to control daylight. Also, the distance between the individual apertures occupies a large part of the system surface, which reduces the efficiency of a fully open system.

Therefore, the aim of this paper is to implement a system that segments the window opening using manually controlled iris diaphragms grouped into clusters, to allow greater control over not only the intensity of the daylight but also the area of the room being affected by it. In order to design such a system, it is necessary to divide it into several phases:

- Creating a parametric iris diaphragm model
- Determining the optimal iris diaphragm settings
- Finding the best performing grid like iris layout
- Finding the best performing disordered iris layout
- Creating clusters of iris diaphragms in a single system, so that the light passing through the opening can be segmented and controlled individually

This paper will focus on the first three phases.

The criteria for evaluating the design of the shading system is based on how much control does the system offer. Moreover, it controls how much light can pass through the system when all of the segments are in fully opened state relative to the surface of the window while keeping the system economically viable in terms of fabrication and assembly times.

2. IRIS DIAPHRAGM-BASED DAYLIGHT CONTROL SYSTEM DESIGN

As mentioned above, this paper explores the first three phases. First it is necessary to make a parametric model of the iris diaphragm, after which a generative design is applied to find the optimal parameter values. The optimal solution entails that a completely opened module blocks as little light as possible. Finally, the module design is used in a, grid like layout across a rectangular window surface. A parametric model was chosen since it allows fast design changes and an efficient iterative process. Programs that were used in the design process are Rhinoceros 6 and Grasshopper for visual programming. Physical models were fabricated in order to test out the proposed designs.

2.1. Creating a parametric iris diaphragm model

There are many types of iris diaphragms. The difference among them is usually indicated by the type of the blade being utilized. The type of iris diaphragm used in this paper is inspired by the iris diaphragm found on Iris calculator website [7]. This type of iris diaphragm consists of blades that are formed by intersecting two rings with the same radius. The ends are rounded and are tied at both ends to the rotating rings (Fig 3a).

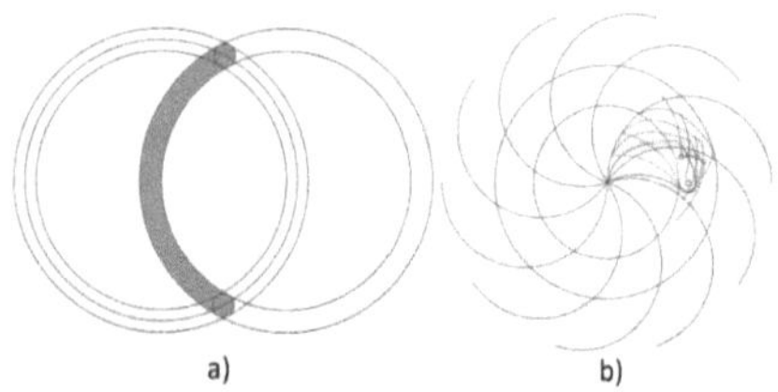

Figure 3
a) Design of the iris diaphragms blade fixed on both sides;
b) Design of the iris diaphragms blade fixed on one side

Unlike the iris diaphragm type being used in the Arab World Institutes south façade (Fig 3b), this type of iris diaphragm is more consistent in opening and closing due to the lack of freestanding blade ends that can intersect and jam at the center during closing. This iris diaphragm consists of multiple parts shown in Figure 4. In addition to the blades (Figure 4a), it also contains two rings, one rotating with holes for the blades (Figure 4c) and a static one with rails (Figure 4b). By rotating the movable ring, blades are rotating, with one side fixed in the hole and the other side sliding along the rail. In this manner, the blades are on top of each other and spaced equally from each other, influencing the daylighting passage of the iris opening. The opening and closing sequences are simulated in Grasshopper and all the parts are modelled in the same environment.

The parametric model is dependent on five main parameters that always interact with each other and control the characteristics of each iris diaphragm: the diameter of the iris diaphragm opening (Figure 4d), the number of blades, the angle of rotation, the width of the blade (Figure 4a) and the casing width (Figure 4e). The diameter of the iris diaphragm opening is an important parameter since it determents how much light passes and the number of modules in a system. By determining the diameter of the iris opening combinations with certain number of blades and their width can be used to cover the opening with that diameter. Number of blades is the base parameter of the system since it influences the remaining parameters. Higher number of blades requires their width to be smaller in order to cover the opening. In fully opened position blades form the outer ring around the opening which is closed inside a casing. Therefore, the casing width is directly proportional to the width of the blade. So, the most important relation for maximizing the performance of the iris is between the number of blades and the width of the blades because the width of the blades determents the width of the casing. Casing width does not let the light through, thus diminishing the maximum amount of light that can reach the interior. Higher number of blades requires a larger angle of rotation but this parameter doesn't affect the performance of the iris diaphragm it is only used to make the simulation of the system in a parametric model, thus it is excluded from the optimisation.

2.2 Determining the optimal iris diaphragm settings

Optimising iris diaphragm settings consists of finding the optimal settings for the base parameter i.e. number of blades and adjusting remaining parameters according to the correlations previously mentioned. Determining the optimal ratio of casing width and number of blades is essential when designing the iris diaphragm. It is necessary to strike a balance between obtaining the narrowest casing possible and an iris diaphragm that can be fabricated in a time-effective manner, with regards to labour and materials. All iris diaphragms have a 160mm diameter opening and were made with minimal blade width for each version to provide the narrowest casing pos-

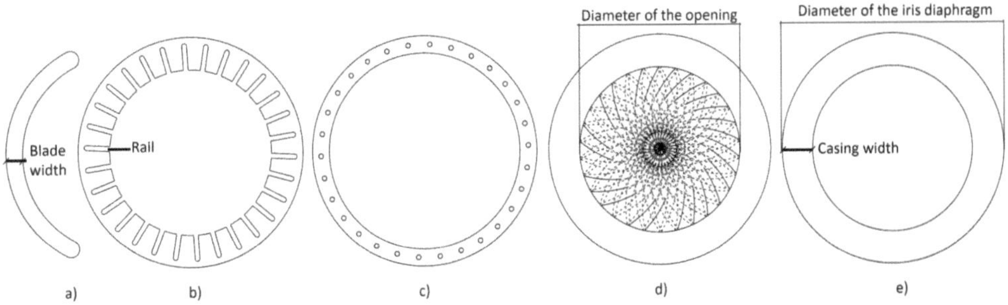

Figure 4
Parts of the iris diaphragm and iris diaphragm in opened and closed position - a) the blade, b) static ring with rails, c) rotating ring with holes, d) fully closed iris diaphragm, e) fully opened iris diaphragm

sible. Even so, the traditional approach has a casing which is wider than the blade width to accommodate the rail length on the rotation ring's inside (Figure 5a).

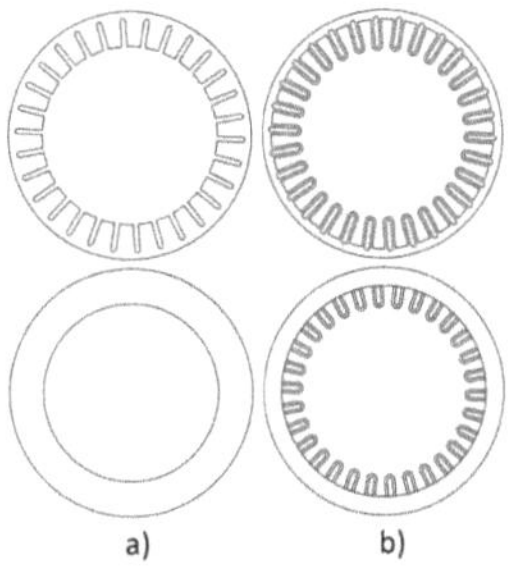

Figure 5
a) Rails inside the casing; b) Optimised rails that protrude in the opening

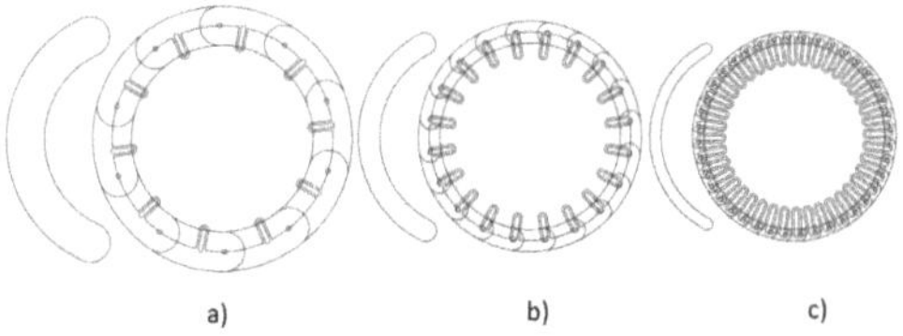

Figure 6
a) Ten, b) twenty and c) forty blade iris diaphragms respectively

However, as shown in Figure 5b, the approach in this paper is to reduce the casing width, leaving the rails protruding inwards and thus allowing more light to pass through. Rails are modified to be only as thick as needed to hold the sliding pins of the blade. In the case of the iris diaphragms shown in Figure 5, rails and casing marked a) are usually used when making iris diaphragms, but they have 51,6% of area that lets the light in. The rails and casing marked b) have 65% of area that lets the light in. This is a 13,4% increase in area which light is passing trough when the casing and opening are designed in such a way.

Reducing the casing to be only as wide as the blades are also simplifies the calculation of the casing width by merging the two factors into one. In order to have as much light passing through the single iris diaphragm as possible, the casing has to be as narrow as possible. But that requires more blades to be used so that the opening can be properly closed. With the addition of more blades, the cost seen through fabrication and assembly times and cost increases, influencing the cost-effectives of the system. A wide range of iris diaphragm were tested, ranging from six blades to forty blades. The maximum number of blades is determinate to be forty, as seen in Figure 6 since the density of the railings prevents the amount to be larger. Minimal number of 6 blades is chosen because it is the first combination of number of blades and blade width worth considering. Figure 6 represents the visual difference between the iris diaphragm with same size opening but with ten, twenty and forty blades with different widths respectively.

Therefore, determining the optimal number of blades requires determining at which point the iris casing width remains similar i.e., at which point the amount of time required for fabricating exceeds the benefits of a narrower iris casing. Chart in Figure 7 in-

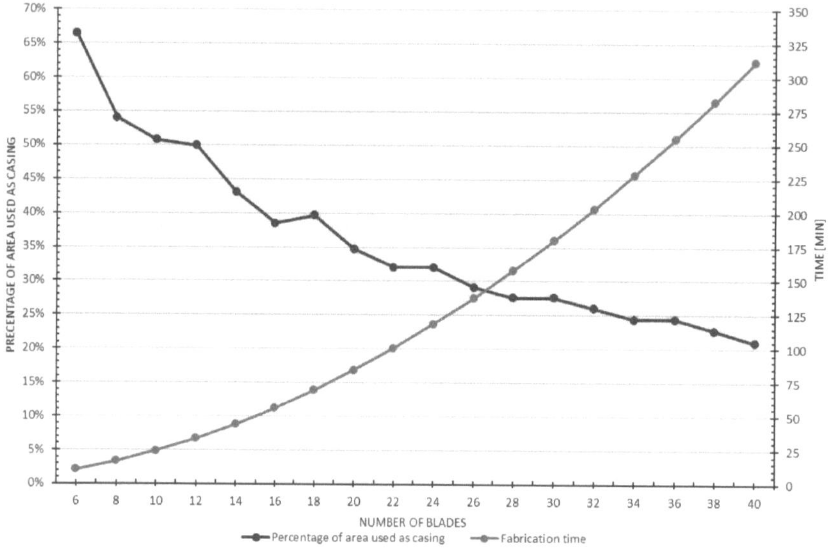

Figure 7
Graph showing comparing of the percentage of openness with occupancy rate

dicates that this number is between 26 and 28 blades. So, in order to maximise the reduction in casing area iris diaphragm with 28 blades was chosen.

This is the optimal number of blades for an iris diaphragm with 160mm diameter. The fabrication time measured on the graph is for the prototype which includes laser cutting the parts, which was an insignificant portion of the time, compared to the assembly, which took a larger portion. Looking at the graph, single iris diaphragm with 28 blades obscures 27,6% of the light indicating that the area is well utilized.

Although the best combination from the graph was chosen, a large number of blades creates a problem in the physical model, as seen in Figure 8a. A large number of blades compressed into a small area creates friction and disables the iris from closing completely.

This problem has been overcome by creating two stacks of 14 blades, like in Figure 8b. This approach allows blades to move unencumbered and prevents them from intersecting, by utilising the same stationary ring and forcing the blades to be on opposite sides of it.

Splitting the blades into two segments does not increase the thickness of the system by much, given that only an additional rail ring is used, measuring 3mm. This increase does not contribute to the light blocking in any way. Once the optimal number of blades and their segmentation is determined, it is possible to implement such an iris system in a larger layout.

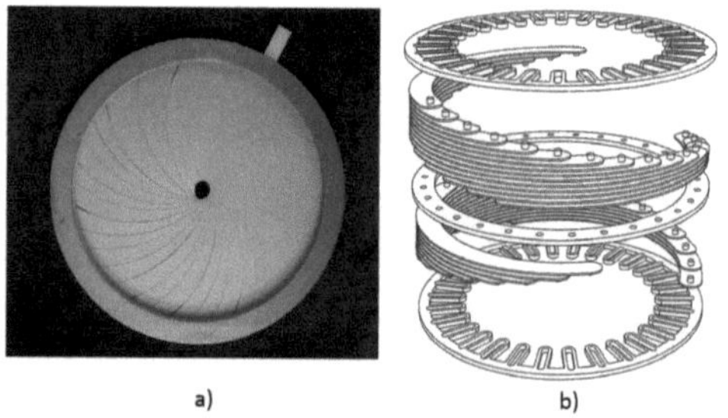

Figure 8
a) Prototype of the iris diaphragm that cannot close due to blade fiction, b) double sided iris diaphragm with two sets of 14 blades

2.3 Finding the best performing grid like iris layout

As the iris diaphragm is circular it is best to implement it inside a module that can tile a rectangular opening of a window in a grid like manner. Modules that are commonly used to tessellate a planar surface are triangles, squares and hexagons, inside which a circle can be inscribed. Apart from squares, triangles and hexagons do not have the opportunity to be tessellated inside a rectangular window opening without trimming the shapes, hence a residual area is bound to form. If the modules are fitted in the opening perfectly, like in Figure 9a., they can utilise their maximal potential. However, most openings are custom or standardised like the opening in Figure 9b (101x141cm) and a larger portion of residual area is generated. The residual area in between the modules can obscure light or it can be left blank to let the light in.

In order to maximize the area used in square layout smaller iris diaphragms can be added as shown in Figure 10. In between the existing iris diaphragms there is a 80mm gap, so the diameter of the iris diaphragm being added is limited to that size. By using the same method for determining the number of blades of the large iris diaphragms, it was determent that the optimal number of blades for the smaller iris diaphragm is 13.

The amount of light that each configuration passes can be seen in the Table 1.

Data from the table indicates that the best performing layout is square layout with small iris diaphragms addition in between the larger ones. If the combination of the different size iris diaphragms is not preferred, then the hexagonal layout is the best option, since it utilizes only one size iris module.

The use of modules, regardless of the layout is very beneficial from the aspect of controlling daylight. These modules can be segmented and then grouped so that the group of modules controls the portion of the opening. Grouping the modules is essential in this system because manually rotating each diaphragm will be very tedious process. Modules are packed one next to each other so by controlling one module all of the adjacent modules can be controlled. By implementing this feature certain segments of the opening can be fully closed and others opened depending on the users needs. This adds another layer of global flexibility to the system on top of the local flexibility from the iris diaphragms. By adding cog teeth to the rings, it is possible to

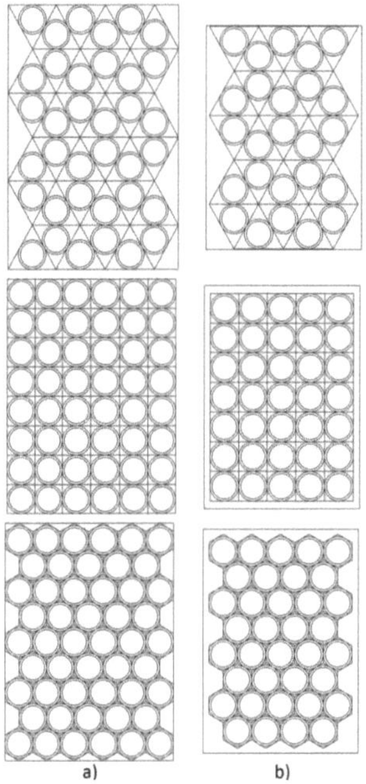

a) b)

Figure 9
a) Triangular, square and hexagonal tessellation that fits the opening perfectly; b) Triangular, square and hexagonal tessellation on standard 101x141cm opening

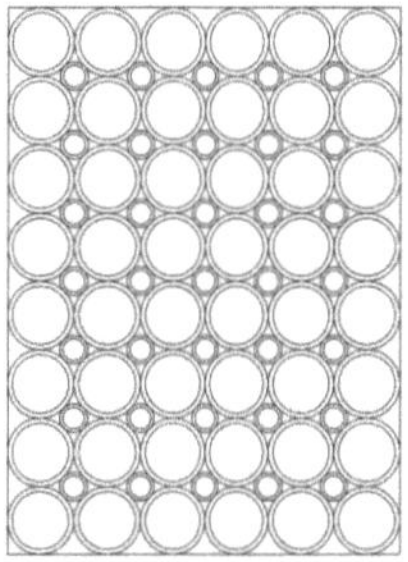

Figure 10
Square layout of iris diaphragms with added iris diaphragm in between existing ones

Type od module	Amount of light passing true the module with perfect fit in the opening	Amount of light passing true the module in 101x141cm opening with extra space obscured	Amount of light passing true the module in 101x141cm opening without extra space obscured
Triangles	37,60%	35,40%	55,23%
Squares	58,45%	51%	62,55%
Hexagons	56,77%	49,60%	73,45%
Squares with added extra iris in between	62,59%	54,34%	67,32%

Table 1
Table with light passing percentage for each system with each variant

connect the rotation between neighboring modules, hence rotating the clusters of diaphragms together instead of rotating each module individually. In this way, number of control dials which control the segments of the opening are equal to the number of segmented regions. This implementation requires more input from the user but it also allows greater control over which parts of the window are dimmed and how much.

3. RESULTS

Combining optimal parameters obtained in sections 2.2 and 2.3 result in a shading system that implements two types of iris diaphragms. One has an opening with diameter of 160mm and 28 blades and the other has opening with a diameter of 60mm and 13 blades, arranged in a square layout. Applying this system on a window opening with a size of 101x141cm and iris diaphragms in fully opened position creates interior conditions with a lot of light, as shown in Figure 11a. If needed, segments of the window can be closed for obtaining a well distributed light coverage in a work environment, like in Figure 11b. Different materials can be used to make the iris diaphragm blades and get different properties from the system. For example, using blades with translucent material properties, can block direct light but still provide diffused lighting in the interior, even in a closed state (Figure 11c). Likewise, all of the system variants have the ability to create interesting and visually pleasing shadows in the interior.

When comparing this system to the existing ones in Arab World Institute, optimisation in iris diaphragm design, finding optimal properties of the iris and improvements in the layout gave this optimised system a wider operational capabilities. The performance of the Arab World Institutes south façade of 10-30% light range was raised to the operation capabilities of the square layout with two size iris diaphragms that has a range from 0 to 54,34%.

Figure 11
a) Fully opened iris diaphragm system, b) iris diaphragm system with segmented control areas, c) iris diaphragm system with translucent blades

4. CONCLUSION AND FUTURE WORK

This paper focused on implementing a system that uses manually controlled iris diaphragms as a basis for a shading system that has a higher level of control over sunlight passing through the window opening, while being economically viable and letting as much light as possible when fully opened. In order to achieve this goal, the application of a parametric model proved to be a very important tool and the most time-efficient solution. The ability to change the design in Grasshopper by simply changing the model parameters has accelerated the lengthy iterative process of testing the optimal iris diaphragm design.

The practice of breaking down the optimisation of the iris diaphragm into individual parts has proven to be very successful as every part had some area to be improved. From choosing the type of the blades and rails that are better for this application, to the choosing an optimal casing width relative to the number of blades. The improvement of every part individually combined into a significant improvement of the whole iris diaphragm altogether. Also, in order to find the optimal iris diaphragm configuration, the digital models were fabricated and tested through physical models. This is noticeable when the digital model has shown that the 28 blades can close but the physical model has shown that the approach of splitting the one set of 28 blades into two equal stacks can provide better functionality.

The implementation of the layout with multiple iris diaphragm sizes has proven to be a better option when compared to the triangular, hexagonal and one sized square model, as indicated by the larger percentage of the light that is passing through the system. This also serves as an indicator for the direction future work can take, exploring disordered implementations to get better performance.

In order to satisfy the needs of users who want to have automatically controlled system this implementation can be switched from manual dials to the step motors which control is influenced by the information provided by photosensors. By keeping the implementation of the cog teeth on the ring, step motors would need to rotate just one diaphragm in the cluster in order to rotate the whole cluster. Therefore, the number of step motors would be directly tied to the number of clusters. Also, in a large configuration a mobile app with the ability to draw a pattern can be configured to control the clusters of diaphragms. Control would be implemented in such a way that controls the clusters of diaphragms contained in set pattern to open while others stay closed, allowing further customisation of the system.

REFERENCES

Aelenei, L, Aelenei, D, Romano, R, Mazzucchelli, E.S, Brzezicki, M and Rico-Martinez, J.M (eds) 2018, *Case studies: adaptive facade network*, TU Delft Open

Altan, H, Ward, I, Mohelnikova, J and Vajkay, F 2008, 'Daylight, solar gains and overheating studies in a glazed office building', *International journal of energy and environment*, 2(2), pp. 129-138

Ashour, AF 2018, 'Islamic architectural heritage: Mashrabiya', *WIT Transactions on The Built Environment*, 177, pp. 245-253

Attia, S 2018, 'Evaluation of adaptive facades: The case study of Al Bahr Towers in the UAE', *QScience Connect*, 2017(2, Special Issue on Shaping Qatar's Sustainable Built Environment-Part I), p. 6

Bakker, L, Hoes-van Oeffelen, E, Loonen, R and Hensen, JL 2014, 'User satisfaction and interaction with automated dynamic facades: A pilot study', *Building and Environment*, 78, pp. 44-52

Boubekri, M 2008, *Daylighting, architecture and health: building design strategies*, Routledge

Foster, M and Oreszczyn, T 2001, 'Occupant control of passive systems: the use of Venetian blinds', *Building and Environment*, 36(2), pp. 149-155

Hamdani, M, Bekkouche, S, Cherier, M, Benouaz, T and Belarbi, R 2016 'Study on effects of window with an external shutters for natural ventilation for buildings in hot climates', *2016 International Renewable and Sustainable Energy Conference (IRSEC)*, pp. 780-784

Hopkinson, RG 1972, 'Glare from daylighting in buildings', *Applied ergonomics*, 3(4), pp. 206-215

Hraska, J 2018, 'Adaptive solar shading of buildings', *International Review of Applied Sciences and Engineering*, 9(2), pp. 107-113

Ip, K, Ylitalo, H and Marshall, D 2013 'Environmental performance of external roller blinds retrofit for offices

in the United Kingdom', *Proceedings of the 19th CIB World Building Congress: Construction and Society, Brisbane Convention \& Exhibition Centre in Queensland, Australia*, pp. 5-9
Jakubiec, JA and Reinhart, CF 2012, 'The 'adaptive zone'– A concept for assessing discomfort glare throughout daylit spaces', *Lighting Research \& Technology*, 44(2), pp. 149-170
Kamal, MA 2013, 'Le Corbusier's solar shading strategy for tropical environment: A sustainable approach', *Journal of Architectural/Planning Research and Studies (JARS)*, 10(1), pp. 19-26
Konstantoglou, M and Tsangrassoulis, A 2016, 'Dynamic operation of daylighting and shading systems: A literature review', *Renewable and Sustainable Energy Reviews*, 60, pp. 268-283
Kuhn, TE 2006, 'Solar control: A general evaluation method for facades with venetian blinds or other solar control systems', *Energy and buildings*, 38(6), pp. 648-660
Meerbeek, B, te Kulve, M, Gritti, T, Aarts, M, van Loenen, E and Aarts, E 2014, 'Building automation and perceived control: a field study on motorized exterior blinds in Dutch offices', *Building and Environment*, 79, pp. 66-77
Murray, S and Murray, SC 2009, *Contemporary curtain wall architecture*, Princeton Architectural Press
Nebia, B and Tabet Aoul, K 2017, 'Overheating and daylighting; assessment tool in early design of london's high-rise residential buildings', *Sustainability*, 9(9), p. 1544
O'Brien, W, Kapsis, K and Athienitis, AK 2013, 'Manually-operated window shade patterns in office buildings: A critical review', *Building and Environment*, 60, pp. 319-338
Osterhaus, WK 2005, 'Discomfort glare assessment and prevention for daylight applications in office environments', *Solar Energy*, 79(2), pp. 140-158
Samuels, W 2011, *Performance and Permeability: An Investigation of the Mashrabiya for use within the Gibson Desert in Australia*, Ph.D. Thesis, School of Architecture and Design of Victoria University, Wellington, New Zealand
Schumacher, M, Vogt, M.M and Krumme, L.A.C. (eds) 2019, *Al Bahr Towers*, Birkh"auser
Tillson, AA, Oreszczyn, T and Palmer, J 2013, 'Assessing impacts of summertime overheating: some adaptation strategies', *Building Research \& Information*, 41(6), pp. 652-661
Tzempelikos, A and Athienitis, AK 2007, 'The impact of shading design and control on building cooling and lighting demand', *Solar energy*, 81(3), pp. 369-382
[1] https://www.merriam-webster.com/dictionary/irisdiaphragm
[2] https://www.adexsi.com/sites/adexsi.com/files/styles/news-large/public/news/new_tellier_adexsi.jpg?itok=bHhJQCzg
[3] https://www.biznisgroup.com/wp-content/uploads/2018/11/15995030_1342820592457717_8487074415441724027_o.jpg
[4] https://images.adsttc.com/media/images/55f8/01c4/d4f7/b7f6/6f00/00b4/slideshow/kiefertechnic_8.jpg?1442316715
[5] https://cdn3.ahr-global.com/images/7_AlBahr_1120x800.jpg
[6] https://images.adsttc.com/media/images/5383/c39e/c07a/8044/af00/004a/large_jpg/JN_GL_PS_AS_PARIS_Institut_Monde_Arabe_GeorgesFessy_int02.jpg?1401144206
[7] https://iris-calculator.com/

Computational Design and Evaluation of Acoustic Diffusion Panels for the Immersive Design Lab

An acoustic design case study

Romana Rust[1], Achilleas Xydis[2], Christian Frick[3], Jürgen Strauss[4], Christoph Junk[5], Jelle Feringa[6], Fabio Gramazio[7], Matthias Kohler[8]
[1,2,5,7,8]ETH Zurich [3]Rocket Science AG [4]Strauss Elektroakustik GmbH [6]Aectual
[1,2,5,7,8]{rust|xydis|junk|gramazio|kohler}@arch.ethz.ch [3]christian.frick@rocket-science.ch [4]info@strauss-elektroakustik.com [6]jelle@aectual.com

Acoustic performance is an important criterion for architectural design. Much is known about sound absorption, but little about sound scattering, although it is equally important for improving the acoustic quality of built spaces. This paper presents an alternative workflow for the computational design and evaluation of acoustic diffusion panels, which have been developed and realized in a real building project - the Immersive Design Lab (IDL). This workflow includes a computational design system, which is integrated with a rough acoustic evaluation method for fast performance feedback, as well as the assessment of acoustic performance with an experimental measurement setup, and the post-processing of a selected design instance for fabricability. The paper illustrates and discusses this workflow on the basis of the presented design study.

Keywords: *Architectural Acoustics, Performance-based Design, Digital Workflow*

INTRODUCTION

In performance-based design, building performance is the guiding factor from early design phases, benefiting both design workflow and outcome. The final design emerges as the design is constantly being evaluated and the computational model is adjusted (Kolarevic 2004; Oxman 2008). Using this design approach, evaluative simulation processes and analysis tools are integrated with digital form generation processes.

In the field of architectural acoustics, the application of such an approach would allow the designer to better combine acoustic performance objectives with architectural goals (Peters 2010; Badino et al. 2020), since they are strictly interlinked: the emitted sound is altered by the architectural space within which it is deployed. The constellation and material of surfaces within that space evoke sound reflection, absorption, and diffusion phenomena. While most architectural acoustics is concerned with sound absorption, sound diffusion is just as important for obtaining an even distribution of sound. It helps to promote spaciousness, prevent flutter echoes, and improve speech intelligibility (Cox and D'Antonio 2004).

Computer simulation software such as e.g. Odeon and Pachyderm Acoustics, which are based on geometrical acoustics (GA), can predict the acoustic performance of architectural spaces before construction with sufficient accuracy. However, despite significant research over the past decades on methods to design, predict, and measure diffusing surfaces, GA methods still lack the ability to accurately model their behaviour (Bork 2005a, 2005b; Brinkmann et al. 2019). To predict the scattering of sound caused by these diffusive surfaces, wave-based acoustic simulations must be used or physical models must be tested. Both of these methods are time-consuming, which is why they cannot be used in an iterative design and evaluation workflow common to performance-based design. Therefore, in architectural practice, design rules for sound scattering (Vomhof et al. 2014) are often applied, or geometries are designed that are similar to tested ones. With using a certain mathematical formulae (Schroeder 1975), the scattering performance for a certain type of geometries can also be predicted.

This paper presents an alternative workflow for the evaluation of acoustic diffusion panels, which have been specifically developed for the Immersive Design Lab (IDL). The lab is an interdisciplinary laboratory at ETH Zurich for future design, architecture, and engineering using extended reality (XR) technologies[1]. It offers 3D spatial auralisation, which is enabled by a total of 75 speakers in an 80 m^2 space (10.6x7.6m) with a height of six meters. Consequently, the room has high acoustic requirements, which had to be taken into account during the planning of the lab. A homogeneous, acoustically isotropic room was to be realised. The acoustics of the laboratory was planned in a 3D model calibrated from a measurement of the existing room using ray-tracing methods. A combination of sound diffusing and sound-absorbing surfaces was chosen, the area proportion of which was determined in the 3D CAD simulation. Absorbers were installed on the walls, floor and ceiling and a sound-absorbing curtain was chosen to prevent specular reflections from the glass façade. The selected proportion of diffusive surfaces is to prevent specular reflections at the listening area. Their staggered mounting also creates a phase grid, which extends the diffusion into lower frequency ranges.

Figure 1
Visualisation of the Immersive Design Lab (IDL) before construction. It shows some of the 75 speakers integrated at different heights in the columns and the ceiling rack. The diffuser panels are planned to create a visually continuous diffusion belt that extends across three walls of the lab. The fourth wall is a glass façade that can be covered with a sound-absorbing curtain to prevent specular reflections.

The particular challenges for the development of the acoustic diffusion panels were to a) improve the acoustic quality of a given space within selected frequency bands, b) fit the aesthetic considerations of the overall design concept of the lab and c) be fabricatable within a tight timeframe using 3D printing. This paper presents the design of sound scattering surfaces through the use of parametric design tools, the integration with a rough acoustic evaluation method (FFT analysis), and measured results obtained from an experimental measurement setup. Additionally, the post-processing of adapting the panels for fabrication, taking the fabrication constraints for a 3D contour printer and the panel mounting into account, is explained.

The project presented in this paper builds upon previous and ongoing research projects conducted together with acoustic experts at the chair of Gramazio Kohler Research. Fields of study have been the design, fabrication, and analysis of wall panels with differentiated spatial and sound-aesthetic properties[2] and an acoustic wall system for office spaces (Vomhof et al. 2014) specifically tailored to sound diffusion. In the ongoing research project Data-Driven Acoustic Design, an acoustic measurement setup for data collection was developed with the goal of studying diffusive surfaces with machine learning (Rust et al. 2021). This experimental measurement setup is also utilized in the presented project.

BACKGROUND

Currently, different acoustic simulation tools are available (e.g. Odeon[3], CATT-Acoustic[4], Pachyderm Acoustics[5], etc.), to estimate the performance of design proposals using the geometrical acoustic (GA) method. In GA, sound is assumed to propagate as rays and the wave-nature of sound is neglected (Savioja and Svensson 2015). Thus, all wave-based phenomena, such as diffraction and interference, are absent. This drawback is usually circumvented by using hybrid GA, which combines ray-tracing with the image source approach that allows for the consideration of diffuse reflections (Vorländer 2013). GA techniques require that absorption and scattering coefficients are assigned to all surfaces in the model in order to calculate the energy loss and the direction of the reflected sound. While the sound absorption properties of many materials are available through acoustic analysis software (Christensen 2005) or can be obtained from material manufacturers, the same is not true for sound scattering properties. Although a number of commercially available diffusers from different manufacturers with known scattering coefficients exists (e.g. RPG, GIK Acoustics, Auralex), for most architectural surfaces these coefficients are unknown. If new surface geometries are developed to be performative as a sound scattering device, their performance will be difficult to predict.

There are standards for measuring directional diffusion coefficient (ISO 2012) and random incidence scattering coefficient (ISO 2004). These processes though, require the fabrication of a prototype surface, a highly specialised setup, are time consuming, labour intensive, and expensive. Therefore, the very limited data-set of scattering coefficients that can be assigned to surfaces in GA models, forces room modellers to rely on empirical guidelines and intuition when assigning scattering coefficients (Wang and Rathsam 2008).

Unlike GA simulations, wave-based simulation methods (e.g. BEM, ISM, FDTD) can accurately simulate the scattering of sound caused by diffusing surfaces. However, these methods are computationally heavy, require long simulation times, and are currently not supported in any commercial acoustic simulation tool (Badino et al. 2020). The FabPod (Peters 2015; Williams et al. 2015) is an example of a research project in which BEM was successfully used to compute the scattering coefficients of different surface proposals and FDTD to visualize the sound waves in order to evaluate different surface geometries. Two different methods had to be used because their FDTD tool lacked the ability to provide a measure of scattering performance. Peters (2015) concluded that the applied workflows are still cumbersome due to the lack of available tools for architects to evaluate the acoustic performance of complex surfaces.

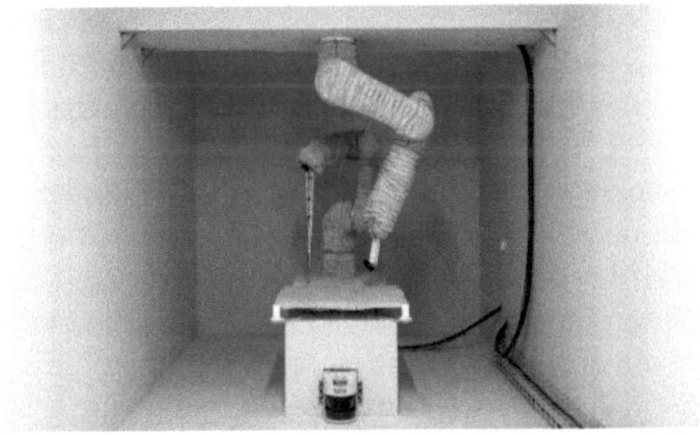

Figure 2
Acoustic data acquisition setup from the DDAD project with two Stäubli TX2-60L robots in an acoustically shielded and absorbent room. The double sided 3D printed panel of dimensions 585x585 mm is placed in a special fixture (Rust et al. 2021).

The research project Data Driven Acoustic Design (DDAD) proposes another approach, for studying the relationship between diffusive surface structures and their acoustic performance using data science methods (Rust et al. 2021). To this end, a robotic data acquisition setup (see Figure 2) was developed that measures 3D-printed surface textures at 1:10 model scale on a daily basis. The setup records 2951 impulse responses in front of these surfaces by repeatedly positioning a microphone and a speaker within a predefined measurement grid of 78 positions. The collected data serves both as an exploratory catalogue of different spatio-temporal acoustic scenarios and as a data set for predicting the acoustic response of digitally designed surface geometries using machine learning. As part of the project, a post-processing method was developed to extract meaningful indicators from the 2951 impulse responses per panel. One of these indicators is the *DDAD absorption coefficient*, which is used in the presented project to assess diffusion properties.

WORKFLOW AND DESIGN SYSTEM

The acoustic panels were developed using a computational design system that generates variable geometric patterns for doubly-curved, undulated surfaces. This design system integrates a rough acoustic assessment method (FFT analysis), which is used to quickly analyse the surface's acoustic performance. It also integrates fabricability analysis and optimization for a 3D contour printing process.

In the beginning, it was necessary to identify the combination of parameters that would generate a particular surface structure, which both fulfils aesthetic and acoustic requirements. This was conducted in a two-step process: First, the geometry generation parameters were manually adjusted and the result of the FFT analysis was observed until a selection of six design instances was found. These designs were then selected for a second, more in-depth acoustic evaluation, for which they were 3D printed at 1:10 scale and measured using the acoustic measurement setup from the DDAD project. A final design selection was then made based on the measurement results. These geometry generation parameters, together with other design-relevant settings, were used to create the 29 individual acoustic diffuser panels for the Immersive Design Lab. In a post-processing step, the geometry of these panels was adapted considering the fabrication constraints for a 3D contour printer and the panel mounting.

DDAD conformity

In order to conform to the DDAD measurement setup (see Figure 2) and the inclusion of the recorded data into the DDAD dataset, two conditions had to be fulfilled. First, the dimensions of the surface, which is evaluated by both acoustic analysis methods, had to be in a rectangular size of 5.85x5.85m, such that it would fit into the measurement fixture at 1:10 scale (585x585mm). Secondly, the geometry generation algorithm had to be reproducible without proprietary software. For this reason, the algorithm was written in Python and only builds upon open source Python libraries such as numpy, scipy and compas nurbs[6]. Via the COMPAS Remote Procedure Call (RPC), the algorithm can be executed from within the Rhinoceros/Grasshopper environment, from which also the remaining components of the computational design system are accessible.

Geometry Generation

The custom geometry generation algorithm creates a NURBS surface that is lofted through planar NURBS curves arranged along the x-axis of a defined frame. It is loosely based on deducted design rules from the research of Cox and D'Antonio (2004) (Vomhof et al. 2014), focusing on differentiated and aperiodic surface depth. It was also conceptualised with one defined direction, i.e. exhibiting the highest undulation along the v-direction (=y-axis of the surface's frame), due to the selected layer-based fabrication method of 3D printing. Apart from project-specific settings, the main parameters controlling the surface undulation are resolution values in u- and v-direction, distortion values u- and v-direction, the panel height, and the degree of the surface in v-direction. The degree in u-direction is set to three. These parameters, together with a random seed value, define the variable location of the surface's control points. The z-value of the control points (in relation to the surface's frame) can be controlled by an additional input, for example, to achieve a flattening at the edges of the surface.

ACOUSTIC PERFORMANCE EVALUATION

Fast Fourier Transform (FFT) analysis

To quickly and roughly assess the acoustic performance of such a generated surface, Fast Fourier Transform (FFT) analysis was integrated into the de-

Figure 3
The workflow elements and information flows of the design system

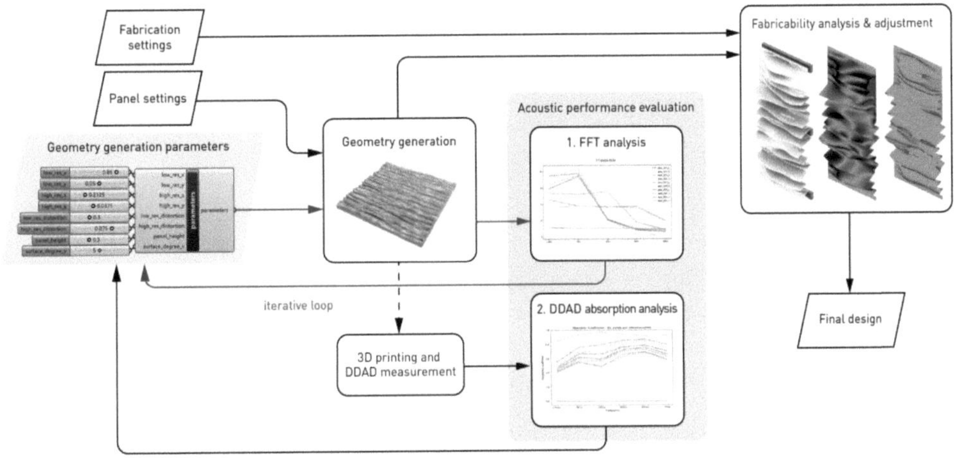

sign tool. For this purpose, a certain number of linear sections (iso-curves) of the surface in both u- and v- directions are analysed by Fourier transform, the spectral characteristics are RMS-averaged and translated into octave band diffusion values. These values are a measure for the 'roughness' of the given surface structure and allow for an estimate of how the surface performs in six octave bands (250, 500, 1000, 2000, and 4000 Hz) (see Figure 5).

Panel selection and reference panels for measurement

In order to make an initial selection of both aesthetically pleasing and acoustically performing designs, the design parameters were manually adjusted and the result of the FFT analysis was observed. This was done until a selection of six design instances was found (see Figure 4a). Note that the labelling of the design instances stems from the DDAD dataset (each surface is labelled successively with a unique identifier and suffixed with 0 or 1 indicating the panel side).

Apart from the six selected design instances (panels *0073-0078*), another six panels have been chosen as reference panels (see Figure 4b) to compare the measurement results. Four of which (*0079-0082*) were generated with the same geometry generation algorithm as the selected panel designs and resemble commonly known diffusers (e.g. RPG Harmonix[7]). The two panels *Flat* and *PRD* are reference panels from the DDAD dataset. *Flat* is the reference for the surface of the highest possible reflection within the dataset and *PRD* the reference for a surface of high and uniform diffusion.

DDAD absorption coefficient

During the DDAD project we developed several methods to compress the information contained in the 2951 captured impulse responses and extract meaningful descriptors therefrom, such that different surfaces can be visually compared to one another and their performances can be analysed at different frequency bands. One of these descriptors is the *DDAD absorption coefficient*.

To evaluate the diffusivity of each panel we observe the amount of reflected energy. For example, a flat reflector produces a specular reflection, redirecting the majority of the energy to a specific direction and a highly diffusive surface redirects the energy in multiple directions. By comparing the two energy values it can be calculated how much energy was not reflected in a specular way, therefore diffused or absorbed.

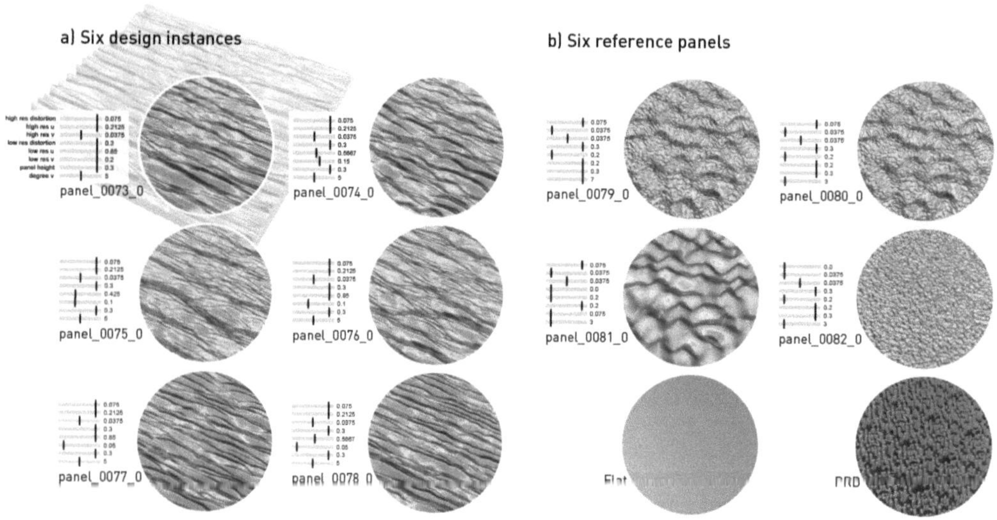

Figure 4
a) Selection of design instances and their parameter settings, b) Six reference panels for comparison

We evaluate a reflection factor $R_j = \sqrt{(E_j)/(Eref_j)}$ or every source-receiver combination j that describes the ratio of sound pressure of the reflected energy with respect to a reference. E_j is the total cumulative energy (TCE) (Rust et al. 2021) of the reflected sound for the diffusive panel and $Eref_j$ is the corresponding TCE of the reflected sound for the reference *Flat* panel. To obtain a global descriptor we calculate the arithmetic mean $\overline{R}$ of all R_j, and from this, the *DDAD absorption coefficient* $\alpha = 1 - \overline{R}^2$ for the whole panel. The same process can be applied for each octave band, providing a more detailed view of the panel's diffusivity over different frequency bands. Panels that perform similar to the flat panel would exhibit values close to 0, and panels with values close to 1 diffuse almost all energy. Note that the final values slightly overestimate the diffusivity of our panels, because a portion of that energy gets absorbed by the panel's material.

Results

The graph in Figure 5a shows the result of the calculated DDAD absorption coefficients for different frequency bands (250, 500, 1000, 2000 and 4000 Hz). The reference panel *Flat* clearly marks the lower line and the reference panel *PRD* the uppermost, such that panels with values on the top can be assumed with higher diffusion. As identified by the acoustic room measurement in the IDL before the installation of acoustic treatment, it is desirable that these curves are as flat as possible, i.e. that they behave similarly at the chosen frequencies. For this reason, panel *0077_-0* was identified as the best performing panel, and *0074_0* as the second best, although panel *0078_0* is higher on average, but it performs worse than *0074_0* in the lower frequencies of 200 and 500 Hz.

Comparing the measurement result with the FFT analysis in Figure 5b, one can discover parallels. The two green curves (panels *0077_0* and *0078_0*) stand out clearly and one could already identify the two as best performing in all selected frequency bands after the FFT analysis. This was however done with caution because the FFT only analyses one surface direction and does not take the acoustic response of the full 3D surface into account. Therefore, the measuring of several different design proposals was still essential in order to validate the results.

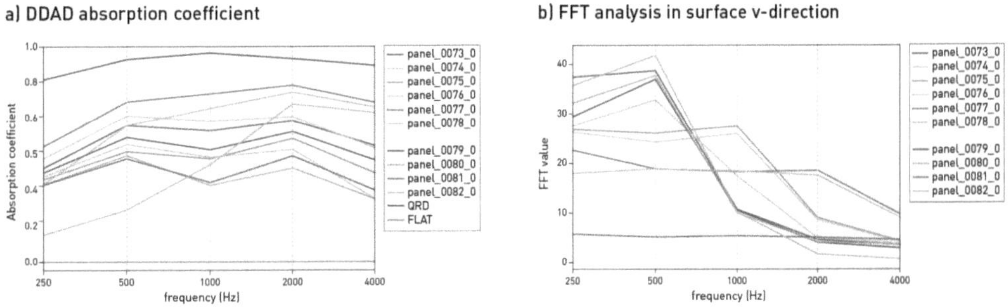

Figure 5
Comparison between DDAD absorption coefficient calculated from measurements (left) and FFT analysis (right)

FABRICATION ADJUSTMENTS

Once the geometry generation parameters for the geometry generation were identified, the next step was to generate 29 individual surfaces: nine, eleven, and nine respectively for three walls of the room, creating a visually continuous diffusion belt that extends across the three walls (see Figure 1). For this, design-specific considerations were taken into account, such as panel arrangements and areas in which the surface depth was reduced, for example in the corners or at the belt's ends. The individual NURBS surfaces were then further processed such that they 1) do not collide with the panel mounting and 2) can be fabricated using a robotic 3D contour printing process. In both cases, an iterative method was implemented in which surface analysis is followed by surface adaptation until the surface fulfils requirements defined for 1) and 2).

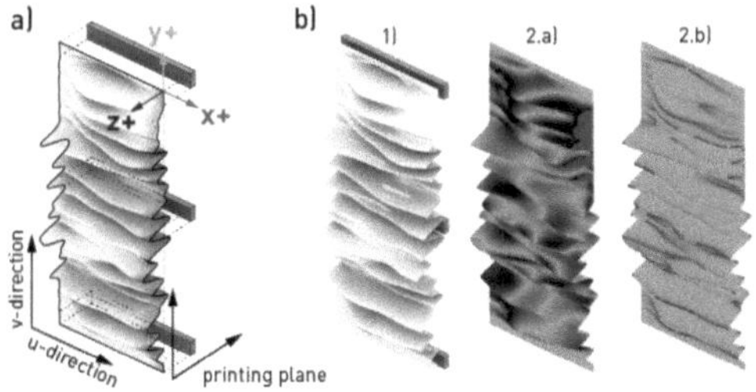

Figure 6
a) Panel build-up, b) Fabrication adjustments: 1) intersection with mounting elements, 2.a) coloured areas with 3D printing overhang and 2.b) coloured areas with curvature radius < 0.028m

The requirement for 1) is simply that there is no intersection between the surface and the mounting elements (see Figure 6b). For 2), two sub-conditions need to be fulfilled. First, the 3D printing overhang angle should not exceed 45°. This is to ensure that each successive printing layer has sufficient support and to avoid droopy filament strands. Another identified 3D printing constraint is the maximum allowed curvature along the printing direction, which constraint derives from the used robotic setup and control. During tests it was found that surface areas with a curvature radius smaller than 0.0028 m could lead to filament artefacts.

A characteristic of the generated surface is that its undulation expands from the surface's frame only along the negative and the positive z-axis (see Figure 6a). To fulfil the identified requirements, a similar strategy of surface adaptation could be applied, namely to make the surface smoother or flatter by moving its control points along the z-axis towards the surface frame. For requirement 1), since the panel mounts are along the negative z-axis of the surface's frame, the control points move incrementally along the positive z-axis. For 2) a smoothing strategy similar to Laplacian smoothing was chosen that proved to be stable, i.e. the error could continuously be reduced: The surface analysis identifies uv point locations that do not fulfil requirements defined for 2). Then, the corresponding control points of the NURBS surface are calculated and grouped per problem area. In each group of N control points P, a new z-value z_i for each control point P_i is calculated as follows:

$$z_i = z_i + \lambda \frac{1}{N} \sum_{j=1}^{N} z_j \quad (1)$$

a) b)

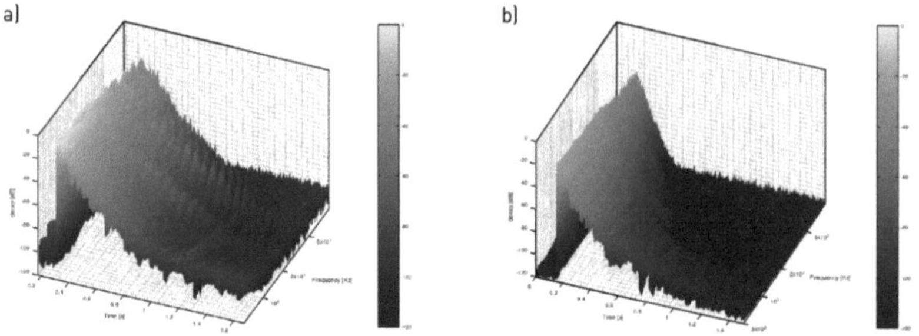

Figure 7
a) Before the installation of the diffusers: Flutter echoes are significantly level-determining and clearly audible towards the end of the impulse decay at mid frequencies and can be seen as spikes towards the tail of the impulse response (dual slope decay). b) After installation of the diffusers: The impulse decays very densely and smoothly. No disturbing spatial artefacts can be measured or heard.

Where z_j is the z-value of the j-th control point P_j in the group and λ a factor that controls the amount of displacement per iteration, which was chosen at 0.05. The process would terminate if less than 0.001% of evaluated uv points would have overhang or curvature problems. This incremental adjustment with a small λ was particularly chosen to avoid unnecessarily smoothing of the surface and losing too much surface depth, otherwise, the effect of diffusion would have been altered. We compared all surfaces before and after the adjustment. Overall, only 5% of all control points moved more than 10 mm along the z-axis. On the most adjusted surface, there was only one area (3% of the total surface) that had larger adjustments of up to 90 mm. This was due to the fact that the bottom peak of the surface wave collided with the mounting part. The adjustments due to 3D printing amounted to a maximum of 4 mm, thus negligible.

RESULTS

Once the surfaces were processed for production, they were passed on to the fabrication partner Aectual[8], who generated the geometry of the panels' support structure considering the panel mounting and for introducing additional stiffness. From this geometry, 3D printing paths were generated, and the final product was fabricated using a robotic 3D printing process.

Validation of the acoustic performance

The performance of the diffuser panels was determined by impulse response analysis of acquired gunshot decay sound samples. For this purpose impulse responses before and after installation of the inhere described diffuser panels were compared using multiple different analysis methods (e.g. cumulative spectral decays, spectrograms with high temporal resolutions). All methods focused on the characteristics of the reverberation time decay slope and did not per se determine panel diffusion parameters. The graphs in Figure 7 visualize the cumulative spectral decay plots using GNU octave. Both impulses were filtered with a digital brick wall high pass filter at 200 Hz, with the initial rising edge being an artefact. During the measurements the room was empty and the sound-absorbing curtains were closed.

Overall, the results show that the set goals were successfully achieved, the room is within the identified specifications. Due to the geometric arrangement of the diffusers and absorbers on the walls, the reverberation time was not significantly reduced by the introduction of the diffusers. Subjective evaluation by carefully listening to the room response validated the mesurement results in Figure 7, no flutter echoes or other types of artefacts resulting from specular reflections could be identified.

DISCUSSION AND CONCLUSION

Empowered through digital communication and new tools, the way how architects, experts, engineers, and fabricators work is dramatically altered. Autonomous processes can be replaced by collective workflows, supported by a common digital infrastructure. Especially for non-standard design projects, such curated digital workflows that span from design, over performance analysis to production are paramount.

This paper presented a design system, which has been successfully validated in a real building project. It integrates acoustic evaluation and fabrication constraints, allowing for a successful collaboration amongst all involved experts from the fields of architecture, acoustics and fabrication. The result is embodied in the feature-rich, full-scale and permanent acoustic panels that adorn the walls of the Immersive Design Lab and have thus become an essential part of its architecture.

The development of the acoustic diffuser panels has created a synthesis with ongoing research projects and produced new findings in a number of aspects. However, a number of limitations were also uncovered during the realisation, highlighting opportunities for improvement and further research:

- While the fast FFT analysis allowed for good selection of design proposals, thus providing an initial evaluation, it is not suitable as a sole acoustic assessment and needs to be complemented with acoustic measurements or wave-based acoustic simulations. Ideally, only wave-based simulations could be used for the purpose presented, but they are too computationally intensive for an iterative design and evaluation process. However, for a specific design system like the one presented, machine learning could be applied by replacing the wave-based simulation with a surrogate simulation and thus decrease the response time for evaluation.
- Another improvement to the presented workflow would be the earlier consideration of fabrication constraints. Rather than trying to adapt the surface in a post-processing step, the acoustic evaluation should be applied to geometries that are fabricatable in the first place.

Projects like the one presented are exemplary how converging interests in academia and start-ups like Aectual can bring academic research and product development in closer continuation of one another: The developed design system provides a lean computational pipeline from design to fabrication and allows the adaptation of surfaces to individual room shapes and custom designs. As a result of this successful partnership, Aectual is launching mass-customizable acoustic diffusion panels that are 3D printed on-demand.

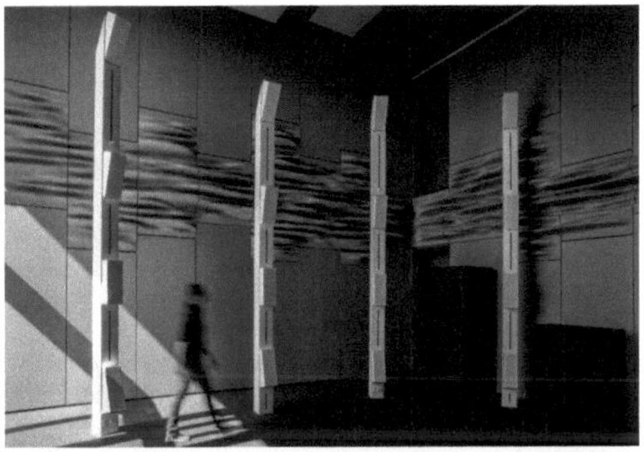

Figure 8
Acoustic panels installed in the Immersive Design Lab.

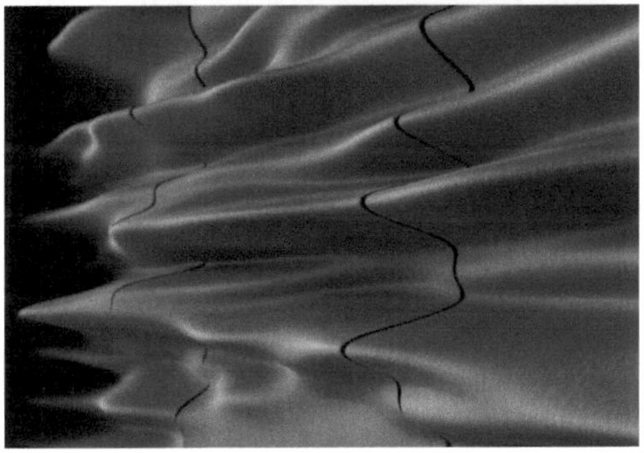

Figure 9
Close up of acoustic diffusor panel.

Acknowledgements

The acoustic diffusion panels have been developed by Gramazio Kohler Research in collaboration with acoustic partners Rocket Science AG and Strauss Elektroakustik GmbH and the fabrication partner Aectual. We thank the extended team of the industry partners for inspiring discussions and help.

Further, the authors want to thank Beat Jäggli for planning the execution on behalf of ETH Real Estate and Michael Lyrenmann for making beautiful images. Kurt Heutschi developed the DDAD absorption coefficient. The realisation of the Immersive Design Laboratory has been made possible as part of the Design++ initiative funded by ETH Zurich through an ETH+ Grant.

REFERENCES

Badino, E, Shtrepi, L and Astolfi, A 2020, 'Acoustic Performance-Based Design: A Brief Overview of the Opportunities and Limits in Current Practice', *Acoustics*, 2(2), pp. 246-278

Bork, I 2005a, 'Report on the 3rd round robin on room acoustical computer simulation–Part I: Measurements', *Acta Acustica united with Acustica*, 91(4), pp. 740-752

Bork, I 2005b, 'Report on the 3rd round robin on room acoustical computer simulation–Part II: Calculations', *Acta Acustica united with Acustica*, 91(4), pp. 753-763

Brinkmann, F, Aspöck, L, Ackermann, D, Lepa, S, Vorländer, M and Weinzierl, S 2019, 'A round robin on room acoustical simulation and auralization', *The Journal of the Acoustical Society of America*, 145(4), pp. 2746-2760

Christensen, CL 2005, 'A new scattering method that combines roughness and diffraction effects', *The Journal of the Acoustical Society of America*, 117(4), pp. 2499-2499

Cox, TJ and D'Antonio, P 2004, *Acoustic Absorbers and Diffusers: Theory, Design and Application*, Spon Press, London

ISO, 17497-1: 2004, *Acoustics - Sound-scattering properties of surfaces - Part 1: Measurement of the random-incidence scattering coefficient in a reverberation room*, International Organization for Standardization

ISO, 17497-2: 2012, *Acoustics - Sound-scattering properties of surfaces - Part 2: Measurement of the directional diffusion coefficient in a free field*, International Organization for Standardization

Kolarevic, B 2004, 'Back to the Future: Performative Architecture', *International Journal of Architectural Computing*, 2(1), pp. 43-50

Oxman, R 2008, 'Performance-Based Design: Current Practices and Research Issues', *International Journal of Architectural Computing*, 6(1), pp. 1-17

Peters, B 2010, 'Acoustic Performance as a Design Driver: Sound Simulation and Parametric Modeling Using SmartGeometry', *International Journal of Architectural Computing*, 8(3), pp. 337-358

Peters, B 2015, 'Integrating acoustic simulation in architectural design workflows: the FabPod meeting room prototype', *Simulation*, 91(9), pp. 787-808

Rust, R, Xydis, A, Heutschi, K, Perraudin, N, Casas, G, Du, C, Strauss, J, Eggenschwiler, K, Perez-Cruz, F, Gramazio, F and Kohler, M 2021, 'A Data Acquisition Setup for Data Driven Acoustic Design', *Building Acoustics*, 28, pp. 1-10

Savioja, L and Svensson, UP 2015, 'Overview of geometrical room acoustic modeling techniques', *The Journal of the Acoustical Society of America*, 138(2), pp. 708-730

Schroeder, MR 1975, 'Diffuse sound reflection by maximum–length sequences', *The Journal of the Acoustical Society of America*, 57(1), pp. 149-150

Vomhof, M, Vasey, L, Gramazio, F, Kohler, M, Bräuer, S and Eggenschwiler, K 2014 'Robotic Fabrication Of Acoustic Brick Walls', *Proceedings of the 34th Annual Conference of the Association for Computer Aided Design in Architecture (ACADIA): Material Agency*, Los Angeles, USA, pp. 555-564

Vorländer, M 2013, 'Computer simulations in room acoustics: Concepts and uncertainties', *The Journal of the Acoustical Society of America*, 133(3), pp. 1203-1213

Wang, LM and Rathsam, J 2008, 'The influence of absorption factors on the sensitivity of a virtual room's sound field to scattering coefficients', *Applied Acoustics*, 69(12), pp. 1249-1257

Williams, N, Burry, J, Davis, D, Peters, P, Pena de Leon, A and Burry, M 2015, 'FabPod: Designing with temporal flexibility & relationships to mass-customisation', *Automation in Construction*, 51, pp. 124–131

[1] https://gramaziokohler.arch.ethz.ch/web/projekte/e/0/0/0/417.html

[2] https://gramaziokohler.arch.ethz.ch/web/forschung/e/0/0/0/85.html

[3] https://odeon.dk

[4] https://www.catt.se

[5] https://www.food4rhino.com/app/pachyderm-acoustical-simulation

[6] https://pypi.org/project/compas-nurbs/

[7] http://www.rpgeurope.com/de/products/product/harmonixk.html

[8] https://www.aectual.com

Smart cities, city modelling and GIS

Visualizing Deep Learning Models for Urban Health Analysis

David Newton[1]
[1] *University of Nebraska-Lincoln*
[1] *david.newton@unl.edu*

As humanity has become increasingly urbanized, physical and mental health problems have increased significantly among urban populations with a combined cost of treating these diseases estimated to be in the trillions of dollars. In parallel to these developments, a growing body of research suggests that the design of the built environment has significant correlations with both physical and mental health outcomes. This research, however, has been limited in its ability to make use of large remote sensing datasets to identify specific design features at the neighborhood scale that correlate with health outcomes. The development of methods that can efficiently find such correlations from ubiquitous remote sensing datasets, such as satellite images, would therefore allow researchers a greater level of insight into how specific urban planning and design features might relate to health. This research contributes knowledge on a novel mixed method workflow to address this issue.

Keywords: *Deep Learning, Urban Planning, Health, Artificial Intelligence, Remote Sensing*

The availability of image-based remote sensing datasets has increased significantly with the proliferation of satellite and aerial sensing platforms. Aerial and satellite photography, light detection and ranging images, hyperspectral images, and thermal images are just a few image-based datasets that are now available to researchers through both governmental and private sources. The bulk of existing research examining the links between the built environment and health, however, relies on traditional quantitative statistical methods to identify correlations (Dumbaugh and Rae 2009, Jackson 2003, Lopez-Zetina, Lee, and Friis 2006, Marshall, Piatkowski, and Garrick 2014). These approaches, while efficacious, are not well suited to quickly process and identify correlations from large image-based datasets. This disadvantage has made it difficult for researchers to make use of a vast array of image-based remote sensing data. Recent work, however, has demonstrated the successful use of methods from the field of deep learning to make progress in addressing this problem.

Deep learning (DL) is an area of research within the field of computer science that explores the use of artificial neural networks to solve a variety of regression and classification problems through the automated analysis of large datasets. DL-based approaches, such as the use of Convolutional Neural

Networks (CNNs), have demonstrated the ability to outperform competing methods significantly in relation to image-based processing and recognition tasks (Simonyan and Zisserman 2015). Researchers have used CNNs to analyze aerial, satellite, and POV imagery of neighborhoods to estimate poverty, obesity, and general health measures with success (Maharana and Nsoesie 2018, Piaggesi et al. 2019, Suel et al. 2019). This previous work, however, has mainly focused on the task of estimation. The analysis of the DL model itself as a source to identify correlations between specific urban design features and health outcomes has largely been unaddressed. Developing methods that can aid in revealing this correlation will help guide urban planning approaches and inform the design of healthier neighborhoods and cities.

This research investigates this problem and contributes knowledge on methods for analyzing DL models in order to identify specific design features that correlate with health outcomes from satellite images. The method presented in this work uses two primary datasets: health survey data from 2017 California Health Interview Survey (CHIS) on rates of obesity, diabetes, and high blood pressure and satellite imagery of all California census tracts. This data is separated into high and low disease incidence categories and passed through a CNN. The neural layers of the CNN are then analyzed using a novel a mixed methods approach to identify design features that are most active for high and low disease incidence. The results are then compared to correlations found by previous work as a means of validating the efficacy of the proposed method.

DATA

The first dataset used in this research is comprised of Health data from 7,949 census tracks provided from the 2017 California Health Interview Survey (CHIS 2017). The CHIS dataset is a self-reported survey that is aggregated at the census tract level providing 7,949 datapoints. The research focused specifically on health data from adults on the following three health measures per census tract: percentage of people that are overweight; percentage of people that are diabetic and borderline diabetic; and the percentage that report being diagnosed with high blood pressure.

The second dataset is comprised of color satellite images of each California census tract from 2017. The images are publicly available through the US Census. Census tract sizes and shapes vary based on population density. Therefore, each satellite image is at a different scale. Each image is cropped to fit within the census tract shape and pixels outside the area of the tract shape are set to white. Each image is scaled non-proportionally to fit within a square pixel area of 299 x 299 pixels. This dimension was found through testing to provide the best trade-off between training time and image resolution. Figure 1 shows two example images from the dataset at the noted resolution. The range of scales between census tracts can be seen in the figure. The scales and image resolution allow buildings, streets, and vegetation to be clearly identified.

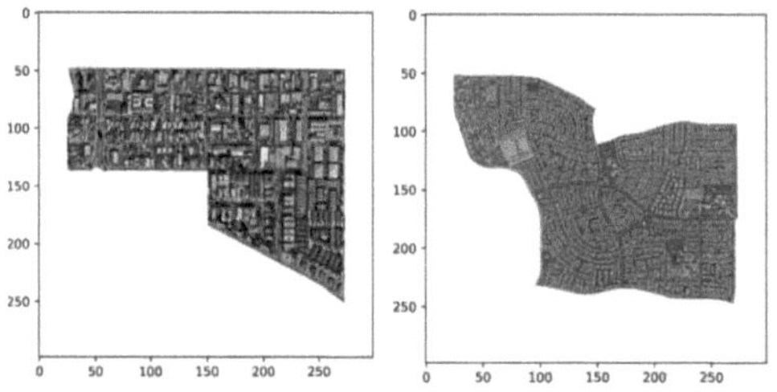

Figure 1
Example California census tract images from the satellite image dataset.

PREVIOUS WORK

DL models are composed of multiple layers of artificial neurons connected together into a network that is able to take in an input value of any data type (e.g., numbers, text, images, etc.) and provide a corresponding output of any data type. DL networks that have greater than three layers are capable of representing any mathematical function. DL networks are therefore used to approximate functions that map an input to an output. Researchers use these abilities (data flexibility and function approximation) to solve regression problems and classification problems through a process that involves training these networks with example input/output combinations (e.g., this is known as supervised learning). For example, a DL network can be trained to recognize whether a cat is present in a picture by showing it example pictures with and without cats and iteratively adjusting weight parameters associated with the neural layers in relation to whether it is guessing correctly or not. These networks can often contain hundreds of thousands, and sometimes millions, of such parameters and it is the iterative adjusting of these weights in an automated fashion which "trains" the model to accurately output "true" when you give it an image of a cat. These models are referred to as "black box" because it is often difficult to make sense of how the thousands to millions of parameters in these models are actually working together to produce a correct result. The development of analytic methods that allow researchers to better understand the correlational patterns the models are learning is, therefore, a pressing problem for disciplines working with DL.

Convolutional Neural Networks (CNNs) are a DL architecture developed for working specifically with images. CNNs take image data as an input and pass that data through a series of neural layers. As the image moves through each neural layer, it is progressively abstracted into sets of visual features that provide a compressed representation of the image data. The layers at the beginning of the model extract low-level features (i.e., vertical lines, corners, etc.) while the layers towards the end of the model extract high-level features (i.e., car wheels, faces, etc.), which are built from the low-level features. CNNs learn which features best define an image for a particular task and how to extract those features from the image data through a training process involving feeding example images into the model along with the desired model output (e.g., a desired classification or regression value).

The analysis of CNN models is a pressing problem for researchers working with image-based datasets. The most widely used approach is the visualization of the neural layers, also known as feature maps, to identify correlated features. This qualitative approach has been used in work using satellite images to estimate health (Jean et al. 2016; Maharana and Nsoesie 2018). A key drawback is that these qualitative methods rely on visual interpretation to identify correlated design features and provide little information on how combinations of features might be correlated with health outcomes. Researchers have also explored quantitative methods of analysis. Zeiler and Fergus (2014) propose a method involving that highlights the portion of an image that is being activated by a particular neural unit. Yosinski et al. (2015) propose the use of optimization techniques to find the highest and lowest neural layer activations. Gatys, Ecker, and Bethge (2016) propose the use of Gram matrices to find the most active combinations of feature maps in relation to particular inputs. These quantitative approaches have not yet been applied to urban analysis, however. Further, no previous research has investigated how they might be combined with the qualitative methods discussed.

This research addresses this gap in previous research and proposes a novel mixed methods approach that combines both qualitative and quantitative methods. Specifically, Gram matrices are calculated following Gatys, Ecker, and Bethge (2016). These are used to quantitatively identify important feature maps in the CNN model. Then, these maps are visually assessed following a qualitative approach similar to Maharana and Nsoesie 2018 to identify specific visual features. This research, therefore, endeavors to test the efficacy of a mixed methods analysis approach for deep learning models in relation to urban analysis.

METHODOLOGY FOR ANALYZING DEEP LEARNING MODELS TO FIND CORRELATIONS

This research proposes a new application and adaptation of Gram matrices (Gatys, Ecker, and Bethge 2016) for the analysis of CNN models using satellite images. For this research, the pre-trained Xception CNN architecture (Chollet 2017) is used. This CNN comes pre-trained to classify images based on the ImageNet database, which is a database comprised of 14 million images spanning 20,000 categories. This means no training has to be done on this CNN model and it can just be used as a feature extractor to find image features that correlate with input images. The Xception architecture is shown in Figure 2 and is composed of 14 convolutional neural layer blocks, a fully connected layer, and an output layer. A key choice in the analysis of the Xception CNN is deciding which convolutional neural layer blocks to analyze. The blocks at the beginning of the model extract low-level image features (e.g., as edge, corners, important colors etc.) that correlate with the outputs of the model. These blocks, if visualized, would allow for visual interpretation because the image data at this point has not been compressed very much. In contrast, the blocks toward the end of the model extract high-level features (e.g., buildings, road networks, etc.). These blocks when visualized do not allow for visual interpretation because the image data is highly compressed at this stage in the model. Block 1 of the Xception architecture is, therefore, chosen as the location for the analysis because this allows the neural layers to be visually assessed and interpreted. Figure 2 shows a visualization of all 32 neural layers (i.e., feature maps) comprising block 1 for an example satellite image of a specific California census tract. In order to find which combination of these feature maps are most active for a particular input, a Gram matrix is calculated for the block. Details on calculating Gram matrices can be found in Gatys, Ecker, and Bethge (2016).

In order to identify the feature maps in the convolutional model that might correlate with specific health measures, the satellite image dataset of California census tracts is first subdivided into sets that represent high and low incidences of diabetes, high blood pressure, and obesity. There are therefore six sets: two sets each representing high and low incidence of obesity; two sets each representing high and low incidence of high blood pressure; two sets each representing high and low incidence of diabetes. Each image of each disease incidence set is then individually passed through the selected CNN architecture and a Gram matrix is calculated using block 1 of the convolutional model for each image. These matrices are then averaged together for all high and low incidence sets. The result is a set of six different average Gram matrices representing high and low disease incidence for diabetes, high blood pressure, and obesity.

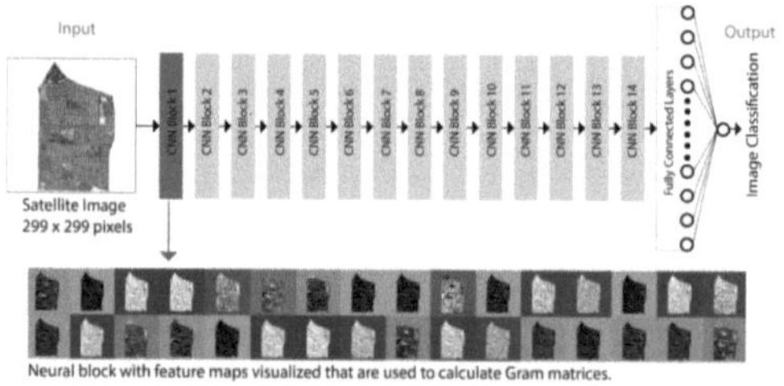

Figure 2
The Xception CNN architecture is shown. The diagram shows that block 1 is visualized for correlational analysis.

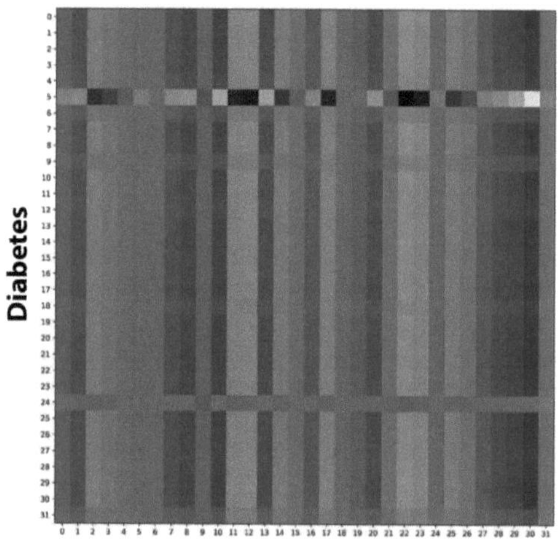

Figure 3
Shows an enlarged view of the average Gram matrix calculated for census tracts with high incidence of diabetes.

Figure 3 shows an enlarged view of the average Gram matrix calculated for census tracts with high incidence of diabetes. The axes of the matrix show identification numbers for the specific feature maps in the first convolutional block. Bright colors in the Gram

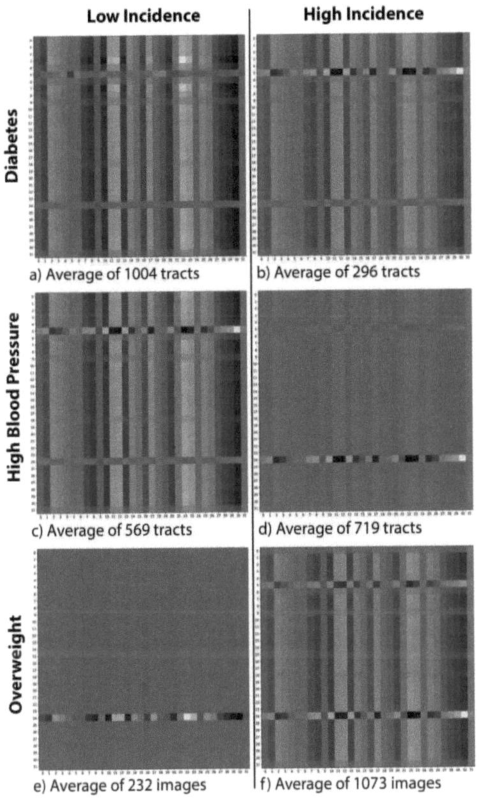

Figure 4
Parts a,c,e show average Gram matrices of low incidence census tracts for health measures. Parts b,d,f show average Gram matrices of high incidence tracts.

matrix represent combinations of feature maps that are most active on average for a particular high or low incidence set. These feature maps can then be visualized and interpreted to identify specific built and natural environment features that are correlated with high and low incidence rates. The results of this analysis are then validated through a comparison with previous work that has identified correlations between these three health outcomes and the built environment as a means of verifying the efficacy of this proposed process.

RESULTS AND DISCUSSION

Figure 4 parts a,c,e show average Gram matrices of low incidence census tracts for diabetes, high blood pressure, and overweight health measures. Parts b,d,f show average Gram matrices of high incidence tracts. The most active feature map combinations identified from the average Gram matrices in Figure 4 for both high and low incidence rates of diabetes, high blood pressure, and overweight adults are presented in Table 1. Comparing the most active feature map combinations of high incidence rates of the three studied health measures reveals several interesting insights. The first, is that census tracts with high incidence of high blood pressure and overweight adults have the same pattern of most active feature map combinations. The highest activating feature maps for both diseases are feature map 30 and 24. Figure 5 and Figure 6 show visualizations of these feature maps for both diseases as well as overlaid analysis. Feature map 30 is a top activating layer for all three diseases and analysis revealed that it activates most when detecting proxies for buildings and streets - such as north south edges and the roofs of buildings - especially lighter roofing materials often associated with larger commercial and residential buildings. In contrast, feature map 24 activates in relation to the space in-between buildings, specifically darker elements in the exterior landscape of the census track, such as asphalt surfaces (e.g., streets and parking lots), vegetation, and shadows.

Table 1
This table shows the top 10% most active feature map combinations identified from the average Gram matrices for both high and low incidence rates of diabetes, high blood pressure, and overweight adults.

Most Active Ranking	Low Incidence Top 10%	High Incidence Top 10%
	Diabetes	
1	22, 3	30,5
2	22,7	10, 5
3	12, 3	29, 5
	High Blood Pressure	
1	30,5	30,24
2	22,0	10,24
3	10,5	29,24
	Overweight	
1	22,24	30,24
2	23,24	10,24
3	12,24	29,24

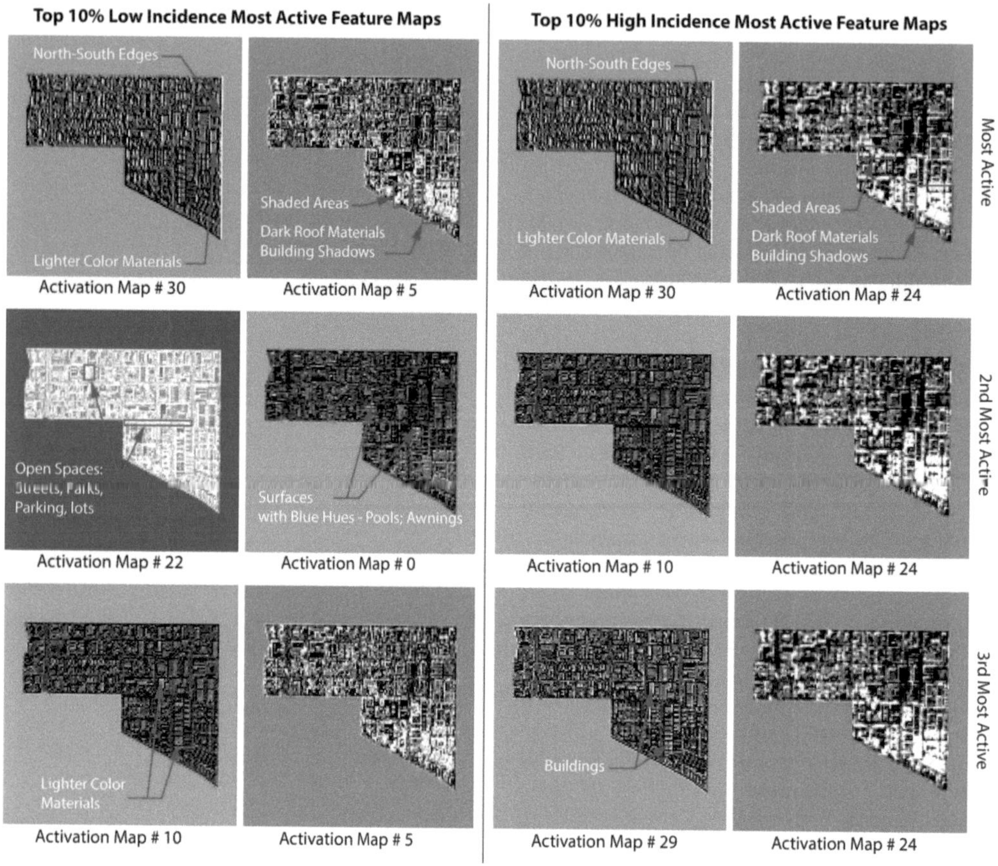

Figure 5
A sample census tract image with a high rate of high blood pressure is used as the input to the CNN Model. (Right) The most active feature maps identified by the Gram matrix analysis are shown for both high and low disease incidences. Qualitative analysis is overlaid on the feature maps to identify specific visual features that are activating the model. Brighter pixel values indicate more activation in that area of the image.

Another insight when looking at the most active feature maps of high incidence cases is that diabetes has one significant difference when compared to the two other diseases. Though diabetes shares feature map 30 with the other diseases, it differs in that it is a combination of feature map 30 and 5 that is most active instead of 30 and 24 with the other two diseases. Figure 7 shows visualizations of these feature maps for diabetes with overlaid analysis. Feature map 5 and 24 seem to activate in relation to dark exterior surfaces (e.g., shadows, asphalt, vegetation), but with one important difference. Feature map 5 is more sensitive to green materials (e.g., parks, natural areas, tree-lined roads, etc.) than 24. This implies that image features correlated with obesity and high-blood pressure are different than those for diabetes. Specifically, it implies that the amount and distribution of vegetation in a census tract is more correlated with high incidence of diabetes than the other two diseases.

The analysis of the most active feature maps for high disease incidence gives insights into correlation, but it is also important to look at the case of low disease incidence and the feature maps associated with those outcomes - as this can help to further shed light on correlation. The left column of Table 1 shows the top 10% most active feature maps for low disease incidence. These results show that - in contrast to the high incidence cases in the right column of the table - no disease shares the exact same feature map combinations. Another insight when comparing all three diseases, is that the most active feature maps for high incidence are different than those for low incidence for all three diseases. Both results imply that the CNN model is looking at different image feature sets for low incidence census tracts than for high incidence ones. This implies that it may not be the presence or absence of one consistent set of image features that may be correlated with both high and low disease incidence but may be combinations of different features that have a more complicated relationship with these diseases. The high blood pressure and overweight measures, for example, show the exact same pattern of feature map activation for high incidence cases but share no feature map combinations for low incidence cases. This could imply that both diseases change their correlation pattern for low disease incidence.

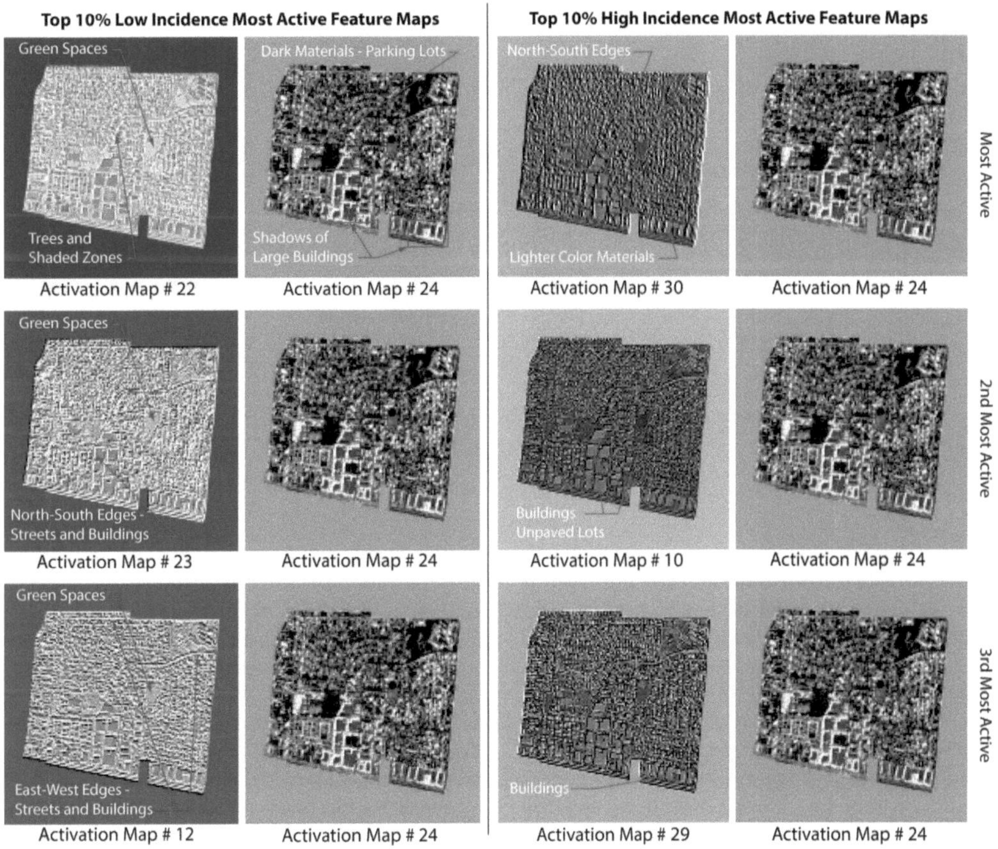

Figure 6
(Left) A sample census tract image with a high rate of overweight adults is used as the input to the CNN Model. (Right) The most active feature maps identified by the Gram matrix analysis are shown for both high and low disease incidences. Qualitative analysis is overlaid on the feature maps to identify specific visual features that are activating the model. Brighter pixel values indicate more activation in that area of the image.

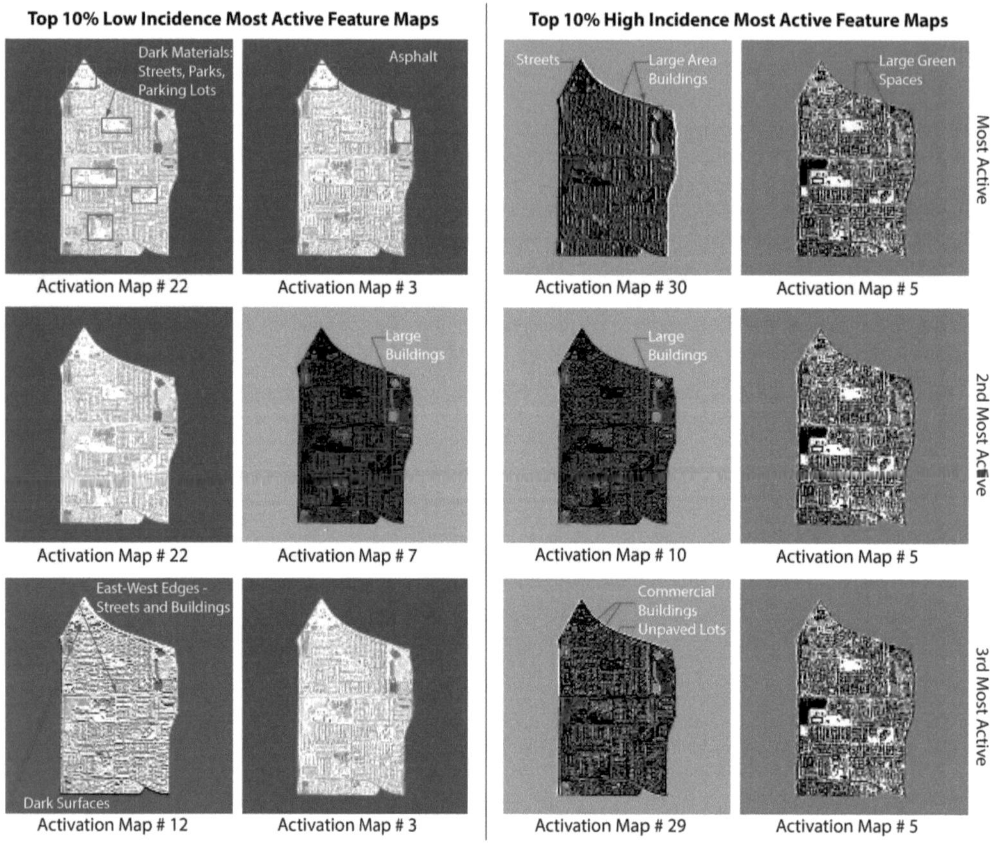

Figure 7
(Left) A sample census tract image with a high rate of diabetes is used as the input to the CNN Model. (Right) The most active feature maps identified by the Gram matrix analysis are shown for both high and low disease incidences. Qualitative analysis is overlaid on the feature maps to identify specific visual features that are activating the model. Brighter pixel values indicate more activation in that area of the image.

In summary, the results suggest that high incidences of diabetes were correlated with feature maps that are sensitive to detecting the distribution of vegetation. The correlation between diabetes and greenspaces is one that has been identified by previous work (Müller et al., 2018). Müller et al. (2018) also found that greenspaces did not have a correlation with high body mass index, which is reflected in the results presented here as well. Another important conclusion from the analysis is that obesity and high blood pressure share the same activation pattern for high incidence cases. Further, the most active feature maps for both diseases are most responsive to proxies for walkability, such as streets, shadow patterns along streets, and parking lots. These results are supported by previous research that has found correlations between walkability and both diseases (Li et al. 2009, Marshall, Piatkowski, and Garrick 2014). The mixed-method approach presented here, therefore, provides another way to verify correlations found by other approaches, adding to the analytic toolkit of researchers.

These results help to demonstrate a DL-driven mixed method to identify correlations between satellite image features and disease incidence, bearing in mind certain limitations. The first major limitation involves the selection of where in the CNN model to calculate the Gram matrices and retrieve the feature maps. In this research, the first convolutional block was chosen because at that stage in the model, images can still be readily interpreted through visual examination. The first blocks of the CNN model have neural layers that learn to find low-level features (e.g., edges, corners, color differences, etc.). While using these early layers from the analysis allows the feature maps to be human-readable, the feature maps at this stage have learned only very basic things. This makes developing insight about how high-level features (e.g., street grid patterns, park distribution patterns, building density differences, etc.) are correlating with specific outcomes more difficult and subject to a greater level of interpretation. There is precedent work that might provide a path to address this issue for those working in the sphere of DL-driven built and natural environment analysis and health estimation. Zeiler and Fergus (2014), for examples, propose one method that addresses this issue.

Another limitation of this mixed methods approach is the degree of interpretation needed to interpret the activation patterns at work in the feature maps identified by the Gram matrices. Identifying the image features that are activating a particular feature map requires a very careful assessment of the feature maps almost on a pixel-by-pixel basis. For some feature maps the activations can be straightforward, but others are difficult to interpret. The results, however, point in directions validated by other quantitative approaches (Li et al. 2009, Marshall, Piatkowski, and Garrick 2014, Müller et al. 2018).

CONCLUSION

The research contributes knowledge on methods to gain insight into the correlation of the visual features represented by satellite images of the built environment and health measures. Specifically, a mixed method approach involving the calculation of Gram matrices and qualitative visual interpretation is presented. The results show that obesity and high blood pressure shared the same pattern of CNN activation for high disease incidence. Specifically, both are most active in relation to proxies for walkability. A result supported by existing research (Li et al. 2009, Marshall, Piatkowski, and Garrick 2014, Müller et al. 2018).

The results further show that diabetes seems to be correlated with greenspaces in a way the other two diseases are not. This result appears to validate findings by other researchers who have identified a similar correlation through other methods (Müller et al., 2018). Lastly, image features correlating with low and high disease incidences were found to be different. For example, the activation patterns for high blood pressure shift from being sensitive to streets for high disease incidence to greenspaces for low disease incidence. This could imply that image features correlating with a low incidence of a particular disease may not be the primary features correlated with high incidences of that same disease, but this result will need to be verified by future work.

In addition to exploring this last point, there are several important areas for future work to address. The first issue involves exploring the effect that image scale might have on this analysis. Future work should analyze satellite images at different zoom scales in order to verify whether correlational results stay consistent in relation to scale. Another avenue of study involves the development of improved quantitative methods that reduce the degree of visual interpretation needed to identify correlated design features. Lastly, future research will need to explore methods that allow for neural layers that are currently not visually interpretable to be mined for correlational insight. Advancements in these areas could greatly impact the ability of researchers in the planning, design, and health disciplines to better understand the relationship between the built environment and human health.

REFERENCES

Chollet, F 2017 'Xception: Deep learning with depthwise separable convolutions', *Proceedings of the IEEE conference on computer vision and pattern recognition*, pp. 1251-1258

Dumbaugh, E and Rae, R 2009, 'Safe urban form: Revisiting the relationship between community design and traffic safety', *Journal of the American Planning Association*, 75(3), pp. 309-329

Jackson, RJ 2003, 'The impact of the built environment on health: an emerging field', *Jackson RJ. The impact of the built environment on health: an emerging field. Am J Public Health. 2003;93(9):1382-1384. doi:10.2105/ajph.93.9.1382*, 93(9), pp. 1382-1384

Li, F, Harmer, P, Cardinal, BJ and Vongjaturapat, N 2009, 'Built environment and changes in blood pressure in middle aged and older adults', *Preventive medicine*, 48(3), pp. 237-241

Lopez-Zetina, J, Lee, H and Friis, R 2006, 'The link between obesity and the built environment. Evidence from an ecological analysis of obesity and vehicle miles of travel in California', *Health \& place*, 12(4), pp. 656-664

M"uller, G, Harhoff, R, Rahe, C and Berger, K 2018, 'Inner-city green space and its association with body mass index and prevalent type 2 diabetes: a cross-sectional study in an urban German city', *BMJ open*, 8(1), p. e019062

Maharana, A and Nsoesie, EO 2018, 'Use of deep learning to examine the association of the built environment with prevalence of neighborhood adult obesity', *JAMA network open*, 1(4), pp. e181535-e181535

Marshall, WE, Garrick, N, Piatkowski, DP and Newton, D 2020, 'Community design, street networks, and public health', in Nieuwenhuijsen, Khreis, M. H. (eds) 2020, *Advances in Transportation and Health*, Elsevier, pp. 371-388

Piaggesi, S, Gauvin, L, Tizzoni, M, Cattuto, C, Adler, N, Verhulst, S, Young, A, Price, R, Ferres, L and Panisson, A 2019 'Predicting city poverty using satellite imagery', *Proceedings of the IEEE/CVF Conference on Computer Vision and Pattern Recognition Workshops*, pp. 90-96

Simonyan, K and Zisserman, A 2014, 'Very deep convolutional networks for large-scale image recognition', *arXiv preprint arXiv:1409.1556*, 7, pp. 112-120

Geometric Parametrization of a New Town

The case study of Lignano Pineta by Marcello D'Olivo

Alberto Sdegno[1], Andrea De Lorenzo[2]
[1] Università degli studi di Udine [2] Università degli studi di Trieste
[1] alberto.sdegno@uniud.it [2] andrea.delorenzo@phd.units.it

This research focuses on the geometric analysis of a project by the architect Marcello D'Olivo, in which the role of parametrization could be a significant part.The first phase was an in-depth study of the compositional syntax of the author, in order to understand the rules adopted by him to design architectures. As he worked between 1950 and 1990, he didn't use digital software for the computation of his projects, but only traditional instruments.The second phase was a description of digital computational procedures to generate models using parametric software. The digitization of some morphologies designed by D'Olivo was converted in shape algorithms.So the aim of the research was to convert his analog procedures into a series of well-defined digital steps, in order to systematize a way to proceed to control complex forms and to attempt to build a bridge between the pencil projects of D'Olivo and parametric design.

Keywords: *Geometric Parametrization, Shape grammar, Marcello D'Olivo*

SHAPE GRAMMARS AND PARAMETRICISM FOR URBAN PLANNING.

The research deals with the theme of parameterization applied to project management at the urban scale. The case examined in this work is Marcello D'Olivo's singular project for the seaside town of Lignano Pineta. The study starts from well-known examples such as: *The logic of architecture. Design, computation, and cognition* (Mitchell, 1994) which describes the forms of design through a careful analysis of the shape grammars underlying both building and thought; and another important research entitled *The Palladian grammar* (Stiny and Mitchell, 1978) which investigates the plans designed by Andrea Palladio through the grammar of forms and spaces. As a comparison with more contemporary research results, the study refers for example to: *Integrated Parametric Urban Design in Grasshopper/Rhinoceros 3D Demonstrated on a Master Plan in Vienna* (Fink, Koenig 2019); *Parametric urbanism as digital methodology. An urban plan in Beijing* (Pinto et al. 2013). In his career, D'Olivo has tackled the theme of city design several times. The urban scale, as we know, recursively returns in his work. One example is the project for the Lido di Classe in Ravenna (fig. 1), where the architect, together with Ludovico Quaroni, designed an entire plan for the city overlooking the sea. The plan is based on a long sinusoid road connecting the various parts of the urbanization. Particularly noteworthy in this drawing are the "Circus", buildings with a semi-circular plan imagined to house up to 6000 people. This kind of architecture would remain a leitmotif of D'Olivo's architecture. In fact, in his "reasoned utopia" (fig. 2) D'Olivo inserts these buildings, later called "Gradiente" (D'Olivo, Mainardis De Campo, 1986), along the main road axis that adapts to the orography of the land but remains indifferent to the context. In fact, this project can be read as a theoretical testament of the author rather than a specific solution. Among the various projects, however, the one for Lignano Pineta was actually realized. A singular case in the history of Italian architecture. The Archimedean spiral-shaped layout is inserted among the trees and dunes of the coast, giving life to a new city. This is why it is of great interest to study this completed work, an example of a parametric city *ante litteram*. It is still unclear how the architect controlled the design of the curvature as it evolved. For example, for another project by D'Olivo, subsequent to that of Lignano - the plan for a satellite city in Rome in 1995 - an underlying function of the entire design has been found. Michele Parrella writes: "We discovered among D'Olivo's notes a formula that we had been looking at for a long time, without grasping its meaning. We had heard him say that the set of curves was contained in a single equation. For those who can taste it, the equation that includes all the sinusoids referred to the horizontal plane x y is the following y=R +[sen x + tg (α/n)]" (Parrella, 1955). However, no similar information has yet been found for this project in Lignano.

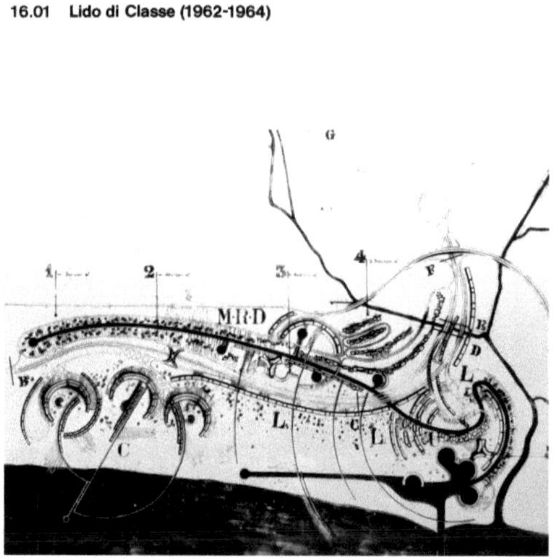

Figure 1
Lido di Classe.
Project by Ludovico Quaroni and Marcello D'Olivo. (From Discorso per un'altra architettura, 1972)

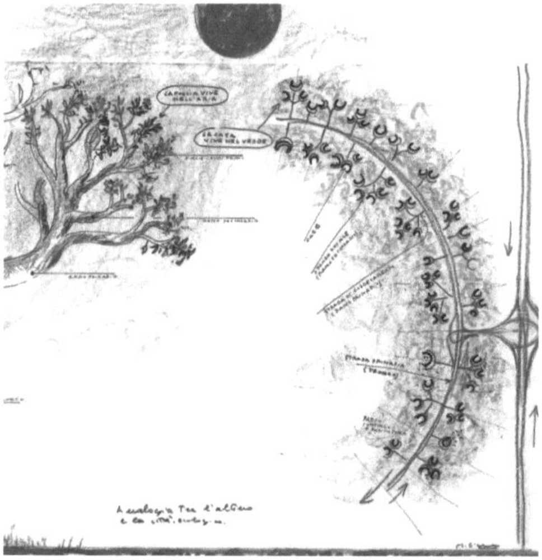

Figure 2
Gradiente. Study of Marcello D'Olivo for the reasoned utopia "Ecotown - Ecoway".

The urban planning of Lignano Pineta: the spiral and the spine

As we have described above, the small town of Lignano Pineta, overlooking the Adriatic Sea and located in the north-east of the Italian peninsula, became a design case of great importance for D'Olivo, who could see the realisation of many studies he had conducted on curved geometries of considerable morphological complexity. In fact it is also one of the rare examples of an urban plan designed and realised by a single architect. The idea of using curved forms for the spatial organisation of the urban intervention was formed in the mind of the architect after a long process of elaboration (fig. 3), which led him to propose, for the competition of ideas, a geometric design of a spiral from which a series of arterial roads branch off, including the spine containing the main shopping avenue. Apparently the design seems to be drawn almost on the spur of the moment, requiring a heuristic process to determine the individual components that is anything but simple, offering an unusual geometric pattern for a city.The use of curved forms is undoubtedly also determined by his interest in nature - and in particular vegetation - and the mathematical rigor with which these forms are regulated. As he would write a few years later: "With or without architects, architecture must approach the world of nature with that humility with which, according to Bacon, 'nature commands itself by obeying it'. The computer is there, and it is a great weapon to be practised because every construction problem, with its direct and indirect effects, can no longer be solved by a single individual, even if he is a genius" (D'Olivo, 1972). The use of computational calculus can therefore make it possible to understand the natural laws that control particular geometries, such as the branched structure of trees and roots. For D'Olivo and his collaborators, therefore, the Lignano Pineta project became an enormous forge for architectural and urban experimentation. The graphic production contains a large number of solutions on both an urban and typological scale. The spiral system layout of Lignano is studded with dwellings and services imagined by the architect. The seaside galaxy of D'Olivo is configured as a utopian expression that seeks to emulate nature. Each design proposal, even the simplest, demonstrates the architect's great capacity for geometric control. But despite the stubbornness of D'Olivo's studio, the project was only partially completed. The architect did not complete his hypothesis in its entirety, both because of the difficult relations with the client and, probably, also because of difficulties connected with the precise control of the geometry of the installation during the construction phase on the building site. One wonders, therefore, whether a truly computational control of the design operation - done with the digital tools currently available - would have allowed a complete verification of the morphology during both the design and construction phases.

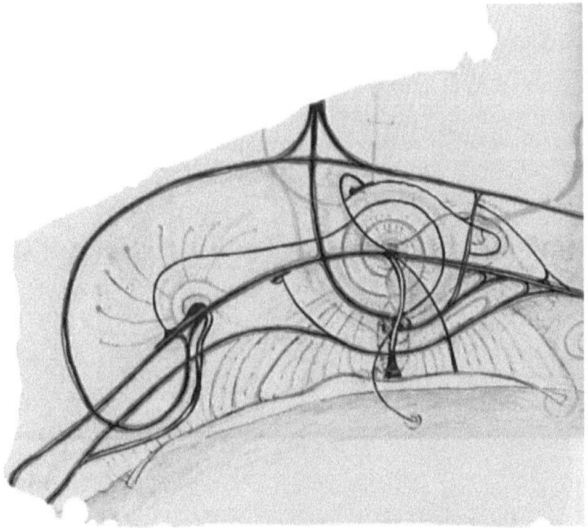

Figure 3
Lignano Pineta: road plan. Marcello D'Olivo 1953. (Private archive Teor)

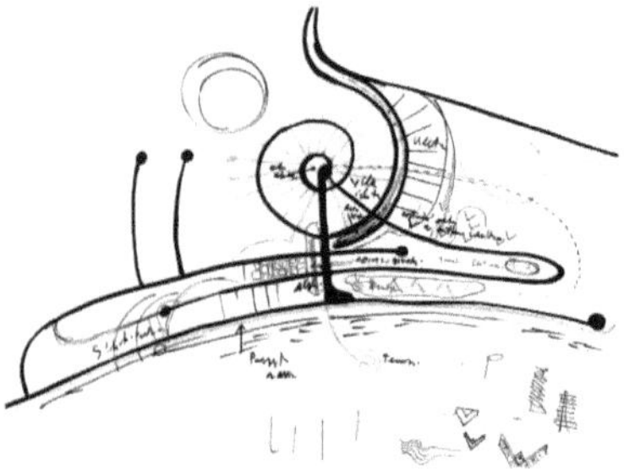

Figure 4
One of the first sketches for Lignano Pineta. The spiral grows in the opposite way and "The Train" is straight. (Private archive Teor)

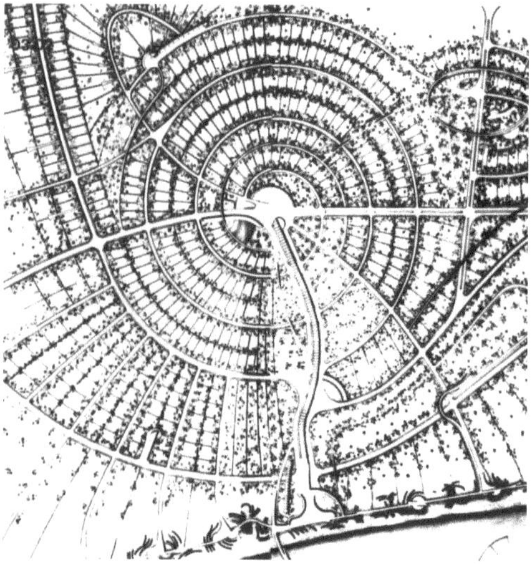

Figure 5
One of the last proposals for the plan of Lignano Pineta. (From Discorso per un'altra architettura, 1972)

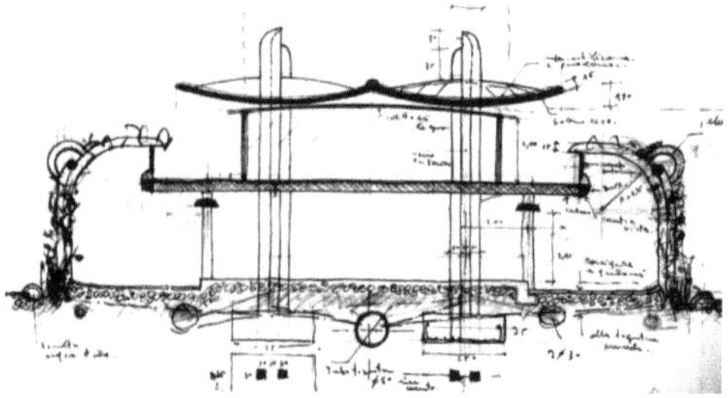

Figure 6
Sketch for the section of "The Train", Marcello D'olivo. (From Discorso per un'altra architettura, 1972)

Parametric algorithm for the drawing of the spine

If on the one hand the geometric form of the spiral does not require great difficulty from the point of view of graphic control - it is an Archimedes spiral which has the characteristic of having a regular distance between the turns of 100 metres - a characteristic element, addressed here with the tools of parametric computation, was the calculation of the spine destined for the commercial/residential avenue that we mentioned in the previous chapter and that is called "The Train" by the architect himself, also due to the fact that it is composed of a series of individual units - the railway cars - spaced out from each other even if irregularly. This spine proceeds from the centre of the spiral, projecting in the direction of the sea. It is interesting to note that the theme of the spine is recurrent in D'Olivo's texts. In 1986 he wrote: "Moving on from the level of house to that of the city, here too, as in the plant world, we have a spine, a trunk to which the gradients are attached. This spine is in circular form with a diameter that can carry according to the exigencies of adaptation to a given place or situation" (D'Olivo, Mainardis de Campo, 1986). The spine of Lignano will undergo different variations: in the first project hypothesis (fig. 4) it turns out to be rectilinear and perpendicular to the coastline, while in the following versions it begins to bend becoming a sinusoid (fig. 5). Since this curve undergoes various modifications in its inflection points during the course of the design, it seemed significant to us to be able to control the design variations of the curvature parametrically, even though we are aware that, in D'Olivo's case, the operation was almost certainly carried out by means of mutual approximations using traditional instruments. We have therefore identified the shape grammar necessary to understand a possible process of geometric parameterization (fig. 7), starting from the construction of a flexible baseline on which to anchor all the building construction present on the spine. The process of geometric control could then be further developed with the use of a Building Information Modeling software, so

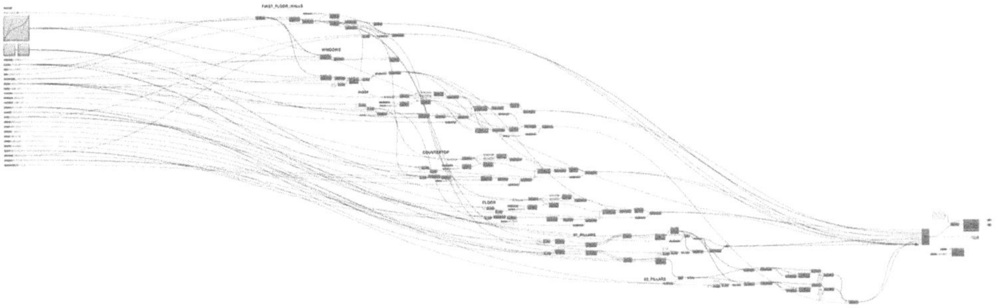

Figure 7
Grasshopper description. Parametric model of "The Train".

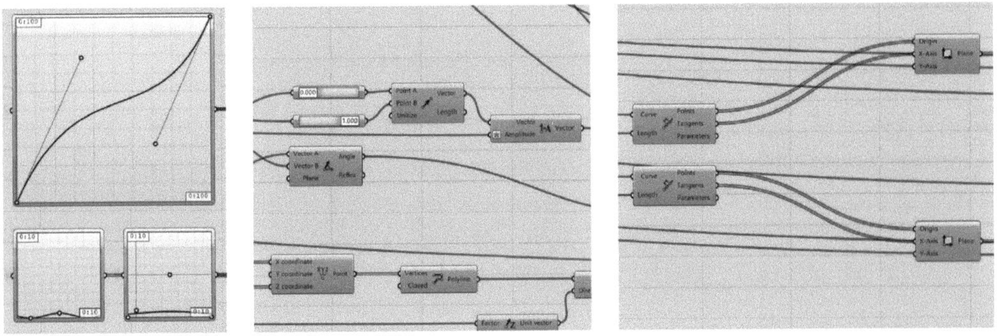

Figure 8
The three Graph Mappers used in Grashopper's description to model the "spine" of the model (up), the section of the roof (bottom left) and the section of the countertop (bottom right). The geometric process to align the section of the roof to the sweep rail. Alining the geometry of the pillars to the tangent of the curve in each point used to set the structure.

that the pure geometric form could convey very detailed architectural information, so that the morphology could be transformed procedurally. In extreme synthesis, it will be possible to use Grasshopper by interfacing it with Revit through the Rhino.inside.Revit procedure, which allows the recognition of architectural attributes inserted within the families of the Autodesk BIM product by the Rhino software, and at the same time it will be possible to exploit the potential of some of the latter's tools by Revit, such as the Graph Mapper command.

Parametric description

From a procedural point of view, the domain within which to insert the points of the sine curve was defined. Then, in order to control the function, we inserted the Graph Mapper command that allows the parametric control of the components in a graphic and immediate way. In fact, the command contains various parametric formulas - such as Bezier, Conic, Parabola, Sine, etc. (fig. 8) - expressed through the graph of the function in a range that can be modified directly by the user, both in terms of values and form. Proceeding in this way, it is possible to intuitively create a large number of different architectural options from a mathematical function (fig. 9,10,11). Even from this initial approach, it is clear that the drawing will be developed according to procedural rather than descriptive logic. Maintaining the design of the basic polygonal as the anchoring element for all the other components, the individual objects - such as the floor slab, the structural elements, the

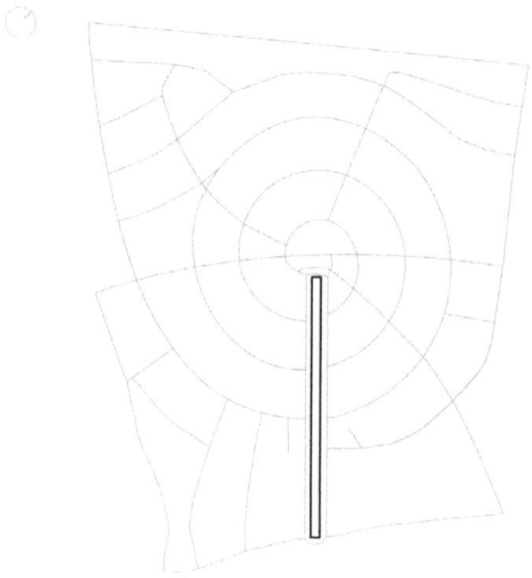

Step 0

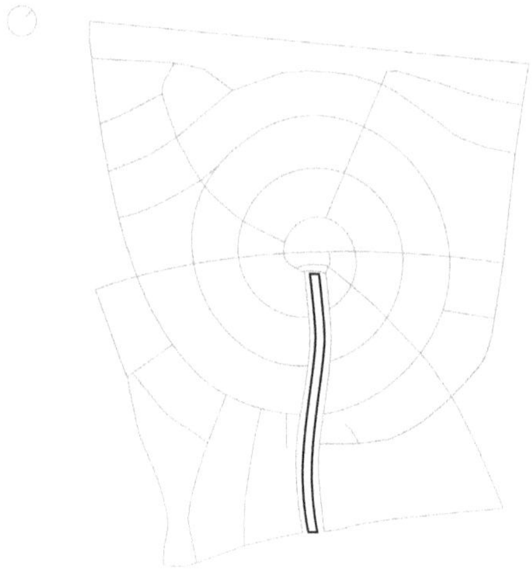

Step 1

Figure 9
Variations based on the original drawings edited by D'Olivo reaching the final shape.

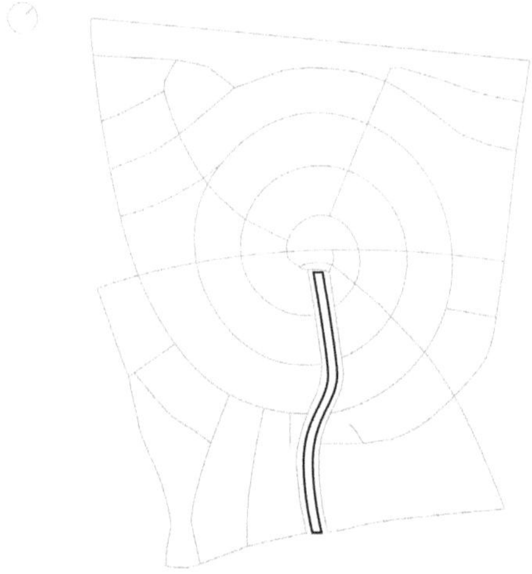

Step 2

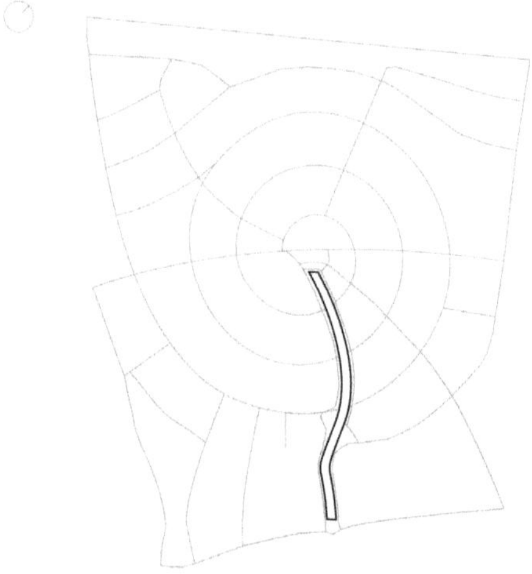

Step 3 - Final shape

Figure 10
Variations based on the original drawings edited by D'Olivo reaching the final shape.

Figure 11
Variations of the elements: roof, pillars, and the first floor.

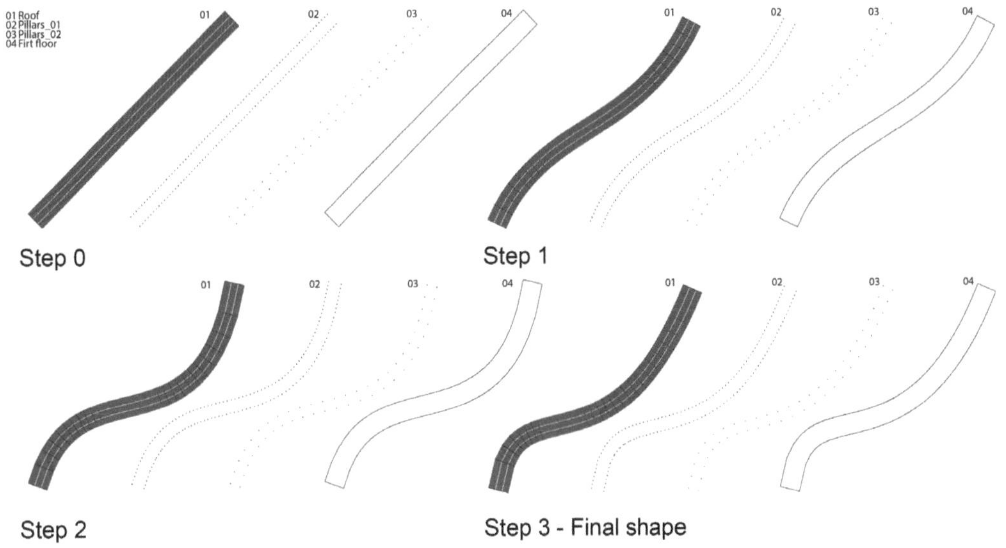

upper floor, the partitions and the roof - were constructed by defining orthogonality constraints to the baseline, so that each individual object could adapt to any formal modifications of the basic geometry, using the Perp Frames option. In this way, each point on the curve becomes the origin of a separate geometric plane with variable local axial coordinates. The x-axis of each plane is then perpendicular to the tangent of the curve at that point. If for some elements - such as the floor or the structural pillars - it was possible to generate them within Grasshopper, thanks to the very simple and linear form determined by a vertical extrusion of a polygonal geometry, in other cases - such as the roof - it was possible to experiment with various hypotheses. As we know, it would be possible to proceed with the im-

Figure 12
Perspective preview of the Grasshopper descrition from Rhinoceros.

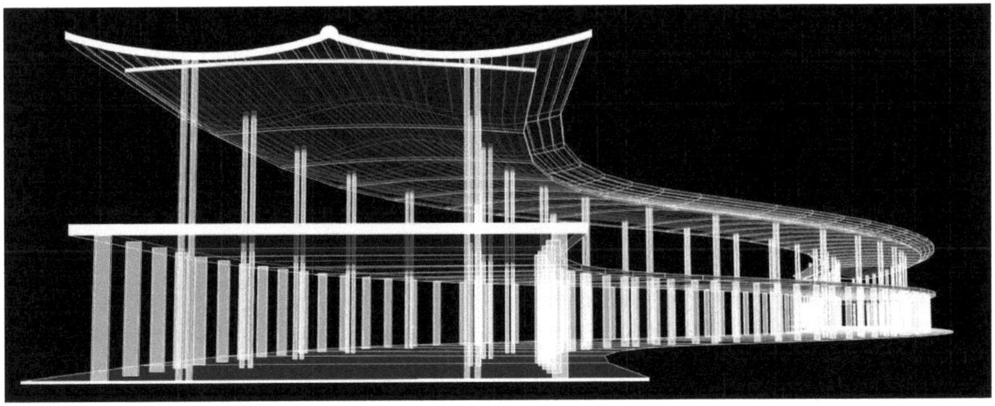

port of a morphology created in the Rhino modeler, making the Grasshopper system recognize it but, in this case too, the use of the Graph Mapper algorithm was experimented with, as already done for the initial baseline curve. The sine function, in the variables Domain and Codomain, succeeds in describing in graphic form the mathematical function relative to the double gull-wing section (fig. 6), conceived by D'Olivo.

CONCLUSIONS

In this way, the control system defined with the baseline relative to the backbone, to which the different parts that constitute the architectural elements of the building are anchored, permits the movement of all the components that determine the project in a coordinated manner, allowing the architect to control the possible formal variations even during the design phase of the project.In this way Marcello D'Olivo, if he had had a parametric procedural system as described here, could have chosen the best configuration by slightly modifying the curvature of the sine wave and immediately seen the results reverberated on the entire geometric system (fig. 12), being able to propose them at the same time during the executive phase thanks to the possible direct connection with the Building Information Modeling system.

REFERENCES

D, M. and Mainardis De Campo, P. 1986, *Ecotown Ecoway. Utopia ragionata*, Rusconi, Milano

D'Olivo, M. 1972, *Discorso per un'altra architettura*, Casamassima, Udine

Fink, T. and Koening, R. 2019 'Integrated Parametric Urban Design in Grasshopper/Rhinoceros 3D Demonstrated on a Master Plan in Vienna', *Proceedings of 37 eCAADe and XXIII SIGraDi Joint Conference*, Porto, pp. 313-322

Finn, E. 2017, *What Algorithms Want. Imagination in the Age of Computing*, The MIT Press, Cambridge MA-London

Koning, H. and Eizenberg, J. 1981, 'The language of the prairie: Frank Lloyd Wright's prairie houses', *Environment and Planning B*, Planning and Design 8, p. 295–324

Luppi, F. and Nicoloso, P. 2002, *Marcello D'Olivo Architetto*, Mazzotta, Milano

March, L. and Steadman, P. 1971, *The Geometry of Environment*, RIBA Publications, London

Mitchell, W.J. 1994, *The logic of architecture. Design, computation, and cognition*, The MIT Press, Cambridge MA-London

Parrella, M. 1955, 'La città a girasole', *La civiltà delle macchine*, 4, pp. 28-29

Pinto, G. M., Vieira, A. and Neto, P. 2013 'Parametric Urbanism as digital methodology. An urban plan in beijing.', *Proceedings of eCAADe 2013*

Schumacher, P. 2016, *Parametricism 2.0*, Architectural Design

Stiny, G. and Mitchell, W. 1978, 'The Palladian grammar', *Environment and Planning B*, Planning and Design(5), p. 5–18

Tedeschi, A. 2014, *AAD_Algorithms-Aided Design*, Le Penseur, Brienza

Zucconi, G. 1997, *Marcello D'Olivo. Architetture e progetti 1947-1991*, Electa, Milano

The Cognition of Residential Convenience Areas Based on Street View Image's Entropy and Complexity

Beijing as an example

Shaoji Wu[1]
[1] *Tianjin University*
[1] *wsjarchitecture@tju.edu.cn*

This paper quantifies the convenience of living in Beijing by calculating street view image's two inherent properties, entropy and complexity. The image's entropy H can measure the degree of disorder in its pixel arrangement, and the complexity C can measure the ``structure" of its pixel arrangement. The study methodology can be divided into four steps as follows. (1) 20,194 Baidu Street View (BSV) images of random geographic coordinates within the study area are crawled as the dataset. (2) Calculate the entropy and complexity of each image separately and plot the entropy-complexity plane. (3) Clustering of data points on the entropy-complexity plane using the K-means algorithm. (4) Analysis of the geographical distribution of the different cluster's data points. The following two conclusions can be drawn from this research. Firstly, low entropy and high complexity street view images can characterize built-up urban areas where the sky occupies a large area, and its buildings are usually more uniform. Conversely, high-entropy and low-complexity images can characterize areas with the more complex built-up environment. Secondly, street view images representing high residential convenience areas in Beijing are characterized by high entropy and low complexity.

Keywords: *Street View Image, Entropy, Complexity, Residential Convenience*

INTRODUCTION

Currently, cities are expanding rapidly in China. For example, Beijing, one of the largest cities in China, its built-up area grew at a rate of 16.11 $km^2/year$ from 2000 to 2017, and its population density went from 13,400 to 17,600 people per km2 during this period (Yu et al. 2020). However, the traditional field research and sampling methods used to study cities do not effectively reflect the city's specific situation due to their high labor cost and low accuracy (Huang et al. 2019). Under the circumstances, we address this problem by proposing a method that uses two values, entropy and complexity of street view images, to measure urban built-up areas quantitatively.

Research Streams

Today, the widespread use of open geospatial data on the web offers new possibilities for solving the issue of data collection. Web maps, such as Google Maps and Baidu Maps, containing massive amounts of street view images, have been developed and widely used. The information in these images provides new opportunities for urban research (Long and Zhou 2017). This study aims to explore the potential of street view images in evaluating cities as an application. This section reviews two types of established studies. The first one is the analysis of cities through street view images, and the other is to evaluate images using entropy and complexity.

Research on Street View Images. Three major research streams have been developed to evaluate built environments using street view images. The first stream studies the urban built environment by using segmentation algorithms, such as SegNet (Badrinarayanan et al. 2017). Xia, Yabuki, and Fukuda proposed a method for assessing street greening rates using Google Street View (GSV) images (2021). Long and Liu analyzed the street greenery of 245 cities in China using one million Tencent Street View (TSV) images and found that the street greenery is higher in the west than in the east in China (2017). Li, Zhang, and Li used GSV to conduct a case study of street greenery in the East Village area of Manhattan, New York, and modified the Green View Index (GVI) formula, which concluded that GSV is well suited for measuring street greenery (2015). Zhang and Dong compared the GVI distribution derived from Beijing's TSV images with the distribution of house prices and found that if all else being equal, the larger the GVI, the higher the house price in the area (2018). Zhou, He, and Cai, et al. used Baidu Street View (BSV) images to identify neighborhoods' walkability in Shenzhen, China. Wang, Lu, and Zhang, et al. used the proportion of visible sky in street view images to quantify the street's walkability (2019).

The second stream uses image recognition algorithms to identify particular objects' numbers or categories in street view images. Huang, Sheng, and Lei, et al. identified and counted pedestrians in street view images of three regions in Beijing and compared the pedestrian's distribution with the integration model based on spatial syntax theory. They found that the street view images can replace the field counted pedestrian flow data when the street view images comprehensively covered the research area (2019). Kang, Körner, and Wang et al. used Convolutional Neural Networks (CNN) to determine the type of buildings in street view images and automatically labeled them on satellite maps taking Vancouver and Fort Worth as examples (2018). Yin, Chen, and Wang et al. used GSV to study the distribution of people in Buffalo and concluded that street view data could essentially replace field counting (2015). Gebru, Krause, and Wang et al. proposed a method for inferring socio-economic attributes such as income, race, education, etc., from cars detected in GSVs using deep learning algorithms (2017).

The third stream analyses the street view images after deformation, usually using Hugin to synthesize them to fisheye images. Carrasco-Hernandez, Smedley, and Webb used fisheye images transformed from GSV to calculate total shortwave global irradiances at street level (2015). Li, Ratti, and Seiferling used GSV to calculate the sky view factor (SVF) and utilized the SVF to quantify the shading effect of street trees in Boston (2018).

These studies show that street view images can measure the built environment based on the idea of taking information from them and analyzing their geographic distribution. However, few studies have analyzed the pixel arrangement of the street view images themselves, which is the research gap that this paper attempts to address.

Research on Image's Entropy and Complexity. An image can be represented by a three-dimensional matrix whose first two dimensions are the height and width, and the third dimension is its RGB value of each pixel. The calculation of the image's entropy and complexity is based on the pixel arrangement of this image. The entropy H of an image can measure the degree of disorder in the image's pixel arrange-

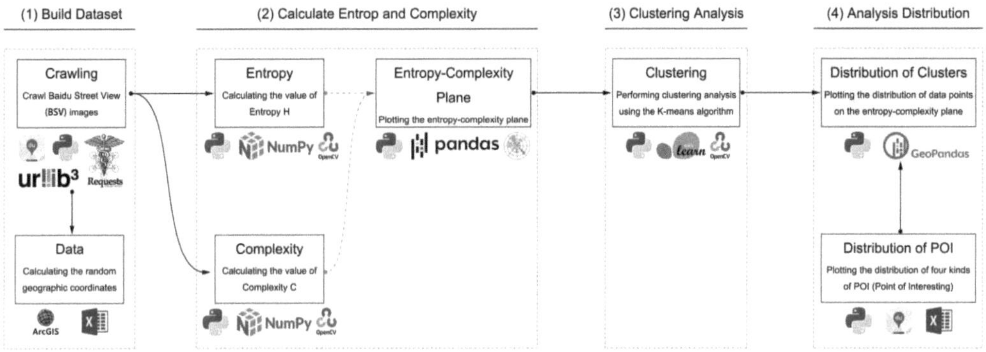

Figure 1
The technology roadmap

ment. Its value is in the interval [0,1], and the closer the entropy is to 1, the more the image's pixel arrangement tends to be disorderly (Bandt and Pompe, 2002). The complexity C of an image can measure the "structure" of the pixel arrangement. This value is zero when the pixel arrangement is completely disordered or ordered, and it is positive when the image's pixel arrangement shows a more complex distribution pattern (Lopez-Ruiz et al. 1995). Existing researches use the "complexity-entropy plane" to visualize image pixel distribution features (Ribeiro et al. 2012). Sigaki, Matja, and Ribeiro proposed a method using the complexity-entropy plane to distinguish paintings from different art schools (2018).

In this context, we ask whether the value defined by extropy H and complexity C is capable of unveiling any properties of convenience for residents in contemporary cities. Following the established studies methodology, this paper uses the complexity-entropy plane to quantify the street view images.

Research Area and Tool
This study takes the area encompassed by the Fifth Ring Road in Beijing as an example to illustrate the method because it is the main built-up area of the city. Baidu Street View (BSV) was selected as the data source, which basically covers the streets within the study area and can provide sufficient data for this research.

METHODOLOGY
Figure 1 illustrates the technology roadmap for this study, which can be divided into the following four steps. (1) Crawl the BSV to construct the dataset for this study using a web crawler. (2) Calculate the complexity and entropy of these images. (3) Clustering analysis of the data points on the complexity-information entropy plane. (4) Analyze the characteristics of the spatial distribution of entropy and complexity.

Crawl the BSV
In this study, 28,000 geographic coordinates were randomly selected within the Fifth Ring Road of Beijing, and the corresponding BSV is automatically downloaded, of which 20,194 are available. These images make up the dataset used in this study, and the images in this dataset all have a size of 512*4096 pixels. Some coordinate points cannot be crawled for effective BSV because they are located in areas inaccessible to Street View collection vehicles such as parks and squares. This section is programmed on Python by Urllib and Requests as web crawler packages.

Calculation of Image's Entropy and Complexity
The entropy and complexity of an image are calculated based on its pixel arrangement. As shown in

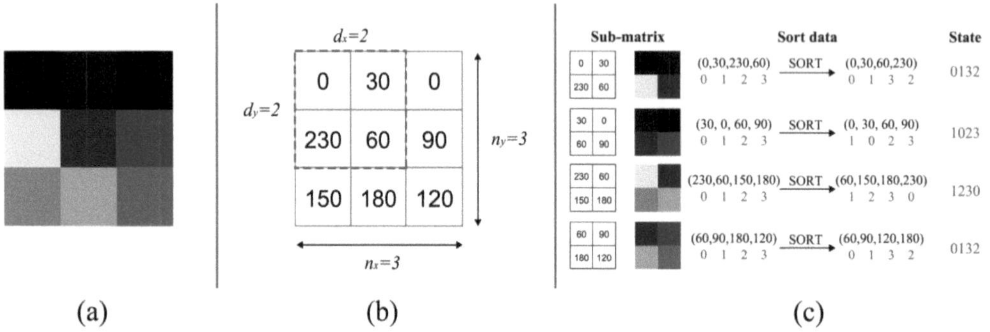

Figure 2
(a) A 3*3 pixel black and white image;
(b) The matrix representing the image; (c) Construction of the accessible states

Figure 2, this section illustrates the process of calculating entropy and complexity through a 3*3 pixel black and white image. This study uses 2*2 pixels sliding partitions with 24 different permutations as image analysis units.

Figure 2(a) shows an image with 3*3 pixels, which can be represented by this matrix in Figure 2(b). After partitioning the matrix in Figure 2(b) using 2*2 sliding partitions, the four sub-matrices in Figure 2(c) are obtained. The probabilities of the patterns of pixel distribution between these sub-matrices are then calculated. The four numbers in the first sub-matrix $(0, 60, 230, 90)$ are ordered as 0132. Similarly, the orders of the other three submatrices are 1023, 1230, and 0132. Based on these four orders, we can calculate the probability $p(\pi)$, i.e. $p(0132) = \frac{2}{4} = 0.5$, $p(1023) = \frac{1}{4} = 0.25$ and $p(1230) = \frac{1}{4} = 0.25$. The entropy H of the image can be calculated according to the following formula.

$$H(P) = \frac{1}{\ln(n)} \sum_{n=0}^{n} p_i \ln\left(\frac{1}{p_i}\right) \tag{1}$$

where $n = (d_x d_y)!$, the value in this image is $(2 \times 2) \neq 4 \times 3 \times 2 \times 1 = 24$. p_i is the probability of each order. This image's entropy is calculated according to this formula as $H \approx 33$, which can indicate its pixels' degree of randomness.

Unlike the entropy, the image's complexity is calculated by the following formula (Martin et al. 2006).

$$C(P) = \frac{D(P,U) \times H(P)}{D^{\star}} \tag{2}$$

where $D(P,U)$ is a relative entropic measure (the Jensen-Shannon divergence). D^{*} is the max value of all $D(P,U)$. The formulas are as follows.

$$D(P,U) = S\left(\frac{P+U}{2}\right) - \frac{S(P)}{2} - \frac{S(U)}{2} \tag{3}$$

$$D^{\star} = -\frac{1}{2}\left[\frac{n+1}{n}\ln(n+1) + \ln(n) - 2\ln(2n)\right] \tag{4}$$

where $\frac{P+U}{2} = \left\{\frac{p_i + \frac{1}{n}}{2}, i = 1, \ldots\ldots, n\right\}$.

However, Martin, Plastino, Rosso, et al. have shown that C(P) is not a trivial function of H(P), which means that for a given value of H(P), there are several corresponding C(P) (2006). This is the reason why we use the entropy-complexity plane. This image's complexity is calculated according to this formula as $C(P \approx 0.27)$, which can indicate the "structure" of the arrangement of its pixels.

The calculated entropy H and complexity C can be plotted in a rectangular coordinate system called the entropy-complexity plane.

Cluster Analysis

This section describes how to cluster data points on the entropy-complexity plane using K-means algorithm, which is based on minimizes Euclidean

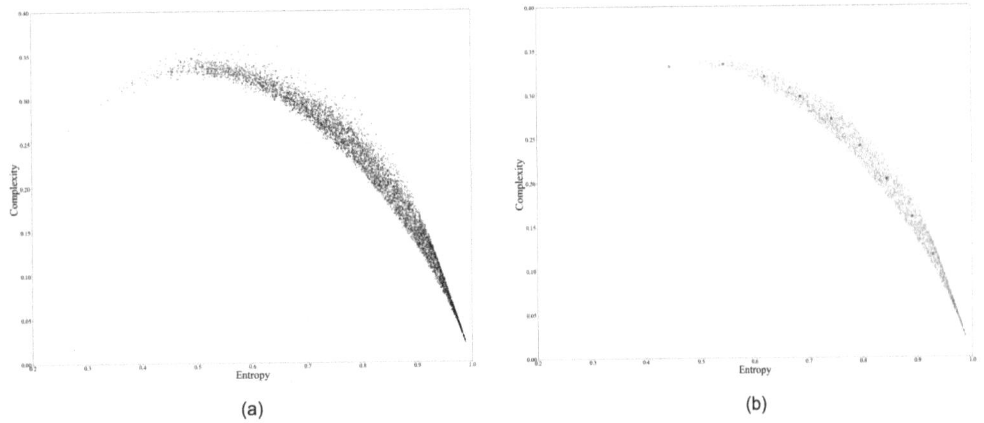

Figure 3
(a) The entropy-complexity plane; (b) The result of clustering analysis;

distances (MacQueen, 1967). This section is programmed on Python by Pandas and Scikit-learn as the statistical package and Matplotlib as the visualization package. This section can be divided into the following three steps.

First, The entropy and complexity of the street view images are imported, and the entropy-complexity plane is created shown in Figure 3. Figure 3(a) illustrates that the complexity is taken in [0.267,0.989], and the entropy is taken in [0.021, 0.362] in the entropy-complexity plane. We can find a correlation between these two kinds of values, although there is no functional relationship.

Second, performing cluster analysis. The number k, the count of classes in which the data needs to be divided, needs to be determined, and in this paper, k=10. Then k central points are randomly generated in the entropy-complexity plane. Every data point in the entropy-complexity plane is assigned by the minimal distance from it to the central points. Once all data points have been allocated, each cluster's center point is recalculated as their geometric center. The algorithm iterates until no more data points are reassigned, or the cluster centers no longer move. Figure 3(b) displays the results of the k-means algorithm, where the data points on the entropy-complexity plane are split into ten parts.

Third, The geographical distribution of the results obtained from the clustering analysis. For further details, we refer to 2.4.

The Geographical Distribution of Street View Image's Entropy and Complexity

This section describes how to visualize the entropy and complexity's geographical distribution. It is programmed on Python by the GeoPandas package.

Figure 4 illustrates the visualization approach. The research area is first rasterized into 4183 units, each with an actual size of approximately 300m*300m. 574 units are removed because they represent areas where street view images do not exist, such as the Forbidden City, the Summer Palace, and other sizeable historical heritage sites or government institutions. There are 3609 units used to visualize the data in this study. Then, the average number of the image entropy and complexity within each unit is calculated, and we use them as the corresponding values for this unit to plot heat maps.

RESULT AND ANALYSIS

This chapter is divided into three main sections. (1) To display examples of images with varying complexity and entropy and explain their characteristics. (2) To describe the geospatial distribution of these data points in the entropy-complexity plane. (3) To analysis the causes of this geographical distribution and what built environment's indicators it can characterize.

The Examples

Entropy	Example
0-20% (0.267612701 -0.4118010128)	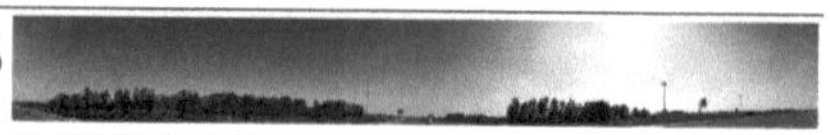
20-40% (0.4118010128- 0.5559893246)	
40-60% (0.5559893246- 0.7001776364)	
60-80% (0.7001776364- 0.8443659482)	
80-100% (0.8443659482 -0.98855426)	

Table 1
Example image of different Entropy

Tables 1 and Table 2 respectively show example images with different entropy and complexity in our dataset. The top 0-20%, 20%-40%, 40%-60%, 60%-80%, and 80%-100% intervals are used in this study to select the images corresponding to different values of entropy and complexity.

Complexity	Example
0-20% (0.021560778 -0.0895995662)	
20-40% (0.0895995662- 0.1576383544)	
40-60% (0.1576383544- 0.2256771426)	
60-80% (0.2256771426- 0.2937159308)	
80-100% (0.2937159308 -0.361754719)	

Table 2
Example image of different Complexity

By comparing the images in Tables 1 and Table 2, the following points can be found. Images with low entropy and high complexity have the following characteristics: (1) They have a larger area occupied by the sky. (2) The surrounding vegetation and buildings are more orderly. (3) The streets are wider, and their D/H ratio values (Ashihara, 1981) are larger, making them more suitable for vehicular traffic. On the contrary, images with high entropy and low complexity have the following characteristics: (1) their sky occupies a smaller area. (2) The surrounding vege-

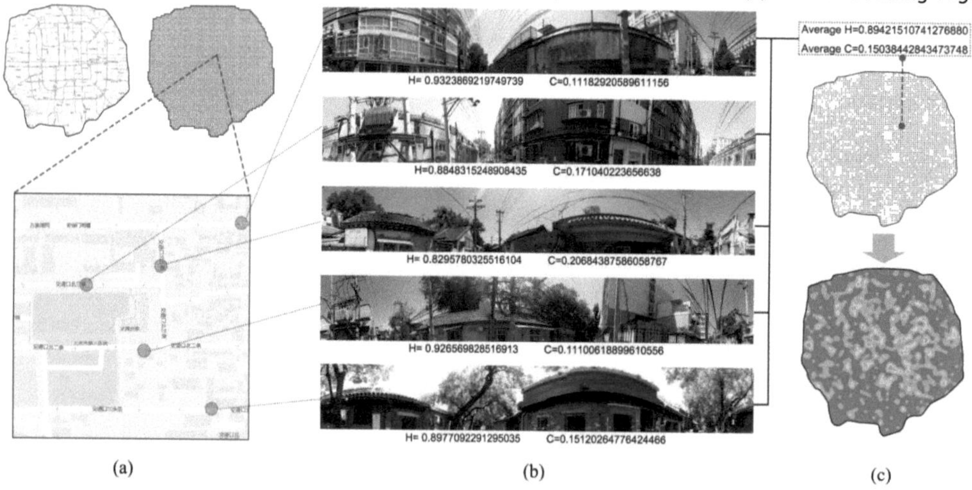

Figure 4
(a) Rasterised the study area; (b) Calculating Entropy and Complexity; (c) Plotting heat maps

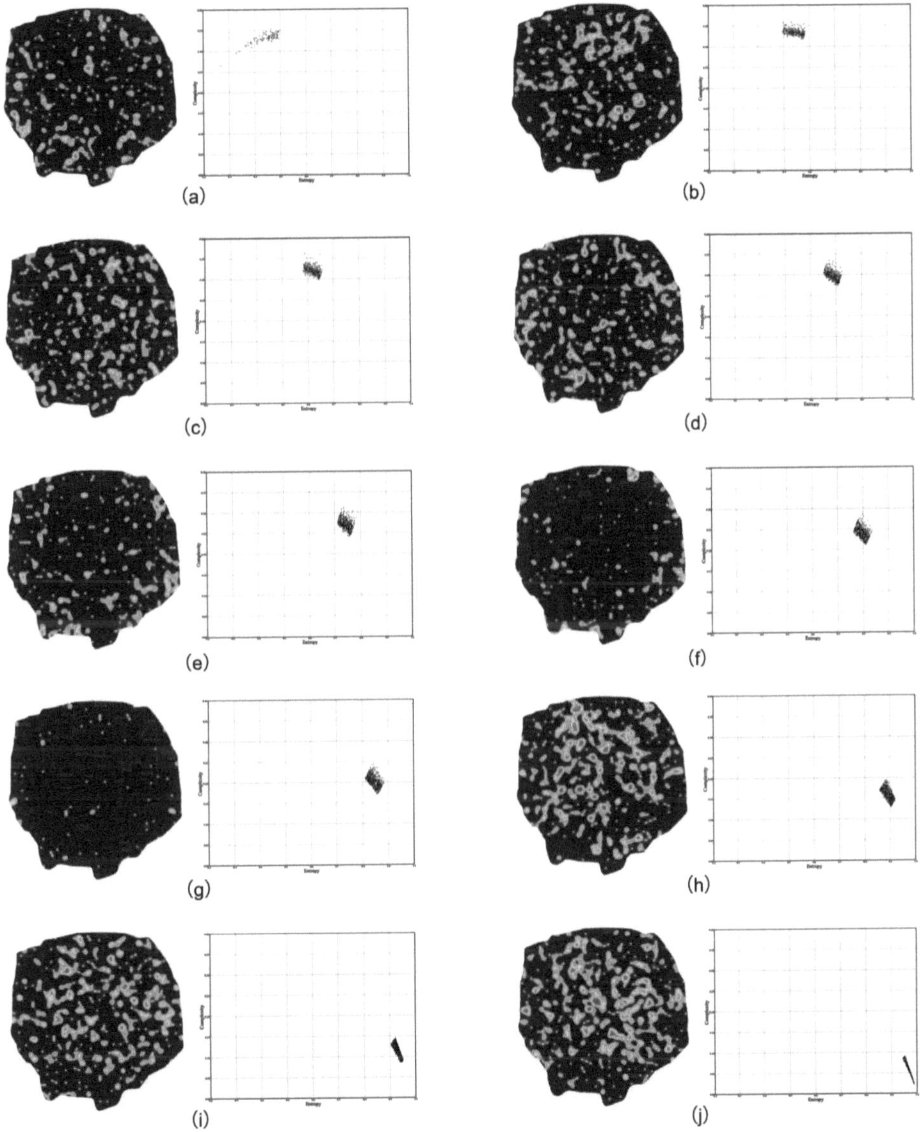

Figure 5
Geographical distribution of data point clusters on the entropy-complexity plane

tation, buildings, etc., are more disorderly. (3) The street's width is narrower, and the value of the D/H ratio is smaller, making it more suitable for pedestrian traffic.

The explanation for the phenomenon is as follows. Images with low entropy and high complexity have a high degree of similarity in their pixel arrangement, and the sky, neatly arranged façade materials, or pure color paint are more consistent with them. Conversely, the more complicated the environment in a street view image, the more complex the arrangement of pixels in the image, and the greater the entropy and lower complexity of it. Therefore, the two values, entropy and complexity of the street view images, can be considered to characterize the urban built-up area.

Geographical Distribution

This section performs geographical spatial visualization based on K-means clustering analysis of the entropy-complexity plane. The clustering coefficient, k, selected is 10 for this study.

Figure 5 shows geographical distribution heat maps of these ten types of data points on the entropy-complexity plane. The distribution is divided into three categories. The data points in Figure 5(a-d) show a uniformly scattered distribution across the study area. In contrast, the data points in Figure 5(e-g) are distributed more towards the urban fringe areas. The data points in Figure 5(h-j) are concentrated in the study area's central and northern areas.

Comparative Analysis

Following the method proposed by Li and Zhang(2021), this paper uses the spatial distribution of POI(Point of Interesting) data to measure the resident's living convenience in the study area. This section analyses the relationship between street view images' entropy and complexity distribution, and the convenience of residents' lives. The POI data is obtained from Baidu Map and using Power Map to draw heat maps.

Figure 6 shows the distribution of the four categories of POIs, which are government agencies, healthcare facilities, educational facilities, and restaurants. The denser the distribution of these facilities in an area, the more convenient for its residents' live. The four types of POI's spatial distribution are similar, i.e., they are mainly located in the central and upper parts of the heat map picture. This indicates that the areas with higher convenience for residents in Beijing are primarily located in the central and northern regions.

In contrast to 3.2, the POI distribution is most similar to Figure 5(h-j), which is the street view images with high entropy and low complexity. This means that street view images corresponding to higher convenience areas are more likely to be located in the lower right part of the entropy-complexity plane. As can be seen from 3.1, such street view images show urban built environments that typically have narrow streets, multiple styles of buildings, and a wide variety of plants, which are usually more suitable for walking. This is in line with the perception of the more convenient locations of the

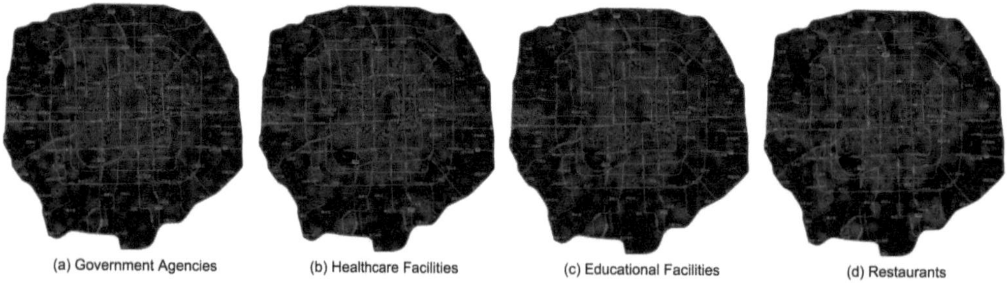

Figure 6
The distribution of the four categories of POI

city.

DISCUSSION
This paper discusses the application of street view image's entropy and complexity to evaluate built-up areas in Beijing. However, three factors might affect the analysis.

First, Although the dataset for this study contains 20,194 street view images of streets, it is not sufficient for Beijing's giant built-up area. This leads to the conclusions of this study still needing further validation using a larger dataset.

Second, there are many chance circumstances present in street view images used in this study, such as pedestrians and cars' presence in a particular image and the characteristics of the vegetation in different seasons, which might lead to errors in the calculations. The use of larger datasets and historical images can alleviate this problem.

Third, this study only calculated the distribution of image entropy and complexity. However, it does not explore the quantitative relationship between the value of entropy and complexity on residents' convenience in built-up urban areas. In the future, we hope to continue our research using quantitative methods such as regression analysis and machine learning algorithms to support preliminary conclusions of this study's qualitative analysis.

CONCLUSION
This paper researches the geographic spatial distribution of entropy and complexity using Baidu Street View in the Fifth Ring Road region of Beijing. The following two conclusions are drawn by comparing the spatial distribution with the four types of POI in the study area.

First, street view images with low entropy and high complexity generally have a large proportion of the sky. The built environment they represent is usually neat and tidy, such as a large-scale collective housing estate. Such areas are more suitable for car traffic. Conversely, images with high entropy and low complexity generally have a lower sky occupation and a more mixed built environment, such as historic districts, which are often more walkable.

Second, high residential convenience areas are mainly located in the central and northern parts of Beijing. By comparing with the geospatial distribution of data points on the entropy-complexity plane, it can be found that the areas with higher entropy and lower complexity pictures correspond to regions with a higher degree of residential convenience.

REFERENCES
Ashihara, Y. 1981, *Exterior design in architecture*, Van Nostrand Reinhold Company, New York

Badrinarayanan, V., Kendall, A. and Cipolla, R. 2017, 'SegNet: A Deep Convolutional Encoder-Decoder Architecture for Image Segmentation', *IEEE Transactions on Pattern Analysis and Machine Intelligence*, vol.39, no.12, pp. 2481-2495

Bandt, C. and Pompe, B. 2002, 'Permutation entropy: a natural complexity measure for time series', *Physical review letters*, 88(17), p. 174102

Carrasco-Hernandez, R., Smedley, A. R. and Webb, A. R. 2015, 'Using urban canyon geometries obtained from Google Street View for atmospheric studies: Potential applications in the calculation of street level total shortwave irradiances', *Energy and Buildings*, 86, pp. 340-348

Gebru, T., Krause, J., Wang, Y., Chen, D., Deng, J., Aiden, E. and Li, F. 2017, 'Using deep learning and Google Street View to estimate the demographic makeup of neighborhoods across the United States', *Proceedings of the National Academy of Sciences*, 114(50), pp. 13108-13113

Huang, Y., Sheng, Q., Lei, H. and Du, J. 2019, 'An Analysis of Substitution on Measured Pedestrian Traffic by Street View Map', *New Architecture*, 2019(04), pp. 137-141

Kang, J., Körner, M., Wang, Y., Taubenböck, H. and Zhu, X. 2018, 'Building instance classification using street view images', *ISPRS journal of photogrammetry and remote sensing*, 145, pp. 44-59

Li, X., Ratti, C. and Seiferling, I. 2018, 'Quantifying the shade provision of street trees in urban landscape: A case study in Boston, USA, using Google Street View', *Landscape and Urban Planning*, 169, pp. 81-91

Li, J. and Zhang, S. 2021, 'Research on Beijing Residential Convenience Index Based on Point of Interest', *Journal of Computer-Aided Design & Computer Graphics*,

2021(1), pp. 1-7
Li, X., Zhang, C., Li, W., Ricard, R., Meng, Q. and Zhang, W. 2015, 'Assessing street-level urban greenery using Google Street View and a modified green view index', *Urban Forestry & Urban Greening*, 14(3), pp. 675-685
Long, Y. and Liu, L. 2017, 'How green are the streets? An analysis for central areas of Chinese cities using Tencent Street View', *PloS one*, 12(2), p. e0171110
Long, Y. and Zhou, Y. 2017, 'Pictorial Urbanism: A New Approach For Human Scale Urban Morphology Study', *Planners*, 33(02), pp. 54-60
López-Ruiz, R., Mancini, H.L. and Calbet, X. 1995, 'A statistical measure of complexity', *Physics Letters A*, 209, pp. 321-326
MacQueen, J. 1967 'Some methods for classification and analysis of multivariate observations', *Proceedings of the fifth Berkeley symposium on mathematical statistics and probability*, pp. Vol. 1, No. 14, pp. 281-297
Martin, M. T., Plastino, A. and Rosso, O. A. 2006, 'Generalized statistical complexity measures: Geometrical and analytical properties', *Physica A: Statistical Mechanics and its Applications*, 369(2), pp. 439-462
Ribeiro, H. V., Zunino, L., Lenzi, E. K., Santoro, P. A. and Mendes, R. S. 2012, 'Complexity-entropy causality plane as a complexity measure for two-dimensional patterns', *PloS one*, 7(8), p. e40689
Sigaki, H. Y., Perc, M. and Ribeiro, H. V. 2018, 'History of art paintings through the lens of entropy and complexity', *Proceedings of the National Academy of Sciences*, 115(37), pp. E8585-E8594
Wang, R., Lu, Y., Zhang, J., Liu, P., Yao, Y. and Liu, Y. 2019, 'The relationship between visual enclosure for neighbourhood street walkability and elders' mental health in China: using street view images', *Journal of Transport & Health*, 13, pp. 90-102
Xia, Y., Yabuki, N. and Fukuda, T. 2021, 'Development of a system for assessing the quality of urban street-level greenery using street view images and deep learning', *Urban Forestry & Urban Greening*, vol.59, p. 126995
Yin, L., Chen, Q., Wang, Z. and Shao, Z. 2015, "Big data'for pedestrian volume: Exploring the use of Google Street View images for pedestrian counts', *Applied Geography*, 63, pp. 337-345
Yu, Y., Chen, P., Qin, F., Liu, B., Huang, Y. and Huang, S. 2020, 'Monitoring and analysis of spatial pattern change of urban expansion in Beijing', *Bulletin of Surveying and Mapping*, 2020(11), pp. 132-136
Zhang, Y. and Dong, R. 2018, 'Impacts of street-visible greenery on housing prices: Evidence from a hedonic price model and a massive street view image dataset in Beijing', *ISPRS International Journal of Geo-Information*, 7(3), p. 104
Zhou, H., He, S., Cai, Y., Miao, W. and Su, S. 2019, 'Social inequalities in neighborhood visual walkability: Using street view imagery and deep learning technologies to facilitate healthy city planning', *Sustainable Cities and Society*, 50, p. 101605

From Streetscape to Data

Semantic segmentation for the prediction of outdoor thermal comfort

Gülin Yazıcıoğlu[1], *İpek Gürsel Dino*[2]
[1,2]*Middle East Technical University*
[1,2]*{gulin.yazicioglu|ipekg}@metu.edu.tr*

In recent years, the increasing pace of urbanization is expected to increase the temperatures in urban contexts and amplify the Urban Heat Island effect. This phenomenon has a negative impact on the urbanites` thermal comfort in outdoor spaces. Modeling and simulation-based approaches can precisely calculate outdoor thermal comfort; however, they are labor-intensive and high in computational cost. This difficulty might discourage decision-makers to consider outdoor thermal comfort conditions, which can affect their strategies at the beginning stage of design. This paper aims to propose a statistical model that can predict outdoor comfort using semantic segmentation of 2D street view images. Firstly, 78 panoramic street images of selected three streets in Istanbul are used to calculate the specific object classes that have an influence on outdoor temperature using semantic segmentation. Following, the streets' outdoor thermal comfort is calculated in Ladybug/Grasshopper. Lastly, two multi-variate regression models are built using the percentages of these object classes in each image and outdoor thermal comfort in given locations on the streets. Initial results show that the proposed regression models can predict UTCI with R2=0.78 and R2=0.80, indicating the semantic segmentation can support the calculation of outdoor comfort.

Keywords: *multivariate linear regression model, semantic segmentation, universal thermal climate index (UTCI)*

INTRODUCTION

The rapid urbanization results in the increasing the difference between the temperature of city centers and their suburbs called the Urban Heat Island (UHI) effect (Oke, 1982). Consequently, thermal comfort conditions in open spaces, especially streets, have been negatively affected by UHI. Therefore, the improvement of outdoor thermal comfort in streets is essential for cities.

Modeling and simulation-based approaches in outdoor thermal comfort can precisely calculate related comfort metrics; however, they are labor-intensive and high in computational cost. This difficulty might discourage decision-makers to integrate outdoor thermal comfort conditions into their strategies at the beginning stage of design. This study aims to develop a new regression-based approach augmented with semantic segmentation to predict thermal comfort in streets. This approach aims to reduce the time and effort in comfort analyses.

The research is conducted under three sections of the methodology. The first section includes obtaining the selected streets' panoramic images and their semantic segmentation. The second section is dedicated to the 3D modeling of streetscapes by referring to images and calculating outdoor thermal comfort by using computational tools. The third section is building multivariate regression models with the outcomes of the first and second sections to predict discomfort in streets (Figure 1). The results of the regression models point to promising results for understanding outdoor thermal comfort in streets without extra computational processes. This prediction model may save designers time to consider outdoor thermal comfort conditions at the early stage of the design.

LITERATURE REVIEW

Streetscapes

Streetscape is a term used to describe the natural and built fabric of a street. It includes buildings, the street surface, fixtures, and fittings that facilitate its use - from bus shelters and signage to planting schemes (Charlwood, 2004). All these features play a role in shaping the character of the streets. Well-planned streetscapes can provide a better quality of pedestrian experience and comfort (Crankshaw, 2009). In addition, maintating and improving outdoor comfort in streets contribute to the planning strategies of streetscapes.

Semantic Segmentation

Semantic segmentation is one of the essential methods in the field of computer vision (Garcia et al. 2018). There are various studies related to street view assessment by taking advantage of semantic segmentation. For instance, the semantic segmentation of street view images is used to show the spatial distribution of street greenery and the openness of street canyons in Boston (Li et al,2017). This study is a good example for mapping rather more green and open streets by street images to see the whole picture of the current situation of urban landscapes. Semantic segmentation of streetscapes is also used to estimate sky view factor, tree view factor and building view factor of street canyons in Hong Kong (Gong et al.,2018). Investigated factors are mapped by using reference data of hemispheric photography from compact high-rise and low-rise areas. Later, correlation analysis is conducted for comparing these three factors. Liang (2019) proposed an assessment of streetscapes by semantic segmentation and correlation analysis with particulate air pollution applied to the city of Milan. This study can associate 2D street images with outdoor air quality.

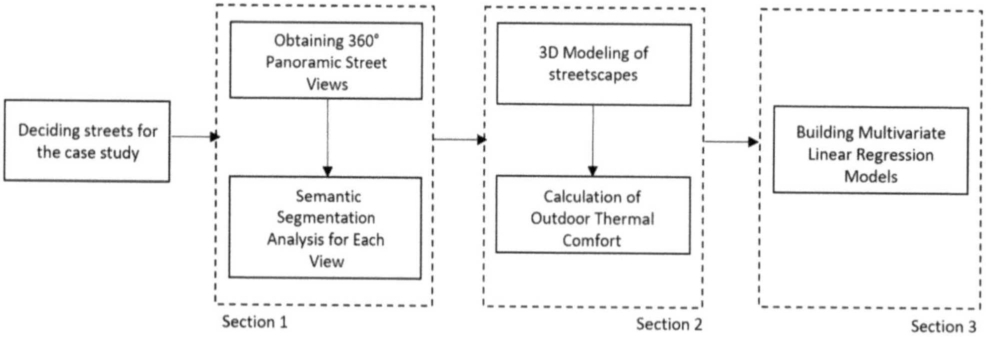

Figure 1
The framework of the study

Table 1
The range of UTCI (Błażejczyk et al. 2013)

UTCI (°C) range	Stress Category
above +46	Extreme heat stress
+38 to +46	Very strong heat stress
+32 to +38	Strong heat stress
+26 to +32	Moderate heat stress
+9 to +26	No thermal stress
+9 to 0	Slight cold stress
0 to -13	Moderate cold stress
-13 to -27	Strong cold stress
-27 to -40	Very strong cold stress
Below -40	Extreme cold stress

Universal Thermal Comfort Index (UTCI)

Universal Thermal Comfort Index (UTCI) is a thermal comfort indicator that combines meteorological and non-meteorological parameters (Błażejczyk et al. 2013). The meteorological inputs are the air temperature (Ta) and mean radiant temperature (Tmrt), wind speed (va), and humidity (vp). The thermal sensation of individuals is based on non-meteorological parameters, such as metabolic rate (MET) and clothing insulation.

As a result of calculations, the values of the UTCI are categorized under ten different thermal stresses. The approach investigates responses to reference conditions and deducts the load caused by the organism's physiological response to real environmental conditions. For instance, there is no thermal stress from +9° C to +26° C. On the other hand, strong heat stress is observed from +32° C to +38° C. The detailed range of UTCI can be seen in Table 1. In this study, the outdoor thermal comfort is calculated based on this thermal comfort indicator.

METHODOLOGY

The study proposes a prediction model that can correlate 2D street view images with outdoor thermal comfort conditions. The model aims to predict thermal discomfort in streets by using 2D street images. The proposed model has mainly three sections (a) semantic segmentation, (b) simulation-based calculation of outdoor thermal comfort, (c) and the development of multivariate regression models. The tools used for this workflow are Rhinoceros3D for 3D modeling, the Ladybug/Grasshopper for UTCI calculation.

1- Semantic Segmentation

Semantic segmentation is performed by using the official repository of the Artificial Intelligence for Resilient Urban Planning workshop by the City Intelligence Lab, Austrian Institute of Technology GmbH [1].

A deep learning model named DeepLab v3+ was developed to classify the street elements of each streetscape into certain classes (Chen et al., 2018). This deep learning model is trained on streetscapes using Cityscapes Dataset (Cordts et al., 2016).

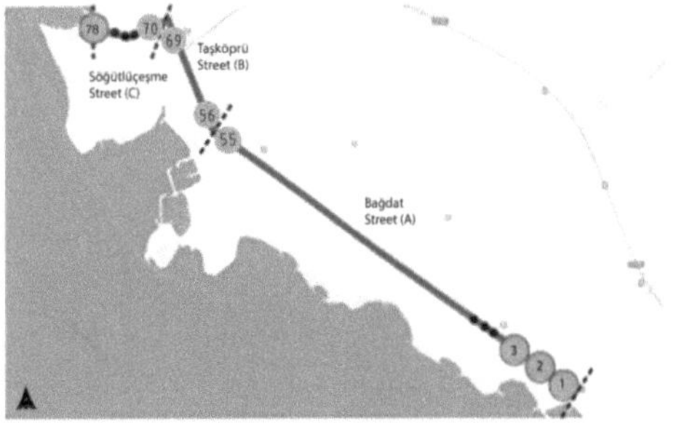

Figure 2
The main route of study (purple line), and the locations from which the images are captured (orange circles)

The Cityscapes Dataset is an image dataset used to label street features such as road, sidewalk, building, wall, fence, pole, traffic light, traffic sign, vegetation, terrain, sky, person, rider, car, motorcycle, and bicycle. After labeling, the percentage values of each label can be obtained. Each label's percentage values are plotted by calculating the ratio between the total number of pixels of the label, and the total number of pixels in the image.

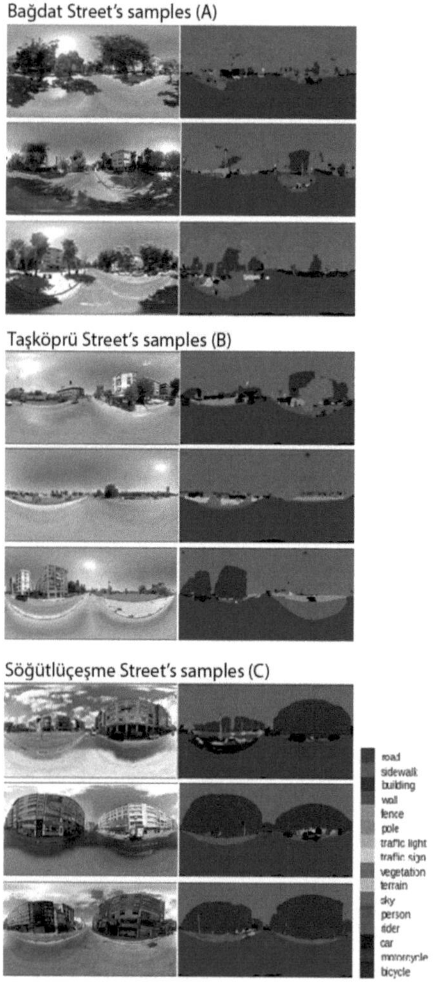

Figure 3
The samples of semantic segmentation

For semantic segmentation, a main route of study is selected, that is Bağdat Street (7 km), Taşköprü Street (1,75 km), and Söğütlüçeşme Street (1 km). This selection is based on these streets' different streetscapes, which are expected to have distinctive thermal sensations.

Initially, 78 panoramic images in the main route are obtained with 100-meter intervals (Figure 2). Panoramic street views are downloaded as 800*1600pixel images, captured from the midpoint of the road. The images are obtained from the 360° Street View downloader collaborated with the iStreetView website (iStreetView, 2017). Following, semantic segmentation of 78 panoramic images is analyzed.

Figure 3 shows panoramic image samples (left) and their semantic segmentation (right).

The urban features that have the highest level of influence on UTCI are identified as (a) road, sidewalk, (b) building, and (c) vegetation. Therefore, only these labels are used in our study, and the percentage values for each image are registered (Figure 4).

The calculated label percentage values indicate a drastic change in the amount of vegetation between the three streets. The average amount of vegetation in Street A, Street B, and Street C is calculated as 26%, 6,4%, and 1,1%. On the other hand, the amount of hard surfaces (road and sidewalks) is approximately the same (40%, 40,5%, and 43% in the same street order). In addition, Street C's streetscapes are dominated by buildings (avg. 20,5%) and hard surfaces (avg. 43,0%).

2- The Calculation of Outdoor Thermal Comfort

The label percentage values for each image, calculated in the previous step, will be used as independent variables in multivariate regression models for the prediction of outdoor thermal comfort.

Outdoor thermal comfort is calculated with UTCI, which is described in detail in the literature review. UTCI is calculated using the Ladybug/Grasshopper.

Initially, a 3D urban model of the selected streets,

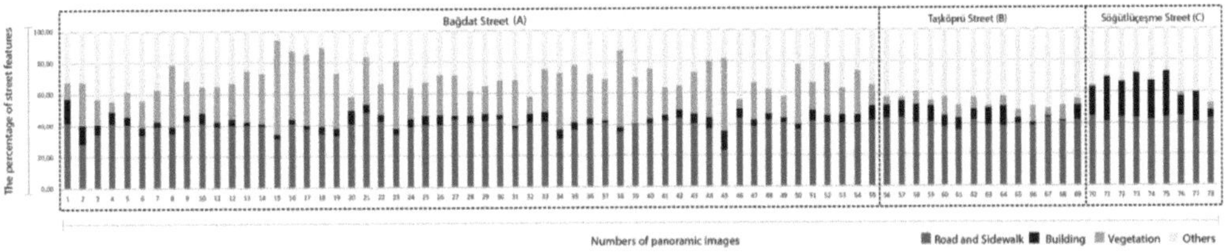

Figure 4
The stacked bar chart of selected street features, as a result of semantic segmentation

with their surrounding buildings and vegetation, should be developed as seen on panoramic images (figure 5). In Istanbul's EPW weather files, the extreme hot week of the year, which is between 13th of July and 19th of July, is selected.

From the EPW file, the hourly values of dry bulb temperature the air temperature (Ta) and mean radiant temperature (Tmrt), wind speed (va) and humidity(vp) radiation are extracted.

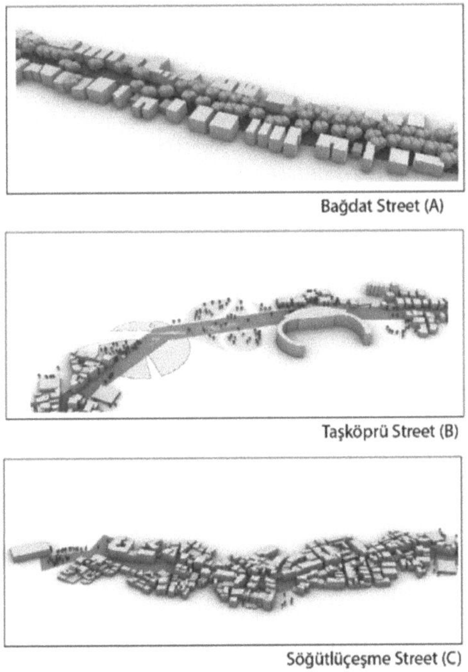

Figure 5
3D models of selected streets

The label percentage values for each image will be used as independent variables in multivariate regression models for outdoor thermal comfort prediction. Outdoor thermal comfort is calculated by using UTCI metric in the Ladybug/Grasshopper.In the process of the calculation, the selected streets with their surrounding buildings and vegetation are modeled initially in Rhinoceros 5 (Figure 5). Then, the hourly values of dry-bulb air temperature (Ta), mean radiant temperature (Tmrt), wind speed (va), and humidity (vp) radiation are given to the calculation of UTCI from Istanbul's EPW weather files. In addition, the analysis period is set for the extreme hot week of the year, between the 13th of July and the 19th of July.

Later, UTCI is calculated for each selected panoramic street image. The weather conditions (from the EPW file) are assumed to be the same, except Tmrt. Tmrt changes concerning the surrounding physical environment; therefore, Tmrt varies throughout the street, due to the changing density of the built environment and the presence of shading objects. Clothing insulation and MET are set to 0.7 and 1.2 respectively.

Figure 6 shows the visualization of a sample result that red boxes represent buildings while green figures are trees. This calculation is performed for each panoramic image (n=78) to understand the general outdoor comfort condition throughout the main route.

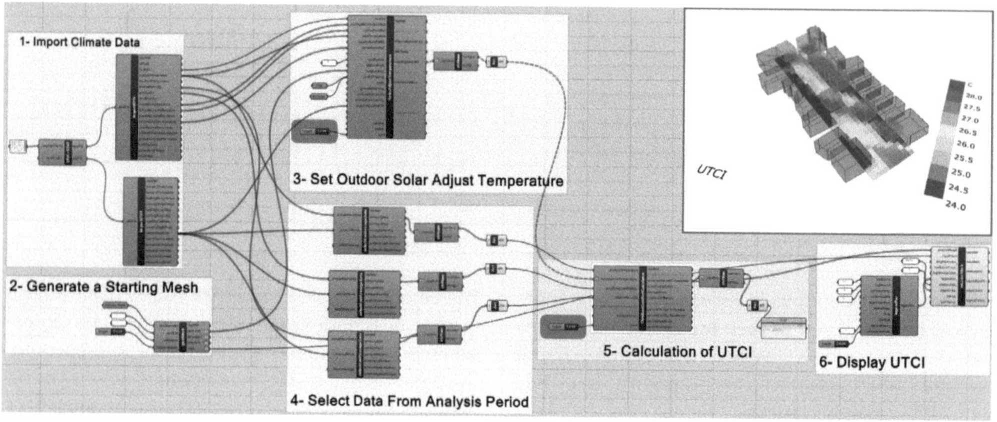

Figure 6
The workflow for the calculation of UTCI in Ladybug/-Grasshopper

3-Developing Multivariate Regression Models

Two regression models with different variables are built for different street characteristics. The reason for building two multivariate regression models is that three streets have different characters in terms of variable percentages. For instance, Street A has the highest amount of vegetation among other streets. However, buildings are more dominant in Street C. Street B is nearly between two streets in the view of the percentage of variables. Therefore, the percentage of variables of panoramic images is analyzed at the beginning. Street A has %40 hard surface; 5% building and 26% vegetation on average. Street B has 40,5% hard surface; 7,40% building and 6,40% vegetation on average. Street C has 43% hard surface; 20,50% building and 1,10% vegetation on average. When the total average values of 78 images are considered, it is 39% for hard surfaces, 7,24% for building, and 19,72% for vegetation (Table 2).

	Average hard surface (road and sidewalk)	Average building	Average vegetation
Street A (1 to 55)	**40%**	5%	**26%**
Street B (56 to 69)	**40,5%**	**7.40%**	6.40%
Street C (70 to 78)	**43%**	**20,50%**	1,10%
Total (1 to 78)	39%	7,24%	19,72%

Table 2
The percentages of selected street features for each street

Following, the vegetation variable is only selected for Street A, on the other hand, the building variable is chosen for Street B and Street C together. Meanwhile, the hard surface variable is common for both two regression models.

Later, the percentage of variables in 2D images should be projected into the variables' surface areas in 3d model because UTCI is calculated in 3d model environment. Therefore, the percentage of variables in 2D images is proportioned to each variable's surface area in the 3D model. In the regression models, these proportioned variable percentages are taken into account.

The multivariate regression model is built by using the formula below.

In the formula, a1 and a2 are coefficients of selected variables, while x1 and x2 are the percentages of selected variables, and b is the intercept. In addition, y is the response variable in the function. This function is repeated for each observation.

$$y = a1x1 + a2x2 + b \quad (1)$$

RESULTS

The first multivariate linear regression model can predict UTCI values with R2=0.78, while the second regression model can predict with R2=0.80 (Table 3).

Table 3
The first and second multivariate regression statistics

Regression Statistics	The First Model	The Second Model
Multiple R	0,886596942	0,897678991
R Square	0,786054137	0,80582757
Adjusted R Square	0,77782545	0,786410327
Standard Error	0,222993371	0,396369094
Observations	55	23

Table 4
The first and second multivariate regression coefficients

		Coefficients
The First Model	Intercept(b)	25,05829986
	Hard Surface Percentage(a_1)	0,017402326
	Vegetation Percentage(a_2)	-0,059933047
The Second Model	Intercept(b)	27,71585246
	Hard Surface Percentage(a_1)	-0,016155844
	Building Percentage(a_2)	-0,013667937

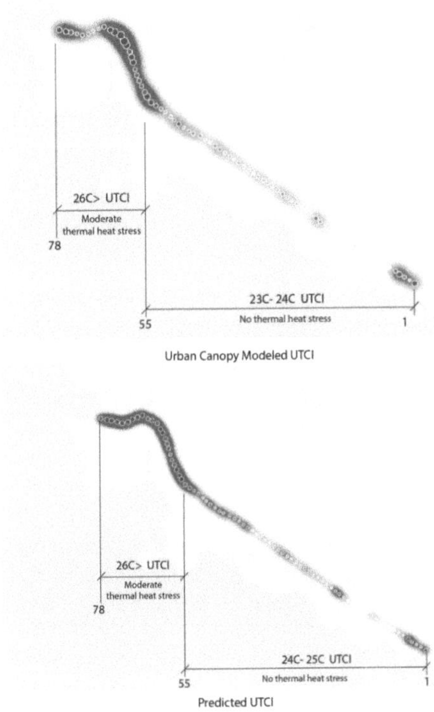

Figure 7
The comparison of urban canopy modeled UTCI and predicted UTCI on the heat map

Moreover, the coefficients of different variables for each regression model can be seen in Table 4.

Visualization

The outcome of this study is visualized by using Mapbox, an open-source mapping platform (Mapbox, n.d).

Figure 7 shows the comparison of urban canopy modeled UTCI and predicted UTCI on the heat map. The UTCI values of each point are represented with colored circles.

As a result of this study, the error is low, and the developed prediction model becomes successful although, this prediction model has a potential for development in the future.

CONCLUSION

This study aims to propose a prediction model to save decision-makers time to analyze outdoor thermal comfort conditions at the early stage of the design. The main reason behind this is that sort of analysis is labor-intensive and has a high computational cost.

The prediction model uses the label percentages calculated by semantic segmentation in 2D streetscape images, which include valuable clues to understand the outdoor thermal comfort, to a statistical model.

This model may encourage decision-makers to focus on outdoor thermal comfort-based design strategies. Moreover, this proposed model is open to be developed in the future.

As a future study, the number of street images can be increased for obtaining more data to analyze streetscapes. This might increase the precision prediction results.

In addition, this study may be used to find spots on solutions to improve outdoor thermal comfort in streets to include fine-tune streetscapes information for a better quality of city life.

REFERENCES

Ash, C, Jasny, BR, Roberts, L, Stone, R and Sugden, AM 2008, 'Reimagining cities', *Science*, 319, p. 739

Błażejczyk, K, Jendritzky, G, Bröde, P, Havenith, G, Epstein, Y and Kampmann, B 2013, 'An introduction to the universal thermal climate index (UTCI)', *Geographia Polonica*, 86, pp. 5-10

Charlwood, C 2004, *Torbay Streetscape Guidelines*, Torbay Council

Chen, LC, Zhu, Y, Papandreou, G, Schroff, F and Adam, H 2018 'Encoder-decoder with atrous separable convolution for semantic image segmentation', *Proceedings of the European conference on computer vision (ECCV)*, pp. 801-818

Cordts, M, Omran, M, Ramos, S, Rehfeld, T, Enzweiler, M, Benenson, R, Franke, U, Roth, S and Schiele, B 2016 'The cityscapes dataset for semantic urban scene understanding', *Proceedings of the IEEE conference on computer vision and pattern recognition*, pp. 3213-3223

Crankshaw, N 2009, *Creating Vibrant Public Spaces; Streetscape Design in Commercial and Historic Districts*, Islandpress

Garcia-Garcia, A, Orts-Escolano, S, Oprea, S, Villena-Martinez, V, Martinez-Gonzalez, P and Garcia-Rodriguez, J 2018, 'A survey on deep learning techniques for image and video semantic segmentation', *Applied Soft Computing*, 70, pp. 41-65

Gong, FY, Zeng, ZC, Zhang, F, Li, X, Ng, E and Norford, LK 2018, 'Mapping sky, tree, and building view factors of street canyons in a high-density urban environment', *Building and Environment*, 134, pp. 155-167

Ji, Q 2019, *Probabilistic Graphical Models for Computer Vision*, Academic Press

Li, X, Ratti, C and Seiferling, I 2017 'Mapping urban landscapes along streets using google street view', *International cartographic conference*, pp. 341-356

Liang, Z 2019, *Urban streetscape assessment through big data imagery processing. Different applications for urban planning in Milan*, Master's Thesis, Politecnico di Milano

Oke, TR 1982, 'The energetic basis of the urban heat island', *Journal of the Royal Meteorological Society*, 108, pp. 1-24

[1] https://github.com/city-intelligence-lab/digital-futures-2020

[2] https://github.com/city-intelligence-lab/digital-futures-2020/blob/master/colab-notebooks/semantic-segmentation.ipynb

[3] https://istreetview.com/1yNemftNP8bOHwnetZV7NQ

[4] https://www.mapbox.com/

Cross-Scale and Density-Driven City Generator

Parametric assistance to designers in prototyping stage

Zihan Mei[1], Yue Pan[2], Jack Cheng[3],
Jose Luis Garcia del Castillo Lopez[4]
[1,2,3,4] Harvard Graduate School of Design
[1,2,3,4] {zmei|pampan|jackcheng|jgarciadelcasti}@gsd.harvard.edu

In the modern urbanization process, urban planners create rules to define urban form and composition of blocks which are greatly impacted by the road network. This research paper proposes a ``city generator", as an urban design toolkit for urban designers to make prototypes of large new town planning and reimagination of city generation. The generator aims to translate planning regulations into three-dimensional urban form and provide users with efficient and intuitive design iterations. Moreover, our generator emphasizes consistency in generation across scales. From a single block to a district, they can be produced in one operation without losing details. Finally, the generator provides a great degree of freedom for users to manipulate, including three aspects - road generation, density mapping and building form. Because of the flexibility of input parameters, generated models can be a rigid urban grid or an organic pattern, which can highly satisfy urban designer's expectations and imagination.

Keywords: *parametric urban design, urban planning, Grasshopper plugin*

INTRODUCTION

Urban form is greatly restrained and defined by zoning regulations. With a set of zoning parameters defining the building density, including the floor area ratio (FAR) and building coverage ratio (BCR), urban designers and architects are required by the city planning departments to articulate the three-dimensional form of buildings. FAR is the ratio of total constructed building floor area to the parcel area, and BCR is the ratio of ground floor area to the parcel area. In large-scale new town planning, it is also essential for urban planners and designers to map the density across the site based on land uses, and vehicle and pedestrian circulations. By understanding city form generation in current planning regulation and design as a holistic process, from road network to building form, our goal is to create a parametric tool that achieves quick prototyping and feedback with consistency in generation across scales, and allows great degree of freedom in user inputs of multiple parameters.

Consistency in generation across scales

We propose the generator that considers the influence of multiple input parameters, such as road network and density mapping, from a single block to an entire city area and does not need to be calculated separately at different city levels. Similar works include CityEngine by ESRI R&D Center Zurich that streamlined the city generation roadmap from multiple historical cases to simulate a virtual city generation with the data input of road systems, population density, land-water boundaries, and topography (Parish, Yoav, and Müller, Pascal 2001). In other words, a user only adjusts the input of parameters once and can get the generation of the entire city including all levels of detail. This makes up for the discontinuity problem of many current computational tools applied in urban design.

For example, some generators can automatically generate a road network based on the main roads input by the user, but there is no way to effectively generate building volume on a city scale, such as large-scale calculation level. Its limitation is that when users want to analyze the 3D model of buildings, the generator can only calculate and generate building volume at a single block level without ability to deal with multiple blocks (Austern et al. 2014).

Another discontinuity problem is that although some generators can produce large-scale road network systems and building volumes, the building can only be adjusted with the height or other single changes in a limited way, which greatly reduces details and authenticity of a single block, that is, the FAR and BSR density information, setback of building and block density according to road level (Arpornwicharnop et al. 2007).

Quick prototyping and feedback

One thing we find important when using digital tools for design is efficiency. Given our targeting at quick prototyping and instant feedback of both urban and building scale generation, we pay additional attention to limit the time consumed for large sites' calculation. Unlike the situations in most related works, where generations tend to take place within a site of around 50 blocks or fewer according to their targets, the test model during our development contains more than 600 blocks, with an area of around 6 million square meters. We manage to optimize the algorithms designed for the density-related calculation and keep the total calculating time below 10 seconds.

The speed of rapid prototyping process is also based on the overall structure of data processing. Instead of applying the Form-Based Coding that specifies the block building form with spatial parameters such as building setback and floors (Schnabel et al. 2017), the data input to generate building form are traditional zoning parameters of density, such as FAR and BCR. In this way, users can manipulate the city form generation intuitively and holistically, without tediously manipulating building form block by block.

Great degrees of freedom in user input of multiple parameters

In our proposal for the tool, it's compatible with inputs in any shape of boundaries and any pattern of main roads. The scope of some other generators is specific to a particular region, with the aim of block generation according to the specific local regulations and lifestyles (Fink & Reinhart 2019). The compatibility in the inputs for our tool is required by the tool's feature of quick prototyping, which means that it needs to deal with random patterns of boundaries and basic urban transportation system in the rapid iteration in the early stage for an urban design or planning project. From some other related works, we also notice that they only generate rigid urban grids, resulting in all outputs being similar as evenly-divided blocks in the overall form - even when the input basic system is not strictly rigid (Beirao et al. 2012). The feature of quick prototyping also requires our tool to contain multiple parameters for quick testing with detailed changes in users' intention. For example, in its first part of network generation, the tool makes use of three groups of parameters, allowing users to choose between organic and rigid urban grids.

METHODOLOGY

Designed for urban designers and planners, our tool is developed on Rhinoceros 7 and Grasshopper 1.0.0007, a computer-aided-design software that is popular with designers worldwide. Designed to be used by designers at will, our algorithms are packed as an open-source, compiled Grasshopper plugin available at GitHub repository https://github.com/saturn-drm/city-generator.

Supposing a boundary and several main roads are used as inputs for a project, the methodology divides the generation into 3 steps (shown in Figure 1):

1. Road network and block generation
2. Density remapping
3. City form generation

Such arrangement generally follows the process in which a designer deals with a project, while considering the overall relationship between the density in urban and building scales. In general, the first step deals with density on an urban scale, while the third step deals with that in a building scale, and the second step acts as a connection in between, making the building scale density based on overall urban scale requirement.

To begin with, the first step generates road networks and blocks with consideration of density variation in different parts of a district. As the urban scale density variation is reflected by the network density and block size, the basic logic for this step is dividing blocks with roads until a chosen target average size. This process can be controlled by multiple parameters, allowing the freedom of the choice between rigid and organic grids, and the significance of the deviation between highest and lowest density in the whole district.

The second step, starting with blocks and roads and ending with FAR, is a process connecting the reflection of density in urban scale and building scale. It calculates a weighted location index by the distances from each block to the roads in all classes and remaps it to a proper domain that is reasonable for FAR in the third step. It contains a series of weighted parameters defining how each class of roads influence the density for the blocks, as well as the remapping index defining the overall FAR distribution across the district.

The third step generates forms of buildings within each block according to FAR, inherited from the density by location (aka zoning to some extent), and BCR. FAR defines the building typologies, while BCR defines the height and additional towers for some typology. This step contains BCR controllers that will define specific building heights and patterns in addition to the overall block density from the urban scale.

Road & Block Generation

As the first step in the generation tool, road and block generation takes in a boundary for the project, with several main roads, and returns the network of main, secondary, and minor roads, as well as the blocks cut by the network.

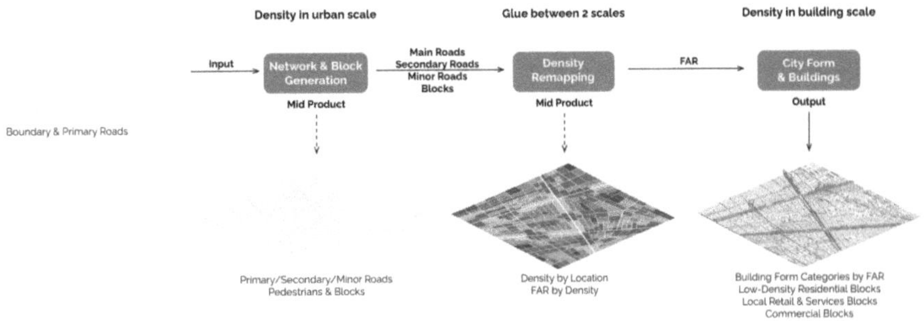

Figure 1
Roadmap of the three steps in the tool

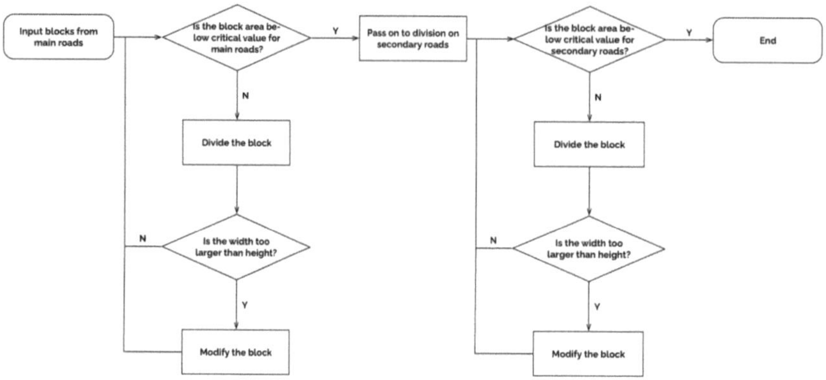

Figure 2
Overall workflow for the looped block-oriented division

Block-oriented generation: Due to the target of density-driven network in the urban scale, this process is based on the looped division of blocks until certain critical values, representing that the block is too small to be divided further, which is unlike some of the related works where random roads are generated evenly by recursion of segment generations. The division is executed as follows (shown in Figure 2):

- Blocks by the boundary and main roads are divided by secondary roads in a loop until all the blocks are smaller than a critical size value decided by the user, representing that such blocks cannot contain additional secondary roads inside.
- Blocks by the secondary roads are divided by minor roads in a loop while compared to another critical size value defined by the user, until all the blocks are too small to be divided further.
- Before each loop of division, check the shape of the blocks, to modify some blocks with too large height-width-deviation by dividing around the mid.

Considering the variation of urban density in different locations between the core and peripheral parts, the critical values for subdivision are not the same for each block. That is, areas nearer to the urban center tend to have higher network density and smaller block size. Therefore, within each step, the critical value whether to divide the blocks further can be controlled by three parameters that are defined by the user (shown in Figure 4, 5, 6, 7):

- Universal size (*uArea*), defining the overall size to stop subdivision.
- Amplitude controller (*AmpC*), defining the deviation in *uArea*.
- Critical distance to main roads (*Dist*), checking if

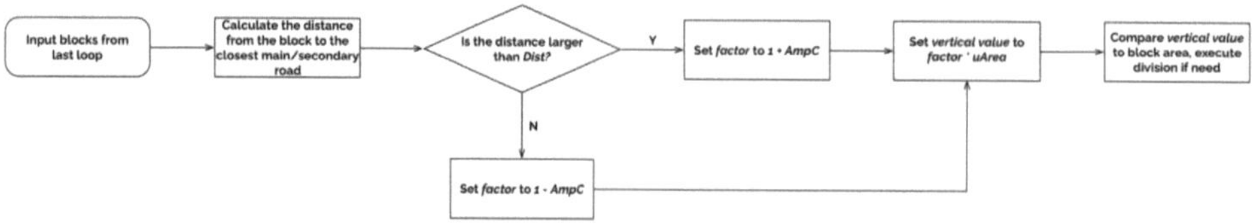

Figure 3
Workflow for calculating customized critical area value for each block to determine further division

the blocks are near the urban center, thus need to be compared to a smaller critical value.

The process that generates the specific critical value for each block can be described as follows (see Figure 3):

1. Calculate the distances from the block's center to all the main roads and get the smallest distance value.
2. Compare the smallest distance value with parameter *Dist*, if smaller (the block is closer to a main road), return *1 - AmpC*; if larger (the block is farther to a main road), return *1 + AmpC*.
3. Return *uArea * [the result from step 2]* as the specific critical size for the block.

Division patterns: While the critical values applied in the process of looped division determine the variation of density all over the district, there are also two patterns (shown in Figure 8) used to execute the divisions, determining the patterns of either organic or rigid grid. The two division patterns share the same random index (Rand Parameter) to control the degree of rigid/organic form (shown in Figure 9).

- **Radius division** generates lines from a random point near the block's center to all the borders. This method is used when the block is not quadrilateral. It's controlled by one parameter defining the random range for the starting point, and another defining the range where the end points should locate on borders.
- **Crossing division** generates lines connecting pairs of random points on opposite borders in each block. It's controlled by one parameter defining the random range where the points should locate on borders.

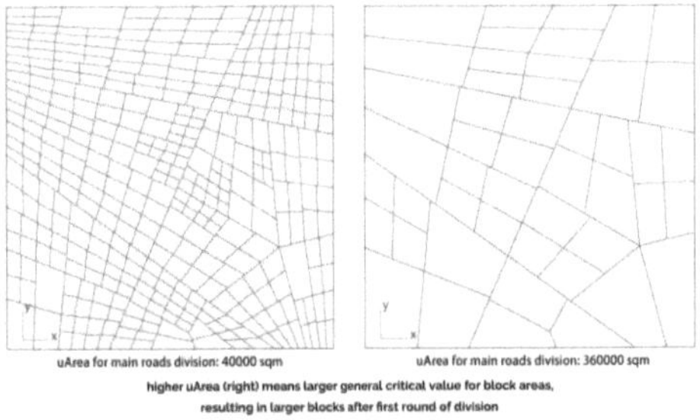

Figure 4
Variation in uArea for main roads

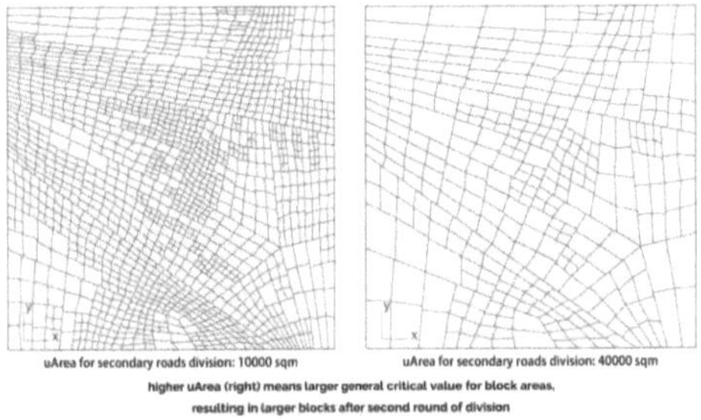

Figure 5
Variation in uArea for secondary roads

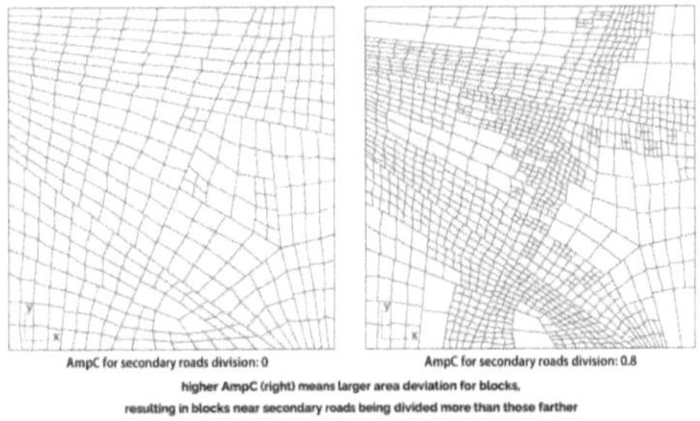

Figure 6
Variation in AmpC for secondary roads

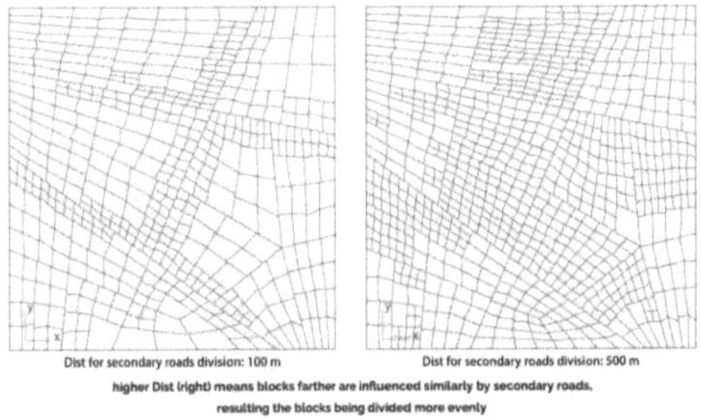

Figure 7
Variation in Dist for secondary roads

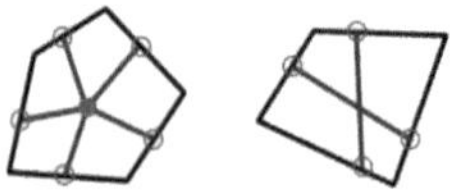

Figure 8
Two division patterns: radius (left) and crossing (right)

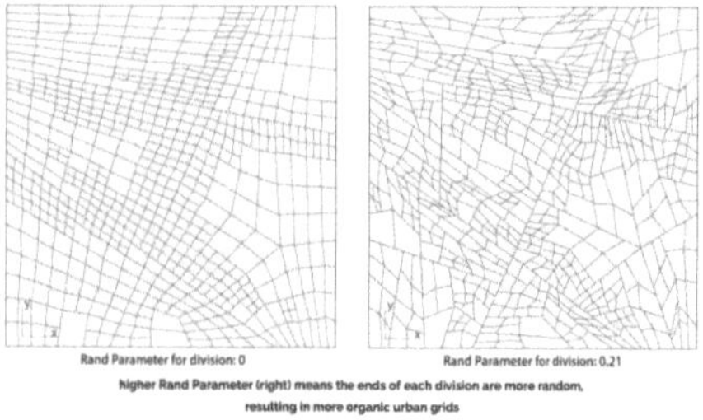

Figure 9
Variation in the random parameter for secondary roads

Density Remapping

In the city generator, the building density of each block is affected by the distance between the block and roads. The method to measure the density of each block is to calculate the minimum distance between the center of the block and all the main, secondary roads on the map respectively. Then, the distance value will be put into three different intervals to evaluate the scores, and all the scores of the block will be summed up. Finally, the summed scores for main roads and secondary roads are weighted into the final density value (shown in Figure 10, 11).
The range of each interval can be determined by the user. The distance value will be assigned a score according to the intervals set by the user. For example, if the user sets three continuous intervals, [1, 10] (starting interval), [10, 20] and [20, 30], they represent 3, 2, and 1 points respectively. When the distance between the block and the main road is 11, then the block will get 2 points. It can be seen that when the block is closer to the main road, the score will be higher, which can reflect higher density.

Since there will be multiple main roads on the map, each block will get multiple points and sum up a total score. Based on the maximum score and minimum score on the entire map, the total score obtained by each block will be remapped to three intervals of FAR, respectively [0.5, 2.0], [2.0, 5.0], and [5.0, 20.0]. In this way, the block score can be used in the next section, city form, to present different functional forms of building volume.

City Form

The generated FAR (Floor Area Ratio) was assigned to each generated urban block from the previous steps. The guiding logic of building form generation in blocks aims to reflect the connection between the FAR regulation and building typologies. We conclude the relationship between building forms and associated block FAR through various zoning documents in the U.S. The block building forms are generalized into three categories, shown in Figure 12: the low-density residential blocks (FAR 0.5 - 2.0), the local retail & service blocks (FAR 2.0 - 5.0), and the commercial blocks (FAR 5.0 - 20.0). There is a unique set of geometry generation rules for each category that takes the density parameter (FAR) generated from the previous step and user-controlled input such as building coverage ratio (BCR) to create block building form. The form reflects its density and uses in an abstract city form. Learning from the building from patterns in cities, we define the number of parcels within each block increases when the block density (FAR) decreases.
Low-density residential blocks are visualized as a group of single-family houses within one block. For each block, with the defined FAR, the number of parcels decreases when the density (FAR) increases. The spacing between each house can be controlled by the user input of BCR. To mimic the form of single-family houses, the height of each house is set as three stories.
Local retail & service blocks are visualized as a group of or a single periphery block that serves as mixed-use housing and local retail buildings. For each block, the area of inner courtyard, the periphery building depth and height are correlated and controlled by the defined FAR and the user-input BCR.
Commercial blocks are visualized as a single periphery block building with tower extrusions on sides that are facing the primary and secondary roads. Differ-

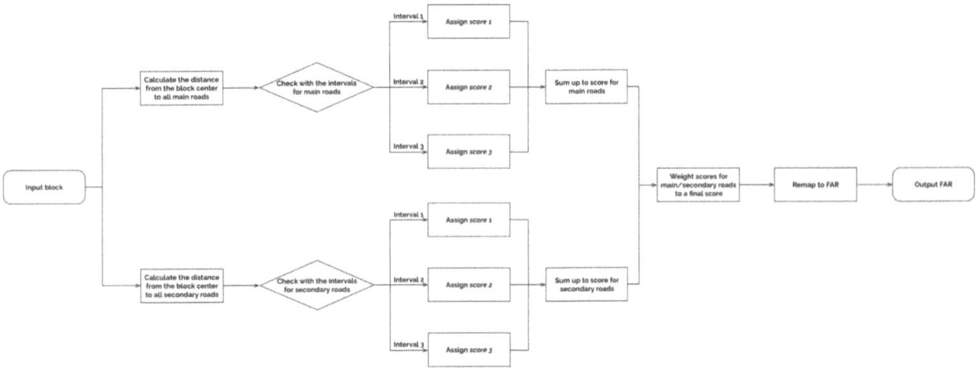

Figure 10
Workflow for density calculation and remapping from distance

ent from the form generation for local retail & service blocks, the building form of commercial blocks is divided into the bottom periphery part, with set building depth and height, and the top tower extrusions, whose height is determined by the FAR and user input BCR and TRatio. BCR controls the tower heights, and TRatio controls the ratio between the heights of towers facing primary streets and secondary streets.

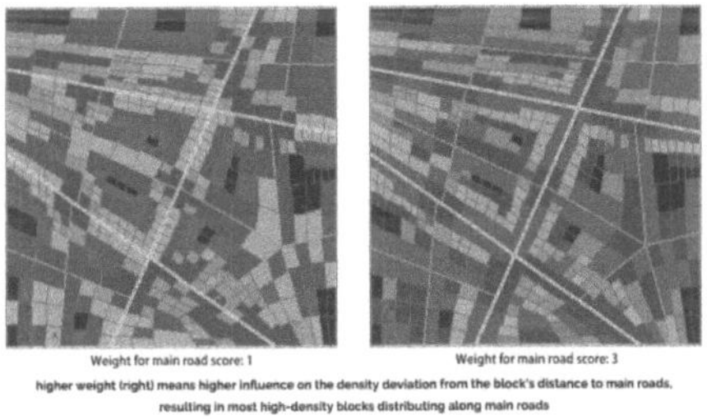

Figure 11
Variation in the weight for the score of main roads

RESULTS

As a test, we compare the output of the tool with an urban design project, the Imperial International Business City (IIBC) in Lagos, Nigeria by Gensler. It is a urban design proposal of a 200-hectare mix-use residential island, with the integration of smart technology. (Gensler, 2014) (shown in Figure 13). In the urban scale, our output shows proper density deviation across blocks in different locations of the city. In the building scale, the tool generates proper building forms according to the block FAR by its location, as well as the heterogeneity in buildings within the same block. However, currently the tool doesn't work with topographic inputs well. It doesn't contain zonal distribution or land use patterns, either.

In conclusion, this tool we presented aims at the density-driven urban and building form generation. The results of this tool show high unity in the cross-scale generation with density. The tool is designed for urban designers in the prototyping stages of projects, and is compatible with complex borders and random input main roads.

FUTURE RESEARCH

The parametric city generator tool described in this paper successfully streamlines the generation process. It has great potential to be integrated into the workflow for urban designers and planners. Currently, the project accomplishes the integration across scales and the efficiency in prototyping. However, as shown in the prototyping result of the IIBC model, the urban modelling is a complicated process and involves various stakeholders.

In our future research, in addition to the existing elements, we plan on integrating the following inputs to enhance to practicality of the tool:

- GIS input: land-water boundary, topography;
- Zoning requirement: land use distribution;
- Special city block: large parks, civic centers, amusement parks, etc.;

- Transportation infrastructure: highways, railways, light rails, etc..

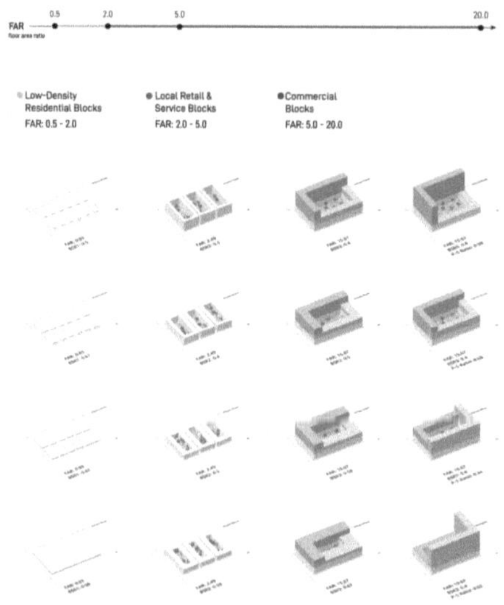

Figure 12
Three types of urban block typology and morphology change with input of FAR and BCR

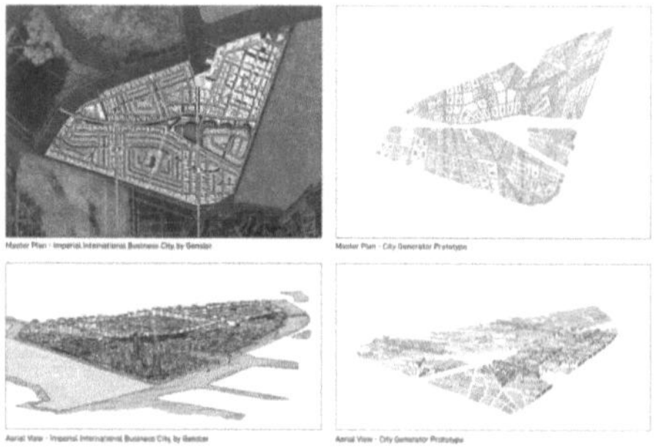

Figure 13
Comparison in master plans and aerial views between the IIBC proposal by Gensler and the generated city form with our grasshopper component

Including the post analysis of the generated city forms would also be a critical next step for this project. Environmental analysis of city forms embedded in Grasshopper includes solar radiation, shadow, wind and surface water analysis. By integrating these post analysis tools to our component, the users can integrate the environmental performance into their decision making process in urban planning.

Moreover, the current product is solely dependent on the Rhino 3D and Grasshopper platform. For future development, the removal of this dependency would allow this product to be more accessible to a greater audience in the design and planning field.

ACKNOWLEDGEMENTS

This research work was conducted as part of the course GSD-6338: Introduction to Computational Design, at the Harvard Graduate School of Design. The authors would like to thank Xiaoshi Wang and Runjia Tian for their help in some typical algorithms and processes of debugging.

REFERENCES

Arpornwicharnop, K, Jinuntuya, P and Kanongchaiyos, P 2007 'Simulation Software Development for Urban Landscape Possibility Analysis', *Proceedings of the 12th International Conference on Computer Aided Architectural Design Research in Asia (CAADRIA 2007)*, Nanjing

Austern, G, Yu, S, Moral, M and Jirathiyut, T 2014 'The Urban Genome', *Rethinking Comprehensive Design: Speculative Counterculture, Proceedings of the 19th International Conference on Computer-Aided Architectural Design Research in Asia (CAADRIA 2014)*, Kyoto, p. 263–272

Beirão, J, Arrobas, P and Duarte, J 2012 'Parametric Urban Design: Joining Morphology and Urban Indicators in a Single Interactive Model', *Achten, Henri; Pavlicek, Jiri; Hulin, Jaroslav; Matejovska, Dana (eds.), Digital Physicality - Proceedings of the 30th eCAADe Conference*, Czech Technical University in Prague, Faculty of Architecture (Czech Republic), pp. 167-175

Fink, T and Koenig, R 2019 'Integrated Parametric Urban Design in Grasshopper / Rhinoceros 3D - Demonstrated on a Master Plan in Vienna', *Sousa, JP, Xavier, JP and Castro Henriques, G (eds.), Architecture in the Age of the 4th Industrial Revolution - Proceedings of the 37th eCAADe and 23rd SIGraDi Conference*, University of Porto, Porto, Portugal, pp. 313-322

Gensler, G (eds) 2014, *The IIBC — Imperial International Business City*, https://www.gensler.com/projects/the-iibc-imperial-international-business-city, Accessed March 23rd 2021.

Parish, YIH and Müller, P 2001 'Procedural Modeling of Cities', *Proceedings of the 28th Annual Conference on Computer Graphics and Interactive Techniques*, p. 301–308

Schnabel, M A, Zhang, Y and Aydin, S 2017, 'Using Parametric Modelling in Form-Based Code Design for High-Dense Cities', *Procedia Engineering*, 180, p. 1379–1387

Index of Authors

V

W

X

Y

Z

CIP - Каталогизација у публикацији
Библиотеке Матице српске, Нови Сад

72.012:004(082)

ECAADE Conference on Education and Research in Computer Aided Architectural Design in Europe (39 ; 2021 ; Novi Sad)

Proceedings : eCAADe 2021 Towards a New, Configurable Architecture : Vol. 1 / 39th eCAADe Conference on Education and Research in Computer Aided Architectural Design in Europe, 8-10th September 2021, Novi Sad ; [editors Bojan Tepavčević, Vesna Stojaković]. - [Bruxelles] : eCAADe [i. e.] Education and research in Computer Aided Architectural Design in Europe ; Novi Sad : Faculty of Technical Sciences, 2021 (Novi Sad : FTN, Grafički centar GRID). - 617 str. : ilustr. ; 20 x 20 cm

Tiraž 150. - Bibliografija uz svaki rad. - Registar.

ISBN 978-86-6022-358-8

a) Архитектонско пројектовање -- Примена рачунара -- Зборници

COBISS.SR-ID 43611657